The Routledge Anthology of Early Modern Drama

The Routledge Anthology of Early Modern Drama is the first new collection of the drama of Shakespeare's contemporaries in over a century.

This volume comprises seventeen accessible, thoroughly glossed, modernized play-texts, intermingling a wide range of unfamiliar works—including the anonymous *Look About You,* Massinger's *The Picture,* Heminge's *The Fatal Contract,* Heywood's *The Four Prentices of London,* and Greene's *James IV*—with more familiar works such as Marlowe's *Doctor Faustus,* Webster's *The Duchess of Malfi,* and Middleton's *Women Beware Women.* Each play is edited by a different leading scholar in the field of early modern studies, bringing specific expertise and context to the chosen play-text.

With an unprecedented variety of plays, and critical introductions that focus on the diversity and strangeness of different early modern approaches to the artistic and commercial enterprise of play-making, *The Routledge Anthology of Early Modern Drama* will offer vital new perspectives on early modern drama for scholars, students, and performers alike.

Jeremy Lopez is Professor of English at the University of Toronto. He is the editor of *Shakespeare Quarterly,* and the author of numerous books and essays on the drama of Shakespeare and his contemporaries.

The Routledge Anthology of Early Modern Drama

Edited by Jeremy Lopez

Routledge
Taylor & Francis Group
LONDON AND NEW YORK

First published 2020
by Routledge
2 Park Square, Milton Park, Abingdon, Oxon OX14 4RN

and by Routledge
52 Vanderbilt Avenue, New York, NY 10017

Routledge is an imprint of the Taylor & Francis Group, an informa business

British Library Cataloguing-in-Publication Data
A catalogue record for this book is available from the British Library

Library of Congress Cataloging-in-Publication Data
Names: Lopez, Jeremy, editor.
Title: The Routledge anthology of early modern drama / edited by Jeremy Lopez.
Description: Abingdon, Oxon ; New York, NY : Routledge, 2020. |
Includes bibliographical references.
Identifiers: LCCN 2019038359 (print) | LCCN 2019038360 (ebook)
Subjects: LCSH: English drama–17th century.
Classification: LCC PR1265.3 .R68 2020 (print) | LCC PR1265.3 (ebook) |
DDC 822/.508–dc23
LC record available at https://lccn.loc.gov/2019038359
LC ebook record available at https://lccn.loc.gov/2019038360

ISBN: 978-1-138-95379-6 (hbk)
ISBN: 978-1-138-95380-2 (pbk)
ISBN: 978-1-315-66718-8 (ebk)

Typeset in Baskerville
by Integra Software Services Pvt. Ltd.

Contents

Acknowledgments

My greatest debt is of course to the seventeen contributing editors, whose careful, imaginative work and unfailing collegiality made this project a pleasure to lead, even in those moments when it seemed like it would never be finished. At Routledge, I am grateful to Polly Dodson and Ben Piggott for their interest in the anthology when I first proposed it, and to Ben for shepherding it along; to Laura Soppelsa and Alaina Christensen for their support in bringing the manuscript to production; and to Tom Bedford for meticulous copyediting. Four students at the University of Toronto—Divna Stojanovic, Jonathan Dick, Katherine Chu, and Samantha Greco—provided invaluable assistance at various stages in the preparation of the texts. Nate Crocker, also at Toronto, did an extraordinary amount of work at the proof-editing stage. On behalf of some of the contributing editors to this volume I would also like to acknowledge, gratefully, the assistance of Melissa Schultheis and Nicole Sheriko (Rutgers University, *Poetaster*); Mary Rose Donahue and Alexa Culshaw (Colorado College, *The Fair Maid of the Exchange*); Amanda Rogus (Mary Baldwin University Shakespeare & Performance, *Look About You*); and (for *Eastward Ho*) Alicia Parker (NYU), Arianna Stucki (NYU Abu Dhabi), and Aiden Selmer and Alexandra Atiya (University of Toronto).

The American Shakespeare Center in Staunton, Virginia not only furnished the image on the cover of the volume, but also produced a number of the plays it contains (in a few cases, theirs is the *only* modern professional production); I hope that the publication of the anthology encourages them to undertake a few more. Four anonymous readers, finally, provided rigorous and encouraging reports on the initial proposal for the anthology. These reports were very important for determining the anthology's scope and structure; I hope that these readers will find the project's promise realized in the final product.

General introduction

Jeremy Lopez

This anthology comprises a representative sample of drama written and performed in England between the 1560s and the 1630s. A few of the plays will be familiar, and have appeared regularly in other anthologies—*Doctor Faustus*, *The Duchess of Malfi*, *Women Beware Women*, and *Eastward Ho*—but most of them will likely be unfamiliar, even to students of the period. More than half of the plays have never been anthologized before, and many have never even been given a modern-spelling edition. Like other volumes of its kind, this anthology represents the remarkable theatrical and verbal creativity, the astonishing range of styles and forms, that characterized early modern English drama. By giving so much space to plays that are so seldom read or written about, we hope that this anthology will also be an opportunity for students and scholars to make new discoveries about the nature of dramatic form, and the interrelation between dramatic forms, in the age of Shakespeare and his contemporaries.

As the word "we" in the previous sentence indicates, this anthology is a collaborative venture. Each of its seventeen texts was selected and prepared by a different editor. While the selection process involved some negotiation, each editor chose his or her text more or less independently of all the others. Each editor chose a text that he or she thought represented something particular and interesting about early modern dramatic form. In following this procedure for determining the table of contents, we had two related goals: one was to present a genuinely eclectic, unexpected array of plays, assembled without regard to pre-determined parameters of authorship or genre. The other was to demonstrate that a broadly historical view of the period could be achieved by starting with the particular features of individual plays. It is in respect of this latter goal that we have not attempted to sketch—either in this general introduction or in the critical introductions to the plays—a history of the late-sixteenth- and seventeenth-century commercial theater in London. Nor have we attempted to articulate, in any systematic way, a contextual argument about the relation between the plays the anthology contains and the most urgent social, political, and economic problems of the period. Accessible, more or less detailed historical overviews of early modern theater history and of the political and social context for early modern drama are readily available in other anthologies, in editions of Shakespeare's plays, and in works of criticism likely to be provided in university courses where readers are most likely to encounter this anthology. It did not seem necessary to provide any further such contextual overview here. Instead, the primary questions each editor was asked to consider in editing and presenting his or her text were: what kind of play is this? Why is it worth reading? What does it tell us about the craft of play-making in the early modern period? The answers to these questions often touch on, or delve into, matters of theater history, or social, political, and economic problems; but they also tend most emphatically toward analysis of form and of the relation between one play and another. The critical introductions are intended primarily to help you get started reading the plays, and to help you read them in relation to other plays—both those that are contained in the volume and those that are not. We hope that your encounters with the unfamiliar, unusual plays represented in this volume will inspire and enable you to see more familiar plays, as well as the historical materials and narratives most typically used to contextualize them, in a new light.

As eclectic as the table of contents is, it does, we think, achieve the goal of broad historical representation. It features plays by most of the period's major authors, and examples of a wide range of genres, including but not limited to comedy, tragedy, English history, classical history, city comedy, estates satire, and romance. Moreover, the plays' known or probable dates of performance are more or less evenly distributed from the 1580s through the 1630s (*Cambises*, c. 1560–61, is an outlier here, though it was reprinted in 1585 and 1595, and may have been revived in 1609). The table of contents also features two fascinating "minor" playwrights of the period, Robert Armin and William Heminge, who are similar in their explicit responsiveness to a wide range of plays (especially those of Shakespeare) that preceded them. Finally, it contains three works by one of the early modern period's most prolific, and still most under-represented playwrights: Anonymous.

But even more important than what the seventeen plays collected here represent about the dramatic authors, genres, and movements of the early modern period is what they represent about the boldness, the inventiveness, and the largeness of conception of early modern playwrights. The plays in this anthology are challenging, and not only because they are unfamiliar. They are dilatory, episodic, and digressive. They feature characters who push actors to the limits of their craft (e.g. the Eunuch in *Fatal Contract*, Redcap in *Look About You*, and Cripple in *Fair Maid*); they revel in implausible incident (e.g. *Four Prentices* and *Sea Voyage*); they push against the boundaries of time and space (e.g. the Cuckold's Haven scene in *Eastward Ho* and Chorus vii in *James IV*); they experiment with different verbal registers and linguistic idioms (e.g. *Cambises* and *Famous Victories*); and they pursue their theatrical ends with a grandeur and grandiosity (e.g. the picture in *The Picture*, the pageant of the seven deadly sins in *Faustus*, the wax figures in *Duchess*, the climactic masque in *Women Beware*, the doubling of Tutch and John in *Two Maids*, and the birdcage in *Bird in the Cage*) that strained the resources of their own theater companies as well as their audiences (see especially the prefatory material to *If This Be Not a Good Play* and *Poetaster*). The challenges presented by the plays collected in this anthology remind us in new and surprising ways that playwriting in the early modern period involved not only a practical, opportunistic understanding of theatrical conventions and audience tastes, but also a willingness to court failure; not only commercial ambition, but also artistic vision.

In deciding how to arrange the plays in this anthology, I (and here I must return to the first-person singular and absolve the contributing editors of responsibility for the decision) sought an alternative to the most common schemes, namely chronological from earliest to latest, or chronological and by author—where, for example, four Jonson plays, dated between 1598 and 1611, might be grouped together and followed by three Middleton plays dated between 1606 and 1621. What I most wanted was an arrangement that would eschew the evolutionary view of the drama implied by chronological ordering and, in doing so, create surprising pairings or sequences of plays. At the same time, I wanted to avoid sheer randomness, and to create an arrangement that would invite readers to reflect upon the importance (or irrelevance) of historical position to the definition of dramatic form and the analysis of intertextuality. The scheme I decided upon was to arrange the plays chronologically, earliest to latest, according to the period in which their action is set. Inevitably, this scheme required some arbitrary decisions, not least thinking about historical setting in a much more verisimilar way than any early modern playwright (including those who wrote history plays) ever did. For example, although Massinger nowhere makes explicit, or important, that he is drawing from actual Hungarian and Polish history for some of the characters in *The Picture*, I have used what is known about his source-materials to justify my assumption that the play is "set" in the mid-fifteenth century. And although there is no definitive evidence that the character John i'th' Hospital in *The Two Maids of More-clacke* actually existed, I have used what scholars have inferred about Armin's likely model for the character (a man named John Smith who died in 1593) to locate the play's historical setting in the 1580s, some two decades before it was performed and published. On the other hand, because of their contemporary allusions or engagement with matters of contemporary interest, I have decided to treat *If This Be Not a Good Play, The Devil Is In It, The Sea Voyage*, and *The Bird in the Cage* as though they are set in roughly the moment of their composition, even though their plots seem almost deliberately to evade historical location.

I take these kinds of decisions to be, if not identical, then certainly analogous to the kinds of decisions that must be made when creating a more truly historical chronology. For example: *Women Beware Women*'s performance date is given, in this volume, as somewhere between 1613 and 1621. Would it be a more accurate representation of the historical relations between works to put it next to *If this Be Not a Good Play* (c. 1611–12) or *The Sea Voyage* (c. 1622)? Would it be more accurate to put *Poetaster* (first performed in 1601) next to *The Fair Maid of the Exchange* (c. 1601–02) or—since the edition included here is based on the 1616 text, which contains material that Jonson added later and that was never performed—next to the *Duchess of Malfi* (1614)? Historical narratives are always at least partly allegorical. The arrangement of plays in this anthology embraces allegory; it suggests that forms give shape to history as much as history gives shape to forms. More importantly, it offers readers the opportunity to make connections between plays by means of both conventional groupings (*Duchess* and *Women Beware*, for example, or *Eastward Ho* and *Fair Maid*) and unconventional (*Poetaster* and *The Fatal Contract*, for example, or *Famous Victories, The Picture*, and *Faustus*).

However unconventional, allegorical, and fundamental to the character of this anthology the arrangement of plays might be, I do not assume that it will determine the order in which readers approach the plays, nor that it will dispel the entirely reasonable desire to have a clear idea of their actual chronology. Below, I provide three lists of the plays: the first gives them in the order in which they appear in this anthology, with brief annotations to indicate the period in which they are (or might be said to be) set; the second gives them in order of first performance; the third gives them in order of publication. All dates, date-ranges, and markers of approximation or uncertainty in the second and third lists are taken from the critical introductions to the plays.

1 *Cambises* mid 5th C BC (Cyrus II)	1 *Cambises*	1560–61 (?)	1 *Cambises*	1570
2 *Poetaster* late 1st C BC (Augustus Caesar)	2 *Faustus*	c. 1588	2 *Famous Victories*	1598
3 *Fatal Contract* late 5th C AD (Clovis I)	3 *Famous Victories*	c. 1588	3 *James IV*	1598
4 *Four Prentices* late 11th C (William I)	4 *James IV*	1588–92	4 *Look About You*	1600
5 *Look About You* late 12th C (Henry II)	5 *Four Prentices*	c. 1594	5 *Poetaster*	1602
6 *Famous Victories* early 15th C (Henry V)	6 *Look About You*	1595–99	6 *Faustus*	1604
7 *Picture* mid 15th C [?] (Wladyslaw III)	7 *Poetaster*	1601	7 *Eastward Ho*	1605
8 *Faustus* late 15th C (Pope Adrian VI)	8 *Fair Maid*	c. 1601–02 (?)	8 *Fair Maid*	1607
9 *James IV* early 16th C (James IV)	9 *Eastward Ho*	1605	9 *Two Maids*	1609
10 *Duchess* 1504 (see II.iii. 57)	10 *Two Maids*	1607–08 (?)	10 *If This Be Not*	1612

11 *Women Beware* 1580s (Bianca Capello)	11 *If This Be Not*	1611–12	11 *Four Prentices*	1615
12 *Two Maids* 1580s (John Smith)	12 *Duchess*	1614	12 *Duchess*	1623
13 *Fair Maid* 1601–02	13 *Women Beware*	c. 1613–21	13 *Picture*	1630
14 *Eastward Ho* 1605	14 *Sea Voyage*	1622	14 *Bird in Cage*	1633
15 *If This Be Not* 1611–12	15 *Picture*	1629	15 *Sea Voyage*	1647
16 *Sea Voyage* 1622	16 *Bird in Cage*	1633	16 *Fatal Contract*	1653
17 *Bird in Cage* 1633	17 *Fatal Contract*	1638–39	17 *Women Beware*	1657

Any anthology is haunted by the ghosts of the many other anthologies it might have been. Users of this one will undoubtedly, and quickly, arrive at their own ideas of which other plays ought to have been included, which could have been left out, and how the principles of selection or the arrangement of the contents could have more effectively represented a new view of the field. To the extent that this anthology is successful in what it sets out to do, it will be in its ability to provide reliable, readable texts of a wide range of interesting, under-studied plays that will broaden and deepen the student's, or theater-practitioner's, or scholar's understanding of the drama of Shakespeare and his contemporaries. All of us who have worked on the volume have approached it as an exciting experiment. We assume that making these plays available in this form will precipitate interesting and productive changes in our understanding of early modern drama, but it is hard to predict what these changes will be. For the changes to occur at all, it will be necessary (to adapt a phrase from the editors of the 1623 Shakespeare Folio) simply to read the plays, and read them again.

***

Like the principles of selection and the table of contents, the editorial principles used to produce the texts in this volume were varied and eclectic. No attempt has been made to establish definitive texts. Editors generally worked from a single exemplar, and in many cases this was a facsimile; each editor indicates the copy-text for his or her edition, and the extent of any collation, in his or her critical introduction. Emendations of the copy-text are recorded in glosses only when they have substantive bearing upon the passage in question.

Different plays make different demands upon both editors and readers, and so there is necessarily some variation across the volume, especially in the presentation of paratextual material (e.g. lists of dramatis personae, authors' epistles, etc.) and in the extent and style of glosses. Stage directions are for the most part handled uniformly, as are act and scene divisions: square brackets are used to indicate when the editor has inserted something that is not in, or has otherwise substantively altered, the copy-text. Indications for words spoken "aside," when they are given in the original texts, are often given in the right-hand margin, rather than before the speech in question; for the most part, this textual feature has been preserved throughout the volume even as editorial asides are presented in the usual way. Important local variations in the handling of stage directions are indicated, as necessary, in the critical introductions.

One of the most pervasive verbal features of early modern texts is the "oath," that is, mild or strong interjections such as "marry" (a compressed form of "by the Virgin Mary"), "God's pity" ("by God's pity"),"Zounds" ("by God's wounds"), "'Slight" ("by God's light"), etc. In order to avoid repetition, we have left these oaths unglossed except in places where they might be difficult to interpret in elided form (e.g. "'Snails" means "by God's nails," i.e. the nails that fastened Christ to the cross). Readers interested in how oaths contributed to the dramatic character of early modern plays might find it useful to read Lucy Munro's essay "'Sblood!': Hamlet's oaths and the editing of Shakespeare's Plays," in *Shakespeare Survey* 70 (2017) 123–34.

All citations of Shakespeare's plays and poems in the introductions and glosses, unless otherwise noted, are from *The Complete Pelican Shakespeare*, edited by Stephen Orgel and A. R. Braunmuller (Penguin, 2002). Unless otherwise noted, all citations of playwrights other than Shakespeare are from *English Renaissance Drama: A Norton Anthology*, edited by David Bevington, Lars Engle, Katharine Eisaman Maus, and Eric Rasmussen (Norton, 2002), with the following exceptions: John Fletcher, *The Mad Lover*, edited by Robert Kean Turner in *The Dramatic Works in the Beaumont and Fletcher Canon*, edited by Fredson Bowers, vol. V (Cambridge, 1982); Christopher Marlowe, *Tamburlaine the Great, Part II*, in *Tamburlaine, Parts One and Two*, edited by Anthony Dawson (Bloomsbury, 2008); and George Peele, *The Battle of Alcazar*, edited by J. Yoklavich in *The Life and Works of George Peele*, edited by C. T. Prouty, vol. II (Yale, 1961).

1 Thomas Preston, *Cambises*

First performed 1560–61?

First printed 1570

Edited by James Siemon

Cambises is either the very first Elizabethan tragedy or among the first. It may have been performed during the Christmas Season of 1560–61 if it is the "huf suff and ruf" offered at Court; it was in print by 1570 (Bevington 60). Two later editions (Q2 c. 1585, Q3 c. 1595) and references to performance c. 1609 suggest enduring popularity. Such apparent popularity should be weighed against the mockery directed its way by professional dramatists, including Shakespeare. Whatever its mixed reputation, *A lamentable tragedy, mixedful of pleasant mirth, conteyning the life of Cambises King of Percia* had much to contribute to later English drama.

In the late 1590s George Chapman, in *An Humorous Day's Mirth*, parodied the stiff dialogue and allegorical characters of *Cambises*: his witty character Lemot evokes "an old fashion play" with "an old King" addressing others "very learnedly" as "my counsell graue, and you my noble peeres" (see Edelman 195). That same year, Shakespeare mocked *Cambises* for histrionic extremity: Falstaff, with reddened eyes, declaims "in King Cambyses' vein" (see *1 Henry IV* II.iv. 373–4 and compare to *Cambises* x. 93–4). The play staged by the artisans of *A Midsummer Night's Dream* mimics *Cambises*'s mix of comic and serious elements, its fourteen-syllable, rhyming lines, and its stagey violence. Mocking Preston's title, the mechanicals announce "tragical mirth" (V.i. 57), while Bottom's ridiculous death throes recall King Cambises's own sword-impaled demise:

> Come, tears, confound,
> Out, sword, and wound
> The pap of Pyramus:
> Ay, that left pap
> Where heart doth hop.
> *[Stabs himself.]*
> Thus die I, thus, thus, thus.
> Now am I dead,
> Now am I fled,
> My soul is in the sky.
> Tongue, lose thy light,
> Moon, take thy flight. *[Exit Moonshine.]*
> Now die, die, die, die, die. *[Dies.]*
> (*Dream* V.i. 290–301)

> KING I feel myself a-dying now; of life bereft am I,
> And death hath caught me with his dart; for want of blood I spy.
> Thus gasping here on ground I lie; for nothing I do care.
> A just reward for my misdeeds my death doth plain declare.
> *Here let him quake and stir.*
> (*Cambises* xi. 37–40)

It was easy to mock, but *Cambises*'s treatment of genre, action, spectacle, language, and even moral complexity was also a resource for the great Elizabethan tragic dramatists.

To begin with genre. Like its narrative contemporary, the *Mirror for Magistrates* (1559), *Cambises* depicts a historical ruler. And, like its dramatic contemporary, the tragedy of *Gorboduc* (performed 1562), *Cambises* represents conflicts involving tyranny, justice, and counsel. But *Cambises* violates virtually all of Sir Philip Sidney's neo-classical standards, portraying not "one action," but events over "many dayes," mingling "Kinges and Clownes," and "representing" such things as "cannot be shewed." "Stately speeches" adjoin comical "scurrilitie" and "doltishness" (see Sidney, *Defense of Poesy*, 1595). Nearly 500 lines of Preston's 1250-line play pass before we encounter Cambises's "odious" acts and the "lamentable pathos" of his victims. Thus, as with Shakespeare's Macbeth, a "noble" protagonist reveals a dark side. We are warned—by the Prologue and by Shame—but until midway through Scene v, we see an effective military leader who follows good counsel and administers justice. Then, abruptly, Cambises defies counsel, drinks heavily, and wantonly slaughters a child.

The play stages the extreme violence of its sources—flaying, skewering with an arrow, bloody stabbing, and bleeding to death—but it is a comical character, "*the Vice*" Ambidexter, who weaves everything, including the tragic events, together. Ostensibly an allegorical embodiment of evil double-dealing, Ambidexter does far more than practice evil or catalyze it in others. Onstage for nearly as many lines (436) as the protagonist (604), Ambidexter resembles Vice characters in morality plays who prompt characters to evil. Also like the traditional Vice, Ambidexter steps outside the action proper to address the audience with witty banter, with warnings about a pickpocket, or with barbed commentary. But he also contributes substantially to a moral complexity that anticipates later Elizabethan drama. Despite its sermonizing Prologue and moral personifications, the play enlists Ambidexter in its provision of contradictory evaluations and perspectives through structural parallels, ambiguities, and ambivalences.

Consider how *Cambises* treats "war the manly art." Scene i acclaims the "manly acts" of Cambises's knights, his own "manly Mars's heart," and his "manly" military campaign (i. 1–49). Yet within a dozen lines of the king's heroic departure to martial drumbeats, Ambidexter enters in ridiculous mock-armor, boasting "To be a man my deeds shall [me] declare" and naming a snail, a butterfly, and a fly as adversaries. (ii. 8–14). "To conquest these fellows the man I will play" he promises (17), predicting that we "shall see" the fly "thrust . . . through the mouth" (16; on the play's martial satire, see Hayes, 57–73). The abrupt shift from heroic admiration to burlesque is surprising, but we next witness yet another—and different—parody. Instead of conquering a fly, Ambidexter brawls with three of Cambises's soldiers; and ultimately, a female vanquishes the swaggering men. Ambidexter "*run[s]*" away "*for fear*" of her "thrust" (iii. 7); Snuf "*fling[s] down his sword and buckler*" to "*run*"; Ruf "*fall[s]*" to the ground pleading for mercy as Meretrix "*falleth upon him and beat[s] him and taketh away his weapon*" (ii. 140 SD).

Thus, in character, language, and action *Cambises* provides irreverent counter-perspectives on the gendered values of its heroical opening. Laughter encourages subversive comparisons between national "honor" and boasting truculence, martial manliness and cowardly aggression, aristocratic war and brawling "*ruffians*," with a character named "whore" ending up on top. A similar reversal of male dominance occurs among the rustics of Scene viii, though without the martial overtones, as "Marian May-be-good" ends the men's stupid quarrel with her broom, calls Ambidexter out for failing to intervene "like a man," and wrestles Ambidexter into yielding her "mastery." Preston's dramaturgy anticipates later plays that subject the aspirations, actions, and language of high characters to low parody. In Marlowe's *Doctor Faustus*, for example, the learned protagonist's pursuit "Of power, of honor, of omnipotence" and his lyrical praise of Helen of Troy are juxtaposed with ignorant servants mangling magical spells, attempting to dominate each other, and offering to trade their souls for a warm meal or for sex. In Shakespeare's *Measure for Measure*, bumbling constables, sketchy gallants, and shifty brothel employees make a comical hash of the main characters' language and attitudes concerning law, justice and sexual morality.

Cambises's parodic comedy suggests some of the play's structural and thematic complexity, but further complexities accompany its spectacular tragic violence. Ignoring classical restraint, the play's polyvalent treatment of stage violence anticipates Thomas Kyd's *Spanish Tragedy*, Marlowe's *Edward II*, or Shakespeare's *Titus Andronicus* and *King Lear*. Preston's first audiences might have witnessed graphic violence in biblical mystery plays. But mystery plays came to their market squares with well-established expectations. By contrast, the stage violence of *Cambises* must have been shocking when first encountered in court, inn yard, dining hall, or academic chamber. Suddenly, right in front of us, Sisamnes is "*flay[ed] . . . with a false skin*"; then Praxaspes's child is "*sh[ot]*" with an arrow, his heart displayed "here" (v. 112–210). Smirdis's stage blood "springs out on the ground" from "*divers places*" (vii. 17–24); "*bleeding*" Cambises "*quake[s] and stir[s]*" (xi. 26 SD; xi. 40 SD). Later playgoers would see Kyd's Hieronimo spitting out his severed tongue, Marlowe's Edward anally penetrated with a hot poker, Shakespeare's Lavinia carrying her father's severed hand in her mouth, and Gloucester's eyes plucked out. But beyond shock and awe, the extreme spectacle of *Cambises* also conveyed multiple thematic significances.

The murder of Smirdis straightforwardly embodies Cambises's tyranny—enacted by the already bloodied "Cruelty" and "Murder." Complications arise, however, with the involvement of Ambidexter. Like other Vices, Ambidexter's moral functions co-exist with his role as comedian. Thus, he prompts Cambises to murder Smirdis, invites us to "weep" at this "wicked deed," but then abruptly directs us instead to "laugh" about it (viii. 1–15). This conjunction of evil tempter, moralizer, and sardonic joker anticipates Shakespeare's Richard III, who similarly tempts, moralizes, weeps fake tears, and invites us to laugh with him, encouraging amoral enjoyment of the misery he incites.

As in Marlowe's *Faustus*, the protagonist's ultimate demise has been predicted by a prologue but remains fraught with ambiguities about agency and causality. Marlowe tells us that Faustus will fall as a result of his "self-conceit" in aspiring to "mount above his reach" but also that the "heavens conspired" his overthrow (*Doctor Faustus* Prologue 20–22). Preston's Prologue suggests that Cambises will either "fall . . . like Icarus" pursuing his own "will," or "Else" he will perish like a fish caught by "subtle bait" (21–8). These alternative causal narratives are compounded by a third: "mighty Jove" will justly punish with "what measure the king did mete" (*Cambises* Prologue 29–33). Cambises's downfall offers no definitive single reading: Ambidexter's offhanded hunch that Cambises "hath shed so much blood that his will be shed" is immediately followed by Cambises's entry proclaiming himself wounded by "chance," before concluding his death a "just reward for my misdeeds" (xi. 24–40). Self-destructive aspiration, divine meddling, mere chance, or just deserts? It is left to us to decide—or not. As with Shakespeare's *Hamlet,* discordant commentary surrounds the protagonist's demise. Ambidexter offers a surprising, perfunctory, lament—"Alas, good King. Alas, he is gone"—before fleeing in fear of arrest. Three lords affirm his death a "just reward" from "God above" but then grant Cambises "princely burial" (xi. 45–63) despite his "misdeeds." Is Hamlet's death due to "accidental judgements," or divinely ordained by "special providence" (V.ii. 368, 197–8)? Does he any more merit burial "like a soldier" than Cambises deserves "princely" interment? Both plays raise more questions—about agency, fate, chance, and divinity—than they resolve.

The most suggestive treatment of violence occurs in *Cambises*'s fifth scene, where spectacular acts of flaying, child murder, and evisceration are accompanied by verbal techniques borrowed from Senecan drama. The play stages extremities that Seneca's *Thyestes* had only evoked verbally, but with the insistent iteration of the term "heart" and its cognates (twenty-four times in Scene v; over ninety times throughout), Preston adopts a Senecan technique of verbal emphasis that appears prominently in Shakespeare's *King John* (eyes), *Titus Andronicus* (hands) and *Richard III* (heart) (see Jones, 267–9). Scene v also displays structural symmetries that anticipate Shakespeare's paired fathers and sons killed in battle (*3 Henry VI* II.v), but Preston differentiates his father-son pairs remarkably. The flaying of Sisamnes is deemed just by himself, by Praxaspes, and ultimately by his son Otian, who cites it as an ethical example: "O King, to me this is a glass; with grief in it I view/ Example that unto your grace I do not prove untrue" (v. 117–18). This stiff rhetorical exemplarity contrasts with the evolving pathos in the treatment of Praxaspes—first doubting that Cambises would kill his "infant" then pleading that his mother would die if he were slain; then weeping while the boy pleads childishly, "Good Master King, do not shoot at me; my mother loves me best of all" (201); and finally silently enduring her highly wrought lamentations. As moving as this pathos may be, Preston cannot resist the irony of the term "heart," as the child's mother expresses her sorrow: "O my heavy heart!/The spiteful pangs that it sustains would make it in two to part" (231–2). Cambises's drunken archery is grotesquely recalled, even here, as impressive theater.

Like the stagey brutalities of Marlowe's Tamburlaine, the arrow through the heart provides a thrilling violation of Christian or classical mores. But this spectacular assertion of self-will returns when the implications could hardly be more different. Scene ix depicts Cambises's incestuous desire as divinely incited: Venus has Cupid—played by the same boy whom Cambises "*shoot[s]*" in Scene v—"*shoot*" Cambises to "wound his heart in lover's wise" (ix. 8). A willful deity wantonly indulges her power over an unsuspecting victim, repeating in inverted form the play's most striking theatrical moment and matching the tyrant's human barbarity with its own. Cambises's incest may violate laws of god and nature, but whose fault is it? The gods who "kill us for their sport" according to Shakespeare's Gloucester (*King Lear* IV.i. 37–8), or the Revenge who "solicit[s]" Kyd's Hieronimo to undertake deeds of slaughter (*Spanish Tragedy* III.xv. 19), lie not that far beyond the imaginative possibilities built into Preston's dramatic form.

Textual note

This text is based on the first quarto edition of Thomas Preston, *A lamentable tragedy mixed ful of pleasant mirth, conteyning the life of Cambises king of Percia* (London: John Allde, c. 1570; STC 20287; Stationers Register 1569–70). I have used the EEBO version of the Huntington Library Q1. Thanks to Adam Smyth I have also consulted photos of the British Library Q1, which provides a few minor corrections in the final leaves; and the Bodleian Library fragmentary second quarto (London: Edward Allde, c. 1585; STC 20287.5). I have examined the Folger Library third quarto (London: Edward Allde, c. 1595; STC 20288) and I have consulted the modern editions of Robert Carl Johnson and Greg Walker. Quarto texts lack scene divisions. I have added them and silently corrected dittography and turned letters, while modernizing spelling and punctuation and regularizing names of characters and speech headings.

Further reading

Editions

Johnson, Robert Carl (ed.) (1975) *A Critical Edition of Thomas Preston's Cambises*, Salzburg: Salzburg Studies in English Literature.
Walker, Greg G. (ed.) (2014) *Cambyses*, in Greg G. Walker (ed.) *The Oxford Anthology of Tudor Drama*, Oxford: Oxford University Press.

Critical and contextual reading

Altman, Joel B. (1978) *The Tudor Play of Mind*, Berkeley: University of California Press.
Bevington, David (1962) *From Mankind to Marlowe: Growth and Structure in the Popular Drama of Tudor England*, Cambridge: Harvard University Press.

Cartwright, Kent (1999) *Theatre and Humanism: English Drama in the Sixteenth Century*, Cambridge: Cambridge University Press.
Cavanagh, Dermot (2009) "Political Tragedy in the 1560s: *Cambises* and *Gorboduc*," in Mike Pincombe and Cathy Shrank (eds), *The Oxford Handbook of Tudor Literature: 1485–1603*, Oxford: Oxford University Press: 488–503.
Edelman, Charles (2007) "Preston's *Cambyses, King of Persia*," *The Explicator* 65: 194–7.
Feuillerat, Albert (ed.) (1908) *Documents Relating to the Office of the Revels in the Time of Queen Elizabeth*, Louvain: A. Uystpruyst.
Hayes, Douglas W. (2004) *Rhetorical Subversion in Early English Drama*, New York: Peter Lang.
Jones, Emrys (1977) *Origins of Shakespeare*, Oxford: Oxford University Press.
Kaplan, Joel H. (1987) "Reopening King Cambises' Vein," *Essays in Theatre* 5: 103–14.
Murakami, Ineke (2011) *Moral Play and Counterpublic: Transformations in Moral Drama, 1465–1599*, New York: Routledge.
Myers, James Phares, Jr. (1973) "The Heart of King Cambises," *Studies in Philology* 70: 367–76.
Norland, Howard B. (1992–93) "'Lamentable tragedy mixed ful of pleasant mirth': The Enigma of 'Cambises'," *Comparative Drama* 26: 330–43.
Rabkin, Norman (1985) "Stumbling Toward Tragedy," in Peter Erickson and Coppélia Kahn (eds), *Shakespeare's Rough Magic: Renaissance Essays in Honor of C.L. Barber*, Cranbury, NJ: Associated University Presses, 28–49.
Weimann, Robert and Robert Schwartz (1978) *Shakespeare and the Popular Tradition in the Theatre: Studies in the Social Dimension of Dramatic Form and Function*, Baltimore: Johns Hopkins University Press.
Wiggins, Martin (2012) "*Cambyses, King of Persia*," in Martin Wiggins and Catherine Richardson (eds), *British Drama 1533–1642: A Catalogue, vol. 2: 1567–1589*, Oxford: Oxford University Press, 45–9.

Cambises (1560–61?)

Dramatis personae[1]

CAMBISES, *son of Cyrus, later* KING *of Persia*
LADY, *wife of Cambises, later* QUEEN
SMIRDIS, *brother of Cambises*
SISAMNES, *a judge*
OTIAN, *son of Sisamnes*
PRAXASPES, *a lord and counselor of Cambises*
YOUNG CHILD, *son of Praxaspes*
MOTHER, *wife of Praxaspes*
AMBIDEXTER, *the Vice*
HUF, SNUF, RUF, *ruffian soldiers*
MERETRIX, *female companion of Huf, Snuf, and Ruf*
HOB *and* LOB, *rustic countrymen*
MARIAN MAY-BE-GOOD, *wife of Hob*
VENUS, *goddess of Love*
CUPID, *son of Venus*
PROLOGUE
COUNSEL
SMALL ABILITY
SHAME
COMMONS' COMPLAINT
PROOF
TRIAL
EXECUTION
ATTENDANCE
DILIGENCE
CRUELTY
MURDER
PREPARATION
EPILOGUE

Lords and Knights attending CAMBISES, *Waiting Maid attending the* LADY/QUEEN, *suitor to the* LADY/QUEEN

The division of the parts.[2]

COUNSEL, HUF, PRAXASPES, MURDER, LOB, 3 LORD: *For one man*
LORD, RUF, COMMONS' CRY, COMMONS' COMPLAINT,
LORD SMIRDIS, VENUS: *For one man*
KNIGHT, SNUF, SMALL ABILITY, PROOF, EXECUTION,
ATTENDANCE, 2 LORD: *For one man*

1 Dramatis personae: not in the early editions
2 This (incomplete) allocation of roles printed in the early editions suggests that the play might be performed by eight actors

CAMBISES, EPILOGUE: *For one man*
PROLOGUE, SISAMNES, DILIGENCE, CRUELTY, HOB,
PREPARATION, 1 LORD: *For one man*
AMBIDEXTER, TRIAL: *For one man*
MERETRIX, SHAME, OTIAN, MOTHER, LADY, QUEEN: *For one man*
YOUNG CHILD, CUPID: *For one man*

[Prologue]

The PROLOGUE *entereth*

[PROLOGUE] Agathon,[3] he whose counsel wise to princes' weal[4] extended,
By good advice unto a prince three things he hath commended:
First, is that he hath government and ruleth over men;
Secondly, to rule with laws, eke[5] justice, saith he, then;
Thirdly, that he must well conceive,[6] he may not always reign.
Lo, thus the rule unto a prince Agathon squarèd plain.[7]
Tully the wise,[8] whose sapience in volumes great doth tell,
Who in wisdom in that time did many men excel,
"A prince," saith he, "is of himself a plain and speaking law;[9]
The law, a schoolmaster divine"[10]—this by his rule I draw.
The sage and witty[11] Seneca[12] his words thereto did frame:[13]
"The honest exercise of kings, men will ensue the same;[14]
But contrariwise, if that a king abuse his kingly seat,
His ignomy[15] and bitter shame in fine[16] shall be more great."
In Persia there reigned a king, who Cyrus hight[17] by name,
Who did deserve, as I do read, the lasting blast of Fame;[18]
But he, when sisters three[19] had wrought to shear his vital thread,
As heir due,[20] to take the crown Cambises did proceed.
He in his youth was trainèd up by trace of[21] virtue's lore;[22]
Yet, being king, did clean[23] forget his perfect race before;[24]
Then, cleaving[25] more unto his will, such vice did imitate

3 1 Agathon: Athenian tragedian (died 401 BC); the passage closely translates his widely cited precepts
4 1 princes' weal: kings' wealth or welfare, and/or kings' virtuous behavior; also referring to realms (weals) ruled by kings
5 4 eke: also
6 5 conceive: realize
7 6 squarèd plain: clearly directed
8 7 Tully the wise: Marcus Tullius Cicero (106–43 BC), highly regarded philosopher and rhetorician
9 9 A ruler's word is the law; adapting a phrase from Cicero's *De Legibus*: "the magistrate is a speaking law"
10 10 The law a schoolmaster divine: law is a divinely instituted instructor
11 11 witty: wise
12 11 Seneca: Lucius Annaeus Seneca (Roman Stoic Philosopher; died 65 AD); playwright, philosopher, tutor and advisor to the emperor Nero
13 11 his words thereto did frame: directed his words by the same principle
14 12 Virtuous royal deeds will prompt subjects to similar acts. There is no known source for these "words" of Seneca, though the sentiments could be found in Senecan works (e.g. *de Clementia* concerning the Emperor Augustus, the "good prince")
15 14 ignomy: dishonor (shortened form of "ignominy")
16 14 in fine: ultimately; or in sum
17 15 who Cyrus hight: who was called Cyrus. Cyrus the Great (c. 590–c. 529 BC), father of Cambises, was the conqueror and founder of the Achaemenid Empire, centered in Persia
18 16 lasting blast of Fame: memorialized by the blast (sound of a trumpet) of Fame
19 17 sisters three: the fates, goddesses in Greek and Roman mythology who spin and cut the "vital thread" to determine one's life and death
20 18 heir due: lineal inheritor (of the crown)
21 19 by trace of: in the path of; or, possibly within the straps of, as in the ropes ("traces") that bind a draught animal to the cart it draws
22 19 lore: doctrine or teaching
23 20 clean: completely
24 20 race before: ancestors; or Cambises's own previous deeds
25 21 cleaving: adhering

As one of Icarus his kind,[26] forewarning[27] then did hate,
Thinking that none could him dismay, ne[28] none his facts[29] could see.
Yet at the last[30] a fall he took, like Icarus to be;
Else,[31] as the fish which oft had take[32] the pleasant bait from hook,
In safe[33] did spring and pierce the streams when fisher fast[34] did look[35]
To hoist up from the wat'ry waves unto the drièd land,
Then scaped,[36] at last by subtle bait come to the fisher's hand;
Even so this King Cambises here, when he had wrought his will,[37]
Taking delight the innocent his guiltless blood[38] to spill,
Then mighty Jove[39] would not permit to prosecute offence;[40]
But, what measure the king did mete, the same did Jove commence[41]
To bring to end with shame his race:[42] two years he did not reign.
His cruelty we will dilate[43] and make the matter plain.
Craving that this may suffice now your patience to win,
I take my way. Behold, I see the players coming in.

[Exit]

FINIS

[Scene i]

First enter CAMBISES *the King,* KNIGHT[, LORD,] *and* COUNSELOR

CAMBISES My counsel grave and sapient,[44] with lords of legal train:[45]
Attentive ears towards bend[46] and mark what shall be sayn.[47]
So you likewise, my valiant knight, whose manly acts doth fly
By bruit[48] of Fame, that sounding trump doth pierce the azure sky.
My sapient words, I say, perpend,[49] and so your skill dilate.[50]
You know that Mors[51] vanquishèd hath Cyrus, that king of state,
And I by due inheritance possess that princely crown,

26 22 As one ... his kind: one resembling Icarus, legendary son who ignored his father Daedalus's warnings and flew too high on his artificial wings; Icarus approached the sun, the wax melted, and he drowned in the Aegean Sea
27 forewarning: advice, counsel
28 23 ne: nor
29 23 facts: actions, deeds
30 24 at the last: finally
31 25 Else: i.e. or else, alternatively
32 25 take: taken
33 26 safe: safety
34 26 fast: readily, with alacrity
35 26 look: hope, intend
36 28 scaped: escaped
37 29 wrought his will: done what he had (perversely) intended to do
38 30 innocent his guiltless blood: blood of the innocent
39 31 Jove: Jupiter, king of the ancient Roman gods
40 31 permit to prosecute offence: omit to punish [his] offence
41 32 By the same measure that Cambises dealt with others, so Jove acted (against him)
42 33 race: life, mode of living
43 34 dilate: set forth at length
44 1 sapient: wise
45 1 of legal train: trained in the law
46 2 towards bend: bend towards me
47 2 sayn: said
48 4 bruit: report, din
49 5 perpend: ponder
50 5 skill dilate: knowledge increase
51 6 Mors: Death

Ruling by sword of mighty force in place of great renown.[52]
You know and often have heard tell my father's worthy facts:
A manly Mars's[53] heart he bare, appearing by his acts.
And what? Shall I to ground let fall my father's golden praise?
No, no, I mean for[54] to attempt this fame more large to raise.[55]
In that[56] that I, his son, succeed his kingly seat as due,[57]
Extend your counsel unto me in that I ask of you.
I am the King of Persia, a large and fertile soil;
The Egyptians against us repugn as[58] varlets,[59] slave and vile.[60]
Therefore I mean with Mars's heart, with wars them to frequent,[61]
Them to subdue as captives mine. This is my heart's intent.
So shall I win honor's delight, and praise of me shall go.[62]
My counsel, speak, and, lordings[63] eke,[64] is it not best do so?
COUNSEL O puissant[65] King, your blissful words deserves abundant praise
That you in this do go about[66] your father's fame to raise.
O blissful day, that king so young such profit should conceive,
His father's praise and his to win from those that would deceive.
Sure, my true and sovereign King, I fall before you prest
Answer to give[67] as duty mine, in that your grace request.
If that your heart addicted[68] be the Egyptians to convince,[69]
Through Mars's aid the conquest won, then deed of happy[70] prince
Shall pierce the skies unto the throne of the supernal seat,[71]
And merit there a just reward of Jupiter the Great.
But then your grace must not turn back from this pretencèd will;[72]
For to proceed in virtuous life, employ endeavor still.[73]
Extinguish vice, and in that cup[74] to drink have no delight.
To martial feats and kingly sport fix all your whole delight.
KING My counsel grave, a thousand thanks with heart I do you render,
That you my case so prosperous entirely do tender.[75]
I will not swerve from those your steps whereto you would me train.[76]
—But now, my lord and valiant knight, with words give answer plain:
Are you content with me to go, the Mars's games[77] to try?

52 8 place of great renown: an office of great honor
53 10 Mars: the Roman god of war
54 12 mean for: intend
55 12 more large to raise: extend even further
56 13 In that: because
57 13 as due: by rightful succession
58 16 us repugn as: contend against us by insulting us as
59 16 varlets: menial male servants
60 16 slave and vile: abject and debased
61 17 frequent: visit repeatedly
62 19 go: spread
63 20 lordings: men of high rank or office (e.g. the Knight) as well as lords (such as the Lord)
64 20 eke: too, also
65 21 puissant: powerful
66 22 go about: undertake
67 25–6 prest/Answer to give: ready to give an answer
68 27 addicted: devoted
69 27 convince: overcome
70 28 happy: successful
71 29 supernal seat: heavenly throne
72 31 pretencèd will: professed intention
73 32 employ endeavor still: strive constantly
74 33 cup: i.e. the cup of vice
75 36 tender: care for
76 37 train: lead
77 39 the Mars's games: i.e. military exploits

LORD Yea, peerless prince, to aid your grace myself will live and die.
KNIGHT And I, for my ability,[78] for fear will not turn back,
But as the ship against the rocks, sustain and bide the wrack.[79]
KING O willing hearts, a thousand thanks I render unto you.
Strike up your drums[80] with courage great; we will march forth even now.
COUNSEL Permit, O King, few words to hear, my duty serves[81] no less;
Therefore give leave to counsel thine[82] his mind[83] for to express.
KING Speak on, my counsel; what it be,[84] you shall have favor mine.
COUNSEL Then will I speak unto your grace, as duty doth me bind.
Your grace doth mean for to attempt of war the manly art;
Your grace therein may hap[85] receive with others for your part
The dint[86] of death: in those affairs all persons are alike.
The heart courageous often times his detriment doth seek.
It's best therefore for to permit a ruler of your land
To sit and judge with equity, when things of right are scanned.[87]
KING My grace doth[88] yield to this your talk; to be thus now it shall:
My knight, therefore prepare yourself Sisamnes for to call.
A judge he is of prudent skill; even he shall bear the sway[89]
In absence mine, when from the land I do depart my way.
KNIGHT Your knight before your grace, even here, himself hath ready prest,[90]
With willing heart for to fulfill, as your grace made request. *Exit*
COUNSEL Pleaseth[91] your grace, I judge of him to be a man right fit,
For he is learnèd in the law, having the gift of wit.
In your grace's precinct,[92] I do not view for it a meeter[93] man.
His learning is of good effect,[94] bring proof thereof I can.
I do not know what is his life,[95] his conscience hid[96] from me;
I doubt not but[97] the fear of God before his eyes to be.[98]
LORD Report declares he is[99] a man that to himself is nigh,[100]
One that favoreth much the world, and too much sets thereby.[101]
But this I say of certainty: if he your grace succeed
In your absence but[102] for a while, he will be warned indeed

78 41 ability: strength, capacity
79 42 bide the wrack: endure shipwreck
80 44 Strike up your drums: it is unclear to whom this command to begin drumming for a march is directed—that is, whether off-stage musicians or on-stage characters play the drums; but the effect of interrupted motion is dramatically registered in Counsel's abrupt interjection at line 45
81 45 serves: prompts, demands
82 46 counsel thine: your counsel
83 46 mind: opinion
84 47 what: whatever
85 50 hap: chance to
86 51 dint: stroke, blow
87 54 when things . . . are scanned: when matters of justice are to be considered
88 55 My grace doth: i.e. "I do"; for the first of many times in the play, Cambises here employs a royal title more typically found in the second and third person forms ("your grace" or "his grace") to refer to himself
89 57 bear the sway: govern
90 59 himself hath ready prest: has eagerly prepared himself
91 61 Pleaseth: i.e. if it might please
92 63 precinct: realm
93 63 meeter: more fitting, appropriate
94 64 His learning . . . good effect: i.e. he is well-accomplished
95 65 life: manner of living
96 65 hid: being hidden
97 66 doubt not but: have no doubt that
98 66 fear of . . . to be: reverence for God is immediately present in him
99 67 Report declares he is: his reputation is
100 67 to himself is nigh: is self-interested, selfish
101 68 too much sets thereby: values (the world and worldly things) too highly
102 70 but: even only

No injustice for to frequent,[103] no partial[104] judge to prove,[105]
But rule all things with equity,[106] to win your grace's love.
KING Of that he shall a warning have, my hests[107] for to obey:
Great punishment for his offence against him will I lay.

[*Enter* SISAMNES]

COUNSEL Behold, I see him now aggress[108] and enter into place.
SISAMNES O puissant Prince and mighty King, the gods preserve your grace.
Your grace's message came to me, your will purporting forth;[109]
With grateful mind I it received, according to mine oath.
Erecting[110] then myself with speed before your grace's eyes,
The tenor[111] of your princely will from you for to agnise.[112]
KING Sisamnes, this the[113] whole effect,[114] the which for you I sent:
Our mind[115] it is to elevate you to great preferment.
My grace and gracious counsel eke hath chose you for this cause:[116]
In judgment you do office bear, which have the skill in laws.
We think that you accordingly by Justice' rule will deal,
That for offence none shall have cause, of wrong you to appeal.[117]
SISAMNES Abundant thanks unto your grace for this benignity;
To you, his counsel, in like case, with lords of clemency.
What so[118] your grace to me permits, if I therein offend,
Such execution[119] then commence, and use it to this end:
That all other by that my deed example so may take
To admonish them to flee the same by fear it may them make.[120]
KING Then according to your words, if you therein offend,
I assure you even from my breast, correction shall extend.[121]
From Persia I mean to go into the Egypt land,
Them to convince by force of arms and win the upper hand.
While I therefore absent shall be, I do you full permit,
As governor in this my right, in that estate[122] to sit,
For to detect and eke correct those that abuse my grace.
This is the total of my will. Give answer in this case.
SISAMNES Unworthy much, O Prince, am I and for this gift unfit;
But sith[123] that it hath pleased your grace that I in it must sit,

103 71 No injustice for to frequent: to practice no injustice
104 71 partial: biased
105 71 prove: turn out to be
106 72 equity: impartiality
107 73 hests: commands
108 75 aggress: approach
109 77 your will purporting forth: expressing your will
110 79 Erecting: rousing
111 80 tenor: substance
112 80 agnise: learn
113 81 this the: i.e. this is the
114 81 effect: sum, reason
115 82 mind: intention
116 83 cause: reason
117 86 appeal: accuse
118 89 What so: whatever
119 90 execution: punishment
120 91–2 That all . . . them make: that all others may be admonished by my example and avoid such deeds for fear (of similar punishment)
121 94 I assure you from my very heart that punishment shall follow
122 98 estate: office
123 102 sith: since

I do avouch unto my death,[124] according to my skill,
With equity for to observe your grace's mind and will,
And nought[125] from it to swerve indeed, but sincerely to stay;[126]
Else let me taste the penalty, as I before did say.
KING Well then, of this authority, I give you full possession.
SISAMNES And I will it fulfill also,[127] as I have made profession.
KING My counsel, then let us depart, a final stay to make;[128]
To Egypt land now forth with speed, my voyage will I take.
Strike up your drums us to rejoice to hear the warlike sound.
Stay you here, Sisamnes; judge, and look well to your bound.[129] *Exeunt* KING, LORD *and* COUNSEL
SISAMNES Even now the king hath me extolled, and set me up aloft.[130]
Now may I wear the brodered guard[131] and lie in down bed soft.
Now may I purchase house and land, and have all at my will.[132]
Now may I build a princely place,[133] my mind for to fulfill.
Now may I abrogate[134] the law, as I shall think it good.
If anyone me now offend, I may demand his blood.
According to the proverb old, my mouth I will up-make.[135]
Now it doth lie all in my hand,[136] to leave or else to take,
To deal with justice to my bound,[137] and so to live in hope.
But oftentimes the birds be gone, while one for nest doth grope.[138]
Do well or ill, I dare avouch, some evil on me will speak—
No, truly.[139] Yet I do not mean the king's precepts to break.
To place[140] I mean for to return my duty to fulfill.

Exit

[Scene ii]

Enter the VICE[141] [AMBIDEXTER] *with an old capcase*[142] *on his head, an old pail about his hips for harness,*[143] *a scummer*[144] *and a potlid by his side and a rake on his shoulder*

AMBIDEXTER Stand away, stand away, for the passion of God![145]

124 103 avouch unto my death: swear upon my death
125 105 nought: not at all
126 105 stay: remain steadfast
127 108 also: in the same manner
128 109 a final stay to make: i.e. to put a final stop to (the acts of the Egyptians)
129 112 look well to your bound: pay careful attention to your oath
130 113 aloft: i.e. in high authority
131 114 brodered guard: embroidered ornamental border or trimming of a garment; often associated with fashion or rank
132 115 all at my will: everything as I desire
133 116 place: palace
134 117 abrogate: reject, deny
135 119 my mouth . . . up-make: fill up my mouth; i.e. have all I want
136 120 it doth . . . my hand: i.e. it's up to me alone
137 121 to my bound: according to my charge
138 122 i.e. opportunity is often elusive
139 123–4 Do well . . . No, truly: whether I perform well or badly, I wager that some will criticize me—No, I mean it
140 125 place: office, role. The sense may be ambiguous, since "place" appears to refer to physical dwelling at line 116; here the sense seems to be political and ethical, reaffirming Sisamnes's commitment to orderly behavior
141 0 SD VICE: character in morality plays who represents a particular vice (see lines 24–5 for Ambidexter's particular vice); also used for a jester at revels
142 0 SD capcase: traveling bag
143 0 SD harness: armor
144 0 SD scummer: shallow ladle for skimming scum or froth from the surface of a liquid; records of Edward VI's court revels include bills "for one vyces dagger & a ladle with a bable pendant [i.e. hanging bauble] . . . garnished & delivered to the Lorde of mysrules foole" and "for a harness of paper boordes" to be worn in a mock combat (Feuillerat, 1908: 73)
145 1 for the passion of God: by the suffering and crucifixion of Jesus (an oath)

Harnessèd I am, preparèd to the field.[146]
I would have been content at home to have bod,[147]
But I am sent forth with my spear and shield.[148]
I am appointed[149] to fight against a snail,[150]
And Wilken Wren[151] the ancient[152] shall bear.
I doubt not but against him[153] to prevail;
To be a man my deeds shall declare.
If I overcome him, then a butterfly takes his part;[154]
His weapon must be a blue speckled hen;
But you shall see me overthrow him with a fart,
So without conquest he shall go home again.
If I overcome him, I must fight with a fly,
And a black pudding[155] the fly's weapon must be.
At the first blow on the ground he shall lie;
I will be sure to thrust him through the mouth to the knee.
To conquest[156] these fellows the man I will play.[157]
Ha, ha, ha! Now ye will make me to smile,
To see if I can all men beguile.[158]
Ha, my name? My name would you so fain[159] know?
Yea, iwis,[160] shall ye, and that with all speed—
I have forgot it; therefore I cannot show[161]—
Ah, ah, now I have it! I have it indeed.
My name is Ambidexter.[162] I signify[163] one
That with both hands finely[164] can play:
Now with King Cambises and by and by[165] gone.
Thus do I run this and that way;
For while[166] I mean with a soldier to be,
Then give I a leap to[167] Sisamnes the judge.
I dare avouch ye shall his destruction see.
To all kind of estates[168] I mean for to trudge.
Ambidexter? Nay, he is a fellow if ye knew all—
Cease for a while; hereafter hear more ye shall.

146 2 field: battlefield
147 3 bod: stayed, abided
148 4 spear and shield: i.e. rake and potlid
149 5 appointed: armed
150 5 fight against a snail: combat between an armed braggart soldier and a snail is staged in the anonymous comical interlude *Thersytes* (performed c. 1537; published c. 1561–3)
151 6 Wilken Wren: small bird named "Wilken"
152 6 ancient: martial flag or standard carried by the "ancient-bearer" or ensign
153 7 him: i.e. the snail
154 9 takes his part: seconds him as the next opponent
155 14 black pudding: sausage made from blood and suet
156 17 conquest: conquer
157 17 the man I will play: "to play the man" meant to act according to notions of "manly" character—i.e., bravely, assertively, etc.
158 19 beguile: charm or cheat
159 20 fain: gladly, eagerly
160 21 iwis: certainly (archaic diction)
161 22 show: reveal (his name)
162 24 Ambidexter: double-dealer (literally right-handed on both sides; in legal discourse, one who takes bribes from both sides in a dispute)
163 24 signify: represent, symbolize
164 25 finely: dexterously (i.e. deceptively)
165 26 and by and by: and then soon
166 28 For while: For a time, temporarily
167 29 give I a leap to: I will leap upon
168 31 kind of estates: sorts of people by rank, order. In England there were three estates: Lords Spiritual (i.e. of the church), Lords Temporal (i.e. the nobles), and Commons (i.e. the people)—traditionally, those who pray, those who fight, and those who labor. "Estate" can also be used in a more specialized sense to mean "office" (see i. 98)

Enter three Ruffians,[169] HUF, RUF *and* SNUF *singing*

HUF Gog's[170] flesh and his wounds, these wars rejoice my heart!
By His wounds, I hope to do well for my part.
By Gog's heart, the world shall go evil[171] if I do not shift;[172]
At some old carl's[173] budget[174] I mean for to lift.[175]
RUF By His[176] flesh, nose, eyes and ears,
I will venture,[177] void of all cares.[178]
He is not a soldier that doth fear any doubt[179]
If that he would bring his purpose about.
SNUF Fear that fear list,[180] it shall not be I.
By Gog's wounds, I will make some neck stand awry.[181]
If I lose my share, I swear by Gog's heart,
Then let another take up my part.[182]
HUF Yet I hope to come the richest soldier away.[183]
RUF If a man ask ye, ye may hap[184] to say nay.
SNUF Let all men get what they can, not to leese[185] I hope;
Wheresoever I go, in each corner[186] I will grope.
AMBIDEXTER What and[187] ye run into the corner of some pretty maid?
SNUF To grope there, good fellow, I will not be afraid.
HUF Gog's wounds, what art thou that with us dost mell?[188]
Thou seemest to be a soldier, the truth to tell;
Thou seemest to be harnessèd,[189] I cannot tell[190] how.
I think he came lately from riding some cow.[191]
Such a deformèd slave[192] did I never see.
Ruf, dost thou know him? I pray thee, tell me.
RUF No, by my troth, fellow Huf, I never see him before.
SNUF As for me, I care not if I never see him more.
Come, let us run his arse against the post.
[AMBIDEXTER] Ah, ye slaves, I will be with you at the 'ost![193]
Here let him swinge them about[194]

169 33 SD *Ruffians*: i.e. rough and disreputable people
170 34 Gog's: by God's
171 36 shall go evil: will go badly (for me)
172 36 shift: make provision (for myself); "shift" could also convey the sense of a fraudulent or evasive device or subterfuge
173 37 carl's: base, miserly fellow's
174 37 budget: purse, wallet
175 37 lift: steal
176 38 His: God's
177 39 venture: take the risk
178 39 void of all cares: recklessly
179 40 doubt: danger, uncertainty
180 42 Fear that fear list: let those who want to fear be afraid
181 43 make some neck stand awry: break someone's neck
182 45 take up my part: grab my portion (of the booty)
183 46 come the richest soldier away: end up as the richest soldier
184 47 hap: happen
185 48 leese: lose
186 49 in each corner: i.e. everywhere
187 50 and: if
188 52 mell: meddle
189 54 harnessèd: armored
190 54 tell: express
191 55 riding some cow: riding a cow like a horse; proverbially suggesting unfitness—also sometimes used satirically to depict inappropriate or ineffectual behavior
192 56 deformèd slave: unsightly, contemptible person (cf. i. 16)
193 61 I will . . . the 'ost: I will be familiar with you (to "be at host" means to be housed)
194 61 SD swinge them about: thrash them, whirl them around

Ah, ye knaves, I will teach ye how ye shall me deride.
Out of my sight! I can ye not abide.
Now, goodman pouch-mouth,[195] I am a slave with you?[196]
Now have at ye afresh again, even now!
Mine arse against the post you will run?
But I will make ye from that saying to turn.[197]
HUF I beseech ye heartily to be content.
RUF I insure[198] you, by mine honesty, no hurt we meant.
Beside that again, we do not know what ye are.
Ye know that soldiers their stoutness will declare;[199]
Therefore, if we have anything[200] offended,
Pardon our rudeness and it shall be amended.
AMBIDEXTER Yea, God's pity, begin ye to entreat me?
Have at ye once again! By the Mass,[201] I will beat ye! *Fight again*
HUF Gog's heart, let us kill him. Suffer[202] no longer. *Draw their swords*
SNUF Thou slave, we will see if thou be the stronger.
RUF Strike off his head at one blow!
That we be soldiers, Gog's heart, let him know.
AMBIDEXTER O the passion of Cod,[203] I have done,[204] by mine honesty.
I will take your part hereafter, verily.
ALL Then content,[205] let us agree.
AMBIDEXTER Shake hands with me, I shake hands with thee.
Ye are full of courtesy, that is the best;
And you take great pain,[206] ye are a mannerly guest.[207]
Why masters, do you not know me? The truth to me tell.
ALL [HUF, SNUF and RUF] No, trust us, not very well.
AMBIDEXTER Why, I am Ambidexter, who many soldiers do love.
HUF Gog's heart, to have thy company needs we must prove.[208]
We must play with both hands with our hostess and host,
Play with both hands and score on the post;[209]
Now and then with our captain for many a delay,[210]
We will not stick[211] with both hands to play.
AMBIDEXTER The honester man ye, ye may me trust.

Enter MERETRIX[212] *with a staff on her shoulder*

MERETRIX What? Is there no lads here that hath a lust

195 64 goodman pouch-mouth: mister big-mouth
196 64 I am . . . with you?: you call me slave?
197 67 from that saying to turn: take those words back
198 69 insure: assure
199 71 their stoutness will declare: will demonstrate their valor
200 72 anything: in any way
201 75 By the mass: an oath by the Eucharist
202 76 Suffer: endure (him)
203 80 Cod: God
204 80 I have done: I quit
205 82 content: (we are) satisfied
206 85 And you take great pain: if you take considerable trouble (i.e. to be courteous)
207 85 mannerly guest: polite person
208 89 to have . . . must prove: with your company we surely will prosper
209 91 score on the post: record our tally by marks cut on a post, i.e. run up debts with innkeepers (whom we will never pay)
210 92 delay: act of procrastination
211 93 stick: hesitate, scruple
212 94 SD MERETRIX: literally, prostitute

To have a passing trull[213] to help at their need?[214]
HUF Gog's heart, she is come, indeed.
What, Mistress Meretrix, by His wounds welcome to me!
MERETRIX What will ye give me, I pray you? Let me see.
RUF By His heart, she looks for gifts by and by.
MERETRIX What, Master Ruf? I cry you mercy.[215]
The last time I was with you I got a broken head
And lay in the street all night for want[216] of a bed.
SNUF Gog's wounds, kiss me, my trull so white![217]
In thee, I swear, is all my delight.
If thou shouldest have had a broken head for my sake,
I would have made his head to ache.
MERETRIX What, Master Ambidexter? Who looked for you?
AMBIDEXTER Mistress Meretrix, I thought not to see you here now.
There is no remedy,[218] at meeting I must have a kiss.
MERETRIX What, man! I will not stick for[219] that, by Gis![220] *Kiss*
AMBIDEXTER So now, gramercy;[221] I pray thee be gone.
MERETRIX Nay soft,[222] my friend, I mean to have one.
Nay soft, I swear, and if[223] ye were my brother,
Before I let go, I will have another. *Kiss, kiss, kiss*
RUF Gog's heart, the whore would not kiss me yet.
MERETRIX If I be a whore, thou art a knave; then it is quit.[224]
HUF But hear'st thou, Meretrix, with who this night wilt thou lie?
MERETRIX With him that giveth the most money.
HUF Gog's heart, I have no money in purse, ne yet[225] in clout.[226]
MERETRIX Then get thee hence and pack,[227] like a lout.[228]
HUF Adieu, like a whore. *Exit* HUF
MERETRIX Farewell, like a knave.
RUF Gog's nails, Mistress Meretrix, now he is gone,
A match[229] ye shall make straight[230] with me:
I will give thee sixpence to lie one night with thee.
MERETRIX Gog's heart, slave, dost thou think I am a sixpenny Jug?[231]
No, wis ye,[232] Jack, I look a little more smug.[233]
SNUF I will give her eighteen pence to serve me first.
MERETRIX Gramercy, Snuf, thou art not the worst.

213 96 trull: prostitute
214 96 help at their need: aid them when necessary
215 101 cry you mercy: beg your pardon
216 103 want: lack
217 104 white: dear, precious
218 110 remedy: alternative
219 111 stick for: refuse
220 111 Gis: Jesus
221 112 gramercy: thank you
222 113 soft: not so fast, wait a second
223 114 and if: even if
224 117 it is quit: we are even
225 120 ne yet: nor also
226 120 clout: (my) clothes
227 121 get thee hence and pack: get out of here, right now
228 121 lout: ill-mannered person; bumpkin
229 125 match: arrangement, bargain
230 125 straight: right away
231 127 Jug: form of "Joan" used as a disparaging term for mistress, i.e. "whore"
232 128 wis ye: know you
233 128 smug: trim, smart

RUF By Gog's heart, she were better be hanged to forsake me and take thee.
SNUF Were she so? That shall we see.
RUF By Gog's heart, my dagger into her I will thrust.
SNUF Ah, ye boy, ye would do it and[234] ye durst.
AMBIDEXTER Peace, my masters, ye shall not fight.
He that draws first, I will him smite.
RUF Gog's wounds, Master Snuf, are ye so lusty?
SNUF Gog's sides, Master Ruf, are ye so crusty?[235]
RUF You may happen to see.
SNUF Do what thou darest to me.

Here draw and fight. Here she must lay on and coil them[236] both; the VICE *must run his way[237] for fear;* SNUF *fling down his sword and buckler,[238] and run his way*

MERETRIX Gog's sides, knaves, seeing[239] to fight ye be so rough,
Defend yourselves, for I will give ye both enough.
I will teach ye how ye shall fall out[240] for me.
Yea, thou slave, Snuf, no more blows wilt thou bide?[241]
To take thy heels a time hast thou spied?[242]
—Thou villain,[243] seeing Snuf is gone away,
A little better I mean thee to pay. *He falleth down; she falleth upon him and beat[s] him and taketh away his weapon*
RUF Alas, good Mistress Meretrix, no more!
My legs, sides, and arms with beating be sore.
MERETRIX Thou a soldier, and lose thy weapon?
Go hence, sir boy; say a woman hath thee beaten.
RUF Good Mistress Meretrix, my weapon let me have;
Take pity on me, mine honesty[244] to save.
If it be known this repulse[245] I sustain,
It will redound to[246] my ignomy[247] and shame.
MERETRIX If thou wilt be my man and wait upon me,
This sword and buckler I will give thee.
RUF I will do all at your commandment;
As servant to you I will be obedient.
MERETRIX Then let me see how before me ye can go.[248]
When I speak to you, ye shall do so:
Off with[249] your cap at place and at board,[250]
"Forsooth,[251] Mistress Meretrix," at every word.
Tut, tut, in the camp such soldiers there be,
One good woman would beat away two or three.

234 134 and: if
235 138 crusty: short-tempered, gruff
236 140 SD *lay on and coil them*: attack vigorously and thrash them
237 140 SD *his way*: away
238 140 SD *buckler*: small round shield
239 141 seeing: seeing that
240 143 fall out: quarrel
241 144 bide: endure
242 145 Have you spotted an opportunity to run away?
243 146 Thou villain: Meretrix now addresses Ruf
244 153 honesty: honor, reputation
245 154 repulse: reproof
246 155 redound to: reflect on to, contribute to
247 155 ignomy: ignominy
248 160 how before . . . can go: how you can conduct yourself as my servant
249 162 Off with: doff
250 162 at place and at board: in the marketplace and at table
251 163 Forsooth: in truth

Well, I am sure customers tarry[252] at home.
Mannerly before,[253] and let us be gone.

Exeunt

[Scene iii]

Enter AMBIDEXTER

AMBIDEXTER O the passion of God! Be they here still or no?
I durst not abide to see her beat them so.
I may say to you I was in such a fright,[254]
Body of me,[255] I see the hair of my head stand upright.
When I saw her so hard upon them lay on,[256]
"O the Passion of God," thought I, "she will be with me anon!"[257]
I made no more ado[258] but avoided the thrust,
And to my legs began for to trust;[259]
And fell a-laughing to myself when I was once gone.
"It is wisdom," quoth I, "by the Mass, to save one!"[260]
Then into this place I intended to trudge,
Thinking to meet Sisamnes the judge.
Behold where he cometh! I will him meet,
And like a gentleman I mean him to greet.

Enter SISAMNES

SISAMNES Since that the king's grace's majesty in office did me set,
What abundance of wealth to me might I get.
Now and then some vantage[261] I achieve; much more yet may I take,
But that[262] I fear unto the king that some[263] complaint will make.
AMBIDEXTER Jesu, Master Sisamnes, you are unwise.
SISAMNES Why so? I pray ye let me agnise.[264]
What, Master Ambidexter, is it you?
Now welcome to me, I make God a vow!
AMBIDEXTER Jesu, Master Sisamnes, with me you are well acquainted.
By me rulers may be trimly painted.[265]
Ye are unwise if ye take not time while ye may;[266]
If ye will not now, when ye would ye shall have nay.[267]
What is he that of you dare make exclamation,
Of your wrong-dealing to make explication?[268]

252 166 tarry: await me
253 167 Mannerly before: walk before me decently
254 3 fright: Q1–Q3 read "flight" here
255 4 Body of me: by my body, a variation on the oath "God's body"
256 5 so hard . . . lay on: beat them so hard
257 6 anon: soon
258 7 made no more ado: did not delay
259 8 And saved myself by running away
260 10 to save one: to look out for oneself
261 17 vantage: advantage, profit
262 18 But that: except for the fact that
263 18 some: some people
264 20 agnise: understand
265 24 trimly painted: accurately represented, pictured
266 25 if ye . . . ye may: if you do not take opportunity when you can
267 26 If you do not act now, when you want to it will not be possible
268 27–8 What is . . . make explication?: who would dare bring accusations, exposing your evil dealing?

Can you not play with both hands and turn with the wind?[269]
SISAMNES Believe me, your words draw deep in my mind.[270]
In color wise[271] unto this day, to bribes I have inclined.
More the same for to frequent, of truth, I am now minded.[272]
Behold, even now[273] unto me suitors do proceed.

[*Enter* SMALL ABILITY]

SMALL ABILITY[274] I beseech you here, good master judge, a poor man's cause to tender.[275]
Condemn me not in wrongful wise[276] that never was offender.
You know right well my right it is;[277] I have not for to give.[278]
You take away from me my due that should my corpse relieve.[279]
The commons[280] of you do complain from them you devocate;[281]
With anguish great and grievous words their hearts do penetrate.
The right you sell unto the wrong, your private gain to win;
You violate the simple man and count it for[282] no sin.
SISAMNES Hold thy tongue, thou prattling knave, and give to me reward;
Else in this wise, I tell thee truth, thy tale will not be heard.
Ambidexter, let us go hence, and let the knave alone.
AMBIDEXTER Farewell, Small Ability, for help now get ye none.
Bribes hath corrupt him good laws to pollute. *Exeunt* [AMBIDEXTER *and* SISAMNES]
SMALL ABILITY A naughty man that will not obey the king's constitute.[283]
With heavy heart I will return[284] till God redress my pain.

Exit

[Scene iv]

Enter SHAME *with a trump black*[285]

SHAME From among the grisly ghosts I come, from tyrants' testy train.[286]
Unseemly[287] Shame, of sooth,[288] I am, procurèd to make plain
The odious facts and shameless deeds that Cambises King doth use:
All piety and virtuous life, he doth it clean[289] refuse;

269 29 turn with the wind: reverse yourself as necessary
270 30 draw deep in my mind: powerfully engage my thoughts
271 31 color wise: cunning deception
272 32 Truly, I now intend to do that more often
273 33 even now: right now
274 34 ABILITY: modernized form of the Q's "Habilitie," meaning capability or capacity for doing something; here possibly referring specifically to authority, wealth, estate, or pecuniary power
275 34 tender: regard or treat with tenderness
276 35 wrongful wise: unjust manner
277 36 right it is: it is my right (to be heard)
278 36 I have . . . to give: I have nothing with which to pay (or bribe)
279 37 my due . . . corpse relieve: my rightful recompense or property that should sustain my body
280 38 commons: common people, i.e. those belonging neither to the nobility nor the gentry
281 38 devocate: meaning uncertain; perhaps make calls or demands (upon); possibly a mistake for "derogate," i.e. disparage
282 41 count it for: consider it
283 47 constitute: ordinance
284 48 return: turn around and leave
285 0 SD *trump black*: black trumpet
286 1 testy train: contentious retinue
287 2 Unseemly: indecent, unbecoming
288 2 of sooth: in truth
289 4 clean: completely, utterly

Lechery and drunkenness, he doth it much frequent;[290]
The tiger's kind[291] to imitate, he hath given full consent.
He nought esteems his counsel grave, ne[292] virtuous bringing-up,[293]
But daily still[294] receives the drink of damnèd Vice's cup.
He can bide[295] no instruction, he takes so great delight
In working of iniquity for to frequent his spite.
As Fame doth sound the royal trump of worthy men and trim,[296]
So Shame doth blow with strainèd[297] blast the trump of shame on him.

Exit

[Scene v]

Enter the KING, LORD, PRAXASPES, *and* SISAMNES

KING My judge, since my departure hence, have you used judgment right?
If faithful steward I ye find, the same I will requite.
SISAMNES No doubt your grace shall not once hear that I have done amiss.
PRAXASPES I much rejoice to hear so good news as this.

Enter COMMONS' CRY *running in[,] speak this verse, go out again hastily*

COMMONS' CRY Alas, alas, how are the commons oppressed
By that vile judge, Sisamnes by name!
I do not know how it should be redressed.
To amend his life no whit he doth frame.[298]
We are undone[299] and thrown out of door,[300]
His damnable dealing doth us so torment.
At his hand we can find no relief nor succor;
God grant him grace for to repent. *Run away crying*
KING What doleful cries be these, my lord, that sound do in mine ear?
Intelligence[301] if you can give, unto your king declare.
To me it seemeth my commons all they do lament and cry
Out of[302] Sisamnes, judge most chief, even now standing us by.
PRAXASPES Even so, O King, it seemed to me, as you rehearsal made:[303]
I doubt[304] the judge culpable be in some respect or trade.[305]
SISAMNES Redoubted[306] King, have no mistrust, no whit your mind dismay;
There is not one that can me charge or aught against me lay.

290 5 frequent: practice
291 6 kind: natural disposition, character
292 7 ne: nor
293 7 bringing-up: (his own) upbringing
294 8 daily still: every day
295 9 bide: abide
296 11 trim: proper, excellent (men)
297 12 strainèd: vehement; melodic
298 8 To reform himself he does not at all undertake
299 9 undone: ruined
300 9 thrown out of door: expelled, rendered destitute
301 14 Intelligence: information
302 15–6 cry / Out of: exclaim upon, rail against
303 17 as you rehearsal made: as you have said
304 18 doubt: suspect
305 18 respect or trade: manner or way
306 19 Redoubted: revered, respected

Enter COMMONS' COMPLAINT *with* PROOF *and* TRIAL

COMMONS' COMPLAINT Commons' Complaint I represent, with thrall[307] of doleful state,[308]
By urgent cause erected forth[309] my grief for to dilate.[310]
Unto the king I will prepare my misery to tell,
To have relief of this my grief and fettered feet so fell.[311]
Redoubted prince and mighty King, myself I prostrate here.
Vouchsafe,[312] O King, with me to bear for this that I appear.[313]
With humble suit I pardon crave of your most royal grace
To give me leave my mind to break[314] before you in this place.
KING Commons' Complaint, keep nothing back; fear not thy tale to tell.
Whate'er he be[315] within this land that hath not used thee well,
As prince's mouth shall sentence give, he shall receive the same.
Unfold the secrets of thy breast, for I extinguish[316] blame.
COMMONS' COMPLAINT God preserve your royal grace and send you blissful days,
That all your deeds might still accord to give the God the praise.
My complaint is, O mighty King, against that judge you by,[317]
Whose careless deeds, gain to receive, hath made the commons cry.
He, by taking bribes and gifts, the poor he doth oppress,
Taking relief[318] from infants young, widows and fatherless.
KING Untrustful traitor and corrupt judge, how likest thou this complaint?
Forewarning I to thee did give of this to make restraint;
And hast thou done this devilish deed mine ire for to augment?
I sentence give, thou Judas[319] judge, thou shalt thy deed repent.
SISAMNES O puissant Prince, it is not so. His complaint I deny.
COMMONS' COMPLAINT If it be not so, most mighty King, in place[320] then let me die.
Behold that I have brought with me both Proof and Trial true,
To stand even here and sentence give, what by him did ensue.
PROOF I, Proof, do him in this appeal:[321] he did the commons wrong;
Unjustly he with them hath dealt, his greedy[322] was so strong.
His heart did covet in to get,[323] he carèd not which way.
The poor did leese[324] their due and right, because they want to[325] pay
Unto him for bribes; indeed, this was his wonted use.[326]
Whereas[327] your grace good laws did make, he did the same abuse.
TRIAL I, Trial, here to[328] verify what Proof doth now unfold,

307 21 thrall: distress, misery; possibly referring to physical fetters (see line 24)
308 21 doleful state: grievous condition
309 22 erected forth: called forth, emboldened to come forth
310 22 dilate: represent
311 24 fettered feet so fell: so cruelly chained feet
312 26 Vouchsafe: grant
313 26 this that I appear: the cause that has brought me before you
314 28 give me . . . to break: permit me to express my thoughts
315 30 Whate'er he be: whatever sort of person he might be
316 32 extinguish: absolve you of
317 35 you by: next to you
318 38 relief: sustenance
319 42 Judas: i.e. corrupt and treacherous (like Judas, who betrayed Christ)
320 44 in place: right here and now
321 47 do him in this appeal: accuse him of this
322 48 greedy: greed
323 49 in to get: to take in, acquire
324 50 leese: lose
325 50 want to: lack (the means) to
326 51 wonted use: usual practice
327 52 Whereas: notwithstanding that; although
328 53 here to: i.e. am here to

To stand against[329] him[330] in his wrong, as now I dare be bold.
KING How likest thou this, thou caitiff[331] vile? Canst thou the same deny?
SISAMNES O noble King, forgive my fact.[332] I yield to thy mercy.
KING Complaint and Proof, redress will I, all this your misery;
Depart with speed from whence you came, and straight command by me[333]
The execution-man to come before my grace with haste.
ALL For to fulfill this your request, no time we mean to waste. *Exeunt they three*
KING My lord, before my grace go call Otian, this judge's son,
And he shall hear and also see what his father hath done.
The father he shall suffer death, the son his room[334] succeed;
And if that he no better prove, so likewise shall he speed.[335]
PRAXASPES As your grace hath commandment given, I mean for to fulfill. *Step aside and fetch him*
KING Accursèd judge, couldst thou consent to do this cursèd ill?
According unto thy demand, thou shalt for this thy guilt
Receive thy death before mine eyes. Thy blood it shall be spilt.
PRAXASPES Behold, O King, Sisamnes' son before you doth appear.

[*Enter* OTIAN]

KING Otian, this is my mind; therefore to me come near:
Thy father here, for judgment wrong, procurèd hath his death,
And thou, his son, shalt him succeed when he hath lost his breath;
And if that thou dost once offend, as thou see'st thy father have,
In like wise thou shalt suffer death; no mercy shall thee save.
OTIAN O mighty King, vouchsafe your grace my father to remit.[336]
Forgive his fault. His pardon I do ask of you as yet.
Alas, although my father hath your princely heart offended,
Amends for miss[337] he will now make, and faults shall be amended.
Instead of his requested life, pleaseth your grace, take mine:
This offer I as tender child, so duty doth me bind.
KING Do not entreat my grace no more, for he shall die the death.
Where is the execution-man him to bereave of breath?

Enter EXECUTION

EXECUTION At hand,[338] and if it like[339] your grace, my duty to dispatch,
In hope that I, when deed is done, a good reward shall catch.
KING Dispatch with sword this judge's life; extinguish fear and cares.
So done, draw thou his cursèd skin straight over both his ears.
I will see the office[340] done, and that before mine eyes.
EXECUTION To do the thing my king commands, I give the enterprise.[341]
SISAMNES Otian, my son, the king to death by law hath me condemned,

329 54 stand against: oppose
330 54 him: i.e. Sisamnes
331 55 caitiff: villain
332 56 fact: deed, crime
333 58 by me: by my authority
334 63 room: office
335 64 speed: fare
336 75 vouchsafe your . . . to remit: grant that my father might be spared
337 78 miss: offences
338 83 At hand: right here
339 83 and if it like: if it please
340 87 office: official act (of execution)
341 88 give the enterprise: readily undertake

And you in room and office mine, his grace's will hath placed.
Use justice, therefore, in this case, and yield unto no wrong,
Lest thou do purchase[342] the like death, or ever[343] it be long.
OTIAN O father dear, these words to hear, that you must die by force,
Bedews my cheeks with stillèd[344] tears. The king hath no remorse.
The grievous griefs and strainèd sighs my heart doth break in twain,
And I deplore, most woeful child, that I should see you slain.
O false and fickle frowning dame[345] that turneth as the wind,
Is this the joy in father's age thou me assignest to find?
O doleful day, unhappy hour, that loving child should see
His father dear before his face thus put to death should be.
Yet, father, give me blessing thine, and let me once embrace
Thy comely corpse[346] in folded arms and kiss thy ancient face.
SISAMNES O child, thou makes mine eyes to run as rivers do by stream.[347]
My leave I take of thee, my son. Beware of this my beam.[348]
KING Dispatch even now, thou man of death; no longer seem to stay.[349]
EXECUTION Come, Master Sisamnes, come on your way.
My office I must pay;[350] forgive therefore my deed.[351]
SISAMNES I do forgive it thee, my friend; dispatch therefore with speed.
Smite him in the neck with a sword to signify his death
PRAXASPES Behold, O King, how he doth bleed, being of life bereft.
KING In this wise he shall not yet be left.
Pull his skin over his ears to make his death more vile.
A wretch he was, a cruel thief, my commons to beguile. *Flay him with a false skin*
OTIAN What child is he of nature's mold could bide[352] the same to see
His father flayèd in this wise? Oh, how it grieveth me!
KING Otian, thou see'st thy father dead, and thou art in his room;[353]
If thou be'st proud, as he hath been, even thereto shalt thou come.
OTIAN O King, to me this is a glass;[354] with grief in it I view
Example that unto your grace I do not prove untrue.
PRAXASPES Otian, convey your father hence to tomb where he shall lie.
OTIAN And if it please your lordship, it shall be done by and by.[355]
Good execution-man, for need help me with him away.[356]
EXECUTION I will fulfill, as you to me did say. *They take him away*
KING My lord, now that my grace hath seen that finished is this deed,
To question mine give 'tentive[357] ear and answer make with speed:
Have not I done a gracious deed, to redress my commons' woe?
PRAXASPES Yea, truly, if it please your grace, ye have indeed done so.
But now, O King, in friendly wise I counsel you in this,

342 92 purchase: bring about
343 92 or ever: before
344 94 stillèd: discharged, distilled
345 97 dame: i.e. Fortune, personified as a woman
346 102 comely corpse: noble body
347 103 do by stream: i.e. flow copiously
348 104 beam: cross; referring metaphorically to Sisamnes's punishment or to his own sinfulness. The word is a reference to Matthew 7:1–5 where a "beam" in one's eye is said to obstruct moral vision
349 105 stay: delay
350 107 pay: perform
351 107 forgive therefore my deed: referring to the customary forgiveness that the doomed were expected to confer upon their executioners
352 113 What child . . . could bide: What naturally born child could endure
353 115 room: office, position
354 117 glass: mirror, i.e. an exemplary image of a vice or virtue
355 120 by and by: immediately
356 121 for need . . . him away: help me, I need assistance to carry him off
357 124 'tentive: attentive

Certain vices for to leave that in you placèd is:
The vice of drunkenness, O King, which doth you sore infect,
With other great abuses which I wish you to detect.[358]
KING Peace, my lord, what needeth this? Of this I will not hear.
To palace now I will return and thereto make good cheer.
God Bacchus[359] he bestows his gifts—we have good store of wine—
And also that the ladies be both passing brave and fine.[360]
But stay, I see a lord now come and eke a valiant knight.
—What news, my lord? To see you here, my heart it doth delight.

Enter LORD *and* KNIGHT *to meet the* KING

LORD No news, O King, but of duty come to wait upon your grace.
KING I thank you, my lord and loving knight. I pray ye with me trace.[361]
My lords and knight, I pray ye tell—I will not be offended—
Am I worthy of any crime once to be reprehended?
PRAXASPES The Persians much praise your grace, but one thing discommend,
In that to wine subject you be, wherein you do offend.
Sith that the might of wine's effect doth oft subdue your brain,
My counsel is, to please their hearts, from it you would refrain.
LORD No, no, my lord, it is not so. For this of prince they tell:
For virtuous proof[362] and princely facts,[363] Cyrus he doth excel.
By that his grace by conquest great the Egyptians did convince,[364]
Of him report abroad doth pass to be a worthy prince.
KNIGHT In person of Croesus[365] I answer make: we may not his grace compare
In whole respect for to be like Cyrus, the king's father,
In so much[366] your grace hath yet no child as Cyrus left behind;
Even you I mean, Cambises King, in whom I favor find.
KING Croesus said well in saying so. But, Praxaspes, tell me why
That to my mouth in such a sort thou should avouch a lie,
Of drunkenness me thus to charge. But thou with speed shalt see
Whether that I a sober king or else a drunkard be.
I know thou hast a blissful babe, wherein thou dost delight;
Me to revenge of these thy words, I will go wreak this spite:[367]
When I the most have tasted wine, my bow it shall be bent;
At heart of him even then to shoot, is now my whole intent.
And if that I his heart can hit, the king no drunkard is.
If heart of his I do not kill, I yield to thee in this.
Therefore, Praxaspes, fetch to me thy youngest son with speed.
There is no way, I tell thee plain, but I will do[368] this deed.
PRAXASPES Redoubted Prince, spare my sweet child; he is mine only joy.
I trust your grace to infant's heart no such thing will employ.
If that his mother hear of this, she is so nigh her flight,[369]

358 130 I wish you to detect: I want to expose in you; or, I want you to see in yourself
359 133 Bacchus: god of wine
360 134 passing brave and fine: surpassingly grand and attractive
361 138 trace: walk, go
362 146 proof: endeavor or substance
363 146 facts: deeds
364 147 convince: conquer
365 149 In person of Croesus: in the assumed voice of Croesus. Croesus was a Lydian king in the sixth century BC famous for his wealth; he was defeated by Cyrus, Cambises's father
366 151 In so much: insofar as
367 158 wreak this spite: avenge this insult
368 164 no way. . . will do: no chance that I will not perform
369 167 nigh her flight: near her death

In clay her corpse will soon be shrined to pass from world's delight.
KING No more ado; go fetch me him. It shall be as I say.
And if that I do speak the word, how dare ye once say nay?
PRAXASPES I will go fetch him to your grace; but so, I trust, it shall not be.
KING For fear of my displeasure great, go fetch him unto me. [*Exit* PRAXASPES]
—Is he gone? Now, by the gods, I will do as I say.
My lord, therefore fill me some wine, I heartily you pray,
For I must drink to make my brain somewhat intoxicate.
When that[370] the wine is in my head, oh, trimly I can prate.[371]
LORD Here is the cup with fillèd wine, thereof to take repast.
KING Give it me to drink it off, and see no wine be waste. *Drink*
Once again enlarge[372] this cup, for I must taste it still. *Drink*
By the gods, I think of pleasant wine I cannot take my fill.[373]
Now drink is in, give me my bow and arrows from Sir Knight.
At heart of child I mean to shoot, hoping to cleave it right.
KNIGHT Behold, O King, where he doth come, his infant young in hand.

[*Enter* PRAXASPES *with the* CHILD]

PRAXASPES O mighty King, your grace' behest with sorrow I have scanned[374]
And brought my child from mother's knee before you to appear;
And she thereof no whit[375] doth know that he in place is here.
KING Set him up, my mark[376] to be. I will shoot at his heart.
PRAXASPES I beseech your grace not so to do. Set this pretense apart.[377]
—Farewell, my dear and loving babe. Come, kiss thy father dear.
A grievous sight to me it is, to see thee slain even here.
Is this the gain[378] now from the king for giving counsel good,
Before my face with such despite to spill my son's heart-blood?
O heavy[379] day to me this is, and mother in like case.[380]
YOUNG CHILD O father, father, wipe your face.
I see the tears run from your eye.
My mother is at home sewing of a band.[381]
Alas, dear father, why do you cry?
KING Before me as mark now let him stand.
I will shoot at him my mind to fulfill.
YOUNG CHILD Alas, alas, father, will you me kill?
Good Master King, do not shoot at me; my mother loves me best of all. *Shoot*
KING I have dispatched him. Down he doth fall.
As right as a line[382] his heart I have hit.
Nay, thou shalt see, Praxaspes, stranger news yet.
My knight, with speed his heart cut out and give it unto me.
KNIGHT It shall be done, O mighty King, with all celerity.[383]

370 176 When that: when
371 176 trimly I can prate: I can chatter cleverly
372 179 enlarge: fill up
373 180 take my fill: get enough
374 184 scanned: understood
375 186 no whit: nothing
376 187 mark: target
377 188 Set this pretense apart: put aside this intention
378 191 gain: reward
379 193 heavy: sorrowful
380 193 in like case: in the same condition
381 196 band: collar, ribbon or strip of cloth for wearing at the neck, or on hats or other clothing
382 203 As right as a line: with a straight shot; straightaway
383 206 celerity: swiftness, speed

LORD My lord Praxaspes, this had not been but your tongue must be walking.
To the king of correction you must needs be talking.[384]
PRAXASPES No correction, my lord, but counsel for the best.
KNIGHT Here is the heart, according to your grace's behest.
KING Behold, Praxaspes, thy son's own heart. Oh, how well the same was hit.
After this wine to do this deed I thought it very fit.
Esteem[385] thou may'st right well thereby no drunkard is the king
That in the midst of all his cups could do this valiant thing.
My lord and knight, on me attend. To palace we will go
And leave him here to take his son when we are gone him fro.[386]
ALL With all our hearts we give consent to wait upon your grace. [*Exeunt all but* PRAXASPES]
PRAXASPES A woeful man, O Lord, am I, to see him in this case.[387]
My days, I deem, desires their end;[388] this deed will help me hence.
To have the blossoms of my field destroyed by violence.

Enter MOTHER

MOTHER Alas, alas, I do hear tell the king hath killed my son.
If it be so, woe worth[389] the deed that ever it was done.
It is even so. My lord I see, how by him he doth weep.
What meant I that from hands of him this child I did not keep?
—Alas, husband and lord, what did you mean to fetch this child away?
PRAXASPES O lady wife, I little thought for to have seen this day.
MOTHER O blissful babe! O joy of womb! Heart's comfort and delight!
For counsel given unto the king is this thy just requite?[390]
O heavy day and doleful time, these mourning tunes to make!
With blubb'rèd[391] eyes into mine arms from earth I will thee take,
And wrap thee in mine apron white.—But, O my heavy heart!
The spiteful pangs that it sustains would make it in two to part,
The death of this my son to see. O heavy mother now,
That from thy sweet and sug'rèd joy to sorrow so shouldst bow!
What grief in womb did I retain before I did thee see!
Yet at the last, when smart[392] was gone, what joy wert thou to me.
How tender[393] was I of thy food, for to preserve thy state!
How stillèd[394] I thy tender heart at times early and late!
With velvet paps[395] I gave thee suck with issue from my breast,
And dancèd thee upon my knee to bring thee unto rest.
Is this the joy of thee I reap?—O King of tiger's brood![396]
O tiger's whelp,[397] hadst thou the heart to see this child's heart-blood?
Nature enforceth me, alas, in this wise to deplore,

384 207–8 i.e. this would not have had to happen had it not been for your wagging tongue. You just felt yourself compelled to chastise the king
385 213 Esteem: judge
386 216 fro: from
387 218 case: condition
388 219 My days . . . their end: my life, I think, is ready to end
389 222 woe worth: may a curse be upon
390 228 requite: reward
391 230 blubb'rèd: flooded with tears
392 236 smart: pain
393 237 tender: careful
394 238 stillèd: calmed
395 239 paps: breasts
396 241 King of tiger's brood: i.e. king born of, or bred by, a tiger
397 242 whelp: offspring

To wring my hands. O wellaway,[398] that I should see this hour!
Thy mother yet will kiss thy lips, silk-soft and pleasant white,
With wringing hands, lamenting for to see thee in this plight.
My lording dear, let us go home, our mourning to augment.
PRAXASPES My lady dear, with heavy heart, to it I do consent,
Between us both the child to bear unto our lordly place.[399]

Exeunt

[Scene vi]

Enter AMBIDEXTER

AMBIDEXTER Indeed, as ye say, I have been absent a long space,[400]
But is not my cousin Cutpurse[401] with you in the mean time?
—To it, to it, cousin, and do your office fine.[402]
—How like you Sisamnes for using of me?[403]
He played with both hands, but he sped ill-favoredly.[404]
The king himself was godly uptrained;[405]
He professed virtue, but I think it was feigned.[406]
He plays with both hands, good deeds and ill;
But it was no good deed Praxaspes' son for to kill.
As he for the good deed on the judge was commended,
For all his deeds else[407] he is reprehended.
The most evil-disposèd person that ever was,
All the state of his life he would not let pass;
Some good deeds he will do, though they be but few.[408]
The like things this tyrant Cambises doth show.
No goodness from him to none is exhibited,
But still malediction abroad is distributed;[409]
And yet ye shall see in the rest of his race[410]
What infamy he will work against his own grace.[411]
Whist,[412] no more words! Here comes the king's brother.

Enter Lord SMIRDIS *with* ATTENDANCE[413] *and* DILIGENCE

SMIRDIS The king's brother by birth am I, issued from Cyrus' loins;
A grief to me it is to hear of this the king's repines.[414]
I like not well of those his deeds that he doth still frequent;[415]
I wish to God that other ways his mind he could content.

398 244 wellaway: alas
399 249 lordly place: noble mansion
400 1 space: time
401 2 Cutpurse: pickpocket
402 3 your office fine: your good occupation (i.e. stealing purses); Ambidexter pretends to address a thief among the audience
403 4 using of me: employing my methods (i.e. double-dealing)
404 5 sped ill-favoredly: fared badly
405 6 godly uptrained: brought up righteously
406 7 feigned: pretended
407 11 else: otherwise
408 12–4 The most . . . but few: i.e. the worst person that ever lived would not live his whole life without doing some good deeds, even if only a few
409 17 Curses (upon him) are constantly distributed
410 18 race: progress through life
411 19 against his own grace: against himself ("his grace"), or against the benevolence divinely bestowed upon him
412 20 Whist: hush
413 20 SD ATTENDANCE: named for the action or condition of an inferior who "attends upon," i.e. serves, a superior
414 22 king's repines: complaints about the king
415 23 still frequent: always practice, use habitually

Young I am and next to him;[416] no mo[417] of us there be.
I would be glad a quiet realm in this his reign to see.
ATTENDANCE My lord, your good awilling[418] heart the gods will recompense,
In that[419] your mind so pensive[420] is for those his great offence.
My lord, his grace shall have a time to pair[421] and to amend.
Happy is he that can escape and not his grace offend.
DILIGENCE If that wicked vice he could refrain, from wasting wine forbear,
A moderate life he would frequent, amending this his square.[422]
AMBIDEXTER My lord, and if your honor it shall please,
I can inform you what is best for your ease.[423]
Let him alone, of his deeds do not talk;
Then by his side ye may quietly walk.
After his death you shall be king;
Then may you reform each kind of thing.
In the meantime live quietly, do not with him deal;
So shall it redound much to your weal.[424]
SMIRDIS Thou sayest true my friend; that is the best.
I know not whether he love me or do me detest.
ATTENDANCE Lean from his company all that you may.[425]
I, faithful Attendance, will your honor obey;
If against your honor he take any ire,
His grace is as like to kindle his fire
To your honor's destruction as otherwise.
DILIGENCE Therefore, my lord, take good advice,
And I, Diligence, your case will so tender[426]
That to his grace your honor shall be none offender.
SMIRDIS I thank you both, entire[427] friends. With my honor still remain.[428]
AMBIDEXTER Behold where the king doth come with his train.[429]

Enter KING *and* 1 LORD

KING O lording dear and brother mine, I joy your state[430] to see,
Surmising much what is the cause you absent thus from me.[431]
SMIRDIS Pleaseth your grace, no absence I,[432] but ready to fulfill,
At all assays,[433] my Prince and King, in that your grace me will.[434]
What I can do in true defence to you, my Prince aright,
In readiness I always am to offer forth my might.
KING And I the like to you again do here avouch the same.

416 25 next to him: immediately after Cambises in the line of succession
417 25 mo: more
418 27 awilling: willing
419 28 In that: because
420 28 pensive: sorrowfully thoughtful
421 29 pair: meaning uncertain. Editors often suggest "repair," but it also might be a form of "appair," i.e. to grow worse, deteriorate, diminish
422 32 square: pattern
423 34 ease: advantage, comfort
424 40 weal: benefit, prosperity
425 43 Avoid him as much as you can.
426 49 your case will so tender: will so represent you
427 51 entire: perfectly beloved
428 51 With my honor still remain: abide with me
429 52 train: attendants
430 53 state: condition
431 54 Wondering a good deal as to the reason why you have been avoiding my presence
432 55 no absence I: I have not been an absentee
433 56 At all assays: at every need
434 56 that your grace me will: whatever you ask of me

ALL[435] For this your good agreement here, now praisèd be God's name.
AMBIDEXTER But hear ye, noble Prince; hark in your ear.
It is best to do as I did declare.
KING My lord and brother Smirdis, now this is my mind and will:
That you to court of mine return and there to tarry still[436]
Till my return within short space your honor for to greet.
SMIRDIS At your behest so will I do till time again we meet.
My leave I take from you, O King; even now I do depart. *Exeunt* SMIRDIS, ATTENDANCE, *and* DILIGENCE
KING Farewell, lord and brother mine; farewell with all my heart.
—My lord, my brother Smirdis is of youth and manly might,
And in his sweet and pleasant face my heart doth take delight.
LORD Yea, noble Prince, if that your grace before his honor die,
He will succeed a virtuous king and rule with equity.
KING As you have said, my lord, he is chief heir next my grace,
And if I die tomorrow, next he shall succeed my place.
AMBIDEXTER And if it please your grace, O King, I heard him say,
For your death unto the God day and night he did pray.
He would live so virtuously and get him such a praise
That Fame by trump his due deserts in honor should upraise.
He said your grace deservèd had the cursing of all men,
That ye should never after him get any praise again.
KING Did he speak thus of my grace in such despiteful wise?
Or else dost thou presume to fill my princely ears with lies?
LORD I cannot think it in my heart that he would report so.
KING How sayest thou? Speak the truth: was it so or no?
AMBIDEXTER I think so, if it please your grace, but I cannot tell.
KING Thou play'st with both hands, now I perceive well.
But, for to put all doubts aside and to make him leese his hope,
He shall die by dint of sword or else by choking rope.
Shall he succeed when I am gone, to have more praise than I?
Were he father, as brother mine,[437] I swear that he shall die.
To palace mine I will therefore, his death for to pursue. *Exit* [KING *with* LORD]
AMBIDEXTER Are ye gone? Straightway I will follow you.
—How like ye now, my masters? Doth not this gear cotton?[438]
The proverb old is verified: "soon ripe and soon rotten."
He will not be quiet till his brother be killed.
His delight is wholly to have his blood spilled.
Marry, sir, I told him a notable lie.
If it were to do again, man, I durst [not] do it, I.[439]
Marry, when I had done, to it I durst not stand;[440]
Thereby ye may perceive I use to play with each hand.
—But how now, cousin Cutpurse, with whom play you?[441]
—Take heed, for his hand is groping even now.
—Cousin, take heed, if ye do secretly grope;
If ye be taken, cousin, ye must look through a rope.[442]

Exit

435 60 SP ALL: it is unclear if Ambidexter joins Diligence, Attendance, and Lord in speaking this line
436 64 tarry still: remain constantly
437 90 Were he . . . brother mine: were he my father, as he is my brother
438 93 gear cotton: trickery go well
439 98 If I had to do it again, I would not dare do it
440 99 When I did do it, I dared not stand up for what I had said (see "I cannot tell" at line 85)
441 101 cousin Cutpurse: here and in the following lines Ambidexter addresses his imaginary "cousin" the pickpocket
442 104 look through a rope: i.e. be hanged

[Scene vii]

Enter Lord SMIRDIS *alone*

SMIRDIS I am wand'ring alone here and there to walk;
The court is so unquiet, in it I take no joy.
Solitary to myself now I may talk.
If I could rule, I wist[443] what to say.

Enter CRUELTY *and* MURDER *with bloody hands*

CRUELTY My co-equal partner Murder, come away.
From me long thou may'st not stay.
MURDER Yes, from thee I may stay, but not thou from me;
Therefore I have a prerogative[444] above thee.
CRUELTY But in this case we must together abide.
Come, come, Lord Smirdis I have spied.
Lay hands on him with all festination[445]
That on him we may work our indignation.[446]
SMIRDIS How now, my friends?[447] What have you to do with me?
MURDER King Cambises hath sent us unto thee,
Commanding us straightly,[448] without mercy or favor,
Upon thee to bestow our behavior,[449]
With cruelty to murder you and make you away.
Strike him in divers[450] places
SMIRDIS Yet pardon me, I heartily you pray.
Consider the king is a tyrant tyrannious,
And all his doings be damnable and pernicious.
Favor me therefore; I did him never offend.
A little bladder of vinegar pricked[451]
CRUELTY No favor at all. Your life is at an end.
—Even now I strike his body to wound.
Behold, now his blood springs out on the ground.
MURDER Now he is dead, let us present him to the king.
CRUELTY Lay to your hand,[452] away him to bring.

Exeunt

[Scene viii]

Enter AMBIDEXTER

AMBIDEXTER O the passion of God, yonder is a heavy[453] court!
Some weeps, some wails, and some make great sport.[454]

443 4 wist: would know
444 8 prerogative: pre-eminence, precedence
445 11 festination: haste
446 12 work our indignation: express our wrath or contempt
447 13 my friends: perhaps the most extreme example of the play's oddly inconsistent mixture of allegorical and representational modes occurs in this scene: two allegorical characters enter with symbolic blood on their hands before committing a crime, debate with one another the ontological priority of their conceptual significances, and are hailed (despite their bloody hands and nature) as "my friends" by a character who is in no way to be taken as previously associated with the violent qualities they embody
448 15 straightly: directly
449 16 behavior: conduct, general practice
450 17 SD divers: different
451 21 SD A little … vinegar pricked: the theatrical means to produce the blood that "springs" in line 24
452 26 Lay to your hand: use your hands
453 1 heavy: sorrowful
454 2 sport: merriment, entertainment

Lord Smirdis by Cruelty and Murder is slain;
But Jesus, for want[455] of him how some do complain!
If I should have had a thousand pound, I could not forbear weeping.
Now Jesus have his blessèd soul in keeping.
Ah, good Lord, to think on him, how it doth me grieve!
I cannot forbear weeping, ye may me believe. *Weep*
O my heart, how my pulses do beat!
With sorrowful lamentations I am in such a heat.
Ah, my heart, how for him it doth sorrow!
Nay, I have done, in faith, now; and God give you good morrow![456]
Ha, ha! Weep? Nay, laugh, with both hands to play!
The king through his cruelty hath made him away;
But hath not he wrought a most wicked deed:
Because king after him he should not proceed,[457]
His own natural brother, and having no more,[458]
To procure his death by violence sore?[459]
In spite, because his brother should never be king,
His heart, being wicked, consented to this thing.
Now he hath no more brothers nor kinred[460] alive;
If the king use this gear still,[461] he cannot long thrive.

Enter HOB *and* LOB[462]

HOB God's hat, neighbor, come away; it's time to market to go.
LOB God's vast,[463] neighbor, zay ye zo?[464]
The clock hath stricken vive,[465] ich[466] think, by Laken,[467]
Bum vay,[468] vrom sleep cham[469] not very wel waken.
But neighbor Hob, neighbor Hob, what have ye to zell?[470]
HOB Bum troth,[471] neighbor Lob, to you I chill[472] tell.
Chave[473] two goslings and a chine[474] of good pork;
There is no vatter[475] between this[476] and York.[477]
Chave a pot of strawberries and a calf's head;
A zennight zince tomorrow,[478] it hath been dead.

455 4 want: lack
456 12 God give you good morrow: good morning to you (said either in greeting or in parting)
457 16 In order that Smirdis should not become king after him
458 17 no more: no other (brother)
459 18 sore: extreme, severely painful
460 21 kinred: alternative form of "kindred"
461 22 use this gear still: continues to act like this
462 22 SD HOB and LOB: generic names for rustic people (Hob was also a familiar name for Robert or Robin)
463 24 God's vast: by God's fast; Hob and Lob speak in stage-rustic accents, substituting "v" for 'f', "z" for "s", using "Ich" for "I", and employing contractions such as "cham" (for "Ich am") and "bum" (for "by my")
464 24 zay ye zo: say you so
465 25 vive: five
466 25 ich: I
467 25 by Laken: by (our) Lady
468 26 Bum vay: by my fay (i.e. faith)
469 26 cham: I am
470 27 zell: sell
471 28 Bum troth: by my truth
472 28 I chill: I will (repeating the personal pronoun)
473 29 Chave: I have
474 29 chine: backbone and its flesh, after the sides are cut off for bacon
475 30 vatter: fatter
476 30 this: here
477 30 York: this and "Watling Street" at xi. 9 are the play's only references to specific places in England
478 32 zennight zince tomorrow: seven nights since tomorrow (a week ago tomorrow)

LOB Chave a score[479] of eggs and of butter a pound;
Yesterday a nest of goodly young rabbits I vound.[480]
Chave vorty[481] things mo, of more and of less:[482]
My brain is not very good them to express.
But, God's hat, neighbor, wot'st[483] what?
HOB No, not well, neighbor, what's that?
LOB Bum vay, neighbor, Master King is a zhrode[484] lad[485]
Zo God help me, and holidam,[486] I think the vool be mad.
Zome zay he deal cruelly: his brother he did kill,
And also a goodly young lad's heart-blood he did spill.[487]
HOB Vorbod of God,[488] neighbor! Has he played[489] zuch a voolish[490] deed?
AMBIDEXTER Goodman[491] Hob and Goodman Lob, God be your speed.[492]
As you two towards market do walk,
Of the king's cruelty I did hear you talk.
I ensure[493] you, he is a king most vile and pernicious.
His doings and life are odious and vicious.
LOB It were a good deed somebody would break his head.
HOB Bum vay, neighbor Lob, I chould[494] he were dead!
AMBIDEXTER So would I, Lob and Hob, with all my heart.
—[*To audience*] Now with both hands will ye see me play my part?
—Ah, ye whoreson[495] traitorly knaves,
Hob and Lob, out upon[496] you, slaves!
LOB And[497] thou call'st me knave, thou art another.
My name is Lob, and Hob my next[498] neighbor.
AMBIDEXTER Hob and Lob! Ah, ye country patches,[499]
Ah, ye fools, ye have made wrong matches.[500]
Ye have spoken treason against the king's grace.
For it I will accuse ye before his face;
Then for the same ye shall be martyrèd.
At the least ye shall be hanged, drawn, and quarterèd.[501]
HOB O gentleman, ye shall have two pear pies, and tell not of me.[502]
LOB By God, a vat goose chill give thee.

479 33 a score: twenty
480 34 vound: found
481 35 vorty: forty
482 35 of more and of less: more or less
483 37 wot'st: do you know
484 39 zhrode: shrewd (malicious, depraved, wicked)
485 39 lad: boy
486 40 holidam: halidom: a holy thing; anything regarded as sacred
487 42 spill: shed
488 43 Vorbod of God: God forbid
489 43 played: done, acted
490 43 voolish: foolish
491 44 Goodman: title of respect to a person below the rank of gentleman, as a yeoman, farmer, or householder; here used with irony as a mock title
492 44 God be your speed: may God cause you to prosper
493 47 ensure: assure, pledge
494 50 I chould: I would (repeating the personal pronoun)
495 53 whoreson: vile, execrable
496 54 out upon: curses upon
497 55 And: if
498 56 next: nearest
499 57 patches: foolish persons, simpletons
500 58 made wrong matches: made bad bets or agreements
501 62 hanged, drawn, and quarterèd: statutory punishment for treason: the criminal was drawn through the streets on a hurdle (a wood frame or sledge), hanged, cut down alive, disemboweled, beheaded, and cut into quarters
502 63 and tell not of me: if you do not tell on me

I think no hurt,[503] by my vather's soul I zwear.
HOB Chave lived well all my lifetime, my neighbors among;
And now chould be loath to come to zuch wrong.
To be hanged and quartered, the grief would be great.
LOB A foul evil on thee, Hob! Who bid thee on it treat?[504]
Vor[505] it was thou that first did him name.
HOB Thou liest like a varlet and thou zayst the same.
It was zuch a voolish Lob as thou.
LOB Speak many words, and by Cod's nails I vow,
Upon thy pate[506] my staff I will lay.
AMBIDEXTER [*Aside*] By the Mass, I will cause them to make a fray.[507]
—Yea, Lob, thou sayest true: all came through him.
LOB Bum vay, thou Hob, a little would make me ye trim.[508]
Give thee a zwap[509] on thy nose till thy heart ache.
HOB If thou darest, do it; else, man, cry "creak!"[510]
I trust,[511] before thou hurt me,
With my staff chill make a lob of thee.

Here let them fight with their staves, not come near another by three or four yards; the VICE *set them on as hard as he can; one of their wives come out and all-to*[512] *beat the* VICE*; he run away*

Enter MARIAN MAY-BE-GOOD, HOB*'s wife, running in with a broom, and part them*

MARIAN O the body of me, husband Hob, what mean you to fight?
For the passion of God, no more blows smite.
Neighbors and friends so long, and now to fall out?[513]
What! In your age[514] to seem so stout?[515]
If I had not parted ye, one had killed another.
LOB I had not cared, I swear by God's mother.
MARIAN Shake hands again at the request of me;
As ye have been friends, so friends still be.
HOB Bum troth, cham content, and zayst word,[516] neighbor Lob.
LOB I am content; agreed, neighbor Hob.

Shake hands and laugh heartily one at another

MARIAN So, get you to market, no longer stay;
And with yonder knave let me make a fray.
HOB Content, wife Marian, chill do as thou dost say.
But buss[517] me, ich pray thee, at going away.

Exeunt HOB, LOB

MARIAN Thou whoreson[518] knave and prick-eared[519] boy, why didst thou let them fight?

503 65 I think no hurt: I mean no harm
504 69 on it treat: speak of it (i.e. talk about the king's cruelty)
505 70 Vor: for
506 74 pate: head
507 75 make a fray: fight
508 77 a little ... ye trim: one more word will make me beat you
509 78 zwap: swap (stroke, blow). This is the Q3 reading; Q1 reads "zawp"
510 79 cry "creak!": say "I give up!" (used in contests and games)
511 80 I trust: I believe
512 81 SD all-to: completely, utterly
513 84 fall out: quarrel
514 85 in your age: at your age
515 85 stout: fierce, furious
516 90 cham content, and zayst word: I am content, if you say the word
517 95 buss: kiss
518 96 whoreson: detestable
519 96 prick-eared: having erect ears (used of animals, esp. dogs) or ears made prominent by a short haircut (used polemically of Catholic priests); also used to characterize presumptuous youths ("prick-eared boy") and, metaphorically, to suggest a readiness to hear anything suspicious

If one had killed another here, couldst thou their deaths requite?
It bears a sign by this thy deed a cowardly knave thou art,[520]
Else wouldst thou draw that weapon thine, like a man them to part.
AMBIDEXTER What, Marian May-Be-Good, are you come prattling?
Ye may hap get a box on the ear with your talking.
If they had killed one another, I had not cared a pease.[521]

Here let her swinge him in[522] *her broom; she gets him down,and he her down; thus one on the top of another make pastime*[523]

MARIAN Ah, villain, myself on thee I must ease.[524]
Give me a box on the ear? That will I try![525]
Who shall be master, thou shalt see by and by.
AMBIDEXTER Oh, no more, no more, I beseech you heartily.
Even now I yield and give you the mastery.

Run his way out while she is down[526]

MARIAN Ah, thou knave, dost thou throw me down and run thy way?
If he were here again, oh how I would him pay!
I will after him, and if I can him meet,
With these my nails his face I will greet.

[*Exit*]

[Scene ix]

Enter VENUS *leading out her son* CUPID, *blind;*[527] *he must have a bow and two shafts, one headed with gold and th'other headed with lead.*[528]

VENUS Come forth, my son. Unto my words attentive ears resign;[529]
What I pretend,[530] see you frequent,[531] to force this game of mine.[532]
The king a kinswoman hath, adorned with beauty store;[533]
And I wish that Diana's gifts[534] they twain[535] shall keep[536] no more,
But use my silver sug'rèd game[537] their joys for to augment.
When I do speak, to wound his heart, Cupid my son, consent,
And shoot at him the shaft of love that bears the head of gold,
To wound his heart in lover's wise,[538] his grief for to unfold.[539]
Though kin she be unto his grace, that nature me expel,[540]

520 98 Your inaction in this matter signifies that you are a cowardly knave
521 102 a pease: a pea; metaphorically anything of very small value
522 102 SD: swinge him in: beat him with
523 102 SD: Walker (2014) suggests the SD provides opportunity for comical sexual actions; "pastime" suggests pleasurable sport or amusement; both meanings are supported by "ease" in 103
524 103 must ease: take pleasure, comfort
525 104 That will I try: I will see about that
526 107 SD she is down: evidently their struggles have culminated with Ambidexter momentarily on top of Marian, making his yielding and flight as well as her subsequent exit "after him" pointedly comical
527 0 SD blind: i.e. probably blindfolded (cf. Romeo and Juliet I.iv. 4 "Cupid hoodwinked with a scarf")
528 0 SD two shafts . . . with lead: Cupid's gold-tipped arrows awaken desire in those they strike; the leaden ones cause aversion
529 1 resign: submit
530 2 pretend: declare
531 2 see you frequent: be sure that you practice
532 2 to force . . . of mine: to further my plans by force
533 3 store: abundant
534 4 Diana's gifts: i.e. chastity (Diana was a virginal Roman goddess)
535 4 twain: both
536 4 keep: observe
537 5 silver sug'rèd game: sweet (erotic) amusement
538 8 in lover's wise: after the manner of a lover
539 8 his grief for to unfold: his pains (of love) to express
540 9 that nature me expel: that natural law (forbidding incest) expel for me (from their attention)

Against the course thereof[541] he may in my game please me well.
Wherefore, my son, do not forget; forthwith pursue the deed.
CUPID Mother, I mean for to obey as you have whole decreed;[542]
But you must tell me, mother dear, when I shall arrow draw,
Else your request to be attained will not be worth a straw.[543]
I am blind and cannot see, but still[544] do shoot by guess.
The poets well, in places store, of my might do express.[545]
VENUS Cupid my son, when time shall serve that thou shalt do this deed,
Then warning I to thee will give; but see thou shoot with speed.[546]

[*Enter*] LORD, LADY, [*and*] WAITING-MAID[547]

[1] LORD Lady dear, to king akin, forthwith let us proceed
To trace abroad the beauty fields, as erst we had decreed.[548]
The blowing[549] buds whose savory[550] scents our sense will much delight,
The sweet smell of musk white rose[551] to please the appetite,
The chirping birds whose pleasant tunes therein shall hear record[552]
That our great joy we shall it find in field to walk abroad;
On lute and cittern[553] there to play a heavenly harmony,
Our ears shall hear, heart to content, our sports to beauty.[554]
LADY Unto your words, most comely lord, myself submit do I;
To trace with you in field so green I mean not to deny. *Here trace up and down,*[555] *playing*[556]
MAID And I, your waiting-maid, at hand with diligence will be,
For to fulfill with heart and hand when you shall command me.

Enter KING, LORD, *and* KNIGHT

KING Come on, my lord and knight, abroad our mirth let us employ.
Since he is dead, this heart of mine in corpse[557] I feel it joy.
Should brother mine have reignèd king when I had yielded breath?
A thousand brothers I rather had, to put them all to death.
But, O behold, where I do see a lord and lady fair.
For beauty she most worthy is to sit in prince's chair.[558]
VENUS Shoot forth, my son! Now is the time that thou must wound his heart.
CUPID Content you, mother. I will do my part. *Shoot there, and go out* VENUS *and* CUPID[559]
KING Of truth, my lord, in eye of mine all ladies she doth excel.

541 10 Against the course thereof: by contradicting the demands (of natural law)
542 12 as you have whole decreed: everything as you have ordered
543 14 Otherwise, your request will be worthless
544 15 still: always
545 16 Poets well express my power in many commonplaces
546 18 with speed: successfully
547 18 SD WAITING-MAID: superior female servant who personally attends a lady
548 20 To walk through the beautiful fields as before we said we would
549 21 blowing: blooming
550 21 savory: pleasant
551 22 musk white rose: probably the aromatic field rose
552 23 therein shall hear record: we shall hear in the fields
553 25 cittern: guitar-like stringed instrument
554 26 beauty: beautify
555 28 SD trace up and down: walk back and forth
556 28 SD playing: perhaps a cue for music of "lute and cittern"
557 32 in corpse: in (my) body
558 36 chair: throne
559 38 SD *Shoot there . . . and* CUPID: i.e. let Cupid shoot at this time and then exit with Venus

Can none report what dame she is, and to my grace it tell?
[2] LORD Redoubted Prince, pleaseth your grace, to you she is akin,
Cousin-german,[560] nigh of birth, by mother's side come in.
KNIGHT And that her waiting-maiden is, attending her upon.
He is a lord of prince's court, and will be there anon.
They sport themselves in pleasant field, to former usèd use.[561]
KING My lord and knight, of truth I speak; my heart it cannot choose
But with my lady I must speak and so express my mind.
—My lord and ladies walking there, if you will favor find,
Present yourselves unto my grace and by my side come stand.
[1] LORD We will fulfill, most mighty King, as your grace doth command.
KING Lady dear, intelligence[562] my grace hath got of late,[563]
You issued out of mother's stock[564] and kin unto my state.[565]
According to rule of birth you are cousin-german mine;
Yet do I wish that farther of[566] this kinred I could find;[567]
For Cupid, he that eyeless boy, my heart hath so enflamed,
With beauty you me to content the like cannot be named;[568]
For since I entered in this place and on you fixed mine eyes,
Most burning fits[569] about my heart in ample wise did rise.
The heat of them such force doth yield,[570] my corpse they scorch, alas!
And burns the same[571] with wasting[572] heat, as Titan[573] doth the grass.
And sith[574] this heat is kindled so, and fresh in heart of me,
There is no way but[575] of the same the quencher you must be.
My meaning is that beauty yours my heart with love doth wound;
To give me love, mind to content, [576] my heart hath you out found;[577]
And you are she must be my wife, else shall I end my days.
Consent to this and be my queen, to wear the crown with praise.
LADY If it please your grace, O mighty King, you shall not this request.
It is a thing that nature's course[578] doth utterly detest,
And high[579] it would the God displease; of all, that is the worst.
To grant your grace to marry so, it is not I that durst.
Yet humble thanks I render now unto you, mighty King,
That you vouchsafe to great estate so gladly would me bring.
Were it not it were[580] offence, I would it not deny,
But such great honor to achieve my heart I would apply.[581]

560 42 Cousin-german: first cousin
561 45 to former usèd use: as has been customary; both "use" and "sport" may have sexual connotations
562 51 intelligence: information
563 51 of late: recently
564 52 mother's stock: my mother's family
565 52 kin unto my state: related to me
566 54 farther of: Qq agree on "of"; modern eds sometimes emend to "farther off", meaning "at greater distance (from me)"
567 54 find: discover
568 56 Nothing could conceivably satisfy me like your beauty
569 58 fits: intense passions
570 59 such force doth yield: is so powerful
571 60 the same: i.e. my body
572 60 wasting: consuming
573 60 Titan: i.e. the sun
574 61 sith: since
575 62 no way but: no alternative but that
576 64 mind to content: to satisfy desire
577 64 out found: discovered
578 68 course: order
579 69 high: highly
580 73 Were it not it were: if it were not
581 74 apply: devote assiduously

Therefore, O King, with humble heart in this I pardon crave;
Mine answer is in this request: your mind[582] ye may not have.
KING May I not? Nay then, I will, by all the gods I vow!
And I will marry thee as wife. This is mine answer now.
Who dare say nay what I pretend,[583] who dare the same withstand,
Shall lose his head and have report as[584] traitor through my land.
There is no nay.[585] I will you have, and you my queen shall be.
LADY Then, mighty King, I crave your grace to hear the words of me:
Your counsel take of lordings' wit,[586] the laws aright peruse;[587]
If I with safe[588] may grant this deed, I will it not refuse.
KING No, no! What I have said to you, I mean to have it so.
For counsel theirs I mean not, I, in this respect to go.[589]
But to my palace let us go, the marriage to prepare;
For to avoid[590] my will in this, I can it not forbear.[591]
LADY O God, forgive me, if I do amiss.
The king by compulsion enforceth me this.[592]
MAID Unto the gods for your estate,[593] I will not cease to pray,
That you may be a happy queen and see most joyful day.
KING Come on, my lords; with gladsome hearts let us rejoice with glee.
Your music show[594] to joy[595] this deed at the request of me.
BOTH[596] For to obey your grace's words our honors do agree.

Exeunt

[Scene x]

Enter AMBIDEXTER

AMBIDEXTER O the passion of me! Marry, as ye say, yonder is a royal court:
There is triumphing and sport upon sport.
Such loyal lords, with such lordly exercise,[597]
Frequenting such pastime[598] as they can devise:
Running at tilt,[599] jousting, with running at the ring,[600]
Masking and mumming,[601] with each kind of thing;
Such dancing, such singing, with musical harmony.
Believe me, I was loath to absent[602] their company.

582 76 mind: desire, intention
583 79 pretend: declare
584 80 have report as: be declared a
585 81 no nay: no denying it
586 83 lordings' wit: noblemen's wisdom
587 83 aright peruse: examine correctly
588 84 safe: safety
589 86 in this respect to go: in this matter to pursue their advice
590 88 avoid: cancel, do away with
591 88 forbear: endure
592 90 this: i.e. to do this
593 91 estate: condition, well-being
594 94 show: perform (perhaps a cue for music to begin playing for the following scene)
595 94 joy: rejoice at
596 95 SP BOTH: this speech prefix appears to include 1 LORD, the suitor of the Lady, in acclaiming the king's assertion of will
597 3 exercise: activity
598 4 pastime: recreation, sport
599 5 Running at tilt: riding on horseback in a sporting combat (like jousting)
600 5 running at the ring: riding on horseback while trying to catch a ring on the point of a lance
601 6 Masking and mumming: masquerading, disguising oneself (for games and festivities)
602 8 absent: leave

But will you believe? Jesu, what haste they made till they were married!
Not for a million of pounds one day longer they would have tarried.
Oh, there was a banquet royal and super-excellent;
Thousands and thousands at that banquet was spent.
I muse of[603] nothing but how they can be married so soon.
I care not if I be married before tomorrow at noon!
If marriage be a thing that so may be had
—How say you, maid? To marry me will ye be glad?[604]
—Out of doubt,[605] I believe it is some excellent treasure;
Else to the same belongs[606] abundant pleasure.
Yet with mine ears I have heard some say:
"That ever I was marrièd, now cursèd be the day!"
Those be they that with curst[607] wives be matched.
That husband for hawk's meat of them is up-snatched,[608]
Head broke with a bedstaff,[609] face all to-be-scratched,[610]
"Knave!", "Slave!", and "Villain!",[611] a coiled[612] coat now and then
When the wife hath given it,[613] she will say, "Alas, good man!"
Such were better unmarrièd, my masters, I trow,[614]
Than all their life after to be matchèd with a shrew.

Enter PREPARATION

PREPARATION With speed I am sent all things to prepare,
My message to do as the king did declare.
His grace doth mean a banquet to make,
Meaning in this place repast for to take.
Well the cloth shall be laid, and all things in readiness,
To court to return when done is my business.
AMBIDEXTER A proper man and also a fit
For the king's estate to prepare a banquet.
PREPARATION What, Ambidexter? Thou art not unknown.
A mischief on all good faces, so that I curse not mine own![615]
Now, in the knave's name, shake hands with me.
AMBIDEXTER Well said, goodman pouch-mouth, your reverence I see.
I will teach ye, if your manners no better be.
Ah, ye slave, the king doth me a gentleman allow;[616]
Therefore I look[617] that to me ye shall bow. *Fight*
PREPARATION Good Master Ambidexter, pardon my behavior;
For this your deeds you are a knave, for your labor![618]

603 13 muse of: wonder about
604 16 This line is addressed to a woman in the audience
605 17 Out of doubt: no doubt
606 18 Else to the same belongs: or else marriage brings
607 21 curst: disagreeable, shrewish
608 22 Such husbands are gobbled up rapaciously by (their wives) as hawks eat meat
609 23 bedstaff: stick or wooden bed slat, well-known as an improvised weapon
610 23 to-be-scratched: scratched
611 24 "Knave . . . Villain!": insults the wife directs at the husband
612 24 coiled: beaten
613 25 it: i.e. the beating
614 26 trow: trust
615 37 A curse upon all handsome faces, provided that I don't curse my own
616 41 allow: acknowledge (as)
617 42 look: expect
618 44 for your labor: as your reward (I call you knave)

AMBIDEXTER Why, ye stale[619] counterly[620] villain, nothing but "knave"? *Fight*
PREPARATION I am sorry your mastership[621] offended I have.
Shake hands that between us agreement may be;
I was overshot with myself,[622] I do see.
Let me have your help this furniture[623] to provide.
The king from this place will not long abide. *Set the fruit on the board*[624]
AMBIDEXTER Content,[625] it is the thing that I would wish.
I myself will go fetch one dish. *Let the* VICE *fetch a dish of nuts, and let them fall in the bringing of them in*
PREPARATION Cleanly,[626] Master Ambidexter, for fair on[627] the ground they lie.
AMBIDEXTER I will have them up again by and by.
PREPARATION To see all in readiness I will put you in trust;
There is no nay,[628] to the court needs I must. *Exit* PREPARATION
AMBIDEXTER Have ye no doubt, but all shall be well.
—Marry, sir,[629] as you say, this gear doth excel.[630]
All things is in a readiness when they come hither,
The king's grace and the queen both together.
I beseech ye, my masters, tell me is it not best
That I be so bold as to bid a guest?[631]
He is as honest a man as ever spurred cow,[632]
My cousin Cutpurse, I mean. I beseech ye, judge you.
—Believe me, cousin, if to be the king's guest ye could be taken,
I trust that offer would not be forsaken.
But, cousin, because to that office[633] ye are not like to come,
Frequent your exercises:[634] a horn on your thumb,[635]
A quick eye, a sharp knife, at hand a receiver.[636]
But then take heed, cousin, ye be a cleanly conveyor.[637]
Content yourself, cousin; for this banquet you are unfit
When such as I at the same am not worthy to sit.

Enter [KING, QUEEN *and* LORDS]

KING My Queen and lords, to take repast let us attempt the same.
Here is the place; delay no time, but to our purpose frame.[638]
QUEEN With willing hearts your whole behest we mind[639] for to obey.

619 45 stale: old, worn-out
620 45 counterly: i.e. fit for debtors' prisons (called "counters" in early modern England)
621 46 your mastership: a title of formal respect, perhaps offered grudgingly or ironically here
622 48 was overshot with myself: went further than I intended (in my speech and action)
623 49 this furniture: these provisions
624 50 SD *board*: table
625 51 Content: agreed
626 53 Cleanly: (do it) properly, neatly
627 53 fair on: right, exactly on
628 56 no nay: no alternative
629 58 Marry, sir: this and the following lines (through 72) are addressed to members of the audience
630 58 gear doth excel: business is going very well
631 62 be so . . . a guest?: be so brave as to invite a guest?
632 63 spurred cow: see ii. 55n
633 67 office: distinction (of being a king's guest)
634 68 Frequent your exercises: pursue your practices (i.e. thieving)
635 68 horn on your thumb: with a horn thimble on your thumb
636 69 at hand a receiver: with an accomplice nearby (to take the purse)
637 70 cleanly conveyor: nimble thief
638 74 delay no . . . purpose frame: do not hesitate, but undertake to do what I have brought us here to do (i.e. eat)
639 75 mind: intend

ALL And we, the rest of prince's train,[640] will do as you do say. *Sit at the banquet*
KING Me think mine ears doth wish the sound of music's harmony;
Here, for to play before my grace, in place I would them spy.[641] *Play at the banquet*
AMBIDEXTER They be at hand, sir, with stick and fiddle;
They can play a new dance called "Hey-diddle-diddle."
KING My Queen perpend:[642] what I pronounce, I will not violate;
But one thing which my heart makes glad I mind to explicate.[643]
You know in court up-trainèd is a lion very young,
Of one litter two whelps beside,[644] as yet not very strong.
I did request one whelp to see and this young lion fight,
But lion did the whelp convince[645] by strength of force and might.
His brother whelp, perceiving that the lion was too good,
And he by force[646] was like to see[647] the other whelp his blood,[648]
With force[649] to lion he did run, his brother for to help.
A wonder great it was to see that friendship in a whelp.
So then the whelps between them both the lion did convince,
Which thing to see before mine eyes did glad the heart of prince. *At this tale told, let the* QUEEN *weep*
QUEEN These words to hear makes stilling[650] tears issue from crystal[651] eyes.
KING What dost thou mean, my spouse, to weep for loss of any price?[652]
QUEEN No, no, O King, but as you see friendship in brother's whelp:
When one was like to have repulse, the other yielded help.
And was this favor showed in dogs to shame of royal king?
Alack, I wish these ears of mine had not once heard this thing.
Even so should you, O mighty King, to brother been[653] a stay,[654]
And not, without offence to you, in such wise him to slay.
In all assays[655] it was your part[656] his cause to have defended,
And whosoever had him misused, to have them reprehended.
But faithful love was more in dog than it was in your grace.
KING O cursèd caitiff, vicious, vile, I hate thee in this place.[657]
This banquet is at an end; take all these things away.
Before my face thou shalt repent the words that thou dost say.
O wretch most vile, didst thou the cause of brother mine so tender[658]
The loss of him should grieve thy heart, he being none offender?[659]
It did me good his death to have; so will it to have thine.
What friendship he had at my hands, the same even thou shalt find.

640 76 rest of prince's train: your other followers
641 78 I would them spy: I would like to see them
642 81 perpend: consider
643 82 mind to explicate: intend to explain
644 84 Of one . . . whelps beside: as well as two puppies from the same litter
645 86 convince: defeat
646 88 by force: by consequence
647 88 like to see: would probably see
648 88 whelp his blood: dog's blood
649 89 With force: violently
650 93 stilling: trickling, distilling
651 93 crystal: shining, bright
652 94 loss of any price: loss of anything precious
653 99 to brother been: to (your) brother have been
654 99 stay: support
655 101 In all assays: in every trial or time of need
656 101 part: proper role
657 104 in this place: right here and now
658 107 didst thou . . . so tender: did you care about my brother's cause?
659 108 he being none offender: i.e. as if he were not so much a wrong-doer

I give consent and make a vow that thou shalt die the death:[660]
By Cruel's sword and Murder fell,[661] even thou shalt lose thy[662] breath.
—Ambidexter, see with speed to Cruelty ye go;
Cause him hither to approach, Murder with him also.
AMBIDEXTER I ready am for to fulfill, if that it be your grace's will.
KING Then nought oblite[663] my message given; absent thyself away.
AMBIDEXTER Then in this place I will no longer stay.
—[*To* QUEEN] If that I durst,[664] I would mourn your case;
But, alas, I dare not, for fear of his grace. *Exit* AMBIDEXTER
KING Thou cursèd jill,[665] by all the gods I take an oath and swear
That flesh of thine these hands of mine, in pieces small could tear.
But thou shalt die by dint of sword; there is no friend ne fee[666]
Shall find remorse at prince's hand to save the life of thee.
QUEEN O mighty King and husband mine, vouchsafe to hear me speak,
And license give to spouse of thine her patient mind to break.[667]
For tender love unto your grace my words I did so frame;
For pure love doth heart of king me violate and blame.
And to your grace is this offence that I should purchase death?[668]
Then cursèd time that I was queen, to shorten this my breath!
Your grace doth know by marriage true I am your wife and spouse,
And one to save another's health at troth-plight made our vows.[669]
Therefore, O King, let loving queen at thy hand find remorse;
Let pity be a mean to quench that cruel raging force,
And pardon, plight[670] from prince's mouth, yield grace unto your queen,
That amity with faithful zeal may ever be us between.
KING Ah, caitiff vile, to pity thee my heart it is not bent;[671]
Ne yet to pardon your offence it is not mine intent.
1 LORD Our mighty prince, with humble suit of your grace this I crave,
That this request it may take place,[672] your favor for to have.
Let mercy yet abundantly the life of queen preserve,
Sith she in most obedient wise your grace's will doth serve.
As yet your grace but while[673] with her hath had cohabitation,
And sure this is no desert why to yield her indignation.[674]
Therefore, O King, her life prolong to joy[675] her days in bliss.
2 LORD Your grace shall win immortal fame in granting unto this.
She is a queen whose goodly hue excels the royal rose;
For beauty bright, Dame Nature she a large gift did dispose;
For comeliness who may compare? Of all she bears the bell.[676]
This should give cause to move your grace to love her very well.

660 111 die the death: be put to death, executed by law
661 112 fell: ruthless
662 112 lose thy: this reading appears only in Q3; in the two versions of Q1, the phrase is given as "dye the breth" and "lose the breth"
663 116 oblite: forget
664 118 durst: dared
665 120 jill: lass, wench (contemptuous)
666 122 ne fee: nor wealth
667 125 mind to break: speak her opinion
668 128 purchase death: die for it
669 131 And we swore at our betrothal to preserve each other's well-being
670 134 plight: pledged
671 136 bent: inclined
672 139 take place: be successful
673 142 but while: only a short time
674 143 desert why . . . her indignation: action deserving wrathful condemnation
675 144 joy: enjoy
676 148 bears the bell: wins the prize

Her silver breast in those your arms to sing the songs of love,
Fine qualities most excellent to be in her you prove;
A precious pearl of price[677] to prince, a jewel passing[678] all.
Therefore, O King, to beg remorse[679] on both my knees I fall:
To grant her grace to have her life, with heart I do desire.
KING You villains twain, with raging force ye set my heart on fire.
If I consent that she shall die, how dare ye crave her life?
You two to ask this at my hand doth much enlarge my strife.
Were it not for shame, you two should die that for her life do sue.
But favor mine from you is gone, my lords, I tell you true.
I sent for Cruelty of late;[680] if he would come away,
I would commit her to his hands, his cruel part to play.
Even now I see where he doth come; it doth my heart delight.

Enter CRUELTY *and* MURDER

CRUELTY Come, Murder, come; let us go forth with might.
Once again the king's commandment we must fulfill.
MURDER I am contented to do it with a good will.
KING Murder and Cruelty, for both of you I sent
With all festination your offices to frequent.[681]
Lay hold on the queen, take her to your power,
And make her away[682] within this hour.
Spare for no fear; I do you full permit.[683]
So I from this place do mean for to flit.[684]
BOTH With courageous hearts, O King, we will obey.
KING Then come, my lords, let us depart away.
BOTH THE LORDS With heavy hearts we will do all your grace doth say. *Exeunt* KING *and* LORDS
CRUELTY Come, lady and queen, now are you in our handling;
In faith, with you we will use no dandling.[685]
MURDER With all expedition I, Murder, will take place;
Though thou[686] be a queen, ye be under my grace.[687]
QUEEN With patience I will you both obey.
CRUELTY No more words, but go with us away.
QUEEN Yet before I die, some psalm[688] to God let me sing.
BOTH We be content to permit you that thing.
QUEEN Farewell, you ladies of the court, with all your masking hue.[689]
I do forsake these brodered guards,[690] and all the fashions new,
The court, and all the courtly train wherein I had delight.
I banished am from happy sport, and all by spiteful spite;

677 152 pearl of price: something of supreme value (cf. Matthew 13: 46)
678 152 passing: surpassing
679 153 beg remorse: plead for pity (for the Queen)
680 160 of late: just now
681 167 Speedily to perform your functions
682 169 make her away: put her to death
683 170 Do not refrain (from killing her) due to any fear; I give you full permission
684 171 flit: go
685 176 with you . . . no dandling: we won't toy with you
686 178 thou: Murder's familiar pronoun ("thou" instead of the more formal "you") expresses his new superiority to the condemned queen
687 178 under my grace: i.e. beneath me; murder here appropriates a title of respect ("my grace") elsewhere employed by King Cambises, who often so refers to himself (cf. line 78)
688 181 psalm: sacred song sung in religious worship
689 183 masking hue: masquerading (as in a courtly masque) or deceptive appearance or complexion
690 184 brodered guards: embroidered trimmings (see i. 114n)

Yet with a joyful heart to God a psalm I mean to sing,
Forgiving all[691] and the king of each kind of thing.

Sing and exeunt

[Scene xi]

Enter AMBIDEXTER *weeping*

AMBIDEXTER Ah, ah, ah, ah! I cannot choose but weep for the queen.
Nothing but mourning now at the court there is seen.
Oh, oh, my heart, my heart! Oh, my bum will break!
Very[692] grief so torments me that scarce I can speak.
Who could but weep for the loss of such a lady?
That cannot I do, I swear by mine honesty.
But, Lord, so the ladies mourn, crying "Alack!"
Nothing is worn now but only black.
I believe all cloth in Watling Street[693] to make gowns would not serve.
If I make a lie, the devil let ye starve!
All ladies mourn, both young and old;
There is not one that weareth a point's worth[694] of gold.
There is a sort for fear for the king do pray
That would have him dead,[695] by the Mass,[696] I dare say.
What a king was he that hath used such tyranny!
He was akin to Bishop Bonner,[697] I think verily.
For both their delights was to shed blood,
But never intended to do any good.
Cambises put a judge to death. That was a good deed;
But to kill the young child was worse to proceed;
To murder his brother, and then his own wife,
So help me God and halidom, it is pity of his life![698]
Hear ye? I will lay[699] twenty thousand pound
That the king himself doth die by some wound.
He hath shed so much blood that his will be shed;
If it come so to pass, in faith, then he is sped.[700]

Enter the KING *without a gown, a sword thrust up into his side, bleeding*

KING Out, alas! What shall I do? My life is finishèd.
Wounded I am by sudden chance; my blood is minishèd.[701]
Gog's heart, what means might I make my life to preserve?
Is there nought to be my help? Nor is there nought to serve?[702]

691 188 all: i.e. all men
692 4 Very: genuine
693 9 Watling Street: London's main street for drapers' shops, where cloth was sold
694 12 point's worth: a very small amount (a "point" was a small ribbon or cord used to lace shoes, to hold up hose, or to attach garments to one another)
695 13–4 There is . . . him dead: there are some who so fear the king that they pray for his good health while secretly wishing him dead
696 14 by the Mass: a particularly ironic oath, swearing in the name used by Catholics for their services, since the following lines invoke a Catholic bishop notorious for persecuting Protestants
697 16 Bishop Bonner: Edmund Bonner, who served as Bishop of London (1540–49 and 1553–59); during the reign of Queen Mary, he was notorious for cruelty, including the trying and burning of Protestants as heretics. Under Queen Elizabeth, he was twice tried for refusing the oath of supremacy; he died in prison in September 1569
698 22 pity of his life: a great pity
699 23 lay: wager
700 26 sped: dispatched, destroyed
701 28 minishèd: diminished
702 30 nought to serve: nothing to be done

Out upon[703] the court and lords that there remain:
To help my grief in this my case will none of them take pain?[704]
Who but I in such a wise[705] his death's wound could have got?
As I on horseback up did leap, my sword from scabbard shot
And ran me thus into the side, as you right well may see.
A marvels[706] chance unfortunate that in this wise should be.
I feel myself a-dying now; of life bereft am I,
And death hath caught me with his dart; for want[707] of blood I spy.[708]
Thus gasping here on ground I lie; for nothing I do care.
A just reward for my misdeeds my death doth plain[709] declare. *Here let him quake and stir*[710]
AMBIDEXTER How now, noble King? Pluck up your heart.
What, will you die, and from us depart?
Speak to me and[711] you be alive!
He cannot speak, but behold how with death he doth strive.
Alas, good King. Alas, he is gone.
The devil take me if for him I make any moan.[712]
I did prognosticate of[713] his end, by the Mass.
Like as I did say, so is it come to pass.
I will be gone; if I should be found here,
That I should[714] kill him it would appear.
For fear with his death they do me charge,
Farewell, my masters, I will go take barge.[715]
I mean to be packing, now is the tide;
Farewell, my masters, I will no longer abide. *Exit* AMBIDEXTER

Enter three LORDS

1 LORD Behold, my lords, it is even so as he[716] to us did tell.
His grace is dead upon the ground, by dint of sword most fell.
2 LORD As he in saddle would have leapt, his sword from sheath did go,
Goring him up into the side; his life was ended so.
3 LORD His blood so fast did issue out that nought could him prolong;
Yet, before he yielded up the ghost, his heart was very strong.
1 LORD A just reward for his misdeeds the God above hath wrought;
For certainly the life he led was to be counted nought.[717]
2 LORD Yet a princely burial he shall have, according[718] his estate;
And more of him here at this time we have not to dilate.[719]

703 31 Out upon: curses upon
704 32 pain: trouble
705 33 wise: manner
706 36 marvels: marvelous, miraculous (meruels Q1–2; maruels Q3)
707 38 want: lack
708 38 spy: see, discover (looking at this bleeding body)
709 40 plain: plainly, clearly
710 40 SD quake and stir: tremble and jerk violently
711 43 and: if
712 46 moan: lament
713 47 prognosticate of: prophesy
714 50 should: did
715 52 take barge: leave on a small ship or ferry-boat
716 55 he: referent unclear
717 62 counted nought: considered worthless or wicked
718 63 according: befitting
719 64 dilate: expound

3 LORD My lords, let us take him up to carry him away.
BOTH Content we are with one accord to do as you do say.

Exeunt all

Epilogus

[*Enter* EPILOGUE]

[EPILOGUE] Right gentle audience, here have you perused
The tragical history of this wicked king.
According to our duty, we have not refused,[720]
But to our best intent expressed every thing.
We trust none is offended for this our doing.

Our author craves likewise, if he have squared amiss,[721]
By gentle admonition to know where the fault is.

His good will shall not be neglected to amend the same,
Praying all to bear, therefore, with his simple deed[722]
Until the time serve a better he may frame.[723]
Thus yielding[724] you thanks, to end we decreed
That you so gently have suffered[725] us to proceed,

In such patient wise[726] as to hear and see,
We can but[727] thank ye therefore; we can do no more, we.

As duty binds us, for our noble Queen[728] let us pray,
And for her honorable Council, the truth that they may use,[729]
To practice justice and defend her grace each day;
To maintain[730] God's word they may not refuse[731]
To correct all those that would her grace and grace's laws abuse;
Beseeching God over us she may reign long,
To be guided by truth and defended from wrong.

Amen. quod[732] Thomas Preston.

Imprinted at London by John Allde.

720 3 refused: declined to accept (our duty)
721 6 squared amiss: fashioned (anything) inappropriately
722 9 simple deed: foolish act (i.e. the play)
723 10 Until the time permits him to fashion a better
724 11 yielding: giving
725 12 suffered: permitted
726 13 wise: manner
727 14 but: only
728 15 our noble Queen: i.e. Queen Elizabeth I
729 16 the truth . . . may use: that they may deal truthfully
730 18 To maintain: in order to uphold
731 18 refuse: decline
732 22 quod: says

2 Ben Jonson, *Poetaster*

First performed 1601

First printed 1602

Edited by Henry S. Turner

Ben Jonson's *Poetaster* has many themes, but its overarching preoccupation is with the status of poetry and theater in Jonson's own period. By the time he wrote *Poetaster*, Jonson had become famous for a type of play he called "comical satire," a genre that brought realistic scenes from London life to the stage in order to poke fun at caricatures of people Jonson observed around him, to model sophisticated urban behavior, and to voice Jonson's own moral and literary philosophy through the mouths of key characters. *Poetaster*, Jonson's fifth play (his fourth to appear in print), has several of these features: young would-be poets collide with their angry fathers, pretentious citizens mix hopefully with sophisticated members of court, colorful street characters invent schemes to defraud their betters and to escape punishment by the authorities. But instead of using a contemporary London backdrop, as he did in his earlier plays, Jonson sets his scene in ancient Rome during the Augustan age, a peak period of imperial power and literary culture that inspired Jonson's own views of poetry, and a period that he and many of his contemporaries—including the soon-to-be King James I—sought to emulate. In a gesture of authorial confidence that borders on grandiosity, Jonson brings the ancient Roman poets Ovid, Horace, and Virgil back to life and models many of the characters, lines, and even entire scenes of his own play directly on their work. Horace acts as the play's literary and moral conscience, and he is an obvious figure for Jonson himself. Among Roman authors, Horace was Jonson's most influential stylistic and moral model. In 1604 or 1605 Jonson translated Horace's famous treatise on poetry, the *Ars Poetica*, into English, and *Poetaster* III.v is a defense of satire lifted straight from one of Horace's own poems. In *Poetaster* the character Horace espouses a vision of virtue that is identical to Jonson's own opinions and, like Jonson, he circulates his epigrams, odes, and elegies among a group of accomplished poet-friends, who include the legendary literary patron Mecoenas and no less a figure than the Emperor Augustus himself.

Poetaster unfolds by following two groups of characters and two converging plots. The first concerns the young poet Ovid (along with Horace and Virgil, one of the three most famous poets of Roman antiquity) his poet friends, and their courtly lovers. These include Ovid's paramour Julia, daughter to the Emperor Augustus Caesar, and her ladies-in-waiting, all of whom pay a social call to the house of the citizen Albius and his wife Chloe, who wish to become better acquainted with the young nobility of the court. At Albius's house Ovid and his friends are joined by characters from the play's second plot: Crispinus, cousin of the courtier Cytheris, who soon falls into the company of the ne'er-do-well rogue, Captain Tucca. Tucca is a classic type on the Renaissance stage, the "braggart soldier" whom Jonson and his contemporaries lifted from the Roman drama of Plautus and Terence. Jonson renders him vividly, giving him a contemporary London idiom peppered with slang and surrounding him with a crowd of dubious characters, from the two boys who facilitate his schemes (the Pyrgi, ironically named after tall Roman siege towers) to the Histrio (Latin for "actor"), whom Tucca convinces to stage a play satirizing Horace, which will be written by the ragged poet-for-hire, Demetrius Fannius. Around this knot of roving, self-interested characters and their hapless opportunism, Jonson adds a spectrum of figures ranging from the angry and foolish (the pharmacist Minos) to the self-important and sinister (the tribune Asinius Lupus). The combined plots of Ovid and his friends and Tucca, Crispinus and their compatriots then culminate in a raucous dinner party held at court, where the young poets, their ladies, and the citizens masquerade as the Pantheon of Roman gods to drink, flirt, and pledge themselves to wanton seduction. The party is suddenly interrupted by the arrival of Caesar, flanked by Horace and Mecoenas and by the informer Lupus and the player Histrio, who have informed Caesar of suspected treason at court. Caesar, scandalized by the impiety of the scene before him, banishes Ovid from Rome, and Jonson writes a brief balcony scene between Ovid and Julia that is probably meant to remind us of Shakespeare's *Romeo and Juliet*.

Poetaster goes further than Jonson's earlier comical satires, however, since it singles out living individuals as objects of insult, notably John Marston and Thomas Dekker, two contemporary playwrights who had recently quarreled publicly with Jonson. Marston is the "poetaster" of the play's title: a minor, struggling, would-be writer named Crispinus who uses pretentious-sounding neologisms and who lacks the moral gravity that Jonson thought was necessary to writing great plays and poems. In fact Marston was an adventurous dramatic satirist in his own right and a sophisticated and accomplished poet. Dekker, for his part, was one of the most prolific writers of Jonson's period and was famous (or infamous) because he wrote for hire: plays for theater companies, pamphlets for book-sellers, pageants for the City of London. Dekker probably represented everything that Jonson despised, and feared, about the profession of playwright. Like the character Demetrius Fannius, who represents Dekker in *Poetaster*, and like many writers who tried to survive exclusively through the commerce of theater and print rather than through patronage, Dekker was chronically poor throughout his life, often borrowing money from theater managers and cycling in and out of debtor's prison. Although Jonson found success in the public theaters, he disliked submitting the fruits of his own literary judgment to popular audiences, whom he found fickle and undiscerning.

Although his unflattering portraits of Marston and Dekker caused controversy at the time, Jonson went on to collaborate with Dekker on an elaborate allegorical entertainment for James I produced by the major livery companies of London (1603) to celebrate the new king's accession to the English throne. In 1605, Jonson then collaborated with Marston and the playwright George Chapman on *Eastward Ho* (included in this anthology), which was also performed at the Blackfriars theater (an indoor theater in a fashionable district of London) by the same company of boy actors who had performed *Poetaster*, the Children of Queen Elizabeth's Chapel. Their satire of Scotsmen and citizens struck too close to their targets (James I was Scottish), and all three writers were questioned by authorities. Both Chapman and Jonson were briefly imprisoned for their involvement. This was the second time Jonson had landed in prison for a writing a controversial play—he had also run afoul of the authorities over a lost play entitled *The Isle of Dogs*, an early satirical collaboration with Thomas Nashe from 1597—and Jonson's early brushes with the law, as well as his persistent interest in contemporary satire, may have contributed to *Poetaster's* thematic concern with libel law and public reputation.

In some ways the plot trajectory of *Poetaster* mirrors the trajectory of Jonson's own career in the first decade of the seventeenth century, or at least the path he seems to have wished for himself. The play's final act shifts our attention from Ovid's love poetry, the pretentious lyrics of Crispinus, and the cheap theater of Histrio and Demetrius to the court of Caesar and to the genres of satire and epic. Horace now takes center stage, surrounded by distinguished patrons and politically connected friends; sitting on a throne above Caesar is no less a figure than Virgil himself, the preeminent poet of ancient Rome and author of the *Aeneid*, the greatest epic poem in Latin (and the source of the soon-to-be King James I's favorite royal iconography). Jonson's portrait of the court in Act V presents a vision of power and poetry as mutually collaborative, and it was a vision he would go on to develop in the many allegorical entertainments, or masques, that he wrote for James's court. Caesar elaborately praises any poetry that celebrates the true virtue that lies within Roman nobles like Cornelius Gallus and Tibullus, or that acts as a living monument to Rome's greatness. In Virgil and his poetry, he proclaims, we see "a human soul made visible in life," and, in a gesture that is as self-serving as it is magnanimous, Caesar symbolically affiliates himself with Virgil by exchanging family names with him and inviting him to read aloud from his recently finished epic. When Lupus interrupts the reading by bursting into the court with Tucca to accuse Horace of libel, Caesar responds by summarily gagging Lupus and having the Histrio whipped offstage. Virgil's approving commentary could stand as a motto for Jonson's entire play: the only true threat to a state is "malicious, ignorant, and base" interpretation that aims to "distort and strain" the work of virtuous authors. In contrast, true satire written in "modest anger" and "wholesome sharp morality" is a great service to the state (V.iii. 110–15), for it "sweeps the cobwebs from unusèd virtue/And makes her shine proportioned to her worth," like the all-powerful "free hand" of Caesar himself (V.ii. 50–52).

As Crispinus and Demetrius Fannius stumble on stage before him, Caesar grants Virgil the power to declare judgment over their "crimes," which turn out to be not only libel against the honest Horace but offenses to the canons of style, taste, and originality that Jonson himself held dear. The final scene of the play, in which Horace administers purgative drugs to Crispinus and forces him to cough up his monstrous vocabulary, is extremely funny, and Jonson took it from a similar scene in a play by the Roman author Lucian, who was influential on English theories of satire in Jonson's period. But the scene must have stung Marston especially sharply. The moment is a climax in what scholars of early modern drama often call the *Poetomachia*, a "Poet's War" or "War of the Theaters" that unfolded over a series of plays written by Jonson, Marston, and Dekker, in which the authors attempted to satirize—and publicly humiliate—one another. Later in life, Jonson claimed that Marston had started the entire quarrel by writing an unflattering portrait of him in his plays, probably the characters Chrisoganus in *Histriomastix* (1599) and Brabant Sr. in *Jack Drum's Entertainment* (1600). Both plays caricatured Jonson's appearance, his vocabulary, his habits, and even the style of satire he wrote for the stage. At some point, Jonson heard rumors that Dekker, too, was planning to write a play making fun of Jonson as "Horace," who would be the play's main character; Jonson said that he worked as quickly as he could to write *Poetaster* in anticipation of Dekker's play and in response to the plays already written by Marston. He succeeded, and Dekker's *Satiromastix* was performed late in 1601 at the Globe theater by the Chamberlain's Men (Shakespeare's playing company) and incorporated references to *Poetaster*, which Dekker had evidently seen. Both *Poetaster* and *Satiromastix* were then published early in 1602.

The 1602 quarto edition of *Poetaster* left out a few passages that had been performed on stage and that Jonson later added back for the second printed edition, the Folio of 1616 (the text below follows this second, fuller edition). Two of the passages—I.ii and III.iv—are strongly satirical of actors and lawyers, and Jonson probably cut them from print because they angered the actors as well as important members of his audience. He may have been forced to remove them by Elizabethan authorities, who reviewed all books before they were published. At the time when Jonson was writing *Poetaster*, all forms of satirical writing, whether drama, poetry, or prose, were being closely watched by the censors because of recent religious controversy and political unrest; Marston's own books of satire had been publicly burned only two years earlier, in 1599. Jonson's dedicatory letter to Richard Martin in the Folio edition of the play tells us that years earlier, when *Poetaster* first appeared, Martin had interceded on the play's behalf and eased its way onto both stage and page. A third additional passage—III.v—consists of Jonson's dramatic adaptation of Horace's *Satire* 2.1, in which Horace and his friend Trebatius discuss what kind of poetry Horace could and should write. Horace argues that he has the right to defend his reputation if he is attacked publicly, using satire that exposes vice and upholds virtue. He also draws a crucial distinction between corrective satire, which speaks in general terms about universal types, and libel, which singles out particular people for judgment and humiliation. Trebatius agrees, and concludes the scene with an observation that takes the argument a step further: if Horace, who is himself above reproach, were to satirize a particular person who deserved it, any objection would be met with laughter, and Horace would walk free of blame.

Jonson probably added the passage to the Folio edition not only because of the earlier controversy his play had caused but because with *Poetaster* he had clearly gone further than an indictment of vice in general. We know he did so not only from his characterization of Crispinus and Demetrius but from a free-standing "Apologetical Dialogue" between three characters, Nasutus, Polyposus, and an unnamed Author, that concludes the play and that also had not appeared in the earlier quarto edition. In a dedicatory letter to the reader placed before the "Apologetical Dialogue" in the Folio, Jonson says it was spoken "only once . . . upon the stage" and that it served as "all the answer I ever gave to sundry impotent libels then cast out (and some yet remaining) against me, and this play" (2–4). Nasutus and Polyposus also call the accusations against the Author "libels," continuing Jonson's thematic attempt in *Poetaster* to distinguish between public utterances that clearly violated laws against defaming a person's reputation and literary compositions that served a larger moral purpose by justly criticizing hypocrisy, pretentiousness, or licentious behavior. The Author provides some important details about the *Poetomachia* that occasioned *Poetaster*. For "three years," he declares, certain unnamed writers "did provoke me with their petulant styles," and to answer them he had chosen Augustan Rome to "show that Virgil, Horace, and the rest/Of those great master-spirits did not want/Detractors" (84–93), thereby establishing a direct line of inheritance between himself and the greatest poets of antiquity and dismissing the criticisms of Marston and Dekker as petty complaint. Polyposus then questions him about the remaining objections—"Why, they say you taxed/The law and lawyers, captains, and the players/By their particular names"—but the Author attributes most of the "slanders" to envy. In this way the "Apologetical Dialogue" returns us to the very opening of *Poetaster*, where the figure of Envy, writhing with poisonous snakes, rises from the stage to speak the play's first Prologue. He will "blast your pleasures and destroy your sports," he declares, by twisting the author's words, deliberately misinterpreting his play, and offering "spy-like suggestions" (Prologue 23–5). But when Envy notices the board hanging over the stage to announce its setting—Rome—he is seized with frustration, since he knows his malicious intent can never flourish in the virtuous atmosphere of Augustan Rome as it can in the literary culture of contemporary London. As Envy sinks back, the play's true Prologue strides on stage in shining armor to stand symbolically on his head and press him into the floor. He delivers a ringing endorsement of the play's author: the best defense against the "pride" and "folly" of malicious detractors who seek to "beslime" one's reputation, he argues, is to rise above them, armed with a "well-erected confidence" that "knows the strength of his own Muse" (75–85). The emblem is a perfect one not only for Horace in *Poetaster* but for Jonson himself, who had his eye on several audiences simultaneously at this moment in his career: the paying customers of the commercial theaters, the actors and companies who supported his work, his professional colleagues and sometime rivals, the royal censors, his would-be noble patrons, even the preferment and power of the throne itself. In the years after writing *Poetaster* Jonson would work hard to distinguish himself as the poet laureate of King James I's court, seeking lucrative commissions for noble entertainments, writing epigrams for aristocratic patrons, and taking pains to display his learning in the printed editions of his works. For in Jonson's period the theater was still a form of popular entertainment, not a high-status profession, and it is one of the enduring paradoxes of Jonson's career that a playwright with such a thorough command of theatrical form, such free-wheeling humor, and so much insight into popular culture could also be so dismissive of actors and theater audiences, so defensive about his public reputation, and so determined to elevate the status of his art.

Textual note

The copy-text for this edition is the 1616 Folio, *The works of Beniamin Ionson* (London: William Stansby, 1616), using the EEBO version of the copy in the British Library, STC 14752, checked against several editions in the Henry E. Huntington Library, and against the EEBO version of the 1602 quarto in the British Library, STC 14781. As noted above, the folio edition includes several passages that did not appear in the 1602 quarto. Both Q and F mark acts and scenes, listing at the start of the scene all of the characters who appear there; rather than "massing" entrances in this way, this edition introduces characters only as they enter, and it marks all entrances and exits in a scene (Q and F do not mark exits consistently). Both Q and F include features that are designed especially for the page and for readers: they mark occasional *sententia*, or memorable phrases in the dialogue, with quotation marks in the margins, so that a reader can copy them into a notebook, and they use occasional marginal annotations to indicate Jonson's classical sources. This edition records these features in the footnotes. I have also consulted the 2012 Cambridge edition of Jonson's *Works*, in both print and online editions, and two other modern editions cited below.

Further reading

Editions

Herford, C. H. and Percy Simpson (eds) (1932) *Poetaster*, in C. H. Herford and Percy Simpson (eds) *The Works of Ben Jonson*, vol. 4, Oxford: Clarendon Press.

Jackson, Gabriel Bernhard (ed.) (2012) *Poetaster*, in David Bevington, Martin Butler, and Ian Donaldson (eds) *The Cambridge Edition of the Works of Ben Jonson*, vol. 2, Cambridge: Cambridge University Press.

Kidnie, Margaret Jane (ed.) (2000) *Poetaster*, in Margaret Jane Kidnie (ed.) *The Devil is an Ass and Other Plays*, Oxford: Oxford University Press.

Critical and contextual reading

Barish, Jonas A. (1958) "Baroque Prose in the Theater: Ben Jonson," *PMLA* 73: 184–95.

Bednarz, James (2001) *Shakespeare and the Poet's War*, New York: Columbia University Press.

Kernan, Alvin (1959) *The Cankered Muse: Satire of the English Renaissance*. New Haven: Yale University Press.

Loewenstein, Joseph (1999) "Personal Material: Jonson and Book-burning," in Martin Butler (ed.), *Re-presenting Ben Jonson: Text, History, Performance*. Houndmills: Macmillian, 93–113.

Loewenstein, Joseph (2003) "Martial, Jonson, and the Assertion of Plagiarism," in Kevin Sharpe and Steven Zwicker (eds), *Reading, Society, and Politics in Early Modern England*, Cambridge: Cambridge University Press, 275–94.

Moss, Ann (1999) "Horace in the Sixteenth Century," in Glyn P. Norton (ed.), *The Cambridge History of Literary Criticism, Vol. III: The Renaissance*, Cambridge: Cambridge University Press, 66–76.

Womack, Peter (1986) *Ben Jonson*, Oxford: Blackwell.

Poetaster, or His Arraignment (1601)

A Comical Satire

Acted in the year 1601 by the then Children of Queen ELIZABETH'S Chapel

The Author B. J.

Mart.

Et mihi nullo de fama rubore placet[1]

To the Virtuous, and My Worthy Friend, Mr. Richard Martin[2]

Sir,

A thankful man owes a courtesy ever, the unthankful but[3] when he needs it. To make mine own mark[4] appear and show by which of these seals I am known,[5] I send you this piece of what may live of mine;[6] for whose innocence, as for the Author's, you were once a noble and timely undertaker to the greatest Justice of this kingdom.[7] Enjoy now the delight of your goodness, which is to see that prosper, you preserved: [8] and posterity to owe the reading of that, without offence, to your name, which so much ignorance and malice of the times then conspired to have suppressed.[9]

Your true lover,[10]

BEN. JONSON.

The Persons of the Play[11]

AUGUSTUS CAESAR,[12] *Emperor of Rome*
MECOENAS,[13] *poet and famous patron*
MARCUS OVID, *Senior, father of Publius Ovid*
LUSCUS, *servant of Ovid Senior and Ovid*
TIBULLUS,[14] *poet and friend of Pub. Ovid*

1 Mart. . . . *placet*: a line from an epigram (7.12.4) by the Roman poet Martial (c.40–c.104 CE): "No fame pleases me that causes anyone to blush"
2 Mr. Richard Martin: 1570–1618, lawyer and statesman
3 2 but: only
4 3 mark: signature
5 3 show by . . . am known: i.e. to show what kind of man I am
6 4 this piece . . . of mine: this play; this part of my work which I claim publicly
7 4–5 for whose . . . this kingdom: Martin had intervened with the Elizabethan authorities to protect Jonson and his play (see Introduction)
8 6 that prosper, you preserved: either "to see this play prosper, which you helped preserve" or "to see this play prosper and your fame preserved"
9 8 suppressed: see Introduction
10 9 lover: friend
11 The Persons of the Play: this is F's heading for the dramatis personae; the list given here is an expanded version of what is given in F
12 CAESAR: Gaius Octavius Thorinus (63 BCE–14 CE), grand-nephew and adopted heir of Julius Caesar, member (with Marcus Lepidus and Mark Antony) of the Triumvirate that ruled Rome after Caesar's death. He presided over a long period of imperial expansion, relative peace, and artistic flowering
13 MECOENAS: Gaius Cilnius Maecenas (c. 70 BCE–8 CE), wealthy nobleman, friend of Augustus, and famous patron of poets, notably Virgil, Horace, and Propertius
14 TIBULLUS: Albius Tibullus (c. 55 BCE–19 CE), Roman elegiac poet

CORNELIUS GALLUS,[15] *poet and friend of Pub. Ovid*
PROPERTIUS,[16] *poet and friend of Pub. Ovid*
FUSCUS ARISTIUS, *scholar, friend of Horace*
PUBLIUS OVID, *Junior,*[17] *poet, son of Marcus Ovid*
VIRGIL,[18] *poet*
HORACE,[19] *poet and critic*
TREBATIUS, *lawyer, friend of Horace*
ASINIUS LUPUS,[20] *Tribune*
PANTILIUS TUCCA,[21] *former soldier, now a man about town*
CRISPINUS,[22] *would-be poet: the "poetaster" of the play's title, cousin of Cytheris*
HERMOGENES, *musician*
DEMETRIUS FANNIUS,[23] *writer for hire, would-be poet and playwright*
ALBIUS, *citizen and husband to Chloe*
MINOS, *apothecary*
HISTRIO,[24] *an actor*
AESOP, *an actor*
PYRGI,[25] *boy pages to Tucca*
JULIA,[26] *daughter of Augustus, love of Ovid*
CYTHERIS, *lady, love of Propertius, cousin of Crispinus*
PLAUTIA, *lady, love of Tibullus*
CHLOE, *gentlewoman, wife of Albius*

Envy, Prologue, Lictors, Equites Romani (Knights of Rome), Maids

The Scene

ROME

[**Induction**]

After the second sounding.[27] ENVY *arising in the midst of the stage*[28]

ENVY Light, I salute thee, but with wounded nerves,
Wishing thy golden splendor pitchy darkness.

15 GALLUS: Gaius Cornelius Gallus (c. 70 BCE–26 CE), Roman elegiac poet, friend of Augustus
16 PROPERTIUS: Sextus Propertius (c. 50 BCE–15 CE). Roman elegiac poet, friend of Gallus and Virgil
17 OVID, *Junior*: Publius Ovidius Naso (43 BCE–18 CE). Along with Virgil and Horace, one of the three most famous poets of Augustan Rome. Author of the *Metamorphoses*, the most significant literary source of classical mythology, as well as of influential books of elegies on many subjects: love, Roman festivals, and the sadness of exile. Augustus banished Ovid from Rome in 8 CE for unknown reasons, and he died in Tomis (modern-day Constanta, Romania)
18 VIRGIL: Publius Vergilius Maro (70 BCE–19 BCE), the most famous poet of the entire Roman period and author of three highly influential literary works: the *Eclogues* (a collection of pastoral poems), the *Georgics* (poems on agriculture and myth), and the *Aeneid*, an epic poem about the hero Aeneas's adventures after the Trojan War, including the founding of Rome
19 HORACE: Quintus Horatius Flaccus (65 BCE–8 CE), a major lyric poet, satirist, and literary critic in Augustan Rome. Educated at Athens, his poetry followed Greek verse models but commented on contemporary Roman society and manners. In *Poetaster* he is a figure for Jonson himself
20 ASINIUS LUPUS: literally "asinine wolf"
21 PANTILIUS TUCCA: his name is suggested by a minor character in one of Horace's *Satires*
22 CRISPINUS: the name "Crispanus" comes from one of Horace's *Satires*, and many of the character's social attributes and speech mannerisms are meant to recall those of John Marston (1576–1634), a contemporary playwright and satirist, also a participant in the so-called "poets' war" (see Introduction)
23 FANNIUS: another combination of names from Horace's satires, the character is a satiric portrait of the playwright Thomas Dekker (1572–1632), the third author contributing to the "poets' war" with Jonson and Marston
24 HISTRIO: literally, "actor"
25 PYRGI: "pyrgus" (plural "pyrgi") is the Latin word for "siege tower"; the name pokes fun at the two boys, probably of diminutive stature, who act as pages for Captain Tucca
26 JULIA: Julia the Elder, daughter of Augustus (39 BCE–14 CE), said to be the lover of Ovid. The historical Julia was banished by Augustus for adultery in 2 BCE
27 0 SD *sounding*: trumpet blast; the action of a play typically began after the third sounding
28 0 SD *in the midst of the stage*: Envy enters through a trap door in the floor of the stage, with snakes curled around his arms

What's here? *Th'Arraignment*?[29] Ay, this, this is it,
That our sunk eyes have waked for all this while:
Here will be subject for my snakes, and me.
Cling to my neck and wrists, my loving worms,
And cast you round, in soft and amorous folds,
Till I do bid uncurl; then break your knots,
Shoot out your selves at length, as[30] your forced stings
Would hide themselves within his maliced[31] sides,
To whom I shall apply you. Stay! The shine
Of this assembly[32] here offends my sight,
I'll darken that first, and outface[33] their grace.
Wonder not, if I stare: these fifteen weeks[34]
(So long as since the plot was but an embryon)[35]
Have I, with burning lights, mixed vigilant thoughts
In expectation of this hated play.
To which (at last) I am arrived as Prologue.
Nor would I you should look for other looks,
Gesture, or compliment from me than what
Th' infected bulk of Envy can afford:[36]
For I am risen here with a covetous[37] hope,
To blast your pleasures and destroy your sports,
With wrestings,[38] comments, applications,[39]
Spy-like suggestions, privy[40] whisperings,
And thousand such promoting sleights[41] as these.
Mark how I will begin: the scene is—hah!
Rome? Rome? and Rome? Crack eye-strings, and your balls[42]
Drop into earth; let me be ever blind.
I am prevented;[43] all my hopes are crossed,
Checked, and abated; fie, a freezing sweat
Flows forth at all my pores, my entrails burn:
What should I do? Rome? Rome? Oh my vexed soul,
How might I force this to the present state?[44]
Are there no players[45] here? No poet-apes[46]
That come with basilisk's eyes,[47] whose forkèd tongues
Are steeped in venom, as their hearts in gall?[48]

29 3 *Th'Arraignment*: Envy glimpses the subtitle of the play that is about to be performed; a sign over the stage would have announced the title and location of the play
30 9 as: as if
31 10 maliced: hated
32 12 assembly: the audience of the theater, whom Envy now notices
33 13 outface: stare down
34 14 fifteen weeks: the length of time it took Jonson to write the play
35 15 embryon: seed
36 19–21 Nor would . . . can afford: nor do I wish you to expect any expression, gesture, or aspect that is not befitting Envy
37 22 covetous: greedy
38 24 wrestings: distortions of meaning
39 24 applications: interpretations
40 25 privy: private
41 26 promoting sleights: provocative tricks
42 28 balls: eyeballs
43 30 prevented: blocked
44 34 force this . . . present state: force an interpretation of play's action so that it seems to apply to the present
45 35 players: actors
46 35 poet-apes: would-be poets, imitators
47 36 basilisk's eyes: the gaze of the basilisk, a mythical reptile, was thought to be fatal
48 37 gall: bitterness

Either of these would help me; they could wrest,[49]
Pervert,[50] and poison all they hear or see,
With senseless glosses[51] and allusions.
Now if you be good devils, fly me not.[52]
You know what dear and ample faculties[53]
I have endowed you with; I'll lend you more.
Here, take my snakes among you, come, and eat,
And while the squeezed juice flows in your black jaws,
Help me to damn the author. Spit it forth
Upon his lines and show your rusty teeth[54]
At every word, or accent; or else choose
Out of my longest vipers to stick down
In your deep throats, and let the heads come forth
At your rank[55] mouths, that he[56] may see you armed
With triple malice, to hiss, sting, and tear
His work, and him; to forge, and then declaim,
Traduce, corrupt, apply, inform, suggest:[57]
Oh, these are gifts wherein your souls are blest.
What? do you hide yourselves? Will none appear?
None answer? What, doth this calm troop affright you?
Nay, then I do despair: down, sink again.
This travail[58] is all lost with my dead hopes.
If in such bosoms spite have left to dwell,[59]
Envy is not on earth, nor scarce in hell. [*Prepares to exit through the floor*]

The third sounding

[*Enter* PROLOGUE]

PROLOGUE Stay, monster, ere thou sink; thus on thy head [*Steps on him*]
Set we our bolder foot, with which we tread
Thy malice into earth. So spite should die,
Despised and scorned by noble industry.[60]
If any muse[61] why I salute the stage,
An armed[62] Prologue, know 'tis a dangerous age:
Wherein who writes had need present his scenes
Fortyfold-proof against the conjuring means
Of base detractors[63] and illiterate apes[64]
That fill up rooms in fair and formal shapes.

49 38 wrest: seize
50 39 pervert: distort
51 40 glosses: interpretations
52 41 fly me not: don't run away from me. Over the next several lines, Envy speaks to the audience
53 42 faculties: powers
54 47 show your rusty teeth: make grimaces
55 51 rank: bad smelling
56 51 he: i.e. the author
57 53–4 to forge . . . inform, suggest: Envy encourages the audience to spit poison at Jonson, to deliberately misinterpret his play, and to spread treacherous and malicious ideas about it to others
58 59 travail: labor
59 60 If even such breasts as yours do not harbor spite
60 65 industry: hard work
61 66 If any muse: if anyone wonders
62 67 armed: the Prologue is dressed in military armor
63 70 detractors: critics
64 70 apes: imitators

'Gainst these have we put on this forced defense;
Whereof the allegory and hid sense
Is, that a well-erected confidence
Can fright their pride, and laugh their folly hence.
Here now, put case[65] our author should, once more,
Swear that his play were good; he doth implore
You would not argue him[66] of arrogance,
Howe'er that common spawn of ignorance,
Our fry of[67] writers, may beslime his fame,
And give his action that adulterate[68] name.
Such full-blown vanity he more doth loathe
Then base dejection: there's a mean 'twixt both,
Which with a constant firmness he pursues,
As one that knows the strength of his own Muse.
And this[69] he hopes all free souls will allow;
Others, that take it with a rugged[70] brow,
Their moods he rather pities, than envies;
His mind it is above their injuries.

Act I, scene i

[LUSCUS *enters to find* OVID *reading at his desk*]

OVID [*Reads*] "Then, when this body falls in funeral fire,
My name shall live, and my best part aspire."[71]
It shall go so.

LUSCUS Young master, master Ovid, do you hear? God's a me! Away with your songs and sonnets, and on with your gown and cap, quickly: here, here, your father will be a man of this room[72] presently. Come, nay, nay, nay, nay be brief. These verses too, a poison on 'hem,[73] I cannot abide 'hem, they make me ready to cast,[74] by the banks of Helicon.[75] Nay look, what a rascally untoward[76] thing this poetry is; I could tear 'hem now.

OVID Give me,[77] how near's my father?

LUSCUS Heart a'man,[78] get a law book in your hand, I will not answer you else. [OVID *picks up a law book*] Why so, now there's some formality in you. By Jove, and three or four of the gods more, I am right of mine old master's humor[79] for that; this villainous poetry will undo you, by the welkin.[80]

OVID What, hast thou buskins[81] on, Luscus, that thou swearest so tragically and high?

LUSCUS No, but I have boots on, sir, and so has your father too by this time, for he called for

65 76 put case: suppose
66 78 argue him: accuse him
67 80 fry of: smallest, most insignificant
68 81 adulterate: debased, i.e. if Jonson declares the play to be good, others may call him prideful
69 86 this: i.e. Jonson's healthy pride in his own play
70 87 rugged: frowning
71 1–2 These are the last lines of Ovid's *Elegy* 1.15, which Jonson has translated into his own English, following Christopher Marlowe's earlier translation of the elegies (c. 1582). In Jonson's scene, the young Ovid has just finished writing the poem; the lines allude to the Roman practice of burning the body after death, while the soul (and name) lives on
72 5–6 man of this room: physically present in your room
73 6 'hem: them
74 7 cast: vomit
75 7 Helicon: the sacred mountain of the Muses
76 8 untoward: stubborn, unruly
77 9 Give me: give those back!
78 10 Heart a'man: Heart of a man (a mild oath)
79 12 right of . . . master's humor: of exactly my master's mood or opinion
80 13 welkin: heavens
81 14 buskins: high boots worn by tragic actors

'hem ere I came from the lodging.

OVID Why? Was he no readier?

LUSCUS Oh no; and there was the mad skeldering[82] captain, with the velvet arms,[83] ready to lay hold on him as he comes down:[84] he that presses every man he meets with an oath, to lend him money, and cries "Thou must do't, old boy, as thou art a man, a man of worship."[85]

OVID Who? Pantilius Tucca?

LUSCUS Ay, he; and I met little master Lupus, the tribune, going thither too.

OVID Nay, and[86] he be under their arrest,[87] I may (with safety enough) read over my elegy before he come. [*Picks up his poem again*]

LUSCUS God sa' me![88] What'll you do? Why, young master, you are not castalian[89] mad, lunatic, frantic, desperate? Ha?

OVID What ailest thou, Luscus?

LUSCUS God be with you, sir, I'll leave you to your poetical fancies, and furies. I'll not be guilty, I. [*Exit*]

OVID Be not, good ignorance. I'm glad th'art gone:
For thus alone, our ear shall better judge
The hasty errors of our morning muse. [*Reads*]
"Envy, why twits thou[90] me, my time's spent ill?
And call'st my verse, fruits of an idle quill?
Or that (unlike the line[91] from whence I sprung)
Wars dusty honors I pursue not young?
Or that I study not the tedious laws;
And prostitute my voice to every cause?
Thy scope is mortal, mine eternal, fame:
Which through the world shall ever chant my name.
Homer will live, whilst Tenedos stands, and Ide,[92]
Or, to the sea, fleet[93] Simois[94] doth slide:
And so shall Hesiod[95] too, while vines do bear,
Or crooked sickles crop the ripened care.
Callimachus,[96] though in invention low,
Shall still be sung: since he in art doth flow.
No loss shall come to Sophocles'[97] proud vein.[98]
With sun, and moon, Aratus[99] shall remain.
Whilst slaves be false, fathers hard, and bawds be whorish,
Whilst harlots flatter, shall Menander[100] flourish.
Ennius,[101] though rude, and Accius's[102] high-reared strain,

82 18 skeldering: begging, swindling
83 18 velvet arms: sword with velvet scabbard, a fashion
84 19 down: downstairs
85 20 man of worship: distinguished person
86 23 and: if
87 23 under their arrest: delayed by them
88 25 God sa' me: God save me
89 25 castalian: from Castalia, the spring of the Muses, hence "in a poetic frenzy"
90 33 why twits thou: why do you reproach. Ovid now reads the poem he just finished, *Elegy* 1.15, in Jonson's own translation
91 35 the line: Ovid was descended from nobility, hence would have been expected to serve in the wars
92 41 Tenedos (an island near Troy) and Ide (Mt. Ida) both appear in Homer's *Iliad*
93 42 fleet: swift
94 42 Simois: a river near Troy
95 43 Hesiod: c. 700 BCE, classical poet of agriculture and farming
96 45 Callimachus: c. 310 BCE, a Libyan Greek poet who wrote epigrams and elegies rather than epics (hence "invention low")
97 47 Sophocles: c. 496 BCE, Greek tragic poet
98 47 proud vein: lofty style
99 48 Aratus: c. 310 BCE, Greek poet of weather and astronomy
100 50 Menander: c. 342 BCE, Greek comic poet who wrote about everyday life
101 51 Ennius: c. 240 BCE, Roman poet of historical epic, thought to have a rough style
102 51 Accius: 170 BCE, Roman tragic poet, was admired for his elegant style ("strain")

A fresh applause in every age shall gain.
Of Varro's[103] name, what ear shall not be told?
Of Jason's Argo?[104] And the fleece of gold?
Then shall Lucretius'[105] lofty numbers[106] die,
When earth, and seas in fire and flames shall fry.
Tytirus,[107] tillage,[108] Aenee[109] shall be read,
Whilst Rome of all the conquered world is head.
Till Cupid's fires be out, and his bow broken,
Thy verses (neat Tibullus[110]) shall be spoken.
Our Gallus shall be known from east to west:
So shall Lycoris,[111] whom he now loves best.
The suffering plough-share, or the flint may wear:
But heavenly poesy no death can fear.
Kings shall give place to it, and kingly shows,
The banks o'er which gold-bearing Tagus[112] flows.
Kneel hinds[113] to trash:[114] me let bright Phoebus[115] swell,
With cups full flowing from the muses' well.
Frost-fearing myrtle[116] shall impale[117] my head,
And of sad lovers I'll be often read.
Envy, the living, not the dead, doth bite:
For after death all men receive their right.[118]
Then, when this body falls in funeral fire,
My name shall live, and my best part aspire."

Act I, scene ii

[*Enter*] OVID SENIOR [*with*] LUSCUS, TUCCA, LUPUS, *and* PYRGUS

OVID SEN Your name shall live indeed, sir; you say true. But how infamously, how scorned and condemned in the eyes and ears of the best and gravest Romans, that you think not on: you never so much as dream of that. Are these the fruits of all my travail and expenses? Is this the scope and aim of thy studies? Are these the hopeful courses, wherewith I have so long flattered my expectation from thee? Verses? Poetry? Ovid, whom I thought to see the pleader,[119] become Ovid the play-maker?
OVID No, sir.
OVID SEN Yes, sir. I hear of a tragedy of yours coming forth for the common players there, called *Medea*.[120] By my household gods, if I come to the acting of it, I'll add one tragic part more than is yet expected to it: believe me when I promise it. What? Shall I have my son

103 53 Varro: 82 BCE, Roman poet who translated the *Argonautica* from Greek to Latin
104 54 Argo: the name of the ship that the mythical hero Jason used to search for the golden fleece
105 55 Lucretius: 99 BCE, Roman poet and philosopher
106 55 numbers: verses
107 57 Tytirus: a character in Vigil's first *Eclogue*
108 57 tillage: Virgil also wrote the Georgics, poems about farming
109 57 Aenee: Aeneas, title character of Virgil's *Aeneid*
110 60 neat: elegant; Tibullus (and Gallus in the next line) are Ovid's contemporaries, and characters in this play
111 62 Lycoris: poetic name for Cytheris, love of Gallus
112 66 Tagus: the largest river in Spain, flowing into Portugal and believed to carry gold in its waters
113 67 hinds: servants, rustics
114 67 trash: bad poetry
115 67 Phoebus: god of the sun
116 69 myrtle: one of the traditional leaves that crowned the poet's head
117 69 impale: encircle
118 71–2 Envy, the … their right: in the 1616 edition of the play, these two lines are marked with quotation marks to signal that they are sententiae, i.e. memorable phrases
119 5 pleader: attorney arguing in court
120 9 *Medea*: here not the play by Euripides but a lost tragedy by Ovid of which only two lines survive

a stager[121] now? An ingle[122] for players? A gull?[123] A rook?[124] A shot-clog?[125] To make suppers, and be laughed at? Publius, I will set thee on the funeral pile first.
OVID Sir, I beseech you to have patience.
LUSCUS Nay, this 'tis to have your ears dammed up to good counsel. I did augur all this to him aforehand, without poring into an ox's paunch[126] for the matter, and yet he would not be scrupulous.[127]
TUCCA [*To* LUSCUS] How now, good man slave?[128] What, roly poly? All rivals,[129] rascal? [*To* OVID SEN] Why my Master of worship, dost hear? Are these thy best projects?[130] Is this thy designs and thy discipline,[131] to suffer knaves to be competitors with commanders and gentlemen? Are we parallels, rascal? Are we parallels?
OVID SEN [*To* LUSCUS] Sirrah,[132] go get my horses ready. You'll still be prating.[133]
TUCCA Do, you perpetual stinkard, do; go, talk to tapsters and ostlers,[134] you slave, they are i' your element, go. Here be the emperor's captains, you raggamuffin[135] rascal, and not your comrades.
LUPUS Indeed, Marcus Ovid, these players are an idle generation, and do much harm in a state, corrupt young gentry very much, I know it. I have not been a tribune thus long, and observed nothing. Besides, they will rob us, us that are magistrates, of our respect, bring us upon their stages, and make us ridiculous to the plebeians; they will play you, or me, the wisest men they can come by still—me!—only to bring us in contempt with the vulgar, and make us cheap.[136]
TUCCA Th'art in the right, my venerable cropshin,[137] they will indeed. The tongue of the oracle never twanged truer. Your courtier cannot kiss his mistress' slippers in quiet for 'hem, nor your white innocent gallant pawn his reveling suit to make his punk[138] a supper. An honest decayed commander cannot skelder, cheat, nor be seen in a bawdy house but he shall be straight in one of their wormwood[139] comedies. They are grown licentious, the rogues, libertines, flat libertines. They forget they are i' the statute,[140] the rascals, they are blazoned[141] there, there they are tricked,[142] they and their pedigrees; they need no other heralds, iwis.[143]
OVID SEN Methinks if nothing else, yet this alone: the very reading of the public edicts[144] should fright thee from commerce with them and give thee distaste enough of their actions. But this betrays what a student you are; this argues your proficiency in the law.[145]
OVID They wrong me, sir, and do abuse you more,

121 11 stager: actor
122 11 ingle: male prostitute
123 11 gull: foolish dupe
124 11 rook: fool
125 11 shot-clog: a hanger-on whom other people tolerate only because he pays for shots (drinks) or "suppers"
126 15 ox's paunch: soothsayers who practiced augury, or the prediction of the future, often looked for signs in the guts of sacrificial cattle
127 16 scrupulous: cautious
128 17 slave: servile person, here a playful epithet, as is "roly poly" and "rascal" (synonyms)
129 17 rivals: equals
130 18 projects: plans, schemes
131 19 discipline: course of study, guiding rule
132 21 Sirrah: term of address used for inferiors
133 21 prating: prattling
134 22 tapsters and ostlers: employees in a tavern or inn who pour drinks (tapster) and handle the horses (ostler)
135 23 raggamuffin: ragged, good-for-nothing
136 25–30 Indeed, Marcus . . . us cheap: Lupus voices many of the common complaints against actors and the public stages in Jonson's time
137 31 cropshin: bad herring
138 33 punk: prostitute
139 35 wormwood: bitter-flavored
140 36 i' the statute: subject to the laws regulating vagrants and men without masters or other employment
141 36 blazoned: pictured or displayed by a heraldic sign; the line compares the legal statutes to a coat of arms for the actors, who are imagined to have a criminal pedigree
142 37 tricked: drawn
143 37 iwis: certainly
144 38 public edicts: laws against playing similar to those passed periodically by the London authorities
145 40 this argues . . . the law: your ignorance of the statutes against playing shows how little you know about the law in general

That blow[146] your ears with these untrue reports.
I am not known unto the open[147] stage,
Nor do I traffic in their theaters.
Indeed, I do acknowledge, at request
Of some near friends, and honorable Romans,
I have begun a poem of that nature.

OVID SEN You have, sir, a poem? And where is't? That's the law you study.

OVID Cornelius Gallus borrowed it to read.

OVID SEN Cornelius Gallus? There's another gallant, too, hath drunk of the same poison, and Tibullus and Propertius. But these are gentlemen of means and revenue now. Thou art a younger brother and hast nothing but thy bare exhibition,[148] which I protest shall be bare indeed, if thou forsake not these unprofitable by-courses,[149] and that timely[150] too. Name me a professed[151] poet that his poetry did ever afford him so much as a competency.[152] Ay, your god of poets there, whom all of you admire and reverence so much, Homer, he whose worm-eaten statue must not be spewed against[153] but with hallowed lips and groveling adoration, what was he? What was he?

TUCCA Marry, I'll tell thee, old swaggerer. He was a poor, blind, rhyming rascal that lived obscurely up and down in booths and tap-houses[154] and scarce ever made a good meal in his sleep,[155] the whoreson hungry beggar.

OVID SEN He says well. Nay, I know this nettles[156] you now, but answer me: is't not true? You'll tell me his name shall live, and that (now being dead) his works have eternized him, and made him divine. But could this divinity feed him, while he lived? Could his name feast him?

TUCCA Or purchase him a senator's revenue? Could it?

OVID SEN Ay, or give him place[157] in the commonwealth? Worship, or attendants? Make him be carried in his litter?

TUCCA Thou speakest sentences,[158] old Bias.[159]

LUPUS All this the law will do, young sir, if you'll follow it.

OVID SEN If he be mine, he shall follow and observe what I will apt him to,[160] or I profess here openly and utterly to disclaim in[161] him.

OVID Sir, let me crave you will forgo these moods;
I will be anything, or study anything;
I'll prove the unfashioned[162] body of the law
Pure elegance, and make her rugged'st strains
Run smoothly as Propertius' elegies.

OVID SEN Propertius' elegies? Good!

LUPUS Nay, you take him too quickly, Marcus.

OVID SEN Why, he cannot speak, he cannot think out of poetry; he is bewitched with it.

LUPUS Come, do not misprize[163] him.

146 42 blow: whisper into
147 43 open: public, commercial
148 52 bare exhibition: small allowance
149 53 by-courses: distractions, minor paths that lie off the main way (to wealth and social distinction)
150 53 timely: quickly
151 54 professed: publicly acknowledged
152 54 competency: sufficient income
153 56 spewed against: spit or vomited upon
154 59 booths and tap-houses: food stalls and taverns
155 59–60 scarce ever . . . his sleep: even in his dreams, Homer ate poorly
156 61 nettles: bothers
157 65 place: office, public distinction
158 67 sentences: memorable phrases, proverbial wisdom
159 67 Bias: one of the seven Sages of antiquity
160 69 apt him to: make him fit for
161 70 disclaim in: disown
162 73 unfashioned: rough
163 79 misprize: misvalue

OVID SEN "Mis-prize"? Ay, marry, I would have him use some such words now. They have some touch, some taste of the law. He should make himself a style out of these, and let his Propertius' elegies go by.

LUPUS Indeed, young Publius, he that will now hit the mark[164] must shoot through the law; we have no other planet reigns, and in that sphere you may sit,[165] and sing with angels. Why, the law makes a man happy, without respecting any other merit.[166] A simple scholar, or none at all, may be a lawyer.

TUCCA He tells thee true, my noble neophyte;[167] my little grammaticaster,[168] he does. It shall never put thee to[169] thy mathematics, metaphysics, philosophy, and I know not what supposed sufficiencies,[170] if thou canst but have the patience to plod enough, talk, and make noise enough, be impudent enough, and 'tis enough.

LUPUS Three books will furnish you.

TUCCA And the less art,[171] the better, besides, when it shall be in the power of thy cheverel[172] conscience to do right, or wrong, at thy pleasure, my pretty Alcibiades.[173]

LUPUS Ay, and to have better men than himself, by many thousand degrees,[174] to observe him, and stand bare.[175]

TUCCA True, and he to carry himself proud, and stately, and have the law on his side for't, old boy.

OVID SEN Well, the day grows old, gentlemen, and I must leave you. Publius, if thou wilt hold my favor, abandon these idle, fruitless studies that so bewitch thee. Send Janus[176] home his back-face again, and look only forward to the law: intend that. I will allow thee what shall suit thee in the rank of gentlemen and maintain thy society with the best, and under these conditions I leave thee. My blessings light upon thee, if thou respect them. If not, mine eyes may drop[177] for thee, but thine own heart will ache for itself, and so farewell.

[*Enter* LUSCUS]

What, are my horses come?

LUSCUS Yes, sir, they are at the gate without.[178]

OVID SEN That's well. Asinius Lupus, a word [*gestures to him*]. Captain, I shall take my leave of you?

TUCCA No, my little old boy, dispatch with Cothurnus[179] there. I'll attend thee, I—

LUSCUS [*Aside*] To borrow some ten drachmas,[180] I know his project.

OVID SEN [*To* LUPUS] Sir, you shall make me beholding[181] to you. [*Exit* LUPUS]

Now Captain Tucca, what say you?

TUCCA Why, what should I say? Or what can I say, my flower o' the order?[182] Should I say,

164 83 mark: target (i.e. for a bow and arrow)
165 84 we have . . . may sit: the law is imagined to have the astrological influence of a powerful planet (it "reigns"), which moves through a particular orbit or transit ("sphere")
166 85 without respecting any other merit: not to mention its other good qualities
167 87 neophyte: novice, beginner
168 87 grammaticaster: little grammar master
169 88 put thee to: demand of you
170 89 sufficiencies: qualifications
171 92 art: skill, pretense
172 92 cheverel: a kind of kid-leather that was especially pliant and flexible
173 93 Alcibiades: young man loved by Socrates whose political allegiances were changeable
174 94 degrees: social ranks
175 95 stand bare: remove their hats (as a sign of deference)
176 99 Janus: the two-faced god, usually pictured as looking both backward and forward
177 103 drop: cry (drop tears)
178 105 without: outside
179 108 Cothurnus: a boot worn by tragic actors, like a buskin; here a nickname for Lupus
180 109 drachmas: Greek coins used as currency in Augustan Rome
181 110 beholding: beholden, obligated
182 112 flower o' the order: distinguished member of an already distinguished group (e.g. knights, officials, etc.—another of Tucca's extravagant, fanciful compliments)

thou art rich? Or that thou art honorable? Or wise? Or valiant? Or learned? Or liberal? Why, thou art all these, and thou knowest it (my noble Lucullus[183]) thou knowest it. Come, be not ashamed of thy virtues, old stump. Honor's a good brooch to wear in a man's hat, at all times. Thou art the man of war's Mecoenas,[184] old boy. Why should'st not thou be graced then by them, as well as he is by his poets? How now, my carrier,[185] what news?

[*Enter* PYRGUS, *who whispers in* TUCCA's *ear*]

LUSCUS [*Aside*] The boy has stayed within for his cue, this half hour.[186]

TUCCA Come, do not whisper to me, but speak it out. What? It is no treason against the state, I hope, is't?

LUSCUS [*Aside*] Yes, against the state of my master's purse.

PYRGUS Sir, Agrippa desires you to forbear him till the next week: his moils[187] are not yet come up.[188]

TUCCA His moils? Now the bots, the spavin, and the glanders,[189] and some dozen diseases more light on him and his moils. What ha' they, the yellows, his moils, that they come no faster? Or are they foundered?[190] Ha? His moils ha' the staggers belike: ha' they?

PYRGUS Oh no, sir. [*Aside*] Then your tongue might be suspected for one of his moils.

TUCCA He owes me almost a talent,[191] and he thinks to bear it away[192] with his moils, does he? Sirrah, you nutcracker,[193] go your ways to him again, and tell him I must ha' money, I. I cannot eat stones and turfs, say. What, will he clem[194] me, and my followers? Ask him, an' he will clem me: do, go. He would have me fry my jerkin,[195] would he? Away, setter,[196] away. [*Calls him back*] Yet stay, my little tumbler: this old boy shall supply[197] now [*gesturing toward* OVID SEN]. I will not trouble him,[198] I cannot be importunate, I. I cannot be impudent.

PYRGUS Alas, sir, no: you are the most maidenly blushing creature upon the earth.

TUCCA [*To* OVID SEN] Dost thou hear, my little six and fifty,[199] or thereabouts? Thou art not to learn[200] the humors and tricks of that old bald cheater, Time. Thou had'st not this chain for nothing.[201] Men of worth have their chimeras,[202] as well as other creatures. And they do see monsters, sometimes. They do, they do, brave boy.

PYRGUS [*Aside*] Better cheap than he shall see you, I warrant him.[203]

TUCCA Thou must let me have six, six drachmas I mean, old boy; thou shalt do it. I tell thee, old boy, thou shalt, and in private too, dost thou see? Go, walk off. [*Pulls him aside*] There, there. Six is the sum. Thy son's a gallant spark, and must not be put out of a sudden.[204] [*To*

183 114 Lucullus: wealthy, generous Roman general and politician

184 116 man of war's Mecoenas: a patron of soldiers (like Tucca) as Mecoenas was a famous patron of poets

185 117 carrier: messenger

186 118 Luscus suggests that Tucca has arranged for the boy to enter at this point to assist in his con of Ovid Senior. Pyrgus pretends that one of Tucca's debtors (Agrippa) is asking for an extension on a loan. This sets up Tucca's request to Ovid Senior for money

187 122 moils: mules

188 123 come up: arrived (presumably carrying a load of valuable commodities, which Agrippa will either sell or use as payment for Tucca's imaginary loan)

189 124 the bots . . . the glanders: like "yellows" and "staggers" in the next lines, diseases carried by horses and other livestock

190 126 foundered: made lame

191 128 talent: a measure of weight in gold or silver, here meant to stand for a considerable sum of money

192 128 bear it away: escape the debt

193 129 nutcracker: sharp, diminutive little fellow

194 130 clem: starve

195 131 jerkin: close-fitting leather jacket

196 131 setter: a hunting dog (as is a "tumbler" in the next line)

197 132 supply: supply the money Tucca needs

198 133 him: here the fictional "Agrippa"

199 135 six and fifty: fifty-six-year-old, i.e. an "old dog"

200 135–6 Thou art not to learn: No one needs to teach you

201 136–7 Thou hadst . . . for nothing: you did what you had to do to get the gold chain you're wearing

202 137 chimeras: mythological monsters combined from several creatures, here "fears"

203 139 His fears will cost him less than the rewards he'll end up giving you

204 142 put out of a sudden: precipitously disowned

OVID] Come hither, Callimachus, thy father tells me thou art too poetical, boy; thou must not be so; thou must leave them,[205] young novice, thou must; they are a sort of poor starved rascals that are ever wrapped up in foul linen, and can boast of nothing but a lean visage, peering out of a seam-rent[206] suit, the very emblems of beggary. No, dost hear? Turn lawyer, thou shalt be my solicitor. [OVID SEN *gives* TUCCA *money*] 'Tis right,[207] old boy, is't?

OVID SEN You were best tell[208] it, Captain.

TUCCA [*To* OVID SEN] No, fare thou well, mine honest horseman, [*To* LUPUS] and thou old beaver. [*To* OVID SEN] Pray thee Roman, when thou comest to town, see me at my lodging, visit me sometimes. Thou shalt be welcome, old boy. Do not balk me, good swaggerer. Jove keep thy chain from pawning. Go thy ways; if thou lack money, I'll lend thee some. I'll leave thee to thy horse, now. Adieu.

OVID SEN Farewell, good Captain.

TUCCA [*Aside*] Boy, you can have but half a share[209] now, boy. [*Exeunt* TUCCA *and* PYRGUS]

OVID SEN 'Tis a strange boldness that accompanies this fellow. [*To* LUSCUS] Come.

OVID I'll give attendance on you to your horse, sir, please you—

OVID SEN No: keep your chamber, and fall to your studies; do so. The gods of Rome bless thee.

[*Exeunt* OVID SENIOR *and* LUSCUS]

OVID And give me stomach to digest this law,
That should have followed sure, had I been he.
Oh sacred poesy, thou spirit of arts,
The soul of science, and the queen of souls,
What profane violence, almost sacrilege,
Hath here been offered thy divinities!
That thine own guiltless poverty should arm
Prodigious ignorance to wound thee thus!
For thence[210] is all their force of argument
Drawn forth against thee, or from the abuse
Of thy great powers in adulterate[211] brains.
When, would men learn but to distinguish spirits,
And set true difference twixt those jaded wits
That run a broken pace for common hire,
And the high raptures of a happy muse
Borne on the wings of her immortal thought,
That kicks at earth with a disdainful heel,
And beats at heaven-gates with her bright hooves;[212]
They would not then with such distorted[213] faces,
And desperate censures stab at poesy.
They would admire bright knowledge, and their minds
Should ne'er descend on so unworthy objects,
As gold, or titles: they would dread far more
To be thought ignorant, than be known poor.
"The time was once, when wit drowned wealth: but now,
Your only barbarism is t' have wit, and want.

205 144 them: the poets
206 146 seam-rent: torn at the seams
207 147 right: the right amount
208 148 tell: count (Ovid Senior replies to Tucca's question whether the money he's just received is the "right" sum)
209 155 half a share: i.e. half of the money Tucca has just received
210 168 thence: from ignorance
211 170 adulterate: base
212 171–7 distinguish spirits . . . bright hooves: distinguish between those old, lame wits that are like poor horses and write bad poetry ("a broken pace") for money and those poets who are truly inspired by the Muses and who fly above the earth toward heaven like Pegasus
213 178 distorted: frowning, angry

No matter now in virtue who excels,
He that hath coin hath all perfection else."[214]

Act I, scene iii[215]

[*Enter*] TIBULLUS

TIBULLUS Ovid?
OVID Who's there? Come in.
TIBULLUS Good morrow, lawyer.
OVID Good morrow, dear Tibullus, welcome. Sit down.
TIBULLUS Not I. What, so hard at it? Let's see, what's here? Nay, I will see it— [*Snatches poem*]
OVID Pray thee away—
TIBULLUS "If thrice in field,[216] a man vanquish his foe,
'Tis after in his choice to serve, or no."
How now Ovid! Law-cases in verse?
OVID In truth, I know not. They run from my pen
Unwittingly,[217] if they be verse. What's the news abroad?
TIBULLUS Off with this gown, I come to have thee walk.
OVID No, good Tibullus, I'm not now in case,[218]
Pray let me alone.
TIBULLUS How? Not in case!
'Slight, thou'rt in too much case, by all this law.
OVID Troth, if I live, I will new dress the law
In sprightly poesy's habiliments.[219]
TIBULLUS The hell thou wilt. What, turn law into verse?
Thy father has schooled thee, I see. Here, read that same. [*Hands him a note*]
There's subject for you, and if I mistake not,
A *supersedeas*[220] to your melancholy.
OVID How! Subscribed[221] Julia! Oh, my life, my heaven! [*Reads to himself*]
TIBULLUS Is the mood changed?
OVID Music of wit! Note for th'harmonious spheres!
Celestial accents, how you ravish me!
TIBULLUS What is it, Ovid?
OVID That I must meet my Julia, the Princess Julia.
TIBULLUS Where?
OVID Why, at—heart,[222] I have forgot. My passion so transports me.
TIBULLUS I'll save your pains. [*Reads the note*] It is at Albius' house,
The jeweler's, where the fair Lycoris[223] lies.
OVID Who? Cytheris, Cornelius Gallus' love?
TIBULLUS Ay, he'll be there too, and my Plautia
OVID And why not your Delia?
TIBULLUS Yes, and your Corinna.

214 184–7 The time . . . perfection else: Jonson's translation of Ovid's *Elegy* 3.8.3–4
215 Act I, scene iii: in the space between scene ii and scene iii, Ovid evidently puts aside his poetry and starts translating a law book into verse
216 7 in field: in battle
217 11 unwittingly: without my realizing it
218 13 in case: in the right outfit (with a pun on law case)
219 17 habiliments: outfits
220 21 *supersedeas*: a legal writ stopping an action: Julia's note will "stay" Ovid from his melancholy
221 22 Subscribed: signed
222 29 heart: i.e. by God's heart
223 31 Lycoris: pseudonym for Cytheris in the next line, used by Gallus in his public poetry to conceal her identity. In the next lines, both Ovid and Tibullus refer to their poetic pseudonyms for their lovers

OVID True, but my sweet Tibullus, keep that secret:
I would not for all Rome it should be thought
I veil bright Julia underneath that name:
Julia the gem, and jewel of my soul,
That takes her honors from the golden sky,
As beauty doth all luster from her eye.
The air respires the pure elysian[224] sweets
In which she breathes. And from her looks descend
The glories of the summer. Heaven she is,
Praised in herself above all praise; and he,
Which hears her speak, would swear the tuneful orbs[225]
Turned in his zenith only. [226]
TIBULLUS Publius, thou'lt lose thy self.
OVID Oh, in no labyrinth can I safelier err,
Than when I lose myself in praising her. [*Thrusts his law books aside*]
Hence, law, and welcome, Muses; though not rich,
Yet are you pleasing: let's be reconciled,
And now made one. Henceforth, I promise faith,
And all my serious hours to spend with you:
With you, whose music striketh on my heart,
And with bewitching tones steals forth my spirit,
In Julia's name; fair Julia. Julia's love
Shall be a law, and that sweet law I'll study,
The law and art of sacred Julia's love.
All other objects will but abjects prove.[227]
TIBULLUS Come, we shall have thee as passionate as Propertius, anon.
OVID Oh, how does my Sextus?
TIBULLUS Faith, full of sorrow, for his Cynthia's death.
OVID What, still?
TIBULLUS Still, and still more his griefs do grow upon him,
As do his hours. Never did I know
An understanding spirit so take to heart
The common work of fate.
OVID Oh my Tibullus,
Let us not blame him: for against such chances,
The heartiest strife of virtue is not proof.
We may read constancy and fortitude
To other souls, but had ourselves been struck
With the like planet, had our loves (like his)
Been ravished[228] from us by injurious death,
And in the height and heat of our best days,
It would have cracked our sinews, shrunk our veins,
And made our very heart-strings jar, like his.
Come, let's go take him forth, and prove[229] if mirth
Or company will but abate his passion.
TIBULLUS Content, and I implore the gods it may.
[*Exeunt*]

224 42 elysian: heavenly
225 46 tuneful orbs: the planets, whose movement was believed to produce celestial harmonies
226 46–47 would swear … zenith only: would swear that the sun and planets turned around him (the zenith was the highest point of the sky as viewed from any single position)
227 60 will but abjects prove: will be rejected
228 74 ravished: stolen
229 78 prove: test

Act II, scene i

[*Enter*] ALBIUS, CRISPINUS

ALBIUS Master Crispinus, you are welcome. Pray, use a stool, sir. Your cousin Cytheris will come down presently. We are so busy for the receiving of these courtiers here, that I can scarce be a minute with myself, for thinking of them. Pray you sit, sir; pray you sit, sir.
CRISPINUS I am very well, sir. Ne'er trust me, but you are most delicately seated[230] here, full of sweet delight and blandishment![231] An excellent air, an excellent air!
ALBIUS Ay, sir, 'tis pretty air. These courtiers run in my mind still; I must look out. For Jupiter's sake, sit, sir. Or please you walk into the garden? There's a garden on the back-side.
CRISPINUS I am most strenuously[232] well, I thank you, sir.
ALBIUS Much good do you,[233] sir.

[*Enter* CHLOE *and her* MAIDS]

CHLOE Come, bring those perfumes forward a little, and strew some roses and violets here. Fie, here be rooms savor[234] the most pitifully rank[235] that ever I felt. I cry the gods mercy, my husband's in the wind[236] of us.
ALBIUS Why this is good, excellent, excellent. Well said, my sweet Chloe. Trim up your house most obsequiously.[237]
CHLOE For Vulcanus'[238] sake, breathe somewhere else. In troth you overcome our perfumes exceedingly, you are too predominant.
ALBIUS Hear but my opinion, sweet wife.
CHLOE A pin for your 'pinion. In sincerity, if you be thus fulsome[239] to me in everything, I'll be divorced. God's my body! You know what you were, before I married you; I was a gentlewoman born, I; I lost all my friends to be a citizen's wife, because I heard indeed they kept their wives as fine as ladies and that we might rule our husbands, like ladies, and do what we listed.[240] Do you think I would have married you, else?
ALBIUS I acknowledge, sweet wife. [*To* CRISPINUS] She speaks the best of any woman in Italy, and moves as mightily, which makes me I had rather she should make bumps on my head as big as my two fingers,[241] than I would offend her. But sweet wife—
CHLOE Yet again? Is't not grace enough for you that I call you husband and you call me wife, but you must still be poking[242] me, against my will, to things?
ALBIUS But you know, wife, here are the greatest ladies, and gallantest gentlemen of Rome, to be entertained in our house now; and I would fain[243] advise thee to entertain them in the best sort, i'faith wife.
CHLOE [*To the rest*] In sincerity, did you ever hear a man talk so idly? [*To* ALBIUS] You would seem to be master? You would have your spoke in my cart?[244] You would advise me to entertain ladies, and gentlemen? Because you can marshal your pack-needles, horse-combs, hobby-horses, and wall-candlesticks in your warehouse better then I, therefore you can tell how

230 4 seated: located (Crispinus praises the location of the house, and puns on the chair he has been offered)
231 5 blandishment: pleasing qualities
232 8 strenuously: extremely (a pretentious phrase)
233 9 Much good do you: much good may it do to you
234 11 savor: smell
235 11 rank: terrible
236 12 in the wind: upwind (Chloe is implying that her husband is the source of the bad smell)
237 14 obsequiously: dutifully
238 15 Vulcanus: Vulcan, god of the forge, who was dirty and thus distasteful to his wife, Venus (Albius's breath smells bad)
239 18 fulsome: full-bodied, abundant, but also disgusting, obnoxious and lewd
240 22 listed: wanted
241 24–5 makes me ... two fingers: I'd rather suffer her blows to my head than offend her. Albius puts two fingers on his head to illustrate the size of the lumps, which would make the audience think of the invisible "horns" that were said to be worn by men whose wives had cuckolded them
242 27 poking: goading, with a sexual suggestion
243 29 fain: gladly
244 32 your spoke in my cart: get in my way, interfere (with a sexual suggestion)

to entertain ladies and gentlefolks better than I?

ALBIUS Oh my sweet wife, upbraid me not with that: "Gain savors sweetly from any thing."[245] He that respects to get[246] must relish all commodities alike, and admit no difference betwixt woad[247] and frankincense, or the most precious balsamum and a tar-barrel.

CHLOE Marry, faugh.[248] You sell snuffers[249] too, if you be remembered, but I pray you let me buy them out of your hand;[250] for I tell you true, I take it highly in snuff[251] to learn how to entertain gentlefolks of[252] you, at these years, i' faith. Alas, man; there was not a gentleman came to your house i' your tother[253] wife's time, I hope? Nor a lady? Nor music? Nor masques?[254] Nor you nor your house were so much as spoken of, before I disbased myself from my hood and my farthingale to these bumrolls and your whalebone bodies.[255]

ALBIUS Look here, my sweet wife; I am mum, my dear mummia,[256] my balsamum, my spermaceti,[257] and my very city of—[*To* CRISPINUS] she has the most best, true, feminine wit in Rome!

CRISPINUS I have heard so, sir, and do most vehemently desire to participate the knowledge[258] of her fair features.

ALBIUS Ah, peace; you shall hear more anon. Be not seen yet, I pray you; not yet. Observe. [*Exit*]

CHLOE 'Sbody, give husbands the head a little more and they'll be nothing but head shortly. [*To her maids*] What's he there? [*Gesturing to* CRISPINUS]

MAID 1 I know not, forsooth.

MAID 2 [*To* CRISPINUS] Who would you speak with, sir?

CRISPINUS I would speak with my cousin Cytheris.

MAID [2] He is one, forsooth, would speak with his cousin Cytheris.

CHLOE Is she your cousin, sir?

CRISPINUS Yes in truth, forsooth, for fault of a better.

CHLOE She is a gentlewoman?

CRISPINUS Or else she should not be my cousin, I assure you.

CHLOE Are you a gentleman born?

CRISPINUS That I am, lady; you shall see mine arms,[259] if't please you.

CHLOE No, your legs do sufficiently show you are a gentleman born, sir. For a man borne upon little legs is always a gentleman borne.

CRISPINUS Yet I pray you, vouchsafe the sight of my arms, mistress; for I bear them about me to have 'hem seen. My name is Crispinus, or Cri-spinas[260] indeed, which is well-expressed in my arms, a face crying *in chief* and beneath it a bloody toe, between three thorns *pungent*.[261]

CHLOE Then you are welcome, sir; now you are a gentleman born, I can find in my heart to welcome you. For I am a gentlewoman born too, and will bear my head high enough,

245 36 "Gain savors ... any thing": from Erasmus's *Adages*, by way of Juvenal
246 37 respects to get: desires to make profit
247 38 woad: a simple plant used to make dye for clothing, contrasted with the preciousness of frankincense, just as the barrel used to hold smelly tar is compared to balsamum, a sweet-smelling resin or sap
248 39 Marry, faugh: an exasperated expression
249 39 snuffers: candle-snuffers
250 40 buy them ... your hand: take them from you
251 40 I take ... in snuff: I'm very offended
252 41 of: from
253 42 tother: other
254 43 masques: elaborate ballet-like entertainments with costumes and music; a court form of entertainment
255 43–4 disbased myself ... whalebone bodies: debased myself by wearing poorer clothes; a "hood" and "farthingale" (a type of large hoop-skirt) were high-status clothes; "bumrolls" (a padded belt around the waist, worn under a dress) and "whalebone bodies" (corsets) were typical of merchants and citizens
256 45 mummia: a tincture made from mummified bodies
257 46 spermaceti: sperm-whale oil, used for perfumes
258 48 participate the knowledge: get to know better (a pretentious phrase)
259 63 arms: coat of arms (proving his gentlemanly status)
260 67 Cri-Spinas: Crispinus spells out the syllables of his name to explain his coat of arms
261 68 *in chief* ... thorns *pungent*: mock-heraldic terms for a crying face at the top of the shield ("in chief") and a toe with three "thorns" (Latin *spinas*) "pricking" it (Latin *pungent*, with a play on "bad-smelling")

though 'twere my fortune to marry a tradesman.
CRISPINUS No doubt of that, sweet feature; your carriage shows it in any man's eye, that is carried[262] upon you with judgment.

ALBIUS *going in and out* [*while preparing the house*]

ALBIUS Dear wife, be not angry.
CHLOE God's my passion!
ALBIUS Hear me but one thing: let not your maids set cushions in the parlor windows, nor in the dining-chamber windows, nor upon stools in either of them, in any case; for 'tis tavern-like; but lay them one upon another in some out-room,[263] or corner of the dining-chamber. [*Exit*]
CHLOE Go, go, meddle with your bed-chamber only, or rather with your bed in your chamber, only, or rather with your wife in your bed only, or on my faith, I'll not be pleased with you only.
ALBIUS [*Enters*] Look here, my dear wife, entertain that gentleman kindly, I pray thee—mum. [*Exit*]

CHLOE Go, I need[264] your instructions indeed; anger me no more, I advise you. Citi-sin,[265] quoth'a![266] She's a wise gentlewoman, i'faith, will marry herself to the sin of the city.
ALBIUS [*Enters*] But this time,[267] and no more (by heaven) wife. Hang no pictures in the hall, nor in the dining-chamber, in any case, but in the gallery only, for 'tis not courtly else, o' my word, wife. [*Exit*]
CHLOE 'Sprecious,[268] never have done![269]
ALBIUS [*Enters*] Wife— [*Exit*]
CHLOE Do I not bear a reasonable corrigible hand[270] over him, Crispinus?
CRISPINUS [*Takes her hand*] By this hand, lady, you hold a most sweet hand over him.
ALBIUS [*Enters*] And then for the great gilt andirons—
CHLOE Again! Would the andirons were in your great guts, for me.
ALBIUS I do vanish, wife. [*Exit*]
CHLOE How shall I do, Master Crispinus? Here will be all the bravest[271] ladies in court presently, to see your cousin Cytheris. Oh the gods! How might I behave myself now, as to entertain them most courtly?
CRIPINUS Marry, lady, if you will entertain them most courtly, you must do thus. As soon as ever your maid or your man brings you word they are come, you must say "A pox on 'hem, what do they here?" And yet when they come, speak them as fair and give them the kindest welcome in words that can be.
CHLOE Is that the fashion of courtiers, Crispinus?
CRISPINUS I assure you, it is, lady, I have observed it.
CHLOE For your pox, sir, it is easily hit on;[272] but 'tis not so easy to speak fair after, methinks?
ALBIUS [*Enters*] Oh wife, the coaches are come, on my word, a number of coaches, and courtiers.
CHLOE A pox on them. What do they here?
ALBIUS How now wife! Wouldst thou not have 'hem come?

262 73 is carried: looks
263 78 out-room: adjacent room
264 83 I need: as if I need
265 83 Citi-sin: a pun on "citizen"
266 84 quoth'a: says he
267 85 But this time: only this one more thing
268 88 'Sprecious: i.e. by God's precious body
269 88 never have done: will he never finish?
270 90 corrigible hand: correcting impulse
271 95 bravest: most elegant
272 104 easily hit on: easily said, with a joke on "easily caught"

CHLOE Come? Come, you are a fool, you. [*To* CRISPINUS] He knows not the trick on't.[273] Call Cytheris, I pray you. And good master Crispinus, you can observe, you say; let me entreat you for all the ladies' behaviors, jewels, jests, and attires, that you marking[274] as well as I, we may put both our marks together when they are gone, and confer of them.
CRISPINUS I warrant you,[275] sweet lady; let me alone to observe, till I turn myself to nothing but observation. [*Enter* CYTHERIS] Good morrow, cousin Cytheris.
CYTHERIS Welcome kind cousin. What? Are they come?
ALBIUS Ay, your friend Cornelius Gallus, Ovid, Tibullus, Propertius, with Julia, the emperor's daughter, and the Lady Plautia, are lighted[276] at the door, and with them Hermogenes Tigellius, the excellent musician.
CYTHERIS Come, let us go meet them, Chloe.
CHLOE Observe, Crispinus.
CRISPINUS At a hair's breadth,[277] lady, I warrant you.

Act II, scene ii

[*Enter*] GALLUS, OVID, TIBULLUS, PROPERTIUS, HERMOGENES, JULIA, PLAUTIA

GALLUS Health to the lovely Chloe. You must pardon me, mistress, that I prefer[278] this fair gentlewoman.
CYTHERIS [*To* GALLUS] I pardon and praise you for it, sir, [*To* JULIA] and I beseech your excellence, receive her beauties into your knowledge and favor.
JULIA Cytheris, she[279] hath favor[280] and behavior that commands as much of me, and sweet Chloe, know I do exceedingly love you, and that I will approve in[281] any grace my father the emperor may show you. Is this your husband?
ALBIUS For fault of a better, if it please your highness.
CHLOE Gods my life! How he shames me!
CYTHERIS Not a whit, Chloe, they all think you politic[282] and witty;[283] wise women choose not husbands for the eye, merit, or birth, but wealth, and sovereignty.[284]
OVID [*To* ALBIUS] Sir, we all come to gratulate for [285] the good report of you.
TIBULLUS And would be glad to deserve your love, sir.
ALBIUS My wife will answer you all, gentlemen; I'll come to you again presently. [*Exit*]
PLAUTIA You have chosen you[286] a most fair companion here, Cytheris, and a very fair house.
CYTHERIS To both which you and all my friends are very welcome, Plautia.
CHLOE With all my heart, I assure your ladyship.
PLAUTIA Thanks, sweet Mistress Chloe.
JULIA You must needs come to court, lady, i' faith, and there be sure your welcome shall be as great to us.
OVID She will well deserve it, madam. I see, even in her looks, gentry[287] and general worthiness.
TIBULLUS I have not seen a more certain character of an excellent disposition.

273 109 trick on't: he doesn't know how to speak to courtiers
274 111 marking: observing
275 113 I warrant you: by all means
276 117 lighted: alighted (from their coaches), arrived
277 121 At a hair's breadth: closely
278 1 prefer: show esteem for
279 5 she: Chloe
280 5 favor: beauty
281 6 in: of
282 10 politic: shrewd
283 10 witty: smart
284 11 sovereignty: power (that wives can have over their husbands)
285 12 gratulate for: congratulate you on
286 15 chosen you: chosen for yourself
287 21 gentry: nobility

[*Enter* ALIBIUS]

ALBIUS Wife.
CHLOE Oh, they do so commend me here, the courtiers! What's the matter now?
ALBIUS For the banquet, sweet wife. [*Exit*]
CHLOE Yes, and I must needs come to court and be welcome, the princess says.
GALLUS [*Taking* OVID *and* TIBULLUS *aside*] Ovid, and Tibullus, you may be bold to welcome your mistresses here.[288]
OVID We find it so, sir.
TIBULLUS And thank Cornelius Gallus.
OVID Nay, my sweet Sextus, in faith thou art not sociable.
PROPERTIUS In faith, I am not, Publius, nor I cannot.
Sick minds are like sick men that burn with fevers,
Who when they drink, please but a present taste,
And after bear a more impatient fit.[289]
Pray, let me leave you; I offend you all,
And my self most.
GALLUS Stay, sweet Propertius.
TIBULLUS You yield too much unto your griefs, and fate,
Which never hurts but when we say it hurts us.
PROPERTIUS Oh peace, Tibullus; your philosophy
Lends you too rough a hand to search my wounds.
Speak they of griefs, that know to sigh and grieve;[290]
The free and unconstrainèd spirit feels
No weight of my oppression.
OVID Worthy Roman!
Methinks I taste his misery, and could
Sit down and chide at[291] his malignant stars.
JULIA Methinks I love him, that[292] he loves so truly.
CYTHERIS This is the perfect'st love, lives after death.
GALLUS Such is the constant ground of virtue still.
PLAUTIA It puts on an inseparable face.
CHLOE [*Aside to* CRISPINUS] Have you marked everything, Crispinus?
CRISPINUS [*Aside to* CHLOE] Everything, I warrant you.
CHLOE What gentlemen are these? Do you know them?
CRISPINUS Ay, they are poets, lady.
CHLOE Poets? They did not talk of me since I went, did they?
CRISPINUS Oh yes, and extolled your perfections to the heavens.
CHLOE Now in sincerity, they be the finest kind of men, that ever I knew. Poets? Could not one get the emperor to make my husband a poet, think you?
CRISPINUS No, lady, 'tis love and beauty make poets: and since you like poets so well, your love and beauties shall make me a poet.
CHLOE What, shall they? And such a one as these?
CRISPINUS Ay, and a better than these. I would be sorry else.
CHLOE And shall your looks change? And your hair change? And all, like these?
CRISPINUS Why, a man may be a poet and yet not change his hair, lady.
CHLOE Well, we shall see your cunning. Yet if you can change your hair, I pray, do.
ALBIUS [*Enters*] Ladies and lordings, there's a slight banquet stays within for you; please you draw near, and accost it.

288 28–9 you may . . . mistresses here: this house is a safe place for you to be with your lovers
289 35–6 please but . . . impatient fit: slake their thirst for a moment, only to become even more thirsty
290 43 Only those who suffer should speak of grief
291 47 chide at: reproach
292 48 that: because

JULIA We thank you, good Albius; but when shall we see those excellent jewels you are commended to have?[293]
ALBIUS At your ladyship's service. [*Aside*] I got that speech[294] by seeing a play last day,[295] and it did me some grace now. I see 'tis good to collect[296] sometimes; I'll frequent these plays more than I have done, now I come to be familiar with courtiers.
GALLUS Why, how now, Hermogenes? What ailest thou, trow?[297]
HERMOGENES A little melancholy; let me alone, pray thee.
GALLUS Melancholy! How so?
HERMOGENES With riding; a plague on all coaches for me.
CHLOE [*Aside*] Is that hard-favored[298] gentleman a poet too, Cytheris?
CYTHERIS [*Aside*] No, this is Hermogenes, as humorous[299] as a poet though: he is a musician.
CHLOE A musician? Then he can sing?
CYTHERIS That he can excellently. Did you never hear him?
CHLOE Oh no. Will he be entreated,[300] think you?
CYTHERIS I know not. [*To* GALLUS] Friend, Mistress Chloe would fain hear Hermogenes sing; are you interested in him? [301]
GALLUS No doubt his own humanity will command him so far to the satisfaction of so fair a beauty, but rather than fail, we'll all be suitors to him.[302]
HERMOGENES 'Cannot sing.
GALLUS Pray thee, Hermogenes.
HERMOGENES 'Cannot sing.
GALLUS For honor of this gentlewoman, to whose house I know thou may'st be ever welcome.
CHLOE That he shall in truth, sir, if he can sing.
OVID What's that?
GALLUS This gentlewoman is wooing Hermogenes for a song.
OVID A song? Come, he shall not deny her. Hermogenes?
HERMOGENES 'Cannot sing.
GALLUS No, the ladies must do it;[303] he stays but to have their thanks acknowledged as a debt to his cunning.[304]
JULIA That shall not want;[305] our self will be the first shall promise to pay him more than thanks, upon a favor so worthily vouchsafed.
HERMOGENES Thank you, madam, but 'will not sing.
TIBULLUS Tut, the only way to win him is to abstain from entreating him.
CRISPINUS [*Aside*] Do you love singing, lady?
CHLOE Oh, passingly.[306]
CRISPINUS Entreat the ladies to entreat me to sing then, I beseech you.
CHLOE [*To the rest*] I beseech your grace, entreat this gentleman to sing.
JULIA That we will Chloe. Can he sing excellently?
CHLOE I think so, madam, for he entreated me to entreat you to entreat him to sing.
CRISPINUS [*Aside*] Heaven, and earth! Would you tell that?
JULIA Good sir, let's entreat you to use your voice.

293 70 commended to have: reputed or renowned for
294 71 that speech: probably referring to his greeting at lines 69–70
295 72 last day: yesterday
296 72 collect: gather and remember choice sayings or phrases
297 74 trow: do you think
298 78 hard-favored: scowling, unpleasant-looking
299 79 humorous: moody
300 82 entreated: persuaded
301 84 are you interested in him: can you convince him?
302 85–6 No doubt . . . to him: her beauty will probably be enough to convince him to sing, but just in case, let's all ask him
303 97 do it: entreat him
304 97–8 stays but . . . his cunning: he's holding back only so he can make them thank him even more warmly for his great skill
305 99 That shall not want: our thanks will not be lacking
306 104 passingly: very much

CRISPINUS Alas, madam, I cannot in truth.

PLAUTIA The gentleman is modest. I warrant[307] you, he sings excellently.

OVID Hermogenes, clear your throat. [*Pointing to* CRISPINUS] I see by him, here's a gentleman will worthily challenge you.

CRISPINUS Not I, sir, I'll challenge no man.

TIBULLUS That's your modesty, sir, but we, out of an assurance[308] of your excellency, challenge him in your behalf.

CRISPINUS I thank you, gentlemen; I'll do my best.

HERMOGENES Let that best be good, sir, you were best.[309]

GALLUS Oh, this contention[310] is excellent. What is't you sing, sir?

CRISPINUS *If I freely may discover, etc.* Sir, I'll sing that.

OVID One of your own compositions, Hermogenes. He offers you vantage[311] enough.

CRISPINUS Nay truly, gentlemen, I'll challenge no man—I can sing but one staff[312] of the ditty neither.[313]

GALLUS The better. Hermogenes himself will be entreated to sing the other.

CRISPINUS [*Sings*] *If I freely may discover*
What would please me in my lover,
I would have her fair and witty,
Savoring more of court, than city,
A little proud, but full of pity,
Light, and humorous in her toying,
Oft building hopes, and soon destroying,
Long,[314] *but sweet in the enjoying,*
Neither too easy, nor too hard;
All extremes I would have barred.

GALLUS Believe me, sir, you sing most excellently.

OVID If there were a praise above excellence, the gentleman highly deserves it.

HERMOGENES Sir, all this doth not yet make me envy you, for I know I sing better than you.

TIBULLUS Attend[315] Hermogenes, now.

HERMOGENES [*Sings*] *She should be allowed her passions,*
So they were but used as fashions;
Sometimes froward,[316] *and then frowning,*
Sometimes sickish, and then swooning,
Every fit with change still crowning.[317]
Purely jealous I would have her,
Then only constant when I crave her.[318]
'Tis a virtue should not save her.[319]
Thus, nor her delicates would cloy me,[320]
Neither her peevishness annoy me.[321]

JULIA Nay, Hermogenes, your merit hath long since been both known and admired of us.

307 112 warrant: guarantee
308 116 assurance: belief in
309 119 You'd better make your "best" be good.
310 120 contention: contest
311 122 vantage: advantage
312 123 staff: stanza
313 124 neither: only
314 133 *Long*: long to seduce
315 139 Attend: listen to
316 142 *froward*: difficult, contrary
317 144 Crowning every fit with further change
318 145–6 *Purely jealous . . . crave her*: I want her to be jealous of my love, but constant in her love for me—but only when I want her
319 147 Constancy won't be a virtue that saves her
320 148 *cloy me*: make me sick of her
321 126–49 The song is based on a satiric poem by Martial

HERMOGENES You shall hear me sing another; now will I begin.
GALLUS We shall do this gentleman's banquet too much wrong, that stays for us, ladies.
JULIA 'Tis true, and well thought on, Cornelius Gallus.
HERMOGENES Why 'tis but a short air; 'twill be done presently, pray stay; strike music.
OVID No, good Hermogenes; we'll end this difference[322] within.
JULIA 'Tis the common disease of all your musicians, that they know no mean to be entreated, either to begin or end.
ALBIUS Please you lead the way, gentles?
ALL Thanks, good Albius. [*Exeunt all but* ALBIUS *and* CRISPINUS]
ALBIUS Oh, what a charm of thanks was here put upon me! Oh Jove, what a setting forth[323] it is to a man to have many courtiers come to his house! Sweetly was it said of a good old housekeeper, "I had rather want meat, than want guests,"[324] especially if they be courtly guests. For never trust me if one of their good legs[325] made in a house be not worth all the good cheer a man can make them. He that would have fine guests, let him have a fine wife; he that would have a fine wife, let him come to me.
CRISPINUS By your kind leave, Master Albius.
ALBIUS What, you are not gone,[326] Master Crispinus?
CRISPINUS Yes faith, I have a design draws me hence. Pray sir, fashion me an excuse to the ladies.
ALBIUS Will you not stay? And see the jewels, sir? I pray you stay.
CRISPINUS Not for a million, sir, now. Let it suffice I must relinquish,[327] and so in a word, please you to expiate[328] this compliment.
ALBIUS Mum.[329] [*Exit*]
CRISPINUS I'll presently go and ingle[330] some broker[331] for a poet's gown, and bespeak a garland;[332] and then, jeweler, look to your best jewel,[333] i'faith.
[*Exit*]

Act III, scene i

[*Enter*] HORACE, CRISPINUS [*at opposite doors*]

HORACE Hmh? Yes; I will begin an ode[334] so, and it shall be to Mecoenas.
CRISPINUS 'Slid,[335] yonder's Horace! They say he's an excellent poet. Mecoenas loves him. I'll fall into his acquaintance if I can; I think he be composing as he goes i' the street! Ha? 'Tis a good humor,[336] and[337] he be. I'll compose too.
HORACE "Swell me a bowl with lusty wine,
Till I may see the plump Lyaeus swim
Above the brim.
I drink, as I would write,

322 156 difference: contest
323 161 setting forth: advantage or advancement
324 163 "I had . . . want guests": proverbial
325 164 good legs: courtly bows
326 168 not gone: you're not leaving, are you?
327 172 relinquish: disappear
328 173 expiate: literally to cleanse or purify; here used pretentiously to mean "deliver, finish off"
329 174 Mum: not a word more
330 175 ingle: coax, fondle; an ingle was a boy sexual partner
331 175 broker: pawnbroker
332 175–6 bespeak a garland: order a poet's wreath
333 176 look to your best jewel: i.e. look out for your wife
334 1 ode: Horace, *Satires* I, 9, from which this scene has been adapted (Jonson's note)
335 2 'Slid: i.e. by God's eyelid
336 4 humor: attitude, way of behaving
337 4 and: if

In flowing measure, filled with flame, and spright."[338]

CRISPINUS [*Meeting him*] Sweet Horace, Minerva and the Muses stand auspicious to thy designs. How fare'st thou, sweet man? Frolic?[339] Rich? Gallant? Ha?

HORACE Not greatly gallant, sir; like my fortunes: well. I'm bold to take my leave, sir, you'd naught else, sir, would you?

CRISPINUS Troth, no, but I could wish thou didst know us, Horace. We[340] are a scholar, I assure thee.

HORACE A scholar, sir? I shall be covetous of your fair knowledge.

CRISPINUS Gramercy, good Horace. Nay, we are new turned poet too, which is more, and a satirist too, which is more than that. I write just in thy vein, I; I am for your odes or your sermons or any thing indeed. We are a gentleman besides; our name is Rufus Laberius Crispinus; we are a pretty Stoic[341] too.

HORACE To the proportion of your beard[342] I think it, sir.

CRISPINUS By Phoebus, here's a most neat fine street, is't not? I protest to thee, I am enamored of this street now, more than of half the streets of Rome, again; 'tis so polite and terse![343] There's the front of a building now. I study architecture too; if ever I should build, I'd have a house just of that prospective.[344]

HORACE [*Aside*] Doubtless this gallant's tongue has a good turn[345] when he sleeps.

CRISPINUS I do make verses when I come in such a street as this. Oh, your city ladies, you shall ha' 'hem sit in every shop like the muses, offering you the Castalian dews and the thespian liquors to as many as have but the sweet grace and audacity to—sip of their lips. Did you never hear any of my verses?

HORACE No, sir. [*Aside*] But I am in some fear I must now.

CRISPINUS I'll tell thee some [*Aside*] (if I can but recover 'hem)—I compos'd e'en now of a dressing[346] I saw a jeweler's wife wear, who indeed was a jewel herself. I prefer that kind of tire[347] now; what's thy opinion, Horace?

HORACE With your[348] silver bodkin,[349] it does well, sir.

CRISPINUS I cannot tell, but it stirs me more than all your court-curls, or your spangles,[350] or your tricks. I affect[351] not these high gable-ends, these tuscan-tops, nor your coronets, nor your arches, nor your pyramids.[352] Give me a fine, sweet, little delicate dressing, with a bodkin, as you say; and a mushroom[353] for all your other ornatures![354]

HORACE [*Aside*] Is't not possible to make an escape from him?

CRISPINUS I have remitted[355] my verses all this while, I think I ha' forgot 'hem.

HORACE [*Aside*] Here's he[356] could wish you had, else.[357]

CRISPINUS Pray Jove, I can entreat 'hem of my memory.

HORACE You put your memory to too much trouble, sir.

CRISPINUS No, sweet Horace, we must not ha' thee think so.

338 9 spright: energy
339 11 Frolic: cheerful
340 14 We: I (a pretentious usage)
341 20 Stoic: a school of philosophy emphasizing self-reliance
342 21 To the . . . your beard: by growing a beard you're trying to look like a philosopher, at least
343 23 polite and terse: elegant
344 25 prospective: appearance, shape
345 26 has a good turn: performs best
346 33 dressing: hairstyle
347 34 tire: headdress
348 35 your: a (a colloquial, casual usage that assumes familiarity with the fashions they are describing)
349 35 bodkin: hairpin
350 36 spangles: sequins (in the hair)
351 37 affect: like
352 37–38 gable-ends . . . your pyramids: elaborate hair-styles
353 39 a mushroom: i.e. I don't give a mushroom
354 39 ornatures: adornments
355 41 remitted: put off
356 42 he: one who (i.e. Horace himself)
357 42 else: if you haven't (forgotten them)

HORACE I cry you mercy. [*Aside*] Then they are my ears
That must be tortured. Well, you must have patience, ears.
CRISPINUS Pray thee, Horace, observe.
HORACE Yes, sir, your satin sleeve begins to fret at the rug[358] that is underneath it, I do observe; and your ample velvet bases[359] are not without evident stains of a hot disposition,[360] naturally.
CRISPINUS Oh, I'll dye them into another color, at pleasure. How many yards of velvet dost thou think they contain?
HORACE [*Aside*] Heart! I have put him now in a fresh way
To vex me more. [*To* CRISPINUS] Faith, sir, your mercer's book[361]
Will tell you with more patience than I can;
[*Aside*] For I am crossed,[362] and so's not that,[363] I think.
CRISPINUS 'Slight, these verses have lost me again. I shall not invite 'hem to mind, now.
HORACE Rack not your thoughts, good sir; rather, defer it
To a new time; I'll meet you at your lodging,
Or where you please. Till then, Jove keep you, sir.
CRISPINUS Nay, gentle Horace, stay. I have it, now.
HORACE Yes, sir. [*Aside*] Apollo, Hermes, Jupiter, look down upon me.
CRISPINUS [*Reciting*] *Rich was thy hap,*[364] *sweet, dainty cap,*
There to be placed:
Where thy smooth black, sleek white may smack,
And both be graced.
"White" is there usurped[365] for her brow, her forehead; and then "sleek" as the parallel to "smooth," that went before. A kind of paranomasy or agnomination:[366] do you conceive,[367] sir?
HORACE Excellent. Troth, sir, I must be abrupt and leave you.
CRISPINUS Why, what haste hast thou? Pray thee, stay a little. Thou shalt not go yet, by Phoebus.
HORACE I shall not? [*Aside*] What remedy? Fie, how I sweat with suffering!
CRISPINUS And then—
HORACE Pray, sir, give me leave to wipe my face a little.
CRISPINUS Yes, do, good Horace.
HORACE Thank you, sir.
[*Aside*] Death! I must crave his leave to piss anon,
Or that I may go hence with half my teeth,[368]
I am in some such fear. This tyranny
Is strange, to take mine ears up by commission,[369]
(Whether I will or no) and make them stalls[370]
To his lewd solecisms and worded trash.
Happy thou, bold Bolanus,[371] now, I say,
Whose freedom and impatience of this fellow,
Would long ere this, have call'd him fool, and fool,

358 49 fret at the rug: rub at the coarse wool
359 50 bases: skirts worn by men
360 50–51 stains of a hot disposition: sweat marks and other stains
361 55 mercer's book: cloth-seller's account book
362 57 crossed: vexed, also crossed-out (of the mercer's account book)
363 57 so's not that: "that" refers to the account book; Crispinus has probably not yet paid the mercer, and so the bill has not been crossed out
364 64 hap: luck
365 68 usurped: substituted
366 69 paranomasy or agnomination: types of rhetorical figures
367 69 conceive: understand
368 79 with half my teeth: i.e. Horace is grinding his teeth in frustration as he tries to think of how to escape from Crispinus
369 81 commission: legal warrant
370 82 stalls: holding places
371 84 Bolanus: a Roman known for his anger

And rank, and tedious fool, and have flung jests
As hard as stones till thou hadst pelted him
Out of the place, whilst my tame modesty
Suffers my wit be made a solemn ass
To bear his fopperies—

CRISPINUS Horace, thou art miserably affected[372] to be gone, I see. But—pray thee, let's prove to enjoy thee[373] awhile. Thou hast no business,[374] I assure me. Whither is thy journey directed? Ha?

HORACE Sir, I am going to visit a friend that's sick.

CRISPINUS A friend? What's he? Do not I know him?

HORACE No, sir, you do not know him. [*Aside*] And 'tis not the worse for him.

CRISPINUS What's his name? Where's he lodged?

HORACE Where I shall be fearful to draw you out of your way, sir, a great way hence. Pray, sir, let's part.

CRISPINUS Nay, but where is't? I pray thee, say.

HORACE On the far side of all Tiber yonder, by Caesar's gardens.

CRISPINUS Oh, that's my course directly; I am for you.[375] Come, go: why stand'st thou?

HORACE Yes, sir, marry, the plague is in that part of the city; I had almost forgot to tell you, sir.

CRISPINUS Fah! It's no matter; I fear no pestilence. I ha' not offended Phoebus.[376]

HORACE I have, it seems, or else this heavy scourge[377]
Could ne'er have lighted on me—

CRISPINUS Come along.

HORACE I am to go down some half mile this way, sir, first, to speak with his physician, and from thence to his apothecary, where I shall stay[378] the mixing of diverse drugs—

CRISPINUS Why, it's all one. I have nothing to do, and I love not to be idle. I'll bear thee company. How call'st thou the pothecary?

HORACE [*Aside*] Oh that I knew a name would fright him now.
Sir, Rhadamanthus, Rhadamanthus,[379] sir.
There's one so called, is a just judge in hell,
And doth inflict strange vengeance on all those
That here on earth torment poor patient spirits.

CRISPINUS He dwells at the three Furies, by Janus' Temple?[380]

HORACE Your pothecary does, sir.

CRISPINUS Heart, I owe him money for sweetmeats,[381] and he has laid[382] to arrest me, I hear, but—

HORACE Sir, I have made a most solemn vow: I will never bail any man.

CRISPINUS Well then, I'll swear and speak him fair if the worst come.[383] But his name is Minos, not Rhadamanthus, Horace.

HORACE That may be, sir. I but guessed at his name by his sign. But your Minos is a judge too, sir.

CRISPINUS I protest to thee, Horace—do but taste me once[384]—if I do know my self and mine own virtues truly, thou wilt not make that esteem of Varius or Virgil or Tibullus or any of 'hem

372 92 miserably affected: desperately wishing
373 92–3 prove to enjoy thee: try enjoying your company
374 93 business: obligations
375 103 I am for you: I'm your man
376 105 Phoebus: Apollo, god of medicine
377 106 scourge: plague (i.e. Crispinus)
378 110 stay: wait for
379 114 Rhadamanthus: Horace tries to scare Crispinus by naming his apothecary after one of the figures who judge the dead when they arrive in the underworld
380 118 dwells at . . . Janus' Temple: Crispinus names the shop of an apothecary he knows, and its location in Rome
381 120 sweetmeats: candied food
382 120 laid: planned
383 123 I'll swear . . . worst come: if he tries to arrest me, I'll flatter him and swear to pay
384 127 do but taste me once: just listen to my opinion (Crispinus changes the subject back to poets)

indeed, as now in thy ignorance thou dost, which I am content to forgive. I would fain see which of these could pen more verses in a day or with more facility than I, or that could court his mistress, kiss her hand, make better sport with her fan, or her dog—

HORACE I cannot bail you yet, sir.

CRISPINUS —or that could move his body more gracefully, or dance better—you should see me, were it not i' the street—

HORACE Nor yet.

CRISPINUS —why, I have been a reveler,[385] and at my cloth-of-silver suit and my long stocking[386] in my time, and will be again—

HORACE If you may be trusted, sir.

CRISPINUS And then for my singing, Hermogenes himself envies me, that[387] is your only master of music you have in Rome.

HORACE Is your mother living, sir?

CRISPINUS Au![388] Convert[389] thy thoughts to somewhat[390] else, I pray thee.

HORACE You have much of the mother[391] in you, sir. Your father is dead?

CRISPINUS Ay, I thank Jove, and my grandfather too and all my kinsfolk, and well composed in their urns.

HORACE [*Aside*] The more their happiness that rest in peace,
Free from th'abundant torture of thy tongue;
Would I were with them too.

CRISPINUS What's that, Horace?

HORACE I now remember me, sir, of a sad fate
A cunning woman, one Sabella sung,
When in her urn[392] she cast my destiny,
I being but a child.

CRISPINUS What was't I pray thee?

HORACE She told me I should surely never perish
By famine, poison, or the enemy's sword;
The hectic fever, cough, or pleurisy
Should never hurt me; nor the tardy gout.
But in my time I should be once surprised
By a strong tedious talker that should vex
And almost bring me to consumption.
Therefore (if I were wise) she warned me shun
All such long-winded monsters as my bane,[393]
For if I could but scape[394] that one discourser,
I might (no doubt) prove an old agèd man.
By your leave, sir?

CRISPINUS Tut, tut. Abandon this idle humor, 'tis nothing but melancholy. For Jove, now I think on't, I am to appear in court here to answer to one that has me in suit. Sweet Horace, go with me, this is my hour. If I neglect it, the law proceeds against me. Thou art familiar with these things—pray thee, if thou lov'st me, go.

HORACE Now, let me die, sir, if I know your laws,
Or have the power to stand still half so long
In their loud courts, as while a case is argued.

385 136 reveler: dancer at court balls
386 136–7 long stocking: tights
387 139 that: who
388 142 Au: Latin exclamation of sorrow or pain
389 142 Convert: turn
390 142 somewhat: something
391 143 the mother: early modern slang for "hysteria," here characterized by heavy breathing or excessive talkativeness
392 152 urn: fortune-telling bowl
393 162 bane: poison
394 163 scape: escape

Besides, you know, sir, where I am to go,
And the necessity—

CRISPINUS 'Tis true—

HORACE [*Aside*] I hope the hour of my release be come; he will upon this consideration discharge me, sure.

CRISPINUS Troth, I am doubtful what I may best do, whether to leave thee or my affairs, Horace?

HORACE Oh Jupiter, me, sir; me, by any means. I beseech you, me, sir.

CRISPINUS No faith, I'll venture[395] those now. Thou shalt see I love thee; come Horace.

HORACE Nay then, I am desperate. [*They walk*] I follow you, sir. [*Aside*] 'Tis hard contending with a man that overcomes thus.

CRISPINUS And how deals Mecoenas with thee? Liberally? Ha? Is he open-handed? Bountiful?

HORACE He's still himself, sir.

CRISPINUS Troth, Horace, thou art exceeding happy in thy friends and acquaintance; they are all most choice spirits and of the first rank of Romans. I do not know that poet, I protest, has[396] used his fortune more prosperously than thou hast. If thou would'st bring me known to Mecoenas, I should second thy desert well;[397] thou should'st find a good sure assistant of me, one that would speak all good of thee in thy absence and be content with the next place, not envying thy reputation with thy patron. Let me not live, but I think thou and I, in a small[398] time, should lift them all out of favor, both Virgil, Varius, and the best of them, and enjoy him wholly to ourselves.

HORACE [*Aside*] Gods, you do know it, I can hold no longer;
This breeze hath pricked my patience. [*To* CRISPINUS] Sir, your silkness
Clearly mistakes Mecoenas and his house,
To think there breathes a spirit beneath his roof
Subject unto those poor affections
Of undermining envy and detraction,
Moods only proper to base, groveling minds.
That place is not in Rome, I dare affirm,
More pure or free from such low common evils.
There's no man grieved that this[399] is thought more rich,
Or this more learnèd; each man hath his place,
And to his merit his reward of grace,
Which with a mutual love they all embrace.

CRISPINUS You report a wonder! 'Tis scarce credible, this.

HORACE I am no torturer to enforce you to believe it, but 'tis so.

CRISPINUS Why, this inflames me with a more ardent desire to be his[400] than before, but, I doubt[401] I shall find the entrance to his familiarity somewhat more than difficult, Horace.

HORACE Tut, you'll conquer him, as you have done me. There's no standing out against you, sir, I see that. Either your importunity,[402] or the intimation of your good parts, or—

CRISPINUS Nay, I'll bribe his porter and the grooms of his chamber, make his doors open to me that way first, and then I'll observe my times.[403] Say he should extrude me[404] his house today; shall I therefore desist, or let fall[405] my suit tomorrow? No. I'll attend him, follow him,

395 181 venture: risk
396 188–9 that poet, I protest, has: any poet . . . who has
397 190 second thy desert well: vouch for your worth
398 193 small: short
399 204 this: another
400 210 his: i.e. Mecoenas's friend
401 211 doubt: fear
402 213 importunity: boldness
403 215 observe my times: watch for my opportunity
404 215 extrude me: kick me out of
405 216 let fall: give up

meet him i' the street, the highways, run by his coach, never leave him. What? Man hath nothing given him in this life without much labor.
HORACE [*Aside*] And impudence.
Archer of heaven, Phoebus, take thy bow,
And with a full drawn shaft, nail to the earth
This python, that I may yet run hence and live;
Or brawny Hercules, do thou come down,
And (though thou mak'st it up thy thirteenth labor)
Rescue me from this hydra of discourse here.

Act III, scene ii[406]

[*Enter*] ARISTIUS

ARISTIUS Horace, well met.
HORACE [*Aside to* ARISTIUS] Oh welcome, my reliever,
Aristius, as thou lov'st me, ransom me.
ARISTIUS What ail'st thou, man?
HORACE [*Aside to* ARISTIUS] Death, I am seized on here
By a land-remora;[407] I cannot stir,
Not move, but as he please.
CRISPINUS Wilt thou go, Horace?
HORACE [*Aside to* ARISTIUS] Heart! He cleaves to me like Alcides' shirt,[408]
Tearing my flesh and sinews. Oh, I have been vexed
And tortured with him beyond forty fevers.
For Jove's sake, find some means to take me from him.
ARISTIUS Yes, I will, but I'll go first and tell Mecoenas.
CRISPINUS Come, shall we go?
ARISTIUS The jest will make his eyes run, i' faith.
HORACE Nay, Aristius!
ARISTIUS Farewell, Horace.
HORACE Death! Will a'[409] leave me? Fuscus Aristius, do you hear? Gods of Rome! You said you had somewhat to say to me in private.
ARISTIUS Ay, but I see you are now employed with that gentleman; 'twere offence to trouble you. I'll take some fitter opportunity; farewell. [*Exit*]
HORACE Mischief and torment! Oh, my soul, and heart,
How are you cramped with anguish! Death itself
Brings not the like convulsions. Oh, this day,
That ever I should view thy tedious face—
CRISPINUS Horace, what passion? What humor is this?
HORACE Away, good prodigy,[410] afflict me not.
[*Aside*] A friend, and mock me thus! Never was man
So left under the axe. [*Spotting* MINOS] How now?

Act III, scene iii

[*Enter*] MINOS [*with two*] LICTORS[411]

406 Act III, scene ii: this scene continues Jonson's dramatic adaptation of Horace, *Satire* 1.9
407 4 remora: a sucking eel that attaches itself to a fish
408 6 Alcides' shirt: Alcides is Hercules, who put on the poisoned shirt or robe of Nessus
409 15 a': he
410 24 prodigy: monster
411 0 SD LICTORS: public officers serving as both bodyguards and policemen

MINOS That's he in the embroidered hat, there, with the ash-colored feather. His name is Laberius Crispinus.

LICTOR Laberius Crispinus, I arrest you in the emperor's name.

CRISPINUS Me, sir? Do you arrest me?

LICTOR Ay, sir, at the suit of Master Minos the pothecary.

HORACE [*Aside*] Thanks, great Apollo. I will not slip[412] thy favor offered me in my escape for my fortunes. [*Exit*]

CRISPINUS Master Minos? I know no master Minos. Where's Horace? Horace? Horace?

MINOS Sir, do not you know me?

CRISPINUS Oh yes; I know you, master Minos, cry you mercy. But Horace? Gods me, is he gone?

MINOS Ay, and so would you too, if you knew how. Officer, look to him.

CRISPINUS Do you hear, master Minos? Pray let's be used like a man of our own fashion. By Janus and Jupiter, I meant to have paid you next week, every drachma. Seek not to eclipse[413] my reputation thus vulgarly.

MINOS Sir, your oaths cannot serve you; you know I have forborne you long.[414]

CRISPINUS I am conscious of it, sir. Nay, I beseech you, gentlemen, do not exhale me[415] thus; remember 'tis but for sweetmeats—

LICTOR Sweet meat must have sour sauce, sir. Come along.

CRISPINUS Sweet master Minos, I am forfeited to eternal disgrace if you do not commiserate. Good officer, be not so officious.

Act III, scene iv

[*Enter*] TUCCA, [*with First and Second*] PYRGUS

TUCCA Why, how now, my good brace of blood-hounds? Whither do you drag the gent'man? You mongrels, you curs, you bandogs,[416] we are Captain Tucca that talk to you, you inhumane pilchers.[417]

MINOS Sir, he is their prisoner.

TUCCA Their pestilence. What are you, sir?

MINOS A citizen of Rome, sir.

TUCCA Then you are not far distant from a fool, sir.

MINOS A pothecary, sir.

TUCCA I knew thou wast not a physician, faugh! Out of my nostrils, thou stink'st of lotium,[418] and the syringe;[419] away, quack-salver.[420] [*To First* PYRGUS] Follower, my sword.

FIRST PYRGUS Here, noble leader. [*Aside*] You'll do no harm with it, I'll trust you.

TUCCA [*To* LICTOR] Do you hear, you, good-man slave? Hook, ram, rogue, catch-pole,[421] loose the gent'man, or by my velvet arms— *The Officer strikes up* [TUCCA'S] *heels*

LICTOR What will you do, sir? [*Grabbing his wrist and taking his sword*]

TUCCA Kiss thy hand, my honorable active varlet, and embrace thee, thus— [*Tries to grab the sword*]

412 6 slip: forget
413 14 eclipse: darken, stain
414 16 forborne you long: waited patiently for your payment
415 17 exhale me: haul me away
416 2 bandogs: vicious guard dogs
417 3 pilchers: worthless people
418 9 lotium: old urine, often used as a hair tonic
419 10 syringe: often used for administering enemas
420 10 quack-salver: quack, charlatan
421 12 Hook, ram ... catch-pole: the "hook" and "catch-pole" were tools used by officers to arrest people; "ram" is a club or battering ram used to break down doors

FIRST PYRGUS [*Aside*] Oh patient metamorphosis!

TUCCA [*To* LICTOR] My sword, my tall rascal.

LICTOR Nay, soft, sir. Some wiser then some.[422]

TUCCA What? And a wit too! By Pluto, thou must be cherished, slave; here's three drachmas for thee, hold.

PYRGUS [*Aside*] There's half his lendings gone.

TUCCA [*Reaches for the sword*] Give me.

LICTOR No, sir, your first word shall stand. I'll hold all.

TUCCA Nay, but, rogue—

LICTOR You would make a rescue of our prisoner, sir, you?

TUCCA I, a rescue? Away inhuman varlet. Come, come, I never relish above one jest at most;[423] do not disgust me, sirrah, do not. Rogue, I tell thee, rogue, do not.

LICTOR How, sir? Rogue?

TUCCA Ay, why! Thou art not angry, rascal? Art thou?

LICTOR I cannot tell, sir; I am little better, upon these terms.

TUCCA Ha! Gods, and fiends! Why, dost hear? [*Offers to make up*] Rogue, thou, give me thy hand; I say unto thee, thy hand, rogue. What? Dost not thou know me? Not me, rogue? Not Captain Tucca, rogue?

MINOS Come, pray surrender the gentleman his sword, officer; we'll have no fighting here.

TUCCA What's thy name?

MINOS Minos, an't please you.

TUCCA Minos? Come, hither, Minos. Thou art a wise fellow, it seems. Let me talk with thee. [*Takes him aside*]

CRISPINUS Was ever wretch so wretched, as unfortunate I?

TUCCA Thou art one of the *centum-viri*,[424] old boy, art not?

MINOS No, indeed, master Captain.

TUCCA Go to, thou shalt be, then. I'll ha' thee one, Minos. Take my sword from those rascals, dost thou see? Go, do it; I cannot attempt with patience. What does this gentleman owe thee, little Minos?

MINOS Fourscore sesterces,[425] sir.

TUCCA What? No more? [*To the rest*] Come, thou shalt release him, Minos. What, I'll be his bail, thou shalt take my word, old boy, and cashier[426] these furies [*gesturing to the* LICTORS]. Thou shalt do't, I say, thou shalt, little Minos, thou shalt.

CRISPINUS Yes, and as I am a gentleman and a reveler, I'll make a piece of poetry and absolve[427] all within these five days.

TUCCA Come, Minos is not to learn how to use[428] a gent'man of quality, I know. My sword. If he pay thee not, I will, and[429] I must, old boy. Thou shalt be my pothecary too; hast good eryngos,[430] Minos?

MINOS The best in Rome, sir.

TUCCA Go to, then. [*To First* PYRGUS] Vermin, know[431] the house.

FIRST PYRGUS I warrant you, Colonel.

TUCCA For[432] this gentleman, Minos?

MINOS I'll take your word, Captain.

TUCCA Thou hast it. My sword.

422 18 Take it easy; I know your tricks
423 26 I never . . . at most: you're taking the joke too far
424 39 *centum-viri*: an important elected jury
425 44 sesterces: Roman coins
426 46 cashier: dismiss
427 49 absolve: redeem
428 50 is not . . . to use: doesn't need any lessons in how to treat
429 51 and: if
430 52 eryngos: candied plant root, often used as an aphrodisiac
431 54 know: remember
432 56 For: And as for

MINOS Yes, sir, but you must discharge[433] the arrest, Master Crispinus.
TUCCA How, Minos? Look in the gentleman's face and but read[434] his silence. Pay, pay; 'tis honor, Minos.
CRISPINUS By Jove, sweet Captain, you do most infinitely endear and oblige me to you.
TUCCA Tut, I cannot compliment, by Mars, but Jupiter love me, as I love good words and good clothes, and there's an end.[435] Thou shalt give my boy that girdle and hangers,[436] when thou hast worn them a little more.
CRISPINUS Oh Jupiter! Captain, he shall have them now, presently. [*To First* PYRGUS] Please you to be acceptive, young gentleman. [*Gives him the belt*]
FIRST PYRGUS Yes, sir, fear not; I shall accept. [*Aside*] I have a pretty foolish humor of taking,[437] if you knew all.
TUCCA Not now; you shall not take, boy.
CRISPINUS By my truth and earnest, but he shall, Captain, by your leave.
TUCCA Nay, and a' sweare by his truth and earnest, take it boy. Do not make a gent'man forsworn.
LICTOR [*To* TUCCA] Well, sir, there is your sword. But thank master Minos. You had not carried it as you do, else. [*Walks away*]
TUCCA Minos is just, and you are knaves, and—
LICTOR [*Returns*] What say you, sir?
TUCCA Pass on, my good scoundrel, pass on, I honor thee. [LICTOR *walks away*] [*To the others*] But that I hate to have action with such base rogues as these, you should ha' seen me unrip their noses now and have sent 'hem to the next barber's,[438] to stitching. For, do you see—[LICTOR *returns*] I am a man of humor, and I do love the varlets, the honest varlets; they have wit, and valor and are indeed good profitable [LICTOR *leaves again*]—errant rogues, as any live in an empire. [*To* CRISPINUS] Doest thou hear, poetaster? Second me. Stand up, Minos, close, gather, yet—so [*Draws them all together*]. [*To* CRISPINUS] Sir [*Aside*] thou shalt have a quarter share,[439] be resolute [*Aloud*] you shall, at my request, take Minos by the hand here; little Minos, I will have it so. All friends, and a health. Be not inexorable.[440] And thou shalt impart[441] the wine, old boy; thou shalt do't, little Minos, thou shalt. Make us pay it in our physic.[442] What? We must live and honor the gods sometimes, now Bacchus, now Comus, now Priapus;[443] every god, a little. [*Enter* HISTRIO] What's he that stalks[444] by there? Boy, Pyrgus, you were best let him pass, sirrah; do, ferret, let him pass, do.
PYRGUS 'Tis a player, sir.
TUCCA A player? Call him, call the lousy slave hither. What, will he sail by and not once strike or vail[445] to a man of war? Ha? Do you hear? [*To* HISTRIO] You, player, rogue, stalker, come back here. No respect to men of worship, you slave? What, you are proud, you rascal, are you proud? Ha? You grow rich, do you? And purchase, you two-penny tear-mouth?[446] You have fortune, and the good year on your side, you stinkard? You have? You have?
HISTRIO Nay, sweet Captain, be confined to some reason;[447] I protest I saw you not, sir.

433 59 discharge: pay the fine for
434 60 read: interpret: "he has no money; honor is more important"
435 64 there's an end: that's the end of it
436 64 girdle and hangers: belt and straps (for wearing a sword)
437 68–9 a pretty . . . of taking: a taste for stealing things
438 80 barber's: as well as cutting hair and shaving beards, barbers acted as doctors and surgeons
439 85 quarter share: of any profits they should make from any schemes
440 86 inexorable: stubborn
441 87 impart: distribute
442 87–8 pay it in our physic: charge us for medicine after we've drunk too much with you
443 88–9 now Bacchus . . . now Priapus: gods of wine and sex
444 89 stalks: walks pretentiously
445 92–3 strike or vail: nautical terms for lowering a sail as a sign of respect to a larger vessel ("man of war"—an appropriate term for the soldier Tucca)
446 95 And purchase . . . tear-mouth: and purchase fine clothes and property, you ranter-for-hire
447 97 be confined to some reason: be reasonable

TUCCA You did not? Where was your sight, Oedipus?[448] You walk with hare's eyes,[449] do you? I'll ha' 'hem glazed,[450] rogue, an you say the word, they shall be glazed for you. Come, we must have you turn fiddler again, slave; get a bass violin at your back and march in a tawny coat, with one sleeve to Goose-fair,[451] and then you'll know us; you'll see us then; you will, gulch,[452] you will? Then [*Mimics*] "wil't please your worship to have any music, Captain?"

HISTRIO [*Laughs*] Nay, good Captain.

TUCCA What? Do you laugh, Owlglass?[453] Death, you perstemptuous[454] varlet, I am none of your fellows.[455] I have commanded a hundred and fifty such rogues, I.

FIRST PYRGUS [*Aside*] Ay, and most of that hundred and fifty have been leaders of a legion.[456]

HISTRIO If I have exhibited wrong, I'll tender satisfaction, Captain.

TUCCA Say'st thou so, honest vermin? Give me thy hand, thou shalt make[457] us a supper one of these nights.

HISTRIO When you please, by Jove, Captain, most willingly.

TUCCA Dost thou swear? Tomorrow then; say and hold,[458] slave. There are some of you players honest gent'man-like scoundrels and suspected to ha' some wit, as well as your poets, both at drinking and breaking[459] of jests, and are companions for gallants. A man may skelder ye, now and then, of half a dozen shillings or so. [*Pointing to* CRISPINUS] Dost thou not know that Pantalabus[460] there?

HISTRIO No, I assure you, Captain.

TUCCA Go and be acquainted with him, then; he is a gent'man parcel-poet,[461] you slave. His father was a man of worship, I tell thee. Go, he pens high, lofty, in a new stalking strain,[462] bigger then half the rhymers i' the town again. He was born to fill thy mouth, Minotaurus,[463] he was. He will teach thee to tear and rand,[464] rascal; to him, cherish his muse, go. Thou hast forty—forty shillings, I mean—stinkard, give him in earnest,[465] do; he shall write for thee, slave. If he pen for thee once, thou shalt not need to travel with thy pumps full of gravel any more after a blind jade and a hamper, and stalk upon boards and barrel heads to an old cracked trumpet—[466]

HISTRIO Troth, I think I ha' not so much about me,[467] Captain.

TUCCA It's no matter; give him what thou hast, stiff-toe,[468] I'll give my word for the rest. Though it lack a shilling or two, it skills[469] not. Go, thou art an honest shifter;[470] I'll ha'

448 98 Oedipus: blinds himself at the end of Sophocles's famous tragedy

449 98 hare's eyes: hares have weak, myopic eyesight

450 99 glazed: made glassy-eyed (with a blow); also "to fill with glass" (the player is possibly wearing little glasses)

451 100–01 turn fiddler . . . Goose-fair: Tucca teases the player that he should become a traveling musician, carrying a "bass violin" (a large guitar-type of instrument) and wearing a coat with the arm removed so he can play more easily. Goose-fair was a fall festival for eating geese

452 102 gulch: glutton

453 104 Owlglass: a reference to the player's wide-eyed appearance, or his glasses. Also the anglicized name for the German jester character Till Eulenspiegel (so, a fool or buffoon)

454 104 perstemptuous: a nonsense word possibly meaning "presumptuous"

455 105 fellows: fellow actors, friends

456 107 legion: i.e. of lice or fleas

457 109 make: buy

458 112 say and hold: give me your word and hold to it

459 114 breaking: cracking

460 116 Pantalabus: a familiar satirical character who sponges off others

461 118 parcel-poet: part-time poet

462 119 stalking strain: tragic and bombastic style

463 121 Minotaurus: a nickname for the player, who ferociously gobbles up the lines written for him

464 121 tear and rand: rage and rant

465 122 in earnest: as a down payment

466 123–5 If he . . . cracked trumpet: Tucca evokes the hardships that faced traveling actors: shoes ("pumps") filled with "gravel" from the road; run-down horses ("blind jade"), and makeshift temporary stages ("boards") held up by barrels

467 126 about me: on me

468 127 stiff-toe: perhaps a reference to the player's stiff gait

469 128 skills: matters

470 128 shifter: cheater

the statute[471] repealed for thee. [*Turning*] Minos, must tell thee, Minos, thou hast dejected[472] yon gent'man's spirit exceedingly, dost observe? Dost note, little Minos?

MINOS Yes, sir.

TUCCA Go to then, raise, recover, do. Suffer him not to droop in prospect of a player,[473] a rogue, a stager; put twenty into his hand, twenty sesterces I mean, and let nobody see; go, do it, the work shall commend it self; be Minos, I'll pay.

MINOS Yes forsooth, Captain.

SECOND PYRGUS [*Aside*] Do not we serve a notable shark?

TUCCA [*To* HISTRIO] And what new matters[474] have you now afoot, sirrah? Ha? I would fain come with my cockatrice[475] one day and see a play if I knew when there were a good bawdy one, but they say you ha' nothing but humors, revels, and satires that gird and fart at the time,[476] you slave.

HISTRIO No, I assure you, Captain, not we. They[477] are on the other side of Tiber. We have as much ribaldry in our plays as can be, as you would wish, Captain. All the sinners i' the suburbs[478] come and applaud our action daily.

TUCCA I hear you'll bring me o' the stage[479] there; you'll play me, they say. I shall be presented by a sort[480] of copper-laced[481] scoundrels of you. Life of Pluto, and you stage me, stinkard, your mansions shall sweat for't, your tabernacles, varlets, your Globes and your triumphs.[482]

HISTRIO Not we, by Phoebus, Captain; do not do us imputation without desert.[483]

TUCCA I wu' not, my good two-penny rascal. Reach me thy neuf.[484] Dost hear? What wilt thou give me a week for my brace[485] of beagles here [*Gesturing to the* PYRGI], my little point-trussers?[486] You shall ha' them act among ye. [*To First* PYRGUS] Sirrah, you, pronounce. Thou shalt hear him speak, in King Darius'[487] doleful strain.

FIRST PYRGUS O doleful days! O direful deadly dump!
O wicked world! And worldly wickedness!
How can I hold my fist from crying "thump,"
In rue of this right rascal wretchedness!

TUCCA In an amorous vein now, sirrah, peace.

FIRST PYRGUS "Oh, she is wilder, and more hard withal,
Then beast, or bird, or tree, or stony wall.
Yet might she love me, to uprear her state,
Ay, but perhaps, she hopes some nobler mate.
Yet might she love me, to content her sire;
Ay, but her reason masters her desire.
Yet might she love me as her beauty's thrall;
Ay, but I fear, she cannot love at all."[488]

471 129 statute: a law prohibiting actors to travel without the sponsorship of a wealthy patron

472 129 dejected: discouraged

473 132 Suffer him . . . a player: don't let him get dejected when a mere player is watching him

474 137 matters: topics (for plays)

475 138 cockatrice: prostitute mistress

476 139–40 gird and . . . the time: sneer at and insult the current times

477 141 they: i.e. other play companies, located on the other side of the river Tiber (as the Thames divided theaters in London into the northern and southern suburbs)

478 143 suburbs: areas outside the legal jurisdiction of the City of London

479 144 bring me o' the stage: make me into a character in a play

480 145 sort: group

481 145 copper-laced: wearing threads in their costumes to imitate gold

482 146–7 your mansions . . . your triumphs: mock-religious language for the theaters, inns, houses, and city pageants where actors performed (the "Globe" was Shakespeare's theater)

483 148 do not . . . without desert: don't falsely accuse us when we don't deserve it

484 149 neuf: hand

485 150 brace: pair

486 151 point-trussers: valets who lace up clothing

487 152 King Darius: an ancient Persian emperor, here a character speaking in a grandiose tragic style, which the First Pyrgus imitates

488 158–65 These lines are adapted from Thomas Kyd's *The Spanish Tragedy* (c. 1592) II.i. 9–28

TUCCA Now, the horrible fierce soldier, you, sirrah.
FIRST PYRGUS What? Will I brave[489] thee? Ay, and beard[490] thee too.
A Roman spirit scorns to bear a brain
So full of base pusillanimity.[491]
HISTRIO Excellent.
TUCCA Nay, thou shalt see that shall ravish thee anon; prick up thine eares, stinkard. The ghost, boys.
FIRST PYRGUS Vindicta![492]
SECOND PYRGUS Timoria![493]
FIRST PYRGUS Vindicta!
SECOND PYRGUS Timoria!
FIRST PYRGUS Veni![494]
SECOND PYRGUS Veni!
TUCCA [*To Second* PYRGUS, *pointing to his drum*] Now thunder, sirrah. [*To First* PYRGUS] You, the rumbling player.
FIRST PYRGUS Ay, but somebody must cry "murder" then, in a small voice.
TUCCA Your fellow sharer[495] there shall do't. Cry, sirrah, cry.
FIRST PYRGUS "Murder, murder!"
SECOND PYRGUS "Who calls out 'murder'? Lady, was it you?"
HISTRIO Oh, admirable good, I protest.[496]
TUCCA Sirrah, boy, brace your drum a little straighter and do the t'other fellow there, he in the—what sha' call him—and yet stay, too.[497]
SECOND PYRGUS "Nay, an thou dalliest, then I am thy foe,
And fear shall force what friendship cannot win;
Thy death shall bury what thy life conceals,
Villain! Thou diest, for more respecting her—"
FIRST PYRGUS "Oh, stay my Lord."
SECOND PYRGUS "Then me, yet speak the truth, and I will guerdon[498] thee,
But if thou dally once again, thou diest."[499]
TUCCA Enough of this, boy.
SECOND PYRGUS "Why then lament therefore; damned be thy guts
Unto King Pluto's hell, and princely Erebus![500]
For sparrows must have food."[501]
HISTRIO Pray, sweet Captain, let one of them do a little of a lady.
TUCCA Oh, he will make thee eternally enamoured of him, there. [*To First* PYRGUS] Do, sirrah, do; 'twill allay your fellow's fury[502] a little.
FIRST PYRGUS [*In a lady's voice*] "Master, mock on. The scorn thou givest me,
Pray Jove, some lady may return on thee."
SECOND PYRGUS No, you shall see me do the Moor.[503] Master, lend me your scarf a little.

489 167 brave: defy
490 167 beard: confront
491 169 base pusillanimity: low cowardice
492 173 Vindicta: Vengeance
493 174 Timoria: Terror
494 177 Veni: Come!
495 182 sharer: actor
496 185 protest: declare
497 186–7 do the . . . stay, too: Tucca directs the little scene, telling the Pyrgi to play several parts at the same time, but gets confused
498 193 guerdon: reward
499 188–94 "Nay, an . . . thou diest": these lines are also adapted from *The Spanish Tragedy* (II.i. 67–75)
500 197 Erebus: God of darkness
501 192–8 an amalgam of lines from several other plays of the period
502 201 allay your fellow's fury: balance the furious speech of the Second Pyrgus
503 204 Moor: probably Muly Mahamet, a character in George Peele's play *The Battle of Alcazar* (1594)

TUCCA Here, 'tis at thy service, boy.

SECOND PYRGUS You, master Minos, hark hither a little. *They* [*Second* PYRGUS *and* MINOS] *withdraw to make themselves ready* [*to perform a brief scene*]

TUCCA [*To* HISTRIO] How dost like him? Art not rapt? Art not tickled now? Dost not applaud, rascal? Dost not applaud?

HISTRIO Yes. What will you ask for 'hem a week, Captain?

TUCCA No, you mangonizing slave,[504] I will not part from 'hem. You'll sell 'hem for ingles, you. Let's ha' good cheer tomorrow-night at supper, stalker, and then we'll talk. Good capon and plover,[505] do you hear, sirrah? And do not bring your eating[506] player with you there; I cannot away with[507] him. He will eat a leg of mutton while I am in my porridge, the lean Poluphagus;[508] his belly is like Barathrum;[509] he looks like a midwife in man's apparel, the slave. Nor the villainous-out-of-tune fiddler Enobarbus,[510] bring not him. What hast thou there? Six and thirty?[511] Ha?

HISTRIO No, here's all I have, Captain, some five and twenty. [*Gives money*] Pray, sir, will you present and accommodate it unto the gentleman? For mine own part, I am a mere stranger to his humor. Besides, I have some business invites me hence, with Master Asinius Lupus, the tribune.

TUCCA Well, go thy ways, pursue thy projects; let me alone with this design. My poetaster shall make thee a play, and thou shalt be a man of good parts[512] in it. But stay, let me see: do not bring your Aesop, your politician, unless you can ram up his mouth with cloves. The slave smells ranker then some sixteen dung-hills and is seventeen times more rotten. Marry, you may bring Frisker, my zany.[513] He's a good skipping swaggerer, and your fat fool there, my Mango, bring him too, but let him not beg rapiers, nor scarves, in his over-familiar playing face, nor roar out his barren bold jests[514] with a tormenting laughter between drunk and dry.[515] Do you hear, stiff-toe? Give him warning, admonition, to forsake his saucy glavering grace[516] and his goggle eye; it does not become him, sirrah; tell him so. I have stood up and defended you, I, to gent'men, when you have been said to prey upon puisnes[517] and honest citizens for socks or buskins, or when they ha' call'd you usurers, or brokers,[518] or said you were able to help to a piece of flesh[519]—I have sworn, I did not think so. Nor that you were the common retreats for punks decayed i' their practice. I cannot believe it of you—

HISTRIO Thank you, Captain. Jupiter and the rest of the gods confine your modern delights without disgust.[520]

TUCCA Stay! [*Pointing at the Second* PYRGUS *and* MINOS] Thou shalt see the Moor ere thou goest. [*Enter* DEMETRIUS] What's he with the half-arms[521] there, that salutes us out of his cloak like a motion?[522] Ha?

HISTRIO Oh sir, his doublet's a little decayed;[523] he is otherwise a very simple honest fellow,

504 210 mangonizing slave: slave-trading rogue
505 212 capon and plover: game birds, eaten as aphrodisiac foods
506 212 eating: hungry
507 213 away with: get rid of
508 214 Poluphagus: from Greek for "great eater"
509 214 Barathrum: a deep pit in Athens
510 215 Enobarbus: literally "wine-beard"
511 215–6 What hast . . . and thirty: Tucca asks Histrio for money to pay Crispanus, hiring him as a writer for his playing company
512 221 thou shalt . . . good parts: you'll look good in it; you'll have a good role
513 224 zany: fool or jester
514 226 barren bold jests: old, coarse jokes
515 226 dry: sober
516 227 glavering grace: flattering politeness
517 229 puisnes: young clerks
518 230 brokers: pawn-brokers
519 230–31 help to a piece of flesh: act as a procurer for prostitutes (these were common charges brought—not always inaccurately—against actors)
520 233–4 Jupiter and . . . without disgust: may the gods preserve your fashionable pleasures without disgust (or ill judgment)
521 236 half-arms: Demetrius wears a cloak with half-length sleeves
522 237 motion: puppet
523 238 decayed: frayed

sir, one Demetrius, a dresser[524] of plays about the town here. We have hired him to abuse[525] Horace and bring him in,[526] in a play, with all his gallants, as[527] Tibullus, Mecoenas, Cornelius Gallus, and the rest.

TUCCA And why so, stinkard?

HISTRIO Oh it will get us a huge deal of money, Captain, and we have need on't, for this winter has made us all poorer than so many starved snakes. Nobody comes at us,[528] not a gentleman, nor a—

TUCCA But you know nothing by[529] him, do you, to make a play of?

HISTRIO Faith, not much, Captain, but our author will devise that that shall serve in some sort.

TUCCA Why, my Parnassus here shall help him, if thou wilt. Can thy author do it impudently enough?

HISTRIO Oh, I warrant you, Captain, and spitefully enough, too; he has one of the most over-flowing rank wits in Rome. He will slander any man that breathes, if he disgust him.

TUCCA I'll know the poor, egregious, nitty rascal; and he have these commendable qualities, I'll cherish him. Stay, here comes the Tartar.[530]

The boy [*Second* PYRGUS] *comes in on* MINOS' *shoulders, who stalks as he acts*

[*To* HISTRIO] I'll make a gathering[531] for him, I, a purse, and put the poor slave in fresh rags. Tell him so, to comfort him. [*To Second* PYRGUS] Well said, boy.

SECOND PYRGUS "Where art thou, boy? Where is Calipolis?
Fight earth-quakes in the entrails of the earth,
And eastern whirlwinds in the hellish shades.
Some foul contagion of th'infected heavens
Blast all the trees and in their cursèd tops
The dismal night-raven and tragic owl
Breed and become forerunners of my fall."[532]

TUCCA [*To* HISTRIO] Well, now fare thee well, my honest penny-biter.[533] Commend me to Seven-shares-and-a-half,[534] and remember tomorrow[535]—if you lack a service,[536] you shall play in my name, rascals, but you shall buy your own cloth,[537] and I'll ha' two shares for my countenance.[538] Let thy author stay with me.

DEMETRIUS Yes, sir.

TUCCA 'Twas well done, little Minos, thou didst stalk well; forgive me that I said thou stunkst, Minos. 'Twas the savor of a poet I met sweating in the street hangs yet in my nostrils.

CRISPINUS Who? Horace?

TUCCA Ay, he, dost thou know him?

CRISPINUS Oh, he forsook[539] me most barbarously, I protest.

TUCCA Hang him, fusty[540] satyr;[541] he smells all goat. He carries a ram under his arm-holes, the slave. I am the worse when I see him. [*Aside*] Did not Minos impart?[542]

CRISPINUS Yes, here are twenty drachmas he did convey.

524 239 dresser: fixer or reviser
525 239 abuse: insult
526 240 bring him in: caricature him
527 240 as: such as
528 244 comes at us: attends our plays
529 246 by: about
530 253 Tartar: i.e. the Moor, played by the Second Pyrgus and Minos
531 254 make a gathering: take up a collection
532 256–62 lines adapted from Peele's *The Battle of Alcazar* (1594) lines 368–77
533 263 penny-biter: coins were sometimes bitten to test their authenticity
534 264 Seven-shares-and-a-half: Tucca's nickname for another actor, presumably one of the leading men in Histrio's company
535 264 tomorrow: the day of their planned supper
536 264 a service: patronage
537 265 cloth: clothing
538 266 countenance: sponsorship
539 272 forsook: left
540 273 fusty: musty
541 273 satyr: a lusty half-man, half goat; also a reference to Horace as a satirist
542 274 impart: give you money

TUCCA Well said, keep 'hem. We'll share anon. [*To* MINOS] Come, little Minos.
CRISPINUS Faith, Captain, I'll be bold to show you a mistress of mine, a jewelers wife, a gallant, as we go along.
TUCCA There spoke my genius. Minos, some of thy eryngoes, little Minos, send. [*To* CRISPINUS, *pointing to* DEMETRIUS] Come hither, Parnassus, I must ha' thee familiar with my little locust, here; 'tis a good vermin, they say. [*Spotting* HORACE *approaching*] See, here's Horace and old Trebatius, the great lawyer, in his company; let's avoid him, now. He is too well-seconded.[543]

[*Exeunt*]

Act III, scene v[544]

[*Enter*] HORACE [*and*] TREBATIUS

HORACE There are[545] to whom I seem excessive sour
And past a satire's law t'extend my power.
Others, that think whatever I have writ
Wants pith,[546] and matter[547] to eternize it,
And that they could, in one day's light, disclose[548]
A thousand verses such as I compose.
What shall I do, Trebatius? Say.
TREBATIUS Surcease.[549]
HORACE And shall my muse admit no more increase?
TREBATIUS So I advise.
HORACE An ill death let me die
If 'twere not best, but sleep avoids mine eye
And I use these,[550] lest nights should tedious seem.
TREBATIUS Rather contend to sleep, and live like them
That holding golden sleep in special price,
Rubbed with sweet oils, swim silver Tiber thrice,
And every ev'n, with neat wine steepèd be.
Or, if such love of writing ravish thee,
Then dare to sing unconquered Caesar's deeds,
Who cheers such actions with abundant meeds.[551]
HORACE That, father,[552] I desire, but when I try,
I feel defects in every faculty.
Nor is't a labor fit for every pen
To paint the horrid troops of armèd men,
The lances burst in Gallia's[553] slaughtered forces,
Or wounded Parthians[554] tumbled from their horses.
Great Caesar's wars cannot be fought with words.
TREBATIUS Yet what his virtue in his peace affords,[555]
His fortitude and justice thou canst show,

543 283 seconded: accompanied and protected
544 Act III, scene v: a dramatic adaptation of Horace, *Satires* 2.1 (Jonson's note). It was not included in the 1602 Quarto edition of the play
545 1 There are: there are some
546 4 pith: importance and energy
547 4 matter: substance
548 5 disclose: issue forth
549 7 Surcease: stop writing
550 11 these: his satiric poems
551 18 meeds: rewards
552 19 father: respectful form of address
553 23 Gallia: France (where Caesar campaigned)
554 24 Parthians: ancient empire located in what is now Iran
555 26 affords: makes possible

As wise Lucilius honored Scipio.[556]
HORACE Of that, my powers shall suffer no neglect,
When such slight labors may aspire respect.
But if I watch not a most chosen time,
The humble words of Flaccus[557] cannot climb
Th'attentive ear of Caesar. Nor must I
With less observance shun gross flattery,
For he, reposèd safe in his own merit,
Spurns back the glozes[558] of a fawning spirit.
TREBATIUS But how much better would such accents sound
Than with a sad and serious verse to wound
Pantolabus, railing in his saucy jests?
Or Nomentanus spent in riotous feasts? [559]
"In satires, each man (though untouched) complains
As he were hurt and hates such biting strains."[560]
HORACE What shall I do? Milonius[561] shakes his heels
In ceaseless dances when his brain once feels
The stirring fervor of the wine ascend,
And that his eyes false number apprehend.
Castor his horse, Pollux[562] loves handy fights, [563]
Thousand heads, a thousand choice delights.[564]
My pleasure is in feet[565] my words to close,[566]
As both our better old Lucilius[567] does.
He, as[568] his trusty friends, his books did trust
With all his secrets; nor in things unjust,
Or actions lawful, ran[569] to other men,
So that the old man's life described was seen
As in a votive table[570] in his lines,
And to his steps my genius inclines—[571]
Lucanian or Apulian, I not whether;[572]
For the Venusian colony[573] plows either.
Sent thither, when the Sabines[574] were forced thence
(As old fame sings) to give the place defence
'Gainst such, as seeing it empty might make road[575]
Upon the empire, or there fix abode,
Whether th'Apulian borderer it were,
Or the Lucanian violence they fear.

556 28 Lucilius was a Roman poet (see lines 104f); Scipio was a Roman general and politician
557 32 Flaccus: i.e. Horace himself
558 36 glozes: flattery
559 39–40 Pantolabus and Nomentanus were figures in Horace's satires
560 41–2 "In satires . . . biting strains": a quotation from Horace's satires, marked for emphasis in F
561 43 Milonius: a character in one of Horace's satires, described as dancing when he drinks wine and losing track of his arithmetic
562 47 Castor and Pollux were half-brothers and mythical heroes transformed into the constellation Gemini
563 47 handy fights: fist-fights
564 48 Every person has his or her own pleasure
565 49 feet: poetic syllables
566 49 close: contain
567 50 Lucilius: another character in Horace's satire
568 51 as: like
569 53 ran: referred
570 55 votive table: a prayer picture
571 56 My talents follow in his footsteps
572 57 I not whether: I know not
573 58 Venusian colony: birthplace of Horace; inhabited by both the Lucanian and Apulian tribes
574 59 Sabines: former occupants of Venusia
575 61 road: invasion

But this,[576] my style no living man shall touch,
If first I be not forced by base reproach,[577]
But, like a sheathèd sword, it shall defend
My innocent life; for, why should I contend
To draw it out, when no malicious thief
Robs my good name, the treasure of my life?
Oh Jupiter, let it with rust be eaten,
Before it touch or insolently threaten
The life of any with the least disease;
So much I love, and woo a general peace.
But, he that wrongs me: better, I proclaim,
He never had assayed to touch my fame,
For he shall weep, and walk with every tongue[578]
Throughout the city, infamously sung.
Servius the praetor[579] threats the laws and urn,[580]
If any at his deeds repine[581] or spurn;
The witch Canidia, that Albucius got,[582]
Denounceth witch-craft where she loveth not;[583]
Thurius, the judge, doth thunder worlds of ill
To such as strive with his judicial will;
All men affright their foes in what they may:
Nature commands it, and men must obey.
Observe with me: the wolf his tooth doth use,
The bull his horn, and who doth this infuse[584]
But nature? There's luxurious[585] Scaeva. Trust
His long-lived mother with him. His so just
And scrupulous right hand no mischief will,[586]
No more than with his heel a wolf will kill,
Or ox with jaw. Marry, let him alone
With tempered poison to remove the crone.
But, briefly, if to age[587] I destined be,
Or that quick death's black wings environ[588] me;
If rich or poor, at Rome, or fate command
I shall be banished to some other land;
What hue[589] soever my whole state[590] shall bear,
I will write satires still, in spite of fear.
TREBATIUS Horace, I fear thou draw'st no lasting breath
And that some great man's friend will be thy death.
HORACE What? When the man[591] that first did satirize

576 65 But this: despite this violent history
577 66 reproach: insult
578 77 with every tongue: with everyone talking about him
579 79 praetor: official judge
580 79 laws and urn: legal judgment (urns were used by juries to cast ballots)
581 80 repine: complain
582 81 got: begot
583 82 Accuses those she hates of witchcraft
584 88 who doth this infuse: who causes these things
585 89 luxurious: self-indulgent
586 91 Romans regarded the right hand as upright and fair, the left hand as treacherous; here Scaeva's right hand refuses to administer poison to his mother (see lines 94–6)—presumably this was done with the left hand
587 95 age: old age
588 96 environ: surround
589 99 hue: quality
590 99 state: condition
591 103 man: Lucilius, an early Roman satirical poet (see below)

Durst[592] pull the skin over the ears of vice
And make who stood in outward fashion clear
Give place as foul within,[593] shall I forbear?
Did Laelius, or the man so great with fame
That from sacked Carthage fetched his worthy name,
Storm that Lucilius did Metellus pierce?
Or bury Lupus quick in famous verse?[594]
Rulers and subjects, by whole tribes he checked,
But virtue and her friends did still protect.
And when from sight or from the judgment seat,[595]
The virtuous Scipio and wise Laelius met,
Unbraced,[596] with him in all light sports they shared,
Till their most frugal suppers were prepared.
Whate'er I am, though both for wealth, and wit,
Beneath Lucilius I am pleased to sit,[597]
Yet envy, spite of her empoisoned breast,
Shall say I lived in grace here with the best,
And seeking in weak trash to make her wound,
Shall find me solid and her teeth unsound—
'Less[598] learned Trebatius' censure disagree.
TREBATIUS No, Horace, I of force must yield to thee.
Only take heed, as being advised by me,
Lest thou incur some danger. Better pause
Than rue thy ignorance of the sacred laws;
There's justice and great action[599] may be sued
'Gainst such as wrong men's fames with verses lewd.
HORACE Ay, with lewd verses, such as libels be,
And aimed at persons of good quality.
I reverence and adore that just decree,
But if they shall be sharp yet modest rhymes
That spare men's persons and but tax[600] their crimes,
Such[601] shall in open court find current pass[602]
Were Caesar judge, and with the maker's grace.[603]
TREBATIUS Nay, I'll add more: if thou thy self being clear,
Shalt tax in person a man fit to bear
Shame and reproach, his suit shall quickly be
Dissolved in laughter, and thou thence set free.

Act IV, scene i

[*Enter*] CHLOE [*with* MAIDS *and*] CYTHERIS

592 104 Durst: dared to
593 105–6 And make ... foul within: make those who appear to be virtuous on the outside admit their true foulness
594 107–10 Did Laelius ... famous verse: Laelius was a statesman and friend of Scipio, "the man" referred to in the same line; they did not get angry ("storm") when their friend, the poet Lucilius, satirized their peers (Metellus and Lupus) in his verse
595 113 And when, in private, away from the courts
596 115 Unbraced: literally with clothes untied or loosened, i.e. relaxed
597 117–18 though both ... to sit: I know I'm not as wealthy or witty as Lucilius
598 123 'Less: unless
599 128 action: legal actions. Trebatius refers to laws against libel
600 134 tax: criticize
601 135 such: such verses
602 135 find current pass: circulate swiftly and easily
603 136 maker's grace: author's honor

CHLOE But, sweet lady, say: am I well enough attired for the court, in sadness?[604]
CYTHERIS Well enough? Excellent well, sweet Mistress Chloe. This straight-bodied[605] city attire, I can tell you, will stir a courtier's blood more than the finest loose sacks the ladies use to be put in;[606] and then you are as well jeweled as any of them; your ruff, and linen about you, is much more pure than theirs. And for your beauty, I can tell you there's many of them would defy the painter if they could change with you.[607] Marry, the worst is you must look to be envied and endure a few court-frumps[608] for it.
CHLOE Oh Jove, madam, I shall buy them too cheap! [*To* MAID] Give me my muff, and my dog there. And will the ladies be anything familiar[609] with me, think you?
CYTHERIS Oh Juno! Why, you shall see 'hem flock about you with their puff wings[610] and ask you where you bought your lawn?[611] And what you paid for it? Who starches you? And entreat you to help 'hem to some pure laundresses[612] out of the city.
CHLOE Oh Cupid! [*To* MAID] Give me my fan and my mask too. And will the lords and the poets there use one well too, lady?
CYTHERIS Doubt not of that. You shall have kisses from them go pit-pat, pit-pat, pit-pat, upon your lips, as thick as stones out of slings at the assault of a city. And then your ears will be so furred with the breath of their compliments that you cannot catch cold of your head (if you would) in three winters after.
CHLOE Thank you, sweet lady. Oh heaven! And how must one behave herself amongst 'hem? You know all.
CYTHERIS Faith, impudently enough, Mistress Chloe, and well enough. Carry not too much under-thought[613] betwixt your self and them. Nor your city mannerly word "forsooth"; use it not too often, in any case, but plain "ay, madam" and "no, madam." Nor never say "your lordship" nor "your honor" but "you" and "you, my lord" and "my lady." The other they count too simple and minsitive.[614] And though they desire to kiss heaven with their titles, yet they will count them fools that give them too humbly.
CHLOE Oh intolerable, Jupiter! By my troth, lady, I would not for a world but you had lyen[615] in my house, and i' faith you shall not pay a farthing for your board nor your chambers.
CYTHERIS Oh, sweet Mistress Chloe!
CHLOE I'faith, you shall not lady; nay, good lady, do not offer it.

Act IV, scene ii

[*Enter*] GALLUS [*and*] TIBULLUS

GALLUS Come, where be these ladies? By your leave, bright stars, this gentleman and I are come to man you[616] to court, where your late[617] kind entertainment is now to be requited with a heavenly banquet.
CYTHERIS A heavenly banquet, Gallus?
GALLUS No less, my dear, Cytheris.
TIBULLUS That were not strange, lady, if the epithet were only given for the company invited

604 1 in sadness: in all seriousness
605 2 straight-bodied: fitted
606 3–4 use to be put in: usually put on
607 5–6 defy the . . . with you: reject their cosmeticians if they had your face
608 7 court-frumps: expressions of indignant displeasure
609 9 familiar: friendly
610 10 puff wings: puffed sleeves
611 11 lawn: fine linen
612 12 pure laundresses: honest laundresses; since prostitutes were sometimes thought to masquerade as laundresses, the line may imply a joke that the court ladies will ask Chloe's advice about how to engage in sexual trysts outside the city
613 21–2 Carry not . . . under-thought: don't think of yourself as beneath them
614 25 minsitive: fawning
615 27 I would not . . . had lyen: I would not have it any other way but to have you lodging
616 2 man you: escort you
617 2 late: recent

thither, yourself and this fair gentlewoman.

CHLOE Are we invited to court, sir?

TIBULLUS You are, lady, by the great princess, Julia, who longs to greet you with any favors that may worthily make you an often courtier.

CHLOE In sincerity, I thank her, sir. You have a coach? Ha' you not?

TIBULLUS The princess hath sent her own, lady.

CHLOE Oh Venus! That's well. I do long to ride in a coach most vehemently.

CYTHERIS But, sweet Gallus, pray you, resolve[618] me, why you give that heavenly praise to this earthly banquet?

GALLUS Because, Cytheris, it must be celebrated by the heavenly powers. All the gods and goddesss will be there, to two of which you two must be exalted.[619]

CHLOE A pretty fiction in truth.

CYTHERIS A fiction indeed, Chloe, and fit for the fit of a poet.

GALLUS Why, Cytheris, may not poets, from whose divine spirits all the honors of the gods have been deduced,[620] entreat so much honor of the gods to have their divine presence at a poetical banquet?

CYTHERIS Suppose that no fiction. Yet where are your abilities to make us two goddesses at your feast?

GALLUS Who knows not, Cytheris, that the sacred breath of a true poet can blow any virtuous humanity up to deity?

TIBULLUS To tell you the female truth, which is the simple truth, ladies; and to show that poets, in spite of the world, are able to deify themselves. At this banquet, to which you are invited, we intend to assume the figures of the gods and to give our several loves the forms of goddesses. Ovid will be Jupiter; the Princess Julia, Juno; Gallus here, Apollo; you Cytheris, Pallas; I will be Bacchus; and my love Plautia, Ceres. And to install you, and your husband, fair Chloe, in honors equal with ours, you shall be a goddess and your husband a god.

CHLOE A god? Oh my god!

TIBULLUS A god, but a lame god, lady, for he shall be Vulcan, and you Venus.[621] And this will make our banquet no less than heavenly.

CHLOE In sincerity, it will be sugared. Good Jove, what a pretty foolish thing it is to be a poet! But hark you, sweet Cytheris, could they not possibly leave out my husband? Methinks a body's husband does not so well at court. A body's friend[622] or so—but husband, 'tis like your clog to your marmoset,[623] for all the world and the heavens.

CYTHERIS Tut, never fear, Chloe. Your husband will be left without in the lobby or the great chamber, when you shall be put in, i' the closet,[624] by this lord and by that lady.

CHLOE Nay, then I am certified: he shall go.

Act IV, scene iii

[*Enter*] HORACE

GALLUS Horace! Welcome.

HORACE Gentlemen, hear you the news?

TIBULLUS What news, my Quintus?

HORACE Our melancholic friend, Propertius
Hath closed himself up in his Cynthia's tomb
And will by no entreaties be drawn thence.

618 14 resolve: explain to

619 17 exalted: raised

620 21 deduced: derived

621 34 he shall . . . you Venus: Vulcan was the Roman god of fire and the forge; he was handicapped by a broken foot that had not healed properly. Venus, his wife, was the goddess of love; she disdained her husband and was often unfaithful to him, especially with Mars, the god of war

622 38 friend: lover

623 39 clog to your marmoset: a clog is a piece of wood, tied to the leg of the marmoset (a small monkey) so that it can't escape

624 40–41 Your husband . . . i'the closet: your husband will be left in the great room while you are seduced secretly in a private one

[*Enter*] ALBIUS, CRISPINUS, TUCCA, [*and*] DEMETRIUS

ALBIUS Nay, good master Crispinus, pray you, bring near the gentleman. [*Pointing to* TUCCA]

HORACE [*Aside*] Crispinus? Hide me, good Gallus. Tibullus, shelter me.
CRISPINUS Make your approach, sweet Captain.
TIBULLUS What means this, Horace?
HORACE I am surprised again; farewell.
GALLUS Stay, Horace.
HORACE What, and be tired on[625] by yond' vulture? No.
Phoebus defend me. [*Exit*]
TIBULLUS 'Slight! I hold my life,
This same is he met him[626] in Holy Street.
GALLUS Troth, 'tis like enough. This act of Propertius' relisheth[627] very strange with me.
TUCCA By thy leave, my neat scoundrel. What, is this the mad boy you talked on?
CRISPINUS Ay. This is master Albius, Captain.
TUCCA Give me thy hand, Agamemnon. We hear abroad, thou art the Hector of citizens. What sayest thou? Are we welcome to thee, noble Neoptolemus?[628]
ALBIUS Welcome, Captain? By Jove, and all the Gods i'the capitol—
TUCCA No more, we conceive[629] thee. Which of these is thy wedlock,[630] Menelaus? Thy Helen? Thy Lucrece? [631] That we may do her honor, mad boy?
CRISPINUS She i' the little fine dressing, sir, is my mistress.
ALBIUS For fault of a better, sir.[632]
TUCCA A better, profane rascal? [*Catches himself*] I cry thee mercy, my good scroyle, was't thou?[633]
ALBIUS No harm, Captain.
TUCCA She is a Venus, a Vesta, a Melpomene. Come hither, Penelope; what's thy name, Iris?[634] [CHLOE *and* TUCCA *speak apart*]
CHLOE My name is Chloe, sir; I am a gentlewoman.
TUCCA Thou art in merit to be an empress, Chloe, for an eye and a lip; thou hast an emperor's nose. [*Kisses her*] Kiss me again. [*She kisses him*] 'Tis a virtuous punk.[635] So. Before Jove, the gods were a sort of goslings[636] when they suffered so sweet a breath to perfume the bed of a stinkard.[637] Thou hadst ill fortune, Thisbe;[638] the fates were infatuate;[639] they were, punk, they were.

625 13 tired on: torn apart
626 16 he met him: the man who met him
627 17 relisheth: feels
628 20–21 Agamemnon . . . noble Neoptolemus: heroic characters from Homer's *Iliad*
629 23 conceive: understand
630 23 wedlock: wife
631 23–4 Menelaus . . . Thy Lucrece: Menelaus, King of Sparta, was the husband of Helen, who was kidnapped by the Trojan prince, Paris; in response, Menelaus and the Greeks attacked Troy, thus starting the Trojan War. Lucrece was a Roman noblewoman who was raped by another nobleman, Tarquin, who was a guest in her home; her rape and suicide was the subject of Shakespeare's poem, *The Rape of Lucrece*
632 26 She's my wife because I don't have a better one
633 27–8 I cry . . . was't thou: Tucca reacts angrily to Albius's exchange with Crispinus and begins to reproach him, but then catches himself and pretends not to have realized that it was Albius who was speaking; Albius waves him away good-naturedly; "scroyle" means scoundrel. See III.iv. 76–83 for another instance of the conflict between Tucca's verbal tempestuousness and his impulse to flatter and ingratiate himself with anyone whom he might turn to his advantage
634 30–31 a Vesta . . . Iris: Vesta was goddess of the home; Melpomene was the Muse of Tragedy; Penelope was the faithful wife of Odysseus; Iris was goddess of the rainbow
635 34 punk: prostitute
636 35 goslings: silly geese
637 36 stinkard: i.e. Albius
638 36 Thisbe: unfortunate heroine in Ovid who married her lover Pyramus; thinking she had been killed by a lion, he killed himself, and she then killed herself in turn (a story recast comically in Shakespeare's *A Midsummer Night's Dream*)
639 36 infatuate: foolish

CHLOE That's sure, sir. Let me crave your name, I pray you, sir.

TUCCA I am known by the name of Captain Tucca, punk; the noble Roman, punk. A gent'man and a commander, punk. [*Goes to kiss her again*]

CHLOE In good time. [*Steps away*] A gentleman and a commander? That's as good as a poet, methinks.

CRISPINUS [*Seeing a viol*] A pretty instrument! It's my cousin Cytheris' viol,[640] this. Is't not?

CYTHERIS Nay, play cousin, it wants but such a voice and hand to grace it as yours is.

CRISPINUS Alas, cousin, you are merrily inspired.

CYTHERIS Pray you play, if you love me.

CRISPINUS Yes, cousin. You know I do not hate you.

TIBULLUS [*Aside*] A most subtle wench! How she hath baited him with a viol yonder, for a song!

CRISPINUS Cousin, pray you call Mistress Chloe; she shall hear an essay[641] of my poetry.

TUCCA I'll call her. [*To* CHLOE] Come hither, cockatrice. Here's one will set thee up,[642] my sweet punk, set thee up.

CHLOE Are you a poet so soon, sir?

ALBIUS Wife, mum.

CRISPINUS [*Sings and plays*] *Love is blind, and a wanton;*
In the whole world there is scant
One such another;
No, not his mother.
He hath plucked her doves and sparrows
To feather his sharp arrows,
And alone prevaileth,
Whilst sick Venus waileth.
But if Cypris once recover
The wag, it shall behoove her
To look better to him,
Or she will undo him.[643]

ALBIUS Oh, most odoriferous[644] music!

TUCCA Aha! Stinkard. Another Orpheus, you slave, another Orpheus! An Arion,[645] riding on the back of a dolphin, rascal!

GALLUS Have you a copy of this ditty, sir?

CRISPINUS Master Albius has.

ALBIUS Ay, but in truth they are my wife's verses;[646] I must not show 'hem.

TUCCA Show 'hem, bankrupt, show 'hem; they have salt[647] in 'hem, and will brook the air, stinkard.

GALLUS [*Takes the poems and reads the titles*] How? "To his bright mistress, Canidia"?

CRISPINUS Ay, sir, that's but a borrowed name, as Ovid's Corinna, or Propertius his Cynthia, or your Nemesis or Delia, Tibullus.

GALLUS It's the name of Horace his witch, as I remember.

TIBULLUS Why the ditty's all borrowed! 'Tis Horace's. Hang him, plagiary![648]

TUCCA How? He borrow of Horace? He shall pawn himself to ten brokers, first. Do you hear, poetasters? I know you to be men of worship.[649] He shall write with Horace for a

640 43 viol: a kind of guitar
641 50 essay: trial, attempt
642 52 set thee up: get you going
643 66 Crispinus's song is about Cupid, son of Venus, whose birds were the dove and the sparrow. Cypris is another name for Venus
644 67 odoriferous: sweet-smelling
645 68 another Orpheus . . . An Arion: mythical Greek poets
646 72 wife's verses: given to his wife
647 73 salt: wit; metaphorically, something that will preserve the poems if they circulate openly
648 79 plagiary: as a plagiarist
649 81 men of worship: gentlemen

talent,[650] and let Mecoenas and his whole college[651] of critics take his part. Thou shalt do't, young Phoebus;[652] thou shalt, Phaeton;[653] thou shalt.

DEMETRIUS Alas, sir, Horace! He is a mere sponge; nothing but humors and observation; he goes up and down sucking from every society, and when he comes home, squeezes himself dry again. I know him, I.

TUCCA Thou sayest true, my poor poetical Fury; he will pen all he knows. A sharp thorny-toothed satirical rascal; fly him,[654] he carries hay in his horn.[655] He will sooner lose his best friend than his least jest. What he once drops upon paper against a man lives eternally to upbraid him in the mouth of every slave tankard-bearer[656] or waterman;[657] not a bawd or a boy that comes from the bake-house but shall point at him. 'Tis all dog and scorpion; he carries poison in his teeth and a sting in his tail. Fough, body of Jove! I'll have the slave whipped one of these days for his satires and his humors, by one cashiered[658] clerk or another.

CRISPINUS We'll undertake him, Captain.

DEMETRIUS Ay, and tickle him i' faith for his arrogancy and his impudence in commending[659] his own things and for his translating. I can trace[660] him i' faith. Oh, he is the most open[661] fellow living; I had as lief as a new suit, I were at it.[662]

TUCCA Say no more then, but do it; 'tis the only way to get thee a new suit; sting him my little newts; I'll give you instructions. I'll be your intelligencer;[663] we'll all join and hang upon him like so many horse-leeches, the players and all. We shall sup together, soon and then we'll conspire, i' faith.

GALLUS [*To* TIBULLUS] Oh, that Horace had stayed still, here.

TIBULLUS So would not I. For both these would have turn'd Pythagoreans,[664] then.

GALLUS What, mute?

TIBULLUS Ay, as fishes i'faith. Come, ladies, shall we go?

CYTHERIS We await you, sir. But Mistress Chloe asks if you have not a god to spare, for this gentleman.

GALLUS Who, Captain Tucca?

CYTHERIS Ay, he.

GALLUS Yes, if we can invite him along, he shall be Mars.

CHLOE Has Mars anything to do with Venus?

TIBULLUS Oh, most of all, lady.

CHLOE Nay, then, I pray let him be invited. And what shall Crispinus be?

TIBULLUS Mercury, Mistress Chloe.

CHLOE Mercury? That's a poet? Is't?

GALLUS No, lady, but somewhat inclining that way. He is a herald at arms.[665]

CHLOE A herald at arms? Good. And Mercury? Pretty. He has to do with Venus, too?

TIBULLUS A little, with her face,[666] lady, or so.

CHLOE 'Tis very well. Pray let's go, I long to be at it.

CYTHERIS Gentlemen, shall we pray your companies along?

650 82 talent: a Roman coin (offered as a reward in the writing contest Tucca is proposing)
651 82 college: group
652 83 Phoebus: god of the sun
653 83 Phaeton: human son of Apollo who tried to drive his chariot—with disastrous results
654 88 fly him: run away from him
655 88 hay in his horn: famers tied hay in the horns of angry cattle as a warning to others
656 90 tankard-bearer: waiter or innkeeper
657 90 waterman: ferryman
658 93 cashiered: bankrupt
659 95 commending: promoting
660 96 trace: track, pursue
661 96 open: brazen
662 97 I had . . . at it: I'd love to get after him as much as I'd love a new suit
663 99 intelligencer: spy
664 103 Pythagoreans: philosophers known for keeping silent
665 116 herald at arms: a clerk who prepares family trees
666 118 with her face: mercury was an ingredient in women's cosmetics

CRISPINUS You shall not only pray but prevail, lady. Come, sweet Captain.
TUCCA Yes, I follow. [*To* ALBIUS] But thou must not talk of this now, my little bankrupt.
ALBIUS Captain, look here: mum.
DEMETRIUS I'll go write, sir.
TUCCA Do, do, stay. There's a drachma, to purchase gingerbread for thy muse.

[*Exeunt*]

Act IV, scene iv

[*Enter*] LUPUS, HISTRIO, [*and a*] LICTOR

LUPUS Come, let us talk here; here we may be private. Shut the door, Lictor. You are a player, you say.
HISTRIO Ay, and't please your worship.
LUPUS Good. And how are you able to give this intelligence?
HISTRIO Marry, sir, they directed a letter to me and my fellow sharers.
LUPUS Speak lower, you are not now i' your theater, stager. My sword, knave. They directed a letter to you, and your fellow sharers. Forward.
HISTRIO Yes, sir, to hire some of our properties: as a scepter, and a crown for Jove, and a caduceus[667] for Mercury, and a petasus—[668]
LUPUS Caduceus? And petasus? Let me see your letter. This is a conjuration, a conspiracy, this. Quickly, on with my buskins. I'll act a tragedy, i' faith. Will nothing but our gods serve these poets to profane? Dispatch.[669] Player, I thank thee. The emperor shall take knowledge of thy good service. [*Knock on the door*] Who's there now? [*To* LICTOR] Look, knave. [*To* HISTRIO] A crown, and a scepter? This is good; rebellion, now?
LICTOR 'Tis your pothecary, sir, master Minos.
LUPUS What tell'st thou me of pothecaries, knave? Tell him I have affairs of state in hand; I can talk to no pothecaries now. Heart of me! Stay the pothecary there. [*Whispers to* HISTRIO] You shall see, I have fished out a cunning piece of plot now: they have had some intelligence that their project is discovered, and now have they dealt with my pothecary to poison me. 'Tis so, knowing that I meant to take physic today. As sure as death, 'tis there. Jupiter, I thank thee that thou hast yet made me so much of a politician.[670] [*To* MINOS] You are welcome, sir. [*Aloud to* LICTOR] Take the potion from him there! [*To* MINOS] I have an antidote more than you wot[671] of, sir! [*To* LICTOR] Throw it on the ground there! [*Breaks the bottle*] So. Now fetch in the dog.[672] And yet we cannot tarry to try experiments, now. [*To* LICTOR] Arrest him! [*To* MINOS] You shall go with me, sir; I'll tickle you, pothecary; I'll give you a glister,[673] i' faith. Have I the letter? Ay 'tis here. Come, your *fasces*,[674] lictors. The half pikes, and the halberds, take them down from the *lares*,[675] there. Player, assist me.

[*Enter* MECOENAS *and* HORACE]

MECOENAS Whither now, Asinius Lupus, with this armory?
LUPUS I cannot talk now; I charge you, assist me. Treason! Treason!
HORACE How? Treason!?
LUPUS Ay. If you love the emperor and the state, follow me.

[*Exeunt*]

667 9 caduceus: winged staff entwined with snakes
668 9 petasus: winged cap
669 12 Dispatch: off you go
670 21 politician: plotter; one skilled in sniffing out plots
671 23 wot: know
672 24 dog: to see if he dies when he licks up the potion from the floor
673 25 glister: enema
674 26 *fasces*: staffs and axe symbolic of authority, the Roman equivalent of the English pikes and halberds
675 27 *lares*: images or statues of household gods, perhaps also a mantelpiece

Act IV, scene v

[*Enter*] OVID [*as Jupiter*], JULIA [*as Juno*], GALLUS [*as Phoebus Apollo*], CYTHERIS [*as Pallas Athena*], TIBULLUS [*as Bacchus*], PLAUTIA [*as Ceres*], ALBIUS [*as Vulcan*], CHLOE [*as Venus*], TUCCA [*as Mars*], CRISPINUS [*as Mercury*], HERMOGENES [*as Momus, and a*] PYRGUS [*as Ganymede*]

OVID Gods, and goddesses, take your several seats. Now, Mercury, move your caduceus, and in Jupiter's name command silence.
CRISPINUS In the name of Jupiter; silence.
HERMOGENES The cryer of the court hath too clarified[676] a voice.
GALLUS Peace, Momus.[677]
OVID Oh, he is the God of reprehension; let him alone. 'Tis his office. Mercury, go forward, and proclaim after Phoebus our high pleasure to all the deities that shall partake this high banquet.
CRISPINUS Yes, sir. [*Stands with* GALLUS *before the banquet table*]
GALLUS The great God, Jupiter,
CRISPINUS The great God, Jupiter,
GALLUS Of his licentious goodness,
CRISPINUS Of his licentious goodness,
GALLUS Willing to make this feast no fast
CRISPINUS Willing to make this feast no fast
GALLUS From any manner of pleasure,
CRISPINUS From any manner of pleasure,
GALLUS Nor to bind any god or goddess
CRISPINUS Nor to bind any god or goddess
GALLUS To be anything the more god or goddess for their names:
CRISPINUS To be anything the more god or goddess for their names:
GALLUS He gives them all free license
CRISPINUS He gives them all free license
GALLUS To speak no wiser than persons of baser titles
CRISPINUS To speak no wiser than persons of baser titles
GALLUS And to be nothing better than common men or women.
CRISPINUS And to be nothing better than common men or women.
GALLUS And therefore no god
CRISPINUS And therefore no god
GALLUS Shall need to keep himself more strictly to his goddess,
CRISPINUS Shall need to keep himself more strictly to his goddess,
GALLUS Than any man does to his wife,
CRISPINUS Than any man does to his wife,
GALLUS Nor any goddess
CRISPINUS Nor any goddess
GALLUS Shall need to keep herself more strictly to her god,
CRISPINUS Shall need to keep herself more strictly to her god,
GALLUS Than any woman does to her husband.
CRISPINUS Than any woman does to her husband.
GALLUS But, since it is no part of wisdom
CRISPINUS But, since it is no part of wisdom
GALLUS In these days to come into bonds,
CRISPINUS In these days to come into bonds,
GALLUS It shall be lawful for every lover
CRISPINUS It shall be lawful for every lover

676 4 clarified: loud
677 5 Momus: god of satire and of criticism

GALLUS To break loving oaths,

CRISPINUS To break loving oaths,

GALLUS To change their lovers, and make love to others,

CRISPINUS To change their lovers, and make love to others,

GALLUS As the heat of everyone's blood

CRISPINUS As the heat of everyone's blood

GALLUS And the spirit of our nectar shall inspire.

CRISPINUS And the spirit of our nectar shall inspire.

GALLUS And Jupiter, save Jupiter.

CRISPINUS And Jupiter, save Jupiter.

TIBULLUS So: now we may play the fools by authority.

HERMOGENES To play the fool by authority is wisdom.

JULIA Away with your mattery sentences, Momus; they are too grave and wise for this meeting.

OVID Mercury, give our jester[678] a stool, let him sit by and reach him of our cates.[679]

TUCCA Dost hear, mad Jupiter? We'll have it enacted. He that speaks the first wise word shall be made cuckold. What say'st thou? Is't not a good motion?

OVID Deities, are you all agreed?

ALL Agreed, great Jupiter.

ALBIUS I have read in a book that to play the fool wisely is high wisdom.

GALLUS How now, Vulcan! Will you be the first wizard?[680]

OVID Take his wife, Mars, and make him cuckold, quickly.

TUCCA Come, cockatrice.

CHLOE No, let me alone with him,[681] Jupiter. [*To* ALBIUS] I'll make you take heed, sir, while you live again: if there be twelve in a company that you be not the wisest of 'hem.

ALBIUS No more, I will not indeed, wife, hereafter; I'll be here, mum.

OVID Fill us a bowl of nectar, Ganymede. We will drink to our daughter Venus.

GALLUS Look to your wife, Vulcan. Jupiter begins to court her.

TIBULLUS Nay, let Mars look to it. Vulcan must do as Venus does, bear.

TUCCA [*To* PYRGUS] Sirrah, boy, catamite![682] Look you play Ganymede well now, you slave. Do not spill your nectar. Carry your cup even, so. You should have rubbed your face with whites of eggs, you rascal, till your brows had shone like our sooty brother's here, as sleek as a horn-book,[683] or ha' steeped your lips in wine till you made 'hem so plump that Juno might have been jealous of 'hem. [*To* CHLOE] Punk, kiss me, punk.

OVID [*Also to* CHLOE] Here, daughter Venus, I drink to thee.

CHLOE Thank you, good father Jupiter.

TUCCA Why, mother Juno! Gods and fiends! What, wilt thou suffer this ocular temptation?

TIBULLUS Mars is enraged; he looks big and begins to stut,[684] for anger.

HERMOGENES Well played, Captain Mars.

TUCCA Well said, minstrel Momus. I must put you in?[685] Must I? When will you be in good fooling of your self,[686] fiddler? Never?

HERMOGENES Oh, 'tis our fashion to be silent when there is a better fool in place, ever.

TUCCA Thank you, rascal.

OVID Fill to our daughter Venus, Ganymede, who fills her father with affection.

JULIA Wilt thou be ranging, Jupiter, before my face?

OVID Why not, Juno? Why should Jupiter stand in awe of thy face, Juno?

678 59 jester: i.e. Hermogenes as Momus

679 59 reach him of our cates: hand delicacies to us

680 65 wizard: wise man (and thus the first cuckold at the party)

681 68 let me alone with him: let me deal with him

682 74 catamite: a boy prostitute

683 75–7 You should … horn-book: egg whites were used as make-up; as the god of fire and the forge, Vulcan was "sooty"; he wears black makeup, with a sheen recalling the translucent horn used to protect a school primer

684 82 stut: stutter

685 84 put you in: include you

686 84–5 be in … your self: be your own joke

JULIA Because it is thy wife's face, Jupiter.
OVID What, shall a husband be afraid of his wife's face? Will she paint it[687] so horribly? We are a king, cotquean,[688] and we will reign in our pleasures and we will cudgel thee to death if thou find fault with us.
JULIA I will find fault with thee, King Cuckold-Maker. What, shall the king of gods turn the king of good fellows, and have no fellow[689] in wickedness? This makes our poets, that know our profaneness, live as profane as we. By my god-head, Jupiter, I will join with all the other gods here, bind thee hand and foot, throw thee down into earth, and make a poor poet of thee if thou abuse me thus.
GALLUS A good smart-tongued goddess, a right Juno.
OVID Juno, we will cudgel thee, Juno. We told thee so yesterday, when thou wert jealous of us for Thetis.[690]
PYRGUS Nay, today she had me in inquisition[691] too.
TUCCA Well said, my fine Phrygian[692] fry; inform, inform. Give me some wine, King of Heralds, I may[693] drink to my cockatrice.
OVID No more, Ganymede, we will cudgel thee, Juno, by Styx,[694] we will.
JULIA Ay, 'tis well, gods may grow impudent in iniquity and they must not be told of it—
OVID Yea, we will knock our chin against our breast and shake thee out of Olympus into an oyster boat for thy scolding.
JULIA Your nose is not long enough to do it, Jupiter, if all thy strumpets thou hast among the stars took thy part. And there is never a star in thy forehead but shall be a horn[695] if thou persist to abuse me.
CRISPINUS A good jest, i' faith.
OVID We tell thee, thou anger'st us, cotquean, and we will thunder thee in pieces for thy cotqueanity.
CRISPINUS Another good jest.
ALBIUS Oh, my hammers and my cyclops! This boy fills not wine enough to make us kind enough to one another.
TUCCA Nor thou hast not collied[696] thy face enough, stinkard.
ALBIUS I'll ply the table with nectar and make them friends.
HERMOGENES Heaven is like to have but a lame skinker,[697] then.
ALBIUS Wine and good livers make true lovers. I'll sentence them together. Here father, here mother, for shame; drink your selves drunk and forget this dissension. You two should cling together before our faces and give us example of unity.
GALLUS Oh, excellently spoken, Vulcan, on the sudden!
TIBULLUS Jupiter may do well to prefer his tongue to some office[698] for his eloquence.
TUCCA His tongue shall be gent'man usher[699] to his wit and still go before it.[700]
ALBIUS An excellent fit office!
CRISPINUS Ay, and an excellent good jest, besides.
HERMOGENES [*To* TUCCA] What, have you hired Mercury to cry your jests you make?
OVID Momus, you are envious.

687 92 paint it: use make-up
688 93 cotquean: vulgar woman
689 96 fellow: equal
690 102 Thetis: sea-goddess and mother of the Greek hero Achilles
691 103 Today she grilled me, too
692 104 Phrygians: an ancient Turkish people who took part in the Trojan War
693 105 I may: so that I may
694 106 Styx: legendary river of the underworld
695 111 horn: i.e. a cuckold's horn
696 119 collied: blackened with coal
697 121 skinker: wine-pourer
698 126 prefer his . . . some office: promote him to some official position
699 127 gent'man usher: head servant or butler
700 127 still go before it: i.e. he'll always speak without thinking

TUCCA [*To* HERMONGENES] Why, you whoreson blockhead, 'tis your only block of wit in fashion nowadays to applaud other folks' jests.
HERMOGENES True, with those that are not artificers themselves. [*To* ALBIUS] Vulcan, you nod[701] and the mirth of the jest droops.
PYRGUS He has filled nectar so long till his brain swims in it.
GALLUS What, do we nod, fellow gods? Sound music and let us startle our spirits with a song.
TUCCA Do, Apollo. Thou art a good musician.
GALLUS What says Jupiter?
OVID Ha? ha?
GALLUS A song.
OVID Why, do, do, sing.
PLAUTIA Bacchus, what say you?
TIBULLUS Ceres?
PLAUTIA But to this song?
TIBULLUS Sing, for my part.
JULIA Your belly weighs down your head, Bacchus. Here's a song toward.
TIBULLUS Begin, Vulcan—
ALBIUS What else? What else?
TUCCA Say, Jupiter—
OVID Mercury—
CRISPINUS Ay, say, say—

Song

Wake, our mirth begins to die.
Quicken it with tunes and wine.
Raise your notes, you're out. Fie, fie,
This drowsiness is an ill sign.
We banish him the queere[702] *of gods,*
That droops again;
Then all are men,
For here's not one but nods.

OVID I like not this sudden and general heaviness amongst our godheads. 'Tis somewhat ominous. Apollo, command us louder music and let Mercury and Momus contend to please, and revive our senses.

Song

HERMOGENES *Then in a free and lofty strain,*
Our broken tunes we thus repair;
CRISPINUS *And we answer them again,*
Running division on the panting air.[703]
BOTH *To celebrate this feast of sense,*
As free from scandal, as offence.
HERMOGENES *Here is beauty for the eye;*
CRISPINUS *For the ear, sweet melody;*
HERMOGENES *Ambrosiac odors for the smell;*
CRISPINUS *Delicious nectar for the taste;*
BOTH *For the touch, a lady's waist*
Which doth all the rest excel!
OVID Ay. This hath wak't us. Mercury, our herald, go from our self, the great god Jupiter, to the great emperor, Augustus Caesar, and command him from us—of whose bounty he hath received his surname, Augustus—that for a thank-offering to our beneficence he presently sacrifice as a dish to this banquet his beautiful and wanton daughter Julia. She's a

701 136 nod: Albius has drunk too much and his head is drooping
702 158 queere: choir
703 168 Singing our parts with panting breaths

cursed quean,[704] tell him, and plays the scold[705] behind his back. Therefore let her be sacrificed. Command him this, Mercury, in our high name of Jupiter Altitonans.[706]

JULIA Stay, feather-footed Mercury, and tell Augustus, from us, the great Juno Saturnia:[707] if he think it hard to do as Jupiter hath commanded him and sacrifice his daughter, that he had better to do so ten times than suffer her to love the well-nosed[708] poet Ovid, whom he shall do well to whip or cause to be whipped about the capitol for soothing[709] her in her follies.

Act IV, scene vi

[*Enter*] CAESAR, MECOENAS, HORACE, LUPUS, HISTRIO, MINOS, [*and*] LICTORS

CAESAR What sight is this? Mecoenas! Horace! Say!
Have we our senses? Do we hear? And see?
Or are these but imaginary objects
Drawn by our fantasy? Why speak you not?
"Let us do sacrifice?" Are they the gods?
Reverence, amaze, and fury fight in me. [OVID, JULIA, *and the rest kneel before* CAESAR]
What? Do they kneel? Nay, then I see 'tis true
I thought impossible. Oh, impious sight!
Let me divert mine eyes; the very thought
Everts[710] my soul with passion. [*To himself*] Look not, man.
There is a panther,[711] whose unnatural eyes[712]
Will strike thee dead. Turn then, and die on her
With her own death.[713] *He* [CAESAR] *offers to kill his daughter* [JULIA]
MECOENAS and HORACE [*Stopping him*] What means imperial Caesar?
CAESAR What, would you have me let the strumpet live,
That, for this pageant, earns so many deaths?
TUCCA [*Whispers to* PYRGUS] Boy, slink, boy.
PYRGUS Pray Jupiter we be not followed by the scent,[714] master. [*Exeunt*]
CAESAR [*To* ALBIUS] Say, sir, what are you?
ALBIUS I play Vulcan, sir.
CAESAR But what are you sir?
ALBIUS Your citizen, and jeweler, sir.
CAESAR [*To* CHLOE] And what are you, dame?
CHLOE I play Venus, forsooth.
CAESAR I ask not what you play but what you are!
CHLOE Your citizen, and jeweler's wife, sir.
CAESAR [*To* CRISPINUS] And you, good sir?
CRISPINUS Your gentleman parcel-poet, sir.
CAESAR Oh, that profanèd name!
And are these seemly company for thee,
Degenerate monster? All the rest I know,
And hate all knowledge for their hateful sakes.[715]

704 181 quean: hussy
705 181 plays the scold: carps and criticizes
706 182 Altitonans: thundering
707 183 Juno Saturnia: daughter of Saturn
708 185 well-nosed: a play on Ovid's family name, Naso
709 186 soothing: encouraging
710 10 Everts: turns upside down
711 11 panther: i.e. Julia
712 11 unnatural eyes: Julia presumably has on gaudy make-up
713 12–13 Turn then . . . own death: you yourself will die inside as you put her to death for (her crime of impiety)
714 18 followed by the scent: pursued by dogs
715 32 I hate what I now know about them, since their profanity makes them hateful to me

Are you that first[716] the deities inspired
With skill of their high natures and their powers,
The first abusers[717] of their useful light,
Profaning thus their dignities, in their forms,
And making them like you, but counterfeits?
Oh, who shall follow virtue and embrace her
When her false bosom is found naught but air?[718]
And yet of[719] those embraces centaurs[720] spring,
That war with human peace and poison men.
Who shall, with greater comforts, comprehend
Her[721] unseen being and her excellence,
When you, that teach and should eternize her,
Live as she were no law unto your lives,
Nor lived her self but with your idle breaths?[722]
If you think gods but feigned[723] and virtue painted,
Know we sustain an actual residence;[724]
And with the title of an emperor
Retain his[725] spirit and imperial power.
By which[726]—in imposition too remiss,[727]
Licentious Naso, for thy violent wrong
In soothing the declined[728] affections
Of our base daughter—we exile thy feet
From all approach to our imperial court
On pain of death, and thy misgotten love[729]
Commit to patronage of iron doors,[730]
Since her soft-hearted sire cannot contain her.
MECOENAS Oh, good my lord, forgive; be like the gods.
HORACE Let royal bounty, Caesar, mediate.
CAESAR There is no bounty to be showed to such
As have no real goodness. Bounty is
A spice of virtue, and what virtuous act
Can take effect on them that have no power
Of equal habitude[731] to apprehend it,
But live in worship of that idol, vice,
As if there were no virtue but in shade
Of strong imagination, merely enforced?[732]
This shows their[733] knowledge is mere ignorance;
Their far-fetched dignity of soul, a fancy;

716 33 that first: that first man
717 35 abusers: i.e. the poets
718 39 naught but air: i.e. the imaginary, insubstantial creations of the poets
719 40 of: from
720 40 centaurs: half-man, half-horse, mythical enemies of men and here an image of the kind of hybrid monsters that poets produce
721 43 Her: virtue's
722 46 As though virtue did not exist except in your imaginary creations
723 47 feigned: imitated, acted
724 48 Know that we actually exist on earth
725 50 his: i.e. an emperor's; Caesar says that he is not emperor in title alone
726 51 By which: by which power
727 51 imposition too remiss: too light a punishment
728 53 declined: degenerate
729 56 misgotten love: i.e. Julia
730 57 patronage of iron doors: the protections of a prison
731 65 habitude: ability
732 68 merely enforced: forced on people by law
733 69 their: poets'

And all their square pretext of gravity
A mere vainglory. Hence, away with 'hem.
I will prefer for knowledge none but such
As rule their lives by it, and can becalm
All sea of humor with the marble trident
Of their strong spirits. Others fight below
With gnats and shadows; others nothing know.

[*Exeunt*]

Act IV, scene vii

[*Enter*] TUCCA, CRISPINUS, [*and the*] PYRGUS

TUCCA What's become of my little punk, Venus! And the polt-foot[734] stinkard, her husband? Ha?
CRISPINUS Oh, they are rid home i' the coach, as fast as the wheels can run.
TUCCA God Jupiter is banished, I hear, and his cockatrice, Juno, locked up. 'Heart, and all the poetry in Parnassus get me to be a player again, I'll sell 'hem my share for a sesterce. But this is Humors,[735] Horace, that goat-footed envious slave; he's turned fawn now, an informer, the rogue; 'tis he has betrayed us all. Did you not see him, with the emperor, crouching?
CRISPINUS Yes.
TUCCA Well, follow me. Thou shalt libel,[736] and I'll cudgel the rascal. [*To* PYRGUS] Boy, provide me a truncheon.[737] Revenge shall gratulate[738] him, *tam Marti, quam Mercurio.*[739]
PYRGUS Ay, but Master, take heed how you give this out;[740] Horace is a man of the sword.
CRISPINUS 'Tis true, in troth; they say, he's valiant.
TUCCA Valiant? So is mine arse, gods and fiends! I'll blow him into air when I meet him next. He dares not fight with a puckfist.[741] HORACE *passes by* [*and exits the stage*]
PYRGUS Master, here he comes.
TUCCA Where? [*Seeing him*] Jupiter save thee, my good poet, my noble prophet, my little fat Horace. [*To the others*] I scorn to beat the rogue i' the court, and I saluted him thus fair because he should suspect nothing, the rascal. Come, we'll go see how forward[742] our journeyman[743] is toward the untrussing[744] of him.
CRISPINUS Do you hear, Captain? I'll write nothing in it but innocence[745] because[746] I may swear I am innocent. [*Exeunt*]

[*Enter* HORACE *and* MECOENAS *on one side,* LUPUS, HISTRIO, *and* LICTORS *on the other*]

HORACE [*Calling to him*] Nay, why pursue you not the emperor for your reward, now, Lupus?
MECOENAS Stay, Asinius; you, and your stager,[747] and your band of lictors.
I hope your service[748] merits more respect

734 1 polt-foot: club foot (Albius played Vulcan, who had a club-foot)
735 6 Humors: here a nickname for Horace; also a playful reference to Jonson himself, who wrote satirical "humors" comedies
736 9 libel: speak against
737 10 truncheon: club
738 10 gratulate: welcome or reward him
739 10–11 *tam Marti, quam Mercurio*: "as Mars does, so also Mercury will do," i.e. "we'll greet Horace with blows as well as with sharp words"
740 12 give this out: boast aloud
741 15 puckfist: a type of puffball mushroom (but metaphorically also a bragging, boastful person, like Tucca himself)
742 19 forward: far along
743 19 journeyman: apprentice, i.e. Demetrius
744 20 untrussing: undoing (through his satire)
745 21 innocence: inoffensive material
746 21 because: so that
747 24 stager: i.e. Histrio
748 25 service: to the emperor

Than thus, without a thanks, to be sent hence?
HISTRIO Well, well, jest on, jest on.
HORACE [*To* HISTRIO] Thou base unworthy groom.
LUPUS Ay, ay, 'tis good.
HORACE [*To* LUPUS] Was this the treason? This the dangerous plot
Thy clamorous tongue so bellowed through the court?
Hadst thou no other project to increase
Thy grace with Caesar but this wolfish train,[749]
To prey upon the life of innocent mirth
And harmless pleasures, bred of noble wit?
Away, I loathe thy presence. Such as thou,
They are the moths and scarabs[750] of a state,
The bane of empires and the dregs of courts;
Who, to endear themselves to any employment
Care not whose fame they blast, whose life they endanger,
And, under a disguised and cobweb mask
Of love unto their sovereign, vomit forth
Their own prodigious malice, and pretending
To be the props and columns of his safety,
The guards unto his person and his peace,
Disturb it most with their false lapwing-cries.[751]
LUPUS Good. Caesar shall know of this; believe it. [*Walks away*]
MECOENAS Caesar doth know it, wolf, and to[752] his knowledge
He will, I hope, reward your base endeavors.
Princes that will but hear or give access
To such officious spies can ne'er be safe;
They take in poison with an open ear
And, free from danger, become slaves to fear.

[*Exeunt*]

Act IV, scene viii

[*Enter*] OVID

OVID Banished the court? Let me be banished life,
Since the chief end of life is there concluded.[753]
Within the court is all the kingdom bounded,
And as her[754] sacred sphere doth comprehend
Ten thousand times so much as so much place
In any part of all the empire else,
So every body, moving in her sphere,
Contains ten thousand times as much in him
As any other her choice orb excludes.
As in a circle a magician then
Is safe[755] against the spirit he excites,
But out of it is subject to his rage

749 33 train: trick, trap
750 37 scarabs: dung-beetles
751 46 lapwing-cries: the lapwing, or peewit, was known for the clever way in which it lured enemies away from its nest by crying far away from it
752 48 to: fitting with
753 2 concluded: contained
754 4 her: i.e. the court's
755 10–11 As in . . . Is safe: magicians were thought to stand inside a conjuring circle drawn on the ground around them in order to protect them from the spirits they called up to serve them

And loseth all the virtue of his art,[756]
So I, exiled the circle of the court,
Lose all the good gifts that in it I joyed.
No virtue current is but with her stamp
And no vice vicious, blanched with her white hand.[757]
The court's the abstract[758] of all Rome's desert,[759]
And my dear Julia th'abstract of the court.
Methinks, now I come near her, I respire[760]
Some air of that late comfort I received,
And while the evening, with her modest veil,
Gives leave to such poor shadows as my self
To steal abroad, I, like a heartless ghost,
Without the living body of my love,
Will here walk and attend her. For I know
Not far from hence she is imprisonèd,
And hopes of her strict guardian to bribe
So much admittance as to speak to me
And cheer my fainting spirits with her breath.

Act IV, scene ix

She [JULIA] *appeareth above, as at her chamber window*

JULIA Ovid? My love?
OVID Here, heavenly Julia.
JULIA Here? And not here? Oh, how that word doth play
With both our fortunes, differing like our selves:
Both one, and yet divided as opposed?
I high, thou low? Oh, this our plight of place
Doubly presents the two lets of[761] our love,
Local and ceremonial[762] height and lowness:
Both ways I am too high and thou too low.
Our minds are even, yet, oh, why should our bodies,
That are their[763] slaves, be so without their rule?
I'll cast my self down to thee. If I die,
I'll ever live with thee; no height of birth,
Of place, of duty, or of cruel power
Shall keep me from thee; should my father lock
This body up within a tomb of brass,
Yet I'll be with thee. If the forms I hold
Now in my soul be made one substance with it,[764]
That soul immortal and the same 'tis now,
Death cannot raze th' affects[765] she[766] now retaineth
And then may she be anywhere she will.
The souls of parents rule not children's souls

756 13 art: magic
757 16–17 No virtue . . . white hand: nothing is virtuous unless the court deems it to be so, and no vice is loathsome if the court forgives it
758 18 abstract: epitome
759 18 desert: excellence
760 20 respire: breathe
761 6 lets of: obstacles to
762 7 Local and ceremonial: both in location and in rank
763 10 their: i.e. the mind's
764 17 it: i.e. my soul
765 19 affects: feelings and powers
766 19 she: the soul

When death sets both in their dissolved estates;[767]
Then is no child, nor father; then eternity
Frees all from any temporal respect.[768]
I come, my Ovid, take me in thine arms
And let me breathe my soul into thy breast. [*Prepares to jump*]
OVID Oh stay, my love; the hopes thou dost conceive
Of thy quick death and of thy future life
Are not authentical. Thou choosest death
So thou might'st joy[769] thy love in th' other life.
But know, my princely[770] love, when thou art dead,
Thou only must survive in perfect soul
And in the soul are no affections.
We pour out our affections with our blood
And with our blood's affections, fade our loves.
No life hath love in such sweet state as this;
No essence is so dear to moody sense
As flesh, and blood, whose quintessence is sense.
Beauty, composed of blood and flesh, moves more
And is more plausible to blood and flesh
Than spiritual beauty can be to the spirit.
Such apprehension as we have in dreams—
When sleep, the bond of senses, locks them up—
Such shall we have, when death destroys them quite.
If love be then thy object, change not life;
Live high, and happy still; I still below,
Close with my fortunes, in thy height shall joy.
JULIA Ay me, that virtue, whose brave eagle's wings
With every stroke blow stars in burning heaven,
Should like a swallow, preying toward storms,
Fly close to earth and with an eager plume
Pursue those objects which none else can see
But seem to all the world the empty air.[771]
Thus thou, poor Ovid, and all virtuous men
Must prey like swallows on invisible food,
Pursuing flies or nothing, and thus love
And every worldly fancy is transposed
By worldly tyranny to what plight[772] it list.
Oh father, since thou gav'st me not my mind,
Strive not to rule it. Take but what thou gav'st
To thy disposure.[773] Thy affections
Rule not in me. I must bear all my griefs;
Let me use all my pleasures; virtuous love
Was never scandal to a goddess' state.
But he's inflexible! And, my dear love,
Thy life may chance be shortened by the length
Of my unwilling speeches to depart.[774]

767 22 estates: conditions
768 24 respect: aspect, but also respectfulness
769 30 joy: enjoy
770 31 princely: noble
771 48–53 Ay me … empty air: it pains me that instead of soaring like an eagle and blowing the stars with the beats of its wings, virtue flies low, like a swallow before a storm, preying on things so insubstantial that they seem invisible
772 58 plight: unfortunate condition (tyranny makes virtuous things into miserable ones)
773 61 disposure: control
774 66–7 Thy life … to depart: the longer I talk, the more chance you'll be discovered and put to death

Farewell, sweet life; though thou be yet exiled
Th'officious court, enjoy me amply still.
My soul, in this my breath, enters thine ears
And on this turret's floor will I lie dead
Till we may meet again. In this proud height,
I kneel beneath thee in my prostrate love,
And kiss the happy sands that kiss thy feet.
Great Jove submits a scepter to a cell[775]
And lovers, ere they part, will meet in hell.
OVID Farewell, all company, and if I could,
All light with thee; hell's shade should hide my brows
Till thy dear beauty's beams redeemed my vows. [*Turns to leave.*] *She calls him back*
JULIA Ovid, my love, alas, may we not stay
A little longer, think'st thou, undiscerned?
OVID For thine own good, fair goddess, do not stay.
Who would engage[776] a firmament of fires,
Shining in thee, for me, a falling star?
Be gone, sweet life-blood; if I should discern
Thyself but touched for my sake, I should die.
JULIA I will be gone then and not heaven itself
Shall draw me back. *He calls her back*
OVID Yet Julia, if thou wilt,
A little longer, stay.
JULIA I am content.[777]
OVID Oh, mighty Ovid! What the sway of heaven
Could not retire, my breath hath turnèd back.
JULIA Who shall go first, my love? My passionate eyes
Will not endure to see thee turn from me.
OVID If thou go first, my soul will follow thee.
JULIA Then we must stay.
OVID Ay me, there is no stay
In amorous pleasures; if both stay, both die.
I hear thy father; hence, my deity! [JULIA *turns and leaves*]
Fear forgeth sounds in my deluded ears;
I did not hear him. I am mad with love.
There is no spirit under heaven that works
With such illusion, yet such witchcraft kill me[778]
Ere a sound mind, without it, save my life.
Here, on my knees, I worship the blest place
That held my goddess and the loving air,
That closed her body in his silken arms.
Vain Ovid! Kneel not to the place, nor air;
She's in thy heart; rise then, and worship there.
The truest wisdom silly men can have
Is dotage on the follies of their flesh.

[*Exit*]

Act V, scene i

[*Enter*] CAESAR, MECOENAS, GALLUS, TIBULLUS, HORACE

775 75 Jove makes a king's commands submit to a prisoner's wishes; that is, Julia's father has no power over her love for Ovid
776 83 engage: wager
777 89 content: happy (to stay)
778 101 yet such witchcraft kill me: I would rather the spell of love should kill me

CAESAR We, that have conquered still[779] to save the conquered
And loved to make inflictions feared, not felt,
Grieved to reprove, and joyful to reward,
More proud of reconcilement than revenge,
Resume into the late state[780] of our love
Worthy Cornelius Gallus and Tibullus.
You both are gentlemen; you, Cornelius,
A soldier of renown, and the first provost[781]
That ever let our Roman eagles fly[782]
On swarthy Egypt, quarried[783] with her spoils.
Yet, not to bear cold forms, nor men's out-terms,[784]
Without the inward fires and lives of men,
You both have virtues shining through your shapes
To show your titles are not writ on posts
Or hollow statues, which the best men are
Without Promethean stuffings[785] reached from heaven!
Sweet poesy's sacred garlands crown your gentry,
Which[786] is, of all the faculties[787] on earth,
The most abstract[788] and perfect; if she be
True born and nursed with all the sciences,[789]
She can so mold Rome and her monuments
Within the liquid marble of her lines
That they shall stand fresh and miraculous
Even when they mix with innovating dust.[790]
In her sweet streams shall our brave Roman spirits
Chase and swim after death with their choice deeds
Shining on their white shoulders, and therein
Shall Tiber and our famous rivers fall[791]
With such attraction that th' ambitious line[792]
Of the round world shall to her center[793] shrink
To hear their[794] music; and, for these high parts,[795]
Caesar shall reverence the Pierian arts.[796]
MECOENAS Your Majesty's high grace to poesy
Shall stand 'gainst all the dull detractions
Of leaden souls, who, for the vain assumings
Of some, quite worthless of her sovereign wreaths,
Contain her worthiest prophets in contempt.[797]

779 1 still: always
780 5 late state: recent condition
781 8 provost: military governor
782 9 fly: on a flag
783 10 quarried: fed
784 11 out-terms: outward appearance
785 16 Promethean stuffings: gifts from the god Prometheus (which fill out the virtuous characters of men, who are like hollow statues without them)
786 18 Which: i.e. poesy
787 18 faculties: skills
788 19 abstract: intellectual, but also able to generalize or epitomize
789 20 sciences: fields of knowledge
790 24 innovating dust: the dust of change
791 28 fall: plunge and run
792 29 ambitious line: the circling equator (from Latin *ambitus*, "a going round, a compass"). Caesar speaks a refined Latinate English
793 30 her center: the world's center (i.e. Rome)
794 31 their: the rivers'
795 31 parts: qualities
796 32 Pierian arts: the arts of the Muses (here poetry)
797 35–7 who, for … in contempt: those who, motivated by vanity to gain favor from others who are themselves undeserving of poetry's rewards, hold the worthiest poets in contempt

GALLUS Happy is Rome of all earth's other states
To have so true and great a president[798]
For her inferior spirits to imitate
As Caesar is, who addeth to the sun
Influence and luster, in increasing thus
His inspirations, kindling fire in us.
HORACE Phoebus[799] himself shall kneel at Caesar's shrine
And deck it with bay[800] garlands dewed with wine
To quite[801] the worship Caesar does to him;
Where[802] other princes, hoisted[803] to their thrones
By fortune's passionate and disordered power,
Sit in their height like clouds before the sun,
Hindering his[804] comforts and—by their excess
Of cold in virtue and cross heat in vice—[805]
Thunder and tempest[806] on those learnèd heads
Whom Caesar with such honor doth advance.
TIBULLUS All human business fortune doth command
Without all order, and with her blind hand
She, blind, bestows blind gifts that still have nursed
They see not who, nor how, but still the worst.[807]
CAESAR Caesar, for his rule, and for so much stuff
As fortune puts in his hand, shall dispose it
As if his hand had eyes and soul in it
With worth and judgment. Hands that part with gifts
Or will restrain their use without desert,
Or with a misery numbed to virtue's right,
Work as they had no soul to govern them
And quite reject her, sev'ring their estates
From human order.[808] Whosoever can,
And will not cherish virtue, is no man.

[*Enter several* EQUITES ROMANI]

FIRST EQUES Virgil is now at hand, imperial Caesar.
CAESAR Rome's honor is at hand then. Fetch a chair,
And set it on our right hand, where 'tis fit
Rome's honor, and our own, should ever sit.
[*A chair is placed next to* CAESAR's *throne, raised on a small dais*]
Now he is come out of Campania,[809]
I doubt not he hath finished all his *Aeneids*,
Which, like another soul, I long t' enjoy.
[*Turns to*] MECOENAS, GALLUS, TIBULLUS

798 39 president: precedent (i.e. Caesar)
799 44 Phoebus: Apollo, god of poetry
800 45 bay: like the laurel, a traditional leaf for the crown ("garland") of the poet
801 46 quite: reward
802 47 Where: whereas
803 47 hoisted: raised
804 50 his: the sun's
805 50–51 by their . . . in vice: because they are so reluctant ("cold") to act virtuously and too quick and passionate ("heat") to act viciously
806 52 Thunder and tempest: bring storms of judgment down
807 56–7 She, blind . . . the worst: blind fortune gives gifts that do not know whom they (the gifts) benefit, nor how they benefit them, but nevertheless always seem to benefit the worst men
808 61–6 Hands that . . . human order: hands that either give or restrict gifts without considering who deserves them, or give in a way that is insensitive to virtue, work as if they had no soul governing them; they completely reject virtue and remove those who receive their gifts from the proper human order (which should depend on virtue, not chance)
809 72 Campania: Virgil's birthplace

What think you three of Virgil, gentlemen—
That are of his profession, though ranked higher—
Or Horace, what sayst thou, that art the poorest,
And likeliest to envy or to detract?
HORACE Caesar speaks after common men in this
To make a difference of me for my poorness,
As if the filth of poverty sunk as deep
Into a knowing spirit as the bane
Of riches doth into an ignorant soul.
No, Caesar, they be pathless, moorish minds
That being once made rotten with the dung
Of damnèd riches, ever after sink
Beneath the steps of any villainy.[810]
But knowledge is the nectar that keeps sweet[811]
A perfect soul, even in this grave of sin,
And for my soul, it is as free as Caesar's,
For what I know is due, I'll give to all.
He that detracts or envies virtuous merit
Is still the covetous and the ignorant spirit.
CAESAR Thanks, Horace, for thy free and wholsome sharpness,
Which pleaseth Caesar more then servile fawns.
A flattered prince soon turns the prince of fools.
And for thy sake, we'll put no difference more
Between the great and good for being poor.
Say then, loved Horace, thy true thought of Virgil.
HORACE I judge him of a rectifièd[812] spirit,
By many revolutions[813] of discourse,
In his bright reason's influence, refined
From all the tartarous[814] moods of common men;
Bearing the nature and similitude
Of a right heavenly body; most severe
In fashion and collection of himself,
And then as clear and confident as Jove.
GALLUS And yet so chaste[815] and tender is his ear
In suffering[816] any syllable to pass
That he thinks may become the honored name
Of issue to his so examined self,[817]
That all the lasting fruits of his full merit
In his own poems he doth still distaste,
As if his mind's piece, which he strove to paint,
Could not with fleshly pencils have her right.[818]
TIBULLUS But to approve[819] his works of sovereign worth,
This observation, methinks, more than serves

810 84–7 they be . . . any villainy: minds rotted by riches are like swamps ("moorish") in which no path or footsteps can be seen (Cambridge)
811 88 sweet: healthy and preserved
812 100 rectifièd: corrected and purified
813 101 revolutions: exchanges
814 103 tartarous: bitter
815 108 chaste: modest
816 109 suffering: allowing
817 110–11 may become . . . examined self: might be worthy of his name and character
818 112–15 That all . . . her right: the good aspects of his poems, which result from his own good character, are never entirely pleasing to him; it is as if his writing can never capture his mind's insights adequately
819 116 approve: prove

And is not vulgar:[820] that which he hath writ,
Is with such judgement labored and distilled
Through all the needful uses of our lives,
That could a man remember but his lines,
He should not touch at any serious point
But he might breathe his spirit out of him.
CAESAR You mean, he might repeat part of his works
As fit for any conference[821] he can use?
TIBULLUS True, royal Caesar.
CAESAR Worthily observed,
And a most worthy virtue in his works.
What thinks material[822] Horace of his learning?
HORACE His learning labors not the school-like gloss
That most consists in echoing words and terms[823]
And soonest wins a man an empty name,
Nor any long or far-fetched circumstance
Wrapped in the curious generalties of arts,[824]
But a direct and analytic sum
Of all the worth and first effects of arts.[825]
And for his poesy, 'tis so rammed[826] with life
That it shall gather strength of life with being,
And live hereafter more admired than now.
CAESAR This one consent, in all your dooms[827] of him
And mutual loves of all your several merits[828]
Argues a truth of merit in you all.

Act V, scene ii

[*Enter*] VIRGIL [*with*] EQUITES ROMANI

CAESAR See, here comes Virgil. [*Stands*] We will rise and greet him.
Welcome to Caesar, Virgil. Caesar and Virgil
Shall differ but in sound; to Caesar, Virgil
Of his expressèd greatness shall be made
A second surname, and to Virgil, Caesar.[829]
Where are thy famous *Aeneids*? Do us grace
To let us see and surfeit[830] on their sight.
VIRGIL Worthless they are of Caesar's gracious eyes
If they were perfect, much more with their wants,[831]
Which yet are more than my time could supply;
And could great Caesar's expectation
Be satisfied with any other service,
I would not show them.

820 118 vulgar: common
821 125 conference: conversation
822 128 material: wise (literally "full of matter")
823 129–30 His learning . . . and terms: his learning doesn't overuse the pedantic technique of simply repeating difficult words and terms
824 132–3 Nor any . . . of arts: Nor does he use longwinded, overly specialized language to describe far-fetched examples
825 134–5 But a . . . of arts: his learning draws on a clear, comprehensive understanding of all the value and most important effects of knowledge
826 136 rammed: stuffed
827 139 dooms: judgments
828 140 several merits: individual good qualities
829 3–5 to Caesar . . . Virgil, Caesar: "Virgil" will become, figuratively speaking, Caesar's surname, because it expresses both of their greatness, and vice versa
830 7 surfeit: feast
831 9 wants: defects

CAESAR Virgil is too modest;
Or seeks, in vain, to make our longings more.
Show them, sweet Virgil.
VIRGIL Then in such due fear
As fits presenters of great works, to Caesar
I humbly show them. [*He hands the book to* CAESAR]
CAESAR Let us now behold
A human soul made visible in life
And more refulgent[832] in a senseless paper
Than in the sensual complement[833] of kings. [CAESAR *returns the book to* VIRGIL]
Read, read, thyself dear Virgil; let not me
Profane one accent with an untuned tongue.
Best matter, badly shown, shows worse than bad. [*Gestures to the chair next to him*]
See then this chair, of purpose set for thee
To read thy poem in. Refuse it not.
Virtue, without presumption, place may take
Above best kings, whom only she should make.
VIRGIL It will be thought a thing ridiculous
To present eyes, and to all future times
A gross untruth, that any poet, void
Of birth, or wealth, or temporal dignity,
Should with decorum transcend Caesar's chair.[834]
Poor virtue raised, high birth and wealth set under,
Crosseth[835] heaven's courses and makes worldlings[836] wonder.
CAESAR The course of heaven and fate itself in this
Will Caesar cross, much more all worldly custom.
HORACE Custom, in course of honor, ever errs,[837]
And they are best whom fortune least prefers.
CAESAR Horace hath but more strictly[838] spoke our thoughts.
The vast rude swinge[839] of general confluence[840]
Is in particular ends[841] exempt from sense,
And therefore reason, which in right should be
The special rector[842] of all harmony,
Shall show we are a man, distinct[843] by it,[844]
From those whom custom rapteth[845] in her press.
[CAESAR *points to the chair on the platform, taking the book and opening it at random*]
Ascend then, Virgil, and where first by chance
We here have turned thy book, do thou first read.
VIRGIL Great Caesar hath his will; I will ascend.
'Twere[846] simple injury to his free hand
That sweeps the cobwebs from unusèd virtue

832 19 refulgent: shining
833 20 sensual complement: physical manifestation (i.e. the human soul is better captured in Virgil's verse than in the body of a king)
834 32 That it should ever be appropriate for a poet to climb above Caesar's chair
835 34 Crosseth: contradicts
836 34 worldlings: those living on earth
837 37 In questions of honor, custom (popular opinion or social convention) always makes mistakes
838 39 strictly: concisely
839 40 rude swinge: vulgar influence
840 40 confluence: opinion
841 41 particular ends: specific cases
842 43 rector: director
843 44 distinct: made distinct
844 44 it: i.e. reason
845 45 rapteth: seizes
846 49 'Twere: it would be

And makes her shine proportioned to her worth,
To be more nice to entertain his grace
Than he is choice and liberal to afford it.[847]
CAESAR [*To the* EQUITES] Gentlemen of our chamber, guard the doors
And let none enter. [*To the rest*] Peace. Begin, good Virgil.
VIRGIL "Meanwhile,[848] the skies 'gan thunder and in tail[849]
Of that fell pouring storms of sleet and hail.
The Tyrian[850] lords and Trojan youth[851] each where,[852]
With Venus' Dardan nephew,[853] now in fear
Seek out for several shelter through the plain,
Whilst floods come rolling from the hills amain.[854]
Dido a cave, the Trojan prince the same
Lighted upon. There, earth and heaven's great dame,
That hath the charge of marriage, first gave sign
Unto this contract; fire and air did shine
As guilty of the match, and from the hill
The nymphs with shriekings do the region fill.
Here first began their bane. This day was ground[855]
Of all their ills. For now nor[856] rumors sound,[857]
Nor nice[858] respect of state moves Dido aught;[859]
Her love no longer now by stealth is sought.
She calls this wedlock, and with that fair name
Covers her fault. Forthwith the bruit[860] and fame
Through all the greatest Lybian towns is gone;
Fame, a fleet[861] evil than which is swifter none,[862]
That moving grows and flying gathers strength;
Little at first and fearful, but at length
She dares attempt the skies, and stalking proud
With feet on ground her head doth pierce a cloud!
This child[863] our parent Earth, stirred up with spite
Of all the gods, brought forth; and, as some[864] write,
She[865] was last sister of that Giant race[866]
That thought to scale Jove's court. Right swift of pace,
And swifter far of wing, a monster vast
And dreadful. Look how many plumes are placed

847 52–3 To be . . . afford it: to be more finicky about receiving his grace than he (Caesar) is judicious and liberal in offering it
848 56 From here to the end of the scene Virgil reads from *Aeneid*, Book IV (in Jonson's own English translation): the Trojan hero Aeneas and Dido, Queen of Carthage, take shelter in a cave and become lovers; rumors of their union then fly throughout the kingdom (Jonson's note on this scene reads "*VIRGIL lib. 4. Aeneid*")
849 56 tail: consequence
850 58 Tyrian: from Tyre (the kingdom of Dido's birth)
851 58 Trojan youth: Aeneas's companions
852 58 each where: everywhere
853 59 nephew: Aeneas's own son Iulus
854 61 amain: violently
855 68 ground: the beginning
856 69 nor: neither
857 69 sound: true
858 70 nice: scrupulous
859 70 aught: at all
860 73 bruit: rumor (literally "noise")
861 75 fleet: swift
862 75 is swifter none: nothing is swifter
863 80 child: i.e. Fame
864 81 some: Jonson's note: "Caeus, Enceladus, &c."
865 82 She: Earth
866 82 Giant race: the Giants, who tried to overthrow the Olympian gods

On her huge corpse:[867] so many waking eyes
Stick underneath and, which may stranger rise
In the report, as many tongues she bears,
As many mouths, as many listening ears.
Nightly, in midst of all the heaven, she flies,
And through the earth's dark shadow, shrieking, cries;
Nor do her eyes once bend to taste sweet sleep.
By day, on tops of houses she doth keep,
Or on high towers, and doth thence affright
Cities and towns of most conspicuous[868] site.
As covetous she is of tales and lies,
As prodigal of truth. This monster— [VIRGIL *breaks off reading*]

Act V, scene iii

[*Enter*] LUPUS, TUCCA, CRISPINUS, DEMETRIUS, LICTORS

LUPUS [*To the* LICTORS] Come, follow me, assist me, second me. Where's the emperor?
FIRST EQUES [*Blocking his way*] Sir, you must pardon us.
SECOND EQUES Caesar is private now, you may not enter.
TUCCA Not enter? [*To* LUPUS] Charge 'hem [869] upon their allegiance,[870] crop-shin.
FIRST EQUES We have a charge to the contrary, sir.
LUPUS I pronounce you all traitors, horrible traitors. What? Do you know my affairs? I have matter of danger and state to impart to Caesar.
CAESAR What noise is there? Who's that names Caesar?
LUPUS A friend to Caesar. One that for Caesar's good would speak with Caesar.
CAESAR Who is't? Look, Cornelius.
FIRST EQUES Asinius Lupus.
CAESAR Oh, bid the turbulent informer hence;
We have no vacant ear now to receive
The unseasoned fruits of his officious tongue.
MECOENAS [*To* EQUITES] You must avoid[871] him there.
LUPUS I conjure[872] thee, as thou art Caesar, or respect'st thine own safety or the safety of the state, Caesar, hear me, speak with me, Caesar; 'tis no common business I come about, but such as, being neglected, may concern the life of Caesar.
CAESAR The life of Caesar? Let him enter. Virgil, keep thy seat.
EQUITES [*To* TUCCA, DEMETRIUS, CRISPINUS, *and* AESOP] Bear back there: whither will you? Keep back.
TUCCA [*Pushes his way in*] By thy leave, good man usher. [*Cuffs him on the head*] Mend thy peruke,[873] so.
LUPUS Lay hold on Horace there and on Mecoenas, lictors. Romans, offer no rescue, upon your allegiance. [*Hands* CAESAR *a paper*] Read, royal Caesar. [*Points at* HORACE] I'll tickle[874] you, satyr.
TUCCA He will, Humors, he will. He will squeeze you, Poet Puckfist.[875]
LUPUS I'll lop you off for an unprofitable[876] branch, you satirical varlet.

867 86 her huge corpse: i.e. Fame's body
868 95 conspicuous: prominent
869 4 Charge 'hem: formally demand that he comply
870 4 allegiance: allegiance to Caesar
871 15 avoid: remove
872 16 conjure: demand
873 23 peruke: wig
874 25 tickle: touch, annoy
875 27 Puckfist: see IV.vii. 15
876 28 unprofitable: dead

TUCCA Ay, and Epaminondas[877] your patron here, with his flagon chain. [*Gestures to* MECOENAS*'s chain*] Come, resign.[878] Though 'twere your great grandfather's, the law[879] has made it mine now, sir. [*To the* LICTORS] Look to him, my particolored[880] rascals; look to him.

CAESAR [*Reads the paper*] What is this, Asinius Lupus? I understand it not.

LUPUS Not understand it? A libel, Caesar. A dangerous, seditious libel. A libel in picture.

CAESAR A libel?

LUPUS Ay, [*Pointing*] I found it in this Horace his[881] study, in Mecoenas his house here; I challenge the penalty of the laws against 'hem.

TUCCA Ay, and remember to beg their land betimes,[882] before some of these hungry court-hounds scent it out.

CAESAR Show it to Horace. Ask him if he know it.

LUPUS Know it? His hand[883] is at it, Caesar.

CAESAR Then 'tis no libel.

HORACE It is the imperfect body of an emblem,[884] Caesar, I began for Mecoenas.

LUPUS An emblem? Right. That's Greek for a "libel." Do but mark how confident he is.

HORACE A just man cannot fear, thou foolish tribune,
Not though the malice of traducing[885] tongues,
The open vastness of a tyrant's ear,[886]
The senseless rigor of the wrested[887] laws,
Or the red eyes of strained authority
Should, in a point, meet all to take his life.
His innocence is armor 'gainst all these.

LUPUS Innocence? Oh, impudence! Let me see, let me see. [*Takes the picture*] Is not here an eagle? And is not that eagle meant by[888] Caesar? Ha? Does not Caesar give the eagle? Answer me; what sayst thou?

TUCCA Hast thou any evasion, stinkard?

LUPUS Now he's turned dumb. I'll tickle you, satyr.

HORACE Pish. [*Starts to laugh*] Ha, ha.

LUPUS Dost thou pish me? [*To* LICTOR] Give me my long-sword.

HORACE With reverence to great Caesar, worthy Romans,
Observe but this ridiculous commenter;
The soul[889] to my device was in this distich:[890]
"Thus oft the base and ravenous multitude
Survive to share the spoils of fortitude."
Which in this body I have figured here,
A vulture—

LUPUS A vulture? Ay; now 'tis a vulture. Oh, abominable! Monstrous! Monstrous! Has not your vulture a beak? Has it not legs? And talons? And wings? And feathers?

877 29 Epaminondas: a Theban warrior
878 30 resign: hand it over
879 30 law: traitors had to surrender their property to the government, and informers sometimes were given a portion of it; both Lupus and Tucca invoke this law
880 31 particolored: a reference to the lictors' multicolored uniforms
881 35 Horace his: i.e. Horace's
882 37 betimes: immediately
883 40 hand: signature
884 42 emblem: an allegorical picture with two parts: the illustration (here the "body") and a caption in verse. Both picture and verse together communicated the idea that the emblem was meant to represent
885 45 traducing: betraying
886 46 vastness of a tyrant's ear: the tyrant's ear is "vast" because it listens to everything
887 47 wrested: misapplied
888 52 by: to be
889 60 soul: the idea that the emblem represents
890 60 distich: rhyming couplet

TUCCA Touch[891] him, old Buskins.[892]
HORACE And therefore must it be an eagle?
MECOENAS Respect him not,[893] good Horace. Say your device.[894]
HORACE A vulture and a wolf—
LUPUS A wolf? Good. That's I; I am the wolf. My name's Lupus; I am meant by the wolf.
On, on; a vulture, and a wolf—
HORACE Preying upon the carcass of an ass—
LUPUS An ass? Good still. That's I, too. I am the ass.
You mean me by the ass—
MECOENAS Pray thee, leave[895] braying then.
HORACE If you will needs take it, I cannot with modesty give it from you.[896]
MECOENAS But by that beast the old Egyptians
Were wont to figure in their hieroglyphics
Patience, frugality, and fortitude,
For none of which we can suspect you, tribune.
CAESAR Who was it, Lupus, that informed you first
This should be meant by us? Or was't your comment?[897]
LUPUS No, Caesar. A player gave me the first light[898] of it, indeed.
TUCCA Ay, an honest sycophant-like slave, and a politician[899] besides.
CAESAR Where is that player?
TUCCA He is without,[900] here.
CAESAR Call him in.
TUCCA [*To the* EQUITES] Call in the player there, Master Aesop, call him.
EQUITES [*Calling offstage*] Player! Where is the player?
[*To* CRISPINUS *and* DEMETRIUS, *who try to crowd in*] Bear back. None but the player enter.

[*Enter* AESOP]

TUCCA Yes, this gent'man and his Achates[901] must. [*Pointing to* CRISPINUS *and* DEMETRIUS]
CRISPINUS Pray you, master usher; we'll stand close, here.
TUCCA [*Pointing to* CRISPINUS] 'Tis a gent'man of quality, this, though he be somewhat out of clothes, I tell ye. Come Aesop, hast a bay leaf[902] i' thy mouth? Well said; be not out, stinkard. Thou shalt have a monopoly of[903] playing confirmed to thee and thy covey[904] under the emperor's broad seal for this service.
CAESAR Is this he? [*Pointing to* AESOP]
LUPUS Ay, Caesar, this is he.
CAESAR Let him be whipped. Lictors, go take him hence.
[*Exeunt* LICTORS *with* AESOP]

891 67 Touch: attack
892 67 Buskins: boots
893 69 Respect him not: don't pay any attention to him
894 69 device: design
895 76 leave: stop
896 77 If you insist on interpreting it that way, I won't prevent you
897 83 comment: interpretation
898 84 light: explanation
899 85 politician: someone who follows court intrigue and policy; see Tucca's description of Aesop at III.iv. 222
900 87 without: outside the door
901 92 Achates: friend of Aeneas in the *Aeneid*
902 95 bay leaf: for bad breath
903 96 monopoly of: exclusive license for
904 96 covey: company

And Lupus, for your fierce[905] credulity,
One[906] fit him with a pair of larger ears;[907]
'Tis Caesar's doom and must not be revoked.
We hate to have our court and peace disturbed
With these quotidian[908] clamors. See it done. [*The* LICTORS *seize* LUPUS]
LUPUS Caesar!
CAESAR Gag him, we may[909] have his silence. [*The* LICTORS *gag* LUPUS]
VIRGIL Caesar hath done like Caesar. Fair and just
Is his award against these brainless creatures.
'Tis not the wholesome sharp morality
Or modest anger of a satiric spirit
That hurts or wounds the body of a state,
But the sinister application
Of the malicious, ignorant, and base
Interpreter, who will distort and strain
The general scope and purpose of an author
To his particular and private spleen.[910]
CAESAR We know it, our dear Virgil, and esteem it
A most dishonest practice in that man[911]
Will seem too witty[912] in another's work. [*Turning to* GALLUS *and* TIBULLUS]
What would Cornelius Gallus and Tibullus? *This while the rest whisper* [*to*] CAESAR[913]
TUCCA [*To* MECOENAS] Nay, but as thou art a man, dost hear? A man of worship and honorable. [*Gives him the chain*] Hold, here, take thy chain again. Resume, mad Mecoenas. What? Dost thou think I meant t' have kept it, bold boy? No, I did it but to fright thee, I, to try how thou would'st take it. What? Will I turn shark upon my friends? Or my friends' friends? I scorn it with my three souls. Come, I love bully Horace as well as thou dost, I. [*Pointing to the paper*] 'Tis an honest hieroglyphic. [*To* HORACE] Give me thy wrist, Helicon.[914] Dost thou think I'll second[915] e'er a rhinoceros[916] of them all against thee? Ha? Or thy noble Hippocrene[917] here? I'll turn stager first and be whipped too. Dost thou see, bully?[918]
CAESAR [*To* GALLUS *and* TIBULLUS] You have your will of Caesar; use it, Romans.
Virgil shall be your praetor,[919] and our self
Will here sit by, spectator of your sports
And think it no impeach of[920] royalty. [*Turning to* VIRGIL]
Our ear is now too much profaned, grave Maro,[921]
With these distastes[922] to take[923] thy sacred lines.
Put up thy book till both the time and we
Be fitted with more hallowed[924] circumstance

905 101 fierce: extreme
906 102 One: One of you
907 102 larger ears: like an ass (also indicating someone who listens too much)
908 105 quotidian: minor
909 107 we may: so that we may
910 117 spleen: bitter anger
911 119 man: man who
912 120 witty: clever
913 121 SD: Jonson's stage direction; "This" refers to the dialogue that follows; the "rest" are Gallus and Tibullus
914 127 Helicon: the mountain of the muses; here a nickname for Horace
915 128 second: support
916 128 rhinoceros: a thick-skinned, angry, charging beast; here an image for informers, libelers, and public opinion
917 128 Hippocrene: the spring sacred to the Muses; here a nickname for Mecoenas
918 129 bully: good fellow
919 131 praetor: judge
920 133 impeach of: challenge to
921 134 Maro: Virgil's family name
922 135 distastes: annoyances
923 135 take: receive
924 137 hallowed: holy

For the receiving so divine a work.
[*To* GALLUS *and* TIBULLUS] Proceed with your design.[925]
MECOENAS, GALLUS, AND TIBULLUS Thanks to great Caesar.
GALLUS Tibullus, draw you the indictment then, whilst Horace arrests them on the statute of calumny.[926] Mecoenas and I will take our places here. Lictors, assist him.
[*The* LICTORS *move to seize* CRISPINUS *and* DEMETRIUS]
HORACE I am the worst accuser under heaven.
GALLUS Tut, you must do't. 'Twill be noble mirth.
HORACE I take no knowledge[927] that they do malign me.
TIBULLUS Ay, but the world takes knowledge.
HORACE Would the world knew
How heartily I wish a fool should hate me.
TUCCA [*Aside*] Body of Jupiter! What? Will they arraign my brisk poetaster and his poor journeyman, ha? Would I were abroad skeldering for a drachma, so I were out of this labyrinth again. I do feel my self turn stinkard already. But I must set the best face I have upon't now.—Well said, my divine, deft Horace, bring the whoreson detracting slaves to the bar, do. Make 'hem hold up their spread golls.[928] I'll give in evidence for thee, if thou wilt. Take courage, Crispinus, would thy man had a clean band.[929]
CRISPINUS What must we do, Captain?
TUCCA Thou shalt see anon; do not make division with thy legs, so.[930]
CAESAR [*Pointing to* TUCCA] What's he, Horace?
HORACE I only know him for a motion,[931] Caesar.
TUCCA I am one of thy commanders, Caesar. A man of service, and action. My name is Pantilius Tucca. I have served i' thy wars against Marc Antony,[932] I.
CAESAR Do you know him, Cornelius?
GALLUS He's one that hath had the mustering or convoy of a company, now and then.[933] I never noted him by any other employment.
CAESAR We will observe him better.
TIBULLUS Lictor, proclaim silence in the court.
LICTORS In the name of Caesar, silence.
TIBULLUS Let the parties, the accuser, and the accused, present themselves.
LICTORS The accuser and the accused, present your selves in court.
CRISPINUS AND DEMETRIUS Here.
VIRGIL Read the indictment.[934]
TIBULLUS "Rufus Laberius Crispinus and Demetrius Fanius, hold up your hands. You are before this time jointly and severally indicted and here presently to be arraigned upon the statute of calumny, or Lex Remmia. The one by the name of Rufus Laberius Crispinus, *aliàs* Crispinas, poetaster and plagiary; the other by the name of Demetrius Fannius, play dresser and plagiary. That you, not having the fear of Phoebus or his shafts before your eyes, contrary to the peace of our liege lord, Augustus Caesar, his crown and dignity, and against the form of a statute in that case made and provided, have most ignorantly, foolishly, and—more like yourselves—maliciously gone about to deprave and calumniate the person and writings of Quintus Horacius Flaccus, here present, poet and priest to the Muses, and to that end have

925 139 design: plan
926 142 calumny: libel
927 145 I take no knowledge: I do not even notice
928 152 golls: hands
929 153 band: collar
930 155 do not . . . legs, so: stop your legs from shaking
931 157 motion: puppet
932 159 wars against Marc Antony: Caesar had made war against Antony, who was one of the two other members of the triumvirate ruling over Rome, and who had exiled himself in Egypt after falling in love with Cleopatra
933 161 mustering or . . . now and then: occasional responsibility for assembling a company in the army
934 169 indictment: what follows is a mock transcript of formal legal charges, for a procedure in which Crispinus and Demetrius are put on trial for their intent to write a slanderous play about Horace

mutually conspired and plotted at sundry times, as by several means and in sundry places, for the better accomplishing your base and envious purpose: taxing him falsely of self-love, arrogancy, impudence, railing, filching[935] by translation, &c. Of all which calumnies, and every of them in manner and form aforesaid, what answer you? Are you guilty, or not guilty?
TUCCA [*Whispers to them*] "Not guilty," say.
CRISPINUS AND DEMETRIUS Not guilty.
TIBULLUS How will you be tried?
TUCCA [*Whispers*] "By the Roman gods, and the noblest Romans."
CRISPINUS and DEMETRIUS By the Roman gods and the noblest Romans.
VIRGIL Here sits Mecoenas and Cornelius Gallus.
Are you contented to be tried by these?
TUCCA [*Whispers*] "Ay, so the noble captain may be joined with them in commission," say.
CRISPINUS AND DEMETRIUS Ay, so the noble captain may be joined with them in commission.
VIRGIL What says the plaintiff?
HORACE I am content.
VIRGIL Captain, then take your place.
TUCCA [TUCCA *joins* MECOENAS *and* GALLUS] Alas, my worshipful praetor! 'Tis more of thy gent'ness than of my deserving, iwis.[936] But since it hath pleased the court to make choice of my wisdom and gravity, come, my calumnious varlets. Let's hear you talk for your selves now, an hour or two. What can you say? Make a noise. Act, act.
VIRGIL [*To* MECOENAS, GALLUS, *and* TUCCA] Stay, turn and take an oath first. You shall swear,
By thunder-darting Jove, the king of gods,
And by the genius of Augustus Caesar,
By your own white and uncorrupted souls
And the deep reverence of our Roman justice,
To judge this case with truth and equity
As bound by your religion and your laws.
Now read the evidence. But first demand
Of either prisoner if that writ[937] be theirs. [*Shows papers*]
TIBULLUS Show this unto Crispinus. Is it yours?
TUCCA Say ay. What? Dost thou stand upon it,[938] pimp? Do not deny thine own Minerva, thy Pallas,[939] the issue of thy brain.
CRISPINUS Yes, it is mine.
TIBULLUS Show that unto Demetrius. Is it yours?
DEMETRIUS It is.
TUCCA There's a father will not deny his own bastard now, I warrant thee.
VIRGIL Read them aloud.
TIBULLUS [*Reading*] "Ramp up, my genius; be not retrograde,[940]
But boldly nominate[941] a spade, a spade.
What, shall thy lubrical and glibbery[942] Muse
Live as she were defunct,[943] like punk in stews?"[944]
TUCCA [*Aside*] Excellent!

935 181 filching: theft
936 198 iwis: certainly
937 209 writ: writings. These are new documents, not the emblem that Lupus has shown to Caesar
938 211 stand upon it: hesitate
939 211–12 Minerva and Pallas are names for Athena, goddess of wisdom, who sprang fully formed from Jove's forehead
940 218 retrograde: contrary. See Introduction for a discussion of the style of this poem
941 219 nominate: call
942 220 lubrical and glibbery: slippery
943 221 defunct: used up
944 221 stews: red-light district

TIBULLUS [*Reading*] "Alas! That were no modern[945] consequence,
To have cothurnal[946] buskins frighted[947] hence.
No, teach thy incubus[948] to poetize,
And throw abroad thy spurious[949] snotteries[950]
Upon that puffed-up lump of barmy[951] froth"—
TUCCA [*Aside*] Ah, ha!
TIBULLUS [*Reading*] "Or clumsy chilblained[952] judgment that, with oath,
Magnificates[953] his merit and bespawls[954]
The conscious[955] time[956] with humorous[957] foam and brawls,
As if his organons[958] of sense would crack
The sinews of my patience. Break his back,
Oh poets all and some. For now we list[959]
Of strenuous vengeance to clutch the fist.
Subscri.[960] Crisp."
TUCCA Ay, marry, this was written like a Hercules in poetry now.
CAESAR Excellently well threatened!
VIRGIL Ay, and as strangely worded, Caesar.
CAESAR We observe it.
VIRGIL The other, now.
TUCCA This's a fellow of a good prodigal tongue too; this'll do well.
TIBULLUS [*Reading*] "Our Muse is in mind for th' untrussing a poet;
I slip by his name, for most men do know it.
A critic that all the world bescumbers[961]
With satirical humors and lyrical numbers."
TUCCA [*Aside*] Art thou there, boy?
TIBULLUS [*Reading*] "And for the most part, himself doth advance
With much self-love and more arrogance."
TUCCA [*Aside*] Good again.
TIBULLUS [*Reading*] "And, but that I would not be thought a prater[962]
I could tell you he were a translator.
I know the authors from whence he has stole,
And could trace him too, but that I understand 'hem not full and whole."
TUCCA [*Aside*] That line is broke loose from all his fellows; chain him up shorter, do.
TIBULLUS [*Reading*] "The best note I can give you to know him by,
Is that he keeps gallants company,
Whom I would wish, in time should him fear,

945 223 modern: ordinary
946 224 cothurnal: tragic
947 224 frighted: frightened ("to have tragedy frightened off the stage")
948 225 incubus: possessing spirit
949 226 spurious: false
950 226 snotteries: filth
951 227 barmy: fermenting (an image for Horace, who is the object of the poem's satire)
952 229 chilblained: rubbed raw
953 230 magnificates: magnifies
954 230 bespawls: spatters saliva on
955 231 conscious: self-conscious
956 231 time: era
957 231 humorous: a reference to Jonson's early "humor" plays, comedies about urban personae and their "humors": foolish habits, moods, and preoccupations
958 232 organons: organs
959 234 list: wish
960 236 Subscri.: Latin abbreviation for "Signed"
961 245 bescumbers: shits upon
962 251 prater: foolish talker

Lest after they buy repentance[963] too dear.
Subscri. Deme. Fan."
TUCCA Well said. This carries palm[964] with it.
HORACE [*To* DEMETRIUS] And why, thou motley gull?[965] Why should they fear?
When hast thou known us wrong[966] or tax a friend?
I dare malice to betray it. Speak. [DEMETRIUS *remains silent*]
Now thou curl'st up, thou poor and nasty snake,
And shrink'st thy pois'nous head into thy bosom.
Out viper, thou that eat'st thy parents, hence.
Rather such speckled creatures as thy self
Should be eschewed and shunned, such as will bite
And gnaw their absent friends, not cure their fame;[967]
Catch at the loosest laughters, and affect
To be thought jesters; such as can devise
Things never seen or heard t'impair men's names
And gratify their credulous adversaries;
Will carry tales, do basest offices,
Cherish[968] divided fires, and still increase
New flames out of old embers; will reveal
Each secret that's committed to their trust.
These be black slaves, Romans, take heed of these.
TUCCA Thou twang'st right, little Horace, they be indeed
A couple of chap-fall'n[969] curs. Come, we of the bench,
Let's rise to the urn and condemn 'hem, quickly.
VIRGIL Before you go together, worthy Romans,
We are to tender our opinion
And give you those instructions that may add
Unto your even[970] judgment in the cause,
Which thus we do commence. First you must know
That where there is a true and perfect merit,
There can be no dejection,[971] and the scorn
Of humble baseness oftentimes so works
In a high soul upon the grosser spirit
That, to his blearèd and offended sense,
There seems a hideous fault blazed in the object,
When only the disease is in his eyes.[972]
Here hence it comes[973] our Horace now stands taxed[974]
Of impudence, self-love, and arrogance
By these who share no merit in themselves,
And therefore think his portion is as small.
For they, from their own guilt, assure their souls
If they should confidently praise their works,
In them it would appear inflation,

963 259 repentance: regret (because Horace will use his familiarity with them to satirize them)
964 261 palm: reward
965 262 motley gull: patchy fool
966 263 wrong: to wrong
967 270 fame: reputation
968 276 Cherish: stoke
969 281 chap-fall'n: gaping, open-mouthed
970 286 even: fair
971 289 dejection: weakening of power
972 289–94 the scorn . . . his eyes: the righteous disdain for low vulgarity, as expressed by a discerning soul, often affects less subtle men in such a way that, misunderstanding what they read, they perceive faults in everything they see, when in fact the fault lies in their own eyes
973 295 comes: comes that
974 295 taxed: criticized

Which, in a full and well-digested man,
Cannot receive that foul abusive name,
But the fair title of erection.[975]
And, for his true use of translating men,
It still hath been a work of as much palm
In clearest judgements as t'invent or make.[976]
His sharpness, that is most excusable,
As being forced out of a suffering virtue,
Oppressèd with the license[977] of the time;
And howsoever fools or jerking[978] pedants,
Players, or such like buffoon,[979] barking wits
May with their beggarly and barren trash
Tickle base vulgar ears in their despite,[980]
This, like Jove's thunder, shall their pride control:
The honest satyr hath the happiest soul.
Now, Romans, you have heard our thoughts. Withdraw, when you please.
TIBULLUS Remove the accused from the bar.
TUCCA Who holds the urn to us? Ha? [*To* CRISPINUS *and* DEMETRIUS] Fear nothing;
I'll quit[981] you, mine honest, pitiful stinkards. I'll do't.
CRISPINUS Captain, you shall eternally girt[982] me to you, as I am generous.
TUCCA Go to.
CAESAR [*Aside*] Tibullus, let there be a case[983] of vizards[984] privately[985] provided; we have found a subject to bestow them on.
TIBULLUS It shall be done, Caesar.
CAESAR [*Pointing to the poems*] Here be words, Horace, able to bastinado[986] a man's ears.
HORACE Ay. Please it great Caesar, I have pills about me,
Mixed with the whitest kind of hellebore,[987]
Would give him a light vomit that should purge
His brain and stomach of those tumorous heats,
Might I have leave to minister unto him.
CAESAR Oh! Be his Aesculapius,[988] gentle Horace;
You shall have leave and he shall be your patient.
Virgil, use your authority; command him forth.
VIRGIL Caesar is careful of your health, Crispinus,
And hath himself chose a physician
To minister unto you: take his pills.
HORACE They are somewhat bitter, sir, but very wholesome. [CRISPINUS *swallows a pill*]
Take yet another, so. Stand by, they'll work anon.
TIBULLUS Romans, return to your several seats. Lictors, bring forward the urn and set

975 299–304 For they . . . of erection: because they have a guilty conscience, they reassure themselves that if they openly praised their own work (and thus acknowledged their authorship) others would view it as vain self-promotion ("inflation"); a self-possessed and well-considered writer could never be described with such an ugly term, but only with the beautiful name of elevated distinction ("erection")

976 305–7 for his . . . or make: as for his skilled ability in translation, good critics recognize that this merits as much reward ("palm") as the original conception ("invent") and creation ("make") of poems

977 310 license: permissiveness

978 311 jerking: whipping

979 312 buffoon: foolish

980 314 despite: spitefulness

981 320 quit: exonerate

982 321 girt: bind

983 323 case: pair

984 323 vizards: masks

985 323 privately: discreetly

986 326 bastinado: beat (as with a stick)

987 328 hellebore: a plant with purgative properties

988 332 Aesculapius: Roman god of healing

the accused at the bar.

TUCCA Quickly, you whoreson egregious varlets. Come forward. What? Shall we sit all day upon you? You make no more haste now than a beggar upon pattens,[989] or a physician to a patient that has no money, you pilchers.

TIBULLUS Rufus Laberius Crispinus and Demetrius Fannius, hold up your hands. You have, according to the Roman custom, put yourselves upon trial to the urn, for diverse and sundry calumnies whereof you have before this time been indicted and are now presently arraigned. Prepare yourselves to harken to the verdict of your triers. [*Reaches into the urn*] Caius Cilnius Mecoenas pronounceth you, by this handwriting, guilty. Cornelius Gallus, guilty. Pantilius Tucca—

TUCCA Parcel-guilty,[990] I.

DEMETRIUS He means himself, for it was he indeed
Suborned[991] us to the calumny.

TUCCA I, you whoreson cantharides?[992] Was't I?

DEMETRIUS I appeal to your conscience, Captain.

TIBULLUS Then you confess it now.

DEMETRIUS I do, and crave the mercy of the court.

TIBULLUS What saith Crispinus?

CRISPINUS Oh, the captain, the captain—

HORACE My physic[993] begins to work with my patient, I see.

VIRGIL Captain, stand forth and answer.

TUCCA Hold thy peace, poet praetor; I appeal from thee to Caesar, I. Do me right, royal Caesar.

CAESAR Marry, and I will, sir. Lictors, gag him, do.
And put a case of vizards o'er his head,
That he may look bi-fronted[994] as he speaks.

TUCCA Gods and fiends! Caesar! Thou wilt not, Caesar? Wilt thou? [*Batting away the* LICTORS] Away, you whoreson vultures, away. You think I am a dead corpse now because Caesar is disposed to jest with a man of mark,[995] or so. Hold your hooked talons out of my flesh, you inhuman harpies. Go to, do't. What? Will the royal Augustus cast away a gent'man of worship, a captain and a commander, for a couple of condemned caitiff[996] calumnious cargoes?[997]

CAESAR Dispatch, Lictors.

TUCCA Caesar! [*The* LICTORS *gag and mask* TUCCA]

CAESAR Forward, Tibullus.

VIRGIL Demand what cause they had to malign Horace.

DEMETRIUS In troth, no great cause, not I, I must confess, but that he kept better company (for the most part) than I, and that better men loved him than loved me, and that his writings thrived better than mine, and were better liked and graced. Nothing else.

VIRGIL Thus envious souls repine[998] at others' good.

HORACE If this be all, faith, I forgive thee freely.
Envy me still, so long as Virgil loves me,
Gallus, Tibullus, and the best-best Caesar,
My dear Mecoenas. While these, with many more,
Whose names I wisely slip, shall think me worthy

989 343 pattens: wooden clogs used for walking in mud
990 351 Parcel-guilty: partly guilty
991 353 Suborned: encouraged or commissioned
992 354 cantharides: a species of fly
993 360 physic: medicine
994 366 bi-fronted: two-faced
995 369 mark: distinction
996 371 caitiff: villainous
997 372 cargoes: wretches
998 380 repine: feel discontent

Their honored and adored society,
And read, and love, prove, and applaud my poems,
I would not wish but such as you should spite them.
CRISPINUS Oh—
TIBULLUS How now, Crispinus?
CRISPINUS Oh, I am sick—
HORACE A basin, a basin, quickly; our physic works. Faint not, man.
CRISPINUS Oh—[*Vomits into the basin*] "retrograde"—"reciprocal"—"incubus."
CAESAR What's that, Horace?
HORACE "Retrograde" and "reciprocal incubus" are come up.
GALLUS Thanks be to Jupiter.
CRISPINUS Oh—[*Continues vomiting*] "glibbery"—"lubrical"—"defunct"—Oh—
HORACE Well said; here's some store.
VIRGIL What are they?
HORACE "Glibbery," "lubrical," and "defunct."
GALLUS Oh, they came up easy.
CRISPINUS Oh—Oh—
TIBULLUS What's that?
HORACE Nothing, yet.
CRISPINUS "Magnificate."
MECOENAS "Magnificate"? That came up somewhat hard.
HORACE Aye. What cheer, Crispinus?
CRISPINUS Oh, I shall cast up my—"spurious"—"snotteries"—
HORACE Good. Again.
CRISPINUS "Chilblained"—Oh—Oh—"clumsy"—
HORACE That "clumsy" stuck terribly.
MECOENAS What's all that, Horace?
HORACE "Spurious snotteries," "chilblained," "clumsy."
TIBULLUS Oh Jupiter!
GALLUS Who would have thought there should ha' been such a deal of filth in a poet?
CRISPINUS Oh—"barmy froth"—
CAESAR What's that?
CRISPINUS —"Puffy"—"inflate"—"turgidous"—"ventositous."
HORACE "Barmy froth," "puffy," "inflate," "turgidous," and "ventositous" are come up.
TIBULLUS Oh, terrible, windy words!
GALLUS A sign of a windy brain.
CRISPINUS Oh—"oblatrant"—"furibund"—"fatuate"—"strenuous"—
HORACE Here's a deal:[999] "oblatrant," "furibund," "fatuate," "strenuous."
CAESAR Now all's come up, I trow.[1000] What a tumult he had in his belly!
HORACE No, there's the often "conscious damp" behind, still.
CRISPINUS Oh—"conscious"—"damp."
HORACE It's come up, thanks to Apollo and Aesculapius. Yet there's another: you were best take a pill more?
CRISPINUS Oh, no. Oh—Oh—Oh—Oh!
HORACE Force your self then a little with your finger.
CRISPINUS Oh—Oh—"prorumped."
TIBULLUS "Prorumped"? What a noise it made! As if his spirit would have prorumped[1001] with it.
CRISPINUS Oh—Oh—Oh.
VIRGIL Help him; it sticks strangely, whatever it is.
CRISPINUS Oh—"clutched."

999 423 deal: great deal
1000 424 trow: think
1001 432 prorumped: burst

HORACE Now it's come: "clutched."
CAESAR "Clutched"? It's well that's come up! It had but a narrow passage.
CRISPINUS Oh—
VIRGIL Again, hold him; hold his head there.
CRISPINUS "Snarling gusts"—"quaking custard."
HORACE How now, Crispinus?
CRISPINUS Oh—"obstupefact."[1002]
TIBULLUS Nay, that are all we, I assure you.
HORACE [*To* CRISPINUS] How do you feel your self?
CRISPINUS Pretty and well,[1003] I thank you.
VIRGIL These pills can but restore him for a time,
Not cure him quite of such a malady,
Caught by so many surfeits,[1004] which have filled
His blood and brain thus full of crudities.[1005]
'Tis necessary, therefore, he observe
A strict and wholesome diet. Look you take
Each morning of old Cato's[1006] principles
A good draught, next your heart; that walk upon[1007]
Till it be well digested. Then come home
And taste a piece of Terence; suck his phrase
Instead of licorice and, at any hand,[1008]
Shun Plautus and old Ennius; they are meats
Too harsh for a weak stomach. Use[1009] to read,
But not without a tutor, the best Greeks,
As Orpheus, Musaeus, Pindarus,
Hesiod, Callimachus, and Theocrite,
High Homer, but beware of Lycophron;
He is too dark and dangerous a dish.
You must not hunt for wild, outlandish terms
To stuff out a peculiar[1010] dialect,
But let your matter run before your words,
And if, at any time, you chance to meet
Some Gallo-belgic[1011] phrase, you shall not straight[1012]
Rack[1013] your poor verse to give it entertainment,[1014]
But let it pass and do not think your self
Much damnified if you do leave it out,
When nor your understanding nor the sense
Could well receive it. This fair abstinence,
In time, will render you more sound and clear,
And this have I prescribed to you in place
Of a strict sentence, which till he perform,

1002 443 obstupefact: stupefied
1003 446 Pretty and well: pretty well
1004 449 surfeits: excesses
1005 450 crudities: raw, undigested material
1006 453 Cato: a classic Roman moralist; Virgil goes on to prescribe other Roman and Greek writers known in Jonson's period as models for morals, style, learning, drama, and poetry
1007 454 that walk upon: walk with that
1008 457 at any hand: by any means
1009 459 Use: make it a habit
1010 466 peculiar: affected
1011 469 Gallo-belgic: French
1012 469 straight: immediately
1013 470 Rack: twist and stretch
1014 470 give it entertainment: put it on display

Attire him in that robe.[1015] And henceforth learn
To bear your self more humbly; not to swell,
Or breathe your insolent and idle spite
On him whose laughter can your worst affright.
TIBULLUS Take him away.
CRISPINUS Jupiter guard Caesar! [*The* LICTORS *seize* CRISPINUS *and hold him aside*]
VIRGIL And for a week or two see him locked up
In some dark place, removed from company;
He will talk idly else after his physic.
[*To* DEMETRIUS] Now, to you, sir. Th' extremity of law
Awards you to be branded in the front[1016]
For this your calumny, but, since it pleaseth
Horace, the party wronged, t' entreat of Caesar
A mitigation of that juster doom,
With Caesar's tongue thus we pronounce your sentence. [*Brings forward a fool's costume*]
Demetrius Fannius, thou shalt here put on
That coat and cap and henceforth think thy self
No other than they make thee. Vow to wear them
In every fair and generous assembly
Till the best sort of minds shall take to knowledge
As well thy satisfaction[1017] as thy wrongs.
HORACE Only, grave praetor, here, in open court,
I crave the oath for good behavior
May be administered unto them both.
VIRGIL Horace, it shall. Tibullus, give it them.

TIBULLUS Rufus Laberius Crispinus and Demetrius Fannius, lay your hands on your hearts. You shall here solemnly attest and swear that never, after this instant, either at booksellers' stalls, in taverns, two-penny rooms,[1018] 'tiring-houses,[1019] noblemen's butteries,[1020] puisnes' chambers—the best and farthest places where you are admitted to come—you shall once offer or dare, thereby to endear yourself the more to any player, ingle, or guilty gull in your company, to malign, traduce, or detract the person or writings of Quintus Horacius Flaccus or any other eminent man transcending you in merit whom your envy shall find cause to work upon, either for that, or for keeping himself in better acquaintance, or enjoying better friends. Or if—transported by any sudden and desperate resolution—you do, that then you shall not, under the baston,[1021] or in the next presence[1022]—being an honorable assembly of his favorers—be brought as voluntary gentlemen to undertake the forswearing of it.[1023] Neither shall you at any time, ambitiously affecting the title of the untrussers or whippers of the age, suffer the itch of writing to overrun your performance in libel, upon pain of being taken up for lepers in wit and, losing both your time and your papers, be irrecoverably forfeited to the hospital of fools. So help you our Roman gods and the genius of great Caesar. [*They swear*]

VIRGIL So. Now dissolve the court.
HORACE, TIBULLUS, GALLUS, MECOENAS, AND VIRGIL And thanks to Caesar
That thus hath exercised his patience.
CAESAR We have, indeed, you worthiest friends of Caesar.
It is the bane and torment of our ears
To hear the discords of those jangling rhymers

1015 478 robe: some kind of ceremonial or distinctive piece of clothing, presumably signifying Crispinus's "tutorial" (and foolish) status
1016 488 front: forehead
1017 498 satisfaction: repentance
1018 505 two-penny rooms: cheap seats at the theater
1019 505 'tiring houses: backstage dressing rooms
1020 505 butteries: pantries
1021 512 baston: threat of the club
1022 512 presence: meeting in person
1023 512–13 be brought . . . of it: put yourself forward as a gentleman and pretend to disavow what you said

That, with their bad and scandalous practices,
Bring all true arts and learning in contempt.
But let not your high thoughts descend so low
As these despisèd objects. Let them fall
With their flat groveling souls. Be you yourselves.
And as with our best favors you stand crowned,
So let your mutual loves be still renowned.
Envy will dwell where there is want of merit,
Though the deserving man should crack his spirit.[1024]

Song[1025]

Blush, folly, blush; here's none that fears
The wagging of an ass's ears,
Although a wolfish case he wears.
Detraction is but baseness' varlet,[1026]
And apes are apes, though clothed in scarlet.

THE END

Rumpatur, quisquis rumpitur invidia.[1027]

TO THE READER.

If by looking on what is past thou hast deserved that name, I am willing thou should'st yet know more by that which follows: an apologetical dialogue,[1028] which was only once spoken upon the stage, and all the answer I ever gave to sundry impotent libels then cast out (and some yet remaining) against me, and this play. Wherein I take no pleasure to revive the times,[1029] but that posterity may make a difference[1030] between their manners that provoked me then, and mine that neglected[1031] them ever. For, in these strifes, and on such persons, were[1032] as wretched to affect[1033] a victory as it is unhappy to be committed[1034] with them. *Non annorum canicies est laudanda, sed morum.*[1035]

[Apologetical Dialogue]

The Persons.

NASUTUS,[1036] POLYPOSUS,[1037] AUTHOR.

NASUTUS I pray you, let's go see him, how he looks
After these libels.

1024 531 crack his spirit: wear himself out (trying to eradicate envy)

1025 531 SD *SONG*: probably to be sung by the entire company on stage. It refers to Aesop's fable in which the ass dresses in a lion's skin to frighten the other animals but is eventually exposed by the fox, who laughs when he hears the ass's braying; so all fools are exposed by their own folly, no matter how grand or terrifying they may appear to others

1026 535 varlet: servant

1027 538 *Rumpatur . . . invidia*: Let him burst, whoever bursts with envy (Martial, 9.97.12)

1028 2 apologetical dialogue: a defense, in the form of a dialogue

1029 4 times: that moment

1030 5 difference: distinction

1031 6 neglected: ignored

1032 6 were: it would be

1033 7 affect: pretend to

1034 7 committed: associated

1035 7–8 *Non annorum . . . sed morum*: Grey hair that evidences not years, but character, is what deserves praise. (St. Ambrose, *Epistles* 1.18)

1036 0 Nasutus: literally "nosed" or "well-nosed"; figuratively a person with good judgment

1037 0 Polyposus: "polypus" or polyp, a fleshy growth in the nose; metaphorically a person with negative judgment

POLYPOSUS Oh, vexed, vexed, I warrant you.
NASUTUS Do you think so? I should be sorry for him,
If I found that.
POLYPOSUS Oh, they are such bitter things,
He cannot choose.[1038]
NASUTUS But is he guilty of 'hem?
POLYPOSUS Fuh! That's no matter.
NASUTUS No?
POLYPOSUS No. Here's his lodging;
We'll steal upon him, or let's listen; stay.
He has a humor oft t' talk t' himself.
NASUTUS They are your manners lead me, not mine own. [*They stand aside to listen*]
AUTHOR [*Talking to himself*] The Fates have not spun him the coarsest thread
That, free from knots of perturbation,
Doth yet so live, although but to himself,
As he can safely scorn the tongues of slaves
And neglect Fortune more than she can him.[1039]
It is the happiest thing, this, not to be
Within the reach of malice. It provides
A man so well to laugh of injuries
And never sends him farther for his vengeance
Than the vexed bosom[1040] of his enemy.
Ay, now, but think how poor their spite sets off[1041]
Who, after all their waste of sulphurous[1042] terms
And burst-out thunder of their chargèd[1043] mouths,
Have nothing left but the unsav'ry smoke
Of their black vomit to upbraid themselves,
Whilst I, at whom they shot, sit here shot-free
And as unhurt of envy, as unhit.
POLYPOSUS [*Stepping forward*] Ay, but the multitude, they think not so, sir;
They think you hit and hurt, and dare give out[1044]
Your silence argues[1045] it, in not rejoining
To this or that late libel!
AUTHOR 'Las, good rout![1046]
I can afford them leave to err so still
And, like the barking students of Bears-College,[1047]
To swallow up the garbage of the time
With greedy gullets, whilst my self sit by
Pleased, and yet tortured with their beastly feeding.
'Tis a sweet madness runs along with them,
To think all that are aimed at still are struck;

1038 5 cannot choose: has no choice
1039 10–14 The Fates … can him: No matter how smoothly your life runs, you can never afford to ignore malicious talk, nor to neglect Fortune, for she will never neglect you
1040 19 vexed bosom: resentful heart
1041 20 sets off: displays them
1042 21 sulphurous: stinky and smoky
1043 22 chargèd: loaded
1044 28 dare give out: dare to say that
1045 29 argues: proves
1046 31 rout: crowd
1047 32 barking students of Bears-College: the dogs trained to attack or "bait" bears in a blood-sport that was popular in Jonson's time; Jonson refers to the bear-baiting arenas as "Bears College" in one of his epigrams (Cambridge)

Then, where the shaft[1048] still lights,[1049] make that the mark[1050]
And so each fear or fever-shaken fool[1051]
May challenge Teucer's[1052] hand in archery.
Good troth, if I knew any man so vile
To act the crimes these whippers[1053] reprehend,
Or what their servile apes[1054] gesticulate,
I should not then much muse their shreds were liked,[1055]
Since ill men have a lust t' hear others' sins
And good men have a zeal to hear sin shamed.
But when it is all excrement, they vent
Base filth and offal, or thefts notable
As ocean piracies or highway stands,
And not a crime there taxed but is their own
Or what their own foul thoughts suggested to them;
And, that in all their heat of taxing others,
Not one of them but lives himself, if known,
Improbior satyram scribente cinaedo.[1056]
What should I say more? Then turn stone with wonder!
NASUTUS I never saw this play bred[1057] all this tumult.
What was there in it could so deeply offend?
And stir so many hornets?
AUTHOR Shall I tell you?
NASUTUS Yes, and ingenuously.[1058]
AUTHOR Then, by the hope
Which I prefer unto all other objects,[1059]
I can profess I never writ that piece
More innocent or empty of offence.
Some salt it had, but neither tooth nor gall,
Nor was there in it any circumstance[1060]
Which, in the setting down, I could suspect
Might be perverted by an enemy's tongue.
Only it had the fault to be called mine.
That was the crime.
POLYPOSUS No? Why they say you taxed
The law and lawyers, captains, and the players
By their particular names.
AUTHOR It is not so.
I used no name. My books have still[1061] been taught
To spare the persons and to speak the vices.
These are mere slanders, and enforced by such
As have no safer ways to men's disgraces
But their own lies and loss of honesty.

1048 39 shaft: arrow-shaft
1049 39 lights: sticks out
1050 39 mark: target
1051 40 And so any fool whose hands, because of fear or fever, are shaking
1052 41 Teucer: a famous Greek archer
1053 43 whippers: detractors, rival satirists
1054 44 apes: actors (who gesture and act out the satirist's "whippings")
1055 45 Then I could understand why their scrappy writing pleases people
1056 55 More shamelessly than a male prostitute writing satire (Latin)
1057 57 bred: that bred
1058 60 ingenuously: frankly
1059 61 objects: goals
1060 65 circumstance: detail
1061 72 still: always

Fellows of practiced and most laxative[1062] tongues,
Whose empty and eager bellies i' the year
Compel their brains to many desp'rate shifts[1063]—
I spare to name 'hem, for their wretchedness
Fury itself would pardon. These, or such,[1064]
Whether of malice or of ignorance
Or itch t' have me their adversary, I know not,
Or all these mixed; but sure I am three years
They did provoke me with their petulant styles
On every stage. And I at last, unwilling,
But weary, I confess, of so much trouble,
Thought I would try if shame could win upon 'hem,
And therefore chose Augustus Caesar's times,
When wit and arts were at their height in Rome,
To show that Virgil, Horace, and the rest
Of those great master-spirits did not want[1065]
Detractors then, or practicers[1066] against them.
And by this line, although no parallel,
I hoped at last they would sit down and blush.
But nothing could I find more contrary.[1067]
And though the impudence of flies be great,
Yet this hath so provoked the angry wasps,
Or as you said, of the next nest, the hornets,
That they fly buzzing, mad, about my nostrils,
And like so many screaming grasshoppers
Held by the wings, fill every ear with noise.
And what? Those former calumnies you mentioned,
First, of the law: indeed, I brought in Ovid,
Chid by his angry father for neglecting
The study of their laws for poetry,
And I am warranted by his own words.
"*Saepe pater dixit, studium quid inutile tentas?*
Maeonides nullas ipse reliquit opes."[1068]
And in far harsher terms elsewhere, as these:
"*Non me verbosas leges ediscere, non me*
Ingrato voces prostituisse foro."[1069]
But how this should relate unto our laws,
Or their just ministers, with least abuse,
I reverence both too much to understand!
Then, for the captain, I will only speak
An epigram I here have made: it is
"Unto true soldiers." That's the *lemma*.[1070] Mark it. [*Reads from a paper*]
"Strength of my country, whilst I bring to view
Such as are miscalled captains and wrong you

1062 77 laxative: loose
1063 79 shifts: devices
1064 81 such: such like them
1065 92 want: lack
1066 93 practicers: plotters
1067 96 contrary: contrary to my expectations
1068 108–9 "*Saepe pater ... reliquit opes*": Father often said, "Why are you putting effort into a useless activity? Homer himself didn't leave any money" (Ovid, *Tristia* 4.10.21–2; Jonson's note) (Cambridge)
1069 111–12 "*Non me ... prostituisse foro*" [Why blame me, that] I do not study the long-winded laws,/That I do not prostitute my utterances in the indifferent forum? (Ovid, *Amores* 1.15; Jonson's note) (Cambridge)
1070 118 *lemma*: theme

And your high names, I do desire that thence[1071]
Be nor put on you, nor you take offence.[1072]
I swear by your true friend, my Muse, I love
Your great profession, which I once did prove,
And did not shame it with my actions, then,
No more than I dare, now, do with my pen.
He that not trusts me, having vowed thus much,
But's angry for the captain still, is such."[1073]
Now, for the players, it is true I taxed 'hem,
And yet but some, and those so sparingly
As all the rest might have sat still, unquestioned,[1074]
Had they but had the wit or conscience
To think well of themselves. But, impotent, they
Thought each man's vice belonged to their whole tribe,
And much good do't 'hem. What th' have done[1075] 'gainst me,
I am not moved with. If it gave 'hem meat
Or got 'hem clothes, 'tis well. That was their end.
Only amongst them, I am sorry for
Some better natures, by the rest so drawn
To run in that vile line.
POLYPOSUS And is this all?
Will you not answer then the libels?
AUTHOR No.
POLYPOSUS Nor the untrussers?
AUTHOR Neither.
POLYPOSUS Y'are undone then.
AUTHOR With whom?
POLYPOSUS The world.
AUTHOR The bawd.
POLYPOSUS It will be taken
To be stupidity or tameness in you.
AUTHOR But they that have incensed me can in soul[1076]
Acquit me of that guilt. They know I dare
To spurn, or baffle 'hem, or squirt their eyes
With ink or urine, or I could do worse,
Armed with Archilochus'[1077] fury, write iambics
Should make the desperate lashers hang themselves.
Rhyme 'hem to death, as they do Irish rats
In drumming tunes. Or, living, I could stamp
Their foreheads with those deep and public brands[1078]
That the whole company of barber-surgeons
Should not take off with all their art and plasters.[1079]
And these my prints[1080] should last, still to be read
In their pale fronts when what they write 'gainst me

1071 121 thence: from that fact (that some people pretend to ranks and experience that they don't actually have)
1072 122 nor you take offence: no offence be placed on you, nor that you take any offence
1073 127–8 He that . . . is such: He who doesn't trust my respect for true military men, even though I've avowed it, and who is still angry about the Captain Tucca in my play, shows himself to be the same as Tucca
1074 131 unquestioned: not called into question
1075 135 done: i.e. their satirical plays
1076 145 in soul: in their souls
1077 149 Archilochus: infamous Greek satirist whose poems were said to have driven their subjects to suicide
1078 153 brands: people found guilty of libel (like Demetrius above) could be branded on the forehead
1079 155 art and plasters: skill and bandages
1080 156 these my prints: these prints of mine

Shall like a figure drawn in water fleet,[1081]
And the poor wretched papers be employed
To clothe tobacco or some cheaper drug.
This I could do, and make them infamous.
But to what end?—when their own deeds have marked 'hem,
And that I know within his guilty breast
Each slanderer bears a whip that shall torment him
Worse than a million of these temporal plagues,
Which to pursue were but a feminine humor,
And far beneath the dignity of a man.
NASUTUS 'Tis true; for to revenge their injuries
Were to confess you felt 'hem. Let 'hem go
And use the treasure of the fool, their tongues,
Who makes his gain by speaking worst of best.
POLYPOSUS Oh, but they lay particular imputations[1082]—
AUTHOR As what?
POLYPOSUS That all your writing is mere railing.
AUTHOR Ha! If all the salt in the old comedy[1083]
Should be so censured, or the sharper wit
Of the bold satire termed scolding rage,
What age could then compare with those for buffoons?
What should be said of Aristophanes?
Persius? Or Juvenal?[1084] —whose names we now
So glorify in schools, at least pretend it.
Ha' they no other?[1085]
POLYPOSUS Yes, they say you are slow,
And scarce bring forth a play a year.
AUTHOR 'Tis true.
I would they could not say that I did that;[1086]
There's all the joy that I take i' their trade,[1087]
Unless such scribes as they might be proscribed[1088]
Th' abusèd theaters. They would think it strange now
A man[1089] should take but colt's-foot[1090] for one day
And, between whiles,[1091] spit out a better poem
Than e'er the master of art or giver of wit,
Their belly, made. Yet this is possible,
If a free mind had but the patience
To think so much together, and so vile.
But that[1092] these base and beggarly conceits[1093]
Should carry it[1094] by the multitude of voices
Against the most abstracted[1095] work, opposed

1081 158 fleet: melt away
1082 172 lay particular imputations: make specific charges
1083 174 old comedy: of Greece (such as by Aristophanes, below)
1084 179 Persius, Juvenal: famous Roman satirists
1085 181 other: other charges
1086 183 did that: did even that
1087 184 trade: playwriting
1088 185 proscribed: prohibited from
1089 187 A man: That a man
1090 187 colt's-foot: a herbal expectorant
1091 188 between whiles: meanwhile
1092 193 But that: But it's outrageous that
1093 193 conceits: ideas for plays
1094 194 carry it: win out
1095 195 abstracted: high-minded and formally composed

To the stuffed nostrils[1096] of the drunken rout!
Oh, this would make a learned and liberal soul
To rive[1097] his stainèd quill up to the back,
And damn his long-watched labors to the fire—
Things that were born when none but the still night
And his dumb candle saw his pinching throes[1098]—
Were not his own free merit a more crown[1099]
Unto his travails than their reeling[1100] claps.
This 'tis, that strikes me silent, seals my lips,
And apts[1101] me rather to sleep out my time
Than I would waste it in contemnèd strifes
With these vile ibides,[1102] these unclean birds
That make their mouths their clysters and still purge
From their hot entrails. But I leave the monsters
To their own fate. And since the comic muse
Hath proved so ominous to me, I will try
If tragedy have a more kind aspect.
Her favors in my next[1103] I will pursue,
Where, if I prove the pleasure but of one,[1104]
So he judicious[1105] be, he shall b'alone[1106]
A theater unto me. Once I'll 'say[1107]
To strike the ear of time in those fresh strains,[1108]
As shall, beside the cunning of their ground,[1109]
Give cause to some[1110] of wonder, some despite,[1111]
And unto more, despair to imitate their sound.
I, that spend half my nights and all my days
Here in a cell,[1112] to get a dark, pale face,
To come forth worth the ivy or the bays,
And in this age can hope no other grace—
Leave me. There's something come into my thought,
That must and shall be sung, high, and aloof,
Safe from the wolf's black jaw and the dull ass's hoof.
NASUTUS I reverence these raptures, and obey 'hem.

1096 196 stuffed nostrils: blocked senses
1097 198 rive: split
1098 201 pinching throes: cramped efforts (to write his work)
1099 202 a more crown: a more fitting reward
1100 203 reeling: wild spinning
1101 205 apts: prepares me
1102 207 ibides: ibis birds; the ibis was infamous for using its beak to give enemas ("clysters") to itself (Cambridge)
1103 213 next: next play (Jonson's next play, *Sejanus*, was in fact a tragedy)
1104 214 one: one reader or audience member
1105 215 judicious: of good judgment
1106 215 b'alone: i.e. be alone
1107 216 'say: essay, try
1108 217 strains: style and voice (of tragedy rather than comedy)
1109 218 ground: plot
1110 219 some: some readers or audience members
1111 219 despite: contempt
1112 222 cell: small room

3 William Heminge, *The Fatal Contract*

First performed 1638–39

First printed 1653

Edited by Andrea Stevens

Little sustained attention has been paid to William Heminge's grisly rape-revenge tragedy *The Fatal Contract*, a play that features one of the more singular characters in early modern drama: the villainous African Eunuch, Castrato, who turns out to be a white woman, Chrotilda, who has disguised herself in order to avenge her own rape. Most scholars have either ignored this play or dismissed it as derivative; Donald McGinn, for example, calls it "the most obvious and detailed example of plagiarism of *Hamlet* in the seventeenth century" (quoted in Morley 22). There is no question that the play is full of passages and motifs from dozens of early modern plays, especially but not exclusively those of Shakespeare. To view it through the anachronistic lens of plagiarism, however, is to misunderstand the play's rich metatheatricality and to ignore its innovative, if also disturbing, take on the convention of racial masquerade on early English stages.

Born in 1602, Heminge was the son of Shakespeare's First Folio editor John Heminge, and thus belonged to the first *second* generation of English theater professionals. Educated at Westminster and later elected as a King's Scholar to Christ Church, Oxford, Heminge clearly grew up watching and reading plays; his biographer, Carol Morley, suggests that he probably also helped his father to prepare the First Folio for publication. Heminge therefore embarked on a career as a dramatist equipped with a set of tools that earlier playwrights such as Thomas Kyd and Christopher Marlowe did not have: a robust archive of plays available to consult in print, to say nothing of his own experience as a playgoer. One way to describe *The Fatal Contract* is as an ingenious mash-up of passages and motifs from literally dozens of early modern plays—*Hamlet, Titus Andronicus*, and *'Tis Pity She's a Whore*, to name just a few. Heminge does not simply echo these earlier texts, but extensively revises them even as he also adapts such non-dramatic sources as Jean de Serres's *Generall Historie of France* (1624) and Ovid's account of the rape of Philomela.

As a "reading" of English theater to date, *The Fatal Contract* offers a vision of that corpus as a rich repository of theatrical bits, special effects, plot devices, and characters to be taken up at will. For the reader, surely part of the pleasure of encountering this play is to recognize familiar quotations and dramatic situations pushed in radical new directions. The character of the Eunuch, for example, combines at least four or five stock characters from medieval to late Caroline drama, including the Vice figure, the African stage villain, and the revenger. It is therefore tempting to think of Heminge the author, in his fondness for recycling and pastiche, as presciently post-modern—and certainly prescient in his apparent recognition of the performativity of such "essential" categories as race and gender. The African servant is "really" an elite white woman; Clotair, the Crown Prince and eventual King of France, is prone to fits of "the mother," as the play names his chronic emotional instability. Far from fixed categories, then, race and gender are shown to require constant performance to be legible. The play was of course written for the all-male English theater at a time when boy actors, who played women's parts, were increasingly the subject of controversy, and the play is preoccupied to the point of obsession with the prosthetics (wigs, breasts, female dress) that create the illusion of femininity (Stevens, "The Eunuch Much Sears," 216–17).

Heminge's eclectic approach to composition creates tonal dissonances that might challenge the expectations of twenty-first century audiences. The dedication printed in the 1653 quarto presents it as a "Curiosity of Wit and Language," implying that the play is an ingeniously crafted work of art—or a novel and strange one (sig A2). To be sure, *The Fatal Contract* sometimes appears to court the audience response of "horrid laughter" as much as the cathartic emotions of pity and fear Aristotle thought proper to the experience of tragedy (Brooke; Dollimore). This problem of tone can, however, be attributed to the play's marriage of two opposing genres: the rape-revenge tragedy and the courtly, comic, and pastoral genre of the Maid-as-Moor play, a sub-genre of English blackface performance that featured in at least six surviving plays from the 1630s, including William Berkeley's *The Lost Lady* (1637) and Richard Brome's *The English Moor* (1637), and a number of elite court theatricals, most notably Walter Montagu's *The Shepherds Paradise* (1633). These comedies and tragicomedies all feature white European female characters who temporarily disguise themselves as Africans, usually to preserve their chastity from unwanted sexual advances or to pursue their own errant lovers without risking detection or injury (Stevens, *Inventions*, 87–120). Importantly, the discovery of the "black" character's essential whiteness typically involves a theatrically striking change in appearance. Off-stage, the character removes the cosmetic disguise and then re-enters as white; such unveilings then pave the way for marriage or the renewal of strained marital bonds. If Heminge models Chrotilda/Castrato on the besieged virgins in these plays, he significantly departs from theatrical practice by shifting her gender along with her race and by not scripting any scene in which we see her restored to whiteness—to say nothing of the fact that he makes her a homicidal revenger. Surely these departures raise at least the possibility that the play was written to parody a popular Caroline theatrical convention.

The Fatal Contract is set in the French court, where the villainous Queen Fredigond is plotting against her husband and two sons, Clotair and Clovis, to install her lover Landrey as King of France. Fredigond's additional grievance is that her own brother was murdered in retaliation for the rape of the aristocratic Chrotilda when in fact it was the queen's eldest son Clotair who committed the act. To avenge her brother, Fredigond had the majority of Chrotilda's family, the Dumains, killed; Chrotilda, who escaped this violence, is presumed to be either dead or lost. We are told that the queen keeps an African servant, the Eunuch Castrato; this is in fact Chrotilda in disguise, possibly the only cross-dressed and black-faced revenger to appear on the early modern stage. Unusually for early modern drama, this disguise deceives not just the characters within the fiction but also the audience (Jonson's *Epicene* is perhaps the most famous example of such a surprise disguise device). For the majority of the action Castrato, also known simply as the "Eunuch," behaves as a typical Vice or villain along the lines of Aaron from *Titus Andronicus* and Iago from *Othello*. Like his Shakespearean predecessors, Castrato confides to the audience in any number of asides, boasting of his intention to "on all sides ... play foul," and declaring his soul to be as black as his face (II.ii. 31–2). In one remarkable scene Castrato, upon hearing the narrative of the lost Chrotilda, wishes for "organs apt and fit for women's service" so that he might rape her himself (I.ii. 55–60). The threat of rape, then, is central to this character's performance of black masculinity (see Little, 2000).

The exposure of the Eunuch's true identity is only disclosed at the play's end and requires a wrenching shift in sympathy to accept. By Act V we've seen him commit various atrocities but for the most part he works at a remove, preferring poison, for example, to more intimate acts of violence. He reserves his most direct torments, however, for Aphelia, who is engaged to the younger prince Clovis (known as the "Monsieur") only to be compelled to marry Clotair, now the King of France, after false reports circulate of Clovis's death. The "fatal contract" of the play's title is Aphelia's pre-engagement to Clovis, which, according to the play's logic, renders her marriage to Clotair incestuous once it is revealed that Clovis is still alive. Aphelia's consent, or lack of consent, to her marriage to Clotair constitutes one of the major cruxes of the play. She has no soliloquies, nor does she ever speak aside to the audience; perhaps her most revealing self-disclosure is when she calls herself a "lamb to slaughter" (V.ii. 117). When Clovis turns up alive, both brothers turn against her for her supposed inconstancy, each fixating on how the outward signs of her beauty—specifically her hair and her breasts—have turned toxic with the revelation of her duplicity (these are, of course, the very prosthetics worn by the boy actor to create the illusion of femininity). Iago-like, the Eunuch convinces Clotair to murder his wife on what is to be their wedding night. It is the Eunuch, though, and not the husband who binds the bride to a chair and then burns her breasts with a red-hot iron, the stage direction in the printed quarto indicating that they "*bind her to the chair,* [and] *the* EUNUCH *much sears her breast*" (V.ii. 261 SD).

In the wake of this graphic, sexually charged violence Castrato starts to peel back his many layers of identity. He first admits to his role plotting against the French royal family and then, via a letter, discloses his true identity as the lost Chrotilda. After these revelations Chrotilda, still in disguise, offers one final confession before dying. Her revenger persona has only extended so far; the woman under the disguise has fallen in love with Clotair:

EUNUCH I should have killed thee, King, and had put on
A masculine spirit to perform the deed;
Alas, how frail our resolutions are!
A woman's weakness conquered my revenge.
....
Thou injured'st me, and yet I spared thy life;
Thou injured'st me, yet I would fall by thee;
And like to my soft sex, I fall and perish
(V.ii. 451–62)

This turn deserves emphasis. In the final moments of the fifth act we are told in rapid succession that the Eunuch is really Chrotilda, and that Chrotilda has fallen in love with her rapist. Neither do we ever see Chrotilda in her own person. Like Viola in *Twelfth Night*, whose retrieval of her woman's weeds is deferred until after the play's end, the truth of the Eunuch's feminine identity is narrated but never shown.

The acknowledgment of the Eunuch's true identity naturalizes femininity as passive, merciful, unthreatening, and forgiving of male sin. Upon hearing this shocking news, the wounded Aphelia affirms her likeness to this "real" woman under the disguise: "Mine injuries and hers are so near kin/That they must bear each other company/In tears of blood and death" (V.ii. 468–70). The play concludes with the prospect of Aphelia, the Eunuch/Crotilda, and Clotair buried together in the same tomb: "Take up the body of the king, and these/That for his love on either hand lie slain;/They shall lie buried in one monument" (V.ii. 530–32). It is difficult to decide what a twenty-first century audience might or should make of this sudden turn to the sentimental. The turn is, however, utterly conventional in the sense that the other Maid-as-Moor plots Heminge draws upon each conclude in the same way: with the restoration of romantic bonds between men and women. But the motif is always a comic one, and by setting this device within a rape-revenge tragedy, Heminge explodes the convention even as he avoids scripting a coup-de-theâtre in which Chrotilda abandons the blackface disguise to re-enter washed white. For a scandalized Fredson Bowers, "such a total confounding of all ethical judgment had never before been found in the Elizabethan tragedy of revenge" (Bowers, 1940: 242). Bowers's indignation notwithstanding, there's no ethical inconsistency here at all, but rather a slavish theatrical consistency: Chrotilda behaves as she does because, among other roles, she's playing both the tragic part of a revenger and the comic part of a Maid-as-Moor. The "scandal," if indeed there is one, is the discordance of these personae.

Simply to see the play as a meditation on antecedent drama, however, or to see it as a clever exercise written by a theatrical insider who wished to subvert well-worn stage conventions even as he showcased his own deep knowledge of English theater, may not satisfy readers troubled by the play's depiction of sexual violence; of the "essential" villainy of blackness; of racial identity as a disguise of convenience; of the fate of Aphelia, that "lamb to slaughter." For some, no matter his intentions, what Heminge shows us might well be unbearable even by the standards of early modern tragedy, and ultimately irreconcilable to the expectation of "horrid laughter" or the aesthetics of camp.

Textual note

The Fatal Contract was first performed by Queen Henrietta's Men at the Salisbury Court theater. The copy-text for this edition is the Folger Shakespeare Library's copy of the first quarto (1653) "printed at London for J.M," the publisher John Marriott; I have also consulted the copies of the 1653 and 1661 editions on EEBO. There are no substantial variations between the earliest quarto and later printings. Throughout I have followed the quarto's act and scene divisions, and I have translated Latin stage directions for ease of reading.

Further reading

Editions

Morley, Carol (2006) *Plays and Poems of William Heminge*, Teaneck: Fairleigh Dickinson University Press.

Critical and contextual reading

Bowers, Fredson (1940) *Elizabethan Revenge Tragedy, 1587–1642*, Princeton: Princeton University Press.

Brooke, Nicholas (1979) *Horrid Laughter in Jacobean Tragedy*, London: Rowman & Littlefield.

Carr, Morwenna (2017) "Material/Blackness: Race and Its Material Reconstructions on the Seventeenth-Century English Stage," *Early Theatre* 20: 77–95.

Dollimore, Jonathan (2001) "The Revenger's Tragedy: Providence, Parody and Black Camp," in Stevie Simkin (ed.), *Revenge Tragedy*, New York: Palgrave, 107–20.

Dressel, Samantha (2016) "'Like to My Soft Sex': Female Revenge and Violence in *The Fatal Contract*," *Quidditas* 37: 8–24.

Little, Arthur, Jr. (2000) *Shakespeare Jungle Fever: National-imperial Re-visions of Race, Rape, and Sacrifice*, Palo Alto: Stanford University Press.

Stevens, Andrea (2010) "'The Eunuch Much Sears Her Breast': Remedying Adulteration in William Heminge's *The Fatal Contract*," in Peter Kanelos and Matthew Kozusko (eds) *Thunder at a Playhouse: Essaying Shakespeare and the Early Modern Stage*, Colombia: Susquehanna Press: 212–33.

Stevens, Andrea (2013) *Inventions of the Skin: The Painted Body in Early English Drama, 1400–1642*, Edinburgh: Edinburgh University Press.

Vaughan, Virginia (2005) *Performing Blackness on English Stages, 1500–1800*, Cambridge: Cambridge University Press.

The Fatal Contract (1638–39)

The Persons of the Play[1]

CHILDERICK, *an old King of France*
CLOTAIR, *the young King*
CLOVIS, *the Monsieur*[2]
LANDREY, *favorite to the Queen, and raised by her favor to be Duke of France and Major of the Palace*
BRISSAC, *an old peer of France*
[CHARLES] *Brissac, his son*
LAMOT
DUMAIN } *banished lords*
MARTELL
BOURBON
LANOVE } *noblemen of France, and friends of the banished lords*
CHROTILDA, [*sister to Dumain*] *by the name of*[3] *Castrato, as an* EUNUCH
FREDIGOND, *the Queen*
APHELIA, *old Brissac's daughter*
ISABELLA, *a lady that waited on Aphelia*
[JULIA, *a lady that waited on Aphelia*]

Lords for attendants, three ladies for attendance, a Cardinal for state when Aphelia is to be beheaded, six young men to bear the hearse, six of the guard, a headsman, musicians, a Page to Brissac, a Lackey

Act I, scene i

Enter LAMOT *and* DUMAIN *like* [*impoverished*] *soldiers*

DUMAIN We are not safe, Lamot. This bawdy peace
Begets a war within me—our swords worn
For ornament, not use; the drum and trumpet
Sing drunken carols, and the cannon speaks
Health, not confusion. Helmets turned to cups,
Our bruisèd arms administer discourse
For tables and for taverns, where the soldier
Oft finds a pity, not relief. I'll tell thee
We're walking images, the signs of men,
And bear about us nothing but the form
Of man that's manly.
LAMOT We're cold indeed.
DUMAIN Yes, and th'ungrateful time
As coldly doth reward us. All our actions,

1 The Persons of the Play: except for the material in square brackets, this list of characters is given as it appears in Q
2 *Monsieur*: title used throughout the play for Clovis, the youngest of King Childerick and Fredigond's two sons; the honorific identifies him with the stock character of lover or romantic lead
3 *by the name of*: i.e. disguised as

Attempts of valor, looked into with eyes
Filled with contempt, when ye gods ye know
It is our gifts they see yet; O, I am mad!
The very bread that lends them life to scorn us
Our blood has paid for. Yet, demand a bit,
Or ask of this old satin-bellied sir[4]
Or madam toothless with her velvet sconce,[5]
And you shall hear their rotten lungs pronounce
"The whip" and "whip-stock!"[6]
LAMOT Prithee contain thyself!
DUMAIN Thou knowest I can.
With what an equal temper did I breathe
Under the frozen climate of the north,
Where in mine arms (the sheets of war) I slept,
My bed being feathered with the down of heaven?
I have lain down a man and rise[7] a snowball.
There these have been my pastimes, which I've borne
As willingly as I received them nobly.
The queen's black envy[8] which doth still remain,
And peeps through every limb she bears about her,
Fated to ruin us, does not swell my gall;
No, nor this willing beggary I wear
To cloud me from her malice. By the gods,
This bastard-getting peace unspirits me,
A greater corrosive to my active soul,
Than all past ills whatever.
LAMOT As you are valiant, be wise, too; this is no time
To vent your passions like a woman in.
Your sword, not tongue, should speak.
DUMAIN You are an expert tutor, and I thank you.
Our wrongs would add a spirit to[9] the dead,
And make them fight our quarrels—but look here,
The minion[10] of our queen; O what a train
The painted peacock bears! Death, were I Jove
But only for this giant.[11]

Enter LANDREY *and two or three insinuating Lords, busy in conference, and three or four* PETITIONERS

PETITIONER 1 Good your honor, our wives and children—
Good your honor, hear us!
LANDREY Where are our slaves? Keep off these dregs of men,
The scum and outcasts of the world. Bring round my chariot
To the postern gate; these bell-mouthed rascals
Split mine ears with noise. Make haste before,

4 19 satin-bellied sir: richly dressed man wearing a satin doublet
5 20 madam toothless . . . velvet sconce: woman wearing a velvet cap, her appearance signifying both vanity and sexual disease (she is "toothless" from the effects of mercury poisoning, a treatment for syphilis)
6 22 whip-stock: whipping post; flogging was a punishment for begging
7 28 rise: i.e. risen
8 31 queen's black envy: the queen's malice against the Dumain family. "Black envy" also potentially points to the queen's minion, the African Eunuch Castrato
9 43 add a spirit to: put life into
10 45 minion: favorite or hanger-on, typically male; also connotes a sexual relationship
11 46–7 were I . . . this giant: king of the Olympian gods; also known as Jupiter and (in Greek myth) as Zeus. The Giants were beings of vast size who rebelled against Jove and were subsequently defeated

Lest my great mistress wait my coming. *Exit*
PETITIONER 2 Good your honor!
PETITONER 1 The devil take your worship; we must follow! *Exeunt* [PETITIONERS]
DUMAIN These are the fruits of base upstarts and flatterers.
Tell me, Lamot, can this same merchpane[12] man
Think, or commit a sin though ne'er so horrid,
But it is candied o'er, and from his vice
Excessive praise and plaudites[13] arise?
Were I the king (but he is willful blind,
And by the horns[14] she rocks him fast asleep),
Before the wanton and hot-blooded queen
Should have the license but to be suspected
With such a knight of gingerbread[15] as this,
A gilded flesh-fly, I would lock her up—
Yea, chain the evil angel in a box
And house her like a silk-worm.[16]
LAMOT Pardon me, sir, the good old king's unable.[17]
DUMAIN And therefore must admit an upstart page,
Now raised to honors by her lawless lust,
Mayor of the palace, and the Duke of France;
The next step is the crown. Now by my life,
'Twere good the king would execute them both.
LAMOT Alas he dares not, for the no-chaste queen
Is as her birth as great in faction,
Followed and sainted by the multitude,
Whose judgment she hath linked unto her purse
And rather bought a love, than found it.
She has a working spirit, an active brain
Apt to conceive, and wary in her wiles;
Besides, her sons, the pillars of the state,
Support her like an Atlas,[18] where she sits
And, like the heavens, commands our fates beneath her.
She is the greater light, the king a star
That only glares but through her influence. *A flourish within*
DUMAIN Hark, the thunder of the world! How out of tune,
This peace corrupting all things makes them speak!
What means this most adulterate noise?
LAMOT Why, are you ignorant?
This is a night of jubilee,[19] and the king
Solemnly feasts for his war's happy success.
Besides, his sons and he are knit again;
We shall have masks and reveling tonight.
DUMAIN Now the great gods confound this pickthank[20] noise,
The drums and trumpets are turned flatterers,

12 58 merchpane: marzipan; Dumain repeatedly derides Landrey as painted or sugar-coated
13 61 plaudites: applause
14 63 horns: cuckold's horns
15 66 knight of gingerbread: i.e. Landrey
16 69 house her like a silk worm: refers to the practice of confining silkworms to be bred and reared for their silk
17 70 unable: impotent
18 84 Atlas: mythical Titan who, upon being turned to stone, became a rock mountain condemned to bear the weight of the heavens
19 92 jubilee: festivity
20 96 pickthank: sycophantic, flattering

And Mars himself a bawd to grace their riot.[21]
O I am mad, this grates my very gall.
LAMOT What, man, bear up;
Although I wish all civil discord hence,
Yet I do hope a time wherein we soldiers
Shall, like a moving wall of living steel,
Defend this city that offends us now.
DUMAIN My thoughts keep not your road, I think.
The devilish spirit of the haughty queen
Will find employment for us yet; her brain
Is very active in exploits that breed
The soldier's harvest: war and dissension.

Enter the EUNUCH *with bags of gold, gives to each of them one, and after a little pause departs*

LAMOT What vision's this? 'Tis gold right and fair,
Sure I dream not.
DUMAIN I cannot tell, but he that takes this from me
Shall soon perceive I do not sleep nor slumber.
LAMOT It was the eunuch.
DUMAIN That needs no deciding.
LAMOT What speaks the paper left behind?
If it be Chorus to this dumb-show,[22] read it, Dumain. [DUMAIN *reads the letter*]

The Letter:
As you are soldiers truly valiant, I honor you; as poor, I pity you, therefore have sent you that will render you as[23] *complete courtiers, as undaunted soldiers. We know your present fortunes shame your parentage, which was not only great in itself, but fortunate in so fair an offspring. Dumain, Lamot, let it suffice we know ye, for our eye is everywhere. Whilst I remember your worths, I shall forget your parents' injuries; fear nothing. For your hitherto concealment I'll get your pardons, and whilst I breathe, breathe your kind Mistress. If you dare trust me, appear at court tonight so adorned, as shall become your honors, our friends.*
—*Fredigond*

LAMOT The queen?
DUMAIN We are betrayed, Lamot—what shall we do?
LAMOT We'll take the gracious proffer of the queen;
She's princely vowed our friend. Besides, what ill
Can we expect from her, who might have sent
Her murdering ministers and slain us here
If she intended foul play? But she's noble.
DUMAIN Noble, grant her so, yet—
LAMOT What yet?
DUMAIN Her murdered brother's memory—
LAMOT When he fell, we were too young for traitors.
DUMAIN But not for torments, had we been apprehended,
For in the high displeasure of the queen
All our posterity was doomed. Some felt the wheel,
Some racked, some hanged, others impaled on stakes,

21 98 Mars, the Roman god of war, has become a pander or go-between whose job it is to facilitate sexual debauchery
22 117 Chorus to this dumb-show: theatrical reference; the "Chorus" is the figure who offers the prologue to a play or explains the plot in advance of the action; "dumb-show" is a short inset play or part of a play performed without speech
23 119 that will render you as: that (i.e. money) which will allow you to be

With divers strange and horrid forms of death,
That you'd have thought—and fitly thought it too—
That all the torments which the poets feign
The damnèd spirits exercise in hell
Had here been put in execution.
And had not we been then in Wittenburg,[24]
Beyond the fury of her mortal spleen,
We had added to the number of the dead;
Then think you still we shall not?
LAMOT Now by my life it's murder to suspect her.
Our lives are all that we can lose; our fame
Not time nor art can murder, so we'll venture.
Exeunt

Act I, scene ii

Enter FREDIGOND *the* QUEEN, *and the* EUNUCH

QUEEN What conference did they maintain with thee?
EUNUCH None farther than the language of their eyes.
They looked on me as if they meant me thanks,
Which their amazement robbed me of.
QUEEN Spoke they not then at all?
EUNUCH No, not a word,
They seemed to me as if they knew no language.
QUEEN You know them not?
EUNUCH No, dearest lady, for th'appeared to me
Like to the silent postures in the arras:[25]
Only the form of men with stranger faces.
QUEEN Take 'em, then, they are our enemies
Whom I have angled[26] with that golden bait;
Their parents waded in my brother's blood,
For which I'll be revenged of all their kin.
Could they increase as oft as I would kill,
I'd ever kill that they might still increase. *Draw the curtain and shows the picture*
This picture drawn by an Italian
(Which still I keep to whet mine anger)
Does represent the murder of my brother,
For ravishing this beauteous piece of ill—[27]
A bloody and a terrible mistake
To murder Clodimir for Clotair's fact,[28]
For which behold how Fredigond's revenged!
This old Dumain and father to this maid,
With all his kindred, 'sociates, and allies,
(This brace of wicked ones, and that ravished whore—
The fair and fatal cause of these events—
Only excepted) [29] are here, here in this picture.

24 144 Wittenburg: famous university founded in 1502 in Wittenburg, Germany and associated with Martin Luther and the Protestant Reformation; Shakespeare's Hamlet attended the same school
25 9 arras: hanging tapestry
26 12 angled: fished for
27 20 beauteous piece of ill: Chrotilda; the Eunuch (Chrotilda in disguise) is present onstage every time the lost Chrotilda is mentioned
28 22 Clotair's fact: Clodimir was blamed and killed for having raped Chrotilda when Clotair was the person responsible
29 26–8 This brace … only excepted: Dumain, Lamot, and Chrotilda are represented in the painting but are the only members of the family to have escaped the queen's revenge

Is't not a brave sight? How doth the object like thee?
How prettily that baby hangs by th'heels,
Sprawling his arms about his mother's womb,
As if again he sought for shelter there?
Here's one bereft of hands, and this of tongue—
Finger thy lute, Maria, sing out Isabel. *Scopticè*[30]
Hark, hark, Castrato, the music of the spheres,[31]
O ravishing touch, hark how the other's voice
Echoes the lute; is it not a divine softness?
Ha, ha, ha, I do expect they now should rail extremely;
I prithee scold at me, good Isabel,
A little of the woman; no, Maria,
Within the clothèd circle of mine eyes
Anchor thy fingers; alas, thy nails are pared,
Nor has poor Isabel a tongue to scold with.
And here's the grand-dam with her glares[32] out;
Saddle her nose with spectacles, or else
She'll miss her way to the infernal pit.
Two hoary gray-beards in this angle lies,
Will find their way to hell without their eyes;
Villains that killed my brother, how does this like thee?
To execute men in picture—is it not rare? *Stabs the picture*
EUNUCH Were but Chrotilda here, and these two youngsters,
It were a pastime for the gods to gaze on.
O, were I but a man as others are,
As kind and open-handed nature made me,
With organs[33] apt and fit for woman's service!
QUEEN What if thou wert?
EUNUCH What if I were, great Queen?
I'd search the deserts, mountains, valleys, plains,
Till I had met Chrotilda, whom by force
I'd make to mingle with these sooty limbs[34]
Till I had got on her one like to me,[35]
Whom I would nourish for the Dumain line;
That time to come might story to the world,
They had the devil to their grandfather.
QUEEN I find thee, Eunuch, apt for my employments,
Therefore I will unclasp my soul to thee;
I've always found thee trusty, and I love thee.
EUNUCH With thanks I ever must acknowledge it,
And lay my life at my great mistress' feet, *Kneels*
To spend it when she pleases.
QUEEN We need it not
As yet, Castrato, but we may hereafter.
See, they're the platform[36] of great Childrick's death;
And they which must be thought his murderers
Our enemies, and now new courtiers

30 34 SD *Scopticè*: spoken scoffingly or mockingly; from the Greek "skoptein," to mock or jest; this direction is given in the right margin in the 1653 text
31 35 music of the spheres: a philosophical concept attributing harmonious music to the movements of the sun, moon, and planets
32 44 glares: eyes
33 55 organs: genitals
34 59 sooty limbs: this is the first reference to the Eunuch's blackness
35 60 one like to me: the Eunuch describes how, if he had functioning genitals, he'd seek out Chrotilda so he could rape her and thereby "pollute" the Dumain line
36 71 platform: i.e. she intends to frame Dumain and Lamot

Whom hitherto I have reserved for policy:
First, that they take away the guilt from us;
Next, being apprehended studying deaths,
The heads of all our engineers shall sit
T'invent unheard-of torments for the slaves.
I long to see them here, here in this frame,
Greeting their kindred's bones.
EUNUCH You are the goddess of invention!
QUEEN Then I'll commend thee to my elder son,[37]
Where thou shalt wind into his secret thoughts.
As for the younger boy,[38] let me alone,
And when we have them on the hip they shall
Follow their father unto hell's black hall.
EUNUCH Still better.
QUEEN Will not this be brave? Ha, how lik'st thou this?
Now by this light I'm taken strangely with thee.
Come kiss me, kiss me sirrah,[39] tremble not. QUEEN *kisses him*
Fie, what a January lip thou hast,
A pair of icicles! Sure thou hast bought
A pair of cast lips of the chaste Diana's.[40]
Thy blood's mere snow-broth; kiss me again. *Again*
Now see if you can find these gallants forth,
And bring them to our presence. *Exit* EUNUCH

Enter LANDREY

O sir y'are welcome!
Your visits have been freer, but I grow old,
And you command the beauties of the time.[41]
LANDREY What means my noble mistress? Think you the blood
Runs so degenerate within these veins,
To stoop to an inferior embrace,
When I enjoy the best?
QUEEN We are betrayed.
I'll tell thee a good jest, Landrey, pray mark:
This morning, dressing my head,[42] my husband came,
And with his switch (for he was then to hunt)
A gentle stroke he gave me on the back.
My fancy busied then to make me fine,
Supposing it was you that sported so
(Not dreaming that the dotard was so near),
Cried "well, my Landrey, in story we still find,
The best knights strike before, and not behind."[43]
The king, who always understood too fast,
Quits suddenly my chamber. What he intends
I cannot guess, unless it be our deaths,

37 82 my elder son: i.e. Clotair
38 84 the younger boy: i.e. Clovis
39 90 sirrah: a term of address for men or boys; implies reprimand, contempt, or condescension, but can also be used more playfully, especially with younger men or boys
40 93 cast lips . . . chaste Diana's: kissing the Eunuch is like kissing the cold bronze (cast) lips of a statue of Diana, the virgin goddess of the hunt
41 99 You can have your pick of the most beautiful young women
42 105 dressing my head: arranging my hair
43 112 strike before, and not behind: the queen makes a joke that the best fighters attack from the front rather than from the rear (with bawdy implications); the joke betrays the affair to the king

Which if he speedily perform not, then
Know he shall never, for this night concludes him.[44]
His sons I weigh like him; they have rebelled
And taken spirit of late t'oppose my will
And contradict my pleasures in thy love,
For which it is not safe that they should live.
The kingdom's heir shall be a boy of thine,
And kings and queens shall follow in thy line.

Enter DUMAIN *and* LAMOT *very brave;*[45] *the* EUNUCH

EUNUCH Madam, here are the gentlemen. [DUMAIN, LAMOT *kneel*]
QUEEN Y'are welcome to the court, and us, brave spirits, y'are welcome.
Take a queen's word y'are welcome.
DUMAIN and LAMOT Your highness is as full of grace as mercy.
QUEEN Rise and follow us, we'll be your guardian and protectress.
LANDREY (*Aside*) What are these?
QUEEN Sheep for my shambles,[46] whom I have fatted up
Only for slaughter; things are on foot decreed,
Shall make some smile tonight, and others bleed.

Exeunt

Act I, scene iii

Enter CLOVIS *at one door,* APHELIA *and a* PAGE *at the other with a torch*

CLOVIS My best mistress,
What angel brought you hither? For I know
Millions attend your goodness.
APHELIA My lord?
CLOVIS Why do you cast such stranger eyes upon me?
You were not wont to clothe your brows with scorn,
Nor dart such deadly looks; can my mistress
Be angry with her servant? My offence,
If slowness in my visits, I'll hereafter
Grow to[47] your threshold; why weep you now?
Trust me, divinest fair, thine eyes seed pearl,
Bracelets for gods to wear about their arms.
APHELIA [*Aside*] I am too fond, and yet he swears he loves me;
I have believed him too, for I have found
A godlike nature in him, and a truth
Hitherto constant.
CLOVIS Sweetest fair, the cause?
APHELIA If this should be dissembled, not your heart,
And having won my soul's affection,
Should on a judgment more retired to state,
Smile at your perjuries, and leave me in love,
What ill-bred tales the world would make of me.
CLOVIS That jealousy I'll strangle; take this ring,
As I that diamond dazzled by thine eyes

44 117 concludes him: sees him dead
45 123 SD *brave*: richly dressed
46 130 shambles: part of town where meat is sold
47 9 Grow to: attach myself to

Whose beauty's sickened 'cause eclipsed by thine;
Be these the mutual pledges of our love,
Our marriage before our marriage;[48]
And cursed be he that separates our love,
Though France be one, or what is greater, Jove.
Are your fears over now?
APHELIA My lord, I dare no ill, and therefore doubt none.

Enter KING, QUEEN, CLOTAIR, LANDREY, DUMAIN, LAMOT, EUNUCH, LORDS, LADIES, GUARD [*reveling*][49]

KING [*To* DUMAIN, LAMOT] Approach our person nearer, for methinks
Y'have honest faces; if your hearts keep touch
T'your outward semblance, y'are a pair
Nothing but death shall force from me.
QUEEN [*Aside*] Good, good, this physic[50] works.
EUNUCH Madam, is it done?
QUEEN Ay, my black genius,[51] such a fatal dram
I have administered will wing his soul
With expedition to the other world.
His part essential,[52] like a wearied ghost,
This night forsakes her inn; when fled and gone,
Who knows where it shall lodge? Mark his looks—
Seest thou not death throned in his hollow eye,
Great tyrant over nature?
EUNUCH With looks inquisitive I have beheld him
But see no alteration.
QUEEN Thou art a fool, and want'st the optic nerves
To pry into my arts. Where I lay trains,
Death comes before the grief; the sulphurous match
Destroys the powder with a motion slow
To what I work with;[53] as autumn-agèd leaf,
In youth the prime and glory of the grove,
Not to be grasped with hand, falls with a puff,
And what we could not touch but now we tread on,
So Childrick—
KING Lend me thine arm, Dumain; I know not what,
But on the sudden— DUMAIN *and* LAMOT *about the* KING
QUEEN How the gnats play and buzz about the fire
Must[54] consume them!
EUNUCH 'Tis rare: observant coxcombs.[55]
CLOTAIR What star's un-sphered[56] and walks upon the earth, [*Sees* APHELIA]
Making our night a noon? Methinks her sight

48 24–5 Be these ... our marriage: this exchange of tokens (Clovis gives Aphelia a ring and takes from her a diamond) and pre-contract of marriage is the "fatal contract" of the play's title

49 29 SD *reveling*: the blocking of this scene is difficult to determine. The implication, though, is that the king, Dumain, Lamot, and company watch a masque or performance (see line 79) during which the queen and the Eunuch speak out of hearing of the others and then later, Clotair and the Eunuch similarly speak apart. Aphelia and Clovis either stand apart or join the revelers

50 34 physic: medicine, here used ironically for the "fatal dram" of poison given to the king

51 36 genius: attendant spirit

52 39 part essential: soul

53 47–50 Where I ... work with: "the queen strikes faster than a gunpowder fuse" (Morley)

54 57–8 the fire ... consume them: i.e. the fire that must consume them

55 59 coxcombs: fools (so called because of the cap worn by a professional fool, which resembled the comb or crest of a rooster)

56 60 un-sphered: fallen from orbit

Does cure blindness, and lend darkness light.
Castrato— *CLOTAIR pulls the EUNUCH aside*
EUNUCH No more, we are observed, my lord.
CLOTAIR What lady's that?
EUNUCH That French India with a mine upon her back,[57]
With whom your brother holds discourse?
CLOTAIR The same.
EUNUCH The chaste and beautiful Aphelia.
CLOTAIR Indeed, she's wondrous fair; nature hath much
Befriended her—art sure she's honest?
EUNUCH Snow's not purer.
No vestal virgin[58] at the altar bears
A soul so incorrupt, so void of flame
That's loosely active.
CLOTAIR Castrato, be as ourself, get but that lady for me—
Thou understand'st me.
EUNUCH She dotes upon your brother, by which means
I'll think upon some plot.
CLOTAIR The masque[59] ended, we will talk further on't.
KING Defer our pastimes till another night,
I am not well at ease.
DUMAIN Lights, lights for his majesty!
CLOTAIR and CLOVIS How is it with your grace our royal father?
EUNUCH [*Aside*] Dumain, Lamot, your feet are in the snare;
Fredigond hunts, and when she hunts, beware. *The EUNUCH talks with APHELIA aside*
LAMOT What says the slave?
DUMAIN No matter what—mind we his majesty.
KING There is an Aetna[60] in me—
The air I draw returns illuminate.
Philosophy, thy element of fire's here!
QUEEN His grace grows worse and worse, support him
Gently, friends; O my dear husband, O my gentle lord!

Exeunt [all except] EUNUCH *and* APHELIA

APHELIA I credit your report, and will obey;
His mind is honorable like his parentage.
His single name has armed me; pray, lead on. *Exeunt* EUNUCH *and* APHELIA

Enter LAMOT

LAMOT O woe, woe, woe!

Enter CLOTAIR

CLOTAIR Horror and death!

Enter CLOVIS, FREDIGOND, LANDRY, DUMAIN, GUARD, ATTENDANTS

CLOVIS O dismal, fatal hour.
QUEEN With Childrick, end the world.

57 66 Aphelia is richly dressed with gold and jewels imported from India, a source of exotic wealth
58 72 vestal virgin: a virgin consecrated to Vesta, the Roman goddess of fire, hearth, and home; the vestal virgins were sworn to vows of chastity
59 79 masque: courtly dramatic entertainment, often allegorical or symbolic in nature; revenge tragedies often included short inset dramas or masques. It is unclear precisely what the royal court is watching or indeed whether the performance was also visible to the audience
60 88 Aetna: Mount Etna, the highest active volcano in Europe; in other words, the king feels as if he's burning up from the effects of the poison

DUMAIN Have patience, gentle queen.
QUEEN Stand from me!
Preach patience to the sea when the rude winds
Swell her ambitious billows[61] 'bove the clouds,
And if thou tutor'st them to peace and silence,
I'll be as calm as they.
CLOTAIR The treason here, and not the traitor,
Quite confounds me.
QUEEN Doubt ye the traitors?
I've brought a pair of vipers to the court,
Warmed and relieved them with a sting to kill us;[62]
Who could be authors of this deed but they?
His new bosom friends have slain him,
Lay hands upon the villains!
DUMAIN We are betrayed, Lamot, basely beset with snares.
LAMOT Justice, fight thou my cause with thine own sword! [DUMAIN, LAMOT *fight off guards, exeunt*]
QUEEN O villains, would ye let them scape?
Two men to pass the strength of all our guard?
This mads me.
CLOTAIR Make after them and bring them back,
Or by my father's soul ye sleep your last.
[*Aside*] Aphelia, O Aphelia, she'll not from my mind—
I may command[63] her now.
—Come mother, brother, friends; come, let us go.
King never received a crown so full of woe.

Exeunt

Act II, scene i

Enter OLD BRISSAC *and the* PAGE

PAGE I left her[64] midst th'amazèd multitude,
Where doubtless frighted with the sudden horror
Of the unlooked-for murder of the king,
She has with other beauties of the court
Retired herself until the morning star.
OLD BRISSAC 'Tis very likely so, yet d'ee hear—
I know not what to say, I'll not to bed,
My thoughts are full of tempests, dismal thinkings;
Where is my son, why went he not to court?
PAGE Your son, Sir Charles, sir, is not yet in bed,
But why he went not to the court I know not.
OLD BRISSAC Perhaps she's safe—then why returns she not?
Why sends she not glad messages of health?
No, no, she's lost, and I undone forever.
Go to your bed. I will not trouble you.
Go take your rest; yet, pray be up betimes— [PAGE] *offers to go*
Yet stay and watch with me, she may come home.

61 102 billows: the surge or swell of the ocean
62 108 them with . . . kill us: those who have the power to kill us
63 119 command: as king, Clotair can now compel Aphelia to marry him
64 1 her: Aphelia

She may come home, it's good to wait for her;
Yet now I've thought on it, get you hence to bed—
And yet not so, run, run unto the court! [PAGE] *offers to go*
O villain how he moves; yet why so fast?
Let me deliberate; that were to give
The courtiers notice I have lost my daughter,
Whom they will then suspect, and call her fame[65]
Into an ill construction; no no no—

Enter CHARLES BRISSAC *and* CLOVIS *the Prince disguised*

O sir you're welcome, where is your sister?
I must have her, sirrah, and I will; where is
She, Charles, where is she?
CHARLES My noble father.
OLD BRISSAC Tut tut tut, noble me no nobles, nor father me
No fathers, where is your sister, sirrah?
CHARLES My sister?
OLD BRISSAC Your sister; this cunning shall not carry it;
Where is she? Speak.
CHARLES Within sir, is she not? Otherwise this gentleman
Has lost his labor; he's come to visit her.
OLD BRISSAC Hoyday,[66] hoyday, hoyday, to visit her?
Plots, plots, mere fetches to delude me. To visit her?
What, at the dead of night, when the whole world
Is sunk in slumber, and our lusty youth
As quiet as the grave? To visit her?
O most ridiculous! To visit her?
Pray, gentlemen, consider, does your sister keep
Times so preposterous for visiting?
Makes she a day of night, or has been bred
As loose as Lais,[67] to love night courtings?
Do not distract me! To visit her?
CHARLES Pray, sir, collect yourself; this gentleman
Even at that horrid point where the king fell—
OLD BRISSAC Ay there's more mischief too; God for his mercy
What a world is this!
CHARLES —saw a ring drop from off my sister's finger,
And at his best advantage took it up,
Which he had then delivered, but that fright
Which renders men forgetful made him so.
But knowing where she lived (so he protests),
He could not sleep until it were delivered.
OLD BRISSAC Pray, let me see the ring; yes, it was hers,
And she would say she'd never part with it
But when she meant to wed. If y'have married her,
Or have her promise riveted to yours,
Tell me but where she is, I'll be content;
For I in losing her, have lost my joy.
CHARLES Is she not then within?

65 24 fame: reputation
66 36 Hoyday: interjection expressing wonder or disbelief
67 45 Lais: Greek courtesan

OLD BRISSAC Yes, too much;[68] O no,
The house contains her not, she is not here,
Nor is,[69] for ought I know, at all.
CLOVIS O my prophetic soul, then 'tis no idle fear. [*Undisguises*]
OLD BRISSAC How, the Monsieur? What makes he here?
CLOVIS There's something whispers me "go not to bed,
Go not to bed till thou hast found her out;"
Be'st thou my genius, or what power else
(Suggesting lawful things), I will obey thee.
Still it cries, "sleep not tonight." Had I ta'en opium,
The drowsy poppy, cold mandragora,[70]
Or all the sleepy syrups of the world,
With such a powerful spell thou work'st upon me
That should I take an everlasting sleep
Thould'st wake my scattered bones, and make them rise
To watch the horror of this fatal night.
Sleep, ever-waking envy and mistrust,
Ye things which never knew what slumber meant:
Ghosts, keep your beds; ye sentinels of night,
Goblins and specters, do not walk your round;
A general lethargy seize on this hour,
Whilst I alone the watchman of the night
Will wake in spite of fate. Argus, thine eyes,[71]
To find Aphelia and her miseries. *Exit*
OLD BRISSAC Pretty, in good sadness,[72] wondrous pretty;
Is he in earnest?
CHARLES Sure he dissembles not; I little thought, when I did
Let him in what person graced our threshold.
OLD BRISSAC Ah, sirrah, what a girl is this to be out of the way.
He is in love, that's certain; let me remember,
When I was first a lover as he is
I'd just such wild vagaries in my brain,
Such midnight madness; this puling baggage[73]
May lose herself forever, and her fortunes,
For this hour's absence. Go, begone,
Follow his royal person, comfort him,
Tell him my daughter will again be found;
And so good angels grant we meet with her.
Exeunt

Act II, scene ii

Enter APHELIA *and the* EUNUCH *with a wax taper*[74]

APHELIA Into what labyrinth do you lead me, sir?
What by-perplexèd[75] ways? I should much fear

68 63 Yes, too much: Old Brissac continues from his earlier speech ("too much lost my joy") before breaking off and answering Charles's question
69 65 is: i.e. is alive
70 73 mandragora: sedative drug made from the mandrake root
71 85 Argus, thine eyes: Argus, let me have your eyes. Argus was a mythological Greek giant with one hundred eyes whom Juno set to watch over the nymph Io, one of her many rivals for Jupiter's love
72 87 in good sadness: in all honesty
73 95 puling baggage: whining or crying girl
74 0 SD *taper*: candle
75 2 by-perplexèd: intricate or confused; the route troubles and confuses her

Had you not used his name—which is to me
A strength 'gainst terror, and himself so good
Occasion cannot vary, nor the night,
Youth, nor his wild desire—otherwise
A silent sorrow from mine eyes would steal
And tell sad stories for me.
EUNUCH You are too tender of your honor, lady,
Too full of anguish trembling; the noble prince
Is, as December, frosty in desire,
Save what is lawful. He not owns that heat
Which, were you snow, would thaw a tear from you.
APHELIA This is the place appointed; pray heavens all things go well.
EUNUCH I will go call him. Please you, rest yourself;
Here lies a book[76] will bear you company
Till I return, which will be presently. APHELIA *reads in the book*
[*Aside*] Hither I'll send the king[77]—not that I mean
To give him leave to cool his burning lust,
For Clovis shall prevent him in the fact,
And thus I shall endear myself to both.
Clovis enraged perhaps will kill the king,
Or by the king will perish; if both fall,
Or either, both ways make for me.
The queen as rootedly does hate her sons
As I her ladyship; to see this fray
She must be brought by me. She'll steel them on
To one another's damage; for her sake
I'll say I set on foot this hopeful brawl,
Whilst she will hug and kiss me for the same.
Thus on all sides the Eunuch will play foul,
And as his face is black he'll have his soul.[78]
APHELIA How witty sorrow has found out discourse
Fitting a midnight season! Here I see
One bathed in virgins' tears, whose purity
Might blanch a blackamoor, turn nature's stream
Back on itself;[79] words pure and of that strain
Might move the Parcae[80] to be pitiful.

Enter CLOTAIR [*with his face muffled*]

CLOTAIR Methinks I stand like Tarquin[81] in the night,
When he defiled the chastity of Rome,
Doubtful of what to do, and like a thief *She still reads on*
I take each noise to be an officer.
She has a ravishing feature, and her mind
Is of a purer temper than her body.

76 16 book: Ovid's *Metamorphoses*
77 18 the king: i.e. Clotair
78 32 The eunuch will make his soul as black as his face (the line draws upon the pervasive color symbolism in medieval art and drama equating external blackness with evil)
79 34–7 Here I . . . on itself: Aphelia reads from Book 6 of the *Metamorphoses* about the rape of Philomela. Aphelia imagines that the tears of a reader sympathetic to Philomela's plight would have the power to "blanch a blackamoor," i.e. turn a black body white, a well-known proverbial expression for impossible labor
80 38 Parcae: the three fates of Greek myth
81 39 Tarquin: Roman prince who raped the virtuous Roman matron Lucretia (or Lucrece), who then committed suicide; public outcry at her suicide led to the expulsion of the monarchy and the founding of the Roman republic

Her virtues more than beauty ravished me,
And I commit even with her piety
A kind of incest with religion.
Though I do know it is a deed of death
Condemned to torments in the other world,
Such tempting sweetness dwells in every limb,
That I must venture my essential parts[82]
For the fruition of a moment's lust—
A pleasure dearly bought. *Exit with a resolve not to do it*
APHELIA Alack poor maid,
Poor ravished Philomel! Thy lot was ill
To meet that violence in a brother,[83] which
I in a stranger doubt not; yet methinks
I am too confident, for I feel my heart
Burdened with something ominous. These men
Are things of subtle nature, and their oaths
Unconstant like themselves. Clovis may prove unkind,
Alack, why not? Say he should offer foul?
The evil counsel of a secret place,
And night his friend, might over-tempt his will—
I dare not stand the hazard.[84] Guide me, light,
To some untrodden place, where poor I may
Wear out the night with sighs till it be day.

Enter CLOTAIR

CLOTAIR [*Aside*] I am resolved. I will be bold and resolute.—
Hail beauteous damsel!
APHELIA Ha, what man art thou
That hast thy countenance clouded with thy cloak,
And hide'st thy face from darkness and the night?
If thy intents deserve a muffler, too,
Withdraw and act them not. What art thou? Speak,
And wherefore cam'st thou hither?
CLOTAIR I came to find one beautiful as thou,
And am a man willing to please a woman.
APHELIA I understand you not.
CLOTAIR But I must you, yea and the right way too,
Or my strength shall fail me.
APHELIA Help, help, help!
CLOTAIR Peace, none of your loud music, lady.
If you raise a note, or beat the air with clamor,
You see your death. *Draws his dagger*
APHELIA What violence is this? Inhuman sir, *Kneels*
Why do you threaten war, fright my soft peace
With most ungentle steel? What have I done
Dangerous, or am like to do? Why do you rack me thus?
Mine arms are guilty of no crimes, do not torment 'um.
Mine heart and they have been heaved up together
For mankind that was holy. If in that act
They have not prayed for you, mend and be good,

82 51 venture my essential parts: risk my soul
83 55 brother: i.e. brother-in-law; Philomela was raped by her sister Procne's husband Tereus
84 64 stand the hazard: take the chance

The fault is none of theirs.
CLOTAIR Come, do not seem
More holy than you are; I know your heart.
APHELIA Let your dagger, too, noble sir, strike home,
And sacrifice a soul to chastity
As pure as is itself, or innocence.
CLOTAIR This is not the way—know you me, beauty? *Discovers himself*
APHELIA The majesty of France!
CLOTAIR Be not afraid.
APHELIA I dare not fear; it's treason to suspect
My king can harbor thoughts that tend to ill.
I know you're godlike good, and have but tried
How far weak women durst be virtuous.[85]
CLOTAIR Cunning simplicity, thou art deceived.
Thy wit as well as beauty wounds me, and thy tongue
In pleading for thee pleads against thyself.
It is thy virtue moves me, and thy good
Tempts me to acts of evil. Wert thou bad,
Or loose in thy desires, I could stand
And only gaze, not surfeit on thy beauty.
But as thou art, there's witchcraft in thy face;
I must enjoy thee, or not thou thy life.

Enter CLOVIS and CHARLES

APHELIA You are my king, and may command my life;
My will to sin you cannot. You may force
Unhallowed deeds upon me, spot my fame,
And make my body suffer—not my mind.
When you have done this unreligious deed,
Conquered a poor weak maid, a trembling maid,
What trophy or what triumph will it bring
More than a living scorn upon your name?
The ashes in your urn shall suffer for't.
Virgins will sow their curses on your grave,
Time blot your kingly parentage, and call
Your birth in question. Do not think
This deed will lie concealed; the faults of kings do
Shine like the fiery beacons[86] on a hill
For all to see, and seeing tremble at.
It's not a single ill which you commit;
What in the subject is a petty fault,
Monsters your actions,[87] and's a foul offence:
You give your subjects license to offend,
When you do teach them how.
CLOTAIR I will endure no longer. Come along,
Or by the curious spinstry[88] of thy head,
Which nature's cunningest finger twisted out,
I'll drag thee to my couch; tempt not my fury.

85 99–100 I know . . . be virtuous: Aphelia suggests that Clotair is merely testing her virtue to see if she's chaste
86 123 fiery beacons: signal fires, usually lit in times of invasion or war
87 127 Monsters your actions: makes your actions monstrous
88 131 spinstry: product of spinning; Clotair refers to Aphelia's elaborate hairdo. The word also suggests that her hair is artificial, which (as a wig on a boy actor) it in fact is

CLOVIS [*Aside*] Hold, hold my heart—can I endure this—
Unhand me, Charles, and render me myself,
Lest I forget my self on thee.
CHARLES Great sir,
Remember 'tis your brother, and the king.

Enter EUNUCH

CLOVIS O that I could forget it, and shake off
Duty at once and consanguinity
That like a whirlwind I might rush upon him,
And bear him to destruction.—Monster of men, [CLOVIS *discovers himself*]
Thou king of darkness down unto thy hell,[89]
I have a spell will lay thy honesty,
And this abusèd goodness. Is't not enough
That thou hast wronged Chrotilda, ravished a maid,
A virgin of that purity of life
Might saint her here on earth, but thou wilt add
Unto the first a second violence the gods must not forgive?
Don't arm your face,[90]
Nor wear a countenance of horror; I can't fear,
Bearing a bosom innocent and pure.
Is't even so? Then guard thyself, O King,
For I am swift as thought that executes. [*They fight*]
CHARLES Hold, hold, my lord, forbear!
EUNUCH Beat down their swords, what do the princes mean?
Ring out the larum bell, call up the court, *Ring the bell*
The princes here will murder one another.
For shame, for shame, forbear!

Enter the QUEEN, *the* GUARD, *and* ATTENDANTS; LANDREY *at the other door*

QUEEN What means this sudden outcry? O my sons,
Hold, hold; part 'um, good gentlemen.
CLOTAIR Braved by a subject's hand?
QUEEN Though nature by precedency of birth
Made thee his king, it therefore follows not
His murderer: wherein is our Clotair
Greater than Clovis? The self-same blood
That spirits thee,[91] makes him as valiant;
The difference lies in *anno domini.*[92]
EUNUCH [*Aside*] Most accurate mischief, most rare crocodile![93]
QUEEN I grant thou art his elder, by which law
Thou art born his subject, not his equal, Clovis.
Know Clotair's thy king, and subject's hands
Without the deep and dangerous traitor's name
May not advance against their sovereign's head.
CLOTAIR Neither shall his without correction;
Upon him, slaves!

89 142 darkness down unto thy hell: evil to your core
90 149 arm your face: Clotair gestures as if to conceal or "muffle" his face once again (see II.ii. 38 SD)
91 166 That spirits thee: that gives you life and spirit
92 167 *anno domini*: in the year of our Lord (Latin—commonly abbreviated to A.D. for dates); in other words, the only difference between the brothers is their ages
93 168 crocodile: proverbially said to shed tears while eating their prey; a symbol of false or insincere sorrow

QUEEN Hold, I command ye hold!
O Clotair, thou art of a valiant soul,
And wilt thou basely thus beset thy brother?
Fear argues spirits most degenerate,
And that thou fear'st, th'advantage argues it.[94]
O set not on thy slaves; if he must die,
Let thy sacrifice not butcher him.
CLOTAIR That argument sounds harsh, does Clotair fear?
CLOVIS Sacrifice me? It is not in his power.
EUNUCH [*Aside*] Exquisite philter,[95] how it operates!
QUEEN We hope so, Clovis; yet thy brother king
Is as an earthly god, his will his law,
His power uncircumscribed, unlimited,
Whose majesty can look a subject dead.
CLOVIS How? Look me dead? I do not fear his frowns.
QUEEN I grant thee as great a basilisk[96] as he,
As thou art merely man. But as thy king,
Divinity doth prop him;[97] he stands firm
That builds on that foundation. Yet I know
Thy sword's as sharp as his, and where it lights[98]
Imprints as much of fate;[99] thine arm's as strong,
Thy spirit as daring, and thy will as prompt
To any action that may write man, "Man."
CLOTAIR He is your darling, you do well to praise him;
When I have slain him, write his epitaph.
CLOVIS My epitaph? This pen of steel shall first
Write on thy heart thine end. *They fight again*
EUNUCH [*Aside*] Still, still better.
The venomed poison of a woman's tongue
Is more sublimed than mercury.[100]
CHARLES Hold, hold.
O dearest madam, your maternal breath
Bears a mandamus[101] in it, and like heaven
Will lay[102] this tempest.
EUNUCH [*Aside*] As the wind the sea,
Which makes it rage the louder.
CLOTAIR Where's our guard
That lets a traitor pull me by the beard?
Upon him, slaves!

The GUARD[S] *fall on* [CLOVIS] *and he falls*

QUEEN O they have slain my son;
Bloody villain, thy hands have made these holes,
Hell take thee for it.

94 177–9 And wilt . . . argues it: ordering your guards to seize your brother makes you seem to be afraid of him, and therefore debased or weak
95 184 philter: love potion or charm, used here to describe the toxic effect of the queen's manipulative words on her sons
96 190 basilisk: mythical reptile whose look was fatal
97 190–92 I grant . . . prop him: considered as men, you are equally lethal; but since he is your king, he's more powerful
98 194 lights: lands
99 195 Imprints as much of fate: is just as lethal
100 203 more sublimed than mercury: sublimation was the chemical term for the process of preparing mercury by heating it to a vapor; mercury (or quick-silver) was a toxic substance that was nevertheless used in cosmetics and medicines, including treatments for syphilis
101 205 mandamus: command
102 206 lay: allay

CLOTAIR Mother, rise and depart,
For I am bent on mischief.
QUEEN Do thy worst,
Thou murderous-minded prince; this blood is mine,
For in some sort I bleed; out, parricide![103]
EUNUCH [*Aside*] How cunningly she spits her poison forth!
I know her soul is light; she's glad he's dead,
And joys in the opportunity to curse the killer,
For which she gains the name of pious mother;
Here's pretty woman-villainy and dissimulation.
APHELIA If they have slain him, wherefore do I live?
O my swollen heart.
CLOTAIR Remove the corpse withal.
Convey this siren[104] from our wandering eyes
And house her in a dungeon. Let no light
Peep through a cranny on her; mask the day,
Put the all-searching eyes of Phoebus[105] out
Lest accidentally he gazing here,
Here fix eternally, and so we may
Despair of night as once we did of day.
Bear her to prison. Reason not the cause.
A king's prerogative's above his laws.
APHELIA Be merciful and lead to earth,[106] away,
Since he is gone, it is to die to stay. *Exeunt some with the* KING, *others leading* APHELIA, *and bearing away the corpse.*
EUNUCH, QUEEN, LANDREY *remain*

QUEEN Now we begin to flourish. This black night
Is only lighted by our stars, which smile
Upon these actions, and rejoice to see
Thee our sole favorite so near a crown.
But tell me, Landrey, how did I play the mother;
Did not I seem a Niobe[107] in passion,
A deluge of salt tears?
LANDREY Most true, you wept.
QUEEN As a good actor in a play would do,
Whose fancy works (as if he waking dreamt)
Too strongly on the object that it copes with,
Shaping realities from mockeries;
And so the queen did weep. By this good night
I think I could become the stage as well
As any she[108] that sells her breath in public;
Come, shall we act, Landrey?
LANDREY Act, lady, what?
QUEEN Nothing that's new; old plays you know are best.
Eunuch, is our bed ready?
EUNUCH Great queen, it is.
QUEEN Come then, my joy, to bed, where we will act
The truth which others doubt,[109] and in that sport

103 214 parricide: person who kills a close relative
104 222 siren: mythical monster, half woman and half bird, whose irresistible voice drew sailors to their destruction; a dangerous or alluring woman
105 225 Phoebus: sun; another name for the sun-god Apollo
106 231 lead to earth: it would be more merciful simply to kill and then bury me
107 238 Niobe: mythical figure of maternal sorrow who, after the murder of her fourteen children, wept herself to death and turned to stone
108 246 she: professional actress
109 251 doubt: suspect

We'll laugh at death which triumphs in the court. *Exeunt* QUEEN *and* LANDREY
EUNUCH Go sleep your last; I'll straight unto the king,
And he shall take them in the very act.
And then to cover my discovery
I'll set on fire the queen's bed-chamber
That so I may disturb them more secure,[110]
And yet the plot not mine; I'll tell the king
Unless he present help, his mother burns.
About it, then, this is a happy night;
The more it works their woe, more's my delight.

Exit

Act III, scene i

Enter KING CLOTAIR *and the* EUNUCH; *the bedchamber on fire*

EUNUCH Look how it flames! I fear some treachery.
Beat at her chamber door, cry it aloud,
And let your voice be thunder to this lightning;
Cry, fire, fire, fire! The court is all a hot-house, fire, fire!
CLOTAIR Great Queen, royal mother, open your door
Lest you do sleep for ever; mother, awake!
The god of sleep lies heavy on her eyes;
Force up the door; fire, fire, fire!
EUNUCH It's fortified 'gainst strength, you must call louder.
CLOTAIR Mother, Queen, mother, awake, awake!
Your sleep was never more like death than now;
Lady, great princess, fire, fire, fire!

Enter QUEEN *above in night attire,* LANDREY

QUEEN What saucy groom
Beats our offenceless doors thus daringly?
He had better roused a sleeping lioness
Than thus t'have broke our slumbers; what art thou?
CLOTAIR Look,
The fire will give you light; 'tis I, your son.
Fly from your chamber else you are but dead,
Your court is all a-bonfire!
QUEEN (*Aside*) Let it burn, I have lost my credit everlastingly,
—I will not move a foot.
CLOTAIR You must be forced, then. *Exit* EUNUCH *busy to quench the fire*
LANDREY (*Aside*) Lady, where is your wit now in necessity?
We shall be taken, and you shamed forever.
Bethink, bethink yourself, what shall we do?
QUEEN I have it, it shall be so. There, put on that, [*Indicates* CLOVIS*'s armor*]
And as the door flies open, meet him full
Appearing in his brother's warlike form.
Thou wilt amaze, and so pass by him safely.
—Do not appear to me, I did not wound thee,
Seek out the beds of those that caused thy death,
And howl to them thy piteous complaints;

110 257 So that I may harry them without fear of detection

O do not look on me, be gone, be gone![111] [*Exit* LANDREY]
CLOTAIR Whom d'ee hold discourse with, with the air?
Bethink yourself, this is no time to dally.
QUEEN O my son, such horrid apparitions full of dread
Have I beheld, have quite unwitted me.
Thy brother's ghost, young Clovis' ghost in arms
Has thrice appeared to me this dismal night;
You heard me speak to't.
CLOTAIR True, I heard you speak,
But what of that?
QUEEN Calls for Aphelia
To bear him company i'th' other world,
Or else he'll nightly haunt us in our sleep.

Enter LANDREY [*below*] *as in the prince's armor*

CLOTAIR O see, it comes!
QUEEN Fear it not, son. [*Exit*]
CLOTAIR What art thou that usurp'st this dead of night,
In metal like the age? Why art thou sent
To cast a horror on me? If thy soul
Walks unrevenged, and the grim ferryman[112]
Deny thy passage, I'll perform thy rites. *The ghost points to his wounds*
O do not wound me with such piteous signs,
Lest I dissolve to air, and like thyself
Affright fool mortals. If that thou desirest
Aphelia's death t'appease thy troubled soul,
Make some consenting sign, and so depart—
Thy sight afflicts my soul!

[LANDREY] *bends*[113] *and so goes off; then at the other door enter* EUNUCH

Enter QUEEN [*below*]

QUEEN How fares our son?
CLOTAIR It was my brother's spirit; nothing but Aphelia?
QUEEN She must die; you see it's requisite
CLOTAIR Would he had asked my life first!
QUEEN Why should you be so fond upon a woman?
CLOTAIR Woman's the least part of her; she's all goddess.
QUEEN 'Twas your offer;
Remember, there's no jesting with the gods.
EUNUCH [*Aside*] What might this mean? Ha, where are my brains?
CLOTAIR I had forgot myself; your pardon, mother.
Bear her from me this jewel I esteem
Equal with life; it was my brother's picture,
And with it, this: that she prepare to die.
Pray her to take it; and in death, but kiss
This sad remembrance for the sender's sake,
Although for his whose form it represents,
And I shall take it for the greatest grace

111 31–4 Do not . . . be gone: in these lines the queen pretends to be terrified by the ghost of Clovis
112 50 ferryman: Charon, the ferryman of Hades who rows the souls of the dead across the rivers Styx and Acheron in the underworld
113 57 SD *bends*: bows to indicate his assent

That she can give, or I ought to desire.
Tell her, and if you can be moved to sorrow
Express it in your tears. It is not I
Pronounce[114] this fatal sentence 'gainst her life
Which needs must ruin mine, but the hid will
And providence of heaven, 'gainst which to rage
It were as impious as not obey.
My brother's funeral is her dying day.
Tell her, though reason and my will do jar,
My soul speaks peace, although my sentence war.
Say I love, and pray her to forgive me. *Exit* QUEEN
Go, all attend my mother; my estate
Delights not in court ceremony. *Exeunt all but the* EUNUCH *and* CLOTAIR
Stay, Castrato stay,
And with thy council cure thy dying prince.
Thou art my bosom, Eunuch, and to thee
I dare unclasp my soul. What's to be done?
This is a damnèd spirit I have seen,
And comes to work my ruin.
EUNUCH What spirit?
CLOTAIR My brother's spirit in arms; I swear it came forth here
Out of my mother's chamber as I knocked.
EUNUCH Was it in armor, said you?
CLOTAIR Yes, in that armor he was used to wear
When we have run at tilt,[115] till our cleft spears
Have with their splinters scarred the element.[116]
EUNUCH [*Aside*] That armor as I well remember I did leave
In the queen's bed-chamber as yesterday,
After the triumphs and the tournaments,
Having unbraced the prince; 'tis even so,
—Ha, ha, ha.
CLOTAIR Why this ridiculous passion?
My state requires thy tears and not thy mirth.
EUNUCH The devil came from your mother's chamber, sir,
She has a circle that can raise a spirit—
A Mars in armor, too. She is a Venus,
And, through your license,[117] Landrey is no Eunuch.
CLOTAIR What killing sense thou utterest?
There's something in it I would understand,
And yet I dare not; Landrey? How know'st thou this?
EUNUCH Since I have gone so far, I'll tell you.
I looked in at the key-hole, and I saw
Him in your mother's arms upon the bed
As sportingly as e'er I saw your father.
CLOTAIR Thou liest, take that! Suspicion double sees; *Strikes him and offers to go out*[118]
Jealous informers ne'er meet better fees.[119]
EUNUCH King, thou hadst better far have struck thy father,

114 78 Pronounce: i.e. who pronounces
115 98 run at tilt: jousted
116 99 element: sky
117 110 through your license: by your leave; if I may say
118 118 SD *offers to go out*: it is clear from the SD at line 122 that Clotair moves some distance from the action after striking the Eunuch but, as this direction indicates, he may not leave the stage entirely
119 119 better fees: i.e. better payment than blows

Digged up his bones and played at logats[120] with them.
—Stroken?[121] *The* KING *returns calmly*
CLOTAIR I know not.
My mother always had a scanted fame;
His thoughts, too, have been mine. I was to blame,
Prithee forgive me; my passion's but like lightning,
Flash and away, dead ere we say it is;[122]
I am not always angry, let that assure.
My mother may be false; she is a woman. *Gives him his purse*
Prithee deliver; come. I will believe thee
Even to the utmost syllable.
EUNUCH Then, she is false.
CLOTAIR And didst thou see him mount my mother's bed?
EUNUCH Else pull these[123] out.
CLOTAIR Thou hast shot poison through me—
False with Landrey, her sometime page?
EUNUCH Even with the same.
CLOTAIR But wherefore would they have Aphelia die?
There lies the mystery.
EUNUCH They fear you will accept her as the queen,
Of whom you may beget a hopeful issue
And frustrate their intents, who but expect
Your hoped-for death, and perhaps plotted, too,
That so they might become what now you cross:
Lawfully man and wife, and govern in your seat.
CLOTAIR [*Aside*] This carries show of truth, or is't a lie
Well shadowed by the slave? I cannot tell.
My mother certainly is not so bad,
It is a sin to think it.—Hence and avoid my sight,
Thou sower of debate![124] Thy seeds are strowed
On sterile ground, and therefore ill-bestowed. *Exit*
EUNUCH Is it even so? Work and about, my brain,
I'm lost forever if not close again.[125]

Exit

Act III, scene ii

Enter DUMAIN, MARTELL, BOURBON, LANOVE

LANOVE Are all your troops well furnished 'gainst resistance?
Are your men bold and daring, resolute
To run your hazard, indifferent rich—not poor,
That only fight for bread? Such oft betray
The sinews of a well-knit plot for gain,
When these as well fight to defend as win.
DUMAIN Noble Lanove,
Mine know nor fear nor death. Souls of that fire,
They'll catch the bullet flying; scale a wall

120 121 logats: a game in which a stake is fixed to the ground and sticks or "logats" are thrown at it
121 122 Stroken: stricken; stunned
122 127 dead ere we say it is: gone before we can even say it is there
123 134 these: i.e. my eyes
124 150 debate: discord
125 153 I'm lost forever if I do not ensnare Clotair once again in my plot

Battled with enemy; stand breaches,[126] laugh
The thunder of a cannon, call it music
Fitter a lady's chamber than the field.
When o'er their heads the element is seeled,[127]
Darkened with darts, they'll fight under the shade,
And ask no other roofs to hide their heads in.
They fear not Jove, and had the Giants been
But half so spirited, they had disthroned him;[128]
Kill till they're killed with killing, and oftener die
Wearied than wounded, being more oppressed
With giving wounds than taking. When they fall,
They fall not vanquished, but by fate betrayed;
Such are the men I lead.
MARTELL They're soldiers fit to sack a kingdom, then,
And share the spoil between them.
BOURBON Were it come to that sport once.
DUMAIN Bourbon, it must, or some of us must fall.
MARTELL Where shall we first attempt?
DUMAIN The Citadel.[129]
LANOVE I say no, it's dangerous.
DUMAIN It is the safest course.
MARTELL Believe it not, it's full of hazard.
DUMAIN So is the general enterprise in hand.
LANOVE But this of certain ruin.
MARTELL Give me a reason why you would invade
The palace first, and I am satisfied.
DUMAIN Then understand: Lamot lives still at court
Disguisèd like a formal surgeon,
To whom the prince, being deliverèd
To be embalmed and bowelled,[130] finding life
Yet in his corpse—which way he's very skillful—
Has balsamed[131] all his wounds and cured him.
LANOVE And what of all this?
DUMAIN Have temperance, and hear the rest:
For this, the prince has promised him the place,
The grand Commander of the Citadel,
Whose aid can stead us infinitely.
LANOVE Is it certain?
DUMAIN I did but even now receive this letter, *Shows the letter*
Which constantly[132] affirms it from himself.
He says it is not known in court yet that the prince lives,
For diverse reasons best known to themselves,
And herein doth require our secrecy.
Therefore, dear friends, be wary to divulge it.
Besides, he says here
That the great Monsieur's supposed funeral
This day's solemnizèd with greatest pomp;
And how Aphelia dies a sacrifice

126 10 stand breaches: push through holes made in enemy fortifications
127 13 seeled: made dark or blind (i.e. when the sky is so full of arrows that it becomes dark)
128 16–17 They fear . . . disthroned him: Lanove claims that his men would have been capable of defeating Jove, unlike the Giants
129 27 Citadel: fortified stronghold; i.e. they will attack the most fortified part of the palace first
130 38 bowelled: have his inner organs removed (in preparation for burial)
131 40 balsamed: healed or soothed
132 48 constantly: faithfully, assuredly

That hour he is burièd on his hearse.
What if we made attempt to save the virgin?
LANOVE It may not be; better she fall alone
Than all of us together. And now, best friends,
Let us behave us bravely; it's no base act
We undertake, but our whole country's freedom
From slavery and bondage. Men of worth stand bare
To pages and gilt butterflies?[133] Besides, the queen
Will grave us[134] all rather than want sport
In spilling human blood. Come, let's withdraw,
And lay the platform of this mighty work.
My soul sits smiling in me; I divine,
Though now it lour,[135] I shall see sun will shine.

Exeunt

Act III, scene iii

Enter CLOVIS *and* LAMOT *both disguised*

CLOVIS Strephon,[136] for so thou nam'st thyself, thou'st made
Thy prince thy subject by thy timely cure;
This is the hour I must be buried living,
And this the hour the fair Aphelia
Dies on my hearse t'appease my wandering ghost;
Say Strephon, is it so?
LAMOT Nay this the very minute: hark, I hear them coming. *Sad solemn music*
CLOVIS Stand close here, we'll observe the mourners.

Enter six of the guard, their halberds[137] *reversed; then a* CARDINAL, LANDREY, OLD BRISSAC*; then the hearse borne by six young men; then* KING, QUEEN, EUNUCH *holding up her train; two or three ladies, these in mourning. At the other door, a headsman; two nuns in white, singing;* APHELIA *with a garland on her head led by two little boys in white; after these, more virgins adorned like the rest. Both troops pass by each other; the song ended, the hearse is set down between both companies,* APHELIA *mourning at one end, and the* KING *at the other, who after a little pause, speaks*

The Song by Nuns
Come blest Virgins come and bring
To this Goddess offering,
Offer to her kisses, such
As make good better by the touch;
Where her eyes let fall a tear,
Another paradise springs there;
It's preposterous cruelty
To sacrifice a deity;
If a true path should be trod,
To her sacrifice a god.

133 64 pages and gilt butterflies: servants and hangers-on at court
134 65 grave us: will kill us
135 69 lour: threatens to storm
136 1 Strephon: conventional name for a pastoral lover (and thus an odd choice for Lamot, who is disguised as a doctor)
137 8 SD *halberds*: military weapon that is a combination of a spear and a battle-axe; the pageant joins Catholic imagery to pagan ritual and serves as an inset spectacle or masque

CLOTAIR Set down, set down your honorable load,
Fitting an Atlas' shoulder; burden of grace
And majesty immense, whose weight doth load
Heaven's stooping porter, under which he groans
More than the spheres, and sweats thy weight, not theirs.
Let me bedew thy hearse with pious tears,
Balm to wounds, repenting ones. Look down
From heaven empyreal[138] and behold me stand
All flood in sorrow, drowned in mine own tears;
Behold this spotless sacrifice, a virgin
As pure in thought as vesture, an oblation
To ransom Jove and heaven had he been taken,[139]
And so we yield her up. *Delivers her to the Headsman*
OLD BRISSAC O my good lord,
This is conspiracy 'gainst an old man's life;
Have you no other way to murder me,
But to begin with her? Are these your plots?
You're weary of my counsel? And my place
May better be supplied by greener heads?
Pray cut off mine—do, do, a weak old man.
My absence were material, since your state
Requires parricides about you.
Alas, I may be spared; why must she die?
Because she's fair? Or that a prince
Once thought her so? The fault is none of hers,
Let nature suffer for't; if it prove art,
Or that with plaistred[140] cunning she did catch
Your brother's love with an adulterate form,
I yield her up as not allied to me;
If not, why should she suffer?
CLOTAIR Brissac, peace. *The* KING *takes the sword from the Executioner*
CLOVIS [*Aside to* LAMOT] What pageant's this?
CLOTAIR Be it no wonder, lords,
To see a prince an executioner;
Far be it from the dignity of France
To let a soul forth so refined as hers
With mercenary hands.
LAMOT [*Aside*] Contain yourself,
You may prevent the danger when you please. *The* KING *kneels, and lays the sword at* APHELIA'S *foot*
CLOTAIR Behold the conquest of thine eyes, Aphelia,
France at thy foot; tread on his royalty,
Or if thy nature knows not to forgive
(Which to believe were impious), take this sword
And search my heart; send me a sacrifice
T'appease the troubled spirit of thy love.
QUEEN (*Aside*) O Eunuch, that she'd take him at his word.
CLOTAIR I find a speaking pity in thine eyes,
Which thence will drop upon thy gentle tongue,

138 26 heaven empyreal: the highest heavens

139 29–30 an oblation . . . been taken: a gift or offering sufficient to ransom even Jove himself had he been captured

140 44 plaistred: plastered or painted, suggesting cosmetic arts and feminine deceit. Brissac argues that if Aphelia used such deceitful tactics to attract Clovis then she deserves to die; if not, she's innocent and should not be executed

And cry in peace, "Long live my Sovereign!"
APHELIA Long live Clotair, long live my sovereign.
CLOTAIR The motions of the spheres move in that tongue.
Turn all your sables to the Tyrian dye,[141]
Your dirges into sprightful wedding airs.
Why looks our court so sad? Is this a time
To anchor your aspects unto the earth?
By my blest self, he's traitor to the height,
That does not straight salute her as his queen.
ALL Long live Aphelia, Queen of France and us.
LAMOT [*Aside*] Do you hear this? What are you, planet-stroken?[142]
Clovis, Prince, Monsieur?
QUEEN What will Clotair do?
CLOTAIR What heaven has pointed for him: marry her.
QUEEN [*Aside*] Thy grave, thy grave first, Clotair.
CLOTAIR Cardinal. *The* CARDINAL *and the* KING *whisper*
QUEEN What evil spirit's crept into my son?
Venomed his noble nature, sickened all
His wholesome faculties, slain's[143] divinity?
Are these your vows? Or canst thou cozen[144] heaven?
Necessity of fate depends on it,
You know she must to earth.
CLOTAIR Ay, but not yet.
Since she has conquered me that could do fate,
Had she joined with me, the awed destinies
Spin her decrees, and what she wills, they act;
Sith then what must be must be, join our hands.[145]
LAMOT [*Aside*] Now, now, prevent them yet, O statue prince,[146]
Thou art undone forever! *The Monsieur stands [forth] amazed*
CLOVIS Where am I?
Awake? Forever rather let me sleep.
Is this a funeral? O that I were a hearse,
And not the mock of what is pageanted.[147]
CLOTAIR Amazement quite confounds me, Clovis alive!
LAMOT Yes sir, by my art he lives, though his desire
Was not to have it known; this chest[148] contains
Nothing but spices sweetly odoriferous.
CLOTAIR Into my soul I welcome thee, dear brother;
This second birth of thine brings me more joy,
Than had Aphelia brought me forth an heir,
Whom now you must remember as a sister.
CLOVIS O that in nature there was left an art,
Could teach me to forget I ever loved
This, her great masterpiece; O well-built frame,[149]

141 67 Change black (sable) clothes for the crimson or purple garments fitter for a celebration
142 74 planet-stroken: stricken or afflicted; made paralyzed by the result of the malign influence of a planet; thunder-struck, bewildered
143 80 slain's: slain his
144 81 cozen: trick, deceive
145 84–7 Since she . . . our hands: Aphelia's power is such that the destinies perform her will, and therefore it is fated that she be married to Clotair rather than slain
146 88 statue prince: Lamot is trying to get Clovis to intervene
147 91–2 O that . . . is pageanted: i.e. I wish I really were dead and that this wasn't merely a sham funeral rite
148 95 chest: coffin
149 103 well-built frame: i.e. Aphelia's beautiful body

Why dost thou harbor such unhallowed guests
To house within thy bosom perjury?
If that our vows are registered in heaven,
Why are they broke on earth? Aphelia,
This was a hasty match, the subtle air
Has not yet cooled the breath with which thou swor'st
Thyself into my soul; and on thy cheeks,
The print and path-way of those tears remain
That wooed me to believe so—fly me not, *She gives back [the ring]*
I am no spirit; taste[150] my active pulse,
And you shall find it make such harmony.
As youth and health enjoy.
EUNUCH The queen, she faints! [APHELIA *faints*]
CLOVIS Is there a god left so propitious
To rid me of my fears? Still[151] let her sleep,
For if she wake (O King) she will appear
Too monstrous a specter for frail eyes
To see and keep their senses.
LAMOT Are you mad?
CLOVIS Nothing so happy, Strephon; would I were.
In time's first progress I despair the hour
That brings such fortune with it; I should then
Forget that she was ever pleasing to me.
I should no more remember she would sit
And sing me into dreams of paradise;
Never more hang about her ivory neck
Believing such a one Diana's was,
Never more dote she breathes Arabia,[152]
Or kiss her coral lip into a paleness.
LAMOT See, she's returned, and with majestic gaze,
In pity rather than contempt beholds you.
CLOVIS Convey me hence, some charitable man, *Admiringly*
Lest this same creature, looking like a saint,
Hurry my soul to hell; she is a fiend,
Appareled like a woman, sent on earth
For man's destruction.
CLOTAIR Rule your disordered tongue.
Clovis, what's past we are content to think
It was our brother spoke, and not our subject.
CLOVIS I had forgot myself, yet well remember
Yon Gorgon[153] has transformed me into stone;
And since that time my language has been harsh,
My words too heavy for my tongue, too earthly;
I was not born so, trust me, Aphelia.
Before I was possessed with these black thoughts
I could sit by thy side, and rest my head
Upon the rising pillows of thy breast,
Whose natural sweetness would invite mine eyes
To sink in pleasing slumbers, wake, and kiss

150 113 taste: feel
151 117 Still: forever
152 129 dote she breathes Arabia: say lovingly that her breath is sweetly scented
153 141 Gorgon: monster of classical mythology with serpents for hair; its gaze turned its victims to stone

The rose buds[154] that afforded me such bliss;
But thou art now a general disease
That eat'st into my marrow, turn'st my blood,
And mak'st my veins run poison, that each sense
Groans at the alteration. Am I the Monsieur?
Does Clovis talk his sorrows, and not act?
O man bewomanized! Wert thou not mine,
How comes it thou art his?
CLOTAIR You have done ill,
And must be taught so; you capitulate[155]
Not with your equal, Clovis; she's thy queen.
CLOVIS Upon my knees I do acknowledge her, *He kneels*
Queen of my thoughts and my affections.
O pardon me, if my ill-tutored tongue
Has forfeited my head; if not, behold
Before the sacred altar of thy feet,
I lie a willing sacrifice.
APHELIA Arise,
And henceforth, Clovis, thus instruct thy soul:
There lies a depth in fate, which earthly eyes
May faintly look into, but cannot fathom.
You had my vow till death to be your wife;
You being dead, my vows were cancelèd,
And I as thus you see bestowed.
CLOVIS Farewell;
I will no more offend you. Would to God
Those cruel hands not enough barbarous
That made these bleeding witnesses of love,
Had set an endless period to my life too.[156]
CLOTAIR Where there's no help, it's bootless to complain.
Clovis, she's mine; let not your spirit war
Or mutiny within you because I say it;
Nor let thy tongue from henceforth dare presume
To say she might, or ever should, be thine.
What's past once more I pardon. 'Tis our wedding day.
CLOVIS A long farewell to love. Thus do I break *He breaks the ring*
Your broken pledge of faith, and with this kiss—
The last that ever Clovis must print here—
Unkiss the kiss that sealed it on thy lips. [*He kisses her*]
Ye powers, ye are unjust, for her wild breath
That has the sacred tie of contract broken,
Is still the same Arabia that it was. *The* KING *pulls him*
Nay, I have done; beware of jealousy.
I would not have you nourish jealous thoughts.
Though she has broke her faith to me, to you
Against her reputation she'll be true.
Farewell my first love lost. I'll choose to have
No wife, till death shall wed me to my grave.
Come, Strephon, come, and teach me how to die,
That gav'st me life so unadvisedly. *Exeunt* CLOVIS *and* LAMOT

154 150 buds: Q reads "beds"
155 158 capitulate: converse
156 172–5 Would to . . . life too: Clovis wishes that he had been killed and not just wounded (his wounds are the "bleeding witnesses" of his love for Aphelia) by Clotair's guards (their "cruel hands" were "not enough barbarous" to finish the job)

CLOTAIR Let Clovis that way go, this way will we;
He's great with grief, we with felicity. *Exeunt all with* CLOTAIR. QUEEN *and* EUNUCH *remain*
QUEEN Mischief grows lean, Castrato; all our plots
Turn head upon themselves. My brains grow weak,
And in this globe the policy's not left
To kill a worm unseen; I am undone,
And all my plots discovered.
EUNUCH This is strange,
Some comic devil crosses our designs;
How else should he revive, or yea prepared,[157]
Nay in the arms of Landrey, when desire
Had made you all a Venus, meet events
So barren in their expectations?
QUEEN Their lies the grief, Castrato; had the court,
So I had quenched these burning flames within,
Been buried in her cinders, I had cared not.
EUNUCH But yet Landrey's escape doth qualify
The non-performance.
QUEEN That sits smiling here,[158]
It set my brains upon the tenters,[159] Eunuch;
Was't not a rare device?
EUNUCH And was not I
As fortunate to leave that armor there?
But now what's to be done?
QUEEN My dull Ethiop,
I will instruct thy blackness. Learn to know
My reputation's sickened, and my fame
Is looked into with narrow eyes at court;
Therefore it's thus decreed, I will remove
And sequester myself from company.
EUNUCH Good.
QUEEN Thou know'st where Childrick kept his concubine
To none discovered but thyself and me,
For which she is no more.[160]
EUNUCH Right.
QUEEN There will I
And my Landrey securely spend our time,
Revel, embrace, and whatnot, my Eunuch.
The cave that leads unto the postern gate,
Which Childrick made, will give him entrance,
No eye acquainted; being thus retired,
What lust inflamed must be by lust unfired.
EUNUCH Excellent mistress, I applaud your brain.
QUEEN I will away tonight. I cannot brook
These loathèd nuptials; they have undone
My hopes on earth forever. Therefore, my Eunuch,
Acquaint Landrey with these designs.

157 205 yea prepared: the meaning of this phrase is difficult to discern. The overall gist of the speech is that the Eunuch is disappointed with the failure of their plotting—for example, the unexpected return of Clovis—even though (unbeknownst to the queen) the Eunuch himself is responsible for the intrusion of Clotair into the queen's bedchamber, where she was very nearly found "in the arms of Landrey"

158 213 that sits smiling here: at least Landrey escaped, and the knowledge of that pleases me

159 214 tenters: wooden framework on which cloth is stretched

160 224–5 To none … no more: this is the only mention of a mistress of the old king that, evidently, Fredigond and the Eunuch had murdered. In the 1653 text, line 224 reads "To none discovered by thyself and me"

EUNUCH What else?
QUEEN If by the engine of thy stronger brain,
Thou couldst remove—
EUNUCH Aphelia or the king,
Monsieur, or all; it is not so, my Queen?
QUEEN Thou hast a brain which doth engender thoughts
As regal as our own, which do beget
A race of rare events; what pity 'tis
Thy body should be sterile, since thy mind
Is of so pregnant and a fruitful kind;
Farewell, remember me. *Exit* QUEEN
EUNUCH Remember you?
Your Gibship[161] shall be thought on, fear it not;
And now bethink thee, Eunuch, all thy plots
Find fruitless issues, only in the king,
His worship walked into the other world,
Like a tame suckling pig that died o'th' pip;[162]
The trouble is behind, my hate extends
To the whole family; I must root them up,
And beldam,[163] first with you. But how? But how?
If (in her proud desire) I do prevent
Her lust this second time, before the third
She may repent and save her loathèd soul,
Which my revenge would damn; yet were she crossed,
Her lust being now at full flood in her,
And no way left to quench her burning flame,
Her dryer bones would make a bonfire
Fit for the devil to warm his hands by.
Stay, stay, Castrato; no, this must not be,
Nor must the high and mighty Queen Aphelia
This night enjoy her bridegroom. I must set
Some mischief instantly on foot to stop it.
If I miscarry in it, story shall tell,
I did attempt it bravely, though I fell.

Enter LAMOT *and* CLOVIS

CLOVIS Dissuade me not—Castrato, I have sought thee
Through every angle of this spacious court:
I've business to impart.
EUNUCH And so have I.
CLOVIS Mine is of honorable consequence,
And doth require thine aid.
EUNUCH So doth mine yours.
CLOVIS Aphelia is—
EUNUCH Your brother's wife, and you
Would fain enjoy her, too. Why sir, you may,
But time must work her.
CLOVIS Eunuch, thou art wide;
Those vanities of love are quite extinct.
Revenge doth swell the Monsieur, and his thoughts

161 246 Gibship: term of reproach for an older woman; gib is a kind of cat; "Your Cattiness" (Morley)
162 250 pip: respiratory disease, but of birds, not swine; also, in comic usage, an illness or malaise of a person
163 253 beldam: aged woman, grandmother; here, derogatory for loathsome old woman, witch or hag

Which burn within him must be quenched with blood.
I have incensed the king with yellowness,[164]
With doubtful phrases on Aphelia's fame;
See'st thou this letter—'tis a script I feigned, *Shows a paper*
For I can counterfeit Aphelia's hand.
The king has banished Landrey from the court,
Because he wore the jewel[165] which he sent
To his Aphelia. Light suspicions,
But this shall aggravate: find thou the king,
Show him this note; it doth express great love
To Landrey from Aphelia, and withal
It mentioneth the jewel as a gift
To gratify her servant. This to[166] the rest
Of poison he has sucked already in
Will so inflame him that the court shall burn
Too hot for his Aphelia.
EUNUCH Think it done;
But now your aid, since that your mind is bent
On honorable ends, here's one will try you.
CLOVIS Thou'dst have me join myself unto the rebels,
And with my person grace their cause, perhaps;
That is not now to plot.
EUNUCH I find you high,
Worthy the name of Monsieur; yet your thoughts
Hit not my purpose—it is such that made
Your brother quake to hear.
CLOVIS What is it, Eunuch ?
If that it bear an honorable sound,
Though death stood gaping wide to swallow me,
I would not shrink nor fear.
EUNUCH Noble. Hear it, then:
Your mother's loose, and this night renders up
Her body unto lust, if not prevented.
I can direct you where and when, with whom.
CLOVIS My soul finds the man; is't not Landrey?
EUNUCH The same.
CLOVIS I'll tear him all to pieces, then.
Whore my mother! Eunuch, lead the way;
In what thou shalt prescribe, we will obey.

Exeunt

Act IV, scene i

Enter CLOTAIR, *alone*

CLOTAIR What vulture gripes me here, ha, what art thou?
If thou be'st jealousy, mount and be gone;
Fly to the vulgar bosom, whose cheap thoughts
Despair their own performance; in a prince

164 279 Clovis has stirred up the king's humors so that he's now imbalanced; yellow is the color associated with the humor of choler or anger

165 284 jewel: this is the jewel or miniature Clotair gave the queen to give to Aphelia at III.i. 68–9, explaining that "it was my brother's picture." This makes it a strange love token for Landrey to be wearing

166 290 This to: this added to

Thou show'st a nature retrograde[167] to honor.
Suppose she gave the jewels, must it follow
She therefore is disloyal? Poor consequence,
A bauble[168] for a boy to play withal.
I am resolved. Hark, I hear her coming;
O Juno,[169] what a look and gait is there! [*Stands aside*]

Enter APHELIA *as going to bed, two or three ladies* [ISABEL, JULIA] *with lights*

APHELIA Mock me not, ladies, with this ceremony,
For I am fitter to attend on you;
I am become a servant and a slave
To every moody passion of my lord.
All that's behind[170] I can perform myself,
Without this complement.
[ISABEL] Sweet lady,
You must not weigh these things so deeply.
Your lord is of a noble spirit,
And you shall see how calm he will return,
Blessing your bridal bed with fruitful issue.
APHELIA No, no;
The saffron-coated Hymen[171] frowns upon us.
These tapers here were lighted at a pile,[172]
As fit attendants on the grave, not bed;
Juno denies her presence at this match,
And all the ill-presaging birds of night
Sing fatal requiems for a bridal song;
O ladies, is not this ominous? [CLOTAIR *comes forward*]
CLOTAIR Yes my Aphelia, if that ragged fate
Lie in a kiss, then it is ominous.
Let me dwell here; I am ravished.
Am I on earth? No, heaven is here,
And all th'unimitable joys that poets feign,
Are bettered in thy goodness.
APHELIA I hope your fears are satisfièd now;
You bear a brow so sweetly pleasant.
CLOTAIR What pretty foolery is this, Aphelia?
I am not jealous, for by all that's good
I cannot think thee evil; kiss me sweet, *Kisses her*
There's no deceit lies here; again, again. *Again kisses*
Her kisses melt upon my lip; if sin
Have so much heaven in't, I'll be a sinner;
Prithee forgive my folly that could be wrought
To such a senseless passion. Come, let's in,
And shake this off as it never been.
[ISABEL] We must a while, my lord, entreat your absence,
We have some certain notions to deliver,
Some pillow counsels; I'll assure your highness

167 5 retrograde: term from astronomy denoting a planet moving in the reverse direction to that which is usual
168 8 bauble: showy trinket that might please a child
169 10 Juno: wife of Jupiter and the most important goddess of Roman mythology; invoked here as the patroness of marriage and motherhood
170 15 All that's behind: all that remains to do
171 22 saffron-coated Hymen: Hymen, the god of marriage, represented as a young man carrying a torch and a veil
172 23 pile: funeral pyre

It shall be no ways prejudicial to you.
[JULIA] You see she's not prepared; till that's performed,
She's ours; that done, we yield her up
To the dark night and mercy of your lordship.
CLOTAIR Go then, unharness your lady for these wars,
For we are of the Camilli, and fight naked.[173] *Exeunt* LADIES *and* APHELIA
Ye powers that favor lovers, infuse apt strength
Through every nerve and sinew of this frame;
Make me all pleasure; and unto the bride
Add every vein a Venus; guide me, light,
Where in one bed lies all the world's delight. *Offers to go out and meets the* EUNUCH
EUNUCH Not yet in bed! O happy, happy minute—
Until this hour I ne'er was fortunate;
I have preserved my king, my prince, my patron,
From the loose ardor of a strumpet's bed.
CLOTAIR What's this?
EUNUCH Be not this second time incredulous,
And scorn my honest heart; or grant you were,
I deal not now on doubts. Your wife is false,
Dishonest as the suburbs.[174] I am loath
To nominate her whore, though it be true.
CLOTAIR True? Ha!
EUNUCH Leave this lethargized passion which benumbs
Your nobler nature; turn your eyes on this: *Shows a letter*
Whose character is this?
CLOTAIR It is Aphelia's hand, the very same
Which I have often seen Clovis peruse
In his love's amorous pursuit. *The bed thrust forth with* APHELIA *asleep*
EUNUCH Read the contents.
CLOTAIR A letter that she loves Landrey, with thanks
For his so frequent visits which she repays
With the rich jewel sent her by the king,
Wishing a perpetuity of embracements.
Ten thousand ravens crook[175] in this black paper;
How came you by it?
EUNUCH I saw it drop from Landrey, but ne'er thought
'Fore I perused it what it did contain;
Which finding, in my duty I was bound
To save my prince from ruin.
CLOTAIR   Hold my heart,
O what shall Clotair do? It cannot be;
Do but behold her face, and thou shalt read
What we call virtue there, and modesty.
Here is a look would persuade cruelty
To sigh and shed a tear, bribe Nemesis[176]
To knot her steely scourge with plume of down,
And Jove himself to call her vice a virtue.
EUNUCH A book of devils may have the cover gilt;
Treason lies cabined in the smoothest brow;
The devil can assume an angel's form;

173 54 The Camilli were a "noble Roman family . . . the 'tradition' of nakedness seems to be Heminge's invention" (Morley, 2006)
174 68 suburbs: London's suburbs lay beyond the authority of the city proper; brothels, theatres, and other venues of vice and entertainment were located there
175 82 crook: croak
176 92 Nemesis: goddess of retribution or vengeance

Your wife is fair, but fair to do you harm.
CLOTAIR O say not so, she is the neatest cut[177]
As e'er was printed by the hand of heaven.
Here is a volume of divinity,
Composed so rarely, that to add to this,
Or take away from hence, were such a sin
Repentance could not expiate. I'll not touch
With hands unhallowed such a purity
Could it change all my thoughts to peace and silence.
EUNUCH My lord—
CLOTAIR Peace, slave, thou that infects all peace!
EUNUCH Why are you thus distempered? Let not truth
Make you so wild a tempest. Were it false,
Or that I sought the ruin of your house,
Your youth and honor, then it were a time
To swell beyond all charming down, but, being truth—
CLOTAIR Truth! Hence and avoid my sight, fly where the world
Promiscuously combines without distinction;
Where every man is every woman's husband,
Or where it's thought a courtesy to have
A fellow laborer in the marriage bed.
These were a people that might bear with thee,
And fit for thee to dwell with; hence, away,
And if thou lov'st thy life, acquaint thy feet
With such by-paths that we may never meet. *Exit*
EUNUCH This prince is of a nature mild and gentle,
His mother's milk's too fluent in his eyes,
And much I fear his resolution.
Yet I will work him forward—she awakes. APHELIA *stirs in the bed*
I'll after him and fetch him back; if then
She scape his hate, hell has no power with men. *Exit* EUNUCH
APHELIA O, O, O, help, help, my lord and husband;
O my father, my lord and husband; help, help!
—Bless me, divinity, is it but a dream! Ha, the light
Gone; who waits there? Isabel, Julia!

Enter ISABEL *with a light*

ISABEL [*Aside*] It was my lady's voice, does she call for help?
I cannot blame her; were I in her place I should
Do so, too; the prince looks like a bungler.
APHELIA Who's there? Isabel?
ISABEL Did you call, madam?
APHELIA Saw'st thou nothing? Where is my lord?
ISABEL [*Aside*] Is he absent? I cannot blame her, then, to cry for help—I should do it myself. A prince? A puppet would have been more manly.—How do you, madam?
APHELIA All stands not well.
ISABEL [*Aside*] I believe that faithfully.[178]
APHELIA O, girl, I've passed the dismall'st part of night,
As ever tortured fancy with extremes.
ISABEL [*Aside*] If all brides should be so tortured, I'd forswear marriage.

177 99 neatest cut: neatest form or shape; heaven fashioned Aphelia well. "Cut" was a term related to the making of clothing; here it is used within a metaphor about the printing of books

178 139 I believe that faithfully: Isabel makes a joke about Clotair being unable to maintain an erection

APHELIA Methoughts I saw my father in a vault,
His silver hair made crimson with his blood;
My brother at his hearse upon his knees,
Taking a solemn oath for his revenge;
Yet all this while fancy so fooled my sense,
Methought that I was here, where on the instant,
My lord in preparation for my bed,
Was by an ugly fiend ravished from hence
And hurried to destruction. Here I awaked,
And trust me, Isabel, I scarce believe
But what I saw was real; heard'st thou nothing?
ISABEL I heard discourse of people in your chamber
Some half an hour since, but they went forth,
And to my seeming, full of discontent,
But know not who they were.
APHELIA O it is too true;
I'll to my father's. My prophetic soul
Sits like a mine of lead within me. Come,
Help me to mourn, my girl, for this sad sight
Befits a funeral, not a bridal night. *Exeunt both*

Enter CLOTAIR *and the* EUNUCH

CLOTAIR I am resolved, Castrato. I'll be cruel
Since she's defiled, and like a crystal well
Has her spring poisoned by the enemy,
For which it's death for the besieged to taste;
Such are adulterate waters. Say, Eunuch,
What read'st thou in our brow?[179] Speak truly, man.
EUNUCH A foolish grudging of the mother still.
CLOTAIR A settled resolution, my black saint,
Not to be altered by the brackish[180] tears
Which flow in pregnant eyes of easy women.
Slack, piety,
And rise, black vengeance, from the depth of hell,
And fate me her destruction![181] Lock up in me
The organs of remorse, all faculties
That write me man, or mankind; create
A spirit of horror in me, apt me to look[182]
Upon such deeds nature would tremble at,
And the discreet composure of the world
Melt and dissolve to nothing, whilst I, unmoved,
Smile at the alteration. Infuse such soul,
And I shall then behold all cruelty
Human invention e'er was guilty of,
And whilst I groan under extremity
Stand and applaud the executioner.
My honor calls for vengeance, and I'll do. Ha— *Draws his dagger and goes to the bed*
How? She gone, and I have lost mine anger. too.
EUNUCH But whither is she gone? To some new groom,

179 168 What readest . . . our brow: Clotair asks the Eunuch if he can see in his forehead the supposed horns of the cuckold
180 171 brackish: salty
181 175 fate me her destruction: choose me as the agent of her destruction
182 178 apt me to look: make me apt to look

Who, being fooled her expectation,[183]
Will make thee cuckold on thy wedding night?
CLOTAIR Thou hast awaked me. I'll know where she is;
Hell, nor her darker deeds, shall hide her from me.
Who waits? Lackey?

Enter LACKEY

LACKEY My lord.
CLOTAIR Where is thy lady? Where's Aphelia?
LACKEY She's even now gone forth.
CLOTAIR Gone forth with whom?
LACKEY There was one with her, but whether man or
Woman I am uncertain; but sure 'twas a man,
She would not dare to venture out so late else.
CLOTAIR Get to thy rest. *Exit* LACKEY
I'll take thy word, Eunuch, for the kingdom's wealth.
EUNUCH O do you begin to credit now,
Now, when perhaps it is too late? This comes of patience.
CLOTAIR Turn patience into fury, love to hate,
My softer temper to a heart of steel;
Respect of wedlock and the sacred vow
Made 'fore the holy altar to the priest,
Thus I do fling ye off. Revenge shall move
About her bridal bed instead of love.

Exeunt

Act IV, scene ii

Enter CLOVIS, LAMOT, *and three or four of the Guard*

CLOVIS Upon your lives let no man pass that way.
GUARDS Your grace shall be obeyed in all.
CLOVIS If he resist or offer violence, knock out his brains.
There's your reward; be careful and begone.
GUARDS God preserve the Monsieur! *Exeunt* GUARDS
CLOVIS You shall possess the cave;[184] myself will in
And visit these night revelers. Such sport
I will administer shall make them dance
Lavoltas[185] in the air; here's that shall fiddle to them.[186]
Have you the habit,[187] Strephon?
LAMOT With these hands
I did disrobe the statue[188] of your father,
And they are ready—
CLOVIS Landrey, blood doth swell
The Monsieur's thoughts to send thy soul to hell.

Exeunt

183 190 being fooled her expectation: the meaning of this phrase is obscure, though the sense of the Eunuch's lines—that Aphelia might be cheating on Clotair on their wedding night—is clear enough
184 6 cave: the secret entrance to the location where the queen is hiding with Landrey
185 9 Lavoltas: a lively, capering dance for two people
186 9 that shall fiddle to them: i.e. Clovis's sword
187 10 habit: costume, disguise
188 11 disrobe the statue: reference to the "gown and robes" in which Clovis will appear at IV.iii. 91 SD

Act IV, scene iii

Enter LANDREY*; music above, and this song*

The Song
Wisdom bids us shun the court;
What great ones do, fame will report.
Here we may enjoy each other,
And no eye our loves discover.
I will make thee choice of poses,
Beds of cassia[189] *mixed with roses,*
Where we'll toy, and kiss, and vary
Pleasures till the morn discloses
All our secrets, if thou'lt tarry.

LANDREY If I will tarry, let me wither here;
Within these sacred walls let me expire,
And spend the remnant of my life that's left
In service of the deity lives here.
The air's perfumed; each room through which I walk
Banquets the senses, courts the appetite
Of every faculty that makes up man,
To complement[190] it into paradise.
If then Elysium's[191] here, where are those shades,[192]
Those blessèd apparitions poets feign?
Appear, my goddess, and out-sing the poets,

Enter QUEEN

Reality of fancy that excell'st
The faint expressions of a lazy tongue
Whose house is roofed with flesh.[193] To tell thy worth,
Tongues tipped with immortality would faint in't.[194] [LANDREY *produces a poem, is seen adding to or amending it*]
QUEEN Excellent servant, what, do you write, too?
Poet and actor both? Why this sudden gaze—
Your cases are too narrow for your eyes?
Pray spare your optics, sir, for Venus' service.[195]
LANDREY No,
I'll play the prodigal with my precious sight
And spend it all on you; to view your second
Were such a happiness, after the which
It were a sin to see more.[196]
QUEEN Bless me, Rabelais,[197]
And all ye softer fancies of the French;

189 6 *cassia*: a fragrant shrub or plant
190 17 complement: to make complete or perfect; Landrey suggests that the queen's presence transforms any space into paradise
191 18 Elysium: in Greek mythology, a paradise in the afterlife
192 18 shades: souls of the dead
193 20–23 Appear, my . . . with flesh: the physical presence of the queen surpasses anything either a mortal or a divine poet could express
194 10–24 If I will . . . in it: Landrey (perhaps self-importantly, perhaps playfully or cynically) is performing the role of the courtly lover who worships his mistress as a goddess or "deity"
195 25–8 Excellent servant . . . Venus' service: i.e "why are you looking at me like that?" The queen is teasing Landrey for his pretension
196 31–3 to view . . . see more: gazing upon you more than I already am would almost be sinful, I'd be so happy
197 34 Rabelais: French writer, scholar, and monk Francois Rabelais (1494–1533), here mentioned for his reputation as a bawdy writer

What ails the man? My Landrey laureate.[198]
LANDREY It is my queen that's laureate, whose blest sight
Creates a poet; this divine feature[199]
Heaven only made to make man ingenious.
QUEEN Is this extempore,[200] or have you hired
Some hackney muse acquainted with the road
Of vulgar exorcisms to charm cheap beauties?[201]
Take up—at this speed else your muse will founder.
LANDREY Founder, and have her founders by?[202] With patience
Hear but these poor expressions of your worth,
Which faintly paint forth your perfections,
And you shall bless my muse.
QUEEN We'll hear your jig.[203]
How is your ballad titled? Come, pronounce.
LANDREY [*Reads*]

From head to foot, Fredigond been
Far excelling beauty's queen;
Had Jason but beheld her hair,
The golden fleece had ne'er seemed fair.[204]
Those stars which mortals suppose eyes,
Were ascendant in the skies,
When it fell to Venus' lot
That little Cupid was begot.
Her tongue in which the spheres do move,
Organ of divinest love,
Was by Apollo framed, that he
From hence might learn more harmony.[205]
Who neats her teeth, and lips discloses,
Walls of pearl and gates of roses;
Two leavèd doors that lead the way
Through her breath t'Arabia,[206]
To which would Cupid grant that bliss,
I'd go a pilgrimage to kiss.
Those hills of snow which on her breast
Rise swelling with their double crest,
Make Parnassus mountain,[207] *whence*
The muses suck their eloquence;
Whose parts which we will not discover
He'll imagine that's a lover.
Like Juno she doth go,
Like Pallas[208] *talk and sow,*

198 36 laureate: crowned or wreathed with laurel; a symbol of distinction, here in poetry
199 38 divine feature: her face and person
200 40 extempore: improvised
201 41–2 Some hackney . . . cheap beauties: hackney or "hackneyed" means stale, shopworn, banal; it is also a derogatory term for a prostitute. The queen teasingly asks Landrey whether he's written the poem he's about to read to her himself or whether he's simply recirculating some unoriginal, overused, "vulgar" (low-class) verse
202 43–4 your muse . . . founders by: Landrey puns on two different meanings of the word "founder," the first "to stumble," and the second "maker" or "creator"
203 47 jig: a jig is a lively, comic, often scurrilous song or ballad
204 51–2 *Had Jason . . . seemed fair*: refers to the story, from Greek mythology, of Jason's quest to claim the Golden Fleece of Colchis
205 58–60 *Organ of . . . more harmony*: her tongue, shaped by the god Apollo, teaches such harmonious eloquence that Apollo himself could learn from her
206 61–4 *Who neats . . . breath t'Arabia*: he who notes her clean teeth and lips will see those teeth as pearls, lips as roses, and her smile a gateway to paradise ("Arabia")
207 69 *Parnassus mountain*: mountain near Delphi, Greece with a summit dedicated to Apollo and the Muses and thus associated with music and poetry
208 74: *Pallas*: Athena, Greek goddess of wisdom

Like Venus in her bliss,
Each kiss a Cupid is,
And her hands as white as snow.
From head to foot my mistress been
Far excelling beauty's queen.

QUEEN Leave these arial viands,[209] taste of that
Is here substantial; how like you the fruit? [*Kisses* LANDREY]
LANDREY Let me forever dwell upon these lips.
QUEEN You are too greedy of these rarities
And must be dieted, lest, surfeiting,
Your appetite should sicken and so die.
LANDREY Die on your lips, O death-bed for a Jove;
Who's buried here, his grave's immortal love;
Here will I dwell, and know no age nor sorrow.
QUEEN Yet Childrick knew them both.
LANDREY A frosty prince
Begot on January by a Dutchman,[210]
And worthy of those flames he now endures.

Enter CLOVIS *from under the stage with his father's gown and robes on*

QUEEN What noise is this? Guard me, divinity! [QUEEN *faints, exit* LANDREY][211]
CLOVIS What has my harshness done? She is my mother;
My conscience tells me I was much to blame
Thus to delude her fancy; she returns. [QUEEN *awakes*]
QUEEN O Childrick I confess 'twas I that killed thee,
These hands administered the fatal draught
That set thy soul on wing.
CLOVIS What do I hear?
QUEEN O do not snatch my soul from out this world
Till I have bathed it in repentant tears,
And made it fit for heaven. [QUEEN *faints*]
CLOVIS She faints again; [CLOVIS] *puts off his robes*
Who waits within? Come forth and lend your aid.

Enter LAMOT [*disguised as Strephon*] *at the trapdoor*

O welcome, Strephon; use thy best of skill
That masters nature, and doth life restore
Beyond the art of Asclepius;[212]
Apply thy gentlest medicines.
LAMOT Let us withdraw;
My life, sir, answer hers if she miscarry.

Enter MUSICIANS

CLOVIS What are ye?
MUSICIANS Musicians, whose obedience

209 80 arial viands: insubstantial meats; airy nothings

210 89–90 A frosty … a Dutchman: Childerick was cold and unloving. For the English, the Dutch were "proverbially phlegmatic" (Morley)—sluggish, apathetic, and lacking in enthusiasm

211 92 SD: I have assigned Landrey an exit here but he could also remain onstage, presumably hidden, until he speaks again at line 116

212 106 Asclepius: Greek god of medicine

Doth here attend the queen.
CLOVIS Bawds, arrant-bawds;
I'll talk with you anon; in, in. *Exeunt* [CLOVIS, LAMOT, QUEEN, MUSICIANS]

Enter the GUARD

1 GUARD Stand close, stand close, I heard a bustling within here while.
2 GUARD [*As drunk*] Bustling, and they come this way here's that shall bustle them.[213]
3 GUARD Fly upon him, he's drunk, and will betray us all.

[*Enter* LANDREY]

LANDREY I am betrayed; that Monsieur seeks my life,
All ways 'gainst my escape are fortified.
O cruel fortune, bawd to time and fate,
That soothe'st us up to make us ruinate;[214]
For now thou know'st no tears, anon no glee,
But only constant in inconstancy.
Ha! What is here? Great goddess pardon me, *Finds the robes*
I have offended 'gainst thy deity.
This shall delude the watch; thrice blessèd hap
That thus deliver'st whom they would entrap. [*Exit* LANDREY *with robes*]
2 GUARD I will not stand, nor I cannot stand; d'ee think
I'm drunk—what's that?

[*Enter* LANDREY *in robes pretending to be a spirit*]

ALL GUARDS Bless us, O bless us; diabolo,[215] diabolo. [*Exeunt* 1 GUARD, 3 GUARD]
2 GUARD The devil, what a devil care I, keep off devil,
I say keep off, I do not fear thee; are you
Sneaking back, you cowardly rogue? D'ee budge?
I hate a cowardly rogue, as I hate, as I hate the devil; take that! [2 GUARD] *knocks* [LANDREY] *down*
LANDREY O, O, O.
2 GUARD O, O, O, I'll make you cry "O";
What devil made you in my way?
I'll now see what money he carries about him;
Men say the prince of darkness is a gentleman.
By'r lady, he has good clothes; but yet for all that,
He may have no money. [2 GUARD, LANDREY *struggle under* LANDREY'S *robes*][216]

Enter QUEEN, CLOVIS, LAMOT *undisguised, musicians*

QUEEN I know not where he is, or if I did,
Before I'd yield him up to thy revenge
I'll die ten thousand deaths.
CLOVIS Thou glorious light, that in thy natural orb
Didst comfortably shine upon this kingdom,

213 113 here's that shall bustle them: "that" could refer either to the guard's sword or to a bottle of alcohol that he is drinking from or gesturing with

214 117–18 Cruel fortune reassures us only later to reduce us to ruin

215 127 diabolo: devil

216 138 SD: the comic spectacle of Landrey and the drunken guard struggling under the robes Clovis initially used to play the ghost of his father is clearly modeled on II.ii of Shakespeare's *Tempest*, and Stephano's discovery of "some monster of the isle with four legs" (Caliban and Trinculo) under Caliban's cloak (II.ii. 64–5)

How is thy worth eclipsed; what a dull darkness
Hangs round about thy fame? In all this piece,
To every limb whereof I once owed duty
I know not where now to find out my mother.
QUEEN The devil and disobedience blinds your eyes.
CLOVIS O that I had no eyes, so you no shame;
Murder your husband to arrive at lust,
And then to lay the blame on innocents?
Blush, blush, thou worse than woman.
QUEEN Ha, ha, ha.
CLOVIS Hold my heart,
You're impudent in sin; has your proud page
Made you thus valiant? Tell me where he is;
For if you dally with me, know this hand
Shall rip him from thy heart, though cabined there.
QUEEN How dar'st thou clothe thy speech in such a phrase
To me, thy natural mother?
CLOVIS My mother!
Adulterate woman, shame of royalty,
I blush to call thee mother; thy foul lusts
Have taught me words of that harsh consequence
That stigmatize obedience, and do brand
With misbecoming accents filial duty.
Deliver quickly where this lecher is;
Here housed he must be, for he cannot 'scape,
Lest wildness, conquering my softer sense,
Thrust forth my hand into an act of horror
And leave you breathless here.
QUEEN What French Neronian[217] spirit have we here?
Insolent boy, wilt thou turn parricide?
CLOVIS The justness of my cause would excuse me
If I should execute; speak, murderess,
Where have you mewed your monster?[218]
QUEEN Here lies the monster, O rare monster; two beards, [*Notes bodies under robes*]
This is a comic monster; a periwig, too—this is a court monster;
D'ee gape? What in the devil's name would you beg now? [LAMOT *discovers* LANDREY, GUARD *under robes*]
LAMOT Behold my lord, the woodcock's in the gin:[219]
Here lies the great Landrey.
QUEEN [*Aside*] O horrid sin.
CLOVIS This habit might have ruined all, Lamot.
But, goblin, now you are caught; what, is he dead?
LAMOT Scarce hurt, my lord; how is it? Look up.

Enter EUNUCH

EUNUCH Where is the queen?
QUEEN Here, Eunuch, as thou seest, in misery.
EUNUCH [*Aside to* QUEEN] O my heart, how came the Monsieur hither? Lamot too?
QUEEN All that I know is that we are betrayed.

217 170 Neronian: like Nero, Roman emperor known for his cruelty, tyranny
218 174 mewed your monster: hidden Landrey; "monster" reinforces the scene's allusion to *The Tempest* II.ii
219 178 woodcock's in the gin: bird is in the trap

EUNUCH I'll set them packing, fear not.—My good lord.
CLOVIS Thou art a faithful servant.
EUNUCH Sir, the rebels—
CLOVIS Give them a nobler title, by my life
I do applaud their courage; come they on?
EUNUCH Yes, and Brissac is made their general.
CLOVIS A hopeful youth, fraught with nobility,
And all the graceful qualities that write
Man truly honorable; my injuries
Have swelled me up to this.
EUNUCH His father's dead.
CLOVIS Trust me I'm sorry; grief has broke his heart,
And mine, Castrato, too. Canst thou imagine
Who was the author of our father's death?
EUNUCH [*Aside*] Am I betrayed? Then lend me impudence,
I'm sure I cannot blush.[220]—Royal sir, whom?
CLOVIS Our mother with Landrey, and this Lamot
They meant should bear the blame; this was Strephon.
EUNUCH Indeed? [*Aside*] Would I were fairly off.[221]
CLOVIS But what news with Aphelia and her bridegroom?
EUNUCH As you could wish. He's full of jealousy;
No Frenchman e'er was more Italian.[222]
I've wrought him bravely on—your physic works.
Hither I've brought Aphelia; tomorrow
You shall hear further sport, I'll warrant you.
In the meanwhile, what will you do with these?
CLOVIS Castrato, thus:
Nature forbids me spill my mother's blood,
And Landrey is unfit for my revenge,
For I must study torments[223] for the slave.
Therefore I give them up to your tuition
Until I shall return victorious.
QUEEN [*Aside to* LANDREY] Observed you that? There is some comfort yet.
CLOVIS Then we'll determine of them; if we fall,
Let Clotair point them out a funeral.
Reward these with the whip, these with my purse;
His merit is two hundred crowns, perform it. [*Gives money to* 2 GUARD]
2 GUARD Drink, I adore thee, drink; good fellows all,
Sometimes we rise by drink, but oftener fall. *Exit* 2 GUARD
CLOVIS A moral drunkard; go away with them,
And on your life let them not stir from hence. *Exeunt* EUNUCH, *musicians,* LANDREY, *and* QUEEN
Now my revenge grows to maturity.
We'll to Dumain, Lamot, and join with him;
Now, France, thou liest a-bleeding; thou shalt prove
What 'tis to cross the Monsieur in his love.

Exeunt

220 200 cannot blush: the Eunuch refers to the supposed opacity and unreadability of black skin which, unlike white skin, cannot show the signs of changing emotions such as the blush (and/or also, because of this opacity, cannot feel the emotions that cause the blush, particularly shame)

221 203 Would I were fairly off: I wish I could get out of here

222 206 Italians were proverbially known for their jealous temperaments

223 214 study torments: decide on the appropriate torments

Act V, scene i

Enter BRISSAC, DUMAIN, BOURBON, LANOVE, MARTEL

DUMAIN For certain, then, the princes are at odds.
BRISSAC Yes, and the ground, the marriage of my sister.
BOURBON The ulcerous state is ripe, and we must lance it.[224]
BRISSAC The king doth whore my sister; she's not his,
But true and lawfully the Monsieur's wife.
DUMAIN Did not one Strephon wait upon the Monsieur?
BRISSAC What's his condition?[225]
DUMAIN A surgeon, and famous for the cure o'th' prince.
BRISSAC Yes, such there was, but little noised[226] at court.
DUMAIN That was Lamot, our fast and noble friend.
MARTEL There's some design on foot that hinders him,
He would not else neglect us. *Within "the Monsieur, the Monsieur, ho, ho, ho"*
BRISSAC What noise is that, Lanove? Step forth and see. [*They shout*] *again*
DUMAIN O death we are surprised, the Monsieur suddenly
Snared; let each man to his charge! *Again*
BOURBON Hark, still the noise increaseth!

Enter LANOVE, [CLOVIS], LAMOT, *and others*

BRISSAC By the sound, this is a shout of joy and not of dread;
Lanove, the news?
CLOVIS Brissac, Dumain, Martel, and you the rest,
Think not I come a traitor to your camp;
I cannot gild my speech with eloquence.
If this will serve you, sir, I am a friend.
BRISSAC The Monsieur's welcome, and his worth will grace
The dignity of this day's work in hand.
CLOVIS My almost-brother once, suffice I thank you,
And fairly greet this brave assembly
Whose souls do look for stirring opposites,[227]
When your resistance I fear will be slender.
But were they centupled,[228] I'll fight your cause;
Kings arm their subjects when they break their laws.
ALL Long live the Monsieur.
CLOVIS Lead on, away.
Exeunt

Act V, scene ii

Enter the EUNUCH, *whilst the waits*[229] *play softly, and solemnly draws the canopy, where the* QUEEN *sits at one end bound with* LANDREY *at the other,*[230] *both as asleep*

EUNUCH Here sits our beldam dieted for venery,[231]

224 3 The state is like an infected or ulcerous wound that must be punctured with a blade (lance) in order to draw out the infection
225 7 Who is he?
226 9 little noised: unknown, not yet reported
227 27 stirring opposites: worthy opponents
228 29 centupled: multiplied by one hundred
229 0 SD *waits*: musicians who play incidental music for the play, most likely woodwind instrumentalists
230 0 SD QUEEN *sits … the other*: the action of the scene suggests that the musicians are stationed "above" in the balcony and the queen and Landrey are positioned in the discovery space such that they can be concealed from, and later revealed to, the others onstage (see "draws the curtain" at line 142 SD)
231 1 dieted for venery: the queen eats to embellish or enhance her sexual pleasure (ironic since she is being starved)

And by her, her Landrey, not surfeited;
Her ladyship's allowed a mouldy crust,
He, stinking water to piece out his life.
Between them both, they banquet like one slave,
Condemned perpetually to the bordello.[232]
They think I know not that they thus are used,
When it is only I that use them thus.
How wickedly they look! O, I could laugh
To hear them rail at other's[233] misery;
He curses her, and she, sooth, curses him,
And both each other damn for their offences.
Learn ye that pamper up your flesh for lust:
The Eunuch in his wickedness is just.
[*To musicians*] Play louder, they sleep too long.
QUEEN A mischief take thee, keeper, hardened dog[234]
Whom no distress can melt or mollify;
The cruel king doth not deny us sleep,
Although the nursers of it: food and ease.
EUNUCH Peace, peace, ye villains, cease that ruder noise
That breaks your softer slumbers. Gentle Queen,
I am not guilty of these harsh-voiced words
Your wilder sense hurl at me. You mistake:
I am your Eunuch, one that weeps for you. [*Steps forward*]
QUEEN O Castrato, waste not those tears in vain!
Come hither and I'll catch those falling drops
Which prodigally over-flow their banks;
There's nectar in thine eye, O let me drink it;
These agèd cisterns are grown dry, and yield
Not one relenting drop to ease my thirst.
Castrato, pity me, my veins are parched,
And this same flesh which walls about my soul
Chops[235] with excessive heat. A little water,
Castrato, but a little, though it hath been
The birth of toads, or what the lepers bathed in.
O show thy love but in a little water,
What can a queen ask less, or subject grant her?
EUNUCH Though I be tortured for it, yet I'll do it. *Exit* EUNUCH
QUEEN It hath quenched half my thirst to find some pity.
LANDREY I cannot bite mine arm; their tyranny
Denies me what's mine own to feed upon.
One mouthful would suffice; I cannot get it.
Poor unfed sides[236] that pass along the street,
I now am sensible of what ye want;
Did I e'er think to die for want of food,
Whose table was the world, from whence I culled
The rarities of nature to delight me,
And more to feed my lust than appetite?
One bit of bread, though it were gray with age,
Hoary and crusted with a second bark,

232 6 bordello: brothel
233 10 other's: i.e. one another's
234 16 keeper, hardened dog: the queen does not yet know that her jailer is Castrato
235 33 Chops: chaps
236 43: unfed sides: starving beggars

Whose loathèd outside would not court a dog
Armed with the edge of appetite, would seem
A rare rich banquet to my empty gorge.
O I am worn to nothing with this want,
Such emptiness has hunger made of me
That you may draw me on another man.[237]
Some bread, some bread!

Enter EUNUCH *with wine and meat, he congees*[238] *with great reverence and ceremony to the* QUEEN

QUEEN O thou art welcome!
Quick, dear Eunuch, quick; what needs this delay?
Away with form and ceremonious duty,
Respect in this is too respectless.
EUNUCH O give me leave, I will begin a health;[239]
It's very good, exceeding pleasant wine.
QUEEN Dost thou deride my sufferance?
EUNUCH No, no, not I.
QUEEN Give me the drink, then, I'm all flame and fire.
EUNUCH Say you so, say you so? Then you must pardon me,
I love your safety, and it's dangerous
To drink while you are hot; pray cool and tarry.
In the meanwhile, I will begin to you:[240]
How tart and pleasing this is to the palate,
A sweeter pheasant Christendom affords not.
LANDREY I thank thee, Eunuch; prithee give it me.
EUNUCH You'll let me taste it for you, will you not?
Are you so sharply set?[241] Fie, this sauce is naught.[242]
LANDREY Prithee make haste, hunger digests no tasters.
EUNUCH Come sir, I must feed you. O, O, not so fast,
Be not so hasty; here, still you are too hasty; *He puts it to* [LANDREY'S] *mouth, and pulls it away again*
Gentle sir, it will digest the better.
LANDREY More, more; O, it is excellent.
EUNUCH Madam, here's for you now.
QUEEN May heaven reward thee for't, O it's rare.
EUNUCH How do you like your banquet, great Landrey?
LANDREY Beyond compare.
EUNUCH And you your drink?
QUEEN The gods taste not the like.
EUNUCH Ha, ha, ha, y'have both eat and drunk abominable poison.
QUEEN Ha!
LANDREY How!
EUNUCH 'Tis true, I tell your oracle;
There's not an hour's life between ye both;
The poison's sure, I did prepare it for ye,
And have myself taken an antidote.
What say now to th'other bout[243] with Landrey?

237 56 draw me on another man: I am grown so thin that I could be sketched or drawn on another man (i.e. I am so empty that I could contain another figure)
238 57 SD *congees*: bows courteously
239 62 begin a health: drink a toast
240 69 begin to you: drink to you first
241 74 sharply set: hungry
242 74 naught: no good, spoiled
243 93 th'other bout: another sexual encounter

I can procure a second meeting for you,
Indeed I can; think you not whoredom sweet
Now you are a-dying? Is not your soul at ease,
The murder of your husband but a toy,
A flea-biting? Alack, you feel it not.
QUEEN Inhumane slave, treacherous rascal. LANDREY *gets loose*
EUNUCH Good words, lady whore, good words. What, are you loose?
Miraculous famine, has your empty guts
Persuaded you to valor? Will it scratch or bite?
I'm sure it has no weapon; Monsieur disarmed it.
[LANDREY] *shows a keen knife which he pulls out of his sleeve, staggers with faintness*
LANDREY He did so, rascal, yet your curious search
Ne'er pried into this sheath; do you see this:
With mine own hands it had let forth mine own life,
Had the proud Monsieur trusted us to any,
Thyself excepted, whom I now perceive
The only author of our misery— *The* EUNUCH *tripped up his heels in scuffle and sits on him* [*also disarms him*]
You're very nimble, hell-hound!
EUNUCH O lord sir, you know the cause,
I'm lighter by a stone[244] or two than you,
Yet I am weight enough to keep you down.
Stir and thou diest—now sir, what say you to me?
How did you like your old queen? Was she gamesome?
Did she apply herself like an apt whore
Unto your loose embraces?
LANDREY Dog, let me rest.
EUNUCH Good my lord, pardon me,
Under your grace's favor be it spoken,
You are our cushion, and I'll sit on you.
I am not very heavy, am I sir? *Jolts upon him*
I do not altogether weigh a man.
QUEEN Villainous traitor,
O let him rise, and wreak thy spite on me.
EUNUCH You cog, now; you'd rather I should kill.[245]
QUEEN O spare him, spare him; Eunuch, save my servant,
And I'll forgive thee all thy sins against me;
There's not an injury thou dost to him,
But wounds me to the soul.
EUNUCH Pray then look here,
How easily this skean[246] is sheathed in him; [*Stabs* LANDREY]
An engine of his own preparing, lady,
And pity it were so brave a gentleman,
Such a neat[247] hopeful whoremaster as he,
Should die by any weapon but his own;
So perish all that love adultery.
There, sit you there again. Once more to you, *He sets him in his chair*
Who, if your poison do not work too fast,
Shall see more sights like these before you die.

244 112 stone: unit of measurement equal to fourteen pounds
245 125 To "cog" is to pretend or to cheat, for example at dice or games; in order to torment the queen the Eunuch suggests that she's only pretending as she pleads for Landrey's life
246 130 skean: knife or dagger
247 133 neat: elegant, finely made

But lest you should prevent us with your tongue,
I will be bold to gag your ladyship;
I'll leave a peeping hole through which you shall
See sights shall kill[248] thee faster than thy poison. *Draws the curtain again*
I am prepared now for Aphelia's death.
All things are ready, and behold the king.
Now for my part.

Enter CLOTAIR *melancholy*

CLOTAIR I am too pitiful; a watery flux,[249]
Which soft and tender-hearted men call tears,
Stand on mine eyes, and does express a nature
Too like my bearer. It is now with me
Full tide in sorrow; my Cynthia[250] governs strongly.
EUNUCH How fares the great Clotair?
CLOTAIR What do the wise,
Castrato, call the moisture which presumes
To meditate betwixt my wrath and me?
EUNUCH Expressions of a weak and silly nature,
Passion of fools and women. Are you a man
And bear so tame a soul, such a smock[251] spirit?
The distaff[252] owns more spleen, more noble anger.
Pray let her live until the pages write
An hopping balladry verse-rhyme upon you:[253]
"Great Clotair had a wife and she was fair,
Yea fairer than the flowery meads in May." *Scoffingly*
O she was fair, yet foul; most riddling sense;
O, it is horrid. Then, to conclude,
In what a high strain you did take revenge,
How like your house and honor, hark, how she dies,
Strangled in tears fall'n from the cuckold's eyes.
You are her husband, sir, and now must own
Her doubtful issue and her lawless lust.
Although a bull should leap her, you must father,
And have a drove of forkèd animals
Shall have their horns born with them to the sound;[254]
'Twill save their prodigal wives the reeky[255] labor.
CLOTAIR Marry a whore? Father a bastard issue?
EUNUCH I tell you truth; there's no avoiding it.
CLOTAIR Come, bring her forth.

Enter APHELIA, *dragged by two ruffians, in her petticoat and hair*[256]

248 142 sights shall kill: sights that shall kill
249 146 flux: abnormally copious discharge
250 150 Cynthia: another name for Artemis, the Greek goddess of the hunt and moon (Diana in Roman mythology); as goddess of the moon, Cynthia had dominion over the tides; in other words, Clothair is visibly weepy
251 156 smock: effeminate, womanish
252 157 distaff: spinning wheel (spinning was women's work)
253 158–9 until the … upon you: until you become the subject of gossip and ridicule, memorialized in a ballad written by servants
254 171 to the sound: to the sound of their birth, i.e. the cries of their laboring mother. The phrase perhaps also plays on the dual sense of "horns," meaning both the horns of an animal and the musical instrument, which could drown out the sound of the mother's cries
255 172 reeky: blackened, filthy
256 175 SD *petticoat and hair*: dressed only in an undergarment and with loose or unbound hair

APHELIA Use not such violence, good gentlemen,
I'll walk a lamb[257] to slaughter, not repine
At any torments you shall put me to,
Only be modest. Commend me to my lord.
I doubt I never shall behold him more,
For by the calculation of your looks
I have not long to live.[258]
CLOTAIR True, Aphelia, confess and turn thy fate; give me to know
With what foul monster thou hast wronged thy soul,
Seam-rent that holy weed,[259] virginity,
And ease me of a load that bears more weight
Than what my youthful sins have heaped upon me.
APHELIA If e'er my lord—
CLOTAIR No more of that, it tends to madness.
I'll force it from thee; bring forth the tortures there.
I'll try if in these fiery instruments *Enter man with pan and irons*
There lie a tongue which better can persuade
Confession from thee; these, red hot, applied
Unto thy breast adulterate, shall extract
All future hope to suckle lawless issue.
The poisonous springs which from these hills arise
Shall have their fountainhead dammed up by these.
APHELIA I've heard you swear that you were poor in words,
And knew not to express the happiness
Which you conceived was habitable here.[260]
How much my lord is altered from himself!
CLOTAIR 'Tis thou art altered. True, Aphelia,
That whilst thy purer thoughts did awe thy will,
I loved like an idolater. I was possessed
That these two twins, these globes of flesh, contained
All that was happy both in earth and heaven.
In this, I could descry the Milky Way,
The maiden zone that girds the waist of heaven;
In this, the seat of paradise, and how
The wanton rivulets played about the isle
Which puzzle yet geography. All this I could,
I could in thee, my sometime-chaste Aphelia,
Find and rejoice in; but thou art now
An undressed[261] wilderness wherein I walk,
Losing my self 'mongst multitude of beasts;
O savage actions! Come, dispatch.
APHELIA Sir—?
CLOTAIR I'll hear no more.
APHELIA Heaven will, then;
And though it bear an ear far distant hence,
Both hear and pity me. O my loved lord,
Should but a dream work on my fancy
That you were thus to suffer as I am,
It would conspire to kill me with more speed

257 177 walk a lamb: walk as a lamb
258 180–82 I doubt . . . to live: based on my interpretation of your expression, I do not believe I will ever see my lord again
259 185 Seam-rent that holy weed: ripped or torn the sacred garment of your virginity
260 200 here: her person, more specifically her breasts
261 214 undressed: disordered, unkempt, unweeded

Than these your threatening ministers. Alas,
I'll force a gentler nature in the steel,
And with my rainy eyes weep out their heat,
Which as it dies, should hiss itself to scorn
For offering to contain but fire to hurt you;
And will you then a bold spectator stand,
Smiling at what I suffer? Shed but one tear,
Or counterfeit a sorrow for my sake,
A little seeming woe, and I shall die
Sick of your kindness, not your cruelty.
CLOTAIR O my soft temper, her sweet harmony
Will melt me into fool. To hear these words,
The mother[262] is too busy in mine eyes;
What shall I do?
EUNUCH Make a new hell,
And if thou canst, create more devils, do,
And they will find employment all on her;
For since the general creation
Time never did produce a fouler sinner,
Or one more beggared hell in punishing.[263]
CLOTAIR Thou hast awaked me. Whore, will you confess?
Do not enforce your death through willfulness; *Drags her by the hair*
Speak, stubborn silence, or I'll break thy heart.
APHELIA My lord and husband, O my lord and husband,
Regard my misery and pity me.
CLOTAIR Thou'rt cruel to thyself, I wrong thee not;
It is not I that tear this precious fleece, *[Drags her] again*
This glorious excrement,[264] in validity
Another Colchis[265] better seeming Jason;
I pull not off these curious sporting tresses, *Again*
Fit braids to captive[266] kings hadst thou been honest.
I wound thee not; confess, and live as free
As mountain air. I will not injure thee.
APHELIA My gracious prince—I dare not call you husband,
Your actions do forbid which write me slave,
And not your equal—if to be your wife
Has plucked this misery upon my head,
Or caused in you this frenzy, put me off,
I will endure it patiently, but if e'er—
CLOTAIR The old tune this, come, come, the irons there. *They bind her to the chair, the* EUNUCH *much sears her breast*
APHELIA O, O, O, cruel, my lord, unmanly;
I will not curse yet heaven, no, nor blaspheme,
Although mine injuries would half persuade
Gods are not, or are deaf to innocents.[267]

Enter a SOLDIER *hastily with his sword drawn*

262 235 The mother: maternal emotion; tears

263 241 Or one who would more exhaust hell's ability to punish her than Aphelia would

264 249 excrement: outgrowth of hair

265 250 Colchis: location of the Golden Fleece won by Jason and the Argonauts; here the location seems to be used to stand for the fleece itself. He suggests that had Aphelia been chaste, her hair would have been more precious than this mythical fleece

266 252 captive: ensnare

267 265 Either no gods exist or if they do, they do not care about the plight of the innocent

SOLDIER Arm, arm, my lord, the castle's walled about
With living clay! Three times ten thousand men,
Approvèd warriors, souls of blood and fire
That only know to do, and not to suffer,
Make head against you. Believe me, sir,
A braver troop, and spirits more resolved,
Life never put in action. Young Brissac,
Now old enough to quit his father's death,
Together with the ruin of his sister,
Has vowed destruction to your name and ashes.
CLOTAIR Let them come on, we'll dare them do their worst;
This castle will endure a fortnight's siege
Before the expiration of which time
My brother with his fellow peers of France
Shall whip these rebels for their insolence.
Know'st thou ought else—why dost thou shake thy head?

Enter another SOLDIER

2 SOLDIER Fly, fly, my lord!
CLOTAIR Villain, it is no language for a prince! *Strikes him*
2 SOLDIER Then stand upon your guard—yet, that's as bad.
The castle's walled about with walking steel,
And you but tempt your death in your escape,
If you stay here—provoke it.
The Monsieur, like the god of war, bestrides
A bounding courser, who is therefore proud
To be so backed, as knowing whom he bears.
So, centaur-like, he's anchored to his seat
As he had twinned with the proud steed he rides on.
He grows unto his saddle all one piece,
And that unto his horse, who thus unmoved
Sits like a Perseus on his Pegasus,[268]
Stable and fleet—who at head of all his troops
With words inflames 'em that did burn before,
But now appear much brighter; their glistering arms
Reflecting 'gainst the sun doth lightning mock,
Unto which blaze, their drums and horses' hooves
Do not want much of thunder. Such is the show,
As if great Mars, angry with humane race,
Did lead the gods to battle 'gainst the earth.
EUNUCH How does your grace? How fares your majesty?
CLOTAIR The Monsieur? Did he not name the Monsieur?
2 SOLDIER I did, my lord.
CLOTAIR Is he joined with them too?
Then doomsday is at hand; I see my ruin.
Go to the castle walls to summon them
To render an account of their intents.
Ask the proud Monsieur (though I know the cause) *Looks on* APHELIA
Why his presumptuous and ambitious feet
Have on the bosom of his mother earth
Made a broad road of treason. Go, begone. *Exeunt* SOLDIERS
Castrato, thou dost love me, I'm sure thou dost;

268 295 Pegasus: the winged horse that sprung from the blood of the Gorgon Medusa when Perseus struck off her head

I have such proofs of thy true hearted-love,
That I must put my life into thy hands.
Thou see'st how all things stand: my wife, she's false;
Her brother seeks my life; the Monsieur's thoughts
(Backed with the ever-factious souls of France)
Aim at the Gallic crown and dignity,
Whilst I a caitiff[269] and neglected prince
Must fall by traitors' hands.
EUNUCH What mean you, sir?
CLOTAIR Look, here's a pistol in whose womb lies death,
A heavy, leaden sleep.
EUNUCH Would you I should
Try the conclusion here? Make her confess
By other instruments her horrid guilt?
In this, there's too much mercy.
CLOTAIR Hear me speak.
I'll trouble her no further; let her sin
Be punished from above. I'll wait heaven's leisure.
Here, Eunuch, take thou this; it was prepared
For the adulterate Landrey. Here, receive it,
And if thou lov'st me, use it upon me.
Come, shoot me through. I know I shall be slain,
(If not by thee, yet by the enemy)
And therefore to prevent the bitter scorn
Of the insulting foe (which is a death
So full of horror to the conquered,
No tyranny is like it) use this handful.
The handsom'st weed that nature can produce
In the large storehouse of her providence,
Can show no simple[270] like it; for this cures
At once the sickness of the mind and body.
Thou shalt, I know thou wilt, I prithee take it;
It is not murder, tender-hearted fool,
Which thou commits; rather, a sacrifice
For which heaven will reward thee.
EUNUCH I do not know the nature of your gods,
Yet on your words I'll try their kindness. [EUNUCH *takes the pistol*]
CLOTAIR Nobly resolved. Come, shoot me quickly, then.
EUNUCH (*Aside*) I never was liker t'express myself
Than at this minute; do not betray me, tears,
The Eunuch's nature must be harsh and cruel.[271]
APHELIA O spare him Eunuch, spare him, save my lord,
And I'll forgive thee all thy sins 'gainst me.
EUNUCH Peace, foolish woman, 'tis thou that kill'st thy lord.
Were't not for thee he might live long and happy;
Pray let me kiss your hand, and take my leave
Of my best, best master.
CLOTAIR Do't and be sudden then. Ah, what means this?
As [EUNUCH] *kisses* [CLOTAIR'S] *hand,* [EUNUCH] *snatches out* [CLOTAIR's] *sword*
EUNUCH Marry sir, this it means,
That if this fail, this shall perform the deed.

269 321 caitiff: wretched
270 341 simple: preparation or concoction of medicinal herbs
271 350–52 I never ... and cruel: this aside is the first obvious indication that the Eunuch may not be what he appears; see Introduction

Think not but I will kill you, do not fear;
I am the excellent'st he alive at these same toys.[272]
Look here, my cozened fool—I do not bungle. [EUNUCH] *shows* LANDREY *and the* QUEEN [*in the discovery space*]
CLOTAIR Are these dead, then?
EUNUCH As sure as you live; pray, ask them else.
Unless this ewe's flesh[273] too intense in heat
Be lingering yet behind; she's scarcely dead,
But in her dying ears I'll howl this noise:
Look, Queen, here's the top-branch of all thy family;
Mark but how kindly for thy sake I'll use him.
CLOTAIR Then I perceive I have been much abused,
So has my chaster queen; O my curst fate!
EUNUCH O, do you so, do you so.[274]
QUEEN O, O, O. QUEEN *dies*
EUNUCH There broke a strumpet's heart. Hear me, King,
Thy mother was a foul adulteress,
A cruel butcherer of innocents.
Witness thy brother, that thy mother's false;
Witness thine own eyes that beheld the fall
And ruin of the Dumain family.
Thy mother's deep in blood, for which she's damned.
You ravished fair Chrotilda; Clodimir,
Your valiant uncle, brother to this queen,
Was for the foul fact slain, for which mistake
Dumain, Lamot, Maria, Isabel,
And the abused Chrotilda (if by flight
She had not saved her life) had fallen with them.
I knowing this, and ever pitying
The wrongs that they endured,
Have found it time thus to revenge them.
CLOTAIR What were their wrongs to thee?
EUNUCH I'll not capitulate[275] mine injuries— *Beat a march softly within*[276]
I hear my time is short.
CLOTAIR How fain would I preserve my life from death
Since my Aphelia's chaste; to think her false
(Not that I fear the foe) made me despair
Of future comfort. Eunuch, spare my life;
I will forgive thee, and reward thee, too.
Remember who it is that sues to thee.
EUNUCH [*Aside*] In that remembrance I have lost myself.
I cannot strike him; my relenting heart
Yearns on his princely person.—Take your sword,
But on condition, Clotair, thou shalt swear
By thy descent, thy princely parentage,
By the wronged souls of all those innocents
To thy lust sacrificed,[277] by Aphelia's self,

272 363 I am the most skilled man alive with these weapons

273 367 ewe's flesh: Fredigond, who burns from the effects of the poison; "ewe" also encompasses the injured Aphelia who earlier compared herself to a "lamb to slaughter" (line 177)

274 374 do you so: the stage action is unclear; the Eunuch is perhaps watching, reacting to, or commenting on the queen's death agonies, Clotair's own despairing actions, or both

275 392 capitulate: specify or enumerate

276 392 SD: the sound of Clovis's approaching soldiers is heard off-stage

277 406 sacrificed: Q reads "satisfied" here, but "sacrificed" makes more sense in context; "perhaps a compositor's error" (Morley, 2006)

Or anything thy soul shall hold more dear,
Upon receipt to guide the fatal point
Directly to my heart.
CLOTAIR Why wouldst thou so?
EUNUCH Pish, I'll teach thee to be speedy in the fact.
Remember how thy royal father fell;
Behold thy mother murdered by this hand;
Into thy bosom cast thine inward eyes
And view the sorrows I have heaped on thee.
Look on Aphelia, and let her wrongs
Prompt thy slow hand to this most timely slaughter;
I cannot brook delay: or do, or suffer.[278]
CLOTAIR A heathen and a traitor die with thee! [CLOTAIR *stabs the* EUNUCH]
EUNUCH A Christian heathen, Clotair, if thou wilt,
Made so by thee; read that, and break thy heart. [*Hands letter to* CLOTAIR]

Enter the Monsieur and his company

CLOVIS Force ope the door, seize on his royal person. Now, Clotair,
Thou are the Monsieur's prisoner; tyrant, say
Where is Aphelia your adulteress? [CLOTAIR] *stands amazed*[279]
CLOTAIR It makes no matter where.
BRISSAC O my dear sister, O my dearest life.
DUMAIN See, noble lords,
Here lies that hell-hound Eunuch; villain, up
And tell us who has done these fatal deeds.
EUNUCH They're near allied to thee that did these acts:
Chrotilda, and a woman.
DUMAIN Villain, thou liest; my sister's gone a weary pilgrimage,
And for this many years, with grief I speak it,
Been traveled none knows where.
CLOTAIR What am I?
What strange and uncouth thing?
EUNUCH A ravisher,
And better to instruct thee in thyself—
Had not Chrotilda been, incestuous.[280] [CLOTAIR *moves to kill himself*]
ALL Hold, hold your royal hand; what will you do?
CLOTAIR What else but follow her? Shall Clotair live
A captive to his brother, slaved to sin,
Enthralled in wedlock that's incestuous,
A ravisher and murderer of his friend?
There's no way left to rid me but my sword
Of all these ills at once. O wronged Chrotilda!
DUMAIN My sister?
CLOTAIR Ay Dumain, no Eunuch she,
No sunburned vagabond of Ethiope
Though entertained for such by Fredigond.
I say here lies thy ravished sister, slain
By me, the ravisher.

278 417 or do, or suffer: either kill me or suffer

279 423 SD *stands amazed*: Morley assigns this stage direction to Clovis; I find it more credible assigned to Clotair as he reads from the letter (note that at III. iii. 89 SD Clovis "*stands [forth] amazed*" as he watches Clotair propose to Aphelia at his sham funeral)

280 436 incestuous: that is, had the Eunuch not prevented the consummation of Clotair's marriage to Aphelia he'd have been guilty of the sin of incest (i.e. having sex with his brother's promised wife)

DUMAIN Hold, hold, my heart.
EUNUCH Lend me thy hand, Clotair, have I thy hand?
CLOTAIR Thou most abused of womankind, thou hast.
EUNUCH I should have killed thee, King, and had put on
A masculine spirit to perform the deed.
Alas, how frail our resolutions are!
A woman's weakness conquered my revenge.
I'd spirit enough to quit my father's wrongs,
And they which should have seen me act that part
Would not believe I should so soon prove haggard.[281]
But there is something dwells upon thy brow
Which did persuade me to humanity;
Thou injured'st me, and yet I spared thy life;
Thou injured'st me, yet I would fall by thee,
And like to my soft sex, I fall and perish. [*Dies*]
CLOTAIR Speak, forever speak; Chrotilda, Chrotilda.
DUMAIN My sister's in mine eyes. This brave revenge
Should have been mine, and not thy act, Chrotilda.
Away salt rheum,[282] Chrotilda laughs at thee,
Her spirit is more manly.
APHELIA I must weep, too.
Mine injuries and hers are so near kin
That they must bear each other company
In tears of blood and death;
For my grieved heart, too long with earth,
Would gladly seek a way to find out rest.
CLOTAIR Art thou joined with her, too, against thyself?
Will my Aphelia leave me? Pardon, sweet,
My love is fatal, and too well thou know'st
The deadly proof in fair Chrotilda's death.
Yet leave me not, though I refrain thy bed,
And must abandon all those thoughts of love
Which married couples use; yet we may sit
And gaze upon each other, tell sad tales
Of ruined princes, wronged virginity,
And when our utterance is tired by speech,
We'll sit and sigh a sad parenthesis,[283]
And then proceed again, then sigh again
A silent chorus to our history.
Our tears shall keep our sorrows ever green,
Still springing, never ripe. Shall we do thus
To lengthen out our grief?
APHELIA Forever, King.
The hand of heaven lies on me, for I feel
My inward and external injuries
Wrestle with life, in which condition
My soul is worried[284] by that tyrant, death.
I must forsake thee, Clotair. [*Dies*]
CLOTAIR Stay awhile; it is unkindly done to leave me thus.

281 457 haggard: wild and intractable person, usually female; a haggard is a hawk caught as an adult and therefore difficult to train. Chrotilda suggests that by veering from her intentions she has failed as a revenger

282 466 salt rheum: tears

283 483 parenthesis: digression

284 492 worried: taken by the throat, choked

O she is gone forever, ever gone;
And I stand prating here between them both,
The fatal cause of death unto them both.
Wilt thou not break, proud heart? I prithee, break;
Prove not a rebel to thy prince like these.
It's well there is some loyalty in thee yet;
Thou art commanded by me— *The* KING *faints [and then revives]*
BRISSAC Gracious my liege.
CLOTAIR Charles, I have injured thee, and thee, Dumain.
Can ye forgive me?
BRISSAC Good your grace,
Call back your spirits; think what's to be done.
CLOTAIR I consider well, and the new king,
The quondam[285] Monsieur, shall not deny me this:
Half of the honors of the dead Landrey
We do confer on thee; the other half
Be thine, Dumain. Charles shall be Duke of France,
Thou of the palace Major.[286] This is our will.
DUMAIN Great king, you are not yet so near your end;
Forfend it, heaven.
BRISSAC Look up, my gracious lord.
CLOVIS My royal brother?
CLOTAIR I begin to faint,
A darkness like to death hangs on mine eyes.
Lend me thine hand, Brissac, and thine, Dumain.
Good gentle souls, when ye shall mention me,
And elder time shall rip these stories up
Dissected and anatomized by you,
Touch sparingly this story; do not read
Too harsh a comment on this loathèd deed
Lest you enforce posterity to blast
My name and memory with endless curses.
Call me an honorable murderer,
And finish there, as I do. *He dies*
DUMAIN O noble lord,
Whose fame was very essence to his soul.
That gone, the other fled, choosing to die
Rather than live a king in infamy.
CLOVIS A heavy spectacle of grief and woe
Have we beheld since our arrival here.
Take up the body of the king, and these
That for his love on either hand lie slain;
They shall lie buried in one monument.
And take up these; this was a royal queen
When virtue steered her thoughts; but we may see,
When we turn foes to good, to vice a friend,
We fall like these, and like these thus we end.
A dead march[287] within

FINIS.

285 506 quondam: former
286 510 of the palace Major: Major (i.e. officer in command) of the palace
287 536 SD *dead march*: funeral march

4 Thomas Heywood, *The Four Prentices of London*

First performed c. 1594

First printed 1615

Edited by William N. West

Thomas Heywood's *The Four Prentices of London* is close to a perfect play: an elaborate, resourceful fantasy that leads its audiences into the far-fetched adventures of its protagonists, satisfying ambitions and desires they might not have known they had. Not many audiences or readers have ventured this opinion—at least not those who left an account of their reactions to it. In *The Knight of the Burning Pestle* (c. 1607) a grocer recommends it as the kind of thing he would like to see more of—"Read the play of *The Four Prentices of London*, where they toss their pikes so"—but the point of the scene seems to be that the grocer's taste is awful. In his prefatory letter to the printed text of *Four Prentices* even Heywood acknowledges that it was done "in my infancy of judgement in this kind of poetry." Later scholars and critics have not been much kinder. But these judgments come from audiences who record their accounts. That the play's spectacular action is explicitly cited in another play means that even then, eight years before any edition we know of, *Four Prentices* had a recognizability matched by only a few other plays of the period: *Tamburlaine*, *The Spanish Tragedy*, *Romeo and Juliet*, *Hamlet*. The earliest extant quarto of *Four Prentices* was published in 1615 (reprinted without significant change in 1631), with Heywood's apologetic letter placing its composition "fifteen or sixteen years ago." If Heywood's letter was written not long after 1610, when the military musters that he praises resumed, *Four Prentices* has a history of demonstrable popularity of nearly four decades, without ever having been enshrined in a fancy folio. While those who wrote down their opinions did not find much to admire in *Four Prentices*, other publics voted with their feet and their pennies, and rewarded it.

For those other playgoers, the "honest and high-spirited Prentices" whom Heywood addresses in his letter as its intended "readers," the play offers just about everything. As apprentices in the great livery companies from which the citizenry and ultimately the government of London was drawn, the titular Four Prentices stand near the bottom of London's civic structure. But although apprenticeship might have been the lowest rung in London's official hierarchy, at least it was on the ladder, and an apprentice could anticipate advancement. He might aspire to become a master of his trade, opening his own shop, employing his own apprentices; he might marry his master's daughter or even his widow, and take over both his business and his household. He could rise in the hierarchy of his company, perhaps someday reaching the level of Alderman or even Lord Mayor of London and thereby earn a knighthood. Apprentices could also expect, after completing their term of indenture to their masters, to become citizens of London and reap the benefits. These were considerable enough that many inhabitants of London (among them numerous playwrights, players, and playhouse entrepreneurs) were affiliated with guilds whose trades they did not practice, solely because of the privileges membership brought. But the pleasure of looking ahead to privileges was purchased by deferring present enjoyments. All the things an apprentice might hope for must have seemed distant from the immediate drudgery of fetching water for his master's household or minding his shop.

Four Prentices expands and shortcuts the apprentice's optimistic but unromantic horizons. Unlike most apprentices, the play's heroes Godfrey, Charles, Guy, and Eustace are brothers of noble birth, turning to their trades after their father, the Earl of Boulogne, unjustly lost his holdings. Settled in London, they adopt the routines of the urban citizenry that must have been familiar to the play's early audiences. From there, though, their trajectory is different, probably unforeseeable except by avid consumers of the chivalric romances in print or on stage: they join an army to free the Holy Land from Muslim rule, survive shipwreck, don disguises and mistake identities, rise by their merits, travel and travail, battle fierce enemies and contend with rivals in their own camp, recognize lost relatives, discover love (Guy, anyway), win crowns, and earn lasting memory in the histories of the livery companies of which the four brothers are members. The play proposes its more exciting path to success through a particular vison of competitive self-assertion of one's superiority to others in every context, but especially in the pleasures of combat as physical exertion and harmless violence. It makes everything a contest. It shows little interest in sexual attractions, despite ample opportunities. Guy hardly knows what to make of the French Lady's description of the courtly love she wants him to offer her. Bella Franca's irresistibility to everyone is a pretext for duels and challenges rather than a more reflective exploration of desire. One word for such solipsistic fantasies of self-promoting competition might be "adolescent." Another, though, might be "chivalric" or "aristocratic." The brothers express their aspirationally aristocratic tastes for violence, honor, and display by yearning after noble entertainments like hawking and hunting. At the same time, they show their good faith as ordinary prentices by liking football or taking up clubs to brawl in the street. It is telling of the prentices' particular formation that when Eustace speaks of jousts and courtly dances, he imagines being a spectator rather than a participant, as someone of higher birth and greater wealth might. The prentices lace their chivalric adventures with the practical values of their masters: they praise the city that "made princes tradesmen" and that is suspicious (even while admiring and envious) of "drone[s]" who can do no work (I.i. 66–70). The hodgepodge climax of the four brothers triumphantly liberating Jerusalem, becoming kings, and then proudly hanging up the arms of their companies so that each "shield may be an honor to my trade" combines two fantasies of success—one reflecting the personal and militaristic codes of romance chivalry, the other the local and communal values of the diligent London tradesmen—and fuses them without a thought to their incongruous fit. To be a hero is to free the Holy Land and (thus) to make a name for oneself in the Guild Hall.

Neither this double consciousness nor the play's capacity to overlook it is especially surprising. The culture of the city and the middling sort whose numbers included the apprentices was openly aspirational of aristocratic culture. Like noble families, the great livery companies bore coats of arms, which feature as a powerful visual reference throughout the play. The arms of the brothers' four livery companies appear on the illustrated title page, and the play ends with them saluting their shields decorated with their companies' arms and probably hanging them up on stage. Each brother expresses a desire to "add/Some honor" (III.ii. 181–2) to his guild's arms, that is, to augment it by adding a new feature commemorating some singular achievement. With the exception of Eustace, these "honors" all appear in the company arms of Heywood's time, allowing the play's early audiences to confirm its version of history by checking the evidence it directs them towards.

Across this armature of fantasies, *Four Prentices* draws a shimmering net of exotic names and events. Like its etiologies of the arms of the livery companies, the play's use of history and geography is almost completely opportunistic. History enters in the form of vivid lists of names—a non-consecutive "chronicle" of crusader kings, eastern empires, and historical figures like William the Conqueror or Tancred of Galilee. These rarely add up in any coherent way. A Godfrey of Boulogne did conquer Jerusalem, and a Guy of Lusignan ruled it, but they were not brothers, and they lived some seventy years apart. Another Guy, of Warwick, was a well-known hero of ballads and other plays. But historical accuracy is not Heywood's aim. Something like a feeling of recognition is, and he fills his story with figures and events that a playgoer might have heard of, if not exactly place. Likewise, the play's world is not to be mapped but enumerated. One shipwreck on Goodwin Sands off the coast of Kent, for instance, improbably washes the four brothers up in the Low Countries, France, Italy, and Ireland. The play's locales are chosen largely for the exotic glamor they provide: Ireland and Jerusalem are equally good at conjuring dreams of new worlds. The Jerusalem the brothers conquer is patched together from phrases dropped in well-known biblical and classical sources. Thomas Platter, a Swiss physician who visited England in 1599 while on a tour of Europe, observed that "for the most part the English don't take the trouble to travel; instead they prefer to watch and experience foreign things in their pastimes while at home." The play's references to London landmarks such as the livery companies' arms or the "London Stone" lend a familiarity to Antiocha Gate or "Jerusalem ye never saw" of the far-off lands in which their adventures take place. But familiarity was by no means the primary effect the plays sought. As the Prologue says: "Had not ye rather, for novelty's sake, see Jerusalem ye never saw, than London that ye see hourly?" (Prologue 25–6). Playgoers to *Four Prentices* could feel at home abroad, and vice versa.

The most consistent commitment of *Four Prentices* is to play itself, to fantasy, amusement, freewheeling but regulated diversions of many kinds, in which it involves and absorbs its beholders. The play is full of references not only to entertainments that an apprentice might watch, such as tiltings, musters, or dances, but also to games in which he might have taken part. The military exercise of tossing the pike is compared to balloon, a more familiar challenge of keeping something aloft; the first assault on Jerusalem turns into a game of king of the mountain, with the Sophy and the Sultan setting up banners and daring the brothers to pull them down. From the frequency with which they occur, it is clear that Heywood thought of the duels and combats among brothers as one of the central attractions of *Four Prentices.* These combats are structured like the fencing contests and prize fights that were often staged in playhouses, with a wide variety of weapons tried and challenge purses staked on the outcome. The plot itself is a kind of game, unfolding for its audiences in surprising ways, showing them new things. It refers often to books, with a literacy that feels popular rather than learned, and solidly anglophone, quoting both Spenser's *Faerie Queene* and Golding's Ovid.

Among the kinds of play that *Four Prentices* explores is the particular kind called a stage-play—its own kind. Perhaps unsurprisingly, *Four Prentices* is full of memories of plays and playing, of the experiences of being a playgoer that seem to have been so much a part of apprenticeship or tenure in the Inns at Court. The high astounding lexicon of the Sultan and the Sophy echoes that of Marlowe's *Tamburlaine* (c. 1590). The brothers' final recognition scene recalls the reunion of Sebastian and Viola in *Twelfth Night*, and when Bella Franca reveals herself to her family, she sounds a lot like Rosalind in *As You Like It*, eager to give nearly everyone what they like. *Four Prentices* also understands the thrill of playgoing, and the importance playgoing had for its audiences. It takes pleasure in reminding its beholders of the experiences of playing they are having as they watch again, now. Its dramaturgy is not innovative, but it exploits a nearly complete range of contemporary possibilities: massed battles, individual duels, presenters, dumbshows, disguises, and rhetorical flourishes. It is full of improbable situations, over and above the journey from Cheapside to Jerusalem. For instance, the brothers, as well as their father and sister, meet repeatedly before they recognize each other, and also frequently muse on how familiar these strangers seem. But *Four Prentices* does not treat the improbabilities of its encounters and disguises as embarrassments. They are moments when the writer celebrates the possibilities of his medium along with its limits, and invites his audience to do the same. Eustace speaks for the audience when he declares that he would leave his master if he could find a drum to follow (I.i. 182). The drum he chooses leads him on crusade, but apprentices watching the play of *Four Prentices* had followed a different one, which customarily paraded through the streets to advertise the beginning of a play.

Four Prentices is confident in its visual power, and the text freely and frequently allows actions on stage to seize the attention and to lead the story forward. The play seems to have found its best eloquence in action. The text abounds in deictics, grammatical markers like "this", "that," or "thus," which rely on gesture and shared reference to something—a far cry from the verbality of much early modern drama, which paints its scenes in words. Stage directions are unusually copious, explaining actions that the dialogue leaves unclear, and key sequences, such as Eustace's and Guy's swapping of identities, or the overthrow of the Sultan and his allies, only make sense if they are visualized. The inclusion of a gorgeous emblematic woodcut on the title pages reflects the play's visual emphasis. It seems at first to capture the brothers at some unspecified moment of action—perhaps when Guy and Eustace toss their pikes, or when Charles and Godfrey are about to fight each other with partisans. In fact it is a scene that appears nowhere but represents everything, like an emblem or a movie poster: four brothers, in armor, spurred for travel, some wearing exotic Eastern scimitars, swinging military weapons. By each brother is his name and the arms of his livery company. Like a tavern sign that allows passersby to identify it and to orient themselves, the title page tells at a glance that this is not just four warriors, but *Four Prentices of London*, striving among themselves and against others, carrying their guild liveries and city values into the foreign East. True and strange.

Textual note

The copy-text for this edition is the quarto of 1615 held in the Newberry Library in Chicago. It was checked against Newberry's copy of the 1631 quarto as well as the EEBO microfilm and transcription of the 1615 quarto.

Further reading

Editions

Gasior, Mary A. (ed.) (1980) *The Four Prentices of London: A Critical Old-Spelling Edition*, New York: Garland.

Critical and contextual reading

Burnett, Mark Thornton (1991) "Apprentice Literature and the 'Crisis' of the 1590s," *The Yearbook of English Studies* 21 (Special Number: Politics, Patronage and Literature in England 1558–1658): 27–38.

Connolly, Annaliese (2011) "Guy of Warwick, Godfrey of Bouillon, and Elizabethan Repertory," in Bernadette Andrea and Linda McJannet (eds), *Early Modern England and Islamic Worlds*, New York: Palgrave Macmillan, 139–58.

Degenhardt, Jane Hwang (2015) "The Metatheatrical Mediterranean: Theatrical Contrivance and Miraculous Reunion in *The Travels of the Three English Brothers, The Four Prentices of London*, and *Pericles*," in Barbara Fuchs and Emily Weissbourd (eds), *Representing Imperial Rivalry in the Early Modern Mediterranean*, Toronto: University of Toronto Press, 163–90.

Howard, Jean (2012) "Thomas Heywood: Dramatist of London and Playwright of the Passions," in Ton Hoenselaars (ed.), *Cambridge Companion to Shakespeare and Contemporary Dramatists*, Cambridge: Cambridge University Press, 120–33.

MacFarlane, Fenella (2001) "To 'Try What London Prentices Can Do': Merchant Chivalry as Representational Strategy in Thomas Heywood's 'The Four Prentices of London'," *Medieval & Renaissance Drama in England* 13: 136–64.

True and Strange, or The Four Prentices of London (c. 1594)

To the honest and high-spirited Prentices, the Readers.[1]

To you (as whom this play most especially concerns) I thought good to dedicate this labor, which though written many years since, in my infancy of judgment in this kind of poetry, and my first practice; yet understanding (by what means I know not) it was in these more exquisite and refined times to come to the press, in such a forwardness ere it came to my knowledge, that it was past prevention, and knowing withal,[2] that it comes short of that accurateness both in plot and style that these more censorious days with greater curiosity acquire, I must thus excuse, that as plays were then some fifteen or sixteen years ago, it was in the fashion.[3] Nor could it have found a more seasonable and fit publication than at this time, when, to the glory of our nation, the security of the kingdom, and the honor of the city, they have begun again the commendable practice of long-forgotten arms,[4] the continuance of which I wish, the discipline approve, and the encouragement thereof even with my soul applaud. In which great and hoped good they deserve not the least attribute of approbation, who, in the dull and sleepy time of peace, first wakened the remembrance of these arms in the Artillery Garden,[5] which, begun out of their voluntary affections, prosecuted by their private industries, and continued at their own proper cost and charge, deserves in my opinion, not only respect and regard, but recompense and reward. But to return again to you, my brave spirited Prentices, upon whom I have freely bestowed these four, I wish you all, that have their courages and forwardness, their noble fates and fortunes,

Yours,

Thomas Heywood.

Dramatis personae[6]

Three PROLOGUES
The OLD EARL OF BULLEN,[7] *sometimes called a Duke*
His four sons
GODFREY *of Bullen, the eldest, apprenticed to the Worshipful Company of Mercers*
GUY, *the second of Old Bullen's sons, apprenticed to the Goldsmiths*
CHARLES, *the third brother, apprenticed to the Haberdashers*

1 1 Prentices, the Readers: the readers may be prentices like the protagonists of the play, but they are also the playwright's prentices in that they are learning this strange and true tale from him
2 5 withal: besides
3 1–8 To you … the fashion: in this tortuous sentence, Heywood apologizes that this play was written long before, when he was an inexperienced writer and when both plays and audiences were less sophisticated. Less convincingly, he explains that it is only being published now because it was given to the printer without Heywood's foreknowledge
4 9–10 they have … long-forgotten arms: this probably refers to the resumption of military musters in the Artillery Garden in Bishopsgate, mentioned in the next sentence, in 1610
5 12–13 they deserve … Artillery Garden: those who organized the musters should be applauded
6 Q includes a list of *dramatis personae*, from which this is adapted
7 BULLEN: pronounced with the accent on the first syllable. Bullen, or Boulogne, is a town in the northern part of France, near the border of Belgium

EUSTACE, *the youngest brother, apprenticed to the Grocers*
BELLA FRANCA, *the daughter of Old Bullen*
An ENGLISH CAPTAIN, *recruiting for Robert of Normandy*
ROBERT OF NORMANDY, *son of William the Conqueror and leader of the Christian army*
A CHORUS, *or Presenter*
The FRENCH KING
A LADY, *the French King's daughter*
The CLOWN, *one of a group of Italian bandits*
[*A* VILLAIN, *another bandit*]
[*An* IRISHMAN, *companion to Eustace*]
TANCRED, *a Prince of Italy, sometimes referred to as the County Palatine*
The SULTAN *of Babylon*[8]
The SOPHY *of Persia*[9]
TURNUS, *a dependent king of the Sophy*
MORETES, *a dependent king of the Sultan*

Mutes, the Bullenois,[10] *Bandits, Irishmen, Ambushes of Pagans, Christian and Muslim soldiers, drummers, trumpeters, and Spaniards*

The Prologue

Enter three [PROLOGUES] *in black cloaks, at three doors*

PROLOGUE 1 What mean you, my masters, to appear thus before your times?[11] Do you not know that I am the Prologue? Do you not see this long black velvet cloak upon my back? Have you not sounded thrice?[12] Do I not look pale, as fearing to be out in my speech? Nay, have I not all the signs of a Prologue about me?[13] Then, to what end come you to interrupt me?
PROLOGUE 2 I have a Prologue to speak, too.
PROLOGUE 3 And I another.
PROLOGUE 1 Oh superfluous, and more than ever I heard of! Three Prologues to one play!
PROLOGUE 2 Have you not seen three ropes to toll one bell, three doors to one house, three ways to one town?
PROLOGUE 1 I grant you: but I never heard of any that had three heads to one body, but Cerberus.[14] But what doth your Prologue mean?
PROLOGUE 2 I come to excuse the name of the play.
PROLOGUE 3 I the errors in the play.
PROLOGUE 1 And I the author that made the play. Touching the name, why is it called, *True and Strange,*[15] *or The Four Prentices of London*? A gentleman that heard the subject discoursed said it was not possible to be true; and none here are bound[16] to believe it.
PROLOGUE 2 'Tis true, that Alexander at thirty years of age conquered the whole world; but strange he should do so. If we should not believe things recorded in former ages, we were not worthy that succeeding times should believe things done in these our ages.
PROLOGUE 1 But what authority have you for your history? I am one of those that will believe nothing that is not in the chronicle.[17]

8 SULTAN *of Babylon*: in this period "Sultan" usually referred to the ruler of the Ottoman Empire, which had its seat in Constantinople and in Heywood's time controlled Jerusalem. Babylon was not a significant center in either the period of the Crusades or the period in which the play was written; Heywood is using the name for its connotations of foreignness
9 SOPHY *of Persia*: ruler of the Persian Empire; "Sophy" is a title derived from "Safi," the name of the ruling dynasty. In Heywood's time, Persia was a rival of the Ottomans and not their ally, but Heywood associates them as Muslim enemies of the European Crusaders
10 *Bullenois*: citizens of the town of Bullen
11 1 before your times: literally, too early, but the First Prologue means that they should not be there at all
12 3 sounded thrice: trumpets were customarily sounded three times at playhouses before the beginning of the show
13 3–4 Nay, have . . . about me?: don't I look like a Prologue?
14 11 Cerberus: gigantic three-headed dog that, in Greek and Roman myth, guarded the realms of the dead
15 15 *Strange*: unusual or surprising, but also foreign
16 16 bound: obligated
17 21 chronicle: a list or narrative of important and less important events from a particular place or institution, proverbially unreliable

PROLOGUE 2 Our authority is a manuscript, a book writ in parchment, which not being public, nor general[18] in the world, we rather thought fit to exemplify to the public censure[19] things concealed and obscured, such as are not common with everyone, than such historical tales as everyone can tell by the fire in winter. Had not ye rather, for novelty's sake, see Jerusalem ye never saw, than London that ye see hourly? So much touching the name of our history.
PROLOGUE 1 You have satisfied me; and, I hope, all that hear me. Now what have you to speak concerning the errors[20] in the play?
PROLOGUE 3 We acknowledge none. For the errors we could find, we would willingly amend; but if these clear-sighted gentlemen,[21] with the eyes of their judgments, looking exactly into us, find any imperfections which are hid from ourselves, our request is, you would rather look over them than through them, not with a troubled eye, that makes one object to seem two, but with a favorable eye, which hath power in itself to make many to seem none at all.
PROLOGUE 1 Oh, now I understand you. Three Prologues to our play—pardon me, y'have need of three hundred, methinks, and all little enough. But to end our beginning in a word, thus much by the patience of these gentlemen.
[ALL] Spectators, should you oppose your judgments against us, where we are three, which some would think too many, were we three thousand,[22] we think ourselves too few. Our Author submits his labors to you, as the authors of all the content[23] he hath within this circumference.[24]
But for your sakes, this only we dare say,
We promised you, and we'll perform, a play.

Act I, scene i

Enter the OLD EARL OF BULLEN *and his daughter* BELLA FRANCA

OLD BULLEN Daughter, thou seest how Fortune turns her wheel.[25]
We that but late were mounted up aloft,
Lulled in the skirt of that inconstant dame,
Are now thrown headlong by her ruthless hand,
To kiss that earth whereon our feet should stand.
What censuring eye that sees me thus deject,
Would take this shape to be that famous Duke,
Which hath made Bullen through the world renowned,
And all our race with fame and honor crowned?
BELLA FRANCA But father, how can you endure a slave
To triumph in your fortunes, and here stand
In soul deject, and banished from your land?
OLD BULLEN I'll tell thee, girl. The French King and myself,
Upon some terms grew in a strange debate,[26]
And taking careful vantage of the time,
Whilst I with all my powers, in aide of William
The Norman Duke, now English Conqueror,
Was busily employed, he seized my right,[27]
Planting another and supplanting me.

18 23 general: widely known; needless to say, this manuscript is fictional
19 23 public censure: judgment of the public, i.e. the audience
20 28 errors: errors of composition, not of fact, which the Second Prologue has tried to dismiss
21 30 clear-sighted gentlemen: i.e. the spectators
22 38 three thousand: if there were three thousand of us; a playhouse might in fact hold three thousand spectators
23 39 content: the audience will be the cause, or author, of contentment for the playwright by enjoying the contents of his play
24 39 circumference: the circle of the playhouse
25 1 Fortune turns her wheel: a medieval emblem showing that human fates rise and fall cyclically. Usually four human figures are shown on a wheel: one atop, one below, one rising, one falling
26 14 strange debate: unexpected or excessive argument
27 18 seized my right: took control of the demesne that was rightfully mine

This is the ground of my extremity.[28]
BELLA FRANCA If for King William's sake, now Conqueror,
You lost your birthright and inheritance,
How comes it that he sees you in this state,
And lifts not up your fortunes ruinate?
OLD BULLEN A conquered kingdom is not easily kept.
He hath so much ado to guard his own
That mine is buried in oblivion,
And I am forced to lose the name of Earl,
And live in London like a citizen.[29]
My four sons are bound prentice to four trades.
Godfrey, my eldest boy, I have made a Mercer;[30]
Guy, my next son, enrolled in Goldsmiths' trade;[31]
My third son Charles bound to an Haberdasher;[32]
Young Eustace is a Grocer:[33] all high born,
Yet of the city-trades they have no scorn.
Thus bare necessity hath made me seek
Some refuge, to sustain our poverty.
And having placed my sons in such a sort,
The little wealth I have left, I leave to thee.
Myself will travel to the Holy Land,
And ere I lie within the earth's vast womb,
Pay my devout vows at my Savior's tomb.
BELLA FRANCA Was that the cause you sent for my four brothers?
OLD BULLEN Their wishèd sight will cheer my agèd heart:
And I will bless them all before I part.

Enter GODFREY, GUY, CHARLES, *and* EUSTACE, *like apprentices*[34]

GODFREY I wonder, brothers, why my father hath sent for us thus early, that, all business set apart, we must meet together this morning.
GUY I know not the reason. I had much ado to get leave of my master to be spared from my attendance in the shop, and serving of customers.
CHARLES 'Faith as soon as I heard but the messenger say my father must speak with me, I left my tankard to guard the Conduit;[35] and away came I.
EUSTACE Aye, beshrew him, I should have been at breakfast with two or three good boys this morning: but that match is disappointed by this meeting.
BELLA FRANCA See where my brothers are already come.
OLD BULLEN Godfrey, Guy, Charles, young Eustace, all at once,
Divide a father's blessing in four parts,
And share my prayers amongst you equally.
First Godfrey: tell me how thou lik'st thy trade?
And knowing in thy thoughts what thou hast been,

28 20 ground of my extremity: reason for my desperate situation

29 29 citizen: while they were not noble, as the Earl and his family are, citizens were nevertheless privileged inhabitants of London. A citizen was a member of one of the livery companies, or tradesmen's guilds, and was allowed to vote for the Aldermen and the City Council; from their ranks the Lord Mayor was chosen. Old Bullen's sons have become apprentices in four notably wealthy livery companies

30 31 Mercer: an importer, exporter, and retailer, especially of cloth

31 32 Goldsmiths': as well as working gold, goldsmiths changed money and served as financial agents, something like modern banks

32 33 Haberdasher: a seller of luxury cloths such as velvet and silk

33 34 Grocer: the grocers sold spices, another luxury item

34 45 SD *like apprentices*: i.e. recognizable as apprentices by their clothing, perhaps wearing flat caps and short blue jackets (see IV.iv)

35 51 I left . . . the Conduit: I set down my water bucket at the Conduit as if it were guarding it. The Great Conduit was the most prominent source bringing potable water into London from a spring in Tyburn to Cheapside, one of the main market areas. There were other similar conduits in London as well. City-dwellers could fill tankards of water at conduits and bring them home for their own use; this chore was often given to apprentices

How canst thou brook[36] to be as thou art now?
GODFREY Bound must obey.[37] Since I have undertook
To serve my master truly for seven years,[38]
My duty shall both answer that desire
And my old master's profit every way.
I praise that City which made princes tradesmen,
Where that man, noble or ignoble born,
That would not practice some mechanic skill,
Which might support his state in penury,
Should die the death; not suffered[39] like a drone[40]
To suck the honey from the public hive.
I hold it no disparage to my birth,
Though I be born an Earl, to have the skill
And the full knowledge of the Mercers' trade.
And were I now to be create anew,[41]
It should not grieve me to have spent my time
The secrets of so rich a trade to know,
By which advantage and much profits grow.
OLD BULLEN Well hast thou done to overcome thy fate,
Making thy mind conformèd to thy state.
How likes my Guy the Goldsmiths' faculty?
GUY As a good refuge in extremity.
Say I be born a prince, and be cast down
By some sinister chance, or fortune's frown;
Say I be banished; when I have a trade
And in myself a means to purchase wealth,
Though my state waste, and towering honors fall,
That still stays with me in the extrem'st of all.
OLD BULLEN What says my third son, Charles?
CHARLES If I should say I would not brook those bonds,
Which God, and fate, and you, have tied me in,
You[42] would be preaching disobedience.
Or should I say the city-trades are base
For such a great man's sons to take on them
Your fatherly regard would straight advise me
To chastise my rebellious thoughts and say,
Son, you by this may live another day.
Therefore, as my two brothers, I reply;
You ask me if I like it. I say aye.
OLD BULLEN What says my youngest boy?
EUSTACE Father, I say hawking is a pretty sport,
And hunting is a princely exercise;
To ride a great horse, oh 'tis admirable!
OLD BULLEN Eustace, I know it is. But to my question.
How canst thou brook to be a prentice, boy?
EUSTACE Methinks I could endure it for seven years,
Did not my master keep me in too much.

36 60 brook: tolerate
37 61 Bound must obey: a familiar saying expressing resignation: you do what you have to do
38 62 seven years: the typical term of apprenticeship
39 69 suffered: grudgingly tolerated
40 69 drone: a male bee, which does not produce honey or keep up the hive; an idle person
41 74 create anew: born again; elevated again to the nobility
42 91 You: what we would expect Charles to say is "I would be preaching disobedience." It is probably a mistake of the writer or compositor. But it also might just be a slip on Charles's part, suggesting that he is critical of his father's choice

I cannot go to breakfast in a morning
With my kind mates and fellow prentices,
But he cries, "Eustace, one[43] bid Eustace come"—
And my name Eustace is in every room.[44]
If I might once a week but see a tilting,[45]
Six days I would fall unto my business close,
And ere the week's end win that idle day.[46]
He will not let me see a mustering,[47]
Nor in a May-day morning fetch in May.[48]
I am no sooner got into the fencing school,
To play a venue[49] with some friend I bring
But "Eustace, Eustace," all the street must ring.
He will allow me not one hour for sport.
I must not strike a football in the street,
But he will frown: not view the dancing school,
But he will miss me straight: not suffer me
So much as take up cudgels[50] in the street,
But he will chide: I must not go to buffets,[51]
No, though I be provoked; that's the hell,
Were't not for this, I could endure it well.
OLD BULLEN Sons, ye must all forget your birth and honors,
And look into the time's necessity.
I know ye are persuaded: think not, sons,
The names of "prentice" can disparage you.
For howsoever of you esteemed they be,[52]
Even kings themselves have of these trades been free.[53]
I made a vow to see the Holy Land,
And in the same my Savior's sepulcher.
Having so well disposed you, I will now
First bless you boys, and then prefer[54] my vow.
GODFREY With much ado do I contain my spirit
Within these bands[55] that have enclosed me round.
Though now this case the noble sun doth shroud;[56]
Time shall behold that sun break through this cloud.
GUY My genius[57] bids my soul have patience,
And says I shall not be a prentice long.
I scorn it not: but yet my spirits aim
To have this hand catch at the crown of Fame.
CHARLES An haberdasher is the trade I use:

43 109 one: someone
44 110 They call for me everywhere
45 111 tilting: a jousting match
46 112–13 Six days . . . idle day: I would work hard six days to get the seventh day off
47 114 mustering: local militias gathering for training, as they did periodically during the Tudor period. See Heywood's dedication letter
48 115 fetch in May: stay out all night to celebrate the return of spring the morning of May 1
49 117 venue: match
50 123 take up cudgels: brawl with clubs
51 124 go to buffets: come to blows
52 130–31 to be called "prentices" does not diminish your worth, whatever you think of the title and position
53 132 free: to be "free of a trade" meant to be a member of one of the liveried companies and thus entitled to all the rights of a citizen. There were stories that members of the royalty had at times been honorary members of some of the livery companies. But "to be free of a trade" might also mean not to have a trade, which seems a better description of kings than of citizens
54 136 prefer: advance, take steps to fulfill
55 138 bands: bonds
56 139 Although my outward appearance as a prentice ("this case") hides my inner nobility
57 141 genius: guiding spirit, conscience, intuition

But the soft wool feels in my hand like steel:
And I could wish each hat comes[58] through my hand
Were turned into an helmet, and each helmet
Upon a soldier's head, for me to lead.
War is the walk which I desire to tread.
EUSTACE I am a grocer, yet had rather see
A fair gilt sword hung in a velvet sheath
Than the best Barbary sugar[59] in the world,
Were it a freight of price inestimable.
I have a kind of prompting in my brain,
That says, though I be bound to a sweet trade,
I must forgo it, I keep too much in.[60]
I would fast from meat and drink a summer's day,
To see swords clash, or view a desperate fray.
OLD BULLEN Bridle these humors,[61] sons, expel them clean,
And your high spirits within your breasts contain,
Whilst I my tedious[62] pilgrimage prepare,
To spend my age in poverty and prayer.
My firstborn, first farewell; my second next;
Charles, Eustace, Daughter. Here my blessings stay,
Your wishes bear me on my sacred way. *Exit*
GODFREY [*To his father*] Even to the place you travel, there to ascend
With those devout prayers you to heaven commend.
[*To his siblings*] Brothers, since we are now as strangers[63] here,
Yet by our father's provident care so placed,
That we may live secure from penury—
So let us please our masters by our care,
That we our ruined fortunes may repair.
GUY Brother, if I knew where to go to war,
I would not stay in London one hour longer.
CHARLES An hour! By heaven I would not stay a minute.
EUSTACE A minute! Not a moment! Would you put a moment
Into a thousand parts, that thousandth part
Would not I linger, might I go to war.
Why, I would presently run from my master,
Did I but hear where were a drum to follow.[64]
BELLA FRANCA Would you so, brother?
EUSTACE Aye, good faith, sweet sister, I would shew him as fine a pair of heels, as light and nimble, as any the neatest cork shoe in all the town turns up. I would, i'faith.
BELLA FRANCA And leave me here alone?
GUY Alone? Why, sister,
Can you be left alone 'mongst multitudes?
London is full of people everywhere.
GODFREY Well, leave this jesting; we forget ourselves.
Sister, we'll have you to our father's house,
T'enjoy the small possessions left you there.

58 147 each hat comes: each hat that comes

59 153 Barbary sugar: sugar from North Africa, which grocers traded in, suggesting a more peaceful interaction with the Muslim world than Eustace is about to take

60 157 keep too much in: stay in the shop too much

61 160 humors: passions

62 162 tedious: difficult, wearying

63 169 strangers: foreigners

64 181 If I only knew where I could march behind a drum. Drums lead soldiers, of course, but a parade of drums through the street could also signal the beginning of a play

Return we to our masters and our charge,
Left seeking this,[65] our loitering to excuse
With forged inventions we their ears abuse.[66] *Sound a drum within, softly*
I hear a drum. I have as much power to sit,
Sort out my wares, and scribble on a shopboard,
When I but hear the music of a drum,
As to abstain from meat when I am hungry.
I'll know what news before I stir a foot.
CHARLES By heaven, I am enamored of this tune,[67]
'Tis the best music in the world to me.
EUSTACE My legs are marching straight when I but hear it.
Ran, tan, tan![68] Oh, I could lead a drum
With a good grace, if I but saw behind me
An hundred soldiers follow in even ranks.
Had I but here a band of men to lead
Methinks I could do wonders! Oh, 'tis brave[69]
To be a captain, and command to have.

Enter after a drum,[70] *a* CAPTAIN *with a Proclamation*

CAPTAIN [*Reading*] All commanders, captains, lieutenants, gentlemen of companies, sergeants, corporals, or common soldiers whatsoever, that will accompany to the holy wars at Jerusalem Robert, Duke of Normandy, the king's son: they shall have pay and place, according to their deserts. And so God save King William, surnamed the Conqueror.
Exit drum and CAPTAIN

EUSTACE *Ran, tan, tan.* Now by St. George, he tells gallant news! I'll home no more; I'll run away tonight.
GUY If I cast bowl, or spoon, or salt again,[71]
Before I have beheld Jerusalem,
Let me turn Pagan.
CHARLES Hats and caps adieu! [*Throwing his cap in the air*]
For I must leave you, if the drum say true.
GODFREY Nay then, have with you brothers! For my spirit
With as much vigor hath burst forth as thine,
And can as hardly be restrained as yours.
Give me your hands, I will consort[72] you, too!
Let's try what London prentices can do!
EUSTACE For my trade's sake, if good success I have,
The Grocers' arms shall in mine ensign wave.[73]
GUY And if my valor bring me to command,
The Goldsmiths' arms shall in my colors stand.
GODFREY So of us all. Then let us in one ship
Launch all together, and as we are brothers,
So let us enter zealous amity,
And still prevail by our united strength.

65 191–2 our charge . . . seeking this: the responsibilities we left to come to our father's summons
66 193 We will make up some false story to explain why we left
67 199 tune: i.e. the sound of a drum
68 202 *Ran, tan, tan*!: Eustace imitates the sound of the drum
69 206 brave: magnificent
70 207 SD *after a drum*: following a drummer
71 214 Guy seems to mix two mock pledges, "may I not toss a ball in bowls" and "may I not eat"
72 221 consort: accompany
73 224 Like noble families, the liveried companies identified themselves with coats of arms. Eustace promises to put the Grocers' coat of arms on his military banner ("ensign") in the crusade

I know our hearts are one. Sister, farewell.
Trust me, in vain you should persuade our stay,
For we are bent.[74] Consort us with your prayers.
ALL [BROTHERS] Farewell!
BELLA FRANCA Farewell.
GODFREY God—
GUY Heaven—
CHARLES Fate—
EUSTACE Fortune![75]
GODFREY Make us happy men! To win—
GUY Wear—[76]
CHARLES Vanquish—
EUSTACE Overcome! *Exeunt*
BELLA FRANCA Amen.
Have you all left me midst a world of strangers,
Here only to myself, not to protect me,
Or to defend me from apparent wrong?
Since it is so, I'll follow after you.
In some disguise I will pursue their steps,
And unto God and fortune yield myself.
Toward sea they are gone, and unto sea must I,
A virgin's unexpected[77] fate to try.

Exit

[Act II, Induction]

Enter marching ROBERT OF NORMANDY, *the* CAPTAIN, *the four brethren, drum, and soldiers*

Enter the PRESENTER[78]

PRESENTER Thus have you seen these brothers shipped to sea,
Bound on their voyage to the Holy Land,
All bent to try their fortunes in one bark.[79]
Now to avoid all dilatory news,[80]
Which might withhold you from the story's pith[81]
And substance of the matter we intend,[82]
I must entreat your patience to forbear,
Whilst we do feast your eye and starve your ear.
For in dumb shews,[83] which, were they writ at large,
Would ask a long and tedious circumstance,
Their infant fortunes[84] I will soon express,
And from the truth in no one point digress.

74 233 we are bent: we have decided
75 234 I have treated this chain of utterances and the next as if they were joined into two quasimetrical lines
76 235 Wear: i.e. achieve a goal and display it. "Win it and wear it" is a conventional challenge
77 244 unexpected: never before experienced, unforeseen
78 0 SD PRESENTER: a figure, like a Prologue or Chorus, who does not participate in the action of the play but instead narrates or explains it. Relatively common in the plays of the 1580s and early 1590s, the convention of the Presenter was revived in many seventeenth-century plays that adopted a deliberately old-fashioned dramaturgy
79 3 bark: boat
80 4 dilatory news: time-consuming accounts
81 5 pith: most important matter
82 6 intend: mean to show
83 9 dumb shews: dumb shows; silent, sometimes symbolic, performances sometimes presented before the main action of a play. They feast the eye because they are acted out, but starve the ear because they do not include dialogue
84 11 Their infant fortunes: the first part of what befell the brothers; *infant* literally means "without speech," also appropriate to dumb shows

Ye have seen the father of these four fair sons,
Already gone his weary pilgrimage;
Godfrey, Guy, Charles, and Eustace, pressed to sea
To follow Robert, Duke of Normandy.
Imagine now ye see the air made thick
With stormy tempests that disturb the sea,
And the four winds at war among themselves:
And the weak barks wherein the brothers sail
Split on strange rocks, and they enforced to swim
To save their desperate lives: where what befell them,
Dispersed to several corners of the world,
We will make bold to explain it in dumb show,
For from their fortunes all our scene must grow.

Enter with a drum on one side certain Spaniards; on the other side certain citizens of Bullen: the Spaniards insult upon[85] *them, and make them do them homage;*[86] *to the citizens enter* GODFREY, *as newly landed and half naked,*[87] *confers with the citizens, and by his instigation they set upon the Spaniards, and beat them away, they come to honor him, and he discloseth himself*[88] *unto them; which done, they crown him, and accept him for their prince: and so exeunt*

Those citizens you see were Bullenoys,[89]
Kept under bondage of that tyrannous earl,
To whom the French King gave that ancient seat,
Which to the wrongèd pilgrim[90] did belong.
But in the height of his ambition,
Godfrey, by shipwreck thrown up on that coast,
Stirs up th'oppressèd city to revolt
And by his valor was th'usurper slain,
The city from base bondage freed again.
The men of Bullen, wondering what strong hand
Had been the means of their deliverance,
Besought him to make known his birth and state:
Which Godfrey did. The people, glad to see
Their natural prince procure their liberty,
Homage[91] to him, create[92] him Earl of Bullen,
And repossess him in[93] his father's seat.
Where we will leave him, having honor won;
And now return unto the second son.

Enter the KING OF FRANCE, *and his daughter walking: to them* GUY, *all wet.*[94] *The* LADY *entreateth her father for his entertainment,*[95] *which is granted; and rich clothes are put about him, and so exeunt*

As the French king did with his daughter walk
By the seaside, from far they might espy

85 25 SD *insult upon*: browbeat
86 25 SD *do them homage*: perform submission to them
87 25 SD *half naked*: this shows that Godfrey has been shipwrecked
88 25 SD *discloseth himself*: reveals his identity, presumably as rightful ruler of Bullen, since he is the oldest son of the deposed earl
89 26 Bullenoys: i.e. the citizens of Bullen; pronounced "Bullen-oyse"
90 29 wrongèd pilgrim: i.e. Old Bullen
91 40 Homage: show honor
92 40 create: the technical term for raising someone to a noble title (see I.i. 75)
93 41 repossess him in: restore him to
94 43 SD *all wet*: like Godfrey's half-nakedness, a sign that Guy has just escaped shipwreck
95 43 SD *entreateth her . . . his entertainment*: asks her father to accept him as a guest

One on a rafter[96] float upon the waves,
Who as he drew more near unto the shore,
They might discern a man, though basely clad,
Yet sparks of honor kindled in his eyes.
Him at first sight the beauteous lady loves
And prays her father to receive him home,
To which the king accords; and in his court
Makes him a great and special officer.
There leave we Guy a gallant courtier proved
And of the beauteous Lady well beloved.

Enter banditos, with the Earl prisoner. Exeunt some of them with him to prison. Enter CHARLES[97] *all wet with his sword; fights with the rest, and kills their captain. They yield and offer to make him their captain, to which he agrees, and sic exeunt omnes*[98]

Charles, the third son, is by the winds and waves
Borne on a plank as far as Italy,[99]
And lands just at a lofty mountain's foot,
Upon whose top a many outlawed thieves,
Bandetti, Bravoes,[100] such as keep in caves,
Made their abode. This crew assails young Charles,
Who in the bickering strikes their captain dead.
They, wondering at his valor, and being now
Without a leader, humbly seek to him
To be their chieftain, and command their strength,
Which at their earnest suit he undertakes.
We leave him there, thinking his brothers drowned,
Nor knowing yet his father there lies bound.

Enter a corse,[101] *after it Irishmen mourning, in a dead march.*[102] *To them enters* EUSTACE, *and talks with the chief mourner, who makes signs of consent, after burial of the corse, and so exeunt*

Eustace, the youngest of the four, was cast
Upon the coast of Ireland: and from thence
He comes to travel to Jerusalem,
Supposing his three brethren drowned by sea.
Thus have you seen these four, that were but now
All in one fleet, a many thousand leagues
Severed from one another: Guy in France,
Godfrey in Bullen, Charles in Italy,
Eustace in Ireland 'mongst the Irish kerns.[103]
Yet, gentlemen, the selfsame wind and fortune
That parted them may bring them altogether.
Their sister follows them with zealous feet:
Be patient, ye will wonder when they meet.
Four London prentices will, ere they die,
Advance their towering fame above the sky,
And win such glorious praise as never fades

96 46 rafter: beam or raft (from the wrecked ship)
97 55 SD *Enter* CHARLES: in another surprising coincidence, Charles washes up in the territory of the same group of bandits who captured his father
98 55 SD *sic exeunt omnes*: so they all go out
99 57 Italy: the geography is growing increasingly improbable
100 60 *Bandetti, Bravoes*: bandits, ruffians. Italian words for Italian villains
101 68 SD *corse*: corpse, in a coffin or shroud, prepared for burial
102 68 SD *dead march*: a funeral procession; also the solemn music that accompanies it
103 77 kerns: lightly armed Irish footsoldiers

Unto themselves and honor of their trades.
Grant them your wonted patience to proceed,
And their keen swords shall make the Pagans bleed.

Exit

[Act II, scene i]

Enter GUY, *and the* LADY OF FRANCE

LADY Fie, stranger, can a skin so white and soft
Cover an heart obdurate, hard as flint?
Since I first saw thee floating on the waves,
The fire of love flew from your radiant eye,
Which like a sunbeam pierced unto my heart.
GUY Sweet lady, all my powers I owe to you,
For by your favor I ascend this height,
Which seats me in the favor of a prince—[104]
A prince, that did he know me, in the stead *Private to himself*[105]
Of doing me honor would cut off my head.
He did exile my father; cast me down;
And, spurred with envious hate, distressed us all.
Since fortune then, and the devouring seas,
Have robbed me of my brothers, and none left
Of all my father's sons alive but I,
Take this advantage, and be secret, Guy;
Meet this occasion, and conclude with fate
To raise again thy father's ruined state.
LADY Fie, niggard,[106] can you spend such precious breath,
Speak to yourself so many words apart,
And keep their sound from my attentive ear,
Which, save[107] your words, no music loves to hear?
GUY What would you have me say?
LADY Would I might teach thee!
Oh, that I had the guidance of thy tongue![108] *Private*
But what would that avail thee, foolish girl?
Small hope in those instructions I should find,
To rule your tongue, if not to guide your mind.
GUY My tongue, my thoughts, my heart, my hand, my sword,
Are all your servants. Who hath done you wrong?
LADY I doubt not of your valor. But resolve me
And tell me one thing truly I shall ask you.
GUY Be't not my birth, no question I'll deny.
Doubt not my truth, for honor scorns to lie.
LADY I do believe you. Fair knight, do you love?
GUY To ride a horse as well as any man;
To make him mount, curvet,[109] to leap, and spring;

104 8 prince: any sovereign ruler, not only the son of a king; here it refers to the King of France

105 9 SD a convention that a character onstage can speak aloud, as if thinking or addressing the playhouse audience, without being overheard by other characters onstage. Generally speeches aside have to be determined from context, but *Four Prentices* marks many instances as "private" or "apart" in stage directions; this edition preserves these editions and their position (typically) in the right margin

106 19 niggard: cheapskate, because Guy is not sharing his words with her. Unusually, the Lady notices that Guy is speaking aside

107 22 save: except for

108 25 I wish I could tell you what to say!

109 37 curvet: a cavalry maneuver in which a horse stands on its hind legs

To chide the bit,[110] to gallop, trot the ring.[111]
LADY I did not ask you if you love to ride.
Some thing I mean, which though my tongue deny,
Look on me, you may read it in mine eye.
But do you love?[112]
GUY To march, to plant a battle,[113] lead an host,[114]
To be a soldier and to go to war,
To talk of flanks,[115] of wings, of sconces,[116] holds,[117]
To see a sally,[118] or to give a charge,[119]
To lead a vaward, rearward, or main host—[120]
By heaven, I love it as mine own dear life.
LADY I know all this; your words are but delays.
Could you not love a lady that loves you?
'Tis hard when women are enforced to woo. *Private*
GUY Where is my man to bring me certain news
The king's commission sends me to the wars?
The villain loiters in my business.
LADY All this is from the matter, gentle knight:
The king's commission may be signed at leisure.
What say you to my question?
GUY You would have me tell you true.
LADY Either speak true, or do not speak at all.
GUY Then as I am true knight, I honor you,
And to your service will espouse my sword.
I wish you as I wish the glorious sun:
That it may ever shine, without whose luster
Perpetual darkness should o'ershade the earth.
But tell me, lady, what you mean by love.
LADY To love a lady is with heart entire
To make her mistress of his whole desire;
To sigh for her, and for her love to weep;
As his own heart her precious favors keep;
Never be from her, in her bosom dwell;
To make her presence heaven, her absence hell;
Write sonnets in her praise, admire her beauty;
Attend her, serve her, count his service duty;
Make her the sole commandress of his powers,
And in the search of love, lose all his hours.[121]
GUY 'Tis pretty for some fool[122] that could endure it:
How near am I unto this love, sweet lady?
I love to mount a steed, whose heavy trot

110 38 chide the bit: resist the bit, a sign of the horse's spirit; the bit is the metal piece that goes in the horse's mouth and to which the bridle and reins are attached. Guy quotes Spenser's *Faerie Queene*, in the opening lines of which Redcrosse's horse "did chide his foaming bit"
111 38 trot the ring: ride in a circle at a moderate pace, a sign of the rider's control over the horse
112 42 Perhaps the Lady's short line implies a pause before Guy again avoids the question
113 43 plant a battle: arrange troops in order for combat
114 43 host: large body of soldiers
115 45 flanks: this and "wings" are words for the ends of a line of battle
116 45 sconces: low earthworks
117 45 holds: fortifications
118 46 sally: a counterattack from a fortified area against a besieging force
119 46 charge: an attack, often a cavalry attack
120 47 vaward, rearward, or main host: the advance force, ahead of the main force of an army; the rearguard, protecting the back of an army; and the main body of soldiers
121 75 hours: with a pun, perhaps, on "whores," which was pronounced similarly
122 76 fool: Guy is thinking not only of someone silly enough to fall in love, but of a court fool or jester who might be a servant to such a lady

Cracks all my sinews, makes my armor crash.
I love to march up to the neck in snow,
To make my pillow of a cake of ice,
That in the morning, when I stretch my limbs,
My hair hangs thick with dropping icicles,
And my bright arms be frozen to the earth.
I love to see my face besmeared in blood,
To have a gaping wound upon my flesh,
Whose very mouth would make a lady sound.[123]
I love no chamber music, but a drum
To give me hunt's-up.[124] Could your grace endure
To lie all night within a sheet of mail,[125]
By a drawn sword that parts not from my side,
Embrace a body full of wounds and scars,
And hear no language but of blood and wars?
Such is my life; such may my honor prove:
Make war a lady, I that lady love.
LADY Fie, fie, you run quite from the bias clean.[126]
To love that dearly, which we hate so deadly.
If love and I be one, you hate us both.
GUY Then can I love no lady by my troth.
Madam, farewell; for under my command
The king your father sends ten thousand men,
To win the holy town Jerusalem.
Thither must I, esteeming your high honor
Like a bright comet and unmatchèd star,
But love no woman in the world, save war. *Exit*
LADY Go, flint;[127] strike fire upon thy enemy's steel,
Whilst I descend one step from Fortune's wheel.
Thou goest before, love bids me follow after:
By thee, the king thy lord must lose his daughter.

Exit

[Act II, scene ii]

Enter CHARLES, *like an outlaw,*[128] *with bandettos and thieves, and with the* CLOWN

CHARLES Thieves, and good fellows, speak—what should I call you?
There's not a rogue among you that fears God,
Nor one that hath a touch of honesty.
Robbers, and knaves, and rascals all together,
Sweet consort of vild[129] villains, list[130] to me.
Am not I well preferred,[131] to become captain
Unto a crew of such pernicious slaves?

123 87 sound: swoon

124 89 hunt's-up: a wake-up call; literally, the sounding of horns to signal the start of a hunt

125 90 mail: metal mesh used for armor

126 96 You are completely changing the subject. Originally referring to an oblique or slanting line (across the weave of a piece of cloth, or the curving path of a weighted ball in bowling), "bias" came to mean a predetermined path

127 106 flint: at the beginning of this scene, the Lady said Guy's heart was "hard as flint"; here she returns to the image. Flint emits sparks when struck against iron and was used to light fire. Touched or provoked, Guy is likely to spark and kindle

128 0 SD: *like an outlaw*: outfitted like a bandit

129 5 vild: vile, with a pun on "wild"

130 5 list: listen

131 6 Am not I well preferred: haven't I been nicely promoted (ironic)

I shall have such a coil to make you Christians,
And bring you to some shape of honesty
That ere I do it, I shall make your bodies
Nothing but scarecrows, to hang round these trees.

CLOWN "Brave Captain courageous, whom death cannot daunt,"[132] we have been all gentlemen and householders. But I was banished for nothing but getting of bastards; but this fellow fled from Venice, for killing a man cowardly on the Rialto; some for one villainy, and some for another. Our captain that you killed, and now supply his place, poisoned a worthy merchant in the city with ratsbane; and flying hither, for his valor we made him our general. But now brave *Cavallero*,[133] to thee alone we sing *Hononονero*.[134]

CHARLES Well, I must have you now turn honest thieves.
He that commits a rape shall sure be hanged;
He that commits a murder shall be murdered
With the same weapon that did act the deed.
He that robs pilgrims, or poor travelers,
That for devotion's sake do pass these mountains,
He shall be naked tied to arms of trees,
And in the day's heat stung with wasps and bees.
Ye slaves, I'll teach you some civility!

CLOWN Captain, what shall he be done withal, that lies with a wench with her will, if he be hung that lies with one against her will?

CHARLES I'll have him whipped.

CLOWN See, see, I think the captain hath been a cook in his time, he can fit sweet meat with sour sauce. But what a fool is our captain, to prescribe laws to outlaws? If we would have kept the laws before in the city, we needed not to have been driven now to lead our lives in the country. But Captain, since you are our captain, we will resign unto you all our treasures and prisoners, and our spoils. Take possession of them in God's name, that came to us in the devil's name.[135]

CHARLES Your prisoners, spoils, and treasure all bring forth,
That I may seize them as mine own by right,
As heir to him whom I have slain in fight.

Enter the Thieves bringing in [OLD BULLEN], *bound*

OLD BULLEN Villains, I know you drag me to my death,
And ye shall do me an exceeding grace.

CHARLES I am deceived but I have seen that face.[136]

VILLAIN Come, come, you old graybeard, you must before our Captain: if he say *Vive*,[137] then live. If not, thou diest, if[138] thou were his father.

CHARLES Villain, thou liest if thou wert my brother!
He shall not die. Upon your low knees fall,
And ask him pardon, or I'll hang you all!

OLD BULLEN 'Tween joy and fear amazed in heart I stand—
Doth my son Charles lead this unruly band?

CHARLES Your only son, and all the sons you have,
And born his father's desperate life to save.

132 12 "Brave Captain ... cannot daunt": the clown remembers the opening line of the ballad "Mary Ambree," "When Captains courageous, whom death could not daunt." The ballad is about a heroic woman warrior who avenges her lover's death at a siege of Ghent by Italian forces, perhaps in 1584

133 17 *Cavallero*: i.e. *Cavaliere*, the Italian word for knight

134 17 *Hononονero*: a slightly different spelling, *Honinonero*, is part of the refrain of a ballad published to celebrate the ascension of James to the throne of England, "The pettigree of our royal King James" (1603)

135 34–5 Take possession ... devil's name: for God's sake, take what we got by behaving devilishly

136 41 I know that face!

137 42 *Vive*: live (Italian)

138 43 if: even if

OLD BULLEN How cam'st thou here? Why dost thou call thy self
My only son, having three brothers more,
Which unto me thy beauteous mother bore?
CHARLES Once we were four, all fellow prentices;
And after fellow soldiers, pressed[139] to serve
The good Duke Robert in his holy wars.
But in a storm, our ships so bravely manned,
Were wrecked; and, save myself,[140] none swam to land.
They perished there. I by the waves and winds
Was driven upon this coast of Italy,
Where landing naked, save my trusty sword,
This crew of bold bandettos set upon me:
But in the dangerous fight, by chance I slew
The luckless captain of this damnèd crew,
Who since have made me captain, here to stay,
Till fortune grant me a more prosperous way.
OLD BULLEN Mine eyes have vowed to die the selfsame death
My sons have done.[141] Son, let me weep a while,
To bring the like destruction to my eyne;[142]
These in salt tears, they in a sea of brine.
CLOWN Is this our captain's father? What villains were we to use him so roughly!
VILLAIN If the old fornicator had but told us so much, we should have had the grace, either to have set him free, or fortune to have used him more gently.
CHARLES Since, father, we have met this happy day,
Secure with me amongst these outlaws stay.
OLD BULLEN Not for the world. Since I have lost my sons,
All outward joys are from my heart removed,
Vain pleasures I abhor, all things defy
That teach not to despair, or how to die.
Yet ere I leave the world I vow to see,
His[143] holy blessèd tomb that died for me.
CHARLES Then take along with you this bag of gold
To bear your charge in every inn you come.
Deny it not, relief is comfortable.
OLD BULLEN Thanks, my dear son, expense it will defray,
And serve to deal to poor men by the way.[144]
And now farewell, sweet Charles, thou all my sons,
For now the last sand in my hourglass runs.
CHARLES Ye two conduct him safe beyond the mountains.
VILLAIN Shall I be one?
CLOWN And I another?
CHARLES Ye know the passages, be it your charge.
VILLAIN I am glad the silly man is weak and old!
By heaven, my fingers tickle at his gold.
CLOWN Old man, is your purse afloat?[145]
I have vowed to cut his throat,
But to have it, every groat.[146] *Exeunt* [*all but* CHARLES]

139 55 pressed: drafted, enforced; it is not strictly true that the brothers were pressed—indeed, they volunteered, eagerly
140 58 save myself: except for me
141 67–8 Mine eyes . . . have done: my eyes are about to drown in tears, as my sons drowned in the ocean
142 69 eyne: eyes
143 81 His: Jesus's
144 85–6 expense it . . . the way: it will cover my expenses and also provide charity to the poor I may meet
145 95 Do you have your wallet handy?
146 97 groat: a farthing, or quarter-penny, i.e. the coin of least value; the Villain and the Clown plan to rob the earl down to the last coin

CHARLES And now return we to survey our cave,
Peruse our treasure got by rape and spoil,
Though won by others, yet possessed by us:
Yet henceforth shall be used no violence.
I'll make these villains work in several trades,
And in these forests make a commonwealth.
When them to civil nurture I can bring,
They shall proclaim me of these mountains king.

Exeunt

[Act II, scene iii]

Enter EUSTACE *and his* IRISHMAN[147]

EUSTACE I think these upright craggy mountain tops
Are (if the truth were known) high way to heaven:
For it is straight, and narrow, and some places
Are for the steepness inaccessible.
Fair fall a rafter and a gale of wind,
Or I had gone to heaven away by water
Nearer than this by land.[148] That way they found,
Who in the salt remorseless seas were drowned:
My brothers, whom I dream on when I sleep;
And my eyes waking at their fortunes weep,
Forgetting them.[149] The friendly Irish coast
Gave me safe harbor; thence I have traveled[150] hither
Even to these lofty hills of Italy
After Prince Robert, Duke of Normandy.
'Tis safer sitting in my master's shop,
Crying, "What lack you?" [151] than 'tis here to stay,
To wolves and wild beasts to be made a prey.

IRISHMAN Master, so Christ save me, I shall wait on thee: wake[152] for thee when thou sleepest, run for thee when thou biddest, and fly a[153] thy errands, like an arrow from a bow, when thou wantest wine, or meat, to drink or eat, or any other necessary provision.
Now I have left my best friend[154] in the grave,
My friendship and my service you shall have.

EUSTACE Well, fortune hath preserved me to some end.
It is for something that I did not sink,[155]
When the salt waves my mouth and ears did drink.
I might have fed the haddocks; but some power
Is my good master, and preserves me still.
Well, sword, in all my troubles stand me by,

147 0 SD *his* IRISHMAN: in a long continuous scene that will require many characters, Heywood seems careful to hold his extras in reserve, giving Eustace only one follower

148 5–7 Fair fall . . . by land: if it had not been for the lucky fall of a beam from the ship and a strong wind, I would have gone to heaven by water, which would have been a more direct route than climbing to it by land, as I am doing now

149 10–11 And my . . . Forgetting them: when I wake up, I cry for what happened to them ("their fortunes"), not recalling that they are now in heaven ("forgetting them")

150 12 traveled: "traveled" and "travailed" were not distinguished in early modern English, so Eustace in one word can say that his journey was laborious. And no wonder—somehow he has walked from Ireland to northern Italy

151 16 "What lack you?": what do you need? This was the customary question of London shopkeepers of all sorts

152 18 wake: keep a watch

153 19 fly a: hasten on, hurry to complete

154 21 best friend: we do not know, or learn, exactly whom the Irishman means, but this must be the corpse that was buried in the dumb show

155 24 There must be some reason I didn't drown

Thou art bound to win me somewhat[156] ere I die.

Enter the CLOWN *and the* VILLAIN, *dragging* [OLD BULLEN] *violently, and rifling*[157] *him*

CLOWN Give us the gold my captain gave you, you old anatomy![158]
VILLAIN Graybeard, deliver, or you are but dead!
OLD BULLEN Take it, my friends; full little needs this strife.
First take the gold, and after take my life.
CLOWN Nay, you old Jack-a-Lent, six weeks and upwards![159] Though you be our captain's father, you cannot stay there, and for surety that you shall not go back and tell him what we have done to you, we'll kill you, and fling you into some coal-pit.
VILLAIN Content,[160] and when we have done, we will return him word we have conducted thee past all danger of the mountains. And now prepare thee for the fatal stroke.
OLD BULLEN Thou dost me a great kindness, let it come.
God take my soul! Now, when thou wilt, strike home!
EUSTACE He strikes his own soul down to Erebus,[161]
That lifts a sword that shall but touch his hair.
IRISHMAN And by St. Patrick, I'll make him garter his hose with his guts, that strikes any stroke here.[162]
CLOWN Whom have we here? A gentleman and his water spaniel?[163] Let's rob them too, and after kill thee.
VILLAIN Content, content. Sirrah,[164] stand.
EUSTACE Yes, I will stand, base wretch, when thou shalt fall;
And strike thee dead, and trampling on thy bulk
By stamping with my foot crush out thy soul.
Take that, you slave, for bidding Eustace stand. *He beats them both away*
Now, father,[165] go in peace.
OLD BULLEN Thanks, my fair son,
By whose stout valor I have freedom won.
I can bestow upon you nought but thanks,
Unless you will divide this gold with me.
EUSTACE No, father, keep it; thou art old and poor:
But when I want, my sword shall purchase more.
OLD BULLEN By viewing him, my former griefs abound, *Apart to himself*
Even such a one was Eustace that was drowned:
Which, had he lived, his stature, years, and all,
Would have resembled his, so straight, so tall,
So fair, so strong, of such a worthy spirit.
But his blest soul, by this, doth heaven inherit.
Grief for his death so near my heart doth dwell
That for my life I cannot say farewell. *Exit*
EUSTACE The captain's father, whom the slaves had killed

156 29 somewhat: something
157 29 SD *rifling*: searching him roughly
158 30 anatomy: skeleton; because of his age, the old Earl is very thin (see Jack-a-Lent, below)
159 34 Jack-a-Lent ... and upwards: a proverbial insult for a thin person; a Jack-a-Lent was a straw figure set up during Lent and used as a target in a child's game. Lent lasted a bit less than six weeks, so the Clown's "Six weeks and upwards" emphasizes how very thin the Earl is
160 37 Content: agreed; fine
161 41 Erebus: in Greek mythology, primordial darkness; or, as here, the realm of the dead
162 43–4 And by ... stroke here: anyone who swings his weapon I'll cut open so he can use his intestines to hold his leggings up
163 45 water spaniel: the Irishman, who is faithful like a dog, and like a spaniel because shaggy-haired. The Clown is making fun of the long forelock traditionally worn by Irish men
164 47 Sirrah: a disrespectful form of address. The Villain gives Eustace an insulting challenge to fight
165 52 father: Eustace and the Earl are using "father" and "son" figuratively, as one might to an older or younger man whom one did not know; they do not yet recognize that they are actually father and son

Had not our coming intervented[166] them,
Resembles mine in gesture, face, and look.
But the old Earl my father is by this[167]
Within the walls of fair Jerusalem,
Else had I surely took this agéd man
T'have asked him blessing. But what next ensues?
I find these mountains will be full of news.

Enter CHARLES, CLOWN, VILLAIN, *and the Crew*

CLOWN Captain, a prize! We two were assailed by two hundred, and of them two hundred, we killed all but these two. These are the remainder of them that are left alive.
CHARLES Go two or three of you, and fetch them in:
If they resist you, take their weapons from them.
CLOWN I had rather somebody else should attempt them than I now. But since there is no other remedy, give me three or four of the stoutest of our crew, and then God and St. Anthony![168]
EUSTACE More thieves and villains have begirt us round.
Now, Eustace, for the honor of thy name,
Return them to their captain back with shame! *He sets upon them all, and beats them*
CHARLES Now by mine honor, the best piece of flesh
That ever in these woods held outlaw play![169]
Even such a spirit had Eustace when he lived:
We must not lose this gallant; if we can,
We'll strive to make him our companion.
EUSTACE Ye slaves, I'll beat you all into a mouse-hole:
And like a baited[170] lion at a stake,
Kill all the curs that come but near to bark.
Ye gulls, have ye no better men amongst you?
Defy your captain from me: here I stand,
To dare him to a combat hand to hand.
CHARLES I were a bastard, not my father's son, should I refuse it.[171]
EUSTACE By all the land I have left me in the world (that's but my grave), Captain, thou honorest me.
CHARLES By all the wealth I brought into these woods (that's but my sword), thou dost the like to me. Thou shalt have fair play, gallant, by mine honor.
EUSTACE False was my mother to my father's bed,
If I should ask more odds of Hercules.[172]
CHARLES He dies upon my sword, disturbs our fray,
Or in the fight dares disadvantage thee.[173]
EUSTACE Were I the world-commanding Alexander,
I would make thee my Ephestion[174] for that word.
I love thee for thy valor, Captain Thief.

166 68 intervented: interrupted, prevented
167 70 by this: by this time
168 80–81 then God and St. Anthony: and after that may God and St. Anthony help us
169 86 play: Charles' use of the word "play" here suggests the similarity of this scene to bouts of fencing that were held in public playhouses and elsewhere
170 91 baited: tormented. In animal baiting, dangerous animals like bears and bulls were tied to stakes while dogs attacked them. Eustace imagines himself as a lion in this situation, killing the much weaker dogs that come too close
171 96 I would show I was unworthy of my ancestry if I didn't accept that challenge
172 102 If I request any additional advantage even of a warrior as powerful as Hercules
173 103–4 He dies … disadvantage thee: I will kill with my sword anyone who tries to interrupt our single combat or puts my opponent at a disadvantage by helping me
174 106 Ephestion: Alexander the Great's closest friend and second-in-command. Eustace shows respect for Charles' fair play, while also pointedly assigning him a subordinate position

CHARLES 'Tis that preserves thee from our violence;
An honored mind lies in this outlaw's shape.
So much I reckon of thy chivalry,
That wert thou master of an Indian mine,
Thou should'st not be diminished one denier.[175]
Securely fight, thy purse is sanctuaried,
And in this place shall beard[176] the proudest thief.
EUSTACE An honor-minded villain, by my sword,
A right good fellow, and an honest thief.
If I should have thee prostrate at my mercy,
I will not kill thee for thy liberal offer.
Yet win it, lad, and take it without fail:
I scorn to have my purse go under bail.
CHARLES He goes beyond me in heroic thoughts.
To thine I stake down this: stand all apart. [*Throws down his own purse*]
He that steps in, be subject to our curses,
And now the better man take both the purses.[177]
EUSTACE It is a match, I'll seize them to thy grief.
Now, true man,[178] try, if thou canst rob a thief.

They fight, as they are fighting, enter BELLA FRANCA, *pursued by an outlaw. She runs betwixt them and parts them*

BELLA FRANCA If ye were born of women, aid a woman.[179]
CHARLES Why, what's the matter?
BELLA FRANCA Oh turn the edges of your swords 'gainst him,
That in the forest would have ravished me.
CHARLES [*To the outlaw*] Cease thy pursuit, and, [*To* EUSTACE] stranger, pause a while,
To hear the tenor of this lady's plaint.
EUSTACE Why, then, king's truce.[180] But let the purses lie:
They'll fall to my advantage by and by.[181]
CHARLES Now tell me lady, what's your suit to me?
BELLA FRANCA To save my life from foul inchastity.
For passing by these countries on my way,
To pay my zealous vows in Golgotha,[182]
Attended only by a little page,
This villain with a crew of ruffian[183] thieves,
Seized what we had first, haled my page from me,
And after would have wracked my chastity.[184]
But being swift of foot, fear lent me wings
Hither (I hope in happy time) to fly,
Either to save mine honor, or to die.
CHARLES Thy honor and thy life are both secured:

175 112 denier: a small coin. The Indian mines of Spanish possession in the New World, or West Indies, were legendarily rich. Charles pledges that even if Eustace were as wealthy as a mine owner, he would not take the smallest amount from him

176 114 beard: defy, challenge; Charles is saying that, in the sanctuary he grants, the purse Eustace has now gotten from the Earl will defy any attempt to steal it

177 124 Going Eustace one better, Charles now bets his own purse against Eustace's. This makes the contest even recognizably like a prize fight, a contest for money staged in the same playhouses where plays were performed, rather than a duel to the death

178 126 Now, true man: Eustace speaks to himself

179 127 aid a woman: Bella Franca is disguised, so her brothers do not recognize her; she is not, as we might have guessed when in I.i she declared her intention to follow her brothers, disguised as a man

180 133 king's truce: the king could command peace between subjects; Eustace is speaking figuratively

181 134 I will get them eventually

182 138 Golgotha: the site of Christ's crucifixion, where Bella Franca is bound as a pilgrim

183 140 ruffian: lawless, violent

184 142 wracked my chastity: raped me

And for a lady's sake you much resemble,[185]
Command my sword, my subjects, and my cave,
Where succor, all offenseless, you shall have.
Sirrah, go you, and scour about the hill.
CLOWN I go.
BELLA FRANCA How like is he to Charles, by shipwreck dead!
And he to Eustace, perished in the waves![186]
But they are both immortal saints in heaven:
Yet I am glad because these shapes are theirs.
My happy coming hath ta'en up[187] their strife,
Preserving mine own honor and my life.
EUSTACE So blushed my sister; and this outlaw thief
Hath a resemblance to my brother Charles.
But she in London lives a virgin pure,
He in some huge whale's belly, too too sure.
CHARLES A pretty wench, i'faith, I'll marry her
And make her queen of all this outlaw crew.
EUSTACE I am half in love already, at first sight:
How will this raging flame increase by might?
CHARLES Fair beauteous maid, resign your love to me;
Mistress of all these forests you shall be.
EUSTACE Love me, I'll kiss away these tears of grief;
Sweet wench, embrace a true man, scorn a thief.
CHARLES How now, Sir Sauce![188] you are as bold methinks,
As if you were a freeman[189] of our trade.
None but myself plead interest in this maid.
EUSTACE My interest is as much; in this 'tis greater,
Because that of the two, I love her better.
CHARLES Proud passenger,[190] I'll make thee eat that word.
EUSTACE If I eat air, thou shalt digest my sword.
CHARLES Revive this quarrel, let the former die:
Fight we for her, and let the purses lie.
Outlaw, I rather love to fight than brawl:
I'll win from thee thy wench, thy purse, and all.
BELLA FRANCA Stay, gentlemen! *She steps between them*
EUSTACE By heaven, I scorn to stay,
Till both the purses I have ta'en away.
CHARLES My sword for me, my mistress, and my gold.[191]
My resolution shall my claim uphold.

Enter the CLOWN *running betwixt them*

CLOWN What do you mean, gentlemen, to fight among yourselves, that should be friends, and had more need to take one another's part, to fight against your enemies. We shall all be slain, killed, murdered, massacred. For my own part, if I had nine lives like a cat, they were all sure to die one dog's death.

185 147 For the sake of a woman whom you resemble—presumably Bella Franca herself, although Charles does not recognize her
186 152–3 It is not clear how Bella Franca could know about the shipwreck that she assumes killed her brothers
187 156 ta'en up: absorbed, interrupted
188 170 Sir Sauce: impudent fellow
189 171 freeman: Charles uses the language of apprenticeship and the trades to describe being a bandit; a freeman of a trade was a master in one of the liveried guilds, such as those to whom the brothers were apprenticed. Only masters could set up their own shops and marry, which Eustace seems intent on doing here
190 175 passenger: traveler
191 183 My sword claims my right to the woman and the gold

CHARLES Why? What's the matter, fellow?
CLOWN Oh, noble captain, we shall all be slain! Tankard,[192] a prince of Italy, with an army, hath beset the foot of the mountains, and hath vowed to make venison of all us poor outlaws, and kill us like deer. God be with you: I'll go shift for one.[193]
CHARLES Dear we will be to him, before he do it,
And dearly sell our desperate carcasses.
Kind stranger, wilt thou[194] take a truce with me,
Thou shalt divide with me my dignity.
We two will jointly o'er these mountains reign,
And by our valors our estates maintain.
EUSTACE Because I hear thy life in jeopardy
And thou hast dealt with me so honorably,
Receive my hand; now I am wholly thine.
And ye mad rogues, I am half your captain now.
Look when ye see me nod, ye crouch and kneel,
Make legs, and curtsies, and keep bare your crowns.
CLOWN 'Tis hard to teach them manners that are clowns.
But for my own part, here's a leg, here's a cap, here's a knee—[195]
All these, sweet half-captain, I reserve for thee.
EUSTACE Speak, do you all accept me?
ALL We do, we do!
EUSTACE Then, brother thief,[196] I am turned outlaw, too,
But to do no man wrong; I make that law
Only to pass this tedious summer here
Till we our downcast fortunes may uprear.
CHARLES You share with me in end, in mind, in all. *Soft march*
But hark, I hear our enemies' drums do brawl.
EUSTACE Their voice is welcome! Oh, that I had with me *Apart*
As many good lads, honest prentices,
From Eastcheap,[197] Canwick Street, and London Stone,[198]
To end this battle, as could wish themselves
Under my conduct if they knew me here;
The doubtful day's success we need not fear.[199]
CHARLES Oh for some Cheapside boys for Charles to lead: *Apart*
They would stick to it, when these outlaws fail.
Wishes are wind—let's think ourselves well manned,
We'll sooner die than fly, so make a stand.

Enter TANCRED *with drum and soldiers*

TANCRED Are these the outlaws that disturb our peace?
Think they these mountain tops can shelter them

192 190 Tankard: the Clown gets Tancred's name wrong, substituting a word for a large mug. In the first scene, Charles left his tankard to answer his father's summons; now a tankard comes for him

193 192: I'll go shift for one: I'm going to go take care of myself

194 195 wilt thou: if thou wilt

195 206 Eustace has demanded from his new troops some of the usual signs of respect shown to superiors: bowing, kneeling, removing a hat. The Clown responds with stage business. This may simply be comical or awkward gestures of courtesy, but since Tancred and his soldiers are entering and the Clown does not reappear in the scene, his leg, knee, and cap may be used to run away

196 210 brother thief: as with "father" and "son" earlier, Eustace says more than he knows

197 218 Eastcheap: the rough neighborhood near one of London's main markets; Cheapside (line 224) was adjacent to it

198 218 London Stone: a large stone set in the ground in Canwick (i.e. Candlewick) Street. Even in Heywood's day no one was quite sure of its significance, although it seems to have been widely known as a landmark and a center of London activity. In Shakespeare's *2 Henry VI* Jack Cade strikes his sword on London Stone to signify his control of the city

199 216–21 Oh, that . . . not fear: Eustace, as Charles will in the next line, wishes to himself that, instead of a band of Italian bravoes, he was accompanied by a group of London prentices, who would certainly be able to overcome the approaching army

From our revenge, and just assembled arms?
CHARLES Come, come, let us prepare to answer them.
TANCRED Which be the chief of these confounded[200] troops?
CHARLES Prince, I am one of them.
EUSTACE And I another.
CHARLES I am his friend.
EUSTACE And I his outlaw brother.
TANCRED How dare you stand contemptuous 'gainst your liege?[201]
Captains, ye are our men.
CHARLES That we deny.
I am a stranger,[202] Tancred.
EUSTACE So am I.
TANCRED Such valor is reported to appear *Apart to his own people*
In the brave deeds of these rude foresters,
That we could rather wish they were our friends,
To dwell in cities than keep out in caves.
Considering now what wars we have in hand,
Their martial spirits might much advantage us,
Would they but keep within some honored bounds.
We'll work them, if we can, to our alliance,
And rather motion[203] love than proud defiance.
CHARLES Why comes the County Palatine[204] in arms,
To fight against unarmèd foresters?
If thou wilt win renown, bend thy brave forces
'Gainst Pagans that besiege Jerusalem.
Small fame and honor canst thou win thee here,
Besides our cheap lives thou shalt purchase dear.
EUSTACE We have reformed these villains since we came,
And taught them manners and civility.
All rape and murder we repay with death:
Amongst us doth not live a ravisher.
TANCRED I have heard no less, but that you weed out such
As pass the bounds of Christian honesty,
Which makes me rather offer peace than war.
But what bright virgin stands so discontent?
CHARLES My life!
EUSTACE My love!
TANCRED [*Aside*] The word had been well spent,
If I had said mine, too: for I protest,
Of all this number I affect her best.[205]
CHARLES Believe me, fellow-partner in my rule,
You offer wrong to impart in this my love.[206]
EUSTACE Half of all's mine, I claim it as my due:
In which, bright virgin, I except not you.
TANCRED I do contain my love with much ado:[207]
For her methinks I could turn outlaw, too.
EUSTACE What, do you think to have a double share?

200 230 confounded: disordered
201 233 liege: a ruler to whom subjects owe allegiance; Tancred assumes Charles and Eustace are locals
202 235 stranger: foreigner (therefore not Tancred's subject)
203 244 motion: show
204 245 County Palatine: a noble, allied to a king or higher noble, who retained independence to rule his territories
205 261 I affect her best: Tancred, too, finds Bella Franca attractive
206 263 You do wrong by insisting on a share of my beloved
207 266 It is only with effort that I resist showing that I love her

Half of her's mine; I will not bate[208] an hair.
CHARLES By thine own words thou gav'st me half at least.
EUSTACE But I'll have all—my title is increased.
TANCRED Stay, captains, for our annual crown's revenues
We would not lose the weakest of you both,[209]
So much do we affect your chivalries.
Let me take up this mutual enmity:
Your quarrel is for her; both would enjoy her.
You claim her as your right. *To* CHARLES
CHARLES 'Tis true, I do.
TANCRED [*To* EUSTACE] And, captain, you say she belongs to you.
EUSTACE True, valiant Prince, my hopes shall his destroy:
Thou art mine own, sweet wench, God give us joy.
TANCRED Then till this strict contention ended be,
Deliver this bright virgin unto me.
Here shall our former hate and discord cease:
This lady shall be hostage of your peace.[210]
Unto thy charge we give ten thousand men. *To* CHARLES
As many soldiers we resign to thee.[211] *To* EUSTACE
Make me her keeper till these wars be done:
Ye have the price, I my content have won.
CHARLES Honor hath taught the Palatine to speak.[212]
EUSTACE Since what we both desire, one can but have,
Take charge of her. Let me receive the charge
Of a great army, and commanding power:
Before I marry, I must win my dower.
CHARLES So say I, too, and outlaw life, adieu!
TANCRED And welcome love, which I must keep for you.
Their drums shall scold, mine shall have time to cease,
And whilst they war, with her I'll make my peace.
Are you content, sweet lady?
BELLA FRANCA I must do
That which amongst you all best pleaseth you.
I am a prisoner; prisoners must obey.
You say I shall, and I must not say nay.
CHARLES Do so, sweet love.
EUSTACE Till these wars ended be
I prithee, sweet love, keep thy heart to me.
TANCRED Come, captain, we bequeath you to your charge,
To march with speed towards the holy wars.
This lady as our life we will esteem
And place her in the honor of a queen.

Exeunt

[Act II, scene iv]

Enter ROBERT OF NORMANDY, GODFREY OF BOULOGNE, *and* GUY OF LESSINGHAM,[213] *with drum and soldiers*

208 269 bate: decrease my claim by
209 272–3 for our . . . you both: we would not want either of you killed, even for a whole year's income
210 284 hostage of your peace: a guarantee that Charles and Eustace will not fight against each other or Tancred
211 286 resign to thee: put in your command
212 289 Tancred speaks honorably
213 0 SD LESSINGHAM: a small village in Norfolk; why Guy is associated with it is not clear, but see note V.iv. 65, where Guy's full name is first announced

GODFREY What art thou with thy brow confrontest me?[214]
GUY One that thinks scorn to give least place to thee.
GODFREY Thou know'st me not, to set my name so light.
GUY I reck thee not, my frown thou canst not fright.[215]
We are no babe; or if we were, yet know
Thy proud face cannot like a bugbear show.[216]
GODFREY Thou hast struck fire upon a flinty[217] spirit.
Think'st thou, because thou lead'st the French king's troops,
And art commander of a few bold French,
That we will yield the upper hand to thee?
I let thee know thou hast dishonored me.
GUY I let thee know thou hast done as much by me.
Think'st thou, thou canst outface me? Proud man, no:
Know I esteem thee as too weak a foe.
GODFREY Now by my knighthood I'll revenge this wrong,
And for that word, thy heart shall curse thy tongue.
ROBERT What mean these hasty princes thus to jar,
And bend their swords against their mutual breasts,
Whose edge were sharpened for their enemies' crests?[218]
GODFREY He shall not march before me.
GUY But I will.
GODFREY Zounds, but thou shalt not, by this blessèd day,
I'll pitch thee like a bar[219] out of my way.
GUY Thy arms want strength, thou canst not toss me so.
GODFREY No, can they not? By heaven, I'll try a throw.
ROBERT Princes, I charge you by the honored zeal,
And love to him[220] for whom ye come to fight,
To cease this envy and abortive jar.[221]
The fields are broad enough for both to march,
And neither have the vantage of the ground.[222]
GUY Robert, mine arm shall act a wondrous thing:
I'll hurl him like a stone out of a sling.
Not have the way? I'll fling thee on the earth,
And then march over thee with all my troops.
GODFREY Robert of Normandy, by all the honor
Thou hop'st t'achieve thee in these holy wars,
Stand from betwixt us, let's but try one fall.[223]
I'll cast his cork-like[224] trunk by wondrous skill,
As Hercules threw Lychas from an hill.[225]
ROBERT For God's sake and our Savior's, in whose book
Ye now are entered as his soldiers pressed,
In whose camp royal if ye mutiny

214 1 Who are you to get in my way?
215 4 I do not consider you at all, and you can't intimidate me
216 5–6 We are . . . bugbear show: even if I were a baby, your face is not a boogie-man that could scare me
217 7 flinty: here, not hard, but combustible; see also II.i. 106
218 17–19 What mean . . . enemies' crests: what do these leaders mean by arguing and pointing their swords at each other? Those swords were meant for their enemies' heads
219 22 pitch thee like a bar: a popular contest in which competitors tried to throw a heavy wooden or iron beam the furthest; Godfrey threatens to heave Guy aside
220 26 him: both Robert and Christ
221 27 abortive jar: uncompleted disagreement
222 29 vantage of the ground: the more privileged position; the bands can march side by side
223 36 let's but try one fall: let's wrestle once, until one of us knocks the other down
224 37 cork-like: because light and soft
225 38 Ovid relates how Hercules threw Lychas over the edge of a cliff while they were wrestling

Ye are found guilty by his martial law,
And worthy death,[226] I charge you princes both
T'abandon this injurious enmity.
Stand you betwixt the soldiers, lest this sting
Of blind seditions reign in this our army
And feed upon our bodies like a plague.
Princes, I charge you by your Savior's blood
Shed for your sins, ye shed none at this time.
GODFREY Well, let him march before, I will resign.[227]
Robert prevails. Frenchman, the right is thine.
GUY I will not march first; but in courtesy
I will resign that honored place to thee.
But what a king should say I should not do
With violent rage that would I run into.[228]
Go on, by heaven you shall, I yield it you;
By heaven, you shall[229]—the place I freely grant.
Friendship can more with me than rude constraint.[230]
GODFREY Thy honored love with honor I return;
What thou wouldst give me, I resign thee back.
This kind reply to me stands like a charm.
Then royally let's march on arm in arm.
ROBERT Such just proportion princes still should keep.
Brave Lord of Bullen, join your troops with ours,
That are by birth approvèd Englishmen:
And Lord of France that under your conduct
Have ready armed ten thousand fighting men,
To fight with us for fair Jerusalem,
Distressed by misbelieving infidels,
Let us unite a friendly Christian league.
We have entered, valiant lords, upon our way
Even to the midst of fertile Lombardy,
By writers termed the garden of the world.
Half of our way we have overcome already:
Then let us here encamp upon these downs.
But stay, what threatening voice of warfare sounds?

Enter, after a trumpet, EUSTACE

GODFREY Had not young Eustace in the seas been drowned,
I should have said, he treads upon this ground.
And, but none scaped the dangerous seas save I,
This Frenchman I should think my brother Guy.
EUSTACE Princes, my master County Palatine,
Wondering what bold foot durst presume to tread
Upon his confines without asking leave,
Sends me to know the cause of your arrive,[231]
Or why the armed hooves of your fiery steeds
Dare wound the forehead of his peaceful land.

226 43 worthy death: deserving capital punishment, but also the eternal death that the damned are said to suffer. Christ is figured as a military commander, Godfrey and Guy disobedient soldiers subject to his punishments
227 50 resign: relinquish my demand to march first
228 54–5 But what . . . run into: if I am ordered not to do something, that makes me want to do it more
229 57 By heaven, you shall: here Godfrey apparently hesitates and Guy insists
230 58 Friendship gets further with me than coercion
231 84 arrive: arrival

GODFREY "Dare"? Sends thy lord in that ambitious key?[232]
GUY Or hath the pride of thy refinèd tongue
Gilded thy message with these words of scorn?[233]
ROBERT Add'st thou unto thy message, knight, or no?
EUSTACE The naked tenor of my master's mind·
Thus I unfold: rash, saucy, insolent,
That by audacious boldness have not feared
To break into my sovereign's royal pale,[234]
I charge you to return the way you came
And step by step tell[235] every tedious stride
That you have measured rashly in his land:
Or by the honor of his name he swears,
To chase you from the margent[236] of his coast,
With an unnumbered[237] army and huge host.
GODFREY March back again? Oh scandal to our names!
Have we deserved to be so censured on?[238]
Though not one man upon my part would stand,
Alone I'll pierce the bowels of his land!
GUY Basely retire, and thirty thousand strong?
Were the whole world's power ambushed in our way[239]
Yet would we on. Return dishonorably?
Forward I'll march, though every step I tread
Plunge me in blood, thus high above my head![240]
ROBERT Princes, have patience, let me answer him.
Knight, I condemn not thee for speaking boldly
The proud defiance that thy master sends,
But mildly we return our pleasures[241] thus.
We do confess it was some oversight
To march so far without some notice given
Unto the lord and prince that owes[242] the land,
And we could wish that we had craved his leave.
But since 'tis thus, that we have marched thus far,
And basely to retire is infamous,
If not with leave,[243] we forward mean to go,
Despite of king or emp'ror shall say no.[244]
EUSTACE I will inform the prince my sovereign so. *Exit*
GUY That young knight's face, methinks, I well should know.
GODFREY I see the swords were sharped 'gainst infidels,
Must be employed to lavish[245] Christian blood.
Upon his soul lie all the heinous guilt,
Who, being a Christian prince, forbids and bars
Our quiet passage to these Pagan wars.

232 87 Was your Lord really so presumptuous as to ask if we *dare* enter?
233 88–9 hath the . . . of scorn: did your pride make you change the words to make them more insulting?
234 94 pale: territory, demesne
235 96 tell: count, go over
236 99 margent: edge, margin
237 100 unnumbered: countless, incalculably numerous
238 102 censured on: judged, insulted
239 106 ambushed in our way: lying in wait
240 108–9 Forward I'll . . . my head: I will go forward even if I step in blood over my head! The words are probably meant to be accompanied with a gesture
241 113 pleasures: desires
242 116 owes: owns
243 120 If not with leave: even without permission
244 121 In defiance of any prince who refuses to allow us
245 125 lavish: spill copiously, waste

GUY This bickering will but keep our arms in ure,[246]
The holy battles better to endure.
ROBERT Well, God for us, for our intent is good.
Charged be their souls with all this Christian blood.[247]

Enter TANCRED, CHARLES, EUSTACE, *drum, colors, and soldiers, marching*

TANCRED What art thou brav'st[248] the County Palatine?
ROBERT My name is Robert, Duke of Normandy.
TANCRED Speak, will ye all retire the way ye came?
ROBERT God keep Duke Robert from so foul a shame.
GODFREY Basely retire when we have marched thus far?
First we'll unpeople this thy land by war.
CHARLES Then will we drive you back by our main force,
And seize upon your troops of foot and horse.
GUY So say you, but should you attempt to do't,
We straight should overthrow you horse and foot.
EUSTACE So said, so done, brave lord, were gallant play.[249]
But you would at the first push[250] shrink away.
ROBERT No, proud Italians—all our spirits are fire,
Which burns not downward, but is made t'aspire.[251]
Prince, we confess we did forget ourselves,
Presuming on that ancient privilege
Which every Christian brother prince should claim
One in the interest of another's name.[252]
An error we confess, though not a fault.
But basely with dishonor back to fly,
And to be held as cowards, we deny.
TANCRED And nothing else can satisfy mine ire,
But whence ye came the same way to retire.
ROBERT And that I'll never do.
GODFREY Nor I.
GUY Nor I.
CHARLES Then shall ye on these Lombard champaigns[253] die.
To arms, brave soldiers!
EUSTACE Strike up warlike drum!
Prepare you, Christian princes, now we come!
GODFREY Stay, brave Prince Tancred! Stay, great Norman Duke!
Out of my zeal to God and Christendom,
To stanch[254] the blood which should be broached[255] this day,
Unto the grief of all that honor Christ,
And joy to such as love idolatry,
I make this challenge general through the host
Of him that interrupts us on our way. [*Throws down a gage*]

246 129 ure: use
247 132 Let them be held accountable for the loss of Christian lives
248 133 What art thou brav'st: who are you to defy
249 143 If you do what you say—beat us easily—that would be a bold accomplishment
250 144 push: assault
251 146 made t'aspire: meant to strive upward
252 147–50 we confess . . . another's name: we admit that we assumed that since we are both Christian rulers, we could give ourselves permission to cross your lands just as well as you could
253 157 champaigns: plains, fields
254 162 stanch: stop the flow of
255 162 broached: made to flow; spilled, as from a container

If any proud Italian dare take up
The honored gage[256] which I have here thrown down
And fight a single combat for our passage,
These shall be made our strict conditions:
If him I conquer, all our host shall march
Without all let and contradiction.[257]
If I be vanquished by thy champion's hand,
Our army shall march back out of thy land.
CHARLES A princely motion to save Christian blood!
Great Prince of Italy, upon my knee
I humbly beg I may thy champion be.
TANCRED Thou hast thy suit; thy valor hath been tried.
With a rough brow see thou confront his pride.
ROBERT Then what ten thousand Christian lives should right,
These two brave lords will end in single fight.
TANCRED It is agreed.
EUSTACE Stand to't, brave outlaw-brother!
Would I were one of them.
GUY And I the other.
CHARLES What weapon wilt thou use?
GODFREY That which next comes.[258]
Give me this partisan.[259] Now strike up, drums!
CHARLES Give me this,[260] soldiers! Trumpet, sound a charge:
I'll stop the passage which he seeks t'enlarge.
GODFREY Princes, stand off! My warlike arm this day
For all your troops shall win a prosperous way.
CHARLES Thou canst not enter though the way stood ope:
My heart, and this, thy passage vows to stop.
GODFREY Yet will I through.
CHARLES Thou shalt not, this says nay.
GODFREY Oh, but behold! I have this to hew my way.
They fight, and are parted by ROBERT *and* TANCRED
TANCRED I would not lose my champion for the world.
ROBERT Nor I this prince. For were these spirits spent,
All Christendom their fortunes might lament.
Part them on equal odds and equal terms.[261]
Both alike valiant, both have honor won,
More valorous live not underneath the sun.
TANCRED We will reserve their haughty chivalries
To exercise against God's enemies.
EUSTACE They have won honor, I have idly stood.
By my good stars, I'll have a challenge, too,
If any in their camp dares answer me!
Give me thy pike,[262] a pike a prince may trail,

256 168 gage: a token, often a glove, dropped to issue a challenge to combat; anyone wishing to accept the challenge may pick the gage up

257 172 Without any hindrance or opposition

258 184 That which next comes: whatever is ready to go

259 185 partisan: a spearlike weapon mounted on a long shaft, with a head that also had shorter blades placed crosswise. Godfrey must take it from one of the soldiers standing by. On the frontispiece of the 1615 text, Godfrey and Charles bear partisans that have heads like a small axe

260 186 this: Charles grabs another partisan. The brothers continue to refer to their weapons as "this" in the scene

261 197 equal odds and equal terms: Robert declares the match a tie

262 205 pike: a long spear, generally used in ranks of soldiers. Long and slow, it was difficult to use one on one, so the stunts that Eustace and Guy engage in are feats of strength and skill. To "trail a pike" was to drag it by the head with the shaft behind when marching; otherwise the long shaft made it difficult to move with. But a nobleman or knight would be unlikely to trail a pike, which was a commoners' weapon, and only really effective when used in massed formation like the "grove of pikes" the Sultan plans to defend Jerusalem. On the frontispiece of the 1615 text, Eustace and Guy wield pikes

And at that weapon will I challenge all.
Great Prince, these fiery princes that came hither
To brave our forces had a champion
To challenge us. Are we as valiant,
And shall we fail to do the like to them?
Give me but leave, my lord, to send one boast
T'affright them, like a devil, through their host.
TANCRED It pleaseth us; then, when thou wilt, begin.[263]
ROBERT What champion shall we have to answer him?
GUY I should esteem him my immortal foe,
That should attempt to take away the honor
Of such a strong encounter from my hand.[264]
Champion, appear betwixt our royal hosts.
Let's see thy strength make good thy haughty boasts.
EUSTACE I am here; stand thou forth on the adverse part!
Survey me well, brave Hector I resemble,
Whose very brow did make the Greeks to tremble.
GUY But I, Achilles, proud ambitious boy,
Will drag thy corse about the walls of Troy.[265]
Give me thy pike, I'll toss it like a reed,
And with this bulrush make mine enemy bleed.
Rapier and pike, is that thy honored play?
Look down, ye gods, this combat to survey.
EUSTACE Rapier and pike this combat shall decide.[266]
Gods, angels, men, shall see me tame thy pride.
GUY Thou dost thyself wrong to o'ercharge thine arm,
With such a weapon as thou canst not wield.
I'll teach thee; thou shalt like my zany[267] be
And feign to do my cunning after me.[268]
EUSTACE Thou wouldst instruct thy master at this play.
Think'st thou this rye-straw[269] can o'errule my arm?
Thus do I bear him when I use to march.
Thus can I fling him up, and catch him thus: *They toss their pikes*
Then thus, to try the sinews of my arm.[270]
GUY But thou should'st charge him thus, advance him thus,
Thus should'st thou take him, when thou see'st from far
The violent horses run to break our ranks.[271]
EUSTACE All that is nothing, I can toss him thus.
GUY I thus: 'tis easier sport than the balloon.[272]

263 213 Issue the challenge whenever you are ready

264 215–17 i.e. Guy demands the honor of facing Eustace; anyone who takes his place would become his enemy

265 221–4 brave Hector … of Troy: Eustace compares himself to Hector, the greatest of Troy's warriors, whose heroism kept the city safe for most of the Trojan War. Guy responds that he is like Achilles, who killed Hector and in rage dragged his dead body around the walls of Troy

266 229 Guy and Eustace seem to agree on "rapier and pike" as weapons, which could mean that one would wield a rapier, a thin, flexible sword, while the other used a pike. These weapons require very different styles of fighting, and such mismatches were often part of fencing displays

267 233 zany: from *zanni*, a servant-character in Italian *commedia dell'arte*, who was typically stupid and comically clumsy

268 234 And merely imitate, badly, my skill

269 236 rye-straw: i.e. the pike. Eustace exaggerates its lightness to emphasize his strength

270 237–9 With each "thus," Eustace shows off a maneuver with his pike ("him"), holding it high to march (a more physically demanding alternative to trailing it) and tossing it, that is, throwing it high into the air and catching it under control

271 240–42 Guy offers a similar tutorial, correcting or supplementing Eustace's maneuvers ("Thus should'st thou"), including demonstrating how to plant the pike to ward off cavalry

272 244 balloon: a game in which players wearing wooden wrist guards knocked an inflated leather ball back and forth

EUSTACE We trifle time, this shall thy rage withstand.
GUY With this, our host shall pierce thy sovereign's land.

They fight. ROBERT *and the Palatine* [TANCRED] *cast their warders*[273] *between them, and part them*

ROBERT That host should lose ten thousand Pagans' lives
With the rich honor of their overthrow,
That should but lose[274] his champion in this combat.
If both should perish, our brave Christian army
Should be more weak by thousands than it was.
TANCRED Their matchless valor have prevailed with[275] us.
Freely enjoy the pleasures of our land;
Our army here we do conjoin with yours,
To lead them to the fair Jerusalem.
ROBERT We pawn our faith to this perpetual league:
And now we shew ourselves that Christian host
In which true peace should flourish and abound.
Unto this peace let drums and trumpets sound.
Champions embrace, and all your stern debate *Flourish*[276]
Pour in abundance on the Pagans' heads.
Princes and lords, let our united bands
Win back Judea from the Pagans' hands. *Exeunt all marching. Manet*[277] *the* FRENCH LADY
LADY Thus have I masked my bashful modesty
Under the habit of a trusty page,
And now my servant's servant am I made.[278]
Love, that transformed the gods to sundry shapes,
Hath wrought in me this metamorphosis.[279]
My love and lord, that honored me a woman,
Loves me a youth,[280] employs me everywhere.
I serve him, wait upon him, and he swears
He favors both my truth and diligence.
And now[281] I have learnt to be a perfect page,
He will have none to truss his points but me,
At board to wait upon his cup but me,
To bear his target in the field but me.
Nay, many a thing, which makes me blush to speak,
He will have none to lie with him but me.[282]
I dream and dream, and things come in my mind,
Only I hide my eyes—but my poor heart

273 246 SD *warders*: gages, here intervening in the duel in order to stop it
274 249 lose: allow to escape, i.e. if either Guy or Eustace were to die here, thousands of Pagan soldiers would survive
275 252 prevailed with: persuaded
276 260 SD *Flourish*: a short triumphant fanfare played on trumpets
277 263 SD *Manet*: remains on stage (Latin)
278 266 When she left the stage in II.i, the French Lady asserted that her father was about to lose a daughter, without specifying how. Now we see: she has disguised herself as a page, taken service with Guy (thus becoming the servant of her servant), and followed the army he leads
279 267–8 Love, that … this metamorphosis: the Lady quotes the beginning of Golding's translation of Ovid's *Metamorphoses*, comparing her disguise as a boy to the "sundry shapes" taken on by the gods in that poem as they pursue the mortals they desire
280 269–70 My love … a youth: my master, who is also the one I love, honored me when I dressed as a woman but loves me now that I am dressed as a young man. When he was refusing to say he loved her, Guy specifically told the Lady that he honored her (see II.i. 60)
281 273 now: now that
282 275–8 At board … but me: these ordinary acts of a subordinate are all charged here with a sexual edge. Trussing points was to tie the laces of garments, especially of trousers. In a famous episode recounted in Ovid and elsewhere, Jupiter was overcome by the beauty of the Trojan boy Ganymede and abducted him to serve as his cupbearer; the story was an emblem of homoerotic desire. Guy even has his page sleep with him at night, which was probably less sexually charged for an Elizabethan than it seems to us; sharing a bed with a friend or servant was a common practice. But as the Lady makes clear, she at least is well aware of the erotic possibilities this common practice entails

Is barred and kept from love's satiety.
Like Tantalus,[283] such is my poor repast,
I see the apples that I cannot taste.
I'll stay my time,[284] and hope yet, ere I die,
My heart shall feast as richly as my eye.

Exit

[Act III, scene i]

Flourish. Enter the old SULTAN, *the young* SOPHY, *tables and forms;*[285] *and* MORETES, TURNUS, *with drum*[286] *and soldiers*

SULTAN Counsel, brave lords! The Christian army marcheth
Even to our gates with paces undisturbed.
The hollow earth resounds with weight of arms
And shrinks to bear so huge a multitude.
They make a valley as they march along,
And raising hills encompass either side.
Counsel, brave lords, these terrors to decide.
SOPHY Jove's great vice-gerent[287] over all the world,
Let us confront their pride, and with our powers
Disperse the strength of their assembled troops.
SULTAN Sion[288] is ours by conquest: all Judea
Is the rich honor of our conquering swords.
Shall we not guard it, then, and make our breasts
The walls that shall defend Jerusalem?
SOPHY They shall march over us, that march this way.
Before the Christians shall attain these walls
With dead men's faces we will pave the earth.
SULTAN I cannot judge[289] the Christians are so mad
To come in way of battle, but of peace.
SOPHY They rather travel in devotion,
To pay their vows at their Messiah's tomb,
And so as pilgrims, not as soldiers, come.
SULTAN Your own power blinds you and hath screened your eyes;
My hairs do wear experience' livery:[290]
But yours, the badge of youth and idleness.
Their army stands upon a mountain top,
Like a huge forest: their tall pikes, like pines,
In height do overpeer the lower trees;
Their horsemen ride like centaurs in the meads,[291]
And scout abroad for pillage and for prey:
Courage is their good captain.
SOPHY Courage! No.
Pale fear and black destruction leads the foe.

283 282 Tantalus: in Greek and Roman myth, a king who was punished for his intemperance during life with insatiable hunger and thirst in the underworld. He was placed in water up to his chest, with an apple tree just out of reach

284 284 stay my time: wait for my moment

285 0 SD *tables and forms*: the tables may be flat surfaces, but could also be notebooks or charts; forms may be plans or models of some kind

286 0 SD: *drum*: a drummer

287 8 vice-gerent: vice-regent, i.e. the Sophy addresses the Sultan as the one who exercises Jupiter's power on earth. As often in the period, English and European writers represent Muslims as worshipping classical gods

288 11 Sion: Zion, i.e. Jerusalem; it also can refer to the Holy Land as a whole

289 18 I cannot judge: I do not think

290 24 My hair is grey (and I am wise) from experience. "Livery" is a uniform that identifies a servant as belonging to a particular household; the Sultan imagines his gray hair as a badge denoting his experience

291 29 meads: fields

SULTAN I say again, the Christian princes lead
An army for their power invincible.[292]
Victorious hope sits hovering on their plumes:
Their gilded armor shines against the sun,
Dazzling our eyes from top of yonder hill
Like the bright streaks that flow from Paradise.
SOPHY Oh, conquest worthy the brave Persian swords![293]
Let us descend from forth the town and meet them!
SULTAN No.
SOPHY Yes.
SULTAN Should Jove himself in thunder answer "aye"
When we say no, we'd pull him from the sky.
SOPHY Should Sultan, Sophy, priest, or presbyter,[294]
Or gods, or devils, or men,[295] gainsay[296] our will,
Him, them, or thee, would the brave Persian kill.
MORETES Quench your hot spleens with drops of sweet advice!
Temper your rage with counsel, mighty kings.
SULTAN I say we will make peace with Christendom.
SOPHY I say the Persian scorns to be colleague,
Or to have part with them of Christendom.
SULTAN Yet hear my age!
SOPHY Yet hearken to my youth!
MORETES My tongue give place unto the Sultan's age.
TURNUS But I applaud the Persian's youthful rage.
SULTAN Stay, lords, our grave experience doth foresee
The mischiefs that attend on this debate.
We tread the path of our destruction.
By our dissensions grow the Christians strong,
Whom our united hearts may easily quell.
Brave Persian Sophy, we commend your hate
To them that have abhorred our Pagan gods—
Yet temper it with wisdom, valiant prince.
'Tis our security I would increase,
When with my words I mention gentle peace.
MORETES Experience doth instruct the Sultan's tongue,
Hearken to him, he speaks judicially.[297]
SOPHY My tongue a while gives license to mine ear.
The depth of your grave wisdoms let us hear.
SULTAN Then thus: let's send unto the Christians' host
To know what cause hath brought them thus far armed.
If peaceably they come to visit here
The ancient relics of their Savior's tomb,
Peace shall conduct them in and guard them out.
But if they come to conquer Sion's Hill,
And make irruption through our triple walls,[298]

292 33–4 the Christian … power invincible: for their army the Christians command a band (a "power") that is invincible; also, the Christian army is invincible because it is very powerful

293 39 Defeating this army would be a deed worthy of our warriors!

294 45 presbyter: elder or minister, generally of a Protestant sect and often distinct from "priest," which suggests Catholicism; it is of course anachronistic for the Sophy to make such a distinction, but it makes sense for Heywood who, as always, is trying to cover a wide spectrum

295 45–6 Sultan, Sophy … or men: the Sophy here rejects all temporal and religious authorities

296 46 gainsay: contradict, hinder

297 67 judicially: with good judgment

298 76 triple walls: Jerusalem was widely said to have three walls, but they were not concentric, as the Sultan's words suggest. Rather, they had been constructed in three separate periods

Death and despair shall ambush in their way
And we will seize the ensigns they display.
SOPHY My youth yields willingly to your grave years,
Let it be so. But whom shall we elect
To be created Lords Ambassadors?
SULTAN Moretes shall be one, for I am sure
He will employ his tongue, peace to procure.
SOPHY Turnus another, he that all things dares,
Will with defiance stir them up to war.
SULTAN Moretes and brave Turnus, speed you straight
Unto the Christian host. Say, if they come
Like pilgrims, to behold the sepulcher,
Our gates stand open to receive them in,
And be you painful[299] to persuade a peace.
But if they stand upon their hostile ground,
Say that our breasts are armed, our swords are keen,
Bold are our hearts, and fiery is our spleen,
And so be gone.
MORETES I to persuade a peace. *Exit*
TURNUS I go the furious rage of war t'increase. *Exit*
SULTAN We will meantime conduct our royal host.
One half is mine, the other you shall lead,
To intercept them ere they win the sight
Of these invincible and high-built walls.
Brave Persians, we will both in ambush lie,
Sure now the Christians are all come to die.[300]

Exeunt

[Act III, scene ii]

Enter TANCRED *with* BELLA FRANCA, *richly attired, she somewhat affecting him, though she makes no shew of it,* ROBERT OF NORMANDY, *the four brethren, and the* FRENCH LADY *like a page*

TANCRED Behold, brave Christian princes, all the glory
That Tancred can inherit in this world.[301]
EUSTACE Part of it's mine.
CHARLES And part belongs to me.
GODFREY An heavenly mixture, now beshrew my heart,
But Godfrey with the rest could cry half part.[302]
GUY I am all hers.
ROBERT That Lady seems to me
The fairest creature ever eye did see.
BELLA FRANCA Tancred, of all, thy face best pleaseth me. *In private*
TANCRED Fair lady!
EUSTACE Madame!
CHARLES Mistress!
GODFREY Beauteous love!
GUY Bright goddess!
ROBERT Nymph!

299 90 be you painful: take pains
300 100–01 Brave Persians . . . to die: it seems that the Sultan either assumes that it will be impossible to negotiate a peace, or that he intends treachery; in either case, this speech is hard to reconcile with his earlier statements
301 1–2 After presenting himself to the brothers as an uninterested guardian of Bella Franca, Tancred here seems to admit that he, too, is attracted to her
302 5 Godfrey also insists that he brings a share of the troops

LADY Love whom ye will, say I:
So ye affect not my beloved Guy![303]
TANCRED Lords, she is mine.
EUSTACE When did my interest cease?
CHARLES When I am here, you brother outlaw, peace.
GODFREY Why should not I enjoy her?
ROBERT Why not I?
GUY She can have none but me.
EUSTACE and CHARLES That we deny!
BELLA FRANCA Princes, what means this frenzy in your hearts?
Or hath some nigromantic[304] conjurer
Raised by his art some fury[305] in my shape,
To work sedition in the Christian camp?
You have confirmed by general parliament
A statute that must stand inviolate,
Namely, that mutiny in prince or peasant
Is death; a kingdom cannot save his life.[306]
Then whence proceed these strange contentions?
CHARLES I seized her first.
EUSTACE I first her thoughts did prove.[307]
TANCRED I plead the composition for my love.[308]
ROBERT If wealth will win the thoughts of that chaste lady,
I'll bid as fair as any for her love.
GODFREY If valor may achieve her, I 'mongst many
Will bid more warlike blows for her then any.
GUY Nay, if you go to scrambling, this for me. *Draw*[309]
LADY Speed they that list, so you repulsèd be.[310]
BELLA FRANCA Yet hear me, princes!
EUSTACE Hence with frivolous words. [*Draw*]
GODFREY Stand we to prate, when others draw their swords? [*Draw*]
CHARLES Speak thou[311] my cause. *Draw*
TANCRED This shall my pleader be. *Draw*
GUY Thou[312] art for us. *Draw*[313]
ROBERT And sword, speak thou for me. [*Draw*]
BELLA FRANCA He that best loves me, pierce me with his sword,
Lest I become your general overthrow!
I do conjure you by the love you bear me,
Either to banish this hostility
Or all at once to act my tragedy.
A blow is death proclaimed by parliament.
Can ye make laws and be the first that break them?
Knew I that this my beauty bred this strife,
With some black poison I would stain my cheeks,

303 11 So long as Guy is not the one whom you like!
304 17 nigromantic: related to black magic
305 18 fury: in Greek and Roman myth, a female deity responsible for inciting rage and vengeance. In the *Aeneid*, Juno directs a fury to possess Turnus to turn against Aeneas and his men; in later poems that imitated it, a fury is often summoned from hell to inspire an antagonist to oppose the course of a hero
306 22–3 mutiny in . . . his life: neither rank nor wealth protects anyone who rises against the leader of an army
307 25 I first . . . did prove: I was the first to find out what she was thinking
308 26 Perhaps Tancred means that he both seized and spoke with Bella Franca
309 31 SD *Draw*: i.e. his sword, to prepare for a fight
310 32 Let whoever wants to do well, so long as you are rejected
311 35 thou: Charles addresses his sword
312 36 Thou: Guy address Tancred: So you are challenging me!
313 36 SD *Draw*: despite the stage direction, Guy has already drawn his sword

Till I looked fouler than an Ethiope.[314]
Still do ye brandish your contentious swords?
This night shall end my beauty, and tomorrow
Look to behold my christall[315] eyes scratched out,
My visage martyred, and my hair torn off:
He that best loves it, ransom it with peace:
I will preserve it, if your fury cease.
But if ye still persist, the heavens I call
As my vow's witness, I will hate ye all.
TANCRED To shew my love, my sword shall sleep in rest. [*Sheathes his sword*]
GODFREY I'll keep mine sharp for the brave Sultan's crest. [*Sheathes*]
GUY Peace, sword. [*Sheathes*]
ROBERT The Norman Robert keeps his keen,
T'abate the fury of the Sultan's spleen. [*Sheathes*]
CHARLES My sword cries truce. [*Sheathes*]
EUSTACE Blade, when thou next art seen·
Thou mak'st thy lord[316] a king, his love a queen. [*Sheathes*]
BELLA FRANCA You have redeemed my beauty. Your last jar
Had made perfection with my face at war.[317]
EUSTACE Lady, the virtuous motions of your heart
Add to the abundant graces of your fame,
It was your beauty that did blind our souls,
And in our close breasts placed oblivion.
'Tis true, we have ordained a strict decree,
That whosoever in our Christian host
Strikes with a sword in hostile enmity
Forfeits his life. Then break off this debate
And keep our own decrees inviolate.

Enter with a tucket[318] *before them* TURNUS, *and* MORETES

MORETES Health to the Christians from the mighty Sultan!
TURNUS Death and destruction from the Persian Sophy.
ROBERT [*To* MORETES] That tongue brings peace, to thee will I attend.
GODFREY [*To* TURNUS] That tongue brings war, thy motions we commend.
TANCRED [*To* MORETES] Speak peace, thy looks are smooth, we'll list to thee.
CHARLES [*To* TURNUS] Speak war, bring war, and we to war agree.
MORETES The Babylonian Sultan, mighty princes,
Sends me to know the cause of this your march
Into a land so far remote from ye.
If ye intend to see your prophet's tomb
As holy pilgrims, peace shall guard your way.
EUSTACE Peace we defy. [*To* TURNUS] Let's hear what thou canst say.
ROBERT Proceed, proceed.
GUY Do; and I'll sound my drum

314 46 Ethiope: an Ethiopian, hence dark-skinned, and proverbially unattractive

315 49 christall: this spelling of "crystal," especially with the word "martyred" below, reminds the reader of the nominally Christian basis for the expedition. As Heywood knew, there were numerous tales of early Christian women martyrs tortured to death by Roman tyrants, figures much like the Sultan or the Sophy, for keeping their faith, their chastity, or both. Bella Franca's irony is multiple: it is the Christians who will force her to accept these tortures

316 60 thy lord: that is, Eustace himself. He is talking to his sword. Where the others defer their own ambitions to join forces in overthrowing the Sultan, Eustace pointedly refuses to subordinate his ambitions to those of the army

317 61–2 Your last … at war: that last argument ("jar") made my face and its perfect beauty oppose each other (i.e. made me wish that I was not so beautiful)

318 71 SD *tucket*: a fanfare on a trumpet, and, in this case, the person who blows the trumpet as well

To drown his voice, that doth for parlance[319] come.
EUSTACE Why, I am born to nothing[320] in this world
But what my sword can conquer. Should we yield
Our fortunes to base composition,
I have no hopes mine honor to increase.
Cursed be his base ear that attends to peace!
MORETES Let me conclude my message.
GODFREY Pagan, no:
[*To* TURNUS] War's friend, speak thou; I am to peace a foe.
TURNUS The Persian Sophy thus instructs my tongue:
That prince amongst you whose heroic breast
Dares shew itself to his triumphant spear,
Excepting but the name of Christian,
Like to the Persian gods he honors him.[321]
But should he know a heart in these proud troops,
And know that heart to be addict to peace,
He'd hate him like a man that should blaspheme.
In Sion towers hangs his victorious flag,
Blowing defiance this way: and it shows
Like a red meteor in the troubled air,
Or like a blazing comet, that foretells
The fall of princes.
CHARLES Thine own prince's fall!
TURNUS Then in one word, destruction to you all.
GODFREY I had not thought such spirits had remained
Within the warlike breasts of infidels.
EUSTACE Dares the majestic spirit of thy king
Answer a challenge? Dares he pawn his crown
Against the hazard of ten thousand lives?[322]
GUY And who should fight against him?
EUSTACE I.
GUY Thou!
EUSTACE Aye, 'gainst him, and thee, and all the world.
That interdicts my honor.
GUY Me!
EUSTACE Thee.
GUY Fire, rage, and fury all my veins do swell.
Be mute my tongue, bright sword my fury tell!
EUSTACE Fire mount 'gainst his mad fury, check his rage,
Burn out then flame, his blood thy heat shall swage.[323] *They fight, and are parted*
GODFREY What have ye done? Injustice stains our crests
If for this act ye have not lost their lives.
ROBERT I will not bear the badge of Christendom
In such a Bedlam-mad[324] society.
CHARLES Cease to determine of their harebrain rage,

319 85 parlance: negotiating (rather than combat)
320 86 born to nothing: this sounds like an exaggeration, but it is largely true. Although Eustace is noble, as the youngest son he would be unlikely to inherit any land or title
321 94–7 That prince … honors him: excepting only the fact that they bear the name of Christians, the Sophy will revere those men who oppose him bravely as he reveres his own gods
322 110–11 Dares he … thousand lives: is he bold enough to stake his kingdom when it will cost him the lives of ten thousand soldiers to defend it?
323 118 swage: temper, assuage
324 122 Bedlam-mad: Bedlam, or Bethlehem, was a London hospital for the mentally ill from the late middle ages. Robert compares the violent pride of Eustace and Guy to behavior of the insane confined there. But they are also "mad" for Bethlehem, the site of Jesus' birth and one of the aims of the Crusades

Till ye have sent the Pagans from our tents.
TANCRED 'Tis well advised. Soldiers, take charge of them,
Till we determine of our embassy.
MORETES I fear me, Turnus, had you known before
The spirits of these haughty Christians,
T'have been so full of envious chivalry,
You would have tempered some part of your rage.
You see they strive and fight amongst themselves,
To practice hate against[325] they meet with us.
TURNUS Moretes, no, we scorn all abject fears,
And they shall know our hearts as great as theirs.
GODFREY It shall be so. Attend me, Pagan lords.
We come not with grey gowns and pilgrims' staves,
Beads[326] at our sides and sandals on our feet,
Fear in our hearts, entreaty in our tongues,
To beg a passage to our prophet's grave.
But our soft beaver fells we have turned to iron,[327]
Our gowns to armor, and our shells to plumes.[328]
Our walking staves we have changed to scimitars,[329]
And so with pilgrims' hearts, not pilgrims' habits,
We come to hew way through your main armies,
And offer at the tomb our contrite hearts,
Made purple with as many Pagans' bloods
As we have in our breasts religious thoughts.
And so be gone, no words in trifling waste;[330]
Death follows after you with wings of haste.
TURNUS That prince speaks music which doth cheer my heart.
MORETES Princes, adieu; with terror I depart. *Exeunt*
CHARLES Now to these other captain-mutineers.
What shall be done with them?
EUSTACE Even what you please.
We have lived with pain, and we can die with ease.
GUY What God hath made, a[331] God's name do you mar.
Death is the least I fear; now to the bar.[332]
ROBERT Lords, give me leave to temper our decree.
The law is death, but such is our regard
Of Christian blood, we moderate it thus.
Because we know your worths, your lives are saved.
Yet that[333] the world shall see we prize our laws,
And are not partial should we sit on kings,[334]
We doom you everlasting banishment

325 132 against: in preparation for when

326 137 Beads: rosaries; with grey robes, walking sticks, and sandals, these were the conventional garb of peaceful pilgrims

327 140 Instead of hats made of beaver pelts, we now wear iron helmets. Godfrey is playing on words, since the visor of a helmet was also called a beaver. Throughout this passage Godfrey takes the typical costume of a peaceful pilgrim to the Holy Land and converts it to the arms of a crusader

328 141 shells to plumes: pilgrims to St. Iago de Compostela in Western Spain customarily carried a scallop shell on their journey to and from the shrine, but Godfrey extends this particular symbol to pilgrimage more broadly. The plumes are the feathers with which a knight might decorate his helmet; see, for instance, the frontispiece of the 1615 text, in which all four brothers wear plumes in their hats

329 142 scimitars: curved swords; this transformation is a little unexpected because scimitars were usually associated with Muslim warriors

330 148 no words in trifling waste: don't waste time with trivial chatter

331 155 a: by, in

332 156 now to the bar: go ahead and kill me. What exactly is meant by "bar" is unclear; the word might refer to the bar at which a case in court was pleaded (so Guy is asking to receive his sentence); or to the barrier that separated duelers or jousters (so Guy is asking to continue the brawl); or to an instrument of torture

333 161 Yet that: but so that

334 162 And do not show favoritism even when we pass judgment on kings

From out the Christian army.
EUSTACE Banishment?
This was your doing; well, I'll be revenged;
By all the hopes that I have lost, I will.
Princes, your dooms are upright,[335] I obey them,
And voluntarily exile myself.
Against my furious spirit I could weep
To leave this royal army, and to lose
The honor promised in the Pagans' deaths.
Farewell to all, with tears of grief I go.
Ye are all my friends, [*To* GUY] thou only art my foe. [*Exit*]
GUY Hold me so still.[336] Where'er I next shall meet thee,
This sword, like thunder, on thy crest shall greet thee.
[*Aside*] Banished the camp I go, but not so far
But I will make one in this Christian war.[337]
Like an unknown knight I will bear a shield,
In it engraven the trade I did profess,
When once I was a goldsmith in Cheapside.[338]
And if I prosper, to these arms I'll add
Some honor,[339] and the scutcheon[340] I shall bear
Shall to the Pagans bring pale death, and fear.
Adieu, brave Christian lords, for I must stray.
A banished man can never miss his way. [*Exit*]
GODFREY Why do you look so sad upon their griefs?
CHARLES Ah, pardon me. My heart begot a thought
At their departure, which had been of force
T'have strained a tear or two from my moist eye.
[*Aside*] How like was he to Eustace! He to Guy!
GODFREY A leaden weight of grief lies at my heart,
And I could wish myself were banished, too,
To bear them in their sorrows company.
ROBERT These, for example's sake, must be removed,
And though their absence will much weaken us,
Yet we had rather put us in God's guard,[341]
Lessening our own strength, than to bear with that
Which might in time lead to our overthrow.
March forward, lords; our love we will defer.
Prince Tancred, till our war's chief heat be spent,
Keep still[342] this beauteous lady [*Indicates* BELLA FRANCA] in your tent. *Exeunt. Flourish. Manent*[343] *two* LADIES
LADY My lord is banished, what shall poor I do?
There is no way, but I must after too.
But ere I go, some cunning I must use,

335 167 your dooms are upright: your judgments are fair
336 174 Hold me so still: continue to consider me your enemy
337 176–7 Banished the . . . Christian war: I will leave the camp, but I will continue to fight in this crusade
338 178–80 Like an . . . in Cheapside: Guy will disguise himself by changing his shield. With his plans for his shield, he returns to the pledge made by all the brothers to bear the arms of their trades to the Holy Land
339 181–2 And if . . . some honor: If I am successful, I will change the Goldsmiths' arms to commemorate my feats. To "add an honor" was the technical term for adding a new device to an existing coat of arms
340 182 scutcheon: escutcheon, shield bearing a coat of arms
341 196 put us in God's guard: give ourselves over to the protection of God
342 201 Keep still: continue to keep
343 201 SD *Manent*: remain on stage (plural; Latin)

To make this lady[344] my lord's love refuse.
BELLA FRANCA Fair youth, why have you singled me along?
Is it to share joy, or partake my moan?
LADY Whether you please. Invention help me now (*Apart*)[345]
To bring her out of love with my sweet lord,
For should she love him I were quite undone.
Madame, in faith, how many suitors have you?
BELLA FRANCA More than I wish I had. First, the French general—
LADY Oh God, I fear, I think I am accursed.
She loves him best, because she names him first.
BELLA FRANCA The English Robert, County Palatine,
Two gentlemen that took me in the woods;
One is now banished, but the other still
Stays in the army; then the Bullen Duke!
LADY And which of all these is the properest man?
BELLA FRANCA Faith, let me hear thy judgment.
LADY Prince Robert is a gallant gentleman,
But the French lord uncomely, and unshaped.
Tancred's a proper man, but the French lord,
He hath no making, no good shape at all.
I could not love a man of his complexion:
I would not love him if I were a lady,
Had he more crowns[346] than Caesar conquerèd.
BELLA FRANCA I see no such defects in that French lord.
LADY [*Aside*] Aye, aye, 'tis so! Upon my life she loves him.
I must devise some plot, or they will use
Some means to meet and marry out of hand.
[*To* BELLA FRANCA] Lady, he was my master, but believe me,
He is the most insatiate man for women,
That ever breathed; nay, madam, which is more,
He loves variety and delights in change.
And I heard him say, should he be married,
He'd make his wife a cuck-quean.[347]
BELLA FRANCA Why though he do, 'tis virtue in a woman
If she can bear[348] his imperfections.
LADY [*Aside*] Upon my life they are made sure already,
She's pleased with any imperfections.
What should I do?
BELLA FRANCA Now fair youth, list to me,
I will acquaint thee with a secrecy.
These lords so trouble me with their vain suits,
That I am tired and wearied, and resolve
To steal away in secret from the camp.
LADY [*Aside*] My Guy is gone, and she would follow him:
I must prevent it, or else lose my love.
BELLA FRANCA Wilt thou consort me, bear me company,
And share with me in joy and misery?
LADY Madame, I will. [*Aside*] She loves him, and no wonder.
I'll go, be't but to keep them still asunder.

344 205 this lady: i.e. Bella Franca
345 208 SD (*Apart*): the parentheses are printed in Q
346 227 crowns: kingships; gold coins (stamped with the image of a crown)
347 237 cuck-quean: a female cuckold; that is, he would take other lovers
348 239 bear: tolerate

BELLA FRANCA Then from their tents this night we'll steal away,
And through the wide woods and the forests stray.

Exeunt

[Act IV, scene i]

Flourish. Enter SULTAN, SOPHY, TURNUS, MORETES, *drums, ensigns, and soldiers*

SULTAN Then your reports sound naught but death and war.
MORETES The Christians would not lend an ear to peace.
SOPHY Since they demean themselves[349] so honorably
This earth shall give them honorable graves.
TURNUS By Pride herself[350] are their proud ensigns borne:
War in their tongues sits, in their faces scorn.
SULTAN Our resolutions shall control base fears.
We are proud as they; our swords shall answer theirs.
SOPHY Didst thou deliver our strict embassy?
TURNUS I did, my lord.
SULTAN Did they not quake to hear it?
TURNUS No more than rocks shake with a puff of breath.
They come resolved, and not in fear of death.
SOPHY Looked they not pale?
TURNUS With fury, not with fear.
They were mad, because your forces were not there.
SULTAN Did you not dash their spirits? Fell not their eyes
Down to the earth, when thou didst speak of us?
Went not a fearful murmur through their host,
When thou didst number our unnumbered power?
Did not their faint swords tremble in their hands,
At that name "Sultan"?
SOPHY Or when thou named'st me,
My power, my strength, my matchless chivalry,
Fell they not flat upon the earth with fear?
TURNUS No, but their proud hearts bounded in their breasts,
Their plumes flew bravely on their golden crests:
And they were ready to have fallen at jar
Which of them first should with the Persian war.[351]
MORETES There was no tongue but breathed defiance forth.
I could not see a face but menaced death,
No hand but brandished a victorious sword.
They all cry "Battle! Battle!," peace defy,
And not a heart but promised victory.
SULTAN There's not an heart shall scape our tyranny;
Since they provoke our indignation,
Like the vast ocean shall our courage rise,
To drown their pride, and all their powers surprise.
SOPHY My scimitar is like the bolt of Jove,
That never toucheth but it strikes with death.
Oh how I long till we with spears in rests[352]
Strike out the lightning from their high-plumed crests.
SULTAN I would burn off this beard in such a flame

349 3 demean themselves: act, behave
350 5 By Pride herself: i.e. as though by the personification of pride (here imagined as female)
351 25–6 fallen at . . . Persian war: come to blows over who would fight with the Persians first
352 38 spears in rests: that is, readied for attack; "rests" supported the weight of cavalry spears in combat

As I could kindle with my puissant[353] blows:
Yet the least hair I value at more worth
Than all the Christian empire.
SOPHY[354] Speak, brave Sultan,
Shall our bard[355] horses climb yond mountain tops,
And bid them battle where they pitch their tents?
SULTAN Courage cries "On!" but good advice saith "Stay!"
Experience bids us fight another way.
Why should we tire our troops in search of them
That with audacious boldness seek out us?
Let us stand to receive them when they come,
And with a grove of pikes growing on this earth
Where now no tree appears, toss up their bodies,
Whose corses by your strong arms kept aloof,
May hang like bloody pendants on your staves.[356]
SOPHY Oh sight best pleasing to the Persian gods!
TURNUS In the sky's forehead[357] shall the bright sun stand
Amazed to view that glorious spectacle,
And with the pleasing sight forget his way,
To grace our trophy with perpetual day.
MORETES But how shall we receive their armèd troops?
What special order will your grace assign
To them that shall command your companies?
SULTAN It shall be thus. This way the Christians march.
The body of our host shall stay behind
To be a strength to fair Jerusalem.
But we with certain soldiers secretly
Will lie in ambush. The great Persian Sophy,
With Turnus and a chief command of men,
Shall guard that way. Myself, and thou, Moretes,
Will keep this passage with a troop select,
To seize on their forerunners, scouts, and spies.
Assist us, fate, ere long the world shall know
Our glories by the Christians' overthrow.
This is my quarter; these my men shall be.
SOPHY Moretes,[358] thou and these shall follow me.

Exeunt

[Act IV, scene ii]

Enter ROBERT OF NORMANDY

ROBERT Oh, whither will blind love conduct my steps?
Prince Tancred's dear, and English Robert's joy,
Is fled in secret, and hath left our tents.

353 41 puissant: powerful
354 43 Q gives this speech to the Sultan, but this is almost certainly an error
355 44 bard: probably short for "barded," equipped with armor
356 54 staves: plural of "staff," a spear meant to be used by a mounted soldier
357 56 forehead: highest, most prominent part
358 75 Moretes: this is the word printed in Q, and it fits the meter of the line; unfortunately, it makes little sense. The Sultan has just said that Moretes would accompany him rather than the Sophy, and the pairing of the Sophy with the equally hot-headed Turnus is more logical. Furthermore, in the next scene, Moretes appears with the Sultan. Possibly this line should be assigned to the Sultan

Thus like an errant[359] and adventurous knight,
I have left the host to follow her fair search,
And durst not trust the air with my intent.
This way, they say, she went; the camp's secure,
This way unknown, in secret I pursue her.

Enter CHARLES

CHARLES This way my love went like a shooting star,
Whose blazing train doth gild the firmament.
Such glorious beauty adds she to the way,
Making the dark night-paths shine bright as day.
Ye honored arms, farewell, and camp, adieu,
I do forsake myself her to pursue.
ROBERT Behold a traveler! I will enquire
If chance hath cast his eye upon my love.
CHARLES I was about to ask of yonder man,
Whether her beauty had enriched his sight,
But 'tis my rival, Robert. Charles, obscure thee.[360]
For should he see thee, he would quickly judge
What adamant[361] had drawn me to these woods.
One case, I see, hath made us errants both.[362]
To be found wandering thus I should be loath.
ROBERT Love that drew me, hath drawn that knight along.
Being but a child, a giant's not so strong.[363]

Enter SULTAN, MORETES, *and soldiers*

SULTAN Stand, Christians, by your crosses on your breasts
Ye're marked for death and base destruction.
ROBERT What are ye, that, like cowards, with such odds
Assault us thus unfurnished[364] for the wars?
SULTAN I am the Sultan, these my men at arms,
That lie to intercept you and prepare
For your accursèd lives this fatal snare.
CHARLES The Sultan, the grand enemy to Christ,
The devil's lieutenant, viceroy[365] under him!
Brave English Robert, since our frowning stars
Have brought us to this narrow exigent,[366]
And trained us hither[367] with a chain of love
To perish by the swords of infidels,
Stand foot to foot.[368]
ROBERT Tush, I am Pagans'-swords-proof,[369] and my stars

359 4 errant: wandering, but also questing, the conventional description of the heroes of chivalric romance, such as Orlando, Amadis of Gaul, and Don Quixote. The Crusades were the nominal setting of many of the most popular of these
360 19 obscure thee: hide yourself
361 21 adamant: magnetic force
362 22 The same situation, i.e. desiring Bella Franca, has sent both of us seeking for her in the woods. "Case" is also slang for "vagina," so the line also contains a sexual pun
363 25 Even though Love is only a child, it is stronger than a giant. Robert is thinking of Cupid, the Roman god of love, often represented as a young boy
364 29 unfurnished: unprepared, unequipped
365 34 lieutenant, viceroy: one who holds a command in another's place, i.e. the Sultan does the devil's work on earth
366 36 narrow exigent: tight squeeze
367 37 trained us hither: led us here
368 39 Charles tells Robert to come close to him so that they can defend one another
369 40 Pagans'-swords-proof: resistant to the swords of Pagans

Have marked me for a conqueror in these wars.
SULTAN Upon them, soldiers; pity they despise,
Scarce can the world afford[370] a richer prize. *Alarum.*[371] *They fight, and are both taken*
CHARLES Thou glorious eye of heaven, be ever blind,
Mask thy bright face in clouds eternally,
Dark vapors and thick mists thy front embrace,
And never shine to look on my disgrace.
ROBERT A prisoner, Robert! This my comfort be:
He makes me bound that best can set me free.[372]
SULTAN Take them to guard! This entrance[373] to our wars
Is full of spirit, and begets much hope.
We will not yet examine what ye are
Till tortures wring it from your slavish tongues.
That done, your bloods these champaigns shall imbrue.[374]
Meantime we'll wait for more of your loose crew.

Enter GUY *with his shield, and a page brings his sword and target,*[375] *in each of his hands a poleax*[376]

GUY I am turned wild man since I used these forests,
And I have won more weapons in these woods,
From outlaws whom my sword hath vanquishèd,
Than I can carry on my back with ease.
I have swords, targets, pikes, and partisans,
Poleaxes, maces, clubs, and horsemen's staves,
Darts,[377] halberds,[378] longswords, pistols, petronels,[379]
All which I have conquered. At this mountain ridge
Two villains with these weapons set upon me,
But with my sword I made them turn their heels,
And leaves[380] these trophies which I thus support,
And bear upon my shoulders, conqueror-like—
What? Do I see an ambush? By their arms
They should be Pagans: Robert, prisoner!
With him a Christian leader! Oh my God,
Thou hast either brought me to revive my name
By rescuing these, or here to die with shame.
Come life, come death, a banished man will try
To live with honor, or with honor die.
Robert, break from thy guard, make them dismayed,
Receive these weapons, God hath sent thee aid.
ROBERT God, and Saint George!
CHARLES Now by the Sultan's crown,

370 43 afford: offer
371 43 SD *Alarum*: alarm, a signal for battle
372 49 God ("He"), who has chosen to make me a prisoner ("bound"), is most able to free me
373 50 entrance: beginning
374 54 imbrue: soak, stain
375 55 SD *target*: small shield; as he pledged earlier (III.ii. 180), the larger shield, which Guy carries, is adorned with the arms of the Goldsmiths, quartered in red (upper left and lower right) and blue, with lions' heads in the red quarters and wreathes in the blue. Guy will later add chalices (V.iv. 90) to the blue quarters, bringing the design up to date for Heywood's audience.
376 55 SD *poleax*: weapon with an axeblade or hammerhead at one end and, generally, a spike at the other. Guy presumably gives these weapons to Charles and Robert, while using a sword himself
377 62 Darts: javelins, spears
378 62 halberds: spearlike weapons with a cutting edge mounted on a long staff
379 62 petronels: heavy pistols; the variety of weapons that Guy displays, and the way in which Charles is challenged to use them skillfully, is reminiscent of some fencing matches, in which opponents might be called upon to use many different weapons, or to match one weapon against another
380 66 leaves: leave (singular verb with plural subject)

If I can wield this weapon, he shall down!
GUY The Christians' God for us!
SULTAN What, are they free?
Alarum drums, the heathen powers for me!

They fight; the Pagans are beaten off, GUY *departs suddenly*

ROBERT Some angel in the habit of a knight,
Hath rescued us; such heavy downright blows
Could never come from any mortal arm.
For every blow he reached was certain death.
CHARLES What is that power, if heavenly power he be,
That we may laud and praise his deity?
ROBERT Departed on a sudden ere we know[381]
To whom our freedoms and our lives we owe!
CHARLES By that inscription graven on his shield,
We may perhaps descry him in the camp.[382]
Cease admiration then; let these events
Hasten our steps back to survey our tents.

[*Exeunt*]

[Act IV, scene iii]

Enter severally[383] GODFREY *and* TANCRED

TANCRED Godfrey!
GODFREY Tancred!
TANCRED Well met, my lord, in these unpeopled paths.
What, hath your love made you to leave the field?
GODFREY Godfrey ne'er dreamt to have met with Tancred here.
The lady that hath fled from our chaste love,
(Whom, Tancred, I do more affectionate
Because she much resembles my fair sister)
Hath caused me so much to forget myself,
And play the wanderer in these unknown woods. *Soft march*
But soft, that drum should speak the Pagans' tongue:
I fear we are betrayed. Aye, aye, 'tis so!
Tancred, we are round compassed by the foe!

SULTAN, SOPHY, *and soldiers encompass the Christian princes. Enter* EUSTACE, *and set them free.* [*They fight off the Pagan soldiers, who go out.* TANCRED *and* GODFREY *exeunt*]

EUSTACE Thank me for this; for, next th'almighty powers,
I have been the means to save your desperate lives.
Now, Christian princes, I am quit with you
For all the grace you have done me in the camp,
And now you owe me for my banishment.
And though you have exiled me from your tents,
You have not power to keep me from the wars.
Upon this shield I bear the Grocers' arms,[384]

381 87 ere we know: before we could learn
382 90 Maybe we will be able to recognize his shield back in camp
383 0 SD *severally*: through separate doors
384 21 Grocers' arms: a red chevron on a white background and peppered with cloves, resembling royal ermine while alluding to the Grocer's origins; like Guy, Eustace is disguising his identity by using the arms of his trade

Unto which trade I was enrolled and bound,
And like a strange knight, I will aid the Christians.
Thou trade[385] which didst sustain my poverty,
Didst helpless help me;[386] though I left thee then,
Yet that the world shall see I am not ingrate,
Or scorning that, which gave my fortunes breath,
I will enlarge these arms and make their name
The original and life of all my fame.
But I am tired with travail.[387] Shield, lie there.
Oh, that I could but see that lusty spirit,
My arch-foe, rival in my banishment,
To be revenged and end my hostile hate!
I'll dream I fight with him to ease my spleen,
And in that thought I lay me on this green. *Sleep*

Enter GUY *with a paper and his shield*

GUY Arms, ye are full of hope and sweet success!
The famous art, whose honored badge ye are,
First, when I lived 'mongst London prentices,
Gave me an honest and a pleasant life,
Now in these woods have won me fame and honor,
And I have rescued princes with this shield.
And princes are indebted to these arms.
And if I live, in memory of this
Within their fair hall[388] shall this scutcheon hang,
Till some smooth pen historify my name.
What object's that? A knight asleep or dead?
Oh, 'tis the base and ground of all my hate!
I'll kill the villain! Oh, dishonored thought!
Art thou not son unto the Bullen Duke,
And canst thou hatch dishonor? Arch-foe, live.
I scorn advantage, should I fight with Mars.[389]
He bears this shield; I will exchange with his
And leave a motto written in mine own
Shall make him quake to read. Be swift, my pen,
T'affright his sense when he shall wake again.
'Tis done. Then go with me,[390] and mine stay here,
Which in despite of thee,[391] base knight, I wear. *Exit*
EUSTACE [*Awakening*] The hours have overrun me with swift pace,
And time hath fastened to him swallows' wings.
Come sword, come shield—but soft, thou art a stranger,[392]
And pardon me, good shield, I know thee not.
What have we here? [*Reads the paper*]

385 24 Thou trade: i.e. the company of the Grocers
386 25 Didst helpless help me: helped me when I was helpless
387 30 travail: labor, but also travel (see II.iii. 12 and note)
388 44 fair hall: the liveried guilds maintained halls for the use of their members; Guy pledges that he will hang his shield in the Goldsmiths' Hall as a monument
389 51 I refuse to take unfair advantage of an enemy, even if I were fighting the god of war himself
390 56 Then go with me: Guy addresses Eustace's shield, which he has picked up
391 57 in despite of thee: to mock you, to your disgrace
392 60 thou art a stranger: like Guy, Eustace speaks to the shield

Ask not who that shield doth owe,[393]
For he is thy mortal foe:
And where'er he sees that shield,
City, borough, grove, or field,
He that bears it, bears his bane;[394]
By his hand[395] *he must be slain.*
Thine, in spite of thee,[396] *he'll bear;*
If thou dar'st, his scutcheon wear.
He writ this, that thy shield will keep,
And might have thine, thee being asleep.
'Tis a fine fellow! By this light, he is
An honest rogue, and hath a good conceit.
Wear it? I'll wear it. If I do not![397] Well,
He needed not to have put in the word "dare"!
For I dare. Dare I? He shall see I dare!
Belike he fears I dare not challenge mine.
Were't fastened to the arm of Beelzebub,[398]
I would fight with him with firebrands for my shield.
But dares he wear mine? On my life he dares!
I love him like my brother for this act,
And I will bear this shield with as much pride
As sat I[399] in a chariot by Jove's side.
Shine bright, my stars, to do me some fair grace,
Bring us to meet in some auspicious[400] place.

[*Exit*][401]

[Act IV, scene iv]

Enter the ladies flying, pursued by the CLOWN

CLOWN Nay, you cowardly lady that run away from the camp and dare not stand to it, I am glad I have light[402] on you! Choose your weapon, choose your weapon! I am a soldier, and a martial man, and I will offer you the right of arms. If you vanquish me, I'll be your captive; if you be cast down I'll carry you back prisoner.
LADY I wear a weapon that I dare not draw.
Fie on this womanish fear, what shall I do?
BELLA FRANCA Some of my father's spirit revives in me.
Give me thy weapon, boy, and thou shalt see.
I for us both will win sweet liberty.
CLOWN I was never so overreached;[403] and, but for shame, and that I am a man at arms, I would run away and take me to my legs. Have at thee, sweet lady.

393 63 owe: own
394 67 He who bears this shield bears the cause of his own destruction
395 68 *his hand*: i.e. the hand of the one who owns the shield
396 69 *in spite of thee*: to insult you
397 75 If I do not!: as if I wouldn't!
398 79 Beelzebub: the devil
399 84 As sat I: as if I sat
400 86 auspicious: favorable; promising of future success
401 86 SD *Exit*: there is no direction here to remove Eustace from the stage, and it is not impossible that he simply remains onstage. But the stage direction at IV.iv. 11 specifies that Eustace "comes in," which suggests that the action is not continuous
402 2 light: i.e. lit, come upon
403 10 overreached: outmatched; the Clown already admits that Bella Franca is better than he is. This is another opportunity for comic business, with the Clown perhaps admitting defeat as soon as Bella Franca draws

As they fight, EUSTACE *comes in*

EUSTACE Base villain, dar'st thou offer violence
Unto a lady? Stay, maintain thy challenge.
CLOWN You think you have a fool in hand? No, by my faith, not I. If you have any business to the camp, farewell—I am running thither as fast as I can. [*Exit*]
EUSTACE Mount up my soul, unto the heighth of joy!
Saving[404] my foe, whose honored shield I bear,
None living did I more desire to meet.
BELLA FRANCA Saving those Christian lords that seek my love,
None living did I more desire to shun.
EUSTACE Well met, brave saint, in these unpeopled paths,
Fear no rude force, for I am civil born,
Descended from a princely parentage·
And though an exile from the Christians' camp,
Yet in my heart I wear the Cross of Christ,
Even in as deep a crimson as the best.
Love me, though I am landless and remote
From the fair clime where first I breathed this air,
Yet know I bear a kingdom in this sword,
And ere I die, look to behold this front
Empaled[405] and circled with a royal crown.
BELLA FRANCA I never marked this gallant half so much.
He hath my brother's eye, my father's brow,
And he is Eustace all from top to toe.
EUSTACE I had a sister, lady, with that red
That gives a crimson tincture to your cheek,
With such a hand hid in a glove of snow,
That spake all music, like your heavenly tongue;
And for her sake, fair saint, I honor you.
BELLA FRANCA I had a brother, had not the rude seas
Deprived me of him, with that manly look,
That grace, that courage, I behold in you.
A prince, whom had the rude seas never seen,
Even such another had young Eustace been.
EUSTACE Eustace! Even such an accent gave her tongue,
So did my name sound in my sister's mouth.
Oh Bella Franca, wert thou not obscured
Within a cloud and mask of poverty,
Such fame ere this had thy rare virtues won,
Thus had thy beauty checked th'all-seeing sun.
BELLA FRANCA It is my brother Eustace!
EUSTACE View her well!
Imagine her but thus attired, and she
Would Bella Franca and my sister be.
BELLA FRANCA But strip my brother from his prentice coat,
His cap, his common soldier's base disguise—
Even such a gallant as this seems to me,
Such would my brother, my sweet Eustace, be.
EUSTACE Sister!
BELLA FRANCA Brother!
EUSTACE Make me immortal then! By heaven I vow,

404 17 Saving: except for
405 31 Empaled: set inside a protective fence or wall

I am richer than the Persian Sophy now.
BELLA FRANCA All Asia flows not with more plenteous treasure,
Than I, to embrace my brother, my heart's pleasure.
How did you scape the waves?
EUSTACE How have you passed
The perilous land and crossed the seas so vast?
BELLA FRANCA Where are my brothers, Eustace?
EUSTACE Oh, those words
Pierce to my heart like darts and pointed swords!
Omit these passions, sister, they are dead.
But to forget these griefs, what youth is this?
LADY Page to the Prince of France.
EUSTACE 'Tis he I hate,
As chief occasion of my banishment.
BELLA FRANCA Yet, my sweet brother, do not blame the youth.
Full well he hath demeaned himself with me.
He never, since we entered in these woods,
Left me in my distress; when we alone
Sit in these deserts, never by rude force
Did do me the least shame, or violence.
LADY A good cause why[406] I lead so chaste a life;
A jealous man may trust me with his wife.
EUSTACE Well, sirrah, for your truth and honesty
I pardon thee, though I detest thy lord.
LADY Then let me change my habit, gentle sir,
Lest in this shape I chance to meet my master.
Then, if you please, I'll clothe me like a lady,
And wait upon your sister in your tent.
EUSTACE Nay, if it please thee; I am well content.
LADY My plot is good; well, howsoe'er it prove,
'Twill either end my life, or win my love.
EUSTACE Come, best part of myself, we now will go
To wail our fortunes and discourse our woe.
I will disguised unto the famous siege,
And in these arms make known my valor's proof.[407]
You shall in secret in my tent abide;
I to achieve fame will my spirits employ.
After this grief my heart divines much joy.

Exit

[Act IV, scene v]

Enter ROBERT, *and* TANCRED, GODFREY, *and* CHARLES, *with their shields and scutcheons, drum and soldiers,* GODFREY's *shield having a maiden head with a crown in it,* CHARLES's *shield the Haberdashers' arms*[408]

ROBERT Behold the high walls of Jerusalem
Which Titus and Vespasian[409] once brake down!
From off these turrets have the ancient Jews
Seen worlds of people mustering on these plains!

406 78 A good cause why: there is a good reason (i.e. because she is actually a woman)
407 91–2 I will go to the siege disguised by a different shield, and show off my bravery and skill in combat
408 0 SD The crowned maiden's head on Godfrey's shield is the arms of the Mercers' guild; the Haberdashers' arms borne by Charles, as he will explain later, is a red diagonal band with a gold lion on it, over a blue and white patterned background
409 2 Titus and Vespasian: son and father Roman generals (and later emperors) who conquered Jerusalem and destroyed the Second Temple in 70 CE after years of resistance to Roman rule

Oh princes, which of all your eyes are dry,
To look upon this temple, now destroyed?
Yonder did stand the great Jehovah's house,
In midst of all his people, there he dwelt.
Vessels of gold did serve his sacrifice,
And with him for the people spake the priests.
There was the ark, the show-bread, Aaron's rod,
Sanctum Sanctorum, and the Cherubins.[410]
Now in that holy place, where God himself
Was personally present, Pagans dwell.
False gods are reared, each temple idols bears.
Oh, who can see this, and abstain from tears?[411]
GODFREY This way, this sacred path our Savior trod,
When he came riding to Jerusalem,
Whilst the religious people spread his way
With flowers, and garments, and "Hosanna" cried.[412]
Yonder did stand the great church, where he taught,
Confuting all the scribes and pharisees.[413]
This place did witness all his miracles:
Within this place did stand the judgment seat,
Where Pontius Pilate with the Elders sat,
Where they condemned him to be whipped and crowned,
To be derided, mocked, and crucified,
His hands bored through with nails, his side with spears.
Oh, who can see this place, and keep his tears?
CHARLES On yond side of the town he died for us:
At whose departure all these walls did shake,
And the destroyèd temple's veil did rend:
The groves are to be seen from which ghosts rose,
There stood the cross, there stands the sepulcher!
The place still bears the name of "Dead men's bones."[414]
And still the tomb our Savior's livery wears.
What eye can see it, and not melt in tears?
TANCRED No soldier but[415] shall look with reverence
Upon these fair and glorious monuments.
To swear, or speak profanely, shall be death.
I cast my heart as low as to this earth
And wish that I could march upon my knees,
In true submission, and right holy zeal.
Oh, since our wars are God's, abandon fears,
But in contrition weep repentant tears.
ROBERT Sound a parley; I see your hearts are fired,
Your souls with victory from heaven inspired.

410 11–12 These lines list the features of the Sanctum Sanctorum (Holy Place of Holy Places), the inner shrine of the Solomonic Temple. The ark was the ark of the covenant, the sacred chest for the tablets given by God to Moses, decorated with gold statues of Cherubim or angels; show-bread were ceremonial loaves that accompanied the ark; Aaron's rod was thought by early modern Christians to have been kept in the ark

411 16 tears: each of the following speeches ends in the word "tears," which in each case completes a rhyming couplet. The four remaining Crusaders offer something like a ritual lament for Jerusalem under Muslim rule

412 17–20 This way … "Hosanna" cried: Robert recalled Jerusalem's Old Testament, Jewish history. Godfrey refers to stories from the New Testament and of Christianity, namely Christ's entry into Jerusalem before his arrest and crucifixion, his first teaching in the Temple as a boy, his trial and death. Charles will discuss its aftermath, and Tancred proper reverence towards its monuments in the present

413 22 scribes and pharisees: interpreters of Jewish law in Jesus' time, and often his opponents in doctrine

414 35 "Dead men's bones": Calvary, or Golgotha, the place where Jesus was crucified, was interpreted in the Gospels of Mark and Matthew to mean "the place of the skull"

415 38 No soldier but: every soldier

Sound a parley.[416] *Enter upon the walls,* SULTAN, SOPHY, TURNUS, MORETES, *soldiers. Flourish*

SULTAN Why swarm these Christians to our city walls?
Look, foreigners, do not the lofty spires,
And these cloud-kissing turrets that you see,
Strike deadly terror in your wounded souls?
Go, Persian, flourish my vermilion flag,[417]
Advance my standard high, the sight whereof
Will drive these stragglers in disordered ranks
And in a hurly-burly throng them hence.
SOPHY See how they quake, to view our martial looks!
As when a sturdy cyclops rears aloft
A boisterous truncheon 'mongst a troop of dwarfs.
GODFREY Sultan and Sophy, ye damned hell-hounds both,
So quakes the eagle to behold a gnat,
The lion to behold a marmoset.[418]
I'll beard and brave you in your own belief,
As when the heathen god, whom you call Jove,
Warred with the giant, great Enceladus,[419]
And flung him from Olympus' two-topped mount,
The swains stood trembling to behold his fall,
That with his weight did make the earth to groan.
So, Sultan, look, when I have scaled these walls,
And won the place where now thou stand'st secure,
To be hurled headlong from the proudest tower,[420]
In scorn of thee, thy false gods, and their power.
CHARLES We will assail you like rebounding rocks,
Bandied[421] against the battlements of heaven!
We'll turn thy city into desert plains,
And thy proud spires that seems[422] to kiss the clouds,
Shall with their gilt tops pave the miry[423] streets,
As all too base for us to march upon.
Seest thou this shield? However this device
Seems not to rank with emperors, Sultan, know
This shield shall give thy fatal overthrow.[424]
SULTAN Such peals of thunder did I never hear.
I think that very words these walls will tear!
GODFREY This shield you see, includes two mysteries:
A virgin crowned, it is the Mercers' arms,
Withal[425] the picture of my love that's fled.

416 47 SD *parley*: a trumpet call signaling a pause in hostilities and a meeting between the opposing forces
417 52 vermilion flag: bright red flag. This might remind playgoers of Marlowe's *Tamberlaine*, where the title character shows a red flag when he will give no quarter to his enemies
418 61 marmoset: small monkey
419 64 Enceladus: in Greek and Roman myth, one of a race of Giants who warred against (and were defeated by) the gods. Enceladus was thrown from heaven and buried under Mt. Etna, the volcano in Sicily
420 68–70 look, when . . . proudest tower: expect to be thrown from the highest tower when I have entered the city. As well as echoing that of the rebellious Enceladus, the Sultan's imagined fate recalls both the killing of Hector's son Astyanax by throwing him from the walls of Troy when the Greeks had taken the city, and Satan's fall from the tower after failing to tempt Christ
421 73 Bandied: hit (like tennis balls)
422 75 seems: i.e. seem (singular verb with plural subject)
423 76 miry: muddy
424 78–80 However this . . . fatal overthrow: the device on Charles's shield seems not to rank with emperors because it is the guild sign of the Haberdashers; even so, Charles will still be able to defeat the Sultan in battle
425 85 withal: and also

Both these I'll grace, and add to them thy head.[426]
SOPHY Methinks I see pale death fly from their words:
Their speech so strong, how powerful are their swords!
CHARLES Since first I bore this shield I quartered it
With this red lion, whom I singly once
Slew in the forest.[427] Thus much have I already
Added unto the Haberdashers' arms.
But ere I leave these fair Judean bounds,
Unto this lion I'll add all your crowns.[428]
TURNUS Send for some prisoners, martyr, torture them
Even in the face of all the Christian host.
SULTAN It shall be so. Moretes, bring them forth.
ROBERT No drop of blood falls from a Christian heart,
But thy heart's blood shall ransom.[429]

Enter some bringing forth OLD BULLEN,[430] *and other prisoners bound*

SULTAN   Bring them forth,
Devise new tortures!
Oh, for some rare artist
That could invent a death more terrible
Than are the everlasting pangs of hell!
OLD BULLEN Oh brethren, let not me move you to ruth![431]
Happy is he that suffers for the truth.
The joys to come exceed the present grief;
Secure yourselves, for Christ is my relief.[432]
GODFREY Why shrinks the warm blood from my troubled heart?
CHARLES Why starts my hair up at this heavy sight?
GODFREY Say, father,[433] are not you the Bullen Earl?
OLD BULLEN Fair son, I was the happen[434] Bullen Earl:
But now my son—
CHARLES   Call no man "son" but me
Father, my sword shall win you liberty!
GODFREY Peace, forgèd bastard, whatsoe'er thou be:[435]
My reverend father, call none "son" but me,
For in this sword doth rest thy liberty!
CHARLES Such mercy as my sword affords to Pagans
He finds that calls me bastard![436] I am Charles,

426 86 add to them thy head: Godfrey promises to add an image of the Sultan's head to his arms once he has defeated him. There is no such image on the actual Mercers' arms

427 90–91 red lion . . . the forest: this is the first we hear of the unlucky lion, but a gold lion on a red diagonal was part of the arms of the company of Haberdashers. Heywood provides a partial etiology for this design. Quartering a shield (line 89) meant to divide it into four fields, two above and two below, as a way of combining two separate coats of arms. The Haberdashers' arms are not quartered, so Charles seems to use the term loosely, to mean he added a lion to the arms

428 94 crowns: royal insignia, but also heads. The Haberdashers' arms do not display crowns

429 98–9 No drop . . . shall ransom: every drop of Christian blood you spill will be paid for with a drop of your own

430 99 SD OLD BULLEN: in the play's first stage direction and in the speech-prefixes of the first scene, Bullen is identified as the "Earl"; in this scene, he is "Old Bullen." This perhaps provides a hint at how the playwright was imagining him in each of these scenes and what affect he is meant to evoke: first, as a nobleman, respect; here, as an old man, pity. Speech prefixes in later scenes split the difference with "Old Duke"

431 104 ruth: sorrow, pity

432 107 Take care of yourselves; I am content to die

433 110 father: as earlier, Heywood plays with the ambiguity of the words "father" and "son" as terms of respect or affection for an older or a younger man and in their proper familial sense for dramatic effect. Godfrey here uses "father" because he knows that Old Bullen is his father, but the Earl calls him "son" as a term of affection for a younger man

434 111 happen: erstwhile

435 114 whatsoe'er thou be: Charles and Godfrey still do not recognize each other, nor does the Earl recognize them until they name themselves

436 117–18 Such mercy . . . me bastard: anyone who says that I am an illegitimate son will get the same treatment I give to my enemies the Pagans

Father, you know me since I rescued you,
I am your only son, the rest are dead.
OLD BULLEN I know thee, Charles.
GODFREY But father, I am Godfrey;
That by my valor have regained your right,
Have got your dukedom from th'insulting French,
And am myself invested Bullen's Duke.
OLD BULLEN I know thee, Godfrey.
CHARLES Godfrey!
GODFREY Brother Charles!
The confident assurance of thy death,
Made me to give the lie to my own thoughts.
CHARLES The selfsame strong opinion blinded me,
Else for my brother I had challenged thee![437]
Brother, you might have known me by the arms
Which I have borne in honor of my trade.[438]
GODFREY Ah, but the resolution of thy death
Made me to lose such thought.
ROBERT Let us rejoice,
And to your plausive[439] fortunes give our voice.
GODFREY Prince Robert, did the time afford us leave,[440]
We would discourse the sum of our escapes—
But to our father's rescue!
CHARLES Yield him, slaves!
SULTAN Tush, we will keep him spite of all your braves.
GODFREY Be that our quarrel.
CHARLES With courage, courage strives,
We fight for Christ, our father, and our lives.
SOPHY Here stands my ensign, and by it a crown,
That you shall know the Persian honorable, *Sets up his standard & crown*
He that can fetch this ensign from the walls,
Which I myself will guard, and leave some token
Behind him, that his sword hath conquered it,
He shall enjoy them both.[441]
SULTAN And here stands mine, *Sets up his standard & crown*
The Babylonian Emperor's royal standard.
By it I plant the rich Sicilian crown,
Guarded by me and my all-conquering troops.
He that but leaves a note he hath been here,[442]
And scapes unslain, although he win them not,
That Christian will I honor.
ROBERT Drums, alarum!
SULTAN As loud and proud defiance our drum sounds.
GODFREY For Christ, my father, conquest, and two crowns! *Exeunt. Alarum*

437 130 I had challenged thee: I would have said you were my brother; there is also a double meaning here, in that Charles did just challenge (take to task) Godfrey for calling him "bastard"

438 131–2 Brother, you . . . my trade: you should have recognized me by the Haberdashers' arms that I carry in honor of my livery company

439 135 plausive: worthy of applause; also (although it is hard to agree with Robert here) plausible

440 136 did the . . . us leave: if we had more time

441 144–7 Although in the fiction of the play the brothers are laying siege to Jerusalem, the scene that the stage directions and the Sophy describe is more like a festive contest or a folklore narrative: whoever can climb the wall and leave his token will be declared victor and win a crown

442 151 If anyone that reaches my banner and leaves evidence that he has done so

The Christians are repulsed. Enter at two several doors GUY *and* EUSTACE, *climb up the walls, beat the Pagans, take away the crowns on their heads, and in the stead hang up the contrary shields,*[443] *and bring away the ensigns, flourishing them, several ways.*[444] *Enter* SULTAN, SOPHY, MORETES, TURNUS, *with soldiers*

SULTAN Now the first wall is won, the ensigns seized,
The crowns surprised, the Christians have the day:
What, shall we leave the town?
ALL Aye, leave the town!
SOPHY 'Tis best, 'tis best to take us to the field.
TURNUS I think 'tis best that we make good the breach[445]
And have no thought of marching towards the field.
We leave a place of much security.
ALL Why then, make good the breach!
SULTAN It shall be so.
Gather our forces to make good the breach.
SOPHY Tush, why should we be pent up in a town?
Let's ope the gates and boldly issue out,
Leaving some few pikes to make good the breach.
What say you, lords?
ALL[446] Then let us issue out!
Set ope the gates, and let us issue out!
SULTAN And so expose us to the general spoil?
Keep the gates shut, defend them manfully.
These Christians fight like devils. Keep fast the gates,
And once again let us make good the wall.
ALL. Make good the walls, make good the walls. [*Exeunt*]

Enter at one door ROBERT *and* CHARLES*; they meet* EUSTACE *with his trophy.*[447] *Enter at another door* GODFREY [*and*] TANCRED*; they meet* GUY *with his trophy*

ROBERT Triumphant honor hovers o'er our arms!
What gallant spirit bravely hath borne hence
The Emperor's standard, slaughtered his proud guard,
And in the stead thereof hung up his shield?
EUSTACE Witness this royal crown upon my head,
I seized the ensign, I hung up that shield.
GODFREY What puissant arm snatched hence the Sophy's standard?
GUY This crown upon my head says it was I.
CHARLES Forgetful Charles, brave Robert, see the knight,[448]
Whose valor freed us from the Sultan's hands!
ROBERT Renownèd Christian, ever honored be!
It was thy sword procured us liberty.
EUSTACE By heaven not I, I never came in place,
Where Robert or that gallant were distressed.
But there are others thankless, whom I freed,

443 155 SD *in the . . . contrary shields*: hang up the shields they have exchanged with each other ("contrary") in place of the ensigns they take

444 155 SD *several ways*: in different directions

445 160 make good the breach: close up the gap in our defenses

446 168 SP ALL: Q divides this half-line from the next line, assigning the first to "Lords" and the next to "All." It is possible that "Lords" designates Turnus and Moretes. What seems most important to signal is that the crowd is confused and undecided, except for the Sultan, the Sophy, and Turnus. Turnus seems to have changed his earlier aggressiveness for caution

447 174 SD *trophy*: the crown and standard he took from the walls. A trophy was originally an enemy's weapons and armor, taken in battle

448 183 see the knight: what happens next is a final case of mistaken identities. Charles recognizes Eustace's shield as that of the knight who rescued Charles and Robert from the ambush, and he and Robert thank him. Godfrey and Tancred similarly give credit to Guy. But because Guy has swapped his shield and Eustace's, Guy and Eustace are mistaken for one another

And now, too proud, forget that honored deed.
GODFREY 'Twas he released us; honored stranger, thanks,
But they are idle offerings from true hearts.
Prince Tancred and myself, owe thee our lives.
GUY You mock me, princes, never did my sword
Drink drop of Pagan's blood to set you free:
But Robert and that prince unthankful be.
CHARLES Whose shield is that? [*Gesturing to* GUY*'s shield that* EUSTACE *set on the walls*]
EUSTACE Mine.
CHARLES Then to you we owe
Thanks for our lives, the Pagans' overthrow.
EUSTACE The shield I challenge, but the act deny,
I never gave you life or liberty.
GODFREY Whose shield is that? [*Gesturing to the other shield*]
GUY Mine.
GODFREY Then by thee we live.
Thou didst our desperate lives and freedom give.
GUY What mean you, princes, to deride a stranger?
These eyes did never see you two in danger.
EUSTACE Who owes[449] that shield? [*Gestures to his own shield, set up by* GUY]
GUY I. And who owes that? [*Gesturing to the other shield*]
EUSTACE I.
GUY Thou know'st me then.
EUSTACE Thanks, fortune, that I do.
GUY Have at thee, slave.
EUSTACE Brave foe, have at thee, too.

Fight, and are parted by the princes

GODFREY Whate'er your quarrel be, contend no more;
He draws his sword 'gainst me that fights again!
For I am foe to all dissension.
CHARLES So are we all. Then end these wars in words,
The Pagans have employment for your swords.
EUSTACE For one blow more, take here my crown amongst you![450]
Now that my spleen is up, it will not down.
I'll give you all I have for one bout more.
GUY Lords, take mine too: by heaven I'll pawn my life
Against the Sultan's head, to bring it you,
So you will let us try this mastery.[451]
ROBERT Kingdoms nor crowns can hire it at our hands,
It shall not be, we say it shall not be.
What are you, lords? We charge you by his honor
Whom in your outward habit you profess[452]
To tell us both what and from whence ye are.
GUY You charge us deeply. I, a banished man,
Whom you for mutiny expulsed the camp,
Yet was I leader of ten thousand French,
But thought by you unworthy of these wars.
Since my exile—Prince Robert, view me well—
I freed you two from base captivity.

449 205 owes: owns
450 213 I will trade the crown I won for one more shot at this Guy
451 218 mastery: the vocabulary—a "bout" to demonstrate "mastery"—is reminiscent of fencing prize fights
452 221–2 We charge . . . you profess: I demand in the name of Christ, whose insignia as Crusaders you wear

'Twas I that brought you weapons in the woods,
And then you termed me some celestial power,
But being now in safety, you forget
Your dangers past, and cancel that great debt.
EUSTACE Nay, I am sure you long to know me too.
I am your outlaw brother, one of your leaders,
Banished with him, that from the Persian's rage
Freed Tancred, and that valiant man at arms,
However now they can forget my prowess.
What need you more? I am he that won this crown
And from these high walls plucked that ensign down.
ROBERT You have redeemed all your offences past,
Deserving best in this society.
But when you freed me, you did bear that shield. [*Points to the shield hung up by* EUSTACE, *originally* GUY*'s*]
GUY I did, but since exchanged it with my foe.
GODFREY And you did bear that shield. [*Points to the other shield*]
EUSTACE True, I did so.
[*To* GUY] Ah, had I been awake, thou know'st my mind:
Thou hadst writ thy ruin in blood.
GUY Thy words are mine.[453]
CHARLES Leave,[454] brother Godfrey, and the Bullen Duke.
EUSTACE How!
GUY What!
CHARLES Do you not know these faces?[455]
GODFREY Brother Charles?
EUSTACE Brother!
GUY Charles!
GODFREY I'll question with them, for may it not be
They might escape the seas as well as we?
I had a brother, sir, resembled you.
EUSTACE I had a brother, too, resembled you.
CHARLES The Bullen Duke, if ever you have heard
Of such a man, had once a son like you.
GUY Aye,[456] and another son as much like you.
GODFREY My brother's name was Eustace.
EUSTACE Godfrey, mine.
GUY That Duke called his son Charles.
CHARLES Mine called his Guy.
GODFREY My brother Eustace!
EUSTACE Godfrey!
CHARLES Guy!
GUY And Charles!
ALL Brothers!
ROBERT This accident[457] breeds wonders in my thoughts.
GODFREY Oh, let me curse that head that envied thee!
GUY Nay, curse my heart that emulated[458] thee!

453 249 I could say the same to you

454 250 Leave: a polite way of interrupting: I beg your permission! Excuse me!

455 253 Do not you know these faces?: what exactly triggers Charles' recognition of Eustace and Guy is not clear from the playtext. His naming of Godfrey and their father seems to be what lets Eustace and Guy know their family at last

456 262 Aye: Q prints "I," which is a conventional spelling in the period. The syllable sounds like both "aye," meaning yes, and "I" the personal pronoun, as if to say "I was that son"

457 267 accident: unlikely, unanticipated occurrence

458 269 emulated: tried to rival or outdo

EUSTACE My brother outlaw, and my own true brother!
CHARLES Forever thus let us embrace each other!
GODFREY When I was cast upon the Bullen strand,[459]
I thought none had escaped the seas but I.
GUY When I was thrown upon the French King's coast,
I thought none had escaped the seas but I.
CHARLES I thought the seas had favored none but me,
When I attained the shores of Italy!
EUSTACE Ireland took me, and there I first touched ground,
Presuming that my brothers all were drowned.
ROBERT Were ye the four young London prentices,
That in the ships were wrecked on Goodwin's Sands[460]
Were said to have perished then, of no repute?[461]
Now come the least of you to lead an host,
And to be found the sons to a great duke?
GODFREY Witness my shield the trade I have professed.
GUY Witness my shield, I am one amongst the rest.
CHARLES Witness thou mine.
EUSTACE And witness thou for me. [*Gesturing towards his shield, hung up*]
ROBERT We witness all your martial chivalry.
EUSTACE And now my foe turned brother, end our hate,
And praise that power divine who guides our state.
GUY Divide we hands and hearts! What hatred rests,[462]
Pour out in thunder on the Pagans' crests.
EUSTACE [*Aside*] Our joys are not at full, they shall not yet
Know where my sister and their love remains,
Until these wars have end. Oh, had our God
Not laid our fortunes open, but a brother
Been brought in triumph to a sister's bed,
Clouds of despair had masked our sun of joy.
Yet will I keep her secret, and the rather,
To crown our haps[463] when we have freed our father.

Enter TURNUS

TURNUS Christians, once more defiance in my tongue
Sounds dismal terror in your fearful ears.
The princes whom I serve grieve they have mured
Such an huge army in a wall of stone,
And they are thus resolved:[464]
To leave all place of scorned advantages
And in a pitched field[465] end this glorious war.
Say, will ye meet them?
ROBERT Though he trust his strength,
Yet will we meet his forces face to face,

459 272 strand: beach
460 281 Goodwin's Sands: a proverbially treacherous area of shallow water and shifting sandbanks off the coast of Kent in England, where many ships were wrecked
461 280–82 Were ye . . . no repute: are you the four prentices, said to be of no particular importance, who were shipwrecked and thought to have died?
462 291 rests: remains
463 300 crown our haps: make the high point of these events
464 303–5 The princes . . . thus resolved: the Sultan and the Sophy regret that they chose to defend the city from within the walls, and have decided to meet the Christians in the field
465 307 pitched field: the site of a battle that has been planned in advance; a particularly violent battle to which all available forces have been committed

When the dry earth shall quaff[466] your bloods apace.
GUY And tell the Sultan from a Christian prince
That won from him these colors, and this crown,
In that pitched field my head this crown shall bear
And scarf-like these athwart my breast I'll wear.[467]
EUSTACE This[468] for the Persian's sake I'll wear in sight,
And under his own ensign this day fight.
CHARLES Go tell the Sultan that he wears my crown.[469]
Fortune hath given it me, it is mine own.
GODFREY If thou hast more to say concerning war,
Omit thy braves[470] and trifling circumstance:[471]
We'll meet you sooner than you can desire.
Be gone, be gone, our hearts are all on fire.
TURNUS Brave lords, our conquests will be honorable
Because we have to deal with honored foes.
Our pikes stand to receive you like a wood;
We'll fleck our white steeds in your Christian blood.
TANCRED Prepare to meet them and appoint our powers,
This day the city and themselves are ours.
ROBERT Thou under whom we fight,[472] this day defend us,
For unto thy protection we commend us.

Exeunt

[Act V, scene i]

Enter at one door with drum and colors, SULTAN, SOPHY, MORETES, TURNUS, *and soldiers*

SULTAN Great monarchs, kings, and princes of the East,
Ye come t'encounter with a valiant foe;
Such as have swum huge rivers, climbed the Alps;
That can endure sharp hunger; such as shrink not
To have their bloods sod[473] with the dog days'[474] heat,
Nor to be curdled[475] with cold Saturn's rod.
What honor were it for an host of giants
To combat with a pygmy nation?
No, lords, the foe we must encounter with,
Is full of spirit and majestic spleen,
Strong, hardy, and their hearts invincible.
Destroy these, and you win yourselves a name
And all the nations of the earth shall fear you.
SOPHY The more renowned the foe is, the more famous
Shall be our conquest, the more great their fall.
Come, lords, divide we our battalions.

466 310 quaff: drink
467 314 these athwart . . . I'll wear: to show his defiance of the Sultan and his earlier success in seizing his crown and ensign, Guy will wear the crown and put the ensign across his chest like a sash
468 315 This: i.e. the crown
469 317 With no crown to wear, Charles simply promises to take the one the Sultan wears. Only Godfrey, who historically and in the literary tradition did become King of Jerusalem, does not participate in this flyting
470 320 braves: taunts, shows of defiance
471 320 trifling circumstance: insignificant, peripheral comments
472 329 Thou under whom we fight: i.e. God, or Christ
473 5 sod: boiled (old past tense of "seethe")
474 5 dog days: the hot days following midsummer; so called because they are distinguished by the reappearance of the "Dog Star" Sirius, the brightest star in the night sky
475 6 curdled: frozen

SULTAN Be yours the vaward.[476]
SOPHY I will give the charge.
SULTAN Turnus, have you the rearward,[477] I the battle,[478]
Moretes, thou this day shalt lead the horse.
Take thou the cornet;[479] Turnus, thou the archers;
Be thine the guidon,[480] I the men-at-arms.
Be mine this ensign.[481]
SOPHY Then mount our cannons, let our flanking pieces[482]
Rail on the Christian army with wide mouths.
For I this day will lead the forlorn hope,[483]
The camisado[484] shall be given by me.
TURNUS Already they have placed their battery,
Their ordinance stand fit to beat the flanks.
SULTAN My cannoneers need no instruction.
Come, let us line our pikes with musketeers,[485]
And so attend the Christians' fatal charge.

Enter marching, ROBERT, TANCRED, GODFREY, GUY, CHARLES, EUSTACE, *drum and soldiers*

ROBERT Princes, this day we are espoused[486] to death:
A better place to die in, than this vale
In which our Savior's sepulcher remains
What man in all our army could desire?
Speak: how have you disposed our officers?
GODFREY Your Grace is Captain General of the army.
GUY And Godfrey you High Marshal[487] and Master of the Camp,
And as assistants you have under you
The Sergeant Major,[488] Quartermaster, Provost,[489]
And Captain of the Spions.[490]
GODFREY My brother Guy chief General of the Horse,
To serve him his Lieutenant Colonel,
Captains, and Scoutmasters.[491]
EUSTACE My brother Charles General of the Artillery,
Under him his Lieutenant Commissaries of Munitions,
Gentlemen of the Artillery, Colonel of Pioners,[492]

476 17 vaward: vanguard, i.e. the first group to attack. The Sophy's response simply restates the Sultan's command

477 18 rearward: the hindmost formation of troops, from where the archers can fire over their forward troops into the enemy

478 18 battle: the middle formation of soldiers

479 20 cornet: the wings or horns of cavalry, so-called because their crescent-shaped formations flanked the slower, rectangular battle formations of footsoldiers

480 21 guidon: war banner; the Sultan probably addresses this line to the Sophy, in whose vaward the guidon will be brandished

481 22 Possibly the Sultan flourishes a banner at the end of this short line

482 23 flanking pieces: artillery, placed at the sides of the formation; the Sophy imagines the cannons shouting insults ("railing") from their open mouths

483 25 forlorn hope: a technical term for a small detachment of soldiers who lead an attack; from Dutch *verloren hoop*, "lost band or squad," but the English phrase suggests a desperate last chance

484 26 camisado: surprise attack, from Spanish *camisado*, "wearing a shirt"; so called because it was imagined to be undertaken in shirt sleeves, that is, lightly armed, whether for speed, stealth, or to help attackers recognize each other

485 30 pikes with musketeers: pikemen were often arrayed with musketeers, to protect them from enemy charges while they reloaded their slow-firing weapons

486 32 espoused: engaged, committed

487 38 High Marshal: Robert is the commander in chief, but Godfrey is responsible for putting the troops in order and supplying them

488 40 Sergeant Major: the equivalent of a modern major general

489 40 Quartermaster, Provost: officers in charge of provisions and collections

490 41 Spions: spies. Note that, like the Sultan's speech above, each brother's speech except the last ends with a short line, perhaps for some gesture or maneuver, or to allow the next brother or his troops to advance

491 44 Scoutmasters: those in charge of scouts, often mounted for speed

492 47 Pioners: soldiers detailed to dig earthworks; accented on the first syllable

Trench Masters, and Carriage Masters.[493]
CHARLES My brother Eustace Treasurer of the Camp,
And under him the Auditors,[494] Muster Masters,[495] and Commissaries.[496]
EUSTACE Prince Tancred is our Royal Secretary,
Without whom nothing is concluded on.
Thus are the special offices disposed.
TANCRED Princes, what order take you for the assault?
ROBERT One half maintain the battery, beat the walls,
Whilst the other keeps them play in the open fields.[497]
GODFREY We shall not need to block the breach with forts,
Victuals and forage are at pleasure ours.
Stockadoes, palisadoes,[498] stop their waters.
Bulwarks[499] and curtains[500] all are battered down
And we are safe entrenched by pioners.
Our casemates,[501] cavaliers,[502] and counterscarps[503]
Are well surveyed by all our engineers,
Fortifications, ramparts, parapets,[504]
That we at pleasure may assault the way
Which leads unto the gate Antiochia.[505]
GUY Whilst you intend[506] the walls, shall my bard horse[507]
Give a brave onset, shivering all their pikes,[508]
Armed with their greaves[509] and maces,[510] and broad swords,
Proof cuirasses,[511] and open burgonets.[512]
CHARLES Yet let us look our battle be well manned
With shot, bills,[513] halberds, and proof targeteers.[514]
EUSTACE No man but knows his charge.[515] Brothers and friends,
See where they stand for us; this night shall hide
All their bright glory which now swells with pride.
SULTAN Christians?

493 48 Trench Masters, and Carriage Masters: officers in charge of earthworks and of transportation
494 50 Auditors: officers responsible for handling payments; accountants
495 50 Muster Masters: officers who maintained lists of available troops
496 50 Commissaries: officers in charge of transportation, food, and other supplies. Somewhat ironically given his temperament, Eustace has been assigned more of a desk job
497 55–6 One half . . . open fields: half the force will fire artillery at the city walls while the rest skirmish in front of them. Robert seems to describe a siege, while the order of battle declared by the Sultan sounds as if the armies will meet in the open
498 59 Stockadoes, palisadoes: fences or walls made of closely set stakes; stockadoes, or stockades, were specifically placed across a water source
499 60 Bulwarks: earthen fortifications
500 60 curtains: plain expanses of wall
501 62 casemates: fortified chambers, sometimes built into a wall
502 62 cavaliers: fortifications that rise above other fortifications to allow for sight, command, and fire
503 62 counterscarps: fortifications protecting a lower ditch or path
504 64 ramparts, parapets: raised walls, towers. The syntax of Godfrey's list of defensive features is vague. Perhaps he means that the fortifications, ramparts and parapets have also been checked by the engineers
505 66 Antiochia: as often, place names seem to be chosen for their evocative potential more than geographical fit. There was no Antioch gate in Jerusalem, although the historical crusaders led by Godfrey of Bouillon reached Jerusalem from Antioch. It is possible that we are to imagine the Sultan's forces falling back to Antioch after being driven from Jerusalem, but in all likelihood the logic here is one of name recognition and not geography
506 67 intend: aim at, approach
507 67 bard horse: horse equipped with protective armor; see IV.i. 44
508 67–8 Whilst you . . . their pikes: Guy promises to direct his cavalry against the enemy's pikemen, "shivering" them into disarray
509 69 greaves: armor for the lower leg
510 69 maces: iron clubs
511 70 Proof cuirasses: armor covering the front and back of the torso; proof armor has been tested for reliability
512 70 open burgonets: light helmets that leave the face uncovered
513 72 bills: a spearlike weapon, similar to a halberd
514 72 targeteers: soldiers who carry targets, that is, small light shields. Targeteers often carried javelins or missiles, so Charles does seem to imagine a formation that will strike from a distance
515 73 No man . . . his charge: everybody here knows his job

EUSTACE Pagans?
SULTAN Behold our camp.
ROBERT Sultan, survey ours, too.
SULTAN From Ganges to the Bay of Calicut
From Turkey and the three-fold Araby,[516]
From Sauxin[517] eastward unto Nubia's bounds,
From Libya and the land of Mauritans,
And from the Red Sea to the wilderness,[518]
Have we unpeopled kingdoms for these wars,
To be revenged on you base Christians.
ROBERT From England, the best brood of martial spirits,
Whose walls the ocean washeth white as snow,
For which you strangers call it Albion,
From France, a nation both renowned and feared,
From Scotland, Wales, even to the Irish coast,
Beyond the pillars great Alcides reared,[519]
At Gades[520] in Spain unto the Pyrene hills,[521]
Have we assembled men of dauntless spirits,
To scourge you hence, ye damnèd infidels.
SOPHY Within our troops are sturdy bands of Moors,
Of Babylonians, Persians, Bactrians,[522]
Of Grecians,[523] Russians, of Tartarians, Turks,
Even from the floods that grow from Paradise[524]
Unto this place where the brook Kedron[525] runs.
GUY Within our troops are English, French, Scotch, Dutch,
Italians of Prince Tancred's regiment.
Even from the seas that wall in Albion,
As far as any river or brook runs
That Christian drinks on, have we people here.
TURNUS To make our streets red with your Christian blood.
CHARLES To drown you slaves in a vermilion flood.
MORETES To burn your bodies o'er your Prophet's grave.
EUSTACE To lead your emperor captive like a slave.
SULTAN To make your guide trot by my chariot wheel.[526]
TANCRED To lash your armor with these rods of steel.
SOPHY Then to extirp[527] you all! Ye Persian powers,
Assist our courage, make the conquest ours.

516 80 three-fold Araby: Europeans customarily divided Arabia into three parts: uncultivated desert; the rocky wilderness where the Israelites received the Law from God; and Arabia Felix, a rich and fertile area

517 81 Sauxin: what this refers to is unclear. There is a river Saux in France and a region named for it; also a Sauxcy in the Netherlands, but neither of these makes much sense

518 79–83 From Ganges … the wilderness: the Sultan's domain spans India, North Africa, and the Nile—in other words, the world of the medieval Muslim conquests. Nubia is the region of the upper Nile, modern Sudan; the land of Mauritans is Mauritania in northwestern Africa. The Red Sea and the wilderness recall the journey of Moses and the Israelites to Canaan and Jerusalem

519 91: pillars great Alcides reared: the Straits of Gibraltar, also known as the Pillars of Hercules, where the Mediterranean opens into the Atlantic; Alcides is another name for Hercules

520 92 Gades: the Roman name for Cádiz

521 92 Pyrene hills: the Pyrenees. Robert balances the Sultan's claim with those of Western Christendom. When the play was written, Spain was a Christian kingdom, but at the time the play takes place it was under Muslim rule

522 96 Bactrians: inhabitants of a region in Central Asia (so too the "Tartarians" in the next line); Heywood wants to suggest that the Sultan and the Sophy have the powers of Asia behind them

523 97 Grecians: in Heywood's time, the territory of Greece was ruled by the Muslim Ottoman Empire; during the first Crusade, it was part of the Byzantine Empire, against whom the Crusaders skirmished on their way to Jerusalem

524 98 Paradise: Eden, which was said to lie between four rivers, and sometimes located in what is now Iraq

525 99 Kedron: a river and a valley beside Jerusalem

526 109 trot by my chariot wheel: run beside my chariot, as a prisoner might

527 111 extirp: destroy completely, root out

ROBERT God match thy might with theirs, protect us, too,
To let this people know what thou canst do.
SULTAN A charge, a charge, rail drums and cannons roar!
Christians, at home your friends abroad deplore.[528]
GODFREY Christians at home abroad our conquests fame;[529]
Thou God of Hosts this day make known thy name.

Alarum. Join battle: The Christians are beaten off. The SULTAN *victoriously leads off his soldiers marching. Enter* CHARLES *and* GODFREY *with pistols*

CHARLES Oh God, that multitude should more than manhood,[530]
That we should thus be borne down with a press,[531]
Be thronged and shouldered from the place we keep!
GODFREY For every man we lead, the foe hath ten,
Their weapons' tops appear above their heads,
In as thick number as the spikes of grain
Upon a well-tilled land: they have more lives
Than all our tired arms could send to death
If they should yield their bare breasts to our swords.
CHARLES What should we do? We are encompassed round,
Girded with thousand thousands in a ring,
And like a man left on a dangerous rock
That waits the climbing tide rise to destroy him,
What way soe'er he looks, sees naught but death,
So we: the bloody tide grows up apace,
Whose waves will swallow us and all our race.
Where's Guy and Eustace?
GODFREY Gone to scale a tower
In which our father lies. Oh, I did see them
Cut down a wood of men upon the sudden.
Their swords cut lances as a scythe cuts grass:
Their valor seems to me miraculous.
Thou Savior of the world, whose cross we bear,
Infuse our hearts with courage, theirs[532] with fear.

Exeunt

[Act V, scene ii]

Enter SULTAN, SOPHY, *and soldiers. Alarum. Enter* GUY *and* EUSTACE *with their father*

EUSTACE A Sion, a Sion!
GUY A Jerusalem!
EUSTACE A father, and in him a crown of joy!
GUY A Sion, a Jerusalem, a father![533]
EUSTACE Through their decurions, centurions, and legions,[534]

528 116 Christians, your friends at home are openly ("abroad") grieving for you!

529 117 fame: make famous

530 119 How terrible that a crowd of soldiers can overcome better, braver ones!

531 120 borne down with a press: overwhelmed by sheer numbers of enemies

532 141 theirs: i.e. the Pagans'

533 1–4 Many battle cries begin with "A!", which sometimes means "For" or "Towards," and sometimes is just a declaration (cf. "A charge!" at V.i. 115). These nuances need not be too precisely calculated; it is first of all a shout

534 5 decurions, centurions, and legions: Roman military terms for, respectively, mid-level cavalry; infantry officers; and a large unit of troops. As often, the brothers conflate ancient Greco-Roman and contemporary Muslim forces

Captains of thousands, and ten thousands guards,[535]
We have ventured even upon the cannon's mouth,
And scaled the bulwarks where their ordinance played.
The strength of armies triumphs in those arms!
We have surprised the fortress and the hold!
My shield I have had cut piecemeal from mine arm.
But now you would have taken me for an archer,
So many arrows were stuck here and here,
The Pagans thought to make a quiver of me.

Alarum. Enter Pagans

See, brother, how the foe fresh forces gather!
A Sion, a Jerusalem, a father!

Every one by turn takes up their father, and carries him: Enter the two brothers, they aid and second them. And with a shout carry him away

[Act V, scene iii]

Alarum. Enter SULTAN, SOPHY

SULTAN An enginer, call forth an enginer!
SOPHY Why, what to do, my lord?
SULTAN I'll make these turrets dance among the clouds[536]
Before the Christians shall inhabit them!
SOPHY Yet there is hope of conquest. Fight, brave Sultan!
SULTAN These Christians rage like spirits conjured up,
Their thund'ring ordinance spit huge clouds of fire,
They run against the walls like iron rams,
And bear them down afore them with their breasts.
SOPHY Fortune, thou art too envious of our glory;
Behold the two great'st emperors of the earth,
The Babylonian Sultan, and great Sophy!
Unveil thine eyes, and look upon our falls.
SULTAN Fortune and fate, and death, the devil and all,

Enter MORETES *and* TURNUS

Oppose themselves against us. Now what news?
MORETES Death.
SOPHY What news bring'st thou?
TURNUS Confusion.
SULTAN That death was once my slave, but now my lord.
SOPHY Confusion was once page unto my sword.
Is the day lost?
TURNUS Lost.
SULTAN Must we needs despair?
MORETES Despair.
SULTAN We will not, we will die resolvedly,
The palace we will make a slaughter-house,

535 6 Eustace likens the Sultan's troops to Philistines, of whom the Book of Samuel records that the Israelites sang "Saul hath slain his thousands, and David his ten thousands" (1 Samuel 18:7)
536 3 The Sultan means to blow up the towers

The streets a shambles,[537] kennels[538] shall run blood
Down from Mount Sion with such hideous noise,
As when great showers of water falls from hills.
SOPHY Through which way did they make irruption first?
TURNUS Through the gate called Antiochia,
The selfsame breach that Roman Titus made
When he destroyed the city, they burst ope.
SULTAN There is some virtue in the cross they wear.
It makes them strong as lions, swift as roes.[539]
Their resolutions[540] make them conquerors.
They have ta'en our royal standard from the walls,
In place whereof they have advanced their cross.
SOPHY I will not I[541] survive so foul a shame.
Once more unite our powers[542]—I mean our selves,
For all powers else have failed us—bravely fight,
That our declining sun may make their night!

Enter the four brethren

SULTAN Christians, base Christians, hear us when we call,
Eternal darkness shall confound you all!

Alarum. The four brethren each of them kill a Pagan king, take off their crowns, and exeunt, two one way, and two another way. Retrait[543]

[Act V, scene iv]

Enter ROBERT, TANCRED, GODFREY, GUY, CHARLES, EUSTACE, [OLD BULLEN], *drum, colors, and soldiers*

ROBERT Now smooth again the wrinkles of your brows,
And wash the blood from off your hands in milk.
With penitential praises laud our God,
Ascribe all glory to the heavenly powers,
Since Sion and Jerusalem are ours.
TANCRED We do abhor a heart puffed up with pride,
That attributes these conquests to our strength.
'Twas God that strengthened us and weakened them,
And gave us Sion and Jerusalem.
GODFREY Thou that dost muster angels in the sky,
That in thy self hast power of victory,
Make thy name shine, bright as the noontide sun,
Since Sion and Jerusalem are won.
OLD BULLEN My former want hath now sufficient store,[544]
For having seen this, I desire no more.
How fair and smooth my stream of pleasure runs,
To look at once on Sion and my sons![545]

537 25 shambles: meat market; in London there was a section near Cheapside called the Shambles, where butchers dressed and sometimes slaughtered animals

538 25 kennels: gutters

539 33 roes: deer

540 34 resolutions: grit and determination; also, possibly, their religious convictions

541 37 I will not I: emphatic for "I will not"

542 38 powers: a grim joke; usually "powers" means troops, but since their troops have all been defeated, the Sophy means their own individual abilities

543 42 SD *Retrait*: a trumpet call signaling a retreat

544 14 The desires I had earlier have been fulfilled

545 17 Sion and my sons: as when, on their first look at Jerusalem, the Crusaders shared a lament for the city with the repetition of the word "tears" (see IV.v. 16), here they describe a triumph, repeating "Jerusalem," "Sion," and "sons"

GUY Showers of abundance rain into our lips,
To make repentance grow within our hearts.
What greater earthly bliss could heaven pour down,
Than Sion, our dear father, and this town?
CHARLES Then to confirm these conquests God hath given us,
Sealed with the blood of kings and emperors,
Let us elect a king, that may maintain
Our honors with the deaths of monarchs slain.[546]
EUSTACE Call forth the Patriarch of Jerusalem;
His right hand must bequeath that dignity.
GODFREY With tears I speak it: lagging in the train
Of the distressèd Sultan he was slain.
ROBERT Praised be our God, we have revenged his death.
Great potentates consort him to his grave.[547]
CHARLES What man, for gravity and sanctity,
May we think worthy of this honored place?
ROBERT Whose years, devotion, and most sacred life
Better can fit that holy place than his
Whose worthy sons have brought to end these wars?
Princes, join hands, invest him all at once. *Flourish*
OLD BULLEN My fervent zeal bids I should not deny.
It brings my soul to heaven before I die.
EUSTACE But, princes, whom will ye elect the king,
To guard this city from succeeding peril?
GODFREY Robert of Normandy.
ROBERT Oh, choose Prince Tancred rather!
TANCRED Too weak is my desert, and I refuse it.
EUSTACE Then put it to most voices.
ALL Robert of Normandy!
ROBERT Princes, we much commend you for your loves:
But letters from England tell me William's dead,
And by succession left the crown to me.[548]
I say Prince Godfrey hath deserved it best.
TANCRED So Tancred says.
ALL And so say all the rest.
GODFREY Princes, ye press me down with too much honors,
And load a soul that cannot bear them up.
Dissuade me not, no counsel I will hear.
Behold a crown which Godfrey means to wear! *A crown of thorns*[549]
This made the blood run from our Savior's brow;
No crown but this can Godfrey's heart allow.
Prayers are my pride, devotion draws my sword,
No pomp but this can Bullen's soul afford.
My vow's irrevocable, state I refuse;
No other crown but this will Godfrey choose.
TANCRED If he refuse the place, elect Prince Guy!
Most voices: shall he have the scepter?
ALL Aye!

546 24–5 that may . . . monarchs slain: i.e. so that he may support our honor according to the high level of our achievements

547 31 He goes to his grave accompanied by the Muslim kings

548 49: by succession . . . to me: Robert did succeed his father as Duke of Normandy upon William's death in 1087, but he never ruled England (another of William's sons, William Rufus, succeeded him there)

549 55 SD *crown of thorns*: Godfrey either holds one up or perhaps puts one on. The historical Godfrey of Bouillon, while ruling Jerusalem, did not officially accept the title of king

ROBERT Then crown him straight, and henceforth let his name
Be through the world called Guy of Lessingham.[550]
All these desire it, I consent with them:
Long live Prince Guy, King of Jerusalem! *Flourish* [*as* GUY *is crowned*]
GUY The crown is burst, and parted from my head;
I fear the heavens are angry with your choice.
OLD BULLEN Son Guy, they are not. By divine instinct
The heavens have lent me a prophetic spirit.
This shews thy troublous reign: mutines[551] from far,
Shall fright thy towns and provinces with war.
GUY If it be nothing else, crown me again.
We have a heart our kingdom to maintain.
What honors do my brothers heads await?
ROBERT Prince Eustace, you shall wear this crown of state,
Be King of Sicil[552] and command that isle.
Lord Charles, the crown of Cyprus[553] longs[554] to you,
That in the fight the King of Cyprus slew.
One general voice at once proclaim them kings. *Flourish*
CHARLES In memory of this solemnity,
Here will I leave this scutcheon borne by me:
That in what coast soe'er my bones be laid,
This shield may be an honor to my trade.
EUSTACE Mine shall hang there, a trophy of my fame,
My trade is famous by King Eustace' name.
GUY In memory a king hath borne this shield,
I add these chalices to this argent field.[555]
GODFREY In honor of my first profession
That shield in all these wars by Godfrey borne,
I crown this maid's head with a wreath of thorn.[556]
OLD BULLEN Oh, were my daughter here this joy to see,
How light her soul, how glad would my heart be!
TANCRED Would I had now my love.
GUY Or I that dame,
That adds to beauty's sun a brighter flame.
ROBERT Were the fair virgin here, I would renown[557]
Her glorious beauty with the English crown.
EUSTACE Princes, I'll fit you all. Lady, come forth.

Enter BELLA FRANCA

BELLA FRANCA The lovely princes.
TANCRED Fair mistress!
CHARLES Lady!
GODFREY Madame!

550 65 Guy of Lessingham: Heywood may be anglicizing the name of Guy of Lusignan, an actual Crusader king whose rule was indeed deeply troubled (see lines 72–3), but who lived about seventy years after Godfrey

551 72 mutines: mutinies

552 78 Sicil: Sicily

553 79 Cyprus: this is the first we hear of this kingdom. Perhaps Moretes and Turnus were kings of Sicily and Cyprus; the Sultan refers to the crown of Sicily when he plants his banner (see IV.v. 149)

554 79 longs: belongs

555 89 Heywood continues to weave his narrative into the contemporary history that his playgoers would have been familiar with. The Goldsmiths' arms used in Elizabethan times were indeed quartered with chalices

556 92 The Virgin on the Mercers' arms is crowned, but not with thorns

557 97 renown: recognize, reward

GUY Honored saint!
BELLA FRANCA Nay, pardon me, love comes not by constraint.
But princes, will you[558] grant me patience,
Before I part, I mean to please you all.
First, holy Patriarch, tell me, of all others,
Whom in the world you most desire to see.
OLD BULLEN My daughter.
BELLA FRANCA Prince Godfrey, Charles, and Eustace,[559] whom say you?
ALL [THREE] Next your self, our sister.
BELLA FRANCA And whom you?
TANCRED My love.
BELLA FRANCA Who's that?
TANCRED Your honored self, fair maid.
BELLA FRANCA Nay, I'll make good the words that I have said. [*Discovers herself*]
Father, I give a daughter to your hand.
Brothers, behold, here doth your sister stand.
Tancred, behold the lady you once seized,
Only I leave Prince Robert here displeased.
OLD BULLEN My daughter Bella Franca!
BROTHERS Sister!
TANCRED Love!
OLD BULLEN I am too happy and too full of joy.
Heaven pours on me more good than I can bear—
I that before was starved now surfeit here.
ROBERT Princes, and Lady, nothing can displease us,
For we partake in all this glad content,
And with applause rejoice this accident.
Tancred, rejoice, your love, and you your friends:
Where you begin with marriage, our love ends.
Kings, and kings' peers, to heaven ascribe the glory,
Whilst we to chronicles report this story.
GUY Make love unto my sister! 'Tis most strange.
Now, Guy, I would thy hadst thy French love here.
My heart should grant her what I then refused.
Now having got this state of dignity,
I grieve that I have so obdurate been,
But for amends would make her Sion's queen.
EUSTACE And well remembered, brother, I must now
Entreat you for a pretty boy, your page,
That hath on some occasion strayed from you.
GUY Oh brother, where's the villain?
EUSTACE Pardon him, and I will tell you.
GUY Great were th'offense I would not clear for you.
EUSTACE The poor boy, brother, stays within my tent,
But so disguised you cannot know him now,
For he's turned wench, and, but I know the wag
To be a boy, to see him thus transformed
I should have sworn he had been a wench indeed.
GUY Pray, let me see him, brother, in that habit—
I would not lose the villain for more gold
Than Sion would be sold for! He will blush
To be ta'en tardy in his maid's attire.

558 103 will you: if you will
559 108 Eustace: we might expect Guy, since Eustace knows Bella Franca's identity. Perhaps even Heywood is having trouble keeping track at this point

EUSTACE You have pardoned him?
GUY I have.
EUSTACE Then, Jack, appear!

Enter the FRENCH LADY

Nay, blush not to be in your woman's gear.
GUY Leap heart, dance spirit, be merry, jocund soul,
'Tis she undoubtedly!
LADY You know me then!
GUY I do, 'twas that disguise,
That all this while hath blinded my clear eyes.
EUSTACE Fie, are you not ashamed to kiss a boy,
And in your arms to grasp him with such joy?[560]
GUY She is no boy, you do mistake her quite.
EUSTACE A boy, a page, a wagtail,[561] by this light!
What say you, sister?
BELLA FRANCA Sure he told me so,
For if he be a maid, I made him one.
EUSTACE Do not mistake the sex, man, for he's none:
It is a rogue, a wag, his name is Jack,
A notable dissembling lad, a crack.[562]
GUY Brother, 'tis you that are deceived in her,
Beshrew her, she hath been my bedfellow
A year and more, yet I had not the grace.[563]
Brothers, receive a sister; reverent[564] father,
Accept a daughter, whilst I take a wife,
And of a great king's daughter make a queen.
This is the beauteous virgin, the French lady
To whom my fortune still remains in debt.
EUSTACE A lady? Then I cry you mercy, brother,
A gallant bride! Would I had such another!
LADY A wondrous change! She that your page hath been
Is now at length transformed to be your queen.
Pardon me, Guy, my love drew me along,
No shameless lust.
GUY Fair saint, I did you wrong.
If fortune had not been your friend in this,
You had not lain thus long without a kiss.
Father, embrace her; brothers, sister, all.
OLD BULLEN This fortune makes our joys mere comical.[565]
The fame of our success all Europe rings:
The father, patriarch, sees his sons all kings.
ROBERT The heavens are full of bounty! Then, brave princes,
First in the temple[566] hang these trophies up

560 154–5 Eustace still believes the Lady is a boy disguised as a lady rather than a lady disguised as a boy

561 157 wagtail: dismissive term for a young man or woman, after a species of bird with a characteristic motion of its tail; the word is probably meant principally to suggest flitting movement, but also carries a suggestion of sexual activity. See also "wag" at line 163

562 162 crack: playful term for a mischievous young man, supposedly from "crack-hemp," someone likely to be hanged. Perhaps also slang for a sexually active woman

563 165 I had not the grace: i.e. to notice that Jack was a Jill, and to benefit from sharing a bed with her

564 166 reverent: "reverend" (i.e. revered) might make more immediate sense, but Old Bullen, as Patriarch of Jerusalem, is reverent (pious) as well

565 180 mere comical: wholly in the manner of a comedy, presumably because now the play will end in marriages

566 184: temple: the Temple of Jerusalem had been destroyed in 70 CE. Probably Heywood is not trying to be specific, but referring generally to a place of worship. The trophies seem to comprise the arms of the livery companies

As a remembrance of your fortunes past.
You, good old father, wear your patriarch's robes,
Prince Godfrey, walk you with your crown of thorns,
Guy with his Lady, Tancred with his wife,
Charles with his crown of Cyprus, and young Eustace
Crowned with the rich Sicilian diadem,
I with the honor of the Pagans' deaths.
So in procession walk we to Christ's tomb
With humble hearts to pay our pilgrims' vows.
Repair we to our countries, that once done,
For Sion and Jerusalem are won.

Exeunt omnes

FINIS.

5 Anonymous, *Look About You*

First performed c. 1595–99

First printed 1600

Edited by Paul Menzer

If I told you that I had just met a man with one arm, you would think that I'd met a man with just one arm. But I also have one arm. And another one. Because a man with two arms is also a one-armed man, though a man with *just* one arm is not a two-armed man. What category of error has been made here? And whose fault is it? Yours or mine? If I told you that I had just met a man with one arm and you think that I've met a man with just one arm, the error is this: you've mistaken an observation for a claim to exclusivity.

Look About You has one author. That is an observation, not an exclusive claim. For to say that a play has one author is not to say that it doesn't have two. For a play with two authors also has one author. In some respects, of course, *Look About You* doesn't even have one author since its authorship is unknown, and anonymity disarms considerations that a play might be a collaboration. And yet *Look About You* "bears all the marks"—as a scholar might say—of collaboration: the play is cleanly cleft between opening and closing scenes at court and comic scenes between that read like an Elizabethan version of *The Keystone Cops*. But within the limited scholarly work on *Look About You*, no one has ever suggested that the play is a collaboration. That is because it takes one known writer to suggest that there might be two. No one has ever suggested that the play might have two authors because no one has ever identified even one. No one has ever suggested that *Look About You*—or any other play—might be a collaboration between anonymous and anonymous.

Look About You is one of the weirdest of all early modern plays, and early modern plays are weird. But its weirdness is a matter of degree, not kind—like a man with three arms. After all, what's weird about this play is what's weird about other plays of this period: tonal disparities, bizarre juxtapositions of incongruous dramatic forms, sloppy treatment of source material, and running gags that have long since lost their bite. The banal cause of such weirdness is often collaboration, the coupling of different writers with different backgrounds, different desires, different notions of what's "appropriate" (and what might be appropriated). Collaboration in the period, as far as we can tell, consisted of writers working separately, not composing together. In many cases, it seems the left hand didn't know what the right hand was up to.

What *Look About You* does that many other plays do not is make this incoherence cohere through the sheer force of theatricality. And it does so by grappling throughout with what Henry Turner has called in another context the "problem of the more-than-one." So far, this introduction has treated the "problem of the more-than-one" only in terms of authorship. But *Look About You* also worries over this problem at the level of plot since it opens with two kings and one hermit, proceeds to a point when it has two kings and two hermits, and terminates with just one king and one hermit (who used to be one of the kings). The play therefore adumbrates one of the central policies of early modern drama, which is a strict one king/one hermit protocol, since even one more than one of either threatens the autonomy of the other. There is something oxymoronic about "two kings," since the wonderful thing about being a king is that you're the only one. Kingship is not to be shared, and we find in this play the deep political, psychic, and civic divisiveness of kingship split into more than one. It's like cleaving the atom and unleashing chaos into the world.

The play therefore argues that there must only ever be one king—and only one hermit, since in the kingdom of the theater, the hermit represents sovereign individuality. But *Look About You* liquefies identity so thoroughly as to undermine the stability of the theatrical enterprise itself. Consider the introduction of a second hermit costume near the end of the play. Just as two kings is an untenable political situation, two hermits is an untenable theatrical one. This is so because, just as only one crown at a time should signify majesty, only one hermit disguise can signify a false hermit, who is the king of the theatrical world. So baffling, so disturbing is the introduction of a second hermit disguise that during the play's late stand-off between two false hermits, it never occurs to anyone that they *both* might be false or *both* true. The hermit stand-off recapitulates the play's opening stand-off between two kings (where it doesn't occur to anyone either that both are true or false), but the hermit stand-off also allows early modern theater to look at itself in the mirror and discover that both images are both true and false.

This playfulness with identities is just part of *Look About You*'s theatricality, and it is the play's theatricality that rationalizes its inclusion in this anthology. "Theatricality" here means the glow that hovers at the edges of a play text—the way that text enables a performance that exceeds its written form. Perversely, though, while *Look About You* enables theatricality, it also threatens to disable it. For the text is an act of theatrical sabotage, a poison pill of a play that might well destroy a company in the act of its own expression. After all, to give a play to a company of actors—the Admiral's servants in the case of its original production—that requires them to imitate one another in a roundelay of swapped identities is just about the worst thing a writer—or writers—can do to a company (although just about the best thing a writer can do for an audience). Because if there's one thing that actors hate, it's discovering that they aren't inimitable. There are dozens of eighteenth-century anecdotes about the greatest actor of the age, David Garrick, being brought to see a man who did a famous impression of him. Garrick watched politely for some time but then allowed that he was baffled; he could see no resemblance whatsoever. He was staring the problem of more-than-one right in the face.

Ultimately, the circuit of swapped identities in *Look About You* has, like an electrical circuit, a ground to which it always returns. That ground is the character named "Redcap" and, more particularly, his stutter, carefully scripted in the 1600 text. Redcap's distinguishing linguistic characteristic makes him easy to mimic but renders him incapable of mimicry. Redcap is therefore the only person in this play incapable of mimicking anyone else. His disability (as we would call it) arms him with an extraordinary stability of identity. Unable to disappear into another persona, Redcap can run but he cannot hide. Redcap therefore represents the end of acting: he is the only character who doesn't suffer the consequences of the problem of more-than-one. Unlike the second hermit disguise, there is only ever one red cap at a time in *Look About You*.

If the play dilates upon the problem of more-than-one—more than one writer, more than one king, more than one hermit, more than one Redcap (but only one red cap, unless, of course, we count Robin's hood)—it is all the more ironic that it opens by staging something that is not there, indeed, something, horses, that are beyond the play's representational abilities: "*Enter ROBERT HOOD, a young nobleman, a SERVANT with him, with riding wands in their hands, as if they had been new lighted*" (i. 0 SD). It would be easy to conclude that the opening stage direction kicks off a play concerned with what is not there—identity in most cases—but to focus on the *limits* of representation would be to mistake the matter since the opening creates surplus out of scarcity (West, 2013). When we read the first line of the play, "Go, walk the horses; wait me on the hill./This is the hermit's cell..." (i. 1–2), we could marvel at the playwright's ingenious method of establishing the play's setting on Blackheath. Or we could say, you've got to be kidding me. This play opens with Robin Hood asking his servant to walk the non-existent horses they rode in on so that he can talk to a hermit? The play is kidding us, of course. This scene isn't set on Blackheath. The scene of this play is a scene of play; the world of this play is a play world. The frame of reference is other plays, and the surplus entertainment that these absent horses create draws upon all the other plays that feature Robin Hood, hermits, and absent horses. The "problem" of the horses is not "more-than-one" but "less-than-any," which is nonetheless productive.

Despite the play's largely comic tenor, there is a handful of serious criticism of *Look About You* as a sub-genre of the history play, a "pseudo-history" since it draws but loosely on chronicle history (Lancashire, 1969). But the temporal framework of this play is not the twelfth century (when the historical Henry II and sons lived) but the early modern theater history of plays past, present, and future that recycle these conventions, gestures, accessories (riding wands), etc. This material is being worked upon and transformed, entered back into the circulatory economy of theatrical matter. The only things that can happen in this play are things that happen in plays. The absent horses are not real horses that are not there, they are fictional horses that also don't appear in other plays without horses.

Tellingly, when theater history has accused *Look About You* of being something, it has accused it of being more than one play. There is a 1600 quarto of *Look About You* that firmly affixes it to the Admiral's players, but the play is not mentioned in the surviving papers of Philip Henslowe, who owned the playhouse where *Look About You* premiered in the late sixteenth century. Henslowe does, however, mention a play called *Disguises* several times in 1595—this play left no text—and some scholars think that this was an alternate name for *Look About You*. The play therefore enters theater history not once but twice. Pinioned between the problem of more-than-one and the problem of less-than-any, between surplus and deficit, *Look About You* finds its sweet spot by the end. With one text, one king, one hermit, one Redcap, one Robin Hood, the play finds its equilibrium—if not its author—in which it has just enough of everything a play needs.

Ultimately, the power of *Look About You* is that little attempt has been made to "norm" the abnormalities, to cohere the incoherencies, to spackle over the rough joins that might have been left by two hands working apart. Instead, *Look About You* highlights rather than hides its tonal fractures, as in the Japanese art of pottery *Kintsugi*, where broken seams are lacquered with gold dust to draw attention to where it all went wrong. If a play like *Look About You* bears all the marks of collaboration, those marks are apparent because the drama has dusted them in gold.

Textual note

Look About You was printed in a quarto of 1600 under the full title, *A Pleasant Commodie Called Looke About You*. The copy-text for this edition is the EEBO copy of the quarto held in the Huntington Library. The play is set mostly in verse and contains ample and descriptive stage directions. Redcap's characteristic stutter is phonetically indicated throughout the text by repetitions of words and letters (e.g. "I I am am Re Redcap, s s sir," ii. 292). The 1600 text contains no internal act or scene divisions. The text here therefore introduces a new scene (but no acts) every time the stage is totally cleared of personnel (this usually indicates a change of setting, but that is incidental). The text was apparently never reprinted.

Further reading

Editions

Hirsch, Richard S. M. (ed.) (1980) *A Pleasant Commodie Called Looke About You*, New York: Garland.

Critical and contextual reading

Gurr, Andrew (2009) *Shakespeare's Opposites: The Admiral's Company 1594–1625*, Cambridge: Cambridge University Press, 51–77.

Hyland, Peter (2006) "Face/Off: Some Speculations on Elizabethan Acting," *Shakespeare Bulletin* 24: 21–9.

Lancashire, Anne (1969) "*Look about You* as a History Play," *Studies in English Literature* 9: 321–34.

Menzer, Paul (forthcoming) "Bowling Alone, or the Whole Point of No Return," in Erika Lin and Gina Bloom (eds), *Games and Theatre*, Amsterdam: ARC/Amsterdam University Press.

Potter, Lois (ed.) (2003) *Playing Robin Hood: The Legend as Performance in Five Centuries*, Newark: University of Delaware Press.

Turner, Henry S. (2006) "The Problem of the More-than-One: Friendship, Calculation, and Political Association in *The Merchant of Venice*," *Shakespeare Quarterly* 57: 413–42.

West, William N. (2013) "Intertheatricality," in Henry S. Turner (ed.), *Early Modern Theatricality*, Oxford: Oxford University Press, 151–72.

Look About You (c. 1595–99)

Dramatis personae[1]

ROBIN HOOD, EARL OF HUNTINGTON
SKINK
HENRY II, *King of England*
HENRY, RICHARD, JOHN, *his sons*
ROBERT, EARL OF GLOUCESTER
EARL OF LANCASTER
EARL OF CHESTER
EARL OF LEICESTER
SIR RICHARD FAUCONBRIDGE
PORTER *of the Fleet*
REDCAP, *son to the Porter of the Fleet*
BLOCK, *servant to Fauconbridge*
LADY FAUCONBRIDGE, *sister to* GLOUCESTER
QUEEN ELINOR, *wife of King Henry*
PURSUIVANT
DRAWER

The Wife of Prince Henry, Isabel wife of Prince John, Humphrey, servant to Fauconbridge, Constable of the Watch, a Page of Lady Rawford's, Two Heralds, Watch, Sheriffs, Officers, Huntsmen, Musicians, Servants

[Scene i]

Enter ROBERT HOOD,[2] *a young nobleman, a* SERVANT *with him, with riding wands in their hands, as if they had been new lighted*[3]

ROBERT Go, walk the horses; wait me on the hill.
This is the hermit's cell; go out of sight.
My business with him must not be revealed
To any mortal creature but himself.
SERVANT I'll wait your honor in the cross highway.[4] *Exit*
ROBERT Do so. Hermit, devout and reverend,
If drowsy age keep not thy stiffened joints
On thy unrestful bed, or if the hours
Of holy orisons[5] detain thee not,
Come forth!

1 Dramatis personae: not in Q
2 0 SD ROBERT HOOD: Consistently named "Robert" or "Robert Hood" in speech prefixes and stage directions, the character is often called "Robin Hood" or "Huntington" by other characters
3 0 SD *lighted*: alighted, as if from a horse
4 5 cross highway: road running between two main roads, a by-road
5 9 orisons: prayers

Enter SKINK *like an hermit*[6]

SKINK Good morrow son, good morrow, and God bless thee Huntington.
A brighter gleam of true nobility
Shines not in any youth more than in thee.
Thou shalt be rich in honor, full of speed,
Thou shalt win foes by fear, and friends by meed.[7]
ROBERT Father, I come not now to know my fate.
Important business urgeth princely Richard *Delivers letters*
In these terms to salute thy reverent age.
Read, and be brief. I know some cause of trust
Made him employ me for his messenger.
SKINK A cause of trust indeed, true honored youth.
Princes had need in matters of import
To make nice[8] choice, fair earl. If I not err,
Thou art the prince's ward.[9]
ROBERT Father, I am
His ward, his chamberlain,[10] and bedfellow.[11]
SKINK Fair fall thee,[12] honorable Robert Hood.
Wend[13] to Prince Richard, say though I am loath
To use my skill in conjuration,
Yet Skink that poisoned red-cheeked Rosamond[14]
Shall make appearance at the parliament.
He shall be there by noon, assure his grace.
ROBERT Good morrow, father, see you fail him not.
For though the villain did a horrible deed,
Yet hath the young king, Richard, and Earl John
Sworn to defend him from his greatest foes.
SKINK God's benison[15] be with thee noble earl.
ROBERT Adieu, good father. Holla there, my horse? *Exit*
SKINK Up, spur the kicking jade,[16] while I make speed
To conjure Skink out of his hermit's weed.
Lie there, religion;[17] keep thy master's grave.
And on the fair trust of these princes' word
To court again, Skink. But, before I go,
Let mischief take advice of villainy
Why to the hermit letters should be sent
To post Skink to the court incontinent.[18]
Is there no trick in this? Ha, let me see?
Or do they know already I am he?
If they do so, faith,[19] westward then with Skink.

6 10 SD *like an hermit*: disguised as a hermit
7 15 meed: desert
8 23 nice: precise, considered
9 24 ward: a minor in the guardianship of an elder
10 25 chamberlain: a male attendant on nobility
11 25 bedfellow: it was not uncommon for men to share beds in the period
12 26 Fair fall thee: may blessings befall you
13 27 wend: make your way
14 29 red-cheeked Rosamond: the old king's mistress, whom Skink killed at the request of Elinor and the young king
15 36 benison: blessing
16 38 jade: insulting term for a horse
17 39–40 To conjure . . . there, religion: Skink sheds his hermit disguise
18 43–5 Let . . . incontinent: be wary and determine why you've been summoned to court so suddenly
19 48 faith: in faith

But what an ass am I to be thus fond.[20]
Here lies the hermit, whom I dying found
Some two months since, when I was hourly charged
With Hugh the crier[21] and with constables.
I saw him[22] in the ready way to heaven;
I helped him forward. 'Twas a holy deed,
And there he lies some six foot in the ground,
Since when, and since, I kept me in his weeds.[23]
Oh, what a world of fools have filled my cell:[24]
For fortunes, runaways, stol'n goods, lost cattle.[25]
Among the number, all the faction
That take the young king's part against the old[26]
Come to myself to harken for myself.[27]
So did the adverse party make enquire,
But either fall full of contrary desire.[28]
The old king's part would kill me, being stained,
The young king's keep me from their violence.
So then thou needst not fear; go boldly on!
Brave Hal,[29] Prince Dick, and my spruce hotspur[30] John!
Here's their safe conduct.[31] Oh, but for Rosamond!
A fig[32] for Rosamond, to this hope I'll lean:
At a queen's bidding I did kill a quean.[33]

Exit

[Scene ii]

Sound trumpets. Enter with a HERALD, *on the one side* [KING] HENRY *II crowned. After him* LANCASTER, CHESTER, SIR RICHARD FAUCONBRIDGE. *On the other part,* KING HENRY *the son crowned;* HERALD *after him; after him* PRINCE RICHARD, PRINCE JOHN, LEICESTER, *being set.*[34] *Enters fantastical* ROBERT OF GLOUCESTER *in a gown girt;*[35] *walks up and down*

KING Why doth not Gloucester take his honored seat?
GLOUCESTER In faith, my liege, Gloucester is in a land
Where neither surety is[36] to sit or stand.
I only do appear as I am summoned,
And will await without[37] till I am called.
HENRY Why, hear you, Gloucester?
GLOUCESTER Henry, I do hear you.

20 49 fond: foolish
21 52 Hugh the crier: pun on "hue and cry," a proclamation for the capture of a criminal
22 53 him: i.e. the dying hermit
23 56 weeds: clothing
24 57 cell: cave
25 58 Skink has been besieged by people seeking oracular advice
26 60 the old: i.e. the old king
27 61 Come to the "Hermit" looking for Skink
28 62–3 So did . . . contrary desire: both factions are looking for Skink, but to opposite ends
29 67 Hal: diminutive of "Henry," the young king
30 67 hotspur: a rash, hot-headed person
31 68 safe conduct: the letter delivered at line 17
32 69 A fig: contemptuous expression
33 70 quean: prostitute
34 0 SD *set*: settled, i.e. taking their place
35 0 SD *fantastical . . . gown girt*: extravagantly dressed in a belted gown
36 3 neither surety is: it isn't safe either
37 5 without: outside the room

HENRY And why not "King"?[38]
GLOUCESTER What's he that sits so near you?
RICHARD King too.
GLOUCESTER Two kings? Ha, ha!
KING Gloucester, sit, we charge thee.
GLOUCESTER I will obey your charge: I will sit down,
But, in this house, on no seat but the ground.
JOHN The seat's too good.[39]
GLOUCESTER I know it, brother John.
JOHN Thy brother?
KING Silence there!
HENRY Pass to the bills,[40] Sir Richard Fauconbridge.
FAUCONBRIDGE My lieges both, old Fauconbridge is proud
Of your right honored charge. He that worst may
Will strain his old eyes;[41] God send peace this day:
[*Reads*] "A bill for the releasement of the Queen, preferred by Henry, the young King; Richard the Prince; John, Earl of Murton; Bohmine, Earl of Leicester; and the commons.
KING Did you prefer this bill?
ALL We did.
CHESTER AND LANCASTER Ye did not well.
GLOUCESTER [*Aside*] Why this is good, now shall we have the hell.
HENRY, RICHARD, JOHN Chester and Lancaster, you wrong the king.
CHESTER AND LANCASTER Our king we do not.
HENRY Do not you see me crowned?
LANCASTER But whilst he[42] lives we to none else are bound.
LEICESTER Is it not wrong, think you, when all the world—
Troubled with rumor of a captive queen
Imprisoned by her husband in a realm
Where her own son doth wear a diadem[43]—
Is like an head[44] of people mutinous,
Still[45] murmuring at the shame done her and us?
Is't not more wrong when her mother[46] zeal—
Sounded through Europe, Africa, Asia—
Tells in the hollow of news-thirsting ears,
Queen Elinor lives in a dungeon
For pity and affection to her son?
But when the true cause, Clifford's daughter's death,[47]
Shall be exposed to stranger nations,
What volumes will be writ, what libels spread?
And in each line, our state dishonorèd.
FAUCONBRIDGE My lord speaks to the purpose. Marry, it may be so.
Pray God it prove not so.
LEICESTER Hear me conclude, and there withal[48] conclude,
It is an heinous and unheard of sin:

38 7 And why not "King"?: Why do you call me "Henry," not "King"?
39 11 too good: i.e. even the ground is too good for you
40 13 bills: legal petitions
41 15–16 He that . . . old eyes: he that is least able (i.e. old Fauconbridge, whose sight is weak) will nevertheless read the bill
42 26 he: i.e. the old king
43 30 diadem: crown
44 31 head: group, as in a "head" of cattle
45 32 Still: always
46 33 mother: native
47 38 Clifford's daughter's death: the death of Rosamond, the old king's mistress
48 44 withal: besides

Queen Elinor—daughter to kingly France,
King Henry's wife, and royal Henry's mother—
Is kept close[49] prisoner for an act of justice
Committed on an odious concubine.
KING Thou wrongst her, Leicester.
LEICESTER Lechers ever praise
The cause of their confusion. She was vile.
FAUCONBRIDGE She was ill-spoken of; it's true, true.
GLOUCESTER [*Aside*] Yonder sits one would do as much for you,
Old fool. Young Richard hath a gift, I know it,
And on your wife, my sister, would bestow it.[50]
Here's a good world: men hate adulterous sin,
Count it a gulf,[51] and, yet, they needs will in.[52]
LEICESTER What answer for the queen?
LANCASTER The king replies:
Your words are foul, slanderous forgeries.
JOHN His highness says not so.
LANCASTER His highness doth,
Tells you it's a shame for such wild youth
To smother any impiety
With show to chastise loose adultery.
Say Rosamond was Henry's concubine;
Had never king a concubine but he?
Did Rosamond begin the fires in France?
Made she the northern borders[53] reek with flames?
Unpeopled she the towns of Picardy?[54]
Left she the wives of England husbandless?
Oh no. She sinned, I grant, so do we all.
She fell herself, desiring none should fall.
But Elinor, whom you so much commend,[55]
Hath been the bellows of seditious fire,
Either through jealous rage or mad desire.
Is't not a shame to think that she hath armed
Four sons' right hands against their father's head;
And not the children of a low-prized wretch,
But one whom God on earth hath deified?
See where he sits with sorrow in his eyes.
Three of his sons, and hers, tutored by her,
Smiles whilst he weeps, and, with a proud disdain,
Embrace blithe mirth while his sad heart complain.
FAUCONBRIDGE Ha? Laugh they? Nay, by the rood,[56] that is not well.
Now fie, young princes, fie!
HENRY Peace, doting fool.
JOHN Be silent, ass.
FAUCONBRIDGE With all my heart, my lords; my humble leave, my lords.
God's mother! "Ass" and "fool" for speaking truth.
'Tis terrible, but fare ye well my lords.

49 48 close: securely
50 53–5 Yonder sits . . . bestow it: i.e. Prince Richard would cuckold Fauconbridge
51 57 Count it a gulf: consider it an abyss
52 57 will in: engage in adultery
53 67 northern borders: the borders of Brittany and Normandy, which Henry II invaded in 1166
54 68 Picardy: region in northwest France
55 72 commend: praise
56 83 rood: cross

RICHARD Nay, stay, good Fauconbridge. Impute it[57] rage
That thus abuses your right reverend age.
My brothers are too hot.
FAUCONBRIDGE Too hot indeed.
"Fool," "ass," for speaking truth? It's more than need.[58]
RICHARD Nay, good Sir Richard, at my kind entreat:[59]
For all the love I bear your noble house,
Let not your absence kindle further wrath.
Each side's at counsel now;[60] sit down I pray.
I'll quite[61] it with the kindest love I may.
GLOUCESTER [*Aside*] Ay, to his wife.
FAUCONBRIDGE Prince Richard, I'll sit down,
But, by the faith I owe fair England's crown,
Had you not been,[62] I would have left the place.
My service merits not so much disgrace.
RICHARD Good Fauconbridge, I thank thee. *Go to their places*
GLOUCESTER [*Aside*] And you'll think of him if you can step into his bower[63] at Stepney.[64]
FAUCONBRIDGE [*Aside*] Prince Richard's very kind. I know his kindness.
He loves me—but he loves my lady better.
No more, I'll watch him. I'll prevent his game.
Young lad, it's ill to halt before the lame.[65] *They break asunder. Papers this while being offered and subscribed[66] between either*
HENRY I'll not subscribe to this indignity!
I'll not be called a king but be a king.
Allow me half the realm. Give me the North,
The provinces that lie beyond the seas,
Wales, and the isles that compass in the main.[67]
GLOUCESTER [*Aside*] Nay, give him all, and he will scant be pleased.
RICHARD Brother, you ask too much.
JOHN Too much? Too little!
He shall have that and more! I swear he shall!
I will have Nottingham and Salisbury,
Stafford and Darby,[68] and some other earldom;
Or, by Saint John (whose blessèd name I bear),
I'll make these places like a wilderness.
Is't not a plague, an horrible abuse,
A king, a king of England, should be father
To four such proper youths—as Hal, and Dick,
My brother Geoffrey,[69] and my proper self—
And yet not give his sons such maintenance[70]

57 89 Impute it: attribute it to
58 92 more than need: excessive
59 93 entreat: entreaty
60 96 at counsel now: speaking among themselves
61 97 quite: requite, reward
62 100 been: been here
63 103 step into his bower: enter his bedroom and sleep with his wife
64 103 Stepney: district in London's East End, location of Fauconbridge's house
65 107 ill to . . . the lame: you cannot fake a limp in front of a lame man (i.e. you cannot fool an expert, proverbial)
66 107 SD *this while . . . and subscribed*: being signed in the meantime
67 110–12 Give me . . . the main: Henry demands Scotland, his territories in Brittany and Normandy, Wales, and, possibly, islands that encircle the English mainland (such as Barrow and the Isle of Wight)
68 116–17 I will . . . and Darby: John demands the earldoms of Nottingham (central England), Salisbury (in the southwest), Stafford (in the West Midlands), and Darby (in the East Midlands)
69 123 Geoffrey: though named here, Geoffrey does not appear in the play
70 124 maintenance: subsistence. Historically, Henry II's sons, led by "young Henry," revolted over their inheritance

As he consumes among his minions?[71]
RICHARD Be more respective,[72] John.
JOHN Respective, Richard?
Are you turned pure? A changing weathercock?[73]
I say it's reason:[74] Henry should be king;
Thou, prince; I, duke, as Geoffrey is a duke.
LANCASTER What shall your father do?
JOHN Live at his prayers,
Have a sufficient pension by the year,
Repent his sins because his end is near.
GLOUCESTER [*Aside*] A gracious son, a very gracious son.
KING Will this content you? I—that have sat still,
Amazed to see my sons devoid of shame,
To hear my subjects, with rebellious tongues,
Wound the kind bosom of their sovereign—
Can no more bear, but, from a bleeding heart,
Deliver all my love for[75] all your hate.
Will this content thee, cruel Elinor?
Your savage mother, my uncivil[76] queen,
The tigress that hath drunk the purple blood
Of three times twenty-thousand valiant men,
Washing her red chaps[77] in the weeping tears
Of widows, virgins, nurses, sucking babes,
And, lastly, sorted with her damned consorts,[78]
Entered a labyrinth to murder love.[79]
Will this content you? She shall be released,
That she may next seize me she most envies.[80]
HENRY Our mother's liberty is some content.[81]
KING What else would Henry have?
HENRY The kingdom.
KING Peruse this bill. Draw near, let us confer.
JOHN Hal, be not answered but with sovereignty,[82]
For glorious is the sway[83] of majesty.
KING What would content you, John?
JOHN Five earldoms, sir.
KING What you, son Richard?
RICHARD Pardon, gracious father,
And the furtherance[84] for my vow of penance.
For I have sworn to God and all his saints,
These arms—erected[85] in rebellious brawls
Against my father and my sovereign—

71 125 minions: favorites of the king, but also male or female mistresses
72 126 respective: respectful
73 127 weathercock: weather vane
74 128 reason: reasonable
75 139 for: in exchange for
76 141 uncivil: barbarous
77 144 chaps: jaws
78 146 consorts: allies
79 147 love: i.e. Rosamond
80 149 That she may next attack me, against whom she holds a grudge
81 150 content: comfort
82 153 sovereignty: the throne
83 154 sway: power
84 157 furtherance: assistance, aid
85 159 erected: raised

Shall fight the battles of the lord of hosts
In wronged Judea[86] and Palestina.
That shall be Richard's penance for his pride:
His blood a satisfaction[87] for his sin;
His patrimony men, munition,
And means to waft them into Syria.[88]
KING Thou shalt have thy desire, heroic son,
As soon as other home-bred brawls are done.
LANCASTER Why weeps old Fauconbridge?
FAUCONBRIDGE I am almost blind,[89]
To hear sons cruel and the father's kind.
Now, well a near[90] that ere I lived to see
Such patience and so much impiety.
GLOUCESTER Brother, content thee; this is but the first.
Worse is a-brewing and yet not the worst.
LEICESTER You shall not stand to[91] this.
HENRY And why, my lord?
LEICESTER The lands of Morton doth belong to John.
HENRY What's that to me? By act of parliament,
If they be mine confirmed, he must be pleased.
JOHN Be pleased, king puppet? Have I stood for thee,
Even in the mouth of death? Opened my arms
To circle in seditious ugly shape?[92]
Shook hands with[93] duty, bade adieu to virtue?
Profaned all majesty in heaven and earth?
Writ in black characters on my white brow,
The name of "rebel John" against his father?
For thee, for thee, thou atomy[94] of honor,
Thou worm of majesty, thou froth, thou bubble?
And must I now be pleased in peace to stand
While statutes make thee owner of my land?
GLOUCESTER [*Aside*] Good pastime, good; now will the thieves fall out?[95]
JOHN Oh, if I do, let me be never held
Royal King Henry's son.[96] Pardon me, father,
Pull down this rebel that hath done thee wrong.
Dick,[97] come and leave his side; assail him, lords.
Let's have no parley[98] but with bills[99] and swords.
KING Peace, John, lay down thy arms.[100] Hear Henry speak;
He minds[101] thee no such wrong.

86 162 Judea: today part of southern Israel; "wronged" because held by the Sunni Muslims at the time
87 164 satisfaction: penance
88 165–6 His patrimony . . . into Syria: the only inheritance he desires is support for his crusade
89 169 blind: i.e. with tears
90 171 well a near: alas
91 175 stand to: follow through on
92 181 circle in seditious ugly shape: embrace rebellion
93 182 Shook hands with: departed from
94 186 atomy: atom, a miniscule amount
95 190 fall out: argue
96 191–2 if I . . . Henry's son: if I put up with the seizure of my land, question my paternity
97 194 Dick: Prince Richard
98 195 parley: debate
99 195 bills: wooden-handled bladed weapons
100 196 arms: the king may speak figuratively, or John may have drawn his sword at "assail him, lords"
101 197 minds: intends

JOHN He were not best.[102]
HENRY Why, hare-brained brother, can ye brook no jest?[103]
I do confirm you Earl of Nottingham.
JOHN And Morton too?
HENRY Ay, and Morton too.
JOHN Why so, now once more I'll sit down by you.
GLOUCESTER Blow, wind! The youngest of King Henry's stock
Would fitly serve to make a weathercock.
JOHN Gape earth! Challenge thine own![104] As Gloucester lies,
Pity such muck is covered with the skies.[105]
FAUCONBRIDGE Be quiet, good my lords, the king commands
You should be quiet, and 'tis very meet.[106]
It's most convenient; how say you, Prince Richard?
RICHARD It is indeed.
FAUCONBRIDGE Why that is wisely said.
You are a very kind, indifferent[107] man,
Marry a God and by my holydam.[108]
[*Aside*] Were not I had a feeling in my head
Of some suspicion twixt my wife and him, [109]
I should affect him more than all the world.
GLOUCESTER Take heed, old Richard, keep thee there mad lad.
My sister's fair, and beauty may turn bad.

Enter ROBERT HOOD, *a paper in his hand*

OFFICER Room there! Make room for young Huntington!
FAUCONBRIDGE A gallant youth, a proper gentleman.
HENRY Richard, I have had wrong about his wardship.[110]
RICHARD You cannot right yourself.
JOHN He can and shall.
RICHARD Not with your help. But, honorable youth,
Have ye performed the business[111] I enjoined?
ROBERT I have, and Skink is come; here is his bill.
HENRY No matter for his bill; let him come in.
KING Let him not enter. His infectious breath
Will poison the assembly.
GLOUCESTER Never doubt
There's more infectious breaths about your throne:
Leicester is there, your envious sons is there.
If them you can endure, no poison fear.
KING Content thee, Gloucester.
GLOUCESTER I must be content
When you, that should mend all, are patient.[112]

102 197 were not best: he had better not wrong me
103 198 brook no jest: take a joke
104 204 Challenge thine own: call your own (i.e. Gloucester) back into yourself
105 205 It isn't fit that filth like Gloucester should live
106 207 meet: appropriate
107 210 indifferent: fair, unbiased
108 211 by my holydam: by my "holy lady," an exclamation
109 212–13 Fauconbridge feels like he might be growing the horns traditionally imagined to sprout on the head of a cuckold—i.e. that his wife might be cheating on him with Richard
110 219 wrong about his wardship: obscure; Henry might mean he's Robert's rightful guardian
111 222 the business: i.e. your errand to Blackheath to fetch Skink
112 230–31 I must . . . are patient: I will be silent since you, who have cause to protest, are patient

[*Enter* SKINK]

HENRY Welcome, good Skink. Thou justly dost complain
Thou standst in dread of death for Rosamond,[113]
Whom thou didst poison at our dread[114] command
And the appointment[115] of our gracious mother.
See here my father's hand unto thy pardon.
SKINK I receive it graciously, wishing his soul sweet peace in heaven for so meritorious a work.
For I fear me I have not his heart, though his hand.
KING Be sure thou hast not, murderous blood-sucker;
To jealous envy, executioner.[116]
HENRY Besides, thou suest to have some maintenance;
We have bethought us how we will reward thee:[117]
Thou shalt have Rowden[118] lordship.
GLOUCESTER Shall he so? Will you reward your murderers with my lands?
HENRY Your lands? It is our gift, and he shall have it.
GLOUCESTER I'll give him seizure[119] first with this and this. *Strikes him*
JOHN Lay hold on Gloucester!
KING Hold that murderous Skink!
GLOUCESTER Villains, hands off! I am a prince, a peer,
And I have borne disgrace while I can bear.
FAUCONBRIDGE Knaves, leave your rudeness. How now, brother Gloucester?
Nay, be appeased; be patient, brother.
RICHARD Shift for thyself, good Skink. There's gold, away.
Here will be parts.[120]
SKINK 'Swounds! I'll make one[121] and stay.
JOHN I prithee,[122] be gone, since thus it falleth out,
Take water,[123] hence, away, thy life I doubt!
SKINK Well, farewell. Get I once out of door,
Skink never will put trust in warrants[124] more. *Exit*
KING Will Gloucester not be bridled?
GLOUCESTER Yes, my liege,
And saddled too, and rid, and spurred, and reined.
Such misery (in your reign) falls[125] your friends.
Let go my arms, you dunghills! Let me speak.
KING Where's that knave Skink? I charge you: see him stayed.[126]
FAUCONBRIDGE The swift-heeled knave is fled.
Body a me,[127] here's rule; here's work indeed.
KING Follow that Skink; let privy search[128] be made.
Let not one pass except he be well known.

113 233 dread of death for Rosamond: fear of execution for killing Rosamond
114 234 dread: awesome
115 235 appointment: direction
116 240 An ironic injunction: the King condemns the executioner to "jealous envy" since he won't get to execute Skink
117 241–2 Besides, thou . . . reward thee: other than your request for subsistence, we plan to reward you further
118 243 Rowden: an area in southwest England
119 246 seizure: pun on the "seizure" of lands, for which Gloucester will give Skink a "seizure," or a fit
120 253 parts: division, dissension
121 253 make one: i.e. join in the dissension
122 254 prithee: pray you, beg of you
123 255 Take water: travel by water
124 257 warrants: legal documents, in this case Skink's pardon
125 260 falls: befalls
126 262 stayed: arrested
127 264 Body a me: i.e. by my body
128 265 privy search: thorough search of every person and place

Let posts be every way sent speedily
For ten miles compass[129] round about the city.
HENRY Take Gloucester to you, Lieutenant of the Tower.
Keep him aside till we confer a while.
Father, you must subscribe to his committing.[130]
LANCASTER Why must he, Henry?
LEICESTER Marry, for this cause:
He hath broke peace and violated laws.
GLOUCESTER So have you all done, rebels as you be.
FAUCONBRIDGE Good words, good brother. Hear me, gracious lords.
HENRY I prithee, Fauconbridge, be patient.
Gloucester must of force[131] answer this contempt.
KING I will not yield[132] he shall unto the Tower.
Warden of th'Fleet,[133] take you the charge of Gloucester.
HENRY Why, be it so, yet stay with him a while,
Till we take order for the company
That shall attend him and resort[134] to him.
GLOUCESTER Warden of the Fleet, I see I am your charge.
Befriend me thus lest, by their command,
I be prevented of what I intend.
KEEPER Command me any service in my power.
GLOUCESTER I pray you call some nimble-footed fellow
To do[135] a message for me to my sister.[136]
KEEPER Call in Redcap. He waiteth with a tipstaff.[137] *Exit one for him*[138]
He stammers, but he's swift and trusty, sir.

Enter REDCAP

GLOUCESTER No matter for his stammering, is this he?
REDCAP I I am am Re Redcap, s s sir.[139]
GLOUCESTER Run Redcap, to Stepney.
REDCAP I'll be at Stepney p p presently.
GLOUCESTER Nay stay. Go to the Lady Fauconbridge, my sister.
REDCAP The La La Lady Fau Fau Faukenbreech? I r r run, sir.
GLOUCESTER But take thy errand: tell her I am prisoner, committed to the Fleet.
REDCAP I am g g glad of th th that: my fa fa father the p p porter sha shall ge ge get a f f fee[140]
by you. *Still runs*[141]
GLOUCESTER Stand still a while. Desire her to make means[142]
Unto Prince Richard for my liberty.
At thy return (make speed), I will reward thee.
REDCAP I am g g gone si sir. [*Exit*]

129 268 compass: circuit
130 271 committing: i.e. to prison
131 277 of force: upon compulsion
132 278 yield: agree
133 279 Fleet: a prison on the east bank of the Fleet River, London
134 282 resort: visit
135 288 do: convey
136 288 sister: Lady Fauconbridge
137 289 tipstaff: a staff capped with metal, the badge of a messenger's office
138 289 SD *for him*: to fetch him
139 292 Redcap's stutter is represented phonetically in the 1600 text and presented here with spelling and punctuation modernized but otherwise unaltered
140 298 get a f f fee: at the time, prisoners paid prison personnel various fees; Redcap's father is a porter (or gatekeeper) at the Fleet, and Gloucester will have to pay him when he goes into the prison
141 299 SD *Still runs*: Redcap starts to run off
142 300 make means: motions, intercessions

RICHARD Commend me to her, gentle Huntington;
Tell her, in these affairs I'll stand her friend.
Her brother shall not long be prisoner.
Say I will visit her immediately.
Be gone, sweet boy, to Marian Fauconbridge.
Thou lookest like love; persuade her to be loving.
ROBERT So far as honor will, I will persuade.
I'll lay love's battery[143] to her modest ears:
Second my mild assault,[144] you may chance win;
Fair parley at the least may hap pass in.[145] *Exit*
HENRY [*To the* KEEPER] Here, take your charge: let no man speak with him
Except our self, our brethren, or Earl Leicester.
FAUCONBRIDGE Not I, my Lord? May not I speak with him?
HENRY Yes, Fauconbridge, thou shalt.
JOHN And why? He[146] is his wife's brother.
FAUCONBRIDGE Earl John, although I be,[147] I am true unto the state, and so is he.
GLOUCESTER What, shall I have no servant of my own?
HENRY No, but[148] the household servants of the Fleet.
GLOUCESTER I thank you, kinsman king. Your father knows,
Gloucester may boldly give a base slave blows.
FAUCONBRIDGE Oh, but not here; it was not well done here.
KING Farewell good Gloucester, you shall hear from us.
GLOUCESTER Even what your sons will suffer[149] you to send.
Is't not a misery to see you stand,
That sometime[150] was the monarch of this land,
Entreating traitors for a subject's freedom?
LEICESTER Let him not speak. Away with him to prison.
GLOUCESTER Here's like[151] to be a well-stayed[152] commonwealth,
Wherein proud Leicester and licentious John
Are pillars for the king to lean upon.
JOHN We'll hear your railing[153] lecture in the Fleet.
HENRY On our displeasure, see he speak no more.
GLOUCESTER On thy displeasure? Well, ye have me here.
Oh, that I were within my fort of Bungay,[154]
Whose walls are washed with the clear streams of Aveney,
Then would not Gloucester pass a half-penny[155]
For all these rebels, and their poor king too.
Laughst thou, King Henry?[156] Thou knows my words are true.
God help thee, good old man, adieu, adieu.
JOHN That castle[157] shall be mine. Where stands it, Fauconbridge?

143 311 battery: attack
144 312 Second my mild assault: follow up on my attack
145 313 Sweet talk might succeed
146 318 He: i.e. Gloucester
147 319 although I be: i.e. although I am his brother-in-law
148 321 but: only
149 326 suffer: allow
150 328 sometime: once
151 331 like: likely
152 331: well-stayed: stable
153 334 railing: complaining
154 337 Bungay: a town in southeast England on a bend of the river Waveney (spelled "Aveney" in the 1600 text)
155 337–9 Oh that . . . half-penny: the three-lines of hypermetrical rhyme are a version of a verse attributed to Hugh Bigod, made when he re-fortified the castle of Bungay around 1165 to defend himself from Henry II. The phrase "pass a half-penny" means "care even a little"
156 341 King Henry: i.e. the young king, spoken ironically
157 343 that castle: i.e. Bungay Castle

FAUCONBRIDGE Far from your reach, sure, under Feckhill ridge.[158]
Five hundred men (England hath few such wight[159])
Keeps it for Gloucester's use both day and night.
But you may easily win it. Wantons' words[160]
Quickly can master men, tongues out-brawl swords.
JOHN Ye are an idiot.
RICHARD I prithee, John, forbear.
JOHN What, shall old winter[161] with his frosty jests
Cross flowery pleasure?
FAUCONBRIDGE Ay, and nip[162] you too.
God's Mary mother, I would tickle[163] you,
Were there no more in place but I and you.
KING Cease these contentions! Forward to the Tower.
Release Queen Elinor—and leave me there
Your prisoner, I am sure, if ye had power.
There's nothing lets you but the commons' fear.[164]
Keep your state,[165] lords; we will by water go,
Making the fresh Thames salt with tears of woe.
HENRY And we'll by land through the city ride,
Making the people tremble at our pride.[166]

Exeunt with trumpets two ways

[Scene iii]

Enter SKINK *solus*[167]

SKINK "Blackheath,"[168] quoth he; and I were king of all Kent I would give it for a commodity of apron-strings to be in my cottage again.[169] Princes' warrants, marry, Skink finds them as sure as an obligation sealed with butter.[170] At King's Bridge,[171] I durst[172] not enter a boat. Through London, the stones were fiery. I have had a good cool way through the fields, and in the high way to Radcliffe[173] stands a heater.[174] Mile-end's covered with "Who goes there?"[175] 'Tis for me, sure. Oh Kent, oh Kent! I would give my part of all Christendom[176] to feel thee as I see thee.[177] If I go forward, I am stayed. If I go backward, there's a rogue in a red cap. He's run from Saint

158 344 Feckhill ridge: unidentified
159 345 such wight: so strong
160 347 Wantons' words: irresponsible words
161 351 old winter: i.e. Fauconbridge
162 352 nip: freeze
163 353 tickle: chastise, beat
164 358 Nothing stops you from imprisoning me except your fear of the common people
165 359 state: status, grandeur
166 362 pride: pomp
167 0 SD *solus*: alone
168 1 "Blackheath": Skink seems to quote either Prince John—who urged him to flee at ii. 254–5—or an unidentified figure who has just told Skink where he is. At the time the play was written, Blackheath was part of northwest Kent; now it is a district in southeast London
169 1–2 and I . . . cottage again: even if I were the king of Kent (a county in southeast England), I would trade the position for relatively worthless wares if I could be safe at home
170 2–3 Princes' warrants . . . with butter: pardons from princes (see ii. 257) are as worthless as legal documents sealed with butter
171 3 King's Bridge: probably what is now called London Bridge
172 3 durst: dared
173 5 Radcliffe: a town outside Manchester
174 5 stands a heater: i.e. the highway to Radcliff is "heater" (hotter) than the "Cool way through the fields"
175 5 Mile-end's covered with "Who goes there?": East London is full of men on the lookout for Skink
176 6 Oh Kent . . . all Christendom: "Neither in Kent nor Christendom" was an ambiguous English proverb meaning something like "neither in the part nor in the whole"
177 6 feel thee as I see thee: obscure; Skink may mean that he hopes Kent turns out to be as safe as it seems

the old king's[178] after me. I were best stay here, lest if he come with hue and cry he stop me yonder. I would slip the collar for fear of the halter.[179] But here comes my runner, and if he run for me his race dies.[180] He is as sure dead as if a parliament of devils had decreed it.

Enter REDCAP

REDCAP Ste Ste Stepney chi church yonder, but I have forgot the La La Lady Fau Fau Fau[181] —plague on her! I mu must b back to the Fle Fle Fleet to kn kn know it. The La the La La Lady Fau, plague on't! G Gloucester will go ne near to st stab me fo for forgetting my errand. He is such a ma ma mad lord. The La Lady Fau Fau—

SKINK Help me device![182] Upon my life, this fool is sent
From Gloucester to his sister Marian.

REDCAP I m must nee needs go back. The La Lady Fau, Fau, Fau—

SKINK God speed, good fellow.

REDCAP Go go god sp sp speed you, sir.

SKINK Why run'st thou from me?

REDCAP Ma Marry sir, I have lo lost a la lady's name, and I am running ba back to se se seek it.

SKINK What lady? I prithee, stay.

REDCAP Why the La Lady Fau Fau—

SKINK Fauconbridge?

REDCAP Ay, the s s same! F f farewell, I th th thank you ha heartily.

SKINK If thou wouldst speak with her, she is in Kent.
I serve her. What's thy business with my lady?

REDCAP I sh sh should do an errand to her f f from my Lord of Gloucester, but a a and[183] she be in K Kent I'll s send it by you.

SKINK Where is my lord?[184]

REDCAP Marry p p prisoner in the Fl Fleet, a a and w would have her speak to P Prince R Richard for his re re release.

SKINK I have much business. Hold, there's thy fare by water; my lady lies this night.

REDCAP Wh wh where, I pray?

SKINK At Gravesend at the Angel.[185]

REDCAP 'Tis devilish co co cold, going by water.

SKINK Why, there's my cloak and hat to keep thee warm.
Thy cap and jerkin will serve me to ride in
By the way. Thou hast wind and tide, take oars.
My lady will reward thee royally.

REDCAP G God a mercy! F fa faith, and ever th thou co co come to the Fl Fl Fleet, I'll give thee tu tu turning of the ke key f for n no nothing.[186]

SKINK Hie thee.[187] Tomorrow morning at Gravesend, I'll wash thy stammering throat with a mug of ale, merrily.

REDCAP God be w with you till s soo soon. What call you the lady? Oh, now I re remember: the La Lady Fa Fauconbridge. At what s sign?

SKINK At the Angel.

REDCAP A Angel, the La La Lady Fa Fa Fauconbridge, Fa Fau Fauconbridge. [*Exit*]

SKINK Farewell and be hanged, good stammering ninny. I think I have set your

178 7–8 Saint John's: the Church of St. John of Jerusalem; near the Fleet prison
179 9 slip the . . . the halter: evade arrest to avoid hanging
180 10 race dies: punning on a footrace, Skink promises to end Redcap's family line
181 11 Ste Ste Stepney . . . Fau Fau: Redcap is near Lady Fauconbridge's Stepney home but has forgotten her name
182 15 device: ingenuity
183 28 and: if
184 30 my lord: i.e. Fauconbridge (whom Skink pretends to serve)
185 35 Gravesend is a town in northwest Kent; the Angel is the name of an inn there
186 41–2 I'll give . . . no nothing: the next time Skink is brought to the Fleet, he'll be let in for free
187 43 Hie thee: go quickly

Redcap's heels a-running. Would your pianet-chattering humor[188] could as sa safely se set me fr from the searchers' walks.[189] Yonder comes someone. Hem,[190] Skink, to your tricks—this tytty tytty a the tongue I believe will fail me.

Enter CONSTABLE *and Watch*

CONSTABLE Come, make up to[191] this fellow; let the other go. He seems a gentleman;[192] what are you, sir?
SKINK Would I had kept my own suit if the countenance carry it away.[193]
CONSTABLE Stand, sirrah,[194] what are you?
SKINK The po po porter's son of the F Fl Fleet, going to Stepney about business to the La La Lady Fa Fa Fauconbridge.
CONSTABLE Well, bring him thither, some two or three of ye honest neighbors, and so back to the Fleet. We'll show ourselves diligent above other officers.
SKINK Wh wh why, le le let me run. I am Re Redcap.
CONSTABLE Well, sure you shall now run no faster than I lead you. Hear ye, neighbor Simmes, I leave my staff[195] with ye. Be vigilant, I pray you. Search the suspicious houses at the town's end; this Skink's a trouncer.[196] Come, will you be gone, sir?
SKINK Yes sir [*Aside*] and the devil go with you and them.—Well, yet have hope mad ha heart. Co co come your way.

Exeunt

[Scene iv]

Enter ROBERT HOOD *and* BLOCK

BLOCK Sweet nobility in reversion,[197] Block, by the commission of his head,[198] conjures you, and withal binds you—by all the tricks that pages pass in time of parliament,[199] as swearing to the pantable,[200] crowning with custards, paper whiffs to the sleepers' noses,[201] cutting of tags,[202] stealing of torches, *cum multis aliis*[203]—tell Block: what block you have cast in the way of my lady's content?
ROBERT Block, by the antiquity of your ancestry, I have given your lady not so much as the least cause of dislike. If she be displeased at any news I bring, it's more than I must blab.
BLOCK Zounds! These pages be so proud, they care not for an old servingman. You are a ward and, so, an earl, and no more. You disquiet our house—that's the most; and I may be even with thee—that's the least.[204]

188 50 pianet-chattering humor: magpie-chattering manner
189 50–51 sa safely . . . searchers' walks: Skink imitates Redcap's stammer
190 51 Hem: an interjection (e.g. "ahem," or "ha")
191 53 make up to: draw near
192 53 let the . . . a gentleman: Redcap is dressed in Skink's "cloak and hat" (line 37) and so is let pass
193 55 If appearances let one escape, I wish I had my own clothes again
194 56 sirrah: contemptuous term of address
195 63 staff: staff of office
196 64 a trouncer: dangerous; also, an odd man
197 1 in reversion: Robert's nobility depends upon the death of another; what follows is a parodic oath, in which Block "swears in" Robert upon a number of juvenile pranks
198 1 commission of his head: ironic, the authority of his office (with a pun on "Block-head")
199 2 tricks that . . . of parliament: the pranks played by young attendants when parliament is in session
200 2–3 swearing to the pantable: proverbial—swearing on a slipper ("pantable")
201 3 paper whiffs to the sleepers' noses: puffs of wind delivered to sleepers' by waved paper
202 3 tags: pieces of stray clothing hanging off garments
203 4 *cum multis aliis*: with many other
204 9–10 I may . . . the least: the least I can do is get even with you for disturbing our house

Enter the LADY FAUCONBRIDGE

LADY FAUCONBRIDGE What, Block? What, Block, I say, what do you there?
BLOCK Making the young lord merry, madam.
LADY FAUCONBRIDGE Go attend the gate. See if you can let in more grief thereat.[205]
BLOCK Zounds! And grief come in there, and I see him once, I'll conjure his gabardine. [206]
LADY FAUCONBRIDGE Will you be gone, sir?
BLOCK Hem, these women, these women! And she be not in love either with Prince Richard or this lad, let Block's head be made a chopping block. *Exit* BLOCK
ROBERT Fair madam, what reply you to my suit?
The prince accepts smiles, welcomes loving looks.
LADY FAUCONBRIDGE The prince, if he give heed to Marian's suit,
Must hear heart-sighs, see sorrow in my eyes,
And find cold welcome to calamities.[207]
ROBERT And why for God's sake?
LADY FAUCONBRIDGE Even for Gloucester's sake.
ROBERT Why, by mine honor, and Prince Richard's faith,
Your brother Gloucester shall have liberty,
Upon condition you release a prisoner
That you have long held in captivity.
LADY FAUCONBRIDGE I have no prisoner.
ROBERT Yes, a world of eyes
Your beauty in a willing bondage ties.
LADY FAUCONBRIDGE Go to, you are disposed to jest my lord.
ROBERT In earnest, I must be an earnest suitor
To you for love, yet you must be my tutor.
LADY FAUCONBRIDGE Are you in love?
ROBERT I dearly love Prince Richard.
LADY FAUCONBRIDGE Then do you love the loveliest man alive,
The princeliest person of King Henry's sons.
ROBERT I like this well.
LADY FAUCONBRIDGE He is virtuous in the mind, his body fair;
His deeds are just, his speeches debonair.[208]
ROBERT Better and better still.
LADY FAUCONBRIDGE Indeed, he is what nobody can deny:
All lovely, beauty all, all majesty.
ROBERT I'll tell his excellence what you report.
No doubt he will be very thankful for't.
LADY FAUCONBRIDGE Nay, hear you, young lord? God's pity, stay.
ROBERT What, have you more in Richard's praise to say?
LADY FAUCONBRIDGE I have said too much if you misconster[209] me.
Duty bids praise him, not unchastity.[210]
ROBERT Unchastity? Holy heavens forfend[211] it,
That he, or I, or you should once intend it!

Enter BLOCK *and* RICHARD

BLOCK They are there, sir, close at it. I leave you, sir; the more room, the less company.

205 13 let in more grief thereat: go let more problems in (said ironically)
206 14 conjure his gabardine: send his gabardine (a loose garment of coarse material, often worn by beggars) away
207 22 calamities: his afflictions
208 38 debonair: gracious, courteous
209 46 misconster: misinterpret
210 47 I praise Richard out of duty to him, not lust for him
211 48 forfend: forbid

RICHARD Drink that,[212] farewell.
BLOCK If that Sir Richard comes, this ties, this binds.[213]
Oh gold, thy power converteth servants' minds. *Exit*
RICHARD How now, fair madam, who hath angered you?
LADY FAUCONBRIDGE Grief at my brother's durance[214] angers me.
RICHARD I had thought my ward, young Huntington, had vexed you.
LADY FAUCONBRIDGE Who he? Alas, good gentleman, he wronged me not. No matter for all this, I'll tell your tale.[215]

A noise within. Enter SKINK [*disguised as* REDCAP], BLOCK, CONSTABLE

BLOCK Sir, there comes no more of you in with him than the constable. Zounds! Here's a beadroll[216] of bills[217] at the gate indeed. Back, ye base![218]
LADY FAUCONBRIDGE Now, sirrah, what's the matter?
BLOCK Marry, here's a stammerer taken clipping[219] the king's English, and the constable and his watch hath brought him to you to be examined.
CONSTABLE No, madam, we are commanded by the king to watch, and, meeting this fellow at Mile-end, he tells us he is the porter's son of the Fleet, that the Earl of Gloucester sent him to you.
SKINK Ay, f f forsooth, h he desire you to speak to the p prince for him.
LADY FAUCONBRIDGE Oh, I conceive thee, bid him blithely fare.[220]
Bear him this ring in token of my care.
SKINK [*Aside*] If I be rid of this evil angel[221] that haunts me, many rings, much Fleet will Skink come unto.[222]
CONSTABLE Madam, if you know this fellow, we'll discharge him.
BLOCK Madam, and you be wise, trust your honest neighbors here. Let them bring this ca ca ca ca to the Fleet, and s see your ring delivered.
SKINK [*Aside*] A plague upon you for a damnèd rogue!
The porter of the Fleet will surely know me.[223]
LADY FAUCONBRIDGE Good neighbors, bring this honest fellow thither.
There's for his pains a crown,[224] if he say true,
And for your labor there's as much for you.
SKINK Why ma ma madam, I am Re Re Redcap, the porter's son.
LADY FAUCONBRIDGE Thou hast no wrong in this; farewell, good fellow.
SKINK Best speaking[225] to Prince Richard? No, I'll try
And face out[226] Redcap if the slave were by.
LADY FAUCONBRIDGE Make them drink, Block.
BLOCK Come to the buttery bar,[227] stitty stitty stammerer. Come, honest constable. Hey, the watch of our town! We'll drink trilill i'faith.[228]

212 51 Drink that: Prince Richard gives Block money
213 52 If Lady Fauconbridge's husband (Richard) shows up, Block will be loyal to Prince Richard since he paid him
214 55 durance: imprisonment
215 58 tell your tale: obscure
216 60 beadroll: list of people to be prayed for; here, figuratively, a group
217 60 bills: either petitions or the weapons carried by the men
218 60 ye base: you lowlifes
219 62 clipping: ruining; counterfeiting
220 68 bid him blithely fare: give him good wishes
221 70 evil angel: i.e. the constable
222 70–71 many rings . . . come unto: Skink will come into great wealth if he can escape the constable. The meaning of "much Fleet" is obscure; possibly Skink imagines becoming head jailer at the Fleet
223 76 The porter will know I'm not his son, Redcap
224 78 crown: a coin worth five shillings
225 82 Best speaking: is it best to speak
226 83 face out: outface
227 85 buttery bar: where liquor is stored in great houses
228 85–6 Hey the . . . trilill i'faith: Block sings a snatch of drinking song, origin unknown. "i'faith": in faith

As they go out, enters Sir RICHARD FAUCONBRIDGE *stealing forward,* PRINCE [RICHARD] *and* LADY [FAUCONBRIDGE] *talking*

ROBERT *Lupus in fabula,*[229] my noble lord:
See the old fox, Sir Richard Fauconbridge.
RICHARD We'll fit him[230] well enough. Second us, Robin.
LADY FAUCONBRIDGE [*Aside*] I'll fit you well enough, for all your hope.

FAUCONBRIDGE *beckons to* BLOCK

FAUCONBRIDGE Leave quaffing,[231] sirrah, listen to their talk.
BLOCK Oh, while you live, beware: two are sooner seen than one. Besides, bear a brain[232] master, if Block should be now spied, my madam would not trust this sconce[233] neither in time nor tide.
FAUCONBRIDGE Well, leave me, now it buds.[234] See, see! They kiss!
BLOCK Adieu, good old sinner. You may recover it with a salad of parsley and the herb patience.[235] If not, sir, you know the worst; it's but even this.[236]
RICHARD Madam, what you desire I not deny,
But promise Gloucester's life and liberty.
I beg but love.
FAUCONBRIDGE [*Aside*] When doth she give her alms?[237]
LADY FAUCONBRIDGE Fair honorable prince.
FAUCONBRIDGE [*Aside*] Nay then, they speed.[238]
LADY FAUCONBRIDGE My soul hath your deserts[239] in good esteem.
FAUCONBRIDGE [*Aside*] Witness these goodly tines[240] that grace my head.
LADY FAUCONBRIDGE But were you the sole monarch of the earth,
Your power were insufficient to invade
My never-yielding heart of chastity.
FAUCONBRIDGE [*Aside*] Sayst thou so Mall?[241] I promise thee, for this
I'll owe thy cherry lips an old man's kiss.
Look how my cockerel droops! [242] 'Tis no matter,
I like it best when women will not flatter.
RICHARD Nay, but sweet lady—
ROBERT Nay, but gracious lord,
Do not so much forget your princely worth,
As to attempt[243] virtue to unchastity.
FAUCONBRIDGE [*Aside*] Oh, noble youth!
ROBERT Let not the lady's dead grief for her brother
Give life to shameless and detested sin.
FAUCONBRIDGE [*Aside*] Sweet child!
ROBERT Consider that she is of high descent.
FAUCONBRIDGE [*Aside*] Most virtuous earl!
ROBERT Wife to the noblest knight that ever breathed.

229 87 *Lupus in fabula*: speak of the devil; literally "wolf in the story" with a possible play on "fox" in the following line
230 89 fit him: punish
231 91 quaffing: drinking
232 92 bear a brain: bear in mind
233 93 sconce: head
234 95 it buds: the romance between Prince Richard and Lady Fauconbridge blossoms
235 96–7 You may . . . herb patience: an abstemious diet will help you recover your patience
236 97 If you're not patient, you'll see yourself cuckolded
237 101 When will she pay the price for his promise?
238 102 speed: proceed
239 103 deserts: deserving
240 104 tines: the forked horns of a cuckold
241 108 Mall: an affectionate diminutive of "Marian"
242 110 my cockerel droops: i.e. Prince Richard looks like a defeated young cock
243 114 attempt: tempt

FAUCONBRIDGE [*Aside*] Now blessing on thee, blessèd Huntington!
ROBERT And would you then first stain your princely stock?[244]
Wrong beauty, virtue, honor, chastity,
And blemish Fauconbridge's untainted arms?[245]
FAUCONBRIDGE [*Aside*] By adding horns unto our falcon's head.[246]
Well thought on, noble youth; 'twas well put in.[247]
LADY FAUCONBRIDGE Besides my gracious lord—
FAUCONBRIDGE [*Aside*] Tickle[248] him, Mall;
Plague him on that side for his hot desire.
LADY FAUCONBRIDGE However secretly great princes sin—
FAUCONBRIDGE [*Aside*] Oh, now the spring![249] She'll do it secretly.
LADY FAUCONBRIDGE —the king of all hearts will have all sins known.
FAUCONBRIDGE [*Aside*] Ah, then, she yields not.
RICHARD Lady, here's my hand.
I did but try[250] your honorable faith.
FAUCONBRIDGE [*Aside*] He did but try her. Would she have been tried,
It had grown hard on this and on this side.[251]
RICHARD And since I see your virtue so confirmed,
As vice can have no entrance in your heart,
I vow, in sight of heaven, never again
To move like question but for love.[252]
FAUCONBRIDGE [*Aside*] My heart is eased.—Hold, Block, take up my cloak.
BLOCK And your cap too, sir?[253]
RICHARD Sir Richard?
FAUCONBRIDGE What, sweet prince? Welcome i'faith.
I see youth quickly gets the start[254] of age.
But welcome, welcome, and young Huntington,
Sweet Robin Hood, honor's best-flow'ring bloom.
Welcome to Fauconbridge[255] with all my heart.
How cheers my love? How fares my Marian, ha?
Be merry, chuck,[256] and Prince Richard, welcome.
Let it go, Mall, I know thy grievances.
Away away, tut, let it pass sweet girl.
We needs must have his help about the earl.[257]
LADY FAUCONBRIDGE Let it not be delayed, dear Fauconbridge.
RICHARD Sir Richard, first make suit unto my father.
I'll follow you to court and second you,
FAUCONBRIDGE [*Aside*] Follow to court, ha? Then I smell a rat.
It's probable he'll have a bout again.[258]
Long siege makes entrance to the strongest fort.
It must not be. I must not leave him here.—

244 123 Would you be the first to stain your family name
245 125 arms: heraldic device, i.e. the insignia on a coat of arms
246 126 adding horns . . . falcon's head: placing a cuckold's horns on the falcon in Fauconbridge's "arms"
247 127 put in: added
248 128 Tickle: torment
249 131 now the spring: now she springs the trap
250 134 try: test
251 135–6 Would she . . . this side: if she had failed the "test," it would have been hard on both of us
252 140 To make similar arguments except for honorable love
253 142 your cap too: an obscure joke, possibly referring to cuckold's horns or to a figurative fool's cap
254 144 gets the start: outpaces
255 147 Fauconbridge: the name of Sir Richard's estate
256 149 chuck: chick, a term of endearment
257 152 the earl: i.e. Gloucester
258 157 He'll probably make an attempt on my wife once more

Prince Richard, if you love my brother's good,
Let's ride back to the court. I'll wait on you.
RICHARD [*Aside*] He's jealous, but I must observe the time—[259]
We'll ride unto the court; I'll leave my boy[260]
Till we return, are you agreed to this?
FAUCONBRIDGE Oh, ay, he is an honorable youth,
Virtuous and modest. Huntington's right[261] heir.
His father, Gilbert, was the smoothest-faced lord
That e'er bare[262] arms in England or in France.
RICHARD [*Aside*] Solicit, Robin;[263] Lady, give good ear,
And of your brother's freedom never fear.
FAUCONBRIDGE Marian farewell. Where's Block? Open the gate!
Come, prince; God send us to prove fortunate.[264] *Exeunt*
LADY FAUCONBRIDGE Why do you stay, sir?
ROBERT Madam, as a lieger,[265] to solicit for your absent love.
LADY FAUCONBRIDGE Walk in the garden; I will follow you.
I'faith, i'faith, you are a noble wag.[266]
ROBERT An honorable wag, and waggish earl.
Even what you will, sweet Lady, I must bear,
Hoping of patience profit will ensue:[267]
That you will bear the prince as I bear you.
LADY FAUCONBRIDGE Well said, well said; I'll have these toys amended.[268]
Go, will you walk into the garden, sir?
ROBERT But will you promise me to bring no maids
To set upon my little manship there?
You threatened whipping, and I am in fear.
LADY FAUCONBRIDGE Upon my word, I'll bring none but myself.
ROBERT You see I am weaponed;[269] do not, I beseech you.
I'll stab them, come there twenty, ere they breech me.[270] *Exit*
LADY FAUCONBRIDGE This youth and Richard think me easily won,
But Marian rather will embrace
The bony carcass of dismaying death[271]
Than prove unchaste to noble Fauconbridge.
Richard's King Henry's son, is light,[272]
Wanton, and loves not humble modesty,
Which makes me (much contrary to my thoughts)
Flatter his humor for my brother's safety.
But I protest I'll dwell among the dead,
Ere I pollute my sacred nuptial bed.

Exit

259 162 observe the time: go along with him for now
260 163 my boy: i.e. Robert
261 166 right: legitimate
262 168 bare: i.e. bore
263 169 Solicit, Robin: i.e. argue in behalf of my suit
264 172 God send . . . prove fortunate: grant that our mission is successful
265 174 lieger: ambassador
266 176 wag: mischievious boy
267 179 In hopes that my patience will eventually pay off
268 181 toys amended: dalliances corrected
269 187 I am weaponed: I have a weapon
270 188 ere they breech me: a) before they penetrate (or "breach") his defenses; b) put him in breeches, which constituted a rite of passage for young men in the period, since young boys and girls were dressed alike in gowns until boys were "breeched" between two and eight; c) Robert seems to be much older than that, so here "breeching" alludes also to sexual rites of passage
271 191 Terrifying skeletons
272 193 light: frivolous, promiscuous

[Scene v]

Enter GLOUCESTER *in his gown, calling*

GLOUCESTER Porter! What, porter? Where's this drowsy ass?

Enter PORTER

PORTER Who calls? My lord of Gloucester, all alone?
GLOUCESTER Alone, and have your wisdom's company.
Pray,[273] where's the stammering chatterer your son?
He's ever running, but he makes small haste.
I'll bring his lither legs in better frame
And if he serve me thus another time.[274] *Knock within*
Hark, sir, your clients' knock. And't be your pie,[275]
Let him vouchsafe[276] to chatter us some news;
Tell him we dance attendance[277] in our chamber. *Exit* PORTER
This John and Henry are so full of hate
That they will have my head by some device.[278]
Gloucester hath plotted means for an escape,
And if it fadge,[279] why so; if not, then well.
The way to heaven is death. This life's a hell.

Enter PORTER *and* SKINK [*disguised as* REDCAP]

PORTER Why should the watchmen come along with thee?
SKINK There's such[280] a que question for yon s same r rogue Skink. P plague,[281] keep far enough from him,[282] that a an honest f fellow ca cannot w w walk the streets.
PORTER Well, sir, dispatch your business with the earl.
He's angry at your stay,[283] I tell ye that. *Exit*
SKINK [*Aside*] 'Sblood! What a frown this Gloucester casts at me.
I hope he means to lend me no more cuffs,[284]
Such as he paid me at the parliament.
GLOUCESTER What mutter you? What tidings from my sister?
SKINK Co commendations, and s she hath s sent ye this r ring.
GLOUCESTER Hold, there's two angels.[285] Shut the chamber door.
You must about some business for me straight.
Come nearer man.
SKINK [*Aside*] I fear I am too near.
GLOUCESTER Hast thou no tidings for my liberty?
SKINK No, b but ye sh shall he hear f from her[286] p p presently.
GLOUCESTER And p presently, sir, off with your coat.

273 4 Pray: I pray you
274 6–7 I'll bring . . . another time: if he takes this long again, I'll fix his rascally ("lither") legs
275 8 And't be your pie: if it's your magpie, i.e. Redcap
276 9 vouchsafe: deign
277 10 dance attendance: wait impatiently
278 12 device: plot
279 14 fadge: succeed
280 17 There's such: that's
281 17 P plague: by the plague
282 17–18 keep far enough from him: keep me away from him
283 20 stay: your delay
284 22 cuffs: blows
285 26 angels: coins; an English "angel" had an image of the archangel Michael stamped upon it
286 30 her: Lady Fauconbridge

Nay, quick, uncase.[287] I am bold to borrow it.
I'll leave my gown; change[288] is no robbery.
Stutterer, it's so. Ne'er flinch, ye cannot pass.[289]
Cry[290] and, by heaven, I'll cut thy coward's throat.
Quickly cashier yourself;[291] you see me stay.[292]
SKINK N n nay, b b but wh wh what m mean ye?
GLOUCESTER To scape, I hope, sir, with your privilege.[293]
How now, who's this? My fine familiar[294] Skink?
Queen Beldam's minion?[295]
SKINK Zounds, you see 'tis I.
GLOUCESTER Time sorts not now to know these mysteries,
How thou camst by this ring or stol'st this coat.
They are mine now in possession, for which kindness,
If I escape, I'll get thee liberty
Or fire[296] the Fleet about the warden's ears.
Mumbudget;[297] not a word as thou lovest thy life,
SKINK Ay, mum, mum, fair; pray God may chance it.[298]
My lord, but that my state is desperate,
I'd see your eyes out ere I would be cheated.
GLOUCESTER Walk like an earl, villain, some are coming.

Enter JOHN *and* PORTER

JOHN Where is this Gloucester?
GLOUCESTER Y y yonder he walks.[299] Fa fa father, l let me out.
PORTER Why, whither[300] must you now?
GLOUCESTER To Je Jericho,[301] I th think, 'tis such a h h humorous[302] earl.
PORTER Well, sir, wilt please you hasten home again?
GLOUCESTER Ay, I'll be h here in a trice.[303] B but, p pray, have ca care of th this madcap. If he g give us the s s slip, s s some of us a are like to m make a sl sl slippery occupation on't.[304]

[All] this while, JOHN *walks and stalks by* SKINK, *never a word between them*

PORTER Look to your business, sir; let me alone.
GLOUCESTER *[Aside]* Alone? Never trust me if I trouble thee.[305]
JOHN Mad Gloucester mute, all mirth turned to despair?
Why, now you see what 'tis to cross a king,
Deal against princes of the royal blood.
You'll snarl and rail, but now your tongue is bedried.[306]

287 32 uncase: undress
288 33 change: exchange
289 34 pass: get out of this
290 35 Cry: cry out
291 36 cashier yourself: resign your position (to me)
292 36 stay: wait (for you)
293 38 To escape using your freedom to come and go
294 39 familiar: a spirit who assists a witch or devil
295 40 Queen Beldam's minion: a beldam is a hag or witch (here used with reference to Queen Elinor); a minion is her attendant or servant
296 45 fire: burn down
297 46 Mumbudget: keep silent
298 47 I'll keep quiet, and let God answer it
299 52 Gloucester takes on Redcap's stutter as part of his disguise
300 53 whither: where
301 54 to Je Jericho: a colloquial exaggeration for a great distance
302 54 humorous: capricious
303 56 in a trice: momentarily
304 56–7 If he … occupation on't: if Gloucester gets away, we'll all be in trouble (with a possible play on the "slip-noose" with which they'll be hanged)
305 59 Once I've escaped, you won't hear from me again
306 63 bedried: i.e. dried out, silent

Come, caper, hay,[307] set all at six and seven![308]
What, musest thou with thought of hell or heaven?
SKINK Of neither, John, I muse at my disgrace,
That I am thus kept prisoner in this place.
JOHN Oh, sir, a number are here prisoners:
My cousin Morton, whom I came to visit,
But he, good man, is at his morrow mass.[309]
But I, that neither care to say[310] nor sing,
Come to seek that preaching hate and prayer;[311]
And while they mumble up their orisons
We'll play a game at bowls.[312] What sayest thou, Gloucester?
SKINK I care not if I do.
JOHN You do not care?
Let old men care for graves, we for our sports.
Off with your gown, there lies my hat and cloak.
[*Calls offstage*] The bowls there, quickly, ho?
SKINK No. My gown stirs not; it keeps sorrow warm,
And she and I am not to be divorced.

Enter PORTER *with bowls* [*and exit*]

JOHN Yes, there's an axe must part your head and you,
And, with your head, sorrow will leave your heart.
But come, shall I begin? A pound a game.[313]
SKINK More pounds and we thus heavy?[314] Well, begin.
JOHN Rub, rub, rub, rub![315]
SKINK Amen. God send it short enough and me
A safe running with them clothes from thee.[316]
JOHN Play Robin.[317] Run, run, run!
SKINK Far enough and well. Fly one foot more,
Would I were half so far without the door.[318]

Enter PORTER

JOHN Now, porter, what's the news?
PORTER Your cousin Morton humbly craves,
Leaving your game, you would come visit him. [*Exit* PORTER]
JOHN Bowl, Gloucester. I'll come presently.
So near, mad Robin? Then have after you![319]
SKINK Would I were gone, make after as you may.

307 64 Come, caper, hay: come, dance!
308 64 at six and seven: in confusion
309 70 morrow mass: morning mass
310 71 say: say my prayers
311 72 The meaning of this line is obscure. The "neither" of line 71 may also govern this line as well, meaning John does not come to prison seeking preaching and prayers
312 74 bowls: early English bowls resembled the Italian game of bocce, where players throw a small ball called the "jack" (see line 97) and then target it with larger balls
313 83 pound a game: a wager of one pound per game
314 84 More pounds . . . thus heavy: i.e. you propose to add more "pounds" to my weighty sorrow
315 85 rub: a cry from a bowler to his ball hoping it will slow down
316 86–7 send it . . . from thee: Skink hopes God will curtail the course of John's ball and bless him with a safe escape in John's clothes
317 88 Robin: a familiarization of Gloucester's first name, Robert
318 89–90 Fly one . . . the door: John's ball has stopped a foot shy of the door; Skink wishes he were at least a half-a-foot outside the door
319 95 Skink bowls after John's "Bowl, Gloucester" (line 94), and his ball rolls so close to John's that John's next roll tries to perfectly follow "after" Skink's, possibly to dislodge Skink's ball

JOHN Well, sir, 'tis yours. One all. Throw but the jack
While I go talk with Morton.[320] I'll not stay.[321]
Keep cloak and hat in pawn;[322] I'll hold out play. [*Exit* JOHN]
SKINK I would be sorry, John, but you should stay
Until my bias[323] run another way.
Now pass, and hey pass,[324] Skink unto your tricks.
'Tis but a chance at hazard.[325] There lies Gloucester,[326]
And here stands Skink. Now, John, play thou thy part,
And, if I scape, I'll love thee with my heart.
So, porter, let me forth!

Enter PORTER

PORTER God bless your grace. Ye spoke with the Lord Morton?
SKINK I have, and must about[327] his business to the court.
It grieves me to break my sport with Gloucester.
The melancholy earl is comfortless.
PORTER I would my grace would comfort him from hence.
The Fleet is weary of his company. REDCAP *knocks*
SKINK Drink that. Some[328] knocks. I prithee, let me out.
His head shall off ere long, never make doubt. *Exeunt*

Enter JOHN *at the other door*

JOHN Now, madcap, thou win'st all—where art thou, Robin?
Uncased?[329] Nay then, he means to play in earnest.
But where's my cloak, my rapier, and my hat?
I hold my birthright to a beggar's scrip:[330]
The bastard is escapèd in my clothes.
'Tis well he left me his to walk the streets.
I'll fire the city, but I'll find him out.
Perchance he hides himself to try my spleen.[331]
I'll to his chamber. Gloucester? Hallo Gloucester? *Exit*

Enter PORTER *and* REDCAP [*in* SKINK's *clothing*]

PORTER I wonder how thou camst so strangely changed?
'Tis not an hour since thou wents from hence.
REDCAP By my Ch Ch Christendom, I ha have not b b been h here this three nights. A p p plague of him that made me such a ch chanting,[332] and s sent me such a ja ja jaunt. Blood! I was st stayed[333] for Skink, that ill fa fa faced rogue.

320 97–8 Throw but . . . with Morton: the scoring is obscure, but John and Skink are tied after the first round. John invites Skink to toss the jack and open the second frame while he exits to speak with Morton
321 98 I'll not stay: I won't be long
322 99 in pawn: John leaves his hat and cloak as collateral against the money he owes Skink (though the game has ended in a tie)
323 101 bias: the curve of a bowled ball
324 102 pass, and hey pass: "hey-pass and re-pass" was a magician's exclamation to make an object move
325 103 'Tis but . . . at hazard: it's just a risky venture
326 103 There lies Gloucester: Skink disrobes, leaving Gloucester's gown on the floor
327 108 must about: must perform, carry out
328 113 some: someone
329 116 uncased: undressed
330 118 I'd wager my birthright against a beggar's wallet
331 122 to try my spleen: as a joke (the spleen was regarded as the seat of laughter)
332 127 chanting: enchantment, i.e. enchanted me to go
333 128 stayed: mistaken

PORTER I pray God there be no practice in this change.
Now I remember! These are Skink's clothes,
That he wore last day at the parliament! *Knock*

Enter at another door JOHN *in* GLOUCESTER*'s gown*

JOHN Porter? You, porter?
PORTER Do you not hear them knock? You must stay, sir.
JOHN Blood! I could eat these rogues.
REDCAP Wh wh what, raw? 'Tis a very harsh mo morsel, ne next your he heart.[334]
JOHN A plague upon your jaunts. What, porter, slave?
REDCAP I have been at G Gravesend, sir.
JOHN What's that to me?
REDCAP And at Ca Ca Canterbury.
JOHN And at the gallows.[335] Zounds, this frets my soul!
REDCAP But I c could not f find your s s sister, the La Lady Fau Fauconbridge.
JOHN You stammering slave, hence. Chat among your daws![336]
Come ye to mad me?[337] While the rogue your father—

Enter PORTER

REDCAP My f fa father.
JOHN Porter? You damnèd slave!
PORTER Is't midsummer?[338] Do you begin to rave?
JOHN Hark, how the traitor flouts me to my teeth.
I would entreat your knaveship let me forth,
For fear I dash your brains out with the keys.
What is become of Gloucester and my garments?
PORTER Alas, in your apparel Gloucester's gone.
I let him out even now. I am undone.[339]
JOHN It was your practice[340] and, to keep me back,
You sent Jack Daw your son with "ca ca ca"
To tell a sleeveless[341] tale. Lay hold on him!
To Newgate[342] with him and you, tut atut,
Run, Redcap and trudge about
Or bid your father's portership farewell.[343] *Exeunt with* PORTER

REDCAP He here's a go good je je jest, by the l lord, to mo mock an ape withal: my fa fa father has brought his ho ho hogs to a fa fa fair m m market.[344] Po po porter, quoth you? P po porter that will for me, and I po po porter it, let them po po post me to heaven in this qua quarter.[345] But I must s s seek this Gl Gl Gloucester and Sk Sk Skink, that co coney-catching[346] ra ra rascal, a pa pa plague co co confound him. Re Re Redcap must ru run he cannot tell wi whither.

Exit

334 135 harsh mo … he heart: an unsavory meal to have in your stomach
335 140 And at the gallows: i.e. go hang yourself
336 142 daws: small birds; simpletons
337 143 mad me: drive me mad
338 145 midsummer: conventionally thought of as a time of madness
339 151 undone: ruined
340 152 practice: deliberate strategy
341 154 sleeveless: trifling, feeble
342 155 Newgate: Newgate Prison, built by Henry II in 1188
343 156–7 Run Redcap … portership farewell: go and find Gloucester or your father is out of his job
344 159 brought his … m market: ironic proverb for things that don't go according to plan
345 161 quarter: quarter-session, local courts held four times a year
346 161 coney-catching: swindling

[Scene vi]

Sound trumpets. Enter HENRY *the younger, on one hand of him* QUEEN ELINOR, *on the other* LEICESTER

HENRY Mother and Leicester, add not oil to fire.
Wrath's kindled with a word and cannot hear
The numberless persuasions you insert.[347]
QUEEN Oh, but my son, thy father favors him.
Richard, that vile, abortive, changeling[348] brat,
And Fauconbridge, are fallen at Henry's feet.
They woo for him.[349] But entreat, my son,
Gloucester may die for this that he hath done.
LEICESTER If Gloucester live, thou wilt be overthrown.
QUEEN If Gloucester live, thy mother dies in moan.
LEICESTER If Gloucester live, Leicester will fly the realm.
QUEEN If Gloucester live, thy kingdom's but a dream.
HENRY Have I not sworn, by that eternal arm
That puts just vengeance'[350] sword in monarch's hands,
Gloucester shall die for his presumption?
What needs more conjuration,[351] gracious Mother?
And, honorable Leicester, mark my words:
I have a beadroll of some threescore[352] lords,
Of Gloucester's faction—
QUEEN Nay, of Henry's faction,
Of thy false father's faction. Speak the truth.
He is the head of factions. Were he down,[353]
Peace, plenty, glory will impale[354] thy crown.
LEICESTER Ay, there's the butt,[355] whose hart-white[356] if we hit
The game is ours.[357] Well, we may rage and rove[358]
At Gloucester, Lancaster, Chester, Fauconbridge,
But he is the upshot.
QUEEN Yet begin with Gloucester.
HENRY The destinies[359] run to the book of fates
And read in never-changing characters[360]
Robert of Gloucester's end. He dies today,
So fate, so heaven, so doth King Henry say.
QUEEN Imperially resolved. *Trumpets far off*
LEICESTER The old king comes.
QUEEN Then comes luxurious[361] lust,
The King of Concubines, the king that scorns
The undefilèd, chaste, and nuptial bed,

347 2–3 Wrath's kindled . . . you insert: anger is deaf to entreaties
348 5 changeling: a child swapped for another at birth; one who changes sides, a turncoat
349 7 him: i.e. Gloucester
350 14 vengeance': i.e. vengeance's
351 16 conjuration: persuasion
352 18 threescore: sixty
353 21 down: defeated
354 22 impale: enclose, encircle
355 23 butt: target
356 23 hart-white: bullseye
357 23–4 if we . . . is ours: if we kill old King Henry, victory is ours
358 24 rove: shoot at; possibly a misprint for "rave"
359 27 destinies: in Roman and Greek mythology, three goddesses who determine fate
360 28 characters: letters
361 32 luxurious: lecherous

The king that hath his queen imprisonèd.
For my sake scorn him, son, call him not father,
Give him the style[362] of a competitor.[363]
HENRY Pride seize upon my heart, wrath fill mine eyes,
Sit lawful majesty upon my front,[364]
Duty fly from me, pity be exiled,
Senses forget that I am Henry's child.
QUEEN I kiss thee, and I bless thee, for this thought.

Enter KING, LANCASTER, RICHARD, FAUCONBRIDGE

KING Oh Lancaster, bid Henry yield some reason
Why he desires so much the death of Gloucester.
HENRY I hear thee Henry, and I thus reply:
I do desire the death of bastard Gloucester
For that he spends the treasure of the crown.
I do desire the death of bastard Gloucester
For that he doth desire to pull me down.
Or were this false (I purpose to be plain),
He loves thee and, for that, I him disdain.
KING Therein thou showest a hate-corrupted mind,
To him the more unjust, to me unkind.
QUEEN He loves you as his father loved his mother.[365]
KING Fie, fie upon thee hateful Elinor!
I thought thou hadst been long since scarlet-dyed.[366]
HENRY She is and therefore cannot change her color.[367]
RICHARD You are too strict. Earl Gloucester's fault
Merits not death.
FAUCONBRIDGE By th'rood, the prince says true.
Here is a statute from the Confessor.[368]
HENRY The Confessor was but a simple fool.
Away with books![369] My word shall be a law;
England her breath shall from this bosom draw.
Gloucester shall die.
LEICESTER Let Gloucester die the death.
LANCASTER Leicester, he shall not.
He shall have law, despite of him and thee.
HENRY What law? Will you be traitors? What's the law?
RICHARD His right hand's loss, and that is such a loss
As England may lament, all Christians weep.
That hand hath been advanced against the Moors,
Driven out the Saracens from Gads and Sicily,[370]
Fought fifteen battles under Christ's red cross.[371]
And is it not (think you) a grievous loss

362 37 style: name, title
363 37 competitor: rival, enemy
364 39 front: forehead
365 54 Henry loves you as much as you used to love me
366 56 scarlet-dyed: dyed red with shame
367 57 change her color: be untrue
368 60 from the Confessor: in existence since the time of Edward the Confessor (reigned 1042–66)
369 62 books: written law
370 70–71 advanced against . . . and Sicily: fought Muslims during crusades through Africa, Spain ("Gads"/Cadiz), and the Mediterranean
371 72 Christ's red cross: a flag with a red cross on a white background, the emblem of the crusades

That, for a slave[372] (and for no other harm),
It should be sundered from his princely arm?
FAUCONBRIDGE More for example, noble Lancaster,
But 'tis great pity, too, too great a pity.
HENRY I'll have his hand and head.
RICHARD Thou shalt have mine then.
QUEEN Well said, stubborn Dick.
Jack[373] would not serve me so, were the boy here.
RICHARD Both John and I have served your will too long.
Mother, repent your cruelty and wrong.
Gloucester, you know, is full of mirth and glee
And never else did your grace injury.
QUEEN Gloucester shall die.
HENRY Fetch him here; I'll see him dead.
RICHARD He that stirs for him shall lay down his head.
FAUCONBRIDGE Oh, quiet, good my lords! Patience, I pray,
I think he comes unsent for, by my fay.[374]

Enter JOHN *in* GLOUCESTER*'s gown*

RICHARD What meanest thou, Gloucester?
HENRY Who brought Gloucester hither?
JOHN Let Gloucester hang and them that [. . .][375]
There lies his case,[376] a mischief on his carcass.
QUEEN My dear son Jack?
JOHN Your dear son Jack-an-apes,[377]
Your monkey, your baboon, your ass, your gull.[378]
LEICESTER What ails Earl John?
JOHN Hence, further from my sight!
My fiery thoughts and wrath have work in hand.
I'll curse ye blacker than the Avernian lake[379]
If you stand wondering at my sorrow thus.
I am with child, big, hugely swollen with rage.
Who'll play the midwife and my throbs assuage?
KING I will, my son.
HENRY I will, high-hearted[380] brother.
JOHN You will, and you? Tut tut, all you are nothing.
'Twill out, 'twill out, myself myself can ease.
You chafe, you swell, ye are commanding king,
My father is your foot stool when he please.
Your word's a law; these lords dare never speak.
Gloucester must die; your enemies must fall.
HENRY What means our brother?
JOHN He means that thou art mad,
She frantic, Leicester foolish, I the babe.

372 74 for a slave: for striking Skink
373 80 Jack: i.e. Prince John
374 88 fay: faith
375 90 [. . .]: there is a lacuna in the 1600 text; the words "follow him" were possibly intended
376 91 There lies his case: Prince John takes off Gloucester's gown
377 92 Jack-an-apes: an apish man, i.e. one who's been made a monkey of
378 93 gull: dupe
379 96 Avernian lake: Lake Avernus in Italy, famed for poisonous vapors; proverbially the entrance to Hades
380 100 high-hearted: angry

These[381] grind us, bite us, vex us, charge, and discharge.
Gloucester, oh, Gloucester!
QUEEN Where is Gloucester, son?
HENRY Where is Gloucester, brother?
KING I hope he be escaped.
JOHN Oh, I could tear my hair and, falling thus upon the
Solid earth, dig into Gloucester's grave, so[382] he were dead
And gone into the depth of under worlds,
Or get sedition's hundred thousand hands,
And, like Briareus,[383] battle with the stars,
To pull him down from heaven if he were there.
FAUCONBRIDGE Look to Earl John; the gentleman is mad.
JOHN Oh, who would not be mad at this disgrace?
Gloucester the fox is fled; there lies his case.
He cozened[384] me of mine; the porter helped him.
HENRY The porter shall be hanged. Let's part[385] and seek him;
Gloucester shall die, all Europe shall not save him.
JOHN He is wise, too wise for us, yet I'll go with you
To get more fools into my company.
QUEEN This is your father's plot; revenge it, son.
HENRY Father, by heaven, if this were your advice,[386]
Your head or heart shall pay the bitter price.
Come mother, brother, Leicester. Let's away.
JOHN Ay, I'll be one, in hope to meet the bastard,
And then no more: myself will be his headsman.[387] *Exeunt* [QUEEN, HENRY, JOHN]
KING Richard and Fauconbridge, follow the search.
You may prevent mischance by meeting Gloucester.
If ye find Skink, see that you apprehend him.
I hear there is a wizard[388] at Blackheath;
Let some enquire of him where Skink remains.[389]
Although I trust not to those fallacies,[390]
Yet now and then such men prove soothsayers.
Will you be gone?
FAUCONBRIDGE With all my heart, with all my heart, my lord.
Come, princely Richard, we are ever yoked.[391]
Pray God there be no mystery[392] in this.
RICHARD Be not suspicious where there is no cause,
FAUCONBRIDGE Nay, nothing, nothing, I am but in jest. *Exeunt* [RICHARD, FAULCONBRIDGE]
KING Call in a pursuivant.[393]
LANCASTER Here's one, my liege. [*Enter Pursuivant*]
KING There is a porter likely to be hanged
For letting Gloucester scape; sirrah, attend,

381 109 These: possibly a misprint for "thou"; alternatively, "these" may refer to the actions John lists at 103–6
382 113 so: if
383 115–16 hundred thousand . . . like Briareus: in Greek mythology, Briareus was one of three one-hundred-armed, fifty-headed sons of Uranus
384 121 cozened: cheated
385 122 part: depart, separate
386 127 if this were your advice: i.e. if you advised Gloucester to escape
387 131 headsman: executioner
388 135 wizard: the dead Hermit whom Skink imitated in Scene i
389 136 remains: resides
390 137 fallacies: predictions, false statements
391 141 ever yoked: always joined
392 142 mystery: hidden meaning; Fauconbridge worries that Richard continues to find ways to gain access to his wife
393 145 pursuivant: warrant officer

You shall have a reprieve to bring him us.[394]
These boys are too, too stubborn, Lancaster,
But 'tis their mother's fault. If thus she move me,
I'll have her head though all the world reprove me.

Exeunt

[Scene vii]

Enter ROBIN HOOD *and* LADY FAUCONBRIDGE

LADY FAUCONBRIDGE Do not deny me, gentle Huntington.
ROBERT My lord will miss me.
LADY FAUCONBRIDGE Tut, let me excuse thee.
ROBERT Turn woman?[395] Oh, it is intolerable!
Except you promise me to play the page.[396]
Do that. Try one night, and you'll laugh forever,
To hear the orisons that lovers use—
Their ceremonious sighs, their idle oaths—
To hear how you are praised and prayed unto,
For you are Richard's saint. They talk of Mary
The blessèd virgin, but upon his beads[397]
He only prays to Marian Fauconbridge.
LADY FAUCONBRIDGE The more his error, but will you agree
To be the Lady Fauconbridge one day?
ROBERT When is't?
LADY FAUCONBRIDGE On Monday.
ROBERT Wherefore is't?[398]
LADY FAUCONBRIDGE Nay, then you do me wrong with inquisition.
And yet I care not greatly if I tell thee.
Thou see'st my husband full of jealousy,
Prince Richard in his suit importunate,[399]
My brother Gloucester threatened by young Henry.
To clear these doubts[400] I will, in some disguise,
Go to Blackheath unto the holy hermit,
Whose wisdom in foretelling things to come
Will let me see the issue[401] of my cares.
If destinies ordain me happiness,
I'll chase these mists of sorrow from my heart
With the bright sun of mirth. If fate agree
It[402] and my friends must suffer misery,
Yet I'll be merry, too, till mischief come.
Only I long to know the worst of ill.
ROBERT I'll once put on a scarlet countenance.[403]
LADY FAUCONBRIDGE Be wary lest ye be discovered, Robin.

394 148 You shall bring him to us for a reprieve
395 3 Turn woman: Lady Fauconbridge has asked Robin to dress as her while she is absent
396 3–4 I won't do it unless you promise to play my attendant
397 10 beads: rosary
398 16 Wherefore: for what reason
399 20 importunate: unrelenting
400 22 clear these doubts: allay my confusion
401 25 issue: outcome
402 29 It: i.e. my heart
403 32 Robin agrees to play a blushing woman

ROBERT Best paint me,[404] then; be sure I shall not blush.

Enter BLOCK *bleeding.* GLOUCESTER [*disguised as* REDCAP *with him*]

BLOCK Beat an officer, Redcap? I'll have ye talked withal. Beat Sir Richard's porter? Help Madam, help!
GLOUCESTER Peace, you damned rogue!
LADY FAUCONBRIDGE Brother,[405] I pray you forbear.
GLOUCESTER Zwounds! A hundred at my heels, almost,
And yet the villain stands on compliment.[406]
BLOCK A bots on you![407] Is't you?
GLOUCESTER Will you to the door you fool? And bar the gate!
Hold, there's an angel for your broken pate.[408]
If any knock, let them not in in haste.
BLOCK Well, I'll do as I see cause. Blood, thou art dear to me, but here's a sovereign plaster[409] for the sore. Gold healeth wounds, gold easeth hearts. What can a man have more? *Exit*
LADY FAUCONBRIDGE Dear brother, tell us how you made escape?
GLOUCESTER You see I am here, but if you would know how—
I cannot scape and tell the manner too.
By this, I know your house is compassèd[410]
With hell-hound search.[411]
LADY FAUCONBRIDGE Brother, I'll furnish you with beard, and hair,
And garments like my husband. How like you that? *Exit* LADY
GLOUCESTER Well, when I have them, quickly then dispatch.
'Sblood! Turn gray beard and hair?
Robin, conceal;[412] this dieteth[413] my mind.
Mirth is the object of my humorous spleen:
Thou high commanding fury, further devise—[414]
Jests are conceited;[415] I long to see their birth.

[*Enter* LADY FAUCONBRIDGE]

What, come ye sister? Robin, a thief's hand,[416]
But, prithee, where hadst thou this beard and hair?
LADY FAUCONBRIDGE Prince Richard wore them hither in a masque.[417]
GLOUCESTER Say'st thou me so? Faith love the princely youth.
Tut, you must taste stol'n pleasure now and then.[418]
ROBERT But if she steal and jealous eyes espy,
She will be sure condemned of burglary.[419]

404 34 paint me: put makeup on me
405 38 Brother: Lady Fauconbridge sees through Gloucester's disguise, or he reveals himself to her
406 39–40 A hundred . . . on compliment: I'm chased by nearly a hundred pursuers and yet Block challenged me at the door
407 41 bots on you: common expression of impatience; "bots" is a parasite that affects horses
408 43 pate: head
409 45 sovereign plaster: excellent bandage; a "sovereign" is also a gold coin, which Gloucester gives to Block
410 50 compassèd: surrounded
411 51 hell-hound search: relentless pursuit
412 56 conceal: keep this secret
413 56 dieteth: feeds
414 57–8 Mirth is . . . further devise: I'm usually governed by mirth, but now I need fury to devise a plan
415 59 conceited: conceived
416 60 thief's hand: provide stealthy aid
417 62 masque: courtly entertainment, often including disguises
418 64 Gloucester accuses his sister of consorting with Prince Richard
419 65–6 But if . . . of burglary: i.e. if her husband catches her with Richard, she'll be arraigned for that "stolen pleasure"

GLOUCESTER Ha, crake?[420] Can your low stumps venter so deep
Into affection's stream?[421] Go to, you wanton.[422]
What want we now? My nightcap. Oh, 'tis here.
So now, no Gloucester, but old Fauconbridge.
Hark, the search[423] knocks; I'll let them in myself.
Welcome, good fellow; ha, what is't you lack?

Enter REDCAP *with another*

REDCAP Ma master co constable, se se search you th that way a and you ho honest man th that way. I'll ru run th this way m my own se self. *They disperse themselves*
GLOUCESTER What search you for? What is it you would have?

Enter BLOCK

BLOCK Madam, what shall I do to these brown-bill fellows?[424] Some run into the wine cellar, some here, some there.
GLOUCESTER Let them alone; let them search their fills.
BLOCK I'll look to their fingers for all that.[425]
GLOUCESTER Do so, good Block; be careful, honest Block.
BLOCK Sir stammerer and your wa watch, y'are pa past,[426] i'faith. *Exit*
GLOUCESTER Will you not speak, knaves, tell me who you seek?
REDCAP Ma marry, sir, we s seek a va va vagabond, a fu fugitive, my la lady's own b brother. But and he were the Po Po Pope's own b brother, I would s search f f for him, for I have a p poor father r ready to be ha ha hanged f f for him.
GLOUCESTER Oh, tis for Gloucester! Marry, search a God's name.
Seek, peace.[427] Will he break prison too?
It's pity he should live; nay, I defy him.
Come, look about, search every little corner.
Myself will lead the way. Pray you, come,
Seek, seek, and spare not though it be labor lost.
He comes not under my roof, hear ye wife?
He comes not hither; take it for a warning.
REDCAP You sp sp speak like an honest ge ge gentleman. Re re rest you me me merry. Co co come my f f friends, I be believe h h he r ran by the g g garden w wall toward the wa water side. *Exeunt running*
GLOUCESTER This fellow is of the humor I would choose my wife: few words and many paces, a word and away, and so must I. Sister, adieu. Pray you for me, I'll do the like for you.
Robin, farewell, commend me to the prince.[428]
LADY FAUCONBRIDGE Can ye not stay here safe?
GLOUCESTER No, I'll not trust the changing humors of old Fauconbridge.
Adieu, young earl; sister, let's kiss and part.
Tush, ne'er mourn, I have a merry heart. *Exit*
LADY FAUCONBRIDGE Farewell, all comfort.
ROBERT What, weeping, lady?

420 67 crake: crow or raven
421 67–8 Can your . . . affection's stream: i.e. Can your youth ("low stumps," i.e. short legs) understand adult affairs so well?
422 68 wanton: naughty boy
423 71 search: searchers
424 76 brown-bill fellows: watchmen carrying halberds painted brown
425 79 I'll make sure they don't steal anything
426 81 y'are pa past: you're done here
427 87 peace: peace officers
428 98 the prince: Prince Richard

Then I perceive you have forgot Blackheath.[429]
LADY FAUCONBRIDGE No, there I'll learn both of his[430] life and death.
ROBERT Till Monday, madam, I must take my leave.
LADY FAUCONBRIDGE You will not miss then?
ROBERT Nay, if Robin fail ye, let him have never favor of fair lady.
LADY FAUCONBRIDGE Meanwhile I'll spend my time in prayers and tears,
That Gloucester may escape these threatened fears.

Exeunt [LADY FAUCONBRIDGE *and* ROBERT]

[Scene viii]

Enter SKINK *like* PRINCE JOHN

SKINK Thus jets[431] my noble Skink along the streets,
To whom each bonnet vails and all knees bend,[432]
And yet my noble humor is too light
By the six shillings.[433] Here are two cracked groats[434]
To helter skelter[435] at some vaulting house.[436]
But who comes yonder? Ha, old Fauconbridge?
Hath a brave[437] chain. Were John and he good friends,
That chain were mine and should unto Blackheath.
I'll venture. It's but trial; luck may fall.[438]
Good morrow, good Sir Richard Fauconbridge.

Enter FAUCONBRIDGE

FAUCONBRIDGE Good morrow, my sweet prince, hearty good morrow!
This greeting well becomes us,[439] marry, does it.
Betterwise then strife and jangling.[440]
Now can I love ye, will ye to the sheriff's?
Your brother Richard hath been there this hour.
SKINK Yes, I am plodding forward as you do.
What cost your chain? It's passing[441] strongly wrought;
I would my goldsmith had a pattern of it.[442]
FAUCONBRIDGE 'Tis at your grace's service; show it him.
SKINK Then dare ye trust me?
FAUCONBRIDGE Who, the princely John?
My sovereign's son? Why what a question's that?
I'll leave you; ye may know I dare trust you.
SKINK I'll bring't ye to the sheriff's; excuse my absence.
FAUCONBRIDGE I will, my noble lord; adieu, sweet prince. *Exit*

429 104 forgot Blackheath: forgot your plan to visit the hermit at Blackheath
430 105 his: Gloucester's
431 1 jets: struts
432 2 Everyone takes off their hat and bends their knee to me (i.e. they think I'm Prince John)
433 3–4 And yet . . . six shillings: despite my "nobility," I'm still broke
434 4 groats: coin worth four pence
435 5 helter skelter: waste
436 5 vaulting-house: brothel
437 7 brave: fancy, valuable
438 9 I'll try to get that chain; it's worth a shot, since luck may befall me
439 12 becomes us: i.e. speaks well of us
440 13 jangling: arguing
441 17 passing: surpassingly
442 18 pattern of it: drawing of it (i.e. so he could make one like it)

SKINK Why, so, this breakfast was well fed upon.[443]
When Skink's devices on Blackheath do fail,
This, and such cheats, would set me under sail.[444]
I'll to the water side. Would it were later,
For still I am afraid to meet Prince John.

Enter GLOUCESTER *like* FAUCONBRIDGE

But what a mischief meant Fauconbridge
To come again so soon? That way he went,
And now comes peeking.[445] Upon my life,
The buzzard hath me in suspicion.
But whatsoever chance, I'll filch a share.[446]
GLOUCESTER Yonder's Prince John. I hope he cannot know me.
There's naught but "Gloucester, Gloucester" in their mouths.
I am half strangled with the garlic breath
Of rascals that exclaim, as I pass by,
"Gloucester is fled, once taken he must die."
But I'll to John. How does my gracious lord?
What tattles rumor[447] now? What news of Gloucester?
SKINK What news could I hear since you left me last?
Were you not here even now, lent me your chain?
I think you dote.
GLOUCESTER Sweet prince, age, age forgets.
[*Aside*] My brother's chain? A pretty accident.[448]
I'll have't and be but in the spite of[449] John.
SKINK [*Aside*] There's more, and more.[450] I'll geld[451] it ere I go. *He breaks the chain*
This same[452] shall keep me in some tavern merry,
Till night's black hand curtain this too clear sky.
GLOUCESTER My sweet prince, I have some cause to use my chain.
Another time (whene'er your lordship please)
'Tis at your service, oh, marry God, it is.
SKINK Here, palsy,[453] take your chain; stoop and be hanged.
[*Aside*] Yet the fish nibbled when she might not swallow;[454]
Gout,[455] I have curtailed what I could not borrow. *Exit*
GLOUCESTER He's gone away in frets.[456] Would he might meet
My brother Fauconbridge in this mad mood,
There would be rare ado. Why, this fits me! [457]
My brain flows with fresh wit and policy.
But, Gloucester, look about: who have we yonder?
Another John, Prince Richard, and the sheriff?

443 25 breakfast was well fed upon: i.e. that went better than anticipated
444 27 set me under sail: put wind in my sails (i.e. sustain me financially)
445 32 peeking: looking for me again
446 34 filch a share: get a bit of the chain's worth
447 41 What tattles rumor: what's the gossip
448 45 pretty accident: a happy coincidence
449 46 in the spite of: just to spite
450 47 more, and more: Skink is breaking the chain into links
451 47 geld: cut
452 48 This same: this piece of chain
453 53 palsy: palsied old man
454 54 I couldn't swallow (steal) the whole thing, so I only took a bite (a few links)
455 55 Gout: as with "palsy" (line 53), Skink addresses "Fauconbridge" with the name of a disease that afflicts the aged
456 56 in frets: angry
457 58 fits me: befits me, suits me

Upon my life, the slave that had the chain
Was Skink, escaped the Fleet by some mad sleight.[458]
Well, farewell he, better and better still,
These seek for me, yet I will have my will.
JOHN Sheriff, in any case, be diligent.
Who's yonder, Fauconbridge?
GLOUCESTER How now sweet chuck? How fares my lovely prince?
JOHN What carest thou? Or[459] well or ill, we crave no help of thee.
GLOUCESTER God's mother, do you scorn me?
JOHN Gout, what then?
RICHARD Fie, leave these idle brawls, I prithee John.
Let's follow that we are enjoined unto.[460]
GLOUCESTER Ay, marry, prince, if now you slip the time,[461]
Gloucester will slip away. Tut, though he[462] hate me,
I have done service; I have found him out.
RICHARD A shame confound thee for thy treachery!
Inconstant dotard,[463] timorous[464] old ass,
That shakes with cowardice, not with years.
GLOUCESTER Go, I have found him; I have winded him.[465]
JOHN Oh, let me hug thee gentle Fauconbridge!
Forgive my oft ill-using of thine age.
I'll call thee "father"; I'll be penitent.
Bring me where Gloucester is; I'll be thy slave.
All that is mine, thou in reward shalt have.
GLOUCESTER Soft, not too hasty, I would not be seen in't.
Marry a God, my wife would chide me dead
If Gloucester by my means should lose his head.
Princely Richard, at this corner make your stand.
[*Aside*] And, for[466] I know you love my sister well,
Know I am Gloucester and not Fauconbridge.
RICHARD [*Aside*] Heaven prosper thee, sweet prince, in thy escape!
GLOUCESTER Sheriff, make this your quarter;[467] make good guard.
John, stay you here; this way he means to turn.
By Thomas,[468] I lack a sword, body a me.
JOHN What wouldst thou with a sword, old Fauconbridge?
GLOUCESTER Oh, sir, to make show in his defense,
For I have left him yonder at a house,
A friend's of mine, an honest citizen.
JOHN We'll fetch him thence.
GLOUCESTER Nay, then you injure me.[469]
Stay till he come; he's in a russet[470] cloak
And must attend me like a servingman.
JOHN Hold, there's my sword, and with my sword my heart.

458 63 sleight: device
459 69 Or: whether
460 72 Let's carry out that which we were urged to do
461 73 slip the time: waste time
462 74 he: i.e. Prince John
463 77 dotard: imbecile
464 77 timorous: timid, easily frightened
465 79 winded him: put out of breath, brought his flight to halt
466 89 for: because
467 92 quarter: area, space
468 94 By Thomas: by St. Thomas
469 99 injure me: i.e. you would insult me by arresting Gloucester at my friend's house
470 100 russet: coarse, reddish-brown cloth

Bring him, for God's sake, and for thy desert
My brother king and mother queen shall love thee.
GLOUCESTER Mark me,[471] good prince, yonder away we come:[472]
I go afore, and Gloucester follows me.
Let not the sheriff nor Richard meddle with us.
Begin you first. Seize Gloucester and arrest him.
I'll draw and lay about me,[473] here and here;
Be heedful that your watchmen hurt me not.
JOHN I'll hang him that doth hurt thee; prithee, away.
I love thee, but thou kill'st me with delay.
GLOUCESTER Well, keep close watch; I'll bring him presently.
JOHN Away then, quickly!
GLOUCESTER Gloucester! Close,[474] master sheriff, Prince Richard.
RICHARD [*Aside*] Gloucester, adieu.
GLOUCESTER I trust you.
RICHARD By my knighthood, I'll prove true. *Exit* GLOUCESTER
JOHN Revenge, I'll build a temple to your name,
And the first offering shall be Gloucester's head.
Thy altars shall be sprinkled with the blood,
Whose wanton current his mad humor fed.
He was a rhymer and a riddler,[475]
A scoffer at my mother, praised my father.
I'll fit him[476] now for all, escape and all.
RICHARD Take heed spite burst not in his proper gall.[477]

Enter FAUCONBRIDGE *and* BLOCK

JOHN How now, what way took Fauconbridge, I wonder?[478]
That is not Gloucester, sure, that attends on him.
FAUCONBRIDGE He[479] came not at the sheriff's by the morrow mass.
I sought the goldsmiths' row[480] and found him not.
Sirrah, y'are sure he sent not home my chain?
BLOCK Who should send your chain sir?
FAUCONBRIDGE The prince, Prince John. I lent it him today.
JOHN What's this they talk?
BLOCK By my truth, sir, and[481] ye lent it him, I think you may go look it.[482] For one of the drawers of the Salutation[483] told me, even now, that he had took up a chamber there till evening, and then he will away to Kent.
FAUCONBRIDGE Body of me, he means to spend my chain!
Come Block, I'll to him.
JOHN Hear you, Fauconbridge?
FAUCONBRIDGE [*To* BLOCK] Why, what a knave art thou? Yonder's Prince John.
BLOCK Then the drawer's a knave; he told me Prince John was at the Salutation.

471 105 Mark me: listen to me
472 105 yonder away we come: from over there we will come
473 109 lay about me: slash with my sword
474 115 Close: keep out of sight
475 122 rhymer and a riddler: a jokester
476 124 fit him: befit him, pay him back
477 125 Be careful that your anger does not explode on account of its own hate
478 126 Fauconbridge has entered at a different spot from where Gloucester exited, confusing John
479 128 He: Prince John
480 129 goldsmith's row: street where goldsmiths' shops are located
481 134 and: if
482 134 look it: look for it
483 135 drawers of the Salutation: barmen at the inn called the Salutation

JOHN Where's Gloucester, Fauconbridge?
FAUCONBRIDGE Sweet prince, I know not.
JOHN Come, jest not with me; tell me where he is.
FAUCONBRIDGE I never saw him since the parliament.
JOHN Impudent liar, didst thou not, even now,
Say thou wouldst fetch him? Hadst thou not my sword?
FAUCONBRIDGE Wert thou a king, I will not bear the lie.[484]
Thy sword? No, boy, thou see'st this sword is mine.
BLOCK My master a liar? Zounds! Wert thou a potentate—
FAUCONBRIDGE I scorn to wear thy arms, untutored child.
I fetch thee Gloucester? Shameless! Did I see thee
Since, as I went this morning to the sheriff's,
Thou borrowedst my gold chain?
JOHN Thy chain?
FAUCONBRIDGE I hope thou wilt not cheat me, princocks[485] John.
JOHN I'll cheat thee of thy life if thou charge me
With any chain.
FAUCONBRIDGE Come,[486] let him come, I pray.
I'll whip ye, boy; I'll teach you to outface.[487]
BLOCK Come, come, come! But one at once, ye dastards,[488] come!
RICHARD Keep the king's peace. I see you are both deceived.
He that was last here was not Fauconbridge.
FAUCONBRIDGE They slander me! Who says that I was here?
RICHARD We do believe ye, sir; nor do you[489] think
My brother John deceived you of a chain.
FAUCONBRIDGE He did! I did deliver it with this hand.
JOHN I'll die upon the slanderer.
FAUCONBRIDGE Let the boy come.
BLOCK Ay, let him come, let him come!
RICHARD [*To* BLOCK] Fellow, thou spake'st, even now, as if Prince John
Had been at some old tavern in the town.
BLOCK Ay, sir, I came up now but from the Salutation,
And a drawer that doth not use to lie told me
Prince John hath been there all this afternoon.
JOHN The devil in my likeness then is there.
FAUCONBRIDGE The devil in thy likeness, or thy self,
Had my gold chain.
JOHN Thou art the devil, for thou
Hadst my good sword. All these can witness it.
FAUCONBRIDGE God's mother thou belie'st me!
JOHN Give me the lie?
RICHARD Nay, calm this fury. Let's down to the tavern.
Or one or both these counterfeits are there.
FAUCONBRIDGE I know him well enough that had my chain.
And there be[490] two Johns, if I find one there,
By'r Lady, I will lay him fast.[491]
RICHARD It is this Skink that mocks us I believe.

484 146 bear the lie: endure being called a liar
485 153 princocks: saucy boy
486 155 Come: come at me
487 156 outface: contradict me
488 157 dastards: cowards
489 161 nor do you: do not
490 180 And there be: if there are
491 181 lay him fast: lay him out

JOHN Alas, poor Skink, it is the devil Gloucester,
Who, if I be so happy once to find,
I'll give contentment to his troubled mind.[492]
RICHARD [*Aside*] I hope he's far enough and free enough.
Yet, these conceits[493] I know delight his soul.
FAUCONBRIDGE Follow me, Block; follow me, honest Block. [*Exeunt* FAUCONBRIDGE, RICHARD, JOHN]
BLOCK Much follow you,[494] I have another piece of work in hand. I hear say Redcap's father shall be hanged this afternoon. I'll see him slip a string[495] though I give my service the slip. Beside, my lady bad me hear his examination[496] at his death. I'll get a good place[497] and pen it word for word, and, as I like it, set out a mournful ditty to the tune of "Labandalashot," or "Row Well Ye Mariners," [498] or somewhat as my muse shall me invoke.[499]

Exit

[Scene ix]

Enter GLOUCESTER *like* FAUCONBRIDGE *with a* PURSUIVANT; GLOUCESTER *having a paper*[500] *in his hand, the* PURSUIVANT *bare*[501]

GLOUCESTER A charitable deed (God bless the king),
He shall be then reprievèd?
PURSUIVANT Ay, sir, some day or two, till the young king and Prince John change it[502]—especially if the good earl be not found, which God forbid.
GLOUCESTER What house is this that we are stepped into to read this warrant in?
PURSUIVANT A tavern sir, the Salutation.
GLOUCESTER A tavern? Then I will turn prodigal.[503]
Call for a pint of sack,[504] good fellow.
PURSUIVANT Drawer?
DRAWER [*Off*] Anon, [505] sir!
GLOUCESTER A pint of thy best sack, my pretty youth!

[*Enter* DRAWER]

DRAWER God bless your worship, sir. Ye shall have the best in London, sir.
GLOUCESTER What, knowst thou me? Knowst thou old Fauconbridge? I am no tavern hunter,[506] I can tell thee.
DRAWER But my master hath taken many a fair pound of your man Block. He was here today, sir, and filled two bottles of nippitate sack.[507]
GLOUCESTER Well, fill us of your nippitate, sir.

492 185 I'll ease his troubles by killing him
493 187 conceits: tricks, confusions
494 189 Much follow you: sarcastic (i.e. "Oh sure, I'll follow you")
495 190 see him slip a string: watch him hang
496 191 bad me hear his examination: bade me to hear his testimony (defense)
497 191 get a good place: i.e. find a good spot from which to view the execution
498 192–3 "Labandalashot" and "Row Well Ye Mariners" were both familiar ballads in sixteenth-century England; Block's plan is to write a ballad about the execution and, potentially, profit from its sale
499 193 somewhat as . . . me invoke: whatever I'm inspired to write
500 0 SD *paper*: Gloucester holds the porter's reprieve
501 0 SD *bare*: without a hat, a sign of respect; also, indicates that the men are indoors
502 3 change it: alter the reprieve
503 7 prodigal: extravagant
504 8 sack: a fortified wine
505 10 Anon: just a minute
506 13–14 tavern hunter: frequenter of bars
507 16 nippitate sack: the best wine

This is well chanced,[508] but hear ye, boy?
Bring sugar in white paper, not in brown,
[*Aside*] For in white paper I have here a trick
Shall make the pursuivant first swoon, then sick. [509]
Thou honest fellow, what's thy name?
PURSUIVANT My name is Winterborne, sir.
GLOUCESTER What countryman, I prithee?
PURSUIVANT Berkshire, and please ye.[510]
GLOUCESTER How long hast thou been sworn a messenger?
PURSUIVANT But yesterday, and please your worship.
This is the first employment I have had.

Enter DRAWER *with wine and sugar*

GLOUCESTER A good beginning. Here, have to thee, fellow.
Thou art my fellow, now thou servest the king.[511]
Nay, take sugar too.[512] God's Lady dear,
I put it in my pocket,[513] but it's here.
Drink a good draught, I prithee, Winterborne. *He drinks and falls over the stool*
DRAWER Oh lord, Sir Richard, the man, the man!
GLOUCESTER What a forgetful beast am I? Peace, boy,
It is his fashion ever when he drinks.
Fellow, he hath the falling sickness.[514]
Run fetch two cushions to raise up his head,
And bring a little key to ope his teeth. *Exit* DRAWER
Pursuivant, your warrant and your box;
These must with me. The shape of Fauconbridge
Will hold no longer water here about.[515]
Gloucester will be a Proteus[516] every hour,
That Elinor and Leicester, Henry, John,
And all that rabble of hate-loving curs
May minister me more mirth to play upon.[517]

Enter DRAWER

DRAWER Here's a key, sir, and one of our folk to help.
GLOUCESTER No matter for a key;[518] help him but in,
And lay him by the fire a little while.
He'll wake immediately, but be heart sick.
There's money for a candle and thy wine.
I'll go but up unto your alderman's,[519]
And come down presently to comfort him. *Exeunt* [GLOUCESTER, DRAWER]

508 18 is well chanced: has turned out well
509 20–21 Gloucester has an emetic wrapped in white paper which he intends to pour in the pursuivant's drink (rather than the sugar the drawer delivers)
510 25 and please ye: if it please you; Berkshire is a county in southeast England
511 30 We are equals since we both serve the king
512 31 take sugar: sack was often sweetened with sugar (an excuse for Gloucester to pour his powder into the pursuivant's drink)
513 31–2 God's Lady . . . my pocket: Gloucester pretends to have sugar in his pocket, giving him an excuse to powder the drink
514 37 falling sickness: epilepsy, seizures
515 41–2 The shape . . . here about: my disguise will soon fail me
516 43 Proteus: Greek god known for his ability to change shape
517 46 May give me more cause to laugh at them
518 48 No matter for a key: Gloucester requests a key at line 39, ostensibly to pry open the pursuivant's mouth. When the drawer hands him a key, he pockets it, since the pursuivant's mouth has opened without it
519 52 alderman: a civic officer

SKINK [*Within*] Drawer? What, drawer? With a vengeance, drawer!
DRAWER [*Within*] Speak in the Crown[520] there.

Enter SKINK *like* PRINCE JOHN

SKINK They be come. The devil crown ye,[521] one by one!
Skink th' art betrayed; that master Fauconbridge,
Missing some of his chain, hath got thee dogged.[522]
Drawer? What, drawer?
DRAWER [*Within*] Anon, anon sir!

[*Enter* DRAWER]

SKINK Was not Sir Richard Fauconbridge below?
DRAWER Yes, and please ye.
SKINK It does not please me well,
Knows he that I am here?
DRAWER No, I protest.
SKINK Come hither, sirrah. I have little money,
But there's some few links of a chain of gold.
Upon your honesty: knows not Sir Richard
That I am here?
DRAWER No, by my holydam.
SKINK Who's that was with him?
DRAWER Why, a pursuivant.
SKINK Where is Sir Richard?
DRAWER At the alderman's.
SKINK A pursuivant and at the alderman's.
What pig, or goose, or capon[523] have you killed
Within your kitchen new?
DRAWER A pig new sticked.[524]
SKINK Fetch me a saucer of the blood. Quick, run! *Exit* [DRAWER]
I'll fit the pursuivant, and alderman,
And Fauconbridge, if Skink have any wit.
Well, Gloucester, I did never love thee yet,
But th'art the maddest lord that e'er I met.
If I scape this, and meet thee once again,
Curse Skink if he die penny in thy debt.[525]

Enter DRAWER

DRAWER Oh, my lord, the house is full of halberts![526] And a great many gentlemen ask for the room where Prince John is!
SKINK Lend me thy apron; run and fetch a pot from the next room. Betrayed, 'swounds! Betrayed by gout, by palsy, by dropsy![527] Oh, brave boy, excellent blood! Up, take my cloak and my hat to thy share; when I come from Kent, I'll pay thee like a king.
DRAWER I thank you, my lord. *Exit*

520 55 the Crown: a room in the Salutation
521 56 crown ye: may the devil crack you on the head, with a play on "the Crown"
522 58 dogged: trapped (i.e. like a quarry bayed by dogs)
523 70 capon: neutered cock
524 71 new sticked: recently killed
525 78 Curse me if I don't pay you back for this
526 79 halberts: men with halberts, long-handled bladed weapons
527 82 by gout . . . by dropsy: i.e. by old Fauconbridge

SKINK Now fortune help or never. [SKINK *smears pig blood on himself*] They come! [*Loudly*] And ye were a prince as ye say ye are, ye would be ashamed to abuse a poor servant thus! But and if you were not of the blood royal, I'd break the neck of ye down the stairs, so would I! I'd teach you to hurt prentices![528]

Enter JOHN, [PRINCE] RICHARD, FAUCONBRIDGE, *Sheriffs and Officers*

RICHARD Who hurt thee, fellow?
SKINK Prince devil or his dam.[529] "Prince John," they call him.
JOHN Gloucester, I hope.
RICHARD I doubt not but it's Skink.
JOHN Where is he?
SKINK Up them stairs; take heed of him.
He's in the Crown.
FAUCONBRIDGE Alas, poor fellow! He hath crowned thee shrewdly.
JOHN In recompense, if it be him I seek,
I'll give thee his whole head to tread upon.
Follow me, brother; come, old Fauconbridge,
Keep the stairs, sheriffs; you see it waxeth[530] dark.
Take heed he slip not by you. *Exeunt* [JOHN, RICHARD, FAUCONBRIDGE]
SKINK Hang yourselves! This darkness shall convey me out of doors.
I'll swim the Thames, but I'll attain[531] Blackheath.
London, farewell! Curse, John; rave, Fauconbridge.
Skink scapes you all by twilight's privilege.[532] [*Exit*]
ALL [*Within*] Where is he? Lights, bring lights, drag out that boy!

Enter all with the [DRAWER]

JOHN This is my cloak, my hat, my rapier,
And either it was Skink or Gloucester.
DRAWER I know not who t'was, sir. He said he was Prince John. He took away my apron and a pottle pot[533] with him, and all to-bloodied[534] his head and face.
FAUCONBRIDGE We met him, by Saint Anthony,[535] we met him!
JOHN The fire of Saint Anthony confound
This changing counterfeit, whatsoever he be!
RICHARD [*Aside*] It makes me laugh at envious greediness,
Who feeds upon her own heart's bitterness.[536]
JOHN Sirrah, you that were born to cry "anon,"
What other copesmates[537] have you in the house?
DRAWER Sir, my master's guests be none of my copesmates.
JOHN Well, your guests; can ye guess who they be?
DRAWER Marry, here's a pursuivant, that this gentleman, Sir Richard Fauconbridge, left sick even now.
FAUCONBRIDGE Marry of God, did I, thou lying knave?
DRAWER I am a poor boy, sir. Your worship may say your pleasure. Our maids have had a foul

528 86–8 And ye . . . hurt prentices: Skink pretends to be fighting Prince John
529 90 his dam: the devil's wife, an insulting term for a woman
530 98 waxeth: grows
531 101 attain: get to
532 103 by twilight's privilege: under cover of darkness
533 108 pottle pot: tankard
534 108 all to-bloodied: thoroughly bloodied
535 109 Saint Anthony: the patron saint of the recovery of lost items
536 112–13 It makes . . . heart's bitterness: John's self-sustaining anger makes me laugh
537 115 copesmates: colleagues, fellow workers

hand with him.[538] You said he would be sick; so he is, with a witness.[539]
JOHN Look about, Fauconbridge; here's work for you.
You have some evil angel in your shape.
Go sirrah, bring us forth that pursuivant.

Enter two leading the PURSUIVANT, *sick*

RICHARD [*Aside*] Gloucester, thou wilt be too, too venturous.
Thou dost delight in those odd humours so,
That much I fear they'll be thy overthrow.
PURSUIVANT Oh, oh, oh! Not too fast. Oh, I am sick! Oh, very sick!
JOHN What picture of the pestilence is this?
PURSUIVANT A poor man sir, a poor man, sir. Down, I pray ye, I pray let me sit down. Ah, Sir Richard, Sir Richard, ah, good Sir Richard: what have I deserved to be thus dealt with all at your worship's hands? A ha, ah, ah!
FAUCONBRIDGE At my hands, knave? At my hands, paltry knave?
DRAWER And I should be brought to my book oath, sir.[540]
WITHIN[541] What, Jeffrey?
DRAWER Anon, anon.
JOHN A plague upon your Jeffring! Is your name Jeffrey?
DRAWER Ay, and't please you, sir.
RICHARD Why, gentle Jeffrey, then stay you awhile.
What can you say if you come to your book?
DRAWER If I be posed[542] upon a book, sir, though I be a poor prentice, I must speak the truth and nothing but the truth, sir.
JOHN And what's your truth, sir?
PURSUIVANT Oh, oh, my heart!
DRAWER Marry, sir, this knight, this man of worship—
FAUCONBRIDGE Well, what of me? What did my worship do?
DRAWER Marry, ye came into the Bell, our room next the bar, with this honest man, as I take it.[543]
FAUCONBRIDGE As thou tak'st it?
PURSUIVANT Oh, sir, 'tis too true, too true, too true. Oh lord.
DRAWER And there he called for a pint of sack, as good sack (I'll be posed upon all the books that ever opened and shut) as any is in all Christendom.
FAUCONBRIDGE Body of me, I come and call for sack?
PURSUIVANT Oh, ye did, ye did, ye did. Oh, oh.
JOHN Well, forward, sirrah.
RICHARD [*Aside*] Gloucester hath done this jest.
DRAWER And you called then for sugar, sir, as good sugar, and as wholesome, as ever came in any cup of sack. You drunk to this man, and you do well,[544] God be thanked, but he no sooner drunk—
PURSUIVANT But I, but I, but I—oh, my head, oh, my heart!
RICHARD [*Aside*] I cannot choose but smile at these conceits.
JOHN I am mad, and yet I must laugh at Fauconbridge.
[*To* PRINCE RICHARD] Brother, look how Sir Richard acts his rage.
FAUCONBRIDGE I came? I call? The man is like to die.

538 121–2 a foul hand with him: have soiled their hands cleaning up after him
539 122 with a witness: I can testify
540 135 I would swear on the Bible
541 136 SP WITHIN: i.e. someone calls the drawer from another room in the tavern (off-stage)
542 142 posed: deposed
543 148–9 as I take it: as I remember
544 159 you do well: as was appropriate

Practice,[545] by the mass, practice by the Mary God!
John loves me not, Prince Richard loves my wife,
I shall be charged here for a poisoned knave!
Practice, by th'lord, practice, I see it clear.
PURSUIVANT And more, Sir Richard. Oh, lord, oh Sir Richard.
FAUCONBRIDGE What, more? What hast thou more? What practice more?
PURSUIVANT Oh, my box, my box, with the king's arms.[546] Oh, my box, oh, my box! It cost me, oh lord, every penny![547] Oh, my box!
RICHARD And what of your box, sir?
DRAWER Marry, sir, it's lost, and 'tis well known my master keeps no thieves in his house. Oh, there was none but you and he.
FAUCONBRIDGE Oh then, belike,[548] thou thinkest I had his box?
PURSUIVANT Oh, Sir Richard I will not—oh, lord—I will not charge you for all the world. But, but, but for the warrant the old king signed to reprieve the porter of the fleet. Oh God, oh God!
JOHN The porter of the Fleet? The old king signed?
PURSUIVANT Ay, my good lord. Oh, oh!
JOHN Is he reprieved then?
PURSUIVANT No, my lord. Oh, Sir Richard took it from me with his own hand, oh.
FAUCONBRIDGE Here's a device to bring me in contempt
With the old king that I ever loved.
Princes and sheriff: you can witness with me
That I have been with you this afternoon,
Only with you, with no body but you.
And now a fellow, whom the king would save
By a reprieve, this fellow says, is hanged.
JOHN If thou hadst done it, I'd have justified it.[549]
But, Richard, I conceit this jest[550] already:
This mad mate Skink, this honest merry knave,
Meeting this pursuivant and, hearing tell
He had a warrant to reprieve a slave
Whom we would hang, stole it away from him.
This is sure the jest, upon my life it is.
PURSUIVANT Oh, but my warrant, how shall I do? Oh!
RICHARD But look about you, hot-brained brother John,
And I believe you'll find it otherwise:
Gloucester hath got the warrant in disguise
And saved the fellow you so fain[551] would hang.
JOHN No, no, how say you, master sheriff? Is he not hanged?
SHERRIF My lord, the gibbet[552] was set up by noon
In the Old Bailey,[553] and I charged my men,
If I return not, though it were by torch light,
To see him executed ere they come.
JOHN I am greedy to hear news.
FAUCONBRIDGE Robbed of my chain, outfaced I had a sword,[554]

545 166 Practice: plots
546 172 king's arms: the pursuivant's warrant box has the insignia of the king upon it
547 173 cost me . . . every penny: positions in the royal household often needed to be purchased
548 177 belike: I suppose
549 191 justified it: answered for it
550 192 conceit this jest: have figured out this trick
551 202 fain: gladly
552 204 gibbet: scaffold
553 205 Old Bailey: central criminal court in London
554 209 outfaced I had a sword: falsely accused of having John's sword

Accused of poisoning, cozenage,[555] seeking blood?
Not to be borne! It is untolerable!
RICHARD Sir Richard, I prithee, have some patience.
FAUCONBRIDGE I'll to Blackheath. Talk not of patience.
It is intolerable, not to be borne!
JOHN It is intolerable, not to be borne.
A warrant, brother? Fauconbridge, a warrant?
FAUCONBRIDGE I saw no warrant; I defy you all.
JOHN A slave, a pursuivant, one Winterborne.
FAUCONBRIDGE I care not for thee, that Winterborne.
PURSUIVANT Oh it is I, sir, that's my warrant!
JOHN Is't you? You rogue! You drunkard! Ye are cheated,
And we are cheated of the prisoner!
Out dog, dog!
PURSUIVANT Oh, oh, oh, oh, my lord! *Exit* [PURSUIVANT] *and* DRAWER
SHERRIF Have patience, and we will have a privy search.
JOHN Go hang, ye blockheads! Get ye from my sight!
Oh, would I were a basilisk,[556] to kill
These gleare-eyed[557] villains.
SHERRIF Come away, let's leave him.
We have a warrant; let him do his worst.[558] *Exeunt* SHERRIF *and Officers*
FAUCONBRIDGE I'll to Blackheath. I'll to the holy hermit.
There shall I know not only these deceivers,
But how my wife plays fast and loose with Richard.
Ha! I shall fit them. I'll tickle them.
I'll do't, I'll hence, I'll to the heath amain.[559] *Exit*
JOHN There shall I know where this damned Gloucester is.
I'll have the devils roused to find that devil,
Or else I'll conjure the old conjurer.
I'll to Blackheath and there with friends conspire,
But I'll have Gloucester's head, my heart's desire. [*Exit*]
RICHARD Would mad earl Robin[560] saw these humorists.[561]
'Twould feed him fat with laughter; oh, 'twould fit him.
Wherever he is, I know the bare conceit[562]
Is better to him than his daintiest food.
Well, and it fits me well; now I have time
To court my Lady Fauconbridge at leisure.
Love, I implore thy aid. Fair Cypria,[563]
Thou sea-born mother at affection's ring,[564]
Shine brightly in thy sphere, that art my star,
My planet; thou, of all lights most beauteous,
Be thou to my desires auspicious.[565]
Exit

555 210 cozenage: swindling
556 227 basilisk: mythical reptile whose look was said to be fatal
557 228 gleare-eyed: possessed of glaring eyes
558 229 However much John curses us, we have a warrant for our search
559 234 amain: at top speed
560 240 mad earl Robin: i.e. Gloucester
561 240 humorists: obsessive men (i.e. governed by humors, or passionate whims)
562 242 bare conceit: the slightest jest
563 246 Cypria: a toponym for Venus, Roman goddess of love, derived from the island of Cyprus, claimed as her birthplace
564 247 affection's ring: meaning obscure, possibly referring to the planet's orbit (see "sphere" in line 248) or to Cyprus as a cultic center of Venus-worship
565 246–50 Fair Cypria … desires auspicious: Richard invokes Venus—born of sea-foam, according to the myth—to bless his pursuit of Lady Fauconbridge

[Scene x]

Enter ROBIN HOOD *in the* LADY FAUCONBRIDGE*'s gown, night attire*[566] *on his head*

ROBERT Oh, for this lady! Was never poor gentleman troubled with gentlewoman as I am with myself. My Lady Fauconbridge hath fitted me a turn.[567] Here I am visited with sleeveless[568] errands and with asking for "this thing, madam," and "that thing, madam," that they make me almost mad in earnest. Whoop, here's another client.

Enter a SERVINGMAN

SERVINGMAN Here's my Lady Rawford's page attends to speak with your ladyship.
ROBERT I pray ye, bid her lordship's page come into my ladyship. Well, Robin Hood, part with these petticoats[569] and cast these loose devices[570] from thy back. I'll ne'er go more untrussed,[571] never be kerchiefed,[572] never have this ado, with "What do you lack?"[573]

Enter PAGE

PAGE Madam, my lady greets your honor kindly,
And sends you the first grapes of her young vine.
ROBERT I am much indebted to her honor. There's an angel for you to drink. Set them up till after supper.[574] Humphrey, pray look about for Block. Humphrey? Trust me, I think the fool be lost.
PAGE No, forsooth, madam. He's upon the green,[575] jesting with a stammerer, one Redcap.
ROBERT It is a lewd fellow. Pray, bid him come in, youth. I'll give him his welcome at the door. Commend me to your lady, I pray ye, heartily. *Exit* PAGE

[*Enter* HUMPHREY]

Humphrey, I marvel where Sir Richard is so late? Truly, truly he does not as beseems[576] a gentleman of his calling.[577] Pray, let some go forth to meet him on the green and send in that blockhead Block. *Exit* HUMPHREY

Enter REDCAP *and* BLOCK *after him*

BLOCK Will ye tell tales, ye ass, will ye?
REDCAP I'll te te tell your la la lady, or I would to G God we were ha hanged else, as my fa father should have been.
ROBERT Now, what's the matter there, I pray you? What company have you there, a God's name? Where spend you the day, I pray?
BLOCK Why, where you gave me leave; at the gallows[578] I was, no farther.
REDCAP A a and you be his la lady, you are the La Lady Fau Fauconbridge, the Earl of Glo Gloucester's sister.
ROBERT I am so fellow.

566 0 SD *night attire*: a head covering worn during sleep
567 2 a turn: for a change (i.e. of gender)
568 2 sleeveless: pointless
569 7 petticoats: underskirts
570 7 devices: garments; also, disguises
571 8 untrussed: dressed in loose garments
572 8 never be kerchiefed: never wear a woman's head dress
573 8 with "What do you lack?": with servants asking me what I need
574 11–12 Set them . . . after supper: i.e. save the grapes for dessert
575 14 green: the lawn
576 17 beseems: becomes
577 18 calling: station, position
578 25 at the gallows: the real Lady Fauconbridge asked Block to take down the porter's "examination" (see viii. 191)

REDCAP Y y your man B B Block, here, does no nothing but f f flout[579] m me, a and cr cries r run Re Redcap and s s see your f f father ha ha hanged. I sh shall g go near[580] to m make m murder and he u use it.[581]

ROBERT Well, sirrah, leave your mocking, you were best. I'll bob your beetle head[582] and if you mock him.

BLOCK He's run,[583] Redcap.

REDCAP La la law,[584] ma madam.

ROBERT Away, ye saucy fool, go wait within.

BLOCK Run Redcap, run Redcap. *Exit*

ROBERT Art thou the porter's son, that was condemned about my brother Gloucester?

REDCAP Ay, G G God be with ye, I am the p p porter's son. I m must r run to s s seeke your b br brother.

ROBERT Well, drink that[585] fellow. If thou find my brother, be not too violent, and I'll reward thee.

REDCAP I th th thank ye h heartily. And I had not been cozened with Sk Skink, I had no nee need of these ja jaunts,[586] for Gl Gloucester was s safe enough.

Enter BLOCK *and the* PORTER *with his cloak muffled*

BLOCK Ah, farewell Redcap.

REDCAP Fa fare we well and be ha hanged. *Exit*

ROBERT You'll never leave your knavery. Who's there more?

BLOCK One, madam, that hath commendations to you from your brother.

ROBERT Com'st thou from Gloucester? Thou art welcome, friend.

BLOCK Oh, it's one of the kindest ladies (though she will now and then have a bout[587] with Block) that ever breathed. And she had been in her mood now, Redcap would have made her such sp sp sport as't a pa pa past.[588]

ROBERT Will you make sport[589] and see who knocks again?

BLOCK Our gates are like an anvil from four to ten, nothing but knick-a-knock upon it. *Exit*

ROBERT Will you be gone, sir? Honest friend, I am glad
My brother Gloucester got thy liberty,
Whose flight was cause of thy captivity.
Nor shall there be in us such negligence,
Though thou have lost thy office and thy house,[590]
But we will see thee better far provided[591]
Than when thou wert porter in the Fleet. [*Exit* PORTER]

Enter BLOCK

BLOCK Madam, your old friend, Prince Richard:
All alone, making moan, fetching many a grievous groan.

ROBERT Prince Richard, come so late? Lights to his chamber,

579 29 flout: mock
580 30 shall g go near: am likely to
581 31 and he u use it: if he keeps it up
582 32 bob your beetle head: beat your thick head
583 34 He's run: your father's dead (i.e. his race is run)
584 35 law: expression of dismay
585 41 drink that: Robert gives Redcap money (with which he might buy himself a drink)
586 44 jaunts: journeys
587 50 have a bout: argue
588 51–2 And she . . . pa past: had she been in the right mood, she would have made fun of Redcap
589 53 make sport: do your job
590 59 office and thy house: job and home (i.e. the porter both kept and lived at the Fleet)
591 60 provided: provided for

Sirrah. In any case, say I am sick.
BLOCK Very sick, sick and like to die. I'll sing it and you will.[592]
ROBERT Away, ye knave; tell him in the morning
I'll humbly wait upon his excellence.
BLOCK That's all his desire, to have ye lowly and humble, and 'tis a courteous thing in a lady. *Exit*
ROBERT Hence, or else I'll set you hence.[593] Go in, good friend.
Come, Lady Fauconbridge,[594] it's time to come;
Robin can hold out no longer, I see,
Hot wooers will be tempters presently.
Exit

[Scene xi]

Enter SKINK *like a hermit*

SKINK Now, holy Skink, in thy religious weed,
Look out for purchase, or thy wonted clients.[595]
"Warrants," quoth you? I was fairly warranted.[596]
Young Robin Hood, the Earl of Huntington,
Shall never fetch me more[597] unto his prince.

Enter LADY FAUCONBRIDGE *in merchant's wife's attire*

But *pauca verba*,[598] Skink, a prize, a prize!
By th'mass, a pretty girl; close, hermit close,
O'erhear, if thou canst, what she desires,
For so my cunning and my credit spreads.[599]
LADY FAUCONBRIDGE See how affection arms my feeble strength
To this so desperate journeying all alone,[600]
While Robin Hood, young Earl of Huntington,
Plays Lady Fauconbridge for me at home.
SKINK What mystery is this? The Lady Fauconbridge?
It's she! Sweet fortune, thou hast sent her well.
I will entice this morsel to my cell.
Her husband's jealous; I will give him cause.
As he believes, I hope it shall succeed;[601]
Nay, swounds, it shall; she's mine in scorn of speed.[602]
LADY FAUCONBRIDGE By this broad beaten path, it should appear,
The holy hermit's cave cannot be far.
And if I err not, this is he himself.
SKINK What honored tongue enquireth for the hermit?
LADY FAUCONBRIDGE What honored tongue?[603]

592 66 Block sings a snatch of a ballad licensed for printing in 1578, which included the line, "Sick, sick, and very sick, and sick and like to die"
593 70 set you hence: dismiss you
594 71 Come, Lady Fauconbridge: Robert addresses his disguise
595 2 Keep your eyes peeled for new and former customers
596 3 Skink facetiously dismisses his pardon, which has not protected him
597 5 fetch me more: summon me again (to Prince Richard)
598 6 *pauca verba*: few words (Latin)
599 9 credit spreads: Skink's credibility (as a soothsayer) increases, since he will learn her secrets
600 10–11 See how . . . all alone: my love for my brother makes me brave enough to make this journey alone
601 18 Since he thinks his wife's cheating on him, I'll make it come true
602 19 scorn of speed: i.e. so quickly it will mock speed itself
603 24 What honored tongue: Lady Fauconbridge is surprised to be addressed as "honored" since she's disguised as a merchant's wife

SKINK Ay, Lady Fauconbridge,
I know ye, and I know for what you come:
For Gloucester, and your husband's jealousy.
LADY FAUCONBRIDGE Oh, thou, whose eye of contemplation
Looks through the windows of the highest heavens,
Resolve thy handmaid[604] where Earl Gloucester lives,
And whether he shall live, and scape the hate,
Of proud young Henry and his brother John.
SKINK I'll have you first in; I'll tell you more, anon.
Madam, they say bushes have ears and eyes,
And these are matters of great secrecy.
And you'll vouchsafe[605] enter my holy cell,
There what you long to know I'll quickly tell.

Enter JOHN *and* FAUCONBRIDGE

LADY FAUCONBRIDGE Stay, here are strangers.
SKINK A plague upon them! Come they in the nick[606]
To hinder Reynard[607] of his fox's trick?
JOHN Good day, old hermit.
FAUCONBRIDGE [*To* LADY FAUCONBRIDGE] So to you, fair dame.
JOHN By Elinor's gray eye,[608] she's fair indeed.
Sweetheart, come ye for holy benisons?[609]
Hermit, hast thou good custom[610] with such clients?
I cannot blame your feats, your juggling[611] tricks.
Plague juggle you!
LADY FAUCONBRIDGE Why curse ye sacred worth?[612]
FAUCONBRIDGE Ill done, in sooth, my lord, very ill done.
Wrong holiness?[613] [*Aside*] A very pretty woman.—
Mock gravity?[614] [*Aside*] By the mass, a cherry lip.—
Ah, it's not well done, deride a holy hermit?
JOHN I have it in my purse shall make amends.[615]
SKINK [*Aside*] His purse, and yours, shall make me some amends.
For hindering me this morning from the lady,
For scaring me at tavern yester night,
For having back your chain, I'll fit you both.
JOHN Hermit, a word.
FAUCONBRIDGE [*To* LADY FAUCONBRIDGE] A word with you, fair mistress.
JOHN Where lie your devils that tell all your news?[616]
Would you would trouble them for half an hour,
To know what's become of traitor Gloucester,
That in my clothes brake prison in the Fleet?
SKINK No, it was Skink.

604 29 Resolve thy handmaid: inform your supplicant
605 35 And you'll vouchsafe: If you'll deign to
606 38 nick: nick of time
607 39 Reynard: a trickster figure of pan-European fables, Reynard the fox took advantage of other animals for his own profit
608 41 By Elinor's gray eye: Prince John swears upon his mother's eyes
609 42 benisons: blessings
610 43 custom: business
611 44 juggling: deceptive
612 45 Why do you curse at this sacred, worthy hermit?
613 47 Wrong holiness: speak ill of a holy man
614 48 Mock gravity: make fun of a grave, serious man
615 50 I'm sure he'll accept money as an apology
616 56 Where are your familiar spirits who help you prognosticate?

JOHN Come, old fool, ye dote.
SKINK But hear me.
FAUCONBRIDGE Hear him, prince.
JOHN [*Aside*] 'Swounds, who hears you? I'll make your lady graft ye for this work[617]—But to your tale, sir.
SKINK Know, thrice-honored prince, that Skink did cozen Redcap of his clothes.
Gloucester did cozen Skink, and so escaped.
JOHN Well done. Fauconbridge?
FAUCONBRIDGE My lord, he tells you true.
JOHN You find it on her lips—but forward, sir.
SKINK 'Twas Skink in Gloucester's gown whom you did visit,
That played at bowls, and after stole your clothes,
While you went into the Lord Morton's chamber.
JOHN This savors of some truth,
FAUCONBRIDGE 'Tis very like.
JOHN Well, Fauconbridge, by heaven I'll tell your wife.
FAUCONBRIDGE She'll much believe you. [*To the* LADY] You will come?
[*To* JOHN] Tell me of my wife? [*To the* LADY] This evening fail me not.
[*To* JOHN] "My wife," quoth you? [*To the* LADY] I'll send my wife from home.
[*To* JOHN] Do tell my wife, Prince John, by my dear mother,
I love her too too well to like another.
LADY FAUCONBRIDGE [*Aside*] It seems so, fox. Oh, what a world is this?
There most sin reigns where least suspicion is.
FAUCONBRIDGE You'll come?
LADY FAUCONBRIDGE I will not fail, I warrant you.
JOHN Hermit, is all this true?
SKINK Himself deliver not so much[618] before ye sleep,
Root me from out the borders of this realm.
JOHN Well, by your leave, Sir Richard Fauconbridge,
Hence, free from fear, you'll melt[619]—you'll melt old man.
FAUCONBRIDGE Nay, take her to you; she is a shrew, I warrant.
I'll to the holy hermit and inquire
About my chain, your sword, the pursuivant,
And other matters that I have to ask.
SKINK You're welcome, good sir Richard.
JOHN [*To the* LADY] Nay, do not stand on terms.[620] I am fire, all life,
Nor never tell me that I have a wife.
I do not mean to marry, ye think so,
But to be merry; you the manner know.[621]
And you will have me, have me, 'point a meeting;[622]
I'll be your true love, you shall be my sweeting.
If you deny to promise, this is plain:
I'll have my will ere you get home again.[623]
LADY FAUCONBRIDGE Most gracious lord.
JOHN Tut, tell not me of grace.
I like no goodness but a beauteous face.
Be therefore brief, give me your hand and swear,

617 64 graft ye for this work: cuckold you (i.e. make horns grow on his forehead); see *Eastward Ho* V.iii. 6
618 84 Himself deliver not so much: if he himself does not say so much
619 87 melt: dwindle; possibly, prove impotent
620 93 stand on terms: insist upon propriety
621 96 you the manner know: you know what I mean
622 97 'point a meeting: appoint a time for an assignation
623 99–100 If you . . . home again: i.e. If you resist, I'll insist

Or I'll away with you[624] into the heath.
Neither shall Fauconbridge nor hermit help,
And what I do I'll answer well enough.
LADY FAUCONBRIDGE Why, then, my lord—
JOHN Nay do not stand on "then,"[625]
But tell me when my lord shall have you, lady.
It's presently I'll venture for a baby.[626]
LADY FAUCONBRIDGE This night, at Stepney, by my summer house,
There is a tavern, which I sometime use,
When we from London come a-gossiping.[627]
It is the Hind.[628]
JOHN Give me thy pretty hand.
Thou'lt meet me at the Hind, I'll be thy roe.[629]
LADY FAUCONBRIDGE One word's enough.
JOHN Suffice, then be it so.
LADY FAUCONBRIDGE [*Aside*] I'll fit my old adulterer and your grace.
I'll send the princess[630] thither, in my place.
FAUCONBRIDGE Prince John, Prince John, the hermit tells me wonders!
He says it was Skink that scaped us at the tavern,
Skink had my chain; nay, sure, that Skink did all.
SKINK I say go but to[631] yonder corner,
And ere the sun be half an hour higher,
There will the thief attempt a robbery.
JOHN Who, Skink?
FAUCONBRIDGE Will Skink?
SKINK Ay, Skink, upon my word.
FAUCONBRIDGE Shall we go seize upon him, good Prince John?
JOHN Nay, we will have him; that's no question,
And yet not hurt the honest rogue.
He'll help us well in quest of changing[632] Gloucester.
Hermit, farewell. Lady, keep your hour.
FAUCONBRIDGE Adieu, old hermit. [*To the* LADY] Soon in th'evening, lass.
[*Exeunt* PRINCE JOHN *and* FAUCONBRIDGE]
LADY FAUCONBRIDGE I'll meet you both, and meet with[633] both of you.
Father, what answer do you give to me?
SKINK Lady, start down I must into my cell,
Where I am curing of a man late[634] hurt.
He dressed,[635] I must unto my orisons.
In half an hour all will be dispatched,
And then I will attend your ladyship. [*Exit* SKINK]
LADY FAUCONBRIDGE At your best leisure[636] father. Oh, the life
That this thrice-reverend hermit leadeth here!

624 104 away with you: i.e. carry you away
625 107 stand on "then": i.e. put me off
626 109 I'm going to impregnate you immediately
627 112 come a-gossiping: assemble with friends to visit and chat
628 113 Hind: a tavern named for a female deer
629 114 roe: male deer
630 117 the princess: Princess Isabel, Prince John's wife
631 121 go but to: go no farther than
632 128 changing: shape-shifting
633 131 meet with: requite
634 134 late: recently
635 135 dressed: bandaged
636 138 At your best leisure: whenever you're ready

How far remote from mortal vanities,[637]
Baits[638] to the soul, enticements to the eye?
How far is he unlike my lustful lord?
Who, being given himself to be unchaste,
Thinks all men like himself in their effects,
And injures me, that never had a thought,
To wrong the sacred rites of spotless faith.[639]

Enter SKINK *with a patch*[640] *on his face, and a falconer's lure*[641] *in his hand*

SKINK Hermit, farewell. I'll pay ye or speak with ye next time I see ye.[642] [*To the* LADY] Sweet mouse, the hermit bids you stay here. He'll visit you anon. [*Aside*] Now, John and Fauconbridge, I'll match ye and[643] I do not say Skink's a wretch, a wren, a worm. When I have tricked them, madam, I will trim[644] you. Commodity[645] is to be preferred before pleasure. About[646] profit, Skink, for crowns, for crowns, that make the kingly thoughts. *Exit*

LADY FAUCONBRIDGE I am assured that man's some murderer.
[*Calls offstage*] Good father hermit, speak and comfort me!
Are ye at prayers, good old man? I pray ye, speak! [*Exit and re-enter*]
What's here, a beard? A counterfeited hair?
The hermit's portesse,[647] garments, and his beads?[648]
Jesus defend me, I will fly this den.
It's some thieves' cave, no haunt[649] for holy men.
What if the murderer (as I guess him one)
Set on my husband! Tush,[650] Prince John and he
Are able to defend their noble selves.
Howe'er, I will not tarry, I'll away.
Lest unto theft and rape, I prove a prey.
Exit

[Scene xii]

Enter SKINK *solus*

SKINK Yonder they are. I'll fit them; here's my ground:
Wa ha how, wa ha how, wa ha how?[651]

Enter FAUCONBRIDGE

FAUCONBRIDGE I warrant ye, my lord, some man's distressed.

637 140 mortal vanities: worldly distractions
638 141 Baits: allurements to sin
639 145–6 injures me . . . spotless faith: i.e. he injures me, who has never even thought about violating my marriage vows
640 146 SD *patch*: bandage (Skink has disguised himself as the man "late hurt" in line 133)
641 146 SD *falconer's lure*: an effigy of a bird swung on a cord to teach a falcon to hunt
642 147 Hermit, farewell . . . see ye: Skink pretends to take leave of the offstage Hermit
643 149 and: if
644 150 trim: rape
645 150 Commodity: profit
646 151 About: seek
647 156 portesse: a small prayer book
648 156 beads: rosary
649 158 haunt: dwelling place
650 160 Tush: dismissive expression
651 2 A hunting cry, perhaps a falconer's call, prompting Fauconbridge's entrance

JOHN Why, man, 'tis a falconer.
FAUCONBRIDGE Marry of me, good fellow, I did think thou hadst been robbed.
SKINK Robbed, sir? No, he that comes to rob me shall have a hard match on't. Yet two good fellows had like to been robbed by one tall thief, had not I stepped in. A bots on him! I lost a hawk by him, and, yet, I cared not to send another after him, so I could find the thief. [652] And here about he is; I know he is squatted.[653]
FAUCONBRIDGE Say'st thou me so?[654] We'll find him, by Saint Mary.
An honest fellow, a good commonwealth's man.[655]
JOHN There are caves hereabout, good fellow, are there not?
SKINK Yes, sir, tread the ground, sir, and you shall hear their hollowness. This way, sir, this way. [JOHN *and* FAUCONBRIDGE *fall into a cave*]
JOHN Help, Fauconbridge!
FAUCONBRIDGE O help me, good Prince John!
SKINK I'll help you both. Deliver,[656] sir deliver! 'Swounds, linger not! Prince John, put up your purse, or I'll throw poniards[657] down upon your pate! Quickly, when?[658] I am Skink that scaped ye yesternight and fled the Fleet in your cloak, carrying me clean[659] out of wind and rain. I broke the bonds and links that fettered your chain amity.[660] This cheat is mine! Farewell, I cannot stay, sweet prince, old knight. I thank ye for this prey.[661]
FAUCONBRIDGE God's Mary mother, here's a jest indeed!
We came to take, a thief takes us.
Where are ye, good my lord?
JOHN No matter where.
I think I was forespoken at the teat.[662]
This damned rogue served me thus? Gloucester and he,
Upon my life, conclude[663] in villainy.
He was not wont to plot these stratagems.
Lend me your hand a little; come, away.
Let's to the cell again; perchance the hermit
Is Skink, and thief, and hermit all in one.
FAUCONBRIDGE Marry a God, then ten to one it's so!
Well thought on, princely John.
He had my chain; no doubt, he had your sword.
JOHN If there be now no hermit at the cell,
I'll swear by all the saints it's none but he.

Exeunt

[Scene xiii]

Enter GLOUCESTER *in the hermit's gown, putting on the beard*

GLOUCESTER This accident[664] hath hit thy humor, Gloucester.
From pursuivant I'll turn a hermit now.

652 7–8 I lost . . . the thief: i.e. the "thief" took one of my hawks during the robbery, but I didn't want to send a hawk after him to recover the first
653 9 squatted: gone to ground
654 10 Say'st thou me so: i.e. you don't say
655 11 commonwealth's man: a man who looks out for the public welfare
656 16 Deliver: hand over your money
657 17 poniards: daggers
658 17 when: exclamation expressing impatience
659 18 clean: safely; cleverly
660 19 chain amity: friendship's bond
661 20 prey: plunder
662 24 forespoken at the teat: meaning obscure, possibly doomed from birth
663 26 conclude: conspire
664 1 accident: i.e. the discovery of the fake beard and hermit's gown

Sure[665] he that keeps this cell is a counterfeit,
Else what does he here with false hair and beard?
Well, howsoe'er it be, I'll seem to be
The holy hermit, for such fame there is
Of one accounted reverend on this heath.

Enter SKINK

SKINK I'll fain unto my cell to my fair lady,
But John and Fauconbridge are at my heels. [*Spies* GLOUCESTER]
And some odd mate[666] is got into my gown
And walks devoutly like my counterfeit.[667]
I cannot stay to question with you now;
I have another gown and all things fit.
These guests once rid, new mate, I'll bum, I'll mark you.[668] [*Exit*]
GLOUCESTER [*Spies* SKINK] What's he, a God's name? He is quickly gone.
I am for him,[669] were he Robin Goodfellow.[670]
Who's yonder? The Prince John and Fauconbridge?
I think they haunt me like my *genii*,[671]
One good, the other ill; by th'mass they pry
And look upon me but suspiciously.[672]
JOHN This is not Skink. The hermit is not Skink.
He is a learnèd reverend holy man.
FAUCONBRIDGE He is, he is, a very godly man.
I warrant ye, he's at his book, at's prayers,
[*To* GLOUCESTER] We should have took you, by my holydam,
Even for a very thief.
GLOUCESTER Now God forfend
Such noblemen as you should guess me so.
I never gave such cause for ought I know.
JOHN Yet thou didst tell us Skink should do a robbery,
Appointed us the place, and there we found him.
FAUCONBRIDGE And he felt us,[673] for he hath robbed us both.
GLOUCESTER He's a lewd fellow, but he shall be taken.
JOHN I had rather hear of Gloucester than of him.
GLOUCESTER Gloucester did cheat him of the same gold chain
That deceived Sir Richard Fauconbridge.
He got your sword, Prince John; 'twas he that saved
The porter and beguiled[674] the pursuivant,
JOHN A vengeance on him!
GLOUCESTER Do not curse, good prince.
He's bad enough; 'twere better pray for him.
JOHN I'll kill thee and[675] thou bid me pray for him.
I'll fell woods, and ring thee round with fire,

665 3 Sure: surely
666 10 mate: man, friend (said ironically)
667 11 my counterfeit: the hermit I impersonated
668 14 I'll bum, I'll mark you: I'll beat you, I'll leave my mark on you
669 16 I am for him: I'm prepared to fight him
670 16 Robin Goodfellow: legendary fairy
671 18 *genii*: attendant spirits
672 20 but suspiciously: with nothing but suspicion
673 31 felt us: knew we were coming
674 37 beguiled: cheated
675 40 and: if

Make thee an offering unto fierce revenge,
If thou have but a thought to pray for him.
GLOUCESTER I am bound to pray for all men, chiefly Christians.
JOHN Ha ha! For Christians? Think'st thou he is one?
For men: hast thou opinion he is a man?
He that changes himself to sundry shapes,
Is he a Christian? Can he be a man?
Oh, irreligious thoughts!
GLOUCESTER Why, worthy prince,
I saw him christened, dipped into the font.
JOHN Then nine times, like the northern Laplanders,
He backward circlèd the sacred font;
And nine times backward said his orisons;[676]
As often cursed the glorious host of heaven
As many times invoked the fiends of hell;
And so turned witch, for Gloucester is a witch.
GLOUCESTER Have patience, gentle prince, he shall appear
Before your kingly father speedily.
JOHN Shall he indeed? Sweet comfort kiss thy cheek;
Peace circle in[677] thy agèd, honored head.
When he is taken, hermit, I protest,
I'll build thee up a chapel and a shrine.
I'll have thee worshipped as a man divine.
Assure he shall come, and Skink shall come.
FAUCONBRIDGE Ay, that same Skink. I prithee send that Skink.
JOHN Send both, and both as prisoners criminate[678]
Shall forfeit their last lives to England's state.
Which way will Fauconbridge?
FAUCONBRIDGE Over the water,
And so, with all speed I may to Stepney.
JOHN I must to Stepney, too, and revel, and be blithe.
Old, wink at my mirth; 't'may make amends,
So thou, and I, and our friends, may be friends.
FAUCONBRIDGE With all my heart, with all my heart, prince.
Old Fauconbridge will wait upon your grace.
Be good to Gloucester for my Marian's sake,
And me and mine you shall your servants make.
GLOUCESTER Of that anon; my pleasure being served,[679]
Gloucester shall have what Gloucester hath deserved.
FAUCONBRIDGE Why, that's well said. Adieu, good honest hermit. *Exit*
JOHN Hermit, farewell. If I had my desire,
I'll make the world thy wondrous deeds admire. *Exit*
GLOUCESTER Still good, still passing good. Gloucester is still
Henry's true hate, foe to John's froward[680] will.
No more of that; for them in better time.
If this same hermit[681] be an honest man,
He will protect me by this simple life.
If not, I care not; I'll be ever Gloucester,

676 51–3 Then nine … his orisons: there is no known source for the image of Laplanders (inhabitants of northern Scandinavia) circling the font backwards, though the reversal of prayers was a common element to ideas of witchcraft in the period
677 60 circle in: enclose
678 66 prisoners criminate: accused prisoners
679 77 my pleasure being served: if I have my way
680 83 froward: perverse, evil
681 85 same hermit: i.e. the hermit he impersonates

Make him my foot stool if he be a slave,[682]
For baseness over worth can have no power.
Robin,[683] bethink thee, thou art come[684] from kings;
Then scorn to be slave to underlings.
Look well about thee,[685] lad, and thou shalt see
Them burst in envy that would injure thee.
Hermit, I'll meet you in your hermit's gown.
Honest,[686] I'll love you; worse, I'll knock you down.

Exit

Scene xiv

Enter PRINCE RICHARD *with music*

RICHARD Kind friends, we have troubled Lady Fauconbridge,
And either she's not willing to be seen,
Or else not well, or with our boldness grieved.
To ease these, I have brought you to this window,
Knowing you are in music excellent.
I have penned a ditty here, and I desire
You would sing it for her love and my content.
MUSICIAN With all my heart, my lord.

Enter ROBIN HOOD *like the* LADY [FAUCONBRIDGE]

ROBERT Your excellence forgets your princely worth.
If I may humbly crave it at your hands,
Let me desire this music be dismissed.
RICHARD Forbear, I pray, and withdraw yourselves. *Exeunt Music*
Be not offended, gracious Marian.
Under the upper heaven, nine goodly spheres
Turn with a motion ever musical.[687]
In palaces of kings, melodious sounds
Offer pleasures to their sovereign's ears.
In temples, milk-white clothèd choristers
Sing sacred anthems, bowing to the shrine,
And in the fields whole choirs of wingèd clerks[688]
Salutes the morning bright and crystalline.[689]
Then blame not me. You are my heaven, my queen,
My saint, my comfort, brighter than the morn.
To you, all music and all praise is due.
For you delight, you for delight was born.[690]
The world would have no mirth, no joy, no day,
If from the world your beauty were away.
ROBERT Fie on love's blasphemy and forgery!
To call that in,[691] that's only misery?

682 88 slave: villain
683 90 Robin: i.e. Robert (Gloucester speaks to himself)
684 90 come: descended
685 92 Look well about thee: be careful
686 95 Honest: if you're honest
687 14–15 nine goodly . . . ever musical: the music of the spheres, allegedly the product of the cosmos moving in perfect harmony
688 20 wingèd clerks: birds, here imagined as "clerks" or clergymen
689 21 crystalline: clear, unsullied
690 25 Delight was made for you and you were made for delight
691 29 call that in: obscure, possibly a compression of "call that in question"

I, that am wedded to suspicious age,[692]
Solicited by your lascivious youth?
I, that have one poor comfort living,
Gloucester, my brother, my high-hearted[693] brother?
He flies for fear, lest he should faint and fall
Into the hands of hate tyrannical.
RICHARD What would you I should do?
ROBERT I would full fain
My brother Gloucester had his peace again.
RICHARD Shall love be my reward if I do bring
A certain token of his good estate,
And after pacify my brothers' wrath?
Say you'll love; we'll be fortunate.[694]
ROBERT I will.
RICHARD No more. I vow to die unblessed
If I perform not this imposèd quest.
But one word, madam, pray can you tell,
Where Huntington my ward is?
ROBERT I was bold[695]
To send young Robin Hood, your noble ward,
Upon some business of import for me.
RICHARD I am glad he is employed in your affairs.
Farewell, kind fair; let not one cloudy frown[696]
Shadow the bright sun of thy beauty's light.
Be confident in this: I'll find thy brother,
Raise power but we'll have peace.[697] Only perform
Your gracious promise at my back return.[698]
ROBERT Well, here's my hand. Prince Richard, that same night
Which secondeth[699] the day of your return
I'll be your bedfellow, and from that hour
Forswear the loathèd bed of Fauconbridge.
Be speedy, therefore, as you hope to speed.[700]
RICHARD Oh, that I were as large-winged as the wind
Then should you see my expeditious will![701]
My most desire, adieu, guess by my haste
Of your sweet promise the delicious taste.[702] *Exit*
ROBERT Why so: I am rid of him by this device.
He would else have tired me with his sighs and songs,

Enter BLOCK [*and* LADY FAUCONBRIDGE *in merchant's wife's attire*]

But now I shall have ease. Here comes the saint
To whom such suit was made.

692 30 suspicious age: a jealous old husband
693 33 high-hearted: passionate, brave
694 41 we'll be fortunate: our love will be blessed; "we'll" is possibly a misprint for "he'll"
695 45 I was bold: I took the liberty
696 49 In the 1600 text, this line reads "Farewell, kind fair; let one cloudy frown"
697 52 Raise power . . . have peace: we'll have peace even if I have to raise an army to secure your brother
698 53 at my back return: when I return
699 55 secondeth: follows
700 58 speed: succeed
701 60 expeditious: swift
702 61–2 guess by . . . delicious taste: i.e. judge by how quickly I bring news of Gloucester how fervently I desire you

BLOCK [*To* LADY FAUCONBRIDGE] My lady gentlewoman is even here in her privity[703] walk. [*To* ROBERT] Madam, here's the merchant's wife was here[704] yesterday would speak with ye. Oh, I was somewhat bold to bring her in.
ROBERT Well, leave us, sir. Y'are welcome, gentlewoman.
BLOCK These women have no liberality in the world in them.[705] I never let in man to my lady, but I am rewarded.
ROBERT Please ye to walk, sir? Wherefore mumble ye? [*Exit* BLOCK]
LADY FAUCONBRIDGE Robin, what news? How hast thou done this night?
ROBERT My ladyship hath done my part, my task,
Lain all alone for lack of company.
I might have had Prince Richard.
LADY FAUCONBRIDGE Was he here?
ROBERT He went away but now.
I have been loved and wooed too simply.
God rid me of the woman once again;[706]
I'll not be tempted so for all the world.
Come, will you to your chamber and uncase?[707]
LADY FAUCONBRIDGE Nay, keep my habit[708] yet a little while.
Old Fauconbridge is almost at the gate.
I met him at Blackheath, just at the hermit's,
And, taking me to be a merchant's wife,
Fell mightily in love, gave me his ring,
Made me protest that I would meet him here.
I told him of his lady. "Oh, tut," quoth he,
"I'll shake her up,[709] I'll pack her out of sight."
He comes! Kind Robin Hood, hold up the jest.

Enter Sir RICHARD FAUCONBRIDGE *and* BLOCK

FAUCONBRIDGE God's Mary, knave, how long hath she been here?
BLOCK Sir, she came but even in afore you.
FAUCONBRIDGE A cunning quean,[710] a very cunning quean.
Go to your business, Block, I'll meet with her.
BLOCK [*Aside*] Ah, old mutton-monger,[711] I believe here's work towards.[712] *Exit*
FAUCONBRIDGE [*To* ROBERT] Do not believe her, Mall, do not believe her.
I only spake a word or two in jest,
But would not for the world have been so mad.[713]
Do not believe her, Mall, do not believe her.
ROBERT What should I not believe? What do you mean?
LADY FAUCONBRIDGE Why, good Sir Richard, let me speak with you.
[*To* FAUCONBRIDGE] Alas, will you undo me? Will you shame me?
Is this your promise? Came I here for this?
To be a laughing-stock unto your lady?
ROBERT How now, Sir Richard, what's the matter there?

703 67 privity: private
704 68 was here: who was here
705 71 These women . . . in them: i.e. women don't tip
706 80 Let me not play a woman any longer
707 82 uncase: undress
708 83 habit: clothing
709 90 up: off
710 94 quean: strumpet
711 96 mutton-monger: lecher; "mutton" was slang for a prostitute or a promiscuous woman
712 96 work towards: trouble brewing
713 99 so mad: i.e. as to have solicited her

FAUCONBRIDGE [*To* ROBERT] I'll talk with you anon. [*To* LADY FAUCONBRIDGE]
Come hither, woman.
Didst not tell my wife what match we made?
LADY FAUCONBRIDGE I, tell your wife? Think ye I am such a beast?
Now, God forgive ye, I am quite undone.
FAUCONBRIDGE Peace duck,[714] peace duck. I warrant all is well.
ROBERT What's the matter? I pray ye, Sir Richard, tell me?
FAUCONBRIDGE Marry, Mall, thus: about some twelve months since,
Your brother Gloucester, that mad prodigal,[715]
Caused me to pass my word unto[716] her husband
For some two thousand pound—or more, perchance—
No matter what it is, you shall not know;
Nay, ye shall never ask to know.
ROBERT And what of this?
FAUCONBRIDGE Marry, the man's decayed,[717]
And I believe a little thing would please her,
A very little thing, a thing of nothing.[718]
Go in, good Mall, and leave us two alone.
I'll deal with ye as simply as I can.[719]
LADY FAUCONBRIDGE [*Aside*] Fox, look about ye; ye are caught i'faith.
ROBERT Deal with her simply? Oh ho, what kind of dealing?
Can ye not deal with her and I be by?[720]
FAUCONBRIDGE Marry a God, what are ye jealous?
Ye teach me what to do.[721] In, get you in.
Oh, I have heard Prince Richard was your guest.
How dealt you then? In, get you in, I say!
Must I take care about your brother's debts
And you stand crossing[722] me? In, or I'll send you in! *Exit* ROBIN
Ha, sirrah, you'll be master;[723] you'll wear the yellow;[724]
You'll be an overseer. Marry, shall ye?
LADY FAUCONBRIDGE Ye are too curst[725] (methinks, sir) to your lady.
FAUCONBRIDGE Ah, wench, content thee. I must bear her hard,[726]
Else she'll be prying into my dalliances.
I am an old man, sweet girl; I must be merry:
All steel, all sprite, keep in health by change,[727]
Men may be wanton, women must not range.
LADY FAUCONBRIDGE You have given good counsel, sir. I'll repent me,
Here's your ring. I'll only love my husband.
FAUCONBRIDGE I mean not so! I think today thou told me
Thy husband was an unthrift and a bankrupt.
And he be so, tut, thou hast favor store.[728]

714 111 duck: term of endearment
715 114 prodigal: spendthrift
716 115 pass my word unto: stand as surety for
717 119 decayed: ruined
718 120–21 little thing . . . of nothing: a trivial amount of money, with a play on "thing" as penis and "nothing" as vagina
719 123 This line is addressed to the disguised Lady Fauconbridge. "Simply" means "straightforwardly" or "honestly"
720 126 and I be by: with me here
721 128 what to do: how to behave
722 132 crossing: quarreling with
723 133 Sirrah, you'll be master: Fauconbridge sarcastically addresses his "wife" as though she were a male servant who would give orders
724 133: wear the yellow: yellow was often associated with jealousy, but in this instance seems to be associated with authority
725 135 curst: cruel
726 136 bear her hard: deal with her firmly
727 139 change: variety (of women)
728 145 favor store: permission stored up

Let the knave beg; beauty cannot be poor.
LADY FAUCONBRIDGE Indeed my husband is a bankrupt,
Of faith, of love, of shame, of chastity,
Dotes upon other women more than me.
FAUCONBRIDGE Ha, do he so? Then give him tit for tat.
Have one so young and fair and loves another?
He's worthy to be cuckolded, by the mass.
What is he, old or young?
LADY FAUCONBRIDGE About your age.
FAUCONBRIDGE An old knave and cannot be content with such a peat?[729]
Come to my closet,[730] girl, make much of me.
We'll appoint a meeting place some twice a week,
And I'll maintain thee like a lady, ha?
LADY FAUCONBRIDGE Oh, but you'll forget me presently,
When you look well upon your lady's beauty.
FAUCONBRIDGE Who? Upon her? Why she is a very dowdy,[731]
A dishcloth, a foul gypsy unto thee!
Come to my closet, lass; there take thy earnest[732]
Of love, of pleasure, and good maintenance.
LADY FAUCONBRIDGE I am very fearful.
FAUCONBRIDGE Come, fool, never fear.
I am lord here; who shall disturb us, then?
Nay come, or by the rood, I'll make you come,
LADY FAUCONBRIDGE Help, Madam Fauconbridge, for God's sake!

Enter ROBIN HOOD *and* BLOCK

FAUCONBRIDGE How now, what mean'st?[733]
LADY FAUCONBRIDGE Help, gentle madam, help!
ROBERT How now, what ail'st thou?
BLOCK Nay, and't be a woman, ne'er fear my master, madam.[734]
ROBERT Why speakst thou not? What ail'st thou?
FAUCONBRIDGE Why, nothing, by the rood, nothing she ails.
LADY FAUCONBRIDGE Oh madam, this vile man would have abused me, and forced me to his closet.
ROBERT [*Aside*] Ah, old cole,[735] now look about, you are catched.
LADY FAUCONBRIDGE Call in your fellows, Block.[736]
FAUCONBRIDGE Do not, thou knave!
LADY FAUCONBRIDGE Do, or I'll crack your crown.
BLOCK Nay, I'll do't. I know she means to shame you. *Exit*
FAUCONBRIDGE Why, Mall, wilt thou believe this paltry woman?
Huswife,[737] I'll have you whipped for slandering me.
ROBERT What, lecher? No, she is an honest woman,
Her husband's well known, all the household knows.[738]

729 154 peat: term of endearment for a young girl or woman
730 155 closet: bed chamber
731 160 dowdy: shabbily dressed woman
732 162 earnest: first installment
733 168 what mean'st: what are you doing
734 171 If you're a woman, my master is no threat (possibly an impotency joke)
735 176 cole: deceiver, cheater
736 177 Call in your fellows, Block: Lady Fauconbridge's disguise as the "merchant's wife" seems briefly to slip here as she addresses Block as her servant (which, of course, he is)
737 181 Huswife: housewife, hussy—a derogatory term for a woman
738 183 knows: i.e. that Fauconbridge is a lecher

[*Enter* BLOCK *and Servants*]

BLOCK Here's some now, to tell all the town your mind.[739]
LADY FAUCONBRIDGE Before ye all, I must sure complain.
You see this wicked man, and ye all know
How oft he hath been jealous of my life,
Suspecting falsehood, being false himself.
BLOCK Oh, master! Oh, master!
FAUCONBRIDGE She slanders me! She is a cozening quean!
Fetch me the constable; I'll have her punished.
LADY FAUCONBRIDGE The constable for me? Fie, fie upon ye!
Madam, do you know this ring?
ROBERT It is Sir Richard's.
BLOCK Oh, ay, that's my master's, too sure.
FAUCONBRIDGE Ay, marry, I did lend it to the false drab[740]
To fetch some money for that bankrupt knave,
Her husband, that lies prisoner in the Fleet.
LADY FAUCONBRIDGE My husband bankrupt? My husband in the Fleet, prisoner? No, no, he is as good a man as you.
ROBERT Ay, that he is, and can spend pound for pound
With thee, i'faith, wert richer[741] than thou art.
I know the gentleman.
LADY FAUCONBRIDGE Nay, madam, he is hard by.[742]
There must be revels at the Hind to night.
Your copesmate's there, Prince John.
ROBERT There's a hot youth.
BLOCK Oh, a fierce gentleman.
LADY FAUCONBRIDGE He was fierce as you, but I have matched him.[743]
The princess[744] shall be there in my attire.
FAUCONBRIDGE A plaguey,[745] crafty quean, marry a God.
I see Prince John courted as well as I,
And since he shall be mocked as well as I
It's some contentment.
BLOCK Mass, he droops. Fellow Humphrey, he is almost taken.[746] Look about ye, old Richard?
FAUCONBRIDGE Hence knaves, get in a little. Prithee, Mall,
Let thou, and I, and she shut up this matter.
ROBERT Away sirs, get in.
BLOCK Come, come let's go. He will be baited[747] now. Farewell, old Richard. *Exit* [*with Servants*]
ROBERT Now, sir, what say you now?
FAUCONBRIDGE Marry, sweet Mall,
I say I met this woman, liked her, loved her,
For she is worthy love, I promise thee.
I say I courted her. Tut, make no brawl
'Twixt thou and I. We'll have amends for all.
ROBERT Had I done such a trick, what then? What then?

739 184 to tell . . . your mind: i.e. servants who will spread gossip about the town
740 196 drab: slattern, prostitute
741 202 wert richer: were you richer
742 204 hard by: close by
743 208 He pursued me as hotly as you did, but I've fooled him as well
744 209 princess: Princess Isabel, John's wife
745 210 plaguey: annoying (one who plagues)
746 214 taken: caught
747 218 baited: tormented, like a bear tied to a stake and attacked by dogs

FAUCONBRIDGE Ah, prithee Mall, tut, bear with men.
ROBERT Ay, we must bear with you. You'll be excused,
When women undeservèd are abused.
FAUCONBRIDGE Nay, do not weep; pardon me, gentle lady.
I know thee virtuous, and I do protest
Never to have an evil thought of thee.
ROBERT Ay, ay, ye swear. Who's that that will believe ye?
FAUCONBRIDGE Now, by my holydam and honest faith,
This gentlewoman shall witness what I swear.
Sweet duck a little help me?
LADY FAUCONBRIDGE Trust him, madam.
FAUCONBRIDGE I will be kind, credulous,[748] constant ever;
Do what thou wilt, I'll be suspicious never.
ROBERT For which I thank noble Fauconbridge. [ROBERT *doffs his disguise*]
FAUCONBRIDGE Body of me! Who's this? Young Huntington?
LADY FAUCONBRIDGE And I your lady, whom you courted last.[749]
Ye looked about you ill, fox; we have caught ye.
I met ye at Blackheath, and ye were hot.[750]
FAUCONBRIDGE I knew thee, Mall; now, by my sword, I knew thee.
I winked at all;[751] I laughed at every jest.
ROBERT Ay, he did wink. The blind man had an eye.
FAUCONBRIDGE Peace, Robin, thou't once be a man as I.[752]
LADY FAUCONBRIDGE Well, I must bear it all.
FAUCONBRIDGE Come, and ye bear, it's but your office.[753] Come, forget, sweet Mall.
LADY FAUCONBRIDGE I do forgive it, and forget it, sir.
FAUCONBRIDGE Why, that's well said. That's done like a good girl.
Ha, sirrah, ha you matched me, pretty earl?
ROBERT I have, ye see sir; I must unto Blackheath
In quest of Richard, whom I sent to seek
Earl Gloucester out. I know he's at the hermit's.
Lend me your coach; I'll shift me[754] as I ride.
Farewell, Sir Richard. *Exit*
FAUCONBRIDGE Farewell, England's pride!
By the matins,[755] Mall, it[756] is a pretty child.
Shall we go meet John? Shall we go mock the prince?
LADY FAUCONBRIDGE We will.
FAUCONBRIDGE Oh, then we shall have sport anon.
Never wear yellow,[757] Mall; 'twas but a trick.
Old Fauconbridge will still be a mad Dick.[758]
Exeunt

[Scene xv]

Enter REDCAP *and* GLOUCESTER [*disguised as the hermit*]

748 235 credulous: inclined to believe you
749 239 last: recently
750 241 hot: i.e. in your pursuit of me
751 243 winked at all: played along
752 245 thou't once . . . as I: you'll be a man like me someday
753 247 and ye . . . your office: putting up with me is your job (as bearing children is women's work)
754 254 shift me: change clothes
755 256 matins: morning prayers
756 256 it: he, Robin Hood
757 259 wear yellow: be jealous (but see line 132)
758 260 mad Dick: crazy Richard

REDCAP Do ye s s say, fa fa father hermit, th that Gl Gloucester is about this heath?
GLOUCESTER He is upon this heath, son, look about it.
Run but the compass, thou shalt find him out,
REDCAP R r run? I'll r run the co compass of all K Kent but I'll f find him out, my f f father (where'er he lays his head), dare ne never co come home, I know, t t till he be fo fo found.
GLOUCESTER Well, thou shalt find him. Knowst thou who's a hunting?
REDCAP M m marry, 'tis the Earls of La La Lancaster and Le Leicester. Fa fa farewell, f father, and I find Skink or Glo Gloucester, I'll g g give thee the pr prize of a penny p p pudding[759] for thy p pains. [*Exit*]
GLOUCESTER Adieu, good friend. This is sure the fellow
I sent on message from the parliament,
The porter's son. He's still in quest of me
And Skink, that cozened him of his red cap.

Enter [PRINCE] RICHARD *like a serving man*

But look about thee, Gloucester; who comes yonder?
Oh, a plain servingman, and yet perhaps
His bags are lined,[760] and my purse now grows thin.
If he have any, I must share with him.

Enter SKINK *like a hermit*

And who's on yond side? Oh, it is my hermit,
Hath got his other suit[761] since I went forth.
SKINK 'Sblood, yonder's company. I'll back again,
Else I would be with you, counterfeit.[762]
I'll leave the rogue till opportunity,[763]
But never eat till I have quit my wrong. *Exit*
RICHARD I saw two men attend like holy hermits;
One's slipped away, the other at his beads.[764]
Now, Richard, for the love of Marian,
Make thy inquiry where mad Gloucester lives.
If England or the verge of Scotland hold him,
I'll seek him thus disguised. If he be passed
To any foreign part, I'll follow him.
Love, thou art lord of hearts, thy laws are sweet;
In every troubled way thou guide'st our feet.
Lovers, enjoined to pass the dangerous sea
Of big-swoll'n sorrow in the bark "Affection,"[765]
The winds and waves of woe need never fear,
While love the helm doth, like a pilot, steer.[766]
GLOUCESTER Here's some lover come; a mischief on him.[767]
I know not how to answer these mad fools,

759 8 pr prize ... p pudding: it was customary to place a coin in a Christmas pudding, the discovery of which conferred good fortune on the finder. Redcap offers Gloucester this "prize"
760 16 lined: i.e. with money
761 19 suit: hermit gown
762 21 counterfeit: i.e. the other, "counterfeit" hermit (ironic since Skink is also counterfeiting)
763 22 till opportunity: i.e. until the opportunity presents itself
764 25 at his beads: counting his rosary
765 34 bark "Affection": a ship named "Affection"
766 33–6 Lovers, enjoined ... pilot, steer: lovers need not fear woe, as long as love guides their course
767 37 a mischief on him: may trouble come to him

But I'll be brief; I'll mar the hermit's tale.[768]
Off gown, hold buckler, slice it bilbo blade.[769]
RICHARD What's this? What should this mean? Old man, good friend!
GLOUCESTER Young fool, deliver, else see your end.
RICHARD I thought thou hadst been holy and a hermit?
GLOUCESTER Whate'er you thought, your purse! Come, quickly sir!
Cast that upon the ground and then confer.[770]
RICHARD There it is.
GLOUCESTER Falls it so heavy? Then my heart is light.
RICHARD Thou't have a heavy heart before thou touch it.
Theft shrined in holy weeds? Stand to't,[771] y'are best.
GLOUCESTER And if I do not, seeing such a prey,
Let this be to me a disaster day. *Fight and part once or twice*
RICHARD Art thou content to breathe?[772]
GLOUCESTER With all my heart.
Take half thy money and we'll friendly part.[773]
RICHARD I will not cherish[774] theft.
GLOUCESTER Then I defy thee. *Fight again and breathe*
RICHARD Alas, for pity, that so stout[775] a man,
So reverend in aspect, should take this course.[776]
GLOUCESTER This is no common man with whom I fight,
And, if he be, he is of wondrous sprite.[777]
Shall we part stakes?[778]
RICHARD Fellow, take the purse,
Upon condition thou wilt follow me.
GLOUCESTER What, wait on you? Wear a turned livery?[779]
Whose man's your master? If I be your man,
My man's man's office will be excellent.[780]
There lies your purse again; win it and wear it.[781] *Fight*

Enter ROBIN HOOD

They breathe, offer again

ROBERT Clashing of weapons at my welcome hither?
Bickering upon Blackheath? Well said, old man,
I'll take thy side; the younger hath the odds.[782]
Stay, end your quarrel, or I promise ye
I'll take the old man's part.
RICHARD You were not wont.[783]
Young Huntington, be still on Richard's side.

768 39 mar the hermit's tale: i.e. curtail the hermit's story, end my impersonation
769 40 Gloucester doffs his gown, and readies his shield ("buckler") and knife ("bilbo blade") for an assault
770 45 Throw your purse on the ground and then we can talk
771 49 Stand to't: prepare to fight
772 52 breathe: pause and catch their breath
773 53 friendly part: part on friendly terms
774 54 cherish: encourage
775 55 stout: brave
776 56 take this course: turn to robbery
777 58 sprite: spirit
778 59 part stakes: divide the money
779 61 turned livery: in the sense of a "turncoat," i.e. Gloucester would be a traitor to his birth by becoming another's servant
780 62–3 Whose man's … be excellent: Gloucester laughs sarcastically at the idea of serving a servingman, and says that if he were to take on such a position it would be an insult to his own servingman ("My man's man")
781 64 win it and wear it: if you want it, you're going to have to work for it (proverbial)
782 67 the odds: the advantage
783 69 wont: accustomed to (fight against me)

ROBERT Pardon, gracious prince, I knew ye not.
GLOUCESTER Prince Richard? Then lie envy at his foot.[784]
Pardon thy cousin Gloucester, valiant lord;
I knew no common force confronted mine.
RICHARD Oh, heaven, I had the like conceit of thine.[785]
I tell thee, Robin, Gloucester, thou art met,
Bringing such comfort unto Richard's heart
As in the foil[786] of war, when dust and sweat,
The thirst of weak,[787] and the sun's fiery heat
Have seized upon the soul of valiance,[788]
And he must faint except[789] he be refreshed.
To me thou com'st as if to him should come
A perry[790] from the north, whose frosty breath
Might fan him coolness in that doubt[791] of death.
With me then meets as he a spring might meet,
Cooling the earth under his toil-parched feet,
Whose crystal moisture in his helmet ta'en,
Comforts his spirits, makes him strong again.
GLOUCESTER Prince, in short terms, if you have brought me comfort,
Know, if I had my pardon in this hand
That smit[792] base Skink in open parliament,
I would not come to court till the high feast
Of your proud brother's birthday be expired.
For as[793] the old king, as he made a vow
At his unlucky coronation,
Must wait upon the boy and fill his cup,
And all the peers must kneel while Henry kneels
Unto his cradle,[794] he shall hang me up
Ere I commit that vile idolatry.[795]
But when the feast is past, if you'll befriend me,
I'll come and brave[796] my proud foes to their teeth.
RICHARD Come, Robin, and if my brothers grace deny,[797]
I'll take thy part, them and their threats defy.
GLOUCESTER Gramercy,[798] princely Dick.
ROBERT I have some power;
I can raise two thousand soldiers in an hour.
GLOUCESTER Gramercy, Robin; gramercy, little wag.
Prince Richard, pray let Huntington
Carry my sister Fauconbridge this ring.
RICHARD I'll carry it myself, but I had rather

784 72 lie envy at his foot: I'll place my anger at his foot, i.e. submit to him
785 75 I had . . . of thine: I thought the same about your strength
786 78 foil: repulse, setback (possibly a misprint for "toil")
787 79 of weak: from weakness
788 80 valiance: valor
789 81 except: unless
790 83 perry: a blast of wind
791 84 doubt: fear
792 91 smit: smote, struck
793 94 For as: because
794 98 his cradle: i.e. the young King Henry
795 99 idolatry: i.e. kneeling to the young king
796 101 brave: defy, challenge
797 102 deny: deny you
798 104 Gramercy: thank you

Had thy kind company. Thou might'st have moved[799]
Thy sister, whom I long have vainly loved.
GLOUCESTER I like her that she shuns temptation,
Prince Richard, but I bear with doting lovers.
I should not take it well that you urge me
To such an office, but I bear with you.
Love's blind and mad. Hie[800] to her boldly; try her.
But if I know she yield, faith, I'll defy her.
RICHARD I like thy honorable resolution,
Gloucester; I pray thee pardon my entreat.[801]
GLOUCESTER It's men's custom. Part, part, gentle prince.
Farewell, good Robin. This gold[802] I will borrow,
Meet you at Stepney, pay you all tomorrow.
ROBERT Adieu, Gloucester.
GLOUCESTER Farewell, be short.[803] You gone, I hope to have a little sport.
RICHARD Take heed, mad coz.[804] *Exeunt* [ROBERT *and* RICHARD]
GLOUCESTER Tut, tell not me of heed,
He that's too wary never hath good speed.

Hallowing within.[805] *Enter* LANCASTER *with a broken staff in his hand*

Whose this? Old Lancaster, my honored friend?
LANCASTER These knaves have served me well,[806] left me alone.
I have hunted fairly, lost my purse, my chain,
My jewels, and been banged[807] by a bold knave
Clad in a hermit's gown like an old man.
Oh, what a world is this?
GLOUCESTER It's ill my lord.
LANCASTER [*Spies* GLOUCESTER] He's come again![808] Oh, knave, 'tis the worse for thee!
Keep from me! Be content with that thou hast[809]
And see thou fly this heath, for, if I take thee,
I'll make thee to all thieves a spectacle.[810]
Had my staff held, thou hadst not scaped me so.
But come not near me; follow not, thou art best.[811]
Holla, Earl Leicester? Holla, huntsman, ho?
GLOUCESTER Upon my life, old Lancaster a-hunting
Hath met my fellow hermit. Could I meet him,
I'd play rob-thief, at least part stakes with him.

[*Enter* SKINK]

SKINK Zounds! He is yonder, alone.
Skink, now revenge thy self on yonder slave.

799 110 moved: petitioned
800 116 Hie: go, hurry
801 119 entreat: entreaty
802 121 This gold: i.e. the purse over which they were fighting
803 124 be short: be brief in your goodbyes
804 125 Take heed, mad coz: be careful, my crazy cousin
805 126 SD *Hallowing within*: offstage shouting
806 128 served me well: sarcastic, done me a good turn
807 130 banged: beaten
808 133 He's come again: Lancaster mistakes Gloucester for the hermit who's beaten him
809 134 that thou hast: i.e. what you've already stolen from me
810 136 a spectacle: an example
811 138 follow not, thou art best: you'd best not follow me

Enter REDCAP *with a cudgel*

'Snails,[812] still prevented? This same Redcap rogue
Runs like hobgoblin[813] up and down the heath.
REDCAP Wh wh wh whoop, he hermit! Ye ha ha ma ma made Re Redcap run a fine co co compass, ha have you not?
SKINK I made thee run?
GLOUCESTER Yonder's my evil angel. Were Redcap gone, Gloucester would conjure him.[814]
REDCAP Je Je Jesus bl bless me! Whoop! To two hermits? I'll ca ca clapperclaw[815] to to t'one of ye for mo mo mocking me, and I d d do not, ha ha hang me. Wh wh which is the fa fa false k k k knave? For I am s s sure the old he he hermit wo would never mo mock an honest man.
GLOUCESTER He is the counterfeit. He mocked thee, fellow.
I did not see thee in my life before.
He wears my garments and has cozened me.
REDCAP Have you co co cozened the he hermit and m made Redcap run to no pu pu purpose?
SKINK No, he's counterfeit; I will tell no lies.
As sure as Skink deceived thee of thy clothes,
Sent thee to Kent, gave thee thy fare by water,
So sure he's false and I the perfect[816] hermit,
GLOUCESTER This villain is a conjurer, I doubt.[817]
Were he the devil, yet I would not budge.
REDCAP Si si sirrah, you are the co counterfeit. Oh, this is the tr tr true he hermit. Sta sta stand still g good man, at that. I'll bu bumbaste[818] you I'faith. I'll make you g give the old m m man his gown. *Offers to strike,* GLOUCESTER *trips up his heels, shifts* SKINK *into his place*
G g god's lid,[819] are ye go good at that? I'll cu cudgel ye f f for this tr tr trick.
SKINK It was not I. 'Twas he that cast thee down.
REDCAP You li li li lie, you ra ra rascal you. I le left ye st standing he here.
SKINK Zounds! Hold you stammerer, or I'll cut your stumps.
GLOUCESTER [*Aside*] He's for me. He's weaponed. I like that.
REDCAP Oh, here's a ro ro rogue in ca ca carnate.[820] Help, mu murder murder!

Enter LANCASTER *and huntsmen at one door,* LEICESTER *and huntsmen at another*

LANCASTER Lay hold upon that thievish counterfeit.
LEICESTER Why, here's another hermit, Lancaster.
GLOUCESTER I am the hermit, sir; that wretched man
Doth many a robbery in my disguise.
SKINK It's he that robs. He slanders me. He lies.
LANCASTER Which set on thee?
REDCAP Th this f f fellow has a s s sword and a buckler.
LANCASTER Search him. This is the thief. Oh, here's my purse,
My chain, my jewels! Oh, thou wicked wretch,
How dar'st thou, under show of holiness,
Commit such actions of impiety?

812 145 'Snails: by God's nails
813 146 hobgoblin: a mischievous spirit
814 150–51 conjure him: beat him away
815 152 clapperclaw: scratch or claw
816 163 perfect: genuine
817 164 doubt: fear
818 167 bumbaste: beat you on the bottom
819 169 G g god's lid: by God's eyelid
820 174 in ca ca carnate: incarnate, in the flesh

Bind him; I'll have him made a public scorn.[821]
SKINK Lay hold upon that other hermit.
He is a counterfeit as well as I.
He stole those clothes from me, for I am Skink.
Search him. I know him not. He is some slave.
GLOUCESTER Thou liest, base varlet.
REDCAP Oh, G God! He has a sword too! S Skink, are you ca catched?[822]
LANCASTER Villain, thou shalt with me unto the court.
LEICESTER And this[823] with me. This is the traitor Gloucester.
GLOUCESTER Thou liest, proud Leicester, I am no traitor.
REDCAP G Gloucester? Oh, b brave![824] Now m my father sh shall be f free.
LANCASTER Earl Gloucester, I am sorry thou art taken.
GLOUCESTER I am not taken yet, nor will I yield
To any here but noble Lancaster.
Let Skink be Leicester's prisoner; I'll be thine.
LEICESTER Thou shalt be mine.
GLOUCESTER First, through a crimson sluice[825]
I'll send thy hated soul to those black fiends[826]
That long have hovered gaping for their part,[827]
When tyrant life should leave thy traitor heart.
Come, Lancaster, keep Skink; I'll go with thee.
Let loose the mad knave,[828] for I praise his shifts.[829]
He shall not start away; I'll be his guide,[830]
And with proud looks outface young Henry's pride.
LEICESTER Look to them Lancaster, upon thy life.
REDCAP Well I'll r r run and get a p pardon of the k k k king. Gl Gloucester and Skink ta ta taken? Oh, b b brave! R r r run Re Re Red ca cap, a and ca ca carry the first n n news to co co court.
LEICESTER Lancaster, I'll help to guard them to the court.
LANCASTER Do as you please.
GLOUCESTER Leicester, do not come near me,
For, if thou do, thou shalt buy it[831] dearly.
LEICESTER I'll have thy hand for this.
GLOUCESTER Not for thy heart.
SKINK Brave earl, had Skink known thou hadst been the noble Gloucester (whose mad tricks have made me love thee), I would have dyed Blackheath red with the blood of millions ere we would have been taken. But what remedy? We are fast[832] and must answer it like gentlemen, like soldiers, like resolutes.
GLOUCESTER Ay, ye are a gallant. Come, old Lancaster,
For thy sake will I go, or else, by heaven,
I'd send some dozen of these slaves to hell.

Exeunt

821 186 scorn: spectacle
822 192 catched: caught
823 194 this: this hermit
824 196 brave: excellent, wonderful
825 201 crimson sluice: spout of blood
826 202 black fiends: devils
827 203 part: share
828 206 mad knave: Skink
829 206 shifts: tricks, devices
830 207 guide: keeper
831 215 buy it: pay for it
832 219 fast: bound, arrested

[Scene xvi]

Enter PRINCE RICHARD, ROBERT HOOD, *and* LADY FAUCONBRIDGE

LADY FAUCONBRIDGE Your travail[833] and your comfortable[834] news,
This ring, the certain sign you met with him,[835]
Binds me in duteous[836] love unto your grace.
But on my knees I fall and humbly crave:
Importune that no more you ne'er can have.[837]
RICHARD Nay, then ye wrong me, Lady Fauconbridge.
Did you not join your fair white hands?[838]
Swore that ye would forswear[839] your husband's bed
If I could but find out Gloucester?
LADY FAUCONBRIDGE I swear so?
RICHARD By heaven.
ROBERT Take heed; it's a high[840] oath my lord.
RICHARD What means thou, Huntington?
ROBERT To save your soul.
I do not love to have my friends forsworn.[841]
She never promised that you urge her with.[842]
RICHARD Go to, provoke me not.
ROBERT I tell you true.
'Twas I in her attire that promised you.
She was gone unto the wizard at Blackheath,
And there had suitors more than a good many.
RICHARD Was I deluded then?
LADY FAUCONBRIDGE No, not deluded,
But hindered from desire unchaste and rude.[843]
Oh, let me woo ye with the tongue of ruth,[844]
Dewing[845] your princely hand with pity's tears,
That you would leave this most unlawful suit.
If e'er we live till Fauconbridge be dead
(As God defend his death I should desire),
Then, if your highness deign so base a match—
And holy laws admit a marriage
Considering our affinity in blood[846]—
I will become your handmaid, not your harlot,[847]
That shame shall never dwell upon my brow.
ROBERT I'faith, my lord, she's honorably resolved.[848]
For shame, no more, importune her no more.
RICHARD Marian, I see thy virtue and commend it.

833 1 travail: labor
834 1 comfortable: comforting
835 2 him: Gloucester
836 3 duteous: dutiful
837 5 Importune . . . have: do not plead any longer for something you can never have
838 7 Did you not put your hands together and vow?
839 8 forswear: renounce
840 10 high: holy
841 12 forsworn: perjured
842 13 urge her with: allege she owes you
843 19 rude: coarse
844 20 ruth: sorrow
845 21 Dewing: covering with dew
846 27 affinity in blood: our distant kinship
847 28 handmaid, not your harlot: wife, not mistress
848 30 honorably resolved: resolved to be honorable

I know my error seeking thy dishonor,
But the respectless, reasonless[849] command
Of my inflamèd love bids me still try
And trample under foot all piety.
Yet, for I will not seem too impious,[850]
Too inconsiderate of thy seeming[851] grief,
Vouchsafe to be my mistress.[852] Use me kindly,
And I protest I'll strive with all my power
That lust himself may in his heat devour.[853]
LADY FAUCONBRIDGE You are my servant, then.
RICHARD Thanks, sacred mistress.
ROBERT What am I?
LADY FAUCONBRIDGE You are my fellow,[854] Robert.

Enter FAUCONBRIDGE *in his hose and doublet*[855]

FAUCONBRIDGE What, Prince Richard? Noble Huntington?
Welcome, i'faith, welcome; by the morrow mass
You are come as fitly as my heart can wish.
Prince John this night will be a reveler;
He hath invited me and Marian.
God's Mary mother, go along with us,
It's but hard by, close by, at our town tavern.
RICHARD Your tavern?
FAUCONBRIDGE Oh, ay, ay, ay, 'tis his own made match.[856]
I'll make you laugh; I'll make you laugh i'faith.
Come, come, he's ready; oh, come, come away.
LADY FAUCONBRIDGE But where's the princess?
FAUCONBRIDGE She's ready too.
Block, my man, must be her waiting man.[857]
Nay, will ye go? For God's sake, let us go.
RICHARD Is the jest so? Nay, then, let us away.
ROBERT Oh, 'twill allay his heat, make dead his fire.
FAUCONBRIDGE Ye bobbed[858] me first; ye first gave me my hire.[859]
But come, a God's name, Prince John stays for us.
Exeunt [FAUCONBRIDGE, LADY FAUCONBRIDGE, RICHARD]
ROBERT This is the world: ever at spendthrifts' feasts,[860]
They are gulled[861] themselves, and scoffed at by their guests.
Exit

[Scene xvii]

Enter JOHN [*with Princess Isabel,* FAUCONBRIDGE, LADY FAUCONBRIDGE, RICHARD, ROBERT, *and* BLOCK]

849 34 respectless, reasonless: disrespectful, irrational
850 37 impious: wicked, profane
851 38 seeming: appropriate, seemly
852 39 mistress: honored beloved; without the modern sexual sense
853 40–41 I'll strive . . . heat devour: I'll try hard to smother my lustful desires
854 43 fellow: companion, peer
855 43 SD *hose and doublet*: i.e. not fully dressed, unready
856 51 made match: i.e. he arranged the meeting with the "Merchant's wife" himself
857 55 waiting man: servant
858 59 bobbed: made a fool of
859 59 gave me my hire: paid me for my behavior
860 61 spendthrifts' feasts: wasteful banquets
861 62 gulled: fooled

JOHN Buffled and scoffed![862] Skink, Gloucester, women, fools, and boys abuse me?
I'll be revenged!
RICHARD Revenged? And why, good child?
Old Fauconbridge hath had a worser basting.[863]
FAUCONBRIDGE Ay, they have bandied me from chase to chase;[864]
I have been their tennis ball since I did court.
RICHARD Come, John, take hand with virtuous Isabel
And let's unto the court like loving friends.
Our kingly brother's birthday's festival
Is forthwith[865] to be kept. Thither, we'll hie,
And grace with pomp that great solemnity.
JOHN Whither ye will,[866] I care not where I go.
If grief will grace it, I'll adorn the show.
FAUCONBRIDGE Come, madam, we must thither; we are bound.[867]
LADY FAUCONBRIDGE I am loath[868] to see the court, Gloucester being from thence,
Or kneel to him that gave us this offence.[869]
FAUCONBRIDGE Body of me, peace woman; I prithee, peace.

Enter REDCAP

REDCAP Go Go God ye, Go God s speed ye.
JOHN Whither run you, sir knave?
REDCAP R r run ye, sir knave? Why I r run to my La Lady Fa Fauconbridge to te te tell her Sk Skink and Gl Gloucester is t taken, and are g gone to the c c court with L Lord Leicester, and L Lord La La Lancaster.
JOHN Is Gloucester taken? Thither will I fly
Upon wrath's wings, not quiet[870] till he die! *Exit with Princess* [*Isabel*]
RICHARD Is Gloucester taken?
REDCAP Ay, he is ta taken, I wa warrant ye, with a wi witness.
RICHARD Then will I to court,
And either set him free or die the death.
Follow me, Fauconbridge. Fear not, fair madam.
You said you had the porter in your house;
Some of your servants bring him. On my life,
One hair shall not be taken from his head,
Nor he, nor you, nor Gloucester injurèd.
FAUCONBRIDGE Come, Mall, and Richard say the word, ne'er fear.
ROBERT Madam, we have twenty thousand at our call.
The most young Henry dares is but to brawl.[871]
LADY FAUCONBRIDGE Pray God it prove so.
RICHARD Follow, Huntington.
Sir Richard, do not fail to send the porter.
FAUCONBRIDGE Block, bring the porter of the Fleet to court.
[*Exeunt* FAUCONBRIDGE, LADY FAUCONBRIDGE, RICHARD, and ROBERT]
BLOCK I will sir.

862 1 Buffled and scoffed: made a fool of
863 3 basting: humiliation
864 4 bandied me … to chase: struck, as in a game of tennis. "Chase" is also a (now archaic) tennis term. In Q this line reads "… bandied from chase to chase"
865 9 forthwith: at once
866 11 Whither ye will: Go where you like
867 13 bound: i.e. by duty, with a play on "bound" as in "heading that direction"
868 14 loath: unwilling
869 15 this offence: i.e. the imprisonment of her brother, Gloucester
870 23 quiet: satisfied
871 35 Henry just wants to bicker, not fight

REDCAP The p p porter of the Fl Fl Fleet to court? What p p porter of the Fl Fl Fleet?
BLOCK What, Redcap? Run Redcap. Wilt thou see thy father?
REDCAP My fa father? Ay, that I w would. S see my f father? And there be a p porter in your ho house, it's my f father.
BLOCK Follow me, Redcap, then. *Exit*
REDCAP And you were to to twenty B Blocks, I'd f f follow ye, s so I would, and r run to the co co court too, and k kneel before the k k king f f for his pa pardon.
BLOCK [*Within*] Come away, Redcap! Run Redcap!
REDCAP I I I r r run as f f fast as I I ca ca can run, I wa warrant ye.

[*Exit*]

[Scene xviii]

Enter [*with*] *a sennet:*[872] *First, two heralds; after them,* LEICESTER *with a scepter;* LANCASTER *with a crown imperial*[873] *on a cushion; after them,* [KING] HENRY *the elder bareheaded, bearing a sword and a globe; after him, young* HENRY *crowned;* ELINOR *the mother queen crowned;* [HENRY's WIFE, *the*] *young queen crowned.* [KING] HENRY *the elder places his son, the two queens, on either hand, himself at his feet;*[874] LEICESTER *and* LANCASTER *below him*

HENRY Herald, fetch Lancaster and Leicester coronets.[875]
Suffer no marquess,[876] earl, nor countess enter
Except their temples circled are in gold, *He delivers coronets to* LEICESTER *and* LANCASTER
Show them our viceroys, by our will controlled:[877]
As at a coronation every peer
Appears in all his pomp, so at this feast,
Held for our birthright, let them be adorned.
Let Gloucester be brought in, crowned like an earl. *Exit* [*Herald*]
This day we'll have no parley of[878] his death,
But talk of jouissance[879] and gleeful mirth.
Let Skink come in; give him a baron's seat.
High is his spirit; his deserts are great.
KING You wrong the honor of nobility
To place a robber in a baron's stead.
QUEEN It's well ye term him not a murderer.
KING Had I mistermed him?[880]
QUEEN Ay, that had you, Henry.
He did a piece of justice at my bidding.
KING Who made you a justice?
HENRY I that had the power.
KING You had none then.

Enter GLOUCESTER *and* SKINK

LEICESTER Yes, he was crowned before.
HENRY Why does not Gloucester wear a coronet?
GLOUCESTER Because his sovereign[881] doth not wear a crown.

872 0 SD *sennet*: offstage trumpet fanfare
873 0 SD *crown imperial*: the sovereign's crown (distinct from the "coronets" called for in line 1)
874 0 SD *himself at his feet*: i.e. Old King Henry sits at the feet of his son
875 1 coronets: small crowns, inferior to the "imperial" crown Henry wears
876 2 marquess: noblemen ranking below a duke
877 4 Their coronets will show that they are viceroys, under our control
878 9 parley of: debate over, negotiation about
879 10 jouissance: delight
880 16 Had I mistermed him?: would it have been inaccurate to call him a murderer?
881 21 his sovereign: i.e. the old King Henry

HENRY By heaven, put on thy coronet, or that heaven,
Which now with a clear[882] lends us this light,
Shall not be curtained with the veil of night
Ere on thy head I clap a burning crown
Of red hot iron that shall sear thy brains.
RICHARD Good Gloucester, crown thee with thy coronet.
LANCASTER Do, gentle earl.
SKINK 'Swounds, do! Would I had one.
QUEEN Do not, I prithee, keep thy proud heart still.
GLOUCESTER I'll wear it but to cross thy froward will.
HENRY Sit down and take thy place.
GLOUCESTER It's the low earth.
To her I must, from her I had my breath.[883]
HENRY We are pleased thou shalt sit there. Skink, take thy place among my nobles.

Enter JOHN *and [Princess] Isabel with coronets*

SKINK Thanks to King Henry's grace.
JOHN John, Earl of Morton and of Nottingham,
With Isabel his countess, bow themselves
Before their brother Henry's royal throne.
HENRY Ascend your seats; live in our daily love.

Enter RICHARD *and* ROBERT *with coronets*

RICHARD Richard, the Prince of England, with his ward,
The noble Robert Hood, Earl Huntington,
Present their service to your majesty.
HENRY Y'are welcome, too, though little be your love.

Enter FAUCONBRIDGE *with his* LADY, *she [with] a coronet*

FAUCONBRIDGE Old Richard Fauconbridge, knight of the cross,
Lord of the Cinque Ports,[884] with his noble wife,
Dame Marian, countess of West Hereford,[885]
Offer their duties at this royal meeting.
HENRY Sit down. Thou art a neuter,[886] she a foe.
Thy love we doubt, her heart too well we know.
What suitors are without? Let them come in.
GLOUCESTER And have no justice where contempt[887] is king.
HENRY Mad man, I give no care to thy loose words.
JOHN [*To* GLOUCESTER] Oh, sir, y'are welcome; you have your old seat.[888]
GLOUCESTER Though thou sit higher, yet my heart's as great.
QUEEN Great heart, we'll make you lesser by the head.
GLOUCESTER Ill comes not ever to the threatenèd.[889]

882 23 clear: a clarity, transparency; alternatively, the word "clear" modifies might be missing (the line is one syllable short)
883 32 breath: possibly a misprint for "birth," which would form a couplet with "earth"
884 44 Cinque Ports: the five ports of Hastings, New Romney, Hythe, Dover, and Sandwich—important coastal towns in Kent and Sussex
885 45 Hereford: cathedral town in southwest England
886 47 neuter: neutral party; impotent
887 50 contempt: lawlessness
888 52 old seat: i.e. on the ground
889 55 Proverbial; "threatened men live long"

Enter BLOCK *and* REDCAP

HENRY What are you two?
REDCAP M m marry and't please you, I am Re Re Redcap.
HENRY And what's your mate?
BLOCK A poor porter sir.
JOHN The porter of the Fleet that was condemned?
BLOCK No, truly sir, I was porter last when I left the door open at the tavern.[890]
JOHN Oh, is't you, sir?
LEICESTER And what would you two have?
REDCAP I co co come to re re re qui quire[891] the young k k king of his go goo goodness: since Glo Gloucester is t t taken, that he wo wo would let my fa fa father have his pa pa pardon.
HENRY Sirrah, your father has his pardon signed.
Go to the office; it shall be delivered.
REDCAP And shall he be p p porter a ga gain?
HENRY Ay, that he shall, but let him be advised[892]
Hereafter how he lets out prisoners.
REDCAP I wa warrant ye, my lord.
HENRY What, hast thou more to say?
REDCAP Marry, I wo would have Skink pu punished for co co coney-catching me.
LEICESTER Is that your business?
REDCAP Ay, by my t t troth, is it.
HENRY Then get away.
GLOUCESTER Against Skink (poor knave) thou gets no right[893] this day.
BLOCK Oh, but run back, Redcap, for the pursuivant.[894]
REDCAP Oh, l lord, s sir, I have another s suit for the p p pursuivant that has l l lost his b b box and his wa wa warrant.
HENRY What means the fellow?
REDCAP Why, the pu pu pursuivant, sir, and the po po porter.
GLOUCESTER The box that I had from him: there it is. [*Produces the box*]
FAUCONBRIDGE Marry a me, and I was charged with it.[895]
Had you it, brother Gloucester? God's good mercy.
HENRY And what have you to say?
BLOCK Nothing, sir, but God bless you. You are a goodly company—except[896] Sir Richard[897] or my lady will command me any more service.
FAUCONBRIDGE Away, you prating[898] knave! Hence, varlet, hence! *Exit* [BLOCK]
LEICESTER Put forth[899] them fellows there.
REDCAP A f fo fore I go go, I b b be s s seech you let Sk Skink and Gl Gloucester be lo lo looked to, for they have p p played the k k knaves too too too b b bad.
HENRY Take hence that stuttering fellow; shut them forth.
REDCAP Nay I'll ru ru run. Faith, you shall not n n need to b b b bid him ta ta take m me away, for Re Re Redcap will r ru run rarely.[900] *Exit*
HENRY The sundry misdemeanors late committed,
As thefts and shifts in other men's disguise,

890 61 The last time I held the door was at the tavern (when Block pretended to be Isabel's servant; see xvi. 55)
891 64 re qui quire: request
892 69 advised: careful
893 76 right: justice
894 77 Turn back and ask pardon for the pursuivant
895 83 charged with it: i.e. accused of stealing it (see ix. 176–7)
896 86 except: unless
897 86 Sir Richard: the 1600 text mistakenly reads "Sir William" here
898 88 prating: prattling, chattering
899 89 put forth: expel
900 94 rarely: excellently

We now must (knave Skink) freely tell[901] thy faults.
SKINK Sweet king, by these two terrors to mine enemies, that lend light to my body's darkness,[902] Cavallero[903] Skink—being beleaguered with an host of leaden heels[904] armed in ring Irish[905]—cheated my stammerer of his red cap and coat, was surprised, brought to the Fleet as a person suspected, passed current[906] till Gloucester stripped me from my counterfeit, clad my back in silk[907] (and my heart in sorrow) and so left me to the mercy of my mother wit.[908] How Prince John released me, he knows. How I got Fauconbridge's chain, I know. But how he will get it again, I know not.
FAUCONBRIDGE Where is it, sirrah, tell me where it is?
GLOUCESTER I got it from him, and I got John's sword.
JOHN I would 'twere to the hilts up in thy heart.
RICHARD Oh, be more charitable, brother John.
LEICESTER My liege, you need not by particulars[909]
Examine what the world knows too plain.
If you will pardon Skink, his life is saved.
If not, he is convicted by the law.
For Gloucester: as you worthily resolved,
First take his hand and afterward his head.
HENRY Skink, thou hast life, our pardon, and our love.
SKINK And your forgiveness for my robbery?
JOHN Tut, never trouble me with such a toy.[910]
Thou hinder'st me from hearing of my joy.
HENRY Bring forth a block, wine, water, and towel,
Knives, and a surgeon to bind up the veins
Of Gloucester's arm when his right hand is off,
His hand that struck Skink at the parliament.
SKINK I shall bear his blows to my grave, my lord.
KING Son Henry, see thy father's palsy hands
Joined like two suppliants, pressing to thy throne.[911]
Look how the furrows of his agèd cheek,
Filled with the rivulets of wet-eyed moan,
Begs mercy for Earl Gloucester. Weigh his guilt.
Why, for a slave, should royal blood be spilt?
SKINK You wrong mine honor. Skink may be revenged.
HENRY Father, I do commend your humble course
But quite dislike the project[912] of your suit.
Good words in an ill cause makes the fact worse.
Of blood or baseness, justice will dispute.[913]
The greater man, the greater his transgression,
Where strength wrongs weakness, it is mere oppression.
LADY FAUCONBRIDGE Oh, but King Henry, hear a sister speak:
Gloucester was wronged, his lands were given away.
They are not justly said just laws to break,

901 97 tell: enumerate
902 98–9 two terrors . . . body's darkness: i.e. my eyes
903 99 Cavallero: horseman, knight
904 99 leaden heels: slow-footed enemies
905 99–100 ring Irish: the phrase is obscure. The general sense is that Skink was surrounded by armed adversaries
906 101 passed current: was taken as the genuine article (as counterfeit currency might be taken for real)
907 102 silk: i.e. Gloucester's gown
908 102 mother wit: native ingenuity
909 109 by particulars: in minute detail
910 117 toy: trifle
911 124–5 see thy . . . thy throne: i.e. see your father's hands raised to you in prayer
912 132 project: purpose
913 134 Justice must contend with both the high- and low-born

That keep their own right with what power they may.[914]
Think, then, thy royal self began the wrong,
In giving Skink what did to him belong.
QUEEN Hear me, son Henry, while thou art a king,
Give, take, prison[915]—thy subjects are thy slaves.
Life, need, thrones, proud hearts in dungeons fling;
Grace[916] men today, tomorrow give them graves.
A king must be like Fortune, ever turning,
The world his football, all her glory spurning.[917]
GLOUCESTER Still your old counsel,[918] Beldam Policy.[919]
You're a fit tut'ress[920] in a monarchy.
RICHARD Mother, you are unjust, savage, too cruel,
Unlike a woman. Gentleness guides their sex,
But you to fury's fire add more fuel.
The vexèd spirit will you delight to vex?
Oh God, when I conceit[921] what you have done,
I am ashamed to be esteemed[922] your son.
JOHN Base Richard, I disdain to call thee brother!
Tak'st thou a traitor's part in our disgrace?
For Gloucester wilt thou wrong our sacred mother?
I scorn thee and defy thee to thy face.
Oh, that we were in field! Then shouldst thou try.[923]
ROBERT How fast Earl John would from Prince Richard fly.
Thou meet a lion in field? Poor mouse,
All thy careers[924] are in a brothel house.
JOHN Zounds, boy!
RICHARD Now, man.
LEICESTER Richard, you wrong Prince John.
RICHARD Leicester, 'twere good you proved his champion.[925]
JOHN Hasten the execution, royal lord;
Let deeds make answer for their worthless words.
GLOUCESTER I know if I respected hand or head
I am encompassed with a world of friends
And could from fury be deliverèd,
But then my freedom hazards[926] many lives.
Henry, perform the utmost of thy hate;
Let thy hard-hearted mother have her will;
Give frantic John no longer cause to prate;
I am preparèd for the worst of ill.
You see my knees kiss the cold pavement's face.
They are not bent to Henry, nor his friends,
But to all you whose blood, fled to your hearts,
Shows your true sorrow in your ashy cheeks.

914 139–40 They are . . . they may: it is unjust to break just laws and maintain one's own possessions by power
915 144 prison: imprison
916 146 Grace: honor
917 148 all her glory spurning: treating even glory scornfully
918 149 old counsel: i.e. the same old advice
919 149 Beldam Policy: "Lady Strategy" (with additional negative connotations, since a "beldam" is a witch)
920 150 tut'ress: teacher
921 155 conceit: think of
922 156 esteemed: regarded as
923 161 Would we were on the field of combat, then I'd like to see you try and cross me
924 164 careers: charges (on horseback)
925 166 proved his champion: fought on his behalf
926 172 hazards: puts at risk

To you I bend my knees, you I entreat,
To smile on Gloucester's resolution.
Whoever loves me will not shed a tear,
Nor breathe a sigh, nor show a cloudy frown.
Look, Henry, here's my hand; I lay it down,
And swear, as I have knighthood, here't shall lie,
Till thou have usèd[927] all thy tyranny.
LADY FAUCONBRIDGE Has no man heart to speak?
GLOUCESTER Let all that love me
Keep silence, or, by heaven, I'll hate them dying.[928]
QUEEN Harry, off with his hand, then with his head.
FAUCONBRIDGE By the red rood,[929] I cannot choose but weep.
Come love or hate, my tears I cannot keep.[930]
QUEEN When comes this lingering executioner?
JOHN An executioner! An executioner!
HENRY Call none till we have drunk. Father, fill wine;
Today your office is to bear our cup.
RICHARD I'll fill it, Henry. *KING kneels down*
HENRY Dick, you are too mean,[931]
So bow unto your sovereign. Gloucester, learn.
GLOUCESTER Kneel? To his child? Oh, hell! Oh, horror!
Who would love life to see this huge dishonor?[932]
HENRY Saturn kneeled to his son;[933] the God was fain
To call young Jove his age's sovereign.
Take now your seat again and wear your crown.
Now shineth Henry like the mid-day's sun
Through his horizon, darting all his beams,
Blinding, with his bright splendor, every eye
That stares against his face of majesty.
The comets, whose malicious[934] gleams
Threatened the ruin of our royalty,
Stands at our mercy. Yet our wrath denies
All favor but extreme extremities.[935]
Gloucester, have to[936] thy sorrow. Chase thy arm,[937]
That I may see thy blood I longed for oft
Gush from thy veins and stain this palace roof.
JOHN 'Twould exceed gilding.[938]
QUEEN Ay, as gold doth ocher.[939]
GLOUCESTER It's well ye count[940] my blood so precious.
HENRY Leicester, reach[941] Gloucester wine.
LEICESTER I reach it him?

927 187 usèd: used up, exhausted
928 189 dying: as I die
929 191 red rood: red cross (see vi. 72)
930 192 keep: keep in, prevent
931 197 too mean: too low (to be my cupbearer)
932 200 Who would want to live to see a sight like this
933 201 Saturn kneeled to his son: in classical myth, Saturn was deposed by his son Jupiter
934 208 malicious: ominous
935 210–11 Yet our . . . extreme extremities: our anger omits all mercy and embraces cruel punishments
936 212 have to: prepare for
937 212 Chase thy arm: obscure, perhaps "prepare" or "bare" your arm
938 215 'Twould exceed gilding: i.e. Gloucester's blood will ornament the ceiling better than gold
939 215 as gold doth ocher: as gold exceeds ochre (a yellow or orange clay) in beauty
940 216 count: account
941 217 reach: fetch

HENRY Proud earl, I'll spurn thee. Quickly, go and bear it.
GLOUCESTER I'll count it poison if his hand come near it.
HENRY Give it him, Leicester, upon our displeasure.
GLOUCESTER Thus Gloucester takes it, thus again he flings it, [GLOUCESTER *throws down the cup of wine*]
In scorn of him that sent it and of him that brought it.
SKINK Oh, brave spirit!
LADY FAUCONBRIDGE Bravely resolved, brother; I honor thee.
QUEEN Hark how his sister joys in his abuse.[942]
Wilt thou endure it, Hal?
FAUCONBRIDGE Peace, good Marian.
HENRY Avoid[943] there, every under-officer.
Leave but us, our peers, and ladies here.
Richard, you love Earl Gloucester; look about.
If you can spy one in this company
That hath but[944] done as great a sin as Gloucester,
Choose him. Let him be the executioner.
RICHARD Thou hast done worse, then. Like rebellious head,
Hast armed ten thousand hands against his life
That loved thee so.[945] As thou wert made a king,
Being his child, now he's thy underling.
I have done worse:[946] thrice I drew my sword,
In three set battles for thy false defense.[947]
John hath done worse: he still hath took thy part.
All of us three have smite our father's heart,
Which made proud Leicester bold to strike his face,[948]
To his eternal shame, and our disgrace.
HENRY Silence, I see thou means[949] to find none fit.
I am sure nor Lancaster, nor Huntington,
Nor Fauconbridge will lay a hand on him.
Mother, wife, brother, let's descend the throne
Where Henry, as the monarch of the west,
Hath sat amongst his princes dignified.
Father, take you the place, see justice.[950]
KING It's injust justice, I must tell thee son.
HENRY Mother, hold you the basin; [*To* WIFE] you, the towel.
I know your French hearts thirst for English blood;
John, take the mallet; I will hold the knife.
And when I bid thee smite, strike for thy life.[951]
Make a mark,[952] surgeon.[953] Gloucester, now prepare thee.
GLOUCESTER Tut, I am ready; to thy[954] worst, I dare thee.
HENRY Then have I done my worst, thrice-honored earl.

942 225 his abuse: i.e. of young Henry and Leicester
943 227 Avoid: leave the room
944 231 but: the 1600 text prints "not," which conflicts with Richard's response
945 233–5 Like rebellious … thee so: like a rebel force, you have turned thousands against the king and father who loves you
946 237 done worse: done worse things than Gloucester ever did
947 237–8 thrice I … false defense: I fought three times for your false cause
948 241 Leicester bold … his face: Richard refers to an occasion when Leicester struck the old king's face, though the play does not depict it
949 243 means: intend
950 249 see justice: administrate the punishment
951 254 for thy life: as if your life depended on it
952 255 a mark: i.e. on Gloucester's arm
953 255 surgeon: there is no entrance direction for the surgeon in Q; presumably he comes on together with the other implements requested by the young king at lines 119–22
954 256 to thy: do your

I do embrace thee in affection's arms.
QUEEN What means thou, Henry? Oh, what means my son?
HENRY I mean no longer to be lullabied
In your seditious arms.
HENRY'S WIFE *Mordieu*[955] Henry!
HENRY *Mordieu,* nor devil, little tit[956] of France,
I know your heart leaps at our heart's mischance.
JOHN 'Swounds, Henry thou art mad!
HENRY I have been mad.
What, stampst thou, John? Knowst thou not who I am?
Come, stamp the devil out, sucked from thy dam.[957]
QUEEN I'll curse thee, Henry.
HENRY You're best be quiet,
Lest where we find you, to the tower we bear you.
For, being abroad,[958] England hath cause to fear ye.
KING I am struck dumb with wonder.
GLOUCESTER I, amazed,
Imagine that I see a vision.
HENRY Gloucester, I give thee first this Skink, this slave;
It's in thy power, his life to spill[959] or save.
SKINK He's a noble gentleman; I do not doubt his usage.[960]
HENRY Stand not thus wondering; princes, kneel all down,
And cast your coronets before his[961] crown.
Down, stubborn Queen, kneel to your wrongèd king.
Down mammet.[962] Leicester, I'll cut off thy legs
If thou delay thy duty. When,[963] proud John?
JOHN Nay, if all kneel, of force[964] I must be one.
FAUCONBRIDGE Now, by my holydam, a virtuous deed.
HENRY Father, you see your most rebellious son,
Stricken with horror of his horrid guilt,
Requesting sentence fitting his desert.
Oh, tread upon his head that trod your heart.
I do deliver up all dignity,
Crown, scepter, sword unto your majesty.
KING My heart surfeits[965] with joy in hearing this.
And, dear son, I'll bless thee with a kiss.
HENRY I will not rise; I will not leave this ground,
Till all these voices, joinèd in one sound,
Cry, "God save Henry, second of that name,
Let his friends live, his foes see death with shame."
ALL God save Henry, second of that name,
Let his friends live, his foes see death with shame.
HENRY Amen, amen, amen.
JOHN Hark, mother, hark?

955 261 *Mordieu*: by God's death
956 262 tit: fool
957 266 dam: mother
958 269 abroad: free to roam
959 273 spill: dispense with
960 274 doubt his usage: fear his verdict
961 276 his: old King Henry's
962 278 mammet: puppet
963 279 When: i.e. when will you kneel?
964 280 of force: by necessity
965 288 surfeits: is filled to excess

My brother is already turnèd clerk.[966]
QUEEN He is a recreant;[967] I am mad with rage.
HENRY Be angry at your envy,[968] gracious mother.
Learn patience and true humility
Of your worst-tutored son, for I am he.
Send hence that Frenchwoman.[969] Give her her dowry.
Let her not speak to trouble my mild soul,
Which of this world hath taken her last leave,[970]
And, by her power, will my proud flesh control.
Off with these silks, my garments shall be gray,
My shirt hard hair,[971] my bed the ashy dust,
My pillow but a lump of hardened clay.
For clay I am, and unto clay I must.
Oh, I beseech ye, let me go alone,
To live where my loose life I may bemoan.
KING Son?
QUEEN Son?
RICHARD Brother?
JOHN Brother?
HENRY Let none call me their son; I am no man's brother.
My kindred is in heaven; I know no other.
Farewell, farewell, the world is yours, pray take it.
I'll leave vexation, and with joy forsake it. *Exit*
LADY FAUCONBRIDGE Wondrous conversion.
FAUCONBRIDGE Admirable good.
Now, by my holydam, Mall, passing good.
RICHARD H'ath fired my soul. I will to Palestine[972]
And pay my vows before the Sepulcher.[973]
Among the multitude of misbelief,
I'll show myself the soldier of Christ,
Spend blood, sweat tears, for satisfaction
Of many, many sins which I lament,
And never think to have them pardonèd
Till I have part of Syria conquerèd.
GLOUCESTER He makes me wonder, and inflames my spirits
With an exceeding zeal to Portugal,[974]
Which kingdom the unchristened Saracens,[975]
The black-faced Africans and tawny moors,
Have got unjustly in possession,
Whence I will fire them[976] with the help of heaven.
SKINK Skink will scorch them, brave Gloucester,
Make carbonadoes[977] of their bacon-fletches,[978]
Deserve to be counted valiant by his valor,

966 297 clerk: priest (pronounced "clark")
967 298 recreant: coward
968 299 envy: greed and jealousy
969 302 that Frenchwoman: i.e. his wife, whom he sends back to France with her dowry
970 304 Which has taken its leave of worldly things
971 307 shirt hard hair: i.e. a monastic hair-shirt
972 322 to Palestine: i.e. to fight in the crusades
973 323 Sepulcher: cave outside Jerusalem where Christ was buried
974 331 Richard inspires me to go fight in Portugal
975 332 unchristened Saracens: unbaptized Muslims
976 335 fire them: drive them out with fire
977 337 carbonadoes: platters of grilled meat
978 337 bacon-fletches: backs and sides

And "Rivo" will he cry, and "Castile," too,[979]
And wonders in the land of Seville[980] do.
ROBERT Oh, that I were a man to see these fights,
To spend my blood amongst these worthy knights!
FAUCONBRIDGE Marry, aye me, were I a boy again,
I'd either to Jerusalem or Spain.
JOHN Faith, I'll keep England;[981] mother, you and I
Will live, for[982] all this fight and foolery.
KING Peace to us all! Let's all for peace give praise,
Unlooked for peace, unlooked for happy days.
Love[983] Henry's birthday, he hath been new born.
I am new crowned, new settled in my seat.
Let's all to the chapel, there give thanks and praise,
Beseeching grace from heaven's eternal throne,
That England never know more prince than one.

Exeunt

FINIS.

979 339 "Rivo" is a cry before drinking; "to Castile" is a toast Skink will make as he heads there to fight
980 340 land of Seville: i.e. Spain
981 345 keep England: stay in England
982 346 for: despite
983 349 Love: cherish, celebrate

6 Anonymous, *The Famous Victories of Henry V*

First performed c. 1588

First printed 1598

Edited by Brian Walsh

From common thief to paragon of a Christian king: the fictionalized version of the historical King Henry V that moves through this play changes about as much as a character can. Or does he? Why, how, and whether the caddish Prince of Wales we meet when *The Famous Victories of Henry V* opens transforms into someone noble by the time it ends is a mystery that gives the play its prevailing tension. Audiences might accept that Henry has genuinely undergone some form of spiritual growth, akin perhaps to the "Everyman" figures in the morality plays of the medieval and Tudor English theater tradition. But the play also raises an uncomfortable question. Is the man who has conquered France on the battlefield and then successfully wooed the French princess in the play's closing moments truly worthy of admiration? Or is he still the wily manipulator and street brawler he was at the start, only now on a bigger scale and with loftier rhetoric?

It is easier to pinpoint *when* Henry changes his behavior than to account for why. In Scene vi, while still Prince of Wales, Henry visits his ailing father, King Henry IV. The wobbly old king frets because his heir is a dissolute tyrant in the making: he robs innocent travelers, riots in the streets with lowlifes, bullies court officials, and flagrantly disregards the rule of law. At the close of their interview the prince announces, in plain language that can serve as a snapshot of the play's matter-of-fact style, "this day, even this day, I am born new again" (vi. 98). It is notable that the prince had entered this scene with an unsheathed dagger in his hand. Just moments before father and son reconcile and the prince claims to be born again as a dutiful child and worthy heir, he was a would-be regicide and parricide.

The play divides roughly in half around this stunning "conversion." Subsequent to the king's death in Scene viii, the freshly crowned Henry V follows an upward trajectory of success that culminates in the great English victory over the French at the Battle of Agincourt. This was an actual event that took place in 1415, and which is here depicted as a triumph engineered by Henry's strategic canniness, his bold determination, and perhaps by divine providence. From one perspective, Henry's sudden transformation is simply an indication of poor literary craftmanship, or that the text of the play as we have it is full of gaps. Perhaps the original version performed on stage sometime in the 1580s included narrative incidents or speeches about Henry's internal state that would better prepare audiences for his change. But from another perspective, the suddenness of this reversal is part of the point of the story, rather than a dramatic or textual defect. In some sense, King Henry V's life *was* miraculous. Just as no one could have predicted that his outnumbered forces would defeat the French army at Agincourt, his emergence as an ideal monarch could not have been anticipated by his degenerate early life. In this way of thinking, his story is rich and worth telling precisely because of its singular implausibility.

This story of King Henry V's life had been told before *The Famous Victories* brought it to the public stage. English chronicles—massive history books that enjoyed something of a vogue in the sixteenth century—included tales of Henry's youthful antics that in some cases were drawn from accounts written during Henry's own lifetime. In the extremely influential *Holinshed's Chronicles*, stories of the prince's wild youth are either dismissed as slander or downplayed as natural outbursts of youthful energy that Henry quickly outgrew. Another chronicler, John Stow, writes that the prince did indeed sometimes wait in disguise with his friends to steal money from government officials. But Stow mitigates his account by assuring his readers that the prince would reveal himself after, return the money, and reward those victims who had fought back most valiantly, as though it were all simply a test, or a rough game.

It is significant that the anonymous author of the *Famous Victories* does not include any such gestures intended to soften or excuse the prince's misdeeds. Indeed, the play seems to parody such attempts. In the opening scene, in what will prove to be a rare instance of self-conscious introspection, the prince asks his companions: "tell me sirs, think you not that it was a villainous part of me to rob my father's receivers?" (i. 7–8). When they answer, in the style of the apologist chroniclers, that it was but a "trick of youth" (9), the prince is satisfied and moves on, unconcerned for the harm he does others. When he confronts the receivers he and his friends have just robbed, far from returning the money or jocularly revealing himself as the thief, he and his cohorts do more than simply keep the money to spend at a tavern; the prince also insults the victims and intimidates them with threats when they hint that they suspect he was the one that robbed them. After they exit, he triumphantly declares to his crew: "Was this not bravely done?" (58). Worse is still to come. In the play's most famous scene, the prince comes to rescue his vicious servant, a thief named Cuthbert Cutter, from being sent to prison. When the Lord Chief Justice of England, one of the highest officials in the King's government, insists on serving justice against Cutter, the prince boxes the ears of the Chief Justice.

When the prince later declares to his father that he is born anew, his rebirth does not clearly involve a new commitment to treat other people better. His main concern now becomes to conquer France and to expand his own power and prestige based on a flimsy claim to the French throne. The Lord Chief Justice stands as a bulwark against the prince's reckless abuse of power when he insists on sending the prince to prison for his actions. He bravely puts principle and the rule of law above deference to tyranny, as do the Mayor and Sherriff of London when they, too, send Henry to prison for his disorderly conduct. The play demonstrates how vulnerable those who stand up to power can be, though. The Mayor and Sherriff are nearly punished by King Henry IV for upholding the law when they imprison the prince, and once the prince becomes king, the Chief Justice, while never wavering or apologizing, does show a very human fear of retribution. He is, however, praised and promoted for his integrity by Henry V in what may be the play's clearest assertion that virtue can be rewarded, and that Henry himself may have sincerely matured.

The action of rewarding the Chief Justice aside, Henry does not exhibit any serious capacity for self-reflection until quite late in the *Famous Victories* when he turns his attentions to his desire to marry the French Princess Katherine: "with what face canst thou seek to gain her love, which hath sought to win her father's crown?" he wonders to himself (xviii. 28–9), hinting at some measure of guilt over his conquest. But he quickly recovers his sense of right, his determination to win, and his sense of sexual entitlement: "Her father's crown said I? No, it is mine own. Aye, but I love her, and must crave her, nay I love her and will have her" (29–30). We are left with an overall portrait of Henry that emphasizes his genuine brilliance once he becomes king. As a general, we see that his battle tactics ensure victory over the French. As a monarch, his ability to rally most (but, as we'll see, not all) of his subjects in support of a common cause is unparalleled. As a statesman, his adept understanding of *realpolitik* allows him to press his military advantage and thoroughly subject France to his will. And despite his presumptuous wooing, the outwardly hesitant princess's asides inform us that she indeed loves him; apparently, he is a brilliant romantic leading man as well.

But even as he progresses toward these pinnacles of success, questions linger about the substance of his being and his moral center. Petulant, arrogant, lawless, and cruel, the prince of the opening scenes forces audiences to confront the debased origin story of a national hero, and to ask whether those days represent a self he discards or one he simply hides beneath majestical bearing and a dazzling military triumph. The *Famous Victories* does not render a clear answer. Rather, it suggests that Henry V's possibly obnoxious swagger and his unrelenting successes are inextricably linked. His charisma is real and no doubt inspired original audiences, as did the chauvinistic portrayal of English manhood compared to French effeteness. But his charisma also invites scrutiny; it asks us to think hard about both what we admire in our leaders and how we define heroism.

Ambivalence amidst an outward celebration of English prowess would become a characteristic of the history play genre as it developed in the 1590s. Scholars have credibly claimed that the *Famous Victories* was in fact the first English history play on the popular stage. The playwright and his company, the Queen's Men, were innovators for recognizing the enormous potential of the chronicles as source material for plays, and for creatively combining historical material with explicitly comic scenes that were based on recognizable, contemporaneous characters and situations from Elizabethan London. The Queen's Men included the most celebrated clown, or comic actor, of the era, a man named Richard Tarlton, who played Derick in the *Famous Victories*. It is vital when reading the text of the play today to try to imagine how this part would have been fleshed out on stage. His scenes (vii or x in particular) might come across awkwardly on the page, but contemporary accounts from the 1580s and 1590s attest that audiences found Tarlton's performances hilariously entertaining for his verbal wit—he was a celebrated improviser, and no doubt added lines to each performance that elude capture in the printed play—as well as for his physical exuberance, which of course can never be satisfactorily represented on the page. Eyewitness accounts include an anecdote about his performance in the *Famous Victories* when, on one occasion, he stepped in for an absent actor and played both his own part and that of the Lord Chief Justice at the moment he gets boxed on the ears, to great comic effect. Tarlton's clowning was a central aspect of the play's popularity in its day, and it did more than just inspire laughs. It could also comment on the historical action around it, as when Derick and his friend John observe that there is one set of rules for nobles like the prince and another for poor men like himself (v. 4–6); or when he jokes about conscription, not caring about Henry's imperial project (x. 11–45); or when, once forced to serve in France, he steals shoes from corpses on the battlefield, revealing the ugly side of "famous victories" (xix. 23–4).

The play's most eminent fan was William Shakespeare, who used it as a working model for three of his own plays: *Henry IV* parts 1 and 2, and *Henry V*. This trilogy covers the same time span as the *Famous Victories*, is also centered on the misspent youth and maturation of Henry V, and is clearly indebted to the earlier play's audacious juxtaposition of comedy and history. Shakespeare's celebrated creation, Falstaff, shares a common historical ancestor with the *Famous Victories'* character Oldcastle. Simultaneously, Falstaff inherits his wit, physical comedy, and dubious morality from Tarlton's Derick. Shakespeare was a poet of the first order whose verbal artistry might make his plays seem distant from the workman-like dialogue we see here. But throughout his many portraits of kings, queens, and other powerful figures across the genres in which he worked,

Shakespeare relentlessly exposed the workings, and questioned the legitimacy, of authority. He may have first been prompted to do so by *The Famous Victories of Henry V*.

Textual note

There are two known copies of the 1598 quarto edition of *The Famous Victories of Henry V*. One is owned by the Bodleian Library, and the other by the Huntington Library. The copy-text for this edition is the Huntington Library copy as it is reproduced in facsimile in the Malone Society Reprint prepared by Chiaki Hanabusa. I have also referred to both copies on the Early English Books Online database. There are no act or scene divisions in the quarto. I have followed previous editors (e.g. Corbin and Sedge) in dividing the play into twenty scenes, with some slight modifications. Some speeches and exchanges from the 1598 quarto are printed as verse, although with no regular beat or rhyme scheme, evidently the result of some transmission or printing house error. (See McMillin and MacLean, 1998: 113–15, for an account of how this may have occurred.) I follow previous editors in setting the play entirely as prose.

Further reading

Editions

Corbin, Peter and Douglas Sedge (eds) (1991) *The Oldcastle Controversy: Sir John Oldcastle, Part I and The Famous Victories of Henry V*, Manchester: Manchester University Press.

Hanabusa, Chiaki (ed.) (2006) *The Famous Victories of Henry V*, Malone Society Reprint 171, New York: Palgrave.

Critical and contextual reading

Bevington, David and David Scott Kastan (eds) (1988) *Henry IV, Part One*, New York: Penguin.

Bryant, Joseph Allen, Jr. (1954) "Shakespeare's Falstaff and the Mantle of Dick Tarlton," *Studies in Philology* 51: 149–62.

Bullough, Geoffrey, (ed.) (1975) *Narrative and Dramatic Sources of Shakespeare*, vol. 4: Later English History Plays, London: Routledge.

Halasz, Alexandra (1995) "'So Beloved that Men use His Picture for Their Signs': Richard Tarlton and the Uses of Sixteenth-Century Celebrity," *Shakespeare Studies* 23: 19–38.

McMillin, Scott and Sally-Beth MacLean (1998) *The Queen's Men and Their Plays*, Cambridge: Cambridge University Press.

Walsh, Brian (2007) "Theatrical Temporality and Historical Consciousness in *The Famous Victories of Henry V*," *Theatre Journal* 59: 57–73.

The Famous Victories of Henry V (c. 1588)

Dramatis personae[1]

HENRY, *Prince of Wales, later* KING HENRY V
HENRY IV, *King of England, his father*
ARCHBISHOP OF CANTERBURY
DUKE OF YORK
OXFORD, *an English lord*
EXETER, *an English lord*
LORD CHIEF JUSTICE OF ENGLAND
CLERK OF THE OFFICE, *assistant to Lord Chief Justice*
SIR JOHN OLDCASTLE (Jockey), *companion of Prince Henry*
NED, *companion of Prince Henry*
TOM, *companion of Prince Henry*
MAYOR OF LONDON
SHERIFF OF LONDON
ENGLISH SECRETARY, *attendant to Henry V*
JOHN COBBLER, *a London tradesman*
ROBIN PEWTERER, *a London tradesman*
LAWRENCE COSTERMONGER, *a London tradesman*
DERICK, *a rustic carrier turned cobbler*
A THIEF (Cutbert Cutter), *servant to Prince Henry*
FRENCH KING (Charles VI)
PRINCE DOLPHIN, *his son and heir to the French throne*
LADY KATHERINE OF FRANCE, *daughter of the King of France*
LORD HIGH CONSTABLE OF FRANCE
DUKE OF BURGUNDY
ARCHBISHOP OF BOURGES
FRENCH HERALD
FRENCH SECRETARY, *attendant to French King*

English Captain, English Soldier, Cobbler's Wife, Vintner's Boy, Jailer, Porter, Two Receivers, Three French Soldiers, French Drummer, French Captain, Attendants, Messengers, Ladies-In-Waiting

[Scene i]

Enter the young PRINCE [HENRY], NED, *and* TOM

PRINCE[2] Come away, Ned and Tom.
BOTH Here my lord.

1 Dramatis personae: not in Q
2 1 PRINCE: this character is identified as "Henry V" throughout the 1598 text, including in these early scenes when he is still Prince of Wales. To make clear his change in status from heir to monarch over the course of the play, he will be PRINCE until his father dies, then KING HENRY V

PRINCE Come away my lads: tell me sirs, how much gold have you got?
NED Faith my lord, I have got five hundred pound.
PRINCE But tell me Tom, how much hast thou got?
TOM Faith my lord, some four hundred pound.
PRINCE Four hundred pounds! Bravely spoken lads. But tell me sirs, think you not that it was a villainous part of me to rob my father's receivers?[3]
NED Why no my lord, it was but a trick of youth.
PRINCE Faith Ned, thou sayest true. But tell me sirs, whereabouts are we?
TOM My lord, we are now about a mile off London.
PRINCE But sirs, I marvel that Sir John Oldcastle comes not away. Zounds, see where he comes.

Enters[4] JOCKEY [OLDCASTLE]

How now Jockey, what news with thee?
OLDCASTLE Faith my lord, such news as passeth: for the town of Deptford[5] is risen with hue and cry after your man, which[6] parted from us the last night, and has set upon, and hath robbed, a poor carrier.[7]
PRINCE Zounds, the villain that was wont to spy out our booties?[8]
OLDCASTLE Aye my lord, even the very same.
PRINCE Now, base-minded rascal, to rob a poor carrier. Well, it skills not.[9] I'll save the base villain's life. Aye, I may. But tell me Jockey, whereabout be the receivers?
OLDCASTLE Faith my lord, they are hard by. But the best is, we are a horseback and they be a foot, so we may escape them.
PRINCE Well, aye, the villains come, let me alone with them. But tell me Jockey, how much got'st thou from the knaves? For I am sure I got something, for one of the villains so belammed[10] me about the shoulders, as I shall feel it this month.
OLDCASTLE Faith my lord, I have got a hundred pound.
PRINCE A hundred pound! Now bravely spoken Jockey. But come sirs, lay all your money before me. Now by heaven, here is a brave show. But, as I am true gentleman, I will have the half of this spent tonight. But sirs, take up your bags, here comes the receivers. Let me alone.

Enters two RECEIVERS

FIRST RECEIVER Alas good fellow, what shall we do? I dare never go home to the court, for I shall be hanged. But look, here is the young prince, what shall we do?
PRINCE How now you villains, what are you?
FIRST RECEIVER Speak you to him.
SECOND RECEIVER No, I pray, speak you to him.
PRINCE Why how now you rascals, why speak you not?
FIRST RECEIVER Forsooth we be—pray speak you to him.
PRINCE Zounds, villains, speak, or I'll cut off your heads.
SECOND RECEIVER Forsooth, he can tell the tale better than I.
FIRST RECEIVER Forsooth, we be your father's receivers.
PRINCE Are you my father's receivers? Then I hope ye have brought me some money.
FIRST RECEIVER Money! Alas sir, we be robbed.

3 8 receivers: treasury officers
4 13 SD *Enters*: a common early modern form for "enter"
5 15 Deptford: area just to the southeast of London
6 16 which: who
7 17 carrier: a messenger or transporter of goods, a courier
8 18 spy out our booties: help us set up our robberies
9 20 skills not: it doesn't matter
10 25 belammed: thrashed, beat

PRINCE Robbed? How many were there of them?

FIRST RECEIVER Marry sir, there were four of them. And one of them had Sir John Oldcastle's bay hobby, and your black nag.

PRINCE Gog's wounds, how like you this Jockey? Blood,[11] you villains! My father robbed of his money abroad, and we robbed in our stables. But tell me, how many were of them?

FIRST RECEIVER If it please you, there were four of them, and there was one about the bigness of you. But I am sure I so belammed him about the shoulders, that he will feel it this month.

PRINCE Gog's wounds you 'lammed[12] them fairly, so that they have carried away your money. But come sirs, what shall we do with the villains?

RECEIVERS I beseech your grace, be good to us.

NED I pray you my lord, forgive them this once.

PRINCE[13] Well, stand up and get you gone, and look that you speak not a word of it, for if there be, zounds, I'll hang you and all your kin. *Exit* [RECEIVERS]

Now sirs, how like you this? Was not this bravely done? For now the villains dare not speak a word of it, I have so feared them with words. Now whither shall we go?

ALL Why my lord, you know our old hostess at Faversham?[14]

PRINCE Our hostess at Faversham, blood, what shall we do there? We have a thousand pound about us, and we shall go to a petty ale house? No, no. You know the old tavern in Eastcheap.[15] There is good wine. Besides, there is a pretty wench that can talk well, for I delight as much in their tongues, as any part about them.

ALL We are ready to wait upon your grace.

PRINCE Gog's wounds, wait![16] We will go altogether. We are all fellows, I tell you sirs, and[17] the king my father were dead, we would be all kings. Therefore, come away.

NED Gog's wounds, bravely spoken Harry.

[*Exeunt*]

[Scene ii]

Enter JOHN COBBLER, ROBIN PEWTERER, LAWRENCE COSTERMONGER[18]

JOHN All is well here, all is well masters.

LAWRENCE How say you, neighbor John Cobbler? I think it best that my neighbor Robin Pewterer went to Pudding Lane End,[19] and we will watch here at Billingsgate Ward.[20] How say you neighbor Robin, how like you this?

ROBIN Marry, well neighbors. I care not much if I go to Pudding Lane's End. But neighbors, and you hear any ado about me, make haste. And if I hear any ado about you, I will come to you. *Exit* ROBIN

LAWRENCE Neighbor, what news hear you of the young prince?

JOHN Marry neighbor, I hear say, he is a toward[21] young prince, for if he meet any by the highway, he will not let to talk with him. I dare not call him thief, but sure he is one of these taking fellows.

11 47 Blood: i.e. "By God's blood"

12 52 'lammed: belammed

13 56 SP PRINCE: this line is assigned to Ned in Q

14 60 hostess at Faversham: proprietress of an inn, with possible suggestion that she is also a "madam" or female pimp. Faversham is a market town some fifty miles southeast of London

15 62 Eastcheap: could refer to a specific street of that name near London Bridge or the general area around the street and market, known for its taverns

16 66 wait: an egalitarian gesture: the prince incredulously dismisses the notion that his "fellows" will "wait" upon, i.e. serve him

17 66 and: if

18 0 SD JOHN COBBLER, etc.: together, these men form part of a "nightwatch," a kind of early police auxiliary force made up of armed citizens who had authority to detain or arrest suspected criminals. Their names indicate their trades: John fixes old shoes, Robin makes pewter utensils, Lawrence sells fruits and vegetables (a coster is a kind of apple)

19 3 Pudding Lane End: London street close to Eastcheap and London Bridge

20 3 Billingsgate Ward: area just north of the river Thames and east of London Bridge, not far from Pudding Lane

21 8 toward: promising

LAWRENCE Indeed neighbor, I hear say he is as lively a young prince as ever was.
JOHN Aye, and I hear say, if he use it long, his father will cut him off from the crown. But neighbor, say nothing of that.
LAWRENCE No, no, neighbor, I warrant you.
JOHN Neighbor, methinks you begin to sleep. If you will, we will sit down, for I think it is about midnight.
LAWRENCE Marry, content[22] neighbor, let us sleep.

Enter DERICK *roving*[23]

DERICK Whoa, whoa there, whoa there! *Exit* DERICK

Enter ROBIN

ROBIN Oh, neighbors, what mean you to sleep, and such ado in the streets?
JOHN and LAWRENCE How now neighbor, what's the matter?

Enter DERICK *again*

DERICK Whoa there, whoa there, whoa there!
JOHN Why, what ail'st thou? Here is no horses.[24]
DERICK Oh alas man, I am robbed. Whoa there, whoa there!
ROBIN Hold him neighbor Cobbler. Why, I see thou art a plain clown.[25]
DERICK Am I a clown? Zounds, masters, do clowns go in silk apparel?[26] I am sure all we gentlemen clowns in Kent scant go so well.[27] Zounds, you know clowns very well. [*To* JOHN] Hear you, are you Master Constable? And you be, speak, for I will not take it at his hands.
JOHN Faith, I am not Master Constable, but I am one of his bad officers,[28] for he is not here.
DERICK Is not Master Constable here? Well it is no matter, I'll have the law at his hands.
JOHN Nay, I pray you, do not take the law of us.
DERICK Well, you are one of his beastly officers.
JOHN I am one of his bad officers.
DERICK Why then I charge thee, look to him.[29]
JOHN Nay but hear ye sir, you seem to be an honest fellow, and we are poor men, and now 'tis night. And we would be loath to have anything ado.[30] Therefore I pray thee, put it up.
DERICK First, thou sayest true, I am an honest fellow, and a proper handsome fellow too. And you seem to be poor men, therefore I care not greatly. Nay, I am quickly pacified. But and you chance to spy the thief, I pray you lay hold on him.
ROBIN Yes, that we will, I warrant you.
DERICK 'Tis a wonderful thing to see how glad the knave is, now I have forgiven him.
JOHN Neighbors, do ye look about you? How now, who's there?

Enter the THIEF

22 17 content: agreed
23 17 SD *roving*: this stage direction indicates that Derick is moving about the stage looking for the thief; his almost immediate exit after one inarticulate line is itself a joke, and part of the comic actor's repertoire, wherein he makes a bumbling entrance and chaotically crosses the stage without doing anything in particular
24 22 Here is no horses: John responds to Derick's cry for help—"whoa there"—which sounds like the traditional calming command given to a horse
25 24 clown: a rustic or country bumpkin; but also points to the fact that Derick was played by Richard Tarlton, the principle comic actor of the playing company
26 25 silk apparel: probably an ironic reference to his humble dress
27 26 scant go so well: can hardly dress so well; Kent is a county in England, southeast of London
28 28 bad officers: means here an officer who was "bidden" or ordered to be on duty, but with obvious joke about his quality
29 33 look to him: do something about him. Derick is offended that Robin called him a clown and wants to see him arrested
30 35 anything ado: any trouble

THIEF Here is a good fellow. I pray you which is the way to the old tavern in Eastcheap?

DERICK Whoop hollo! Now Gad's Hill,[31] knowest thou me?

THIEF I know thee for an ass.

DERICK And I know thee for a taking fellow, upon Gad's Hill in Kent: a bots[32] light upon ye.

THIEF The whoreson villain would be knocked.

DERICK Masters! Villain! And ye be men stand to him, and take his weapon from him, let him not pass you.

JOHN My friend, what make you abroad now? It is too late to walk now.

THIEF It is not too late for true men to walk.

LAWRENCE We know thee not to be a true man.

THIEF Why, what do you mean to do with me? Zounds, I am one of the king's liege people.[33]

DERICK Hear you sir, are you one of the king's liege people?

THIEF Aye, marry am I sir, what say you to it?

DERICK Marry sir, I say you are one of the king's filching people.

JOHN Come, come, let's have him away.

THIEF Why, what have I done?

ROBIN Thou hast robbed a poor fellow, and taken away his goods from him.

THIEF I never saw him before.

DERICK Masters, who comes here?

Enter the VINTNER'S BOY

VINTNER'S BOY How now good man Cobbler?

JOHN How now Robin,[34] what makes thou abroad at this time of night?

VINTNER'S BOY Marry, I have been at the Counter.[35] I can tell such news as never you have heard the like.

JOHN What is that Robin, what is the matter?

VINTNER'S BOY Why this night about two hours ago, there came the young prince, and three or four more of his companions, and called for wine good store.[36] And then they sent for a noise[37] of musicians, and were very merry for the space of an hour. Then whether their music liked them not, or whether they had drunk too much wine or no, I cannot tell, but our pots flew against the walls, and then they drew their swords, and went into the street and fought. And some took one part, some took another. But for the space of half an hour, there was such a bloody fray as passeth, and none could part them until such time as the mayor and sheriff were sent for, and then at the last with much ado, they took them. And so the young prince was carried to the Counter, and then about one hour after, there came a messenger from the court in all haste from the king, for my Lord Mayor and the sheriff, but for what cause I know not.

JOHN Here is news indeed, Robert.

LAWRENCE Marry neighbor, this news is strange indeed. I think it best, neighbor, to rid our hands of this fellow first.

THIEF What mean you to do with me?

JOHN We mean to carry you to the prison, and there to remain till the sessions day.[38]

THIEF Then, I pray you, let me go to the prison where my master is.

31 43 Gad's Hill: Derick sarcastically addresses the thief by the name of the place where he plies his trade, Gad's Hill, a spot on the route to London near Rochester, in Kent, where robberies frequently occurred

32 45 bots: parasitic worms; Derick wishes that the Thief will contract a gastrointestinal illness

33 52 liege people: those who owe service to a nobleman

34 62 Robin: like one of the watchmen, the boy is named Robin (a nickname for Robert)

35 63 Counter: "counter" was a generic name (from "compter") for debtors' prisons in London; based on the locales mentioned here, the boy probably refers to the Poultry Counter or the Wood Street Counter, both located in Cheapside

36 67 good store: a large quantity of

37 68 noise: a collective noun for musicians

38 80 sessions day: periodic court dates

JOHN Nay thou must go to the country prison, to Newgate,[39] therefore come away.
THIEF I prithee, be good to me honest fellow.
DERICK Aye marry will I, I'll be very charitable to thee, for I will never leave thee, till I see thee on the gallows.

[*Exeunt*]

[Scene iii]

Enter [KING] HENRY [IV], *with the* EARL of EXETER, *and the* LORD of OXFORD

OXFORD And[40] please your majesty, here is my Lord Mayor and the sheriff of London, to speak with your majesty.
KING HENRY IV Admit them to our presence.

Enter the MAYOR *and the* SHERIFF

Now my good Lord Mayor of London, the cause of my sending for you at this time, is to tell you of a matter which I have learned of my council. Herein, I understand that you have committed my son to prison without our leave and license. What although[41] he be a rude youth, and likely to give occasion, yet you might have considered that he is a prince, and my son, and not to be hauled to prison by every subject.
MAYOR May it please your majesty to give us leave to tell our tale?
KING HENRY IV Or else God forbid, otherwise you might think me an unequal judge, having more affection to my son, than to any rightful judgement.
MAYOR Then I do not doubt but we shall rather deserve commendations at your majesty's hands, than any anger.
KING HENRY IV Go to, say on.
MAYOR Then if it please your majesty, this night betwixt two and three of the clock in the morning, my lord the young prince with a very disordered company, came to the old tavern in Eastcheap. And whether it was that their music liked them not, or whether they were overcome with wine, I know not, but they drew their swords, and into the street they went. And some took my lord the young prince's part, and some took the other, but betwixt them there was such a bloody fray for the space of half an hour, that neither watchmen nor any other could stay them, till my brother the sheriff of London and I were sent for. And at the last with much ado we stayed them, but it was long first, which was a great disquieting to all your loving subjects thereabouts. And then my good lord, we knew not whether your grace had sent them to try us, whether we would do justice, or whether it were of their own voluntary will or not, we cannot tell. And therefore in such a case we knew not what to do, but for our own safeguard we sent him to ward,[42] where he wanteth nothing that is fit for his grace, and your majesty's son. And thus most humbly beseeching your majesty to think of our answer.
KING HENRY IV Stand aside until we have further deliberated on your answer. *Exit* MAYOR [*and* SHERIFF]
KING HENRY IV Ah Harry, Harry, now thrice accursed Harry,[43] that hath gotten a son, which with grief will end his father's days. Oh my son, a prince thou art, aye, a prince indeed, and to deserve imprisonment. And well have they done, and like faithful subjects. Discharge them and let them go.
EXETER I beseech your grace, be good to my lord the young prince.
KING HENRY IV Nay, nay, 'tis no matter, let him alone.

39 82 Newgate: a prominent prison in London, at the corner of Newgate Street and Old Bailey Street. It held prisoners from outside of London who had been arrested in the city, hence the "country prison"
40 1 And: if it
41 6 What although: even though
42 26 to ward: to prison
43 29 Harry: King Henry addresses himself by the nickname Harry

OXFORD Perchance the mayor and the sheriff have been too precise[44] in this matter.
KING HENRY IV No, they have done like faithful subjects. I will go myself to discharge them, and let them go.

Exit omnes[45]

[Scene iv]

Enter LORD CHIEF JUSTICE,[46] CLERK OF THE OFFICE, JAILOR, [OFFICERS OF THE COURT], JOHN COBBLER, DERICK, *and the* THIEF

CHIEF JUSTICE Jailer, bring the prisoner to the bar.[47]
DERICK Hear you my lord, I pray you bring the bar to the prisoner.
CHIEF JUSTICE Hold thy hand up at the bar.
THIEF Here it is my lord.
CHIEF JUSTICE Clerk of the Office, read his indictment.
CLERK What is thy name?
THIEF My name was known before I came here, and shall be when I am gone, I warrant you.
CHIEF JUSTICE Aye, I think so, but we will know it better before thou go.
DERICK Zounds, and you do but send to the next jail, we are sure to know his name, for this is not the first prison he hath been in, I'll warrant you.
CLERK What is thy name?
THIEF What need you to ask, and have it in writing?
CLERK Is not thy name Cutbert Cutter?[48]
THIEF What the devil need you ask, and know it so well?
CLERK Why then Cutbert Cutter, I indict thee by the name of Cutbert Cutter, for robbing a poor carrier the twentieth day of May last past, in the fourteenth year of the reign of our sovereign lord King Henry the Fourth, for setting upon a poor carrier upon Gad's Hill in Kent, and having beaten and wounded the said carrier, and taken his goods from him.
DERICK Oh, masters stay there, nay let's never belie the man, for he hath not beaten and wounded me also, but he hath beaten and wounded my pack,[49] and hath taken the great raze[50] of ginger that bouncing Bess with the jolly buttocks should have had. That grieves me most.
CHIEF JUSTICE Well, what sayest thou, art thou guilty, or not guilty?
THIEF Not guilty, my lord.
CHIEF JUSTICE By whom wilt thou be tried?
THIEF By my lord the young prince, or by myself, whether you will.

Enter the young PRINCE, *with* NED *and* TOM

PRINCE Come away my lads, Gog's wounds ye villain, what make you here? I must go about my business myself, and you must stand loitering here?
THIEF Why my lord, they have bound me, and will not let me go.
PRINCE Have they bound thee villain? Why, how now my lord?
CHIEF JUSTICE I am glad to see your grace in good health.
PRINCE Why my lord, this is my man.[51] 'Tis marvel you knew him not long before this. I tell

44 35 precise: strict
45 37 SD *omnes*: all (Latin)
46 0 SD LORD CHIEF JUSTICE: a high-ranking government official, essentially the head of the judiciary
47 1 to the bar: the bar is a wooden barrier that separates the judge from the public areas of a courtroom. Those with business before the court must be called to the bar to be officially addressed or to address the judge
48 13 Cutbert Cutter: the name, like "Cobbler" or "Costermonger," denotes his profession. Thieves were known to "cut" the purse strings of their victims
49 20 pack: either his packhorse or his bag of deliverables
50 21 raze: root
51 32 man: servant

you, he is a man of his hands.[52]
THIEF Aye, Gog's wounds, that I am, try me who dare.
CHIEF JUSTICE Your grace shall find small credit by acknowledging him to be your man.
PRINCE Why my lord, what hath he done?
CHIEF JUSTICE And it please your majesty, he hath robbed a poor carrier.
DERICK Hear you sir, marry it was one Derick, Goodman Hobling's man, of Kent.
PRINCE What, was't you, button-breech?[53] Of my word my lord, he did it but in jest.
DERICK Hear you sir, is it your man's quality to rob folks in jest? In faith, he shall be hanged in earnest.
PRINCE Well my lord, what do you mean to do with my man?
CHIEF JUSTICE And please your grace, the law must pass on him, according to justice, then he must be executed.
DERICK Hear you sir, I pray you, is it your man's quality to rob folks in jest? In faith, he shall be hanged in jest.
PRINCE Well my lord, what mean you to do with my man?
CHIEF JUSTICE And please your grace, the law must pass on him, according to justice, then he must be executed.[54]
PRINCE Why then, belike you mean to hang my man?
CHIEF JUSTICE I am sorry that it falls out so.
PRINCE Why my lord, I pray ye, who am I?
CHIEF JUSTICE And please your grace, you are my lord the young prince, our king that shall be after the decease of our sovereign lord, King Henry the Fourth, whom God grant long to reign.
PRINCE You say true my lord. And you will hang my man.
CHIEF JUSTICE And like[55] your grace, I must needs do justice.
PRINCE Tell me my lord, shall I have my man?
CHIEF JUSTICE I cannot, my lord.
PRINCE But will you not let him go?
CHIEF JUSTICE I am sorry that his case is so ill.
PRINCE Tush, case me no casings. Shall I have my man?
CHIEF JUSTICE I cannot, nor I may not, my lord.
PRINCE Nay, and "I shall not" say, and then I am answered.
CHIEF JUSTICE No.
PRINCE No! Then I will have him. *He* [*the* PRINCE] *giveth him* [*the* LORD CHIEF JUSTICE] *a box on the ear*
NED Gog's wounds my lord, shall I cut off his head?
PRINCE No, I charge you draw not your swords, but get you hence. Provide a noise of musicians. Away, be gone.[56] *Exeunt* [NED *and* TOM]
CHIEF JUSTICE Well my lord, I am content to take it at your hands.
PRINCE Nay and you be not, you shall have more.
CHIEF JUSTICE Why, I pray you my lord, who am I?
PRINCE You? Who knows not you? Why man, you are Lord Chief Justice of England.
CHIEF JUSTICE Your grace hath said truth. Therefore, in striking me in this place, you greatly abuse me, and not me only, but also your father, whose lively person here in this place I do represent. And therefore, to teach you what prerogatives mean, I commit you to the Fleet,[57] until

52 33 man of his hands: literally means a manual laborer, but the prince bluntly indicates the thief's real profession as a pickpocket, for which he must be adept at using his hands

53 39 button-breech: an obscure insult, probably to do with Derick's rustic dress

54 49 The near repetition of the exchanges between lines 40–49 may be a compositor's error, and so lines 45–9 could be safely cut without any plot being lost. But the variation in Derick's remarks at 45–6, where he shifts to irony, is interesting, and repetition is an effective way to represent resistance—here, both Derick's and the Chief Justice's. The drawing out of the exchange, then, is just as likely intentional

55 57 And like: if it please

56 69 In what may be a misprint, Q has the thief exit here, although he is still evidently in the court's control, because the Chief Justice commands he be taken to prison, and we learn later that he has in fact been sent there.

57 76 Fleet: London prison east of the river Fleet, north of the Thames

we have spoken with your father.
PRINCE Why then, belike you mean to send me to the Fleet?
CHIEF JUSTICE Aye, indeed, and therefore carry him away.

Exeunt [PRINCE] *with the officers* [*and* JOHN *and* DERICK]

CHIEF JUSTICE Jailer, carry the prisoner to Newgate again, until the next assizes.[58]
JAILER At your commandment my lord, it shall be done.

[*Exeunt*]

[Scene v]

Enter DERICK *and* JOHN COBBLER

DERICK Zounds, masters,[59] here's ado, when princes must go to prison! Why John, didst ever see the like?
JOHN Oh Derick, trust me, I never saw the like.
DERICK Why, John, thou mayest see what princes be in choler! A judge a box on the ear! I'll tell thee, John, oh John, I would not have done it for twenty shillings.
JOHN No nor I, there had been no way but one with us, we should have been hanged.
DERICK Faith John, I'll tell thee what, thou shalt be my Lord Chief Justice, and thou shalt sit in the chair, and I'll be the young prince, and hit thee a box on the ear. And then thou shalt say, "to teach you what prerogatives mean, I commit you to the Fleet."
JOHN Come on, I'll be your judge. But thou shalt not hit me hard? [JOHN *sits in the chair*]
DERICK No, no.
JOHN What hath he done?
DERICK Marry, he hath robbed Derick.
JOHN Why then, I cannot let him go.
DERICK I must needs have my man.
JOHN You shall not have him.
DERICK Shall I not have my man, say no and[60] you dare. How say you, shall I not have my man?
JOHN No, marry, shall you not.
DERICK Shall I not John?
JOHN No, Derick.
DERICK Why then, take you that till more come. [*Gives* JOHN *a box on the ear*]
Zounds, shall I not have him?
JOHN Well I am content to take this at your hand. But I pray you, who am I?
DERICK Who art thou? Zounds, dost not know thyself?
JOHN No.
DERICK Now away, simple fellow. Why man, thou art John the cobbler.
JOHN No, I am my Lord Chief Justice of England.
DERICK Oh John, mass,[61] thou sayest true, thou art indeed.
JOHN Why then, to teach you what prerogatives mean, I commit you to the Fleet.
DERICK Well, I will go, but i'faith you gray beard knave, I'll course[62] you. *Exit. And straight enters again*
Oh John, come, come out of thy chair, why what a clown wert thou, to let me hit thee a box on the ear. And now thou see'st they will not take me to the Fleet. I think that thou art one of these worenday[63] clowns.

58 80 assizes: court sessions; "the prisoner" here means the thief
59 1 masters: probably directed at the audience
60 17 and: if
61 29 mass: short for "by the mass," a mild oath
62 31 course: thrash, beat
63 34 worenday: an uncertain word. Possibly "working day," that is, ordinary, basic, simple; or, it could be "wordeyned," an old spelling of "ordained," i.e. "you were fated to be a clown" (Bevington and Kastan, 1988)

JOHN But I marvel, what will become of thee?
DERICK Faith, I'll be no more a carrier.
JOHN What wilt thou do then?
DERICK I'll dwell with thee and be a cobbler.
JOHN With me? Alas, I am not able to keep thee. Why, thou wilt eat me out of doors.
DERICK Oh John, no John, I am none of these great slouching fellows, that devour these great pieces of beef and brewis.[64] Alas, a trifle serves me: a woodcock, a chicken, or a capon's leg,[65] or any such little thing serves me.
JOHN A capon! Why man, I cannot get a capon once a year, except it be at Christmas, at some other man's house, for we cobblers be glad of a dish of roots.
DERICK Roots? Why, are you so good at rooting? Nay, cobbler, we'll have you ringed.[66]
JOHN But Derick, though we be so poor, yet will we have in store a crab in the fire, with nut-brown ale, that is full stale, which will a man quail, and lay in the mire.[67]
DERICK A bots on you, and be but[68] for your ale, I'll dwell with you. Come, let's away as fast as we can.

Exeunt

[Scene vi]

Enter the young PRINCE, *with* NED *and* TOM

PRINCE Come away sirs. Gog's wounds Ned, didst thou not see what a box on the ear I took[69] my Lord Chief Justice?
TOM By Gog's blood, it did me good to see it! It made his teeth jar in his head.

Enter SIR JOHN OLDCASTLE

PRINCE How now Sir John Oldcastle, what news with you?
OLDCASTLE I am glad to see your grace at liberty. I was come, I, to visit you in prison.
PRINCE To visit me? Didst thou not know that I am a prince's son? Why, 'tis enough for me to look into a prison, though I come not in myself. But here's such ado nowadays, here's prisoning, here's hanging, whipping, and the devil and all. But I tell you sirs, when I am king, we will have no such things. But my lads, if the old king my father were dead, we would be all kings.
OLDCASTLE He is a good old man. God take him to his mercy the sooner.
PRINCE But Ned, so soon as I am king, the first thing I will do, shall be to put my Lord Chief Justice out of office. And thou shalt be my Lord Chief Justice of England.
NED Shall I be Lord Chief Justice? By Gog's wounds, I'll be the bravest Lord Chief Justice that ever was in England.
PRINCE Then Ned, I'll turn all these prisons into fence schools,[70] and I will endow thee with them, with lands to maintain them withal. Then I will have a bout with my Lord Chief Justice. Thou shalt hang none but pick-purses and horse-stealers, and such base-minded villains. But that fellow that will stand by the highway-side courageously with his sword and buckler[71] and take a purse—that fellow, give him commendations. Beside that, send him to me and I will give him an annual pension out of my exchequer, to maintain him all the days of his life.
OLDCASTLE Nobly spoken Harry. We shall never have a merry world till the old king be dead.

64 41 beef and brewis: boiled beef with broth and vegetables
65 41–2 capon's leg: Derick is casually suggesting that he expects a fairly rich diet. A capon is a castrated rooster
66 45 Derick suggests that John must be a pig ("good at rooting") and so should have a ring put in his nose
67 47 in the mire: John probably sings the little rhyme here, starting with "yet we will." A "crab" is an apple, "full stale" means strong, and "quail and lay in the mire" means the ale is strong enough to knock a man out
68 48 and be but: and if not for
69 1 took: gave
70 16 fence schools: fencing schools
71 19 sword and buckler: buckler is a type of round shield; the phrase "sword and buckler" connotes a lower-class, boastful brawler

NED But whither are ye going now?

PRINCE To the court, for I hear say my father lies very sick.

TOM But I doubt[72] he will not die.

PRINCE Yet will I go thither, for the breath shall be no sooner out of his mouth, but I will clap the crown on my head. [The PRINCE *produces a cloak with needles*[73] *attached and puts it on*]

OLDCASTLE Will you go to the court with that cloak so full of needles?

PRINCE Cloak, eyelet-holes, needles, and all was of mine own devising, and therefore I will wear it.

TOM I pray you my lord, what may be the meaning thereof?

PRINCE Why man, 'tis a sign that I stand upon thorns, till the crown be on my head.

OLDCASTLE Or that every needle might be a prick to their hearts that repine at your doings.

PRINCE Thou sayest true Jockey. But there's some will say, the young prince will be a well-toward young man and all this gear,[74] that I had as lief they would break my head with a pot, as to say any such thing. But we stand prating here too long. I must needs speak with my father. Therefore, come away. [*They cross the stage and knock at the castle door.* A PORTER *answers*]

PORTER What a rapping keep you at the king's court gate?

PRINCE Here's one that must speak with the king.

PORTER The king is very sick, and none must speak with him.

PRINCE No? You rascal, do you not know me?

PORTER You are my lord the young prince.

PRINCE Then go and tell my father that I must and will speak with him. [*Exit* PORTER]

NED Shall I cut off his head?

PRINCE No, no! Though I would help you in other places, yet I have nothing to do here. What, you are in my father's court.

NED I will write him in my tables,[75] for so soon as I am made Lord Chief Justice, I will put him out of his office. *The trumpet sounds*

PRINCE Gog's wounds sirs, the king comes. Let's all stand aside. [*Exeunt* PRINCE *and others*]

Enter the KING [HENRY IV], *with the* LORD OF EXETER

KING HENRY IV And is it true my lord, that my son is already sent to the Fleet? Now truly that man is more fitter to rule the realm than I, for by no means could I rule my son, and he by one word hath caused him to be ruled. Oh my son, my son, no sooner out of one prison, but into another. I had thought once whiles I had lived, to have seen this noble realm of England flourish by thee my son, but now I see it goes to ruin and decay. *He weepeth*

Enters LORD of OXFORD

OXFORD And please your grace, here is my lord your son, that cometh to speak with you. He saith he must and will speak with you.

KING HENRY IV Who, my son Harry?

OXFORD Aye, and please your majesty.

KING HENRY IV I know wherefore he cometh. But look that none come with him.

OXFORD A very disordered company, and such as make very ill rule in your majesty's house.

72 25 doubt: fear

73 27 SD *cloak with needles*: the prince might be wearing this strange garment from the start of the scene; Oldcastle might be referring to a cloak he knows about but that is not present on stage yet; or, as this suggested stage direction indicates, he might have just now put it on and thus prompted Oldcastle's question

74 35 gear: stuff or nonsense

75 47 tables: literally a notebook, but used here metaphorically as a vow to remember something

KING HENRY IV Well let him come, but look that none come with him.

[OXFORD] *goeth* [*toward where* PRINCE *exited and calls*]

OXFORD And please your grace, my lord the king sends for you.

[PRINCE *and companions re-enter*]

PRINCE Come away sirs, let's go all together.

OXFORD And please your grace, none must go with you.

PRINCE Why I must needs have them with me. Otherwise I can do my father no countenance.[76] Therefore come away.

OXFORD The king your father commands there should none come.

PRINCE Well sirs, then be gone. And provide me three noise of musicians.

Exeunt knights [NED, TOM, OLDCASTLE]

[*The*] PRINCE [*steps forward*] *with a dagger in his hand*

KING HENRY IV Come my son, come on a God's name, I know wherefore thy coming is. Oh my son, my son, what cause hath ever been, that thou shouldst forsake me, and follow this vild[77] and reprobate[78] company, which abuseth youth so manifestly. Oh my son, thou knowest that these thy doings will end thy father's days. (*He weeps*) Aye, so, so, my son, thou fearest not to approach the presence of thy sick father, in that disguised sort, I tell thee my son, that there is never a needle in thy cloak, but it is a prick to my heart. And never an eyelet-hole, but it is a hole to my soul. And wherefore thou bringest that dagger in thy hand I know not, but by conjecture. *He weeps*

PRINCE My conscience accuseth me, most sovereign lord, and well-beloved father, to answer first to the last point. That is, whereas you conjecture that this hand and this dagger shall be armed against your life—No! Know my beloved father, far be the thoughts of your son—son said I? An unworthy son for so good a father. But far be the thoughts of any such pretended mischief. And I most humbly render it to your majesty's hand, and live my lord and sovereign forever. And with your dagger arm show like vengeance upon the body of that your son! I was about to say and dare not! Ah, woe is me, therefore that, your wild slave.[79] 'Tis not the crown that I come for, sweet father, because I am unworthy. And those vild and reprobate company[80] I abandon, and utterly abolish their company forever. Pardon sweet father, pardon. The least thing and most desire.[81] And this ruffianly cloak, I here tear from my back, and sacrifice it to the devil, which is master of all mischief. Pardon me, sweet father, pardon me. Good my Lord of Exeter speak for me. Pardon me, pardon good father. Not a word! Ah, he will not speak one word. Ah Harry, now thrice unhappy Harry. But what shall I do? I will go take me into some solitary place, and there lament my sinful life, and when I have done, I will lay me down and die. *Exit*

KING HENRY IV Call him again, call my son again.

[PRINCE *re-enters*]

PRINCE And doth my father call me again? Now Harry, happy be the time that thy father calleth thee again. [PRINCE *kneels*]

KING HENRY IV Stand up my son, and do not think thy father, but at the request of thee, my son, I will pardon thee. And God bless thee, and make thee his servant.

PRINCE Thanks good my lord, and no doubt but this day, even this day, I am born new again.

KING HENRY IV Come my son and lords, take me by the hands.

Exeunt omnes

76 66 can do . . . no countenance: cannot show my father respect

77 72 vild: archaic form of vile, perhaps also meaning here and elsewhere in the play "wild"

78 72 reprobate: sinful

79 83 I was . . . wild slave: I was about to call myself your son, but dare not given my behavior; call me instead your wild slave

80 85 company: companions

81 86 most desire: sense uncertain. Perhaps it should read "most desired," i.e. abandoning the bad companions is the least he can do, and the thing the king most wants of him

[Scene vii]

Enter DERICK

DERICK Thou art a stinking whore, and a whoreson stinking whore! Doest think I'll take it at thy hands?

Enter JOHN COBBLER *running*

JOHN Derick, D, D![82] Hearest 'a?[83] Do D, never while thou livest use that.[84] Why, what will my neighbors say, and thou go away so?
DERICK She's an arrant whore, and I'll have the law on you, John.
JOHN Why, what hath she done?
DERICK Marry, mark thou John. I will prove it, that I will.
JOHN What wilt thou prove?
DERICK That she called me in to dinner. John, mark the tale well, John. And when I was set, she brought me a dish of roots and a piece of barrel butter[85] therein. And she is a very knave, and thou a drab[86] if thou take her part.
JOHN Hearest 'a Derick, is this the matter? Nay, and it be no worse, we will go home again, and all shall be amended.
DERICK Oh John, hearest 'a John, is all well?
JOHN Aye, all is well.
DERICK Then I'll go home before, and break all the glass windows.

[*Exeunt*]

[Scene viii]

Enter the KING [HENRY IV] *with his* LORDS [OXFORD *and* EXETER]

KING HENRY IV Come my lords. I see it boots me not[87] to take any physic,[88] for all the physicians in the world cannot cure me, no not one. But good my lords, remember my last will and testament concerning my son. For truly my lords, I do not think but[89] he will prove as valiant and victorious a king as ever reigned in England.
BOTH LORDS Let heaven and earth be witness between us, if we accomplish not thy will to the uttermost.
KING HENRY IV I give you most unfeigned thanks, good my lords. Draw the curtains and depart my chamber a while, and cause some music to rock me asleep.

Exeunt LORDS, [*music plays*]. *He sleepeth* [*music stops*]

Enter the PRINCE

PRINCE Ah Harry, thrice unhappy, that hath neglect so long from visiting of thy sick father. I will go. Nay but why do I not go to the chamber of my sick father, to comfort the melancholy soul of his body? His soul said I? Here is his body indeed, but his soul is whereas it needs no body.[90] Now thrice accursed Harry, that hath offended thy father so much, and could not I crave pardon for all. Oh my dying father, cursed be the day wherein I was born, and accursed be the hour wherein I was begotten! But what shall I do? If weeping tears which come

82 3 D: John calls Derick by the first letter of his name
83 3 Hearest 'a?: do you hear me?
84 3 use that: act that way
85 10 barrel butter: preserved butter (Derick would prefer fresh)
86 11 knave, and thou a drab: a drab is an untidy woman, usually implied to be a prostitute or sexually loose. Derick has, for comic effect, mixed up his insults, calling John a "drab" and his wife a "knave" (fool, or rogue, an insult usually reserved for men)
87 1 boots me not: does me no good
88 1 physic: medicine
89 3 I do not think but: a double negative meaning "I have no doubt"
90 12: needs no body: the prince believes his father is dead, so that his soul is free (and so "needs no body")

too late may suffice the negligence neglected[91] to some, I will weep day and night until the fountain be dry with weeping. *Exit [with crown]*

Enter LORDS OF EXETER *and* OXFORD

EXETER Come easily[92] my lord, for waking of[93] the king.
KING HENRY IV [*Wakes*] Now my lords.
OXFORD How doth your grace feel yourself?
KING HENRY IV Somewhat better after my sleep. But good my lords, take off my crown, remove my chair a little back, and set me right.
BOTH And please your grace, the crown is taken away.
KING HENRY IV The crown taken away! Good my Lord of Oxford, go see who hath done this deed. [*Exit* OXFORD] No doubt 'tis some vild traitor that hath done it, to deprive my son. They that would do it now, would seek to scrape and scrawl[94] for it after my death.

Enter LORD OF OXFORD *with the* PRINCE

OXFORD Here, and please your grace, is my lord the young prince with the crown.
KING HENRY IV Why, how now my son? I had thought the last time I had you in schooling, I had given you a lesson for all, and do you now begin again? Why, tell me my son, dost thou think the time so long, that thou would'st have it before the breath be out of my mouth?
PRINCE Most sovereign lord, and well-beloved father, I came into your chamber to comfort the melancholy soul of your body. And finding you at that time past all recovery, and dead to my thinking, God is my witness! And what should I do, but with weeping tears lament the death of you, my father, and after that, seeing the crown, I took it. And tell me, my father, who might better take it than I, after your death? But seeing you live, I most humbly render it into your majesty's hands. And the happiest man alive, that my father live! And live my lord and father, forever.
KING HENRY IV Stand up my son, thine answer hath sounded well in mine ears. For I must need confess that I was in a very sound sleep, and altogether unmindful of thy coming. But come near my son, and let me put thee in possession whilst I live, that none deprive thee of it after my death.
PRINCE Well may I take it at your majesty's hands, but it shall never touch my head, so long as my father lives. *He taketh the crown*
KING HENRY IV God give thee joy my son, God bless thee and make thee his servant, and send thee a prosperous reign. For God knows my son, how hardly I came by it, and how hardly I have maintained it.
PRINCE Howsoever you came by it, I know not. But now I have it from you, and from you I will keep it. And he that seeks to take the crown from my head, let him look that his armor be thicker than mine, or I will pierce him to the heart, were it harder than brass or bullion.
KING HENRY IV Nobly spoken, and like a king. Now trust me my lords, I fear not but[95] my son will be as warlike and victorious a prince, as ever reigned in England.
BOTH His former life shows no less.
KING HENRY IV Well my lords, I know not whether it be for sleep, or drawing near of drowsy summer[96] of death, but I am very much given to sleep. Therefore, good my lords, and my son, draw the curtains, depart my chamber, and cause some music to rock me asleep.

[*Music resumes*]
Exeunt [*all but* KING HENRY IV]
The KING *dieth*

91 14–15 If weeping . . . negligence neglected: meaning uncertain, but seems to indicate some hope for God's (unmerited) grace through contrition
92 17 easily: softly
93 17 for waking of: to avoid waking
94 25 scrape and scrawl: scratch and scramble
95 48 I fear not but: I have no doubt
96 52 summer: possibly a misprint for "slumber" or "summoner"

[Scene ix]

Enter the THIEF

THIEF Ah God, I am now like to a bird which hath escaped out of the cage. For so soon as my Lord Chief Justice heard that the old king was dead, he was glad to let me go, for fear of my lord the young prince. But here comes some of his companions. I will see and I can get anything of them, for old acquaintance.

Enter Knights [TOM, NED, OLDCASTLE] *ranging*[97]

TOM Gog's wounds, the king is dead.
OLDCASTLE Dead! Then Gog's blood, we shall be all kings.
NED Gog's wounds, I shall be Lord Chief Justice of England.
TOM [*Notices the* THIEF] Why, how are you broken out of prison?
NED Gog's wounds, how the villain stinks.
OLDCASTLE Why, what will become of thee now? Fie upon him, how the rascal stinks.
THIEF Marry, I will go and serve my master again.
TOM Gog's blood, dost think that he will have any such scabbed knave as thou art? What man, he is a king now.
NED Hold thee, here's a couple of angels[98] for thee, and get thee gone, for the king will not be long before he come this way. And hereafter, I will tell the king of thee. *Exit* THIEF
OLDCASTLE Oh, how it did me good, to see the king when he was crowned. Methought his seat[99] was like the figure of heaven, and his person like unto a god.
NED But who would have thought, that the king would have changed his countenance so?
OLDCASTLE Did you not see with what grace he sent his embassage[100] into France, to tell the French king that Harry of England hath sent for the crown, and Harry of England will have it?
TOM But 'twas but a little to make the people believe that he was sorry for his father's death. *The trumpet sounds*
NED Gog's wounds, the king comes. Let's all stand aside.

Enter [*the* PRINCE, *now as*] KING [HENRY V] *with the* ARCHBISHOP [OF CANTERBURY] *and the* LORD OF OXFORD

OLDCASTLE How do you, my lord?
NED How now Harry? Tut my lord, put away these dumps,[101] you are a king, and all the realm is yours. What man, do you not remember the old sayings? You know I must be Lord Chief Justice of England. Trust me my lord, methinks you are very much changed, and 'tis but with a little sorrowing, to make folks believe the death of your father grieves you, and 'tis nothing so.
KING HENRY V I prithee Ned, mend thy manners, and be more modester in thy terms. For my unfeigned grief is not to be ruled by thy flattering and dissembling talk. Thou sayest I am changed. So I am indeed, and so must thou be, and that quickly, or else I must cause thee to be changed.
OLDCASTLE Gog's wounds, how like you this? Zounds, 'tis not so sweet as music.
TOM I trust we have not offended your grace no way.
KING HENRY V Ah Tom, your former life grieves me, and makes me to abandon and abolish your company forever. And therefore, not upon pain of death to approach my presence by ten miles' space. Then, if I hear well of you, it may be I will do somewhat for you. Otherwise look

97 4 SD *ranging*: walking across the stage
98 15 angels: coins (so-called for being stamped with St. Michael the archangel)
99 18 seat: perhaps the throne, or Henry's bearing and posture as he sat in it
100 20 embassage: embassy
101 26 these dumps: this melancholy

for no more favor at my hands, than at any other man's. And therefore be gone, we have other matters to talk on. *Exeunt Knights* [TOM, NED, OLDCASTLE]
Now my good Lord Archbishop of Canterbury, what say you to our embassage into France?
CANTERBURY Your right to the French crown of France, came by your great grandmother Isabel, wife to King Edward the Third, and sister to Charles the French king. Now if the French king deny it, as likely enough he will, then must you take your sword in hand, and conquer the right. Let the usurped[102] Frenchman know, although your predecessors have let it pass, you will not. For your countrymen are willing with purse and men, to aid you. Then my good lord, as it hath been always known, that Scotland hath been in league with France, by a sort of pensions which yearly come from thence, I think it therefore best to conquer Scotland, and then I think that you may go more easily into France. And this is all that I can say, my good lord.
KING HENRY V I thank you, my good Lord Archbishop of Canterbury. What say you my good Lord of Oxford?
OXFORD And please your majesty, I agree to my Lord Archbishop, saving in this: he that will Scotland win, must first with France begin, according to the old saying. Therefore my good lord, I think it best first to invade France, for in conquering Scotland, you conquer but one: and conquer France, and conquer both.[103]

Enter LORD OF EXETER

EXETER And please your majesty, my Lord Ambassador is come out of France.
KING HENRY V Now trust me my lord, he was the last man that we talked of. I am glad that he is come to resolve us of our answer; commit him to our presence.

Enter DUKE OF YORK

YORK God save the life of my sovereign lord the King.
KING HENRY V Now my good lord the Duke of York, what news from our brother the French king?
YORK And please your majesty, I delivered him my embassage, whereof I took some deliberation. But for the answer he hath sent my Lord Ambassador of Bourges,[104] the Duke of Burgundy, Monsieur le Cole, with two hundred and fifty horsemen, to bring the embassage.
KING HENRY V Commit my Lord Archbishop of Bourges into our presence.

Enter ARCHBISHOP OF BOURGES

Now my Lord Archbishop of Bourges, we do learn by our Lord Ambassador, that you have our message to do from our brother the French king. Here my good lord, according to our accustomed order, we give you free liberty and license to speak, with good audience.
BOURGES God save the mighty King of England. My lord and master, the most Christian King Charles the Sixth,[105] the great and mighty King of France, as a most noble and Christian king, not minding[106] to shed innocent blood, is rather content to yield somewhat to your unreasonable demands. That if fifty thousand crowns a year, with his daughter the said Lady Katherine, in marriage, and some crowns which he may well spare, not hurting of his kingdom, he is content to yield so far to your unreasonable desire.
KING HENRY V Why, then belike your lord and master thinks to puff me up with fifty thousand crowns a year! No, tell thy lord and master, that all the crowns in France shall not serve me, except

102 45 usurped: usurping
103 54–5 and conquer France, and conquer both: i.e. by conquering France, you simultaneously conquer Scotland
104 63 Lord Ambassador of Bourges: this character is both the Archbishop of Bourges and an ambassador for the French King, and is referred to both ways
105 70 Sixth: in Q the king is referred to here as the "seventh," although historically the king is the sixth. The Dolphin of this play would eventually become Charles VII
106 71 minding: wishing

the crown and kingdom itself. And perchance hereafter I will have his daughter.

BOURGES And it please your majesty, my lord Prince Dolphin[107] greets you well, with this present. *He* [BOURGES] *delivereth a tun*[108] *of tennis balls*

KING HENRY V What, a gilded tun? I pray you my Lord of York, look, what is in it?

YORK And it please your grace, here is a carpet and a tun of tennis balls.

KING HENRY V A tun of tennis balls? I pray you good my Lord Archbishop, what might the meaning thereof be?

BOURGES And it please you my lord, a messenger you know, ought to keep close his message,[109] and specially an ambassador.

KING HENRY V But I know that you may declare your message to a king. The law of arms allows no less.

BOURGES My lord, hearing of your wildness before your father's death, sent you this my good lord, meaning that you are more fitter for a tennis court than a field, and more fitter for a carpet[110] than the camp.

KING HENRY V My lord Prince Dolphin is very pleasant with me. But tell him, that instead of balls of leather, we will toss him balls of brass and iron,[111] yea such balls as never were tossed in France. The proudest tennis court shall rue it. Aye, and thou, Prince of Bourges, shall rue it. Therefore get thee hence, and tell him thy message quickly, lest I be there before thee. Away priest, be gone.

BOURGES I beseech your grace, to deliver me your safe conduct under your broad seal manual.[112]

KING HENRY V Priest of Bourges, know, that the hand and seal of a king, and his word, is all one. And instead of my hand and seal, I will bring him my hand and sword. And tell thy lord and master that I, Harry of England, said it, and I, Harry of England, will perform it. My Lord of York, deliver him our safe conduct, under our broad seal manual.

Exeunt ARCHBISHOP [OF BOURGES], *and the* DUKE OF YORK

Now my lords, to arms, to arms, for I vow by heaven and earth, that the proudest Frenchman in all France shall rue the time that ever these tennis balls were sent into England. My lord, I will ye there be provided a great navy of ships, with all speed, at Southampton,[113] for there I mean to ship my men. For I would be there before him, if it were possible. Therefore come. But stay! I had almost forgot the chiefest thing of all, with chafing with this French ambassador. Call in my Lord Chief Justice of England.

Enters LORD CHIEF JUSTICE OF ENGLAND

EXETER Here is the king, my lord.

CHIEF JUSTICE God preserve your majesty.

KING HENRY V Why, how now my lord, what is the matter?

CHIEF JUSTICE I would it were unknown to your majesty.

KING HENRY V Why, what ails you?

CHIEF JUSTICE Your majesty knoweth my grief well.

KING HENRY V Oh my lord, you remember you sent me to the Fleet, did you not?

CHIEF JUSTICE I trust your grace have forgotten that.

KING HENRY V Aye, truly my lord, and for revengement, I have chosen you to be my Protector[114] over my realm, until it shall please God to give me speedy return out of France.

CHIEF JUSTICE And if it please your majesty, I am far unworthy of so high a dignity.

107 78 Dolphin: the French heir was traditionally titled the *Dauphin*, French for dolphin, after an emblem that appeared on the heir's coat of arms; the English often used the translated title rather than the French term

108 79 SD *tun*: cask or barrel

109 84–5 keep close his message: say no more than he has been instructed to

110 90 carpet: indoors, in a comfortable place

111 92 brass and iron: that is, instead of tennis balls (made from leather), cannon balls

112 96–7 seal manual: a seal that has been signed by the king

113 104 Southampton: port city southwest of London

114 117 Protector: head of the government in the king's absence

KING HENRY V Tut my lord, you are not unworthy, because I think you worthy. For you that would not spare me, I think will not spare another. It must needs be so, and therefore come, let us be gone, and get our men in a readiness.

Exeunt omnes

[Scene x]

Enter a CAPTAIN, JOHN COBBLER, *and his* [COBBLER's] WIFE

CAPTAIN Come, come, there's no remedy. Thou must needs serve the king.
JOHN Good master Captain, let me go, I am not able to go so far.
WIFE I pray you good master Captain, be good to my husband.
CAPTAIN Why, I am sure he is not too good to serve the king?
JOHN Alas no. But a great deal too bad. Therefore, I pray you, let me go.
CAPTAIN No, no, thou shalt go.
JOHN Oh sir, I have a great many shoes at home to cobble.
WIFE I pray you let him go home again.
CAPTAIN Tush, I care not, thou shalt go.
JOHN Oh wife, and you had been a loving wife to me, this had not been, for I have said many times, that I would go away, and now I must go against my will. *He weepeth*

Enters DERICK [*with a potlid*]

DERICK How now ho, *basillus manus* for an old codpiece.[115] Master Captain shall we away? Zounds, how now John, what, a-crying? What make you and my dame there? I marvel whose head you will throw the stools at, now we are gone.
WIFE I'll tell you, come, ye cloghead. What do you with my potlid? Hear you, will you have it rapped about your pate? *She beateth him with her potlid*
DERICK Oh good dame! *Here he shakes her*
And I had my dagger here, I would worry[116] you all to pieces, that I would.
WIFE Would you so? I'll try that.[117] *She beateth him*
DERICK Master Captain, will you suffer her? Go to, dame, I will go back as far as I can. But and you come again, I'll clap the law on your back, that's flat. I'll tell you, master Captain, what you shall do: press her for a soldier, I warrant you, she will do as much good as her husband and I, too.

Enters the THIEF

Zounds, who comes yonder?
CAPTAIN How now good fellow, dost thou want a master?
THIEF Aye, truly sir.
CAPTAIN Hold thee then, I press thee for a soldier to serve the king in France.
DERICK How now Gads, what, dost know'st? Think'st?[118]
THIEF Aye, I knew thee long ago.
DERICK Hear you, master Captain?
CAPTAIN What sayest thou?
DERICK I pray you let me go home again.
CAPTAIN Why what wouldst thou do at home?
DERICK Marry I have brought two shirts with me, and I would carry one of them home again,

115 12 *basillus manus* . . . old codpiece: a vulgar, impertinent salutation. The italicized portion is a corruption of the Spanish phrase "besar los manos," i.e. "kiss the hands," a form of greeting; a "codpiece" is a prominent pouch or flap of material that covers a man's genitals

116 18 worry: here, cut; technically, to tear the neck with the teeth, as a dog or wolf might

117 19 I'll try that: a taunt, basically, "I'd like to see you try"

118 28 know'st? Think'st?: Derick sarcastically asks: "Do you know me *now*? What do you think?"

for I am sure he'll steal it from me, he is such a filching fellow.
CAPTAIN I warrant thee, he will not steal it from thee. Come let's away.
DERICK Come master Captain, let's away. Come follow me.
JOHN Come wife, let's part lovingly.
WIFE Farewell, good husband.
DERICK Fie, what a kissing and crying is here? Zounds, do ye think he will never come again? Why John come away, dost think that we are so base-minded to die among Frenchmen? Zounds, we know not whether they will lay us in their church or no. Come master Captain, let's away.
CAPTAIN I cannot stay no longer, therefore come away.

Exeunt omnes

[Scene xi]

Enter the [FRENCH] KING, PRINCE DOLPHIN, *and* LORD HIGH CONSTABLE[119] OF FRANCE

FRENCH KING Now my Lord High Constable, what say you to our embassage into England?
HIGH CONSTABLE And it please your majesty, I can say nothing, until my lords ambassadors be come home. But yet me thinks, your grace hath done well, to get your men in so good a readiness, for fear of the worst.
FRENCH KING Aye, my lord, we have some in a readiness, but if the King of England make against us, we must have thrice so many more.
DOLPHIN Tut my lord. Although the King of England be young and wild-headed, yet never think he will be so unwise to make battle against the mighty King of France.
FRENCH KING Oh my son, although the King of England be young and wild-headed, yet never think but he is ruled by his wise counselors.

Enter ARCHBISHOP OF BOURGES

BOURGES God save the life of my sovereign lord the King.
FRENCH KING Now my good Lord Archbishop of Bourges, what news from our brother the English king?
BOURGES And please your majesty, he is so far from your expectation, that nothing will serve him but the crown and kingdom itself. Besides, he bade me haste quickly, lest he be there before me, and, so far as I hear, he hath kept promise, for they say he is already landed at Kidcocks[120] in Normandy, upon the river of Seine, and laid his siege to the garrison town of Harfleur.[121]
FRENCH KING You have made great haste in the meantime, have you not?
DOLPHIN I pray you my lord, how did the King of England take my presents?
BOURGES Truly my lord, in very ill part. For these your balls of leather, he will toss you balls of brass and iron. Trust me my lord, I was very afraid of him, he is such a haughty and high-minded prince. He is as fierce as a lion.
HIGH CONSTABLE Tush, we will make him as tame as a lamb, I warrant you.

Enters a MESSENGER

MESSENGER God save the mighty King of France.
FRENCH KING Now messenger, what news?
MESSENGER And it please your majesty, I come from your poor distressed town of Harfleur, which is so beset on every side, if your majesty do not send present aid, the town will be yielded to the English king.

119 0 SD LORD HIGH CONSTABLE: a high ranking noble, traditionally the commander-in-chief of the French army
120 16 Kidcocks: Chef de Caux, a point near the port city Le Havre
121 17 Harfleur: seaport town in Normandy, on the northwest French coast

FRENCH KING Come my lords, come, shall we stand still till our country be spoiled under our noses? My lords, let the Normans, Brabants, Picardies, and Danes be sent for with all speed. And you, my Lord High Constable, I make general over all my whole army. Monsieur le Cole, master of the bows, Signor Devens, and all the rest, at your appointment.
DOLPHIN I trust your majesty will bestow some part of the battle on me. I hope not to present any otherwise than well.
FRENCH KING I tell thee my son, although I should get the victory, and thou lose thy life, I should think myself quite conquered, and the Englishmen to have the victory.
DOLPHIN Why my lord and father, I would have the petty King of England to know, that I dare encounter him in any ground of the world.
FRENCH KING I know well my son, but at this time I will have it thus.[122] Therefore, come away.

Exeunt omnes

[Scene xii]

Enters [KING] HENRY V, *with his* LORDS [YORK *and* OXFORD]

KING HENRY V Come my lords of England, no doubt this good luck of winning this town, is a sign of an honorable victory to come. But good my lord, go and speak to the captains with all speed, to number the host of the Frenchmen, and by that means we may the better know how to appoint the battle.
YORK And it please your majesty, there are many of your men sick and diseased, and many of them die for want of victuals.
KING HENRY V And why did you not tell me of it before? If we cannot have it for money, we will have it by dint of sword. The law of arms allows no less.
OXFORD I beseech your grace, to grant me a boon.
KING HENRY V What is that my good lord?
OXFORD That your grace would give me the avant-garde[123] in the battle.
KING HENRY V Trust me my Lord of Oxford, I cannot, for I have already given it to my uncle the Duke of York. Yet I thank you for your good will. (*A trumpet sounds*) How now, what is that?
YORK I think it be some herald of arms.[124]

Enters a [FRENCH] HERALD

FRENCH HERALD King of England, my Lord High Constable, and others of the noblemen of France, sends me to defy thee, as open enemy to God, our country, and us, and hereupon, they presently bid thee battle.
KING HENRY V Herald, tell them that I defy them as open enemies to God, my country, and me, and as wrongful usurpers of my right. And whereas thou sayest they presently bid me battle, tell them that I think they know how to please me. But I pray thee, what place hath my lord Prince Dolphin here in battle?
FRENCH HERALD And it please your grace, my lord and king his father will not let him come into the field.
KING HENRY V Why then he doth me great injury. I thought that he and I should have played at tennis together. Therefore, I have brought tennis balls for him, but other manner of ones than he sent me. And herald, tell my lord Prince Dolphin, that I have inured[125] my hands with other kind of weapons than tennis balls ere this time a day, and that he shall find it ere it be long. And

122 39 I will have it thus: I will not allow you to participate in the battle
123 11 avant-garde: the lead position of the attack
124 15 herald of arms: a messenger/diplomat whose safe passage between armies was traditionally guaranteed by codes of medieval warfare
125 27 inured: practiced

so adieu my friend. And tell my lord, that I am ready when he will. *Exit* [FRENCH] HERALD
Come my lords, I care not and I go[126] to our captains, and I'll see the number of the French army myself. Strike up the drum!

Exeunt omnes

[Scene xiii]

Enter [THREE] FRENCH SOLDIERS

1 FRENCH SOLDIER Come away Jack Drummer,[127] come away all, and me will tell you what me will do.[128] Me will tro[129] one chance on the dice, who shall have the King of England and his lords.
2 FRENCH SOLDIER Come away Jack Drummer, and tro your chance, and lay down your drum.

Enter [FRENCH] DRUMMER

FRENCH DRUMMER Oh, the brave apparel that the Englishmans hay broth[130] over, I will tell you what me ha done, me ha provided a hundreth trunks, and all to put the fine 'parel[131] of the Englishmans in.
1 FRENCH SOLDIER What do thou mean by trunks?
2 FRENCH SOLDIER A shest[132] man, a hundred shests.
1 FRENCH SOLDIER Ah *oui*, ah *oui*, ah *oui*, me will tell you what, me ha put five shildren out of my house, and all too little to put the fine apparel of the Englishmans in.[133]
FRENCH DRUMMER Oh the brave, the brave apparel that we shall have anon. But come, and you shall see what we will tro at the king's drummer and fife.[134] [*Rolls dice*] Ha, me ha no good luck, tro you.
THIRD FRENCH SOLDIER Faith, me will tro at the Earl of Northumberland and my Lord a Willoughby, with his great horse: snorting, farting, oh brave horse. [*Rolls dice*]
FIRST FRENCH SOLDIER Ha, by'r lady, you ha reasonable good luck, now I will tro at the king himself: Ha, me have no good luck. [*Rolls dice*]

Enters a [FRENCH] CAPTAIN

FRENCH CAPTAIN How now, what make you here, so far from the camp?
SECOND FRENCH SOLDIER Shall me tell our captain what we have done here?
FRENCH DRUMMER Ah *oui*, ah *oui*. *Exeunt* [FRENCH] DRUMMER, *and* [FIRST FRENCH] SOLDIER
SECOND FRENCH SOLDIER I will tell you what we have done. We have been troing our shance on the dice, but none can win the king.
FRENCH CAPTAIN I think so! Why, he is left behind for me. And I have set three or four chair-makers a work, to make a new disguised[135] chair to set that womanly King of England

126 30 I care . . . I go: I wouldn't mind going
127 1 Jack Drummer: "Jack Drum" was part of a proverbial expression for harsh treatment, probably military in origin. Here, it seems to be adapted as a generic, perhaps joking, name for the French drummer
128 2 me will do: I will do; unlike the French nobility introduced in previous scenes, the lower-class French characters in this and some ensuing scenes speak at times in broken English, probably with an exaggerated accent, an attempt by the playwright to highlight their foreignness for comic effect
129 2 tro: throw
130 6 hay broth: have brought
131 7 'parel: apparel
132 10 shest: chest
133 11–12 me ha . . . Englishmans in: the French soldier hyperbolically claims that even though he has evicted five of his children to make room for all the clothes he plans to confiscate from defeated English soldiers, there will still not be enough space
134 14 tro at . . . and fife: i.e. throw for the apparel of the English drummer and fife player
135 26 disguised: elaborately designed

in, that all the people may laugh and scoff at him.
SECOND FRENCH SOLDIER Oh brave captain!
FRENCH CAPTAIN I am glad, and yet with a kind of pity to see the poor king. Why, who ever saw a more flourishing army in France in one day, than here is? Are not here all the peers of France? Are not here the Normans with their fiery handguns, and flaunching curtle-axes?[136] Are not here the Brabantians[137] with their bard horses,[138] and launching spears? Are not here Picardes with their crossbows and piercing darts? The Henves with their cutting glaives and sharp carbuncles.[139] Are not here the lance knights of Burgundy? And on the other side, a sight of poor English scabs? Why, take an Englishman out of his warm bed, and his stale drink, but one month, and alas what will become of him? But give the Frenchman a radish root, and he will live with it all the days of his life. *Exit*
2 FRENCH SOLDIER Oh, the brave apparel that we shall have of the Englishmans.

Ex[eunt omnes]

[Scene xiv]

Enters the KING OF ENGLAND [HENRY V] *and his* LORDS [OXFORD *others*]

KING HENRY V Come my lords and fellows of arms, what company is there of the Frenchmen?
OXFORD And it please your majesty, our captains have numbered them. And so near as they can judge, they are about threescore thousand horsemen, and forty thousand footmen.
KING HENRY V They threescore thousand, and we but two thousand. They threescore thousand footmen, and we twelve thousand. They are a hundred thousand, and we forty thousand, ten to one.[140] My lords and loving countrymen, though we be few and they many, fear not, your quarrel is good, and God will defend you. Pluck up your hearts, for this day we shall either have a valiant victory, or an honorable death. Now my lords, I will that my uncle, the Duke of York, have the avant-garde in the battle. The Earl of Derby, the Earl of Oxford, the Earl of Kent, the Earl of Nottingham, the Earl of Huntington, I will have beside the army, that they may come fresh upon them. And I myself with the Duke of Bedford, the Duke of Clarence, and the Duke of Gloucester, will be in the midst of the battle. Furthermore, I will that my Lord of Willoughby, and the Earl of Northumberland, with their troops of horsemen, be continually running like wings on both sides of the army. My Lord of Northumberland, on the left wing. Then I will that every archer provide him a stake of a tree, and sharp it at both ends, and at the first encounter of the horsemen, to pitch their stakes down into the ground before them, that they may gore themselves upon them, and then to recoil back, and shoot wholly altogether, and so discomfit them.
OXFORD And it please your majesty, I will take that in charge, if your grace be therewith content.
KING HENRY V With all my heart, my good Lord of Oxford. And go and provide quickly.
OXFORD I thank your highness. *Exit*
KING HENRY V Well, my lords, our battles are ordained. And the French making of bonfires, and at their banquets.[141] But let them look, for I mean to set upon them. *The trumpet sounds*
Soft, here comes some other French message.

Enters [FRENCH] HERALD

136 31–2 flaunching curtle-axes: meaning uncertain. Perhaps "slashing." A curtle-axe is a cutlass, a short, curved sword
137 32 Brabantians: Q reads "Barbarians" but previous mention of "Brabants" in Scene xi makes this emendation likely
138 32 bard horses: armored horses
139 33–4 Henves with … sharp carbuncles: "Henues" or "Henves" probably refers to soldiers from Hainault. Glaives are single-edged blades affixed to the end of a pole. Carbuncles are red gems that can be embedded in a shield
140 5–7 They threescore … to one: textual corruption may account for the king's bad calculations and poor attempt at parallelism. The point is that, as was reported in the records of the time, the English army was greatly outnumbered
141 24–5 making of bonfires, and at their banquets: the French are now making bonfires and eating

FRENCH HERALD King of England, my Lord High Constable, and other of my lords, considering the poor estate of thee and thy poor countrymen, sends me to know what thou wilt give for thy ransom? Perhaps thou mayest agree better cheap now, than when thou art conquered.
KING HENRY V Why then, belike your High Constable sends to know what I will give for my ransom? Now trust me, herald, not so much as a tun of tennis balls, no, not so much as one poor tennis ball. Rather shall my body lie dead in the field to feed crows, than ever England shall pay one penny ransom for my body.
FRENCH HERALD A kingly resolution.
KING HENRY V No herald, 'tis a kingly resolution, and the resolution of a king. Here take this for thy pains.

[*Gives money*]
Exit [FRENCH] HERALD

But stay my lords, what time is it?
ALL Prime,[142] my lord.
KING HENRY V Then it is good time no doubt, for all England prayeth for us. What, my lords, methinks you look cheerfully upon me? Why, then with one voice and like true English hearts, with me throw up your caps, and for England, cry "Saint George," and "God and Saint George help us." Strike, drummer![143]

Exeunt omnes

[Scene xv]

The FRENCHMEN *cry within "Saint Denis, Saint Denis, Mountjoy, Saint Denis"* [144]
The Battle

Enters KING OF ENGLAND [HENRY V], *and his* LORDS [OXFORD *and* YORK]

KING HENRY V Come my lords, come, by this time our swords are almost drunk with French blood! But my lords, which of you can tell me how many of our army be slain in the battle?
OXFORD And it please you majesty, there are of the French army slain above ten thousand. Twenty-six hundred whereof are princes and nobles bearing banners. Besides, all the nobility of France are taken prisoners. Of your majesty's army are slain none but the good Duke of York, and not above five or six and twenty common soldiers.
KING HENRY V For the good Duke of York my uncle, I am heartily sorry, and greatly lament his misfortune. Yet the honorable victory which the Lord hath given us, doth make me much rejoice. But stay, here comes another French message.

Sound trumpet. Enters a [FRENCH] HERALD *and kneeleth*

FRENCH HERALD God save the life of the most mighty conqueror, the honorable King of England.
KING HENRY V Now, herald, methinks the world is changed with you now. What, I am sure it is a great disgrace for a herald to kneel to the King of England! What is thy message?
FRENCH HERALD My lord and master, the conquered King of France, sends thee long health, with hearty greeting.
KING HENRY V Herald, his greetings are welcome, but I thank God for my health. Well, herald, say on.
FRENCH HERALD He hath sent me to desire your majesty, to give him leave to go into the field to view his poor countrymen, that they may all be honorably buried.

142 38 Prime: the first hour of daylight, when the first prayers of the Divine Office were offered

143 42 Strike, drummer!: printed in Q as a stage direction. A version of this phrase is said earlier by Henry at the close of Scene xii, and so is more likely the climax of Henry's battle cry here

144 0 SD *Saint Denis*: a (possibly legendary) third-century Christian martyr and the patron saint of France, here invoked as a battlecry, the equivalent of the traditional English shout of "St. George." It is unclear what Mountjoy ("Mount Ioy" in Q) means here. It is clearly also a battle cry. Perhaps it is meant to be the name of one of the French generals leading the battle

KING HENRY V Why herald, doth thy lord and master send to me to bury the dead? Let him bury them a[145] God's name. But I pray thee herald, where is my Lord High Constable, and those that would have had my ransom?

FRENCH HERALD And it please your majesty, he was slain in the battle.

KING HENRY V Why you may see, you will make yourselves sure before the victory be won. But herald, what castle is this so near adjoining to our camp?

FRENCH HERALD And it please your majesty, 'tis called the Castle of Agincourt.[146]

KING HENRY V Well then my lords of England, for the more honor of our Englishmen, I will that this be forever called the Battle of Agincourt.

FRENCH HERALD And it please your majesty, I have a further message to deliver to your majesty.

KING HENRY V What is that, herald? Say on.

FRENCH HERALD And it please your majesty, my lord and master craves to parley[147] with your majesty.

KING HENRY V With a good will, so some of my nobles view[148] the place, for fear of treachery and treason.

FRENCH HERALD Your grace needs not to doubt[149] that.

KING HENRY V Well, tell him then, I will come. *Exit* [FRENCH] HERALD

Now my lords, I will go into the field myself, to view my countrymen, and to have them honorably buried. For the French king shall never surpass me in courtesy whiles I am Harry, King of England. Come on my lords.

Exeunt omnes

[Scene xvi]

Enters JOHN COBBLER *and* ROBIN PEWTERER

ROBIN Now, John Cobbler, didst thou see how the king did behave himself?

JOHN But Robin, didst thou see what a policy the king had, to see how the Frenchmen were killed with the stakes of the trees?

ROBIN Aye John, there was a brave policy.

Enters an ENGLISH SOLDIER, *roaming*

ENGLISH SOLDIER What are you, my masters?

BOTH Why, we be Englishmen.

ENGLISH SOLDIER Are you Englishmen? Then change your language, for the king's tents are set afire, and all they that speak English will be killed.

JOHN What shall we do Robin? Faith, I'll shift, for I can speak broken French.

ROBIN Faith so can I. Let's hear how thou canst speak.

JOHN *Commodevales, monsieur.*[150]

ROBIN That's well. Come let's be gone.

[*Exeunt*] *Drum and trumpet sounds*

[Scene xvii]

Enters DERICK *roaming. After him a* FRENCHMAN,[151] [*who*] *takes* [DERICK] *prisoner*

145 21 a: in

146 26 Castle of Agincourt: the site of the battle was in the northwest of France, not far from the port of Calais

147 32 parley: speak, negotiate

148 134 so some . . . nobles view: as long as some of my nobles can first view

149 136 doubt: suspect

150 11 *Commodevales*: nonsense French, probably a garbled version of the phrase "comment allez-vous," i.e. "how are you?"

151 0 SD FRENCHMAN: presumably also a solider, so this part could be taken by any of the French soldiers from Scene xiii

DERICK Oh, good *mounser*.[152]
FRENCHMAN Come, come, you villeaco.[153]
DERICK Oh, I will sir, I will.
FRENCHMAN Come quickly, you peasant.
DERICK I will sir, what shall I give you?
FRENCHMAN Marry thou shalt give me one, two, tre, four, hundred crowns.
DERICK Nay sir, I will give you more. I will give you as many crowns as will lie on your sword.
FRENCHMAN Wilt thou give me as many crowns as will lie on my sword?
DERICK Aye, marry will I, aye, but you must lay down your sword, or else they will not lie on your sword.

Here the FRENCHMAN *lays down his sword, and* [DERICK] *the clown takes it up, and hurls him down*

DERICK Thou villain, darest thou look up?
FRENCHMAN Oh, good monsieur, *comparteve*![154] Monsieur, pardon me.
DERICK Oh, you villain, now you lie at my mercy, doest thou remember since thou 'lammest me in thy short ell?[155] Oh villain, now I will strike off thy head.

Here, whiles he turns his back, the FRENCHMAN *runs his ways*

DERICK What, is he gone? Mass, I am glad of it. For if he had stayed, I was afraid he would have stirred again, and then I should have been spilt.[156] But I will away, to kill more Frenchmen.

[*Exit*]

[Scene xviii]

Enters KING [CHARLES VI] OF FRANCE, KING [HENRY V] OF ENGLAND, *and* ATTENDANTS [*including* ENGLISH SECRETARY]

KING HENRY V Now, my good brother of France, my coming into this land was not to shed blood, but for the right of my country, which if you can deny, I am content peaceably to leave my siege, and to depart out of your land.
FRENCH KING What is it you demand, my loving brother of England?
KING HENRY V My secretary hath it written. Read it.
ENGLISH SECRETARY Item, that immediately Henry of England be crowned King of France.
FRENCH KING A very hard sentence, my good brother of England.
KING HENRY V No more but right, my good brother of France.
FRENCH KING Well, read on.
ENGLISH SECRETARY Item, that after the death of the said Henry, the crown remain to him and his heirs forever.
FRENCH KING Why then, you do not only mean to dispossess me, but also my son.
KING HENRY V Why, my good brother of France, you have had it long enough. And as for Prince Dolphin, it skills not, though he sit beside the saddle.[157] Thus I have set it down, and thus it shall be.
FRENCH KING You are very peremptory, my good brother of England.
KING HENRY V And you as perverse, my good brother of France.
FRENCH KING Why then belike, all that I have here is yours.
KING HENRY V Aye, even as far as the kingdom of France reaches.
FRENCH KING Aye, for by this hot beginning, we shall scarce bring it to a calm ending.

152 1 *mounser*: Derick's attempt at "monsieur"
153 2 villeaco: villain
154 13 *comparteve*: probably a corruption of French, meant to convey "have compassion" (Bullough 1975: 337)
155 14–15 'lammest me in thy short ell: beat me with your little sword
156 17 spilt: possibly a misprint for "split," but in either case it means wounded
157 14 it skills ... the saddle: it doesn't matter that he is being pushed aside

KING HENRY V It is as you please. Here is my resolution.
FRENCH KING Well, my brother of England, if you will give me a copy, we will meet you again tomorrow.
KING HENRY V With a good will, my good brother of France.

Exit KING OF FRANCE, *and* [*all the* FRENCH] ATTENDANTS

Secretary deliver him a copy. My lords of England go before, and I will follow you.

Exeunt [ENGLISH SECRETARY *and*] LORDS

[KING HENRY] *speaks to himself*

KING HENRY V Ah Harry, thrice unhappy Harry. Hast thou now conquered the French King, and begins a fresh supply[158] with his daughter? But with what face canst thou seek to gain her love, which hath sought to win her father's crown? Her father's crown said I? No, it is mine own. Aye, but I love her, and must crave her, nay I love her and will have her.

Enters LADY KATHERINE *and her* LADIES

But here she comes. How now fair lady, Katherine of France, what news?
KATHERINE And it please your majesty, my father sent me to know if you will debate any of these unreasonable demands which you require.
KING HENRY V Now trust me Kate, I commend thy father's wit greatly in this, for none in the world could sooner have made me debate it, if it were possible. But tell me, sweet Kate, canst thou tell how to love?
KATHERINE I cannot hate, my good lord. Therefore, far unfit were it for me to love.
KING HENRY V Tush Kate, but tell me in plain terms, canst thou love the King of England? I cannot do as these countries[159] do, that spend half their time in wooing. Tush wench, I am none such. But wilt thou go over to England?
KATHERINE I would to God that I had your majesty as fast in love, as you have my father in wars. I would not vouchsafe so much as one look, until you had abated[160] all these unreasonable demands.
KING HENRY V Tush Kate, I know thou wouldst not use me so hardly. But tell me, canst thou love the King of England?
KATHERINE How should I love him, that hath dealt so hardly with my father?
KING HENRY V But I'll deal as easily with thee, as thy heart can imagine, or tongue can require. How sayest thou, what will it be?
KATHERINE If I were of my own direction, I could give you answer. But seeing I stand at my father's direction, I must first know his will.
KING HENRY V But shall I have thy good will in the mean season?
KATHERINE Whereas I can put your grace in no assurance, I would be loath to put you in any despair.
KING HENRY V Now before God, it is a sweet wench.

She goes aside, and speaks as followeth

KATHERINE I may think myself the happiest in the world, that is beloved of the mighty King of England.
KING HENRY V Well Kate, are you at host with me?[161] Sweet Kate, tell thy father from me, that none in the world could sooner have persuaded me to it than thou, and so tell thy father from me.
KATHERINE God keep your majesty in good health.

Exit [*with* LADIES]

158 28 fresh supply: new "attack," that is, a campaign to woo her
159 39 countries: Henry probably means other monarchs rather than whole nations
160 42 abated: Q reads "related"; I follow previous editors in emending to "abated" in the archaic sense of "put an end to a condition"
161 57 at host with me: in agreement

KING HENRY V Farwell sweet Kate, in faith, it is a sweet wench. But if I knew I could not have her father's good will, I would so rouse the towers over his ears,[162] that I would make him be glad to bring her me, upon his hands and knees.

Exit KING [HENRY V]

[Scene xix]

Enters DERICK, *with his girdle*[163] *full of shoes*

DERICK How now? Zounds, it did me good to see how I did triumph over the Frenchmen.

Enters JOHN COBBLER *roving, with a pack full of apparel*

JOHN Whoop, Derick, how dost thou?
DERICK What John, *comedevales*, alive yet?
JOHN I promise thee Derick, I 'scaped hardly, for I was within half a mile when one was killed.
DERICK Were you so?
JOHN Aye, trust me, I had like been slain.[164]
DERICK But once killed, why, 'tis nothing. I was four or five times slain.
JOHN Four or five times slain? Why, how couldst thou have been alive now?
DERICK Oh John, never say so, for I was called the bloody soldier amongst them all.
JOHN Why, what didst thou?
DERICK Why, I will tell thee John. Every day, when I went into the field, I would take a straw and thrust it into my nose, and make my nose bleed. And then I would go into the field, and when the captain saw me, he would say, "peace, a bloody soldier," and bid me stand aside, whereof I was glad. But mark the chance John. I went and stood behind a tree, but mark then John. I thought I had been safe, but on a sudden, there steps to me a lusty tall Frenchman. Now he drew, and I drew. Now I lay here, and he lay there. Now I set this leg before, and turned this backward, and skipped quite over a hedge, and he saw me no more there that day. And was not this well done John?
JOHN Mass Derick, thou hast a witty head.
DERICK Aye, John, thou mayest see, if thou hadst taken my counsel. But what hast thou there? I think thou hast been robbing the Frenchmen.
JOHN I'faith Derick, I have gotten some reparrel[165] to carry home to my wife.
DERICK And I have got some shoes, for I'll tell thee what I did. When they were dead, I would go take off all their shoes.
JOHN Aye, but Derick, how shall we get home?
DERICK Nay zounds, and they take thee, they will hang thee. Oh John, never do so. If it be thy fortune to be hanged, be hanged in thy own language whatsoever thou dost.
JOHN Why Derick, the wars is done, we may go home now.
DERICK Aye, but you may not go before you ask the king leave. But I know a way to go home, and ask the king no leave.
JOHN How is that Derick?
DERICK Why John, thou knowest the Duke of York's funeral must be carried[166] into England, dost thou not?
JOHN Aye, that I do.
DERICK Why then thou knowest we'll go with it.
JOHN Aye, but Derick, how shall we do for to meet them?

162 62: rouse the … his ears: the expression is obscure, but seems to be a threat of further violence and destruction against the French king, i.e. "I'll bring the whole city down on his head"
163 0 SD *girdle*: a large belt, often used to hang a purse on
164 6 had like been slain: was almost killed
165 22 reparrel: apparel
166 32 funeral must be carried: out of respect for the Duke's high rank, there will be a continuous funeral procession for him as the army transports his body back to England

DERICK Zounds, if I make not shift to meet them, hang me. Sirrah, thou knowest that in every town there will be ringing,[167] and there will be cakes and drink. Now I will go to the clerk and sexton[168] and keep a-talking, and say, "Oh this fellow rings well." And thou shalt go and take a piece of cake, then I'll ring, and thou shalt say, "Oh this fellow keeps a good stint."[169] And then I will go drink to thee all the way. But I marvel what my dame will say when we come home, because we have not a French word to cast at a dog[170] by the way?

JOHN Why what shall we do Derick?

DERICK Why John, I'll go before and call my dame whore, and thou shalt come after and set fire on the house. We may do it John, for I'll prove it, because we be soldiers. *The trumpets sound*

JOHN Derick, help me to carry my shoes and boots.

[*Exeunt*]

[Scene xx]

Enters KING [HENRY V] OF ENGLAND, LORD[S] OF OXFORD *and* EXETER, *then the* KING [CHARLES VI] OF FRANCE, [*his* SECRETARY,] PRINCE DOLPHIN, *and the* DUKE OF BURGUNDY, PRINCESS KATHERINE *and* ATTENDANTS

KING HENRY V Now, my good brother of France, I hope by this time you have deliberated of your answer?

FRENCH KING Aye, my well-beloved brother of England. We have viewed it over with our learned council, but cannot find that you should be crowned King of France.

KING HENRY V What? Not King of France, then nothing! I must be king. But, my loving brother of France, I can hardly forget the late injuries offered me, when I came last to parley. The Frenchmen had better 'a[171] raked the bowels out of their fathers' carcasses, than to have fired my tents.[172] And if I knew thy son Prince Dolphin for one, I would so rouse him, as he was never so roused.

FRENCH KING I dare swear for my son's innocency in this matter. But if this please you, that immediately you be proclaimed and crowned heir and Regent of France, not King, because I myself was once crowned king.

KING HENRY V Heir and Regent of France, that is well. But that is not all that I must have.

FRENCH KING The rest my secretary hath in writing.

FRENCH SECRETARY Item, that Henry King of England, be crowned Heir and Regent of France, during the life of King Charles, and after his death, the crown with all rights, to remain to King Henry of England, and to his heirs forever.

KING HENRY V Well, my good brother of France, there is one thing I must needs desire.

FRENCH KING What is that, my good brother of England?

KING HENRY V That all your nobles must be sworn to be true to me.

FRENCH KING Whereas they have not stuck with greater matters, I know they will not stick with such a trifle. Begin you, my lord Duke of Burgundy.

KING HENRY V Come my Lord of Burgundy, take your oath upon my sword.

BURGUNDY I, Philip, Duke of Burgundy, swear to Henry, King of England, to be true to him, and to become his liegeman. And that if I, Philip, hear of any foreign power coming to invade the said Henry or his heirs, then I, the said Philip, to send him word, and aid him with all the power I can make. And thereunto I take my oath. *He kisseth the sword*

KING HENRY V Come Prince Dolphin, you must swear too. [PRINCE DOLPHIN] *kisseth the sword*

167 38 ringing: of church bells

168 38–9 clerk and sexton: clerk means here an assistant to the parish priest; the sexton was a church caretaker and sometimes bell-ringer

169 40 stint: the usage here is unclear, but Derick seems to mean to echo the previous line's, "this fellow rings [the bells] well"

170 42 not a . . . a dog: Derick seems to worry that, since they have not learned any French, John's wife may doubt that they really served in the war in France. In his next line, Derick says that he will prove it by setting her house on fire (as soldiers would burn enemy houses)

171 7 'a: have

172 6–8 I can . . . my tents: Henry recalls the "injuries" the French inflicted when they set fire to his tents (xvi. 7–8) after he had agreed with the Herald to a negotiation ("parley") with the French King (xv. 32–37)

Well my brother of France, there is one thing more I must needs require of you.
FRENCH KING Wherein is it that we may satisfy your majesty?
KING HENRY V A trifle, my good brother of France. I mean to make your daughter Queen of England, if she be willing, and you therewith content. How sayest thou Kate, canst thou love the King of England?
KATHERINE How should I love thee, which is my father's enemy?
KING HENRY V Tut, stand not upon these points, 'tis you must make us friends. I know, Kate, thou art not a little proud that I love thee. What, wench, the King of England?
FRENCH KING Daughter, let nothing stand betwixt the King of England and thee. Agree to it.
KATHERINE [*Aside*] I had best whilst he is willing, lest when I would, he will not.—I rest at your majesty's command.
KING HENRY V Welcome sweet Kate. But my brother of France, what say you to it?
FRENCH KING With all my heart I like it. But when shall be your wedding day?
KING HENRY V The first Sunday of the next month, God willing.

Sound trumpets. Exeunt omnes

FINIS.

7 Philip Massinger, *The Picture*

First performed 1629

First printed 1630

Edited by Lucy Munro

Once upon a time, there was a heroic warrior, his wise and witty wife, an imperious queen, and her complacent husband. The warrior carried with him a magical picture of his wife, given to him with these instructions:

Carry it still about you, and as oft
As you desire to know how she's affected
With curious eyes peruse it. While it keeps
The figure it now has, entire and perfect,
She is not only innocent in fact
But unattempted; but if once it vary
From the true form, and what's now white and red
Incline to yellow, rest most confident
She's with all violence courted but unconquered.
But if it turn all black, 'tis an assurance
The fort by composition or surprise
Is forced or with her free consent surrendered.
(I.i. 174–85)

Massinger's tragicomedy *The Picture*, licensed for performance by the King's Men on 8 June 1629, tells a story that can be traced as far back as Buddhist narratives of around the third century CE (Edwards and Gibson, 1976: 183). But if its characters and its magical picture lend it a fairy-tale quality, this is a very adult fairy tale. The play depicts a marriage that is threatened on two fronts. Mathias leaves his wife, Sophia, and his home in Bohemia in order to seek his fortune by fighting in the wars of Ladislaus, King of Hungary, against the Ottoman Empire. At the Hungarian court he catches the attention of Honoria, Ladislaus's wife, whose jealousy is provoked by Mathias's boasts about his wife's beauty, virtue, and chastity. Honoria schemes both to win Mathias for herself and to ruin Sophia, sending a pair of dissolute courtiers, Ubaldo and Ricardo, to corrupt her.

The picture, given to Mathias by his scholar-friend Julio Baptista, is the pivot on which the two sections of the narrative turn. Designed as a portrait miniature, the picture resembles a perverted love-token, the focus of a set of male anxieties about female sexuality and the extent to which women or their desires can be known or understood (see Obermueller; Rochester, 110–12). As a representation of Sophia, it also has much in common with the ways in which women are displayed in early modern lyric poetry as "painted" because they make up their faces with cosmetics. Like the poems, the picture effaces Sophia's own body and agency even as it claims to represent them, subjecting her to the scrutiny and control of her husband. But, as Kim F. Hall has said of the lyric, the male claim to "dominion is always in struggle" (1995: 91), and in the final scene of Massinger's play Sophia denies the picture's power to offer any insight into her thoughts or behavior, telling her startled husband "We did not deal like you in speculations/On cheating pictures" (V.ii. 95–6).

The picture also crystalizes and gives physical form to a network of ideas about race, religion, and beauty in which the play's imaginary is steeped. The word "mammet," which Massinger uses twice with a range of meanings that include "puppet," "false idol," "fool," and "grotesque" (see I.i. 106, III.iv. 60), originally derives from a corruption of "Mahomet," reflecting the medieval and early modern Christian belief that the prophet was worshipped as a god; the word "Termagaunt" (II.i. 118) refers to another supposed deity of Muslims and other non-Christians. As these words suggest, the Ottoman Empire is a powerful off-stage presence in the play, not least because many early spectators of *The Picture* would have known that Székesfehérvár, the old Hungarian capital, and the Alba Regalis, where Ladislaus's court is located, had been under Ottoman rule almost continuously since 1543.

Moreover, the capacity of the picture to turn Sophia's skin from "white and red," to "yellow," and finally "all black" reflects a set of racist and classist assumptions about female beauty. These assumptions are rendered most explicit when

Ladislaus tells Honoria that the goddess Venus "compared to you in my/Opinion is a negro" (II.ii. 329–30), but they run though the play. In its original state, the picture is referred to as Sophia's "fair figure" (II.ii. 326), while the term "luster" is twice used with reference to Sophia herself. Both terms invoke what Farah Karim-Cooper calls the "arousing glister of the fair face" in early modern writing on beauty and cosmetics, where "fairness" is entwined with whiteness but not always coterminous with it (2006: 12). It is notable that the picture does not turn immediately from white to black: instead, there is an intermediate stage in which it turns yellow. This in-between color distresses Mathias because it suggests that Sophia has been assailed or tempted to infidelity, but it also had other important connotations in early modern English culture. To be "yellow" was to be tanned by the sun, a condition which was strongly associated with lower class status and sometimes with religious and racial alterity. In a series of poems, Massinger's younger contemporary, John Collop, likens his "Yellow Skin'd" mistress's skin to "Gilt pictures Papists for devotion use," and to the gold brought by the Spanish to Europe from South America. Yet he finally tells his mistress "Scorn but my fancy, thou again art poor [. . .] I made thee gold, 'tis I can make thee brasse,/Currant with Tinkers thou shalt onely passe." Like Collop's suntanned mistress, the yellowed Sophia is rendered socially and sexually ambiguous. Similarly, while Sophia's picture becomes marked with "lines/Of a dark color" (IV.i. 33–4), it is noticeable that Honoria is rhetorically blackened because her pride and self-assertion threaten to upset the status quo: she is compared with the Assyrian queen Semiramis (I.ii.189–218) and the Egyptian queen Cleopatra (II.ii. 247), and Mathias reprovingly describes her as "virtuous, though somewhat darkened/With pride and self-opinion" (IV.iv. 32–3). Whiteness, yellowness, and blackness thus move across lines of race and status, anchored by the central image of the shifting picture.

The questions about theatrical representation that the picture raises also inflect the play's construction and casting. The 1630 edition includes not only a *dramatis personae* but a list of "The Actors names" that indicates which members of the King's Men played which roles. While early modern playing companies did not depend on simple or consistent type-casting, the list indicates that Massinger tailored roles to his performers and capitalized on their skills. For example, John Shank's role as company clown is alluded to in a meta-theatrical fashion when his character, Hilario, appears in the character of a chivalric knight and declares "I have played the fool before" (II.i. 3). Thomas Pollard, who played Ubaldo, was also famed for his comic roles, while Elliard Swanston, who played Ricardo, was a rising star in the company who went on to play roles such as Othello and Richard III. The pair are named together in the 1639 will of Richard Benfield—a kinsman of another King's Man, Robert Benfield—as his "Gossipp[s]," and they may have been known as a double-act offstage as well as on it (Honigmann and Brock, 1993: 195).

The play is also unusual for the attention that it pays to the age of characters and the ways in which these fictional ages tally with those of the actors. The 53-year-old John Lowin, who played the "old counselor" Eubulus, appears to have been the oldest of the actors, while Honoria's comments that Mathias has a "pretty, promising presence" but is past his "May of youth" (III.v. 127–30) reflects—somewhat unflatteringly—the fact that the actor who played him, Joseph Taylor, was probably in his early 40s. Lowin and Taylor had led the King's Men for a number of years, and their position was being challenged in the early 1630s by a much younger performer, Richard Sharpe, who played the lead in John Clavell's *The Soddered Citizen* (c. 1630) and important roles in Lodowick Carlell's *The Deserving Favorite* (c. 1629) and Arthur Wilson's *The Swisser* (1631). His star quality is likely to have lent the general, Ferdinand, more glamor on stage than his somewhat under-written role provides.

Questions about the relationship between actor and role are most pressing in relation to female roles, all of which were played by boy actors. John Honeyman (Sophia) was aged sixteen, while John Thompson (Honoria), was probably a few years older; both had been performing with the King's Men since at least 1626, when they took roles in Massinger's *The Roman Actor* (see Kathman, 255–8). Spectators would thus have been used not only to seeing boy actors in general take female roles, but to viewing the women of the King's Men's plays through these particular actors. Female roles seem generally not to have been tailored to individual actors as much as adult male roles, but Thompson is required to sing in two other roles, Domitia in *The Roman Actor* and Panopia in *The Swisser*, suggesting that he may have performed the "*song of pleasure*" that Mathias hears in III.v.

As this discussion indicates, cultural, political, and theatrical concerns are intertwined in *The Picture*, and they also inflect its narrative structure and style. The play is described in the 1630 edition as "A True Hungarian History" and "A Tragicomedy," terms that convey some of the ways in which it deals with genre and form. "History," which could mean both a narrative recounting events from the past and, more simply, a story, reflects quite accurately the mixture of historical and fictive elements that Massinger would have found in sources such as William Painter's "The Lady of Boeme," itself a translation of the Italian writer Matteo Bandello's "Mirabil Beffa fatta da una Gentildonna a dui Baroni del Regno d'Ongaria." "Tragicomedy," meanwhile, had been used increasingly frequently since the early seventeenth century to describe plays in which comedy and tragedy are intermingled, as they are in *The Picture*.

Massinger's handling of tragicomic form is epitomized in some respects by two great scenes of sexual temptation at the end of the third act. In III.v, Honoria tries to seduce Mathias but he resists with the help of the picture, and in III.vi, Ubaldo and Ricardo besiege Sophia with false stories of her husband's sexual exploits at court. The former scene is largely serious in tone, employing visual spectacle and alluring music; the latter is comic, with Ubaldo and Ricardo playing out a cynical double act in which Sophia is forced to serve as the butt of their jokes. Yet the stakes are just as high in each scene, as the marriage of Mathias and Sophia is presented as depending on their mutual loyalty, and Mathias's possession of the picture raises the tension still further. These tensions are maintained into the final scene, when Mathias's doubts about Sophia's fidelity are dispelled, but his furious wife demands that Ladislaus grant her a divorce from Mathias. Although Sophia eventually declares herself "reconciled" when Mathias vows to destroy the picture, we might reasonably have doubts about the future health of the marriage as we read the final lines of this complex and tough-minded exploration of sexual paranoia and integrity.

Textual note

The Picture survives in one seventeenth-century edition, published in quarto in 1630 by Thomas Walkley and printed by John Norton. Two issues of this edition survive, later copies having an updated title-page, in which some changes have been made to layout, capitalization and spelling, and corrections to pages in III.vi and IV.i. Despite these changes, many misprints, turned letters, errors in punctuation, and other inadequacies persist throughout the edition. (The running title, "*The Picture*," actually appears upside-down on one page in III.v.) At least 40 copies have survived. One of them, Folger Shakespeare Library STC 17640.5 copy 3, has manuscript corrections in Massinger's hand in Acts I and II. The copy-text for this edition is British Library 644.e.75, a copy of the second issue. Scene divisions follow the quarto, but I have corrected errors in their numbering (for instance, III.iii is labelled as "*Actus tertij, scaena prima*" in the quarto). The most significant intervention that I have made is in rearranging some of the stage directions for the inset masque in II.ii to make the action clearer. I have also incorporated Massinger's own corrections in Acts I and II.

Further reading

Editions

Edwards, Philip, and Colin Gibson (eds) (1976) "*The Picture*," in Philip Edwards and Colin Gibson (eds), *The Plays and Poems of Philip Massinger*, vol. 3, Oxford: Clarendon Press.

Mason, John Monck (ed.) (1779) "*The Picture*," in John Monck Mason (ed.), *The Dramatick Works of Philip Massinger*, vol. 1, London: T. Davies.

Critical and contextual reading

Clark, Ira (1993) *The Moral Art of Philip Massinger*, Lewisburg: Bucknell University Press.

Collop, John (1656) *Poesis Rediviva, Or, Poesie Reviv'd*, London: Humphrey Moseley.

Hall, Kim F. (1995) *Things of Darkness: Economies of Race and Gender in Early Modern England*, Ithaca: Cornell University Press.

Hila, Marina (2017) "'To Heighten Your Desire': Sexual Politics in Massinger's *The Picture* (1629)," *Cahiers Élisabéthains* 92: 68–81.

Honigmann, E.A.J., and Susan Brock (eds) (1993) *Playhouse Wills*, 1558–1642, Manchester: Manchester University Press.

Hutson, Lorna (2009) "Probable Infidelities from Bandello to Massinger," in Mary Ellen Lamb and Valerie Wayne (eds), *Staging Early Modern Romance: Prose Fiction, Dramatic Romance, and Shakespeare*, New York and London: Routledge, 219–35.

Karim-Cooper, Farah (2006) *Cosmetics in Shakespearean and Renaissance Drama*, Edinburgh: Edinburgh University Press.

Kathman, David (2005) "How Old Were Shakespeare's Boy Actors?" *Shakespeare Survey* 58: 220–46.

Mukherji, Subha (2006) "False Trials in Shakespeare, Massinger, and Ford," *Essays in Criticism* 56: 219–40.

Obermueller, Erin V. (2007) "'On Cheating Pictures': Gender and Portrait Miniatures in Philip Massinger's *The Picture*," *Early Theatre* 10: 87–107.

Rochester, Joanne (2010) *Staging Spectatorship in the Plays of Philip Massinger*, Farnham: Ashgate.

Ryner, Bradley D. (2013) *Performing Economic Thought: English Drama and Mercantile Writing* 1600–1642, Edinburgh: Edinburgh University Press.

The Picture (1629)

To my Honored and Selected Friends of the Noble Society of the Inner Temple[1]

It may be objected[2] my not inscribing their names, or titles, to whom I dedicate take this poem, proceedeth either from my diffidence[3] of their affection to me, or their unwillingness to be published the patrons of a trifle.[4] To such as shall make so strict an inquisition of me, I truly answer: the play in the presentment[5] found such a general approbation[6] that it gave me assurance of their favor to whose protection it is now sacred, and they have professed they so sincerely allow[7] of it, and the maker, that[8] they would have freely granted that in the publication, which for some reasons I denied myself. One, and that is a main one: I had rather enjoy (as I have done) the real proofs of their friendship than mountebank-like[9] boast their numbers in a catalogue. Accept it, noble gentlemen, as a confirmation of his service who hath nothing else to assure you, and witness to the world how much he stands engaged for your so frequent bounties,[10] and in your charitable opinion of me believe that you now may and shall ever command,

Your servant

Philip Massinger

To his Worthy Friend Master Philip Massinger upon his Tragicomedy Styled *The Picture*

Methinks I hear some busy[11] critic say,
"Who's this that singly[12] ushers on this play?"
'Tis boldness, I confess, and yet perchance
It may be constered[13] love, not arrogance.
I do not here upon this leaf[14] intrude
By praising one to[15] wrong a multitude.
Nor do I think that all are tied to be
(Forced by my vote) in the same creed[16] with me.

1 0 Inner Temple: one of the four Inns of Court, where lawyers practiced and were trained
2 1 It may be objected: people may complain that
3 2 diffidence: distrust
4 3 trifle: something unimportant
5 3 presentment: performance
6 4 approbation: approval
7 5 allow: approve
8 5 that: i.e. the publication of their names
9 7 mountebank-like: like a charlatan
10 10 bounties: acts of generosity
11 1 busy: interfering
12 2 singly: alone
13 4 constered: interpreted as
14 5 leaf: page
15 6 to: i.e. in order to
16 8 creed: belief

Each man hath liberty to judge, free will
At his own pleasure to speak good or ill.
But yet your Muse already's[17] known so well
Her worth will hardly find an infidel.[18]
Here she[19] hath drawn a picture, which shall lie
Safe for all future times to practice by.
Whate'er shall follow are but copies; some
Preceding works were types of this to come.
'Tis your own lively image and sets forth[20]
When we are dust[21] the beauty of your worth.
He that shall dully read and not advance[22]
Aught[23] that is here betrays his ignorance.
Yet whosoever beyond desert[24] commends[25]
Errs more by much than he that reprehends,[26]
For praise misplaced, and honor set upon
A worthless subject, is detraction.
I cannot sin so here unless I went
About to style you only[27] excellent.
Apollo's[28] gifts are not confined alone
To your dispose; he hath more heirs than one,
And such as do derive from his blessed hand
A large inheritance in the poets' land
As well as you. Nor are you—I assure
Myself—so envious, but you can endure
To hear their praise whose worth long since was known
And justly, too, preferred before[29] your own.
I know you would take it for an injury[30]
(And 'tis a well-becoming[31] modesty)
To be paralleled[32] with Beaumont,[33] or to hear
Your name by some too-partial[34] friend writ near
Unequaled Jonson,[35] being men whose fire[36]
At distance and with reverence you admire.
Do so, and you shall find your gain will be
Much more by yielding them priority
Than with a certainty of loss to hold
A foolish competition. 'Tis too bold

17 11 already's: already is
18 12 infidel: skeptic
19 13 she: i.e. the Muse
20 17 sets forth: i.e. will preserve
21 18 dust: long dead
22 19 advance: promote
23 20 Aught: anything
24 21 desert: its own merit
25 21 commends: praises
26 22 reprehends: finds fault
27 26 only: alone
28 27 Apollo: Roman god of poetry and music
29 34 preferred before: liked more than (and/or earlier than)
30 35 injury: insult to the other writer
31 36 well-becoming: suitable, attractive
32 37 paralleled: compared
33 37 Beaumont: Francis Beaumont (1584–1616), dramatist and poet
34 38 too-partial: biased
35 39 Jonson: Ben Jonson (1572–1637), dramatist and poet
36 39 fire: genius, creative inspiration

A task, and to be shunned, nor shall my praise
With too much weight ruin what it would raise.

Thomas Jay[37]

Dramatis personae[38]

MATHIAS, *a knight of Bohemia*
SOPHIA, *wife to Mathias*
CORISCA, *Sophia's maidservant*
HILARIO, *servant to Mathias and Sophia*
JULIO BAPTISTA, *a great scholar*
UBALDO, *an older wild courtier*
RICARDO, *a younger wild courtier*
LADISLAUS, *King of Hungary*
EUBULUS, *an old counselor*
HONORIA, *Queen of Hungary*
SILVIA,[39] *a maid of honor to Honoria*
ACANTHE, *a maid of honor to Honoria*
POST, *a messenger to the Hungarian court*
FERDINAND, *general of the Hungarian army*

Masquers, Servants, Attendants to the Hungarian court, Captains, Guide

Act I, scene i

Enter MATHIAS *in armor,* SOPHIA *in a riding suit,*[40] CORISCA, [*and*] HILARIO, *with other Servants*

MATHIAS Since we must part, Sophia, to pass further[41]
Is not alone[42] impertinent but dangerous.
We are not distant from the Turkish[43] camp
Above five leagues,[44] and who knows but some party
Of his timariots[45] that scour the country
May fall upon us. Be now as thy name
Truly interpreted hath ever spoke thee,
Wise and discreet,[46] and to thy understanding
Marry thy constant patience.
SOPHIA You put me, sir,
To the utmost trial of it.
MATHIAS Nay, no melting,[47]
Since the necessity[48] that now separates us
We have long since disputed,[49] and the reasons

37 47 Thomas Jay: Sir Thomas Jay (1585–1636), magistrate and Member of Parliament, one of the dedicatees of Massinger's *The Roman Actor* (1626) and author of dedicatory verses for *The Roman Actor* and *A New Way to Pay Old Debts* (1633)
38 Dramatis personae: adapted from the list of characters given in Q
39 SILVIA: makes two appearances attending Honoria (I.ii and II.ii), and has no lines
40 0 SD *riding suit*: clothing suitable for riding
41 1 pass further: continue talking
42 2 alone: only
43 3 Turkish: Ottoman
44 4 league: measurement of distance equal to about three miles
45 5 timariots: tenants and supporters of the Ottoman emperor
46 6–8 Be now . . . and discreet: Sophia means "wisdom" in Greek
47 10 melting: showing emotion
48 11 necessity: poverty
49 12 disputed: argued over

Forcing me to it too oft washed in tears.
I grant that you in birth were far above me,
And great men, my superiors, rivals for you,
But mutual consent of heart, as hands
Joined by true love, hath made us one, and equal.
Nor is it in me mere desire of fame
Or to be cried up by the public voice
For a brave soldier that puts on my armor;
Such airy tumors[50] take not me. You know
How narrow our demeans are[51] and, what's more,
Having as yet no charge of children on us
We hardly can subsist.
SOPHIA In you alone, sir,
I have all abundance.
MATHIAS For my mind's content
In your own language I could answer you.
You have been an obedient wife, a right[52] one,
And to my power, though short of your desert,[53]
I have been ever an indulgent husband.
We have long enjoyed the sweets of love, and though
Not to satiety[54] or loathing, yet
We must not live such dotards[55] on our pleasures
As still to hug them to the certain loss
Of profit and preferment. Competent[56] means
Maintains a quiet bed; want breeds dissension
Even in good women.
SOPHIA Have you found in me, sir,
Any distaste or sign of discontent
For want of what's superfluous?
MATHIAS No, Sophia.
Nor shalt thou ever have cause to repent
Thy constant course in goodness if heaven bless
My honest undertakings: 'tis for thee
That I turn soldier and put forth, dearest,
Upon this sea of action as a factor[57]
To trade for rich materials to adorn
Thy noble parts, and show 'em in full luster.[58]
I blush that other ladies less in beauty
And outward form, but in the harmony
Of the soul's ravishing music the same age
Not to be named with thee,[59] should so outshine thee
In jewels and variety of wardrobes,
While you—to whose sweet innocence both Indies[60]
Compared are of no value—wanting these

50 21 tumors: swellings (as if puffed up by ambition)
51 22 How narrow our demeans are: i.e. our behavior is not extravagant
52 27 right: virtuous
53 28 desert: deservings, worth
54 31 satiety: exhaustion of desire
55 32 live such dotards: be so foolishly attached to
56 34 Competent: sufficient
57 43 factor: commercial agent
58 45 luster: brilliance, glory
59 47–9 but in . . . with thee: i.e. except in their prospects of divine salvation not worthy of comparison with you
60 51 both Indies: India and the West Indies

Pass unregarded.
SOPHIA If I am so rich, sir,
In your opinion, why should you borrow
Additions for me?
MATHIAS Why? I should be censured
Of[61] ignorance, possessing such a jewel,
Above all price, if I forbear to give it
The best of ornaments. Therefore, Sophia,
In few words know my pleasure and obey me,
As you have ever done. To your discretion
I leave the government of my family[62]
And our poor fortunes, and from these[63] command
Obedience to you as to myself.
To the utmost[64] of what's mine live plentifully,
And ere the remnant of our store be spent,
With my good sword I hope I shall reap for you
A harvest in such full abundance, as
Shall make a merry winter.
SOPHIA Since you are not
To be diverted, sir, from what you purpose,
All arguments to stay you here are useless.
Go when you please, sir. Eyes, I charge you waste not
One drop of sorrow, look[65] you hoard all up
Till in my widowed bed I call upon you,
But then be sure you fail not. You blessed angels,
Guardians of human life, I at this instant
Forbear t'invoke[66] you; at our parting 'twere
To personate devotion.[67] My soul
Shall go along with you and, when you are
Circled with death and horror, seek and find you,
And then I will not leave a saint unsued to[68]
For your protection. To tell you what
I will do in your absence would show poorly;
My actions shall speak me. 'Twere to doubt you
To beg I may hear from you, where you are
You cannot live obscure,[69] nor shall one post[70]
By night or day pass unexamined by me.
[*Kisses him*] If I dwell long upon your lips, consider
After this feast the griping[71] fast that follows
And it will be excusable. Pray turn from me.
All that I can is spoken. *Exit* SOPHIA
MATHIAS Follow your mistress.
Forbear[72] your wishes for me, let me find 'em

61 56 Of: for
62 61 family: household and servants
63 62 these: Hilario, Corisca and the other servants
64 64 utmost: upper limit
65 72 look: ensure that
66 76 Forbear t'invoke: refuse to call upon
67 77 personate devotion: parody religious ritual
68 80 unsued to: not called upon
69 85 obscure: inconspicuously
70 85 post: bearer of letters
71 88 griping: painful
72 91 Forbear: spare

At my return in your prompt will to serve her.
HILARIO For my part, sir, I will grow lean with study
To make her merry.
CORISCA Though you are my lord,
Yet being her gentlewoman, by my place
I may take my leave: your hand, or if you please
To have me fight so high, I'll not be coy
But stand a-tiptoe for't. [*Kisses him*]
MATHIAS O farewell, girl.
HILARIO A kiss well begged, Corisca.
CORISCA 'Twas my fee.
Love,[73] how he melts! I cannot blame my lady's
Unwillingness to part with such marmalade[74] lips.
There will be scrambling for 'em in the camp,
And were it not for my honesty I could wish now
I were his leaguer laundress.[75] I would find
Soap of mine own, enough to wash his linen,
Or I would strain hard for't.[76]
HILARIO How the mammet[77] twitters!
Come, come, my lady stays for us.
CORISCA Would I had been
Her ladyship the last night.
HILARIO No more of that, wench. *Exeunt* HILARIO [*and* CORISCA *with Servants*]
MATHIAS I am strangely troubled. Yet why should I nourish
A fury[78] here—and with imagined food,
Having no real grounds[79] on which to raise
A building of suspicion—she[80] was ever
Or can be false hereafter? I in this
But foolishly inquire the knowledge of
A future sorrow, which if I find out,
My present ignorance were a cheap purchase
Though with my loss of being. I have already
Dealt with a friend of mine, a general scholar,[81]
One deeply read in nature's hidden secrets,
And though with much unwillingness have won him
To do as much as art[82] can to resolve me
My fate that follows. To my wish, he's come.

Enter BAPTISTA

Julio Baptista, now I may affirm
Your promise and performance walk together.

73 100 Love: i.e. "O Cupid"
74 101 marmalade: sweet
75 104 leaguer laundress: i.e. the person in charge of his linen while he is in the military camp
76 105–6 Soap of . . . hard for't: i.e. the means to do him (sexual) service, no matter what the cost was
77 106 mammet: puppet, fool
78 110 fury: furious conviction
79 111 grounds: foundation
80 112 she: that she
81 118 a general scholar: skilled in all kinds of learning
82 121 art: cunning, magic

And therefore, without circumstance,[83] to the point:
Instruct me what I am.
BAPTISTA I could wish you had
Made trial of my love some other way.
MATHIAS Nay, this is from the purpose.[84]
BAPTISTA If you can
Proportion your desire to any mean,[85]
I do pronounce you happy. I have found
By certain rules of art your matchless wife
Is to this present hour from all pollution[86]
Free and untainted.
MATHIAS Good.
BAPTISTA In reason, therefore,
You should fix here and make no further search
Of what may fall hereafter.
MATHIAS O Baptista,
'Tis not in me to master so my passions.
I must know further or you have made good
But half your promise. While my love stood by,
Holding her[87] upright, and my presence was
A watch[88] upon her, her desires being met, too,
With equal ardor from me, what one proof
Could she give of her constancy, being untempted?
But when I am absent, and my coming back
Uncertain, and those wanton heats in women
Not to be quenched by lawful means, and she
The absolute disposer of herself,
Without, control, or curb—nay, more, invited
By opportunity and all strong temptations—
If then she hold out—
BAPTISTA As no doubt she will.
MATHIAS Those doubts must be made certainties, Baptista,
By your assurance, or your boasted art
Deserves no admiration. How you trifle[89]
And play with my affliction! I am on
The rack[90] till you confirm me.
BAPTISTA Sure, Mathias,
I am no god, nor can I dive into
Her hidden thoughts or know what her intents are.
That is denied to art, and kept concealed
Even from the devils themselves. They can but guess
Out of long observation what is likely,
But positively to foretell that this shall be
You may conclude impossible. All I can,
I will do for you: when you are distant from her
A thousand leagues, as if you then were with her
You shall know truly when she is solicited,

83 125 circumstance: further delay
84 128 from the purpose: irrelevant
85 129 mean: moderate level
86 132 pollution: sexual corruption
87 139 her: i.e. herself
88 140 watch: guard
89 152 trifle: waste time
90 154 rack: instrument of torture on which victims were stretched

And how far wrought on.
MATHIAS I desire no more.
BAPTISTA [*Giving him a picture*] Take then this little model of Sophia,
With more than human skill limned[91] to the life,
Each line and lineament[92] of it in the drawing
So punctually[93] observed that had it motion
In so much 'twere herself.[94]
MATHIAS It is indeed
An admirable piece, but if it have not
Some hidden virtue that I cannot guess at,
In what can it advantage me?
BAPTISTA I'll instruct you.
Carry it still about you and, as oft
As you desire to know how she's affected,
With curious eyes peruse it. While it keeps
The figure it now has, entire and perfect,
She is not only innocent in fact[95]
But unattempted; but if once it vary
From the true form, and what's now white and red
Incline to yellow, rest most confident
She's with all violence courted but unconquered.
But if it turn all black, 'tis an assurance
The fort[96] by composition[97] or surprise
Is forced or with her free consent surrendered.
MATHIAS How much you have engaged[98] me for this favor
The service of my whole life shall make good.
BAPTISTA We will not part so; I'll along with you.
And it is needful: with the rising sun
The armies meet, yet ere the fight's begun
In spite of opposition I will place you
In the head of the Hungarian general's troop
And near his person.
MATHIAS As my better angel[99]
You shall direct and guide me.
BAPTISTA As we ride
I'll tell you more.
MATHIAS In all things I'll obey you.

Exeunt

Act I, scene ii

Enter UBALDO [*and*] RICARDO

RICARDO When came the post?
UBALDO The last night.
RICARDO From the camp?

91 167 limned: painted
92 168 lineament: feature
93 169 punctually: minutely
94 169–70 had it . . . 'twere herself: i.e. if it could move it would be indistinguishable from Sophia
95 178 fact: deed
96 184 fort: fortress, i.e. Sophia herself
97 184 composition: capitulation
98 186 engaged: obliged
99 193 better angel: spiritual guide, moral exemplar

UBALDO Yes, as 'tis said, and the letter writ[100] and signed
By the General Ferdinand.
RICARDO Nay, then, sans[101] question
It is of moment.[102]
UBALDO It concerns the lives
Of two great armies.
RICARDO Was it cheerfully
Received by the king?
UBALDO Yes, for being assured
The armies were in view of one another,
Having proclaimed a public fast and prayer
For the good success, dispatched[103] a gentleman
Of his privy chamber[104] to the general
With absolute authority from him
To try the fortune of a day.[105]
RICARDO No doubt, then,
The general will come on and fight it bravely.
Heaven prosper him! This military art
I grant to be the noblest of professions
And yet—I thank my stars for't—I was never
Inclined to learn it, since this bubble,[106] honor—
Which is indeed the nothing soldiers fight for
With the loss of limbs or life—is in my judgment
Too dear a purchase.
UBALDO Give me our court-warfare;
The danger is not great in the encounter
Of a fair mistress.
RICARDO Fair and sound[107] together
Do very well, Ubaldo. But such are
With difficulty to be found out and, when they know
Their value, prized too high. By thy own report
Thou wast at twelve a gamester,[108] and since that
Studied all kinds of females, from the night-trader[109]
I' the street, with certain danger to thy pocket,
To the great lady in her cabinet,[110]
That spent upon thee more in cullises[111]
To strengthen thy weak back than would maintain
Twelve Flanders mares[112] and as many running horses,[113]
Besides apothecaries' and chirurgeons'[114] bills
Paid upon all occasions, and those frequent.
UBALDO You talk, Ricardo, as if yet you were

100 2 writ: written
101 3 sans: without
102 4 of moment: important
103 9 dispatched: he dispatched
104 9–10 a gentleman . . . privy chamber: one of his personal servants; the privy chamber is the monarch's private apartment
105 12 To try . . . a day: to see whether fortune would favor them that day
106 17 bubble: illusion
107 22 sound: healthy
108 26 gamester: sexual player
109 27 night-trader: prostitute
110 29 cabinet: private chamber or apartment
111 30 cullises: strong, meaty broths fed to invalids
112 32 Flanders mares: strong horses used to pull coaches
113 32 running horses: racehorses
114 33 chirurgeons: surgeons

A novice in those mysteries.
RICARDO By no means;
My doctor can assure the contrary.
I lose no time; I have felt the pain and pleasure,
As he that is a gamester and plays often
Must sometimes be a loser.
UBALDO Wherefore then
Do you envy me?
RICARDO It grows not from my want,
Nor thy abundance, but being as I am
The likelier[115] man, and of much more experience,
My good parts[116] are my curses: there's no beauty[117]
But yields ere it[118] be summoned, and as[119] nature
Had signed[120] me the monopoly[121] of maidenheads,[122]
There's none can buy till I have made my market.[123]
Satiety[124] cloys[125] me; as I live,[126] I would part with
Half my estate, nay, travel[127] o'er the world
To find that only phoenix[128] in my search
That could hold out against me.
UBALDO Be not rapt[129] so;
You may spare that labor. As she is a woman
What think you of the queen?
RICARDO I dare not aim at
The petticoat[130] royal; that is still excepted.
Yet were she not my king's, being the abstract
Of all that's rare, or to be wished in woman,
To write her in my catalogue,[131] having enjoyed her,
I would venture my neck to a halter.[132] But we talk of
Impossibilities: as[133] she hath a beauty
Would make old Nestor[134] young, such majesty
Draws forth a sword of terror to defend it
As would fright Paris,[135] though the Queen of Love[136]
Vowed her best furtherance[137] to him.
UBALDO Have you observed

115 43 likelier: more qualified or vigorous
116 44 parts: looks
117 44 beauty: beautiful woman
118 45 it: she
119 45 as: as if
120 46 signed: assigned
121 46 monopoly: exclusive trade
122 46 maidenheads: virginities, virginal women
123 47 market: choice
124 48 Satiety: abundance, fulfilment
125 48 cloys: wearies, disgusts
126 48 as I live: i.e. truly
127 49 travel: with a pun on "travail" (labor)
128 50 phoenix: unique woman, paragon
129 51 rapt: enraptured
130 54 petticoat: undergarment
131 57 catalogue: list of conquests
132 58 I would . . . a halter: I would risk hanging; a "halter" is a noose
133 59 as: just as
134 60 Nestor: Greek hero famous for his wisdom and age
135 62 Paris: Trojan prince who, with Venus's help, abducted Helen from Greece
136 62 Queen of Love: Venus
137 63 furtherance: assistance

The gravity[138] of her language mixed with sweetness?
RICARDO Then, at what distance she reserves herself
When the king himself makes his approaches to her.
UBALDO As she were still a virgin, and his life
But one continued wooing.
RICARDO She well knows
Her worth, and values it.
UBALDO And so far the king is
Indulgent to her humors,[139] that he forbears
The duty of a husband[140] but[141] when she calls for't.
RICARDO All his imaginations and thoughts
Are buried in her, the loud noise of war
Cannot awake him.
UBALDO At this very instant,
When both his life and crown are at the stake,
He only studies her content, and when
She's pleased to show herself, music and masques [142]
Are with all care and cost provided for her.
RICARDO This night she promised to appear.
UBALDO You may
Believe it by the diligence[143] of the king,
As if he were her harbinger.[144]

Enter LADISLAUS, EUBULUS, *and Attendants with perfumes*

LADISLAUS These rooms
Are not perfumed as we directed.
EUBULUS Not, sir?
I know not what you would have; I am sure the smoke[145]
Cost treble the price of the whole week's provision[146]
Spent in your majesty's kitchens.
LADISLAUS How![147] I scorn
Thy gross[148] comparison. When my Honoria,
Th'amazement[149] of the present time and envy
Of all succeeding ages, does descend
To sanctify a place, and in her presence
Makes it a temple to me, can I be
Too curious,[150] much less prodigal,[151] to receive her?
But that the splendor of her beams of beauty
Hath struck thee blind—
EUBULUS As dotage[152] hath done you.

138 64 gravity: seriousness, authority
139 70 humors: physical needs, moods
140 71 duty of a husband: i.e. sexual intercourse
141 71 but: except for
142 77 masques: courtly theatrical entertainments
143 80 diligence: careful attention
144 81 harbinger: forerunner, herald
145 83 smoke: perfume, produced by burning fragrant substances
146 84 provision: supply
147 85 How!: an indignant exclamation
148 86 gross: coarse, materialistic
149 87 amazement: wonder
150 91 curious: attentive, careful
151 91 prodigal: extravagant
152 93 dotage: excessive love, foolishness

LADISLAUS Dotage? Oh, blasphemy! Is it in me
To serve her to her merit? Is she not
The daughter of a king?
EUBULUS And you the son
Of ours, I take it; by what privilege else
Do you reign over us? For my part I know not
Where the disparity lies.
LADISLAUS Her birth, old man—
Old in the kingdom's service, which protects thee[153]—
Is the least grace in her, and though her beauties
Might make the Thunderer[154] a rival for her
They are but superficial ornaments
And faintly speak her. From her heavenly mind,
Were all antiquity and fiction lost,
Our modern poets could not in their fancy
But fashion a Minerva[155] far transcending
Th'imagined one, whom Homer[156] only dreamt of.
But then add this: she's mine, mine, Eubulus,
And though she know[157] one glance from her fair eyes
Must make all gazers her idolaters,[158]
She is so sparing of their influence
That to shun superstition in others
She shoots her powerful beams[159] only at me.
And can I then, whom she desires to hold
Her kingly captive above all the world,
Whose nations and empires if she pleased
She might command as slaves, but gladly pay
The humble tribute of my love and service?
Nay, if I said of adoration to her
I did not err!
EUBULUS Well, since you hug your fetters,[160]
In love's name wear 'em. You are a king, and that
Concludes[161] you wise, your will a powerful reason
Which we that are foolish subjects must not argue,
And what in a mean man I should call folly
Is in your majesty remarkable wisdom.
But for me I subscribe.[162]
LADISLAUS Do, and look up
Upon this wonder.

Loud music.[163] [*Enter*] HONORIA *in state*[164] *under a canopy,*[165] *her train borne up by* SILVIA *and* ACANTHE

RICARDO Wonder? It is more, sir.

153 100 Because of your long service to the kingdom, you will not be punished for speaking freely
154 102 Thunderer: Jupiter, king of the Roman gods, renowned for his sexual assaults on mortal women
155 107 Minerva: Roman name for Athena, the Greek goddess of the arts, wisdom, and warfare
156 108 Homer: ancient Greek author or compiler of *The Iliad* and *The Odyssey*
157 110 know: knows
158 111 idolaters: worshippers
159 114 shoots her powerful beams: eyes were thought to work by projecting beams of light
160 121 fetters: chains
161 123 Concludes: proves
162 127 subscribe: submit
163 128 SD *Loud music*: a fanfare
164 128 SD *in state*: with ceremonial pomp
165 128 SD *canopy*: covering held over a high-status person

UBALDO A rapture, an astonishment!
RICARDO What think you, sir?
EUBULUS As the king thinks; that is the surest guard
We courtiers ever lie at.[166] Was prince ever
So drowned in dotage? Without spectacles
I can see a handsome woman, and she is so,
But yet to admiration[167] look not on her. [LADISLAUS *kisses* HONORIA*'s hand as* EUBULUS *speaks*]
Heaven, how he fawns,[168] and, as it were his duty,
With what assured gravity she receives it!
Her hand again! [HONORIA *kisses* LADISLAUS]
Oh, she at length vouchsafes[169]
Her lip, and as[170] he had sucked nectar from it
How he's exalted! Women in their natures [171]
Affect command,[172] but this humility
In a husband and a king marks[173] her the way
To absolute tyranny. [LADISLAUS *places* HONORIA *in his throne*]
So Juno's[174] placed
In Jove's tribunal[175] and, like Mercury[176]
Forgetting his own greatness, he attends
For her employments.[177] She prepares to speak;
What oracles[178] shall we hear now?
HONORIA That you please, sir,
With such assurances of love and favor
To grace your handmaid[179]—but[180] in being yours, sir,
A matchless queen, and one that knows herself so—
Binds me in retribution[181] to deserve
The grace conferred upon me.
LADISLAUS You transcend
In all things excellent, and it is my glory,
Your worth weighed truly, to depose myself
From absolute command, surrendering up
My will and faculties[182] to your disposure.
And here I vow, not for a day or year,
But my whole life, which I wish long to serve you,
That whatsoever I in justice may
Exact from these my subjects, you from me
May boldly challenge. And when you require it,
In sign of my subjection, as your vassal,[183]

166 130–31 that is . . . lie at: i.e. to agree with the king is a courtier's safest option
167 134 to admiration: with amazement
168 135 fawns: grovels, flatters
169 137 vouchsafes: condescends to offer
170 138 as: as if
171 139 in their natures: naturally
172 140 affect command: love to be in charge
173 141 marks: shows
174 142 Juno: queen of the Roman gods and Jupiter's wife
175 143 Jove's tribunal: Jupiter's throne, or seat of judgement
176 143 Mercury: Roman god of commerce, eloquence, and thievery, who often disguised himself to deceive mortals
177 145 employments: service
178 146 oracles: wise or authoritative statements
179 148 handmaid: servant
180 148 but: only
181 150 retribution: recompense, return
182 155 faculties: powers, abilities
183 161 vassal: servant, slave

Thus I will pay my homage. [*He kisses the hem of her robe*]
HONORIA Oh forbear, sir.
Let not my lips envy my robe: on them
Print your allegiance often; I desire
No other fealty.[184]
LADISLAUS Gracious sovereign,
Boundless in bounty!
EUBULUS [*Aside*] Is not here fine fooling?
He's questionless[185] bewitched; would I were gelt[186]
So that would disenchant him. Though I forfeit
My life for it I must speak.—By your good leave,[187] sir,
I have no suit[188] to you, nor can you grant one,
Having no power. You are, like me, a subject,
Her more-than-serene majesty being present,
And I must tell you 'tis ill[189] manners in you,
Having deposed yourself, to keep your hat on
And not stand bare as we do, being no king
But a fellow subject with us. Gentlemen ushers,[190]
It[191] does belong to your place, see it reformed:[192]
He has given his crown and cannot challenge
The privilege of his bonnet.
LADISLAUS Do not tempt me.
EUBULUS Tempt you in what? In following your example?
If you are angry, question me hereafter,
As Ladislaus should do Eubulus,
On equal terms. You were of late[193] my sovereign
But weary of it; I now bend my knee
To her divinity, and desire a boon[194]
From her more than magnificence.
HONORIA Take it freely.
[*To* LADISLAUS] Nay, be not moved,[195] for our mirth'[196] sake let us hear him.
EUBULUS 'Tis but to ask a question: have you ne'er[197] read
The story of Semiramis and Ninus?[198]
HONORIA Not as I remember.
EUBULUS I will then instruct you,
And 'tis to the purpose. This Ninus was a king,
And such an impotent loving king as this was,
But now he's none. This Ninus—pray you observe me—
Doted on this Semiramis, a smith's wife—
I must confess there the comparison holds not:

184 165 fealty: sign of the vassal's loyalty
185 167 questionless: surely
186 167 gelt: gelded, castrated
187 169 leave: permission
188 170 suit: petition
189 173 ill: bad
190 176 Gentlemen ushers: court officials
191 177 It: the king's refusal to remove his hat
192 177 see it reformed: i.e. see that he removes his hat
193 183 of late: until recently
194 185 boon: favor
195 187 moved: angered
196 187 mirth' amusement's
197 188 ne'er: never
198 189 Semiramis and Ninus: Semiramis was a legendarily power-hungry Assyrian queen; Ninus was her husband

You are a king's daughter, yet, under your correction,[199]
Like her a woman—this Assyrian monarch,
Of whom this is a pattern,[200] to express
His love and service, seated her—as you are—
In his[201] regal throne and bound by oath his nobles,
Forgetting all allegiance[202] to himself,
One day to be her subjects and to put
In execution[203] whatever she
Pleased to impose upon 'em. Pray you command him
To minister the like to us and then
You shall hear what followed.
LADISLAUS Well, sir, to[204] your story.
EUBULUS You have no warrant,[205] stand by.[206] Let me know
Your pleasure, goddess.
HONORIA Let this nod assure you.
EUBULUS Goddess-like indeed; as I live, a pretty idol.
She,[207] knowing her power, wisely made use of it,
And fearing his inconstancy, and repentance
Of what he had granted—as in reason, madam,
You may do his—that[208] he might never have
Power to recall his grant, or question her[209]
For her short[210] government, instantly gave order
To have his head struck off.
LADISLAUS Is't possible?
EUBULUS The story says so, and commends her wisdom
For making use of her authority.
And it is worth your imitation, madam;
He loves subjection, and you are no queen
Unless you make him feel the weight of it.
You are more than all the world to him, and that
He may be so to you, and not seek change
When his delights are sated, mew[211] him up
In some close[212] prison if you let him live—
Which is no policy[213]—and there diet[214] him
As you think fit to feed your appetite,
Since there ends his ambition.[215]
UBALDO Devilish counsel.
RICARDO The king's amazed.
UBALDO The queen appears too full

199 196 under your correction: unless you correct me
200 198 this is a pattern: Ladislaus is a copy
201 200 his: Ninus's
202 201 allegiance: duty, service
203 203 In execution: into effect
204 206 to: get on with
205 207 warrant: authorization (i.e. from Honoria)
206 207 by: aside
207 210 She: Semiramis
208 213 that: in order that
209 214 question her: challenge her, call her to account
210 215 short: hasty, irascible
211 224 mew: shut
212 225 close: enclosed, hidden
213 226 no policy: not a good strategy
214 226 diet: starve, discipline
215 228 there ends his ambition: i.e. this is what he wants

Of deep imaginations.[216] Eubulus
Hath put both to it.[217]
RICARDO Now she seems resolved;
I long to know the issue. HONORIA *descends* [*from the throne*]
HONORIA Give me leave,
Dear sir, to reprehend[218] you for appearing
Perplexed with what this old man, out of envy
Of your unequaled graces showered upon me,
Hath in his fabulous[219] story saucily[220]
Applied to me. Sir, that you only nourish
One doubt[221] Honoria dares abuse the power
With which she is invested by your favor
Or that she ever can make use of it
To the injury of you, the great bestower,[222]
Takes from your judgment.[223] It was your delight
To seek to[224] me with more obsequiousness[225]
Than I desired, and stood it[226] with my duty
Not to receive what you were pleased to offer?
I do but act the part you put upon me,
And though you make me personate a queen
And you my subject, when the play your pleasure[227]
Is at a period,[228] I am what I was
Before I entered, still your humble wife,
And you my royal sovereign.
RICARDO Admirable!
HONORIA I have heard of captains taken more with danger
Than the rewards, and if in your approaches
To those delights which are your own, and freely
To heighten your desire, you make the passage[229]
Narrow and difficult, shall I prescribe[230] you?
Or blame[231] your fondness? Or can that swell[232] me
Beyond my just proportion?[233]
UBALDO Above wonder!
LADISLAUS Heaven make me thankful for such goodness.
HONORIA Now, sir,
The state[234] I took to satisfy your pleasure
I change to this humility, and the oath
You made to me of homage I thus cancel,

216 230 imaginations: thoughts, schemes
217 231 put both to it: put them both at a loss
218 233 reprehend: rebuke
219 236 fabulous: ridiculous, false
220 236 saucily: insolently
221 237–8 only nourish/One doubt: i.e. cherish even the slightest suspicion
222 241 bestower: giver
223 242 Takes from your judgment: would damage your reputation for good sense
224 243 seek to: pursue
225 243 obsequiousness: diligence, servility
226 244 stood it: was it consistent
227 248 the play your pleasure: the act I have put on to please you
228 249 at a period: comes to an end
229 255 passage: way through
230 256 prescribe: limit, restrict
231 257 blame: reprove, find fault with
232 257 swell: inflate
233 258 just proportion: natural shape, appropriate limits
234 260 state: mode of behavior, power

And seat you in your own. [*She seats* LADISLAUS *in his throne*]
LADISLAUS I am transported
Beyond myself.
HONORIA And now to your wise lordship.
Am I proved a Semiramis? Or hath
My Ninus, as maliciously you made him,
Cause to repent th'excess of favor to me,
Which you call dotage?
LADISLAUS Answer, wretch.
EUBULUS I dare, sir,
And say however the event[235] may plead
In your defense, you had a guilty cause;[236]
Nor was it wisdom in you—I repeat it—
To teach a lady, humble in herself,
With the ridiculous dotage of a lover
To be ambitious.
HONORIA Eubulus, I am so,
'Tis rooted in me. You mistake my temper.
I do profess myself to be the most
Ambitious of my sex, but not to hold
Command over my lord: such a proud torrent[237]
Would sink me in my wishes. Not that I
Am ignorant how much I can deserve
And may with justice challenge—
EUBULUS [*Aside*] This I looked for;
After this seeming humble ebb[238] I knew
A gushing tide would follow.
HONORIA By my birth
And liberal gifts of nature, as of fortune,
From you, as things beneath me, I expect
What's due to majesty, in which I am
A sharer with your sovereign.
EUBULUS [*Aside*] Good again!
HONORIA And as I am most eminent[239] in place,[240]
In all my actions I would appear so.
LADISLAUS You need not fear a rival.
HONORIA I hope not;
And till I find one, I disdain to know
What envy is.
LADISLAUS You are above it, madam.
HONORIA For beauty without art,[241] discourse,[242] and free[243]
From affectation,[244] with what graces[245] else
Can in the wife and daughter of a king
Be wished, I dare prefer[246] myself.

235 269 event: outcome
236 270 cause: intention
237 278 torrent: violently flowing stream
238 282 ebb: receding tide
239 288 eminent: exalted
240 288 place: rank
241 293 art: cosmetics
242 293 discourse: powers of reason and/or conversation
243 293 free: i.e. freedom
244 294 affectation: artificiality in behavior or manner
245 294 graces: virtues, marks of divine favor
246 296 prefer: present, recommend

EUBULUS As I
Blush for you, lady. Trumpet[247] your own praises?
This spoken by the people had been heard
With honor to you. Does the court afford
No oil-tongued parasite,[248] that you are forced
To be your own gross flatterer?
LADISLAUS Be dumb,[249]
Thou spirit of contradiction.
HONORIA The wolf
But barks against the moon, and I contemn[250] it.
The masque you promised. *A horn [sounds]*
LADISLAUS Let 'em enter.

Enter a POST

How!
EUBULUS Here's one, I fear, unlooked for.[251]
LADISLAUS From the camp?
POST The general, victorious in your fortune,
Kisses your hand in this,[252] sir. [*Gives him a letter, which* LADISLAUS *reads*]
LADISLAUS That great power[253]
Who at his pleasure does dispose of battles,
Be ever praised for't! Read, sweet, and partake it.
The Turk is vanquished, and with little loss
Upon our part, in which our joy is doubled.
EUBULUS But let it not exalt you.[254] Bear it, sir,
With moderation, and pay what you owe for't.
LADISLAUS I understand thee, Eubulus; I'll not now
Enquire particulars. Our delights deferred,
With[255] reverence to the temples; there we'll tender[256]
Our souls' devotions to his dread[257] might
Who edged our swords and taught us how to fight.

Exeunt omnes

The end of the first act

Act II, scene i

Enter HILARIO [*and*] CORISCA

HILARIO You like my speech?
CORISCA Yes, if you give it action[258]
In the delivery.

247 297 Trumpet: proclaim, celebrate
248 300 parasite: hanger-on, sycophant
249 301 dumb: silent
250 303 contemn: despise
251 305 unlooked for: not expected, unwelcome
252 307 Kisses your hand in this: greets you in this letter
253 307 That great power: i.e. God
254 312 exalt you: i.e. fill you with pride
255 316 With: let us go with
256 316 tender: offer
257 317 dread: revered
258 1 action: appropriate gestures and facial expressions

HILARIO If? I pity you.
I have played the fool before; this is not the first time,
Nor shall be I hope the last.
CORISCA Nay, I think so too.[259]
HILARIO And if I put her not out of her dumps[260] with laughter,
I'll make her howl for anger.
CORISCA Not too much
Of that, good fellow Hilario. Our sad lady
Hath drank too often of that bitter cup;
A pleasant one must restore her. With what patience
Would she endure to hear of the death of my lord,
That merely out of doubt he may miscarry[261]
Afflicts[262] herself thus?
HILARIO Um. 'Tis a question
A widow only can resolve. There be some
That in their husbands' sicknesses have wept
Their pottle[263] of tears a day, but being once certain
At midnight he was dead, have in the morning
Dried up their handkerchers and thought no more on't.
CORISCA Tush![264] She is none of that race. If her sorrow
Be not true and perfect, I against my sex
Will take my oath woman ne'er wept in earnest.
She has made herself a prisoner to her chamber,
Dark as a dungeon, in which no beam
Of comfort enters. She admits no visits,
Eats little, and her nightly music is
Of sighs and groans tuned to such harmony
Of feeling grief, that I against my nature
Am made one of the consort.[265] This hour only
She takes the air, a custom every day
She solemnly observes, with greedy hopes
From some that pass by to receive assurance
Of the success and safety of her lord.
Now if that your device will take—
HILARIO Ne'er fear it.
I am provided cap à pie,[266] and have
My properties[267] in readiness.
SOPHIA [*Within*] Bring my veil there.
CORISCA Be gone, I hear her coming.
HILARIO If I do not
Appear and, what's more, appear perfect,[268] hiss me. *Exit* HILARIO

259 3–4 I have . . . so too: an in-joke, as Hilario is played by the company clown, John Shank
260 5 dumps: depression
261 11 miscarry: suffer misfortune
262 12 Afflicts: torments, makes herself ill
263 15 pottle: pot (technically measuring a half-gallon or about two liters)
264 18 Tush: an exclamation signaling disagreement or disgust
265 27 consort: band of musicians
266 33 cap à pie: head to foot
267 34 properties: props
268 36 perfect: knowing all my lines

Enter SOPHIA [*wearing black*][269]

SOPHIA I was flattered once I was[270] a star, but now
Turned[271] a prodigious[272] meteor, and, like one,
Hang in the air between my hopes and fears,
And every hour the little stuff burnt out
That yields a waning[273] light to dying comfort.
I do expect my fall and certain ruin.
In wretched things more wretched is delay,
And hope a parasite[274] to me, being unmasked[275]
Appears more horrid than despair, and my
Distraction[276] worse than madness. E'en my prayers
When with most zeal sent upward, are pulled down
With strong imaginary doubts and fears,
And in their sudden precipice[277] o'erwhelm me.
Dreams and fantastic[278] visions walk the round
About my widowed bed, and every slumber
Broken[279] with loud alarms.[280] Can these be then
But sad presages,[281] girl?
CORISCA You make 'em so,
And antedate[282] a loss shall ne'er fall on you.
Such pure affection, such mutual love,
A bed, and undefiled on either part,
A house without contention, in two bodies
One will and soul, like to the rod of concord[283]
Kissing each other, cannot be short-lived
Or end in barrenness. If all these, dear madam—
Sweet in your sadness—should produce no fruit,
Or leave the age no models[284] of yourselves
To witness to posterity[285] what you were,
Succeeding times, frighted with the example[286]
But hearing of your story,[287] would instruct
Their fairest issue[288] to meet sensually,[289]
Like other creatures,[290] and forbear to raise

269 36 SD *wearing black*: at III.ii. 60 Ricardo refers to her "widow's garments"
270 37 I was: that I was
271 38 Turned: I have turned into
272 38 prodigious: portentous, appalling
273 41 waning: diminishing
274 44 parasite: deceiver
275 44 being unmasked: which, being unmasked
276 46 Distraction: mental disturbance
277 49 precipice: headlong fall
278 50 fantastic: imaginary
279 52 Broken: is broken
280 52 alarms: disturbance, warnings of danger
281 53 presages: omens, signs
282 54 antedate: anticipate
283 58 rod of concord: wand with two serpents winding about it, carried by Mercury
284 62 models: miniature imitations, sketches (i.e. children)
285 63 posterity: future generations
286 64 frighted with the example: frightened by your example
287 65 But hearing of your story: i.e. only hearing a report of these events
288 66 issue: children
289 66 meet sensually: have sex
290 67 other creatures: non-human animals

True love or Hymen altars.[291]
SOPHIA O Corisca,
I know thy reasons are like to thy wishes,
And they are built upon a weak foundation
To raise[292] me comfort. Ten long days are past—
Ten long days, my Corisca—since my lord
Embarked himself upon a sea of danger
In his dear care of me. And if his life
Had not been shipwracked on the rock of war,
His tenderness[293] of me—knowing how much
I languish[294] for his absence—had provided
Some trusty friend from whom I might receive
Assurance of his safety.
CORISCA Ill news, madam,
Are swallow-winged,[295] but what's good walks on crutches.
With patience expect it, and ere long
No doubt you shall hear from him. *A sowgelder's horn*[296] *blown*
SOPHIA Ha! What's that?
CORISCA [*Aside*] The fool has got a sowgelder's horn.—A post
As I take it, madam.
SOPHIA It makes this way still,
Nearer and nearer.
CORISCA From the camp, I hope.

Enter HILARIO, *with a long white hair and beard, in an antique*[297] *armor,* [a *Servant*] *with a horn before him*

SOPHIA The messenger appears and in strange armor.
Heaven,[298] if it be thy will!
HILARIO It is no boot[299]
To strive; our horses[300] tired, let's walk on foot.
And that the castle, which is very near us,
To give us entertainment[301] may soon hear us,
Blow lustily,[302] my lad, and drawing nigh-a,[303]
Ask for a lady which is cleped[304] Sophia.
CORISCA He names you, madam.
HILARIO For to her I bring,
Thus clad in arms, news of a pretty[305] thing
By name Mathias.
SOPHIA From my lord? O sir,
I am Sophia, that Mathias' wife.

291 67–8 forbear to . . . Hymen altars: i.e. reject marriage altogether; Hymen is the Roman god of marriage
292 71 raise: provide
293 76 tenderness: loving care
294 77 languish: suffer, pine
295 80 Are swallow-winged: travels quickly
296 82 SD *sowgelder's horn*: blown to mark the arrival of the traveling sowgelder (someone who castrates pigs); its sound appears to have been notably loud and harsh
297 85 SD *antique*: old; interchangeable with "antic" (eccentric or extravagant)
298 87 Heaven: i.e. O God
299 87 no boot: useless
300 88 our horses: because our horses are
301 90 entertainment: welcome, a fine meal
302 91 lustily: vigorously
303 91 nigh-a: near
304 92 cleped: named (a deliberately old-fashioned word)
305 94 pretty: brave, gallant

So may Mars favor you in all your battles,
As you with speed unload me of the burthen[306]
I labor under, till I am confirmed[307]
Both where and how you left him.
HILARIO If thou art,
As I believe, the pigsney[308] of his heart,
Know he's in health and, what's more, full of glee.
And so much I was willed to say to thee.
SOPHIA Have you no letters from him?
HILARIO No more words;
In the camp we use no pens, but write with swords.
Yet as I am enjoined,[309] by word of mouth
I will proclaim his deeds from north to south.
But tremble not while I relate the wonder,
Though my eyes like lightning shine, and my voice thunder.
SOPHIA This is some counterfeit braggart.
CORISCA Hear him, madam.
HILARIO The rear marched first, which, followed by the van[310]
And winged[311] with the battalia,[312] no man
Durst stay to shift[313] a shirt or louse himself;[314]
Yet ere the armies joined,[315] that hopeful elf,[316]
Thy dear, my dainty duckling, bold Mathias,
Advanced, and stared like Hercules[317] or Golias.[318]
A hundred thousand Turks—it is no vaunt[319]—
Assailed him, every one a Termagaunt.[320]
But what did he then? With his keen-edge spear
He cut and carbonadoed[321] 'em—here and there
Lay legs and arms—and—as 'tis said truly
Of Bevis[322]—some he quartered all in three.
SOPHIA This is ridiculous.
HILARIO I must take breath,
Then like a nightingale I'll sing his death.
SOPHIA His death?
HILARIO [*To* CORISCA] I am out.[323]
CORISCA [*To* HILARIO] Recover, dunderhead.[324]
HILARIO How he escaped I should have sung, not died;
For, though[325] a knight, when I said so I lied.

306 98 burthen: burden
307 99 confirmed: assured, informed
308 101 pigsney: darling
309 106 enjoined: required
310 111 van: vanguard, foremost division of the army
311 112 winged: supported on either side
312 112 battalia: host of soldiers
313 113 Durst stay to shift: dared to change
314 113 louse himself: check himself for lice
315 114 joined: met in battle
316 114 elf: knight (an imitation of Spenser's *Faerie Queene*)
317 116 Hercules: classical hero possessing incredible strength
318 116 Golias: i.e. Goliath, a Biblical giant killed by David
319 117 vaunt: exaggeration, boast
320 118 Termagaunt: a god imagined by Christians to be worshipped by Muslims
321 120 carbonadoed: cut across and grilled (used of meat and fish)
322 122 Bevis: Bevis of Hampton, a hero of Elizabethan fiction
323 125 am out: have forgotten my lines
324 125 dunderhead: idiot
325 127 though: although I am

Weary he was, and scarce could stand upright
And looking round for some courageous knight
To rescue him, as one perplexed in woe
He called to me, "Help, help, Hilario,
My valiant servant, help!"
CORISCA [*Aside*] He has spoiled all.
SOPHIA Are you the man of arms, then? I'll make bold
To take off your martial beard; you had fool's hair
Enough without it. Slave, how durst thou make
Thy sport[326] of what concerns me more than life,
In such an antic[327] fashion? Am I grown
Contemptible to those I feed? You, minion,[328]
Had a hand in it too, as it appears;
Your petticoat serves for bases[329] to this warrior.
CORISCA We did it for your mirth.
HILARIO For myself, I hope,
I have spoke like a soldier.
SOPHIA Hence, you rascal.
I never but with reverence name my lord,
And can I hear it by thy tongue profaned[330]
And not correct thy folly? But you are
Transformed and turned knight-errant;[331] take your course[332]
And wander where you please, for here I vow
By my lord's life—an oath I will not break—
Till his return, or certainty of his safety,
My doors are shut against thee. *Exit* SOPHIA
CORISCA You have made
A fine piece of work on't. How do you like the quality?[333]
You had a foolish itch[334] to be an actor,
And may stroll[335] where you please.
HILARIO Will you buy my share?[336]
CORISCA No, certainly, I fear I have already
Too much of mine own. I'll only as a damsel
(As the books[337] say) thus far help to disarm you. [*She removes his helmet or another part of his armor*]
And so, dear Don Quixote,[338] taking my leave,
I leave you to your fortune. *Exit* CORISCA [*and* SERVANT]
HILARIO Have I sweat
My brains out for this quaint[339] and rare invention,
And am I thus rewarded? I could turn

326 136 sport: entertainment
327 137 antic: grotesque, indecorous (with a pun on "antique")
328 138 You, minion: i.e. Corisca; a "minion" is a servant or underling
329 140 bases: skirts worn with armor
330 144 profaned: defiled
331 146 knight-errant: a traveling or questing knight
332 146 course: path
333 151 quality: profession of an actor
334 152 itch: longing
335 153 stroll: travel in the manner of a touring actor
336 153 share: share in a playing company
337 156 books: i.e. chivalric romances
338 157 Don Quixote: hero of Cervantes's parodic chivalric novel, *Don Quixote*
339 159 quaint: ingenious, courtly

Tragedian and roar[340] now, but that I fear
'Twould get me too great a stomach,[341] having no meat
To pacify colon.[342] What will become of me?
I cannot beg in armor, and steal I dare not;
My end must be to stand in a cornfield
And fright away the crows for bread and cheese,
Or find some hollow tree in the highway,
And there until my lord return sell switches.[343]
No more Hilario, but Dolorio[344] now.
I'll weep my eyes out and be blind of purpose[345]
To move compassion. And so I vanish.

Exit HILARIO

Act II, scene ii

Enter EUBULUS, UBALDO, RICARDO, *and others*

EUBULUS Are the gentlemen sent before, as it was ordered
By the king's direction, to entertain
The general?
RICARDO Long since. They by this[346] have met him
And given him the bienvenue.[347]
EUBULUS I hope I need not
Instruct you in your parts.[348]
UBALDO How! Us, my lord?
Fear not, we know our distances and degrees[349]
To the very inch where we are to salute him.
RICARDO The state were miserable if the court had none
Of her own breed familiar with all garbs [350]
Gracious[351] in England, Italy, Spain, or France,
With form and punctuality[352] to receive
Stranger[353] ambassadors. For the general,
He's a mere native[354] and it matters not
Which way we do accost[355] him.
UBALDO 'Tis great pity
That such as sit at the helm[356] provide no better
For the training up of the gentry.[357] In my judgment,
An academy erected, with large pensions

340 161 roar: shout, lament
341 162 stomach: passion, appetite
342 163 pacify colon: appease my appetite
343 168 switches: sticks
344 169 Dolorio: Hilario changes his name from one signifying mirth to one signifying sorrow
345 170 of purpose: deliberately
346 3 by this: by this time
347 4 bienvenue: welcome
348 5 parts: roles in the court ceremony
349 6 distances and degrees: positions (i.e. the gaps between soldiers when standing in formation), social ranks
350 9 garbs: customs, manners
351 10 Gracious: pleasing, of high status
352 11 form and punctuality: good order and ceremoniousness, attention to detail
353 12 Stranger: foreign
354 13 native: i.e. Hungarian
355 14 accost: approach, address
356 15 sit at the helm: i.e. rule; the helm is the tiller of a ship
357 16 gentry: social rank immediately below the nobility

To such as in a table[358] could set down
The congees,[359] cringes,[360] postures,[361] methods,[362] phrase[363]
Proper to every nation—
RICARDO Oh, it were
An admirable piece of work!
UBALDO And yet rich fools
Throw away their charity on hospitals
For beggars and lame soldiers, and ne'er study
The due regard to compliment[364] and courtship,[365]
Matters of more import, and are[366] indeed
The glories of a monarchy.
EUBULUS These no doubt
Are state-points,[367] gallants, I confess. But, sure,
Our court needs no aids this way, since it is
A school of nothing else: there are some of you,
Whom I forbear to name, whose coining[368] heads
Are the mints[369] of all new fashions, that have done
More hurt to the kingdom by superfluous[370] bravery,[371]
Which the foolish gentry imitate, than a war
Or a long famine. All the treasure by[372]
This foul excess is got into the merchant's,
Embroiderer's, silk-man's, jeweler's, tailor's hand,
And the third part of the land, too, the nobility
Engrossing titles[373] only.
RICARDO My lord, you are bitter.

Enter a SERVANT. *A trumpet [sounds]*

SERVANT The general is alighted[374] and now entered.
RICARDO Were he ten generals I am prepared,
And know what I will do.
EUBULUS Pray you what, Ricardo?
RICARDO I'll fight at compliment with him.
UBALDO I'll charge home too.
EUBULUS And that's a desperate[375] service if you come off well.[376]

Enter FERDINAND, MATHIAS, BAPTISTA, *[and] two Captains*

358 18 table: notebook
359 19 congees: bows
360 19 cringes: obsequious bows
361 19 postures: poses, positions of the body
362 19 methods: rules, procedures
363 19 phrase: language, mode of expression
364 24 compliment: formal praise
365 24 courtship: behavior appropriate to a courtier
366 25 are: that are
367 27 state-points: subjects of political importance
368 30 coining: inventive, forging
369 31 mints: places where money is produced, sites of innovation
370 32 superfluous: excessive, trivial
371 32 bravery: ostentatious show, fine clothing
372 34 by: by means of
373 38 Engrossing titles: keeping possession of signs of rank
374 39 alighted: arrived, dismounted (from his horse)
375 43 desperate: reckless, outrageous
376 43 come off well: succeed

FERDINAND Captain, command the officers to keep
The soldier as he[377] marched, in rank and file,[378]
Till they hear further from me.
EUBULUS Here's one speaks
In another key; this is no canting[379] language
Taught in your academy.[380]
FERDINAND [*To* MATHIAS] Nay, I will present you
To the king myself.
MATHIAS A grace[381] beyond my merit.
FERDINAND You undervalue what I cannot set
Too high a price on.
EUBULUS [*To* FERDINAND] With a friend's true heart
I gratulate[382] your return.
FERDINAND Next to the favor
Of the great king, I am happy in your friendship.
UBALDO By courtship! Coarse on both sides.[383]
FERDINAND Pray you receive
This stranger to your knowledge; on my credit
At all parts[384] he deserves it.
EUBULUS Your report
Is a strong assurance to me. Sir, most welcome.
MATHIAS This said by you, the reverence of your age
Commands me to believe it.
RICARDO [*To* UBALDO] This was pretty,
But second[385] me now. [*To* FERDINAND, *bowing*] I cannot stoop too low
To do your excellence that due observance[386]
Your fortune claims.
EUBULUS He ne'er thinks on his[387] virtue.
RICARDO For being, as you are, the soul of soldiers,
And bulwark[388] of Bellona[389]—
UBALDO The protection
Both of the court and king—
RICARDO And the sole minion
Of mighty Mars[390]—
UBALDO One that with justice[391] may
Increase the number of the Worthies[392]—
EUBULUS Hoy day![393]
RICARDO It being impossible in my arms to circle

377 45 soldier as he: i.e. soldiers as they
378 45 rank and file: military formation
379 47 canting: affected, cheating (as if they speak thieves' "cant" or jargon)
380 48 academy: school of manners
381 49 grace: mark of favor, privilege
382 52 gratulate: welcome
383 54 Ubaldo swears ("By courtship") in astonishment at how unsophisticated ("coarse") both Eubulus and Ferdinand are
384 56 at all parts: in all respects
385 60 second: support (as if in combat)
386 61 due observance: appropriate display of respect or good manners
387 62 his: Ferdinand's
388 64 bulwark: fortification, defense
389 64 Bellona: Roman goddess of war
390 66 Mars: Roman god of war
391 66 with justice: justly, with good reason
392 67 Worthies: the exemplary Nine Worthies of medieval tradition (Hector, Alexander the Great, Julius Caesar, Joshua, David, Judas Maccabeus, King Arthur, King Charlemagne, and Godfrey of Bouillon)
393 67 Hoy day: a scornful exclamation

Such giant worth—
UBALDO At distance we presume
To kiss your honored gauntlet.[394]
EUBULUS What reply now
Can he make to this foppery?[395]
FERDINAND You have said,
Gallants, so much, and hitherto done so little,
That till I learn to speak and you to do
I must take time to thank you.[396]
EUBULUS As I live,
Answered as I could wish. How the fops gape now!
RICARDO This was harsh, and scurvy.[397]
UBALDO We will be revenged
When he comes to court the ladies, and laugh at him.
EUBULUS Nay, do your offices, gentlemen, and conduct
The general to the presence.[398]
RICARDO Keep your order!
UBALDO Make way for the general! *Exeunt omnes praeter* EUBULUM[399]
EUBULUS What wise man
That with judicious eyes looks on a soldier
But must[400] confess that fortune's swinge[401] is more
O'er that profession than all kinds else
Of life pursued by man. They[402] in a state
Are but as chirurgions[403] to wounded men
Even[404] desperate in their hopes: while pain and anguish
Make them[405] blaspheme and call in vain for death,
Their wives and children kiss the chirurgion's knees,
Promise him mountains if his saving hand
Restore the tortured wretch to former strength;
But when grim death by Aesculapius'[406] art
Is frighted from the house, and health appears
In sanguine[407] colors on the sick man's face,
All is forgot, and asking[408] his reward[409]
He's paid with curses, often receives wounds
From him whose wounds he cured; so soldiers—
Though of more worth and use—meet the same fate,
As it is too apparent. I have observed
When horrid Mars—the touch of whose rough hand
With palsies[410] shakes a kingdom—hath put on

394 70 gauntlet: armored glove
395 71 foppery: folly, absurdity
396 74 take time to thank you: postpone thanking you
397 76 scurvy: discourteous, rude
398 79 presence: the presence of the king
399 80 SD *Exeunt omnes praeter* EUBULUM: they all leave except for Eubulus (Latin)
400 82 But must: can't help but
401 82 swinge: power, authority
402 84 They: i.e. soldiers
403 85 chirurgions: surgeons
404 86 Even: utterly
405 87 them: the wounded men
406 91 Aesculapius: Roman god of medicine and healing
407 93 sanguine: rosy, hopeful (i.e. the blood returns to his face)
408 94 asking: when he asks for
409 94 reward: payment
410 100 palsies: paralysis, often accompanied by shaking; oppression

His dreadful helmet and with terror fills
The place where he, like an unwelcome guest,
Resolves to revel,[411] how the lords of acres,[412]
The tradesman, merchant, and litigious pleader[413]—
And such like scarabs[414] bred i' th' dung of peace—
In hope of their protection humbly offer
Their daughters to their beds,[415] heirs to their service,
And wash with tears their sweat, their dust, their scars.
But when those clouds of war that menacèd[416]
A bloody deluge[417] to th'affrighted state
Are by their breath dispersed and overblown,[418]
And famine, blood, and death, Bellona's pages,[419]
Whipped from the quiet continent to Thrace,[420]
Soldiers, that like the foolish hedge-sparrow
To their own ruin hatch this cuckoo peace,[421]
Are straight thought burdensome, since want of means,
Growing from want of action,[422] breeds contempt;
And that the worst of ills fall to their lot,[423]
Their service with the danger soon forgot.

Enter a SERVANT

SERVANT The queen, my lord, hath made choice of this room
To see the masque.
EUBULUS I'll be a looker-on;[424]
My dancing days are past.

Loud music as they pass, a song in the praise of war. [*Enter*] UBALDO, RICARDO, LADISLAUS, FERDINAND *and* HONORIA [*who seat themselves*], MATHIAS, SILVIA, ACANTHE, BAPTISTA, *and others*

LADISLAUS This courtesy
To a stranger, my Honoria, keeps fair rank[425]
With all your rarities.[426] [*To* FERDINAND] After your travail[427]
Look on our court delights, but first from your
Relation with erected[428] ears I'll hear
The music of your war, which must be sweet,
Ending in victory.
FERDINAND Not to trouble

411 103 revel: make merry, amuse himself
412 103 lords of acres: landowning men, landlords
413 104 litigious pleader: lawyer
414 105 scarabs: dung beetles
415 107 to their beds: i.e. to be sexually exploited by the soldiers
416 109 menacèd: threatened
417 110 deluge: flood, downpour
418 111 overblown: blown away
419 112 pages: boy servants
420 113 Thrace: a former Roman province in southeastern Europe, now divided between Bulgaria, Greece, and Turkey
421 114–15 like the . . . cuckoo peace: hedge-sparrows are among the species of smaller birds in whose nests cuckoos lay their own eggs
422 117 action: military activity
423 118 That which is worst of all becomes their fate
424 121 looker-on: observer
425 123 keeps fair rank: is equal in virtue
426 124 rarities: precious qualities, exceptional characteristics
427 124 travail: labor (with a potential pun on "travel")
428 126 erected: pricked up, attentive

Your majesties with description of a battle
Too full of horror for the[429] place—and to
Avoid particulars, which, should I deliver,[430]
I must trench[431] longer on your patience than
My manners will give way to—in a word, sir,
It was well fought on both sides, and almost
With equal fortune, it continuing doubtful[432]
Upon whose tents plumed[433] victory would take
Her glorious stand. Impatient of delay,
With the flower of our prime gentlemen[434] I charged
Their main battalia, and with their assistance
Brake in; but when I was almost assured
That they were routed, by a stratagem
Of the subtle[435] Turk, who opening his gross body,[436]
And rallying[437] up his troops on either side,
I found myself so far engaged[438]—for I
Must not conceal my errors—that I knew not
Which way with honor to come off.
EUBULUS I like
A general that tells his faults, and is not
Ambitious to engross unto himself
All honor, as some have in which[439] with justice
They could not claim a share.
FERDINAND Being thus hemmed in,
Their scimitars[440] raged among us and, my horse
Killed under me, I every minute looked for
An honorable end—and that was all
My hope could fashion to me, circled thus
With death and horror—as one sent from heaven
This man of men, with some choice horse[441] that followed
His brave example, did pursue the tract[442]
His sword cut for 'em. And but that I see him
Already blush to hear what he, being present,
I know would wish unspoken,[443] I should say, sir,
By what he did we boldly may believe
All that is writ of Hector.[444]
MATHIAS General,
Pray[445] spare these strange hyperboles.

429 130 the: i.e. this
430 131 deliver: recount
431 132 trench: cut into, encroach
432 135 doubtful: to be uncertain
433 136 plumed: feathered (as if wearing a military helmet)
434 138 flower of our prime gentlemen: the very best of our soldiers
435 142 subtle: shrewd, cunning
436 142 opening his gross body: i.e. engaging the entire army
437 143 rallying: reassembling
438 144 engaged: exposed to risk, unable to retreat
439 149 which: that which
440 151 scimitars: short swords with curved blades
441 156 choice horse: excellent soldiers mounted on horses
442 157 tract: path
443 159–60 what he . . . wish unspoken: i.e. that which he would rather not have said in his presence
444 162 Hector: Trojan hero, one of the "Worthies" mentioned at line 67
445 163 Pray: please

EUBULUS Do not blush
To hear a truth; here are a pair of monsieurs[446]
Had they[447] been in your place would have run away
And ne'er changed countenance.[448]
UBALDO We have your good word[449] still.
EUBULUS And shall while you deserve it.
LADISLAUS Silence! On.
FERDINAND He, as I said, like dreadful lightning thrown
From Jupiter's shield[450] dispersed the armèd gyre[451]
With which I was environed,[452] horse and man
Shrunk under his strong arm, more with his looks
Frighted, the valiant fled; with which encouraged,
My soldiers—like young eaglets preying[453] under
The wings of their fierce dam,[454] as if from him
They took both spirit and fire—bravely came on.[455]
By him I was remounted and inspired
With treble courage, and such as[456] fled before
Boldly made head[457] again and, to confirm[458] 'em,
It suddenly was apparent that the fortune
Of the day was ours. Each soldier and commander
Performed his part, but this[459] was the great wheel[460]
By which the lesser moved, and all rewards
And signs of honor, as the civic garland,[461]
The mural wreath,[462] the enemy's prime horse,
With the general's sword, and armor—the old honors
With which the Romans crowned their several leaders—
To him alone are proper.[463]
LADISLAUS And they shall
Deservedly fall on him. Sit, 'tis our pleasure.
FERDINAND Which I must serve, not argue. [*He sits*]
HONORIA [*To* MATHIAS] You are a stranger,[464]
But in your service for the king a native,
And though a free queen I am bound in duty
To cherish virtue wheresoe'er I find it:
This place[465] is yours.
MATHIAS It were presumption in me

446 164 monsieurs: affectedly courtly men
447 165 Had they: who if they had
448 166 changed countenance: blushed
449 166 good word: approval, flattery (said ironically)
450 168–9 dreadful lightning . . . Jupiter's shield: the god Jupiter uses lightning bolts as a weapon
451 169 gyre: circle, vortex
452 170 environed: surrounded
453 173 preying: hunting
454 174 dam: mother
455 175 came on: advanced
456 177 such as: those who
457 178 made head: advanced
458 178 confirm: strengthen
459 181 this: i.e. Mathias
460 181 wheel: cog-wheel
461 183 civic garland: victory wreath awarded by the city
462 184 mural wreath: wreath awarded in ancient Rome to the first soldier to climb the walls ("murus") of a besieged town
463 187 proper: merited, appropriate
464 189 stranger: foreigner
465 193 place: seat

To sit so near you.
HONORIA Not having our warrant.[466] [MATHIAS *sits*]
LADISLAUS Let the masquers[467] enter. [*To* FERDINAND *and* MATHIAS] By the preparation
'Tis a French brawl,[468] an apish[469] imitation
Of what you really perform in battle.
And Pallas[470] bound up in a little volume,[471]
Apollo with his lute[472] attending on her,
Serve for the induction.[473]

Enter the [MASQUERS *and*] *two boys, one* [APOLLO] *with his lute, the other like*[474] PALLAS. [PALLAS *sings*] *a song in the praise of soldiers, especially being victorious*

PALLAS *Though we contemplate*[475] *to express*
The glory of your happiness,
That by your powerful arm have been
So true a victor, that no sin
Could ever taint you with a blame
To lessen your deservèd fame,

Or though we contend[476] *to set*
Your worth in the full height, or get
Celestial[477] *singers crowned with bays*[478]
With flourishes[479] *to dress*[480] *your praise,*
You know your conquest, but your story
Lives in your triumphant glory. [*The* MASQUERS *dance.*] *The song* [*and dance*] *ended the* KING *goes on*
LADISLAUS Our thanks to all.
To[481] the banquet that's prepared to entertain 'em! [*Exeunt* MASQUERS, PALLAS, and APOLLO]
What would my best Honoria?
HONORIA May it please
My king that I, who by his suffrage[482] ever
Have had power to command, may now entreat
An honor from him.
LADISLAUS Why should you desire
What is your own? Whate'er it be you are
The mistress of it.

466 194 warrant: permission
467 195 masquers: courtiers dancing in the masque
468 196 brawl: a kind of dance
469 196 apish: trifling, silly
470 198 Pallas: Pallas Athena, Greek goddess of wisdom and war
471 198 bound up in a little volume: i.e. played by a child
472 199 lute: a stringed musical instrument
473 200 induction: introductory sequence in a theatrical entertainment
474 200 SD *like*: costumed as (probably wearing a helmet and carrying a spear)
475 201 contemplate: study how
476 207 contend: struggle
477 209 Celestial: heavenly, divinely excellent
478 209 bays: laurel wreaths signifying victory
479 210 flourishes: fine words, decorative additions to the music
480 210 dress: adorn
481 213 To: let us go to
482 215 suffrage: approval, consent

HONORIA I am happy[483] in
Your grant. My suit,[484] sir, is that your commanders,
Especially this stranger, may—as I
In my discretion[485] shall think good—receive
What's due to their deserts.[486]
LADISLAUS What you determine
Shall know no alteration.
EUBULUS The soldier
Is like to have good usage when he depends
Upon her pleasure! Are all the men so bad
That to give satisfaction we must have
A woman treasurer? Heaven help all.
HONORIA [*To* MATHIAS] With you, sir,
I will begin and as in my esteem
You are most eminent, expect to have
What's fit for me to give and you to take,
The favor in the quick dispatch being double.
[*To* ACANTHE] Go fetch my casket, and with speed. *Exit* ACANTHE
EUBULUS The kingdom
Is very bare of money, when rewards
Issue from the queen's jewel-house. Give him gold
And store,[487] no question the gentleman wants it.
Good madam, what shall he do with a hoop-ring[488]
And a spark of diamond in it? Though[489] you took it

Enter ACANTHE [*with the casket*]

For the greater honor from your majesty's finger
'Twill not increase the value. He must purchase
Rich suits, the gay caparison[490] of courtship,
Revel, and feast, which, the war ended,[491] is
A soldier's glory, and 'tis fit that way
Your bounty should provide for him.
HONORIA You are rude,
And by your narrow thoughts proportion mine.
What I will do now shall be worth the envy
Of Cleopatra.[492] HONORIA *descends* [*and gives* MATHIAS *the casket*]
Open it, see here.
The lapidary's[493] idol, gold, is trash
And a poor salary fit for grooms;[494] wear these
As studded stars[495] in your armor, and make the sun
Look with jealousy of a greater light

483 219 happy: fortunate
484 220 suit: plea, request
485 222 discretion: good judgement
486 223 deserts: merits, worthy actions
487 236 store: ample supply
488 237 hoop-ring: finger-ring encircled with gemstones
489 238 Though: even if
490 241 gay caparison: showy equipment
491 242 the war ended: now that the war is over
492 247 Cleopatra: renowned queen of Egypt
493 248 lapidary: jeweler
494 249 grooms: menial servants
495 249–50 wear these . . . stars: suggests that Honoria's gift consists of diamonds

Than his beams gild[496] the day with. When it is
Exposed to view, call it Honoria's gift,
The Queen Honoria's gift that loves a soldier,
And to give ornament and luster to him
Parts freely with her own. Yet not to take
From[497] the magnificence of the king, I will
Dispense his bounty too, but as a page
To wait on mine.[498] For other trifles take
A hundred thousand crowns.[499] [*To* LADISLAUS] Your hand, dear sir,
And this shall be thy warrant. *Takes off the* KING's *signet*[500]
EUBULUS I perceive
I was cheated in this woman. Now she is
I' th' giving vein[501] to soldiers, let her be proud
And the king dote,[502] so she go on,[503] I care not.
HONORIA This done, our pleasure is that all arrearages[504]
Be paid in to the captains and their troops,
With a large donative[505] to increase their zeal
For the service of the kingdom.
EUBULUS Better still!
Let men of arms be used thus: if they do not
Charge desperately upon the cannon's mouth
Though the devil roared,[506] and fight like dragons, hang me.
Now they may drink sack,[507] but small[508] beer, with a passport[509]
To beg with as they travel, and no money,
Turns their red blood to buttermilk.[510]
HONORIA Are you pleased, sir,
With what I have done?
LADISLAUS Yes, and thus confirm it
With this addition of mine own: you have, sir,
From our loved queen received some recompense
For your life hazarded in the late action,
And that we may follow her great example,
In cherishing valor without limit, ask
What you from us can wish.
MATHIAS If it be true,
Dread sir, as 'tis affirmed, that every soil
Where he is well is to a valiant man
His natural country, reason may assure me
I should fix[511] here, where blessings beyond hope

496 252 gild: make golden
497 256–7 take/From: diminish
498 258–9 but as . . . on mine: i.e. an inferior gift to mine
499 260 hundred thousand crowns: £250,000 (worth approximately 30 million pounds today)
500 261 SD *signet*: signet ring
501 263 vein: mood
502 264 dote: love excessively, be infatuated
503 264 so she go on: as long as she proceeds like this
504 265 arrearages: overdue wages
505 267 donative: gift
506 271 devil roared: i.e. the cannon fired
507 272 sack: white wine
508 272 small: weak
509 272 passport: permit
510 272–4 Now they . . . to buttermilk: i.e. now that they are getting paid they can drink wine, but when they are forced to beg because they have not been paid, and have only weak beer to drink, they turn cowards
511 285 fix: stay, settle

From you, the spring,[512] like rivers flow unto me.
If wealth were my ambition, by the queen
I am made rich already, to the amazement
Of all that see or shall hereafter read
The story of her bounty. If to spend
The remnant of my life in deeds of arms,
No region is more fertile of good knights
From whom my knowledge that way may be bettered
Than this your warlike Hungary. If favor
Or grace in court could take me, by your grant,
Far, far beyond my merit, I may make
In yours a free election.[513] But alas, sir,
I am not mine own, but by my destiny—
Which I cannot resist—forced to prefer
My country's smoke before the glorious fire
With which your bounties warm me. All I ask, sir,
Though I cannot be ignorant it must relish[514]
Of foul ingratitude, is your gracious license
For my departure.
LADISLAUS Whither?
MATHIAS To my own home, sir,
My own poor home, which will at my return
Grow rich by your magnificence. I am here
But a body without a soul, and till I find it[515]
In the embraces of my constant wife,
And, to set off[516] that constancy, in her beauty
And matchless excellencies without a rival,
I am but half myself.
HONORIA And is she then
So chaste and fair as you infer?[517]
MATHIAS O madam,
Though it must argue weakness in a rich man
To show his gold before an armèd thief,
And I in praising of my wife but feed
The fire of lust in others to attempt her,
Such is my full-sailed[518] confidence in her virtue
Though in my absence she were now besieged
By a strong army of lascivious wooers,
And every one more expert in his art
Than those that tempted chaste Penelope,[519]
Though they raised batteries[520] by prodigal gifts,
By amorous letters, vows made for her service,
With all the engines[521] wanton appetite
Could mount to shake the fortress of her honor,
Here, here is my assurance she holds out

512 286 spring: source
513 297 election: choice (of office at court)
514 302 relish: taste, have a touch
515 307 it: i.e. my soul
516 309 set off: show to advantage
517 312 infer: allege
518 317 full-sailed: unimpeded, whole-hearted
519 321 Penelope: legendarily faithful wife of the Greek hero Odysseus
520 322 batteries: bombardments
521 324 engines: devices (literally, weapons such as battering rams or catapults)

And is impregnable.[522] *[Takes out and] kisses the picture*
HONORIA What's that?
MATHIAS Her fair figure.[523]
LADISLAUS As I live, an excellent face!
HONORIA You have seen a better.
LADISLAUS I ever except yours.[524] Nay, frown not, sweetest;
The Cyprian queen[525] compared to you in my
Opinion is a negro.[526] As you ordered
I'll see the soldier paid, and in my absence
Pray you use your powerful arguments to stay
This gentleman in our service.
HONORIA I will do
My parts.
LADISLAUS On to the camp.
Exeunt LADISLAUS, FERDINAND, EUBULUS, BAPTISTA, CAPTAINS[, *and Servant*]
HONORIA [*Aside*] I am full of thoughts,
And something there is here I must give form to,
Though yet an embryon.[527]—You seigniors[528]
Have no business with the soldier, as I take it,
You are for other warfare. Quit[529] the place,
But be within call.
RICARDO Employment, on my life,[530] boy.
UBALDO If it lie in our road we are made forever. *Exeunt* UBALDO, RICARDO[, ACANTHE, *and* SILVIA]
HONORIA You may perceive the king is no way tainted
With the disease of jealousy, since he leaves me
Thus private with you.
MATHIAS It were in him, madam,
A sin unpardonable to distrust such pureness,
Though I were an Adonis.[531]
HONORIA I presume
He neither does, nor dares, and yet the story
Delivered of you by the general,
With your heroic courage—which sinks deeply
Into a knowing[532] woman's heart—besides
Your promising presence,[533] might beget some scruple[534]
In a meaner[535] man. But more of this hereafter.[536]
I'll take another theme now, and conjure[537] you
By the honors you have won, and by the love

522 327 impregnable: capable of withstanding all attacks
523 327 figure: image
524 329 I ever except yours: i.e. I always make an exception for your face
525 330 Cyprian queen: Venus, who, in classical mythology, emerged from the sea near Paphos, Cyprus
526 331 negro: black woman (reflecting the racist assumption that blackness is less attractive than whiteness)
527 337 embryon: embryo
528 337 seigniors: lords
529 339 Quit: leave
530 340 on my life: an oath (i.e. "I swear")
531 346 Adonis: handsome youth loved by Venus
532 350 knowing: shrewd, worldly wise
533 351 presence: demeanor, bearing
534 351 scruple: doubt
535 352 meaner: less noble
536 352 hereafter: later
537 353 conjure: entreat, invoke by supernatural power

Sacred to your dear wife, to answer truly
To what I shall demand.
MATHIAS You need not use
Charms[538] to this purpose, madam.
HONORIA Tell me then—
Being yourself assured 'tis not in man
To sully with one sport[539] th'immaculate whiteness
Of your wife's honor—if you have not since
The Gordian[540] of your love was tied by marriage
Played false with her?[541]
MATHIAS By the hopes of mercy, never.
HONORIA It may be, not frequenting[542] the converse[543]
Of handsome ladies, you were never tempted
And so your faith's[544] untried yet.
MATHIAS Surely, madam,
I am no woman-hater; I have been
Received to the society of the best
And fairest of our climate,[545] and have met with
No common entertainment,[546] yet ne'er felt
The least heat[547] that way.
HONORIA Strange. And do you think still
The earth can show no beauty that can drench
In Lethe[548] all remembrance of the favor
You now bear to your own?
MATHIAS Nature must find out
Some other mold to fashion a new creature
Fairer than her Pandora[549] ere I prove
Guilty or in my wishes or[550] my thoughts
To my Sophia.
HONORIA Sir, consider better.
Not one in our whole sex?
MATHIAS I am constant to
My resolution.
HONORIA But dare you stand
The opposition,[551] and bind yourself
By oath for the performance?
MATHIAS My faith else
Had but a weak foundation.
HONORIA I take hold
Upon your promise, and enjoin[552] your stay
For one month here.

538 357 Charms: spells, enchantments
539 359 sport: sexual act
540 361 Gordian: strong knot tied by King Gordius, which Alexander the Great eventually cut
541 362 played false with her: been unfaithful to her
542 363 frequenting: habitually attending
543 363 converse: society
544 365 faith: sexual fidelity
545 368 climate: region, nation
546 369 entertainment: reception, treatment
547 370 heat: inclination, desire
548 372: Lethe: a river in the underworld; drinking its waters produced forgetfulness
549 375 Pandora: the first woman in classical mythology, on whom all the gods bestowed gifts
550 376 or . . . or: either . . . or
551 379–80 stand/The opposition: i.e. resist temptation
552 383 enjoin: require

MATHIAS I am caught.
HONORIA And if I do not
Produce a lady in that time that shall
Make you confess your error, I submit
Myself to any penalty you shall please
T'impose upon me. In the mean space[553] write
To your chaste wife, acquaint her with your fortune;
The jewels that were mine you may send to her
For better confirmation. I'll provide you
Of[554] trusty messengers. But how far distant is she?
MATHIAS A day's hard riding.
HONORIA There's no retiring;[555]
I'll bind you to your word.
MATHIAS Well, since there is
No way to shun it I will stand the hazard,
And instantly make ready my dispatch.[556]
'Till then, I'll leave your majesty. *Exit* MATHIAS
HONORIA How I burst
With envy that there lives besides myself
One fair and loyal woman! 'Twas the end[557]
Of my ambition to be recorded
The only wonder of the age, and shall I
Give way to a competitor? Nay, more,
To add to my affliction, the assurances
That I placed in my beauty have deceived me.
I thought one amorous glance of mine could bring
All hearts to my subjection, but this stranger,
Unmoved as rocks, contemns me. But I cannot
Sit down so[558] with any honor. I will gain
A double victory by working[559] him
To my desire and taint her in her honor,
Or lose myself. I have read that sometime poison
Is useful: to supplant her I'll employ
With any cost Ubaldo and Ricardo,
Two noted courtiers of approvèd cunning
In all the windings of lust's labyrinth,
And in corrupting him I will outgo
Nero's Poppaea.[560] If he shut his ears
Against my siren[561] notes, I'll boldly swear
Ulysses[562] lives again, or that I have found
A frozen cynic,[563] cold in spite of all

553 388 mean space: meantime
554 392 Of: with
555 393 retiring: retreating, returning home
556 396 dispatch: letter
557 399 end: aim, culmination
558 408 Sit down so: settle, be content
559 409 working: converting, transforming
560 417 Nero's Poppaea: Nero was a Roman emperor who reigned 54–68 CE; Poppea was his second wife, represented by Tacitus and later writers as unscrupulous and sexually voracious
561 418 siren: alluring (the sirens in classical mythology lured men to their deaths with their beautiful singing)
562 419 Ulysses: Roman name for the Greek hero Odysseus, who escaped the sirens by having his men tie him to the mast of their ship and block their own ears
563 420 cynic: one who rejects luxury and pleasure

Allurements, one whom beauty cannot move
Nor softest blandishments[564] entice to love.

Exit HONORIA

The end of the second act

Act III, scene i

Enter HILARIO

HILARIO Thin,[565] thin provision! I am dieted
Like one set to watch hawks,[566] and to keep me waking
My croaking guts make a perpetual larum.[567]
Here I stand sentinel,[568] and though I fright
Beggars from my lady's gate in hope to have
A greater share, I find my commons[569] mend not.
I looked this morning in my glass,[570] the river,
And there appeared a fish called a Poor John,[571]
Cut with a Lenten[572] face in my own likeness,
And it seemed to speak, and say, "Good morrow,[573] cousin."
No man comes this way but has a fling at[574] me,
A chirurgion passing by asked at what rate[575]
I would sell myself; I answered, "For what use?"
"To make," said he "a living anatomy[576]
And set thee up in our hall,[577] for thou art transparent
Without dissection." And, indeed, he had reason,
For I am scoured with this poor purge to nothing.
They say that hunger dwells in the camp,[578] but till
My lord returns, or certain tidings of him,
He[579] will not part with me. But sorrow's dry
And I must drink howsoever.

Enter UBALDO *and* RICARDO [*with a*] GUIDE

GUIDE That is her castle
Upon my certain knowledge.
UBALDO Our horses held out.
To my desire: I am afire to be at it!

564 422 blandishments: flatteries, enticements
565 1 Thin: scanty, insufficient
566 2 set to watch hawks: hawks were kept awake in order to tame them
567 3 larum: call to arms, uproar
568 4 sentinel: on guard
569 6 commons: supply or quality of food
570 7 glass: looking-glass, mirror
571 8 Poor John: usually refers to salt-dried hake, eaten during Lent
572 9 Lenten: thin, dismal
573 10 morrow: morning
574 11 has a fling at: mocks
575 12 rate: price
576 14 anatomy: skeleton
577 15 hall: livery hall, where the members of a trade (in this case the barber-surgeons) met
578 18 camp: military camp
579 20 He: i.e. hunger

RICARDO Take the jades[580] for thy reward; before I part hence
I hope to be better carried![581] Give me the cabinet.[582]
So leave us now.
GUIDE Good fortune to you, gallants. *Exit* GUIDE
UBALDO Being joint agents, in a design of trust[583] too,
For the service of the queen and our own pleasure,
Let us proceed with judgment.
RICARDO If I take not
This fort at the first assault, make me an eunuch!
So I may have precedence.[584]
UBALDO On no terms.
We are both to play one prize.[585] He that works best
I' th' searching this mine[586] shall carry it
Without contention.
RICARDO Make you your approaches[587]
As I directed.
UBALDO I need no instruction.
I work not on your anvil.[588] I'll give fire
With my own linstock; if the powder be dank[589]
The devil rend[590] the touch-hole.[591] Who have we here?
What skeleton's this?
RICARDO A ghost! Or the image of famine!
Where dost thou dwell?
HILARIO Dwell, sir? My dwelling is
I' th' highway. That goodly house was once
My habitation, but I am banished
And cannot be called home 'till news arrive
Of the good knight Mathias.
RICARDO If that will
Restore thee, thou art safe.
UBALDO We come from him
With presents to his lady.
HILARIO But are you sure
He is in health?
RICARDO Never so well. Conduct us
To the lady.
HILARIO Though a poor snake I will leap
Out of my skin for joy. Break, pitcher,[592] break,
And wallet,[593] late my cupboard, I bequeath thee
To the next beggar. Thou, red herring,[594] swim

580 24 jades: inferior horses
581 25 be better carried: find a better mount (i.e. in sex)
582 25 cabinet: casket
583 27 design of trust: plan that requires discretion
584 31 have precedence: be first in line
585 32 prize: sporting contest
586 33 searching this mine: finding or penetrating a passage dug under an enemy fortress
587 34 approaches: advances to Sophia
588 36 I work . . . your anvil: i.e. I am not reliant on you
589 37 dank: damp
590 38 rend: tear, split
591 36–8 I'll give . . . the touch-hole: an extended and violent image of sexual intercourse, referring to the explosives that might be placed in a "mine": a linstock is a long staff holding a match at the end, used to fire a cannon; a touch-hole is the hole through which the powder in the cannon is ignited
592 49 pitcher: pot (used to collect alms)
593 50 wallet: beggar's bag
594 51 red herring: dried, smoked fish

To the Red Sea[595] again. Methinks I am already
Knuckle deep in the flesh-pots[596] and, though waking, dream
Of wine and plenty.
RICARDO What's the mystery
Of this strange passion?[597]
HILARIO My belly, gentlemen,
Will not give me leave to tell you. When I have brought you
To my lady's presence I am disenchanted;
There you shall know all. Follow. If I outstrip[598] you,
Know I run for my belly.
UBALDO A mad fellow.

Exeunt

Act III, scene ii

Enter SOPHIA [*and*] CORISCA

SOPHIA Do not again delude me.
CORISCA If I do,
Send me a-grazing with my fellow Hilario.
I stood, as you commanded, in the turret,
Observing all that passed by, and even now
I did discern a pair of cavaliers,[599]
For such their outside spoke them, with their guide
Dismounting from their horses. They said something
To our hungry sentinel that made him caper
And frisk[600] i' th' air for joy, and to confirm this
See, madam, they are in view.

Enter HILARIO, UBALDO, [*and*] RICARDO

HILARIO News from my lord!
Tidings of joy! These are no counterfeits,
But knights indeed. Dear madam, sign my pardon,
That I may feed again and pick up my crumbs;
I have had a long fast of it.
SOPHIA Eat, I forgive thee.
HILARIO O comfortable words: "Eat, I forgive thee."
And if in this I do not soon obey you,
And ram in[601] to the purpose, billet[602] me again
I' the highway. Butler and cook be ready,
For I enter like a tyrant. *Exit* HILARIO
UBALDO Since mine eyes
Were never happy in so sweet an object,
Without injury[603] I presume you are

595 52 Red Sea: inlet of the Indian ocean, between Africa and Asia
596 53 flesh-pots: cooking pots in which meat is boiled
597 55 passion: outburst
598 58 outstrip: outrun
599 5 cavaliers: courtly gentlemen
600 8–9 caper/And frisk: leap and dance
601 17 ram in: i.e. cram myself with food
602 17 billet: lodge
603 21 Without injury: respectfully

The lady of the house, and so salute you. [UBALDO *bows or kisses* SOPHIA]
RICARDO This letter with these jewels from your lord
Warrant my boldness, madam. [RICARDO *kisses* SOPHIA. *She reads the letters and opens the casket*]
UBALDO [*To* CORISCA] In being a servant
To such rare beauty, you must needs deserve
This courtesy from a stranger. [UBALDO *kisses* CORISCA]
RICARDO [*To* UBALDO] You are still
Beforehand with[604] me.—Pretty one, I descend
To take the height of your lip, and if I miss
In the altitude hereafter, if you please
I will make use of my Jacob's staff.[605] [RICARDO *kisses* CORISCA]
CORISCA These gentlemen
Have certainly had good breeding, as it appears
By their neat kissing: they hit me so pat on the lips
At the first sight.
SOPHIA [*Kneeling*] Heaven in thy mercy make me
Thy thankful handmaid for this boundless blessing
In thy goodness showered upon me.
UBALDO [*To* RICARDO] I do not like
This simple[606] devotion in her; it is seldom
Practiced among my mistresses.
RICARDO Or mine.
Would they kneel to I-know-not-who for the possession
Of such inestimable[607] wealth before
They thanked the bringers of it? The poor lady
Does want instruction, but I'll be her tutor
And read her another lesson.
SOPHIA [*Rising*] If I have
Shown want of manners, gentlemen, in my slowness
To pay[608] the thanks I owe you for your travail[609]
To do my lord and me—howe'er unworthy
Of such a benefit—this noble favor,
Impute it in your clemency[610] to the excess
Of joy that overwhelmed me.
RICARDO She speaks well.
UBALDO Polite, and courtly.
SOPHIA And howe'er it may
Increase th'offence to trouble you with more
Demands touching my lord, before I have
Invited you to rest such[611] as the coarseness
Of my poor house can offer, pray you connive
On[612] my weak tenderness though I entreat
To learn from you something he hath, it may be,
In his letter left unmentioned.
RICARDO I can only

604 27 Beforehand with: ahead of
605 30 Jacob's staff: instrument used to measure the altitude of the sun (with double entendre)
606 36 simple: innocent, unpretentious
607 39 inestimable wealth: i.e. the jewels in the casket
608 44 pay: recompense
609 44 travail: exertion (with a pun on "travel")
610 47 clemency: mercy, generosity
611 52 rest such: i.e. such accommodation
612 53–4 connive/On: treat indulgently

Give you assurance that he is in health,
Graced[613] by the king and queen.
UBALDO And in the court
With admiration looked on.
RICARDO You must therefore
Put off these widow's garments, and appear
Like to yourself.
UBALDO And entertain all pleasures
Your fortunes marks out for you.
RICARDO There are other
Particular privacies[614] which on occasion
I will deliver to you.
SOPHIA You oblige me
To your service ever.
RICARDO [*To* UBALDO] Good! "Your service." Mark that.
SOPHIA In the meantime, by your good acceptance make
My rustic entertainment relish[615] of
The curiousness of the court.[616]
UBALDO Your looks, sweet madam,
Cannot but make each dish a feast.
SOPHIA It shall be
Such in the freedom of my will to please you.
I'll show you the way; this is too great an honor
From such brave guests to me so mean an hostess.

Exeunt

Act III, scene iii

Enter ACANTHE [*with*] *two, four, or five* [SERVANTS] *with vizards*[617]

ACANTHE You know your charge.[618] Give it action and expect
Rewards beyond your hopes.
FIRST SERVANT If we but eye[619] 'em
They are ours, I warrant[620] you.
SECOND SERVANT May we not ask why
We are put upon this?
ACANTHE [*Giving him money*] Let that stop your mouth,
And learn more manners, groom. 'Tis upon the hour
In which they use[621] to walk here; when you have 'em
In your power, with violence carry them to the place
Where I appointed. There I will expect you.
Be bold and careful. *Exit* ACANTHE

Enter MATHIAS *and* BAPTISTA

FIRST SERVANT These are they.

613 58 Graced: favored
614 63 privacies: private matters
615 67 relish: taste
616 66–8 by your . . . the court: i.e. behave as if my humble meal is as exquisite as what you would eat at court
617 0 SD *vizards*: masks
618 1 charge: task
619 2 eye: see
620 3 warrant: assure
621 6 use: are accustomed

SECOND SERVANT Are you sure?
FIRST SERVANT Am I sure I am myself?
SECOND SERVANT Seize on him strongly. If he have but means
To draw his sword, 'tis ten to one we smart for't.[622]
Take all advantages.[623]
MATHIAS I cannot guess
What her intents are, but her carriage[624] was
As I but now related.
BAPTISTA Your assurance
In the constancy of your lady is the armor
That must defend you. Where's the picture?
MATHIAS Here.
And no way altered.
BAPTISTA If she be not perfect,
There is no truth in art.
MATHIAS By this[625] I hope
She hath received my letters.
BAPTISTA Without question.
These courtiers are rank[626] riders when they are
To visit a handsome lady.
MATHIAS Lend me your ear.
One piece of her[627] entertainment will require
Your dearest privacy.
FIRST SERVANT Now they stand fair.[628]
Upon 'em!
MATHIAS Villains!
FIRST SERVANT [*Aside*] Stop their mouths.—We come not
To try your valors. [*Aside*] Kill him if he offer[629]
To open his mouth.—We have you; 'tis in vain
To make resistance. [*Aside*] Mount 'em[630] and away.

Act III, scene iv

Enter Servants with lights, LADISLAUS, FERDINAND, [*and*] EUBULUS

LADISLAUS 'Tis late, go to your rest, but do not envy
The happiness I draw near to.
EUBULUS If you enjoy it
The moderate way, the sport[631] yields, I confess,
A pretty titillation,[632] but too much oft

622 12 smart for't: will suffer as a result
623 13 advantages: favorable positions for attack
624 14 carriage: manner, behavior
625 19 by this: by this time
626 21 rank: swift, eager
627 23 her: Honoria's
628 24 stand fair: are in the right position
629 26 offer: attempts
630 28 Mount 'em: put them on the backs of (offstage) horses
631 3 sport: sexual exertion
632 4 titillation: mild sexual excitement

Will bring you on your knees. In my younger days
I was myself a gamester,[633] and I found
By a sad experience there is no such soaker[634]
As a young, spongy[635] wife. She keeps a thousand
Horse-leeches[636] in her box,[637] and the thieves will suck out
Both blood and marrow.[638] I feel a kind of cramp
In my joints[639] when I think on't. But it may be queens—
And such a queen as yours is—has the art—
FERDINAND You take leave
To talk, my lord.
LADISLAUS He may since he can do nothing.
EUBULUS If you spend this way too much of your royal stock[640]
Ere long we may be pew-fellows.[641]
LADISLAUS The door shut?
Knock gently. Harder! So, here comes her woman.
Take off my gown.

Enter ACANTHE

ACANTHE My lord, the queen by me
This night desires your pardon.
LADISLAUS How, Acanthe!
I come by her appointment. 'Twas her grant;[642]
The motion[643] was her own.
ACANTHE It may be, sir,
But by her doctors since she is advised
For her health[644] sake to forbear.[645]
EUBULUS [*Aside*] I do not like
This physical[646] lechery, the old downright[647] way
Is worth a thousand on't.
LADISLAUS [*Holding out a jewel*] Prithee, Acanthe,
Mediate for me.
EUBULUS [*Aside*] O the fiends of hell!
Would any man bribe his servant to make way
To his own wife? If this be the court state[648]
Shame fall on such as use it.
ACANTHE By this jewel,
This night I dare not move her, but tomorrow
I will watch all occasion.

633 6 gamester: sexually promiscuous person
634 7 soaker: absorber, exhauster
635 8 spongy: draining
636 9 Horse-leeches: medicinal leeches that suck a patient's blood
637 9 box: medicine chest (puns on the sexual sense of "box," i.e. vagina)
638 10 marrow: bodily tissue
639 10–11 cramp/In my joints: exhaustion (also a symptom of venereal disease)
640 14 stock: goods, capital (i.e. sexual potency)
641 15 pew-fellows: companions
642 19 grant: consent
643 20 motion: suggestion
644 22 health: health's
645 22 forbear: refrain (from sexual activity)
646 23 physical: medicinal
647 23 downright: plain, straightforward
648 27 state: manner

LADISLAUS Take this
To be mindful of me. *Exit* ACANTHE
EUBULUS [*Aside*] 'Slight, I thought a king
Might have took up any woman at the king's price,
And must he buy his own at a dearer rate[649]
Than a stranger in a brothel?
LADISLAUS What is that
You mutter, sir?
EUBULUS No treason to your honor.
I'll speak it out though it anger you. If you pay for
Your lawful pleasure in some kind, great sir,
What do you make the queen? Cannot you clicket[650]
Without a fee, or when she has a suit
For you to grant?
FERDINAND Oh hold, sir.
LADISLAUS Off with his head!
EUBULUS Do when you please. You but blow out a taper[651]
That would light your understanding, and in care of't
Is burnt down to the socket. Be as you are, sir,
An absolute monarch. It did show more kinglike
In those libidinous[652] Caesars that compelled
Matrons[653] and virgins of all ranks to bow
Unto their ravenous lusts, and did admit
Of more excuse[654] than I can urge for you,
That slave yourself to th'imperious humor
Of a proud beauty.
LADISLAUS Out of my sight!
EUBULUS I will, sir,
Give way to your furious passion, but when reason
Hath got the better of it I much hope
The counsel that offends now will deserve
Your royal thanks. Tranquility of mind
Stay with you, sir. [*Aside*] I do begin to doubt[655]
There's something more in the queen's strangeness[656] than
Is yet disclosed, and I'll find it out
Or lose myself in the search. [*Exit*]
FERDINAND Sure, he is honest,
And from your infancy hath truly served you.
Let that plead for him and impute[657] this harshness
To the forwardness[658] of his age.
LADISLAUS I am much troubled
And do begin to stagger. Ferdinand, good night.
Tomorrow visit us. [*To Servants*] Back to our own lodgings.

649 33 dearer rate: higher price
650 38 clicket: have sex (originally used of animals)
651 41 taper: candle
652 45 libidinous: lustful
653 46 Matrons: married women
654 47–8 did admit . . . more excuse: was more excusable
655 55 doubt: fear
656 56 strangeness: coldness
657 60 impute: attribute
658 61 forwardness: perversity, contrariness

Act III, scene v

Enter ACANTHE, *the vizarded* SERVANTS, MATHIAS, [*and*] BAPTISTA[, *blindfolded*]

ACANTHE You have done bravely.[659] Lock this[660] in that room.
There let him ruminate;[661] I'll anon[662] unhood him. *They carry off* BAPTISTA
The other must stay here. As soon as I
Have quit the place give him the liberty
And use of his eyes. That done, disperse yourselves
As privately as you can, but on your lives
No word of what hath passed. *Exit* ACANTHE
FIRST SERVANT If I do, sell
My tongue to a tripe-wife.[663] Come, unbind his arms.
[*To* MATHIAS] You are now at your own disposure,[664] and however
We used you roughly I hope you will find here
Such entertainment as will give you cause
To thank us for the service. And so I leave you. *Exeunt* SERVANTS
MATHIAS If I am in a prison 'tis a neat[665] one.
What Oedipus[666] can resolve this riddle? Ha!
I never gave just cause to any man
Basely[667] to plot against my life. But what is
Become of my true friend? For him I suffer
More than myself.
ACANTHE [*Within*] Remove that idle fear;
He's safe as you are.
MATHIAS Whosoe'er thou art,
For him I thank thee. I cannot imagine
Where I should be, though I have read the table[668]
Of errant[669] knighthood, stuffed with the relations[670]
Of magical enchantments. Yet I am not
So sottishly[671] credulous to believe the devil
Hath that way power. *Music above, a song of pleasure*
Ha? Music!
[HONORIA][672] [*Singing within*] *The blushing rose and purple flower*
Let grow too long are soonest blasted.[673]
Dainty fruits, though sweet, will sour
And rot in ripeness, left untasted.
Yet here is one more sweet than these;
The more you taste, the more she'll please.

659 1 bravely: well
660 1 this: Baptista
661 2 ruminate: meditate
662 2 anon: soon
663 8 tripe-wife: woman who prepares or sells tripe
664 9 disposure: disposal
665 13 neat: elegant
666 14 Oedipus: mythological king of Thebes, who solved the riddle of the Sphinx
667 16 Basely: dishonorably
668 21 table: summary, synopsis
669 22 errant: wandering, roving
670 22 relations: reports, stories
671 24 sottishly: foolishly
672 26 SP [HONORIA]: no speech prefix is given for this song in Q; Mathias's comments (lines 38–40) suggest that it is Honoria; the actor playing her, John Thompson, sings in two other plays
673 27 blasted: withered

Beauty though enclosed with ice
Is a shadow chaste as rare,
Then how much those sweets entice
That have issue[674] *full as fair.*
Earth cannot yield from all her powers
One equal for Dame Venus' bowers.[675]
MATHIAS A song too! Certainly, be it he or she
That owes[676] this voice, it hath not been acquainted
With much affliction. Whosoe'er you are
That do inhabit here, if you have bodies
And are not mere aerial[677] forms appear
And make me know your end[678] with me.

Enter HONORIA [*masked*]

Most strange!
What have I conjured up? Sure, if this be
A spirit 'tis no damned one. What a shape's here!
Then with what majesty it moves. If Juno
Were now to keep her state among the gods,
And Hercules to be made again her guest,
She could not put on a more glorious habit
Though her handmaid Iris[679] lent her various colors
Or old Oceanus[680] ravished from the deep
All jewels shipwracked in it. As you have
Thus far made known yourself, if that your face
Have not too much divinity about it
For mortal eyes to gaze on, perfect what
You have begun with wonder and amazement
To my astonished senses. [*He*] *kneels; she pulls off her mask*
How! The queen!
HONORIA Rise, sir, and hear my reasons in defense
Of the rape,[681] for so you may conceive,[682] which I
By my instruments[683] made upon you. You perhaps
May think what you have suffered for my lust
Is a common practice with me, but I call
Those ever-shining lamps[684] and their great maker
As witnesses of my innocence. I ne'er looked on
A man but your best self on whom I ever—
Except the king—vouchsafed an eye of favor.
MATHIAS The king indeed, and only such a king,
Deserves your rarities, madam, and but he[685]
'Twere giant-like ambition in any

674 35 issue: produce, profits
675 37 bowers: bed-chambers, arbors
676 39 owes: owns
677 42 aerial: immaterial
678 43 end: purpose
679 50 Iris: Roman goddess of the rainbow
680 51 Oceanus: god of the sea
681 59 rape: abduction
682 59 conceive: believe it
683 60 instruments: servants
684 63 ever-shining lamps: stars
685 68 but he: except for him

In his wishes only[686] to presume to taste
The nectar[687] of your kisses, or to feed
His appetite with that ambrosia[688] due
And proper to a prince and, what binds more,
A lawful husband. For myself, great Queen,
I am a thing obscure,[689] disfurnished[690] of
All merit that can raise me higher than—
In my most humble thankfulness for your bounty—
To hazard my life for you, and that way
I am most ambitious.
HONORIA I desire no more
Than what you promise. If you dare expose
Your life, as you profess,[691] to do me service,
How can it better be employed than in
Preserving mine? Which only you can do,
And must do with the danger of your own.
A desperate danger too: if private men
Can brook[692] no rivals in what they affect,
But to the death pursue such as invade
What law makes their inheritance, the king—
To whom you know I am dearer than his crown,
His health, his eyes, his after-hopes,[693] with all
His present blessings—must fall on that man
Like dreadful lightning that[694] is won by prayers,
Threats, or rewards to stain his bed or make
His hoped-for issue doubtful.[695]
MATHIAS If you aim
At what I more than fear you do, the reasons
Which you deliver should in judgment rather
Deter me than invite a grant[696] with[697] my
Assurèd ruin.
HONORIA True, if that you were
Of a cold temper, one whom doubt or fear
In the most horrid forms they could put on
Might teach to be ingrateful.[698] Your denial
To me, that have deserved so much, is more
If it can have addition.[699]
MATHIAS I know not
What your commands are.
HONORIA Have you fought so well
Among armed men, yet cannot guess what lists[700]

686 70 In his wishes only: even in his imagination
687 71 nectar: the drink of the gods in classical mythology
688 72 ambrosia: the food of the gods
689 75 obscure: humble, undistinguished
690 75 disfurnished: deprived
691 81 profess: claim
692 86 brook: tolerate
693 90 after-hopes: hopes of eternal life
694 92 that: who
695 93–4 make . . . issue doubtful: make the children he hopes for open to accusations that they are illegitimate
696 97 grant: consent
697 97 with: that is accompanied by
698 101 ingrateful: ungrateful, displeasing
699 101–3: Your denial . . . have addition: i.e. your refusal will be worth even more if you can continue to resist me
700 105 lists: place of combat

You are to enter when you are in private
With a willing lady? One that to enjoy
Your company this night denied the king
Access to what's his own, if you will press me
To speak in plainer language.
MATHIAS Pray you, forbear.[701]
I would I did not understand too much
Already. By your words I am instructed
To credit[702] that which, not confirmed by you,
Had bred suspicion in me of untruth
Though an angel had affirmed it.[703] But suppose
That, cloyed[704] with happiness—which is ever built
On virtuous chastity—in the wantonness
Of appetite[705] you desire to make trial
Of the false delights proposed by vicious lust,
Among ten thousand every way more able
And apter[706] to be wrought on,[707] such as owe you
Obedience, being your subjects, why should you
Make choice of me, a stranger?
HONORIA Though yet reason
Was ne'er admitted in the court of love,
I'll yield you one unanswerable. As I urged
In our last private conference, you have
A pretty, promising presence, but there are
Many in limbs and feature who may take
That way the right-hand file of[708] you. Besides,
Your May[709] of youth is passed, and the blood spent
By wounds, though bravely taken, renders you
Disabled for love's service, and that valor,
Set off with better fortune—which it may be
Swells you above your bounds[710]—is not the hook
That hath caught me. Good sir, I need no champion
With his sword to guard my honor or my beauty;
In both I can defend myself, and live
My own protection.
MATHIAS If these advocates,[711]
The best that can plead for me, have no power,
What can you find in me else that may tempt you
With irrecoverable loss unto yourself
To be a gainer from me?
HONORIA You have, sir,
A jewel of such matchless[712] worth and luster
As does disdain comparison, and darkens

701 110 forbear: desist
702 113 credit: believe
703 112–15 By your ... affirmed it: I must believe what you are telling me, even though I would have thought it was a lie had I heard it from an angel
704 116 cloyed: glutted, bored
705 117–18 wantonness/Of appetite: i.e. wild passions provoked by lust
706 121 apter: more suitable
707 121 wrought on: persuaded
708 128–9 may take ... file of: i.e. are superior to
709 130 May: springtime, height
710 133–4 which it ... your bounds: which, perhaps, makes you transgress your limits
711 138 advocates: things that intercede or protect
712 143 matchless: incomparable

All that is rare in other men. And that
I must or win or lessen.
MATHIAS You heap more
Amazement on me. What am I possessed of
That you can covet? Make me understand it,
If it have a name.
HONORIA Yes, an imagined one,
But is in substance nothing, being a garment
Worn out of fashion, and long since given o'er
By the court and country: 'tis your loyalty
And constancy to your wife. 'Tis that I dote on
And does deserve my envy, and that jewel
Or by fair play or foul, I must win from you.
MATHIAS These are mere contraries.[713] If you love me, madam,
For my constancy, why seek you to destroy it?
In my keeping it, preserve me worth your favor.
Or if it be a jewel of that value
As you with labored rhetoric would persuade me,
What can you stake[714] against it?
HONORIA A queen's fame[715]
And equal honor.
MATHIAS So whoever wins
Both shall be losers.
HONORIA That is that I aim at.
Yet on the by[716] I lay my youth, my beauty,
This moist palm, this soft lip, and those delights
Darkness should only judge of. Do you find 'em
Infectious in the trial[717] that you start,[718]
As frighted with their touch?
MATHIAS Is it in man
To resist such strong temptations?
HONORIA [*Aside*] He begins
To waver.
MATHIAS Madam, as you are gracious,
Grant this short night's deliberation to me
And with the rising sun from me you shall
Receive full satisfaction.
HONORIA Though extremes[719]
Hate all delay, I will deny you nothing.
[*Giving him a key*] This key will bring you to your friend. You are safe, both,
And all things useful that could be prepared
For one I love and honor wait upon you.
Take counsel of your pillow;[720] such a fortune
As with affection's swiftest wings flies to you
Will not be often tendered.[721] *Exit* HONORIA
MATHIAS How my blood

713 156 contraries: contradictions
714 161 stake: wager, bet
715 161 fame: reputation
716 164 on the by: as a side-wager
717 167 in the trial: when you try them
718 167 start: flinch, recoil; Honoria probably tries to clasp Mathias's hand or to kiss him as she speaks
719 173 extremes: extremes of emotion
720 178 Take counsel of your pillow: i.e. sleep on it
721 180 tendered: offered

Rebels! I now could call her back, and yet
There's something stays[722] me. If the king had tendered
Such favors to my wife 'tis to be doubted[723]
They had not been refused, but being a man
I should not yield first or prove an example
For her defense of frailty.[724] By this, sans question,
She's tempted too, and here I may examine
How she holds out. *Looks on the picture*
She's still the same, the same
Pure crystal rock of chastity. Perish all
Allurements that may alter me! The snow
Of her sweet coldness hath extinguished quite
The fire that but even now began to flame,
And I by her confirmed,[725] rewards, nor titles,
Nor certain death from the refusèd queen
Shall shake my faith, since I resolve to be
Loyal to her, as she is true to me. *Exit* MATHIAS

Act III, scene vi

Enter UBALDO *[and]* RICARDO

UBALDO What we spake on the volley[726] begins to work;
We have laid a good foundation.
RICARDO Build it up,
Or else 'tis nothing. You have by lot[727] the honor
Of the first assault, but as it is conditioned[728]
Observe the time proportioned.[729] I'll not part with
My share in the achievement; when I whistle
Or hem,[730] fall off.

Enter SOPHIA *[richly dressed]*

UBALDO She comes. Stand by; I'll watch
My opportunity.
SOPHIA I find myself
Strangely distracted with the various stories
Now well, now ill, then doubtfully by my guests
Delivered of my lord. And like poor beggars
That in their dreams find treasure by reflection
Of a wounded fancy make it questionable
Whether they sleep or not,[731] yet, tickled[732] with
Such a fantastic hope of happiness,

722 182 stays: stops
723 183 doubted: feared
724 185–6: prove … frailty: i.e. give her a precedent for her weakness
725 193 confirmed: strengthened, reassured
726 1 on the volley: spontaneously
727 3 lot: the casting of lots
728 4 as it is conditioned: i.e. as the terms of our agreement state
729 5 proportioned: allotted to you
730 7 hem: cough, clear my throat
731 12–14 in their … or not: i.e. dream of wealth so vividly that they wonder if they are awake or asleep
732 14 tickled: pleased

Wish they may never wake, in some such measure,[733]
Incredulous of what I see and touch,
As[734] 'twere a fading apparition,[735] I
Am still perplexed and troubled; and when most
Confirmed 'tis true,[736] a curious jealousy[737]
To be assured by what means and from whom
Such a mass of wealth was first deserved, then gotten,
Cunningly[738] steals[739] into me. I have practiced[740]
For my certain resolution with these courtiers,
Promising private conference to either,
And at this hour, if in search of the truth
I hear or say more than becomes my virtue,
Forgive me, my Mathias.
UBALDO [*Aside*] Now I make in—
Madam, as you commanded, I attend
Your pleasure.
SOPHIA I must thank you for the favor.
UBALDO I am no ghostly father,[741] yet if you have
Some scruples touching your lord you would be resolved of,
I am prepared.
SOPHIA But will you take your oath
To answer truly?
UBALDO On the hem of your smock, if you please,
A vow I dare not break, it being a book[742]
I would gladly swear on.
SOPHIA To spare, sir, that trouble,
I'll take your word, which in a gentleman
Should be of equal value. Is my lord then
In such grace with the queen?
UBALDO You should best know,
By what you have found from him, whether he can
Deserve a grace or no.
SOPHIA What grace do you mean?
UBALDO That special grace—if you'll have it[743]—he labored so hard for
Between a pair of sheets on your wedding night,
When your ladyship lost you-know-what.[744]
SOPHIA Fie! Be more modest
Or I must leave you.
UBALDO I would tell a truth
As cleanly as I could, and yet the subject
Makes me run out a little.[745]
SOPHIA You would put now
A foolish jealousy in my head my lord

733 16 in some such measure: in a similar fashion
734 18 As: as if
735 18 apparition: specter, ghost
736 19–20 and when . . . 'tis true: and when I am most certain of my happiness
737 20 jealousy: anxiety, eagerness
738 23 Cunningly: craftily, stealthily
739 23 steals: sneaks, creeps
740 23 practiced: negotiated with
741 31 ghostly father: priest
742 36 book: Ubaldo likens Sophia's hem to the Bible, used in swearing formal oaths
743 43 if you'll have it: i.e. if you'll hear me out, if you would call it that
744 45 you-know-what: i.e. your virginity
745 48 run out a little: speak rather boldly

Hath gotten a new mistress.
UBALDO One? A hundred!
But under seal[746] I speak it; I presume
Upon your silence,[747] it being for your profit.
They talk of Hercules' back[748] for fifty in a night;
'Twas well, but yet to yours he was a piddler.[749]
Such a soldier and a courtier never came
To Alba Regalis![750] The ladies run mad for him,
And there is such contention among 'em
Who shall engross him wholly, that the like
Was never heard of.
SOPHIA Are they handsome women?
UBALDO Fie, no! Coarse mammets, and what's worse they are old too—
Some fifty, some threescore,[751] and they pay dear[752] for't,
Believing that he carries a powder[753] in his breeches
Will make 'em young again, and these suck shrewdly.[754]
RICARDO Sir, I must fetch you off. [RICARDO] *whistles*
UBALDO I could tell you wonders
Of the cures he has done—but a business of import
Calls me away, but that dispatched I will
Be with you presently. [UBALDO] *steps aside;* [RICARDO *comes forward*]
SOPHIA There is something more
In this than bare suspicion.
RICARDO Save you,[755] lady.
Now you look like yourself! I have not looked on
A lady more complete, yet have seen a madam
Wear a garment of this fashion, of the same stuff too,
One just of your dimensions. [*Aside*] Sate the wind there,[756] boy.
SOPHIA What lady, sir?
RICARDO Nay, nothing. And methinks
I should know this ruby. Very good! 'Tis the same.
This chain of orient[757] pearl and this diamond too
Have been worn before, but much good may they do you.
Strength to the gentleman's back! He toiled hard for 'em
Before he got 'em.
SOPHIA Why? How were they gotten? UBALDO *hems*
RICARDO Not in the field with his sword, upon my life;
He may thank his close stiletto.[758] Plague upon it!
Run the minutes so fast? Pray you excuse my manners;
I left a letter in my chamber window,
Which I would not have seen on any terms. Fie on it,
Forgetful as I am, but I straight attend you. RICARDO *steps aside*

746 51 under seal: in confidence (like a letter closed with a seal)
747 51–2 presume/Upon your silence: assume that you will keep quiet
748 53 back: i.e. strong back (indicating his sexual resilience)
749 54 piddler: dilettante, amateur
750 56 Alba Regalis: the Latin name of the medieval Hungarian capital Székesfehérvár; both names mean "royal white castle"
751 61 threescore: sixty
752 61 dear: high prices
753 62 powder: medicinal substance
754 63 suck shrewdly: violently drain him (i.e. through sexual activity)
755 68 Save you: a greeting (short for "God save you")
756 72 Sate the wind there: a difficult phrase that may mean something like "fill the sails", i.e. pursue this course, capitalize on this approach; "sate" might alternatively be a misprint for "sat" or "sits," giving a phrase meaning "is this the direction things are taking?"
757 75 orient: Indian, precious (because Indian pearls were of better quality)
758 80 close stiletto: hidden short dagger (with a sexual suggestion)

SOPHIA This is strange. His letters said these jewels were
Presented him by the queen, as a reward
For his good service, and the trunks of clothes
That followed them this last night, with haste[759] made up
By his direction. UBALDO [*comes forward*]
UBALDO I was telling you
Of wonders, madam.
SOPHIA If you are so skillful,[760]
Without premeditation answer me:
Know you this gown and these rich jewels?
UBALDO Heaven,
How things will come out! But that I should offend you,
And wrong my more-than-noble friend, your husband—
For we are sworn brothers—in the discovery[761]
Of his nearest secrets, I could—
SOPHIA By the hope of favor
That you have from me, out with it.
UBALDO 'Tis a potent spell
I cannot resist. Why, I will tell you, madam,
And to how many several women you are
Beholding for your bravery. This was
The wedding gown of Paulina, a rich strumpet,[762]
Worn but a day when she married old Gonzago
And left off trading.[763]
SOPHIA O my heart!
UBALDO This chain
Of pearl was a great widow's, that invited
Your lord to the masque, and the weather proving foul
He lodged in her house all night, and merry they were.
But how he came by it I know not.
SOPHIA Perjured[764] man!
UBALDO This ring was Julietta's, a fine piece,[765]
But very good at the sport; this diamond
Was Madam Acanthe's, given him for a song
Pricked[766] in a private arbor—as she said—
When the queen asked for it, and she heard him sing, too,
And danced to his hornpipe,[767] or there are liars abroad.
There are other toys about you the same way purchased,
But paralleled with these not worth the relation.
You are happy in a husband: never man
Made better use of his strength. Would you have him waste
His body away for nothing? If he holds out,
There's not an embroidered petticoat in the court
But shall be at your service.
SOPHIA I commend him;

759 88 with haste: hurriedly
760 90 skillful: expert in these matters
761 95 discovery: revelation
762 101 strumpet: prostitute
763 103 trading: selling sex
764 107 Perjured: unfaithful, deceitful
765 108 fine piece: splendid item of jewelry, refined woman
766 111 Pricked: played (with a sexual pun on "penetrated")
767 113 danced to his hornpipe: (figuratively) had sex with him; a hornpipe is a lively tune, and/or the wind instrument (made of horn) on which it is played

It is a thriving trade. But pray you leave me
A little to myself.
UBALDO You may command
Your servant, madam. [*To* RICARDO] She's stung unto the quick,[768] lad.
RICARDO I did my part. If this potion work not, hang me.
Let her sleep as well as she can tonight; tomorrow
We'll mount new batteries.
UBALDO And till then leave her. *Exeunt* UBALDO [*and*] RICARDO
SOPHIA You powers that take into your care the guard
Of innocence, aid me, for I am a creature[769]
So forfeited[770] to despair, hope cannot fancy[771]
A ransom to redeem me. I begin
To waver in my faith, and mark[772] it doubtful
Whether the saints that were canonized for
Their holiness of life sinned not in secret,
Since my Mathias is fallen from his virtue
In such an open fashion. Could it be else
That such a husband, so devoted to me,
So vowed to temperance, for lascivious hire
Should prostitute himself to common harlots?
Old and deformed, too? Was't for this he left me?
And in a feigned pretense for want of means
To give me ornament?[773] Or to bring home
Diseases to me? Suppose these[774] are false
And lustful goats, if he were true and right
Why stays he so long from me being made rich
And that the only reason why he left me?
No, he is lost. And shall I wear the spoils[775]
And salaries of lust? They cleave[776] unto me
Like Nessus' poisoned shirt![777] No, in my rage
I'll tear 'em off, and from my body wash
The venom with my tears. Have I no spleen[778]
Nor anger of a woman? Shall he build
Upon my ruins and I unrevenged
Deplore[779] his falsehood? No! With the same trash[780]
For which he hath dishonored me, I'll purchase
A just revenge. I am not yet so much
In debt to years, nor so misshaped that all
Should fly from my embraces. Chastity,
Thou only art a name, and I renounce thee;
I am now a servant to voluptuousness.[781]

768 123 unto the quick: to her very core
769 128 creature: wretch
770 129 forfeited: lost, given up
771 129 fancy: imagine
772 131 mark: consider
773 141 ornament: fine clothing and jewelry
774 142 these: Ubaldo and Ricardo
775 146 spoils: plunder
776 147 cleave: cling
777 148 Nessus' poisoned shirt: Nessus was a centaur killed by Hercules with a poisoned arrow; the poisoned shirt was a shirt dipped in Nessus's blood, given to Hercules by his wife, Deianeira
778 150 spleen: courage, angry pride
779 153 Deplore: grieve, lament
780 153 trash: i.e. the clothes and jewelry
781 159 voluptuousness: sexual indulgence

Wantons[782] of all degrees and fashions welcome!
You shall be entertained, and if I stray
Let him condemn himself that lead the way.

Exit

The end of the third act

Act IV, scene i

Enter MATHIAS [*and*] BAPTISTA

BAPTISTA We are in a desperate strait, there's no evasion[783]
Nor hope left to come off but[784] by your yielding
To the necessity. You must feign a grant[785]
To her violent passion, or—
MATHIAS What, my Baptista?
BAPTISTA We are but dead else.
MATHIAS Were the sword now heaved[786] up,
And my neck upon the block, I would not buy
An hour's reprieve with the loss of faith and virtue
To be made immortal here. Art thou a scholar—
Nay, almost without parallel—and yet fear
To die, which is inevitable? You may urge
The many years that by the course of nature
We may travel[787] in this tedious pilgrimage,[788]
And hold it as a blessing, as it is
When innocence is our guide; yet know, Baptista,
Our virtues are preferred before[789] our years
By the great judge.[790] To die untainted[791] in
Our fame and reputation is the greatest,[792]
And to lose that can we desire to live?
Or shall I for a momentary pleasure,
Which soon comes to a period, to all times
Have breach of faith and perjury remembered
In a still-living epitaph? No, Baptista,
Since my Sophia will go to her grave
Unspotted in her faith, I'll follow her
With equal loyalty. But[793] look on this,
Your own great work, your masterpiece, and then,
She being still the same, teach me to alter. *The picture altered*[794]
Ha! Sure I do not sleep, or if I dream
This is a terrible vision! I will clear

782 160 Wantons: lechers
783 1 evasion: means of escape, subterfuge
784 2 come off but: meet with success except
785 3 a grant: acquiescence, submission
786 5 heaved: lifted
787 12 travel: with a pun on "travail" (labor)
788 12 this tedious pilgrimage: i.e. life
789 15 preferred before: valued more highly
790 16 great judge: God
791 16 untainted: undamaged, pure
792 17 greatest: i.e. the greatest virtue
793 25 But: merely
794 27 SD *altered*: indicated either by a new prop picture or the reactions of Mathias and Baptista

My eyesight;[795] perhaps melancholy[796] makes me
See that which is not.
BAPTISTA It is too apparent;
I grieve to look upon't. Besides the yellow
That does assure she's tempted, there are lines
Of a dark color that disperse themselves
O'er every miniature[797] of her face, and those
Confirm—
MATHIAS She is turned whore.
BAPTISTA I must not say so.
Yet, as a friend to truth, if you will have me
Interpret it, in her consent and wishes
She's false, but not in fact[798] yet.
MATHIAS Fact, Baptista?
Make not yourself a pander to her looseness
In laboring to palliate[799] what a vizard[800]
Of impudence cannot cover. Did e'er woman
In her will decline from chastity but found[801] means
To give her hot lust fuel? It is more
Impossible in nature for gross[802] bodies,
Descending of themselves, to hang in the air,
Or with my single arm to underprop[803]
A falling tower, nay, in its violent course
To stop the lightning, than to stay a woman
Hurried by two furies[804]—lust and falsehood—
In her full career[805] to wickedness.
BAPTISTA Pray you temper
The violence of your passion.
MATHIAS In extremes
Of this condition,[806] can it be in man
To use a moderation? I am thrown
From a steep rock headlong into a gulf
Of misery, and find myself past hope
In the same moment that I apprehend
That I am falling. And this the figure of
My idol few hours since,[807] while she continued
In her perfection—that was late a mirror[808]
In which I saw miraculous shapes of duty,
Staid[809] manners, with all excellency a husband
Could wish in a chaste wife—is on the sudden
Turned to a magical glass, and does present

795 29–30 clear/My eyesight: i.e. rub my eyes
796 30 melancholy: sadness, hardship
797 35 miniature: feature, detail
798 40 fact: action
799 42 palliate: mitigate, disguise
800 42 vizard: mask
801 44 but found: who did not find
802 46 gross: material, physical
803 48 underprop: prop up, support
804 51 furies: wild passions
805 52 career: gallop, race
806 54 condition: kind
807 60 few hours since: a few hours ago
808 61 mirror: model, example
809 63 Staid: steadfast, dignified

Nothing but horns[810] and horror.
BAPTISTA You may yet—
And 'tis the best foundation—build up comfort
On your own goodness.
MATHIAS No, that hath undone me.
For now I hold my temperance a sin
Worse than excess, and what was vice a virtue.
Have I refused a queen, and such a queen,
Whose ravishing beauties at the first sight had tempted
A hermit from his beads[811] and changed his prayers
To amorous sonnets, to preserve my faith
Inviolate to thee,[812] with the hazard[813] of
My death with torture since she could inflict
No less for my contempt? And have I made
Such a return from thee?[814] I will not curse thee,
Nor for thy falsehood rail[815] against the sex.
'Tis poor[816] and common.[817] I'll only with wise men
Whisper unto myself, "Howe'er they seem,
Nor present, nor past times, nor the age to come
Hath heretofore, can now, or ever shall
Produce one constant woman."
BAPTISTA This is more
Than the satirists[818] wrote against 'em.
MATHIAS There's no language
That can express the poison of these aspics,[819]
These weeping crocodiles, and all too little
That hath been said against 'em. But I'll mold
My thoughts into another form, and if
She can outlive the report of what I have done
This hand when next she comes within my reach
Shall be her executioner.

Enter HONORIA [*with Servants*]

BAPTISTA The queen, sir.
HONORIA [*To Servants*] Wait our command at distance. [*To* BAPTISTA] Sir, you have
Free liberty to depart.
BAPTISTA I know my manners,
And thank you for the favor. *Exit* BAPTISTA
HONORIA Have you taken
Good rest in your new lodgings? I expect now
Your resolute answer, but advise[820] maturely
Before I hear it.
MATHIAS Let my actions, madam—

810 66 horns: the invisible horns of the cuckold
811 73 beads: prayers, rosary beads
812 75 thee: Mathias probably addresses the picture directly here
813 75 hazard: risk
814 77–8 made . . . from thee: been repaid by you in this manner
815 79 rail: rant
816 80 poor: contemptible, unworthy (of me)
817 80 common: ordinary, generally known
818 85 satirists: authors of anti-feminist verse
819 86 aspics: asps, venomous snakes
820 97 advise: reflect

For no words can dilate[821] my joy in all
You can command with cheerfulness to serve you—
Assure your highness, and in sign of my
Submission, and contrition for my error,
My lips, that but the last night shunned the touch
Of yours as poison, taught humility now,
Thus on your foot—and that too great an honor
For such an undeserver—seals my duty.[822] [*He kisses her foot*]
A cloudy mist of ignorance equal to
Cimmerian[823] darkness would not let me see then
What now with adoration and wonder,
With reverence, I look up to. But those fogs
Dispersed and scattered by the powerful beams
With which yourself, the sun of all perfection,
Vouchsafe to cure my blindness, like a suppliant
As low as I can kneel I humbly beg
What you once pleased to tender.
HONORIA This is more
Than I could hope. What find you so attractive
Upon my face in so short time to make
This sudden metamorphosis? Pray you rise;
I for your late neglect thus sign your pardon.
[*Kisses him*] Ay, now you kiss like a lover, and not as brothers
Coldly salute their sisters.
MATHIAS I am turned
All spirit and fire.
HONORIA Yet to give some allay[824]
To this hot fervor, 'twere good to remember
The king, whose eyes and ears are everywhere,
With the danger too that follows, this discovered.
MATHIAS Danger? A bugbear,[825] madam. Let me ride once
Like Phaeton[826] in the chariot of your favor,
And I contemn Jove's[827] thunder. Though the king
In our embraces stood a looker-on,
His[828] hangmen, and with studied[829] cruelty, ready
To drag me from your arms, it should not fright me
From the enjoying that[830] a single life is
Too poor a price for. Oh, that now all vigor
Of my youth were recollected[831] for an hour,
That my desire might meet with yours and draw[832]
The envy of all men in the encounter!
Upon my head,[833] I should—but we lose[834] time.

821 99 dilate: amplify
822 106 seals my duty: confirms my willingness to serve you
823 108 Cimmerian: of the Cimmerii, an ancient people of Asia Minor who were fabled to live in darkness
824 122 allay: calming influence
825 126 bugbear: needless fear
826 127 Phaeton: son of the sun-god, who borrowed the chariot with which his father pulled the sun across the sky, with disastrous consequences
827 128 Jove: Jupiter
828 130 His: with his
829 130 studied: deliberate, premeditated
830 132 that: that which
831 134 recollected: summoned again
832 135 draw: provoke
833 137 Upon my head: of my own accord
834 137 lose: waste

Be gracious, mighty Queen.
HONORIA Pause yet a little.
The bounties of the king, and—what weighs more—
Your boasted constancy to your matchless wife,
Should not soon be shaken.
MATHIAS The whole fabric[835]
When I but look on you is in a moment
O'erturned and ruined and, as rivers lose
Their names when they are swallowed by the ocean,
In you alone all faculties of my soul
Are wholly taken up; my wife and king
At the best as things forgotten.
HONORIA [*Aside*] Can this be?
I have gained my end now.
MATHIAS Wherefore stay you,[836] madam?
HONORIA In my consideration[837] what a nothing
Man's constancy is.
MATHIAS Your beauties make it so
In me, sweet lady.
HONORIA And it is my glory.
I could be coy now as you were, but I
Am of a gentler temper. Howsoever,
And in a just return of what I have suffered
In your disdain, with the same measure[838] grant me
Equal deliberation.[839] I ere long
Will visit you again and when I next
Appear, as[840] conquered by it, slave-like wait
On my triumphant beauty. *Exit* HONORIA [*and Servants*]
MATHIAS What a change[841]
Is here, beyond my fear,[842] but by thy falsehood,
Sophia, not her beauty. Is it denied me
To sin but in my wishes? What a frown
In scorn at her departure she threw on me!
I am both ways lost; storms of contempt and scorn
Are ready to break on me, and all hope
Of shelter doubtful. I can neither be
Disloyal, nor yet honest; I stand guilty
On either part. At the worst, death will end all,
And he must be my judge to right my wrong,
Since I have loved too much and lived too long.
Exit MATHIAS

Act IV, scene ii

Enter SOPHIA *sola*[843] *with a book and a note*

835 141 fabric: structure (of marriage and loyalty)
836 148 wherefore stay you: why do you hesitate
837 149 In my consideration: I am considering
838 155 with the same measure: i.e. in return
839 156 deliberation: time to make a decision
840 158 as: as if you are
841 159 change: change in me
842 160 my fear: what I feared
843 0 SD *sola*: alone

SOPHIA Nor custom[844] nor example,[845] nor vast numbers
Of such as do offend, make less the sin.
For each particular crime a strict accompt[846]
Will be exacted, and that comfort which
The damned pretend, fellows in misery,[847]
Takes nothing from their torments. Everyone
Must suffer in himself the measure of
His wickedness. If so, as I must grant,
It being unrefutable in reason,
Howe'er my lord offend it is no warrant
For me to walk in his forbidden paths.
What penance then can expiate[848] my guilt
For my consent—transported then with passion—
To wantonness? The wounds I give my fame
Cannot recover his, and though I have fed
These courtiers with promises and hopes
I am yet in fact untainted. And I trust
My sorrow for it, with my purity
And love to goodness for itself made powerful,
Though all they[849] have alleged prove true or false,
Will be such exorcisms as shall command
This fury, jealousy, from me. What I have
Determined touching[850] them I am resolved
To put in execution. Within there!
Where are my noble guests?

Enter HILARIO [*and*] CORISCA *with other* SERVANTS

HILARIO The elder,[851] madam,
Is drinking by himself to your ladyship's health
In muscadine[852] and eggs, and for a rasher[853]
To draw his liquor down he hath got a pie
Of marrowbones, potatoes, and eryngoes,[854]
With many such ingredients, and 'tis said
He hath sent his man in post to the next town
For a pound of ambergris[855] and half a peck[856]
Of fishes called cantharides.[857]
CORISCA The younger[858]
Prunes[859] up himself as if this night he were
To act a bridegroom's part, but to what purpose

844 1 custom: tradition
845 1 example: precedent
846 3 accompt: reckoning, judgment
847 4–5 that comfort . . . in misery: i.e. the solace that sinners find in knowing that others have sinned
848 12 expiate: alleviate, make amends for
849 20 they: Ubaldo and Ricardo
850 23 touching: regarding
851 25 elder: Ubaldo
852 27 muscadine: white wine made from muscat grapes
853 27 rasher: something that stimulates thirst
854 29 eryngoes: candied roots of sea holly
855 32 ambergris: waxy substance produced in the intestines of sperm whales
856 32 peck: unit of measurement equivalent to eight dry quarts or around 8–9 liters
857 29–33 marrowbones, potatoes . . . called cantharides: all of these substances were thought to be aphrodisiacs
858 33 younger: Ricardo
859 34 Prunes: preens, smartens

I am ignorance itself.
SOPHIA Continue so. *Gives [the* SERVANTS*] a paper*
Let those lodgings be prepared as this directs you,
And fail not in a circumstance,[860] as you
Respect my favor.
FIRST SERVANT We have our instructions.
SECOND SERVANT And punctually[861] will follow 'em. *Exeunt* SERVANTS

Enter UBALDO

HILARIO Here comes, madam,
The Lord Ubaldo.
UBALDO [*To* CORISCA] Pretty one, there's gold
To buy thee a new gown. [*To* HILARIO] And there's for thee;
Grow fat and fit for service. I am now
As I should be: at the height and able to
Beget a giant. O my better angel,
In this you show your wisdom when you pay
The lecher in his own coin![862] Shall you sit puling[863]
Like a patient Grizel[864] and be laughed at? No,
This is a fair revenge! Shall we to it?
SOPHIA To what, sir?
UBALDO The sport you promised.
SOPHIA Could it be done with safety?
UBALDO I warrant you, I am sound as a bell, [865] a tough
Old blade, and steel to the back,[866] as you shall find me
In the trial on your anvil.[867]
SOPHIA So. But how, sir,
Shall I satisfy your friend to whom by promise
I am equally engaged?[868]
UBALDO I must confess
The more the merrier, but of all men living
Take heed of him; you may safer run upon
The mouth of a cannon when it is unlading,[869]
And come off colder.
SOPHIA How! Is he not wholesome? [870]
UBALDO Wholesome? I'll tell you for your good: he is
A spittle[871] of diseases and, indeed,
More loathsome and infectious. The tub[872] is
His weekly bath. He hath not drank this seven year
Before he came to your house but[873] compositions

860 38 a circumstance: any detail
861 40 punctually: precisely
862 46–7 you pay . . . own coin: i.e. you beat Mathias at his own game
863 47 puling: whining
864 48 patient Grizel: Griselda, the famously patient heroine of Chaucer's *Clerk's Tale*
865 51 sound as a bell: strong, healthy
866 52 steel to the back: made of steel throughout, possessing a strong back (for sexual exertion)
867 53 In the . . . your anvil: i.e. if we have sex; the image is of testing a sword's hardness and strength
868 55 engaged: committed
869 58 unlading: discharging
870 59 wholesome: healthy
871 61 spittle: inferior hospital
872 62 tub: sweating tub, used to treat venereal disease
873 64 but: anything except

Of sassafras[874] and guacum,[875] and dry mutton[876]
His daily portion. Name what scratch[877] soever
Can be got by women, and the surgeons will resolve you
At this time or at that Ricardo had it.
SOPHIA Bless me from him!
UBALDO 'Tis a good prayer, lady,
It being a degree unto[878] the pox[879]
Only to mention him; if my tongue burn not hang me,
When I but name Ricardo.[880]
SOPHIA Sir, this caution[881]
Must be rewarded.
UBALDO [*Aside*] I hope I have marred his market.—
But when?
SOPHIA Why, presently. Follow my woman;
She knows where to conduct you, and will serve
Tonight for a page. [*To* CORISCA] Let the waistcoat I appointed,
With the cambric shirt perfumed, and the rich cap,
Be brought into his chamber.
UBALDO Excellent lady!
And a caudle,[882] too, in the morning.
CORISCA I will fit you.[883] *Exeunt* UBALDO *and* CORISCA

Enter RICARDO

SOPHIA So, hot on the scent here comes the other beagle.[884]
RICARDO [*To* HILARIO] Take purse and all.
HILARIO If this company would come often
I should make a pretty term on't.[885]
SOPHIA For your sake
I have put him off. He only begged a kiss;
I gave it and so parted.
RICARDO [*Aside*] I hope better.—
He did not touch your lips?
SOPHIA Yes. I assure you,
There was no danger in it.
RICARDO No? [*Taking out a bag or box*] Eat presently
These lozenges,[886] of forty crowns[887] an ounce,
Or you are undone.
SOPHIA What is the virtue[888] of 'em?

874 65 sassafras: dried bark of the sassafras tree, used as a purging agent
875 65 guacum: resin from the guacum tree, used medicinally
876 65 dry mutton: i.e. the blandest of foods
877 66 scratch: itch, disease
878 70 degree unto: step towards
879 70 the pox: syphilis
880 71–2 if my … name Ricardo: I'll be damned ("hang me") if my tongue doesn't burn when I merely speak Ricardo's name (a burning sensation is a symptom of venereal disease)
881 72 caution: warning
882 79 caudle: a warm drink made of sweetened or spiced oatmeal mixed with wine or ale
883 79 fit you: provide for you, punish you
884 80 beagle: hunting dog
885 82 pretty term on't: have a good time of it
886 87 lozenges: tablets
887 87 of forty crowns: worth forty crowns (equivalent to £10)
888 88 virtue: goodness, power

RICARDO They are preservatives[889] against stinking breath[890]
Rising from rotten lungs.
SOPHIA If so, your carriage
Of such dear antidotes in my opinion
May render yours[891] suspected.
RICARDO Fie, no! I use 'em
When I talk with him; I should be poisoned else.
But I'll be free[892] with you. He was once a creature
It may be of God's making, but long since
He is turned to a druggist's shop. The spring and fall
Hold all the year with him.[893] That he lives he owes
To art not nature; she has given him o'er.[894]
He moves like the Fairy King,[895] on screws and wheels
Made by his doctor's recipes, and yet still
They are out of joint, and everyday repairing.
He has a regiment of whores he keeps
At his own charge in a lazar-house,[896] but the best is
There's not a nose among 'em. [897] He's acquainted
With the green water[898] and the spitting pill's[899]
Familiar to him; in a frosty morning
You may thrust him in a pottle pot.[900] His bones
Rattle in his skin like beans tossed in a bladder[901]
If he but hear a coach.[902] The fomentation,[903]
The friction,[904] with fumigation,[905] cannot save him
From the chine evil.[906] In a word, he is
Not one disease but all; yet being my friend
I will forbear[907] his character, for I would not
Wrong him in your opinion.
SOPHIA The best is,
The virtues you bestow on him to me
Are mysteries I know not. But, however,
I am at your service. [*To* HILARIO] Sirrah,[908] let it be your care
T'unclothe the gentleman, and with speed; delay
Takes from[909] delight.
RICARDO Good! There's my hat, sword, cloak—

889 89 preservatives: protection
890 89 stinking breath: another symptom of venereal disease
891 92 yours: i.e. your breath/lungs
892 94 free: open, frank
893 96–7 The spring . . . with him: i.e. the changes of the seasons mean nothing to him
894 98 given him o'er: abandoned him
895 99 the Fairy King: i.e. a puppet of Oberon, the king of fairyland
896 103 lazar-house: hospice
897 104 not a nose among 'em: syphilis attacks the flesh and cartilage of the nose
898 105 green water: a medicinal liquid containing verdigris (copper acetate), used to treat venereal disease
899 105 spitting pill: a tablet used to aid the production of saliva
900 107 pottle pot: half-gallon pot or tankard
901 108 bladder: bag-pipe
902 109 coach: i.e. one bringing women to him
903 109 fomentation: application of hot flannels
904 110 friction: chafing or rubbing
905 110 fumigation: exposure to fumes for medicinal purposes
906 111 chine evil: a disease especially affecting horses
907 113 forbear: refrain from discussing
908 117 Sirrah: form of address used by those of higher rank to their inferiors
909 119 Takes from: reduces

A vengeance on[910] these buttons! Off with my doublet.
I dare show my skin; in the touch you will like it better.
[*To* HILARIO] Prithee cut my codpiece point,[911] and for this service
When I leave them[912] off they are thine.
HILARIO I'll take your word, sir.
RICARDO Dear lady, stay not long.
SOPHIA I may come too soon, sir.
RICARDO No, no, I am ready now.
HILARIO This is the way, sir. *Exeunt* HILARIO *and* RICARDO
SOPHIA I was much to blame to credit their reports
Touching my lord that so traduce[913] each other,
And with such virulent malice, though I presume
They are bad enough. But I have studied for 'em
A way for their recovery.

The noise of clapping[914] *a door.* UBALDO [*enters*] *above in his shirt*[915]

UBALDO What dost thou mean, wench?
Why dost thou shut the door upon me? Ha!
My clothes are ta'en away too! Shall I starve here?
Is this my lodging? I am sure the lady talked of
A rich cap, a perfumed shirt, and a waistcoat,
But here is nothing but a little fresh straw,
A petticoat for a coverlet,[916] and that torn, too,
And an old woman's biggin[917] for a nightcap.

Enter CORISCA [*and Servants carrying implements for spinning*]

'Slight, 'tis a prison or a pigsty! Ha!
The windows grated with iron;[918] I cannot force 'em,
And if I leap down here I break my neck.
I am betrayed. Rogues, villains, let me out!
I am a lord, and that's no common title.
And shall I be used thus?
SOPHIA Let him rave. He's fast.[919]
I'll parley[920] with him at leisure.

RICARDO *enter*[*s*] *with a great noise above, as fallen*

RICARDO Zounds! Have you trapdoors?
SOPHIA The other bird's i' th' cage too. Let him flutter.
RICARDO Whither am I fallen? Into hell?
UBALDO Who makes that noise there?
Help me if thou art a friend!

910 120 a vengeance on: exclamation expressing anger or impatience
911 122 codpiece point: a codpiece is a piece of fabric or bag covering a man's genitals; the point is the lace tying it to the breeches
912 123 them: my clothes
913 127 traduce: malign, slander
914 130 SD *clapping*: slamming
915 130 SD *shirt*: linen shirt worn as an undergarment
916 136 coverlet: counterpane, quilt
917 137 biggin: hood, headgear
918 139 windows grated with iron: the windows are covered with iron grates
919 143 fast: securely imprisoned
920 144 parley: speak, discuss terms (as if in combat)

RICARDO A friend? I am where
I cannot help myself. Let me see thy face.
UBALDO How, Ricardo! Prithee throw me thy cloak,
If thou canst, to cover me; I am almost
Frozen to death.
RICARDO My cloak? I have no breeches!
I am in my shirt as thou art, and here's nothing
For myself but a clown's cast suit.[921]
UBALDO We are both undone.
Prithee roar a little. Madam!

Enter HILARIO *in* RICARDO*'s suit*

RICARDO Lady of the house!
UBALDO Grooms of the chamber!
RICARDO Gentlewomen! Milkmaids!
UBALDO Shall we be murdered?
SOPHIA No, but soundly punished
To your deserts.[922]
RICARDO You are not in earnest, madam?
SOPHIA Judge as you find and feel it. And now hear
What I irrevocably purpose to you.
Being received as guests into my house,
And with all it afforded entertained,[923]
You have forgot all hospitable[924] duties,
And with the defamation of my lord
Wrought on my woman-weakness in revenge
Of[925] his injuries,[926] as you fashioned[927] 'em to me,
To yield my honor to your lawless lust.
HILARIO Mark that, poor fellows.
SOPHIA And so far you have
Transgressed against the dignity of men—
Who should, bound to it by virtue, still defend
Chaste ladies' honors—that it was your trade
To make 'em[928] infamous. But you are caught
In your own toils[929] like lustful beasts, and therefore
Hope not to find the usage of[930] men from me.
Such mercy you have forfeited, and shall suffer
Like the most slavish[931] women.
UBALDO How will you use us?
SOPHIA Ease and excess in feeding made you wanton;
A pleurisy[932] of ill blood you must let out
By labor and spare diet that way got too,

921 154 clown's cast suit: peasant's discarded clothing
922 158 To your deserts: as you deserve
923 162 Made welcome with everything it had to offer
924 163 hospitable: appropriate to a guest
925 165–6 in revenge/Of: to take revenge for
926 166 his injuries: his wrongful treatment of me
927 166 fashioned: counterfeited
928 172 'em: i.e. ladies' honors
929 173 toils: nets
930 174 usage of: treatment appropriate for
931 176 slavish: low-status, subordinate
932 178 pleurisy: excess

Or perish for hunger.[933] [*To Servants*] Reach him up that distaff[934]
With the flax upon it.—Though no Omphale,[935]
Nor you a second Hercules, as I take it,
As you spin well at my command, and please me,
Your wages in the coarsest bread and water
Shall be proportionable.[936]
UBALDO I will starve first.
SOPHIA That's as you please.
RICARDO What will become of me now?
SOPHIA You shall have gentler work. I have oft observed
You were proud to show the fineness of your hands
And softness of your fingers; you should reel[937] well
What he spins, if you give your mind to it, as I'll force you.
[*To Servants*] Deliver him his materials.—Now you know
Your penance, fall to work; hunger will teach you.
And so, as slaves to your lust, not me, I leave you. *Exeunt* SOPHIA[, CORISCA,] *and Servants*
UBALDO I shall spin a fine thread out[938] now.
RICARDO I cannot look
On these devices but they put me in mind
Of rope-makers.[939]
HILARIO Fellow, think of thy task.
Forget such vanities. My livery[940] there
Will serve thee to work in.
RICARDO Let me have my clothes yet;
I was bountiful to thee.
HILARIO They are past your wearing[941]
And mine by promise, as all these[942] can witness.
You have no holidays coming, nor will I work
While these and this[943] lasts. And so when you please
You may shut up your shop windows. *Exit* HILARIO
UBALDO I am faint
And must lie down.
RICARDO I am hungry too, and cold.
O cursèd women!
UBALDO This comes of our whoring.
But let us rest as well as we can tonight,
But not o'ersleep ourselves lest[944] we fast tomorrow. *They draw the curtains*[945]

Act IV, scene iii

Enter LADISLAUS, HONORIA, EUBULUS, FERDINAND, ACANTHE, [*and*] *Attendants*

933 178–80 A pleurisy . . . for hunger: you must cure yourself through hard work and the plain diet that you will earn through that work, or you will starve
934 180 distaff: staff around which wool or flax is wound in spinning
935 181 Omphale: Lybian queen who enslaved Hercules and made him do women's work
936 185 proportionable: commensurate, appropriate
937 189 reel: wind wool onto a reel
938 194 spin a fine thread out: spend a good deal of time to no effect
939 196 rope-makers: i.e. manufacturers of ropes for hanging
940 197 livery: clothing, uniform
941 199 past your wearing: no longer suitable for you to wear
942 200 all these: i.e. the playhouse audience
943 202 these and this: i.e. the fine clothes
944 207 lest: in case
945 207 SD *curtains*: curtains around the playhouse balcony

HONORIA Now you know all, sir, with the motives why
I forced him to my lodging.
LADISLAUS I desire
No more such trials, lady.
HONORIA I presume, sir,
You do not doubt my chastity.
LADISLAUS I would not,
But these are strange inducements.
EUBULUS By no means, sir.
Why, though he were with violence seized upon,
And still detained, the man, sir, being no soldier,
Nor used to charge his pike when the breach is open,[946]
There was no danger in't. You must conceive,[947] sir,
Being religious, she chose him for a chaplain
To read old homilies[948] to her in the dark;
She's bound to it by her canons.[949]
LADISLAUS Still tormented
With thy impertinence.
HONORIA By yourself,[950] dear sir,
I was ambitious only to overthrow
His boasted constancy in his consent,[951]
But for fact[952] I contemn him. I was never
Unchaste in thought; I labored to give proof
What power dwells in this beauty you admire so,
And when you see how soon it hath transformed him,
And with what superstition[953] he adores it,
Determine as you please.
LADISLAUS I will look on
This pageant,[954] but—
HONORIA When you have seen and heard, sir,
The passages[955] which I myself discovered,
And could have kept concealed had I meant basely,
Judge as you please.
LADISLAUS Well, I'll observe the issue.[956]
EUBULUS How had you took this, general, in your wife?
FERDINAND As a strange curiosity;[957] but queens
Are privileged above subjects, and 'tis fit, sir.

Act IV, scene iv

Enter MATHIAS [*and*] BAPTISTA

946 8 charge his ... is open: another violent image of sexual penetration; a pike is a staff with a point or spike on the end; a breach is a gap in fortifications
947 9 conceive: believe
948 11 homilies: religious writings
949 12 canons: rules, religious principles
950 13 By yourself: by your authority
951 15 consent: feeling (i.e. for Sophia)
952 16 fact: his actions
953 20 superstition: credulity, irrational belief
954 22 pageant: show
955 23 passages: incidents
956 25 issue: result
957 27 curiosity: novelty

BAPTISTA You are much altered, sir, since the last night,
When the queen left you, and look cheerfully,
Your dullness[958] quite blown over.
MATHIAS I have seen a vision
This morning makes[959] it good, and never was
In such security[960] as at this instant.
Fall what can fall,[961] and when the queen appears,
Whose shortest absence now is tedious to me,
Observe th'encounter.

Enter HONORIA [*below*], LADISLAUS, EUBULUS, FERDINAND, [*and*] ACANTHE, *with others, above*

BAPTISTA She already is
Entered the lists.
MATHIAS And I prepared to meet her.
BAPTISTA I know my duty. [*He moves to leave*]
HONORIA Not so. You may stay now
As a witness of our contract.
BAPTISTA I obey
In all things, madam.
HONORIA Where's that reverence,
Or rather superstitious adoration,
Which captive-like to my triumphant beauty
You paid last night? No humble knee? Nor sign
Of vassal[962] duty? Sure, this is the foot
To whose proud cover[963]—and then happy in it—
Your lips were glued, and that the neck then offered,
To witness your subjection, to be trod on.
Your certain loss of life in the king's anger
Was then too mean[964] a price to buy my favor,
And that false glow-worm fire of constancy
To your wife extinguished by a greater light
Shot from our eyes, and that,[965] it may be—being
Too glorious to be looked on—hath deprived you
Of speech and motion. But I will take off
A little from the splendor and descend
From my own height, and in your lowness hear you
Plead as a suppliant.
MATHIAS I do remember
I once saw such a woman.
HONORIA How!
MATHIAS And then
She did appear a most magnificent queen
And, what's more, virtuous, though somewhat darkened
With pride and self-opinion.[966]
EUBULUS Call you this courtship?

958 3 dullness: depression
959 4 makes: that makes
960 5 security: freedom from anxiety
961 6 Fall what can fall: i.e. let whatever happens happen
962 16 vassal: servile
963 17 proud cover: i.e. shoe
964 21 mean: low
965 24 that: the "light" of Honoria's eyes
966 33 self-opinion: self-regard

MATHIAS And she was happy in a royal husband,
Whom envy could not tax,[967] unless it were
For his too much indulgence to her humors.[968]
EUBULUS Pray you, sir, observe that touch.[969] 'Tis to the purpose.
I like the play the better for't.
MATHIAS And she lived
Worthy her birth and fortune; you retain yet
Some part of her angelical form. But when
Envy to the beauty of another woman,
Inferior to hers—one she never
Had seen but in her picture—had dispersed
Infection through her veins, and loyalty,
Which a great queen as she was should have nourished,
Grew odious to her—
HONORIA I am thunderstruck.
MATHIAS And lust in all the bravery it could borrow
From majesty, howe'er disguised, had took
Sure footing in the kingdom of her heart—
The throne of chastity once—how in a moment
All that was gracious, great, and glorious in her,
And won upon all hearts, like seeming[970] shadows,
Wanting true substance, vanished.
HONORIA How his reasons
Work on my soul.
MATHIAS Retire[971] into yourself
Your own strengths,[972] madam, strongly manned[973] with virtue,
And be but as you were, and there's no office
So base, beneath the slavery that men
Impose on beasts, but I will gladly bow to.
But as you play and juggle with[974] a stranger,
Varying your shapes like Thetis,[975] though the beauties
Of all that are by poets' raptures[976] sainted
Were now in you united, you should pass[977]—
Pitied by me, perhaps, but not regarded.
EUBULUS If this take not I am cheated.
MATHIAS To slip once
Is incident,[978] and excused by human frailty,
But to fall ever[979] damnable. We were both
Guilty, I grant, in tendering our affection,
But, as I hope you will do, I repented.
When we are grown up to ripeness, our life is
Like to this picture. [*Takes out the picture*]
While we run

967 35 tax: find fault with
968 36 humors: whims
969 37 touch: rebuke
970 52 like seeming: i.e. as if they were
971 54 Retire: pull back
972 55 strengths: sources of moral or mental strength, (figuratively) armed forces
973 55 manned: guarded
974 59 juggle with: play tricks on, deceive
975 60 Thetis: a sea-nymph who could transform herself
976 61 raptures: ecstatic writings
977 62 pass: leave unnoticed
978 65 incident: natural, probable
979 66 ever: forever, continually

A constant race in goodness, it retains
The just proportion. But the journey being
Tedious, and sweet temptations in the way,
That may in some degree divert us from
The road that we put forth[980] in ere we end
Our pilgrimage,[981] it may like this turn yellow
Or be with blackness clouded. But when we
Find we have gone astray, and labor to
Return unto our never-failing guide,[982]
Virtue, contrition with unfeignèd tears,
The spots of vice washed off will soon restore it[983]
To the first pureness.
HONORIA I am disenchanted.[984]
Mercy, O mercy, heavens! *[She] kneels*
LADISLAUS I am ravished[985] with
What I have seen and heard.
FERDINAND Let us descend and hear
The rest below.
EUBULUS This hath fallen out beyond
My expectation. *They descend*[986]
HONORIA How have I wandered
Out of the tract of piety, and misled
By overweening pride and flattery
Of fawning sycophants—the bane[987] of greatness—
Could never meet till now a passenger[988]
That in his charity would set me right
Or stay[989] me in my precipice to ruin.
How ill have I returned your goodness to me?
The horror in my thought oft turns me marble,
But if it may be yet prevented—

Enter [LADISLAUS] *the king and others* [*including* EUBULUS, FERDINAND *and* ACANTHE]

O sir,
What can I do to show my sorrow or
With what brow[990] ask your pardon?
LADISLAUS Pray you rise.
HONORIA Never, till you forgive me, and receive
Unto your love and favor a changed woman.
My state[991] and pride, turned to humility, henceforth
Shall wait on your commands, and my obedience
Steered[992] only by your will.
LADISLAUS And that will prove

980 75 put forth: set off
981 75–6 ere we end/Our pilgrimage: i.e. before we die
982 79 never-failing guide: i.e. God
983 81 it: i.e. life
984 82 disenchanted: set free from a magic spell
985 83 ravished: transported, entranced
986 86 SD *descend*: exit the upper stage
987 89 bane: curse
988 90 passenger: traveler
989 92 stay: stop, hold
990 97 brow: expression of shame, confidence
991 100 state: greatness, pomp
992 102 Steered: will be guided

A second and a better marriage to me.
All is forgot.
HONORIA Sir, I must not rise yet,
Till with a free confession of a crime
Unknown to you yet and a following suit
Which thus I beg be granted—
LADISLAUS I melt[993] with you.
'Tis pardoned, and confirmed thus. [*He embraces* HONORIA *and raises her to her feet*]
HONORIA Know then, sir,
In malice to this good knight's wife I practiced[994]
Ubaldo and Ricardo to corrupt her.
BAPTISTA [*To* MATHIAS] Thence grew the change of the picture.
HONORIA And how far
They have prevailed I am ignorant. Now if you, sir,
For the honor of this good man may be entreated
To travel thither, it being but a day's journey,
To fetch 'em off—
LADISLAUS We will put on[995] tonight.
BAPTISTA I,[996] if you please, your harbinger.
LADISLAUS I thank you.
[*To* MATHIAS] Let me embrace you in my arms; your service
Done on the Turk compared with this weighs nothing.
MATHIAS I am still your humble creature.[997]
LADISLAUS My true friend.
FERDINAND And so you are bound to hold him.
EUBULUS Such a plant
Imported to your kingdom, and here grafted,[998]
Would yield more fruit than all the idle weeds
That suck up your reign of favor.
LADISLAUS In my will[999]
I'll not be wanting. Prepare for our journey.
[*To* HONORIA] In act[1000] be my Honoria now, not name,
And to all aftertimes[1001] preserve thy fame.
Exeunt

The end of the fourth act

Act V, scene i

SOPHIA, CORISCA, [*and*] HILARIO

SOPHIA Are they then so humble?
HILARIO Hunger and hard labor
Have tamed 'em, madam. At the first they bellowed
Like stags ta'en in a toil, and would not work
For sullenness,[1002] but when they found without it

993 107 melt: am softened by emotion
994 109 practiced: employed
995 115 put on: leave in haste
996 116 I: I will be
997 119 creature: servant
998 121 grafted: inserted (like a shoot from one tree grafted onto another)
999 123 will: willingness to do what I intend
1000 125 act: deeds, behavior
1001 126 aftertimes: posterity
1002 4 sullenness: ill humor, sulking

There was no eating, and that to starve to death
Was much against their stomachs,[1003] by degree[1004]
Against their wills they fell to it.
CORISCA And now feed on
The little pittance[1005] you allow with gladness.
HILARIO I do remember that they stopped[1006] their noses
At the sight of beef and mutton as coarse feeding
For their fine palates, but now, their work being ended,
They leap at a barley-crust[1007] and hold cheese parings[1008]
With a spoonful of palled[1009] wine poured in their water,
For festival exceedings.[1010]
CORISCA When I examine
My spinster's[1011] work he trembles like a prentice
And takes a box on the ear when I spy faults
And botches in his labor as a favor
From a curst[1012] mistress.
HILARIO The other,[1013] too, reels well
For his time,[1014] and if your ladyship would please
To see 'em for your sport, since they want airing,[1015]
It would do well, in my judgment. You shall hear
Such a hungry dialogue from 'em.
SOPHIA But suppose
When they are out of prison they should grow
Rebellious?
HILARIO Never fear't. I'll undertake
To lead 'em out by the nose[1016] with a coarse thread
Of the one's spinning and make the other reel after,
And without grumbling, and, when you are weary of
Their company, as easily return 'em.
CORISCA Dear madam, it will help to drive away
Your melancholy.
SOPHIA Well, on this assurance
I am content. Bring 'em hither.
HILARIO I will do it
In stately equipage.[1017] *Exit* HILARIO
SOPHIA They have confessed, then,
They were set on by the queen to taint me in
My loyalty to my lord?
CORISCA 'Twas the main cause
That brought 'em hither.
SOPHIA I am glad I know it,

1003 6 against their stomachs: (literally) to the detriment of their health, (figuratively) against their wishes
1004 6 by degree: gradually
1005 8 pittance: small amount of food
1006 9 stopped: held
1007 12 barley-crust: scraps of bread made from barley
1008 12 parings: shavings, rinds
1009 13 palled: stale
1010 14 festival exceedings: extra food served on holidays
1011 15 spinster: i.e. Ubaldo
1012 18 curst: disagreeable, demanding
1013 18 other: Ricardo
1014 19 For his time: considering how little practice he has had
1015 20 airing: exercise in the open air
1016 25 by the nose: in an obedient fashion
1017 32 equipage: ceremony, formality

And, as I have begun, before I end
I'll at the height[1018] revenge it. Let us step aside;
They come. The object's[1019] so ridiculous,
In spite of my sad thoughts I cannot but
Lend a forced smile to grace[1020] it.

Enter HILARIO [*with*] UBALDO *spinning* [*and*] RICARDO *reeling*

HILARIO Come away!
Work as you go and lose no time—'tis precious;
You'll find it in your commons.[1021]
RICARDO Commons, call you it?
The word is proper: I have grazed so long
Upon your commons I am almost starved here.
HILARIO Work harder and they shall be bettered.
UBALDO Bettered?
Worser they cannot be. Would I might lie
Like a dog under her table and serve for a footstool,
So I might have my belly full of that[1022]
Her Iceland cur[1023] refuses.
HILARIO How do you like
Your airing? Is it not a favor?
RICARDO Yes,
Just such a one as you use[1024] to a brace[1025] of greyhounds
When they are led out of their kennels to scumber.[1026]
But our case is ten times harder: we have nothing
In our bellies to be vented.[1027] If you will be
An honest yeoman fewterer,[1028] feed us first
And walk us after!
HILARIO Yeoman fewterer?
Such another word to your governor,[1029] and you go
Supperless to bed for't.
UBALDO Nay, even as you please.
The comfortable[1030] names of breakfasts, dinners,
Collations,[1031] supper, beverage, are words
Worn out of our remembrance.
RICARDO Oh, for the steam
Of meat in a cook's shop!
UBALDO I am so dry
I have not spittle enough to wet my fingers
When I draw my flax from my distaff.

1018 37 at the height: in the most severe manner
1019 38 object: sight
1020 40 grace: favor, lend approval to
1021 42 You'll find … your commons: i.e. you will have your food allowance reduced. Hilario uses the word "commons" in the sense "rations," and Ricardo uses it in the sense "shared land where livestock graze"
1022 48 that: that which
1023 49 Iceland cur: Icelandic sheepdog, popular as a lapdog
1024 51 use: grant
1025 51 brace: pair
1026 52 scumber: defecate
1027 54 vented: discharged
1028 55 yeoman fewterer: servant in charge of greyhounds
1029 57 governor: keeper
1030 59 comfortable: comforting, sustaining
1031 60 Collations: light meals

RICARDO Nor I strength
To raise my hand to the top of my reeler. Oh,
I have the cramp[1032] all over me!
HILARIO What do you think
Were best to apply to it? A cramp-stone,[1033] as I take it,
Were very useful.
RICARDO Oh, no more of stones!
We have been used too long like hawks[1034] already.
UBALDO We are not so high in our flesh[1035] now to need casting.[1036]
We will come to an empty fist.[1037]
HILARIO Nay, that you shall not.
[*Throwing them food*] So ho, birds! How the eyases[1038] scratch and scramble.
Take heed of a surfeit; do not cast your gorges.[1039]
This is more than I have commission for.[1040] Be thankful.
SOPHIA Were all that study the abuse of women
Used thus, the city would not swarm with cuckolds
Nor so many tradesmen break.[1041]
CORISCA Pray you, appear now
And mark the alteration. [SOPHIA *and* CORISCA *move forward*]
HILARIO To your work!
My lady is in presence; show your duties
Exceeding well.
SOPHIA How do your scholars profit?
HILARIO Hold up your heads demurely.[1042] Prettily
For young beginners.
CORISCA And will do well in time
If they be kept in awe.
RICARDO In awe? I am sure
I quake like an aspen leaf.
UBALDO No mercy, lady?
RICARDO Nor intermission?[1043]
SOPHIA Let me see your[1044] work.
Fie upon't! What a thread's here? A poor cobbler's wife
Would make a finer to sew a clown's rent.[1045] Start up![1046]
And here you reel as you were drunk.
RICARDO I am sure
It is not with wine.
SOPHIA Oh, take heed of wine!
Cold water is far better for your healths,
Of which I am very tender;[1047] you had foul bodies

1032 66 cramp: hunger pangs
1033 67 cramp-stone: stone or pebble carried to ward off cramp
1034 69 like hawks: hawks eat small stones to aid their digestion
1035 70 high in our flesh: accustomed to luxurious food
1036 70 casting: purging, being made to vomit
1037 71 an empty fist: i.e. without a lure
1038 72 eyases: untrained hawks
1039 73 cast your gorges: make yourselves sick
1040 74 This is . . . commission for: giving you this food is more than I have permission to do
1041 77 break: be made bankrupt
1042 81 demurely: meekly, quietly
1043 85 intermission: respite
1044 85 your: Ubaldo's
1045 87 rent: tear
1046 87 Start up: stir yourself
1047 91 I am very tender: I am taking very good care

And must continue in this physical[1048] diet
Till the cause of your disease be ta'en away
For fear of a relapse, and that is dangerous.
Yet I hope already that you are in some
Degree recovered, and that way to resolve[1049] me
Answer me truly—nay, what I propound[1050]
Concerns both nearer.[1051] What would you now give
If your means were in your hands to lie all night
With a fresh and handsome lady?
UBALDO How! A lady?
Oh, I am past it! Hunger with her razor
Hath made me an eunuch.
RICARDO For a mess of porridge[1052]
Well sopped,[1053] with a bunch of radish and a carrot,
I would sell my barony.[1054] But for women? Oh,
No more of women! Not a doit[1055] for a doxy
After this hungry voyage.
SOPHIA These are truly
Good symptoms. Let them not venture too much in the air
Till they are weaker.
RICARDO This is tyranny!
UBALDO Scorn upon scorn!
SOPHIA You were so
In your malicious intents to me.
And therefore 'tis but justice.

Enter a SERVANT

What's the business?
SERVANT My lord's great friend, Signor Baptista, madam,
Is newly lighted from his horse with certain
Assurance of my lord's arrival.
SOPHIA How!
And stand I trifling[1056] here? Hence with the mongrels
To their several kennels; there let them howl in private.
I'll be no further troubled. *Exeunt* SOPHIA *and* SERVANT
UBALDO Oh, that ever
I saw this fury![1057]
RICARDO Or looked on a woman
But as a prodigy[1058] in nature.
HILARIO Silence!
No more of this.
CORISCA Methinks you have no cause
To repent your being here.

1048 92 physical: medicinal
1049 96 resolve: reassure
1050 97 propound: propose
1051 98 nearer: more directly
1052 102 mess of porridge: dish of thick soup or stew
1053 103 sopped: steeped in liquid
1054 104 barony: rank or lands of a baron
1055 105 doit: small Dutch coin worth half an English farthing
1056 115 trifling: wasting time
1057 118 fury: avenging female deity
1058 119 prodigy: monster, aberration

HILARIO Have you not learnt
When your states[1059] are spent your several trades to live by
And never charge the hospital?[1060]
CORISCA Work but tightly[1061]
And we will not use a dishclout[1062] in the house
But of your spinning.
UBALDO Oh, I would this hemp
Were turned to a halter!
HILARIO Will you march?
RICARDO A soft[1063] one,
Good general, I beseech you.
UBALDO I can hardly
Draw my legs after me.
HILARIO For a crutch you may use
Your distaff; a good wit makes use of all things.

Exeunt

Act V, scene ii

Enter SOPHIA [*and*] BAPTISTA

SOPHIA Was he jealous of me?
BAPTISTA There's no perfect love
Without some touch of't, madam.
SOPHIA And my picture,
Made by your devilish art, a spy upon
My actions? I never sat to be drawn,
Nor had you, sir, commission for't,
BAPTISTA Excuse me;
At his earnest suit I did it.
SOPHIA Very good!
Was I grown so cheap in his opinion of me?
BAPTISTA The prosperous events that crowned his fortunes
May qualify[1064] the offence.
SOPHIA Good! The "events,"
The sanctuary fools and madmen fly to
When their rash and desperate undertakings thrive well.
But good and wise men are directed by
Grave counsels, and with such deliberation
Proceed in their affairs that chance has nothing
To do with 'em. Howsoe'er, take the pains, sir,
To meet the honor in the king and queen's
Approaches to my house that breaks[1065] upon me;
I will expect them with my best of care.
BAPTISTA To entertain such royal guests—
SOPHIA I know it.
Leave that to me, sir. *Exit* BAPTISTA

1059 122 states: estates, inheritances
1060 121–3: Have you . . . the hospital: you each have learned a trade so when you have wasted all your money you will not have to depend on charity
1061 123 tightly: vigorously, effectively
1062 124 dishclout: dishcloth
1063 126 soft: leisurely
1064 9 qualify: mitigate
1065 17 breaks: rushes

What should move[1066] the queen,
So given to ease and pleasure, as fame speaks her,[1067]
To such a journey? Or work on my lord
To doubt my loyalty? Nay, more, to take
For the resolution of his fears a course
That is by holy writ denied a Christian?
'Twas impious in him, and perhaps the welcome
He hopes in my embraces may deceive
His expectation. [*Trumpets play in the distance*]
The trumpets speak
The king's arrival. Help a woman's wit, now,
To make him know his fault and my just anger.
Exit SOPHIA

Act V, scene iii

Loud music. Enter MATHIAS, EUBULUS, LADISLAUS, FERDINAND, HONORIA, BAPTISTA, [*and*] ACANTHE, *with Attendants*

EUBULUS Your majesty must be weary.
HONORIA No, my lord,
A willing mind makes a hard journey easy.
MATHIAS Not Jove, attended on by Hermes,[1068] was
More welcome to the cottage of Philemon
And his poor Baucis[1069] than your gracious self,
Your matchless queen, and all your royal train
Are to your servant and his wife.
LADISLAUS Where is she?
HONORIA I long to see her as my now-loved rival.
EUBULUS And I to have a smack at her.[1070] 'Tis a cordial[1071]
To an old man, better than sack and a toast[1072]
Before he goes to supper.
MATHIAS Ha! Is my house turned
To a wilderness? Nor wife nor servants ready
With all rites due to majesty to receive
Such unexpected blessings? [*To* BAPTISTA] You assured me
Of better preparation. Hath not
Th'excess of joy transported her beyond
Her understanding?
BAPTISTA I now[1073] parted from her,
And gave her your directions.
MATHIAS How shall I beg
Your majesties' patience? Sure, my family's drunk,
Or by some witch in envy of my glory
A dead sleep thrown upon 'em.

1066 20 move: provoke
1067 21 fame speaks her: her reputation suggests
1068 3 Hermes: the Greek name for Mercury
1069 3–5 Philemon and Baucis were a husband and wife who welcomed the disguised Jupiter and Mercury when other residents of their town rejected them
1070 9 smack at her: the chance to kiss her
1071 9 cordial: restorative medicine
1072 10 toast: browned bread often put into wine
1073 17 now: just now

Enter HILARIO *and* SERVANTS

FIRST SERVANT Sir—
MATHIAS But that
The sacred presence of the king forbids it,
My sword should make a massacre among you.
Where is your mistress?
HILARIO First, you are welcome home, sir,
Then know she says she's sick, sir. [*Aside*] There's no notice
Taken of my bravery.[1074]
MATHIAS Sick at such a time?
It cannot be. Though she were on her deathbed,
And her spirit even now departed, here stand they
Could call it back again, and in this honor
Give her a second being. Bring me to her.
I know not what to urge, or how to redeem
This mortgage of her manners.[1075] *Exeunt* MATHIAS *and* HILARIO
EUBULUS There's no climate
On the world I think where one jade's trick[1076] or other
Reigns not in women.
FERDINAND You were ever bitter
Against the sex.
LADISLAUS This is very strange.
HONORIA Mean women
Have their faults as well as queens.
LADISLAUS Oh, she appears now.

Enter MATHIAS, SOPHIA[, *and* HILARIO]

MATHIAS The injury that you conceive I have done you
Dispute hereafter, and in your perverseness[1077]
Wrong not yourself and me.
SOPHIA I am past my childhood
And need no tutor.
MATHIAS This is the great king,
To whom I am engaged till death for all
I stand possessed of.
SOPHIA My humble roof is proud, sir,
To be the canopy of so much greatness,
Set off with goodness.
LADISLAUS My own praises flying
In such pure air as your sweet breath, fair lady,
Cannot but please me.
MATHIAS This is the queen of queens
In her magnificence[1078] to me.
SOPHIA In my duty
I kiss her highness's robe.
HONORIA You stoop too low
To her whose lips would meet with yours.

1074 26 bravery: fine clothing
1075 32 mortgage of her manners: i.e. her lost honor
1076 33 jade's trick: unmannerly or disruptive behavior
1077 38 perverseness: contrariness, stubbornness
1078 47 magnificence: generosity, bounty

SOPHIA How'er
It may appear preposterous[1079] in women
So to encounter, 'tis your pleasure, madam,
And not my proud ambition. [*Kisses her; turns to* MATHIAS]
Do you hear, sir?
Without a magical picture, in the touch
I find your print of close and wanton kisses
On the queen's lips.
MATHIAS Upon your life, be silent.
And now salute these lords.
SOPHIA Since you'll have me,[1080]
You shall see I am experienced at the game
And can play it tightly. [*To* FERDINAND] You are a brave man, sir,
And do deserve a free and hearty welcome;
Be this the prologue to it. [*Kisses him*]
EUBULUS An old man's turn
Is ever last in kissing. I have lips too,
However cold ones, madam.
SOPHIA I will warm 'em
With the fire of mine. [*Kisses him*]
EUBULUS And so she has, I thank you,
I shall sleep the better all night for't.
MATHIAS You express
The boldness of a wanton courtesan,
And not a matron's modesty. Take up,[1081]
Or you are disgraced forever.
SOPHIA How? With kissing
Feelingly, as you taught me? Would you have me
Turn my cheek to 'em, as proud ladies use
To their inferiors, as if they intended
Some business should be whispered in their ear
And not a salutation? What I do
I will do freely; now I am in the humor
I'll fly at[1082] all. Are there any more?
MATHIAS Forbear,
Or you will raise my anger to a height
That will descend in fury.
SOPHIA Why? You know
How to resolve yourself what my intents are[1083]
By the help of Mephistopheles[1084] and your picture.
Pray you look upon't again. I humbly thank
The queen's great care of me while you were absent;
She knew how tedious 'twas for a young wife,
And being for that time a kind of widow
To pass away her melancholy hours
Without good company, and in charity therefore
Provided for me. Out of her own store
She culled[1085] the Lords Ubaldo and Ricardo,

1079 50 preposterous: unnatural, ridiculous
1080 56 have me: ask me do this
1081 66 Take up: hold back
1082 74 fly at: rush upon, attack
1083 77 How to find out what I intend to do
1084 78 Mephistopheles: Baptista (referring to the devil summoned in Marlowe's *Doctor Faustus*)
1085 86 culled: picked

Two principal courtiers for ladies' service,
To do me all good offices, and as such
Employed by her. I hope I have received
And entertained 'em, nor shall they depart
Without the effect[1086] arising from the cause
That brought 'em hither.
MATHIAS Thou dost belie[1087] thyself.
I know that in my absence thou wert honest,
However now turned monster.
SOPHIA The truth is,
We did not deal like you in speculations
On cheating pictures; we knew shadows were
No substances and actual performance
The best assurance. I will bring 'em hither
To make good in this presence. So much for me.
Some minute's space I beg your majesties' pardon.
[*To* MATHIAS] You are moved now; champ upon this bit a little,
Anon you shall have another.—Wait[1088] me, Hilario. *Exeunt* SOPHIA *and* HILARIO
LADISLAUS How now? Turned statue, sir?
MATHIAS Fly, and fly quickly
From this cursed habitation, or this Gorgon[1089]
Will make you all as I am. In her tongue
Millions of adders hiss, and every hair
Upon her wicked head a snake more dreadful
Than that Tisiphon[1090] threw on Athamas,
Which in his madness forced him to dismember
His proper issue.[1091] Oh, that ever I
Reposed[1092] my trust in magic, or believed
Impossibilities, or that charms had power
To sink and search into the bottomless hell
Of a false woman's heart![1093]
EUBULUS These are the fruits
Of marriage; an old bachelor, as I am,
And what's more will continue so, is not troubled
With these fine fegaries.[1094]
FERDINAND Till you are resolved,[1095] sir,
Forsake not hope.
BAPTISTA Upon my life this is
Dissimulation.
LADISLAUS And it suits not with
Your fortitude and wisdom to be thus
Transported with your passion.
HONORIA You were once
Deceived in me, sir, as I was in you,
Yet the deceit pleased both.

1086 91 effect: consequences
1087 92 belie: slander, misrepresent
1088 102 Wait: attend upon
1089 104 Gorgon: in Greek myth, one of a group of women with snakes for hair, who turned everyone who met their eyes to stone
1090 108 Tisiphon: i.e. Tisiphone, one of the mythical furies, who punished the crime of murder
1091 108–10 Athamas . . . proper issue: Athamas was a Boeotian king who, having been driven mad by Tisiphone, killed his own son, Learchus
1092 111 Reposed: placed
1093 114 Of a false woman's heart: this reading is Mason's emendation of Q's "For a false woman's heart"
1094 117 fegaries: pranks, whims
1095 117 resolved: freed from uncertainty

MATHIAS She hath confessed all,
What further proof should I ask?
HONORIA Yet remember
The distance that is interposed between
A woman's tongue and her heart, and you must grant
You build upon no certainties.

Enter SOPHIA, CORISCA, HILARIO, UBALDO *and* RICARDO, [*spinning and reeling*] *as before*

EUBULUS What have we here?
SOPHIA You must come on and show yourselves.
UBALDO The king!
RICARDO And queen too! Would I were as far under the earth
As I am above it.
UBALDO Some poet will
From this relation, or in verse or prose,
Or both together blended, render us
Ridiculous to all ages.
LADISLAUS I remember
This face when it was in a better plight.[1096]
Are not you Ricardo?
HONORIA And this thing, I take it,
Was once Ubaldo.
UBALDO I am now I know not what.
RICARDO We thank your majesty for employing us
To this subtle Circe.[1097]
EUBULUS How, my lord? Turned spinster?
Do you work by the day or by the grate?[1098]
FERDINAND Is your theorbo[1099]
Turned to a distaff, signor, and your voice
With which you chanted "Room for a lusty gallant!"
Turned to the note of "Lachrimae"?[1100]
EUBULUS Prithee tell me,
For I know thou art free,[1101] how often and to the purpose
Have you been merry with this lady.
RICARDO Never, never!
LADISLAUS Howsoever, you should say so for your credit,
Being the only court bull.[1102]
UBALDO Oh, that ever
I saw this kicking heifer![1103]
SOPHIA You see, madam,
How I have cured your servants, and what favors
They with their rampant[1104] valor have won from me.
You may, as they are physicked,[1105] I presume,
Trust a fair virgin with 'em. They have learned

1096 134 plight: condition
1097 138 Circe: sorceress encountered by Ulysses who enslaved men and turned them into pigs
1098 139 grate: fireplace (i.e. at night)
1099 139 theorbo: base lute
1100 142 "Lachrimae": a famous Elizabethan lute song by John Dowland
1101 143 free: uninhibited
1102 146 bull: stud
1103 147 heifer: young cow
1104 149 rampant: unrestrained
1105 150 physicked: cured, disciplined

Their several[1106] trades to live by, and paid nothing
But cold and hunger for 'em, and may now
Set up for themselves, for here I give 'em over.
[*To* MATHIAS] And now to you, sir. Why do you not again
Peruse your picture and take the advice
Of your learned consort?[1107] These are the men, or none,
That made you, as the Italian says, a *becco*.[1108]
MATHIAS I know not which way to entreat your pardon,
Nor am I worthy of it, my Sophia,
My best Sophia. Here before the king,
The queen, these lords, and all the lookers-on,
I do renounce my error, and embrace you
As the great example to all aftertimes
For such as would die chaste, and noble wives
With reverence to imitate.
SOPHIA Not so, sir.
I yet hold off. However I have purged
My doubted innocence, the foul aspersions
In your unmanly doubts cast on my honor
Cannot so soon be washed off.
EUBULUS Shall we have
More jiggumbobs[1109] yet?
SOPHIA When you went to the wars
I set no spy upon you to observe
Which way you wandered; though our sex by nature
Is subject to suspicions and fears,
My confidence in your loyalty freed me from 'em.
But to deal as you did 'gainst your religion,
With this enchanter to survey my actions,
Was more than woman's weakness. Therefore know,
And 'tis my boon[1110] unto the king, I do
Desire a separation from your bed,
For I will spend the remnant[1111] of my life
In prayer and meditation.
MATHIAS Oh, take pity
Upon my weak condition, or I am
More wretched in your innocence than if
I had found you guilty! Have you shown a jewel
Out of the cabinet of your rich mind
To lock it up again? She turns away.
Will none speak for me? Shame and sin hath robbed me
Of the use of my tongue.
LADISLAUS Since you have conquered, madam,
You wrong the glory of your victory
If you use it not with mercy.
FERDINAND Any penance
You please to impose upon him I dare warrant
He will gladly suffer.
EUBULUS Have I lived to see

1106 152 several: respective
1107 157 consort: partner (i.e. Baptista)
1108 158 *becco*: cuckold
1109 171 jiggumbobs: thingamabobs, knick-knacks
1110 179 boon: request
1111 181 remnant: rest, remaining part

But one good woman, and shall we for a trifle
Have her turn nun? I will first pull down the cloister.
To the old sport[1112] again with a good luck to you;
'Tis not alone enough that you are good,
We must have some of the breed of you. Will you destroy
The kind and race of goodness? I am converted,
And ask your pardon, madam, for my ill opinion
Against the sex, and show me but two such more
I'll marry yet, and love 'em.
HONORIA She that yet
Ne'er knew what 'twas to bend[1113] but to the king,
Thus begs remission for him. [*She kneels*]
SOPHIA O dear madam,
Wrong not your greatness so.
OMNES[1114] We all are suitors.
UBALDO I do deserve to be heard among the rest.
RICARDO And we have suffered for it.
SOPHIA I perceive
There's no resistance.[1115] But suppose I pardon
What's past, who can secure[1116] me he'll be free
From jealousy hereafter?
MATHIAS I will be
My own security. Go ride where you please,
Feast, revel, banquet, and make choice with whom.
I'll set no watch upon you, and for proof of't
This cursèd picture I surrender up
To a consuming fire.[1117]
BAPTISTA As I abjure
The practice of my art.
SOPHIA Upon these terms
I am reconciled, and for these[1118] that have paid
The price of their folly I desire your mercy.
LADISLAUS At your request they have it.
UBALDO Hang all trades now.
RICARDO I will find a new one, and that is to live honest.
HILARIO These[1119] are my fees.
UBALDO Pray you take 'em, with a mischief.[1120]
LADISLAUS So all ends in peace now,
And to all married men be this a caution,
Which they should duly tender[1121] as their life,
Neither to dote too much nor doubt a wife.

Exeunt omnes

FINIS.

1112 196 old sport: sex, procreation
1113 203 bend: kneel
1114 205 SP OMNES: all (Latin)
1115 208 resistance: resisting
1116 209 secure: guarantee
1117 214–15 I surrender … consuming fire: setting fire to the picture on stage would make a spectacular finale; necromantic books are destroyed by fire in the anonymous play *The Two Noble Ladies* (*c.* 1619–23), and a copy of the Koran is burned in the second part of Christopher Marlowe's *Tamburlaine* (c. 1587)
1118 217 these: Ubaldo and Ricardo
1119 221 These: Ricardo's clothes
1120 221 with a mischief: an expletive (compare "and be damned")
1121 224 tender: cherish

8 Christopher Marlowe, *The Tragical History of Doctor Faustus*

First performed c.1588

First printed 1604

Edited by Peter Kirwan

Doctor Faustus is many things to many people. In his opening speech, he tells us that he has achieved fame as a physician, a theologian, and a philosopher. In the course of Marlowe's play he raises spirits, offers political advice, provides (and takes away) food, even deals in horses. In broader culture, Faustus is a warning, a moral fable against hubris, a condemnation of a life lived in defiance of God; or, conversely, a critique of a God who stacks the deck against a foolish soul. But above and beyond all this, Faustus might best be thought of as the consummate performer.

When the acclaimed actor Edward Alleyn stood on the stage of the Rose theater, drew his magic circle, put on his magic garment, and began reading an incantation in Latin from a hefty tome, he *was* performing magic; at least, that is, he was going through all the motions of a magical conjuration, written out in full in the early texts, and helpfully illustrated in a woodcut on the title page of the 1616 edition. Alleyn presumably had no intention of literally raising a spirit, but anecdotal evidence suggests that successful conjuration was not dependent on intention. The anti-theatrical pamphleteer William Prynne described a Tudor performance of *Faustus* when an actual devil appeared on stage, causing "distraction"; another commentator described a performance that ended in chaos when the actors onstage suddenly realised that "there was one devil too many amongst them." Such anecdotes are apocryphal, of course, but their existence is indicative of the transgressive potential of the playgoing experience. Words are power, and early modern actors were extraordinary manipulators of words. Actors invited audiences to join them in conjuring worlds through shared imaginative power; what would happen if this power was sufficient to make the fictional real? Speaking words might result in unintended consequences; this is what happens to Rafe and Robin, who fumble their way through a stolen book and pay dearly for summoning Mephistopheles.

Doctor Faustus takes place in a world where the barriers between the natural and the supernatural are stretched very thin indeed. Early modern confessional and superstitious practices were organized around these thin barriers, from the liminal space of the communion rail or saint's grave to the commonplace understanding that devils and angels attended the beds of the dying. The theater itself was constructed on supernatural lines, with actors suspended in the amphitheater between the "heavens"—the roof of the theater from which descended the gods —and "hell," the space beneath the stage accessed by trapdoor, where bodies were laid and from which demons emerged. The proximity of heaven and hell to the stage, which in the *theatricum mundi* metaphor itself represented the world, made the actor both the summoner and the victim of supernatural forces.

When Faustus first summons Mephistopheles, he demands of the devil "Did not my conjuring speeches raise thee?" Mephistopheles's reply is that this is *per accidens*—by happenstance—for "when we hear one rack the name of God . . . We fly, in hope to get his glorious soul" (iv. 43–7). That is, Mephistopheles was already listening for the words. Both Faustus and Mephistopheles identify the words spoken as the key to their meeting, and the importance of words reappears throughout the play. Once he has agreed to sell his soul to Lucifer, Faustus writes out his terms as a "deed of gift" (vi. 34) written in his own blood. His blood rebels at the action, however, and needs to be warmed by fire in order to flow again; even once he has signed, though, Faustus notes that the cuts on his arm have formed the words "*Homo fuge*" (vi. 74): "Fly, man." First his blood resists being turned into words, then the scars form their own. Even if none of these words is actually visible on the stage, their macabre evoked presence places text at the level of blood and skin, Faustus himself becoming both the ink and the parchment for the words that bridge the divide between earth and hell.

The importance of words in their physical manifestation is made explicit in the opening scene of the play, when Faustus is discovered leafing through his books. These books are introduced only to be dismissed, and indeed it is hard to be sure how closely Faustus is paying attention to them. For instance, when he picks up his Bible, he says the following:

Jerome's Bible, Faustus, view it well.
Stipendium peccati mors est. Ha! *Stipendium* etc.
The reward of sin is death. That is hard.
Si peccasse negamus, fallimur,
Et nulla est in nobis veritas.

If we say that we have no sin,
We deceive ourselves, and there's no truth in us.
(ii. 38–44)

In this edition, as is typical for editions of *Doctor Faustus*, the Latin text is in italics; but does that mean Faustus is reading it? The "etc." in line 39 is particularly revealing. Does Faustus actually say "etc.," showing that he is dismissing the rest? The Biblical passage referred to here, Romans 6:23, concludes with "but the gift of God is eternal life through Jesus Christ our Lord," a promise of hope that Faustus either deliberately or accidentally fails to read. Similarly, lines 41–2 (taken from 1 John 1:8) also leave out the source passage's promise of salvation. More to the point, these passages are from different ends of the New Testament, and the Latin for both does not match any extant Latin version. Is Faustus, like some contemporary preachers, merely holding up the book without actually checking to see if he has read it properly? For all of his scholarly accreditation, his failure to read accurately is telling.

While the written word is integral to the truth claims of *Doctor Faustus*, however, Marlowe also uses theatrical space to illustrate Faustus's dilemma. In the earlier medieval morality plays such as *Everyman* and *Mankind*, the central protagonist becomes the target of competing forces looking to tempt or save him. In some of *Doctor Faustus*'s most memorable scenes, these morality plays are evoked by the Good Angel and the Evil Angel, who appear and "buzzeth in mine ears" (viii. 14). The rhetorical back-and-forth between the competing angels, most likely with Faustus between them, mimics the earlier appearance of Valdes and Cornelius, with whom the angels are sometimes doubled in performance, and sets up the equivocation that leads to Faustus's fall.

GOOD ANGEL Faustus, repent yet; God will pity thee.
EVIL ANGEL Thou art a spirit; God cannot pity thee.
FAUSTUS Who buzzeth in mine ears I am a spirit?
Be I a devil, yet God may pity me.
Aye, God will pity me, if I repent.
EVIL ANGEL Aye, but Faustus never shall repent.
(viii. 12–17)

The Good Angel promises that God "will" pity Faustus; the Evil Angel, blasphemously, retorts that God "cannot," placing a restriction on God's agency. A wavering Faustus takes the spatial and confessional middle ground, allowing that God "may" forgive him, according to God the agency, but then rephrases this in the conditional: "*if*" he repents, God "*will*" pity him. The Evil Angel picks up immediately on the trap that Faustus has set for himself, now reversing its previous statement to agree that God "will"—or rather, *would*—pity Faustus, but that Faustus will never repent. Faustus is outflanked physically and outwitted verbally by the flexible Evil Angel, unrestricted to this temporal plane, who leads Faustus into traps created by his own limited use of words.

For a man who begins the play focusing entirely on the written word, Faustus is easily won over by visuals. Marlowe makes extensive use of the special effects available in the early modern amphitheaters. When Faustus seems to be paying too much attention to the words of warning on his arm, Mephistopheles shows him a dance of devils. When he wants marriage, Mephistopheles offers a devil in woman's clothes "*with fireworks*" (vi. 135 SD) and this distracts him from pursuing the matter. And when Faustus openly rebels against Mephistopheles, Lucifer and Beelzebub themselves appear to present Faustus with the pageant of the Seven Deadly Sins. This serio-comic set-piece is a highlight of the play, the brief sketches of the Sins witty and full of character, but as he delights in them, Faustus forgets that these will be his companions for eternity. Again, for all his learnedness, Faustus is as limited as any human when it comes to imagining unending time, still assuming that he might "see hell, and return again" (viii. 139). In this short scene, Marlowe once again foregrounds the institution of theater, perhaps holding up a mirror to spectators who are likewise enjoying their brief flirtation with the infernal without considering the lasting consequences.

What Faustus learns, he puts into action. The second half of *Doctor Faustus* sees Faustus traveling the world and associating with all ranks. It is here that the two early texts of *Doctor Faustus*, the 1604 (A) text and 1616 (B) text, begin to diverge significantly. The B-text, which probably represents a version revised after Marlowe's death, creates a narrative of Faustus intervening in European politics and rescuing a rival candidate for the Pope, but the A-text—probably closer to the play as it was first staged—treats Faustus's uses of his powers as petty and even childish, mimicking the grotesque pageantry he has witnessed in his study. He becomes invisible in order to steal the Pope's food and box him on the ears; he calls up spirits mimicking Alexander the Great and Helen of Troy for the amusement of others; he puts horns on the head of a knight who mocks him; he sells a bewitched horse to a horse-courser, and then terrifies the man when his leg magically detaches. It is of note that the more powerful Faustus becomes, the less consequential his party tricks become, and by the time he summons up some grapes for the Duchess of Vanholt, he is indistinguishable from a stage magician, performing on demand. The "tragedy" of Doctor Faustus is ostensibly his damnation, but the A-text allows for a different reading, suggesting that the real tragedy is that a man who began the play as a healer and a thinker of consequence has become little more than a court performer, bringing the same kind of pleasure to his noble patrons that the actors performing *Doctor Faustus* do.

Faustus is, then, a consummate performer; he is also, ultimately, no more than a performer, and a performer who has forgotten what play he is in. The final scenes repeatedly stage opportunities for Faustus to repent and escape his fate, while simultaneously denying those opportunities, and his fate is contrasted with that of the Old Man, menaced to death by devils but embracing God as he dies. Faustus's last monologue aligns the end of the play with the end of his life (a point made vividly in the Latin motto that closes the printed text, "*Terminat hora diem, terminat author opus*"—the hour ends the day; the author ends the work). Faustus, who has been suspended between the competing forces of good and evil for the whole play, is finally and categorically dragged down to hell. The play's overt moral message is clear, although the sheer scale of the forces stacked up against Faustus may provoke legitimate critique of how far his fate was pre-determined. His final cry of "I'll burn my books" (xvi. 103) offers a last alignment of the written word with an act of performance; Faustus is at this point capable only of imagining an act of spectacle reminiscent of the fires of hell, not of uttering the words that might, indeed that would, redeem him. Whether Faustus needs to burn his books or to read them more carefully may be the play's most searching question.

Textual note

Published in nine quarto editions between 1604 and 1631, *Doctor Faustus* was one of the most frequently reprinted of early modern plays. The fourth quarto (1616) presented a radically different version of the play from that which had previously been published, with longer comic set-pieces and more substantial interconnections between the different episodes. This version is referred to by scholars as the B-text. The 1604 text, on which this edition is based, is shorter and more episodic, and is known as the A-text. In the wake of the textual scholarship of the New Bibliography in the early twentieth century, scholars tended to treat the A-text as a corrupt or partial version of the longer, more authoritative B-text. More recently, work by Eric Rasmussen and Leah Marcus (among others) has rehabilitated the A-text, suggesting that both versions represent the play at different points in its theatrical life, with the B-text incorporating revisions made during the play's performance history.

The copy-text for this edition is the EEBO copy of the 1604 quarto in the Bodleian Library, STC 17429, with occasional emendations from the 1616 text. This quarto is printed in black letter and, as is conventional for early quartos, has no scene divisions. Given the episodic nature of the play, and the irregular placement of Choruses, this edition divides the play into scenes only, without imposing act divisions. The primary difficulty posed by the A-text is its placement of the comic scenes featuring Wagner, Rafe, and Robin, which are grouped together out of sequence with the rest of the play. This is the first edition to put Scene xiii in its current location, noting the need for passage of time between Scenes xii and xiv.

Further reading

Editions

Bevington, David, and Eric Rasmussen (eds) (1993) *Doctor Faustus: A- and B-texts (1604, 1616)*, Manchester: Manchester University Press.
Gill, Roma (ed.) (2008) *Doctor Faustus*, revised edition by Ros King, London: Methuen.
Hanabusa, Chiaki (ed.) (2018) *Doctor Faustus 1604*, Manchester: Malone Society.
Menzer, Paul (ed.) (2019) *Doctor Faustus*, London: Methuen.

Critical and contextual reading

Deats, Sara Munson (2008) "'Mark this show': Magic and Theater in Marlowe's *Doctor Faustus*," in Sara Munson Deats and Robert A. Logan (eds), *Placing the Plays of Christopher Marlowe*, London: Routledge: 13–24.
Guenther, Genevieve (2011) "Why Devils Came when Faustus Called Them," *Modern Philology* 109: 46–70.
Healy, Thomas (2004) "*Doctor Faustus*" in Patrick Cheney (ed.), *The Cambridge Companion to Christopher Marlowe*, Cambridge: Cambridge University Press, 174–92.
Loehlin, James N. (2016) *Doctor Faustus: The Shakespeare Handbooks*, London: Palgrave Macmillan.
Love, Genevieve (2018) "Doctor Faustus's Leg," in Kirk Melnikoff and Roslyn L. Knutson (eds), *Christopher Marlowe, Theatrical Commerce, and the Book Trade*, Cambridge: Cambridge University Press: 81–92.
Marcus, Leah S. (1996) *Unediting the Renaissance: Shakespeare, Marlowe, Milton*, London: Routledge.
Poole, Kristen (2011) *Supernatural Environments in Shakespeare's England: Spaces of Demonism, Divinity, and Drama*, Cambridge: Cambridge University Press.
Rasmussen, Eric (1993) *A Textual Companion to Doctor Faustus*, Manchester: Manchester University Press.
Sofer, Andrew (2009) "How to Do Things with Demons: Conjuring Performatives in *Doctor Faustus*," *Theatre Journal* 61: 1–21.
Thomson, Leslie (2005) "Marlowe's Staging of Meaning," *Medieval and Renaissance Drama in England* 18: 19–36.
Woods, Gillian (2013) "Marlowe and Religion," in Emily C. Bartels and Emma Smith (eds), *Christopher Marlowe in Context*, Cambridge: Cambridge University Press, 222–31.

The Tragical History of Doctor Faustus (c. 1588)

Dramatis personae[1]

CHORUS
DOCTOR FAUSTUS
WAGNER, *Faustus' servant*
VALDES, *a scholar*
CORNELIUS, *a scholar*
ROBIN *the clown, an ostler*
RAFE, *an ostler*
POPE Adrian VI
CARDINAL *of Lorraine*
The HOLY ROMAN EMPEROR, *Charles V*
KNIGHT *at Charles V's court*
DUKE *of Vanholt*
DUCHESS *of Vanholt*
HORSE-COURSER
VINTNER
OLD MAN
MEPHISTOPHELES
GOOD ANGEL
BAD ANGEL
LUCIFER

Friars, Attendants, Three Scholars, Beelzebub, The Seven Deadly Sins (Pride, Covetousness, Wrath, Envy, Gluttony, Sloth, Lechery), Alexander the Great, Alexander's Paramour, Helen of Troy, Devils

[Scene i]

Enter CHORUS

CHORUS Not marching now in fields of Trasimene,[2]
Where Mars did mate[3] the Carthaginians,
Nor sporting in the dalliance[4] of love,
In courts of kings where state is overturned,
Nor in the pomp of proud audacious deeds,
Intends our muse to daunt[5] his heavenly verse.
Only this, gentlemen, we must perform:
The form of Faustus' fortunes, good or bad.

1 Dramatis personae: not in Q
2 1 Trasimene: Lake Trasimeno in Italy, where the Carthaginian general Hannibal won a famous victory over the Romans in 217 BC
3 2 mate: ally with
4 3 dalliance: frivolity
5 6 daunt: tame, exhaust

To patient judgments we appeal our plaud,[6]
And speak for Faustus in his infancy.
Now is he born, his parents base of stock,
In Germany, within a town called Rhodes.[7]
Of riper years to Württemberg[8] he went,
Whereas[9] his kinsmen chiefly brought him up.
So soon he profits in divinity,[10]
The fruitful plot of scholarism graced,[11]
That shortly he was graced with doctor's name,
Excelling all whose sweet delight disputes[12]
In heavenly matters of theology;
Till, swollen with cunning of a self-conceit,[13]
His waxen wings[14] did mount above his reach,
And melting heavens conspired his overthrow.
For, falling to a devilish exercise,
And glutted more with learning's golden gifts,
He surfeits upon cursed necromancy.[15]
Nothing so sweet as magic is to him,
Which he prefers before his chiefest bliss,[16]
And this the man that in his study sits.

Exit

[Scene ii]

Enter FAUSTUS *in his study*

FAUSTUS Settle thy studies, Faustus, and begin
To sound[17] the depth of that thou wilt profess.
Having commenced, be a divine[18] in show,
Yet level at[19] the end of every art
And live and die in Aristotle's works:
Sweet *Analytics*,[20] 'tis thou hast ravished me.
Bene disserere est finis logices.[21]
Is to dispute well logic's chiefest end?
Affords this art no greater miracle?
Then read no more, thou hast attained the end;
A greater subject fitteth Faustus' wit.
Bid *on kai me on*[22] farewell. Galen,[23] come!

6 9 appeal our plaud: appeal for applause
7 12 Rhodes: Roda, now Stadtroda, in Germany
8 13 Württemberg: part of the Holy Roman Empire, a dukedom in what is now south-west Germany
9 14 Whereas: Where
10 15 divinity: theology
11 16 The most favored area of scholarship
12 18 sweet delight disputes: chief pleasure is in debating
13 20 cunning of a self-conceit: pride in his skill
14 21 waxen wings: a reference to the myth of Icarus, who fashioned wings from wax but fell into the sea when he flew too close to the sun
15 25 necromancy: literally communication with the dead, but more broadly black magic or sorcery
16 27 his chiefest bliss: eternal life
17 2 sound: measure
18 3 divine: theologian
19 4 level at: aim for
20 6 *Analytics*: the Greek philosopher Aristotle's works on logic and deductive reasoning
21 7 The end of logic is to dispute well
22 12 *on kai me on*: being and not being, a Greek phrase
23 12 Galen: ancient Greek physician

Seeing *ubi desinit philosophus, ibi incipit medicus,*[24]
Be a physician,[25] Faustus, heap up gold,
And be eternized[26] for some wondrous cure.
Summum bonum medicinae sanitas:[27]
The end of physic is our bodies' health.
Why Faustus, hast thou not attained that end?
Is not thy common talk sound aphorisms?[28]
Are not thy bills hung up as monuments,
Whereby whole cities have escaped the plague,
And thousand desperate maladies been eased?
Yet art thou still but Faustus, and a man.
Wouldst thou[29] make man to live eternally
Or, being dead, raise them to life again,
Then this profession were to be esteemed.
Physic, farewell. Where is Justinian?[30]
Si una eadamque res legatur duobus,
Alter rem, alter valorem rei,[31] etc.
A pretty case of paltry legacies.
Exhaereditare filium non potest pater nisi:[32]
Such is the subject of the Institute
And universal body of the church.[33]
This study fits a mercenary drudge[34]
Who aims at nothing but external trash.
Too servile and illiberal[35] for me.
When all is done, divinity is best.
Jerome's Bible,[36] Faustus, view it well.
Stipendium peccati mors est.[37] Ha! *Stipendium* etc.
The reward of sin is death. That's hard.
Si peccasse negamus, fallimur,
Et nulla est in nobis veritas.[38]
If we say that we have no sin,
We deceive ourselves, and there's no truth in us.
Why then belike we must sin,
And so consequently die.
Aye, we must die an everlasting death.
What doctrine call you this? *Che serà, serà,*
What will be, shall be? Divinity, adieu.
These metaphysics of magicians,
And necromantic books are heavenly.
Lines, circles, scenes,[39] letters, and characters:

24 13 *ubi desinit philosophus, ibi incipit medicus*: where the philosopher ends, there the physician begins
25 14 physician: medical doctor
26 15 eternized: remembered eternally
27 16 The greatest good of medicine is health
28 19 sound aphorisms: accepted principles, sayings
29 24 Wouldst thou: were you to
30 27 Justinian: Roman emperor whose legacy was the recodifying of Roman law, including in his *Institutes*
31 28–9 *Si una . . . valorem rei*: if one and the same thing is bequeathed to two persons, one [shall be given] the thing, the other the value of the thing
32 31 It is not possible for a father to disinherit his son, unless . . .
33 33 church: i.e. church law
34 34 mercenary drudge: hack
35 36 illiberal: unrefined, by contrast with the "liberal" arts that Faustus professes
36 38 Jerome's Bible: the Vulgate Bible, in Latin; the canonical scripture of this period
37 39 *Stipendium peccati mors est*: the wages of sin is death
38 41–2 *Si peccasse . . . nobis veritas*: if we deny to have sinned, we are deceived and there is no truth in us
39 52 scenes: pictures

Aye, these are those that Faustus most desires.
O, what a world of profit and delight,
Of power, of honor, of omnipotence,
Is promised to the studious artisan!
All things that move between the quiet poles
Shall be at my command. Emperors and kings
Are but obeyed in their several provinces,
Nor can they raise the wind, or rend the clouds;
But his dominion that exceeds in this
Stretcheth as far as doth the mind of man.
A sound magician is a mighty god.
Here, Faustus, try thy brains to gain a deity.[40]

Enter WAGNER

Wagner, commend me to my dearest friends,
The German Valdes and Cornelius.
Request them earnestly to visit me.
WAGNER I will, sir. *Exit*
FAUSTUS Their conference will be a greater help to me
Than all my labors, plod I ne'er so fast.

Enter the GOOD ANGEL *and the* EVIL ANGEL

GOOD ANGEL O Faustus, lay that damnèd book[41] aside
And gaze not on it, lest it tempt thy soul
And heap God's heavy wrath upon thy head.
Read, read the scriptures; that is blasphemy.
EVIL ANGEL Go forward, Faustus, in that famous art
Wherein all nature's treasury is contained.
Be thou on earth as Jove[42] is in the sky:
Lord and commander of these elements. *Exeunt* [ANGELS]
FAUSTUS How am I glutted with conceit[43] of this!
Shall I make spirits fetch me what I please,
Resolve me of all ambiguities,
Perform what desperate enterprise I will?
I'll have them fly to India for gold,
Ransack the ocean for orient pearl,
And search all corners of the new-found world
For pleasant fruits and princely delicates.
I'll have them read me strange philosophy
And tell the secrets of all foreign kings.
I'll have them wall all Germany with brass,
And make swift Rhine circle fair Württemberg.[44]
I'll have them fill the public schools with silk,
Wherewith the students shall be bravely clad.[45]
I'll levy[46] soldiers with the coin they bring,

40 64 gain a deity: gain the powers of a god
41 71 that damnèd book: i.e. a book of necromancy
42 77 Jove: Jupiter, king of the gods in Roman mythology
43 79 glutted with conceit: overwhelmed by the thought
44 90 Rhine circle fair Württemberg: the River Rhine flowed along the western border of the duchy of Württemberg
45 92 bravely clad: splendidly dressed
46 93 levy: enlist

And chase the Prince of Parma[47] from our land,
And reign sole king of all our provinces;
Yea, stranger engines for the brunt of war
Than was the fiery keel at Antwerp's bridge[48]
I'll make my servile spirits to invent.
Come, German Valdes and Cornelius,
And make me blessed with your sage conference.

Enter VALDES *and* CORNELIUS

Valdes, sweet Valdes, and Cornelius,
Know that your words have won me at the last
To practice magic and concealèd arts:
Yet not your words only, but mine own fantasy,[49]
That will receive no object,[50] for my head
But[51] ruminates on necromantic skill.
Philosophy is odious and obscure;
Both law and physic are for petty wits;
Divinity is basest[52] of the three,
Unpleasant, harsh, contemptible, and vile.
'Tis magic, magic that hath ravished me.
Then, gentle friends, aid me in this attempt,
And I, that have with concise syllogisms[53]
Graveled[54] the pastors of the German Church,
And made the flow'ring pride[55] of Württemberg
Swarm to my problems as the infernal spirits
On sweet Musaeus[56] when he came to hell,
Will be as cunning as Agrippa[57] was,
Whose shadows made all Europe honor him.
VALDES Faustus, these books, thy wit, and our experience
Shall make all nations to canonize us.
As Indian Moors obey their Spanish lords,
So shall the subjects of every element
Be always serviceable to us three.
Like lions shall they guard us when we please,
Like Almaine rutters with their horsemen's staves,[58]
Or Lapland giants[59] trotting by our sides;
Sometimes like women, or unwedded maids,
Shadowing more beauty in their airy brows
Than in the white breasts of the queen of love.[60]
From Venice shall they drag huge argosies,[61]

47 94 Prince of Parma: Alexander Farnese, governor of the Spanish Netherlands from 1578–92
48 97 fiery keel at Antwerp's bridge: a fireship used to destroy a bridge during a battle in Antwerp in 1585
49 104 fantasy: imagination
50 105 receive no object: think about nothing else; entertain no objection
51 106 But: only
52 109 basest: lowest in rank
53 113 concise syllogisms: deductive reasoning
54 114 Graveled: perplexed
55 115 flow'ring pride: the youthful best
56 117 Musaeus: Musaeus of Athens is seen surrounded by spirits when Aeneas visits the underworld in Book VI of Virgil's *Aeneid*
57 118 Agrippa: renaissance necromancer, active in the early sixteenth century.
58 126 Almaine rutters with their horsemen's staves: German mounted soldiers with lances
59 127 Lapland giants: men from the polar regions, reputed to be unusually "tall and sturdy" (*2 Tamburlaine* I.i. 27)
60 130 queen of love: Aphrodite (Greek) or Venus (Roman)
61 131 argosies: merchant ships, loaded with wealth

And from America the golden fleece[62]
That yearly stuffs old Philip's[63] treasury,
If learnèd Faustus will be resolute.
FAUSTUS Valdes, as resolute am I in this
As thou to live; therefore object it not.
CORNELIUS The miracles that magic will perform
Will make thee vow to study nothing else.
He that is grounded in astrology,
Enriched with tongues, well seen[64] in minerals,
Hath all the principles magic doth require.
Then doubt not, Faustus, but to be renowned,
And more frequented for this mystery
Than heretofore the Delphian Oracle.[65]
The spirits tell me they can dry the sea,
And fetch the treasure of all foreign wracks;
Aye, all the wealth that our forefathers hid
Within the massy entrails of the earth.
Then tell me, Faustus, what shall we three want?[66]
FAUSTUS Nothing, Cornelius. O, this cheers my soul.
Come, show me some demonstrations magical,
That I may conjure in some lusty[67] grove
And have these joys in full possession.
VALDES Then haste thee to some solitary grove,
And bear wise Bacon's and Albanus' works,[68]
The Hebrew Psalter,[69] and New Testament;
And whatsoever else is requisite
We will inform thee ere our conference cease.
CORNELIUS Valdes, first let him know the words of art,
And then, all other ceremonies learned,
Faustus may try his cunning by himself.
VALDES First I'll instruct thee in the rudiments,[70]
And then wilt thou be perfecter than I.
FAUSTUS Then come and dine with me, and after meat
We'll canvas every quiddity[71] thereof;
For ere I sleep I'll try what I can do.
This night I'll conjure, though I die therefore.

Exeunt

[Scene iii]

Enter two SCHOLARS

FIRST SCHOLAR I wonder what's become of Faustus, that was wont to make our

62 132 golden fleece: in Greek mythology, the golden sheepskin that Jason and his Argonauts sailed in quest of to establish his right to the throne. In idiomatic use, any object of great value, here the treasures of the New World
63 133 old Philip: King Philip II of Spain
64 140 well seen: well versed
65 144 Delphian Oracle: the Oracle at Delphi, proverbial fount of wisdom
66 149 want: lack
67 152 lusty: pleasant
68 155 Bacon's and Albanus' works: Roger Bacon and Pietro d'Abano, thirteenth-century philosophers known for their conjuring
69 156 Psalter: the book of Psalms
70 162 rudiments: basics
71 165 quiddity: subtlety

schools ring with "*sic probo*."[72]

SECOND SCHOLAR That shall we know, for see, here comes his boy.

Enter WAGNER

FIRST SCHOLAR How now sirrah,[73] where's thy master?

WAGNER God in heaven knows.

SECOND SCHOLAR Why, dost not thou know?

WAGNER Yes, I know, but that follows not.

FIRST SCHOLAR Go to, sirrah, leave your jesting and tell us where he is.

WAGNER That follows not necessary by force of argument, that you, being licentiate,[74] should stand upon't. Therefore acknowledge your error, and be attentive.

SECOND SCHOLAR Why, didst thou not say thou knew'st?

WAGNER Have you any witness on't?

FIRST SCHOLAR Yes, sirrah, I heard you.

WAGNER Ask my fellow if I be a thief.

SECOND SCHOLAR Well, you will not tell us.

WAGNER Yes sir, I will tell you. Yet if you were not dunces, you would never ask me such a question, for is not he *corpus naturale*, and is not that *mobile*?[75] Then wherefore should you ask me such a question? But that I am by nature phlegmatic,[76] slow to wrath, and prone to lechery—to love, I would say—it were not for you to come within forty foot of the place of execution, although I do not doubt to see you both hanged the next sessions.[77] Thus, having triumphed over you, I will set my countenance like a precisian,[78] and begin to speak thus: truly, my dear brethren, my master is within at dinner with Valdes and Cornelius, as this wine, if it could speak, it would inform your worships. And so the Lord bless you, preserve you, and keep you, my dear brethren, my dear brethren. *Exit*

FIRST SCHOLAR Nay, then I fear he is fall'n into that damned art for which they two are infamous through the world.

SECOND SCHOLAR Were he a stranger, and not allied to me, yet should I grieve for him. But come, let us go and inform the rector,[79] and see if he, by his grave counsel, can reclaim him.

FIRST SCHOLAR O, but I fear me nothing can reclaim him.

SECOND SCHOLAR Yet let us try what we can do.

Exeunt

[Scene iv]

Enter FAUSTUS *to conjure*

FAUSTUS Now that the gloomy shadow of the earth,[80]
Longing to view Orion's drizzling look,[81]
Leaps from th'Antarctic world unto the sky
And dims the welkin[82] with her pitchy breath,
Faustus, begin thine incantations,
And try if devils will obey thy hest,[83]

72 2 *sic probo*: I prove it thus
73 4 sirrah: a contemptuous or patronizing form of address
74 9 licentiate: licenced to dispute, as scholars
75 17 *corpus naturale* . . . that *mobile*: a natural body, and therefore mobile
76 18 phlegmatic: in humoral theory, a person with an abundance of phlegm was calm and imperturbable
77 20 sessions: term
78 21 precisian: one who is pedantic or rigid in matters of form or religious observance
79 28 rector: head of the university
80 1 shadow of the earth: night
81 2 Orion's drizzling look: in the Northern hemisphere, the constellation Orion is most visible in winter
82 4 welkin: sky
83 6 hest: command

Seeing thou hast prayed and sacrificed to them.
Within this circle is Jehovah's[84] name,
Forward and backward, and anagrammatized,[85]
The 'breviated names of holy saints,
Figures of every adjunct[86] to the heavens,
And characters of signs and erring stars[87]
By which the spirits are enforced to rise.
Then fear not, Faustus, but be resolute,
And try the uttermost magic can perform.
Sint mihi dei Acherontis propitii. Valeat numen triplex Jehovae. Ignei, aerii, aquatici spiritus saluete. Orientis princeps Beelzebub, inferni ardentis monarcha, et Demogorgon, propitiamus vos ut apariat et surgat Mephistopheles. Quid tu moraris? Per Jehovam, Gehennam et consecratam aquam quam nunc spargo, signumque crucis quod nunc facio, et per vota nostra, ipse nunc surgat nobis dicatis Mephistopheles.[88]

Enter a DEVIL

I charge thee to return and change thy shape;
Thou art too ugly to attend on me.
Go and return an old Franciscan friar;
That holy shape becomes a devil best. *Exit* DEVIL
I see there's virtue in my heavenly words.
Who would not be proficient in this art?
How pliant is this Mephistopheles,
Full of obedience and humility!
Such is the force of magic and my spells.
No, Faustus, thou art conjurer laureate,[89]
That canst command great Mephistopheles.
Quin redis, Mephistopheles, fratris imagine?[90]

Enter MEPHISTOPHELES [*in habit of friar*]

MEPHISTOPHELES Now, Faustus, what wouldst thou have me do?
FAUSTUS I charge thee, wait upon me whilst I live,
To do whatever Faustus shall command,
Be it to make the moon drop from her sphere
Or the ocean to overwhelm the world.
MEPHISTOPHELES I am a servant to great Lucifer,
And may not follow thee without his leave;
No more than he commands must we perform.
FAUSTUS Did not he charge thee to appear to me?
MEPHISTOPHELES No, I came now hither of mine own accord.
FAUSTUS Did not my conjuring speeches raise thee? Speak.
MEPHISTOPHELES That was the cause, but yet *per accidens*,[91]

84 8 Jehovah: a Hebrew name for God
85 9 anagrammatized: made into anagrams
86 11 Figures of every adjunct: charts of astrological bodies
87 12 signs and erring stars: signs of the Zodiac and planets ("erring" means "wandering," i.e. the planets seem to wander through the sky)
88 16–20 *Sint mihi … dicatis Mephistopheles*: the gods of Acheron [a river in the underworld] be propitious to me. May the triple power of Jehovah be strong. Spirits of fire, air, and water, welcome. Beelzebub, Prince of the East, monarch of burning hell, and Demogorgon, we ask your favor that Mephistopheles may appear and rise. Why do you delay? By Jehovah, Gehenna [Hell], and the holy water which I now sprinkle, and by the sign of the cross which I now make, and by our prayers, let Mephistopheles himself now arise at our words
89 30 laureate: crowned with laurels; pre-eminent
90 32 Why not return in the image of a friar, Mephistopheles?
91 44 *per accidens*: by happenstance

For when we hear one rack[92] the name of God,
Abjure the scriptures and his savior, Christ,
We fly, in hope to get his glorious soul.
Nor will we come, unless he use such means
Whereby he is in danger to be damned.
Therefore, the shortest cut to conjuring
Is stoutly to abjure the Trinity[93]
And pray devoutly to the prince of hell.
FAUSTUS So Faustus hath already done, and holds this principle:
There is no chief but only Beelzebub,
To whom Faustus doth dedicate himself.
This word damnation terrifies not him,
For he confounds hell in Elysium.[94]
His ghost be with the old philosophers.
But, leaving these vain trifles of men's souls,
Tell me, what is that Lucifer, thy lord?
MEPHISTOPHELES Arch-regent and commander of all spirits.
FAUSTUS Was not that Lucifer an angel once?
MEPHISTOPHELES Yes, Faustus, and most dearly loved of God.
FAUSTUS How comes it then that he is prince of devils?
MEPHISTOPHELES O, by aspiring pride and insolence,
For which God threw him from the face of heaven.
FAUSTUS And what are you that live with Lucifer?
MEPHISTOPHELES Unhappy spirits that fell with Lucifer,
Conspired against our God with Lucifer,
And are for ever damned with Lucifer.
FAUSTUS Where are you damned?
MEPHISTOPHELES In hell.
FAUSTUS How comes it then that thou art out of hell?
MEPHISTOPHELES Why, this is hell, nor am I out of it.
Think'st thou that I, who saw the face of God
And tasted the eternal joys of heaven,
Am not tormented with ten thousand hells
In being deprived of everlasting bliss?
O Faustus, leave these frivolous demands,
Which strike a terror to my fainting soul.
FAUSTUS What, is great Mephistopheles so passionate
For being deprivèd of the joys of heaven?
Learn thou of Faustus manly fortitude,
And scorn those joys thou never shalt possess.
Go, bear these tidings to great Lucifer:
Seeing Faustus hath incurred eternal death
By desp'rate thoughts against Jove's deity,
Say he surrenders up to him his soul,
So he will spare him four-and-twenty years,
Letting him live in all voluptuousness,[95]
Having thee ever to attend on me,
To give me whatsoever I shall ask,
To tell me whatsoever I demand,
To slay mine enemies, and aid my friends,

92 45 rack: abuse, torture
93 51 Trinity: the Holy Trinity
94 57 He rejects hell along with the classical afterlife
95 90 voluptuousness: enjoyment of sensual pleasures

And always be obedient to my will.
Go, and return to mighty Lucifer,
And meet me in my study at midnight,
And then resolve me of thy master's mind.
MEPHISTOPHELES I will, Faustus. *Exit*
FAUSTUS Had I as many souls as there be stars,
I'd give them all for Mephistopheles.
By him I'll be great emperor of the world,
And make a bridge through the moving air
To pass the ocean with a band of men.
I'll join the hills that bind the Afric shore,
And make that land continent to Spain,[96]
And both contributory to my crown.
The Emperor[97] shall not live but by my leave,
Nor any potentate[98] of Germany.
Now that I have obtained what I desire,
I'll live in speculation of[99] this art,
Till Mephistopheles return again.

Exit

[Scene v]

Enter WAGNER *and* [ROBIN] *the clown*

WAGNER Sirrah boy, come hither.

ROBIN How, "boy"? 'Swounds, "boy"? I hope you have seen many boys with such *pique-devants*[100] as I have. "Boy," quoth'a?[101]

WAGNER Tell me, sirrah, hast thou any comings-in?[102]

ROBIN Aye, and goings-out too, you may see else.

WAGNER Alas, poor slave, see how poverty jesteth in his nakedness. The villain is bare and out of service, and so hungry that I know he would give his soul to the Devil for a shoulder of mutton, though it were blood-raw.

ROBIN How, my soul to the Devil for a shoulder of mutton though 'twere blood-raw? Not so, good, friend; by'r Lady, I had need have it well roasted, and good sauce to it, if I pay so dear.

WAGNER Well, wilt thou serve me, and I'll make thee go like *Qui mihi discipulus*?[103]

ROBIN How, in verse?

WAGNER No sirrah, in beaten silk and stavesacre.[104]

ROBIN How, how, "knave's acre"? Aye, I thought that was all the land his father left him. Do ye hear, I would be sorry to rob you of your living.

WAGNER Sirrah, I say in stavesacre.

ROBIN O ho, O ho, stavesacre; why then, belike if I were your man, I should be full of vermin.

WAGNER So thou shalt, whether thou be'st with me, or no. But sirrah, leave your jesting and bind[105] yourself presently unto me for seven years, or I'll turn all the lice about thee into familiars,[106] and they shall tear thee in pieces.

96 105–6 I'll join . . . to Spain: Faustus will join the North African coast to that of Spain
97 108 Emperor: the Holy Roman Emperor, Charles V
98 109 potentate: ruler, person of power
99 111 live in speculation of: spend my time studying
100 3 *pique-devants*: small pointed beards
101 3 quoth'a?: said he?
102 4 comings-in: income
103 12 *Qui mihi discipulus*: he who is my disciple
104 14 stavesacre: the seed of a plant used to kill vermin and lice (with which Robin is riddled)
105 20 bind: apprentice
106 21 familiars: evil spirits attendant on a witch or conjurer

ROBIN Do you hear, sir? You may save that labor; they are too familiar with me already. 'Swounds, they are as bold with my flesh as if they had paid for my meat and drink.

WAGNER Well, do you hear, sirrah? Hold, take these guilders.[107]

ROBIN Gridirons? What be they?

WAGNER Why, French crowns.

ROBIN Mass, but for the name of French crowns, a man were as good have as many English counters,[108] and what should I do with these?

WAGNER Why, now sirrah, thou art at an hour's warning whensoever or wheresoever the Devil shall fetch thee.

ROBIN No, no, here, take your gridirons again.

WAGNER Truly, I'll none of them.

ROBIN Truly, but you shall.

WAGNER [*To audience*] Bear witness I gave them him.

ROBIN Bear witness I give them you again.

WAGNER Well, I will cause two devils presently to fetch thee away: Baliol and Belcher.[109]

ROBIN Let your Balio and your Belcher come here, and I'll knock them; they were never so knocked since they were devils. Say I should kill one of them, what would folks say? "Do ye see yonder tall fellow in the round slop?[110] He has killed the Devil." So I should be called "kill-devil" all the parish over.

Enter two DEVILS, *and* [ROBIN] *the clown runs up and down crying*

WAGNER Baliol and Belcher, spirits away. *Exeunt* [DEVILS]

ROBIN What, are they gone? A vengeance on them, they have vile long nails. There was a he-devil and a she-devil. I'll tell you how you shall know them: all he-devils has horns, and all she-devils has clefts[111] and cloven feet.

WAGNER Well, sirrah, follow me.

ROBIN But do you hear? If I should serve you, would you teach me to raise up Banios and Belcheos?

WAGNER I will teach thee to turn thyself to anything, to a dog, or a cat, or a mouse, or a rat, or anything.

ROBIN How? A Christian fellow to a dog or a cat, a mouse or a rat? No, no sir, if you turn me into anything, let it be in the likeness of a little pretty frisking flea, that I may be here and there and everywhere. O, I'll tickle the pretty wenches' plackets.[112] I'll be amongst them, i'faith.

WAGNER Well sirrah, come.

ROBIN But do you hear, Wagner?

WAGNER How?[113] Baliol and Belcher!

ROBIN O Lord, I pray sir, let Banio and Belcher go sleep.

WAGNER Villain, call me Master Wagner, and let thy left eye be diametrically fixed upon my right heel, with *quasi vestigiis nostris insistere.*[114] *Exit*

ROBIN God forgive me, he speaks Dutch fustian.[115] Well, I'll follow him, I'll serve him, that's flat. *Exit*

107 24 guilders: coins, identified as French crowns by Wagner. The Clown repeatedly misspeaks the word

108 28 English counters: valueless tokens

109 36 Baliol and Belcher: names of two devils, here carrying comic associations with gluttony (belly and belch). The Clown repeatedly misspeaks the names

110 39 round slop: baggy breeches

111 44 clefts: the gap in a cloven foot, here associated with female genitals

112 52 plackets: openings in women's underskirts, again associated with the genitals

113 56 How?: expression of annoyance at the Clown's apparent insubordination

114 59 *quasi vestigiis nostris insistere*: as if to follow in our footsteps

115 60 Dutch fustian: inappropriately lofty (and thus nonsensical) language

[Scene vi]

Enter FAUSTUS *in his study*

FAUSTUS Now, Faustus, must thou needs be damned,
And canst thou not be saved?
What boots it[116] then to think of God or heaven?
Away with such vain fancies and despair;
Despair in God, and trust in Beelzebub.
Now, go not backward; no, Faustus, be resolute.
Why waverest thou? O, something soundeth in mine ears:
"Abjure this magic, turn to God again."
Aye, and Faustus will turn to God again.
To God? He loves thee not.
The god thou servest is thine own appetite,
Wherein is fixed the love of Beelzebub.
To him I'll build an altar and a church,
And offer lukewarm blood of new-born babes.

Enter GOOD ANGEL *and* EVIL [ANGEL]

GOOD ANGEL Sweet Faustus, leave that execrable[117] art.
FAUSTUS Contrition, prayer, repentance: what of them?
GOOD ANGEL O, they are means to bring thee unto heaven.
EVIL ANGEL Rather illusions, fruits of lunacy,
That makes men foolish that do trust them most.
GOOD ANGEL Sweet Faustus, think of heaven, and heavenly things.
EVIL ANGEL No, Faustus, think of honor and wealth. *Exeunt* [ANGELS]
FAUSTUS Of wealth—
Why, the signory of Emden[118] shall be mine
When Mephistopheles shall stand by me.
What God can hurt thee, Faustus? Thou art safe;
Cast no more doubts. Come, Mephistopheles,
And bring glad tidings from great Lucifer.
Is't not midnight? Come, Mephistopheles,
Veni, veni Mephistophile.[119]

Enter MEPHISTOPHELES

Now tell, what says Lucifer thy Lord?
MEPHISTOPHELES That I shall wait on Faustus whilst he lives,
So he will buy my service with his soul.
FAUSTUS Already Faustus hath hazarded that for thee.
MEPHISTOPHELES But Faustus, thou must bequeath it solemnly
And write a deed of gift with thine own blood,
For that security[120] craves great Lucifer.
If thou deny it, I will back to hell.
FAUSTUS Stay, Mephistopheles, and tell me, what good will my soul do thy lord?
MEPHISTOPHELES Enlarge his kingdom.
FAUSTUS Is that the reason he tempts us thus?

116 3 What boots it: what use is it
117 15 execrable: accursed
118 22 signory of Emden: the lordship of Emden, a trade port in Germany
119 28 Come, come Mephistopheles
120 35 security: a deposit as guarantee of payment of a debt

MEPHISTOPHELES *Solamen miseris socios habuisse doloris.*[121]
FAUSTUS Have you any pain, that tortures others?
MEPHISTOPHELES As great as have the human souls of men.
But tell me, Faustus, shall I have thy soul?
And I will be thy slave, and wait on thee,
And give thee more than thou hast wit to ask.
FAUSTUS Aye Mephistopheles, I give it thee.
MEPHISTOPHELES Then stab thine arm courageously
And bind thy soul, that at some certain day
Great Lucifer may claim it as his own,
And then be thou as great as Lucifer.
FAUSTUS Lo, Mephistopheles, for love of thee
I cut mine arm, and with my proper blood
Assure my soul to be great Lucifer's,
Chief Lord and regent of perpetual night.
View here the blood that trickles from mine arm,
And let it be propitious[122] for my wish.
MEPHISTOPHELES But Faustus, thou must write it in manner of a deed of gift.
FAUSTUS Aye, so I will. But Mephistopheles,
My blood congeals and I can write no more.
MEPHISTOPHELES I'll fetch thee fire to dissolve it straight. *Exit*
FAUSTUS What might the staying[123] of my blood portend?
Is it unwilling I should write this bill?
Why streams it not, that I may write afresh?
"Faustus gives to thee his soul": ah, there it stayed.
Why shouldst thou not? Is not thy soul thine own?
Then write again: "Faustus gives to thee his soul."

Enter MEPHISTOPHELES *with a chafer*[124] *of coals*

MEPHISTOPHELES Here's fire. Come, Faustus, set it on.
FAUSTUS So, now the blood begins to clear again,
Now will I make an end immediately.
MEPHISTOPHELES [*Aside*] O, what will not I do to obtain his soul?
FAUSTUS *Consummatum est*:[125] this bill is ended,
And Faustus hath bequeathed his soul to Lucifer.
But what is this inscription on mine arm?
"*Homo fuge*."[126] Whither should I fly?
If unto God, he'll throw thee down to hell.
My senses are deceived; here's nothing writ.
I see it plain! Here in this place is writ,
"*Homo fuge*," yet shall not Faustus fly.
MEPHISTOPHELES [*Aside*] I'll fetch him somewhat to delight his mind. *Exit*

Enter [MEPHISTOPHELES] *with* DEVILS, *giving crowns and rich apparel to* FAUSTUS, *and dance, and then* [DEVILS] *depart*

FAUSTUS Speak, Mephistopheles, what means this show?
MEPHISTOPHELES Nothing, Faustus, but to delight thy mind withal,

121 40 It is a comfort to those who are miserable to have had allies in pain
122 56 propitious: advantageous
123 61 staying: stopping of the flow
124 66 SD *chafer*: a portable heating vessel
125 71 *Consummatum est*: it is finished (an allusion to the last words of Jesus on the cross)
126 74 *Homo fuge*: fly, man

And to show thee what magic can perform.
FAUSTUS But may I raise up spirits when I please?
MEPHISTOPHELES Aye Faustus, and do greater things than these.
FAUSTUS Then there's enough for a thousand souls.
Here, Mephistopheles, receive this scroll,
A deed of gift of body and of soul;
But yet conditionally, that thou perform
All articles prescribed between us both.
MEPHISTOPHELES Faustus, I swear by hell and Lucifer
To effect all promises between us made.
FAUSTUS Then hear me read them, on these conditions following.
"First, that Faustus may be a spirit in form and substance.
Secondly, that Mephistopheles shall be his servant, and at his command.
Thirdly, that Mephistopheles shall do for him, and bring him whatsoever.
Fourthly, that he shall be in his chamber or house invisible.
Lastly, that he shall appear to the said John Faustus at all times, in what form or shape soever he please. I, John Faustus of Württemberg, doctor, by these presents,[127] do give both body and soul to Lucifer, Prince of the East, and his minister Mephistopheles, and furthermore grant unto them, that four-and-twenty years being expired, the articles above written inviolate, full power to fetch or carry the said John Faustus, body and soul, flesh, blood, or goods, into their habitation wheresoever.

By me, John Faustus."

MEPHISTOPHELES Speak, Faustus, do you deliver this as your deed?
FAUSTUS Aye, take it, and the Devil give thee good on't.[128]
MEPHISTOPHELES Now Faustus, ask what thou wilt.
FAUSTUS First will I question with thee about hell.
Tell me, where is the place that men call hell?
MEPHISTOPHELES Under the heavens.
FAUSTUS Aye, but where about?
MEPHISTOPHELES Within the bowels of these elements,[129]
Where we are tortured and remain forever.
Hell hath no limits, nor is circumscribed[130]
In one self place, for where we are is hell,
And where hell is, must we ever be:
And to conclude, when all the world dissolves,
And every creature shall be purified,
All places shall be hell that is not heaven.
FAUSTUS Come, I think hell's a fable.
MEPHISTOPHELES Aye, think so still, till experience change thy mind.
FAUSTUS Why? Think'st thou then that Faustus shall be damned?
MEPHISTOPHELES Aye, of necessity, for here's the scroll
Wherein thou hast given thy soul to Lucifer.
FAUSTUS Aye, and body too, but what of that?
Think'st thou that Faustus is so fond[131]
To imagine that after this life there is any pain?
Tush, these are trifles and mere old wives' tales.
MEPHISTOPHELES But Faustus, I am an instance to prove the contrary,
For I am damned, and am now in hell.

127 98 by these presents: by the articles now under discussion
128 105 the Devil . . . good on't: may the Devil reward you (a common oath)
129 110 these elements: earth, air, fire, and water, which make up the natural world
130 112 circumscribed: measured out, demarcated
131 124 fond: foolish

FAUSTUS How? Now in hell? Nay, and[132] this be hell, I'll willingly be damned here: what, walking, disputing, etc.? But leaving off this, let me have a wife, the fairest maid in Germany, for I am wanton and lascivious, and cannot live without a wife.
MEPHISTOPHELES How, a wife? I prithee[133] Faustus, talk not of a wife.
FAUSTUS Nay, sweet Mephistopheles, fetch me one, for I will have one.
MEPHISTOPHELES Well, thou wilt have one. Sit there till I come;
I'll fetch thee a wife in the Devil's name. [*Exit*]

Enter [MEPHISTOPHELES] *with a devil dressed like a woman, with fireworks*

Tell, Faustus, how dost thou like thy wife?
FAUSTUS A plague on her for a hot whore!
MEPHISTOPHELES Tut, Faustus, marriage is but a ceremonial toy; if thou lovest me, think no more of it.
I'll cull thee out the fairest courtesans,[134]
And bring them ev'ry morning to thy bed.
She whom thine eye shall like, thy heart shall have,
Be she as chaste as was Penelope,[135]
As wise as Saba,[136] or as beautiful
As was bright Lucifer before his fall.
Hold, take this book, peruse it thoroughly;
The iterating[137] of these lines brings gold;
The framing[138] of this circle on the ground
Brings whirlwinds, tempests, thunder, and lightning.
Pronounce this thrice devoutly to thyself,
And men in armor shall appear to thee,
Ready to execute what thou desir'st.
FAUSTUS Thanks Mephistopheles, yet fain would I have a book wherein I might behold all spells and incantations, that I might raise up spirits when I please.
MEPHISTOPHELES Here they are in this book. *There turn to them*
FAUSTUS Now would I have a book where I might see all characters and planets of the heavens, that I might know their motions and dispositions.[139]
MEPHISTOPHELES Here they are too. *Turn to them*
FAUSTUS Nay, let me have one book more, and then I have done, wherein I might see all plants, herbs, and trees that grow upon the earth.
MEPHISTOPHELES Here they be.
FAUSTUS O, thou art deceived.
MEPHISTOPHELES Tut, I warrant thee. *Turn to them*
[*Exeunt*]

[Scene vii]

Enter ROBIN *the ostler*[140] *with a book in his hand*

ROBIN O, this is admirable! Here I ha' stol'n one of Doctor Faustus' conjuring books, and

132 129 and: if
133 132 prithee: pray thee
134 140 courtesans: prostitutes
135 143 Penelope: in Homer's *Odyssey*, the wife of Odysseus who refused to accept new suitors while waiting for her husband to return
136 144 Saba: in the Old Testament, the Queen of Sheba, who tested King Solomon's wisdom
137 147 iterating: reciting
138 148 framing: drawing
139 157 motions and dispositions: movements and positions
140 0 SD *ostler*: stableman

i'faith I mean to search some circles[141] for my own use; now will I make all the maidens in our parish dance at my pleasure stark naked before me, and so by that means I shall see more than e'er I felt or saw yet.

Enter RAFE, *calling* ROBIN

RAFE Robin, prithee come away. There's a gentleman tarries[142] to have his horse, and he would have his things rubbed and made clean. He keeps such a chafing[143] with my mistress about it, and she has sent me to look thee out. Prithee, come away.

ROBIN Keep out, keep out, or else you are[144] blown up, you are dismembered, Rafe. Keep out, for I am about a roaring[145] piece of work.

RAFE Come, what dost thou with that same book? Thou can'st not read.

ROBIN Yes, my master and mistress shall find that I can read: he for his forehead,[146] she for her private study. She's born to bear with me,[147] or else my art fails.

RAFE Why, Robin, what book is that?

ROBIN What book? Why, the most intolerable[148] book for conjuring that e'er was invented by any brimstone[149] devil.

RAFE Can'st thou conjure with it?

ROBIN I can do all these things easily with it: first, I can make thee drunk with hippocras[150] at any tavern in Europe for nothing; that's one of my conjuring works.

RAFE Our master parson says that's nothing.

ROBIN True, Rafe, and more,[151] Rafe, if thou hast any mind to Nan Spit, our kitchen maid, then turn her and wind her to thy own use, as often as thou wilt, and at midnight.

RAFE O brave Robin, shall I have Nan Spit, and to mine own use? On that condition I'll feed thy devil with horse-bread[152] as long as he lives, of free cost.

ROBIN No more, sweet Rafe. Let's go and make clean our boots, which lie foul upon our hands, and then to our conjuring in the Devil's name.

Exeunt

[Scene viii]

[*Enter* FAUSTUS *and* MEPHISTOPHELES]

FAUSTUS When I behold the heavens, then I repent
And curse thee, wicked Mephistopheles,
Because thou hast deprived me of those joys.
MEPHISTOPHELES Why, Faustus,
Think'st thou heaven is such a glorious thing?
I tell thee, 'tis not half so fair as thou,
Or any man that breathes on earth.
FAUSTUS How provest thou that?
MEPHISTOPHELES It was made for man, therefore is man more excellent.
FAUSTUS If it were made for man, 'twas made for me;

141 2 search some circles: look up some magic circles (with a pun, where "circles" means female genitals)
142 5 tarries: who waits
143 6 chafing: scolding, but playing on its alternate meaning of "rubbing"
144 8 are: will be
145 9 roaring: bold, noisy
146 11 forehead: an allusion to the proverbial horns sprouting from the forehead of a cuckolded husband
147 12 bear with me: carry my weight during sex, carry my child
148 14 intolerable: banned, not allowed (though Robin perhaps means "incomparable")
149 15 brimstone: sulphur, associated with the fires of hell
150 17 hippocras: a spiced wine drink
151 20 more: moreover
152 23 horse-bread: bread made out of beans or bran for feeding horses

I will renounce this magic, and repent.

Enter GOOD ANGEL *and* EVIL ANGEL

GOOD ANGEL Faustus, repent yet; God will pity thee.
EVIL ANGEL Thou art a spirit;[153] God cannot pity thee.
FAUSTUS Who buzzeth in mine ears I am a spirit?
Be I a devil, yet God may pity me.
Aye, God will pity me, if I repent.
EVIL ANGEL Aye, but Faustus never shall repent. *Exeunt* [ANGELS]
FAUSTUS My heart's so hardened I cannot repent.
Scarce can I name salvation, faith, or heaven,
But fearful echoes thunder in mine ears:
"Faustus, thou art damned," then swords and knives,
Poison, guns, halters,[154] and envenomed steel[155]
Are laid before me to dispatch myself,
And long ere this I should have slain myself,
Had not sweet pleasure conquered deep despair.
Have not I made blind Homer sing to me,
Of Alexander's love, and Oenone's death?[156]
And hath not he that built the walls of Thebes[157]
With ravishing sound of his melodious harp
Made music with my Mephistopheles?
Why should I die then, or basely despair?
I am resolved Faustus shall ne'er repent.
Come Mephistopheles, let us dispute again,
And argue of divine astrology.
Tell me, are there many heavens above the moon?
Are all celestial bodies but one globe,[158]
As is the substance of this centric earth?[159]
MEPHISTOPHELES As are the elements, such are the spheres:
Mutually folded in each other's orb,[160]
And, Faustus, all jointly move upon one axletree,[161]
Whose terminine[162] is termed the world's wide pole.
Nor are the names of Saturn, Mars, or Jupiter
Feigned, but are erring stars.[163]
FAUSTUS But tell me, have they all one motion, both *situ et tempore*?[164]
MEPHISTOPHELES All jointly move from east to west in four-and-twenty hours upon the poles of the world, but differ in their motion upon the poles of the Zodiac.[165]

153 13 spirit: devil
154 22 halters: nooses
155 22 envenomed steel: poisoned blades
156 27 Alexander's love, and Oenone's death: in Greek mythology, Paris (Alexander) left his first wife, Oenone (here pronounced "Enon") for Helen of Troy, the outcome of which is the subject of Homer's *Iliad*
157 28 he that . . . of Thebes: Amphion and his twin brother Zethus fortified the city of Thebes, Amphion playing his lyre so that the stones moved of their own accord
158 36 Do the heavenly bodies form a globe about the earth?
159 37 centric earth: in the Ptolemaic system, the earth sat at the center of the universe
160 39 Each of the planets forms a globe within that of the next
161 40 axletree: fixed bar on which wheels turn
162 41 terminine: endpoint
163 42–3 Nor are . . . stars: Saturn, Mars, and Jupiter are rightly called "planets" (derived from the Greek word for "wanderers") because their paths wander through those of the other stars. There may also be an allusion to the tendency of the gods after whom the planets are named to "err" morally
164 44 *situ et tempore*: in place and in time
165 46 poles of the Zodiac: the axis on which the planets appear to move through constellations, creating their "double motion" (line 49)

FAUSTUS Tush, these slender trifles[166] Wagner can decide.
Hath Mephistopheles no greater skill?
Who knows not the double motion of the planets?
The first is finished in a natural day,[167]
The second thus: as Saturn in thirty years, Jupiter in twelve, Mars in four, the Sun, Venus, and Mercury in a year, the moon in eight-and-twenty days. Tush, these are freshmen's[168] suppositions. But tell me, hath every sphere a dominion or *intelligentia*?[169]
MEPHISTOPHELES Aye.
FAUSTUS How many heavens or spheres are there?
MEPHISTOPHELES Nine: the seven planets, the firmament,[170] and the imperial heaven.
FAUSTUS Well, resolve me in this question: why have we not conjunctions, oppositions, aspects, eclipses,[171] all at one time, but in some years we have more, in some less?
MEPHISTOPHELES *Per inaequalem motum respectu totius.*[172]
FAUSTUS Well, I am answered. Tell me who made the world?
MEPHISTOPHELES I will not.
FAUSTUS Sweet Mephistopheles, tell me.
MEPHISTOPHELES Move me not, for I will not tell thee.
FAUSTUS Villain, have I not bound thee to tell me anything?
MEPHISTOPHELES Aye, that is not against our kingdom, but this is.
Think thou on hell, Faustus, for thou art damned.
FAUSTUS Think Faustus upon God that made the world.
MEPHISTOPHELES Remember this. *Exit*
FAUSTUS Aye, go, accursèd spirit, to ugly hell;
'Tis thou hast damned distressèd Faustus' soul.
Is't not too late?

Enter GOOD ANGEL *and* EVIL [ANGEL]

EVIL ANGEL Too late.
GOOD ANGEL Never too late, if Faustus can repent.
EVIL ANGEL If thou repent, devils shall tear thee in pieces.
GOOD ANGEL Repent, and they shall never raze[173] thy skin. *Exeunt* [ANGELS]
FAUSTUS Ah, Christ my Savior, seek to save distressèd Faustus' soul.

Enter LUCIFER, BEELZEBUB, *and* MEPHISTOPHELES

LUCIFER Christ cannot save thy soul, for he is just.
There's none but I have interest[174] in the same.
FAUSTUS O, who art thou that look'st so terrible?
LUCIFER I am Lucifer, and this is my companion prince in hell.
FAUSTUS O Faustus, they are come to fetch away thy soul.
LUCIFER We come to tell thee thou dost injure us.
Thou talk'st of Christ, contrary to thy promise.
Thou should'st not think of God; think of the Devil,
And of his dame[175] too.

166 47 slender trifles: simple matters
167 50 finished in a natural day: the planets appear to move around the earth in twenty-four hours
168 52 freshmen: first-year university students
169 53 dominion or *intelligentia*: governing intelligence
170 56 firmament: the sphere of the stars
171 57–8 conjunctions, oppositions, aspects, eclipses: astronomical phenomena in which planets and stars appear in unusual positions relative to one another
172 59 Because of their unequal motion in respect to the whole
173 75 raze: wound
174 78 interest: an investment
175 85 dame: wife or mother; a proverbial phrase

FAUSTUS Nor will I henceforth. Pardon me in this,
And Faustus vows never to look to heaven,
Never to name God or to pray to him,
To burn his scriptures, slay his ministers,
And make my spirits pull his churches down.
LUCIFER Do so, and we will highly gratify[176] thee.

Faustus, we are come from hell to show thee some pastime: Sit down, and thou shalt see all the seven deadly sins appear in their proper shapes.

FAUSTUS That sight will be as pleasing unto me, as paradise was to Adam,[177] the first day of his creation.

LUCIFER Talk not of paradise, nor creation, but mark this show; talk of the Devil, and nothing else. Come away.

Enter the SEVEN DEADLY SINS

Now Faustus, examine them of[178] their several names and dispositions.[179]

FAUSTUS What art thou, the first?

PRIDE I am Pride. I disdain to have any parents. I am like to Ovid's flea;[180] I can creep into every corner of a wench. Sometimes, like a periwig,[181] I sit upon her brow; or, like a fan of feathers, I kiss her lips, indeed I do; what do I not? But fie, what a scent is here? I'll not speak another word, except the ground were perfumed and covered with cloth of arras.[182]

FAUSTUS What art thou, the second?

COVETOUSNESS I am Covetousness, begotten of an old churl,[183] in an old leathern bag:[184] and, might I have my wish, I would desire that this house, and all the people in it, were turned to gold, that I might lock you up in my good chest. O, my sweet gold!

FAUSTUS What art thou, the third?

WRATH I am Wrath. I had neither father nor mother; I leapt out of a lion's mouth when I was scarce half an hour old, and ever since I have run up and down the world, with this case[185] of rapiers, wounding myself when I had nobody to fight withal. I was born in hell, and look to it, for some of you shall be my father.[186]

FAUSTUS What art thou, the fourth?

ENVY I am Envy, begotten of a chimney-sweeper and an oyster wife.[187] I cannot read, and therefore wish all books were burned. I am lean with seeing others eat—O, that there would come a famine through all the world, that all might die and I live alone; then thou should'st see how fat I would be. But must thou sit and I stand? Come down, with a vengeance.[188]

FAUSTUS Away, envious rascal. What art thou, the fifth?

GLUTTONY Who, I sir? I am Gluttony. My parents are all dead, and the Devil a penny[189] they have left me but a bare pension, and that is thirty meals a day, and ten bevers:[190] a small trifle to suffice nature.[191] O, I come of a royal parentage: my grandfather was a gammon of

176 91 gratify: reward
177 94 Adam: in the Bible, the first human created by God
178 98 examine them of: question them about
179 98 several names and dispositions: individual names and personalities
180 100 Ovid's flea: from a poem wrongly attributed to Ovid, which muses on the ability of a flea to go wherever it wishes
181 101 periwig: wig, perhaps to cover a defect
182 103 cloth of arras: rich tapestries
183 105 churl: miser
184 105 leathern bag: moneybag
185 111 case: pair
186 112 my father: the cause of anger
187 114 oyster-wife: woman who sells oysters
188 117 with a vengeance: a mild oath
189 119 the Devil a penny: barely any money
190 120 bevers: snacks taken between meals
191 121 suffice nature: satisfy natural appetite

bacon, my grandmother a hogshead[192] of claret wine. My godfathers were these: Peter Pickle-herring and Martin Martlemas-beef.[193] O, but my godmother, she was a jolly gentlewoman, and well beloved in every good town and city; her name was Mistress Margery March-beer.[194] Now Faustus, thou hast heard all my progeny;[195] wilt thou bid me to supper?

FAUSTUS No, I'll see thee hanged. Thou wilt eat up all my victuals.[196]

GLUTTONY Then the Devil choke thee.

FAUSTUS Choke thyself, glutton. What art thou, the sixth?

SLOTH I am Sloth. I was begotten on a sunny bank, where I have lain ever since, and you have done me great injury to bring me from thence. Let me be carried thither again by Gluttony and Lechery. I'll not speak another word for a king's ransom.

FAUSTUS What are you, mistress minx, the seventh and last?

LECHERY Who, I sir? I am one that loves an inch of raw mutton better than an ell of fried stockfish,[197] and the first letter of my name begins with lechery.

LUCIFER Away, to hell, to hell. *Exeunt the* SINS

Now Faustus, how dost thou like this?

FAUSTUS O, this feeds my soul.

LUCIFER But Faustus, in hell is all manner of delight.

FAUSTUS O, might I see hell, and return again, how happy were I then?

LUCIFER Thou shalt. I will send for thee at midnight. In meantime, take this book; peruse it thoroughly, and thou shalt turn thyself into what shape thou wilt.

FAUSTUS Great thanks, mighty Lucifer. This will I keep as chary[198] as my life.

LUCIFER Farewell Faustus, and think on the Devil.

FAUSTUS Farewell great Lucifer. Come, Mephistopheles.

Exeunt omnes

[Scene ix]

Enter WAGNER *solus*[199]

WAGNER Learnèd Faustus,
To know the secrets of astronomy
Graven[200] in the book of Jove's high firmament,
Did mount himself to scale Olympus' top,[201]
Being seated in a chariot burning bright,
Drawn by the strength of yoky[202] dragons' necks.
He now is gone to prove cosmography[203]
And, as I guess, will first arrive at Rome
To see the Pope and manner of his court,
And take some part of holy Peter's feast,[204]
That to this day is highly solemnized.

Exit WAGNER

192 122 hogshead: large cask
193 122–3 Peter Pickle-herring and Martin Martlemas-beef: personifications of pickled herring and salted beef
194 124 March-beer: a strong beer
195 125 progeny: ancestry
196 126 victuals: food and drink
197 133–4 an inch … fried stockfish: a small amount of good meat (with "raw mutton" proverbially referring to prostitutes) rather than a large amount (an ell is forty-five inches) of a proverbially limp and beaten fish (referring here to sexual inadequacy)
198 142 chary: carefully
199 0 SD *solus*: alone
200 3 Graven: engraved
201 4 Olympus' top: the peak of Mount Olympus in Greece, residence of the gods
202 6 yoky: yoked
203 7 prove cosmography: try his skill in the mapping of the universe
204 10 holy Peter's feast: held on 29 June in honor of St. Peter's martyrdom

[Scene x]

Enter FAUSTUS *and* MEPHISTOPHELES

FAUSTUS Having now, my good Mephistopheles,
Passed with delight the stately town of Trier,[205]
Environed round with[206] airy mountain tops,
With walls of flint and deep entrenchèd lakes,
Not to be won by any conquering prince;
From Paris next, coasting[207] the realm of France,
We saw the river Main fall into Rhine,[208]
Whose banks are set with groves of fruitful vines.
Then up to Naples, rich Campania,[209]
Whose buildings fair and gorgeous to the eye,
The streets straight forth and paved with finest brick,
Quarters the town in four equivalents.
There saw we learnèd Maro's[210] golden tomb,
The way he cut an English mile in length
Thorough[211] a rock of stone in one night's space.
From thence to Venice, Padua, and the rest,
In midst of which a sumptuous temple[212] stands,
That threats the stars with her aspiring top.
Thus hitherto hath Faustus spent his time.
But tell me now, what resting place is this?
Hast thou as erst[213] I did command,
Conducted me within the walls of Rome?
MEPHISTOPHELES Faustus, I have, and because we will not be unprovided, I have taken up his Holiness' privy chamber[214] for our use.
FAUSTUS I hope his Holiness will bid us welcome.
MEPHISTOPHELES Tut, 'tis no matter, man; we'll be bold with his good cheer.[215]
And now, my Faustus, that thou may'st perceive
What Rome containeth to delight thee with,
Know that this city stands upon seven hills
That underprops the groundwork[216] of the same.
Just through the midst runs flowing Tiber's stream,[217]
With winding banks that cut it in two parts,
Over the which four stately bridges lean,
That makes safe passage to each part of Rome.
Upon the bridge called Ponte Angelo,[218]
Erected is a castle passing strong,[219]

205 2 Trier: a town in western Germany on the Moselle river
206 3 Environed round with: surrounded by
207 6 coasting: skirting
208 7 Rhine: the tributary river Main feeds into the Rhine at Wiesbaden; having initially gone west from Trier to Paris, Faustus is now heading further east
209 9 Naples, rich Campania: modern Naples is the capital city of the southern Italian region of Campania; during the sixteenth and seventeenth centuries, the Kingdom of Naples was a separate entity under Spanish control
210 13 Maro: the Roman poet Virgil (Publius Vergilius Maro), said to be buried at the entrance to a tunnel connecting ancient Naples to the small towns of Pozzuouli and Baiae. Medieval legend credited Virgil with carving out the tunnel magically
211 15 Thorough: through
212 17 a sumptuous temple: most likely the opulent St. Mark's Basilica in Venice
213 21 erst: earlier
214 24 his Holiness' privy chamber: the private apartments of the Pope, Adrian VI
215 26 good cheer: welcoming disposition; food and drink
216 30 underprops the groundwork: holds up the foundations
217 31 Tiber's stream: the primary river of Rome, dividing the city
218 35 Ponte Angelo: the Ponte Sant'Angelo, or Bridge of the Holy Angel
219 36 a castle passing strong: an especially strong castle, the Castel Sant'Angelo, or Mausoleum of Hadrian

Within whose walls such store of ordnance[220] are,
And double cannons,[221] framed of carvèd brass,
As match the days within one complete year,[222]
Besides the gates and high pyramides[223]
Which Julius Caesar brought from Africa.
FAUSTUS Now, by the kingdoms of infernal rule,
Of Styx, Acheron, and the fiery lake
Of ever-burning Phlegethon,[224] I swear
That I do long to see the monuments
And situation of bright splendent[225] Rome.
Come therefore, let's away.
MEPHISTOPHELES Nay Faustus, stay. I know you'd fain[226] see the Pope
And take some part of holy Peter's feast,
Where thou shalt see a troupe of bald-pate[227] friars,
Whose *summum bonum*[228] is in belly-cheer.[229]
FAUSTUS Well, I am content to compass[230] then some sport,
And by their folly make us merriment.
Then charm me that I may be invisible, to do what I please unseen of[231] any whilst I stay in Rome.
MEPHISTOPHELES So, Faustus, now do what thou wilt, thou shalt not be discerned.[232]

Sound a sennet.[233] *Enter the* POPE *and the* CARDINAL *of Lorraine*[234] *to the banquet, with* FRIARS *attending*

POPE My lord of Lorraine, wilt please you draw near?
FAUSTUS Fall to, and the Devil choke you and you spare.[235]
POPE How now, who's that which spake? Friars, look about.
FRIAR Here's nobody, if it like[236] your Holiness.
POPE My lord, here is a dainty dish was sent me from the Bishop of Milan.
FAUSTUS I thank you, sir. [FAUSTUS] *snatch[es] it*
POPE How now, who's that which snatched the meat from me? Will no man look? My lord, this dish was sent me from the Cardinal of Florence.
FAUSTUS You say true, I'll ha't.[237] [FAUSTUS *snatches dish*]
POPE What, again? My lord, I'll drink to your grace.
FAUSTUS I'll pledge[238] your grace. [FAUSTUS *snatches drink*]
LORD My lord, it may be some ghost newly crept out of purgatory[239] come to beg a pardon of your Holiness.

220 37 ordnance: military supplies
221 38 double cannons: large cannons, perhaps capable of firing multiple projectiles
222 38–9 And double . . . complete year: Mephistopheles speaks figuratively here to indicate a large number of cannons, rather than a literal count of 365
223 40 pyramides: obelisks
224 43–4 Styx, Acheron . . . ever-burning Phlegethon: three of the five rivers of the classical underworld
225 46 splendent: resplendent; magnificent
226 48 fain: gladly
227 50 bald-pate: bald-headed
228 51 *summum bonum*: greatest good
229 51 belly-cheer: eating and drinking
230 52 compass: devise
231 54 of: by
232 56: discerned: seen
233 56 SD *sennet*: set of notes played on the trumpet for a processional entrance
234 56 SD *Lorraine*: a region of France
235 58: and you spare: if you eat lightly
236 60 like: please
237 65 ha't: have it
238 67 pledge: drink to
239 68 purgatory: in Catholic belief, the place in which souls waited to have their sins cleansed before progressing to heaven; a pardon from the Pope would decrease the waiting time

POPE It may be so. Friars, prepare a dirge[240] to lay[241] the fury of this ghost. Once again, my lord, fall to.

The POPE *crosseth himself*[242]

FAUSTUS What, are you crossing of yourself?
Well, use that trick no more, I would advise you.

[POPE] *crosse[s himself] again*

Well, there's the second time; aware[243] the third,
I give you fair warning.

[POPE] *crosse[s himself] again, and* FAUSTUS *hits him a box of*[244] *the ear, and they all run away*

Come on Mephistopheles, what shall we do?
MEPHISTOPHELES Nay, I know not. We shall be cursed with bell, book, and candle.[245]
FAUSTUS How? Bell, book and candle, candle, book, and bell,
Forward and backward to curse Faustus to hell.
Anon[246] you shall hear a hog grunt, a calf bleat, and an ass bray,[247] because it is St. Peter's holy day.

Enter all the FRIARS *to sing the dirge*

FRIAR Come brethren, let's about our business with good devotion.

[FRIARS] *sing this*

Cursèd be he that stole away his Holiness' meat from the table.
Maledicat dominus.[248]
Cursèd be he that struck his Holiness a blow on the face.
Maledicat dominus.
Cursèd be he that took[249] Friar Sandelo a blow on the pate.[250]
Maledicat dominus.
Cursèd be he that disturbeth our holy dirge.
Maledicat dominus.
Cursèd be he that took away his Holiness' wine.
Maledicat dominus.
Et omnes sancti.[251] *Amen.*

[FAUSTUS and MEPHISTOPHELES] *beat the* FRIARS, *and fling fireworks among them, and so exeunt*

[Scene xi]

Enter CHORUS

CHORUS When Faustus had with pleasure ta'en the view
Of rarest things and royal courts of kings,
He stayed his course,[252] and so returnèd home,
Where such as bear his absence but with grief—
I mean his friends and nearest companions—

240 70 dirge: song sung in commemoration of the dead
241 70 lay: allay
242 71 SD *crosseth himself*: blesses himself by making the sign of the cross, a protection against evil
243 74 aware: beware
244 75 SD *a box of*: a blow on
245 77 bell, book, and candle: a Catholic rite of excommunication, here used for exorcism. Bells are rung, the Bible is closed, and candles extinguished
246 80 Anon: shortly
247 80 hog grunt . . . ass bray: Faustus compares the chanting to the meaningless noises of animals
248 84 May the Lord curse him
249 87 took: gave
250 87 pate: head, perhaps referring to an action that has just taken place
251 93 *Et omnes sancti*: and all the saints (curse him)
252 3 stayed his course: ended his journey

Did gratulate[253] his safety with kind words.
And in their conference of what befell[254]
Touching[255] his journey through the world and air,
They put forth questions of astrology,
Which Faustus answered with such learnèd skill,
As[256] they admired and wondered at his wit.[257]
Now is his fame spread forth in every land.
Amongst the rest the Emperor[258] is one,
Carolus the Fifth, at whose palace now
Faustus is feasted 'mongst his noblemen.
What there he did in trial of[259] his art
I leave untold: your eyes shall see[260] performed.

Exit

[Scene xii]

Enter EMPEROR, FAUSTUS, *and a* KNIGHT, *with* ATTENDANTS

EMPEROR Master Doctor Faustus, I have heard strange report of thy knowledge in the black art, how that none in my empire, nor in the whole world, can compare with thee for the rare[261] effects of magic. They say thou hast a familiar[262] spirit, by whom thou canst accomplish what thou list.[263] This, therefore, is my request: that thou let me see some proof of thy skill, that mine eyes may be witnesses to confirm what mine ears have heard reported. And here I swear to thee, by the honor of mine imperial crown, that whatever thou doest, thou shalt be no ways prejudiced or endamaged.[264]

KNIGHT I'faith, he looks much like a conjurer. *Aside*

FAUSTUS My gracious sovereign, though I must confess myself far inferior to the report men have published, and nothing answerable to[265] the honor of your imperial majesty, yet—for that love and duty binds me thereunto—I am content to do whatsoever your majesty shall command me.

EMPEROR Then, Doctor Faustus, mark what I shall say.
As I was sometime solitary set[266]
Within my closet,[267] sundry[268] thoughts arose
About the honor of mine ancestors:
How they had won by prowess such exploits,
Got such riches, subdued so many kingdoms,
As[269] we that do succeed,[270] or they that shall
Hereafter possess our throne, shall,

253 6 gratulate: express joy at
254 7 conference of what befell: discussion of what had happened
255 8 Touching: concerning
256 11 As: that
257 11 wit: knowledge
258 13 Emperor: the Holy Roman Emperor, Charles V
259 16 in trial of: to demonstrate
260 17 see: see it
261 2 rare: of uncommon excellence or merit
262 3 familiar: attendant
263 4 list: desire
264 7 prejudiced or endamaged: prejudiced against or discredited
265 10 nothing answerable to: not worthy of
266 14 was sometime solitary set: recently sat alone
267 15 closet: private room
268 15 sundry: various
269 19 As: so that (also line 27)
270 19 succeed: inherit, follow

I fear me, never attain to that degree
Of high renown and great authority;
Amongst which kings is Alexander the Great,
Chief spectacle of the world's pre-eminence,[271]
The bright shining of whose glorious acts
Lightens the world with his reflecting beams,
As, when I hear but motion[272] made of him,
It grieves my soul I never saw the man.
If, therefore, thou, by cunning[273] of thine art,
Canst raise this man from hollow vaults[274] below
Where lies entombed this famous conqueror,
And bring with him his beauteous paramour,[275]
Both in their right[276] shapes, gesture, and attire
They used to wear during their time of life,
Thou shalt both satisfy my just desire
And give me cause to praise thee whilst I live.

FAUSTUS My gracious Lord, I am ready to accomplish your request, so far forth as[277] by art and power of my spirit I am able to perform.

KNIGHT (*Aside*) I'faith, that's just nothing at all.

FAUSTUS But, if it like your grace, it is not in my ability to present before your eyes the true substantial[278] bodies of those two deceased princes,[279] which long since are consumed to dust.

KNIGHT (*Aside*) Aye, marry, Master Doctor, now there's a sign of grace[280] in you, when you will confess the truth.

FAUSTUS But such spirits as can lively[281] resemble Alexander and his paramour shall appear before your grace, in that manner that they best lived in, in their most flourishing estate,[282] which I doubt not shall sufficiently content your imperial majesty.

EMPEROR Go to, Master Doctor, let me see them presently.[283]

KNIGHT Do you hear, Master Doctor? You bring Alexander and his paramour before the emperor?

FAUSTUS How then,[284] sir?

KNIGHT I'faith, that's as true as Diana turned me to a stag.[285]

FAUSTUS No sir, but when Actaeon died, he left the horns for you. Mephistopheles, be gone.

Exit MEPHISTOPHELES

KNIGHT Nay, and you go to conjuring, I'll be gone.

Exit KNIGHT

FAUSTUS I'll meet with you anon[286] for interrupting me so. Here they are, my gracious lord.

Enter MEPHISTOPHELES *with* ALEXANDER *and his* PARAMOUR

EMPEROR Master Doctor, I heard this lady, while she lived, had a wart or mole in her neck.

271 24 of the world's pre-eminence: of those pre-eminent in the world
272 27 motion: a suggestion
273 29 cunning: skill
274 30 hollow vaults: the graves, crypts
275 32 paramour: lover
276 33 right: correct
277 37 so far forth as: as far as
278 41 substantial: physical
279 41 princes: monarchs (here, of both genders)
280 43 grace: virtue
281 45 lively: in motion
282 46 estate: condition, time of life
283 48 presently: immediately
284 51 How then?: so what?
285 52 Diana turned . . . a stag: Diana, Roman goddess of hunting, turned Actaeon into a stag when he saw her bathing
286 55 anon: shortly

How shall I know whether it be so or no?
FAUSTUS Your highness may boldly go and see. *Ex[eun]t* ALEX[ANDER *and* PARAMOUR]
EMPEROR Sure, these are no spirits, but the true substantial bodies of those two deceased princes.
FAUSTUS Wilt please your highness now to send for the knight that was so pleasant with me here of late?
EMPEROR One of you call him forth.

Enter the KNIGHT *with a pair of horns on his head*

EMPEROR How now, sir knight? Why I had thought thou had'st been a bachelor, but now I see thou hast a wife that not only gives thee horns, but makes thee wear them—feel on thy head.
KNIGHT Thou damnèd wretch, and execrable dog,
Bred in the concave[287] of some monstrous rock,
How dar'st thou thus abuse a gentleman?
Villain, I say, undo what thou hast done.
FAUSTUS O, not so fast sir—there's no haste but good.[288] Are you remembered how you crossed me in my conference with the Emperor? I think I have met[289] with you for it.
EMPEROR Good Master Doctor, at my entreaty release him; he hath done penance sufficient.
FAUSTUS My gracious lord, not so much for the injury he offered me here in your presence, as to delight you with some mirth, hath Faustus worthily requited[290] this injurious knight: which, being all I desire, I am content to release him of his horns—and, sir knight, hereafter speak well of scholars. Mephistopheles, transform him straight. Now, my good lord, having done my duty, I humbly take my leave.
EMPEROR Farewell Master Doctor, yet ere you go, expect from me a bounteous reward.
[*Exeunt*] EMPEROR[, KNIGHT *and* ATTENDANTS]
FAUSTUS Now, Mephistopheles, the restless course[291]
That time doth run with calm and silent foot,
Short'ning my days and thread[292] of vital life,
Calls for the payment of my latest years.[293]
Therefore, sweet Mephistopheles, let us make haste to Württemberg.
MEPHISTOPHELES What, will you go on horseback or on foot?
FAUSTUS Nay, till I am past this fair and pleasant green,[294]
I'll walk on foot.

Enter a HORSE-COURSER

HORSE-COURSER I have been all this day seeking one Master Fustian.[295] Mass, see where he is. God save you, Master Doctor.
FAUSTUS What, horse-courser, you are well met.
HORSE-COURSER Do you hear, sir? I have brought you forty dollars[296] for your horse.
FAUSTUS I cannot sell him so:[297] if thou lik'st him for fifty, take him.
HORSE-COURSER Alas, sir, I have no more. [*To* MEPHISTOPHELES] I pray you, speak for

287 67 concave: hollow space
288 70 there's no haste but good: rash actions lead to no good (proverb)
289 71 met: got even
290 74 requited: repaid
291 79 restless course: journey without pause
292 81 thread: in mythology, the thread of fate that measured a person's life
293 82 my latest years: last years of my life
294 85 green: grassy land
295 87 Fustian: error for "Faustus," meaning inflated or inappropriately lofty language
296 90 dollars: large silver coins
297 91 so: at that price

me.

MEPHISTOPHELES I pray you, let him have him; he is an honest fellow, and he has a great charge,[298] neither wife nor child.

FAUSTUS Well, come, give me your money. My boy will deliver him to you. But I must tell you one thing before you have him: ride him not into the water at any hand.[299]

HORSE-COURSER Why sir, will he not drink of all waters?

FAUSTUS O yes, he will drink of all waters, but ride him not into the water. Ride him over hedge or ditch, or where thou wilt, but not into the water.

HORSE-COURSER Well sir, now am I made man for ever. I'll not leave[300] my horse for forty. If he had but the quality of "hey ding, ding, hey ding, ding,"[301] I'd make a brave living[302] on him; he has a buttock as slick as an eel.[303] Well, goodbye sir, your boy will deliver him me. But hark ye sir, if my horse be sick or ill at ease, if I bring his water[304] to you, you'll tell me what it is?

FAUSTUS Away, you villain; what, dost think I am a horse doctor? *Exit* HORSE-COURSER

What art thou Faustus, but a man condemned to die?
Thy fatal time doth draw to final end.
Despair doth drive distrust unto my thoughts.
Confound[305] these passions with a quiet sleep.
Tush, Christ did call the thief upon the cross.[306]
Then rest thee, Faustus, quiet in conceit.[307] [FAUSTUS *goes to*] *sleep in his chair*

Enter HORSE-COURSER *all wet, crying*

HORSE-COURSER Alas, alas, Doctor Fustian quoth'a? Mass, Doctor Lopus[308] was never such a doctor. H'as[309] given me a purgation[310] has purged me of forty dollars—I shall never see them more. But yet, like an ass as I was, I would not be ruled by him, for he bade me I should ride him into no water. Now I, thinking my horse had had some rare quality that he would not have had me known of, I, like a venturous youth, rid him into the deep pond at the town's end. I was no sooner in the middle of the pond, but my horse vanished away, and I sat upon a bottle[311] of hay, never so near drowning in my life. But I'll seek out my doctor and have my forty dollars again, or I'll make it the dearest[312] horse. O, yonder is his snipper-snapper[313]—do you hear? You, hey-pass,[314] where's your master?

MEPHISTOPHELES Why sir, what would you? You cannot speak with him.

HORSE-COURSER But I will speak with him.

MEPHISTOPHELES Why, he's fast asleep. Come some other time.

HORSE-COURSER I'll speak with him now, or I'll break his glass windows[315] about his ears.

298 95 charge: burden (ironic)
299 97 at any hand: for any reason
300 101 I'll not leave: I would not sell
301 102: the quality . . . ding, ding: the ability to thrust. "Hey ding, ding" was a sexual refrain in contemporary ballads
302 102 brave living: a good living (by selling him as a stallion)
303 103 slick as an eel: suggests virility, and/or attractiveness to mares
304 104 water: urine
305 109 Confound: dismiss
306 110 Christ did . . . the cross: Faustus remembers the words of comfort that Jesus offered to a repentant thief crucified alongside him, promising him a place in paradise
307 111 conceit: this idea
308 112 Doctor Lopus: Doctor Roderigo Lopez, personal physician to Queen Elizabeth I, executed in 1594 for plotting to poison the queen
309 113 H'as: he has
310 113 purgation: drug designed to empty the system, e.g. a laxative
311 117 bottle: bale
312 119 dearest: most expensive
313 119 snipper-snapper: young, insignificant person
314 120 hey-pass: a command by a juggler to will something into motion
315 124 glass windows: glasses

MEPHISTOPHELES I tell thee he has not slept this eight nights.
HORSE-COURSER And[316] he have not slept this eight weeks, I'll speak with him.
MEPHISTOPHELES See where he is fast asleep.
HORSE-COURSER Aye, this is he. God save ye, Master Doctor, Master Doctor, Master Doctor Fustian—forty dollars, forty dollars for a bottle of hay.
MEPHISTOPHELES Why, thou see'st he hears thee not.
HORSE-COURSER So, ho, ho: so, ho, ho![317] *Hallow*[*s*][318] *in his ear*
No, will you not wake? I'll make you wake ere I go. [HORSE-COURSER] *pull*[*s*] *him by the leg, and pull*[*s*] *it away*
Alas, I am undone![319] What shall I do?
FAUSTUS O my leg, my leg! Help, Mephistopheles, call the officers! My leg, my leg!
MEPHISTOPHELES Come villain, to the constable.
HORSE-COURSER O lord, sir, let me go, and I'll give you forty dollars more.
MEPHISTOPHELES Where be they?
HORSE-COURSER I have none about me. Come to my ostry,[320] and I'll give them you.
MEPHISTOPHELES Begone quickly. HORSE-COURSER *runs away*
FAUSTUS What, is he gone? Farwell, he. Faustus has his leg again, and the horse-courser, I take it, a bottle of hay for his labor. Well, this trick shall cost him forty dollars more.

Enter WAGNER

How now, Wagner, what's the news with thee?
WAGNER Sir, the Duke of Vanholt[321] doth earnestly entreat your company.
FAUSTUS The Duke of Vanholt! An honorable gentleman, to whom I must be no niggard of my cunning.[322] Come Mephistopheles, let's away to him.

Exeunt

[Scene xiii]

Enter ROBIN *and* RAFE *with a silver goblet*

ROBIN Come, Rafe, did not I tell thee we were for ever made[323] by this Doctor Faustus' book? *Ecce signum*![324] Here's a simple[325] purchase for horse keepers; our horses shall eat no hay[326] as long as this lasts.

Enter the VINTNER[327]

RAFE But Robin, here comes the vintner.
ROBIN Hush, I'll gull[328] him supernaturally. Drawer,[329] I hope all is paid, God be with you. Come, Rafe.
VINTNER Soft, sir, a word with you. I must yet have a goblet paid from you ere you go.

316 126 Even if
317 131 A shout used when hunting
318 131 SD *Hallows*: shouts
319 133 undone: ruined, in trouble
320 138 ostry: hostelry, inn
321 144 Vanholt: Anhalt, in eastern Germany
322 145–6 niggard of my cunning: miser with my skill
323 1 were for ever made: have success assured for life
324 2 *Ecce signum*: behold the sign (of our success)
325 2 simple: straightforward, sensible
326 2 eat no hay: eat well (though perhaps with the accidental joke that Rafe and Robin will forget their job to feed the horses)
327 3 SD VINTNER: a wine-merchant, perhaps also one who is an innkeeper
328 5 gull: trick
329 5 Drawer: one who (merely) serves drinks in a tavern, and thus an insult to the vintner

ROBIN I, a goblet, Rafe? I, a goblet? I scorn you, and you are but a etc.[330] I, a goblet? Search me.
VINTNER I mean so, sir, with your favor.[331] [VINTNER *searches* ROBIN]
ROBIN How say you now?[332]
VINTNER I must say somewhat to your fellow, you, sir.
RAFE Me, sir? Me, sir? Search your fill. [VINTNER *searches* RAFE] Now sir, you may be ashamed to burden[333] honest men with a matter of truth.[334]
VINTNER Well, one of you hath this goblet about you.
ROBIN You lie, drawer, 'tis afore me.[335] Sirrah you, I'll teach ye to impeach[336] honest men: stand by, I'll scour[337] you for a goblet. Stand aside, you had best, I charge you in the name of Beelzebub. Look to the goblet, Rafe.
VINTNER What mean you, sirrah?
ROBIN I'll tell you what I mean. *He reads [from the book]*
Sanctobulorum, Periphrasticon—nay, I'll tickle you, vintner—look to the goblet Rafe—
Polypragmos Belseborams framanto pacostiphos tostu Mephistopheles, etc.[338]

Enter MEPHISTOPHELES[, *who*] *sets squibs*[339] *at their backs. They run about*

VINTNER *O nomine Domine*,[340] what meanest thou Robin? Thou hast no goblet.
RAFE *Peccatum peccatorum*,[341] here's thy goblet, good vintner.
ROBIN *Misericordia pro nobis*,[342] what shall I do? Good devil, forgive me now, and I'll never rob thy library more.[343]

Enter to them[344] MEPH[ISTOPHELES]

MEPHISTOPHELES Vanish, villains, th'one like an ape; another like a bear, the third an ass, for doing this enterprise.
Monarch of hell,[345] under whose black survey[346]
Great potentates do kneel with awful fear,
Upon whose altars thousand souls do lie,
How am I vexèd with these villains' charms?[347]
From Constantinople[348] am I hither come,
Only for pleasure of these damnèd slaves.
ROBIN How, from Constantinople? You have had a great journey. Will you take sixpence in your purse to pay for your supper, and be gone?
MEPHISTOPHELES Well, villains, for your presumption, I transform thee into an ape, and thee

330 8 etc.: an insult is implied here. The actor may either be intended to improvise their own, or to say the word "et cetera" as a joke
331 10 with your favor: if you permit me
332 11 What do you have to say now?
333 14 burden: accuse
334 14 matter of truth: dispute over truth (though also a joking admission that the vintner is correct)
335 16 'tis afore me: it is before me. There are many staging possibilities here; the most literal interpretation is that the goblet is now somewhere where Robin can see it but the vintner cannot
336 16 impeach: discredit
337 17 scour: beat; also cleanse or purge (suggesting taking the goblet from the vintner)
338 21–2 *Sanctobulorum Periphrasticon . . . Mephistopheles*, etc.: nonsense words based on Latin
339 22 SD *squibs*: fireworks
340 23 *O nomine Domine*: O, in the name of God
341 24 *Peccatum peccatorum*: sin of sins; i.e. the worst sin possible
342 25 *Misericordia pro nobis*: mercy on us
343 26 more: again
344 26 SD *Enter to them*: Mephistopheles reveals himself to them
345 29 Monarch of hell: identified earlier as Beelzebub, but perhaps here referring to Lucifer
346 29 black survey: fearful oversight
347 32 charms: spells, conjurations
348 33 Constantinople: Istanbul, in Turkey

into a dog, and so be gone. *Exit*

ROBIN How, into an ape? That's brave. I have fine sport with the boys, I'll get nuts and apples enough.

RAFE And I must be a dog.

ROBIN I'faith thy head will never be out of the pottage pot.[349]

Exeunt

[Scene xiv]

Enter [FAUSTUS *and* MEPHISTOPHELES, *and*] *to them the* DUKE [*of Vanholt*] *and the* DUCHESS. *The* DUKE *speaks*

DUKE Believe me, Master Doctor, this merriment hath much pleased me.

FAUSTUS My gracious lord, I am glad it contents you so well. But it may be, madam, you take no delight in this. I have heard that great-bellied[350] women do long for some dainties or other. What is it, madam? Tell me, and you shall have it.

DUCHESS Thanks, good Master Doctor. And, for I see your courteous intent to pleasure me, I will not hide from you the thing my heart desires: and were it now summer, as it is January and the dead time of the winter, I would desire no better meat than a dish of ripe grapes.

FAUSTUS Alas, madam, that's nothing. Mephistopheles, be gone. *Exit* MEPH[ISTOPHELES]

Were it a greater thing than this, so it would content you, you should have it.

Enter MEPHISTOPHELES *with the grapes*

Here they be, madam. Wilt please you taste on[351] them?

DUKE Believe me, Master Doctor, this makes me wonder above the rest; that being in the dead time of winter and in the month of January, how you should come by these grapes.

FAUSTUS If it like your grace, the year is divided into two circles over the whole world, that when it is here winter with us, in the contrary circle it is summer with them, as in India, Saba,[352] and farther countries in the east, and by means of a swift spirit that I have, I had them brought hither, as ye see. How do you like them, madam? Be they good?

DUCHESS Believe me, Master Doctor, they be the best grapes that e'er I tasted in my life before.

FAUSTUS I am glad they content you so, madam.

DUKE Come madam, let us in,[353]
Where you must well reward this learnèd man
For the great kindness he hath showed to you.

DUCHESS And so I will, my lord, and whilst I live,
Rest beholding[354] for this courtesy.

FAUSTUS I humbly thank your grace.

DUKE Come, Master Doctor, follow us and receive your reward.

Exeunt

[Scene xv]

Enter WAGNER *solus*

WAGNER I think my master means to die shortly,
For he hath given to me all his goods.

349 42 pottage pot: porridge pot. Proverbially, a dog's head was always in the porridge pot

350 3 great-bellied: pregnant

351 10 taste on: taste

352 14 Saba: Sheba, in modern Yemen

353 20 in: go in

354 24 Rest beholding: remain indebted

And yet methinks, if that death were near,
He would not banquet, and carouse, and swill[355]
Amongst the students, as even now he doth,
Who are at supper with such belly-cheer
As Wagner ne'er beheld in all his life.
See where they come: belike[356] the feast is ended.

[*Exit*]

Enter FAUSTUS *with two or three* SCHOLARS

FIRST SCHOLAR Master Doctor Faustus, since our conference about fair ladies, which was the beautifullest in all the world, we have determined with ourselves that Helen of Greece[357] was the admirablest lady that ever lived. Therefore, Master Doctor, if you will do us that favor, as to let us see that peerless dame of Greece, whom all the world admires for majesty, we should think ourselves much beholding[358] unto you.

FAUSTUS Gentlemen,
For that I know your friendship is unfeigned,
And Faustus' custom is not to deny
The just requests of those that wish him well,
You shall behold that peerless dame of Greece,
No otherways for[359] pomp and majesty
Than when Sir Paris crossed the seas with her
And brought the spoils[360] to rich Dardania.[361]
Be silent then, for danger is in words.

Music sounds, and HELEN *passeth over the stage*

SECOND SCHOLAR Too simple is my wit to tell her praise
Whom all the world admires for majesty.
THIRD SCHOLAR No marvel though the angry Greeks pursued[362]
With ten years' war the rape[363] of such a queen,
Whose heavenly beauty passeth all compare.
FIRST SCHOLAR Since[364] we have seen the pride of nature's works,
And only paragon[365] of excellence,

Enter an OLD MAN

Let us depart, and for this glorious deed
Happy and blessed be Faustus evermore.
FAUSTUS Gentlemen, farewell; the same I wish to you.

Exeunt SCHOLARS

OLD MAN Ah, Doctor Faustus, that I might prevail
To guide thy steps unto the way of life,[366]
By which sweet path thou mayest attain the goal
That shall conduct thee to celestial rest.[367]
Break heart, drop blood,[368] and mingle it with tears,

355 4 carouse, and swill: drink freely and greedily
356 8 belike: presumably
357 10 Helen of Greece: more popularly known as Helen of Troy. Helen was Queen of Sparta as the wife of Menelaus, and her abduction by Paris, Prince of Troy, instigated the ten-year Trojan war
358 13 beholding: indebted
359 19 No otherways for: no less in
360 21 spoils: that which has been stolen (here, Helen)
361 21 Dardania: Troy
362 25 pursued: avenged
363 26 rape: abduction
364 28 Since: now that
365 29 paragon: model
366 34 way of life: (correct) manner of living; path to heaven
367 36 celestial rest: eternal life
368 37 Break heart, drop blood: may your heart break and bleed (in repentance)

Tears falling from repentant heaviness
Of thy most vile and loathsome filthiness,
The stench whereof corrupts the inward soul
With such flagitious[369] crimes of heinous sins,
As no commiseration[370] may expel,
But mercy, Faustus, of thy savior sweet,
Whose blood alone must wash away thy guilt.
FAUSTUS Where art thou, Faustus? Wretch, what hast thou done?
Damned art thou, Faustus, damned—despair and die.
Hell calls for right,[371] and with a roaring voice
Says, "Faustus, come, thine hour is come," MEPHISTOPHELES *gives him a dagger*
And Faustus will come to do thee right.
OLD MAN Ah, stay, good Faustus, stay thy desperate steps.[372]
I see an angel hovers o'er thy head,
And with a vial full of precious grace
Offers to pour the same into thy soul.
Then call for mercy and avoid despair.
FAUSTUS Ah, my sweet friend, I feel thy words
To comfort my distressèd soul.
Leave me awhile to ponder on my sins.
OLD MAN I go, sweet Faustus, but with heavy cheer,
Fearing the ruin of thy hopeless soul. [*Exit*]
FAUSTUS Accursèd Faustus, where is mercy now?
I do repent, and yet I do despair.
Hell strives with grace for conquest in my breast.
What shall I do to shun the snares of death?
MEPHISTOPHELES Thou traitor, Faustus, I arrest thy soul
For disobedience to my sovereign lord.
Revolt,[373] or I'll in piecemeal[374] tear thy flesh.
FAUSTUS Sweet Mephistopheles, entreat thy lord
To pardon my unjust presumption,
And with my blood again I will confirm
My former vow I made to Lucifer.
MEPHISTOPHELES Do it then quickly, with unfeignèd heart,
Lest greater danger do attend thy drift.[375]
FAUSTUS Torment, sweet friend, that base and crooked age[376]
That durst dissuade me from thy Lucifer
With greatest torments that our hell affords.
MEPHISTOPHELES His faith is great; I cannot touch his soul,
But what I may afflict his body with
I will attempt, which is but little worth.
FAUSTUS One thing, good servant, let me crave of thee
To glut[377] the longing of my heart's desire:
That I might have unto my paramour[378]
That heavenly Helen which I saw of late,

369 41 flagitious: extremely wicked
370 42 commiseration: pity
371 47 right: justice
372 50 stay thy desperate steps: pause in your desperate actions
373 66 Revolt: return (to Lucifer); abandon God
374 66 in piecemeal: into pieces
375 72 drift: going off course
376 73 age: i.e. the old man
377 80 glut: satisfy
378 81 unto my paramour: as my lover

Whose sweet embracings may extinguish clean
These thoughts that do dissuade me from my vow,
And keep mine oath I made to Lucifer.
MEPHISTOPHELES Faustus, this, or what else thou shalt desire,
Shall be performed in twinkling of an eye.

Enter HELEN

FAUSTUS Was this the face that launched a thousand ships,
And burnt the topless towers of Ilium?[379]
Sweet Helen, make me immortal with a kiss.
Her lips sucks forth my soul—see where it flies.
Come Helen, come, give me my soul again.
Here will I dwell, for heaven be in these lips,
And all is dross[380] that is not Helena.

Enter OLD MAN

I will be Paris and, for love of thee,
Instead of Troy shall Württemberg be sacked,
And I will combat with weak Menelaus
And wear thy colors[381] on my plumèd crest.[382]
Yea, I will wound Achilles in the heel,[383]
And then return to Helen for a kiss.
O, thou art fairer than the evening air,
Clad[384] in the beauty of a thousand stars.
Brighter art thou than flaming Jupiter
When he appeared to hapless Semele;[385]
More lovely then the monarch of the sky[386]
In wanton Arethusa's azured arms,[387]
And none but thou shalt be my paramour. *Exeunt* [*all except* OLD MAN]
OLD MAN Accursèd Faustus, miserable man,
That from thy soul exclud'st[388] the grace of heaven
And fliest[389] the throne of His tribunal seat.

Enter the DEVILS

Satan begins to sift[390] me with his pride,
As in this furnace God shall try my faith.
My faith, vile hell, shall triumph over thee.
Ambitious fiends, see how the heavens smiles

379 89 Ilium: Troy
380 94 dross: worthless
381 98 colors: livery; tokens of favor
382 98 plumèd crest: helmet
383 99 wound Achilles in the heel: the Greek warrior Achilles was legendarily invulnerable except at the back of his heel. Paris killed him with an arrow during the Trojan war
384 102 Clad: dressed
385 104 Semele: a mortal lover of Jupiter, who asked to see him in his true form of flaming gold and was consumed
386 105 monarch of the sky: Jupiter
387 106 wanton Arethusa's azured arms: the blue arms of Arethusa, a nymph. Arethusa had no association with Jupiter in classical mythology
388 109 exclud'st: keeps out
389 110 fliest: runs away from
390 111 sift: make trial of

At your repulse,[391] and laughs your state[392] to scorn.
Hence, hell, for hence I fly unto my God.

Exeunt

[Scene xvi]

Enter FAUSTUS *with the* SCHOLARS

FAUSTUS Ah, gentlemen.
FIRST SCHOLAR What ails Faustus?
FAUSTUS Ah, my sweet chamber-fellow![393] Had I lived with thee, then had I lived still, but now I die eternally. Look, comes he not? Comes he not?
SECOND SCHOLAR What means Faustus?
THIRD SCHOLAR Belike[394] he is grown into some sickness, by being ever solitary.
FIRST SCHOLAR If it be so, we'll have physicians to cure him. 'Tis but a surfeit;[395] never fear, man.
FAUSTUS A surfeit of deadly sin that hath damned both body and soul.
SECOND SCHOLAR Yet Faustus, look up to heaven. Remember, God's mercies are infinite.
FAUSTUS But Faustus' offence can ne'er be pardoned. The serpent that tempted Eve may be saved, but not Faustus. Ah, gentlemen, hear me with patience, and tremble not at my speeches, though my heart pants and quivers to remember that I have been a student here these thirty years. O, would I had never seen Württemberg, never read book. And what wonders I have done, all Germany can witness; yea, all the world, for which Faustus hath lost both Germany and the world; yea, heaven itself—heaven the seat of God, the throne of the blessed, the kingdom of joy—and must remain in hell forever. Hell, ah, hell forever, sweet friends; what shall become of Faustus, being in hell forever?
THIRD SCHOLAR Yet Faustus, call on God.
FAUSTUS On God, whom Faustus hath abjured? On God, whom Faustus hath blasphemed? Ah, my God, I would weep, but the Devil draws in my tears. Gush forth blood instead of tears; yea, life and soul. O, he stays my tongue. I would lift up my hands, but see, they hold them, they hold them.
ALL SCHOLARS Who, Faustus?
FAUSTUS Lucifer and Mephistopheles.
Ah, Gentlemen! I gave them my soul for my cunning.[396]
ALL SCHOLARS God forbid!
FAUSTUS God forbade it indeed, but Faustus hath done it: for vain pleasure of four-and-twenty years hath Faustus lost eternal joy and felicity.[397] I writ them a bill with mine own blood: the date is expired, the time will come, and he will fetch me.
FIRST SCHOLAR Why did not Faustus tell us of this before, that divines might have prayed for thee?
FAUSTUS Oft have I thought to have done so, but the Devil threatened to tear me in pieces if I named God, to fetch both body and soul if I once gave ear to divinity, and now 'tis too late. Gentlemen away, lest you perish with me.
SECOND SCHOLAR O, what shall we do to save Faustus?
FAUSTUS Talk not of me, but save yourselves, and depart.
THIRD SCHOLAR God will strengthen me; I will stay with Faustus.
FIRST SCHOLAR Tempt not God, sweet friend, but let us into the next room, and

391 115 repulse: being driven back
392 115 state: power
393 3 chamber-fellow: roommate
394 6 Belike: probably
395 7 surfeit: excess (in humoral theory, a cause of mental illnesses was an excess or deficit of one of the humors, or bodily fluids)
396 27 for my cunning: in payment for my skill
397 30 felicity: happiness

there pray for him.

FAUSTUS Aye, pray for me, pray for me, and what noise soever ye hear, come not unto me, for nothing can rescue me.

SECOND SCHOLAR Pray thou, and we will pray that God may have mercy upon thee.

FAUSTUS Gentlemen, farewell. If I live till morning, I'll visit you; if not, Faustus is gone to hell.

ALL SCHOLARS Faustus, farewell. *Exeunt* SCHOLARS. *The clock strikes eleven*

FAUSTUS Ah, Faustus,
Now hast thou but one bare hour to live,
And then thou must be damned perpetually.
Stand still, you ever-moving spheres of heaven,[398]
That time may cease and midnight never come.
Fair Nature's eye,[399] rise, rise again, and make
Perpetual day, or let this hour be but a year,
A month, a week, a natural day,
That Faustus may repent and save his soul.
O lente, lente curite noctis equi:[400]
The stars move still, time runs, the clock will strike,
The Devil will come, and Faustus must be damned.
O, I'll leap up to my God—who pulls me down?
See, see, where Christ's blood streams in the firmament.[401]
One drop would save my soul, half a drop. Ah, my Christ!
Ah, rend not my heart for naming of my Christ.
Yet will I call on him; O, spare me Lucifer!
Where is it now? 'Tis gone, and see where God
Stretcheth out his arm and bends his ireful brows.
Mountains and hills, come, come and fall on me,
And hide me from the heavy wrath of God.
No, no, then will I headlong run into the earth.
Earth, gape! O no, it will not harbor me.
You stars that reigned at my nativity,[402]
Whose influence hath allotted[403] death and hell,
Now draw up Faustus like a foggy mist
Into the entrails of yon lab'ring cloud,
That when you vomit forth into the air,
My limbs may issue from your smoky mouths,[404]
So that my soul may but ascend to heaven.
Ah, half the hour is past: *The watch*[405] *strikes*
'Twill all be past anon.
O God, if thou wilt not have mercy on my soul,
Yet for Christ's sake, whose blood hath ransomed me,
Impose some end to my incessant pain;
Let Faustus live in hell a thousand years,
A hundred thousand, and at last be saved.
O, no end is limited to damnèd souls.
Why wert thou not a creature wanting[406] soul?

398 51 spheres of heaven: the stars and planets, in constant motion
399 53 Fair Nature's eye: the sun
400 57 O, run slowly, slowly, horses of the night
401 61 streams in the firmament: flows in the sky
402 71 stars that . . . my nativity: alluding to the idea that the position of the stars and planets at birth determines one's destiny
403 72 allotted: destined me for
404 73–6 Now draw . . . smoky mouths: pull me as a mist into the wisps of that stormy cloud, so that in a storm my body will be expelled
405 78 SD *watch*: clock
406 86 wanting: lacking

Or why is this immortal that thou hast?
Ah, Pythagoras' *metempsychosis*;[407] were that true,
This soul should fly from me, and I be changed
Unto some brutish beast: all beasts are happy, for when they die,
Their souls are soon dissolved in elements,[408]
But mine must live still to be plagued in hell.
Cursed be the parents that engendered me.
No, Faustus, curse thyself, curse Lucifer,
That hath deprived thee of the joys of heaven. *The clock striketh twelve*
O it strikes, it strikes! Now, body, turn to air,
Or Lucifer will bear thee quick to hell; *Thunder and lightning*
O soul, be changed into little water drops
And fall into the ocean, ne'er be found.
My God, my God, look not so fierce on me!

Enter DEVILS

Adders and serpents, let me breathe a while!
Ugly hell gape not; come not Lucifer!
I'll burn my books. Ah, Mephistopheles!

Exeunt [DEVILS] *with him*

[Scene xvii]

Enter CHORUS

CHORUS Cut is the branch that might have grown full straight,
And burnèd is Apollo's laurel bough[409]
That sometime[410] grew within this learnèd man.
Faustus is gone: regard his hellish fall,
Whose fiendful fortune may exhort the wise
Only to[411] wonder at unlawful things,
Whose deepness doth entice such forward wits[412]
To practice more than heavenly power permits.

Terminat hora diem, terminat author opus.[413]

407 88 Pythagoras' *metempsychosis*: the Greek philosopher Pythagoras' theory of the transmigration of souls, in which the soul passes into a new body at the moment of death
408 91 dissolved in elements: dispersed into nature
409 2 Apollo's laurel bough: a wreath of laurel leaves marking distinction in poetry
410 3 sometime: once
411 6 Only to: to do no more than
412 7 forward wits: those whose intelligence makes them presumptuous
413 The hour ends the day, the author ends the work. This motto is separate from the Chorus's speech

9 Robert Greene, *The Scottish History of James the Fourth*

First performed 1588–92

First printed 1598

Edited by Kirk Melnikoff

The Scottish History of James the Fourth (hereafter *James IV*) has long been praised for its energetic exposition, its complex plotting, its comic routines, and its ground-breaking examination of gender and sexual norms through Dorothea's assumption of a male disguise. Written by Robert Greene towards the end of his relatively short career as a professional writer, the play is conversant with Greene's popular print pamphlets and with the plays and dramatic styles of the professional theater in the late 1580s and early 1590s.

The earliest extant record of *James IV* comes from London's Stationers' Company. On 14 May 1594, the printer Thomas Creede entered both it and *The Famous Victories of Henry the Fifth* in the Stationers' Register. *James IV* most likely was not brought to press until 1598. In that year, Creede published a quarto edition with the full title *The Scottish historie of Iames the fourth, slaine at Flodden. Entermixed with a pleasant comedie, presented by Oboram King of Fayeries.* Creede's edition advertises that the play was "Written by *Robert Greene*, Maister of Arts," and that it "*hath bene sundrie times publikely plaide*"—though it does not say which playing company or companies played it. Henslowe's diary does not record the play in its lists of play performances between 1592 and 1597, suggesting that it was not owned by Strange's Men, Sussex's Men, or the Admiral's Men. Gerald M. Pinciss and others have argued that *James IV* was most likely a Queen's Men play. This attribution, however, is somewhat questionable in light of Creede's advertising habits. Between 1594 and 1599, Creede published editions of nine different professional plays; unlike he does with *James IV*, on the title pages of four, he makes a point of touting Queen's Men credentials. No matter which playing company owned *James IV*, the fact that Creede procured it in 1594 likely indicates that the play had proven a valuable commodity in the professional theater and that it continued to be staged in the immediate years after it was first composed. Creede's assurance that the play had been "*sundrie times . . . plaide*" may very well document an even longer stage life, extending at least to 1598 when the first edition of the play was published.

Years of popularity means that *James IV* would have been entangled with a number of trends in the Elizabethan professional theater. One of these, emerging at the end of the 1580s, was the production of plays having to do with English history. Early examples of this fashion include *The Famous Victories of Henry V* (included in this anthology), *The Troublesome Reign of King John*, Shakespeare's Henry VI plays, and Marlowe's *Edward II*. As has been pointed out by a number of commentators, however, *James IV* seems best understood as a romance or a romantic comedy—or even a tragi-comedy (Braunmuller, 1973)—because nothing of its plot is drawn from actual historical events. Indeed, the main plot of the play is taken from a story in the Italian author Cinthio's collection *Hecatommithi* (1565). Greene either read the Italian original or a French translation published in the mid-1580s. Even *James IV*'s advertisement of James IV's killing at the Battle of Flodden in 1513 proves disingenuous. The play appears, in other words, to be a history play in title alone. It does, nevertheless, make use of motifs that would have been immediately recognizable to playgoers drawn to staged English history, including a weak king, unreliable counsel, and a teetering state. Like the history plays in the Queen's Men repertory, it is energized by a style consisting of allegorical characters, clowning, dialects, dumb shows, songs, dancing, and an interplay between the low and high (see McMillin and MacLean). It also contains conventional scenes such as the opening dynastic spectacle of Dorothea's crowning, the airing of the nobility's grievances against James IV (II.ii), the English King's siege of Dunbar (V.iii), and James IV and the English King's dueling military processions (V.vi). These help Greene suggest larger social and political stakes for a monarch's personal transgressions. Greene's title, induction (where the action is said to occur "[i]n the year 1520," line 75), and protagonist may have been anemic gestures toward the kind of true chronicle history fashioned by Marlowe and Shakespeare, but the play's mixed style was also very much in line with other English history plays from this period (Knutson, 2008).

In the late 1580s, the Elizabethan professional theater also witnessed a burst of framed (or "induction") plays: that is, plays that include characters who, in a separate narrative, comment upon and in some cases watch the main action of the play (see Young, 1969). Extant today are more than a dozen of these dramas written between 1587 and 1595, and it stands to reason that at least a few more have been lost. Tudor interest in framed dramas has been connected with native church rituals and with the emblem-book tradition (Greenfield, 1969), and the presence of permanent playhouses after the 1570s in London—affording a host of staging possibilities as well as larger cast sizes—could be taken to have been a significant factor in their increase in the Elizabethan period. Even before he turned to the professional theater, Greene had often worked with literary versions of this device. In 1584, the year after he took his M.A. from Cambridge, Greene began producing volumes of stories with framing narratives populated by taletellers: Venus and Saturn in *Planetomachia* (1585) and humble tradespeople in *Perimedes the Blacksmith* (1588). Over the next four years, he would pen seven such works. Influenced in structure and tone by Boccaccio and Bandello, these offered framed tales in the vein of the Italian novelle and attempted to build on the popularity of similar material in the bookstalls of London. It is thus the twin contexts of the Elizabethan professional theater and the Elizabethan pamphlet market that Greene's production of framed dramas like *James IV* as well as *Alphonsus King of Aragon* and *A Looking Glass for London and England* should be understood.

In print, framing dialogues can draw attention to the rhetorical methods of tale-tellers and to the interpretive strategies of auditors. In the theater, frame material can foster a double awareness in an audience; auditors witness action in both a frame and a titular sequence of events, and in so doing are encouraged to develop a metatheatrical perspective. *James IV* traffics in metatheatricality. Its opening frame sequence casts the titular narrative as a "demonstration" by Bohan of why he "hate[s] the world" (Induction 74). Thereafter, the audience is treated to a number of short scenes in which Oberon and Bohan each respond to what they have seen performed. At times, Oberon reacts with theatrical demonstrations of his own, and as such the frame presents a dramatic competition of sorts: Oberon's dumb shows, songs, and dances pitted against Bohan's historical romance (see Gieskes, 2008). All of this comes to a conclusion with Bohan ironically insisting that Dorothea's happy reunion with James IV tells "in mirkest terms . . ./The loath of sins and where corruption dwells" (Chorus viii. 5–6). At the end the play, then, Bohan is shown to be a misguided spectator wholly absorbed by his own misanthropy. Greene's frame, though, facilitates other perspectives as well in that its relationship with the titular narrative is unstable at best. Bohan may call it *his* "demonstration," but as it unfolds we witness not only a number of moments when Bohan's actors address the audience, but also, towards the end, Bohan worrying about the safety of his actor-son Slipper ("What, hang my son? I think not, Oberon" [Chorus vii. 11]) and Oberon carrying the clown away in order to "stand his friend" (Chorus vii. 9). In these moments, Greene puts pressure on the conventions of the framed play—creating shifting ontologies and fashioning both a mediated and unmediated relationship between audience and titular narrative—even as he takes advantage of them (Braunmuller, 1973).

It is often supposed that by the late 1580s and early 1590s, allegorical drama in the form of the morality play and the interlude had been largely superseded by dramatic realism on the professional stage. This assumption, though, is belied by the many allegorical plays that were written during these years; some of these, like *A Knack to Know a Knave*, were frequently performed at Henslowe's Rose. *James IV*'s debt to this dramatic tradition is most apparent in the late exchange between the Lawyer, Merchant, and Divine, characters in the vein of *Cambises*'s Commons' Cry and Commons' Complaint (this play is also included in this anthology). The tense finger-pointing here is never resolved and is only put to rest by the entrance of a Scottish-army scout. Ateukin also belongs to the allegorical tradition in that his malevolence, buffoonish actions, and Machiavellian tactics are strongly reminiscent of Vice-figures like *Cambises*'s Ambidexter and *Clyomon and Clamydes*'s Subtle Shift. At first lurking at the edge of James IV's court, Ateukin steps out of the shadows with a rhymed knavish aside directed to the audience: "And now's my time by wiles and words to rise,/Greater than those that think themselves more wise" (I.i. 158–9). Like most Vices, Ateukin targets an everyman, in this case James IV. Slipper and Andrew may subsequently join Ateukin as Vice-lieutenants, but their knavery is balanced out by the actions of Dorothea, Ida, the Countess, and Nano as virtues (Lavin: xvi–xviii; Sanders: xlvi–xlvii). Ateukin's rise is at first shown to be a function of his "art," that is, his knowledge of astrology and his "charms and spells" (I.i. 264). In this, Greene's play can be linked to a number of late 1580s and early 1590s plays concerned with magical powers and pacts with the devil—including most of Greene's other plays as well as blockbusters like Marlowe's *Doctor Faustus* (see Knutson, "Marlowe in Repertory," 31–3). As Bohan's "demonstration" continues, though, Ateukin increasingly sheds his necromantic and Vice-figure edge until he escapes from Scotland with what might be described as a moralizing whimper: "Thus God doth work with those that purchase fame/By flattery and make their prince their gain" (V.ii. 37–8). Here, Bohan's play eschews the spectacular final exits of other Vice figures for the happy endings of romantic comedy.

While Bohan's play ultimately follows the conventional course of romantic comedy, the frame inflects the larger whole with a persistent strand of romance. Magical, mischievous, artistic, and adjudicating, Oberon can be traced back to the medieval Germanic tradition having to do with the fairy "Alberich." Greene's "little King" (Chorus ii. 1) has a more immediate source in Auberon, fairy ruler in the French romance *Huon de Bordeaux* (Aydelotte). Ten appearances give Oberon with his spells, shows, and antic assistants a pervasive presence in *James IV*, one that goes some way towards explaining Dorothea's wondrous forgiveness of her husband at the end of the play. At this point, after all, Oberon has aggressively extended his magical influence to Bohan's play in saving Slipper from James IV's order to "hang [him and Ateukin] as traitors to the king" (V.vi. 49). Greene's orientation towards the wonderful actions and endings of romance can be explained with reference to his work on both the page and the stage. Throughout the 1580s, Greene continued to experiment with the genre in his print productions, veering ultimately towards the shipwrecks, happenstance encounters, and magical reunions of Greek romance in pamphlets like *Menaphon* and the bestseller *Pandosto*. The characters and themes of these pamphlets were simultaneously being reenacted in a number of professional plays like Greene's own *Friar Bacon and*

Friar Bungay, the now-lost "Valentine and Orson," and Munday's *John a Kent and John A Cumber* to name just a few. A few years later, Greene's play would have competed for audiences with dramas like the now-lost "Huon of Bordeaux," Chapman's *The Blind Beggar of Alexandria*, and Shakespeare's *A Midsummer Night's Dream*. Indeed, Shakespeare was likely inspired by 1590s productions of *James IV* in fashioning his own Oberon play.

Textual note

This edition is based on the EEBO copy of the 1598 quarto held at the Huntington Library. Norman Sanders's collation of this text with the other three copies held at the Folger Shakespeare Library, the British Library, and the Victoria and Albert Museum has been consulted. Spelling and punctuation have been modernized throughout, and scene divisions have been added. Bohan's Scottish diction has been standardized in terms of pre-1700 usage as specified by the online *Dictionary of the Scots Language* (www.dsl.ac.uk); his and other characters' Scotticisms have been retained. Throughout the play Jaques speaks with a mixture of French, English, and Italian; his French has been corrected, modernized, and italicized throughout, and his Italianisms have been retained. Names have been modernized and standardized in speech-prefixes, in dialogue, and in stage directions. Speech-prefix errors have been silently corrected. For clarity's sake, stage directions have been added for asides and directed speech, and existing stage directions have in a few instances been moved. Abbreviations and contractions have mostly been expanded, and italicization and capitalization of proper names and place names have been removed. In a few cases, Greene's iambic pentameter has been regularized by addition or subtraction of words and by the addition of grave accents. As Oberon's three dumb shows along with his final exchange with Bohan are wrongly positioned after the first act in the 1598 first edition of the play, this edition has put the first dumb show after I.i, the second after II.i, and the third after III.ii; it has moved the final exchange to the end of the play. Other textual corruptions or variants, where significant, have been indicated in the notes. Sanders's 1970 *James IV* has proven to be enormously helpful; my punctuation, glosses, and emendations are greatly indebted to this important scholarly edition.

Further reading

Editions

Collins, J. Churton (ed.) (1905) *The Plays and Poems of Robert Greene*, vol. 1, Oxford: Clarendon Press.
Dickinson, T.H. (ed.) (1910) *The Scottish History of James the Fourth*, London: New Mermaids.
Dyce, Alexander (ed.) (1831) *The Dramatic Works of Robert Greene*, vol. 2, London: William Pickering.
Grosart, Alexander (ed.) (1881–86) *Life and Complete Works of Robert Greene*, vol. 13, London: Printed for private circulation.
Lavin, J.A. (ed.) (1967) *The Scottish History of James the Fourth*, London: New Mermaids.
Sanders, Norman (ed.) (1970) *The Scottish History of James the Fourth*, London: Methuen.
Swaen, A.E.H. (ed.) (1921) *The Scottish History of James the Fourth*, Oxford: Malone Society Reprints.

Critical and contextual reading

Aydelotte, Laura (2012) "'A Local Habitation and a Name': The Origins of Shakespeare's Oberon," *Shakespeare Survey* 65: 1–11.
Braunmuller, A.R. (1973) "The Serious Comedy of *James IV*," *English Literary Renaissance* 3: 335–50.
Crupi, Charles (1986) *Robert Greene*, New York: Twayne.
Foakes, R.A. (ed.) (2002) *Henslowe's Diary*, 2nd edn, Cambridge: Cambridge University Press.
Gieskes, Edward (2008) "Staging Professionalism in Greene's *James IV*," in Kirk Melnikoff and Edward Gieskes (eds), *Writing Robert Greene: Essays on England's First Notorious Professional Writer*, Aldershot: Ashgate: 53–72.
Greenfield, Thelma N. (1969) *The Induction in Elizabethan Drama*, Eugene: University of Oregon Press.
Hudson, Ruth (1932) "Greene's *James IV* and Contemporary Allusions to Scotland," *PMLA* 47: 652–67.
Knutson, Roslyn L. (1997) "Marlowe in Repertory, 1587–1593," in Kirk Melnikoff and Roslyn L. Knutson (eds), *Christopher Marlowe, Theatrical Commerce, and the Book Trade*, Cambridge: Cambridge University Press: 26–40.
Knutson, Roslyn L. (2008) "The History Play, *Richard II*, and Repertorial Commerce," in Jeremy Lopez (ed.), *Richard II: New Critical Essays*, New York: Routledge, 74–94.
McMillin, Scott and Sally Beth MacLean (1998) *The Queen's Men and Their Plays*, Cambridge: Cambridge University Press.
Melnikoff, Kirk (2011) *Robert Greene*, Aldershot: Ashgate.
Pinciss, G.M. (1970) "Thomas Creede and the Repertory of the Queen's Men, 1583–1592," *Modern Philology* 67: 321–30.
Syme, Holger Schott (2012) "Thomas Creede, William Barley, and the Venture of Printing Plays," in Marta Straznicky (ed.), *Shakespeare's Stationers: Studies in Cultural Bibliography*, Philadelphia: University of Pennsylvania Press: 28–46.
Young, Steven C. (1969) "A Check List of Tudor and Stuart Induction Plays," *Philological Quarterly* 48: 131–4.

The Scottish History of James IV (1588–92)

Dramatis personae[1]

OBERON, *King of the Fairies*
BOHAN
SLIPPER, *a clown, son of Bohan*
NANO, *a dwarf, son of Bohan*
JAMES IV, *King of Scotland*
KING OF ENGLAND
DOROTHEA, *Queen of Scotland, daughter of the King of England*
COUNTESS *of Arran*
IDA, *daughter of the Countess*
ATEUKIN
ANDREW *Snoord*
BARTRAM, *a Scottish Lord*
EUSTACE, *an English Lord*
SERVANT *to the Countess*
BISHOP *of St. Andrews*
DOUGLAS, *a Scottish Lord*
MORTON, *a Scottish Lord*
PURVEYOR, *servant to James IV*
JAQUES, *a French soldier*
ROSS, *a Scottish Lord*
SIR CUTHBERT ANDERSON, *a Scottish Lord*
LADY ANDERSON, *wife of Sir Cuthbert*

Huntsmen, Ladies, Tailor, Shoemaker, Cutler, Lawyer, Merchant, Divine, Scottish Scout, Lady Douglas (a Scottish Lady), Sir Egmond (a Scottish Lord), Percy (an English Lord), Antics, Fairies, Scottish Lords, English Lords, Revelers, Soldiers, English Herald, Servants

[Induction]

Music playing within. Enter after OBERON, *King of Fairies, an antic*[2] *who dances about a tomb placed conveniently*[3] *on the stage, out of the which suddenly starts up as they dance* BOHAN, *a Scot attired like a Redesdale man,*[4] *from whom the antic flies.* OBERON *manet*[5]

BOHAN Ay[6] say, what's[7] thou?
OBERON Thy friend, Bohan.

1 Dramatis personae: not in Q
2 0 SD *antic*: a performer, grotesquely attired
3 0 SD *conveniently*: in a suitable position
4 0 SD *Redesdale man*: violent marauder
5 0 SD *manet*: remains (Latin)
6 1 Ay: I; this edition retains Q's somewhat free movement, in Bohan's speech, between "I" and "ay" for the first-person singular pronoun
7 1 what's: what are

BOHAN What wot[8] I or reck[9] I that? Whey,[10] guid[11] man, I reck no friend nor ay reck no foe: al's ene[12] to me. Git thee ganging[13] and trouble not may quyat[14] or ay's gar[15] thee reckon me nene of thay[16] friend; by the mary mass,[17] sall I.[18]

OBERON Why, angry Scot, I visit thee for love; then what moves thee to wrath?

BOHAN The de'el awhit reck I thy love.[19] For I know too well that true love took her flight twenty winter sence[20] to heaven, whither till ay can, weel[21] I wot, ay sall ne'er find love. An[22] thou lov'st me, leave me to myself. But what were those puppits[23] that hopped and skipped about me year whayle?[24]

OBERON My subjects.

BOHAN Thay subjects? Whey, art thou a king?

OBERON I am.

BOHAN The de'el thou art! Whey, thou look'st not so big as the king of clubs, nor so sharp as the king of spades, nor so fain[25] as the king a daymonds. Be[26] the mass, ay take thee to be the king of false hearts; therefore, I rid[27] thee away, or ay's so curry[28] your kingdom that you's[29] be glad to run to save your life.

OBERON Why, stoical[30] Scot, do what thou dar'st to me. Here is my breast; strike!

BOHAN Thou wilt not threap[31] me! This whinyard has garred[32] many better men to lope[33] than thou. [*Tries to draw sword*] But how now? Go's seyds,[34] what, will't not out? Whey, thou witch! Thou de'el! Gad's fute,[35] may[36] whinyard!

OBERON Why, pull man! But what an 'twere[37] out? How then?

BOHAN This then! Thou wert best be gone first, for ay'll so lop thy limbs that thou's go with half a knave's carcass to the de'el.

OBERON Draw it out. [BOHAN *draws sword*] Now strike, fool! Canst thou not?

BOHAN Bread ay god,[38] what de'el is in me? Whey, tell me, thou skipjack;[39] what art thou?

OBERON Nay, first tell me what thou wast from thy birth, what thou hast passed hitherto, why thou dwellest in a tomb and leavest the world. And then I will release thee of these bonds; before, not.

8 3 wot: know
9 3 reck: care about
10 3 Whey: why
11 3 guid: good
12 4 al's ene: all's one
13 4 Git thee ganging: Get going
14 4 may quyat: my quiet
15 4 ay's gar: I'll make
16 5 nene of thay: none of thy
17 5 by the mary mass: by the mass of the Virgin Mary (expression)
18 5 sall I: shall I
19 7 The de'el . . . thy love: I do not care the least bit for your love (de'el: devil)
20 8 sence: since
21 8 weel: well
22 9 An: If
23 9 puppits: inferior actors
24 10 year whayle: erewhile, a little while ago
25 15 fain: glad
26 15 Be: by
27 16 rid: dismiss
28 16 ay's so curry: I will so batter
29 16 you's: you will
30 18 stoical: unaffected, austere
31 19 threap: quarrel with, fall out with
32 19 This whinyard has garred: this short sword has made
33 19 lope: jump away
34 20 Go's seyds: by God's sides
35 21 Gad's fute: by God's foot
36 21 may: my
37 22 an 'twere: if it were
38 26 Bread ay god: by the bread of God
39 26 skipjack: conceited dandy

BOHAN And not before? Then needs must, needs sall.[40] I was born a gentleman of the best bloud[41] in all Scotland, except the king. When time brought me to age[42] and death took my parents, I became a courtier, where, though ay list not praise[43] myself, ay engraved the memory of Bohan[44] on the skin-coat[45] of some of them and reveled with the proudest.
OBERON But why, living in such reputation, didst thou leave to be[46] a courtier?
BOHAN Because my pride was vanity, my expense loss, my reward fair words and large promises, and my hopes spilled, for that after many years' service, one outran[47] me. And what the de'el should I then do there? No, no, flattering knaves that can cog and prate[48] fastest speed[49] best in the court.
OBERON To what life didst thou then betake thee?
BOHAN I then changed the court for the country and the wars for a wife. But I found the craft[50] of swains[51] more vile than the knavery of courtiers, the charge of[52] children more heavy than servants, and wives' tongues worse than the wars itself. And therefore I gave o'er that and went to the city to dwell, and there I kept a great house with small cheer,[53] but all was ne'er the near.[54]
OBERON And why?
BOHAN Because in seeking friends, I found table guests to eat me and my meat, my wife's gossips[55] to bewray[56] the secrets of my heart, kindred to betray the effect[57] of my life; which, when I noted the court ill, the country worse, and the city worst of all, in good time my wife died. Ay would she had died twenty winter sooner, by the mass. Leaving my two sons to the world, I now shut myself into this tomb, where if I die, I am sure I am safe from wild beasts, but, whilst I live, cannot be free from ill company. Besides, now I am sure, gif[58] all my friends fail me, I sall have a grave of mine own providing. This is all. Now, what art thou?
OBERON Oberon, King of Fairies, that loves thee because thou hatest the world; and to gratulate[59] thee, I brought those antics to show thee some sport in dancing, which thou hast loved well.
BOHAN Ha, ha, ha! Thinkest thou those puppits can please me? Whey, I have two sons that with one Scottish jig[60] shall break the neck of thy antics.
OBERON That would I fain[61] see.
BOHAN Why thou shalt. Ho, boys! (*Enter* SLIPPER *and* NANO) Haud your clacks,[62] lads! Trattle[63] not for thy life, but gather up your legs and dance me forthwith a jig worth the sight.
SLIPPER Why, I must talk an[64] I die for't; wherefore was my tongue made?

40 30 needs must, needs sall: I must, I shall
41 31 bloud: blood
42 31 When time . . . to age: when I became a man
43 32 list not praise: desire not to praise
44 32–3 engraved the memory of Bohan: left scars
45 33 skin-coat: skin
46 34 leave to be: stop being
47 36 outran: got ahead of
48 37 cog and prate: cheat and boast
49 37 speed: fare
50 41 craft: fraud
51 41 swains: countrymen
52 41 charge of: responsibility for
53 43 small cheer: limited entertainments
54 43–4 ne'er the near: never the nearer to what I aspired
55 47 gossips: friends
56 47 bewray: expose
57 47 betray the effect: malign the accomplishments
58 51 gif: if
59 54 gratulate: gratify
60 57 jig: dance
61 58 fain: gladly
62 59 Haud your clacks: hold your tongues
63 60 Trattle: talk idly
64 62 an: even if

BOHAN Prattle, an thou darest, ene[65] word more and ay's dab[66] this whinyard in thy wemb![67]
OBERON Be quiet, Bohan. I'll strike him dumb and his brother, too. Their talk shall not hinder our jig. Fall to it! Dance, I say man!
BOHAN Dance, hummer![68] Dance, ay rid thee![69] *The two dance a jig devised for the nonce*[70]
Now get you to the wide world with more than my father gave me: that's learning enough, both kinds, knavery and honesty; and that I gave you spend at pleasure.
OBERON Nay, for their sport[71] I will give them this gift: to the dwarf I give a quick wit, pretty of body, and awarrant[72] his preferment to a prince's service where by his wisdom he shall gain more love than common. And to loggerhead,[73] your son, I give a wandering life and promise he shall never lack; and avow that, if in all distresses he call upon me, to help him. Now let them go. *Exeunt* [SLIPPER *and* NANO] *with curtsies*
BOHAN Now, King, if thou be a king, I will show thee whey I hate the world by demonstration. In the year 1520 was in Scotland a king overruled with parasites, misled by lust and many circumstances too long to trattle on now, much like our court of Scotland this day. That story have I set down.[74] Gang[75] with me to the gallery,[76] and I'll show thee the same in action by guid fellows of our countrymen. And then, when thou seest that, judge if any wise man would not leave the world if he could.
OBERON That will I see. Lead and I'll follow thee.
Exeunt

Act I, scene i[77]

Enter the KING of ENGLAND, JAMES IV, DOROTHEA *his queen, the* COUNTESS, *Lady* IDA, *with other lords, and* ATEUKIN *with them aloof*

JAMES IV Brother of England,[78] since our neighboring land
And near alliance doth invite our loves,
The more I think upon our last accord,
The more I grieve your sudden parting hence.
First, laws of friendship did confirm our peace;
Now, both the seal of faith and marriage bed,
The name of father,[79] and the style[80] of friend,
These force in me affection full confirmed,
So that I grieve—and this my hearty grief
The heavens record, the world may witness well—
To lose your presence who are now to me
A father, brother, and a vowèd friend.
KING OF ENGLAND Link all these lovely styles, good King, in one.
And since thy grief exceeds in my depart,[81]

65 63 ene: one
66 63 ay's dab: I'll stab, pierce
67 63 wemb: belly
68 66 hummer: talker, possibly "humor" (a whimsical person)
69 66 ay rid thee: away with you!
70 66 SD *nonce*: occasion
71 69 for their sport: in recompense for their dancing
72 70 awarrant: pledge his employment in
73 71 loggerhead: blockhead
74 77 set down: written down in the form of a play
75 77 Gang: walk
76 77 gallery: upper seating area in an amphitheatre playhouse
77 Act I, scene i: in Q, the first act is headed with "*Laus Deo detur in Eternum*" (Let praise be given to God forevermore; Latin)
78 1 Brother of England: during the period, monarchs commonly addressed one another as siblings
79 7 father: father-in-law
80 7 style: title
81 14 depart: departure

I leave my Dorothea to enjoy
Thy whole compact[82] of loves and plighted vows.
Brother of Scotland, this is my joy, my life,
Her father's honor and her country's hope,
Her mother's comfort, and her husband's bliss.
I tell thee, King, in loving of my Doll,[83]
Thou bindst her father's heart and all his friends
In bands of love that death cannot dissolve.
JAMES IV Nor can her father love her like to me.
My life's light and the comfort of my soul,
Fair Dorothea, that wast England's pride,
Welcome to Scotland; and, in sign of love,
Lo, I invest thee with the Scottish crown.
Nobles and ladies, stoop unto your queen,
And trumpets sound that heralds may proclaim
Fair Dorothea peerless Queen of Scots!
ALL Long live and prosper our fair Queen of Scots! *Install and crown her*
DOROTHEA Thanks to the King of kings[84] for my dignity;
Thanks to my father that provides so carefully;
Thanks to my lord and husband for this honor;
And thanks to all that love their king and me.
ALL Long live fair Dorothea, our true queen!
KING OF ENGLAND Long shine the sun of Scotland in her pride,
Her father's comfort and fair Scotland's bride.
But Dorothea, since I must depart
And leave thee from thy tender mother's charge,[85]
Let me advise my lovely daughter first
What best befits her in a foreign land.
Live, Doll, for many eyes shall look on thee;
Have care of honor and the present state,
For she that steps to height of majesty
Is ever the mark whereat the enemy aims:
Thy virtues shall be construèd to[86] vice,
Thine affable discourse to abject mind;
If coy, detracting tongues will call thee proud.
Be therefore wary in this slippery state;[87]
Honor thy husband; love him as thy life.
Make choice of friends as eagles of their young,[88]
Who soothe no vice, who flatter not for gain,
But love such friends as do the truth maintain.
Think on these lessons when thou art alone,
And thou shalt live in health when I am gone.
DOROTHEA I will engrave these precepts in my heart,
And as the wind with calmness woos you hence,[89]
Even so I wish the heavens in all mishaps
May bless my father with continual grace.
KING OF ENGLAND Then, son, farewell;

82 16 compact: contract
83 20 Doll: nickname for Dorothea
84 32 King of kings: i.e. Jesus Christ
85 40 charge: oversight
86 47 construèd to: interpreted as
87 50 slippery state: difficult to manage nation
88 52 as eagles of their young: as eagles cull their weak fledglings
89 58 As calm wind invites your departure

The favoring winds invite us to depart.
Long circumstance[90] in taking princely leaves
Is more officious than convenient.
Brother of Scotland, love me in my child;
You greet[91] me well, if so you will[92] her good.
JAMES IV Then, lovely Doll and all that favor me,
Attend to see our English friends at sea;
Let all their charge depend upon my purse:
They are our neighbors, by whose kind accord[93]
We dare attempt[94] the proudest potentate.
Only, fair Countess and your daughter, stay;
With you I have some other things to say.
Exeunt all—save JAMES IV, *the* COUNTESS, IDA, [*and*] ATEUKIN—*in all royalty*[95]
[*Aside*] So let them triumph that have cause to joy;
But, wretched King, thy nuptial knot is death,
Thy bride the breeder of thy country's ill,
For thy false heart dissenting from thy hand,
Misled by love, has made another choice;
Another choice, even when thou vow'dst thy soul
To Dorothea, England's choicest pride,
Oh then thy wandering eyes bewitched thy heart.
Even in the chapel did thy fancy change,
When, perjured man, though fair Doll had thy hand,
The Scottish Ida's beauty stole thy heart.
Yet fear and love have tied thy ready tongue
From blabbing forth the passions of thy mind,
Lest fearful silence has in subtle looks
Bewrayed[96] the treason of my new vowed love.
Be fair and lovely, Doll, but here's the prize
That lodgeth here[97] and entered through mine eyes.
Yet howsoe'er I love, I must be wise.
—Now, lovely Countess, what reward or grace
May I employ[98] on you for this your zeal
And humble honors done us in our court
In entertainment of the English king?
COUNTESS It was of duty, prince, that I have done,
And what in favor may content me most
Is that it please your grace to give me leave
For to return unto my country home.
JAMES IV But, lovely Ida, is your mind the same?
IDA I count of court, my lord, as wise men do:
'Tis fit for those that know what longs[99] thereto;
Each person to his place: the wise to art,
The cobbler to his clout,[100] the swain to cart.

90 63 circumstance: ceremony
91 66 greet: treat
92 66 will: aspire for
93 70 by whose kind accord: with whose friendly alliance
94 71 attempt: defy
95 73 SD *in all royalty*: with great pomp
96 88 Bewrayed: divulged, betrayed
97 90 here: in my heart
98 93 employ: bestow
99 102 longs: belongs
100 104 clout: piece of leather used for mending

JAMES IV But, Ida, you are fair, and beauty shines
And seemeth best where pomp her pride refines.
IDA If beauty (as I know there's none in me)
Were sworn my love, and I his life should be,
The farther from the court I were removed,
The more I think of heaven I were beloved.
JAMES IV And why?
IDA Because the court is counted Venus' net,[101]
Where gifts and vows for stales[102] are often set;
None, be she chaste as Vesta,[103] but shall meet
A curious tongue to charm her ears with sweet.
JAMES IV Why, Ida, then I see you set at naught[104]
The force of love.
IDA In sooth,[105] this is my thought,
Most gracious King, that they that little prove[106]
Are mickle[107] blessed from bitter sweets of love;
And weel I wot, I heard a shepherd sing,
That like a bee, love hath a little sting:
He lurks in flowers; he percheth on the trees;
He on kings' pillows bends his pretty knees;
The boy[108] is blind, but when he will not spy,[109]
He has a leaden foot and wings to fly.
Beshrew me yet[110] for all these strange effects,
If I would like the lad that so infects.
JAMES IV [*Aside*] Rare wit, fair face, what heart could more desire?
But Doll is fair and doth concern thee near.
Let Doll be fair; she is won, but I must woo
And win fair Ida; there's some choice in two.[111]
—But, Ida, thou art coy.
IDA And why, dread King?
JAMES IV In that you will dispraise so sweet a thing
As love. Had I my wish—
IDA What then?
JAMES IV Then would I place
His arrow here, his beauty in that face.
IDA And were Apollo[112] moved and ruled by me,
His wisdom should be yours and mine his tree.[113]

Enter the train back

JAMES IV But here returns our train. Welcome, fair Doll.
How fares our father? Is he shipped and gone?
DOROTHEA My royal father is both shipped and gone.

101 112 Venus' net: the web of Venus, Roman goddess of love
102 113 stales: traps; also, unchaste women
103 114 Vesta: Roman goddess of the hearth and household
104 116 set at naught: do not take seriously
105 117 sooth: truth
106 118 little prove: barely test it
107 119 mickle: greatly
108 124 The boy: Cupid
109 124 when he will not spy: though he cannot see
110 126 Beshrew me: evil befall me
111 131 there's some choice in two: with two, I have a choice
112 137 Apollo: Greek god of wisdom, son of Zeus
113 138 his tree: pursued by Apollo, Daphne was transformed into the laurel tree in order to protect her virginity

God and fair winds direct him to his home.
JAMES IV Amen, say I. [*Aside*] Would thou wert with him too;
Then might I have a fitter time to woo.
—But Countess, you would be gone; therefore, farewell.
Yet Ida, if thou wilt, stay thou behind
To accompany my queen.
But if thou like the pleasures of the court—
[*Aside*] Or if she liked me, though she left the court.
What should I say? I know not what to say.
—You may depart; and you, my courteous queen,
Leave me a space; I have a weighty cause
To think upon. [*Aside*] Ida, it nips me near;[114]
It came from thence; I feel it burning here.[115]

Exeunt all, saving JAMES IV *and* ATEUKIN

Now am I free from sight of common eye,
Where to myself I may disclose the grief
That hath too great a part in mine affects.[116]
ATEUKIN [*Aside*] And now is my time by wiles and words to rise,
Greater than those that think themselves more wise.
JAMES IV And first, fond King, thy honor doth engrave
Upon thy brows the drift of thy disgrace.
Thy new vowed love in sight of God and men
Links thee to Dorothea during life,
For who more fair and virtuous than thy wife?
Deceitful murtherer[117] of a quiet mind,
Fond love, vile lust, that thus misleads us men
To vow our faiths and fall to sin again.
But kings stoop not to every common thought:
Ida is fair and wise, fit for a king;
And for fair Ida will I hazard life,
Venture my kingdom, country, and my crown:
Such fire hath love to burn a kingdom down.
Say Doll dislikes that I estrange[118] my love;
Am I obedient to a woman's look?
Nay, say her father frown when he shall hear
That I do hold fair Ida's love so dear.
Let father frown and fret, and fret and die,
Nor earth[119] nor heaven shall part my love and I.
Yea, they shall part us, but we first must meet,
And woo, and win, and yet the world not see't.[120]
Yea, there's the wound, and wounded with that thought,
So let me die, for all my drift is naught.[121]
ATEUKIN Most gracious and imperial majesty!
[*Aside*] A little flattery more were but too much.
JAMES IV Villain, what art thou that thus
Darest interrupt a prince's secrets?
ATEUKIN Dread King, thy vassal is a man of art,[122]

114 153 nips me near: upsets me greatly
115 154 here: in my heart
116 157 affects: affections
117 165 murtherer: murderer (this edition follows Q's "murther" for "murder" throughout)
118 173 estrange: withdraw
119 178 Nor earth: neither earth
120 180 see't: see it
121 182 all my drift is naught: all of what I have talked about here is in vain
122 187 man of art: scholar

Who knows by constellation of the stars,
By oppositions[123] and by dire aspects,[124]
The things are past[125] and those that are to come.
JAMES IV But where's thy warrant to approach my presence?
ATEUKIN My zeal and ruth[126] to see your grace's wrong
Makes me lament I did detract[127] so long.
JAMES IV If thou know'st thoughts, tell me what I mean now?
ATEUKIN I'll calculate the cause
Of those your highness' smiles and tell your thoughts.
JAMES IV But lest thou spend thy time in idleness
And miss the matter that my mind aims at,
Tell me, what star was opposite when that[128] was thought? *He strikes him on the ear*
ATEUKIN 'Tis inconvenient,[129] mighty potentate,
Whose looks resemble Jove[130] in majesty,
To scorn the sooth of science[131] with contempt.
I see in those imperial looks of yours
The whole discourse of love: Saturn, combust,
With direful looks at your nativity,
Beheld fair Venus in her silver orb.[132]
I know by certain axioms I have read
Your grace's griefs and further can express her name
That holds you thus in fancy's bands.[133]
JAMES IV Thou talkest wonders.
ATEUKIN Naught but truth, O King.
'Tis Ida is the mistress of your heart,
Whose youth must take impression of affects,[134]
For tender twigs will bow and milder minds
Will yield to fancy, be they followed well.
JAMES IV What god art thou composed in human shape,
Or bold Trophonius,[135] to decide[136] our doubts?
How know'st thou this?
ATEUKIN Even as I know the means
To work your grace's freedom and your love.
Had I the mind, as many courtiers have,
To creep into your bosom for your coin
And beg rewards for every cap and knee,[137]
I then would say, "if that your Grace would give
This lease,[138] this manor, or this patent sealed,[139]
For this or that I would effect your love."

123 189 oppositions: the position of heavenly bodies in relation to one another
124 189 dire aspects: the position of heavenly bodies in relation to an observer on earth (sometimes appearing "dire," i.e. portending ill)
125 190 The things are past: the causes of things that have happened
126 192 ruth: sorrow
127 193 detract: delay, stray from my purpose
128 199 that: i.e. the blow that James IV just gave him
129 200 inconvenient: unreasonable
130 201 Jove: Jupiter, king of the gods
131 202 sooth of science: truth of knowledge
132 204–6 Saturn, combust . . . silver orb: Ateukin here contends that astrological configurations at James IV's birth portend love between him and Ida
133 209 fancy's bands: love's bonds
134 212 must take impression of affects: is necessarily subject to affections
135 216 Trophonius: ancient Greek hero or god around which an oracular cult developed
136 216 decide: resolve
137 221 cap and knee: act of deference
138 223 lease: land grant
139 223 patent sealed: an official document conferring privilege, right, office, or title

But Ateukin is no parasite, O Prince;
I know your grace knows scholars are but poor,
And therefore as I blush to beg a fee,
Your mightiness is so magnificent
You cannot choose but cast some gift apart[140]
To ease my bashful need that cannot beg.
As for your love, oh might I be employed,
How faithfully would Ateukin compass[141] it.
But princes rather trust a smoothing tongue
Than men of art that can accept the time.[142]
JAMES IV Ateukin, if so thy name, for so thou sayst,
Thine art appears in entrance[143] of my love;
And since I deem thy wisdom matched with truth,
I will exalt thee, and thyself alone
Shalt be the agent to dissolve my grief.
Sooth is, I love, and Ida is my love,
But my new marriage nips me near, Ateukin:
For Dorothea may not brook th'abuse.[144]
ATEUKIN These lets[145] are but as motes[146] against the sun—
Yet not so great—like dust before the wind—
Yet not so light. Tut, pacify your grace;
You have the sword and scepter in your hand.
You are the king: the state depends on you;
Your will is law. Say that the case were mine:
Were she my sister whom your highness loves,
She should consent, for that our lives, our goods,
Depend on you; and if your queen repine,
Although my nature cannot brook of blood,
And scholars grieve to hear of murtherous deeds,
But if the lamb should let[147] the lion's way,
By my advice the lamb should lose her life.
Thus am I bold to speak unto your grace,
Who am too base to kiss your royal feet:
For I am poor, nor have I land, nor rent,
Nor countenance[148] here in court; but for my love,
Your grace shall find none such within the realm.
JAMES IV Wilt thou effect my love?[149] Shall she be mine?
ATEUKIN I'll gather moly,[150] crocus,[151] and the herbs
That heal the wounds of body and the mind;
I'll set out charms and spells; naught else shall be left[152]
To tame the wanton if she shall rebel.
Give me but tokens of your highness' trust.
JAMES IV Thou shalt have gold, honor, and wealth enough;

140 229 cast some gift apart: give some gift
141 232 compass: accomplish
142 234 accept the time: accept their lot
143 236 entrance: knowing
144 242 brook th'abuse: endure the ill treatment
145 243 lets: obstacles
146 243 motes: particles of dust
147 254 let: hinder
148 259 countenance: reputation
149 261 effect my love: cause my love to be reciprocated
150 262 moly: herb thought to have magical powers
151 262 crocus: flower sometimes used for love spells
152 264 left: neglected

Win my love, and I will make thee great.
ATEUKIN These words do make me rich, most noble prince.
I am more proud of them than any wealth.
Did not your grace suppose I flatter you,[153]
Believe me, I would boldly publish this:
Was never eye that saw a sweeter face,
Nor never ear that heard a deeper wit.
O God, how I am ravished in your worth!
JAMES IV Ateukin, follow me; love must have ease.
ATEUKIN I'll kiss your highness' feet; march when you please.

Exeunt

[Chorus i][154]

[*Enter* OBERON *and* BOHAN]

OBERON Here see I good fond[155] actions in thy jig
And means to paint the world's inconstant ways.
But turn thine eye; see which I can command.

Enter two [sides] strongly fighting, the one [led by] Semiramis, the other [by] Stabrobates; [Semiramis] flies and her crown is taken and she hurt; [exeunt both sides]

BOHAN What gars this din[156] of mirk and baleful[157] harm
Where everywean[158] is all betaint[159] with bloud?
OBERON This shows thee, Bohan, what is worldly pomp.
Semiramis, the proud Assyrian queen,
When Ninus[160] died, did tend[161] in her wars
Three millions of footmen to the fight,
Five hundred thousand horse, of armèd chars[162]
A hundred thousand more; yet in her pride
Was hurt and conquered by Stabrobates.[163]
Then what is pomp?
BOHAN I see thou art thine ene,[164]
Thou bonny[165] King; if[166] princes fall from high,
My fall is past, until I fall to die.
Now mark my talk and prosecute[167] my jig.

[*Exeunt*]

153 271 If you would not just assume I was flattering you
154 Chorus i: mistakenly printed at the end of Act I in Q
155 1 fond: foolish
156 4 din: noise
157 4 mirk and baleful: obscure and deadly
158 5 everywean: everyone
159 5 betaint: stained
160 8 Ninus: king of Assyria, Semiramis' second husband
161 8 tend: lead
162 10 chars: chariots
163 12 Stabrobates: Indian king
164 13 ene: own
165 14 bonny: term expressing fondness
166 14 if: even if
167 16 prosecute: continue with

[Act I, scene ii]

Enter SLIPPER, NANO, *and* ANDREW *with their bills*[168] *ready written in their hands*

ANDREW Stand back, sir; mine shall stand highest.

SLIPPER Come under mine arm, sir, or get a footstool; or else by the light of the moon, I must come to it.[169]

NANO Agree, my masters, every man to his height: though I stand lowest, I hope to get the best master.

ANDREW Ere I will stoop to a thistle, I will change turns,[170] as good luck comes on the right hand as the left: here's for me. [*Posts bill*]

SLIPPER And me. [*Posts bill*]

NANO And mine. [*Posts bill*]

ANDREW But tell me, fellows, till better occasion come, do you seek masters?

SLIPPER AND NANO We do.

ANDREW But what can you do worthy preferment?

NANO Marry, I can smell a knave from a rat.

SLIPPER And I can lick a dish before a cat.

ANDREW And I can find two fools unsought. How like you that? But in earnest, now tell me of what trades are you two?

SLIPPER How mean you that, sir, of what trade? Marry, I'll tell you, I have many trades: the honest trade when I needs must, the filching trade[171] when time serves, the cozening trade[172] as I find occasion. And I have more qualities: I cannot abide a full cup unkissed,[173] a fat capon[174] uncarved, a full purse unpicked, nor a fool to prove a justice[175] as you do.

ANDREW Why, sot, why call'st thou me fool?

SLIPPER For examining wiser than thyself.

ANDREW So doth many more than I in Scotland.

NANO Yea, those are such as have more authority than wit and more wealth than honesty.

SLIPPER This is my little brother with the great wit.[176] 'Ware[177] him. But what canst thou do, tell me, that art so inquisitive of us?

ANDREW Anything that concerns a gentleman to do, that can I do.

SLIPPER So you are of the gentle trade?[178]

ANDREW True.

SLIPPER Then, gentle sir, leave us to ourselves, for here comes one as if he would lack a servant ere he went.[179]

Enter ATEUKIN

ATEUKIN Why so, Ateukin? This becomes thee best:
Wealth, honor, ease, and angels[180] in thy chest.
Now may I say, as many often sing,
"No fishing to the sea nor service to the king."[181]
Unto this high promotion doth belong

168 0 SD *bills*: advertisements (they are seeking employment)
169 3 come to it: get the most opportune position for his advertisement
170 6 Ere I . . . change turns: before I will put my advertisement below Nano's, I will find another position on the wall
171 18 filching trade: thievery
172 18 cozening trade: cheating
173 19 unkissed: not drunk
174 19 capon: castrated rooster
175 20 justice: judge
176 25 great wit: brilliant mind
177 25 'Ware: beware
178 28 gentle trade: shoemaking
179 30–31 as if . . . he went: who will come to realize he needs a servant before he goes any further
180 33 angels: ten-shilling gold coins
181 35 Nothing is better than fishing in the sea or serving a king (proverbial)

Means to be talked of in the thickest throng.
And first, to fit the humors[182] of my lord,
Sweet lays[183] and lines of love I must record;
And such sweet lines and love lays I'll indite[184]
As men may wish for and my liege delight;
And next a train of gallants[185] at my heels
That men may say, "the world doth run on wheels";[186]
For men of art that rise by indirection
To honor and the favor of their king
Must use all means to save what they have got
And win their favors whom they never knew.[187]
If any frown to see my fortunes such,
A man must bear a little, not too much.[188]
But in good time, these bills portend, I think,
That some good fellows do for service seek.

[ATEUKIN] *read[s]. If any gentleman, spiritual or temporal,*[189] *will entertain out of his service*[190] *a young stripling*[191] *of the age of 30 years that can sleep with the soundest, eat with the hungriest, work with the sickest, lie with the loudest, face*[192] *with the proudest, etc., that can wait in a gentleman's chamber when his master is a mile off, keep his stable when 'tis empty, and his purse when 'tis full, and has many qualities worse than all these, let him write his name and go his way and attendance shall be given.*

By my faith, a good servant. Which is he?

SLIPPER Truly, sir, that am I.

ATEUKIN And why doest thou write such a bill? Are all these qualities in thee?

SLIPPER Oh lord, ay, sir, and a great many more: some better, some worse, some richer, some poorer. Why, sir, do you look so? Do they not please you?

ATEUKIN Truly, no, for they are naught and so art thou; if thou hast no better qualities, stand by.

SLIPPER O sir, I tell the worst first, but if you lack a man, I am for you; I'll tell you the best qualities I have.

ATEUKIN Be brief then.

SLIPPER If you need me in your chamber, I can keep the door at a whistle;[193] in your kitchen, turn the spit, and lick the pan, and make the fire burn; but if in the stable—

ATEUKIN Yea, there would I use thee.

SLIPPER Why, there you kill me;[194] there am I. And turn me to[195] a horse and a wench, and I have no peer.

ATEUKIN Art thou so good in keeping a horse? I pray thee tell me how many good qualities hath a horse?

SLIPPER Why so, sir, a horse hath two properties of a man, that is a proud heart and a hardy stomach; four properties of a lion, a broad breast, a stiff docket[196]—hold your nose,[197] master—a

182 38 humors: inclinations
183 39 lays: poems to be sung
184 40 indite: write
185 42 train of gallants: entourage of fashionable gentlemen and gentlewomen
186 43 the world . . . on wheels: all is prosperous (proverbial)
187 47 And ingratiate themselves with people that they did not know previously
188 49 A successful man must be willing to take some disdain from others
189 52 *spiritual or temporal*: a divine or a layperson
190 52–3 *entertain out of his service*: support in exchange for service
191 53 *stripling*: adolescent passing into manhood
192 54 *face*: swagger
193 68 at a whistle: at your beck and call
194 71 you kill me: you have it
195 71 turn me to: direct my attentions to
196 76 docket: tail
197 76 hold your nose: possibly because the lion's tail is near the anus

wild countenance, and four good legs; nine properties of a fox, nine of a hare, nine of an ass, and ten of a woman.
ATEUKIN A woman? Why, what properties of a woman hath a horse?
SLIPPER O master, know you not that? Draw your tables[198] and write what wise[199] I speak. First, a merry countenance; second, a soft pace;[200] third, a broad forehead; fourth, broad buttocks; fifth, hard of ward;[201] sixth, easy to leap upon; seventh, good at long journey; eighth, moving under a man; ninth, always busy with the mouth; tenth, ever chewing on the bridle.
ATEUKIN Thou art a man for me. What's thy name?
SLIPPER An ancient name, sir, belonging to the chamber and the nightgown. Guess you that.
ATEUKIN What's that, "Slipper"?
SLIPPER By my faith, well guessed and so 'tis indeed. You'll be my master?
ATEUKIN I mean so.
SLIPPER Read this first.
[ATEUKIN *reads*]. *Pleaseth it any gentleman to entertain a servant of more wit than stature, let them subscribe and attendance shall be given.*
What of this?
SLIPPER He is my brother, sir, and we two were born together, must serve together, and will die together, though[202] we be both hanged.
ATEUKIN What's thy name?
NANO Nano.
ATEUKIN The etymology of which word is "a dwarf." Art not thou the old stoic's son that dwells in his tomb?
SLIPPER AND NANO We are.
ATEUKIN Thou art welcome to me. Wilt thou give thyself wholly to be at my disposition?[203]
NANO In all humility I submit myself.
ATEUKIN Then will I deck thee princely, instruct thee courtly, and present thee to the queen as my gift. Art thou content?
NANO Yes, and thank your honor, too.
SLIPPER Then welcome brother and fellow now.
ANDREW May it please your honor to abase your eye so low as to look either on my bill or myself?
ATEUKIN What are you?
ANDREW By birth a gentleman, in profession a scholar, and one that knew your honor in Edinburgh[204] before your worthiness called you to this reputation,[205] by name Andrew Snoord.
ATEUKIN Andrew, I remember thee. Follow me, and we will confer further, for my weighty affairs for the king commands me to be brief at this time. Come on Nano; Slipper follow.

Exeunt

[Act I, scene iii]

Enter BARTRAM *with* EUSTACE *and others, booted*[206]

BARTRAM But tell me, lovely Eustace, as thou lov'st me,
Among the many pleasures we have passed,
Which is the rifest[207] in thy memory

198 80 Draw your tables: take out your commonplace book (i.e. a notebook for writing down wise sayings)
199 80 wise: wisdom
200 81 pace: footstep
201 82 hard of ward: difficult to master
202 94 though: even if
203 100–01 at my disposition: under my control
204 111 Edinburgh: capital of Scotland
205 111 called you to this reputation: led to your current prominence in court
206 0 SD *booted*: wearing riding boots
207 3 rifest: most prevalent

To draw thee over to[208] thine ancient friend?
EUSTACE What makes Sir Bartram thus inquisitive?
Tell me, good knight, am I welcome or no?
BARTRAM By sweet Saint Andrew[209] and may sale[210] I swear,
As welcome is my honest Dick[211] to me
As morning's sun or as the wat'ry moon
In mirkest[212] night when we the borders track.[213]
I tell thee, Dick, thy sight hath cleared my thoughts
Of many baneful troubles that there wound.
Welcome to Sir Bartram as his life.
Tell me, bonny Dick, hast got a wife?
EUSTACE A wife? God shield,[214] Sir Bartram, that were ill
To leave my wife and wander thus astray;
But time and good advice ere many years
May chance to make my fancy bend that way.
What news in Scotland? Therefore came I hither,
To see your country and to chat together.
BARTRAM Why man, our country's blithe, our king is well,
Our queen so-so, the nobles well, and worse
And weel are they that were about the king,
But better are the country gentlemen.[215]
And I may tell thee, Eustace, in our lives,
We old men never saw so wondrous change.
But leave this trattle and tell me what news
In lovely England with our honest friends?
EUSTACE The king, the court, and all our noble friends
Are well, and God in mercy keep them so.
The northern lords and ladies hereabouts,
That know I came to see your queen and court,
Commend them to my honest friend, Sir Bartram,
And many others that I have not seen;
Among the rest, the Countess Elinor
From Carlisle,[216] where we merry oft have been,
Greets well my lord and hath directed me
By message this fair lady's face to see. [EUSTACE *shows portrait of* IDA]
BARTRAM I tell thee, Eustace, lest mine old eyes daze,[217]
This is our Scottish moon and evening's pride,
This is the blemish of your English bride.[218]
Who sails by her are sure of wind at will;
Her face is dangerous; her sight is ill.[219]
And yet in sooth, sweet Dick, it may be said,
The king hath folly; there's virtue in the maid.
EUSTACE But knows my friend this portrait? Be advised.[220]

208 4 draw thee over to: encourage you to visit
209 7 Saint Andrew: patron saint of Scotland
210 7 may sale: my soul
211 8 Dick: nickname for Eustace
212 10 mirkest: gloomiest
213 10 track: cross
214 15 God shield: God forbid
215 24 i.e. better because not in court
216 36 Carlisle: town in southern Scotland
217 39 daze: are confounded with light
218 41 the blemish . . . English bride: that which has created a blot on Dorothea's situation
219 43 Her beauty is tempting; it is dangerous to see her
220 46 Be advised: think it over

BARTRAM Is it not Ida, the Countess of Arran's daughter?
EUSTACE So was I told by Elinor of Carlisle.
But tell me, lovely Bartram, is the maid
Evil inclined, misled, or concubine
Unto the king or any other lord?
BARTRAM Should I be brief and true? Then thus, my Dick:
All England's grounds yield not a blither[221] lass;
Nor Europe can match her for her gifts
Of virtue, honor, beauty, and the rest;
But our fond[222] king, not knowing sin in lust,
Makes love by endless means and precious gifts,
And men that see it dare not say't, my friend,
But we may wish that it were otherwise.
But I bid thee to view the picture still,
For by the person's sights there hangs some ill.[223]
EUSTACE O good Sir Bartram, you suspect I love;
Then were I mad—she whom I never saw!
But howsoe'er, I fear not enticings;
Desire will give no place unto a king.[224]
I'll see her whom the world admires so much
That I may say with them, "there lives none such."
BARTRAM Be Gad,[225] and shall both[226] see and talk with her,
And when th'hast done, whate'er her beauty be,
I'll warrant thee her virtue may compare
With the proudest she[227] that waits upon your queen.

[*Enter* SERVANT]

[SERVANT] My lady entreats your worship in to supper.
BARTRAM Guid bonny Dick, my wife will tell thee more;
Was never no man in her book before;[228]
Be Gad, she's blithe, fair, luwely,[229] bonny, etc.[230]

Exeunt

[Chorus ii]

Enter BOHAN *and* OBERON *after the first act, to them a round*[231] *of fairies or some pretty dance*[*; exeunt fairies*]

BOHAN Be Gad, gramercy,[232] little King, for this;
This sport is better in my exile life
Than ever the deceitful world could yield.
OBERON I tell thee, Bohan, Oberon is king

221 53 blither: more kindly
222 56 fond: foolish and in love
223 61 Seeing Ida in person could be dangerous, since she is loved by the king
224 65 will give . . . a king: will not be thwarted even by a king
225 68 Be Gad: by God
226 68 shall both: you shall both
227 71 she: woman
228 74 She has never been interested in a man as of yet
229 75 luwely: lovely
230 75 etc.: indication that characters should exit talking
231 0 SD *round*: circular dance
232 1 gramercy: thanks

Of quiet, pleasure, profit, and content,
Of wealth, of honor, and of all the world;
Tied to no place, yet all are tied to one.[233]
Live thou in this life, exiled from world and men,
And I will show thee wonders ere we part.
BOHAN Then mark my story and the strange doubts[234]
That follow flatterers, lust, and lawless will,
And then say I have reason to forsake
The world and all that are within the same.
Go shroud[235] us in our harbor[236] where we'll see
The pride[237] of folly as it ought to be.

Exeunt

Act II, scene i

Enter the COUNTESS *of Arran with* IDA *her daughter in*[238] *their porch, sitting at work.*[239] *A song*

COUNTESS Fair Ida, might you choose the greatest good
'Midst all the world in blessings that abound,
Wherein, my daughter, should your liking be?
IDA Not in delights, or pomp, or majesty.
COUNTESS And why?
IDA Since these are means to draw the mind
From perfect good and make true judgment blind.
COUNTESS Might you have wealth and fortune's richest store?
IDA Yet would I (might I choose) be honest poor,
For she that sits at Fortune's feet a-low[240]
Is sure she shall not taste a further woe;
But those that prank[241] on top of Fortune's ball[242]
Still fear a change and, fearing, catch a fall.
COUNTESS Tut, foolish maid, each one condemneth need.[243]
IDA Good reason why, they know not good indeed.
COUNTESS Many marry then on whom distress doth lour.[244]
IDA Yes, they that virtue deem an honest dower.[245]
Madam, by right this world I may compare
Unto my work, wherein with heedful care,
The heavenly workman plants with curious hand,
As I with needle draw each thing one land;[246]
Even as he list,[247] some men, like to the rose,
Are fashioned fresh; some in their stalks do close
And born do sudden die; some are but weeds,

233 7 Tied nowhere while everyone else is tied somewhere
234 10 doubts: apprehensions
235 14 shroud: hide
236 14 harbor: i.e. the gallery
237 15 pride: prideful nature
238 0 SD *in*: on
239 0 SD *at work*: at needlework
240 9 a-low: without advantage
241 11 prank: prance
242 11 Fortune's ball: ever-turning globe or wheel held by Fortune, representing change and unpredictability
243 13 need: poverty
244 15 lour: frown
245 16 dower: dowry
246 20 draw each thing one land: embroider each thing with its own place
247 21 he list: God chooses

And yet from them a secret good proceeds.
I with my needle, if I please, may blot[248]
The fairest rose within my cambric plot;[249]
God with a beck[250] can change each worldly thing,
The poor to earth, the beggar to the king.
What then hath man wherein he well may boast,
Since by a beck he lives, a lour[251] is lost?

Enter EUSTACE *with letters*

COUNTESS Peace, Ida, here are strangers near at hand.
EUSTACE Madam, God speed.
COUNTESS I thank you, gentle squire.
EUSTACE The country[252] Countess of Northumberland
Doth greet you well and hath requested me
To bring these letters to your ladyship. *He [offers] the letters*
COUNTESS I thank her honor and yourself, my friend. *She receives and peruseth them*
I see she means you good, brave gentleman;
Daughter, the Lady Elinor salutes
Yourself as well as me; then for her sake
'Twere good you entertained that courtier well.
IDA As much salute[253] as may become[254] my sex,
And he in virtue can vouchsafe[255] to think,
I yield him for the courteous countess' sake.
Good sir, sit down; my mother here and I
Count time misspent an endless vanity.
EUSTACE [*Aside*] Beyond report, the wit, the fair, the shape.
—What work you here, fair mistress? May I see it?
IDA Good sir, look on. How like you this compact?[256]
EUSTACE Methinks in this I see true love in act:
The woodbines[257] with their leaves do sweetly spread,
The roses blushing prank them[258] in their red,
No flower but boasts the beauties of the spring;
The bird hath life indeed, as it[259] could sing.
What means, fair mistress, had you in this work?
IDA My needle, sir.
EUSTACE In needles then there lurks
Some hidden grace I deem beyond my reach.
IDA Not grace in them, good sir, but those that teach.[260]
EUSTACE Say that your needle now were Cupid's sting—
[*Aside*] But ah, her eye must be no less,[261]
In which is heaven and heavenliness,

248 25 blot: disfigure
249 26 cambric plot: fine white linen
250 27 beck: slight nod
251 30 lour: frown
252 33 country: rurally located
253 41 salute: greeting
254 41 may become: is appropriate to
255 42 vouchsafe: be prepared
256 48 compact: embroidered picture
257 50 woodbines: climbing plant
258 51 prank them: prance, show themselves off
259 53 as it: as if it
260 57 The grace does not lie in the needles but in what can be taught by the images they sew
261 59 Ida's eye is like Cupid's love arrow

In which the food of God is shut,
Whose powers the purest minds do glut.[262]
IDA What if it were?
EUSTACE Then see a wondrous thing:
I fear me you would paint in Tereus' heart
Affection in his power and chiefest parts.[263]
IDA Good Lord sir, no, for hearts but prickèd soft[264]
Are wounded sore, for so I hear it oft.
EUSTACE What recks[265] the wound, where but your happy eye
May make him live whom Jove hath judged to die?
IDA Should life and death within this needle lurk,
I'll prick no hearts; I'll prick upon my work.

Enter ATEUKIN *with* SLIPPER *the clown*

COUNTESS Peace, Ida, I perceive the fox at hand.
EUSTACE The fox? Why, fetch your hounds and chase him hence.
COUNTESS O sir, these great men bark at small offence.
Come, will it please you to enter, gentle sir? [COUNTESS, IDA, *and* EUSTACE] *offer to exeunt*
ATEUKIN Stay, courteous ladies; favor me so much
As to discourse a word or two apart.
COUNTESS Good sir, my daughter learns this rule of me:
To shun resort[266] and strangers' company;
For some are shifting mates[267] that carry letters,
Some, such as you, too good because our betters.
SLIPPER Now I pray you, sir, what a kin are you to a pickerel?[268]
ATEUKIN Why, knave?
SLIPPER By my troth, sir, because I never knew a proper situation fellow[269] of your pitch[270] fitter to swallow a gudgeon.[271]
ATEUKIN What mean'st thou by this?
SLIPPER "Shifting fellow," sir, these be thy words:[272] "shifting fellow." This gentlewoman, I fear me, knew your bringing up.
ATEUKIN How so?
SLIPPER Why sir, your father was a miller that could shift for a peck of grist in a bushel,[273] and you a fair-spoken gentleman that can get more land by a lie than an honest man by his ready money.
ATEUKIN Caitiff,[274] what sayest thou?
SLIPPER I say, sir, that if she call you "shifting knave," you shall not put her to the proof.[275]
ATEUKIN And why?

262 62 the purest minds do glut: can overcome the most virtuous minds
263 64–5 in Tereus' ... chiefest parts: Tereus raped Philomela and cut out her tongue; Eustace fears that Ida would paint "Affection" as his "chiefest" characteristic
264 66 prickèd soft: barely pricked
265 68 recks: matters
266 79 resort: a crowd
267 80 shifting mates: knaves
268 82 pickerel: young pike (a fish)
269 84 proper situation fellow: man in a good situation
270 84 pitch: status
271 85 gudgeon: small fish used for bait
272 87 thy words: words applying to you
273 90–91 shift for ... a bushel: steal a peck out of every bushel of unground corn (a peck is a quarter bushel)
274 93 Caitiff: villain
275 94 put her to the proof: contest her accusation

SLIPPER Because, sir, living by your wits as you do, shifting is your letters patents;[276] it were a hard matter for me to get my dinner that day wherein my master had not sold a dozen of devices,[277] a case of cogs,[278] and a suit of shifts[279] in the morning. I speak this in your commendation, sir, and I pray you so take it.
ATEUKIN If I live, knave, I will be revenged! What gentleman would entertain a rascal thus to derogate from[280] his honor?
IDA My lord, why are you thus impatient?
ATEUKIN Not angry, Ida, but I teach this knave
How to behave himself among his betters.
Behold, fair countess, to assure your stay,[281]
I here present the signet[282] of the king,
Who now by me, fair Ida, doth salute you;
And since in secret I have certain things
In his behalf, good madam, to impart,
I crave your daughter to discourse apart.
COUNTESS She shall in humble duty be addressed
To do his highness' will in what she may. [IDA *and* ATEUKIN *talk apart*]
IDA Now, gentle sir, what would his grace with me?
ATEUKIN Fair, comely nymph, the beauty of your face,
Sufficient to bewitch the heavenly powers,
Hath wrought so much in him that now of late
He finds himself made captive unto love,
And though his power and majesty require[283]
A straight command before an humble suit,
Yet he his mightiness doth so abase,
As to entreat your favor, honest maid.
IDA Is he not married, sir, unto our queen?
ATEUKIN He is.
IDA And are not they by God accursed
That sever them whom he hath knit in one?
ATEUKIN They be. What then? We seek not to displace
The princess from her seat; but since by love
The king is made your own, he is resolved
In private to accept your dalliance,[284]
In spite of war, watch, or worldly eye.
IDA Oh how he talks as if he should not die,
As if that God in justice once could wink[285]
Upon that fault I am ashamed to think.
ATEUKIN Tut, mistress, man at first was born to err.
Women are all not formèd to be saints;
'Tis impious for to kill our native king,
Whom by a little favor we may save.
IDA Better than live unchaste to live in grave.
ATEUKIN He shall erect your state and wed you well.[286]

276 96 shifting is your letters patents: stealing and cheating is your official business
277 98 devices: tricks
278 987 cogs: dice scams
279 98 shifts: subterfuges
280 101 derogate from: denigrate
281 105 assure your stay: make certain you do not depart
282 106 signet: a small, authorized seal
283 118 require: necessitate
284 128 dalliance: secret love
285 131 wink: turn a blind eye
286 138 wed you well: find you a husband of stature

IDA But can his warrant keep my soul from hell?
ATEUKIN He will enforce, if you resist his suit.
IDA What though the world may shame to him account[287]
To be a king of men and worldly pelf,[288]
Yet hath no power to rule and guide himself.
ATEUKIN I know you, gentle lady, and the care,
Both of your honor and his grace's health,
Makes me confusèd[289] in this dangerous state.
IDA So counsel him, but soothe thou not his sin;
'Tis vain allurement that doth make him love.
I shame to hear; be you ashamed to move.[290]
COUNTESS [*Aside*] I see my daughter grows impatient;
I fear me he pretends[291] some bad intent.
ATEUKIN Will you despise the king and scorn him so?
IDA In all allegiance I will serve his grace
But not in lust; Oh how I blush to name it!
ATEUKIN [*Aside*] An endless work is this; how should I frame it? *They discourse privately*
SLIPPER O mistress, may I turn a word upon[292] you?
COUNTESS Friend, what wilt thou?

SLIPPER Oh, what a happy gentlewoman be you truly; the world reports this of you, mistress, that a man can no sooner come to your house, but the butler comes with a black jack[293] and says, "Welcome, friend, here's a cup of the best for you." Verily, mistress, you are said to have the best ale in all Scotland.

COUNTESS Sirrah,[294] go fetch him drink. [*Servant brings drink*] How likest thou this?

SLIPPER Like it, mistress? Why, this is quincy quarie pepper de watchet, single goby,[295] of all that ever I tasted: I'll prove in this ale and toast[296] the compass[297] of the whole world. First, this[298] is the earth; it ties[299] in the middle a fair brown toast, a goodly country for hungry teeth to dwell upon; next this is the sea, a fair pool for a dry tongue to fish in; now come I and seeing the world is naught,[300] I divide it thus, and because the sea cannot stand without the earth, as Aristotle[301] say'th, I put them both into their first chaos[302] which is my belly; and so, mistress, .you may see your ale is become a miracle.[303]

EUSTACE A merry mate, madam, I promise you. [SLIPPER *moans*]

COUNTESS Why sigh you, sirrah?

SLIPPER Truly, madam, to think upon the world, which since I denounced,[304] it keeps such a rumbling in my stomach, that unless your cook give it a counterbuff[305] with some of your roasted capons or beef, I fear me I shall become a loose body, so dainty[306] I think, I shall neither hold

287 141 may shame to him account: may consider it shameful
288 142 pelf: stolen goods
289 146 confusèd: disconcerted
290 149 move: implore
291 151 pretends: asserts
292 156 turn a word upon: talk to
293 159 black jack: tar coated beer jug
294 162 Sirrah: term of address expressing authority of speaker
295 163 quincy quarie . . . single goby: nonsense words
296 164 ale and toast: bread was traditionally served in a mug of beer
297 164 compass: measure
298 165 this: the drinking vessel
299 165 ties: holds
300 167 naught: worthless
301 168 Aristotle: ancient Greek philosopher
302 168 first chaos: state of disorder before God made the earth
303 169 miracle: because it renders the "first chaos"
304 172 since I denounced: alluding to "the world is naught" at line 167
305 173 counterbuff: a returned blow
306 174 dainty: delicate in constitution

fast before nor behind.[307]
COUNTESS Go, take him in and feast this merry swain.
Sirrah, my cook is your physician;
He hath a purge[308] for to digest the world. [*Exeunt* SLIPPER *and Servant*]
ATEUKIN Will you not, Ida, grant his highness this?
IDA As I have said, in duty I am his;
For other lawless lusts that ill beseem him,
I cannot like, and good I will not deem him.
COUNTESS Ida, come in; [*To* EUSTACE] and sir, if so you please,
Come take a homely widow's entertain.
IDA If he hath no great haste, he may come nigh;
If haste, though he be gone, I will not cry. *Exeunt* [COUNTESS, IDA, *and* EUSTACE]
ATEUKIN I see this labor lost, my hope in vain,
Yet will I try another drift[309] again.
[*Exit*]

[Chorus iii][310]

[*Enter* OBERON *and* BOHAN]

OBERON How should these crafts[311] withdraw thee from the world?
But look, my Bohan, pomp allureth.

Enter Cyrus, kings humbling themselves, himself crowned by olive [leaves], that at last dying [is] laid in a marble tomb with this inscription: "Whoso thou be that passest, for I know one shall pass, know I am Cyrus of Persia and I prithee [312] *leave me not thus like a clod of clay wherewith my body is covered"; [kings] exeunt*

Enter [a] king in great pomp who reads [the inscription] and [exits, crying] "ver meum!"[313]

BOHAN What meaneth this?
OBERON Cyrus of Persia,
Mighty in life, within a marble grave
Was laid to rot, whom Alexander[314] once
Beheld entombed and weeping did confess
Nothing in life could 'scape from wretchedness.
Why then boast men?
BOHAN What reck I then of life[315]
Who makes the grave my home, the earth my wife?
But mark me more.
[*Exeunt*]

[Act II, scene ii]

Enter the BISHOP *of St. Andrews,*[316] *Earl* DOUGLAS, MORTON, *with others one way,* DOROTHEA *with* NANO *another way*

307 174–5 shall neither … nor behind: will become openly gaseous, belching ("before") and farting ("behind")
308 178 purge: treatment
309 188 drift: scheme
310 Chorus iii: mistakenly printed at the end of Act I in Q
311 1 crafts: deceits
312 2 SD *I prithee* : I pray thee
313 2 SD *ver meum*: my spring (i.e. my youth; Latin)
314 5 Alexander: Alexander the Great, ancient Greek king and conqueror
315 8 What reck I then of life: why am I concerned about life
316 0 SD *St. Andrews*: small town on the east coast of Scotland

BISHOP [*Aside*] O wrack of commonweal! O wretched state!
DOUGLAS [*Aside*] O hapless flock whereas[317] the guide is blind!
MORTON [*Aside*] O heedless youth when counsel is despised! *They all are in a muse*[318]
DOROTHEA Come, pretty knave, and prank it by my side.
Let's see your best attendance[319] out of hand.[320]
NANO Madam, although my limbs are very small,
My heart is good; I'll serve you therewithal.
DOROTHEA How if I were assailed, what couldst thou do?
NANO Madam, call help and boldly fight it too;
Although a bee be but a little thing,
You know, fair queen, it has a bitter sting.
DOROTHEA How couldst thou do me good were I in grief?
NANO Counsel, dear princess, is a choice relief:
Though Nestor[321] wanted force, great was his wit,
And though I am but weak, my words are fit.
BISHOP [*Aside*] Like to a ship upon the ocean seas,
Tossed in the doubtful stream without a helm,[322]
Such is a monarch without good advice.
I am o'erheard; cast rein upon thy tongue,
Andrews beware, reproof[323] will breed a scar.
MORTON Good day, my lord.
BISHOP Lord Morton, well ymet.[324]
Whereon deems Lord Douglas all this while?
DOUGLAS Of that which yours and my poor heart doth break,
Although fear shuts our mouths; we dare not speak.
DOROTHEA [*Aside*] What means these princes sadly to consult?
Somewhat, I fear, betideth them amiss;[325]
They are so pale in looks, so vexed in mind.
—In happy hour, you noble Scottish peers,
Have I encountered you; what makes you mourn?
BISHOP If we with patience may attention gain,
Your grace shall know the cause of all our grief.
DOROTHEA Speak on, good father, come and sit by me;
I know thy care is for the common good.
BISHOP As fortune, mighty princess, reareth some
To high estate and place in commonweal,
So by divine bequest to them is lent
A riper judgment and more searching eye,
Whereby they may discern the common harm;
For where our fortunes in the world are most,
Where all our profits rise and still increase,
There is our mind, thereon we meditate.[326]
And what we do partake of good advice,[327]

317 2 whereas: where
318 3 SD *in a muse*: lost in their own thoughts
319 5 best attendance: best work as a servant
320 5 out of hand: at once
321 14 Nestor: wise, old king who served on the side of the Greeks in the Trojan War
322 17 helm: steering mechanism
323 20 reproof: censure
324 21 well ymet: I am happy to meet you
325 26 Some bad news worries them, I fear
326 40–41 Where all . . . we meditate: when we are successful we only think of our successes
327 42 And what good advice we can offer

That we employ for to concern the same.[328]
To this intent these nobles and myself,
That are (or should be) eyes of commonweal,
Seeing his highness' reckless course of youth,
His lawless and unbridled vain[329] in love,
His too attentive trust to flatterers,
His abject[330] care of counsel and his friends,
Cannot but grieve; and since we cannot draw
His eye or judgment to discern his faults,
Since we have spake and counsel is not heard,
I for my part (let others as they list[331])
Will leave the court and leave him to his will,
Lest with a ruthful eye I should behold
His overthrow, which sore,[332] I fear, is nigh.
DOROTHEA Ah, father, are you so estranged from love,
From due allegiance to your prince and land,
To leave your king when most he needs your help?
The thrifty husbandmen[333] are never wont,[334]
That see their lands unfruitful, to forsake them;
But when the mould[335] is barren and unapt,[336]
They toil, they plow, and make the fallow fat;[337]
The pilot in the dangerous seas is known,
In calmer waves the silly sailor strives.[338]
Are you not members, lords of commonweal,
And can your head, your dear anointed king,
Default, ye lords, except yourselves do fail?
Oh stay your steps; return and counsel him.
DOUGLAS Men seek not moss upon a rolling stone,
Or water from the sieve, or fire from ice,
Or comfort from a reckless monarch's hands.
Madam, he sets us light that served in court,
In place of credit in his father's days;[339]
If we but enter presence of his grace,
Our payment is a frown, a scoff, a frump,[340]
While flattering Gnatho[341] pranks it by his side,
Soothing the careless king in his misdeeds.
And if your grace considers your estate,
His life should urge you too,[342] if all be true.
DOROTHEA Why, Douglas, why?
DOUGLAS As if you have not heard

328 43 That which we employ for the sake of the commonweal
329 47 vain: vanity
330 49 abject: base, poor
331 53 list: like
332 56 sore: injury
333 60 husbandmen: farmers
334 60 wont: accustomed
335 62 mould: top soil
336 62 unapt: unfit
337 63 fallow fat: ploughed land fertile
338 64–5 The pilot … sailor strives: the pilot understands the ins and outs of treacherous oceans, but even on calm seas the simple sailor needs the help of the pilot
339 74 his father's days: the time of King James III
340 76 frump: sneer
341 77 Gnatho: conventional name for a flatterer
342 80 His life … you too: his actions should cause you to leave as well

His lawless love to Ida grown of late,
His careless estimate of your estate.
DOROTHEA Ah, Douglas, thou misconstr'est his intent;
He doth but tempt his wife; he tries my love.
This injury pertains to me, not to you.
The king is young, and if he step awry,
He may amend, and I will love him still.
Should we disdain our vines because they sprout
Before their time? Or young men, if they strain
Beyond their reach? No, vines that bloom and spread
Do promise fruits, and young men that are wild
In age grow wise. My friends and Scottish peers,
If that an English princess may prevail,
Stay, stay with him! Lo, how my zealous prayer
Is pled with tears. Fie, peers, will you hence?
BISHOP Madam, 'tis virtue in your grace to plead,
But we that see his vain untoward course[343]
Cannot but fly the fire before it burn
And shun the court before we see his fall.
DOROTHEA Will you not stay? Then lordings, fare you well;
Though you forsake your king, the heavens, I hope,
Will favor him through mine incessant prayer.
NANO Content you, madam; thus old Ovid[344] sings,
"'Tis foolish to bewail recureless[345] things."
DOROTHEA Peace, dwarf! These words my patience move.
NANO Although you charm[346] my speech, charm not my love. *Exeunt* NANO *and* DOROTHEA

Enter JAMES IV; *the nobles, spying him, return*

JAMES IV Douglas, how now? Why changest thou thy cheer?[347]
DOUGLAS My private troubles are so great, my liege,
As I must crave your license for a while
For to attend mine own affairs at home.
JAMES IV You may depart. [*Exit* DOUGLAS] But why is Morton sad?
MORTON The like occasion doth import[348] me too,
So I desire your grace to give me leave.
JAMES IV Well, sir, you may betake you to your ease. [*Exit* MORTON]
[*Aside*] When such grim sirs are gone, I see no let[349]
To work my will.
BISHOP What? Like the eagle then,
With often flight wilt thou thy feathers lose?[350]
O King, canst thou endure to see thy court
Of finest wits and judgments dispossessed,
Whilst cloaking craft[351] with soothing[352] climbs so high

343 98 untoward course: inept path
344 104 Ovid: Roman poet
345 105 recureless: hopeless
346 107 charm: subdue
347 108 Why changest thou thy cheer: why do you look unhappy now
348 113 import: concern
349 116 let: impediment
350 117–18 Like the . . . feathers lose: like the eagle, will you lose your feathers (supports, counselors) with frequent flights (indulgent acts of hubris)
351 121 cloaking craft: concealed plotting
352 121 with soothing: by flattering

As each bewails ambition is so bad?[353]
Thy father left thee, with estate and crown,
A learnèd counsel to direct thy court;
These, carelessly, O King, thou castest off
To entertain a train of sycophants.
Thou well may'st see, although thou wilt not see,
That[354] every eye and ear both sees and hears:
The certain signs of thine incontinence.[355]
Thou art allied unto the English king
By marriage, a happy friend indeed,
If usèd well; if not, a mighty foe.
Thinketh your grace he can endure and brook
To have a partner in his daughter's love?
Thinketh your grace the grudge of privy wrongs
Will not procure him change[356] his smiles to threats?
Oh, be not blind to good: call home your lords;
Displace these flattering Gnathos; drive them hence;
Love and with kindness take your wedlock wife,[357]
Or else (which God forbid) I fear a change;
Sin cannot thrive in courts without a plague.[358]
JAMES IV Go pack thou too, unless thou mend thy talk.
On pain of death, proud bishop, get you gone,
Unless you headless mean to hop away.
BISHOP Thou God of heaven, prevent my country's fall. [*Exit*]
JAMES IV These stays and lets to pleasure plague my thoughts,
Forcing my grievous wounds anew to bleed;
But care that hath transported me so far,
Fair Ida, is dispersed in thought of thee,
Whose answer yields me life or breeds my death.
Yond comes the messenger of weal[359] or woe.

Enter ATEUKIN

Ateukin, what news?
ATEUKIN The adamant, O King, will not be filed
But by itself,[360] and beauty that exceeds
By some exceeding favor[361] must be wrought.[362]
Ida is coy as yet and doth repine,[363]
Objecting marriage, honor, fear, and death.
She's holy, wise, and too precise[364] for me.
JAMES IV Are these thy fruits of wit, thy sight in art?
Thine eloquence? Thy policy? Thy drift,
To mock thy prince? Then, caitiff, pack thee hence,

353 122 Even as everyone laments that the ambitious are a bad lot
354 128 That: that which
355 129 incontinence: lack of self-restraint
356 136 procure him change: induce him to change
357 139 wedlock wife: wife in wedlock
358 141 without a plague: without bringing on a plague
359 151 weal: happiness
360 153–4 The adamant . . . by itself: a diamond cannot be cut by anything other than another diamond
361 155 exceeding favor: great gift
362 155 wrought: won over
363 156 doth repine: is yet dissatisfied
364 158 precise: religiously strict

And let me die devoured in my love.
ATEUKIN Good lord, how rage gainsayeth[365] reason's power.
My dear, my gracious, and beloved prince,
The essence of my suit,[366] my god on earth,
Sit down and rest yourself; appease your wrath,
Lest with a frown ye wound me to the death.
Oh, that I were included in my grave,
That either now, to save my prince's life,
Must counsel cruelty or lose my king.
JAMES IV Why, sirrah, are there means to move her mind?
ATEUKIN Oh, should I not offend my royal liege?
JAMES IV Tell all; spare naught,[367] so I may gain my love.
ATEUKIN Alas, my soul, why art thou torn in twain,[368]
For fear thou talk a thing that should displease?
JAMES IV Tut, speak what so thou wilt; I pardon thee.
ATEUKIN How kind a word, how courteous is his grace;
Who would not die to succor such a king?
My liege, this lovely maid of modest mind
Could well incline to love but that she fears
Fair Dorothea's power; your grace doth know
Your wedlock is a mighty let to love.
Were Ida sure to be your wedded wife,
That then the twig would bow,[369] you might command.
Ladies love presents, pomp, and high estate.
JAMES IV Ah, Ateukin, how should we displace this let?
ATEUKIN Tut mighty prince, oh that I might be whist.[370]
JAMES IV Why dalliest thou?
ATEUKIN I will not move my prince;
I will prefer his safety before my life.
Hear me, O King, 'tis Dorothea's death
Must do you good.
JAMES IV What, murther of my queen?
Yet to enjoy my love, what is my queen?
Oh, but my vow and promise to my queen;
Ay, but my hope to gain a fairer queen.
With how contrarious[371] thoughts am I withdrawn;[372]
Why linger I 'twixt[373] hope and doubtful fear?
If Dorothea die, will Ida love?
ATEUKIN She will, my lord.
JAMES IV Then let her die. Devise, advise the means;
All likes me well[374] that lends me hope in love.
ATEUKIN What, will your grace consent? Then let me work.
There's here in court a Frenchman, Jaques called,
A fit performer of our enterprise,
Whom I by gifts and promise will corrupt

365 163 gainsayeth: denies
366 165 essence of my suit: the subject of my appeal to Ida
367 173 naught: nothing
368 174 in twain: in two
369 184 That then . . . would bow: then Ida would obey
370 187 whist: silent
371 195 contrarious: contrary
372 195 withdrawn: distracted
373 196 'twixt: between
374 199 All likes me well: I like everything well

To slay the queen, if that your grace will seal
A warrant for the man to save his life.[375]
JAMES IV Naught shall he want; write thou and I will sign.
And gentle Gnatho, if my Ida yield,
Thou shalt have what thou wilt; I'll give thee straight
A barony, an earldom for reward.
ATEUKIN Frolic, young King; the lass shall be your own;
I'll make her blithe and wanton by my wit.

Exeunt

[Chorus iv]

Enter BOHAN *with* OBERON

BOHAN So Oberon, now it begins to work in kind:[376]
The ancient lords, by leaving him alone,
Disliking of his humors and respite,[377]
Let him run headlong till his flatterers,
Sweeting[378] his thoughts of luckless lust
With vile persuasions and alluring words,
Make him make way by murther to his will.
Judge, fairy king, hast heard a greater ill?
OBERON Nor found more virtue in a country maid.
I tell thee, Bohan, it doth make me sorry[379]
To think the deeds the king means to perform.
BOHAN To change that humor, stand and see the rest;
I think my son Slipper will show's a jest.[380]

Enter SLIPPER *with a companion, boy, or wench, dancing a hornpipe,*[381] *and dance out again*

Now, after this beguiling of our thoughts,
And changing them from sad to better glee,
Let's to our cell[382] and sit and see the rest,
For I believe this jig will prove no jest.

Exeunt

Act III, scene i

Enter SLIPPER *one way and Sir* BARTRAM *another way*

BARTRAM Ho fellow! Stay and let me speak with thee.
SLIPPER Fellow? Friend, thou dost disbuse[383] me; I am a gentleman.
BARTRAM A gentleman, how so?
SLIPPER Why, I rub horses, sir.
BARTRAM And what of that?
SLIPPER Oh simple witted, mark my reason: they that do good service in the commonweal are

375 204–5 if that . . . his life: Ateukin asks for a warrant guaranteeing that Jaques will not be punished for the murder
376 1 work in kind: transpire as expected
377 3 respite: leisure
378 5 Sweeting: making sweet
379 10 sorry: Q reads "merrie" here
380 13 show's a jest: perform for us an amusing entertainment
381 13 SD *hornpipe*: a vigorous dance associated with sailors
382 16 cell: gallery
383 2 disbuse: abuse

gentlemen, but such as rub horses do good service in the commonweal; ergo,[384] tarbox[385] master courtier, a horse keeper is a gentleman.
BARTRAM Here is overmuch wit in good earnest. But sirrah, where is thy master?
SLIPPER Neither above ground nor underground, drawing out red into white,[386] swallowing that down without chawing[387] that was never made without treading.
BARTRAM Why, where is he then?
SLIPPER Why, in his cellar, drinking a cup of neat and brisk claret[388] in a bowl of silver; O sir, the wine runs trillil down his throat which cost the poor vintner many a stamp[389] before it was made. But I must hence, sir; I have haste.
BARTRAM Why, whither now, I prithee?
SLIPPER Faith sir, to Sir Sylvester, a knight hard by, upon my master's errand, whom I must certify this: that the lease of East Spring[390] shall be confirmed[391] and therefore must I bid him provide trash,[392] for my master is no friend without money.
BARTRAM [*Aside*] This is the thing for which I sued so long;
This is the lease which I, by Gnatho's[393] means,
Sought to possess by patent from the king.
But he, injurious man, who lives by crafts
And sells kings' favors for who will give most,
Hath taken bribes of me yet covertly,
Will sell away the thing pertains to me.
But I have found a present help, I hope,
For to prevent his purpose and deceit.
—Stay, gentle friend.
SLIPPER A good word,[394] thou hast won me; this word is like warm caudle[395] to a cold stomach.
BARTRAM Sirrah, wilt thou, for money and reward,
Convey me certain letters out of hand[396]
From out thy master's pocket?
SLIPPER Will I, sir? Why, were it to rob my father, hang my mother, or any such like trifles, I am at your commandment, sir. What will you give me, sir?
BARTRAM A hundred pounds.
SLIPPER I am your man; give me earnest.[397] I am dead at a pocket,[398] sir. Why, I am a lifter, master, by my occupation.
BARTRAM A lifter, what is that?
SLIPPER Why, sir, I can lift a pot as well as any man and pick a purse as soon as any thief in my country.
BARTRAM Why, fellow, hold; here is earnest, ten pounds to assure thee. Go, dispatch and bring it me to yonder tavern thou seest; and assure thyself, thou shalt both have thy skin[399] full of wine and the rest of thy money.

384 7 ergo: therefore (Latin)
385 7 tarbox: stinking fellow
386 10 drawing out red into white: pouring red wine into a silver ("white") vessel
387 11 chawing: chewing
388 13 neat and brisk claret: undiluted, crisp-tasting wine
389 14 many a stamp: wine grapes were stamped upon for their juice
390 18 East Spring: a parcel of land
391 18 confirmed: transferred to Sir Sylvester
392 19 trash: money
393 21 Gnatho's: i.e. Ateukin's
394 30 A good word: i.e. "gentle"
395 30 caudle: medicinal drink
396 33 Steal certain letters at once
397 38 earnest: a down payment
398 38 dead at a pocket: great at pickpocketing
399 44 skin: wine carrier made out of animal skin

SLIPPER I will, sir. Now room for a gentleman, my masters.[400] Who gives me money for a fair new angel, a trim new angel?

Exeunt

[Act III, scene ii]

Enter ANDREW and PURVEYOR[401]

PURVEYOR Sirrah, I must needs have your master's horses; the king cannot be unserved.[402]
ANDREW Sirrah, you must needs go without them because my master must be served.
PURVEYOR Why, I am the king's purveyor, and I tell thee I will have them.
ANDREW I am Ateukin's servant, Signor Andrew, and I say thou shall not have them.
PURVEYOR Here's my ticket;[403] deny it if thou dar'st.
ANDREW There is the stable; fetch them out if thou dar'st.
PURVEYOR Sirrah, sirrah, tame your tongue lest I make you.
ANDREW Sirrah, sirrah, hold your hand lest I bum[404] you.
PURVEYOR I tell thee, thy master's geldings[405] are good and therefore fit for the king.
ANDREW I tell thee, my master's horses have galled[406] backs and therefore cannot fit the king. Purveyor, purveyor, purvey thee of more wit; dar'st thou presume to wrong my Lord Ateukin, being the chiefest man in the court?
PURVEYOR The more unhappy commonweal where flatterers are chief in court.
ANDREW What sayest thou?
PURVEYOR I say thou art too presumptuous, and the officers shall school thee.
ANDREW A fig[407] for them and thee, purveyor; they seek a knot in a ring[408] that would wrong my master or his servants in this court.

Enter JAQUES

PURVEYOR The world is at a wise pass[409] when nobility is afraid of a flatterer.
JAQUES Sirrah, what be you that *parle contra monsieur,*[410] my Lord Ateukin? *En bonne foi,*[411] prate you[412] against Sir *Altesse*?[413] Me maka your *tête*[414] to leap from your shoulders; *par ma foi, c'y ferai-je.*[415]
ANDREW O Signor Captain,[416] you show yourself a forward and friendly gentleman in my master's behalf. I will cause him to thank you.
JAQUES *Poltron,*[417] speak me one *parole*[418] against my *bon gentilhomme,*[419] I shall *estampe*[420]

400 46 my masters: Slipper is addressing the audience
401 0 SD PURVEYOR: officer responsible for requisitioning supplies for a monarch
402 1 cannot be unserved: go without horses
403 5 ticket: warrant, directive
404 8 bum: beat
405 9 geldings: castrated horses
406 10 galled: swollen
407 16 A fig: contemptuous expression, usually accompanied by a rude gesture
408 16 a knot in a ring: unnecessary difficulties
409 18 at a wise pass: in an unfortunate state
410 19 *parle contra monsieur*: speak against my lord (French; Jacques mixes French words and phrases with accented English, and the occasional Italian word, throughout his time on stage)
411 19 *En bonne foi*: In good faith
412 20 prate you: do you talk foolishly
413 20 *Altesse*: highness
414 20 maka your *tête*: make your head
415 21 *par ma foi, c'y ferai-je*: upon my word, I will do it
416 22 Captain: Jaques is a soldier
417 24 *Poltron*: coward
418 24 *parole*: word
419 24 *bon gentilhomme*: good gentleman
420 24 *estampe*: stamp

your guts and thumpa your backa that you *ne point mange*[421] this ten hours.
PURVEYOR Sirrah, come open me the stable and let me have the horses. And fellow, for all your French brags, I will do my duty.
ANDREW I'll make garters of thy guts, thou villain, if thou enter this office.[422]
JAQUES *Mort dieu,*[423] take me that cappa *pour votre labeur.*[424] Be gone villain in the *mort.*[425]
PURVEYOR What, will you resist me then? Well, the council,[426] fellow, shall know of your insolence.

Exit [PURVEYOR]

ANDREW Tell them what thou wilt and eat that I can best spare from my back parts[427] and get you gone with a vengeance.

Enter ATEUKIN

ATEUKIN Andrew.
ANDREW Sir.
ATEUKIN Where be my writings I put in my pocket last night?
ANDREW Which, sir, your annotations upon Machiavelli?[428]
ATEUKIN No, sir, the letters-patents for East Spring.
ANDREW Why, sir, you talk wonders to me, if you ask that question.
ATEUKIN Yea, sir, and will work wonders too with you, unless you find them out. Villain, search me them out and bring them me, or thou art but dead.
ANDREW A terrible word in the latter end of a sessions.[429] Master, were you in your right wits yesternight?
ATEUKIN Dost thou doubt it?
ANDREW Ay, and why not, sir, for the greatest clerks[430] are not the wisest, and a fool may dance in a hood[431] as well as a wise man in a bare frock; besides, such as give themselves to *philautia*[432] as you do, master, are so choleric of complexion[433] that that which they burn in fire overnight they seek for with fury the next morning. Ah, I take care of your worship; this commonweal should have a great loss of so good a member as you are.
ATEUKIN Thou flatterest me.
ANDREW Is it flattery in me, sir, to speak you fair? What is it then in you to dally[434] with the king?
ATEUKIN Are you prating, knave? I will teach you better nurture.[435] Is this the care you have of my wardrobe, of my accounts, and matters of trust?
ANDREW Why alas, sir, in times past your garments have been so well inhabited[436] as your tenants would give no place to a moth to mangle them; but since you are grown greater and your garments more fine and gay, if your garments are not fit for hospitality, blame your pride and commend my cleanliness.[437] As for your writings, I am not for them, nor they for me.
ATEUKIN Villain go, fly, and find them out; if thou losest them, thou losest my credit.

421 25 *ne point mange*: do not eat
422 28 enter this office: undertake to fulfill your duty
423 29 *Mort dieu*: God's death (an oath)
424 29 cappa *pour votre labeur*: trifle for your labor; here and elsewhere, Jaques mixes an Italian accent ("cappa") with his French
425 29 in the *mort*: i.e. *a la mort*, forever
426 30 council: king's council
427 32 eat that . . . back parts: eat my shit
428 37 Machiavelli: fifteenth- and sixteenth-century Italian political theorist, historian, diplomat, and playwright. His most famous work, *The Prince*, argued that rulers sometimes had to act unscrupulously in order to maintain their power
429 42 A terrible . . . a sessions: unsettling verdict ("thou art but dead") at the end of a trial
430 45 clerks: clergymen or lay officers in a church
431 46 dance in a hood: be hanged
432 47 *philautia*: self love (Greek)
433 47 choleric of complexion: volatile of temperament
434 51 dally: talk idly
435 53 nurture: upbringing
436 55 well inhabited: full of lice
437 57–8 if your . . . my cleanliness: "pride" perhaps because too fine, "cleanliness" perhaps because clean garments are seldom seen among the elite

ANDREW Alas, sir, can I lose that you never had?
ATEUKIN Say you so? Then hold, feel you that you never felt. [ATEUKIN *beats* ANDREW]
JAQUES O *monsieur, ayez* patient;[438] pardon your poor valet. Me be at your *commandement.*[439]
ATEUKIN Signor Jaques, well met; you shall command me. [*To* ANDREW] Sirrah, go cause my writings be proclaimed in the marketplace. Promise a great reward to them that finds them. Look where I supped and everywhere.
ANDREW I will, sir. [*Aside*] Now are two knaves well met and three well parted,[440] if you conceive mine enigma. Gentlemen,[441] what shall I be then, faith, a plain harp shilling?[442]

[*Exit*]

ATEUKIN Sieur[443] Jaques, this our happy meeting rids
Your friends and me of care and grievous toil;
For I, that look into deserts of men
And see among the soldiers in this court
A noble forward mind and judge thereof,
Cannot but seek the means to raise them up
Who merit credit in the commonweal.
To this intent, friend Jaques, I have found
A means to make you great and well esteemed,
Both with the king and with the best in court;
For I espy in you a valiant mind,
Which makes me love, admire, and honor you.
To this intent (if so your trust and faith,
Your secrecy be equal with your force),
I will impart a service to thyself,
Which if thou dost effect, the king, myself,
And whate'er he, and I with him, can work,
Shall be employed in what thou wilt desire.
JAQUES Me sweara by my ten bones, my *signor*, to be loyal to your lordship's intents, affairs; yea, my *monseigneur, que non ferai-je pour*[444] your pleasure? By my sworda, me be no baby, lord.
ATEUKIN Then hoping on thy truth, I prithee see
How kind Ateukin is to forward thee.
Hold, take this earnest penny[445] of my love,
And mark my words: the king by me requires
No slender service, Jaques, at thy hands.
Thou must by privy practice make away[446]
The queen, fair Dorothea, as she sleeps,
Or how thou wilt, so she be done to death.
Thou shalt not want promotion here in court.
JAQUES Stabba the woman, *par ma foi*;[447] *monseigneur*, me thrusta my weapon into her belly, so me may be guard *par la roi.*[448] Me do your service. But me no be hanged *per*[449] my labor?
ATEUKIN Thou shalt have warrant, Jaques, from the king;

438 62 *ayez* patient: mixing French and bad English Jaques means to say "have patience"
439 62 *commandement*: command
440 66 Now are . . . well parted: Ateukin and Jaques are "knaves"; all three of them have good "parts" (i.e. penises)
441 67 Gentlemen: Andrew is addressing the audience
442 67 plain harp shilling: Irish brass coin worth about a penny in England
443 68 Sieur: respectful form of address
444 87 *monseigneur, que non ferai-je pour*: my lord, what will not I do for
445 91 earnest penny: down payment
446 94 by privy practice make away: secretly kill
447 98 *par ma foi*: by my faith
448 99 *par la roi*: by the king
449 99 *per*: for

None shall outface, gainsay,[450] and wrong my friend.
Do not I love thee, Jaques? Fear not, then;
I tell thee, who so toucheth thee in aught[451]
Shall injure me. I love, I tender[452] thee;
Thou art a subject fit to serve his grace.
Jaques, I had a written warrant once,
But that by great misfortune late is lost.
Come, wend[453] we to St. Andrews, where his grace
Is now in progress,[454] where he shall assure
Thy safety and confirm thee to the act.
JAQUES We will attend your nobleness.

Exeunt

[Chorus v][455]

[*Enter* BOHAN *and* OBERON]

BOHAN I can no more; my patience will not warp[456]
To see these flatterers, how they scorn and carp.[457]
OBERON Turn but thy head.

Enter four kings carrying crowns, ladies presenting odors[458] *to* [*a*] *potentate enthroned who suddenly is slain by his servants and thrust out; and so they eat;* [*these e*]*xeunt*

BOHAN Sik[459] is the world, but whilke[460] is he I saw?
OBERON Sesostris[461] who was conqueror of the world,
Slain at the last and stamped on by his slaves.
BOHAN How blessed are peur[462] men then that know their grave.
Now mark the sequel of my jig.

[*Exeunt*]

[Act III, scene iii]

Enter Sir BARTRAM, DOROTHEA *the Queen,* NANO, *Lord* ROSS, *ladies,* [*and*] *attendants*

DOROTHEA Thy credit, Bartram, in the Scottish court,
Thy reverend years, the strictness of thy vows,[463]
All these are means sufficient to persuade;
But love, the faithful link of loyal hearts,
That hath possession of my constant mind,
Exiles all dread, subdueth vain suspect.[464]

450 101 outface, gainsay: stand up to, oppose
451 103 toucheth thee in aught: injures you for any reason
452 104 tender: have great affection for
453 108 wend: proceed
454 109 in progress: on a royal tour of Scotland
455 Chorus v: mistakenly printed at the end of Act I in Q
456 1 warp: endure
457 2 scorn and carp: jeer and boast foolishly
458 3 SD *odors*: incense, spices, ointments
459 4 Sik: such
460 4 whilke: what
461 5 Sesostris: ancient Egyptian king
462 7 peur: poor
463 2 strictness of thy vows: strictness with which you keep your vows
464 6 suspect: suspicion

Methinks no craft[465] should harbor in that breast
Where majesty and virtue are installed.
Methinks my beauty should not cause my death.
BARTRAM How gladly, sovereign princess, would I err
And blind my shame[466] to save your royal life.
'Tis princely in yourself to think the best,
To hope his grace is guiltless of this crime;
But if in due prevention you default,
How blind are you that were forewarned before?
DOROTHEA Suspicion without cause deserveth blame.
BARTRAM Who sees and shuns not harms deserves the same;[467]
[*Shows warrant*] Behold the tenor of this traitorous plot.
DOROTHEA What, should I read? Perhaps he wrote it not.
BARTRAM Here is his warrant, under seal and sign,
To Jaques born in France to murther you.
DOROTHEA Ah, careless King, would God this were not thine.
What though I read? Ah, should I think it true?
ROSS The hand[468] and seal confirms the deed is his.
DOROTHEA What know I, though, if now he thinketh this?[469]
NANO Madam, Lucretius[470] say'th that to repent
Is childish, wisdom to prevent.[471]
DOROTHEA What though?[472]
NANO Then cease your tears that have dismayed you,
And cross the foe before he has betrayed you.
BARTRAM What needs these long suggestions[473] in this cause,
When every circumstance confirmeth truth?
First, let the hidden mercy from above
Confirm your grace, since by a wondrous means
The practice of your dangers came to light.
Next, let the tokens of approvèd truth
Govern and stay your thoughts, too much seduced,
And mark the truth and listen the intent:
Your highness knows, and these my noble lords
Can witness this, that whilst your husband's sire[474]
In happy peace possessed the Scottish crown,
I was his sworn attendant here in court;
In dangerous fight I never failed my lord;
And since his death and this your husband's reign,
No labor, duty have I left undone
To testify my zeal unto the crown.
But now my limbs are weak; mine eyes are dim;
Mine age unwieldy[475] and unmeet for[476] toil.
I came to court in hope, for service past,

465 7 craft: treachery
466 11 blind my shame: blind myself to the king's shameful behavior
467 17 the same: i.e. blame
468 24 hand: handwriting
469 25 If the king is capable of this then everything I believe is untrue
470 26 Lucretius: Roman poet and philosopher
471 26–7 to repent . . . to prevent: it is wiser to prevent mischief than to regret its having occurred
472 27 What though: what if I work to prevent
473 30 long suggestions: many prompts
474 39 sire: father
475 47 unwieldy: infirm
476 47 unmeet for: unequal to

To gain some lease to keep[477] me, being old.
There found I all was upsy-turvy turned,[478]
My friends displaced, the nobles loth to crave.[479]
Then sought I to the minion of the king,
Ateukin, who, allurèd by a bribe,
Assured me of the lease for which I sought.
But see the craft: when he had got the grant,
He wrought[480] to sell it to Sir Sylvester,
In hope of greater earnings from his hands.
In brief, I learned his craft and wrought the means,
By one his needy servants for reward,[481]
To steal from out his pocket all the briefs,[482]
Which he performed and with reward resigned.
Them when I read (now mark the power of God),
I found this warrant sealed among the rest
To kill your grace, whom God long keep alive.
Thus, in effect, by wonder are you saved;
Trifle not, then, but seek a speedy flight;
God will conduct your steps and shield the right.
DOROTHEA What should I do, ah poor, unhappy queen,
Born to endure what fortune can contain?
Alas, the deed is too apparent now;
But oh, mine eyes, were you[483] as bent to hide[484]
As my poor heart is forward[485] to forgive.
Ah, cruel King, my love would thee acquit.
Oh, what avails to be allied and matched
With high estates that marry but in show?
Were I baser born, my mean estate
Could warrant[486] me from this impendent[487] harm;
But to be great and happy, these are twain.[488]
Ah, Ross, what shall I do? How shall I work?
ROSS With speedy letter to your father send,
Who will revenge you and defend your right.
DOROTHEA As if they kill not me who with him[489] fight?
As if his breast be touched, I am not wounded?
As if he wailed, my joys were not confounded?
We are one heart, though rent by hate in twain,
One soul, one essence doth our weal contain.
What then can conquer him that kills not me?
ROSS If this advice displease, then, madam, flee.
DOROTHEA Where may I wend[490] or travel without fear?
NANO Where not, in changing this attire you wear?

477 49 keep: financially support
478 50 upsy-turvy turned: topsy-turvy
479 51 crave: ask for favors
480 56 wrought: plotted
481 58–9 wrought the . . . for reward: arranged, by bribing his poor servant
482 60 briefs: lease documents
483 71 were you: I wish you were
484 71 bent to hide: willing to close (i.e. not see the warrant)
485 72 forward: ready
486 77 warrant: protect
487 77 impendent: impending
488 78 are twain: must be separate
489 82 him: James IV
490 89 wend: go

DOROTHEA What, shall I clad me like a country maid?
NANO The policy is base,[491] I am afraid.
DOROTHEA Why, Nano?
NANO Ask you why? What, may a queen
March forth in homely weed[492] and be not seen?
The rose, although in thorny shrubs she spreads,
Is still the rose, her beauties wax[493] not dead.
And noble minds, although the coat be bare,
Are by their semblance[494] known how great they are.
BARTRAM The dwarf say'th true.
DOROTHEA What garments lik'st thou then?
NANO Such as may make you seem a proper[495] man.
DOROTHEA He makes me blush and smile, though I am sad.
NANO The meanest coat for safety is not bad.[496]
DOROTHEA What, shall I jet[497] in breeches like a squire?
Alas, poor dwarf, thy mistress is unmeet.[498]
NANO Tut, go me thus, your cloak before your face,
Your sword upreared[499] with quaint and comely grace.
If any come and question what you be,
Say you, "a man," and call for witness me.
DOROTHEA What, should I wear a sword? To what intent?
NANO Madam, for show, it is an ornament.
If any wrong you, draw, a shining blade
Withdraws[500] a coward thief that would invade.[501]
DOROTHEA But if I strike, and he should strike again,
What should I do? I fear I should be slain.
NANO No, take it single[502] on your dagger so;
I'll teach you, madam, how to ward a blow.
DOROTHEA How little shapes much substance may include.
Sir Bartram, Ross, ye ladies, and my friends,
Since presence yields me death and absence life,
Hence will I fly, disguisèd like a squire,
As one that seeks to live in Irish wars.[503]
You, gentle Ross, shall furnish my depart.[504]
ROSS Yea prince,[505] and die with you with all my heart.
Vouchsafe[506] me then in all extremest states[507]
To wait on you and serve you with my best.
DOROTHEA To me pertains the woe; live then in rest.[508]

491 92 base: faulty (with pun on low)
492 94 weed: clothing
493 96 wax: grow
494 98 semblance: expression in a person's appearance
495 100 proper: complete
496 102 The poorest coat is not bad if it provides safety
497 103 jet: move about
498 104 unmeet: unfit
499 106 upreared: raised up
500 112 Withdraws: scares away
501 112 invade: assail
502 115 take it single: receive the blow singly
503 121 Irish wars: anachronistic reference to the Irish wars that occurred throughout Elizabeth I's reign
504 122 furnish my depart: outfit me for my journey
505 123 prince: during the period, the term can refer to a male or female ruler
506 124 Vouchsafe: accept
507 124 extremest states: the worst conditions
508 126 rest: comfort

Friends, fare you well; keep secret my depart;
Nano alone shall my attendant be.
NANO Then, madam, are you manned, I warrant ye.
Give me a sword, and if there grow debate,
I'll come behind and break your enemy's pate.[509]
ROSS How sore we grieve to part so soon away.
DOROTHEA Grieve not for those that perish if they stay.
NANO The time in words misspent is little worth;
Madam, walk on, and let them bring us forth.

Exeunt

[Chorus vi]

Enter BOHAN; [OBERON *remains in the gallery*[510] *asleep*]

BOHAN So these sad motions[511] make the fairy sleep,
And sleep he shall in quiet and content,
For it would make a marble[512] melt and weep
To see these treasons 'gainst the innocent.
But since she 'scapes by flight to save her life,
The king may chance repent; she was his wife.
The rest is ruthful,[513] yet to beguile the time,
'Tis interlaced with merriment and rhyme.

[*Exit*]

Act IV, scene i

After a noise of horns and shoutings, enter certain HUNTSMEN, *if you please, singing one way, another way* ATEUKIN *and* JAQUES

ATEUKIN Say, gentlemen, where may we find the king?
HUNTSMAN Even here at hand and bent on hunting.
And at this hour he taken hath a stand[514]
To kill a deer.
ATEUKIN A pleasant work in hand.
Follow your sport, and we will seek his grace.
HUNTSMAN [*Aside*] When such him seek,[515] it is a woeful case.

Exeunt HUNTSMEN *one way,* ATEUKIN *and* JAQUES *another*

[Act IV, scene ii]

Enter EUSTACE, IDA, *and the* COUNTESS

COUNTESS Lord Eustace, as your youth and virtuous life
Deserves a far more fair and richer wife,
So since I am a mother and do wit[516]
What wedlock is and that which longs to it,
Before I mean my daughter to bestow,

509 131 pate: head
510 0 SD *gallery*: see Induction 77
511 1 motions: shows
512 3 marble: marble statue
513 7 ruthful: lamentable
514 3 stand: raised platform
515 6 When such him seek: when people like Ateukin seek the king
516 3 wit: understand

'Twere meet that she and I your state did know.
EUSTACE Madam, if I consider Ida's worth,
I know my portions merit none so fair,
And yet I hold, in farm and yearly rent,
A thousand pound, which may her state content.
COUNTESS But what estate,[517] my lord, shall she possess?
EUSTACE All that is mine, grave countess, and no less.
But Ida, will you love?
IDA I cannot hate.
EUSTACE But will you wed?
IDA 'Tis Greek to me,[518] my lord.
I'll wish you well and thereon take my word.
EUSTACE Shall I some sign of favor then receive?
IDA Ay, if her ladyship will give me leave.
COUNTESS Do what thou wilt.
IDA Then noble English peer,
Accept this ring, wherein my heart is set,
A constant heart with burning flames befret;[519]
But under written this: *O morte dura.*[520]
Hereon when so you look with eyes *pura*,[521]
The maid you fancy most will favor you.
EUSTACE I'll try this heart in hope to find it true.

Enter certain HUNTSMEN *and* LADIES

HUNTSMEN Widow countess, well ymet;
Ever may thy joys be many.
Gentle Ida, fair beset,[522]
Fair and wise, not fairer any.
Frolic[523] huntsmen of the game
Will you well and give you greeting.
IDA Thanks, good woodsmen, for the same.
And for our sport and merry meeting.
HUNTSMEN Unto thee we do present
Silver hart[524] with arrow wounded.
EUSTACE [*Aside*] This doth shadow[525] my lament,
Both fear and love confounded.[526]
LADIES To the mother of the maid,
Fair as th'lilies, red as roses,
Even so many goods are said
As herself in heart supposes.[527]
COUNTESS What are you, friends, that thus doth wish us well?
HUNTSMAN Your neighbors nigh that have on hunting been,
Who understanding of your walking forth,

517 11 estate: property
518 14 'Tis Greek to me: it is something I know nothing about
519 20 befret: gnawing away at it
520 21 *O morte dura*: O cruel death (Latin)
521 22 *pura*: chaste (Latin)
522 27 fair beset: endowed with fairness
523 29 Frolic: frolicsome, joyful
524 34 Silver hart: ornamental stag made of silver
525 35 shadow: represent, give shape to
526 36 Confused by feelings of fear and love; Eustace identifies with the wounded stag
527 39–40 Even so … heart supposes: as much good is said of you as you assume of others

Prepare this train[528] to entertain you with:
This Lady Douglas, this Sir Egmond is.
COUNTESS Welcome ye ladies, and thousand thanks for this.
Come, enter you a homely widow's house,
And if mine entertainment please you, let us feast.
HUNTSMEN A lovely lady never wants a guest.

Exeunt, manent[529] EUSTACE *and* IDA

EUSTACE Stay, gentle Ida. Tell me what you deem;
What doth this hart, this tender heart beseem?[530]
IDA Why not, my lord, since nature teaches art,
To senseless[531] beasts to cure their grievous smart.
Dictamnum[532] serves to close the wound again.
EUSTACE What help for those that love?
IDA Why, love again—[533]
EUSTACE Were I the hart—
IDA Then I the herb would be.
You shall not die for help; come, follow me.

Exeunt

[Act IV, scene iii]

Enter ANDREW *and* JAQUES

JAQUES *Mon dieu,*[534] what *malheur*[535] be this? Me come *à* the chamber, *Signor* Andrew, *mon dieu*, take my *poignard en ma main*[536] to give the *estocade*[537] to the *damoiselle*; *par ma foi,*[538] there was no person; *elle s'est en alle.*[539]
ANDREW The worse luck, Jaques, but because I am thy friend I will advise thee somewhat towards the attainment of the gallows.
JAQUES "Gallows," what be that?
ANDREW Marry, sir, a place of great promotion,[540] where thou shalt by one turn[541] above ground rid the world of a knave and make a goodly example for all bloody villains of thy profession.
JAQUES *Que dite vous,*[542] *Monsieur* Andrew?
ANDREW I say, Jaques, thou must keep this path and hie thee,[543] for the queen, as I am certified,[544] is departed with her dwarf, appareled like a squire. Overtake her, Frenchman; stab her. I'll promise thee, this doublet shall be happy.[545]
JAQUES *Pourquoi?*[546]

528 44 train: group
529 49 SD *manent*: remain (Latin; plural form of *manet*)
530 51 Does this ornamental stag resemble my own heart?
531 53 senseless: without reason
532 54 Dictamnum: healing herb; Ida, in this exchange, is telling Eustace that he should not, as "senseless beasts," "cure" his "wound" with an actual healing herb; she will play the part of the herb
533 55 love again: love as well
534 1 *Mon dieu*: my god
535 1 *malheur*: misfortune
536 2 *poignard en ma main*: dagger in my hand
537 2 *estocade*: thrust
538 2 *damoiselle*; *par my foi*: damsel; by my faith
539 3 *elle s'est en alle*: she had gone
540 7 promotion: social rising, elevation
541 7 turn: i.e. being "turned off" the scaffold and hanged
542 10 *Que dite vous*: what are you saying
543 11 hie thee: make haste
544 12 certified: assured
545 13 doublet shall be happy: vest-like piece of clothing; it will be "happy" to have Jaques' hangman as its new owner (executioners were entitled to the clothing of the prisoners they executed)
546 14 *Pourquoi?*: why?

ANDREW It shall serve a jolly gentleman, Sir Dominus Monsignor Hangman.
JAQUES *C'est tout un*;[547] me will rama *pour le monnaie.*[548] [*Exit*]
ANDREW Go, and the rot[549] consume thee! Oh, what a trim[550] world is this. My master lives by cozening the king, I by flattering him, Slipper, my fellow, by stealing, and I by lying. Is not this a wily accord,[551] gentlemen?[552] This last night our jolly horsekeeper,[553] being well steeped in liquor, confessed to me the stealing of my master's writings and his great reward. Now, dare I not bewray him lest he discover my knavery, but this have I wrought: I understand he will pass this way to provide him necessaries,[554] but if I and my fellows fail not, we will teach him such a lesson as shall cost him a chief place on penniless bench[555] for his labor. But yond[556] he comes.

Enter SLIPPER *with a* TAILOR, *a* SHOEMAKER, *and a* CUTLER

SLIPPER Tailor!
TAILOR Sir.
SLIPPER Let my doublet be white northern,[557] five groats[558] the yard. I tell thee, I will be brave.[559]
TAILOR It shall, sir.
SLIPPER Now, sir, cut it me like the battlements of a custard,[560] full of round holes; edge me the sleeves with Coventry blue,[561] and let the linings be of ten-penny lockram.[562]
TAILOR Very good, sir.
SLIPPER Make it the amorous cut, a flap before.[563]
TAILOR And why so? That fashion is stale.[564]
SLIPPER O friend, thou art a simple fellow. I tell thee, a flap is a great friend to a storre:[565] it stand him in stead of clean napery;[566] and if a man's shirt be torn, it is a present penthouse[567] to defend him from a clean housewife's scoff.[568]
TAILOR You say sooth, sir.
SLIPPER Hold, take thy money; there is seven shillings for the doublet and eight for the britches; seven and eight, byr'lady, thirty-six[569] is a fair deal of money.
TAILOR Farewell, sir.
SLIPPER Nay, but stay, tailor.
TAILOR Why, sir?
SLIPPER Forget not this special make: let my back parts be well lined, for there come many

547 16 *C'est tout un*: that's all one
548 16 rama *pour le monnaie*: ram (i.e. thrust his sword) for the money
549 17 the rot: syphilis
550 17 trim: sound (ironic)
551 19 wily accord: harmony of knavery
552 19 gentlemen: Andrew is addressing the audience
553 19 horsekeeper: i.e. Slipper
554 22 to provide him necessaries: to outfit himself
555 23 penniless bench: seat for the destitute (colloquial)
556 23 yond: here
557 27 white northern: cloth made in northern England
558 27 groats: coins of low value
559 28 brave: finely dressed
560 30 battlements of a custard: pinched crust of a custard pie
561 31 Coventry blue: vibrant blue thread
562 31 ten-penny lockram: fine linen
563 33 the amorous ... flap before: with a flap on the front, allowing quick access to the genitalia
564 34 stale: out of date
565 35 storre: rough fellow (this is Sanders's (1970) gloss on Q's "storrie")
566 36 stand him ... clean napery: serves in place of clean underwear
567 36 present penthouse: can be folded up over the tear
568 37 scoff: scorn (because Slipper's shirt is torn)
569 40 thirty-six: Slipper pays with thirty-six coins, some of differing value; or, he cannot add

winter storms[570] from a windy belly, I tell thee. [*Exit* TAILOR] Shoemaker!
SHOEMAKER Gentleman, what shoe will it please you to have?
SLIPPER A fine, neat[571] calf's leather, my friend.
SHOEMAKER O sir, that is too thin; it will not last you.
SLIPPER I tell thee, it is my near kinsman, for I am Slipper, which hath his best grace in summer to be suited in lambs' skins. Goodwife Calf was my grandmother and Goodman Neatherleather[572] mine uncle, but my mother, good woman, alas, she was a Spaniard and being well tanned and dressed[573] by a good fellow, an Englishman, is grown to some wealth: as when I have but my upper parts[574] clad in her husband's costly Spanish leather, I may be bold to kiss the fairest lady's foot in this country.
SHOEMAKER You are of high birth, sir, but have you all your mother's marks[575] on you?
SLIPPER Why, knave?
SHOEMAKER Because if thou come of the blood of the Slippers, you should have a shoemaker's awl[576] thrust through your ear.
SLIPPER Take your earnest,[577] friend, and be packing, and meddle not with my progenitors. *Exit* [SHOEMAKER]
Cutler!
CUTLER Here, sir.
SLIPPER I must have a reaper and digger.
CUTLER A rapier and a dagger you mean, sir?
SLIPPER Thou sayest true, but it must have a very fair edge.
CUTLER Why so, sir?
SLIPPER Because it may cut by himself,[578] for truly, my friend, I am a man of peace and wear weapons but for fashion.
CUTLER Well, sir, give me earnest; I will fit[579] you.
SLIPPER Hold, take it. I betrust[580] thee, friend; let me be well armed.
CUTLER You shall. *Exit* CUTLER
SLIPPER Now, what remains? There, twenty crowns[581] for a house, three crowns for household stuff, six pence to buy a constable's staff; nay, I will be the chief of my parish. There wants nothing but a wench, a cat, a dog, a wife, and a servant to make an whole family. Shall I marry with Alice, goodman Grimshave's daughter? She is fair, but indeed her tongue is like clocks on Shrove Tuesday,[582] always out of temper.[583] Shall I wed Cicely of the Whighton?[584] Oh no, she is like a frog in a parsley bed, as skittish as an eel; if I seek to hamper her, she will horn[585] me. But a wench must be had, Master Slipper. Yea and shall be, dear friend.
ANDREW [*Aside*] I now will drive him from his contemplations. O my mates, come forward. The lamb is unpent; the fox shall prevail.

Enter three antics who dance round and take[586] SLIPPER *with them*

570 45 winter storms: loud, powerful farts
571 47 neat: elegant
572 51 Neatherleather: leather covering for the legs
573 52 dressed: prepared
574 53 upper parts: chest and arms
575 55 mother's marks: possibly a subtle reference to the scars of syphilis (i.e. the Spanish pox)
576 58 awl: shoemaker's tool for cutting holes
577 59 earnest: down payment
578 66 Because it . . . by himself: so sharp that it will cut with no effort
579 68 fit: outfit
580 69 betrust: trust
581 71 crowns: English coins worth five shillings or sixty pence
582 74–5 clocks on Shrove Tuesday: ringing church bells on the day before Ash Wednesday
583 75 out of temper: disorderly, not in unison
584 75 Whighton: town in southwest Scotland
585 76 horn: cuckold, cheat on
586 79 SD *take*: pull

SLIPPER I will, my friend, and I thank you heartily. Pray, keep your courtesy;[587] I am yours in the way of an hornpipe. They are strangers;[588] I see they understand not my language. Wee, wee.[589] *While they are dancing,* ANDREW *takes away his money and* [*with*] *the other antics depart*[*s*]
Nay, but my friends, one hornpipe further, a refluence back, and two doubles forward; what, not one cross point[590] against[591] Sundays? What ho, sirrah? You gone? You with the nose like an eagle and you, be a right Greek,[592] one turn more. Thieves, thieves! I am robbed! Thieves! Is this the knavery of fiddlers? Well, I will then bind the whole credit of their occupation on a bagpiper,[593] and he for my money. But I will after and teach them to caper in a halter[594] that have cozened[595] me of my money.

[*Exit*]

[Act IV, scene iv]

Enter NANO [*and*] DOROTHEA, [*the latter*] *in man's apparel*

DOROTHEA Ah, Nano, I am weary of these weeds,[596]
Weary to wield this weapon that I bear,
Weary of love from whom my woe proceeds,
Weary of toil, since I have lost my dear.
O weary life, where wanteth no distress,[597]
But every thought is paid with heaviness.
NANO Too much of "weary," madam; if you please,
Sit down; let "weary" die and take your ease.
DOROTHEA How look I, Nano? Like a man or no?
NANO If not a man, yet like a manly shrew.[598]
DOROTHEA If any come and meet us on the way,
What should we do if they enforce us stay?
NANO Set cap a-huff[599] and challenge him the field.
Suppose[600] the worst; the weak may fight to yield.[601]
DOROTHEA The battle, Nano, in this troubled mind
Is far more fierce than ever we may find.
The body's wounds by medicines may be eased,
But griefs of minds by salves are not appeased.[602]
NANO Say, Madam, will you hear your Nano sing?
DOROTHEA Of woe, good boy, but of no other thing.
NANO What if I sing of fancy,[603] will it please?
DOROTHEA To such as hope success, such notes breed ease.
NANO What if I sing like Damon to my sheep?

587 80 keep your courtesy: do not be indecorous
588 81 strangers: foreigners
589 82 Wee, wee: oui, oui (yes, yes)
590 83–4 refluence back . . . cross point: dance steps
591 84 against: in preparation for
592 85 be a right Greek: act like a Greek person (Greeks were proverbially associated with merriness)
593 86–7 bind the . . . a bagpiper: rate them as low as bagpipers
594 87 caper in a halter: dance in a hangman's noose; be hanged
595 88 cozened: cheated
596 1 these weeds: male clothes
597 5 where wanteth no distress: where no distress is lacking
598 10 shrew: complaining woman
599 13 a-huff: at an angle like a swashbuckler
600 14 Suppose: prepare for
601 14 to yield: to make the attacker surrender
602 18 by salves are not appeased: by healing ointments are not cured
603 21 fancy: love

DOROTHEA Like Phillis, I will sit me down to weep.[604]
NANO Nay, since my songs afford such pleasure small,
I'll sit me down and sing you none at all.
DOROTHEA Oh be not angry, Nano.
NANO Nay, you loathe
To think on that which doth content us both.
DOROTHEA And how?
NANO You scorn disport[605] when you are weary,
And loathe my mirth who lives to make you merry.
DOROTHEA Danger and fear withdraw me from delight.
NANO 'Tis virtue to condemn false fortune's spite.
DOROTHEA What should I do to please thee, friendly squire?
NANO A smile a day is all I will require;
And if you pay me well the smiles you owe me,
I'll kill this cursèd care or else beshrew[606] me.

Enter JAQUES, *his sword drawn*

DOROTHEA We are descried! O Nano, we are dead!
NANO Tut, yet you walk: you are not dead, indeed.
Draw me your sword, if he your way withstand.
And I will seek for rescue out of hand.[607]
DOROTHEA Run, Nano, run; prevent thy prince's death.
NANO Fear not; I'll run all danger out of breath. [*Exit*]
JAQUES Ah, you calletta,[608] you strumpet, *tu, maitresse Dorothea, vous êtes surpris.*[609] Come, say your paternoster[610] *car vous êtes mort, par ma foi.*[611]
DOROTHEA Callest me strumpet, caitiff as thou art—
But even[612] a princess born who scorns thy threats?
Shall never Frenchman say an English maid
Of threats of foreign force will be afraid.
JAQUES You no *dire votre prières? Morbleu, méchante femme,*[613] guarda your breasta; there me make you die on my morglay.[614]
DOROTHEA God shield me, hapless[615] princess and a wife,
And save my soul, although I lose my life. *They fight and she is sore wounded*
Ah, I am slain; some piteous power repay
This murtherer's cursèd deed that doth me slay.
JAQUES *Elle est tout mort.*[616] Me will run *pour* a wager[617] for fear me be *surpris* and *pendu*[618] for my labor. *Bien, je m'en allerai au roi citer mes affaires; Je ferra un chevalier*[619] for this day's travail.[620] *Exit*

604 23–4 "Damon" and "Phillis" were stock names for shepherds and shepherdesses in pastoral literature
605 29 disport: diversion
606 36 beshrew: abuse
607 40 out of hand: immediately
608 43 calletta: callet, i.e. whore
609 43 *tu, maitresse Dorothea, vous êtes surpris*: you, mistress Dorothea, you are surprised
610 44 paternoster: Lord's Prayer
611 44 *car vous êtes mort, par ma foi*: because you are dead, by my faith
612 46 even: equal to
613 49 *dire votre prières? Morbleu, méchante femme*: say your prayers? God's wounds, malicious woman
614 50 morglay: mythical sword belonging to the romance hero Bevis of Hampton
615 51 hapless: unfortunate
616 55 *Elle est tout mort*: she is all dead
617 55 Me will . . . a wager: I will run as if for a wager
618 55 *pendu*: hanged
619 56 *Bien, je . . . un chevalier*: good, I will go to the king to tell of my business; I will be made a knight
620 57 travail: work

Enter NANO [*and*] SIR CUTHBERT ANDERSON [*with*] *his sword drawn*

SIR CUTHBERT Where is this poor distressèd gentleman?
NANO Here laid on ground and wounded to the death.
Ah, gentle heart, how are these beauteous looks
Dimmed by the tyrant cruelties of death.
O weary soul, break thou from forth my breast,
And join thee with the soul I honored most.
SIR CUTHBERT Leave mourning, friend; the man is yet alive.
Come, help me to convey him to my house;
There will I see him carefully recured[621]
And send privy search[622] to catch the murtherer.
NANO The God of heaven reward thee, courteous knight.

Exeunt [*bearing out*] DOROTHEA

[Act IV, scene v]

Enter JAMES IV, JAQUES, ATEUKIN, [*and*] ANDREW; JAQUES *running with his sword one way,* JAMES IV *with his train another way*

JAMES IV Stay, Jaques. Fear not: sheath thy murthering blade.
Lo, here thy king and friends are come abroad
To save thee from the terrors of pursuit.
What, is she dead?
JAQUES *Oui, monsieur, elle* is *blessée par la tete* over *les épaules;*[623] I warrant,[624] she no trouble you.
ATEUKIN Oh then, my liege, how happy art thou grown,
How favored of the heavens and blessed by love.
Methinks I see fair Ida in thine arms,
Craving remission for her late attempt;[625]
Methinks I see her, blushing, steal a kiss,
Uniting both your souls by such a sweet,[626]
And you, my King, suck nectar from her lips.
Why then delays your grace to gain the rest
You long desired? Why lose we forward time?[627]
Write, make me spokesman now; vow marriage.
If she deny your favor, let me die.
ANDREW Mighty and magnificent potentate,[628] give credence to[629] mine honorable good lord, for I heard the midwife swear at his nativity[630] that the fairies gave him the property of the Thracian stone:[631] for who toucheth it is exempt from grief, and he that heareth my master's counsel is already possessed of happiness; nay, which is more miraculous, as the nobleman in his infancy lay in his cradle, a swarm of bees laid honey on his lips in token of his eloquence for *melle dulcior fluit oratio.*[632]
ATEUKIN Your grace must bear with imperfections:

621 66 recured: restored to health
622 67 send privy search: make a thorough search
623 5 *blessée par . . . les épaules*: wounded on the head over her shoulders
624 5 warrant: assure you
625 10 attempt: effort to resist the king's advances
626 12 sweet: delight
627 15 forward time: opportunity
628 18 potentate: powerful ruler
629 18 give credence to: believe
630 19 nativity: birthday
631 20 Thracian stone: magical stone
632 23 *melle dulcior fluit oratio*: honey flowing speech (Latin; from Cicero)

This is exceeding love that makes him speak.
JAMES IV Ateukin, I am ravished in conceit[633]
And yet depressed again with earnest thoughts:
Methinks this murther soundeth in mine ear
A threatening noise of dire and sharp revenge.
I am incensed with grief yet fain would joy.[634]
What may I do to end me of these doubts?
ATEUKIN Why, prince, it is no murther in a king[635]
To end another's life to save his own;
For you are not as common people be,
Who die and perish with a few man's tears.
But if you fail, the state doth whole default,[636]
The realm is rent in twain in such a loss.
And Aristotle holdeth this for true:
Of evils needs we must choose the least.[637]
Then better were it that a woman died,
Than all the help of Scotland should be blent.[638]
'Tis policy, my liege, in every state,
To cut off members[639] that disturb the head;
And by corruption generation grows,
And contraries maintain the world and state.[640]
JAMES IV Enough, I am confirmed. Ateukin come;
Rid me of love[641] and rid me of my grief;
Drive thou the tyrant from this tainted[642] breast,
Then may I triumph in the height of joy.
Go to mine Ida; tell her that I vow
To raise her head[643] and make her honors great.
Go to mine Ida; tell her that her hairs
Shall be embellishèd with orient pearls,
And crowns of sapphires compassing her brows
Shall wear[644] with those sweet beauties of her eyes.
Go to mine Ida; tell her that my soul
Shall keep her semblance[645] closèd in my breast,
And I in touching of her milk-white mold[646]
Will think me deified in such a grace.
I like no stay;[647] go write, and I will sign.
Reward me[648] Jaques; give him store of crowns.
And sirrah, Andrew, scout thou here in court,
And bring me tidings[649] if thou canst perceive

633 26 in conceit: by my imagination
634 30 fain would joy: gladly would rejoice
635 32 in a king: for a king
636 36 default: collapse
637 39 It is necessary to choose the least of two evils
638 41 blent: troubled
639 43 members: body parts (metaphor of the body politic), see II.ii. 66–8
640 44–5 And by . . . and state: negative actions often have positive consequences for the state
641 47 love: my love for Dorothea
642 48 tainted: infected
643 51 raise her head: promote her
644 55 shall wear: shall she wear
645 57 semblance: image
646 58 milk-white mold: alabaster body
647 60 stay: delay
648 61 Reward me: give a reward from me to
649 63 tidings: news

The least intent of muttering[650] in my train;
For either those that wrong thy lord or thee
Shall suffer death.
ATEUKIN How much, O mighty King,
Is thy Ateukin bound to honor thee;
Bow thee, Andrew; bend thine sturdy knees;
See'st thou not here thine only God on earth?
[*Exit* JAMES IV]
JAQUES *Mais où est mon argent, Signor?*[651]
ATEUKIN Come, follow me; his grace, I see, is mad[652]
That thus on sudden[653] he has left us here.
Come, Jaques; we'll have our packet[654] soon dispatched,
And you shall be my mate upon the way.
JAQUES *Comme vous plaira, monsieur.*[655]
Exeunt [ATEUKIN *and* JAQUES]
ANDREW Was never such a world I think before
When sinners seem to dance within a net;[656]
The flatterer and the murtherer, they grow big;[657]
By hook or crook,[658] promotion now is sought.
In such a world, where men are so misled,
What should I do but as the proverb say'th:
Run with the hare and hunt with the hound;[659]
To have two means[660] beseems[661] a witty man.
Now here in court I may aspire and climb
By subtlety 'fore my master's death.
And if that fail, well fare another drift:[662]
I will in secret certain letters send
Unto the English King and let him know
The order of[663] his daughter's overthrow,
That if my master crack[664] his credit here,
(As I am sure long flattery cannot hold[665])
I may have means within the English court
To 'scape the scourge that waits on[666] bad advice.
Exit

[Chorus vii]

Enter BOHAN *and* OBERON

OBERON Believe me, bonny Scot, these strange events

650 64 intent of muttering: intention to complain
651 70 But where is my money, my lord?
652 71 mad: about the possibility of his "train" "muttering" against him
653 72 on sudden: suddenly
654 73 packet: letter to Ida
655 75 As you please, my lord
656 77 sinners seem. . .a net: sinners enjoy themselves in a trap (proverbial)
657 78 big: successful
658 79 by hook or crook: by any means
659 82 Support both sides of a conflict
660 83 two means: two paths to success
661 83 beseems: is appropriate for
662 86 well fare another drift: I hope another plan will work
663 89 The order of: of the command for
664 90 crack: wreck
665 91 long flattery cannot hold: even his flattery cannot help him forever
666 93 scourge that waits on: punishment that always follows

Are passing[667] pleasing; may they end as well.
BOHAN Else say that Bohan hath a barren skull,
If better motions yet then any passed
Do not more glee to make the fairy greet.[668]
But my small son made pretty handsome shift[669]
To save the queen, his mistress, by his speed.
OBERON Yea, and your laddie,[670] for his sport[671] he made,
Shall see, when least he hopes, I'll stand his friend,
Or else he capers in a halter's end.
BOHAN What, hang my son? I trow not, Oberon;
I'll rather die than see him woebegone.[672]

Enter a round or some dance at pleasure[673] [*and exeunt*]

OBERON Bohan, be pleased; for do they what they will,
Here is my hand; I'll save thy son from ill.

[*Exeunt*]

Act V, scene i

Enter DOROTHEA *in a nightgown,*[674] LADY ANDERSON, *and* NANO

LADY ANDERSON My gentle friend, beware in taking air[675]
Your walks grow not offensive to[676] your wounds.
DOROTHEA Madam, I thank you for your courteous care;
My wounds are well-nigh[677] closed, though sore they are.
LADY ANDERSON Methinks these closèd wounds should breed more grief,
Since open wounds have cure and find relief.
DOROTHEA Madam, if undiscovered wounds you mean,
They are not cured because they are not seen.
LADY ANDERSON I mean the wounds which do the heart subdue.
NANO Oh, that is love, madam; speak I not true?

[SIR CUTHBERT *enters and*] *overhears*

LADY ANDERSON Say it were true; what salve[678] for such a sore?
NANO Be wise and shut such neighbors[679] out of door.
LADY ANDERSON How if I cannot drive him from my breast?
NANO Then chain him well and let him do his best.
SIR CUTHBERT [*Aside*] In ripping up[680] their wounds, I see their wit,[681]
But if these wounds be cured, I sorrow it.[682]

667 2 passing: extremely
668 5 Do not give you more happiness
669 6 shift: maneuver
670 8 laddie: young son (i.e. Slipper)
671 8 sport: pleasant diversion
672 12 woebegone: in despair
673 12 SD *at pleasure*: at the actors' discretion
674 0 SD *in a nightgown*: in a man's nightgown; still disguised as a man
675 1 beware in taking air: be careful in going outside that
676 2 grow not offensive to: do not aggravate
677 4 well-nigh: almost
678 11 salve: healing ointment
679 12 such neighbors: i.e. love
680 15 ripping up: painfully exposing
681 15 wit: thinking
682 16 But if Lady Anderson's love be reciprocated, I am sorry for it

DOROTHEA Why are you so intentive[683] to behold
My pale and woeful looks by care controlled?
LADY ANDERSON Because in them a ready way is found
To cure my care and heal my hidden wound.
NANO [*To* DOROTHEA] Good master, shut your eyes; keep that conceit;[684]
Surgeons give quoive[685] to get a good receipt.
DOROTHEA [*To* NANO] Peace, wanton son, this lady did amend[686]
My wounds; mine eyes her hidden grief shall end.
NANO Look not too much; it is a weighty case
Whereas[687] a man puts on a maiden's face:[688]
For many times, if ladies wear them not,
A nine month's wound with little work is got.[689]
SIR CUTHBERT [*Aside*] I'll break off their dispute, lest love proceed
From covert smiles to perfect love indeed.
NANO The cat's abroad. Stir not; the mice be still.
LADY ANDERSON Tut, we can fly such cats when so we will.
SIR CUTHBERT How fares my guest? Take cheer, naught shall default[690]
That either doth concern your health or joy.
Use me, my house, and what is mine is yours.
DOROTHEA Thanks, gentle knight, and if all hopes be true,
I hope ere long to do as much for you.
SIR CUTHBERT Your virtue doth acquit me of that doubt.[691]
But courteous sir, since troubles call me hence,
I must to Edinburgh unto the king,
There to take charge and wait[692] him in his wars.
Meanwhile, good madam, take this squire in charge,[693]
And use[694] him so as if it were myself.
LADY ANDERSON Sir Cuthbert, doubt not of my diligence.
Meanwhile, till your return, God send you health.
DOROTHEA God bless his grace, and if his cause be just,
Prosper his wars; if not, he'll mend,[695] I trust.
Good sir, what moves the king to fall to[696] arms?
SIR CUTHBERT The King of England forageth his land[697]
And hath besieged Dunbar[698] with mighty force.
What other news is common in the court,[699]
Read you these letters. [*Gives letters to* LADY ANDERSON] Madam, tell the squire
The whole affairs of state, for I must hence. *Exit*
DOROTHEA God prosper you and bring you back from thence.
Madam, what news?

683 17 intentive: heedful
684 21 conceit: idea (i.e. pretend to be asleep)
685 22 quoive: meaning uncertain; this probably has something to do with contraceptives
686 23 amend: take care of
687 26 Whereas: when
688 26 puts on a maiden's face: pretends chastity
689 27–8 if ladies ... is got: if women are not chaste (i.e. they do not wear a "maiden's face"), they will be impregnated
690 33 default: be lacking
691 38 acquit me of that doubt: erase any doubt
692 41 wait: serve
693 42 take this squire in charge: attend to this squire (i.e. Dorothea)
694 43 use: treat
695 47 mend: amend his behavior
696 48 fall to: take up
697 49 forageth: ravages
698 50 Dunbar: town on the east coast of Scotland
699 51 For other news from the court

LADY ANDERSON They say the queen is slain.
DOROTHEA Tut, such reports more false than truth contain.
LADY ANDERSON But these reports have made his nobles leave him.
DOROTHEA Ah, careless men,[700] and would they so deceive him?
LADY ANDERSON The land is spoiled; the commons[701] fear the cross;[702]
All cry against the king, their cause of loss.
The English king subdues and conquers all.
DOROTHEA Alas, this war grows great on causes small.
LADY ANDERSON Our court is desolate, our prince alone,
Still dreading death.
DOROTHEA Woe's me, for him I moan.
Help me, now help me, for a sudden qualm[703]
Assails my heart.
NANO Good madam, stand her friend;
Give us some liquor to refresh his heart.[704]
LADY ANDERSON Daw[705] thou him up, and I will fetch thee forth
Potions of comfort to repress his pain. *Exit*
NANO Fie, princess, faint on every fond[706] report?
How well nigh had you opened your estate.[707]
Cover these sorrows with the veil of joy,
And hope the best, forwhy[708] this war will cause
A great repentance in your husband's mind.
DOROTHEA Ah, Nano, trees live not without their sap;
And Clytia[709] cannot blush but on the sun;
The thirsty earth is broke with many a gap;
And lands are lean where rivers do not run;
Where soul is reft[710] from that it loveth best,
How can it thrive or boast of quiet rest?
Thou knowest the prince's loss[711] must be my death;
His grief, my grief; his mischief[712] must be mine.
Oh, if thou love me, Nano, hie[713] to court;
Tell Ross, tell Bartram that I am alive;
Conceal thou yet the place of my abode;
Will them, even as they love their queen,
As they are chary of[714] my soul and joy,
To guard the king, to serve him as my lord;
Haste thee, good Nano, for my husband's care[715]
Consumeth me and wounds me to the heart.
NANO Madam, I go, yet loathe to leave you here. [*Exit*]

700 58 careless men: men without compassion or a sense of duty
701 59 commons: people
702 59 the cross: English banner with the red cross of St. George
703 65 qualm: faintness
704 67 his heart: Q reads "her heart" here
705 68 Daw: rouse
706 70 fond: credulous
707 71 You very nearly revealed yourself
708 73 forwhy: for the reason that
709 76 Clytia: sea nymph deserted by Apollo and transformed into a heliotrope, a flower that always faces the sun
710 79 reft: separated
711 81 prince's loss: death of James IV
712 82 mischief: misfortune
713 83 hie: hasten
714 87 chary of: concerned with
715 89 care: worries

DOROTHEA Go thou with speed; even as thou hold'st me dear,
Return in haste.

Enter LADY ANDERSON

LADY ANDERSON Now sir, what cheer? Come taste this broth I bring.
DOROTHEA My grief is past; I feel no further sting.
LADY ANDERSON Where is your dwarf? Why hath he left you, sir?
DOROTHEA For some affairs; he is not traveled far.
LADY ANDERSON If so you please, come in and take your rest.
DOROTHEA Fear keeps awake a discontented breast.

Exeunt

[Act V, scene ii]

After a solemn service, enter from the COUNTESS' *house a service, musical songs of marriages, or a masque,*[716] *or what pretty triumph*[717] *you list;*[718] *to them,* ATEUKIN *and* JAQUES

ATEUKIN What means this triumph, friend? Why are[719] these feasts?
SERVANT Fair Ida, sir, was married yesterday
Unto Sir Eustace, and for that intent,
We feast and sport[720] it thus to honor them.
And if you please, come in and take your part;
My lady is no niggard of her cheer. *Exit* [SERVANT]
JAQUES *Monseigneur,*[721] why be you so sadda? *Faites bonne chère; foutre de ce monde.*[722]
ATEUKIN What? Was I born to be the scorn of kin,
To gather feathers like to a hopper crow,[723]
And lose them in the height of all my pomp?
Accursèd man, now is my credit[724] lost.
Where are my vows I made unto the king?
What shall become of me if he shall hear
That I have caused him kill a virtuous queen,
And hope in vain for that which now is lost?
Where shall I hide my head? I know the heavens
Are just and will revenge; I know my sins
Exceed compare. Should I proceed in this?
This Eustace must amain[725] be made away.
Oh, were I dead, how happy should I be.
JAQUES *Est-ce donc a point à tel point, votre état?*[726] Faith, then, *adieu* Scotland; *adieu Signor* Ateukin. Me will homa[727] to France and no be hanged in a strange country. *Exit*
ATEUKIN Thou dost me good to leave me thus alone,
That galling[728] grief and I may yoke in one.[729]

716 0 SD *masque*: courtly allegorical drama
717 0 SD *triumph*: pageant
718 0 SD *list*: like
719 1 Why are: what is the occasion for
720 4 sport: celebrate
721 7 *Monseigneur*: my lord
722 7 *Faites bonne . . . ce monde*: make good cheer; fuck this world
723 9 hopper crow: crow that follows a farmer who is sowing seeds; Ateukin complains of the demeaning work he must perform in order to raise himself socially
724 11 credit: reputation
725 19 amain: hastily
726 21 *Est-ce donc . . . votre état*: has it come to such a point, your state
727 22 homa: go home
728 24 That galling: so that offensively irritating
729 24 yoke in one: be bound together

Oh what[730] are subtle means to climb on high
When every fall swarms with exceeding shame?
I promised Ida's love unto the prince,
But she is lost, and I am false forsworn;[731]
I practiced Dorothea's hapless[732] death,
And by this practice have commenced a war.
O cursèd race of men that traffic guile,[733]
And, in the end, themselves and kings beguile.
Ashamed to look upon my prince again,
Ashamed of my suggestions and advice,
Ashamed of life, ashamed that I have erred,
I'll hide myself, expecting for my shame.[734]
Thus God doth work with those that purchase fame
By flattery and make their prince their gain.

[*Exit*]

[Act V, scene iii]

Enter the KING OF ENGLAND, *Lord Percy, and others*

KING OF ENGLAND Thus far, you English peers, have we displayed
Our waving ensigns[735] with a happy war;
Thus, nearly has our furious rage revenged
My daughter's death upon the traitorous Scot.
And now before Dunbar our camp is pitched,
Which, if it yield not to our compromise,[736]
The place shall furrow[737] where the palace stood,
And fury shall envy so high a power
That mercy shall be banished from our swords.[738]

[*Enter* DOUGLAS *and others above*]

DOUGLAS What seeks the English King?
KING OF ENGLAND Scot, open those gates and let me enter in;
Submit thyself and thine unto my grace,
Or I will put each mother's son to death
And lay this city level with the ground.
DOUGLAS For what offence? For what default[739] of ours
Art thou incensed so sore against our state?
Can generous hearts in nature[740] be so stern
To prey on those that never did offend?
What though the lion, king of brutish race,
Through[741] outrage sin, shall lambs be therefore slain?
Or is it lawful that the humble die

730 25 what: what good
731 28 I am false forsworn: I have perjured myself
732 29 hapless: unlucky
733 31 traffic guile: trade in deceit
734 36 expecting for my shame: awaiting my humiliation
735 2 waving ensigns: flags
736 6 compromise: offer of compromise
737 7 furrow: be plowed (because the town has been razed)
738 8–9 And fury . . . our swords: for our swords, fury will take precedence over mercy
739 15 default: transgression
740 17 generous hearts in nature: naturally generous hearts
741 20 Through: with

Because the mighty do gainsay the right?[742]
O English King, thou bearest in thy breast
The king of beasts that harms not yielding ones;
The roseal cross[743] is spread within thy field,
A sign of peace, not of revenging war.
Be gracious, then, unto this little town,
And though we have withstood thee for a while,
To show allegiance to our liefest liege,[744]
Yet since we know no hope of any help,
Take us to mercy, for we yield ourselves.
KING OF ENGLAND What, shall I enter then and be your lord?
DOUGLAS We will submit us to the English King. *They descend down, open the gates, and humble them[selves]*
KING OF ENGLAND Now life and death dependeth on my sword;
This hand now reared, my Douglas, if I list,
Could part thy head and shoulders both in twain.
But since I see thee wise and old in years,
True to thy king and faithful in his wars,
Live thou and thine; Dunbar is too too small
To give an entrance[745] to the English King.
I, eagle-like, disdain these little fowls
And look on none but those that dare resist.
Enter your town[746] as those that live by me;[747]
For others that resist, kill, forage, spoil
Mine English soldiers; as you love your king,
Revenge his daughter's death and do me right.

Exeunt

[Act V, scene iv]

Enter the LAWYER, *the* MERCHANT, *and the* DIVINE

LAWYER My friends, what think you of this present state?
Were ever seen such changes in a time?
The manners and the fashions of this age
Are like the ermine[748] skin, so full of spots;
As soon may the Moor[749] be washèd white,
Than these corruptions banished from this realm.
MERCHANT What sees Mas. Lawyer in this state amiss?
LAWYER A wresting[750] power that makes a nose of wax[751]
Of grounded[752] law, a damned and subtle drift[753]
In all estates to climb by others' loss,
An eager thirst for wealth, forgetting truth.

742 22 gainsay the right: deny what is right
743 25 roseal cross: red cross, see V.i. 59
744 29 liefest liege: most beloved lord
745 40 To give an entrance: to give a sufficiently glorious welcome
746 43 Enter your town: the English king now addresses his troops
747 43 as those . . . by me: as you would enter (i.e. peacefully) any town that chooses to submit to me
748 4 ermine: a white, spotted, weasel-like animal
749 5 the Moor: dark-skinned inhabitant of North Africa
750 8 wresting: twisting, distorting
751 8 nose of wax: something easily manipulated
752 9 grounded: well-established
753 9 drift: tendency

Might I ascend unto the highest states
And by discant discover[754] every crime,
My friends, I should lament, and you would grieve
To see the hapless ruins of this realm.
DIVINE O lawyer, thou hast curious[755] eyes to pry
Into the secret maims[756] of their estate,
But if thy veil of error were unmasked,
Thyself should see your sect[757] do maim her most.
Are you not those that should maintain the peace
Yet only are the patrons[758] of our strife?
If your profession has its ground and spring
First from the laws of God, then country's right,
Not any ways[759] inverting nature's power,
Why thrive you by contentions? Why devise you
Clauses and subtle reasons to except?[760]
Our state was first, before you grew so great,
A lantern to[761] the world for unity.
Now they that are befriended[762] and are rich
Oppress the poor; come Homer without coin,
He is not heard.[763] What shall we term this drift,
To say the poor man's cause is good and just,
And yet the rich man gains the best in law?
It is your guise[764] (the more the world laments)
To coin provisos[765] to beguile your laws,
To make a gay pretext of due proceeding[766]
When you delay your common pleas[767] for years.
Mark what these dealings lately here have wrought:
The crafty[768] men have purchased great men's lands;
They poll,[769] they pinch, their tenants are undone;
If these complain by you, they are undone;
You fleece[770] them of their coin, their children beg,
And many want because[771] you may be rich.
This scar is mighty, Master Lawyer.
Now war hath gotten head within this land,[772]
Mark but the guise: the poor man that is wronged
Is ready to rebel; he spoils, he pills.[773]

754 13 by discant discover: by pointed commentary publish to the world
755 16 curious: snooping
756 17 maims: defects
757 19 sect: profession
758 21 patrons: supporters
759 24 any ways: in any way
760 26 to except: to make objections
761 28 lantern to: bright example for
762 29 befriended: friends with powerful people
763 30–31 come Homer . . . not heard: even Homer (Greek epic poet) would need to pay to be heard
764 34 guise: practice
765 35 provisos: formal exceptions, stipulations in a legal document
766 36 Render proper procedures into flippant pretenses
767 37 common pleas: civil law suits
768 39 crafty: deceitful (with pun on "crafts" as in artisan trades)
769 40 poll: plunder
770 42 fleece: rob
771 43 because: so that
772 45 Now that war has taken this land over
773 47 pills: pillages

"We need no foes to forage[774] that we have;
The law," say they, "in peace consumèd us,
And now in war we will consume the law."
Look to this mischief, lawyer. Conscience knows
You live amiss; amend it, lest you end.
LAWYER Good lord, that these divines should see so far
In others' faults without amending theirs!
Sir, sir, the general defaults in state
(If you would read before you did correct),[775]
Are by a hidden working from above,
By their successive changes still removed;
Were not the law by contraries maintained[776]
How could the truth from falsehood be discerned?
Did we not taste the bitterness of war,
How could we know the sweet effects of peace?
Did we not feel the nipping winter frosts,
How should we know the sweetness of the spring?
Should all things still remain in one estate?[777]
Should not in greatest arts some scars[778] be found?
Were all upright and changed,[779] what world were this?
A chaos made of quiet yet no world
Because the parts thereof did still accord.
This matter craves a variance,[780] not a speech.
But, Sir Divine, to you: look on your maims,
Divisions, sects, your simonies[781] and bribes,
Your cloaking[782] with the great, for fear to fall;
You shall perceive you are the cause of all.
Did each man know there were a storm at hand,
Who would not clothe him[783] well to shun the wet?
Did prince and peer, the lawyer, and the least
Know what were sin without a partial gloss,[784]
We need no long discovery then of crimes,
For each would mend, advised by holy men.
This but slightly shadows out[785] your sins,
But if they were depainted out for life,[786]
Alas, we both had[787] wounds enough to heal.
MERCHANT None of you both, I see, but are in fault.[788]
Thus simple men as I do swallow flies.[789]
This grave divine can tell us what to do,
But we may say, "Physician, mend thyself."

774 48 forage: take
775 56 If you would understand before you spoke
776 59 by contraries maintained: conducted by arguments and counter arguments
777 65 estate: condition
778 66 scars: imperfections
779 67 changed: perfected
780 70 a variance: debate
781 72 simonies: selling of ecclesiastical offices
782 73 cloaking: dissembling
783 76 clothe him: clothe himself
784 78 a partial gloss: your prejudiced understanding
785 81 shadows out: hints at
786 82 depainted out for life: fully described
787 83 had: would have
788 84 Neither of you, I see, is at fault (a sarcastic observation)
789 85 do swallow flies: are fed lies

This lawyer hath a pregnant wit[790] to talk,
But all are words; I see no deeds of worth.
LAWYER Good merchant, lay your fingers on your mouth;
Be not a blab for fear you bite yourself.
What should I term your state, but even the way
To every ruin in this commonweal?
You bring us in the means of all excess;
You rate it and retail it[791] as you please;
You swear, forswear, and all to compass[792] wealth.
Your money is your god, your hoard your heaven.
You are the groundwork[793] of contention.
First, heedless youth by you is overreached;
We are corrupted by your many crowns;[794]
The gentlemen, whose titles you have bought,
Lose all their father's toil within a day,
Whilst Hob, your son, and Sib,[795] your nutbrown child,
Are gentlefolks,[796] and gentles are beguiled;[797]
This makes so many noble maids to stray
And take sinister courses in the state.[798]

Enter a SCOUT

SCOUT My friends, be gone, and if you love your lives.
The King of England marcheth here at hand.
Enter the camp[799] for fear you be surprised.
DIVINE Thanks, gentle scout. God mend that is amiss[800]
And place true zeal whereas[801] corruption is.

Exeunt

[Act V, scene v]

Enter DOROTHEA [*in man's apparel,*] LADY ANDERSON, *and* NANO

DOROTHEA What news in court, Nano? Let us know it.
NANO If so you please, my lord, I straight will show it.
The English king hath all the borders spoiled,[802]
Hath taken Morton prisoner, and hath slain
Seven thousand Scottish lads not far from Tweed.[803]
DOROTHEA A woeful murther and a bloody deed.
NANO The king, our liege, hath sought by many means
For to appease his enemy by prayers;
Naught will prevail unless he can restore

790 88 pregnant wit: ready intelligence
791 95 rate it and retail it: price it and sell it
792 96 compass: obtain
793 98 groundwork: foundation
794 100 crowns: coins
795 103 Hob, your son, and Sib: stereotypical names for rustic men and women; Sib is "nutbrown" from manual labor
796 104 Are gentlefolks: presume to be gentlemen and gentlewomen
797 104 gentles are beguiled: real gentlefolk are cheated of their position
798 105–6 This makes . . . the state: this leads noblewomen to choose corrupt paths and marry beneath themselves
799 109 the camp: the camp of James IV
800 110 that is amiss: that which is amiss
801 111 zeal whereas: righteousness where
802 3 spoiled: ravaged
803 5 Tweed: river in southern Scotland

Fair Dorothea long supposèd dead.
To this intent he has proclaimèd late
That whosoever return the queen to court
Shall have a thousand marks[804] for his reward.
LADY ANDERSON He loves her then, I see, although enforced,
That would bestow such gifts for to regain her.
Why sit you sad, good sir?[805] Be not dismayed.
NANO I'll lay my life, this man would be a maid.
DOROTHEA [*Aside*] Fain would I show myself and change my tire.[806]
LADY ANDERSON [*To* NANO] Whereon divine you,[807] sir?
NANO Upon desire.
Madam, mark but my skill: I'll lay my life
My master here will prove a married wife.
DOROTHEA [*To* NANO] Wilt thou bewray[808] me, Nano?
NANO [*To* DOROTHEA] Madam, no.
You are a man, and like a man you go.
But I that am in speculation seen[809]
Know you would change your state to be a queen.
DOROTHEA [*To* NANO] Thou art not, dwarf, to learn thy mistress' mind;
Fain would I with thyself disclose my kind,
But yet I blush.
NANO [*To* DOROTHEA] What, blush you, madam, then
To be yourself who are a feignèd man?
Let me alone.[810]
DOROTHEA [*To* NANO] Good Nano, Stay awhile.
Were I not sad, how kindly could I smile
To see how fain I am to leave this weed;
And yet I faint to show myself indeed.
But danger hates delay; I will be bold.
—Fair lady, I am not, as you suppose,
A man, but even that queen, more hapless I,
Whom Scottish king appointed hath to die.
I am that hapless princess for whose right
These kings in bloody wars revenge despite.[811]
I am that Dorothea whom they seek,
Yours bounden[812] for your kindness and relief.
And since you are the means that saved my life,
Yourself and I will to the camp repair,[813]
Whereas[814] your husband shall enjoy reward
And bring me to his highness once again.
LADY ANDERSON Deceitful beauty, hast thou scorned me so?
NANO Nay, muse not, madam, for she tells you true.
LADY ANDERSON Beauty bred love, and love hath bred my shame.
NANO And women's faces work more wrongs than these.

804 13 marks: coins valued somewhat less than pounds
805 16 good sir: the disguised Dorothea
806 18 tire: attire
807 19 Whereon divine you: on what basis do you conjecture
808 22 bewray: expose
809 24 speculation seen: known for his probing mind
810 30–45 In Q, this line and Dorothea's speech that follows were mistakenly set after line 59
811 39 revenge despite: take vengeance on spitefulness
812 41 Yours bounden: bound to you
813 43 repair: go
814 44 Whereas: where

Take comfort, madam, to cure your disease.
And yet he loves a man as well as you;
Only this difference: he cannot fancy two.
LADY ANDERSON Blush, grieve, and die in thine own insatiate lust.
DOROTHEA Nay, live and joy that thou hast won a friend
That loves thee as her life by good desert.
LADY ANDERSON I joy, my lord, more than my tongue can tell;
Although not as I desired, I love you well.
But modesty, that never blushed before,
Discovers[815] my false heart. I say no more.
Pardon, most gracious princess, if you please,
My rude discourse and homely entertain;[816]
And if my words may savor any worth,[817]
Vouchsafe[818] my counsel in this weighty cause:
Since that our liege has so unkindly dealt,
Give him no trust; return unto your sire,
There may you safely live in spite of him.
DOROTHEA Ah, lady, so would worldly counsel work,
But constancy, obedience, and my love,
In that my husband is my lord and chief,
These call me to compassion of his estate.[819]
Dissuade me not, for virtue will not change.
LADY ANDERSON What wondrous constancy is this I hear?
If English dames their husbands love so dear,
I fear me in the world they have no peer.
NANO Come, princess, wend, and let us change your weed;
I long to see you now a queen indeed.

Exeunt

[Act V, scene vi]

Enter JAMES IV*, the English Herald, and lords*

JAMES IV He[820] would have parley,[821] lords. Herald, say he shall.
And get thee gone. Go, leave me to myself. [*Exeunt English Herald and lords*]
'Twixt love and fear, continual is the wars:
The one assures me of my Ida's love,
The other moves me for my murthered queen.
Thus find I grief of that whereon I joy
And doubt in greatest hope and death in weale.[822]
Alas, what hell may be compared with mine,
Since in extremes my comforts do consist?
War then will cease when dead ones are revived;
Some then will yield when I am dead for hope.[823]
Who doth disturb me? Andrew?

815 59 Discovers: reveals
816 61 homely entertain: simple hospitality
817 62 savor any worth: be worth anything
818 63 Vouchsafe: take
819 70 estate: circumstances
820 1 He: the King of England
821 1 parley: temporary truce in battle in order to discuss terms of surrender or peace
822 7 weale: prosperity
823 11 The attacks will stop when my hope is dead

ANDREW *enter with* SLIPPER

ANDREW Ay, my liege.
JAMES IV What news?
ANDREW I think my mouth was made at first
To tell these tragic tales, my liefest lord.
JAMES IV What, is Ateukin dead? Tell me the worst.
ANDREW No, but your Ida—shall I tell him all?
—Is married late—Ah, shall I say to whom?
—My master sad—For why[824] he shames the court—
Is fled away. Ah, most unhappy flight.
Only myself—ah, who can love you more?—
To show my duty—duty past belief—
Am come unto your grace—O, gracious liege—
To let you know—oh, would it were not thus—
That love is vain, and maids soon lost and won.
JAMES IV How have the partial[825] heavens then dealt with me,
Boding my weal for[826] to abase my power?
Alas, what thronging[827] thoughts do me oppress?
Injurious love is partial in my right,[828]
And flattering tongues, by whom I was misled,
Have laid a snare to spoil my state and me.
Methinks I hear my Dorothea's ghost
Howling revenge for my accursèd hate.
The ghosts of those my subjects that are slain
Pursue me, crying out, "Woe, woe to lust!"
The foe pursues me at my palace door;
He breaks my rest and spoils me in my camp.
Ah, flattering brood of sycophants, my foes,
First shall my dire revenge begin on you.
I will reward thee, Andrew.
SLIPPER Nay, sir, if you be in your deeds of charity, remember me. I rubbed[829] Master Ateukin's horse heels when he rid to the meadows.
JAMES IV And thou shalt have thy recompense for that:
Lords, bear them to the prison; chain them fast
Until we take[830] some order for their deaths.
ANDREW If so, your grace in such sort gives[831] rewards,
Let me have naught: I am content to want.
SLIPPER Then I pray, sir, give me all; I am as ready for a reward as an oyster for a fresh tide. Spare not me, sir.
JAMES IV Then hang them both as traitors to the king.
SLIPPER The case is altered,[832] sir; I'll none of your gifts. What, I take a reward at your hands? Master, faith sir, no. I am a man of better conscience.
JAMES IV Why dally you? Go draw them hence away!

824 18 For why: because
825 25 partial: prejudiced
826 26 Boding my weal for: presaging my happiness only
827 27 thronging: gathering
828 28 partial in my right: prejudiced against me
829 40 rubbed: massaged
830 44 take: give
831 45 in such sort gives: gives such
832 50 The case is altered: I've changed my mind

Enter OBERON *and antics and carry away* [SLIPPER] *the clown;* [SLIPPER] *makes pots,*[833] *and sports,*[834] *and scorns*

SLIPPER Why, alas, sir, I will go away. I thank you, gentle friends; I pray you, spare your pains;
I will not trouble his honor's mastership; I'll run away. [*Exit*]
JAMES IV Why stay you? Move me not! Let search be made
For vile Ateukin; whoso finds him out
Shall have five hundred marks for his reward.
Away with them; lords, troops about my tent;
Let all our soldiers stand in battle 'ray,[835]
For lo, the English to their parley come.

March over bravely first the English host, [*his*] *sword carried before the* KING OF ENGLAND *by Percy. The Scottish army on the other side with all their pomp bravely*

JAMES IV What seeks the King of England in this land?
KING OF ENGLAND False traitorous Scot, I come for to revenge
My daughter's death; I come to spoil[836] thy wealth,
Since thou hast spoiled me of my marriage joy;[837]
I come to heap thy land with carcasses
That this thy thirsty soil, choked up with blood,
May thunder forth revenge upon thy head;
I come to quit[838] thy loveless love with death.
In brief, no means of peace shall e'er be found
Except[839] I have my daughter or thy head.
JAMES IV My head, proud King? Abase thy pranking 'plaints,[840]
So striving fondly[841] may'st thou catch thy grave.
But if true judgment do direct thy course,
These lawful reasons should divide[842] the war:
Faith, not by my consent thy daughter died.
KING OF ENGLAND Thou liest, false Scot; thy agents have confessed it.
These are but fond delays; thou canst not think
A means for to reconcile me for thy friend;[843]
I have thy parasite's confession penned.
What then canst thou allege in thy excuse?
JAMES IV I will repay the ransom[844] for her blood.
KING OF ENGLAND What, think'st thou, caitiff, I will sell my child?
No, if thou be a prince and man-at-arms,[845]
In single combat come and try thy right,
Else will I prove thee recreant[846] to thy face.
JAMES IV I brook no combat,[847] false injurious King,
But since thou needless art inclined to war,
Do what thou darest; we are in open field.

833 52 SD *makes pots*: makes faces
834 52 SD *sports*: taunts
835 59 'ray: array
836 63 spoil: plunder
837 64 spoiled me . . . marriage joy: deprived me of my joy in your marriage
838 68 quit: requite
839 70 Except: unless
840 71 Abase thy pranking 'plaints: humble your swaggering complaints
841 72 fondly: foolishly
842 74 divide: break up
843 77–8 thou canst . . . thy friend: you cannot come up with an excuse to make me again your friend
844 81 repay the ransom: pay a monetary settlement
845 83 man-at-arms: soldier
846 85 prove thee recreant: call you a coward
847 86 brook no combat: will endure no single combat

Arming my battles,[848] I will fight with thee.
KING OF ENGLAND Agreed. Now trumpets sound a dreadful charge!
Fight for your princess, brave Englishmen!
JAMES IV Now for your lands, your children, and your wives,
My Scottish peers, and lastly for your king!

Alarum[849] *sounded. Both* [*the armies*] *offer to meet; and as the kings are joining battle, enter* SIR CUTHBERT [*and*] *his* LADY ANDERSON *with the Queen* DOROTHEA [*veiled and*] *richly attired*[850] [*and* NANO]

SIR CUTHBERT Stay princes! Wage not war! A private grudge
'Twixt such as you (most high in majesty)
Afflicts both nocent[851] and the innocent.
How many swords, dear princes, see I drawn?
The friend against his friend, a deadly friend;
A desperate division in those lands,[852]
Which if they join in one, command the world.
Oh stay, with reason mitigate your rage,
And let an old man humbled on his knees
Entreat a boon,[853] good princes, of you both. [*Kneels*]
KING OF ENGLAND I condescend,[854] for why[855] thy reverend years
Import some news of truth and consequence.
JAMES IV I am content, for Anderson I know
Thou art my subject and dost mean me good.
SIR CUTHBERT But by your gracious favors grant me this:
To swear upon your swords to do me right.
KING OF ENGLAND See, by my sword and by a prince's faith,
In every lawful sort[856] I am thine own.
JAMES IV And by my scepter and the Scottish crown,
I am resolved to grant thee thy request.
SIR CUTHBERT I see you trust me, princes, who repose[857]
The weight of such a war upon my will.
Now mark my suit. A tender lion's whelp[858]
This other day came straggling in the woods,
Attended by a young and tender hind,[859]
In courage haughty yet 'tired[860] like a lamb.
The prince of beasts had left this young in keep[861]
To foster up as lovemate and compeer[862]
Unto the lion's mate, a neighbor friend.
This stately guide, seducèd by the fox,
Sent forth an eager wolf bred up in France

848 89 battles: battalions
849 93 SD *Alarum*: call to arms
850 93 SD *richly attired*: wearing rich clothes
851 96 nocent: guilty
852 99 those lands: England and Scotland
853 103 boon: favor
854 104 condescend: agree
855 104 for why: because
856 111 sort: way
857 114 repose: place
858 116 whelp: cub (i.e. Dorothea)
859 118 hind: female deer (i.e. Nano)
860 119 'tired: attired
861 120 in keep: in possession
862 121 compeer: equal

That gripped[863] the tender whelp and wounded it.
By chance as I was hunting in the woods,
I heard the moan the hind made for the whelp.
I took them both and brought them to my house;
With chary care I have recured the one.
And since I know the lions are at strife
About the loss and damage of the young,
I bring her home. Make claim to her who list. *He discovereth[864] her*
DOROTHEA I am the whelp, bred by this lion up,
This royal English King, my happy sire;
Poor Nano is the hind that tended me.
My father, Scottish King, gave me to thee,
A hapless wife. Thou, quite misled by youth,
Hast sought sinister[865] loves and foreign[866] joys.
The fox Ateukin, cursèd parasite,
Incensed your grace to send the wolf abroad,
The French-born Jaques, for him to end my days.
He, traitorous man, pursued me in the woods
And left me wounded, where this noble knight
Both rescued me and mine, and saved my life.
Now keep thy promise: Dorothea lives;
Give Anderson his due and just reward;
And since, you kings, your wars began by me,
Since I am safe returned, surcease[867] your fight.
JAMES IV Durst I presume to look upon those eyes
Which I have tired with a world of woes?
Or did I think[868] submission were enough
Or sighs might make an entrance to thy soul,
You heavens, you know how willing I would weep;
You heavens can tell how glad[869] I would submit;
You heavens can say how firmly I would sigh.
DOROTHEA Shame me not, prince, companion in thy bed.
Youth has misled; tut, but a little fault.
'Tis kingly to amend what is amiss.
Might I with twice as many pains as these
Unite our hearts, then should my wedded lord
See how incessant labors I would take.
My gracious father, govern your affects;[870]
Give me that hand that oft has blessed this head,
And clasp thine arms that have embracèd this[871]
About the shoulders of my wedded spouse.
Ah, mighty prince, this king and I am one:
Spoil thou[872] his subjects, thou despoilest me;
Touch thou his breast, thou dost attaint[873] this heart.

863 125 gripped: seized
864 132 SD *discovereth*: unveils
865 138 sinister: underhanded
866 138 foreign: extramarital
867 148 surcease: end
868 151 Or did I think: if only I thought
869 154 glad: gladly
870 162 affects: emotions
871 164 this: this body
872 167 Spoil thou: if you destroy
873 168 attaint: condemn

Oh be my father then in loving him.
KING OF ENGLAND Thou provident, kind mother of increase,[874]
Thou must prevail; ah, nature, thou must rule.
Hold, daughter; join my hand and his in one;
I will embrace him for to favor thee;
I call him friend and take him for my son.
DOROTHEA Ah, royal husband, see what God hath wrought:
Thy foe is now thy friend. Good men at arms,
Do you the like.[875] These nations, if they join,
What monarch with his liegemen in this world
Dare but[876] encounter you in open field?
JAMES IV All wisdom joined with godly piety.
Thou English King, pardon my former youth,
And pardon, courteous Queen, my great misdeed.
And for assurance of mine after life,[877]
I take religious vows before my God
To honor thee for father, her for wife.
SIR CUTHBERT But yet my boons, good princes, are not past.[878]
First, English King, I humbly do request
That by your means our princess may unite
Her love unto mine aldertruest[879] love.
Now you will love, maintain, and help them both.
KING OF ENGLAND Good Anderson, I grant thee thy request.
SIR CUTHBERT But you, my prince, must yield me mickle[880] more.
You know your nobles are your chiefest stays[881]
And long time have been banished from your court;
Embrace and reconcile them to yourself;
They are your hands whereby you ought to work.
As for Ateukin and his lewd compeers[882]
That soothed[883] you in your sins and youthly pomp,
Exile, torment, and punish such as they,
For greater vipers never may be found
Within a state than such aspiring heads
That reck not how they climb so that they climb.
JAMES IV Guid knight, I grant thy suit. First, I submit
And humble[884] crave a pardon of your grace.
Next, courteous Queen, I pray thee by thy loves
Forgive mine errors past and pardon me.
My lords and princes, if I have misdone
(As I have wronged indeed both you and yours),
Hereafter, trust me; you are dear to me.
As for Ateukin, whoso finds the man,
Let him have martial law and straight be hanged,

874 170 mother of increase: the king invokes Mother Nature
875 177 Do you the like: join hands and embrace
876 179 Dare but: would even dare
877 183 after life: future actions
878 186 past: yet granted
879 189 aldertruest: truest of all (i.e. James IV, his king)
880 192 mickle: much
881 193 stays: props
882 197 compeers: fellows
883 198 soothed: encouraged
884 204 humble: i.e. humbly

As all his vain abettors now are divided.[885]
And Anderson, our treasurer shall pay
Three thousand marks for friendly recompense.
NANO But princes, while you friend it thus in one,[886]
Methinks of friendship Nano shall have none.
DOROTHEA What would my dwarf that I will not bestow?[887]
NANO My boon, fair queen, is this: that you would go.
Although my body is but small and neat,[888]
My stomach after toil requireth meat.
An easy suit, dread princess, will you wend?[889]
JAMES IV Art thou a pigmy[890] born, my pretty friend?
NANO Not so, great King, but nature when she framed me
Was scant of[891] earth and "Nano" therefore named me;
And when she saw my body was so small,
She gave me wit to make it big withal.[892]
JAMES IV Till time when—
DOROTHEA Eat then.
JAMES IV My friend, it stands with wit[893]
To take repast[894] when stomach serveth[895] it.
DOROTHEA Thy policy, my Nano, shall prevail:
Come, royal father, enter we my tent;
And soldiers feast it, frolic it[896] like friends.
My princes, bid this kind and courteous train
Partake some favors of our late accord.[897]
Thus wars have end, and after dreadful hate,
Men learn at last to know their good estate.[898]

Exeunt

[Chorus viii][899]

[*Enter* BOHAN *and* OBERON]

BOHAN An[900] here we'll make ends: the mirk and sable[901] night
Doth leave[902] the peering[903] morn to pry[904] abroad.
Thou nill me stay.[905] Hail then, thou pride of kings,

885 212 divided: condemned to death
886 215 in one: together
887 217 What could you ask for that I would not give?
888 219 neat: agreeable
889 221 wend: go
890 222 pigmy: mythical African race of small humans
891 224 Was scant of: had a limited amount of
892 226 withal: in spite of all
893 227 it stands with wit: it makes sense
894 228 repast: nourishment
895 228 serveth: demands
896 231 frolic it: make merry
897 233 favors of our late accord: gifts as a result of our treaty
898 235 good estate: happy condition
899 Chorus viii: mistakenly printed at the end of Act I in Q
900 1 An: and
901 1 mirk and sable: gloomy and dark
902 2 leave: allow
903 2 peering: appearing
904 2 pry: look
905 3 nill me stay: will not get me to stay

I ken[906] the world and wot well worldly things.
Mark thou my jig in mirkest terms that tells
The loath[907] of sins and where corruption dwells.
Hail me ne mere[908] with shows of guidly[909] sights;
My grave is mine that rids me from despites.[910]
Accept my jig, guid King, and let me rest;
The grave with[911] guid men is a gay-built[912] nest.
OBERON The rising sun doth call me hence away.
Thanks for thy jig; I may no longer stay.
But if my train did wake thee from thy nest,
So shall they sing thy lullaby to rest.

[*Enter antics who sing a lullaby; exit* BOHAN *into tomb; exeunt*]

FINIS.

906 4 ken: know
907 6 loath: hatefulness
908 7 Hail me ne mere: greet me no more
909 7 guidly: goodly
910 8 despites: injuries
911 10 with: to
912 10 gay-built: happily constructed

10 John Webster, *The Duchess of Malfi*

First performed 1614

First printed 1623

Edited by Farah Karim-Cooper

The Duchess of Malfi is John Webster's most celebrated play. Ahead of its time in its sympathetic portrayal of female strength and courage, it dramatizes the story of Giovanna d'Aragona (c. 1478–1513), a widowed noblewoman who secretly married her household steward. Departing from his primary source for the play—William Painter's novella, *The Palace of Pleasure*, an English translation of the French *Histoires Tragiques* (1565) by Francois de Belleforest—which represents the Duchess's remarriage as immoral, Webster represents the Duchess's brothers, Duke Ferdinand and the Cardinal, as vengeful, somewhat psychopathic patriarchs who attempt to control and contain their sister, body and soul. At the time this play was staged, King James I was on the throne and female monarchy was a thing of the recent past (Elizabeth I had died in 1603). In some ways, the question of Elizabethan authority haunts Webster's play, which meditates upon how powerful female sexuality was perceived to be a threat, particularly when a woman prominent in the state and nobility unapologetically pursues her heart's desire. By engaging in a secret courtship and marriage with Antonio, the steward of her household, the Duchess risks her reputation and that of the family she represents. Her brothers' concerns about her sexual behavior reflect this fear about family reputation that was particularly important to the nobility, but Ferdinand, her twin, becomes perversely obsessed with her sexual status; his threats toward her become disturbingly incestuous and tyrannical. This is clearly shown in Act IV, when, with the help of his spy, the malcontent Bosola, he engineers a sequence of psychological tortures designed to punish and weaken the Duchess. These involve a "dead hand" made of wax and the macabre display of the waxen figures of her husband and children, intended to make the Duchess believe that they are dead. Even Bosola, who is commissioned to enact the tortures, struggles with their horrifying nature. Nevertheless, until the very moment of her death, the Duchess maintains her composure and independence. In what is perhaps the play's most famous line, "I am Duchess of Malfi still," spoken just before she is killed (IV.ii. 120), the Duchess affirms her sense of self and identity, and insists on her courage and virtue.

Webster's fascination with female agency is evident not only in his portrayal of the Duchess. Julia, the Cardinal's mistress, is also a unique and remarkable character. While she is not virtuous (she is having an affair with a man of the clergy), she is nevertheless a strong-minded woman who is not afraid to use her sexuality or her voice to gain advancement and seek her own pleasure. The Duchess is heroic; Julia is sexually aggressive. Both are bold and both suffer consequences because they live in a world fraught with misogyny and rigid rules under which women were expected to live. The misogyny of this world is voiced mainly by Bosola and Ferdinand. Bosola's outburst against the Old Lady, for example, is deeply troubling. He rages against women's cosmetic practices, echoing many misogynistic tirades against female vanity and going so far as to suggest that the dressing table of a woman is like a "shop of witchcraft" (II.i. 27). The fact that the Duchess is seen at her dressing table later suggests that Bosola's view is only one side of the debate; Webster was interested in presenting female identity in all of its complexity.

In addition to its proto-feminist sensibilities, *The Duchess of Malfi* is preoccupied with a number of themes including the relationship between social classes; sibling relationships; mental health or "madness" (highlighted by Ferdinand's degenerating temperament and the eight madmen he sends to torment his sister); the rituals and potential corruption of Catholicism; and political surveillance or spying. One theme that stands out in particular is Webster's fascination with death and dying. In its imagery and action the play meditates upon the various attitudes to death in the Jacobean period, including the difference between a good and bad death—drawing, in this case, upon contemporary books and sermons that instructed people how to die well. The Duchess's death and that of her lady, Cariola, seem to be deliberately juxtaposed so that we can contrast their attitudes towards mortality in their final moments. While Cariola fights and tries to stall her death, the Duchess accepts hers stoically; aware that death must come to all, she retains her dignity in the face of her ultimate calamity.

The play was performed by the King's Men in 1614, first in the Blackfriars playhouse in the winter before its summer performances in the Globe on Bankside. The Globe was an outdoor theater built originally in 1599, but it burned down in 1613 when a spark from the theater's cannon lit the thatched roof on fire during a performance of Shakespeare and John Fletcher's play *Henry VIII, or All is True*. The company rebuilt the Globe in 1614 on the foundations of the original and it is thus the second Globe where Webster's play was performed. The Blackfriars and the Globe were quite different theaters: one was an indoor playhouse, the other was an amphitheater. Webster's play seems tailor-made for the indoor theater, which would have been lit with candles and which therefore provided more opportunities to create illusion and special effects. Given the play's attention to changes in light and darkness (particularly in Act IV when all the candles are removed from the scene and the Duchess is left in complete darkness); its interest in special effects such as the wax figures and the dead hand; and its preoccupation with death, Catholic ritual, and domestic life, it is not difficult to imagine a candlelit former Dominican monastery providing an appropriate environment for *The Duchess of Malfi*'s earliest performances.

Textual note

This edition is based on the British Library copy of the 1623 quarto, which exists in two states: a first state and a corrected state. Most editors agree that Webster was personally involved in making the corrections. The main difference between the two states occurs in III.iv when, in a dumbshow, the Cardinal is divested of his robes and attired in military regalia. In the uncorrected quarto, the song that accompanies this moment is entitled "The Hymne" and is accompanied by a stage direction that reads: "This hymne is sung to very solemn music, by divers churchmen" (7–9). In the corrected text, the word "hymne" has been removed and, in the stage direction, has been changed to "ditty." A marginal note has been added, noting that "the author disclaims this ditty to be his." It appears that for whatever reason Webster did not want to associate his authorship with the "hymne"; editors remain uncertain about the reasons behind the change, or Webster's note. Three further quarto editions were published in 1640, 1678, and 1708. I have consulted the 1640 edition to examine variants.

Further reading

Editions

Brown, John Russell (ed.) (1997) *The Duchess of Malfi*, Manchester: Manchester University Press.
Marcus, Leah (ed.) (2009) *The Duchess of Malfi*, London: Bloomsbury.

Critical and contextual reading

Callaghan, Dympna (ed.) (2000) *The Duchess of Malfi: John Webster*, New York: Macmillan.
Carnegie, David (2014) *Webster: The Duchess of Malfi*, New York: Palgrave Macmillan.
Coleman, David (2010) *John Webster: Renaissance Dramatist*, Edinburgh: Edinburgh University Press.
Jankowski, Theodora A. (1990) "Defining/Confining the Duchess: Negotiating the Female Body in John Webster's *The Duchess of Malfi*," *Studies in Philology* 87: 221–45.
Karim-Cooper, Farah (2016) *The Hand on the Shakespearean Stage: Gesture, Touch and the Spectacle of Dismemberment*, London: Bloomsbury.
Luckyj, Christina (2011) *The Duchess of Malfi: A Critical Guide*, London: Bloomsbury.
Oakes, Elizabeth (1999) "*The Duchess of Malfi* as a Tragedy of Identity," *Studies in Philology* 96: 51–67.
Tricomi, Albert H. (2004) "The Severed Hand in Webster's *The Duchess of Malfi*," *Studies in English Literature* 44: 347–58.
White, Martin (2014) "'When torchlight made an artificial noon': Light and Darkness in the Indoor Jacobean Theatre," in Andrew Gurr and Farah Karim-Cooper (eds), *Moving Shakespeare Indoors: Performance and Repertoire in the Jacobean Playhouse*, Cambridge: Cambridge University Press, 115–36.

The Duchess of Malfi (1614)

The Actors' Names[1]

Bosola	J. Lowin
Ferdinand	1. R. Burbage, 2. J. Taylor
Cardinal	1. H. Condell, 2. R. Robinson
Antonio	1. W. Ostler, 2. R. Benfield
Delio	J. Underwood
Forobosco	N. Towley
Malateste	
The Marquis of Pescara	J. Rice
Silvio	T. Pollard
The several mad men	N. Towley, J. Underwood, etc.
The Duchess	R. Sharpe
The Cardinal's Mistress	J. Tomson
The Doctor,	R. Pallant
Cariola	R. Pallant
Court Officers	R. Pallant
Three young Children	
Two Pilgrims	

To the Right Honorable, George Harding,[2] Baron Berkeley of Berkeley Castle and Knight of the Order of the Bath, to the illustrious Prince Charles

My Noble Lord,

That I may present my excuse why, being a stranger to your lordship, I offer this poem to your patronage, I plead this warrant: men who never saw the sea, yet desire to behold that regiment of waters, choose some eminent river to guide them thither, and make that, as it were, their conduct or postilion.[3] By the like ingenious means has your fame arrived at my knowledge, receiving it from some of worth who, both in contemplation and practice, owe to your honor their clearest service.[4] I do not altogether look up at your title, the ancientest nobility being but a relic of time past and the truest honor indeed being for a man to confer honor on himself, which your learning strives to propagate and shall make you arrive at the dignity of a great example. I am confident this work is not unworthy your honor's perusal; for by such poems as this, poets have kissed the hand of great princes and drawn their gentle eyes to look down upon

1 The Actors' Names: This is the first time a list of the names of the actors who performed in a play's original performances was published in a play text. The King's Men, who owned the outdoor Globe and the indoor Blackfriars playhouses, performed the play in both, as the title page tells us. The names with a 1 next to them represent the sharers and players in the first performances of the play in 1613–14. The names with a 2 next to them refer to those who replaced the original players in subsequent performances through to the Caroline period

2 George Harding: the son of Elizabeth Carey, who was the daughter of George Cary, 2nd Baron Hunsdon. Her father and grandfather were both patrons of Shakespeare's company, the Lord Chamberlain's Men, known as the King's Men by the time Webster wrote *Malfi*. Harding was a literary and theatrical patron; other authors, such as Philip Massinger, Robert Burton, and James Shirley also dedicated work to him. This dedication shows Webster's attempt to acquire an important and prolific patron

3 4 conduct or postilion: conductor or driver

4 6 owe to . . . clearest service: are indebted to you for your patronage

their sheets of paper when the poets themselves were bound up in their winding-sheets. The like courtesy from your lordship shall make you live in your grave and laurel[5] spring out of it when the ignorant scorners of the Muses (that, like worms in libraries, seem to live only to destroy learning) shall wither, neglected and forgotten. This work and myself I humbly present to your approved censure.[6] It being the utmost of my wishes to have your honorable self my weighty and perspicuous[7] comment, which grace so done me shall ever be acknowledged.

By your lordship's in all duty and observance,
John Webster

In the just worth of that well deserver, Mr John Webster, and upon this masterpiece of tragedy

In this thou imitat'st one rich and wise,
That sees his good deeds done before he dies;
As he by works, thou by this work of Fame
Hast well provided for thy living name.
To trust to others' honorings is worth's crime;[8]
Thy monument is raised in thy lifetime.
And 'tis most just; for every worthy man
Is his own marble, and his merit can
Cut him to any figure and express
More art than Death's cathedral palaces,
Where royal ashes keep their court.[9] Thy note
Be ever plainness,[10] 'tis the richest coat.
Thy epitaph only the title be:
Write, "Duchess," that will fetch a tear for thee.
For who e'er saw this Duchess live and die,
That could get off under[11] a bleeding eye?

In Tragediam

Ut lux ex tenebris ictu percussa Tomantis,
Illa, ruina malis, claris fit vita poetis.[12]

Thomas Middletonus
Poeta & Chron: Londiniensis[13]

To his friend Mr John Webster Upon his Duchess of Malfi

I never saw thy Duchess till the day
That she was lively bodied in thy play.
Howe'er she answered[14] her low-rated love,
Her brothers' anger did so fatal prove.
Yet my opinion is, she might speak more,
But never in her life so well before.[15]

William Rowley[16]

5 12 laurel: evergreen shrub used in ancient Greece and Rome to crown a victor; a laurel wreath became symbolic of poetic achievement
6 14 approved censure: approval; good judgement
7 15 perspicuous: easily understood; clearly expressed
8 5 It is characteristic of people of great worth and achievement to mistakenly assume others will honor them after their deaths
9 7–11 for every . . . their court: worthy men do not need elaborate funeral monuments cut out of alabaster or marble to memorialize their deeds
10 11–12 Thy note/Be ever plainness: write always in a simple, truthful style
11 16 get off under: come away with less than
12 17–19 *In Tragediam . . . vita poetis*: As light springs from darkness at the Thunderer's stroke, so may she [Tragedy], the ruin of the wicked, be life for illustrious poets. (Latin, translation from Marcus)
13 21 *Poeta & Chron: Londiniensis*: Poet and chronologer of London (Latin)
14 3 answered: answered for
15 5–6 she might . . . well before: the Duchess could never speak so well in past depictions of her story as she does in Webster's play
16 7 William Rowley: Jacobean playwright, most famous for his collaborations with other writers, including *The Changeling* with Thomas Middleton (1622) and *A Cure for a Cuckold* (1624) with John Webster

To the reader of the author and his **Duchess of Malfi**

Crown him a poet, whom nor Rome nor[17] Greece
Transcend in all theirs for a masterpiece;
In which, whiles words and matter change, and men
Act one another, he, from whose clear pen
They all took life, to memory hath lent
A lasting fame, to raise his monument.[18]
JOHN FORD[19]

Dramatis personae[20]

DUCHESS OF MALFI, *ruler of Malfi, sister to Ferdinand and the Cardinal, later wife to Antonio*
ANTONIO, *steward in the Duchess's household, later her husband*
FERDINAND, *Duke of Calabria, twin brother of the Duchess and brother of the Cardinal*
CARDINAL, *brother of the Duchess and Duke Ferdinand*
BOSOLA, *malcontent and spy for Ferdinand, later Master of Horse to the Duchess*
CARIOLA, *lady-in-waiting to the Duchess*
DELIO, *Antonio's friend, a courtier*
MARQUIS OF PESCARA, *nobleman and soldier*
COUNT MALATESTE, *a courtier in Rome*
JULIA, *wife to Castruchio, mistress to the Cardinal*
CASTRUCHIO, *an old man, husband to Julia*
SILVIO, *a courtier in Malfi and Rome*
RODERIGO, *a courtier*
GRISOLAN, *a courtier*
THREE CHILDREN
DOCTOR
OLD LADY

Officers of the Court, Servants, Soldiers, Attendants, Ladies-in-Waiting, Churchmen, Eight Madmen (Astrologer, Lawyer, Priest, Doctor, English Tailor, Gentleman Usher, Farmer and Broker), Three Children, Two Pilgrims, Executioners

Act I, scene i

[*Enter*] ANTONIO [*and*] DELIO

DELIO You are welcome to your country, dear Antonio.
You have been long in France, and you return
A very formal Frenchman in your habit.[21]
How do you like the French court?
ANTONIO I admire it;
In seeking to reduce[22] both state and people
To a fixed order, their judicious king
Begins at home: quits[23] first his royal palace
Of flattering sycophants, of dissolute
And infamous persons, which[24] he sweetly terms

17 1 nor . . . nor: neither . . . nor
18 6 monument: i.e. memorial
19 7 JOHN FORD: Jacobean and Caroline playwright, known for plays such as *The Broken Heart* (c. 1624) and *'Tis Pity She's a Whore* (c. 1629–34)
20 Dramatis personae: not in the 1623 text
21 3 habit: clothing, fashion or style; demeanor
22 5 reduce: restore
23 7 quits: rids
24 9 which: i.e. his royal palace

His master's masterpiece, the work of heaven,
Considering duly that a prince's court
Is like a common fountain, whence should flow
Pure silver drops in general. But if't chance
Some cursed example poison't near the head,
"Death and diseases through the whole land spread."[25]
And what is't makes this blessèd government
But a most provident council, who dare freely
Inform him the corruption of the times?
Though some o'th' court hold it presumption[26]
To instruct princes what they ought to do,
It is a noble duty to inform them
What they ought to foresee.

[*Enter*] BOSOLA

Here comes Bosola,
The only court-gall.[27] Yet I observe his railing
Is not for simple love of piety.
Indeed, he rails at those things which he wants,[28]
Would be as lecherous, covetous or proud,
Bloody, or envious as any man
If he had means to be so.

[*Enter*] CARDINAL

Here's the cardinal.
BOSOLA I do haunt you still.
CARDINAL So.
BOSOLA I have done you
Better service than to be slighted thus.
Miserable age,[29] where only the reward
Of doing well is the doing of it.
CARDINAL You enforce your merit too much.
BOSOLA I fell into the galleys[30] in your service,
Where, for two years together, I wore two towels instead of
A shirt, with a knot on the shoulder after the fashion of a
Roman mantle.[31] Slighted thus? I will thrive some way:
Blackbirds fatten best in hard weather; why not I
In these dog days?[32]
CARDINAL Would you could become honest.
BOSOLA With all your divinity, do but direct me the way to it. I have known many travel far for it and yet return as arrant knaves as they went forth because they carried themselves always along with them.[33] [*Exit* CARDINAL] Are you gone? Some fellows, they say, are

25 15 "Death and … land spread": Webster's play contains many of these moral reflections or aphorisms, known as *sententiae*, which sometimes seem artificial or oddly out of place. Some editors mark these by printing them in italics; this edition uses quotation marks, which follows the practice of the 1623 text
26 19 hold it presumption: think it presumptuous
27 23 court-gall: a person who irritates the court with skepticism and satire. A "gall" is a painful blister or sore; to "gall" is to make sore by rubbing. Here, both senses of the word are appropriate to the description of Bosola
28 25 wants: lacks
29 31 age: times
30 34 fell into the galleys: punishment for murder in which a prisoner is sentenced to be an oarsman on a ship
31 35–7 two towels … Roman mantle: Bosola sarcastically compares the galley slave to a noble Roman in a toga
32 39 dog days: the hottest time of summer
33 40–42 I have … with them: many have traveled far to seek honesty but never found it because they are inherently dishonest themselves

possessed with the devil, but this great fellow were able to possess the greatest devil and make him worse.

ANTONIO He hath denied thee some suit?

BOSOLA He and his brother are like plum trees that grow crooked over standing pools: they are rich and o'erladen with fruit, but none but crows, pies,[34] and caterpillars feed on them. Could I be one of their flattering panders,[35] I would hang on their ears like a horse-leech[36] till I were full and then drop off. I pray, leave me. Who would rely upon these miserable dependencies in expectation to be advanced tomorrow? What creature ever fed worse than hoping Tantalus?[37] Nor ever died any man more fearfully than he that hoped for a pardon. There are rewards for hawks and dogs when they have done us service, but for a soldier that hazards his limbs in a battle, nothing but a kind of geometry is his last supportation.[38]

DELIO Geometry?

BOSOLA Ay, to hang in a fair pair of slings, take his latter swinge[39] in the world upon an honorable pair of crutches, from hospital to hospital. Fare ye well, sir. And yet do not you scorn us, for places in the court are but like beds in the hospital, where this man's head lies at that man's foot, and so lower and lower. [*Exit*]

DELIO I knew this fellow seven years in the galleys
For a notorious murder, and 'twas thought
The cardinal suborned it.[40] He was released
By the French General, Gaston de Foux,[41]
When he recovered[42] Naples.
ANTONIO 'Tis great pity
He should be thus neglected; I have heard
He's very valiant. This foul melancholy
Will poison all his goodness; for I'll tell you,
If too immoderate[43] sleep be truly said
To be an inward rust unto the soul,
It then doth follow want of action
Breeds all black malcontents,[44] and their close rearing,
Like moths in cloth, do hurt for want of wearing.[45]

Act I, scene ii

DELIO The presence[46] 'gins to fill; you promised me
To make me the partaker of the natures
Of some of your great courtiers.
ANTONIO The Lord Cardinal's
And other strangers' that are now in court,
I shall.

34 47 pies: magpies

35 48 panders: a go-between in secret love affairs; a pimp or procurer

36 48 horse-leech: a blood-sucking worm

37 51 Tantalus: king of Lydia who killed his son Pelops and served his body parts as food at a banquet for the gods. He was punished in the underworld with an insatiable thirst and hunger and placed up to the chin in the midst of a pool of water which would recede when he reached to take a drink; above him was a tree with low-hanging fruit, which would rise or be blown away by wind when he reached to pluck one

38 53 supportation: physical support or help

39 55 swinge: movement through, with a pun on "swing"

40 61 suborned it: hired him to do it

41 62 Gaston de Foux: (Foix) noted French military commander 1489–1511, also known as the "thunderbolt of Italy"

42 63 recovered: re-occupied; in 1501 the French King Louis XII renewed an earlier French claim on Naples, occupying it briefly

43 67 too immoderate: excessive

44 70 malcontents: people who are discontented with the status quo and the politics of the age and who voice their dissatisfaction, often satirically. Bosola is a malcontent (see line 23)

45 70–71 their close . . . of wearing: the phrasing is obscure, but the sense of these lines seems to be that the discontented thoughts of the malcontent are dangerous because they are hidden and nurtured by his inactivity—in the same way that a moth thrives in unworn clothes

46 1 presence: presence chamber; a room in a palace where the monarch or ruler receives guests

[*Enter*] FERDINAND

Here comes the great Calabrian duke.

FERDINAND Who took the ring[47] oft'nest?

SILVIO Antonio Bologna, my lord.

FERDINAND Our sister Duchess's great master of her household?
Give him the jewel. [ANTONIO *receives the jewel*]
When shall we leave this sportive action,
And fall to action indeed? [ANTONIO *and* DELIO *stand aside*]

CASTRUCHIO Methinks, my lord
You should not desire to go to war in person.

FERDINAND Now, for some gravity—why, my lord?

CASTRUCHIO It is fitting a soldier arise to be a prince, but not necessary a prince descend to be a captain.

FERDINAND No?

CASTRUCHIO No, my lord. He were far better do it by a deputy.

FERDINAND Why should he not as well sleep or eat by a deputy? This might take idle, offensive and base office from him, whereas the other deprives him of honor.

CASTRUCHIO Believe my experience: that realm is never long in quiet, where the ruler is a soldier.

FERDINAND Thou toldst me thy wife could not endure fighting.

CASTRUCHIO True, my lord.

FERDINAND And of a jest she broke of a captain she met full of wounds; I have forgot it.

CASTRUCHIO She told him, my lord, he was a pitiful fellow to lie like the children of Ishmael, all in tents.[48]

FERDINAND Why, there's a wit were able to undo all the surgeons o'th city, for although gallants should quarrel and had drawn their weapons, and were ready to go to it, yet her persuasions would make them put up.[49]

CASTRUCHIO That she would, my lord. How do you like my Spanish jennet?[50]

RODERIGO He is all fire.

FERDINAND I am of Pliny's[51] opinion: I think he was begot by the wind. He runs as if he were ballasted with quicksilver.[52]

SILVIO True, my lord, he reels from the tilt[53] often.

RODERIGO, GRISOLAN Ha, ha, ha!

FERDINAND Why do you laugh? Methinks you that are courtiers should be my touchwood: take fire when I give fire; that is, laugh when I laugh, were the subject never so witty.

CASTRUCHIO True, my lord, I myself have heard a very good jest, and have scorned to seem to have so silly a wit as to understand it.

FERDINAND But I can laugh at your fool, my lord.

CASTRUCHIO He cannot speak, you know, but he makes faces. My lady cannot abide him.

FERDINAND No?

CASTRUCHIO Nor endure to be in merry company; for she says too much laughing and too much company fills her too full of the wrinkle.[54]

47 6 took the ring: used his lance (while riding on horseback) to carry away a ring suspended in the air; this game was popular at the court of James I

48 23–4 to lie … in tents: "tents" is a pun meaning both "bandages" and the dwellings of soldiers on a battlefield. The Biblical reference is to the bastard son of Abraham, Ishmael who with his children led a nomadic existence and therefore would have lived in tents (*Genesis*, 21: 1–21)

49 27 put up: literally, put down their weapons; there is also a sexual suggestion in "up," i.e. "get an erection"

50 28 Spanish jennet: a special breed of horse popular in the middle ages and early modern period, known for its style and smooth ride

51 30 Pliny: Pliny the Elder, ancient Roman author and natural philosopher. Pliny writes that Portuguese mares can be impregnated by the west wind

52 31 ballasted with quicksilver: ballast is a heavy material used to weigh a ship down and quicksilver refers to mercury, which is associated with quickness. The ballast should slow the horse down, but the quicksilver makes him run faster

53 32 reels from the tilt: a jousting reference, meaning dodging a lance. "Tilt" is a reference to sexual intercourse. It is possible that Silvio separately makes a sexual joke about Antonio, which is why Roderigo and Grisolan laugh and Ferdinand cannot understand what is so funny

54 42 fills her … the wrinkle: a joke about the presumed vanity of women not wanting to move their faces too much (especially by laughing) so as to avoid wrinkles

FERDINAND I would then have a mathematical instrument made for her face, that she might not laugh out of compass.[55] I shall shortly visit you at Milan, Lord Silvio.

SILVIO Your grace shall arrive most welcome. [ANTONIO *comes forward*]

FERDINAND You are a good horseman, Antonio. You have excellent riders in France; what do you think of good horsemanship?

ANTONIO Nobly, my lord. As out of the Grecian horse[56] issued many famous princes, so out of brave horsemanship arise the first sparks of growing resolution that raise the mind to noble action.

FERDINAND You have bespoke it worthily.

[*Enter*] CARDINAL, DUCHESS, CARIOLA, JULIA [*and* Attendants]

SILVIO Your brother, the Lord Cardinal, and sister Duchess.
CARDINAL Are the galleys come about?
GRISOLAN They are, my lord.
FERDINAND Here's the lord Silvio, is come to take his leave.
DELIO [*Aside to* ANTONIO] Now, sir, your promise. What's that cardinal?
I mean his temper?[57] They say he's a brave[58] fellow—
Will play his five thousand crowns at tennis, dance,
Court ladies—and one that hath fought single combats.

ANTONIO Some such flashes superficially hang on him for form. But observe his inward character: he is a melancholy churchman; the spring in his face is nothing but the engendering of toads.[59] Where he is jealous of any man, he lays worse plots for them than ever was imposed on Hercules,[60] for he strews in his way flatterers, panders, intelligencers,[61] atheists, and a thousand such political monsters. He should have been Pope, but instead of coming to it by the primitive decency of the church,[62] he did bestow bribes so largely and so impudently, as if he would have carried it away[63] without heaven's knowledge. Some good he hath done—

DELIO You have given too much of him. What's his brother?
ANTONIO The duke there? A most perverse and turbulent nature.
What appears in him mirth is merely outside:
If he laugh heartily, it is to laugh
All honesty out of fashion.
DELIO Twins?
ANTONIO In quality.
He speaks with others' tongues and hears men's suits
With others' ears; will seem to sleep o'th bench[64]
Only to entrap offenders in their answers;
Dooms men to death by information,[65]
Rewards by hearsay.
DELIO Then the law to him
Is like a foul black cobweb to a spider:
He makes it his dwelling and a prison
To entangle those shall feed him.

55 44 out of compass: excessively

56 48 Grecian horse: the wooden horse built by the Greeks and presented as a gift to the Trojans which enabled the Greeks to enter and sack the city of Troy

57 56 temper: temperament

58 56 brave: gorgeously dressed; flamboyant

59 60–61 his face . . . of toads: the cardinal's face is good for nothing but immoral or dirty purposes

60 62 Hercules: Roman name for the Greek hero Heracles, son of Zeus and Alcmene; known for his superhuman strength and for completing the twelve labors

61 62 intelligencers: spies

62 64 primitive decency of the church: i.e. before the church had been corrupted by Catholic ritual and hierarchy

63 65 carried it away: brought it off with success or gotten away with it

64 72 sleep o'th bench: he pretends to sleep during a trial while serving as a judge

65 74 by information: for things he learns about them from informants

ANTONIO Most true.
He ne'er pays debts unless they be shrewd turns,
And those he will confess that he doth owe,
Last. For his brother there, the cardinal,
They that do flatter him most say oracles
Hang at his lips,[66] and verily, I believe them,
For the devil speaks in them.
But for their sister, the right noble Duchess—
You never fixed your eye on three fair medals[67]
Cast in one figure of so different temper:
For her discourse, it is so full of rapture
You only will begin, then, to be sorry
When she doth end her speech, and wish, in wonder,
She held it less vainglory to talk much
Than your penance to hear her.[68] Whilst she speaks,
She throws upon a man so sweet a look
That it were able raise one to a galliard[69]
That lay in a dead palsy,[70] and to dote
On that sweet countenance;[71] but in that look
There speaketh so divine a continence[72]
As cuts off all lascivious[73] and vain hope.
Her days are practiced in such noble virtue,
That, sure, her nights—nay more, her very sleeps—
Are more in heaven than other ladies' shrifts.[74]
Let all sweet ladies break their flattering glasses,[75]
And dress themselves in her.
DELIO Fie, Antonia![76]
You play the wire-drawer[77] with her commendations.
ANTONIO I'll case the picture up;[78] only thus much,
All her particular worth grows to this sum:
She stains the time past, lights the time to come.

[*Enter*] CARIOLA

CARIOLA You must attend my lady in the gallery[79]
Some half an hour hence.
ANTONIO I shall. [*Exeunt* ANTONIO *and* DELIO]
FERDINAND Sister, I have a suit to you.
DUCHESS To me, sir?

66 82–3 oracles/Hang at his lips: he speaks with oracular authority
67 86 medals: bronze medallions popular amongst the aristocracy in this period. The suggestion is the three siblings look alike
68 88–92 For her . . . hear her: her conversation is so extraordinary that you will be sorry when she stops speaking, and wish that she thought it even less vain to speak than it is a punishment for you to hear her (i.e. the Duchess is needlessly modest in speaking, and makes every listener want to hear more)
69 94 galliard: a vigorous, athletic dance, consisting of leaps and hops
70 95 palsy: paralysis
71 96 countenance: face and/or facial expression; a look
72 97 continence: chastity
73 98 lascivious: immorally lustful
74 101 shrifts: penance as instructed by a priest after confession
75 102 flattering glasses: mirrors backed with crystal that showed a more flattering image than a steel backed mirror
76 103 Antonia: most editors assume "Antonia" to be an error in Q1, but like Leah Marcus, I suggest this feminization of Antonio's name is deliberate as Delio mocks him for getting carried away in his praise of the Duchess. It is obviously a sexist slur that suggests that doting is effeminate
77 104 wire-drawer: one who draws metal into a wire. Delio suggests Antonio spends too much time on the Duchess's character; he "draws out" her description
78 105 case the picture up: stop describing her character vividly
79 108 gallery: a long room in a palace used for accessing other parts of the house; it will be a private place where they won't be detected

FERDINAND A gentleman here, Daniel de Bosola,
One that was in the galleys—
DUCHESS Yes, I know him.
FERDINAND A worthy fellow h'is; pray, let me entreat for
The provisorship of your horse.[80]
DUCHESS Your knowledge of him
Commends him and prefers him.
FERDINAND Call him hither. [*Exit Attendant*]
We now, upon parting, good lord Silvio
Do us commend[81] to all our noble friends
At the leaguer.[82]
SILVIO Sir, I shall.
FERDINAND You are for Milan?
SILVIO I am.
DUCHESS Bring the caroches.[83] We'll bring you down to the haven.
[*Exeunt all but* CARDINAL *and* FERDINAND]
CARDINAL Be sure you entertain that Bosola
For your intelligence.[84] I would not be seen in't,
And therefore many times I have slighted him
When he did court our furtherance, as this morning.
FERDINAND Antonio, the great master of her household,
Had been far fitter.
CARDINAL You are deceived in him,
His nature is too honest for such business,
He comes; I'll leave you. [*Exit*]

[*Enter*] BOSOLA

BOSOLA I was lured to you.
FERDINAND My brother here, the cardinal, could never abide you.
BOSOLA Never since he was in my debt.
FERDINAND Maybe some oblique character[85] in your face
Made him suspect you.
BOSOLA Doth he study physiognomy?[86]
There's no more credit to be given to th' face,
Than to a sick man's urine,[87] which some call
The physician's whore because she cozens him.
He did suspect me wrongfully.
FERDINAND For that,
You must give great men leave to take their times.
Distrust doth cause us seldom be deceived.
You see, the oft shaking of the cedar tree
Fastens it more at root.
BOSOLA Yet, take heed:
For to suspect a friend unworthily
Instructs him the next way to suspect you

80 114 provisorship of your horse: master of the horse; an important role in the royal household
81 117 Do us commend: commend us, i.e. give our regards
82 118 leaguer: military camp
83 120 caroches: luxurious or stately coaches
84 121–2 Be sure . . . your intelligence: employ Bosola as a spy
85 131 oblique character: difficult to read, or crooked, feature
86 132 physiognomy: the study of the face in order to understand someone's character
87 134 sick man's urine: physicians examined the urine to determine what was wrong with a patient; much like physiognomy, it was not a reliable diagnostic method

And prompts him to deceive you.
FERDINAND There's gold. [*Gives him a pouch filled with coins*]
BOSOLA So,
What follows? Never rained such showers as these
Without thunderbolts i'th' tail of them—
Whose throat must I cut?
FERDINAND Your inclination to shed blood rides post
Before[88] my occasion to use you; I give you that
To live i'th court here and observe the Duchess,
To note all the particulars of her 'havior:
What suitors do solicit her for marriage
And whom she best affects. She's a young widow;
I would not have her marry again.
BOSOLA No, sir?
FERDINAND Do not you ask the reason, but be satisfied.
I say I would not.
BOSOLA It seems you would create me
One of your familiars.
FERDINAND Familiar? What's that?
BOSOLA Why, a very quaint[89] invisible devil in flesh:
An intelligencer.
FERDINAND Such a kind of thriving thing
I would wish thee, and ere long, thou mayest arrive
At a higher place by't.
BOSOLA [*Attempts to give the coins back*] Take your devils
Which hell calls angels![90] These cursed gifts would make
You a corrupter, me an impudent traitor,
And, should I take these, they'd take me to hell.
FERDINAND Sir, I'll take nothing from you that I have given.
There is a place that I procured for you
This morning: the provisorship o'th' horse.
Have you heard on't?[91]
BOSOLA No.
FERDINAND 'Tis yours; is't not worth thanks?
BOSOLA I would have you curse yourself now, that your bounty,
Which makes men truly noble, e'er should make
Me a villain. Oh, that to avoid ingratitude
For the good deed you have done me, I must do
All the ill man can invent. Thus, the devil
Candies all sins o'er, [92] and what heaven terms vild,[93]
That names he complemental.[94]
FERDINAND Be yourself:
Keep your old garb of melancholy; 'twill express
You envy[95] those that stand above your reach,
Yet strive not to come near 'em. This will gain
Access to private lodgings where yourself

88 147–8 rides post/Before: gets ahead of
89 157 quaint: curious
90 161 angels: gold coins that had the image of angels stamped on them
91 167 on't: of it
92 173 Candies all sins o'er: makes sin seem sweet
93 173 vild: vile
94 174 complemental: necessary (i.e. something that completes); possibly "complimental," i.e. "complimentary"
95 175–6 express/You envy: suggest that you envy

May, like a politic dormouse[96]—
BOSOLA As I have seen some
Feed in a lord's dish[97] half asleep, not seeming
To listen to any talk, and yet these rogues
Have cut his throat in a dream. What's my place?
The provisorship o'th horse? Say then my corruption
Grew out of horse dung. I am your creature.
FERDINAND Away!
BOSOLA Let good men for good deeds covet good fame,
Since place and riches oft are bribes of shame—
Sometimes the devil doth preach. *Exit* BOSOLA

[*Enter*] CARDINAL [*and*] DUCHESS

CARDINAL We are to part from you, and your own discretion
Must now be your director.
FERDINAND You are a widow.
You know already what man is, and therefore,
Let not youth, high promotion, eloquence—
CARDINAL No, nor anything without the addition honor[98]—
Sway your high blood.
FERDINAND Marry, they are most luxurious
Will wed twice.
CARDINAL Oh, fie!
FERDINAND Their livers[99] are more spotted
Than Laban's sheep.[100]
DUCHESS Diamonds are of most value,
They say, that have passed through most jewelers' hands.
FERDINAND Whores, by that rule, are precious.
DUCHESS Will you hear me?
I'll never marry.
CARDINAL So most widows say,
But commonly that motion[101] lasts no longer
Than the turning of an hourglass; the funeral sermon
And it end both together.
FERDINAND Now hear me:
You live in a rank[102] pasture here i'th court.
There is a kind of honeydew[103] that's deadly:
'Twill poison your fame. Look to't; be not cunning.
For they whose faces do belie their hearts
Are witches ere they arrive at twenty years,
Ay, and give the devil suck.
DUCHESS This is terrible good counsel.
FERDINAND Hypocrisy is woven of a fine small thread,

96 179 politic dormouse: "politic" means prudent shrewd; a "dormouse" is a small rodent, known for hibernating throughout winter and emerging refreshed in the spring. Ferdinand suggests that a spy is like a dormouse, that is, he can remain hidden until he can be of service

97 180 Feed in a lord's dish: eat at a lord's table

98 192 addition honor: i.e. the name of honor, the quality of being honorable

99 194 livers: the liver was proverbially the seat of passion and sexual desire

100 195 Laban's sheep: in the Bible (Genesis 30: 25–43) Jacob agreed to tend the flocks of Laban, separating the spotted ones out for himself; in so doing, he bred more spotted sheep so as to increase his wealth

101 199 motion: resolution

102 202 rank: overgrown; also, rotten. Ferdinand suggests that the Duchess has an excess of men to choose from at court, but that they all lack virtue

103 203 honeydew: nectar

Subtler than Vulcan's engine[104]—yet, believe't,
Your darkest actions, nay, your privat'st thoughts,
Will come to light.
CARDINAL You may flatter yourself,
And take your own choice: privately be married
Under the eaves of night.
FERDINAND Think't the best voyage
That e'er you made, like the irregular crab,
Which though't goes backward, thinks that it goes right
Because it goes its own way. But, observe:
Such weddings may more properly be said
To be executed than celebrated.[105]
CARDINAL The marriage night
Is the entrance into some prison.
FERDINAND And those joys,
Those lustful pleasures, are like heavy sleeps
Which do forerun man's mischief.
CARDINAL Fare you well.
Wisdom begins at the end: remember it. [*Exit*]
DUCHESS I think this speech between you both was studied,[106]
It came so roundly off.
FERDINAND You are my sister.
This was my father's poniard:[107] do you see? [*Shows her his poniard*]
I'll be loath to see't look rusty 'cause 'twas his.
I would have you to give o'er these chargeable revels:[108]
A visor and a mask are whispering rooms
That were ne'er built for goodness. Fare ye well.
And women like that part, which, like the lamprey,
Hath ne'er a bone in't.[109]
DUCHESS Fie, Sir!
FERDINAND Nay,
I mean the tongue, variety of courtship;
What cannot a neat knave with a smooth tale[110]
Make a woman believe? Farewell, lusty widow. [*Exit*]
DUCHESS Shall this move me? If all my royal kindred
Lay in my way unto this marriage,
I'll make them my low footsteps. And even now,
Even in this hate, as men in some great battles
By apprehending danger have achieved
Almost impossible actions—I have heard soldiers say so—
So I, through frights and threatenings, will assay
This dangerous venture. Let old wives report
I winked and chose a husband—

[*Enter*] CARIOLA

Cariola,

104 209 Vulcan's engine: Vulcan was the Roman god of fire and metalwork. His wife, Venus, goddess of love, was caught committing adultery with Mars by a very fine bronze net engineered by Vulcan
105 218 merely performed rather than celebrated (with the double sense of "executed" as "put to death")
106 223 studied: rehearsed
107 225 poniard: dagger
108 227 chargeable revels: expensive performances, lavish parties
109 230–31 the lamprey . . . bone in't: a lamprey is an eel; the Duchess thinks her brother makes a lewd joke about penises
110 233 tale: a pun on "tail," which has sexual connotations

To thy known secrecy I have given up
More than my life: my fame.[111]
CARIOLA Both shall be safe
For I'll conceal this secret from the world
As warily as those that trade in poison
Keep poison from their children.
DUCHESS Thy protestation
Is ingenious[112] and hearty; I believe it.
Is Antonio come?
CARIOLA He attends you.
DUCHESS Good. Dear soul,
Leave me, but place thyself behind the arras[113]
Where thou may'st overhear us. Wish me good speed,
For I am going into a wilderness,
Where I shall find no path nor friendly clew[114]
To be my guide. [CARIOLA *goes behind the arras*]

[*Enter*] ANTONIO

I sent for you; sit down.
Take pen and ink, and write. Are you ready?
ANTONIO Yes.
DUCHESS What did I say?
ANTONIO That I should write somewhat.
DUCHESS Oh, I remember:
After these triumphs[115] and this large expense
It's fit, like thrifty husbands,[116] we enquire
What's laid up for tomorrow.
ANTONIO So please your beauteous excellence.
DUCHESS Beauteous?
Indeed, I thank you. I look young for your sake.
You have ta'en my cares upon you.
ANTONIO I'll fetch your grace
The particulars of your revenue and expense.
DUCHESS Oh, you are an upright treasurer, but you mistook;
For when I said I meant to make enquiry
What's laid up for tomorrow, I did mean
What's laid up yonder for me.
ANTONIO Where?
DUCHESS In heaven.
I am making my will, as 'tis fit princes should
In perfect memory, and I pray, sir, tell me,
Were not one better make it smiling thus
Than in deep groans and terrible ghastly looks,
As if the gifts we parted with procured
That violent destruction?[117]

111 245 fame: reputation
112 249 ingenious: politic, wise
113 251 arras: expensive, richly woven tapestry
114 254 clew: ball of thread; alludes to the Greek myth in which Theseus was able to find his way out of the Labyrinth after killing the minotaur with the help of Ariadne, who gave him thread and told him to unravel it as he entered the maze
115 259 triumphs: festivities (see line 228)
116 260 husbands: stewards; also, perhaps, "husbandmen," i.e. farmers
117 272–5 Were not … violent destruction: isn't it better to make a will while one is healthy and of sound mind, rather than waiting until we are in the throes of death—as if the act of making bequests could actually bring about our destruction?

ANTONIO Oh, much better.
DUCHESS If I had a husband now, this care were quit.
But I intend to make you overseer.
What good deed shall we first remember, say?
ANTONIO Begin with that first good deed began i'th' world,
After man's creation: the sacrament of marriage.
I'd have you first provide for a good husband:
Give him all.
DUCHESS All?
ANTONIO Yes, your excellent self.
DUCHESS In a winding sheet?[118]
ANTONIO In a couple.[119]
DUCHESS Saint Winifred![120] That were a strange will.
ANTONIO 'Twere strange if there were no will in you
To marry again.
DUCHESS What do you think of marriage?
ANTONIO I take't as[121] those that deny purgatory:[122]
It locally contains or heaven or[123] hell,
There's no third place in't.
DUCHESS How do you affect it?
ANTONIO My banishment feeding my melancholy
Would often reason thus—
DUCHESS Pray, let's hear it.
ANTONIO Say a man never marry nor have children,
What takes that from him? Only the bare name
Of being a father or the weak delight
To see the little wanton[124] ride a cock-horse
Upon a painted stick,[125] or hear him chatter
Like a taught[126] starling.
DUCHESS Fie, fie! What's all this?
One of your eyes is bloodshot; use my ring to't,[127] [*Gives him her ring*]
They say 'tis very sovereign;[128] 'twas my wedding ring.
And I did vow never to part with it,
But to my second husband.
ANTONIO You have parted with it now.
DUCHESS Yes, to help your eyesight.
ANTONIO You have made me stark blind.
DUCHESS How?
ANTONIO There is a saucy and ambitious devil
Is dancing in this circle.[129]
DUCHESS Remove him.
ANTONIO How?

118 282 winding sheet: sheet which corpses are wrapped in for burial
119 283 couple: a pair, but also that which unites, or a brace or leash for holding two dogs together
120 283 Saint Winifred: a seventh-century Welsh saint whose suitor decapitated her when she decided to become a nun
121 286 I take't as: I think of it in the same way as
122 286 purgatory: in Catholic doctrine, the place where one's sins were purged by fire before going to heaven
123 287 or . . . or: either . . . or
124 294 wanton: unruly boy
125 294–5 cock-horse . . . painted stick: a child's toy, a stick with a horse's head
126 296 taught: trained
127 297 use my ring to't: the Duchess tells Antonio to take her wedding ring and use it to heal his eye (gold was thought to have healing properties); she is also telling him that she wants to marry him
128 298 sovereign: powerful, effective
129 302–3 There is . . . this circle: Antonio expresses his fears about the clandestine nature of their relationship by imagining he sees a devil conjured up within the circumference of the ring

DUCHESS There needs small conjuration when your finger
May do it: thus—is it fit? [*Places the ring on his finger*]
ANTONIO What said you? *He kneels*
DUCHESS Sir,
This goodly roof of yours is too low built;
I cannot stand upright in't, nor discourse,
Without[130] I raise it higher. Raise yourself,
Or, if you please, my hand to help you— [*Raises him*] so.
ANTONIO Ambition, madam, is a great man's madness,
That is not kept in chains and close-pent[131] rooms,
But in fair, lightsome lodgings, and is girt[132]
With the wild noise of prattling[133] visitants,
Which makes it lunatic beyond all cure.
Conceive not I am so stupid, but I aim
Whereto your favors tend. But he's a fool
That, being a-cold,[134] would thrust his hands i'th' fire
To warm them.
DUCHESS So, now the ground's broke.
You may discover what a wealthy mine
I make you lord of.
ANTONIO Oh, my unworthiness!
DUCHESS You were ill to sell yourself;
This darkening of your worth is not like that
Which tradesmen use i'th' city; their false lights
Are to rid bad wares off. And I must tell you,
If you will know where breathes a complete[135] man—
I speak it without flattery—turn your eyes
And progress through yourself.
ANTONIO Were there nor heaven nor hell,
I should be honest: I have long served virtue,
And never ta'en wages of her.
DUCHESS Now she pays it.
The misery of us that are born great—
We are forced to woo because none dare woo us.
And as a tyrant doubles with his words
And fearfully equivocates,[136] so we
Are forced to express our violent passions
In riddles and in dreams, and leave the path
Of simple virtue, which was never made
To seem the thing it is not. Go, go brag
You have left me heartless, mine is in your bosom;
I hope 'twill multiply love there. You do tremble:
Make not your heart so dead a piece of flesh
To fear more than to love me. Sir, be confident.
What is't distracts you? This is[137] flesh and blood, sir,
'Tis not the figure cut in alabaster

130 308 Without: unless
131 311 close-pent: dark, closed up
132 312 girt: surrounded by
133 313 prattling: gossiping; Antonio suggests ambition cannot be contained
134 317 a-cold: cold
135 325 complete: perfect; perfectly accomplished
136 333 equivocates: speaks with deliberate ambiguity
137 342 This is: I am

Kneels at my husband's tomb.[138] Awake, awake man!
I do here put off all vain ceremony,
And only do appear to you a young widow
That claims you for her husband, and like a widow,
I use but half a blush in't.
ANTONIO Truth speak for me.
I will remain the constant sanctuary[139]
Of your good name.
DUCHESS I thank you, gentle love.
And 'cause you shall not come to me in debt,
Being now my steward, here upon your lips
I sign your *Quietus est:*[140] [*Kisses him*]
This[141] you should have begged now—
I have seen children oft eat sweetmeats[142] thus,
As fearful to devour them too soon.
ANTONIO But for your brothers?
DUCHESS Do not think of them,
All discord without this circumference,[143]
Is only to be pitied and not feared.
Yet, should they know it, time will easily
Scatter the tempest.
ANTONIO These words should be mine,
And all the parts you have spoke, if some part of it
Would not have savored flattery.
DUCHESS Kneel. [CARIOLA *comes forward*]
ANTONIO Ha?
DUCHESS Be not amazed; this woman's of my counsel.
I have heard lawyers say a contract in a chamber,
Per verba presenti,[144] is absolute marriage. [*They kneel*]
Bless, heaven, this sacred Gordian,[145] which let violence
Never untwine.
ANTONIO And may our sweet affections, like the spheres,[146]
Be still[147] in motion—
DUCHESS Quickening, and make
The like soft music[148]—
ANTONIO That we may imitate the loving palms,
Best emblem of a peaceful marriage,
That ne'er bore fruit divided.[149]
DUCHESS What can the church force more?
ANTONIO That Fortune may not know an accident
Either of joy or sorrow, to divide

138 343–4 figure cut ... husband's tomb: funerary effigies were popular in the seventeenth century; the Duchess is protesting that she is alive and full of passion
139 349 constant sanctuary: loyal keeper; place of refuge
140 353 *Quietus est*: release from a debt
141 354 This: i.e. this kiss
142 355 sweetmeats: cakes or candy
143 358 without this circumference: outside of this circle (presumably of the ring she has given him signifying their union)
144 366 *Per verba presenti*: literally, by words in the present; the practice was not condoned, but exchanging marriage vows clandestinely, in the presence of a witness, was still considered a binding contract in Jacobean England
145 367 Gordian: an intricately tied knot; Gordius, king of Gordium in Phrygia tied this knot, which was notoriously difficult to untie
146 368 spheres: celestial bodies
147 369 still: always
148 370 soft music: the music of the spheres; alluding to the Pythagorean theory that, as the heavenly bodies moved, they made a harmonious music that could not be heard by the ear, but only by an enlightened or divinely touched intellect
149 370–73 loving palms ... fruit divided: an emblem of marriage based on Pliny's suggestion that palms only produce fruit in pairs

Our fixed wishes.
DUCHESS How can the church bind faster?
We now are man and wife, and 'tis the church
That must but echo this. [*They rise*] Maid, stand apart,
I now am blind.
ANTONIO What's your conceit in this?
DUCHESS I would have you lead your fortune by the hand[150]
Unto your marriage bed.
You speak in me this, for we now are one.[151]
We'll only lie and talk together, and plot
T'appease my humorous kindred;[152] and, if you please,
Like the old tale in Alexander and Lodowick,[153]
Lay a naked sword between us, keep us chaste.
Oh, let me shroud my blushes in your bosom,
Since 'tis the treasury of all my secrets. [*Exeunt* DUCHESS and ANTONIO]
CARIOLA Whether the spirit of greatness or of woman
Reign most in her, I know not, but it shows
A fearful madness. I owe her much of pity.

Exit

Act II, scene i

[*Enter*] BOSOLA [*and*] CASTRUCHIO

BOSOLA You say you would fain[154] be taken for an eminent courtier?
CASTRUCHIO 'Tis the very main[155] of my ambition.
BOSOLA Let me see—you have a reasonable good face for't already, and your nightcap[156] expresses your ears sufficient largely. I would have you learn to twirl the strings of your band[157] with a good grace; and in a set speech[158] at th' end of every sentence to hum three or four times, or blow your nose till it smart again, to recover your memory. When you come to be a president[159] in criminal causes, if you smile upon a prisoner, hang him, but if you frown upon him and threaten him, let him be sure to 'scape the gallows.[160]
CASTRUCHIO I would be a very merry president—
BOSOLA Do not sup a-nights; 'twill beget you an admirable wit.
CASTRUCHIO Rather it would make me have a good stomach[161] to quarrel, for they say your roaring boys[162] eat meat seldom, and that makes them so valiant. But how shall I know whether the people take me for an eminent fellow?
BOSOLA I will teach a trick to know it: give out you lie a-dying, and if you hear the common people curse you, be sure you are taken for one of the prime nightcaps—

150 380 lead your . . . the hand: alluding to the fact that the goddess Fortune was blind
151 382 You say this (i.e. that I am your fortune) in my voice, because, in marriage, we now speak with one voice
152 384 humorous kindred: her brothers full of ill-humors; alludes to the ancient Galenic theory of the four humors or temperaments: sanguine, phlegmatic, melancholic or choleric; illness was thought to be due to an imbalance in the humors
153 385 Alexander and Lodowick: the story of two friends who looked so alike that no one could tell them apart; Lodowick married the Princess of Hungaria as Alexander and laid each night with a sword between them so as not to wrong his friend
154 1 fain: gladly
155 2 main: aim, goal
156 3 nightcap: a lawyer's white skullcap, which would be tight fitting, perhaps overemphasizing the ears
157 5 band: collar worn by a lawyer with a string attached to it; may also refer to it as an elaborate collar, fashionable in the seventeenth century
158 5 set speech: a speech that has been prepared and memorized for delivery
159 7 president: a presiding judge
160 8 gallows: a device for inflicting death by hanging
161 11 stomach: guts, strength or courage
162 12 roaring boys: rowdy youths

[*Enter*] *an* OLD LADY

You come from painting now?
OLD LADY From what?
BOSOLA Why, from your scurvy face-physic[163]—to behold thee not painted inclines somewhat near a miracle. [*Pointing to her wrinkles*] These in thy face here were deep ruts and foul sloughs[164] the last progress.[165] There was a lady in France that, having had the small pox, flayed the skin off her face[166] to make it more level; and, whereas before she looked like a nutmeg grater, after she resembled an abortive hedgehog.
OLD LADY Do you call this painting?
BOSOLA No, no, but careening of an old morphewed lady to make her disembogue again;[167] there's roughcast phrase to your plastic.[168]
OLD LADY It seems you are well acquainted with my closet.[169]
BOSOLA One would suspect it for a shop of witchcraft, to find in it the fat of serpents, spawn of snakes, Jews' spittle, and their young children's ordures[170]—and all these for the face. I would sooner eat a dead pigeon taken from the soles of the feet of one sick of the plague, than kiss one of you fasting.[171] Here are two of you whose sin of your youth is the very patrimony of the physician, makes him renew his foot-cloth[172] with the spring and change his high-prized courtesan with the fall of the leaf.[173] I do wonder you do not loathe yourselves.
Observe my meditation now:
What thing is in this outward form of man
To be beloved? We account it ominous
If nature do produce a colt or lamb,
A fawn or goat in any limb resembling
A man, and fly from't as a prodigy.[174]
Man stands amazed to see his deformity
In any other creature but himself.
But in our own flesh, though we bear diseases
Which have their true names only ta'en from beasts,
As the most ulcerous wolf and swinish measle;[175]
Though we are eaten up of lice and worms,
And though continually we bear about us
A rotten and dead body, we delight
To hide it in rich tissue.[176] All our fear—
Nay all our terror—is lest our physician

163 16–18 You come … face-physic: Bosola, like a typical stage malcontent, misogynistically mocks the use of makeup by women; "face-physic" refers to the act of putting on makeup ("physic" means medicine or cure)
164 20 sloughs: ditches
165 20 progress: elaborate, ceremonial journey of the monarch throughout the country
166 21 flayed the … her face: an aggressive form of exfoliation, like a modern chemical peel, sometimes effected with harmful ingredients such as turpentine and lemon juice
167 24 careening of … disembogue again: Bosola uses conventional language of anti-cosmetic satire; a popular image of comparison was that of a weatherbeaten ship ("morphewed [i.e. discolored, covered with lesions] lady") that needed to be turned on its side and scraped down ("careened") before going back out to sea ("disembogue")
168 25 there's roughcast phrase to your plastic: i.e. there's the harsh truth beneath the smoothness you insist upon with makeup
169 26 closet: dressing table; private chamber
170 28 ordures: excrement; feces
171 28–30 I would … you fasting: dead pigeons were used to draw infection from the wounds of plague victims; Bosola is expressing his disgust with women's cosmetics, which at the time would have consisted of lots of odd ingredients, including parts of animals, fats, and poisonous minerals
172 31 foot-cloth: a large cloth, richly embroidered or ornamented, that would be draped over the back of a horse so as to protect the rider from mud; a sign of status and wealth
173 30–32 two of you … the leaf: Bosola points out that both Castruchio and the Old Lady have in their youth been sinful through sexual pleasure or vanity, both of which would have made their doctor wealthy and allowed him to spend time with highly paid courtesans
174 38 prodigy: a rare occurrence or thing, taken as an omen
175 42–3 true names … swinish measle: referring to diseases suffered by humans such as "the wolf," which was a flesh-eating virus, and the measles, named after a skin ailment in pigs
176 47 rich tissue: expensive fabrics

Should put us in the ground to be made sweet.
[*To* CASTRUCHIO] Your wife's gone to Rome: you two couple, and get you
To the wells at Lucca[177] to recover your aches. [*Exeunt* CASTRUCHIO *and* OLD LADY]
I have other work on foot. I observe our Duchess
Is sick a-days: she pukes, her stomach seethes;[178]
The fins of her eyelids look most teeming blue;[179]
She wanes i'th' cheek and waxes fat i'th' flank,[180]
And, contrary to our Italian fashion,
Wears a loose-bodied gown;[181] there's somewhat in't![182]
I have a trick may chance discover it—
A pretty one. I have bought some apricocks,[183]
The first our spring yields.

[*Enter*] ANTONIO [*and*] DELIO [*talking apart*]

DELIO And so long since married?
You amaze me!
ANTONIO Let me seal your lips forever,
For did I think that anything but th'air
Could carry these words from you, I should wish
You had no breath at all. [*To* BOSOLA] Now, sir, in your contemplation?[184]
You are studying to become a great, wise fellow?
BOSOLA Oh, sir, the opinion of wisdom is a foul tetter[185] that runs all over a man's body. If simplicity direct us to have no evil, it directs us to a happy being: for the subtlest folly proceeds from the subtlest wisdom.[186] Let me be simply honest.
ANTONIO I do understand your inside.[187]
BOSOLA Do you so?
ANTONIO Because you would not seem to appear to th' world
Puffed up with your preferment,[188] you continue
This out-of-fashion melancholy. Leave it, leave it!
BOSOLA Give me leave to be honest in any phrase, in any compliment whatsoever—shall I confess myself to you? I look no higher than I can reach. They are the gods that must ride on winged horses; a lawyer's mule of a slow pace will both suit my disposition and business. For mark me, when a man's mind rides faster than his horse can gallop, they quickly both tire.
ANTONIO You would look up to heaven, but I think
The devil that rules i'th' air stands in your light.
BOSOLA Oh, sir, you are lord of the ascendant,[189] chief man with the Duchess, a duke was your cousin-german removed;[190] say you were lineally descended from King

177 51 Lucca: a town in Tuscany known in the seventeenth century for its natural hot springs
178 53 seethes: quickens, gets agitated, swollen
179 54 She has dark circles around her eyes
180 55 wanes i'th' ... i'th' flank: using imagery of the moon (wax and wane) to describe the paleness of the Duchess's complexion and the increase in her body weight
181 57 loose-bodied gown: a gown without a corset, worn by pregnant and older women in the seventeenth century
182 57 somewhat in't: something going on here
183 59 apricocks: apricots, thought to cause illness in pregnant women
184 64 in your contemplation: in deep thought, musing, cogitation
185 66 tetter: sore resulting from a skin disease, such as impetigo, ringworm, or even herpes
186 66–8 If simplicity ... subtlest wisdom: being dull of wit can make one happy because one is too simple for evil; so being foolish is a kind of wisdom (taken from French philosopher Michel de Montaigne's essay, "An Apology for Raymond Sebond")
187 69 your inside: what you really mean
188 71 preferment: advancement, promotion
189 79 ascendant: according to astrology, the zodiacal sign that rises on the eastern horizon at a specific time, such as at the birth of a child
190 80 cousin-german removed: first cousin once removed

Pepin,[191] or he himself,[192] what of this? Search the heads of the greatest rivers in the world, you shall find them but bubbles of water. Some would think the souls of princes were brought forth by some more weighty cause than those of meaner persons; they are deceived. There's the same hand to them, the like passions sway them; the same reason that makes a vicar go to law for a tithe-pig[193] and undo his neighbors, makes them spoil a whole province and batter down goodly cities with the cannon.

[*Enter*] DUCHESS [*with Ladies and Attendants*], RODERIGO [*and*] GRISOLAN

DUCHESS Your arm, Antonio; do I not grow fat?
I am exceeding short-winded. Bosola,
I would have you, sir, provide for me a litter,[194]
Such a one as the Duchess of Florence rode in.
BOSOLA The duchess used one when she was great with child.
DUCHESS I think she did. [*To one of her Ladies*] Come hither, mend my ruff,
Here, when? Thou art such a tedious lady, and
Thy breath smells of lemon peels;[195] would thou hadst done!
Shall I swoon[196] under thy fingers? I am
So troubled with the mother![197]
BOSOLA [*Aside*] I fear too much—
DUCHESS I have heard you say that the French courtiers
Wear their hats on 'fore the king.
ANTONIO I have seen it.
DUCHESS In the presence?
ANTONIO Yes.
DUCHESS Why should not we bring up that fashion?
'Tis ceremony more than duty that consists
In the removing of a piece of felt.
Be you the example to the rest o'th' court:
Put on your hat first.
ANTONIO You must pardon me.
I have seen, in colder countries than in France,
Nobles stand bare to th' prince, and the distinction,
Methought, showed reverently.[198]
BOSOLA I have a present for your grace.
DUCHESS For me, sir?
BOSOLA Apricocks, madam.
DUCHESS Oh, sir, where are they?
I have heard of none to year.[199]
BOSOLA [*Aside*] Good, her color rises.
DUCHESS Indeed, I thank you; they are wondrous fair ones.
What an unskillful fellow is our gardener?
We shall have none this month.

191 81 Pepin: eighth-century king of the Germanic peoples known as the Franks
192 81 or he himself: i.e. say that you were even King Pepin himself
193 85 tithe-pig: in early modern England Anglican priests were entitled to one tenth or "tithe" of the incomes of those who lived in their parish; farm animals such as pigs might constitute income
194 89 litter: a bed that would be carried on the shoulders of servants
195 94 lemon peels: lemons were eaten for all sorts of medicinal purposes including to fight diseases and to fortify the brain or heart; lemon peels could stave off bad breath
196 95 swoon: faint
197 96 the mother: hysteria, thought to be a disease of the womb
198 104–7 Put on … showed reverently: the Duchess asks Antonio to wear his hat in her presence, as would befit a social equal; he is cautious and asks to keep his head bare to honor publicly the social distinction between them
199 110 to year: so far this year

BOSOLA Will not your grace pare[200] them?
DUCHESS No, they taste of musk, methinks; indeed they do.
BOSOLA I know not, yet I wish your grace had pared 'em.
DUCHESS Why?
BOSOLA I forgot to tell you the knave gardener,
Only to raise his profit by them the sooner,
Did ripen them in horse dung.
DUCHESS Oh, you jest!
You shall judge; pray, taste one.
ANTONIO Indeed, madam,
I do not love the fruit.
DUCHESS Sir, you are loath
To rob us of our dainties. 'Tis a delicate fruit;
They say they are restorative.[201]
BOSOLA 'Tis a pretty art,
This grafting.[202]
DUCHESS 'Tis so: a bettering of nature.
BOSOLA To make a pippin grow upon a crab,
A damson on a blackthorn.[203] [*Aside*] —How greedily she eats them!
A whirlwind strike off these bawd-farthingales,[204]
For, but for that, and the loose-bodied gown,
I should have discovered apparently
The young springald[205] cutting a caper[206] in her belly—
DUCHESS I thank you, Bosola. They were right good ones.
If they do not make me sick.
ANTONIO How now, madam?
DUCHESS This green fruit and my stomach are not friends;
How they swell me!
BOSOLA [*Aside*] —Nay, you are too much swelled already—.
DUCHESS Oh, I am in an extreme cold sweat!
BOSOLA I am very sorry.
DUCHESS Lights to my chamber! Oh, good Antonio,
I fear I am undone. *Exit* DUCHESS [*Ladies and Attendants, with* BOSOLA, RODERIGO *and* GRISOLAN]
DELIO Lights there, lights!
ANTONIO Oh my most trusty Delio, we are lost!
I fear she's fallen in labor, and there's left
No time for her remove.[207]
DELIO Have you prepared
Those ladies to attend her, and procured
That politic safe conveyance for the midwife
Your Duchess plotted?
ANTONIO I have.
DELIO Make use then of this forced occasion:

200 113 pare: peel
201 122 restorative: medicinal
202 123 grafting: Bosola both refers to the cross-breeding of the fruit, and alludes cryptically to the child he assumes the Duchess is carrying
203 123–5 'Tis so . . . a blackthorn: Bosola and the Duchess engage in a familiar argument about the virtues of art over nature; a pippin is a type of apple and a crab-apple is inedible, so cross-breeding these two would adulterate the pippin; similarly, the damson is a valued type of plum while the blackthorn is a thorny bush that produces small, less palatable plums. Bosola does not yet suspect that Antonio is the Duchess's lover, but his images here suggest that he suspects that she has been impregnated by a social inferior
204 126 farthingales: hooped petticoats worn under the skirts of a gown
205 129 springald: young man
206 129 cutting a caper: dancing friskily
207 139 remove: confinement (typical during and for a time after labor)

Give out that Bosola hath poisoned her
With these apricocks; that will give some color[208]
For keeping her close.
ANTONIO Fie, fie! The physicians
Will then flock to her.
DELIO For that you may pretend
She'll use some prepared antidote of her own,
Lest the physicians should re-poison her.
ANTONIO I am lost in amazement! I know not what to think on't.

Exeunt

Act II, scene ii

[*Enter*] BOSOLA

BOSOLA So, so: there's no question but her tetchiness and most vulturous eating of the apricocks are apparent signs of breeding— ([*Enter*] OLD LADY) Now?
OLD LADY I am in haste, sir.
BOSOLA There was a young waiting-woman had a monstrous desire to see the glass house[209]—
OLD LADY Nay, pray let me go—
BOSOLA And it was only to know what strange instrument it was should swell up a glass to the fashion of a woman's belly.
OLD LADY I will hear no more of the glass house. You are still abusing women!
BOSOLA Who, I? No, only by the way, now and then, mention your frailties. The orange tree bears ripe and green fruit and blossoms altogether, and some of you give entertainment for pure love, but more for precious reward. The lusty spring smells well, but drooping autumn tastes well. If we have the same golden showers that rained in the time of Jupiter[210] the thunderer, you have the same Danaes still, to hold up their laps to receive them.[211] Didst thou never study the mathematics?
OLD LADY What's that, sir?
BOSOLA Why, to know the trick how to make a many lines meet in one center.[212] Go, go! Give your foster-daughters[213] good counsel: tell them that the devil takes delight to hang at a woman's girdle,[214] like a false rusty watch, that she cannot discern how the time passes.

[*Exit* OLD LADY]

[*Enter*] ANTONIO, DELIO, RODERIGO [*and*] GRISOLAN

ANTONIO Shut up the court gates!
RODERIGO Why, sir? What's the danger?
ANTONIO Shut up the posterns[215] presently[216] and call
All the officers o'th' court.
GRISOLAN I shall, instantly. [*Exit*]
ANTONIO Who keeps the key o'th' park gate?

208 145 color: excuse; cover
209 4 glass house: place where glass is manufactured
210 12 Jupiter: Roman name for the king of the gods
211 12–13 If we ... receive them: Danäe was the daughter of Acrisius, king of Argos, who kept her locked in a tower; Jupiter turned himself into shower of gold in order to enter the tower and rape her
212 13–16 Didst thou ... one center: Bosola belittles the Old Lady's ignorance of mathematics in order to make another sexual joke. Mathematics, he suggests, is like a pander that brings lovers together for sex
213 17 foster-daughters: pregnant women; the Old Lady is presumably midwife to the Duchess
214 18 girdle: belt or band worn at the waist
215 20 posterns: back or side doors
216 20 presently: immediately

RODERIGO Forobosco.[217]
ANTONIO Let him bring't presently.

[*Enter* GRISOLAN *and the Servants*][218]

1 SERVANT Oh, Gentlemen o'th' court, the foulest treason!
BOSOLA If that these apricocks should be poisoned now
Without my knowledge!
1 SERVANT There was taken even now a Switzer[219] in the Duchess' bed-chamber.
2 SERVANT A Switzer?
1 SERVANT With a pistol in his great cod-piece![220]
BOSOLA Ha, ha, ha!
1 SERVANT The cod-piece was the case for't.
2 SERVANT There was a cunning traitor. Who would have searched his cod-piece?
1 SERVANT True, if he had kept out of the ladies' chambers; and all the moulds of his buttons[221] were leaden bullets.
2 SERVANT Oh, wicked cannibal! A firelock[222] in's cod-piece?
1 SERVANT 'Twas a French plot,[223] upon my life!
2 SERVANT To see what the devil can do—
ANTONIO All the officers here?
1 SERVANT We are.
ANTONIO Gentlemen,
We have lost much plate,[224] you know, and but this evening,
Jewels, to the value of four thousand ducats,
Are missing in the Duchess' cabinet[225]—
Are the gates shut?
1 SERVANT Yes.
ANTONIO 'Tis the Duchess's pleasure
Each officer be locked into his chamber
'Till the sun-rising, and to send the keys
Of all their chests and of their outward doors,
Into her bedchamber. She is very sick.
RODERIGO At her pleasure.
ANTONIO She entreats you take't not ill. The innocent
Shall be approved[226] by it.
BOSOLA Gentlemen o'th' wood yard,[227] where's your Switzer now?
1 SERVANT By this hand, 'twas credibly reported by one o'th' blackguard.[228] [*Exeunt all but* ANTONIO *and* DELIO]
DELIO How fares it with the Duchess?
ANTONIO She's exposed
Unto the worst of torture, pain and fear.

217 22 Forobosco: a courtier who is named in the list of actors in Q1, but who doesn't have any speaking parts in the play
218 23 SD *Servants*: Grisolan is meant to return with "officers" (line 22) but Q1 has "*Servants*." Some editors emend the speech prefixes to "Officer"
219 27 Switzer: Swiss Guardsman or mercenary, often used by Italian noblemen to settle scores
220 29 cod-piece: an appendage to the front of close-fitting hose or breeches worn by men; they were sometimes exaggerated and ornamented, especially as symbols of wealth and masculinity
221 33–4 moulds of his buttons: the wooden or hard material of a button covered with cloth
222 35 firelock: a gunlock used in muskets or firearms using gunpowder with which sparks are produced to ignite the charge; this is one in a series of sexual jokes
223 36 French plot: a scheme by the French; continues the sexual jokes as syphilis was known as the "French pox"
224 41 plate: precious metalware, such as gold or silver, used for serving in banquets
225 43 cabinet: private bedchamber or closet; a woman's casket where she would keep her precious items
226 51 approved: favored
227 52 Gentlemen o'th' wood yard: people who frequent lowly places; referring to the servants and mocking them for referring to themselves as gentlemen of the court
228 53 blackguard: kitchen servants

DELIO Speak to her all happy comfort.
ANTONIO How I do play the fool with mine own danger!
You are this night, dear friend, to post to Rome;
My life lies in your service.
DELIO Do not doubt me.
ANTONIO Oh, 'tis far from me: and yet fear presents me
Somewhat that looks like danger.
DELIO Believe it,
'Tis but the shadow of your fear; no more.
How superstitiously we mind our evils!
The throwing down salt or crossing of a hare,
Bleeding at nose, the stumbling of a horse,
Or singing of a cricket, are of power
To daunt whole man in us.[229] Sir, fare you well.
I wish you all the joys of a blessed father,
And, for my faith, lay this unto your breast:
Old friends, like old swords, still are trusted best.

[*Enter*] CARIOLA

CARIOLA Sir, you are the happy father of a son.
Your wife commends him to you.
ANTONIO Blessèd comfort!
For heaven's sake, tend her well: I'll presently
Go set a figure for's nativity.[230]

Exeunt

Act II, scene iii

[*Enter*] BOSOLA, [*with a dark lantern*[231]]

BOSOLA Sure I did hear a woman shriek. List,[232] ha?
And the sound came, if I received it right,
From the Duchess' lodgings. There's some stratagem
In the confining all our courtiers
To their several[233] wards: I must have part of it;
My intelligence will freeze else.[234] List again!
It may be 'twas the melancholy bird,
Best friend of silence and of solitariness,
The owl, that screeched so.[235] Ha? [*Enter* ANTONIO] Antonio?
ANTONIO I heard some noise! Who's there? What art thou? Speak!
BOSOLA Antonio? Put not your face nor body
To such a forced expression of fear.
I am Bosola, your friend.
ANTONIO Bosola?
[*Aside*] —This mole does undermine me[236]—Heard you not
A noise even now?

229 64–7 The throwing . . . in us: Delio lists commonplace events that were seen as ominous
230 74 set a figure for's nativity: draw an astrological chart to assess the exact position of the planets at the moment of the child's birth
231 0 SD *dark lantern*: a lantern with a shutter used so the light can be obscured but not blown out
232 1 List: listen
233 5 several: separate
234 6 My intelligence will freeze else: otherwise, my spying can go no further
235 1–9: Sure I . . . screeched so: throughout this speech, a production of the play might choose to deploy sound effects
236 14 undermine me: threaten to bring me down by tunneling beneath me (i.e. by subterfuge)

BOSOLA From whence?
ANTONIO From the Duchess' lodging.
BOSOLA Not I. Did you?
ANTONIO I did, or else I dreamed.
BOSOLA Let's walk towards it.
ANTONIO No! It may be 'twas
But the rising of the wind—
BOSOLA Very likely.
Methinks 'tis very cold, and yet you sweat.
You look wildly.
ANTONIO I have been setting a figure
For the Duchess' jewels.
BOSOLA Ah! And how falls your question?
Do you find it radical?[237]
ANTONIO What's that to you?
'Tis rather to be questioned what design,
When all men were commanded to their lodgings,
Makes you a night-walker.
BOSOLA In sooth[238] I'll tell you:
Now all the court's asleep, I thought the devil
Had least to do here. I came to say my prayers,
And if it do offend you I do so,
You are a fine courtier.
ANTONIO [*Aside*] —This fellow will undo me—
You gave the Duchess apricocks today:
Pray heaven they were not poisoned.
BOSOLA Poisoned? A Spanish fig[239]
For the imputation!
ANTONIO Traitors are ever confident
Till they are discovered. There were jewels stol'n too.
In my conceit, none are to be suspected
More than yourself.
BOSOLA You are a false steward.
ANTONIO Saucy slave! I'll pull thee up by the roots!
BOSOLA Maybe the ruin will crush you to pieces.
You are an impudent snake indeed, sir:
Are you scarce warm and do you show your sting?
ANTONIO You libel well, sir.
BOSOLA No, sir. Copy it out,
And I will set my hand to't.
ANTONIO [*Aside*] —My nose bleeds:
One that were superstitious would count
This ominous when it merely comes by chance.
Two letters that are wrought here for my name
Are drowned in blood![240]
Mere accident.—For you, sir, I'll take order:
I'th' morn you shall be safe.[241] [*Aside*] —'Tis that must color
Her lying in.—Sir, this door you pass not.

237 21–2 how falls … it radical?: using astrological terminology, Bosola asks Antonio how he has attempted to calculate the answer to his question in relation to the position of the stars

238 25 In sooth: in truth; truly

239 31 Spanish fig: a rude gesture that requires making a fist and placing the thumb between the index and middle finger; undoubtedly, the gesture would accompany the phrase here

240 44–5 Two letters … in blood: Antonio wipes his bloody nose on his handkerchief embroidered with his initials

241 46–7 For you … be safe: you shall be safely put away (i.e. imprisoned) for night walking

I do not hold it fit that you come near
The Duchess' lodgings till you have quit[242] yourself.
"The great are like the base; nay, they are the same—
When they seek shameful ways to avoid shame." *Exit*
BOSOLA Antonio hereabout did drop a paper;
Some of your help, false friend![243] Oh, here it is.
What's here? A child's nativity calculated?
[*Reads*] "*The Duchess was delivered of a son 'tween the hours twelve and one in the night, Anno domini 1504*"—that's this year—"*decimo nono Decembris*"[244]—that's this night—"*taken according to the meridian*[245] *of Malfi*"—that's our Duchess! Happy discovery!—"*The lord of the first house being combust in the ascendant*[246] *signifies short life, and Mars, being in a human sign,*[247] *joined to the tail of the Dragon,*[248] *in the eighth house, doth threaten a violent death. Caetera non scrutantur.*"[249]
Why now 'tis most apparent; this precise fellow
Is the Duchess' bawd.[250] I have it to my wish.
This is a parcel of intelligency[251]
Our courtiers were cased up for! It needs must follow
That I must be committed on pretence
Of poisoning her, which I'll endure and laugh at.
If one could find the father now! But that,
Time will discover. Old Castruchio
I'th morning posts to Rome; by him I'll send
A letter that shall make her brothers' galls
O'er-flow their livers.[252] This was a thrifty way.[253]
"Though lust do mask in ne'er so strange disguise,
She's oft found witty, but is never wise."
[*Exit*]

Act II, scene iv

[*Enter*] CARDINAL *and* JULIA

CARDINAL Sit. Thou art my best of wishes. Prithee tell me,
What trick didst thou invent to come to Rome
Without thy husband?
JULIA Why, my lord, I told him
I came to visit an old anchorite[254]
Here, for devotion.
CARDINAL Thou art a witty, false one!—
I mean to him.
JULIA You have prevailed with me
Beyond my strongest thoughts. I would not now

242 50 quit: acquitted; exonerated
243 54 false friend: the dark lantern he is holding; it can conceal things from others but reveal things to Bosola
244 57 *decimo nono Decembris*: the nineteenth of December (Latin)
245 58 *meridian*: refers to the midpoint of the heavens; also used as a name for the devil
246 58–59 *The lord . . . the ascendant*: rising planet that is too close to the sun and gets burned
247 60 *human sign*: the signs of the zodiac that take part or all human form: Gemini, Aquarius, Virgo, and Sagittarius
248 60 *tail of the Dragon*: the place in the heavens where the moon crosses the path of the rising sun
249 61 *Caetera non scrutantur*: the rest remains unexamined (Latin)
250 63 bawd: pimp; Bosola still has not worked out that Antonio is the father of the Duchess's child
251 64 intelligency: new information
252 71–2 brothers' galls . . . their livers: according to humoral theory most yellow bile is stored in the gall bladder. Bosola suggests the intelligence he has discovered will aggravate the brothers so much it will cause an overproduction of yellow bile, making them excessively choleric
253 72 This was a thrifty way: Bosola refers to his luck at finding the dropped horoscope
254 4 anchorite: one who lives in seclusion, usually for the purposes of religious devotion

Find you inconstant.
CARDINAL Do not put thyself
To such a voluntary torture, which proceeds
Out of your own guilt.
JULIA How, my lord?
CARDINAL You fear
My constancy because you have approved
Those giddy and wild turnings[255] in yourself.
JULIA Did you e'er find them?[256]
CARDINAL Sooth, generally for women![257]
A man might strive to make glass malleable
Ere he should make them fixed.[258]
JULIA So, my lord.
CARDINAL We had need go borrow that fantastic glass[259]
Invented by Galileo the Florentine,[260]
To view another spacious world i'th' moon,
And look to find a constant woman there.
JULIA This is very well, my lord!
CARDINAL Why do you weep?
Are tears your justification? The self-same tears
Will fall into your husband's bosom, lady,
With a loud protestation that you love him
Above the world. Come, I'll love you wisely,
That's jealously, since I am very certain
You cannot make me a cuckold.[261]
JULIA I'll go home
To my husband.
CARDINAL You may thank me, lady.
I have taken you off your melancholy perch,
Bore you upon my fist, and showed you game,
And let you fly at it.[262] I prithee, kiss me. [*He kisses her*]
When thou wast with thy husband, thou wast watched
Like a tame elephant.[263] Still you are to thank me:
Thou hadst only kisses from him and high feeding,[264]
But what delight was that? 'Twas just like one
That hath a little fingering on the lute,
Yet cannot tune it.[265] Still you are to thank me.
JULIA You told me of a piteous wound i'th' heart
And a sick liver when you wooed me first,
And spake like one in physic.[266]

255 12 giddy and wild turnings: dizzy and untamed emotions; changing affections; the cardinal says Julia accuses him of inconstancy because she is herself unfaithful to her husband
256 13 Did you e'er find them?: Julia asks whether the cardinal has ever found her to be inconstant to him
257 13 Sooth, generally for women: the cardinal expresses the misogynistic commonplace that all women are changeable in their affections
258 14–15 A man . . . them fixed: it would be easier to make glass bendable than it would be to find a woman who is faithful
259 16 fantastic glass: telescope
260 17 Galileo the Florentine: Galileo Galilei (1564–1642), Italian astronomer and physicist. After learning about a Dutch telescope, he developed one of his own. His discovery that Venus had phases like the moon, which meant that it rotated around the sun, overturned the widespread belief that the Earth was the center of the universe
261 26 cuckold: a man whose wife has been unfaithful to him
262 28–30 I have . . . at it: an image of falconry; falcons wore hoods while they perched on the arm of their trainers; they were then let loose to catch their prey
263 32 tame elephant: no elephant can be entirely tame and so must be watched
264 33 high feeding: luxurious banquets
265 34–6 like one . . . tune it: Julia's husband cannot fulfil her sexual needs and is therefore as unsatisfying and dull as one who knows the fingering (which notes belong to which strings) of a lute but does not have the skill to play a melody
266 39 in physic: receiving medical care

CARDINAL Who's that?
Rest firm; for my affection to thee,
Lightning moves slow to't.[267]

[*Enter*] SERVANT

SERVANT Madam, a gentleman
That's come post from Malfi desires to see you.
CARDINAL [*To* JULIA] Let him enter. I'll withdraw. *Exit*
SERVANT He says
Your husband, old Castruchio, is come to Rome
Most pitifully tired with riding post.

[*Enter*] DELIO

JULIA Signior Delio?—'Tis one of my old suitors. [*Exit* SERVANT]
DELIO I was bold to come and see you.
JULIA Sir, you are welcome.
DELIO Do you lie[268] here?
JULIA Sure, your own experience
Will satisfy you. No, our Roman prelates[269]
Do not keep lodging for ladies.
DELIO Very well.
I have brought you no commendations from your husband,
For I know none by him.
JULIA I hear he's come to Rome?
DELIO I never knew man and beast, of a horse and a knight,
So weary of each other. If he had a good back,
He would have undertook to have borne his horse,
His breech[270] was so pitifully sore.
JULIA Your laughter
Is my pity.
DELIO Lady, I know not whether
You want money, but I have brought you some.
JULIA From my husband?
DELIO No, from mine own allowance.
JULIA I must hear the condition ere I be bound to take it.
DELIO Look on't; 'tis gold. Hath it not a fine color?
JULIA I have a bird more beautiful.
DELIO Try the sound on't.[271]
JULIA A lute-string far exceeds it.
It hath no smell, like cassia[272] or civet;[273]
Nor is it physical, though some fond doctors
Persuade us seeth't[274] in cullisses.[275] I'll tell you,
This is a creature bred by—

267 41 to't: compared to it
268 48 lie: stay, reside; likely with a sexual implication and with the sense "tell a lie"
269 49 prelates: high-ranking clergy or officials of the church, like the cardinal
270 56 breech: backside, buttocks
271 63 Try the sound on't: test it or sound it out to make sure it is genuine
272 64 cassia: less delicate, cheaper form of cinnamon
273 64 civet: perfume made from the secretions found in the anal glands of the African civet cat or musk cat
274 66 seeth't: boil it
275 66 cullisses: broths made from a gamey or strong meat

[*Enter* SERVANT]

SERVANT Your husband's come—
Hath delivered a letter to the Duke of Calabria, that,
To my thinking, hath put him out of his wits. [*Exit*]
JULIA Sir, you hear.
Pray let me know your business and your suit
As briefly as can be.
DELIO With good speed—I would wish you,
At such time as you are non-resident
With your husband, my mistress.
JULIA Sir, I'll go ask my husband if I shall,
And straight return your answer. *Exit*
DELIO Very fine.
Is this her wit or honesty that speaks thus?
I heard one say the duke was highly moved
With a letter sent from Malfi. I do fear
Antonio is betrayed. How fearfully
Shows his ambition now. Unfortunate Fortune!
"They pass through whirlpools and deep woes do shun,
Who the event weigh, ere the action's done."
Exit

Act II, scene v

[*Enter*] CARDINAL *and* FERDINAND, *with a letter*

FERDINAND I have this night digged up a mandrake.[276]
CARDINAL Say you?
FERDINAND And I am grown mad with't.
CARDINAL What's the prodigy?
FERDINAND Read there: a sister damned. She's loose i'th' hilts—[277]
Grown a notorious strumpet!
CARDINAL Speak lower!
FERDINAND Lower?
Rogues do not whisper't now, but seek to publish't,
As servants do the bounty of their lords,
Aloud; and with a covetous searching eye,
To mark who note them. Oh, confusion seize her!
She hath had most cunning bawds to serve her turn,
And more secure conveyances for lust
Than towns of garrison for service.[278]
CARDINAL Is't possible?
Can this be certain?
FERDINAND Rhubarb![279] Oh, for rhubarb
To purge this choler! Here's the cursèd day
To prompt my memory and here't shall stick
Till of her bleeding heart I make a sponge
To wipe it out!

276 1 mandrake: a poisonous plant with potentially narcotic effects; assumed to have magical properties as well as medicinal value
277 3 loose i'th' hilts: unreliable; sexually unfaithful
278 9–11 She hath … for service: Ferdinand imagines his sister has carefully hidden her promiscuity; she has been as strategic in procuring lovers as a fortified town is in supplying itself
279 12 Rhubarb: a plant with medicinal properties, thought to purge choler and other humoral imbalances

CARDINAL Why do you make yourself
So wild a tempest?
FERDINAND Would I could be one,[280]
That I might toss her palace 'bout her ears,
Root up her goodly forests, blast her meads,
And lay her general territory as waste
As she hath done her honors!
CARDINAL Shall our blood,
The royal blood of Aragon and Castile,
Be thus attainted?[281]
FERDINAND Apply desperate physic.[282]
We must not now use balsamum,[283] but fire—
The smarting[284] cupping-glass,[285] for that's the means
To purge infected blood, such blood as hers.
There is a kind of pity in mine eye;
I'll give it to my handkercher.[286] [*Wipes his eyes*]
And now 'tis here.
I'll bequeath this to her bastard.
CARDINAL What to do?
FERDINAND Why, to make soft lint[287] for his mother's wounds
When I have hewed her to pieces.
CARDINAL Cursed creature!
Unequal nature, to place women's hearts
So far upon the left side.[288]
FERDINAND Foolish men,
That e'er will trust their honor in a bark
Made of so slight, weak bulrush[289] as is woman,
Apt every minute to sink it.
CARDINAL Thus ignorance, when it hath purchased honor,
It cannot wield it.
FERDINAND Methinks I see her laughing.
Excellent hyena!—Talk to me somewhat—quickly,
Or my imagination will carry me
To see her in the shameful act of sin.
CARDINAL With whom?
FERDINAND Happily,[290] with some strong-thighed bargeman,
Or, one th' wood yard that can quoit the sledge,[291]
Or toss the bar;[292] or else some lovely squire
That carries coals up to her privy lodgings.
CARDINAL You fly beyond your reason.
FERDINAND Go to, mistress!

280 17 one: i.e. a tempest
281 23 attainted: tainted, stained
282 23 physic: medicine; medical care
283 24 balsamum: an exotic, resinous herb used to soothe skin ailments, but could also be ingested to calm the nerves
284 25 smarting: painful
285 25 cupping-glass: a glass vessel or cup used to purge blood through the use of vacuum pressure
286 28 handkercher: handkerchief; Ferdinand has tears in his eyes
287 30 lint: soft material made from flax; in another of Ferdinand's violent fantasies, he imagines using it as a bandage for the Duchess's wounds after he hacks her to pieces
288 32–3 Unequal nature … left side: a misogynistic suggestion that women's hearts sit farther on the left side than men's (the left being the "sinister" side of the body)
289 35 bulrush: a marsh or waterside plant known for being very fragile
290 43 Happily: perhaps
291 44 quoit the sledge: throw a sledgehammer
292 45 toss the bar: throw an iron bar; this and "quoit the sledge" are rustic sports that require brute strength

'Tis not your whore's milk that shall quench my wildfire,[293]
But your whore's blood!
CARDINAL How idly shows this rage, which carries you,
As men conveyed by witches, through the air
On violent whirlwinds;[294] this intemperate noise
Fitly resembles deaf men's shrill discourse,
Who talk aloud, thinking all other men
To have their imperfection.
FERDINAND Have not you
My palsy?[295]
CARDINAL Yes. I can be angry
Without this rupture.[296] There is not in nature
A thing that makes man so deformed, so beastly
As doth intemperate anger. Chide yourself!
You have divers men, who never yet expressed
Their strong desire of rest, but by unrest,
By vexing of themselves. Come, put yourself
In tune.[297]
FERDINAND So. I will only study to seem
The thing I am not. I could kill her now,
In you or in myself, for I do think
It is some sin in us. Heaven doth revenge
By her!
CARDINAL Are you stark mad?
FERDINAND I would have their bodies
Burnt in a coal-pit with the ventage stopped
That their cursed smoke might not ascend to heaven;
Or dip the sheets they lie in, in pitch[298] or sulphur,
Wrap them in't and then light them like a match;
Or else to boil their bastard to a cullis,
And give't his lecherous father to renew
The sin of his back.[299]
CARDINAL I'll leave you.
FERDINAND Nay, I have done.
I am confident, had I been damned in hell,
And should have heard of this, it would have put me
Into a cold sweat. In, in; I'll go sleep;
Till I know who leaps my sister, I'll not stir.
That known, I'll find scorpions to string my whips,
And fix her in a general[300] eclipse.

Exeunt

Act III, scene i

[*Enter*] ANTONIO *and* DELIO

293 48 wildfire: rage; also, an inflammatory skin rash that burned and spread quickly
294 51–2 As men . . . violent whirlwinds: alludes to the folklore belief that witches would kidnap men and carry them away on their broomsticks; such are Ferdinand's wild thoughts
295 56 palsy: weakness in the body that causes shaking or tremors
296 57 rupture: break from reason and calmness
297 62–3 put yourself/In tune: calm your excessive choler; rebalance yourself
298 70 pitch: a sticky black substance that turns to liquid when it gets hot
299 74 sin of his back: copulation; Ferdinand imagines the Duchess's lover to be worn out from having sex, and then imagines administering him a cure ("renew . . . his back") in the form of a cullis made from the child he and the Duchess have produced
300 80 general: total, i.e. the Duchess's light will be put out forever

ANTONIO Our noble friend, my most belovèd Delio!
Oh, you have been a stranger long at court.
Came you along with the Lord Ferdinand?
DELIO I did, sir, and how fares your noble Duchess?
ANTONIO Right fortunately well. She's an excellent
Feeder of pedigrees:[301] since you last saw her,
She hath had two children more, a son and daughter.
DELIO Methinks 'twas yesterday. Let me but wink
And not behold your face, which to mine eye
Is somewhat leaner, verily I should dream
It were within this half hour.
ANTONIO You have not been in law, friend Delio,
Nor in prison, nor a suitor at the court,
Nor begged the reversion of some great man's place,
Nor troubled with an old wife, which doth make
Your time so insensibly[302] hasten.
DELIO Pray, sir, tell me,
Hath not this news arrived yet to the ear
Of the Lord Cardinal?
ANTONIO I fear it hath.
The Lord Ferdinand, that's newly come to court,
Doth bear himself right dangerously.[303]
DELIO Pray why?
ANTONIO He is so quiet that he seems to sleep
The tempest out, as dormice[304] do in winter.
Those houses that are haunted are most still,
Till the devil be up.
DELIO What say the common people?
ANTONIO The common rabble do directly say
She is a strumpet.
DELIO And your graver heads,
Which would be politic, what censure they?
ANTONIO They do observe I grow to infinite purchase
The left-hand way,[305] and all suppose the Duchess
Would amend it if she could. For, say they,
Great princes, though they grudge their officers
Should have such large and unconfinèd means
To get wealth under them, will not complain
Lest thereby they should make them odious
Unto the people.[306] For other obligation
Of love or marriage between her and me,
They never dream of.

[*Enter*] FERDINAND, DUCHESS[, *and*] BOSOLA [*who stands apart*]

DELIO The Lord Ferdinand
Is going to bed?
FERDINAND I'll instantly to bed,

301 6 pedigrees: lineages, i.e. the Duchess has had more children
302 16 insensibly: unconsciously; imperceptibly
303 20 right dangerously: in a rage; Ferdinand is a danger
304 22 dormice: see I.ii. 179 and note
305 29 The left-hand way: illegally or suspiciously
306 31–5 Great princes … the people: although princes do not like their officers to use their offices for self-enrichment, they don't complain when it happens because they don't want the people to turn against those officers

For I am weary. I am to be—bespeak
A husband for you.
DUCHESS For me, sir? Pray, who is't?
FERDINAND The great Count Malateste.
DUCHESS Fie upon him!
A count? He's a mere stick of sugar candy:[307]
You may look quite through him. When I choose
A husband I will marry for your honor.
FERDINAND You shall do well in't. How is't, worthy Antonio?
DUCHESS But, sir, I am to have private conference with you
About a scandalous report is spread
Touching mine honor.
FERDINAND Let me be ever deaf to't:
One of Pasquil's[308] paper bullets, court calumny,
A pestilent air, which princes' palaces
Are seldom purged of. Yet, say that it were true—
I pour it in your bosom—my fixed love
Would strongly excuse, extenuate, nay, deny
Faults, were they apparent in you. Go, be safe
In your own innocency.
DUCHESS Oh, blessed comfort!
This deadly air is purged. *Exeunt* [*all but* FERDINAND]
FERDINAND Her guilt treads on
Hot burning coulters.[309] [BOSOLA *comes forward*] Now, Bosola,
How thrives our intelligence?
BOSOLA Sir, uncertainly.
'Tis rumored she hath had three bastards, but
By whom, we may go read i'th' stars.
FERDINAND Why some
Hold opinion all things are written there.
BOSOLA Yes, if we could find spectacles to read them.
I do suspect there hath been some sorcery
Used on the Duchess.
FERDINAND Sorcery? To what purpose?
BOSOLA To make her dote on some desertless fellow
She shames to acknowledge.
FERDINAND Can your faith give way
To think there's power in potions or in charms
To make us love whether we will or no?
BOSOLA Most certainly.
FERDINAND Away! These are mere gulleries,[310] horrid things
Invented by some cheating mountebanks[311]
To abuse us. Do you think that herbs or charms
Can force the will? Some trials have been made
In this foolish practice, but the ingredients
Were lenitive[312] poisons, such as are of force
To make the patient mad; and straight the witch
Swears, by equivocation, they are in love.

307 42 a mere … sugar candy: trivial, insubstantial
308 49 Pasquil: Pasquino, a fifteenth-century Roman shoemaker who wrote bitter satires against the elite
309 57 coulters: iron blades fixed on the front of the large pointed blade on a plough
310 70 gulleries: deceptions, trickery
311 71 mountebanks: con artists; charlatans who travel around selling supposed medicines
312 75 lenitive: soothing; laxative

The witchcraft lies in her rank blood. This night
I will force confession from her. You told me
You had got within these two days a false[313] key
Into her bed chamber.
BOSOLA I have.
FERDINAND [*Gives him the key*] As I would wish.
BOSOLA What do you intend to do?
FERDINAND Can you guess?
BOSOLA No—
FERDINAND Do not ask then.
He that can compass me and know my drifts
May say he hath put a girdle 'bout the world[314]
And sounded all her quicksands.
BOSOLA I do not
Think so.
FERDINAND What do you think then, pray?
BOSOLA That you
Are your own chronicle[315] too much, and grossly
Flatter yourself.
FERDINAND Give me thy hand; I thank thee.
I never gave pension but to flatterers
Till I entertained thee.[316] Farewell:
"That friend a great man's ruin strongly checks
Who rails into his belief all his defects."[317]

Exeunt

Act III, scene ii

[*Enter*] DUCHESS, ANTONIO[, *and*] CARIOLA

DUCHESS [*To* CARIOLA] Bring me the casket hither, and the glass.[318]
You get no lodging here tonight, my lord.
ANTONIO Indeed, I must persuade one.
DUCHESS Very good.
I hope in time 'twill grow into a custom
That noblemen shall come with cap and knee[319]
To purchase a night's lodging of their wives.
ANTONIO I must lie here.
DUCHESS Must? You are a Lord of Misrule.[320]
ANTONIO Indeed, my rule is only in the night.
DUCHESS To what use will you put me?
ANTONIO We'll sleep together.
DUCHESS Alas! What pleasure can two lovers find in sleep?
CARIOLA My lord, I lie with her[321] often, and I know
She'll much disquiet you—
ANTONIO See, you are complained of!

313 80 false: duplicate
314 85 put a . . . the world: circumnavigated the world
315 88 chronicle: history
316 90–91 I never . . . entertained thee: before I hired you, the only people I employed were flatterers
317 92–3 "That friend . . . his defects": the friend who best articulates a great man's faults helps keep his defects in check
318 1 The Duchess is sitting at her dressing table in her private chamber; a casket is a box that might contain jewelry or cosmetics
319 5 cap and knee: a doffed cap and bended knee were signs of subservience or supplication
320 7 Lord of Misrule: during Christmas or midsummer revels, a person of low rank chosen to be in charge of the festivities
321 11 lie with her: share a bed with her

CARIOLA —For she's the sprawling'st bedfellow!
ANTONIO I shall like her the better for that.
CARIOLA Sir, shall I ask you a question?
ANTONIO I pray thee, Cariola.
CARIOLA Wherefore still when you lie with my lady,
Do you rise so early?
ANTONIO Laboring men,
Count the clock oftenest, Cariola,
Are glad when their task's ended.
DUCHESS I'll stop your mouth! [*Kisses him*]
ANTONIO Nay, that's but one. Venus[322] had two soft doves
To draw her chariot. I must have another. [*Kisses her*]
When wilt thou marry, Cariola?
CARIOLA Never, my lord.
ANTONIO Oh fie upon this single life! Forgo it.
We read how Daphne,[323] for her peevish flight,
Became a fruitless bay tree; Syrinx[324] turned
To the pale, empty reed; Anaxarete[325]
Was frozen into marble; whereas those
Which married or proved kind unto their friends
Were, by a gracious influence, transshaped
Into the olive, pomegranate, mulberry;
Became flowers, precious stones, or eminent stars.
CARIOLA This is a vain poetry. But I pray you, tell me,
If there were proposed me wisdom, riches, and beauty
In three several young men, which should I choose?
ANTONIO 'Tis a hard question. This was Paris'[326] case
And he was blind in't, and there was great cause;
For how was't possible he could judge right
Having three amorous goddesses in view,
And they stark naked? 'Twas a motion
Were able to benight the apprehension
Of the severest counselor of Europe.
Now I look on both your faces, so well formed,
It puts me in mind of a question I would ask.
CARIOLA What is't?
ANTONIO I do wonder why hard-favored[327] ladies,
For the most part, keep worse-favored waiting women
To attend them and cannot endure fair ones.
DUCHESS Oh, that's soon answered.
Did you ever in your life know an ill painter
Desire to have his dwelling next door to the shop
Of an excellent picture-maker?[328] 'Twould disgrace

322 21 Venus: Roman goddess of Love

323 25 Daphne: daughter of the river god Peneus, pursued by the god Apollo because of her beauty. She begged her father to help her, so he transformed her into a laurel tree

324 26 Syrinx: a nymph in Greek mythology known for her virtue. She was pursued by Pan and she begged the river nymphs to help her; they transformed her into water reeds

325 27 Anaxarete: a Greek virgin who resisted the courtship of Iphis, a shepherd. She mocked him and he committed suicide on her doorstep; unmoved even by this, she was punished when Venus turned her into a statue

326 36 Paris: in Greek mythology, the child of Priam and Hecuba; he was tasked by Zeus to decide whether Hera (Zeus's wife), Athena (goddess of wisdom), or Aphrodite (goddess of Love) was more beautiful. Paris was bribed by Aprhodite to choose her. In return, she promised him the love of Helen of Sparta, who was already married; Paris stole her from her husband Menelaus and started the Trojan war

327 46 hard-favored: unattractive

328 52 picture-maker: portrait artist

His face-making and undo him. I prithee,
When were we so merry? My hair tangles!
ANTONIO [*Aside*] —Pray thee, Cariola, let's steal forth the room,
And let her talk to herself. I have divers times
Served her the like when she hath chafed[329] extremely:
I love to see her angry. Softly, Cariola. *Exeunt*
DUCHESS Doth not the color of my hair 'gin to change?
When I wax grey, I shall have all the court
Powder their hair with arras,[330] to be like me.

[*Enter* FERDINAND *unseen*]

You have cause to love me: I entered you into my heart
Before you would vouchsafe to call for the keys.
We shall one day have my brothers take you napping.
Methinks his presence, being now in court,
Should make you keep your own bed; but you'll say
Love mixed with fear is sweetest. I'll assure you
You shall get no more children till my brothers
Consent to be your gossips. Have you lost your tongue? [*Turns and sees* FERDINAND]
'Tis welcome.
For know, whether I am doomed to live or die,
I can do both like a prince. FERDINAND *gives her a poniard*
FERDINAND Die then, quickly!
Virtue, where art thou hid? What hideous thing
Is it that doth eclipse thee?
DUCHESS Pray, sir, hear me—
FERDINAND Or is it true, thou art but a bare name
And no essential thing?
DUCHESS Sir—
FERDINAND Do not speak!
DUCHESS No sir,
I will plant my soul in mine ears to hear you.
FERDINAND Oh, most imperfect light of human reason,
That mak'st so unhappy to foresee
What we can least prevent. Pursue thy wishes
And glory in them; there's in shame no comfort,
But to be past all bounds and sense of shame.
DUCHESS I pray, sir, hear me. I am married.
FERDINAND So—
DUCHESS Happily[331] not to your liking, but for that,
Alas, your shears do come untimely now
To clip the bird's wings that's already flown.
Will you see my husband?
FERDINAND Yes, if I could change
Eyes with a basilisk![332]
DUCHESS Sure you came hither
By his confederacy?
FERDINAND The howling of a wolf
Is music to the screech-owl; prithee, peace!

329 57 chafed: raged with anger
330 61 arras: orris powder, made from the root of iris; used to color as well as perfume the hair
331 85 Happily: perhaps
332 89 basilisk: mythical reptile (also called a cockatrice) whose look was said to be fatal

Whate'er thou art that hast enjoyed my sister,—
For I am sure thou hear'st me—for thine own sake,
Let me not know thee. I came hither prepared
To work thy discovery; yet, am now persuaded
It would beget such violent effects
As would damn us both. I would not for ten millions
I had beheld thee; therefore, use all means
I never may have knowledge of thy name.
Enjoy thy lust still and a wretched life
On that condition. And for thee, vile woman,
If thou do wish thy lecher may grow old
In thy embracements, I would have thee build
Such a room for him, as our anchorites
To holier use inhabit. Let not the sun
Shine on him till he's dead. Let dogs and monkeys
Only converse with him, and such dumb[333] things
To whom nature denies use to sound his name;
Do not keep a paraquito[334] lest she learn it.
If thou do love him, cut out thine own tongue
Lest it bewray[335] him.
DUCHESS Why might not I marry?
I have not gone about, in this, to create
Any new world or custom.
FERDINAND Thou art undone.
And thou hast ta'en that massy[336] sheet of lead
That hid thy husband's bones, and folded it
About my heart.
DUCHESS Mine bleeds for't.
FERDINAND Thine? Thy heart?
What should I name't, unless a hollow bullet
Filled with unquenchable wildfire?
DUCHESS You are, in this,
Too strict, and were you not my princely brother,
I would say too willful. My reputation
Is safe.
FERDINAND Dost thou know what reputation is?
I'll tell thee, to small purpose, since th'instruction
Comes now too late.
Upon a time, Reputation, Love, and Death
Would travel o'er the world, and it was concluded
That they should part and take three several ways.
Death told them they should find him in great battles,
Or cities plagued with plagues. Love gives them counsel
To enquire for him 'mongst unambitious shepherds,
Where dowries were not talked of, and sometimes
'Mongst quiet kindred that had nothing left
By their dead parents. "Stay," quoth Reputation,
"Do not forsake me, for it is my nature
If once I part from any man I meet
I am never found again." And so, for you:

333 107 dumb: mute
334 109 paraquito: parrot or parakeet; talking bird
335 111 bewray: betray
336 114 massy: solid; heavy

You have shook hands with Reputation
And made him invisible. So fare you well.
I will never see you more.
DUCHESS Why should only I,
Of all the other princes of the world,
Be cased up like a holy relic? I have youth,
And a little beauty.
FERDINAND So you have[337] some virgins
That are witches—I will never see thee more. *Exit*

Enter ANTONIO *with a pistol* [*and* CARIOLA]

DUCHESS You saw this apparition?[338]
ANTONIO Yes. We are
Betrayed! How came he hither? [*To* CARIOLA] I should turn
This to thee[339] for that?
CARIOLA Pray, sir, do! And when
That you have cleft my heart, you shall read there
Mine innocence.
DUCHESS That gallery gave him entrance.
ANTONIO I would this terrible thing would come again,
That, standing on my guard, I might relate
My warrantable love. *She shows the poniard*
Ha! What means this?
DUCHESS He left this with me—
ANTONIO And, it seems, did wish
You would use it on yourself?
DUCHESS His action seemed
T'intend so much.
ANTONIO This hath a handle to't
As well as a point; turn it towards him
And so fasten the keen edge in his rank gall![340] [*Knocking within*]
How now? Who knocks? More earthquakes?
DUCHESS I stand,
As if a mine beneath my feet were ready
To be blown up.
CARIOLA 'Tis Bosola.
DUCHESS Away!
Oh misery! Methinks unjust actions
Should wear these masks and curtains, and not we.
You must instantly part hence. I have fashioned it[341] already. *Exit* ANTONIO

[*Enter*] BOSOLA

BOSOLA The duke your brother, is ta'en up in a whirlwind,
Hath took horse and's rid post to Rome.
DUCHESS So late?
BOSOLA He told me, as he mounted into the saddle,
You were undone.

337 141 So you have: the same can be said of
338 143 apparition: vision, specter
339 144–5 turn/This to thee: i.e. point the pistol at you
340 155 gall: bile (secretion from the liver), bitterness
341 161 fashioned it: come up with an explanation for your departure.

DUCHESS Indeed, I am very near it.
BOSOLA What's the matter?
DUCHESS Antonio, the master of our household
Hath dealt so falsely with me in's accounts.
My brother stood engaged with me for money
Ta'en up of certain Neapolitan Jews,
And Antonio lets the bonds be forfeit.[342]
BOSOLA [*Aside*] Strange. This is cunning.—
DUCHESS And hereupon
My brother's bills at Naples are protested
Against. Call up our officers!
BOSOLA I shall. *Exit*

[*Enter*] ANTONIO

DUCHESS The place that you must fly to is Ancona.[343]
Hire a house there. I'll send after you
My treasure and my jewels. Our weak safety
Runs upon enginous wheels: short syllables
Must stand for periods. I must now accuse you
Of such a feignèd crime as Tasso calls
Magnanima mensogna:[344] a noble lie,
'Cause it must shield our honors. Hark! They are coming.

[*Enter*] BOSOLA [*and*] OFFICERS

ANTONIO Will your grace hear me?
DUCHESS I have got well by you; you have yielded me
A million of loss. I am like to inherit
The people's curses for your stewardship.
You had the trick in audit-time[345] to be sick,
Till I had signed your *quietus*,[346] and that cured you
Without help of a doctor. [*To* OFFICERS] Gentlemen,
I would have this man be an example to you all:
So shall you hold my favor. I pray, let him,
For h'as done that, alas, you would not think of,
And, because I intend to be rid of him,
I mean not to publish.[347] Use your fortune elsewhere.
ANTONIO I am strongly armed to brook[348] my overthrow,
As commonly men bear with a hard year:
I will not blame the cause on't, but do think
The necessity of my malevolent star
Procures this, not her humor. Oh, the inconstant
And rotten ground of service![349] You may see—
'Tis e'en like him, that in a winter night

342 168–70: My brother acted as surety for me for some money I borrowed from the Jews of Naples, and Antonio failed to pay them back
343 174 Ancona: an independent state out of the Duchess's brothers' jurisdiction
344 180 *Magnanima mensogna*: Italian poet Torquato Tasso's epic *Gerusalemme liberata*, translated into English in 1600 by Edward Fairfax, is alluded to here in its famous use of a "noble lie": the character Sophronia lies in order to save other Christians
345 186 audit-time: formal time to go through household accounts; Antonio is being accused of feigning illness so that the Duchess's accounts could not be examined thoroughly
346 187 *quietus*: release from a debt
347 193 publish: make his crimes publicly known
348 194 brook: endure
349 199 service: i.e. service to a prince

Takes a long slumber o'er a dying fire,
As loath to part from't, yet parts thence as cold
As when he first sat down.
DUCHESS We do confiscate,
Towards the satisfying of your accounts,
All that you have.
ANTONIO I am all yours, and 'tis very fit
All mine should be so.
DUCHESS So, sir; you have your pass.
ANTONIO You may see, gentlemen, what 'tis to serve
A prince with body and soul. *Exit*
BOSOLA Here's an example for extortion: what moisture is drawn out of the sea when foul weather comes, pours down and runs into the sea again.
DUCHESS I would know what are your opinions
Of this Antonio.
2 OFFICER He could not abide to see a pig's head gaping.[350]
I thought your grace would find him a Jew.
3 OFFICER I would you had been his officer for your own sake.
4 OFFICER You would have had more money.
1 OFFICER He stopped his ears with black wool and, to those came to him for money, said he was thick of hearing.
2 OFFICER Some said he was an hermaphrodite,[351] for he could not abide a woman.
4 OFFICER How scurvy proud he would look when the treasure was full. Well, let him go.
1 OFFICER Yes, and the chippings of the buttery[352] fly after him to scour[353] his gold chain.
DUCHESS Leave us. *Exeunt [OFFICERS]*
What do you think of these?
BOSOLA That these are rogues that in's prosperity
But to have waited on his fortune could have wished
His dirty stirrup riveted through their noses
And followed after's mule, like a bear in a ring;[354]
Would have prostituted their daughters to his lust;
Made their first-born intelligencers; thought none happy
But such as were born under his blessed planet,
And wore his livery:[355] and do these lice[356] drop off now?
Well, never look to have the like again.
He hath left a sort[357] of flattering rogues behind him;
Their doom must follow; princes pay flatterers
In their own money; flatterers dissemble their vices
And they dissemble their lies. That's justice—
Alas, poor gentlemen!
DUCHESS Poor? He hath amply filled his coffers.[358]
BOSOLA Sure, he was too honest: Pluto, the god of riches,
When he's sent by Jupiter to any man,
He goes limping, to signify that wealth
That comes on God's name comes slowly: but when he's sent

350 213 pig's head gaping: anti-Semitic comment about the fact that the Jews don't eat pork
351 219 hermaphrodite: person with characteristics of both sexes
352 222 chippings of the buttery: bread crusts that have been thrown away; a "buttery" is a pantry or storeroom for household provisions
353 222 scour: polish
354 227 bear in a ring: a bear that is captive and led by a ring pierced through his nose
355 231 livery: uniform indicating employment in a particular household
356 231 lice: commonplace term for flatterers, sycophants
357 233 sort: gang, pack
358 238 coffers: chests or boxes for holding money or valuables

On the devil's errand, he rides post and comes in by scuttles.[359]
Let me show you what a most unvalued[360] jewel
You have in a wanton[361] humor thrown away
To bless the man shall find him.[362] He was an excellent
Courtier, and most faithful, a soldier that thought it
As beastly to know his own value too little,
As devilish to acknowledge it too much:
Both his virtue and form deserved a far better fortune.
His discourse rather delighted to judge itself than show itself.
His breast was filled with all perfection,
And yet it seemed a private whispering room,
It made so little noise of't.
DUCHESS But he was basely descended.
BOSOLA Will you make yourself a mercenary herald,[363]
Rather to examine men's pedigrees than virtues?
You shall want him.
For know, an honest statesman to a prince,
Is like a cedar planted by a spring:
The spring bathes the tree's root; the grateful tree
Rewards it with his shadow: you have not done so.
I would sooner swim to the Bermoothes[364] on two politicians'
Rotten bladders tied together with an intelligencer's[365] heart-string
Than depend on so changeable a prince's favor.
Fare thee well, Antonio; since the malice of the world
Would needs down with thee, it cannot be said yet
That any ill happened unto thee,
Considering thy fall was accompanied with virtue.
DUCHESS Oh, you render me excellent music!
BOSOLA Say you?
DUCHESS This good one that you speak of is my husband.
BOSOLA Do I not dream? Can this ambitious age
Have so much goodness in't as to prefer
A man merely for worth without these shadows
Of wealth and painted honors?[366] Possible?
DUCHESS I have had three children by him.
BOSOLA Fortunate lady!
For you have made your private nuptial bed
The humble and fair seminary[367] of peace.
No question but many an unbenificed scholar
Shall pray for you, for this deed and rejoice
That some preferment in the world can yet
Arise from merit. The virgins of your land
That have no dowries, shall hope your example
Will raise them to rich husbands. Should you want
Soldiers, 'twould make the very Turks and Moors

359 243 scuttles: large baskets
360 244 unvalued: priceless
361 245 wanton: careless
362 246 To bless … find him: to the advantage of the man who hires him next
363 255 herald: an officer of the court who conferred titles upon people based on their lineage; heralds were criticized for being susceptible to bribery and for the corrupt sale of pedigrees
364 262 Bermoothes: Bermudas
365 263 intelligencer's: spy's
366 274 painted honors: false status symbols
367 277 seminary: seed plot or nursery; also a pun alluding to male reproductive organs

Turn Christians and serve you for this act.
Last, the neglected poets of your time,
In honor of this trophy of a man,
Raised by that curious engine,[368] your white hand,
Shall thank you in your grave for't, and make that
More reverend than all the cabinets[369]
Of living princes. For Antonio,
His fame shall likewise flow from many a pen,
When heralds shall want coats[370] to sell to men.
DUCHESS As I taste comfort in this friendly speech,
So would I find concealment.
BOSOLA Oh, the secret of my prince,
Which I shall wear on th'inside of my heart.
DUCHESS You shall take charge of all my coin and jewels
And follow him, for he retires himself
To Ancona.
BOSOLA So.
DUCHESS Whither, within few days,
I mean to follow thee.
BOSOLA Let me think:
I would wish your grace to feign a pilgrimage
To our Lady of Loreto,[371] scarce seven leagues
From fair Ancona; so may you depart
Your country with more honor and your flight
Will seem a princely progress, retaining
Your usual train[372] about you.
DUCHESS Sir, your direction
Shall lead me by the hand.
CARIOLA In my opinion,
She were better progress to the baths
At Lucca, or go visit the Spa
In Germany;[373] for, if you will believe me,
I do not like this jesting with religion,
This feignèd pilgrimage.
DUCHESS Thou art a superstitious fool!
Prepare us instantly for our departure.
Past sorrows, let us moderately lament them,
For those to come, seek wisely to prevent them. *Exit* DUCHESS [*and* CARIOLA]
BOSOLA A politician is the devil's quilted anvil:[374]
He fashions all sins on him, and the blows
Are never heard. He may work in a lady's chamber,
As here for proof. What rests, but I reveal
All to my lord? Oh, this base quality
Of intelligencer! Why every quality i'th'world
Prefers but[375] gain or commendation.

368 288 curious engine: ingenious instrument
369 290 cabinets: curiosity cabinets or cabinets of wonder containing exotic and strange objects
370 293 coats: coats of arms
371 303 Lady of Loreto: a famous shrine and site of pilgrimage near Ancona in Italy, believed to contain the house of the Virgin Mary (the faithful believe that the house was transported by angels from Jerusalem to Italy in the thirteenth century)
372 307 train: retinue, entourage
373 310–11 Spa/In Germany: a natural spa also known for its healing; actually located in Belgium
374 317 quilted anvil: used to quietly pound an object into shape
375 323 Prefers but: seeks nothing but

Now for this act I am certain to be raised,
"And men that paint weeds to the life are praised."[376]

Exit

Act III, scene iii

[*Enter*] CARDINAL, FERDINAND, MALATESTE, PESCARA, SILVIO [*and*] DELIO

CARDINAL Must we turn soldier then?
MALATESTE The emperor,
Hearing your worth that way, ere you attained
This reverend garment, joins you in commission
With the right fortunate soldier, the Marquis of Pescara
And the famous Lannoy.
CARDINAL He that had the honor
Of taking the French king prisoner?[377]
MALATESTE The same.
Here's a plot drawn for a new fortification at Naples. [MALATESTE *and* CARDINAL *speak aside*]
FERDINAND This great Count Malateste, I perceive,
Hath got employment?
DELIO No employment, my lord.
A marginal note in the muster book[378] that he is
A voluntary lord.[379]
FERDINAND He's no soldier?
DELIO He has worn gunpowder in's hollow tooth
For the toothache.[380]
SILVIO He comes to the leaguer with a full intent
To eat fresh beef and garlic, means to stay
Till the scent be gone and straight return to court.
DELIO He hath read all the late service,
As the city chronicle relates it,
And keeps two pewterers[381] going, only to express
Battles in model.
SILVIO Then he'll fight by the book.
DELIO By the almanac,[382] I think, to choose good days
And shun the critical. That's his mistress' scarf.
SILVIO Yes, he protests he would do much for that taffeta.[383]
DELIO I think he would run away from a battle
To save it from taking prisoner.
SILVIO He is horribly afraid
Gunpowder will spoil the perfume on't.
DELIO I saw a Dutchman break his pate[384] once

376 325 Men are praised for putting their talents to use, even if it is to a base end

377 5–6 the famous … king prisoner: Charles de Lannoy (1487–1527) was a soldier to the Hapsburg emperors and member of the council of Charles of Burgundy; he was famous for defeating the French army and taking King Francoise I prisoner at the battle of Pavia in 1525

378 10 muster book: record of troops in service

379 11 voluntary lord: he is not a real soldier and has no military record

380 12–13 He has … the toothache: a remedy for toothache was to place a little gunpowder in a linen cloth. Delio suggests that Malateste's closest brush with battle was applying this remedy to a sore tooth

381 19 pewterers: tradespeople who make pewter; referring here to the toy soldiers for Malateste's miniature model army

382 21 almanac: book forecasting the weather and providing astrological advice

383 23 taffeta: a fine, lustrous silk

384 27 pate: head

For calling him potgun;[385] he made his head
Have a bore in't like a musket.
SILVIO I would he had made a touch-hole[386] to't.
He is indeed a guarded sumpter cloth
Only for the remove of the court.[387]

[*Enter*] BOSOLA, [*stands apart to speak with the* CARDINAL *and* MALATESTE]

PESCARA Bosola arrived? What should be the business?
Some falling out amongst the cardinals?
These factions amongst great men, they are like foxes:
When their heads are divided,
They carry fire in their tails and all the country
About them goes to wrack[388] for't.
SILVIO What's that Bosola?
DELIO I knew him in Padua—a fantastical[389] scholar, like such who study to know how many knots was in Hercules' club, of what color Achilles'[390] beard was, or whether Hector[391] were not troubled with the toothache. He hath studied himself half blear-eyed to know the true symmetry of Caesar's nose by a shoeing-horn, and this he did to gain the name of a speculative[392] man.
PESCARA Mark Prince Ferdinand—
A very salamander[393] lives in's eye,
To mock the eager violence of fire.
SILVIO That cardinal hath made more bad faces with his oppression than ever Michelangelo[394] made good ones: he lifts up's nose, like a foul porpoise before a storm.[395]
PESCARA The lord Ferdinand laughs—
DELIO Like a deadly cannon
That lightens ere it smokes.
PESCARA These are your true pangs of death:
The pangs of life that struggle with great statesmen.
DELIO In such a deformèd silence, witches whisper their charms.
CARDINAL [*To* FERDINAND] Doth she make religion her riding hood[396]
To keep her from the sun and tempest?
FERDINAND That!
That damns her! Methinks her fault and beauty
Blended together show like leprosy:
The whiter, the fouler. I make it a question
Whether her beggarly brats were ever christened.
CARDINAL I will instantly solicit the state of Ancona
To have them banished.
FERDINAND You are for Loreto?
I shall not be at your ceremony: fare you well. [*Exit* CARDINAL]
Write to the Duke of Malfi, my young nephew

385 28 potgun: cannon or mortar shell; a satirical jab at the Dutch, proverbially heavy drinkers, for loving their "pots" of ale
386 30 touch-hole: in a musket or firearm the hole where powder is inserted
387 31–2 a guarded . . . the court: a "sumpter cloth" is a saddle cloth; they mock Malateste by suggesting he's only good for moving with the court from one place to the next, not for military service
388 38 wrack: ruin
389 39 fantastical: full of fancy or imagination; strange or bizarre
390 40 Achilles: Greek general in the Trojan war
391 41 Hector: son of King Priam of Troy and Queen Hecuba; killed by Achilles in the Trojan war
392 43 speculative: full of thought and insight
393 45 salamander: mythical lizard said to live in fire
394 47 Michelangelo: Italian Renaissance artist who painted the Sistine Chapel in the Vatican in Rome
395 48 porpoise before a storm: it was believed that seeing a porpoise playing on the surface of the water was an omen of storms to come
396 54 Does she use religion as a cover

She had by her first husband, and acquaint him
With's mother's honesty.
BOSOLA I will.
FERDINAND Antonio?
A slave that only smelled of ink and counters[397]
And never in's life looked like a gentleman,
But in the audit time! Go, go presently,
Draw me out an hundred and fifty of our horse,
And meet me at the fort bridge.
Exeunt

Act III, scene iv

[*Enter*] TWO PILGRIMS *to the shrine of Our Lady of Loreto*

1 PILGRIM I have not seen a goodlier shrine than this,
Yet I have visited many.
2 PILGRIM The Cardinal of Aragon
Is this day to resign his cardinal's hat.
His sister Duchess likewise is arrived
To pay her vow of pilgrimage; I expect
A noble ceremony.
1 PILGRIM No question.—They come!

Here the ceremony of the CARDINAL's *installment in the habit of a soldier, performed in delivering up his cross, hat, robes, and ring at the shrine, and investing him with sword, helmet, shield, and spurs. Then* ANTONIO, *the* DUCHESS, *and their children, having presented themselves at the shrine, are, (by a form of banishment in dumb show, expressed towards them by the* CARDINAL *and the State of Ancona) banished. During all which ceremony, this ditty is sung to very solemn music by divers churchmen and then exeunt*

Arms and honors deck thy story,
To thy Fame's eternal glory.
Adverse fortune ever fly thee,
No disastrous fate come nigh thee.

The author disclaims this ditty to be his.[398]

I alone will sing thy praises,
Whom to honor, virtue raises,
And thy study, that divine is,
Bent to martial discipline is.
Lay aside all those robes lie by thee;
Crown thy arts with arms: they'll beautify thee.

O worthy of worthiest name, adorned in this manner,
Lead bravely thy forces on under war's warlike banner.
O may'st thou prove fortunate in all martial courses;
Guide thou still, by skill in arts and forces:

Victory attend thee nigh whilst fame sings loud thy powers;
Triumphant conquest crown thy head, and blessings pour down showers.

397 66 counters: tokens used for counting; with "ink" (used for keeping the accounts), the word emphasizes Antonio's social inferiority

398 9–10 The author . . . be his: the Quarto of 1623 exists in two states, suggesting a correction was made before a second printing. In the first state the song sung is referred to as "The Hymne" and there is no marginal note; in the second state (the one represented here) the verses are not entitled "The Hymne" and the marginal note instead refers to the song as a "ditty," a song much less solemn than a hymn. Most editors agree that Webster visited the printer and insisted on the correction to disclaim (i.e. deny) his authorship of the song

1 PILGRIM Here's a strange turn of state! Who would have thought
So great a lady would have matched herself
Unto so mean[399] a person? Yet the cardinal
Bears himself much too cruel.
2 PILGRIM They are banished.
1 PILGRIM But I would ask what power hath this state
Of Ancona to determine of a free prince?[400]
2 PILGRIM They are a free state, sir, and her brother showed
How that the Pope, forehearing of her looseness,
Hath seized into the protection of the church
The dukedom, which she held as dowager.[401]
1 PILGRIM But by what justice?
2 PILGRIM Sure, I think by none,
Only her brother's instigation.
1 PILGRIM What was it with such violence he took
Off from her finger?
2 PILGRIM 'Twas her wedding ring,
Which he vowed shortly he would sacrifice
To his revenge.[402]
1 PILGRIM Alas, Antonio!
If that a man be thrust into a well,
No matter who sets hand to't, his own weight
Will bring him sooner to th'bottom.[403] Come, let's hence.
Fortune makes this conclusion general:
"All things do help th'unhappy man to fall."

Exeunt

Act III, scene v

[*Enter*] DUCHESS, ANTONIO, CARIOLA, *Children*, [*and*] *Servants*

DUCHESS Banished Ancona?
ANTONIO Yes, you see what power
Lightens in great men's breath.
DUCHESS Is all our train
Shrunk to this poor remainder?
ANTONIO These poor men,
Which have got little in your service, vow
To take your fortune. But your wiser buntings,[404]
Now they are fledged, are gone.
DUCHESS They have done wisely.
This puts me in mind of death. Physicians thus,
With their hands full of money, use to give o'er[405]
Their patients.
ANTONIO Right the fashion of the world!
From decayed fortunes every flatterer shrinks;
Men cease to build where the foundation sinks.
DUCHESS I had a very strange dream tonight.

399 25 mean: of low social status
400 28 determine of a free prince: sit in judgment of a monarch with sovereign power
401 30–32 the Pope . . . as dowager: influenced by the cardinal, the Pope has seized the Duchess's power
402 37–8 sacrifice/To his revenge: destroy as an act of vengeance
403 40–41 No matter . . . to th'bottom: no matter who pushes a man down a well, he is brought to the bottom by his own weight
404 5 buntings: small birds, here used to refer to the followers of the Duchess who have flown from her in her distress
405 8 give o'er: abandon

ANTONIO What was't?
DUCHESS Methought I wore my coronet of state,
And on a sudden[406] all the diamonds
Were changed to pearls.
ANTONIO My interpretation
Is you'll weep shortly; for to me the pearls
Do signify your tears.
DUCHESS The birds that live i'th field
On the wild benefit of nature, live
Happier than we; for they may choose their mates,
And carol[407] their sweet pleasures to the spring.

[*Enter*] BOSOLA [*with a letter*]

BOSOLA You are happily o'er-ta'en.
DUCHESS [*Takes the letter*] From my brother?
BOSOLA Yes, from the Lord Ferdinand, your brother,
All love and safety.
DUCHESS Thou dost blanch mischief—
Wouldst make it white.[408] See, see, like to calm weather
At sea before a tempest, false hearts speak fair
To those they intend most mischief.
[*Reads letter*] *Send Antonio to me. I want his head in a business.*
A politic equivocation!
He doth not want your counsel, but your head;
That is, he cannot sleep till you be dead.
And here's another pitfall that's strewed o'er
With roses: mark it; 'tis a cunning one:
[*Reads*] *I stand engaged for your husband for several debts at Naples. Let not that trouble him. I had rather have his heart than his money.*
And I believe so too!
BOSOLA What do you believe?
DUCHESS That he so much distrusts my husband's love,
He will by no means believe his heart is with him
Until he see it. The devil is not cunning enough
To circumvent us in riddles.
BOSOLA Will you reject that noble and free league
Of amity and love which I present you?
DUCHESS Their league is like that of some politic kings,
Only to make themselves of strength and power
To be our after-ruin.[409] Tell them so.
BOSOLA And what from you?
DUCHESS Thus tell him: I will not come.
BOSOLA And what of this?
ANTONIO My brothers[410] have dispersed
Bloodhounds abroad, which, till I hear are muzzled,
No truce, though hatched with ne'er such politic skill,
Is safe that hangs upon our enemies' will.
I'll not come at them.

406 14 on a sudden: suddenly
407 20 carol: sing
408 23–4 Thou dost … it white: you are trying to make his bad intentions seem good
409 42–4 Their league … after-ruin: their offer of friendship is intended only to make them strong enough to destroy me
410 46 brothers: i.e. brothers-in-law

BOSOLA This proclaims your breeding.
Every final thing draws a base mind to fear,
As the adamant[411] draws iron. Fare you well, sir.
You shall shortly hear from's. *Exit*
DUCHESS I suspect some ambush.
Therefore, by all my love I do conjure you
To take your eldest son and fly towards Milan.
Let us not venture all this poor remainder[412]
In one unlucky bottom.[413]
ANTONIO You counsel safely.
Best of my life, farewell, since we must part.
Heaven hath a hand in't, but no otherwise
Than as some curious artist takes in sunder
A clock or watch, when it is out of frame,
To bring't in a better order.[414]
DUCHESS I know not which is best,
To see you dead or part with you. [*To her son*] Farewell, boy.
Thou art happy that thou hast not understanding
To know thy misery, for all our wit
And reading brings us to a truer sense
Of sorrow.[415] [*To* ANTONIO] In the eternal church,[416] sir,
I do hope we shall not part thus.
ANTONIO Oh, be of comfort!
Make patience a noble fortitude,
And think not how unkindly we are used:
"Man, like to cassia, is proved best being bruised."[417]
DUCHESS Must I, like to a slave-born Russian,[418]
Account it praise to suffer tyranny?
And yet, oh heaven, thy heavy hand is in't.
I have seen my little boy oft scourge his top
And compared myself to't: naught made me e'er
Go right, but heaven's scourge-stick.[419]
ANTONIO Do not weep.
Heaven fashioned us of nothing and we strive
To bring ourselves to nothing. Farewell, Cariola,
And thy sweet armful;[420] [*To the* DUCHESS] if I do never see thee more,
Be a good mother to your little ones,
And save them from the tiger; fare you well.
DUCHESS [*To* ANTONIO] Let me look upon you once more, for that speech
Came from a dying father. [*Kisses him*] Your kiss is colder
Than that I have seen an holy anchorite
Give to a dead man's skull.[421]
ANTONIO My heart is turned to a heavy lump of lead,

411 52 adamant: magnet
412 56 venture all this poor remainder: risk what little we have left
413 57 unlucky bottom: doomed vessel
414 60–62 some curious . . . better order: a skilled mechanic takes apart a broken clock or watch in order to fix it
415 65–7 all our . . . sorrow: the more we know, the more we know of sorrow
416 67 eternal church: heaven
417 71 people grow stronger through adversity, just as the best property of cassia (its fragrance) is realized when the spice is broken or ground up
418 72 slave-born Russian: it was common at the time to compare the freedom of the English man with the enchained serfs or "unfree peasants" of the early Russian Empire
419 77 scourge-stick: a stick used to whip a spinning top to make it go faster
420 80 sweet armful: the child or children Cariola is holding
421 86 dead man's skull: a skull served as a *memento mori* (reminder of death); kissing it was a medieval tradition

With which I sound my danger: fare you well. *Exit [with their elder son]*
DUCHESS My laurel is all withered.
CARIOLA Look, Madam, what a troop of armèd men
Make toward us!

Enter BOSOLA *with a guard [of soldiers wearing vizards]*

DUCHESS Oh, they are very welcome.
When Fortune's wheel[422] is overcharged with princes,
The weight makes it move swift. I would have my ruin
Be sudden. [*To* BOSOLA] I am your adventure,[423] am I not?
BOSOLA You are. You must see your husband no more.
DUCHESS What devil art thou, that counterfeits heaven's thunder?
BOSOLA Is that terrible? I would have you tell me
Whether is that note worse that frights the silly birds
Out of the corn, or that which doth allure them
To the nets? You have hearkened to the last too much.
DUCHESS Oh misery! Like to a rusty o'ercharged[424] cannon,
Shall I never fly in pieces?[425] Come, to what prison?
BOSOLA To none.
DUCHESS Whither then?
BOSOLA To your palace.
DUCHESS I have heard that Charon's[426] boat serves to convey
All o'er the dismal lake, but brings none back again.
BOSOLA Your brothers mean you safety and pity.
DUCHESS Pity? With such a pity men preserve alive
Pheasants and quails, when they are not fat enough
To be eaten.
BOSOLA These are your children?
DUCHESS Yes.
BOSOLA Can they prattle?[427]
DUCHESS No.
But I intend, since they were born accursed,
Curses shall be their first language.
BOSOLA Fie, madam!
Forget this base, low fellow—
DUCHESS Were I a man,
I'd beat that counterfeit face[428] into thy other.
BOSOLA —One of no birth.
DUCHESS Say that he was born mean,
Man is most happy when's own actions
Be arguments[429] and examples of his virtue.
BOSOLA A barren, beggarly virtue.
DUCHESS I prithee, who is greatest? Can you tell?
Sad tales befit my woe. I'll tell you one:
A salmon, as she swam unto the sea,

422 92 Fortune's wheel: symbol of fate; humans are tied to this wheel and Fortune (usually a woman blindfolded) spins it: sometimes one is at the top, but another spin could place one at the bottom
423 94 adventure: prize; assignment; target
424 101 o'ercharged: overloaded
425 102 fly in pieces: break up, as an artillery piece (or perhaps even the gun itself) might when fired from an old, overloaded cannon
426 104 Charon: in classical myth, Charon was the ferryman of Hades, who would row the newly dead across the rivers of Styx and Acheron
427 110 prattle: talk
428 114 counterfeit face: i.e. Bosola's mask
429 117 arguments: evidence

Met with a dogfish,[430] who encounters her
With this rough language: "Why art thou so bold
To mix thyself with our high state of floods,
Being no eminent courtier, but one
That for the calmest and fresh time o'th' year
Dost live in shallow rivers? Rank'st thyself
With silly smelts[431] and shrimps? And darest thou
Pass by our Dogship without reverence?"
"Oh," quoth the salmon, "sister, be at peace.
Thank Jupiter we both have passed the net;
Our value never can be truly known
Till in the fisher's basket we be shown.
I'th' market, then, my price may be the higher,
Even when I am nearest to the cook and fire."
So to great men the moral may be stretched:
"Men oft are valued high when they're most wretch'd."
But come, whither you please. I am armed 'gainst misery,
Bent to all sways of the oppressor's will.
"There's no deep valley but near some great hill."
Exeunt

Act IV, scene i

[*Enter*] FERDINAND [*and*] BOSOLA

FERDINAND How doth our sister Duchess bear herself
In her imprisonment?
BOSOLA Nobly. I'll describe her:
She's sad, as one long used to't, and she seems
Rather to welcome the end of misery
Than shun it, a behavior so noble,
As gives a majesty to adversity.
You may discern the shape of loveliness
More perfect in her tears than in her smiles.
She will muse four hours together, and her silence,
Methinks, expresseth more than if she spake.
FERDINAND Her melancholy seems to be fortified
With a strange disdain.
BOSOLA 'Tis so. And this restraint,
Like English mastiffs[432] that grow fierce with tying,
Makes her too passionately apprehend
Those pleasures she's kept from.
FERDINAND Curse upon her!
I will no longer study in the book
Of another's heart. Inform her what I told you. *Exit*

[*Enter*] DUCHESS

BOSOLA All comfort to your grace.
DUCHESS I will have none.
Pray thee, why dost thou wrap thy poisoned pills

430 122 dogfish: a species of shark
431 128 smelts: tiny fish
432 13 mastiffs: very large dogs, often used as guard dogs or fighting dogs

In gold and sugar?
BOSOLA Your elder brother, the lord Ferdinand,
Is come to visit you, and sends you word,
'Cause once he rashly made a solemn vow
Never to see you more, he comes i'th' night,
And prays you gently neither torch nor taper[433]
Shine in your chamber. He will kiss your hand
And reconcile himself; but, for[434] his vow,
He dares not see you.
DUCHESS At his pleasure.
Take hence the lights.[435] [*Exit* BOSOLA *with lights*]

[*Enter*] FERDINAND

He's come.
FERDINAND Where are you?
DUCHESS Here, sir.
FERDINAND This darkness suits you well.
DUCHESS I would ask you pardon.
FERDINAND You have it.
For I account it the honorabl'st revenge,
Where I may kill, to pardon.[436] Where are your cubs?[437]
DUCHESS Whom?
FERDINAND Call them your children;
For though our national law distinguish bastards
From true legitimate issue, compassionate nature
Makes them all equal.
DUCHESS Do you visit me for this?
You violate a sacrament o'th' church[438]
Shall[439] make you howl in hell for't!
FERDINAND It had been well,
Could you have lived thus always, for indeed
You were too much i'th' light.[440] But no more.
I come to seal my peace with you: here's a hand,
To which you have vowed much love. The ring upon't
You gave. *Gives her a dead man's hand*[441]
DUCHESS I affectionately kiss it.
FERDINAND Pray do, and bury the print[442] of it in your heart.
I will leave this ring with you for a love token.[443]
And the hand, as sure as the ring; and do not doubt
But you shall have the heart too. When you need a friend,
Send it to him that owed[444] it. You shall see
Whether he can aid you.

433 25 taper: small wax candle
434 27 for: because of
435 29 Take hence the lights: in the original performance at the Blackfriars Theater, the scene would likely have been shrouded in near-complete darkness
436 33 Where I may kill, to pardon: i.e. to grant a pardon when I ought to kill
437 33 cubs: children
438 39 sacrament o'th' church: the sacrament of marriage; by suggesting her children are bastards, Bosola is denying that the Duchess and Antonio were married
439 40 Shall: that shall
440 42 too much i'th' light: too public in your behavior; lustful ("light" could also mean "promiscuous")
441 45 SD *dead man's hand*: this prop hand was, presumably, made out of wax (see line 55), but hard to distinguish from the real thing
442 46 print: imprint, such as a ring imprinted into a wax seal
443 47 love token: gift given in courtship rituals, such as a ring, brooch, handkerchief or pair of gloves
444 50 owed: owned

DUCHESS You are very cold.
I fear you are not well after your travel.
Ha?—lights! Oh horrible!
FERDINAND Let her have lights enough! *Exit*

[*Enter* BOSOLA *with a light*]

DUCHESS What witchcraft[445] doth he practice that he hath left
A dead man's hand here?

Here is discovered, behind a traverse, the artificial figures of Antonio and his children, appearing as if they were dead[446]

BOSOLA Look you, here's the piece[447] from which 'twas ta'en.
He doth present you this sad spectacle
That,[448] now you know directly they are dead,
Hereafter you may wisely cease to grieve
For that which cannot be recoverèd.
DUCHESS There is not between heaven and earth one wish
I stay for after this; it wastes me more
Than were't my picture[449] fashioned out of wax,
Stuck with a magical needle[450] and then buried
In some foul dunghill. And yond's an excellent property[451]
For a tyrant, which I would account mercy—
BOSOLA What's that?
DUCHESS If they would bind me to that lifeless trunk,
And let me freeze to death.
BOSOLA Come, you must live.
DUCHESS That's the greatest torture souls feel in hell—
In hell: that they must live and cannot die.
Portia,[452] I'll new kindle thy coals again,
And revive the rare and almost dead example
Of a loving wife.
BOSOLA Oh fie! Despair? Remember
You are a Christian.
DUCHESS The church enjoins fasting;
I'll starve myself to death.
BOSOLA Leave this vain sorrow.
Things being at the worst begin to mend.
The bee, when he hath shot his sting into your hand,
May then play with your eyelid.[453]
DUCHESS Good comfortable fellow,
Persuade a wretch that's broke upon the wheel[454]
To have all his bones new set; entreat him live
To be executed again. Who must dispatch[455] me?

445 54 witchcraft: witches were believed to use the amputated hands of dead criminals for magical purposes
446 55 SD The figures would be revealed behind a curtain in either the discovery space (the area within the central opening at the back of the main stage) or the upper stage gallery. While Webster probably wanted the audience to share the Duchess's belief that these were the actual dead bodies of her husband and children, it is unlikely that the figures were "played" by the actors (as in some modern productions) and more likely that they were made out of wax
447 56 here's the piece: the hand Ferdinand gave the Duchess was cut from the artificial figure of Antonio
448 58 That: so that
449 63 picture: effigy
450 64 magical needle: witches were thought to stick needles or pins into an effigy in order to injure the person represented
451 65 property: prop (referring to the figure of Antonio)
452 71 Portia: the wife of Brutus, one of Julius Caesar's assassins; she swallowed hot coals to kill herself when her husband died
453 77–8 The bee . . . your eyelid: a proverb meaning that things are not as bad as they seem; once a bee has stung, it cannot sting again
454 79 wheel: torture device that fractures the limbs when a body is stretched upon it
455 81 dispatch: execute; release from suffering

I account this world a tedious theater,
For I do play a part in't 'gainst my will.
BOSOLA Come, be of comfort. I will save your life.
DUCHESS Indeed, I have not leisure to tend so small a business.
BOSOLA Now, by my life, I pity you.
DUCHESS Thou art a fool then,
To waste thy pity on a thing so wretched
As cannot pity it. I am full of daggers.
Puff! Let me blow these vipers[456] from me.

[*Enter*] SERVANT

What are you?
SERVANT One that wishes you long life.
DUCHESS. I would thou wert hanged for the horrible curse
Thou hast given me. I shall shortly grow one
Of the miracles[457] of pity. I'll go pray.
No, I'll go curse. [*Exit* SERVANT]
BOSOLA Oh, fie!
DUCHESS I could curse the stars—
BOSOLA Oh, fearful!
DUCHESS And those three smiling seasons[458] of the year
Into a Russian winter, nay, the world
To its first chaos.[459]
BOSOLA Look you, the stars shine still.
DUCHESS Oh, but you must
Remember my curse hath a great way to go.
Plagues that make lanes through[460] largest families
Consume them!
BOSOLA Fie, lady!
DUCHESS Let them, like tyrants,
Never be remembered but for the ill they have done.
Let all the zealous prayers of mortifièd[461]
Churchmen forget them.
BOSOLA Oh, uncharitable!
DUCHESS Let heaven, a little while, cease crowning martyrs
To punish them.
Go, howl them this, and say I long to bleed.
"It is some mercy when men kill with speed." *Exit*

[*Enter*] FERDINAND

FERDINAND Excellent! As I would wish; she's plagued in art.[462]
These presentations are but framed in wax
By the curious master in that quality,
Vincentio Lauriola,[463] and she takes them

456 89 vipers: an image for the grief tormenting the Duchess; possibly "vipers" is a printing error for "vapors" (which one might more easily "blow" away than vipers)
457 93 miracles: extraordinary or legendary examples
458 95 smiling seasons: spring, summer, and autumn
459 97 first chaos: state of disorder that preceded the existence of the world
460 100 make lanes through: cause destruction to (literally, leave large gaps in)
461 103 mortifièd: pious
462 109 plagued in art: tormented by artificial figures
463 112 Vincentio Lauriola: fictional name, invented by Webster

For true substantial bodies.
BOSOLA Why do you do this?
FERDINAND To bring her to despair.
BOSOLA Faith, end here,
And go no farther in your cruelty.
Send her a penitential garment[464] to put on
Next to her delicate skin, and furnish her
With beads and prayer books.
FERDINAND Damn her! That body of hers,
While that my blood ran pure in't, was more worth
Than that which thou wouldst comfort called a soul.
I will send her masques of common courtesans,[465]
Have her meat served up by bawds[466] and ruffians,[467]
And, 'cause she'll needs be mad, I am resolved
To remove forth the common hospital[468]
All the mad folk, and place them near her lodging.
There let them practice together, sing and dance,
And act their gambols to the full o'th' moon.[469]
If she can sleep the better for it, let her.
Your work is almost ended.
BOSOLA Must I see her again?
FERDINAND Yes.
BOSOLA Never.
FERDINAND You must.
BOSOLA Never in mine own shape,
That's forfeited by my intelligence
And this last cruel lie. When you send me next,
The business shall be comfort.
FERDINAND Very likely!
Thy pity is nothing of kin to thee. Antonio
Lurks about Milan; thou shalt shortly thither
To feed a fire as great as my revenge,
Which ne'er will slack till it have spent his fuel.
"Intemperate agues[470] make physicians cruel."

Exeunt

Act IV, scene ii

[*Enter*] DUCHESS [*and*] CARIOLA. [*A noise of singing and shouting within*]

DUCHESS What hideous noise was that?
CARIOLA 'Tis the wild consort[471]
Of madmen, lady, which your tyrant brother
Hath placed about your lodging. This tyranny,
I think, was never practiced till this hour.

464 116 penitential garment: clothing, such as the hair shirts worn by zealous Catholics, that scratches or aggravates the skin constantly, reminding the wearer of the need to repent the sins of the flesh
465 121 courtesans: prostitutes
466 122 bawds: women who run brothels
467 122 ruffians: criminals; pimps
468 124 remove forth the common hospital: release from the hospital—here an asylum for the mentally ill; the most famous one in Webster's London was Bethlehem ("Bedlam") hospital
469 127 act their . . . o'th' moon: it was thought that madmen would become more frenzied during a full moon
470 138 agues: fevers
471 1 consort: group; company of musicians

DUCHESS Indeed, I thank him: nothing but noise and folly
Can keep me in my right wits; whereas, reason
And silence make me stark mad. Sit down—
Discourse to me some dismal tragedy.
CARIOLA Oh, 'twill increase your melancholy.
DUCHESS Thou art deceived.
To hear of greater grief would lessen mine.
This is a prison?
CARIOLA Yes, but you shall live
To shake this durance[472] off.
DUCHESS Thou art a fool.
The robin redbreast and the nightingale
Never live long in cages.
CARIOLA Pray, dry your eyes.
What think you of, madam?
DUCHESS Of nothing.
When I muse thus, I sleep.
CARIOLA Like a madman, with your eyes open?
DUCHESS Dost thou think we shall know one another
In th' other world?
CARIOLA Yes, out of question.
DUCHESS Oh that it were possible we might
But hold some two days' conference with the dead.
From them I should learn somewhat, I am sure,
I never shall know here. I'll tell thee a miracle:
I am not mad yet, to my cause of sorrow.
Th' heaven o'er my head seems made of molten brass,
The earth of flaming sulphur, yet I am not mad.
I am acquainted with sad misery,
As the tanned galley slave is with his oar:
Necessity makes me suffer constantly,
And custom makes it easy. Who do I look like now?
CARIOLA Like to your picture in the gallery:
A deal of[473] life in show, but none in practice;
Or rather like some reverend monument
Whose ruins are even pitied.
DUCHESS Very proper;
And Fortune seems only to have her eyesight
To behold my tragedy.—How now!
What noise is that?

[*Enter* SERVANT]

SERVANT I am come to tell you
Your brother hath intended you some sport.
A great physician, when the Pope was sick
Of a deep melancholy, presented him
With several sorts of madmen, which wild object,
Being full of change and sport, forced him to laugh,
And so th' impostume[474] broke. The selfsame cure
The duke intends on you.

472 12 durance: imprisonment
473 32 A deal of: much
474 43 impostume: festering sore

DUCHESS Let them come in.
SERVANT There's a mad lawyer and a secular priest,[475]
A doctor that hath forfeited his wits
By jealousy; an astrologian[476]
That in his works said such a day o'th' month
Should be the day of doom[477] and, failing of't,
Ran mad; an English tailor crazed i'th' brain
With the study of new fashion; a gentleman usher[478]
Quite beside himself with care to keep in mind
The number of his lady's salutations,
Or "how do you" she employed him in each morning;
A farmer too, an excellent knave in grain,[479]
Mad 'cause he was hindered transportation.[480]
And let[481] one broker[482] that's mad loose to these,
You'd think the devil were among them.
DUCHESS Sit, Cariola. [*To* SERVANT] Let them loose when you please,
For I am chained to endure all your tyranny.

[*Enter* MADMEN]

Here, by a madman, this song is sung to a dismal kind of music

Oh, let us howl some heavy note,
Some deadly, dogged howl,
Sounding as from the threatening throat
Of beasts and fatal fowl.
As ravens, screech owls, bulls, and bears,
We'll bill and bawl our parts,
Till yerksome[483] *noise have cloyed*[484] *your ears,*
And corrosived your hearts.
At last, whenas our choir wants breath,
Our bodies being blest,
We'll sing like swans to welcome death,
And die in love and rest.

1 MADMAN Doomsday not come yet? I'll draw it nearer by a perspective,[485] or make a glass[486] that shall set all the world on fire upon an instant. I cannot sleep; my pillow is stuffed with a litter of porcupines.
2 MADMAN Hell is a mere glasshouse, where the devils are continually blowing up women's souls on hollow irons and the fire never goes out.
3 MADMAN I will lie with every woman in my parish the tenth night. I will tithe[487] them over

475 45 secular priest: i.e. a priest who lives and works in the world, not in monastic seclusion
476 47 astrologian: astrologer
477 49 day of doom: judgement day
478 51 gentleman usher: servant who kept the door of a household and was responsible for introducing guests as they arrived
479 55 knave in grain: dishonest in the business of selling grain; "in grain" also meant "dyed," and so was used colloquially to describe indelible qualities—the farmer is a knave "by nature"
480 56 hindered transportation: stopped from exporting grain
481 57 And let: if you let
482 57 broker: a middleman
483 67 *yerksome*: irksome; vexing
484 67 *cloyed*: pierced; overloaded
485 73 perspective: telescope
486 74 glass: magnifying glass
487 78 tithe: a priest's right to ten percent of a parishioner's land

like haycocks.[488]

4 MADMAN Shall my 'pothecary[489] outgo me because I am a cuckold? I have found out his roguery. He makes alum[490] of his wife's urine and sells it to Puritans[491] that have sore throats with over-straining.

1 MADMAN I have skill in heraldry.

2 MADMAN Hast?

1 MADMAN You do give for your crest[492] a woodcock's[493] head with the brains picked out on't; you are a very ancient gentleman.

3 MADMAN Greek is turned Turk. We are only to be saved by the Helvetian translation.[494]

1 MADMAN Come on, sir, I will lay the law to you.

2 MADMAN Oh, rather lay a corrosive; the law will eat to the bone.

3 MADMAN He that drinks but to satisfy nature is damned.

4 MADMAN If I had my glass here, I would show a sight should make all the women here call me mad doctor.

1 MADMAN What's he, a ropemaker?

2 MADMAN No, no, no, a snuffling[495] knave that, while he shows the tombs,[496] will have his hand in a wench's placket.[497]

3 MADMAN Woe to the caroche that brought home my wife from the masque at three o'clock in the morning; it had a large feather-bed in it.[498]

4 MADMAN I have pared[499] the devil's nails forty times, roasted them in raven's eggs, and cured agues with them.

3 MADMAN Get me three hundred milch-bats[500] to make possets[501] to procure sleep.

4 MADMAN All the college may throw their caps at me. I have made a soap-boiler costive;[502] it was my masterpiece.

Here the dance consisting of eight madmen, with music answerable thereunto, after which, BOSOLA, *like an old man, enters*

DUCHESS Is he mad too?

SERVANT Pray question him: I'll leave you. [*Exeunt* SERVANT *and* MADMEN]

BOSOLA I am come to make thy tomb.

DUCHESS Ha! My tomb?

Thou speak'st as if I lay upon my death bed

Gasping for breath! Dost thou perceive me sick?

BOSOLA Yes, and the more dangerously, since thy sickness is insensible.[503]

DUCHESS Thou art not mad sure. Dost know me?

BOSOLA Yes.

DUCHESS Who am I?

488 79 haycocks: haystacks

489 80 'pothecary: apothecary; a druggist or pharmacist

490 81 alum: mineral salt used in dyeing and tanning

491 81 Puritans: Protestant zealots who sought to purify the English church of all practices and remnants of Catholicism

492 85 crest: symbol placed on a coat of arms

493 85 woodcock: bird that is easily caught; a symbol of gullibility

494 87 Helvetian translation: Geneva Bible preferred by Calvinists

495 94 snuffling: breathing heavily through one's nose

496 94 shows the tombs: referring to the priest who gives tours of graveyards

497 95 placket: opening slit in a skirt (with sexual suggestion)

498 96–7 Woe to . . . in it: large, private coaches were commonly thought to enable sexual liaisons

499 98 pared: trimmed

500 100 milch-bats: bats used for milking

501 100 possets: drinks made with hot milk flavored with spices and combined with ale or liquor

502 101 made a soap-boiler costive: caused a soap-boiler to be constipated; soap-makers were proverbially known for having diarrhea because of the animal fat used in soaps

503 107 insensible: undetectable, i.e. something you do not feel

BOSOLA Thou art a box of wormseed,[504] at best, but a salvatory[505] of green mummy.[506] What's this flesh? A little crudded[507] milk, fantastical puff paste.[508] Our bodies are weaker than those paper prisons boys use to keep flies in: more contemptible, since ours is to preserve earthworms. Didst thou ever see a lark in a cage? Such is the soul in the body. This world is like her little turf of grass and the heaven o'er our heads, like her looking glass, only gives us a miserable knowledge of the small compass of our prison.

DUCHESS Am not I thy Duchess?

BOSOLA Thou art some great woman, sure, for riot begins to sit on thy forehead, clad in grey hairs, twenty years sooner than on a merry milkmaid's. Thou sleep'st worse than if a mouse should be forced to take up her lodging in a cat's ear. A little infant that breeds its teeth,[509] should it lie with thee, would cry out as if thou wert the more unquiet bedfellow.

DUCHESS I am Duchess of Malfi still.
BOSOLA That makes thy sleeps so broken:
"Glories, like glow-worms, afar off shine bright,
But looked too near have neither heat nor light."
DUCHESS Thou art very plain.[510]
BOSOLA My trade is to flatter the dead, not the living.
I am a tomb-maker.
DUCHESS And thou com'st to make my tomb?
BOSOLA Yes.
DUCHESS Let me be a little merry:
Of what stuff wilt thou make it?
BOSOLA Nay, resolve me first, of what fashion?
DUCHESS Why, do we grow fantastical in our death bed?
Do we affect fashion in the grave?
BOSOLA Most ambitiously. Princes' images on their tombs
Do not lie, as they were wont, seeming to pray
Up to heaven, but with their hands under their cheeks,
As if they died of the toothache; they are not carved
With their eyes fixed upon the stars, but as their
Minds were wholly bent upon the world,
The selfsame way they seem to turn their faces.[511]
DUCHESS Let me know fully, therefore, the effect
Of this thy dismal preparation,
This talk, fit for a charnel.[512]
BOSOLA Now I shall.
Here is a present from your princely brothers,
And may it arrive welcome, for it brings
Last benefit, last sorrow.

[*Enter*] EXECUTIONERS [*with*] *a coffin, cords,*[513] *and a bell*

DUCHESS Let me see it—

504 109 wormseed: literally, dried flower heads of a plant used to destroy intestinal worms in humans—as in his next image, Bosola is thinking of the Duchess's body as a box of medicine; here he also suggests that human flesh, destined for the earth, is merely something that allows worms to flourish
505 109 salvatory: ointment box
506 109 green mummy: "mummy" was a medicine made from mummified corpses; with "green," Bosola presumably refers to the fact that the Duchess is not yet dead
507 110 crudded: curdled
508 110 fantastical puff paste: puff pastry designed in delicate, extravagant shapes
509 118 breeds its teeth: is teething
510 124 plain: direct
511 133–9 Princes' images … their faces: refers to the latest fashion in tomb-making, effigies of the dead lying on their sides resting their heads on their hands, rather than kneeling in prayer. Bosola's cites this as an example of the vanity of the age
512 142 charnel: cemetery or mortuary
513 145 SD *cords*: rope

I have so much obedience in my blood,
I wish it in their veins to do them good.
BOSOLA This is your last presence chamber.[514]
CARIOLA Oh, my sweet lady!
DUCHESS Peace! It affrights not me.
BOSOLA I am the common bellman[515]
That usually is sent to condemned persons
The night before they suffer.
DUCHESS Even now thou said'st,
Thou wast a tomb-maker?
BOSOLA 'Twas to bring you
By degrees to mortification.[516] Listen: [*Rings the bell*]

Hark! Now everything is still.
The screech owl and the whistler[517] *shrill,*
Call upon our dame aloud
And bid her quickly don her shroud.[518]
Much you had of land and rent;
Your length in clay's[519] *now competent.*[520]
A long war disturbed your mind;
Here your perfect peace is signed.
Of what is't fools make such vain keeping?
Sin their conception, their birth weeping,[521]
Their life a general mist of error,
Their death, a hideous storm of terror.
Strew your hair with powders sweet,
Don clean linen, bathe your feet,
And, the foul fiend more to check,
A crucifix let bless your neck.
'Tis now full tide 'tween night and day;
End your groan and come away.[522]

CARIOLA Hence villains, tyrants, murderers! Alas,
What will you do with my lady? Call for help!
DUCHESS To whom, to our next neighbors? They are mad folks.
BOSOLA Remove that noise.[523] [1 EXECUTIONER *seizes* CARIOLA]
DUCHESS Farewell, Cariola,
In my last will, I have not much to give:
A-many hungry guests have fed upon me;
Thine will be a poor reversion.[524]
CARIOLA I will die with her.
DUCHESS I pray thee, look thou giv'st my little boy

514 148 presence chamber: room in a palace where a monarch receives visitors

515 150 common bellman: one who would ring a hand bell at midnight in prisons to remind condemned prisoners of their looming deaths and to pray for salvation

516 154 By degrees to mortification: gradually to a state of spiritual purity

517 156 *whistler*: a bird whose whistle betokens the death of the one who hears it

518 158 *don her shroud*: put on the white sheet that will wrap her corpse for burial

519 160 *length in clay*: grave

520 160 *competent*: sufficient

521 164 *birth weeping*: refers to the conventional idea that babies cry when they are born because they have entered the world of sin and death

522 155–72 It is possible that Bosola's invocation of the various rituals associated with the preparation for death, written in rhyming couplets, is meant to be sung

523 176 that noise: i.e. Cariola

524 179 There won't be much left over for you (referring to the custom whereby servants ate after their masters). "Reversion" was also a legal term referring to property granted to someone upon the death of the grantee; the Duchess is saying that everything has been taken from her and there is nothing left for Cariola to have

Some syrup for his cold, and let the girl
Say her prayers ere she sleep. [1 EXECUTIONER *forces* CARIOLA *off*]
Now, what you please.
What death?
BOSOLA Strangling. Here are your executioners.
DUCHESS I forgive them.
The apoplexy,[525] catarrh,[526] or cough o'th' lungs[527]
Would do as much as they do.
BOSOLA Doth not death fright you?
DUCHESS Who would be afraid on't?
Knowing to meet such excellent company
In th' other world.[528]
BOSOLA Yet, methinks
The manner of your death should much afflict you,
This cord should terrify you.
DUCHESS. Not a whit.
What would it pleasure me to have my throat cut
With diamonds? Or to be smothered
With cassia? Or to be shot to death with pearls?
I know death hath ten thousand several[529] doors
For men to take their exits, and 'tis found
They go on such strange geometrical hinges,[530]
You may open them both ways. Any way, for heaven sake,
So I were out of your whispering.[531] Tell my brothers
That I perceive death, now I am well awake,
Best gift is[532] they can give or I can take.
I would fain put off my last woman's fault[533]—
I'd not be tedious to you.
2 EXECUTIONER We are ready.
DUCHESS Dispose my breath how please you, but my body
Bestow upon my women, will you?[534]
3 EXECUTIONER Yes. [*Places cord around her neck*]
DUCHESS Pull, and pull strongly, for your able strength
Must pull down heaven upon me.
Yet stay! Heaven's gates are not so highly arched
As princes' palaces; they that enter there
Must go upon their knees. [*Kneels*] Come, violent death,
Serve for mandragora[535] to make me sleep.
Go tell my brothers when I am laid out,
They then may feed[536] in quiet. *They strangle her*
BOSOLA Where's the waiting woman?
Fetch her! Some other strangle the children. [*Exeunt* EXECUTIONERS]

525 186 apoplexy: stroke
526 186 catarrh: cerebral hemorrhage
527 186 cough o'th' lungs: pneumonia
528 188–90 Who would . . . other world: the Duchess still believes that Antonio and their children are dead
529 196 several: separate
530 198 geometrical hinges: the kind of hinges that would enable a door to swing in both directions; the doors to death are also the doors to life
531 200 out of your whispering: away from your spying
532 201–2 I perceive . . . gift is: I see that death is the best gift that
533 203 woman's fault: i.e. talking too much (a misogynist commonplace)
534 205–6 my body . . . will you?: the Duchess requests that her corpse be given to her servants for proper burial
535 212 mandragora: mandrake, a poisonous plant with a soothing, narcotic effect
536 214 feed: i.e. on her estate

[*Enter* EXECUTIONERS *with* CARIOLA]

Look you, there sleeps your mistress.
CARIOLA Oh you are damned
Perpetually for this! My turn is next,
Is't not so ordered?
BOSOLA Yes, and I am glad
You are so well prepared for't.
CARIOLA You are deceived, sir,
I am not prepared for't; I will not die!
I will first come to my answer and know
How I have offended.
BOSOLA Come, dispatch her!
You kept her counsel; now you shall keep ours.
CARIOLA I will not die! I must not; I am contracted[537]
To a young gentleman!
EXECUTIONER Here's your wedding ring. [*Shows her a noose*]
CARIOLA Let me but speak with the duke! I'll discover
Treason to his person.
BOSOLA Delays. Throttle her.
EXECUTIONER She bites and scratches.
CARIOLA If you kill me now
I am damned. I have not been at confession
This two years!
BOSOLA When.[538]
CARIOLA I am quick with child![539]
BOSOLA Why then,
Your credit's saved.[540] [*They strangle her*] Bear her in to th' next room.
Let this lie still.[541] [*Exeunt* EXECUTIONERS *with* CARIOLA'S *body*]

[*Enter*] FERDINAND

FERDINAND Is she dead?
BOSOLA She is what
You'd have her. But here begin your pity. [*Opens the tiring house curtain*]
Shows the children strangled
Alas, how have these offended?
FERDINAND The death
Of young wolves is never to be pitied.
BOSOLA Fix your eye here.[542]
FERDINAND Constantly.
BOSOLA Do you not weep?
Other sins only speak; murder shrieks out.
The element of water moistens the earth,
But blood flies upwards and bedews the heavens.
FERDINAND Cover her face. Mine eyes dazzle; she died young.
BOSOLA I think not so; her infelicity[543]
Seemed to have years too many.

537 224 contracted: engaged
538 231 When: an exclamation of impatience
539 231 quick with child: pregnant
540 232 Your credit's saved: i.e. you are being spared the shame of bearing a child out of wedlock
541 233 Let this lie still: let the Duchess's dead body remain where it is
542 237 here: on the Duchess's body
543 242 infelicity: misfortune; bad luck

FERDINAND She and I were twins,
And should I die this instant I had lived
Her time to a minute.
BOSOLA It seems she was born first.
You have bloodily approved the ancient truth
That kindred commonly do worse agree
Than remote strangers.
FERDINAND Let me see her face again.
Why didst not thou pity her? What an excellent
Honest man might'st thou have been
If thou hadst borne her to some sanctuary?
Or, bold in a good cause, opposed thy self
With thy advancèd sword above thy head,
Between her innocence and my revenge?
I bade thee, when I was distracted of my wits,
Go kill my dearest friend, and thou hast done't.
For let me but examine well the cause:
What was the meanness of her match to me?
Only, I must confess, I had a hope,
Had she continued widow, to have gained
An infinite mass of treasure by her death,
And that was the main cause—her marriage—
That drew a stream of gall quite through my heart.
For thee, as we observe in tragedies
That a good actor many times is cursed
For playing a villain's part, I hate thee for't;
And, for my sake, say thou hast done much ill well.
BOSOLA Let me quicken your memory; for I perceive
You are falling into ingratitude. I challenge
The reward due to my service.
FERDINAND I'll tell thee,
What I'll give thee—
BOSOLA Do!
FERDINAND I'll give thee a pardon
For this murder.
BOSOLA Hah?
FERDINAND Yes, and 'tis
The largest bounty I can study to do thee.
By what authority did'st thou execute
This bloody sentence?
BOSOLA By yours—
FERDINAND Mine? Was I her judge?
Did any ceremonial form of law[544]
Doom her to not-being? Did a complete jury
Deliver her conviction up i'th' court?
Where shalt thou find this judgment registered
Unless in hell? See, like a bloody fool
Th' hast forfeited thy life, and thou shalt die for't.
BOSOLA The office of justice is perverted quite
When one thief hangs another. Who shall dare
To reveal this?
FERDINAND Oh, I'll tell thee:
The wolf shall find her grave and scrape it up,

544 276 ceremonial form of law: legitimate trial

Not to devour the corpse, but to discover
The horrid murder.
BOSOLA You, not I, shall quake for't.
FERDINAND Leave me.
BOSOLA I will first receive my pension.[545]
FERDINAND You are a villain.
BOSOLA When your ingratitude
Is judge, I am so.
FERDINAND Oh horror!
That not the fear of him, which binds the devils
Can prescribe man obedience.
Never look upon me more!
BOSOLA Why, fare thee well.
Your brother and yourself are worthy men.
You have a pair of hearts are hollow graves,
Rotten, and rotting others; and your vengeance,
Like two-chained bullets,[546] still goes arm in arm.
You may be brothers; for treason, like the plague,
Doth take much in a blood.[547] I stand like one
That long hath ta'en a sweet and golden dream.
I am angry with myself now that I wake.
FERDINAND Get thee into some unknown part o'th' world
That I may never see thee.
BOSOLA Let me know
Wherefore I should be thus neglected? Sir,
I served your tyranny, and rather strove
To satisfy yourself than all the world;
And though I loathed the evil, yet I loved
You that did counsel it, and rather sought
To appear a true servant than an honest man.
FERDINAND I'll go hunt the badger by owl-light.[548]
'Tis a deed of darkness. *Exit*
BOSOLA He's much distracted.[549] Off, my painted honor![550]
While with vain hopes our faculties we tire,[551]
We seem to sweat in ice, and freeze in fire.
What would I do, were this to do again?
I would not change my peace of conscience
For all the wealth of Europe. She stirs! Here's life—
Return, fair soul, from darkness and lead mine
Out of this sensible[552] hell. She's warm; she breathes!
Upon thy pale lips I will melt my heart
To store[553] them with fresh color.—Who's there?
Some cordial[554] drink. Alas! I dare not call,
So pity would destroy pity. Her eye opes,

545 288 pension: payment for the murders
546 297 two-chained bullets: cannon balls connected by chains so that when fired together the results are doubly destructive
547 299 take much in a blood: afflicts members of the same family
548 310 hunt the badger by owl-light: the best light to hunt badgers in is moonlight; badger hunting was a notoriously cruel sport, as they were baited with dogs
549 312 distracted: unhinged; mad
550 312 painted honor: disguise
551 313 our faculties we tire: we exhaust ourselves
552 319 sensible: palpable
553 321 store: restore
554 322 cordial: revitalizing, restorative

And heaven in it seems to ope, that late was shut,
To take me up to mercy.
DUCHESS Antonio—
BOSOLA Yes, madam, he is living.
The dead bodies you saw were but feigned statues.
He's reconciled to your brothers; the Pope hath wrought
The atonement.[555]
DUCHESS Mercy! *She dies*
BOSOLA Oh, she's gone again. There the cords of life broke.
Oh sacred innocence that sweetly sleeps
On turtles'[556] feathers, whilst a guilty conscience
Is a black register,[557] wherein is writ
All our good deeds and bad. A perspective[558]
That shows us hell! That we cannot be suffer'd
To do good when we have a mind to it!
This is manly sorrow.[559]
These tears, I am very certain, never grew
In my mother's milk. My estate is sunk
Below the degree of fear. Where were
These penitent fountains[560] while she was living?
Oh, they were frozen up. Here is a sight
As direful to my soul as is the sword
Unto a wretch hath slain[561] his father. Come,
I'll bear thee hence,
And execute thy last will: that's deliver
Thy body to the reverend dispose
Of some good women; that the cruel tyrant
Shall not deny me. Then I'll post to Milan,
Where somewhat I will speedily enact
Worth my dejection.[562]
Exit [with the body of the DUCHESS*]*

Act V, scene i

[Enter] ANTONIO *[and]* DELIO

ANTONIO What think you of my hope of reconcilement
To the Aragonian brethren?[563]
DELIO I misdoubt[564] it,
For though they have sent their letters of safe conduct
For your repair to Milan, they appear
But nets to entrap you. The Marquis of Pescara,
Under whom you hold certain land in 'cheat,[565]
Much 'gainst his noble nature hath been moved

555 328 atonement: reconciliation
556 331 turtles: turtle doves, symbolic of faithful marriages
557 332 register: record-book
558 333 perspective: a glass or telescope
559 336 manly sorrow: appropriate or suitable since it is caused by remorse
560 340 penitent fountains: repentant tears
561 343 hath slain: who hath slain
562 350 dejection: sorrow; lowered social condition
563 2 Aragonian brethren: i.e. Duke Ferdinand and the Cardinal
564 2 misdoubt: doubt
565 6 'cheat: escheat, i.e. if Antonio were to be imprisoned, or die without any heirs, Pescara would automatically receive Antonio's property

To seize those lands, and some of his dependants
Are at this instant making it their suit
To be invested in your revenues.[566]
I cannot think they mean well to your life
That do deprive you of your means of life—
Your living.
ANTONIO You are still an heretic
To any safety I can shape myself.

[*Enter* PESCARA]

DELIO Here comes the Marquis. I will make myself
Petitioner for some part of your land,
To know whether it is flying.
ANTONIO I pray do. [*Stands apart*]
DELIO Sir, I have a suit to you.
PESCARA To me.
DELIO An easy one:
There is the citadel[567] of St Bennet,
With some demesnes[568] of late in the possession
Of Antonio Bologna. Please you bestow them on me?
PESCARA You are my friend, but this is such a suit,
Nor fit for me to give, nor you to take.
DELIO No sir?
PESCARA I will give you ample reason for't
Soon, in private—

[*Enter* JULIA]

—Here's the cardinal's mistress.
JULIA My lord, I am grown your poor petitioner,
And should be an ill beggar, had I not
A great man's letter here, the cardinal's,
To court you in my favor. [*Gives* PESCARA *a letter*]
PESCARA He entreats for you
The citadel of St Bennet that belonged
To the banished Bologna.
JULIA Yes.
PESCARA I could not have thought of a friend I could
Rather pleasure with it: 'tis yours.
JULIA Sir, I thank you.
And he shall know how doubly I am engaged
Both in your gift and speediness of giving,
Which makes your grant the greater. *Exit*
ANTONIO [*Aside*] —How they fortify
Themselves with my ruin!
DELIO Sir, I am
Little bound to you.
PESCARA Why?
DELIO Because you denied this suit, to me and gave't

566 10 To take possession of the revenue your land yields
567 19 citadel: fortress or stronghold
568 20 demesnes: possessions or property

To such a creature.[569]
PESCARA Do you know what it was?
It was Antonio's land, not forfeited
By course of law, but ravished from his throat[570]
By the cardinal's entreaty. It were not fit
I should bestow so main a piece of wrong
Upon my friend: 'tis a gratification
Only due to a strumpet. For it is injustice!
Shall I sprinkle the pure blood of innocents
To make those followers I call my friends
Look ruddier[571] upon me? I am glad
This land, ta'en from the owner by such wrong,
Returns again unto so foul a use
As salary for his lust. Learn, good Delio,
To ask noble things of me and you shall find
I'll be a noble giver.
DELIO You instruct me well.
ANTONIO [*Aside*] —Why, here's a man now would fright impudence
From sauciest[572] beggars!
PESCARA Prince Ferdinand's come to Milan
Sick, as they give out, of an apoplexy,
But some say 'tis a frenzy;[573] I am going
To visit him. *Exit*
[ANTONIO *comes forward*]

ANTONIO 'Tis a noble old fellow.
DELIO What course do you mean to take, Antonio?
ANTONIO This night, I mean to venture all my fortune,
Which is no more than a poor lingering life,
To the cardinal's worst of malice. I have got
Private access to his chamber and intend
To visit him about the mid of night
As once his brother did our noble Duchess.
It may be that the sudden apprehension
Of danger, for I'll go in mine own shape,
When he shall see it, freight with[574] love and duty,
May draw the poison out of him and work
A friendly reconcilement. If it fail,
Yet, it shall rid me of this infamous calling;[575]
For better fall once, than be ever falling.
DELIO I'll second you in all danger, and howe'er,
My life keeps rank with yours.
ANTONIO You are still my loved and best friend.
Exeunt

Act V, scene ii

[*Enter*] PESCARA [*and*] *a* DOCTOR

569 41 creature: i.e. Julia
570 43 ravished from his throat: stolen
571 50 ruddier: redder, i.e. healthier (and covered with the "blood of innocents")
572 57 sauciest: rudest, most insolent
573 59 frenzy: mania or madness
574 70 freight with: fraught with; full of
575 73 calling: position; occupation

PESCARA Now Doctor, may I visit your patient?
DOCTOR If't please your lordship, but he's instantly
To take the air here in the gallery
By my direction.
PESCARA Pray thee, what's his disease?
DOCTOR A very pestilent[576] disease, my lord,
They call lycanthropia.
PESCARA What's that?
I need a dictionary to't.
DOCTOR I'll tell you:
In those that are possessed with't there o'erflows
Such melancholy humor, they imagine
Themselves to be transformèd into wolves,
Steal forth to churchyards in the dead of night
And dig dead bodies up. As two nights since
One met the duke 'bout midnight in a lane
Behind St. Mark's Church, with the leg of a man
Upon his shoulder, and he howled fearfully;
Said he was a wolf, only the difference
Was, a wolf's skin was hairy on the outside,
His on the inside; bade them take their swords,
Rip up his flesh and try.[577] Straight I was sent for,
And having ministered to[578] him, found his grace
Very well recovered.
PESCARA I am glad on't.
DOCTOR Yet not without some fear
Of a relapse. If he grow to his fit again,
I'll go a nearer way to work with him
Than ever Paracelsus[579] dreamed of. If
They'll give me leave I'll buffet[580] his madness out of him.
Stand aside—he comes.

[*Enter*] FERDINAND, CARDINAL, MALATESTE [*and*] BOSOLA, [*who stands apart and observes*]

FERDINAND Leave me.
MALATESTE Why doth your lordship love this solitariness?
FERDINAND Eagles commonly fly alone; they are crows, daws, and starlings that flock together.—Look, what's that follows me?
MALATESTE Nothing, my Lord.
FERDINAND Yes—
MALATESTE 'Tis your shadow.
FERDINAND Stay[581] it! Let it not haunt me!
MALATESTE Impossible, if you move and the sun shine.
FERDINAND I will throttle[582] it. [*Throws himself down upon his shadow*]
MALATESTE Oh, my lord, you are angry with nothing!
FERDINAND You are a fool. How is't possible I should catch my shadow unless I fall upon't? When I go to hell, I mean to carry a bribe; for look you, good gifts evermore make way for the worst persons.

576 5 pestilent: toxic
577 19 try: see if he was telling the truth
578 20 ministered to: examined
579 25 Paracelsus: Swiss astrologer, physician, and philosopher of alchemy (c. 1493–1541)
580 26 buffet: whip
581 34 Stay: stop
582 36 throttle: strangle, choke

PESCARA Rise, good my lord.
FERDINAND I am studying the art of patience.
PESCARA 'Tis a noble virtue.
FERDINAND To drive six snails before me, from this town to Moscow; neither use goad[583] nor whip to them, but let them take their own time—the patientest man i'th' world match me for an experiment[584]—and I'll crawl after like a sheep-biter.[585]
CARDINAL Force him up. [PESCARA *and* MALATESTE *raise him up*]
FERDINAND Use me well, you were best! What I have done, I have done: I'll confess nothing.
DOCTOR Now let me come to him. Are you mad, my lord?
Are you out of your princely wits?
FERDINAND What's he?
PESCARA Your doctor.
FERDINAND Let me have his beard sawed off and his eyebrows filed more civil.
DOCTOR I must do mad tricks with him for that's the only way on't. I have brought your grace a salamander's skin to keep you from sun-burning.
FERDINAND I have cruel, sore eyes.
DOCTOR The white of a cockatrice's[586] egg is present remedy.
FERDINAND Let it be a new-laid one, you were best:—
Hide me from him! Physicians are like kings:
They brook no contradiction.
DOCTOR Now he begins to fear me; now let me alone with him.
CARDINAL How now, put off your gown?[587]
DOCTOR Let me have some forty urinals[588] filled with rose-water: he and I'll go pelt one another with them. Now he begins to fear me: can you fetch a frisk,[589] sir? Let him go, let him go upon my peril. I find by his eye, he stands in awe of me. I'll make him as tame as a dormouse.
FERDINAND Can you fetch your frisks, sir? I will stamp him into a cullis, flay off his skin to cover one of the anatomies![590] This rogue hath set i'th' cold yonder in Barber-Surgeons' Hall.[591] Hence! hence! You are—all of you—like beasts for sacrifice! There's nothing left of you but tongue and belly, flattery and lechery! [*Exit*]
PESCARA Doctor, he did not fear you throughly.[592]
DOCTOR True, I was somewhat too forward.[593]
BOSOLA Mercy upon me, what a fatal judgement
Hath fall'n upon this Ferdinand!
PESCARA Knows your grace
What accident hath brought unto the Prince,
This strange distraction?[594]
CARDINAL [*Aside*] —I must feign somewhat—Thus they say it grew:
You have heard it rumored for these many years,
None of our family dies but there is seen
The shape of an old woman, which is given
By tradition to us to have been murdered
By her nephews for her riches; such a figure
One night, as the prince sat up late at's book,

583 44 goad: stick with a sharp, pointed end
584 45–6 the patientest ... an experiment: let even the most patient man in the world try to outdo me
585 46 sheep-biter: sheepdog
586 56 cockatrice: basilisk (see III.ii. 89 and note)
587 61 gown: doctor's robe; the doctor removes it in preparation for fighting with Ferdinand
588 62 urinals: vials for holding urine
589 63 fetch a frisk: cut a caper, dance
590 66 anatomies: dissected bodies displayed as medical specimens in the Barber-Surgeons' Hall museum
591 66–7 Barber-Surgeons' Hall: the hall on Monkwell Street in London where the company of the barber-surgeons met and where, after 1540, anatomical dissections took place
592 69 throughly: thoroughly
593 70 forward: pushy
594 75 distraction: madness

Appeared to him; when crying out for help,
The gentlemen of's chamber found his grace
All on a cold sweat, altered much in face
And language; since which apparition,
He hath grown worse and worse, and I much fear
He cannot live. [BOSOLA *comes forward*]
BOSOLA Sir, I would speak with you.
PESCARA We'll leave your grace,
Wishing to the sick prince, our noble lord,
All health of mind and body.
CARDINAL You are most welcome. [*Exeunt all but* CARDINAL *and* BOSOLA]
[*Aside*] —Are you come? So. This fellow must not know
By any means I had intelligence
In our Duchess' death. For, though I counseled it,
The full of all th' engagement seemed to grow
From Ferdinand.—Now sir, how fares our sister?
I do not think but sorrow makes her look
Like to an oft-dyed garment. She shall now
Taste comfort from me. Why do you look so wildly?
Oh, the fortune of your master here, the prince,
Dejects you; but be you of happy comfort.
If you'll do one thing for me, I'll entreat,
Though he had a cold tombstone o'er his bones,
I'd make you what you would be.
BOSOLA Anything.
Give it me in a breath, and let me fly to't.
They that think long, small expedition win,
For musing much o'th' end, cannot begin.[595]

[*Enter*] JULIA

JULIA Sir, will you come in to supper?
CARDINAL I am busy! Leave me.
JULIA [*Aside*] What an excellent shape hath that fellow![596] *Exit*
CARDINAL 'Tis thus: Antonio lurks here in Milan.
Enquire him out and kill him. While he lives,
Our sister cannot marry and I have thought
Of an excellent match for her. Do this and style me
Thy advancement.
BOSOLA But by what means shall I find him out?
CARDINAL There is a gentleman called Delio
Here in the camp[597] that hath been long approved
His loyal friend. Set eye upon that fellow;
Follow him to mass. Maybe Antonio,
Although he do account religion
But a school-name, for fashion of the world,[598]
May accompany him; or else go enquire out
Delio's confessor,[599] and see if you can bribe
Him to reveal it. There are a thousand ways

595 106–7 Those who think too much about what they hope to achieve have a hard time getting started, and so achieve very little
596 109 that fellow: i.e. Bosola
597 116 camp: military settlement
598 120 for fashion of the world: because it is fashionable to treat religion trivially
599 122 confessor: the priest who hears his confession

A man might find to trace[600] him; as to know
What fellows haunt[601] the Jews for taking up[602]
Great sums of money, for sure he's in want;
Or else to go to th' picture-makers[603] and learn
Who bought her picture lately—some of these
Happily may take—
BOSOLA Well, I'll not freeze i'th' business.
I would see that wretched thing, Antonio,
Above all sights i'th' world.
CARDINAL Do, and be happy. *Exit*
BOSOLA This fellow doth breed basilisks in's eyes;
He's nothing else but murder, yet he seems
Not to have notice of the Duchess' death;
'Tis his cunning.[604] I must follow his example.
There cannot be a surer way to trace
Than that of an old fox.[605]

[*Enter*] JULIA, [*aiming a pistol at him*]

JULIA So, sir, you are well met.
BOSOLA How now?
JULIA Nay, the doors are fast[606] enough.
Now, sir, I will make you confess your treachery.
BOSOLA Treachery?
JULIA Yes, confess to me
Which of my women 'twas you hired to put
Love powder into my drink?
BOSOLA Love powder?
JULIA Yes, when I was at Malfi.
Why should I fall in love with such a face else?
I have already suffered for thee so much pain;
The only remedy to do me good
Is to kill my longing.
BOSOLA Sure your pistol holds
Nothing but perfumes or kissing comfits.[607]
Excellent lady, you have a pretty way on't to discover
Your longing. Come, come, I'll disarm you,
And arm you thus— [*Embraces her*] —yet this is wondrous strange.
JULIA Compare thy form and my eyes together,
You'll find my love no such great miracle. Now you'll say
I am wanton; this nice modesty in ladies
Is but a troublesome familiar[608]
That haunts them.
BOSOLA Know you me? I am a blunt soldier.
JULIA The better!
Sure, there wants fire where there are no lively sparks

600 124 trace: seek
601 125 haunt: visit frequently
602 125 taking up: borrowing
603 127 picture-makers: artists who paint miniature portraits
604 135 cunning: trick, deception
605 136–7 There cannot . . . old fox: if you want to be cunning, you should follow the example of an old fox
606 138 fast: locked
607 148 kissing comfits: sweetmeats; nuts or seeds coated in sugar, eaten to make the breath sweet
608 155 familiar: a spirit that attends on witches

Of roughness.[609]
BOSOLA And I want compliment.[610]
JULIA Why, ignorance
In courtship cannot make you do amiss,
If you have a heart to do well.
BOSOLA You are very fair.
JULIA Nay, if you lay beauty to my charge,
I must plead unguilty.
BOSOLA Your bright eyes
Carry a quiver of darts in them, sharper
Than sunbeams.
JULIA You will mar me with commendation,
Put yourself to the charge of courting me,
Whereas now I woo you.
BOSOLA [*Aside*] —I have it! I will work upon this creature—
Let us grow most amorously familiar.
If the great cardinal now should see me thus,
Would he not count me a villain?
JULIA No, he might count me a wanton,
Not lay a scruple[611] of offence on you.
For if I see and steal a diamond,
The fault is not i'th' stone, but in me, the thief
That purloins[612] it. I am sudden with you.
We that are great women of pleasure[613] use to cut off
These uncertain wishes and unquiet longings,
And in an instant join the sweet delight
And the pretty excuse together. Had you been in'th' street,
Under my chamber window, even there
I should have courted you.
BOSOLA Oh, you are an excellent lady!
JULIA Bid me do somewhat for you presently[614]
To express I love you.
BOSOLA I will, and if you love me,
Fail not to effect it.
The cardinal is grown wondrous melancholy.
Demand the cause; let him not put you off
With feigned[615] excuse; discover the main ground on't.[616]
JULIA Why would you know this?
BOSOLA I have depended on him,
And I hear that he is fall'n in some disgrace
With the emperor;[617] if he be, like the mice
That forsake falling houses, I would shift
To other dependence.[618]
JULIA You shall not need follow the wars.

609 158–9 there wants . . . Of roughness: there can be no fire without a rough surface to ignite the match
610 159 want compliment: lack refinement, courtesy
611 173 scruple: doubt
612 176 purloins: steals
613 177 great women of pleasure: women who enjoy pleasure and luxury; courtesans
614 183 presently: immediately
615 188 feigned: pretended
616 188 ground on't: reason for it
617 192 emperor: Charles V, Holy Roman Emperor from 1519 to 1558
618 193–4 shift/To other dependence: change my allegiance

I'll be your maintenance.[619]
BOSOLA And I your loyal servant—
But I cannot leave my calling.[620]
JULIA Not leave an
Ungrateful general for the love of a sweet lady?
You are like some cannot sleep in feather beds,
But must have blocks for their pillows.
BOSOLA Will you do this?
JULIA Cunningly.
BOSOLA Tomorrow I'll expect th' intelligence.
JULIA Tomorrow? Get you into my cabinet.[621]
You shall have it with you; do not delay me
No more than I do you. I am like one
That is condemned: I have my pardon promised,
But I would see it sealed. Go, get you in.
You shall see me wind my tongue about his heart,
Like a skein[622] of silk. [BOSOLA *hides behind a curtain*]

[*Enter*] CARDINAL [*and* SERVANTS]

CARDINAL Where are you?
SERVANT Here.
CARDINAL Let none upon your lives
Have conference with the Prince Ferdinand,
Unless I know it. [*Exeunt* SERVANTS] —In this distraction
He may reveal the murder.
Yond's my lingering consumption.[623]
I am weary of her, and by any means
Would be quit of—
JULIA How now, my Lord?
What ails you?
CARDINAL Nothing.
JULIA Oh, you are much altered.
Come, I must be your secretary,[624] and remove
This lead from off your bosom; what's the matter?
CARDINAL I may not tell you.
JULIA Are you so far in love with sorrow
You cannot part with part of it? Or think you
I cannot love your grace when you are sad
As well as merry? Or do you suspect
I, that have been a secret to your heart
These many winters, cannot be the same
Unto your tongue?
CARDINAL Satisfy thy longing.
The only way to make thee keep my counsel
Is not to tell thee.
JULIA Tell your echo this,
Or flatterers, that like echoes, still report

619 196 maintenance: financial support
620 198 calling: profession; assignment
621 203 cabinet: closet; private chamber
622 209 skein: reel
623 214 consumption: wasting disease (i.e. Julia causes the cardinal to waste time and fortune in sinful behavior)
624 218 secretary: confidant (keeper of secrets)

What they hear, though most imperfect, and not me:
For if that you be true unto yourself,
I'll know.
CARDINAL Will you rack[625] me?
JULIA No, judgment shall
Draw it from you. It is an equal fault
To tell one's secrets unto all or none.
CARDINAL The first argues folly.
JULIA But the last tyranny.
CARDINAL Very well—why imagine I have committed
Some secret deed, which I desire the world
May never hear of?
JULIA Therefore, may not I know it?
You have concealed for me as great a sin
As adultery. Sir, never was occasion
For perfect trial of my constancy
Till now. Sir, I beseech you.
CARDINAL You'll repent it.
JULIA Never.
CARDINAL It hurries thee to ruin; I'll not tell thee.
Be well advised and think what danger 'tis
To receive a prince's secrets: they that do
Had need have their breasts hooped with adamant[626]
To contain them. I pray thee yet be satisfied.
Examine thine own frailty; 'tis more easy
To tie knots than unloose them. 'Tis a secret
That, like a lingering poison, may chance lie
Spread in thy veins and kill thee seven year hence.
JULIA Now you dally with me.
CARDINAL No more; thou shalt know it.
By my appointment,[627] the great Duchess of Malfi
And two of her young children, four nights since,
Were strangled.
JULIA Oh heaven! Sir, what have you done?
CARDINAL How now? How settles this? Think you your
Bosom will be a grave dark and obscure enough
For such a secret?
JULIA You have undone yourself, sir.
CARDINAL Why?
JULIA It lies not in me to conceal it.
CARDINAL No? Come, I will swear you to't upon this book.
JULIA Most religiously.
CARDINAL Kiss it. [*She kisses the book*]
Now you shall never utter it; thy curiosity
Hath undone thee. Thou'rt poisoned with that book.
Because I knew thou couldst not keep my counsel,
I have bound thee to't by death. [BOSOLA *comes forward*]
BOSOLA For pity sake, hold!
CARDINAL Ha, Bosola!
JULIA I forgive you
This equal piece of justice you have done.

625 232 rack: instrument of torture that stretched the body in order to force a confession or reveal intelligence
626 246 hooped with adamant: protected by the strongest metal
627 253 appointment: order or arrangement

For I betrayed your counsel to that fellow;
He overheard it. That was the cause I said—
It lay not in me to conceal it.
BOSOLA Oh, foolish woman,
Couldst not thou have poisoned him?
JULIA 'Tis weakness
Too much to think what should have been done.
I go I know not whither. [*She dies*]
CARDINAL Wherefore com'st thou hither?
BOSOLA That I might find a great man like yourself,
Not out of his wits as the Lord Ferdinand,
To remember my service.
CARDINAL I'll have thee hewed[628] in pieces.
BOSOLA Make not yourself such a promise of that life
Which is not yours to dispose of.
CARDINAL Who placed thee here?
BOSOLA Her lust, as she intended.
CARDINAL Very well.
Now you know me for your fellow murderer.
BOSOLA And wherefore should you lay fair marble colors[629]
Upon your rotten purposes to me?
Unless you imitate some that do plot great treasons,
And when they have done, go hide themselves i'th' graves
Of those were actors in't?
CARDINAL No more. There is a fortune attends thee.
BOSOLA Shall I go sue to Fortune any longer?
'Tis the fool's pilgrimage.
CARDINAL I have honors in store for thee.
BOSOLA There are a-many ways that conduct to seeming
Honor, and some of them very dirty ones.
CARDINAL Throw to the devil
Thy melancholy. The fire burns well;
What need we keep a-stirring of 't and make
A greater smother?[630] Thou wilt kill Antonio?
BOSOLA Yes.
CARDINAL Take up that body. [*Points to* JULIA'S *body*]
BOSOLA I think I shall
Shortly grow the common bier[631] for churchyards.
CARDINAL I will allow thee some dozen of attendants
To aid thee in the murder.
BOSOLA Oh, by no means. Physicians that apply horse-leeches to any rank swelling use to cut off their tails, that the blood may run through them the faster. Let me have no train when I go to shed blood, lest it make me have a greater when I ride to the gallows.[632]
CARDINAL Come to me after midnight to help to remove that body to her own lodging. I'll give out she died o'th' plague; 'twill breed the less enquiry after her death.
BOSOLA Where's Castruchio, her husband?
CARDINAL He's rode to Naples to take possession
Of Antonio's citadel.

628 276 hewed: chopped
629 281 fair marble colors: an artificial finish to make wood appear like marble; such finishes were commonly found in early modern amphitheatres, and can be seen today on the oak pillars at the new Globe Theatre in London
630 292–4 The fire … greater smother?: why stop to worry when everything is going according to plan?
631 296 bier: moveable platform on which a corpse is placed before burial
632 299–301 Physicians that … the gallows: Physicians who use leeches to reduce swelling cut off their tails so that they can draw blood more efficiently. Let me commit this murder by myself ("have no train") so that I am less likely to be caught—or, if I am caught, others are not punished with me

BOSOLA Believe me, you have done a very happy turn.
CARDINAL Fail not to come. There is the master key
Of our lodgings— [*Gives him the key*] —and by that you may conceive
What trust I plant in you. *Exit*
BOSOLA You shall find me ready.
Oh poor Antonio! Though nothing be so needful
To thy estate[633] as pity, yet I find
Nothing so dangerous. I must look to my footing.
In such slippery ice-pavements, men had need
To be frost-nailed[634] well; they may break their necks else.
The precedent's here afore me. How this man
Bears up in blood![635] Seems fearless! Why, 'tis well.
Security some men call the suburbs of hell,
Only a dead wall between.[636] Well, good Antonio,
I'll seek thee out, and all my care shall be
To put thee into safety from the reach
Of these most cruel biters that have got
Some of thy blood already. It may be
I'll join with thee in a most just revenge.
The weakest arm is strong enough that strikes
With the sword of justice. Still, methinks the Duchess
Haunts me. There! There!—'Tis nothing but my melancholy.
Oh penitence, let me truly taste thy cup
That throws men down, only to raise them up.
Exit

Act V, scene iii

[*Enter*] ANTONIO [*and*] DELIO [*and* ECHO *from the* DUCHESS' *grave*]

DELIO Yond's the cardinal's window. This fortification
Grew from the ruins of an ancient abbey;
And to yond side o'th' river lies a wall,
Piece of a cloister,[637] which, in my opinion,
Gives the best echo that you ever heard.
So hollow and so dismal, and withal
So plain in the distinction of our words
That many have supposed it is a spirit
That answers.
ANTONIO I do love these ancient ruins.
We never tread upon them, but we set
Our foot upon some reverend history,
And questionless, here in this open court,
Which now lies naked to the injuries
Of stormy weather, some men lie interred
Loved[638] the church so well, and gave so largely to't,
They thought it should have canopied their bones
Till doomsday. But all things have their end:

633 312 estate: condition, situation
634 315 To be frost-nailed: to have nails on the soles of their boots
635 317 Bears up in blood: maintains his courage
636 318–19 Security some . . . wall between: it is dangerous to be too secure in one's salvation; the image is of an unbroken ("dead") wall that obscures the view of hell when one feels secure
637 4 cloister: a covered walkway that runs along the outer walls of a monastery or church
638 15 Loved: who loved

Churches and cities, which have diseases like to men,
Must have like death that we have.
ECHO [*From within*][639] *Like death that we have.*
DELIO Now the echo hath caught you.
ANTONIO It groaned, methought, and gave
A very deadly accent.[640]
ECHO *Deadly accent.*
DELIO I told you 'twas a pretty one. You may make it[641]
A huntsman or a falconer, a musician,
Or a thing of sorrow.
ECHO *A thing of sorrow.*
ANTONIO Ay, sure, that suits it best.
ECHO *That suits it best.*
ANTONIO 'Tis very like my wife's voice.
ECHO *Ay, wife's voice.*
DELIO Come, let's us walk farther from't;
I would not have you go to th' cardinal's tonight.
Do not.
ECHO *Do not.*
DELIO Wisdom doth not more moderate wasting sorrow
Than time. Take time for't. Be mindful of thy safety.
ECHO *Be mindful of thy safety.*
ANTONIO Necessity compels me.
Make scrutiny throughout the passes
Of your own life; you'll find it impossible
To fly your fate.
ECHO *Oh, fly your fate.*
DELIO Hark! The dead stones seem to have pity on you
And give you good counsel.
ANTONIO Echo, I will not talk with thee;
For thou art a dead thing.
ECHO *Thou art a dead thing.*
ANTONIO My Duchess is asleep now,
And her little ones, I hope sweetly. Oh, heaven!
Shall I never see her more?
ECHO *Never see her more.*
ANTONIO I marked not one repetition of the echo
But that; and on the sudden, a clear light
Presented me a face folded in sorrow.
DELIO Your fancy,[642] merely.
ANTONIO Come, I'll be out of this ague.
For to live thus is not indeed to live.
It is a mockery and abuse of life.
I will not henceforth save myself by halves:
Lose all, or nothing.
DELIO Your own virtue save you!
I'll fetch your eldest son and second you.
It may be that the sight of his own blood
Spread in so sweet a figure may beget

639 19 SD *From within*: it may be the Duchess speaking these lines (as is sometimes the case in modern productions); the actor who played the Duchess could be in the tiring house at stage or upper stage level
640 22 deadly accent: death-like voice
641 23 make it: imagine that it is
642 47 fancy: imagination

The more compassion.[643] However, fare you well.
Though in our miseries fortune have a part,
Yet in our noble sufferings she hath none.
Contempt of pain, that we may call our own.

Exeunt

Act V, scene iv

[*Enter*] CARDINAL, PESCARA, MALATESTE, RODERIGO [*and*] GRISOLAN [*with torches*]

CARDINAL You shall not watch tonight by the sick prince;
His grace is very well recovered.
MALATESTE Good my lord, suffer[644] us.
CARDINAL Oh, by no means.
The noise and change of object in his eye
Doth more distract him. I pray, all to bed,
And though you hear him in his violent fit,
Do not rise, I entreat you.
PESCARA So sir, we shall not.
CARDINAL Nay, I must have you promise
Upon your honors, for I was enjoined to't
By himself, and he seemed to urge it sensibly.
PESCARA Let our honors bind this trifle.[645]
CARDINAL Nor any of your followers.
MALATESTE Neither.
CARDINAL It may be to make trial of your promise,
When he's asleep, myself will rise and feign
Some of his mad tricks, and cry out for help,
And feign myself in danger.
MALATESTE If your throat were cutting,[646]
I'd not come at you, now I have protested against it.
CARDINAL Why, I thank you. [*Stands apart*]
GRISOLAN 'Twas a foul storm tonight.
RODERIGO The lord Ferdinand's chamber shook like an osier.[647]
MALATESTE 'Twas nothing but pure kindness in the devil
To rock his own child.[648] *Exeunt* [*all but the* CARDINAL]
CARDINAL The reason why I would not suffer these
About my brother is because at midnight
I may with better privacy, convey
Julia's body to her own lodging. Oh, my conscience!
I would pray now, but the devil takes away my heart
For having any confidence in prayer. [*Enter* BOSOLA *unseen*]
About this hour, I appointed Bosola
To fetch the body. When he hath served my turn,
He dies. *Exit*
BOSOLA Hah? 'twas the cardinal's voice. I heard him name,
"Bosola" and my death. Listen! I hear one's footing.[649]

643 53–5 It may . . . more compassion: perhaps if Ferdinand sees his own nephew, he will be moved to compassion
644 3 suffer: allow
645 11 We swear on our honors to respect this small request
646 16 cutting: being cut
647 19 osier: a type of willow tree
648 21 his own child: i.e. Ferdinand
649 32 footing: footsteps

[*Enter* FERDINAND]

FERDINAND Strangling is a very quiet death.
BOSOLA [*Aside*] —Nay then I see, I must stand upon my guard.
FERDINAND What say to that? Whisper, softly, do you agree to't?
So it must be done i'th' dark. The cardinal
Would not for a thousand pounds the doctor should see it. *Exit*
BOSOLA My death is plotted; here's the consequence of murder.
"We value not desert, nor Christian breath,
When we know black deeds must be cured with death."

[*Enter*] ANTONIO [*and*] SERVANT

SERVANT Here stay, sir, and be confident, I pray.
I'll fetch you a dark lantern. *Exit*
ANTONIO Could I take him at his prayers,
There were hope of pardon.
BOSOLA [*Aside*] —Fall right my sword:
I'll not give thee so much leisure, as to pray. [*Stabs* ANTONIO]
ANTONIO Oh, I am gone! Thou hast ended a long suit,
In a minute.
BOSOLA What art thou?[650]
ANTONIO A most wretched thing
That only have thy benefit in death,
To appear myself.[651]

[*Re-Enter*] SERVANT [*with a dark lantern*]

SERVANT Where are you, sir?
ANTONIO Very near my home. Bosola?
SERVANT Oh, misfortune.
BOSOLA Smother thy pity, thou art dead else. Antonio?
The man I would have saved 'bove mine own life!
We are merely the stars' tennis-balls: struck and banded[652]
Which way please them. Oh, good Antonio,
I'll whisper one thing in thy dying ear
Shall make thy heart break quickly. Thy fair Duchess
And two sweet children—
ANTONIO Their very names
Kindle a little life in me.
BOSOLA —Are murdered!
ANTONIO Some men have wished to die
At the hearing of sad tidings; I am glad
That I shall do't in sadness. I would not now
Wish my wounds balmed[653] nor healed; for I have no use
To put my life to. In all our quest of greatness,
Like wanton boys, whose pastime is their care,[654]
We follow after bubbles blown in th'air.

650 47 What art thou?: In this moment, Bosola thinks he has stabbed Ferdinand; because it is so dark, he mistakenly kills Antonio. It is only when the servant returns with a lantern that Bosola can see whom he has killed

651 47–9 A most … appear myself: a most wretched thing, allowed to experience the benefit you've conferred upon me—to see myself for what I am—only in death

652 53 banded: bandied

653 62 balmed: anointed with healing ointments

654 64 whose pastime is their care: whose only worry is the game they are playing

Pleasure of life, what is't? Only the good hours
Of an ague, merely a preparative to rest,
To endure vexation. I do not ask
The process of my death; only commend me
To Delio.
BOSOLA Break, heart!
ANTONIO And let my son fly the courts of princes. [*He dies*]
BOSOLA Thou seem'st to have loved Antonio?
SERVANT I brought him hither
To have reconciled him to the cardinal.
BOSOLA I do not ask thee that.
Take him up, if thou tender[655] thine own life,
And bear him where the Lady Julia
Was wont to lodge. Oh, my fate moves swift.
I have this cardinal in the forge[656] already;
Now I'll bring him to th' hammer. Oh direful misprision![657]
I will not imitate things glorious,
No more than base. I'll be mine own example. [*To* SERVANT]
On, on and look thou represent, for silence,
The thing thou bear'st.

Exeunt [*with the body of* ANTONIO]

Act V, scene v

[*Enter*] CARDINAL, *with a book*

CARDINAL I am puzzled in a question about hell:
He[658] says in hell there's one material fire,
And yet it shall not burn all men alike.
Lay him by. [*Puts book down*] How tedious is a guilty conscience?
When I look into the fishponds in my garden,
Methinks I see a thing armed with a rake[659]
That seems to strike at me— [*Enter* BOSOLA] Now? Art thou come?
Thou look'st ghastly.
There sits in thy face some great determination,
Mixed with some fear.
BOSOLA Thus it lightens[660] into action;
I am come to kill thee.
CARDINAL Ha? Help! Our guard!
BOSOLA Thou art deceived. They are out of thy howling.
CARDINAL Hold, and I will faithfully divide
Revenues with thee.
BOSOLA Thy prayers and proffers[661]
Are both unseasonable.
CARDINAL Raise the watch!
We are betrayed!
BOSOLA I have confined your flight.
I'll suffer your retreat to Julia's chamber,

655 76 tender: care for
656 79 forge: blacksmith's furnace or workshop
657 80 direful misprision: dreadful error
658 2 He: the author of the book the cardinal is reading
659 6 rake: sharp iron instrument
660 10 lightens: flashes
661 14 proffers: offers; proposals

But no further.
CARDINAL Help! We are betrayed!

[*Enter above*] MALATESTE, PESCARA, RODERIGO [*and*] GRISOLAN, [*with torches*]

MALATESTE Listen!
CARDINAL My dukedom for rescue!
RODERIGO Fie upon his counterfeiting!
MALATESTE Why, 'tis not the cardinal.
RODERIGO Yes, yes, 'tis he.
But I'll see him hanged ere I'll go down to him.
CARDINAL Here's a plot upon me! I am assaulted! I am lost
Unless some rescue!
GRISOLAN He doth this pretty well,
But it will not serve to laugh me out of mine honor.
CARDINAL The sword's at my throat!
RODERIGO You would not bawl[662] so loud then.
MALATESTE Come, come, let's go to bed. He told us thus much aforehand.[663]
PESCARA He wished you should not come at him, but believe't,
The accent of the voice sounds not in jest.
I'll down to him, howsoever, and with engines
Force ope the doors. [*Exit* PESCARA, *above*]
RODERIGO Let's follow him aloof,[664]
And note how the cardinal will laugh at him.
[*Exeunt* MALATESTE, RODERIGO *and* GRISOLAN, *above*]

[*Enter*] *Servant with* ANTONIO's *body*

BOSOLA There's for you first,
'Cause you shall not unbarricade the door
To let in rescue. *He kills the Servant*
CARDINAL What cause hast thou to pursue my life?
BOSOLA Look there!
CARDINAL Antonio?
BOSOLA Slain by my hand unwittingly.
Pray and be sudden.[665] When thou killed'st thy sister,
Thou took'st from Justice her most equal balance,
And left her naught but her sword.[666]
CARDINAL Oh, mercy!
BOSOLA Now it seems thy greatness was only outward—
For thou fall'st faster of thyself than calamity
Can drive thee. I'll not waste longer time— [*Stabs him*] There!
CARDINAL Thou hast hurt me:
BOSOLA Again! [*Stabs him again*]
CARDINAL Shall I die like a leveret?[667]
Without any resistance? Help! Help! Help!
I am slain!

662 25 bawl: cry out
663 26 He told us thus much aforehand: he told us earlier that he might test us in this way
664 30 aloof: at a distance
665 36 be sudden: do it quickly
666 37–8 Thou took'st … her sword: a traditional image of Justice was a blindfolded woman holding a set of scales ("most equal balance") in one hand and a sword in the other
667 42 leveret: young hare; one without a spirit

[*Enter*] FERDINAND

FERDINAND Th'alarum? Give me a fresh horse.
Rally the vanguard[668] or the day is lost.
Yield, yield! I give you the honor of arms,
Shake my sword over you. Will you yield?
CARDINAL Help me! I am your brother.
FERDINAND The devil?
My brother fight upon the adverse party?[669]

He wounds the CARDINAL *and in the scuffle gives* BOSOLA *his death wound*

There flies your ransom!
CARDINAL Oh, justice!
I suffer now for what hath former been,
"Sorrow is held the eldest child of sin."
FERDINAND Now you're brave, fellows! Caesar's fortune was harder than Pompey's: Caesar died in the arms of prosperity, Pompey at the feet of disgrace.[670] You both died in the field. The pain's nothing. Pain many times is taken away with the apprehension of greater, as the toothache with the sight of a barber that comes to pull it out.[671] There's philosophy for you.
BOSOLA Now my revenge is perfect. Sink, thou main cause
Of my undoing! (*He kills* FERDINAND) The last part of my life,
Hath done me best service.
FERDINAND Give me some wet hay[672]—I am broken-winded.
I do account this world but a dog kennel.
I will vault credit[673] and affect[674] high pleasures
Beyond death.
BOSOLA He seems to come to himself
Now he's so near the bottom.
FERDINAND My sister! Oh, my sister! There's the cause on't.
"Whether we fall by ambition, blood, or lust,
Like diamonds, we are cut with our own dust." [*He dies*]
CARDINAL Thou hast thy payment too.
BOSOLA Yes, I hold my weary soul in my teeth,
'Tis ready to part from me. I do glory
That thou, which stood'st like a huge pyramid
Begun upon a large and ample base,
Shalt end in a little point—a kind of nothing.

[*Enter below*] PESCARA, MALATESTE, RODERIGO [*and*] GRISOLAN

PESCARA How now, my lord?
MALATESTE Oh, sad disaster!
RODERIGO How comes this?
BOSOLA Revenge for the Duchess of Malfi, murdered
By th'Aragonian brethren; for Antonio,
Slain by his hand; for lustful Julia,
Poisoned by this man; and lastly, for myself
That was an actor in the main of all,

668 45 vanguard: the military division at the forefront of an attack
669 49 upon the adverse party: for the enemy
670 53–4 Caesar's fortune … of disgrace: Caesar's death was harder than Pompey's because he died at the height of his power; Pompey died after being defeated by Caesar and fleeing ignominiously to Egypt
671 56 barber that comes to pull it out: tooth-pulling was one of many medical tasks performed by early modern barbers
672 60 wet hay: medicinal for horses who had difficulty breathing
673 62 vault credit: exceed what would be expected of or believed about me
674 62 affect: aspire to

Much 'gainst mine own good nature, yet i'th' end
Neglected.[675]
PESCARA How now, my lord?
CARDINAL Look to my brother.
He gave us these large wounds as we were struggling
Here i'th' rushes.[676] And now, I pray, let me
Be laid by and never thought of. [*He dies*]
PESCARA How fatally, it seems, he did withstand
His own rescue!
MALATESTE Thou wretched thing of blood,
How came Antonio by his death?
BOSOLA In a mist.[677] I know not how.
Such a mistake, as I have often seen
In a play. Oh, I am gone,
We are only like dead walls[678] or vaulted graves,
That, ruined, yields no echo. Fare you well.
It may be pain but no harm to me to die
In so good a quarrel. Oh, this gloomy world—
In what a shadow or deep pit of darkness
Doth womanish and fearful mankind live?
Let worthy minds ne'er stagger in distrust
To suffer death or shame for what is just.
Mine is another voyage. [*He dies*]
PESCARA The noble Delio, as I came to th' palace,
Told me of Antonio's being here and showed me
A pretty gentleman, his son and heir.

[*Enter* DELIO *with the* DUCHESS's *eldest son*]

MALATESTE Oh sir, you come too late.
DELIO I heard so, and
Was armed for't ere I came. Let us make noble use
Of this great ruin,[679] and join all our force
To establish this young hopeful gentleman
In's mother's right.[680] These wretched eminent things[681]
Leave no more fame[682] behind 'em than should one
Fall in a frost and leave his print in snow:
As soon as the sun shines, it ever melts,
Both form and matter. I have ever thought
Nature doth nothing so great for great men,
As when she's pleased to make them lords of truth:
"Integrity of life is fame's best friend,
Which nobly, beyond death, shall crown the end."

Exeunt

FINIS.

675 80–81 yet i'th' end/Neglected: which [i.e. his good nature] I ultimately neglected
676 83 rushes: dried stalks of waterside plants that were strewn on the floors of rooms in early modern English houses
677 88 mist: confusion
678 91 dead walls: walls without openings
679 105 this great ruin: this tragic situation
680 107 In's mother's right: as his mother's rightful heir
681 107 wretched eminent things: the Aragonian brothers
682 108 fame: legacy, reputation; it is also implied that the brothers leave no heirs

11 Thomas Middleton, *Women Beware Women*

First performed c. 1613–21

First printed 1657

Edited by Roberta Barker

At the climax of Thomas Middleton's *Women Beware Women*, deadly mayhem infiltrates the stately rhythms of court theater. The performance in question is a "marriage-triumph": a masque staged by a group of aristocratic performers to celebrate the "hasty nuptials" of the Duke of Florence to his recently widowed mistress, Bianca (IV.ii. 150–51). With its lofty goddess, heartsick shepherds, and beautiful nymph—not to mention its bow-bearing cupids and showers of divine largesse—the masque appears at first sight to be a predictable compendium of spectacle, flattery, and neoclassical romance. As it unfolds, however, all hell breaks loose. The goddess slays the nymph with a hail of burning gold, not realizing that the nymph has already poisoned her with a cloud of toxic incense. As the ducal couple watches, one lovesick shepherd is shot by the cupids' poisoned arrows, while the other unexpectedly falls to his death through a trap door. Finally, just as this fatal performance seems to be winding down, the duke himself is felled by a gulp of poisoned wine—unwittingly administered, as it transpires, by his new bride, who had meant to murder his brother. The marriage-triumph, designed to affirm established norms of class and gender, turns out to be a stage upon which, as the duke puts it, "great mischiefs/Mask in expected pleasures" (V.ii. 171–2). As such, it squares perfectly with the complex Jacobean tragedy to which it serves as denouement—for although *Women Beware Women* appears to affirm the "expected pleasures" of familiar theatrical tropes and moral precepts, both its form and its content permit a far more subversive reading.

The many debates surrounding *Women Beware Women* begin with its theatrical origins. The play was first published in a small, affordable octavo edition in 1657. At this time, London's public theaters were closed by order of Oliver Cromwell's government; one can imagine some shoppers buying the little volume with nostalgia for the outrageous scenes of sex and violence they had once enjoyed on the now-illicit stage. The volume, entitled *Two New Playes*, featured *Women Beware Women* alongside the tragicomedy *More Dissemblers Besides Women*; the author was noted on the title page as *Tho. Middleton, Gent.* Unfortunately, unlike many others in the period, this title page fails to mention the acting company that first performed these plays. We know that the King's Men, the most celebrated company of early modern London, played *More Dissemblers Besides Women* at the court of King James I in 1624 (Wiggins, 2016: 363). Since their prestigious name is not offered as a selling point on the title page of the 1657 octavo, it seems reasonable to guess that they did not also perform in *Women Beware Women*.

One likely candidate for that honor is the Lady Elizabeth's Men, which was founded in 1611 and had the distinction of being composed largely of former boy players from both the King's Men and a number of children's companies. *Women Beware Women* shares many traits with Thomas Middleton's London comedy *A Chaste Maid in Cheapside*, which was first performed by the Lady Elizabeth's Men in about 1613. The company had recently absorbed a troupe of boys, the Children of Whitefriars, and *Chaste Maid*'s large cast, which features many prominent female roles, could reflect this influx of new boy players. Some scholars, including Richard Dutton, have theorized that *Women Beware Women* may have been written for this same large group of actors around 1613/14 (Dutton, 1999: xxi). Others, such as John Jowett, have pointed to allusions in *Women Beware Women* that seem to indicate sources that post-date this era (Jowett, 2007: 416). Like many previous scholars, Jowett suggests 1618–21 as the most likely dates for its premiere. If so, the play's text may contain discernable traces of its early actors. For instance, in Act III of *Women Beware Women* the Ward declares of Isabella, "The ape's so little/I shall scarce feel her; I have seen almost/As tall as she sold in the fair for ten pence" (III.ii. 68–70). In *The Spanish Gypsy*, a tragicomedy written for the Lady Elizabeth's Men by a group of collaborators including Middleton and performed in 1623, Pretiosa is similarly described as a "little ape" (I.v. 115) and "little fairy" (I.v. 120). Might these very similar descriptors reflect the presence of a single boy player—slightly built but prodigiously gifted, especially in singing and dancing—who played both Isabella and Pretiosa? The other main female roles in *The Spanish Gypsy*—Eugenia, the old mother of the gypsies; Cardochia, the scheming hostess; and Clara, the victim of a savage rape who marries her attacker—closely parallel those of the Widow, Livia, and Bianca in *Women Beware Women*. Still, such links remain inconclusive. Like the many other arguments adduced in favor of one date or the other for *Women Beware Women*, neither the play's parallels with *A Chaste Maid in Cheapside* nor its ties to *The Spanish Gypsy* allow us definitively to pinpoint its first performance.

Perhaps most interesting in this context is the fact that both arguments hinge on the importance of female characters—and of the boys who played them on the early modern English stage—to Middleton's tragedy and the theater for which he wrote it. As Jowett writes in his introduction to the play, "Middleton must have been especially confident in the strength of the envisaged company's boy actors, for few plays of the period have three more demanding female roles" (Jowett, 2007: 1488). The role of Livia, the witty and cynical widow who engineers many of the play's intrigues, offers a particularly rich set of histrionic opportunities, and it is one that has proved attractive to a number of leading actresses of the modern stage, including most recently Penelope Wilton (Royal Shakespeare Company, 2006) and Harriet Walter (Royal National Theatre, 2010). At 581 lines, Livia's is the largest part in the play. The scene in which she seduces the bewildered young clerk Leantio (one of the few male characters whose part comes close to hers in size) suggests that Middleton must have had considerable faith in the charisma of the boy who created her, who is called upon to stand up to—and eventually to overwhelm—his older male colleague. But why, the talents of such young actors notwithstanding, should Middleton have chosen to focus this tragedy so closely on the figures and fates of women?

We might begin to answer this question by considering the play's title. From the first, it suggests a sensationalist emphasis on female viciousness, treachery, and cruelty that is corroborated by the tragedy's plot. Livia cons Isabella into incest with Hippolito and betrays Bianca into the hands of the lascivious duke. The Widow cluelessly plays chess and chomps sweetmeats while her daughter-in-law is raped and debauched. Once driven to sin, Bianca and Isabella prove just as capable at it as their elders, not only committing adultery but also plotting murder. As the play's skullduggeries reach their peak, the women themselves condemn their gender's supposed duplicity. Isabella, called upon to conceal her loathing for Livia, mutters, "Well, I had a mother;/I can dissemble too" (IV.ii. 170-71). Dying, Bianca apologizes to the husband who tried to possess her and mourns the duke who raped her; she reserves her blame for Livia, declaring, "In this belief I die:/Like our own sex, we have no enemy, no enemy" (V.ii. 214–15). The presence of boy actors on the early modern English stage has often been ascribed to English society's terror of just such "feminine" characteristics: of women's corruptibility, sensuality, and talent for dissembling. Better maintain an all-male theater, the logic is supposed to have run, than risk placing female actors onstage to seduce audiences with the deceptive arts of the performer. Significantly, Middleton's imagined version of a dark, Medici-ruled Florence is a world not unlike that of James I's court, in which women *did* perform. Here as in the Jacobean court, noble ladies wield power behind the scenes. Eventually, they appear onstage in their own persons in the "marriage-triumph," just as James I's spouse, Anna of Denmark, and her ladies did in a sequence of lavish court masques. Middleton thus offers a tragic view of women's performance traditions that would later shape the comic vision of Shirley's *The Bird in a Cage*. Moving from covert sin to brazen display of themselves as actresses and adulteresses, the anti-heroines of *Women Beware Women* seem at first sight to bear out all the anti-feminist clichés that worked to keep actresses off of the early modern English public stage.

A closer look at the play's structure and rhetoric, however, hints at a more complicated approach to gender relations. The men of this world are no more virtuous than the women; indeed, the social order they promote does more to force women into vice than to protect them from it. Far from being represented simply as depraved temptresses, the young women, Bianca and Isabella, begin *Women Beware Women* by protesting their allegiance to strict patriarchal definitions of feminine virtue. Leaving her wealthy family for the impoverished Leantio, Bianca protests that she is "rich" in her husband's love (I.i. 128) even as he declares his intention to hide her from the world like a valuable possession. Forced into a lucrative marriage with the idiotic Ward by her equally foolish father, Isabella sighs that she is "born with that obedience/ That must submit unto a father's will" (II.i. 86–7). She laments that "[m]en buy their slaves, but women buy their masters" (II.i. 173)—though the Ward treats her frankly as *his* purchase when he inspects her like a horse at market in III.iii. Trapped in this marriage, Isabella decides to exploit it in order to pursue her affair with the man she temporarily allows herself to believe is not her uncle. Bianca, having suffered the duke's assault, similarly decides that she has no choice but to embrace her enforced dishonor, crying, "Come, poison all at once!" (II.ii. 424). Rape traps her—like Chrotilda in Heminge's later *Fatal Contract* (included in this anthology), which *Women Beware Women* may have influenced—in a fatal cycle of desire, hatred, and revenge. The twice-widowed Livia, who implies that she has seen her fill of such usage, sums up the logic of the women's actions when she declares that men taste

> many sundry dishes
> That we poor wretches never lay our lips to:
> As obedience, forsooth, subjection, duty, and such kickshaws,
> All of our making, but served in to them.
> And if we lick a finger then sometimes,
> We are not to blame: your best cooks use it.
>
> (I.ii. 40–45)

In the end, she implies, women embrace sin out of sheer frustration with their own subservience. When she herself engages in an affair with Leantio, her low-born lover is quickly killed by her brother Hippolito, who is hardly innocent of sexual misdemeanors. All of Middleton's characters are fallen, but the women (and the lower-class man) bear more than their fair share of punishment and condemnation.

In these terms, the play's violent climax can be read as the product of female rage. Billed as a performative celebration of love, marriage, and noble status, the culminating masque mutates into a savage parody of itself in which women do the lion's share of the killing and the nobility of Florence is "brought to nothing" (V.ii. 147). Arguably, *Women Beware Women* is founded upon a similarly subversive dramaturgical logic. Even as it appears to condemn women's evil deeds, Middleton's tragedy reveals the self-defeating cruelty of the patriarchal hierarchies that drive women to sin. Even as it is structured by the social conventions that exclude female actors from the stage, it gives female characters lines that expose the despair and fury of women trapped in a system that excludes them. Like the marriage-triumph whose "expected pleasures" mask a storm of vengeance, it hides a stinging and wide-ranging social critique beneath its façade of glib misogyny. If it bids women beware women, it also bids its Jacobean audience beware the deadly fruits of a society that oppresses, objectifies, and assaults them.

Textual note

The copy-text for this edition is the octavo volume printed by Thomas Newcomb for Humphrey Moseley in 1657, in which *Women Beware Women* appears after *More Dissemblers Besides Women*. My text is based upon the more complete of the two versions held by the British Library (shelfmark 643 b.37). As the play's previous editors have noted, *Women Beware Women* was generally very well printed in its first edition, which may be based upon a scribal copy of the author's manuscript (Carroll, 1994: xxxv). Act and scene divisions are consistently and clearly marked in the 1657 octavo; this edition follows these divisions. Stage directions, too, are generally clear and relatively copious in the 1657 octavo, at least until the final masque scene, when they become rarer and less lucid. I have tried to add editorial directions sparingly and only where necessary to clarify the action for the reader. The octavo consistently uses some rather idiosyncratic contractions—"ev'r" rather than "e'er," for example—that I have chosen to retain in the belief that they fit a play whose music is more hard-edged than soft. The modern editions that proved of special assistance in the preparation of this text are cited below.

Further reading

Editions

Carroll, William C. (ed.) (1994) *Women Beware Women*, London: A & C Black.

Dutton, Richard (ed.) (1999) *Women Beware Women and Other Plays*, Oxford: Oxford University Press.

Gill, Roma (ed.) (1968) *Women Beware Women*, London: New Mermaids.

Jowett, John (ed.) (2007) "*Women, Beware Women*," in Gary Taylor and John Lavagnino (eds), *Thomas Middleton: The Collected Works*, Oxford: Clarendon Press.

Mulryne, J. R. (ed.) (1975) *Women Beware Women*, London: Methuen.

Critical and contextual reading

Dawson, Anthony B. (1987) "*Women Beware Women* and the Economy of Rape," *Studies in English Literature* 27: 303–20.

Detmer-Goebel, Emily (2007) "What More Could Woman Do?: Dramatizing Consent in Heywood's *Rape of Lucrece* and Middleton's *Women Beware Women*," *Women's Studies* 36: 141–59.

Jowett, John (2007) "*Women, Beware Women*: Summer 1621," in Gary Taylor and John Lavagnino (eds), *Thomas Middleton and Early Modern Textual Culture: A Companion to The Collected Works*, Oxford: Clarendon Press, 414–16.

Middleton, Thomas, with John Ford, Thomas Dekker, and William Rowley (2007) "*The Spanish Gypsy*," in Gary Taylor and John Lavagnino (eds), *Thomas Middleton: The Collected Works*, Oxford: Clarendon Press, 1723–65.

Mulryne, J.R. and Margaret Shewring (2007) "Dancing Towards Death: Masques and Entertainments in London and Florence as Precedents for Thomas Middleton's *Women Beware Women*," *Dance Research* 25: 134–43.

Nicol, David (2012) *Middleton and Rowley: Forms of Collaboration in the Jacobean Playhouse*, Toronto: University of Toronto Press.

Potter, John (1982) "'In Time of Sports': Masques and Masking in Middleton's *Women Beware Women*," *Papers on Language and Literature* 18: 368–83.

Tricomi, Albert H. (1989) "Middleton's 'Women Beware Women' as Anticourt Drama," *Modern Language Studies* 19: 65–77.

Wiggins, Martin with Catherine Richardson (2016) *British Drama, 1533–1642: A Catalogue*, vol. VII: 1617–1623, Oxford: Oxford University Press.

Women Beware Women (c. 1613–21)

Dramatis personae[1]

DUKE OF FLORENCE
LORD CARDINAL, *brother to the Duke*
FABRITIO, *father to Isabella; brother to Livia and Hippolito*
HIPPOLITO, *brother to Fabritio and Livia; uncle to Isabella*
GUARDIANO, *uncle to the foolish Ward*
The WARD, *a rich young heir*
LEANTIO, *a factor,*[2] *husband to Bianca*[3]
SORDIDO, *the Ward's man*
LIVIA, *sister to Fabritio and Hippolito; aunt to Isabella*
ISABELLA, *daughter of Fabritio; niece to Livia and Hippolito*
BIANCA, *Leantio's wife*
The WIDOW, *Leantio's mother*

Two Cardinals more, A Lord, States[4] *of Florence, Citizens, A Prentice,*[5] *Boys, A Messenger, Servants, Two Ladies, Lords, Pages, Guards, and, in the masque, Hymen, Ganymede, Hebe, Two Nymphs, Cupids*

Act I, scene i

Enter LEANTIO *with* BIANCA, *and* MOTHER

MOTHER Thy sight was never yet more precious to me!
Welcome, with all the affection of a mother
That comfort[6] can express[7] from natural love.
Since thy birth-joy—a mother's chiefest gladness
After she's undergone her curse of sorrows[8]—
Thou wast not more dear to me than this hour
Presents thee to my heart. Welcome, again!
LEANTIO [*Aside*] 'Las, poor affectionate soul, how her joys speak to me!
I have observed it often, and I know it is
The fortune commonly of knavish children
To have the loving'st mothers.
MOTHER What's this gentlewoman?

1 Dramatis personae: adapted from the 1657 octavo edition (hereafter O)
2 *factor*: commercial agent for a merchant
3 *Bianca*: spelled "Brancha" throughout O. The character is based upon the real-life mistress of Francesco de' Medici, Bianca Capello (1548–87). Since the meter of Middleton's verse frequently demands that the name cover three syllables, all modern editors have assumed that Middleton intended "Bianca"
4 *states*: nobility
5 *Prentice*: apprentice
6 3 comfort: relief
7 3 express: distill or press out
8 5 curse of sorrows: the pains of childbirth, inflicted on women as punishment after Adam and Eve's original sin

LEANTIO Oh, you have named the most unvalued'st[9] purchase
That youth of man had ever knowledge of.
As often as I look upon that treasure
And know it to be mine—there lies the blessing!—
It joys me that I ever was ordained
To have a being, and to live 'mongst men:
Which is a fearful living, and a poor one,
Let a man truly think on't.
To have the toil and griefs of fourscore years
Put up in a white sheet, tied with two knots![10]
Methinks it should strike earthquakes in adulterers,
When ev'n the very sheets they commit sin in
May prove, for aught they know, all their last garments.
Oh, what a mark[11] were there for women then!
But beauty, able to content a conqueror
Whom earth could scarce content, keeps me in compass.[12]
I find no wish in me bent sinfully
To this man's sister, or to that man's wife;
In love's name let 'em keep their honesties[13]
And cleave to their own husbands, 'tis their duties.
Now, when I go to church, I can pray handsomely,[14]
Not come like gallants only to see faces,
As if lust went to market still[15] on Sundays.
I must confess I am guilty of one sin, mother,
More than I brought into the world with me;[16]
But that I glory in: 'tis theft, but noble
As ever greatness yet shot up withal.[17]
MOTHER How's that?
LEANTIO Never to be repented, mother,
Though sin be death;[18] I had died if I had not sinned.
And here's my masterpiece: do you now behold her![19]
Look on her well, she's mine. Look on her better;
Now say if't be not the best piece of theft
That ever was committed—and I have my pardon for't,
'Tis sealed[20] from heaven by marriage.
MOTHER Married to her!
LEANTIO You must keep counsel,[21] mother, I am undone else.
If it be known, I have lost her; do but think now
What that loss is: life's but a trifle to't.
From Venice her consent and I have brought her
From parents great in wealth, more now in rage.
But let storms spend their furies; now we have got
A shelter o'er our quiet innocent loves,

9 12 unvalued'st: invaluable; priceless
10 21 white sheet . . . two knots: a winding sheet or burial shroud, fastened by knots at head and feet
11 25 mark: example or model to follow
12 26–7 beauty, able . . . in compass: beauty, which can satisfy even the most ambitious conqueror, keeps me in check
13 30 honesties: good reputations; chastity
14 32 handsomely: properly; admirably
15 34 still: even
16 35–6 one sin . . . with me: one sin beyond original sin, of which all are guilty
17 37–8 'tis theft . . . up withal: as noble a theft as any great man has yet perpetrated in order to rise in the world
18 40 though sin be death: see Romans 6:23: "The wages of sin is death"
19 41 do you now behold her: have a look at her now
20 45 sealed: approved
21 46 keep counsel: keep our secret

We are contented. Little money sh'as brought me:
View but her face, you may see all her dowry,
Save that which lies locked up in hidden virtues,
Like jewels kept in cabinets.
MOTHER Y'are to blame,
If your obedience will give way to a check,[22]
To wrong such a perfection.
LEANTIO How?
MOTHER Such a creature,
To draw her from her fortune, which no doubt
At the full time might have proved rich and noble!
You know not what you have done. My life can give you
But little helps, and my death lesser hopes,
And hitherto your own means has but made shift
To keep you single, and that hardly too.[23]
What ableness have you to do her right, then,
In maintenance fitting her birth and virtues?
Which ev'ry woman of necessity looks for,
And most to go above it, not confined
By their conditions, virtues, bloods, or births,
But flowing to affections, wills, and humors.[24]
LEANTIO Speak low, sweet mother! You are able to spoil as many
As come within the hearing. If it be not
Your fortune to mar[25] all, I have much marvel.
I pray, do not you teach her to rebel
When she's in a good way to obedience:
To rise with other women in commotion[26]
Against their husbands for six gowns a year,
And so maintain their cause, when they're once up,[27]
In all things else that require cost enough.
They are all of 'em a kind of spirits soon raised,
But not so soon laid,[28] mother. As for example,
A woman's belly is got up in a trice;
A simple charge[29] ere it be laid down again!
So ever in all their quarrels and their courses.
And I'm a proud man, I hear nothing of 'em;[30]
They're very still, I thank my happiness,
And sound asleep. Pray, let not your tongue wake 'em.
If you can but rest quiet, she's contented
With all conditions that my fortunes bring her to:
To keep close[31] as a wife that loves her husband;
To go after the rate of my ability,
Not the licentious swinge of her own will,[32]

22 57 If your . . . a check: if you are obedient enough to listen to a rebuke
23 63–4 your own . . . hardly too: your own means have scarcely managed to maintain you as a bachelor
24 68–70 most to . . . and humors: most women seek to rise above their own social station; not satisfied with the condition they are born to, they follow their own wills, desires, and fancies
25 73 mar: ruin
26 76 commotion: rebellion; resistance
27 78 when they're once up: once they've gained power
28 80–81 spirits soon . . . soon laid: Leantio compares women's "spirits"—their tempers or desires—with "spirits" like ghosts and demons: easy to summon or "raise" (i.e. to incite to anger or desire) but hard to "lay" (i.e. to dismiss or satisfy)
29 83 A simple charge: an easy thing
30 85 I'm proud to say I hear none of these complaints
31 90 keep close: stay in seclusion
32 91–2 To go . . . own will: live within my means, rather than giving free rein ("swinge") to her own desires

Like some of her old school-fellows. She intends
To take out other works in a new sampler,
And frame the fashion of an honest love,[33]
Which knows no wants, but mocking poverty
Brings forth more children to make rich men wonder
At divine providence, that feeds mouths of infants
And sends them none to feed, but stuffs their rooms[34]
With fruitful bags,[35] their beds with barren wombs.
Good mother, make not you things worse than they are
Out of your too much openness; pray take heed on't,
Nor imitate the envy of old people
That strive to mar good sport because they are perfect.[36]
I would have you more pitiful to youth,
Especially to your own flesh and blood.
I'll prove an excellent husband, here's my hand:
Lay in provision, follow my business roundly,[37]
And make you a grandmother in forty weeks.
Go, pray salute her, bid her welcome cheerfully.
MOTHER Gentlewoman, thus much is a debt of courtesy
Which fashionable strangers pay each other
At a kind meeting [*Kisses* BIANCA]; then there's more than one,
Due to the knowledge I have of your nearness.[38] [*Kisses* BIANCA *again*]
I am bold to come again, and now salute you
By the name of daughter, which may challenge more
Than ordinary respect. [*Kisses* BIANCA *again*]
LEANTIO Why, this is well now,
And I think few mothers of threescore will mend it.[39]
MOTHER What I can bid you welcome to is mean,[40]
But make it all your own; we are full of wants,[41]
And cannot welcome worth.
LEANTIO Now this is scurvy,[42]
And spake as if a woman lacked her teeth.[43]
These old folks talk of nothing but defects,
Because they grow so full of 'em themselves.
BIANCA Kind mother, there is nothing can be wanting
To her that does enjoy all her desires.
Heaven send a quiet peace with this man's love,
And I am as rich as virtue can be poor,
Which were enough, after the rate of mind,
To erect temples for content placed here.[44]
I have forsook friends, fortunes, and my country,
And hourly I rejoice in't. Here's my friends,

33 94–5 take out . . . honest love: a sampler is a piece of embroidery that serves as a model to be copied. Bianca will offer a new model of feminine behavior, building ("framing") it upon honest love for her husband
34 99 their rooms: the rooms of childless rich people
35 100 fruitful bags: money-bags
36 104 perfect: blameless; chaste
37 108 follow my business roundly: pursue my work wholeheartedly
38 114 nearness: familial relationship with me
39 118 mend it: improve upon it
40 119 mean: poor; scanty
41 120 full of wants: full of defects; lacking in comforts
42 121 scurvy: rude; shabby
43 122 lacked her teeth: a sign of extreme age; also, a symptom of the disease scurvy
44 129–30 Which were . . . placed here: Bianca suggests that the riches of peace and her husband's love, if measured intellectually and not economically, will build her temples of happiness in this poor house

And few is the good number. Thy successes,
Howev'r they look, I will still name my fortunes;
Hopeful or spiteful, they shall all be welcome.
Who invites many guests has of all sorts,
As he that traffics[45] much drinks of all fortunes,
Yet they must all be welcome, and used[46] well.
I'll call this place the place of my birth now,
And rightly too, for here my love was born,
And that's the birthday of a woman's joys.
[*To* LEANTIO] You have not bid me welcome since I came.
LEANTIO That I did, questionless.
BIANCA No, sure. How was't?
I have quite forgot it.
LEANTIO [*Kissing her*] Thus.
BIANCA Oh sir, 'tis true;
Now I remember well: I have done thee wrong.
Pray take't again, sir. [*She kisses him*]
LEANTIO How many of these wrongs
Could I put up[47] in an hour? And turn up the glass[48]
For twice as many more!
MOTHER Will't please you to walk in, daughter?
BIANCA Thanks, sweet mother;
The voice of her that bare me is not more pleasing. *Exeunt* [MOTHER *and* BIANCA]
LEANTIO Though my own care[49] and my rich master's trust
Lay their commands both on my factorship,[50]
This day and night I'll know no other business
But her and her dear welcome. 'Tis a bitterness
To think upon tomorrow: that I must leave her
Still to the sweet hopes of the week's end;
That pleasure should be so restrained and curbed
After the course of[51] a rich work-master,
That never pays till Saturday night.
Marry, it comes together in a round sum then,
And does more good, you'll say. Oh fair-eyed Florence!
Didst thou but know what a most matchless jewel
Thou now art mistress of, a pride would take thee
Able to shoot destruction through the bloods
Of all thy youthful sons. But 'tis great policy[52]
To keep choice treasures in obscurest places;
Should we show thieves our wealth, 'twould make 'em bolder.
Temptation is a devil will not stick[53]
To fasten upon a saint; take heed of that.
The jewel is cased up[54] from all men's eyes.
Who could imagine, now, a gem were kept

45 137 traffics: trades
46 138 used: treated
47 147 put up: bear with; store
48 147 turn up the glass: turn over the hour-glass
49 151 care: conscientiousness; self-interest
50 152 factorship: job as a merchant's agent
51 158 After the course of: upon the bidding of
52 165 policy: cunning
53 168 will not stick: will not scruple
54 170 cased up: hidden in its case or box

Of that great value under this plain roof?
But how in times of absence? What assurance
Of this restraint then? Yes, yes: there's one with her.[55]
Old mothers know the world; and such as these,
When sons lock chests, are good to look to[56] keys.

Exit

Act I, scene ii

Enter GUARDIANO, FABRITIO, *and* LIVIA

GUARDIANO What, has your daughter seen him yet? Know you that?
FABRITIO No matter, she shall love him.
GUARDIANO Nay, let's have fair play.
He has been now my ward[57] some fifteen year,
And 'tis my purpose, as time calls upon me,[58]
By custom seconded and such moral virtues,
To tender[59] him a wife. Now, sir, this wife
I'd fain elect out of a daughter of yours.
You see my meaning's fair; if now this daughter
So tendered (let me come to your own phrase, sir)
Should offer to refuse him, I were hanseled.[60]
[*Aside*] Thus am I fain to calculate all my words
For the meridian[61] of a foolish old man,
To take[62] his understanding.—What do you answer, sir?
FABRITIO I say still she shall love him.
GUARDIANO Yet again?
And shall she have no reason for this love?
FABRITIO Why, do you think that women love with reason?
GUARDIANO [*Aside*] I perceive fools are not at all hours foolish,
No more than wise men wise.
FABRITIO I had a wife;
She ran mad for me. She had no reason for't,
For aught I could perceive. What think you, lady sister?
GUARDIANO [*Aside*] 'Twas a fit match, that,
Being both out of their wits.—A loving wife, it seemed
She strove to come as near you[63] as she could.
FABRITIO And if her daughter prove not mad for love too,
She takes not after her; nor after me,
If she prefer reason before my pleasure.
You're an experienced widow, lady sister,
I pray let your opinion come amongst us.
LIVIA I must offend you then, if truth will do't,
And take my niece's part, and call't injustice
To force her love to one she never saw.

55 174 one with her: Leantio trusts that his mother will guard Bianca
56 176 look to: look after
57 3 ward: minor child, usually an orphan, placed under the protection of a legal guardian
58 4 as time calls upon me: the Ward is almost at the legal age of majority, twenty-one; to profit financially from his marriage to a wealthy heiress, his guardian must arrange the match before the Ward reaches that age
59 6 tender: offer; sell
60 10 hanseled: given a lucky present (said ironically)
61 12 meridian: specific capacities or measure
62 13 take: catch
63 23 come as near you: be as like you

Maids should both see and like: all little enough!
If they love truly after that, 'tis well.
Counting[64] the time she takes one man, till death,
That's a hard task, I tell you; but one may
Enquire at three years' end, amongst young wives,
And mark how the game goes.
FABRITIO Why, is not man
Tied to the same observance, lady sister,
And in one woman?
LIVIA 'Tis enough for him.
Besides, he tastes of many sundry dishes
That we poor wretches never lay our lips to:
As obedience, forsooth, subjection, duty, and such kickshaws,[65]
All of our making, but served in to them.
And if we lick a finger then sometimes,
We are not to blame: your best cooks use it.[66]
FABRITIO Th'art a sweet lady, sister, and a witty—
LIVIA A witty! Oh, the bud of commendation
Fit for a girl of sixteen! I am blown,[67] man,
I should be wise by this time; and for instance,
I have buried my two husbands in good fashion,
And never mean more to marry.
GUARDIANO No? Why so, lady?
LIVIA Because the third shall never bury me.
I think I am more than witty; how think you, sir?
FABRITIO I have paid often fees to a counsellor
Has had a weaker brain.
LIVIA Then I must tell you,
Your money was soon parted.[68]
GUARDIANO Light her[69] now, brother!
LIVIA Where is my niece? Let her be sent for straight.
If you have any hope 'twill prove a wedding,
'Tis fit, i'faith, she should have one sight of him,
And stop upon't,[70] and not be joined in haste
As if they went to stock a new-found land.[71]
FABRITIO Look out[72] her uncle, and y'are sure of her.
Those two are nev'r asunder; they've been heard
In argument[73] at midnight; moonshine nights
Are noon days with them; they walk out their sleeps,[74]
Or rather at those hours appear like those
That walk in 'em,[75] for so they did to me.
Look you, I told you truth! They're like a chain:
Draw but one link, all follows.

64 34 counting: considering
65 42 kickshaws: fancy dishes
66 45 your best cooks use it: a proverb states that it is "an ill cook that cannot lick his own fingers." Livia suggests that since women are always serving things like obedience to men, they should have a chance to "taste" their own wares
67 48 blown: in full bloom
68 56 soon parted: evokes the proverb, "a fool and his money are soon parted"
69 56 Light her: enlighten her (Guardiano is again ironic)
70 60 stop upon't: pause on it; take time to reflect
71 61 stock a new-found land: poor colonists bound for newly settled territories were often married hastily in order to encourage propagation
72 62 Look out: find
73 64 argument: discussion
74 65 walk out their sleeps: go out walking together instead of sleeping
75 66–7 appear like … in 'em: appear like sleepwalkers

Enter HIPPOLITO *and* ISABELLA *the niece*

GUARDIANO Oh affinity,[76]
What piece of excellent workmanship art thou!
'Tis work clean wrought,[77] for there's no lust, but love, in't,
And that abundantly: when[78] in stranger things[79]
There is no love at all, but what lust brings.
FABRITIO [*To* ISABELLA] On with your mask,[80] for 'tis your part to see now,
And not be seen. Go to, make use of your time.
See what you mean to like; nay, and I charge you,
Like what you see. Do you hear me? There's no dallying:
The gentleman's almost twenty, and 'tis time
He were getting lawful heirs, and you a-breeding on 'em.
ISABELLA Good father!
FABRITIO Tell not me of tongues and rumors![81]
You'll say the gentleman is somewhat simple:
The better for a husband, were you wise,
For those that marry fools live ladies' lives.[82]
On with the mask, I'll hear no more. He's rich;
The fool's hid under bushels.[83]
LIVIA Not so hid, neither;
But here's a foul great piece of him, methinks.
What will he be, when he comes altogether?[84]

Enter the WARD *with a trap-stick,*[85] *and* SORDIDO *his man*

WARD Beat him?
I beat him out o'th'field with his own cat-stick,
Yet gave him the first hand.[86]
SORDIDO Oh strange!
WARD I did it!
Then he set jacks on me.[87]
SORDIDO What, my lady's tailor?[88]
WARD Ay, and I beat him too.
SORDIDO Nay, that's no wonder;
He's used to beating.[89]
WARD Nay, I tickled him[90]
When I came once to my tippings.[91]

76 69 affinity: kinship
77 71 clean wrought: flawlessly made
78 72 when: whereas
79 72 stranger things: beings not bound by kinship
80 74 mask: ladies often wore masks in public to avoid sunburn or to conceal their identities
81 80 tongues and rumors: gossip (about the Ward)
82 83 Marrying a rich fool allows you to live like a great lady
83 85 bushels: large quantities of money
84 87 What will . . . comes altogether?: some "foul" part of the Ward's anatomy (or a sound, such as flatulence, suggesting his approach) may emerge at this point; alternatively, the Ward's "trapstick" may appear on stage before he does, suggesting a phallus
85 87 SD *trap-stick*: also called a "cat-stick," this was a wooden stick used in the popular game of "tip-cat," in which a wooden "cat" shaped like an hourglass was batted into the air like a ball
86 90 hand: stroke
87 91 set jacks on me: encouraged scoundrels to compete with or attack me
88 91 my lady's tailor: Sordido may mistake the Ward's reference to "jacks" for a reference to "Jacques," the tailor's proper name
89 93 used to beating: a pun; tailors worked with "beaten" or embroidered cloth
90 93 tickled him: beat him thoroughly
91 94 tippings: actions in the game of tip-cat

SORDIDO Now you talk on 'em,
There was a poulterer's wife made a great complaint of you last night to your guardianer,[92] that you struck a bump in her child's head as big as an egg.
WARD An egg may prove a chicken then in time: the poulterer's wife will get by't.[93] When I am in game, I am furious; came my mother's eyes in my way, I would not lose a fair end; no, were she alive but with one tooth in her head, I should venture the striking out of that. I think of nobody when I am in play, I am so earnest. Coads-me,[94] my guardianer!
Prithee lay up my cat and cat-stick safe.
SORDIDO Where, sir, i'th' chimney corner?
WARD Chimney corner?
SORDIDO Yes, sir, your cats[95] are always safe i'th' chimney corner,
Unless they burn their coats.[96]
WARD Marry, that I am afraid on.
SORDIDO Why, then I will bestow your cat i'th' gutter,[97]
And there she's safe, I am sure.
WARD If I but live
To keep a house, I'll make thee a great man,
If meat and drink can do't. I can stoop gallantly,
And pitch out, when I list: I'm dog at a hole.[98]
I mar'l[99] my guardianer does not seek a wife for me!
I protest I'll have a bout with the maids else,
Or contract myself at midnight[100] to the larderwoman,
In presence of[101] a fool[102] or a sack-posset.[103]
GUARDIANO Ward!
WARD I feel myself after any exercise
Horribly prone.[104] Let me but ride, I'm lusty:
A cock-horse[105] straight,[106] i'faith.
GUARDIANO Why, Ward, I say!
WARD I'll forswear[107] eating eggs in moonshine nights;[108]
There's never a one I eat, but turns into a cock[109]
In four and twenty hours. If my hot blood
Be not took down in time, sure 'twill crow shortly.
GUARDIANO Do you hear, sir? Follow me, I must new school you.[110]
WARD School me? I scorn that now, I am past schooling.
I am not so base to learn to write and read;

92 95 guardianer: guardian
93 97 get by't: gain money from it; be impregnated
94 100 Coads-me: i.e. God's me, an exclamation of surprise
95 103 cats: Sordido uses the phallically shaped wooden "cat" as a metaphor for the penis
96 103–4 chimney corner … their coats: the "chimney" is a euphemism for female genitalia. Sordido implies that a man may safely have sex with a woman unless she is "burned," that is, suffers from venereal disease
97 105 bestow your cat i'th'gutter: refers to the proverbial phrase, "to agree like two cats in a gutter." The "gutter" may allude to the anus, suggesting that anal sex is safer for the male partner
98 108–9 can stoop … a hole: the Ward alludes to his prowess at tip-cat, while also evoking his ability to "pitch out" or ejaculate when faced with the "hole" or female genitalia
99 110 mar'l: marvel
100 112 contract myself at midnight: secretly promise myself in marriage
101 113 In presence of: legally witnessed by
102 113 fool: a dessert of whipped cream and fruit
103 113 sack-posset: a sweet alcoholic drink of mixed wine, milk, eggs, and sugar
104 115 prone: ready for sexual activity
105 116 cock-horse: a hobby horse; also a euphemism for a prostitute
106 116 straight: immediately
107 117 forswear: give up
108 117 eating eggs in moonshine nights: eggs were believed to be aphrodisiacs, while moonlit nights were thought to be times of high fertility
109 118 cock: male fowl, with punning suggestion of an erect penis
110 121 new school you: teach you to behave better

I was born to better fortunes in my cradle.[111] *Exit* [WARD *with* SORDIDO]
FABRITIO How do you like him, girl? This is your husband.
Like him or like him not, wench, you shall have him,
And you shall love him.
LIVIA Oh, soft there, brother! Though you be a justice,[112]
Your warrant cannot be served out of your liberty.[113]
You may compel, out of the power of father,
Things merely[114] harsh to a maid's flesh and blood.
But when you come to love, there the soil alters;
Y'are in another country, where your laws
Are no more set by than the cacklings
Of geese in Rome's great Capitol.[115]
FABRITIO Marry him she shall, then;
Let her agree upon love afterwards. *Exit*
LIVIA You speak now, brother, like an honest mortal
That walks upon th'earth with a staff; you were
Up i'th'clouds before. You'd command love,
And so do most old folks that go without it.
[*To* HIPPOLITO] My best and dearest brother, I could dwell here;[116]
There is not such another seat[117] on earth
Where all good parts[118] better express themselves.
HIPPOLITO You'll make me blush anon.
LIVIA 'Tis but like saying grace before a feast, then,
And that's most comely; thou art all a feast,
And she that has thee a most happy guest.
Prithee, cheer up thy niece with special counsel.[119] [*Exit*]
HIPPOLITO [*Aside*] I would 'twere fit to speak to her what I would; but
'Twas not a thing ordained. Heaven has forbid it,
And 'tis most meet that I should rather perish
Than the decree divine receive least blemish.
Feed inward, you my sorrows, make no noise;
Consume me silent, let me be stark dead
Ere the world know I'm sick. You see my honesty;
If you[120] befriend me, so.
ISABELLA Marry a fool!
Can there be greater misery to a woman
That means to keep her days true to her husband,
And know no other man? So virtue wills it.
Why, how can I obey and honor him,
But I must needs commit idolatry?[121]
A fool is but the image of a man,
And that but ill-made neither. Oh, the heart-breakings
Of miserable maids where love's enforced!

111 123–4 I am . . . my cradle: as a rich man, the Ward believes that he has no need to be literate
112 128 justice: justice of the peace
113 129 liberty: area of a magistrate's legal jurisdiction
114 131 merely: completely
115 134–5 the cacklings . . . great Capitol: in ancient Rome, geese sacred to Juno were kept on the Capitoline Hill. Livia contrasts the august setting of the Capitol with the loud but little-regarded noise of the geese
116 141 dwell here: Livia may suggest that her eyes could gaze on Hippolito forever; or she may embrace him at this point
117 142 seat: home
118 143 parts: gifts of mind and body
119 148 special counsel: advice fitted to her situation
120 156 you: Hippolito continues to address his sorrows, asking them to "befriend" him by killing him
121 161 idolatry: worship of a false god

The best condition is but bad enough:
When women have their choices, commonly
They do but buy their thraldoms, and bring great portions[122]
To men to keep 'em in subjection—
As if a fearful prisoner should bribe
The keeper to be good to him, yet lies in still,[123]
And glad of a good usage, a good look
Sometimes. By'r Lady, no misery surmounts a woman's!
Men buy their slaves, but women buy their masters.
Yet honesty and love makes all this happy,
And, next to angels', the most blest estate.
That providence that has made ev'ry poison
Good for some use, and sets four warring elements[124]
At peace in man, can make a harmony
In things that are most strange to human reason.
Oh, but this marriage! What, are you sad too, uncle?
Faith, then there's a whole household down[125] together.
Where shall I go to seek my comfort now,
When my best friend's distressed? What is't afflicts you, sir?
HIPPOLITO Faith, nothing but one grief that will not leave me,
And now 'tis welcome; ev'ry man has something
To bring him to his end, and this will serve,
Joined with your father's cruelty to you
That helps it forward.
ISABELLA Oh, be cheered, sweet uncle!
How long has't been upon you? I nev'r spied it.
What a dull sight have I! How long, I pray, sir?
HIPPOLITO Since I first saw you, niece, and left Bologna.
ISABELLA And could you deal so unkindly with my heart,
To keep it up so long hid from my pity?
Alas, how shall I trust your love hereafter?
Have we passed through so many arguments,[126]
And missed of that still, the most needful one?
Walked out whole nights together in discourses,
And the main point forgot? We are to blame both;
This is an obstinate, willful forgetfulness,
And faulty on both parts. Let's lose no time now:
Begin, good uncle, you that feel't. What is it?
HIPPOLITO You of all creatures, niece, must never hear on't;
'Tis not a thing ordained for you to know.
ISABELLA Not I, sir! All my joys that word cuts off.
You made profession once you loved me best;
'Twas but profession![127]
HIPPOLITO Yes, I do't too truly,
And fear I shall be chid for't. Know the worst, then:
I love thee dearlier than an uncle can.
ISABELLA Why, so you ever said, and I believed it.
HIPPOLITO [*Aside*] So simple is the goodness of her thoughts,

122 167 portions: dowries
123 170 lies in still: remains stuck in prison
124 177 four warring elements: the four contrasting elements (earth, air, fire, and water) were believed to make up the world, and also (in the form of the four humors) to make up each human being's nature
125 181 down: laid low
126 195 arguments: topics of discussion
127 206 but profession: merely words

They understand not yet th' unhallowed[128] language
Of a near sinner: I must yet be forced—
Though blushes be my venture—to come nearer.—
As a man loves his wife, so love I thee.
ISABELLA What's that?
Methought I heard ill news come toward me,
Which commonly we understand too soon.
Then, over-quick at hearing, I'll prevent it,
Though my joys fare the harder. Welcome it?[129]
It shall nev'r come so near mine ear again.
Farewell, all friendly solaces and discourses!
I'll learn to live without ye, for your dangers
Are greater than your comforts. What's become
Of truth in love if such we cannot trust,
When blood that should be love is mixed with lust? *Exit*
HIPPOLITO The worst can be but death, and let it come:
He that lives joyless, ev'ry day's his doom.
Exit

Act I, scene iii

Enter LEANTIO, *alone*

LEANTIO Methinks I'm ev'n as dull now at departure
As men observe great gallants the next day
After a revels;[130] you shall see 'em look
Much of my fashion, if you mark 'em well.
'Tis ev'n a second hell to part from pleasure
When man has got a smack on't.[131] As many holidays
Coming together makes your poor heads idle
A great while after, and are said to stick
Fast in their fingers' ends,[132] ev'n so does game[133]
In a new-married couple for the time:
It spoils all thrift, and indeed lies abed
To invent all the new ways for great expenses.[134]

[*Enter*] BIANCA *and* MOTHER *above*[135]

See and[136] she be not got on purpose now
Into the window to look after me!
I have no power to go now, and[137] I should be hanged.
Farewell, all business! I desire no more
Than I see yonder. Let the goods at quay[138]
Look to themselves; why should I toil my youth out?

128 211 unhallowed: unholy
129 218 Welcome it?: Isabella briefly considers, then rejects, the "joys" of accepting Hippolito's love
130 3 a revels: a night of partying
131 6 smack on't: taste of it
132 6–9 As many . . . fingers' ends: just as too many holidays blunt workers' ability to work effectively
133 9 game: fun; sexual activity
134 11–12 lies abed . . . great expenses: while in bed, new-married lovers find ways to "spend" themselves both financially and sexually
135 12 SD *above*: looking down from a window or balcony
136 13 and: if
137 15 and: even if
138 17 goods at quay: goods newly arrived or about to depart by ship, which Leantio is tasked with managing

It is but[139] begging two or three year sooner,
And stay with her continually; is't a match?[140]
Oh fie, what a religion have I leapt into!
Get out again, for shame! The man loves best
When his care's most: that shows his zeal to love.
Fondness is but the idiot to affection,[141]
That plays at hot-cockles[142] with rich merchants' wives:
Good to make sport withal when the chest's full
And the long warehouse cracks.[143] 'Tis the time of day
For us to be more wise; 'tis early with us,
And if they[144] lose the morning of their affairs,
They commonly lose the best part of the day.
Those that are wealthy and have got enough,
'Tis after sunset with 'em: they may rest,
Grow fat with ease, banquet, and toy and play,[145]
When such as I enter the heat o'th' day;
And I'll do't cheerfully.
BIANCA [*Above*] I perceive, sir,
Y'are not gone yet. I have good hope you'll stay now.
LEANTIO Farewell, I must not.
BIANCA Come, come, pray return.
Tomorrow, adding but a little care more,
Will dispatch all as well; believe me, 'twill, sir.
LEANTIO I could well wish myself where you would have me!
But love that's wanton must be ruled awhile
By that that's careful, or all goes to ruin.
As fitting is a government[146] in love
As in a kingdom; where 'tis all mere lust,
'Tis like an insurrection in the people
That, raised in self-will, wars against all reason.
But love that is respective for increase[147]
Is like a good king that keeps all in peace.
Once more, farewell.
BIANCA But this one night, I prithee.
LEANTIO Alas, I'm in for twenty if I stay,
And then for forty more, I have such luck to flesh:
I never bought a horse but he bore double.[148]
If I stay any longer, I shall turn
An everlasting spendthrift; as you love
To be maintained well, do not call me again,
For then I shall not care which end goes forward.[149]
Again, farewell to thee! *Exit*
BIANCA Since it must, farewell too.
MOTHER Faith, daughter, y'are to blame; you take the course

139 19 It is but: it's only a matter of
140 20 match: deal
141 24 Besotted infatuation is only a parody of—or court jester to—true love
142 25 hot-cockles: a game like blind man's buff (from the French *hautes-coquilles*)
143 27 the long warehouse cracks: the warehouse bursts at the seams because it is so full
144 29 they: people
145 33 toy and play: fondle and dally with lovers
146 43 government: rational order and control
147 47 respective for increase: concerned with gaining wealth (and possibly with procreation)
148 51–2 I have . . . bore double: Leantio's puns hint that Bianca will quickly become pregnant
149 56 I shall . . . goes forward: I won't care what happens next (with a sexual double entendre)

To make him an ill husband, troth you do;
And that disease is catching, I can tell you—
Ay, and soon taken by a young man's blood,
And that with little urging. Nay, fie, see now,
What cause have you to weep? Would I had no more,
That have lived threescore years; there were a cause,
And[150] 'twere well thought on. Trust me, y'are to blame;
His absence cannot last five days at utmost.
Why should those tears be fetched forth? Cannot love
Be ev'n as well expressed in a good look,
But it must see her face still in a fountain?[151]
It shows like a country maid dressing her head
By a dish of water.[152] Come, 'tis an old custom
To weep for love.

Enter two or three BOYS *and a* CITIZEN *or two with an* APPRENTICE

BOYS Now they come, now they come!
BOY 2 The duke!
BOY 3 The state![153]
CITIZEN How near, boy?
BOY 1 I'th' next street, sir, hard at hand.
CITIZEN You, sirrah, get a standing[154] for your mistress,
The best in all the city.
APPRENTICE I have't for her, sir!
'Twas a thing I provided for her overnight;
'Tis ready at her pleasure.[155]
CITIZEN Fetch her to't, then. Away, sir!
BIANCA What's the meaning of this hurry?
Can you tell, mother?
MOTHER What a memory
Have I! I see by that years come upon me.[156]
Why, 'tis a yearly custom and solemnity,[157]
Religiously observed by th'duke and state,
To St. Mark's Temple, the fifteenth of April.
See if my dull brains had not quite forgot it!
'Twas happily questioned of thee; I had gone down else,
Sat like a drone below, and never thought on't.
I would not, to be ten years younger again,
That you had lost the sight; now you shall see
Our duke, a goodly gentleman of his years.
BIANCA Is he old, then?
MOTHER About some fifty-five.
BIANCA That's no great age in man; he's then at best
For wisdom and for judgment.
MOTHER The Lord Cardinal,
His noble brother: there's a comely gentleman,

150 65 And: if
151 69 still in a fountain: always bathed in a fountain of tears
152 70–71 dressing her . . . of water: doing her hair by using a bowl of water as a mirror
153 73 The state: the nobles or high officials of the realm
154 75 standing: place to stand
155 78 at her pleasure: the apprentice jokes that he has already provided a "standing" (an erection) to pleasure his mistress at night
156 81 I see . . . upon me: I can tell by my forgetfulness that I am getting old
157 82 solemnity: festival; ceremonial procession

And greater in devotion than in blood.[158]
BIANCA He's worthy to be marked.
MOTHER You shall behold
All our chief states of Florence; you came fortunately
Against[159] this solemn day.
BIANCA I hope so always.

Music

MOTHER I hear 'em near us now, do you stand easily?[160]
BIANCA Exceeding well, good mother.
MOTHER Take this stool.
BIANCA I need it not, I thank you.
MOTHER Use your will, then.[161]

Enter in great solemnity six Knights bare-headed, then two Cardinals, and then the LORD CARDINAL, *then the* DUKE; *after him the States of Florence by two and two, with variety of music and song. Exit*

MOTHER How like you, daughter?
BIANCA 'Tis a noble state.
Methinks my soul could dwell upon the reverence
Of such a solemn and most worthy custom.
Did not the duke look up? Methought he saw us.
MOTHER That's everyone's conceit[162] that sees a duke;
If he look steadfastly, he looks straight at them;
When he perhaps, good careful[163] gentleman,
Never minds any, but the look he casts
Is at his own intentions, and his object
Only the public good.
BIANCA Most likely so.
MOTHER Come, come, we'll end this argument below.

Exeunt

Act II, scene i

Enter HIPPOLITO *and Lady* LIVIA *the widow*

LIVIA A strange affection, brother, when I think on't!
I wonder how thou cam'st by't.
HIPPOLITO Ev'n as easily
As man comes by destruction, which oft-times
He wears in his own bosom.
LIVIA Is the world
So populous in women, and creation
So prodigal in beauty and so various,
Yet does love turn thy point[164] to thine own blood?
'Tis somewhat too unkindly.[165] Must thy eye
Dwell evilly on the fairness of thy kindred,
And seek not where it should? It is confined

158 95 greater in . . . in blood: even more admirable for his piety than for his noble birth
159 98 Against: in time for
160 99 easily: comfortably
161 101 Use your will, then: as you please
162 106 conceit: belief; fancy
163 108 careful: full of cares or duties
164 7 thy point: the point of your compass needle (with a sexual double entendre)
165 8 unkindly: against kin or kind; unnatural

Now in a narrower prison than was made for't.
It is allowed a stranger;[166] and where bounty[167]
Is made the great man's honor, 'tis ill husbandry
To spare,[168] and servants shall have small thanks for't.
So he heaven's bounty seems to scorn and mock,
That spares free means, and spends of his own stock.[169]
HIPPOLITO Never was man's misery so soon sewed up,
Counting how truly.[170]
LIVIA Nay, I love you so
That I shall venture much to keep a change from you
So fearful as this grief will bring upon you.
Faith, it even kills me when I see you faint
Under a reprehension;[171] and I'll leave it,
Though I know nothing can be better for you.
Prithee, sweet brother, let not passion[172] waste
The goodness of thy time and of thy fortune.
Thou keep'st[173] the treasure of that life I love
As dearly as mine own; and if you think
My former words too bitter, which were ministered[174]
By truth and zeal, 'tis but a hazarding[175]
Of grace and virtue, and I can bring forth
As pleasant fruits as sensuality wishes
In all her teeming[176] longings. This I can do.
HIPPOLITO Oh, nothing that can make my wishes perfect![177]
LIVIA I would that love of yours were pawned to't, brother,
And as soon lost that way as I could win.[178]
Sir, I could give as shrewd a lift[179] to chastity
As any she that wears a tongue in Florence.
Sh'ad need be a good horsewoman, and sit fast,
Whom my strong argument could not fling[180] at last.
Prithee, take courage, man! Though I should counsel
Another to despair, yet I am pitiful
To thy afflictions, and will venture hard—
I will not name for what, 'tis not handsome.[181]
Find you the proof,[182] and praise me.
HIPPOLITO Then I fear me
I shall not praise you in haste.
LIVIA This is the comfort:
You are not the first, brother, has attempted

166 12 allowed a stranger: permitted to love someone outside the family
167 12 bounty: generosity
168 14 spare: be parsimonious
169 16 Refuses to spend what is freely offered to him (other women) and instead spends his love (and semen) on his own family
170 17–18 Never was . . . how truly: a man's pain was never summed up so concisely, considering how truly you've described it
171 22 reprehension: reprimand
172 24 passion: sorrow
173 26 Thou keep'st: you hold in yourself
174 28 ministered: administered (like a medicine)
175 29 a hazarding: an experiment; a test
176 32 teeming: fertile, abundant
177 33 perfect: satisfied.
178 34–5 I would . . . could win: I wish your love were bet on my success in making Isabella love you, and could be lost as easily as I can win
179 36 give as shrewd a lift: lend as cunning a helping hand
180 39 fling: unseat
181 43 handsome: appropriate
182 44 Find you the proof: see me accomplish it

Things more forbidden than this seems to be.
I'll minister all cordials[183] now to you,
Because I'll cheer you up, sir.
HIPPOLITO I am past hope.
LIVIA Love, thou shalt see me do a strange cure, then,
As ev'r was wrought on a disease so mortal[184]
And near akin to shame. When shall you see her?
HIPPOLITO Never in comfort more.
LIVIA Y'are so impatient, too.
HIPPOLITO Will you believe? 'Death,[185] sh' has forsworn my company,
And sealed it with a blush.
LIVIA So, I perceive
All lies upon my hands, then; well, the more glory
When the work's finished.

Enter SERVANT

How now, sir, the news?
SERVANT Madam, your niece, the virtuous Isabella,
Is lighted[186] now to see you.
LIVIA [*To* HIPPOLITO] That's great fortune.
Sir, your stars bless.[187] [*To* SERVANT] You, simple, lead her in. *Exit* SERVANT
HIPPOLITO What's this to me?
LIVIA Your absence, gentle brother.
I must bestir my wits for you.
HIPPOLITO Ay, to great purpose. *Exit* HIPPOLITO
LIVIA Beshrew you,[188] would I loved you not so well!
I'll go to bed, and leave this deed undone.
I am the fondest where I once affect,[189]
The carefull'st of their healths and of their ease, forsooth,
That I look still but slenderly[190] to mine own.
I take a course to pity him so much now
That I have none left for modesty and myself.
This 'tis to grow so liberal![191] Y'ave few sisters
That love their brothers' ease 'bove their own honesties.
But if you question my affections,
That will be found my fault.

Enter ISABELLA *the niece*

Niece, your love's welcome.
Alas, what draws that paleness to thy cheeks?
This enforced marriage towards?[192]
ISABELLA It helps, good aunt,

183 48 cordials: stimulating or comforting medicines
184 51 mortal: fatal; worthy of damnation
185 54 'Death: i.e. by God's death
186 59 lighted: alighted; arrived
187 60 bless: i.e. bless you
188 63 Beshrew you: curse you (generally used playfully or affectionately)
189 65 I am most foolishly tender once I love someone
190 67 slenderly: slightly
191 70 liberal: generous
192 75 towards: impending

Amongst some other griefs; but those I'll keep
Locked up in modest silence, for they're sorrows
Would shame the tongue more than they grieve the thought.
LIVIA Indeed, the Ward is simple.
ISABELLA Simple! That were well;
Why, one might make good shift[193] with such a husband.
But he's a fool entailed; he halts downright in't.[194]
LIVIA And knowing this, I hope 'tis at your choice
To take or refuse, niece.
ISABELLA You see it is not.
I loathe him more than beauty can hate death,
Or age, her spiteful neighbor.
LIVIA Let't appear, then.
ISABELLA How can I, being born with that obedience
That must submit unto a father's will?
If he command, I must of force[195] consent.
LIVIA Alas, poor soul! Be not offended, prithee,
If I set by[196] the name of niece awhile,
And bring in pity in a stranger fashion.
It lies here in this breast would cross[197] this match.
ISABELLA How, cross it, aunt?
LIVIA Ay, and give thee more liberty[198]
Than thou hast reason yet to apprehend.
ISABELLA Sweet aunt, in goodness keep not hid from me
What may befriend my life.
LIVIA Yes, yes, I must,
When I return to reputation,
And think upon the solemn vow I made
To your dead mother, my most loving sister.[199]
As long as I have her memory 'twixt mine eyelids,[200]
Look for no pity now.
ISABELLA Kind, sweet, dear aunt!
LIVIA No, 'twas a secret I have took special care of,
Delivered by your mother on her deathbed—
That's nine years now—and I'll not part from't yet,
Though nev'r was fitter time, nor greater cause for't.
ISABELLA As you desire the praises of a virgin—
LIVIA Good sorrow! I would do thee any kindness,
Not wronging secrecy or reputation.
ISABELLA Neither of which, as I have hope of fruitfulness,
Shall receive wrong from me.
LIVIA Nay, 'twould be your own wrong,
As much as any's, should it come to that once.[201]
ISABELLA I need no better means to work persuasion, then.
LIVIA Let it suffice, you may refuse this fool,
Or you may take him, as you see occasion

193 80 make good shift: cope well
194 81 he's a . . . downright in't: he's a born fool whose qualities stop at that
195 88 I must of force: I am compelled to
196 90 set by: put aside
197 92 would cross: that would thwart
198 93 liberty: freedom; sexual license
199 99 sister: sister-in-law
200 100 'twixt mine eyelids: in my mind's eye
201 111 come to that once: ever come to that

For your advantage; the best wits will do't.
Y'have liberty enough in your own will.
You cannot be enforced; there grows the flower,
If you could pick it out, makes[202] whole life sweet to you.
That which you call your father's command's nothing;
Then your obedience must needs be as little.
If you can make shift here to taste your happiness,
Or pick out aught that likes[203] you, much good do you.[204]
You see your cheer, I'll make you no set dinner.[205]
ISABELLA And, trust me, I may starve for all the good
I can find yet in this! Sweet aunt, deal plainlier.
LIVIA Say I should trust you now upon an oath,
And give you in a secret that would start you,[206]
How am I sure of you in faith and silence?
ISABELLA Equal assurance may I find in mercy,[207]
As you for that in me.
LIVIA It shall suffice.
Then know, however custom has made good,
For reputation's sake, the names of niece
And aunt 'twixt you and I, w'are nothing less.[208]
ISABELLA How's that?
LIVIA I told you I should start your blood.
You are no more allied to any of us,
Save what the courtesy of opinion casts
Upon your mother's memory and your name,[209]
Than the mere'st stranger is, or one begot
At Naples when the husband lies at Rome;
There's so much odds betwixt us. Since your knowledge
Wished more instruction, and I have your oath
In pledge for silence, it makes me talk the freelier.
Did never the report of that famed Spaniard,
Marquis of Coria,[210] since your time was ripe
For understanding, fill your ear with wonder?
ISABELLA Yes, what of him? I have heard his deeds of honor
Often related when we lived in Naples.
LIVIA You heard the praises of your father then.
ISABELLA My father!
LIVIA That was he. But all the business[211]
So carefully and so discreetly carried
That fame[212] received no spot by't, not a blemish.
Your mother was so wary to her end,
None knew it but her conscience and her friend[213]
Till penitent confession made it mine,

202 118 makes: that makes
203 122 likes: pleases
204 122 much good do you: much good may it do you
205 123 You can see the food set before you; I won't tell you what to eat
206 127 start you: startle you
207 129 mercy: God's mercy on Judgment Day
208 133 w'are nothing less: we are not at all related
209 137 name: surname; family reputation
210 144 Coria: a town in Spain
211 149 business: affair
212 151 fame: reputation
213 153 friend: lover

And now my pity yours. It had been long else,[214]
And I hope care and love alike in you,
Made good by oath, will see it take no wrong now.
How weak his commands now whom you call father?
How vain all his enforcements, your obedience?
And what a largeness in your will and liberty,
To take, or to reject, or to do both?
For fools will serve to father wise men's children.[215]
All this y'have time to think on. Oh my wench!
Nothing o'erthrows our sex but indiscretion;
We might do well else of a brittle people
As any under the great canopy.[216]
I pray, forget not but to call me aunt still—
Take heed of that; it may be marked in time else.
But keep your thoughts to yourself, from all the world,
Kindred or dearest friend—nay, I entreat you,
From him that all this while you have called uncle,
And though you love him dearly, as I know
His deserts claim as much ev'n from a stranger,
Yet let not him know this, I prithee do not.
As ever thou hast hope of second pity[217]
If thou shouldst stand in need on't, do not do't.
ISABELLA Believe my oath, I will not.
LIVIA Why, well said!
[*Aside*] Who shows more craft t'undo a maidenhead,[218]
I'll resign my part to her.

Enter HIPPOLITO

[*To him*] She's thine own, go. *Exit*
HIPPOLITO [*Aside*] Alas, fair flattery cannot cure my sorrows!
ISABELLA [*Aside*] Have I passed so much time in ignorance,
And never had the means to know myself
Till this blest hour? Thanks to her virtuous pity
That brought it now to light—would I had known it
But one day sooner! He had then received
In favors what (poor gentleman) he took
In bitter words: a slight and harsh reward
For one of his deserts.
HIPPOLITO [*Aside*] There seems to me now
More anger and distraction[219] in her looks.
I'm gone; I'll not endure a second storm;
The memory of the first is not past yet.
ISABELLA [*Aside*] Are you returned, you comforts of my life,
In this man's presence? I will keep you fast now,
And sooner part eternally from the world
Than my good joys in you. [*To* HIPPOLITO] Prithee, forgive me.
I did but chide in jest; the best loves use it

214 155 It had been long else: otherwise, it would have stayed hidden for a long time
215 162 Fools can do the job of passing for the fathers of cleverer men's illegitimate children
216 165–6 We might . . . great canopy: without indiscretion, we might profit as well from frail humanity as any other sinners under heaven
217 175 second pity: further help from Livia
218 178 undo a maidenhead: talk a virgin into giving up her virginity
219 189 distraction: fury

Sometimes. It sets an edge upon affection.[220]
When we invite our best friends to a feast,
'Tis not all sweetmeats that we set before them;
There's somewhat[221] sharp and salt, both to whet appetite
And make 'em taste their wine well. So, methinks,
After a friendly, sharp, and savory chiding
A kiss tastes wondrous well, and full o'th' grape.[222] [*She kisses him*]
How think'st thou, does't not?
HIPPOLITO 'Tis so excellent
I know not how to praise it, what to say to't.
ISABELLA This marriage shall go forward.
HIPPOLITO With the Ward!
Are you in earnest?
ISABELLA 'Twould be ill for us else.
HIPPOLITO [*Aside*] For us? How means she that?
ISABELLA Troth, I begin
To be so well, methinks, within this hour,
For all[223] this match able to kill one's heart,
Nothing can pull me down now; should my father
Provide a worse fool yet—which I should think
Were a hard thing to compass[224]—I'd have him either;[225]
The worse the better, none can come amiss now
If he want wit enough. So discretion love me,
Desert and judgment,[226] I have content sufficient.
She that comes once to be a housekeeper
Must not look every day to fare well, sir,
Like a young waiting-gentlewoman in service,[227]
For she feeds commonly[228] as her lady does:
No good bit passes her but she gets a taste on't;[229]
But when she comes to keep house for herself,
She's glad of some choice cates[230] then once a week,
Or twice at most, and glad if she can get 'em.
So must affection learn to fare with thankfulness.
Pray make your love no stranger, sir, that's all—
[*Aside*] Though you be one[231] yourself, and know not on't;
And I have sworn you must not. *Exit*
HIPPOLITO This is beyond me!
Never came joys so unexpectedly
To meet desires in man. How came she thus?
What has she[232] done to her? Can any tell?
'Tis beyond sorcery, this, drugs, or love-powders:

220 197 sets an edge upon affection: gives piquancy to desire
221 200 somewhat: something
222 203 full o'th' grape: delicious; as rich as wine
223 210 For all: in spite of
224 213 compass: manage
225 213 either: in place of the other
226 215–16 So discretion . . . and judgment: the qualities Isabella sees in Hippolito
227 217–19 a housekeeper . . . in service: a married woman who sets up her own house must not expect to be pampered like an unmarried girl who serves a great lady
228 220 commonly: usually
229 221 on't: of it
230 223 choice cates: fine delicacies
231 227 one: a stranger, i.e. not related to Isabella
232 231 she: Livia

Some art that has no name, sure, strange to me
Of all the wonders I ev'r met withal
Throughout my ten years' travels; but I'm thankful for't.
This marriage now must of necessity forward;
It is the only veil wit can devise
To keep our acts hid from sin-piercing eyes.

Exit

Act II, scene ii

Enter GUARDIANO *and* LIVIA

LIVIA How, sir, a gentlewoman so young, so fair
As you set forth,[233] spied from[234] the widow's window?
GUARDIANO She!
LIVIA Our Sunday-dinner woman?
GUARDIANO And Thursday-supper woman, the same still.[235]
I know not how she came by her, but I'll swear
She's the prime gallant for a face in Florence,[236]
And no doubt other parts follow their leader.[237]
The duke himself first spied her at the window;
Then in a rapture, as if admiration
Were poor when it were single,[238] beckoned me,
And pointed to the wonder warily,
As one that feared she would draw in her splendor
Too soon if too much gazed at. I nev'r knew him
So infinitely taken with a woman;
Nor can I blame his appetite, or tax
His raptures of slight folly:[239] she's a creature
Able to draw a state from serious business,
And make it their best piece[240] to do her service.
What course shall we devise? H'as spoke twice now.
LIVIA Twice?
GUARDIANO 'Tis beyond your apprehension
How strangely that one look has catched his heart!
'Twould prove but too much worth in wealth and favor
To those should work his peace.[241]
LIVIA And if I do't not,
Or at least come as near it—if your art
Will take a little pains and second me—
As any wench in Florence of my standing,
I'll quite give o'er, and shut up shop in[242] cunning.
GUARDIANO 'Tis for the duke, and if I fail your purpose,
All means to come by riches or advancement
Miss me and skip me over!

233 1–2 so young . . . set forth: as young and beautiful as you've described
234 2 spied from: seen looking out from
235 3–4 These lines suggest that the Widow is given a meal at Livia's house on Sundays and Thursdays as an act of charity toward a poor neighbor
236 6 the prime . . . a face: the most beautiful person in Florence when it comes to her face
237 7 follow their leader: are as beautiful as her face
238 9–10 as if . . . were single: as if wonder were lesser when unshared
239 15–16 tax/His . . . slight folly: criticize his desire for being trivial and foolish
240 18 piece: accomplishment
241 23 work his peace: satisfy his desire
242 27 shut up shop in: renounce my reputation for

LIVIA Let the old woman then
Be sent for with all speed; then I'll begin.
GUARDIANO A good conclusion follow, and a sweet one,
After this stale beginning with old ware.[243]
Within there!

Enter SERVANT

SERVANT Sir, do you call?
GUARDIANO Come near, list hither. [*Talks with* SERVANT *aside*]
LIVIA I long myself to see this absolute[244] creature
That wins the heart of love and praise so much.
GUARDIANO Go, sir, make haste.
LIVIA Say I entreat her company.
Do you hear, sir?
SERVANT Yes, madam. *Exit*
LIVIA That brings her quickly.
GUARDIANO I would 'twere done; the duke waits the good hour,
And I wait the good fortune that may spring from't.
I have had a lucky hand these fifteen year
At such court-passage with three dice in a dish.[245]

Enter FABRITIO

Signor Fabritio!
FABRITIO Oh sir, I bring an alteration in my mouth now.
GUARDIANO An alteration! [*Aside*] No wise speech, I hope;
He means not to talk wisely, does he, trow?[246]
—Good! What's the change, I pray, sir?
FABRITIO A new change.[247]
GUARDIANO Another yet! Faith, there's enough already.
FABRITIO My daughter loves him now.
GUARDIANO What, does she, sir?
FABRITIO Affects him beyond thought—who but the Ward, forsooth!
No talk but of the Ward; she would have him
To choose 'bove all the men she ever saw.
My will goes not so fast as her consent now;
Her duty gets before my command still.
GUARDIANO Why, then, sir, if you'll have me speak my thoughts,
I smell[248] 'twill be a match.
FABRITIO Ay, and a sweet young couple,
If I have any judgment.
GUARDIANO [*Aside*] 'Faith, that's little.
—Let her be sent to tomorrow before noon,
And handsomely tricked up;[249] for 'bout that time
I mean to bring her in and tender her to him.
FABRITIO I warrant you for handsome; I will see

243 33 old ware: old goods; Guardiano likens the Widow to stale foodstuffs
244 35 absolute: perfect
245 42 court-passage . . . a dish: "passage" is a two-person dice game, played with three dice. Guardiano implies that he is good at managing love triangles and similar affairs at court
246 46 trow: I think; I suppose
247 47 new change: a laughable redundancy, as Guardiano points out
248 56 smell: predict
249 59 tricked up: adorned

Her things laid ready, every one in order,
And have some part of her tricked up tonight.
GUARDIANO Why, well said.
FABRITIO 'Twas a use[250] her mother had
When she was invited to an early wedding;
She'd dress her head[251] o'ernight, sponge up herself,
And give her neck three lathers.
GUARDIANO [*Aside*] Nev'r a halter?[252]
FABRITIO On with her chain of pearl, her ruby bracelets,
Lay ready all her tricks and jiggam-bobs.[253]
GUARDIANO So must your daughter.
FABRITIO I'll about it straight, sir. *Exit* FABRITIO
LIVIA How he sweats in the foolish zeal of fatherhood,
After[254] six ounces an hour, and seems
To toil as much as if his cares were wise ones!
GUARDIANO Y'have let his folly blood in the right vein, lady.[255]
LIVIA And here comes his sweet son-in-law that shall be.
They're both allied in wit before the marriage;
What will they be hereafter, when they are nearer?
Yet they can go no further than the fool:
There's the world's end in both of 'em. [256]

Enter WARD *and* SORDIDO, *one with a shuttlecock, the other a battledore*[257]

GUARDIANO Now, young heir!
WARD What's the next business after shittlecock[258] now?
GUARDIANO Tomorrow you shall see the gentlewoman
Must be your wife.
WARD There's ev'n[259] another thing[260] too
Must be kept up with a pair of battledores.
My wife! What can she do?
GUARDIANO Nay, that's a question you should ask yourself, Ward,
When y'are alone together.
WARD That's as I list.[261]
A wife's to be asked anywhere, I hope!
I'll ask her in a congregation, if I have a mind to it, and so save a licence.[262] My guardianer has no more wit than an herb-woman that sells away all her sweet herbs and nosegays, and keeps a stinking breath for her own pottage.[263]
SORDIDO Let me be at the choosing of your beloved,
If you desire a woman of good parts.[264]

250 64 use: habit
251 66 dress her head: do her hair
252 67 halter: a noose or bridle made of leather; Guardiano implies that Fabritio's wife was unhappily yoked to him
253 69 tricks and jiggam-bobs: ornaments and finery
254 72 After: at the rate of
255 74 Referring to the medical practice of blood-letting, Guardiano suggests that Livia has correctly diagnosed Fabritio's folly
256 79 Both have reached the limits of idiocy
257 79 SD *a shuttlecock . . . a battledore*: the birdie and racket used in a game that prefigured badminton
258 80 shittlecock: the Ward characteristically mispronounces or misuses objects' names so that they take on excretory and sexual meanings
259 82 ev'n: yet
260 82 thing: the phallus, which must be kept "up" for a wife
261 86 list: desire
262 88 I'll ask . . . a licence: the Ward determines to have his marriage banns publicly proclaimed so that he need not pay for a special licence
263 90 pottage: soup
264 92 parts: qualities; body parts

WARD Thou shalt, sweet Sordido.
SORDIDO I have a plaguey guess;[265] let me alone to see what she is. If I but look upon her—
'way,[266] I know all the faults to a hair that you may refuse her for.
WARD Dost thou? I prithee, let me hear 'em, Sordido.
SORDIDO Well, mark 'em, then; I have 'em all in rhyme.
The wife your guardianer ought to tender
Should be pretty, straight, and slender;
Her hair not short, her foot not long,
Her hand not huge, nor too, too loud her tongue;
No pearl in eye,[267] nor ruby[268] in her nose,
No burn[269] or cut but what the catalogue shows.[270]
She must have teeth, and that no black ones;
And kiss most sweet when she does smack once;
Her skin must be both white and plump,
Her body straight, not hopper-rumped,[271]
Or wriggle sideways like a crab;
She must be neither slut nor drab,[272]
Nor go too splay-foot with her shoes,
To make her smock lick up the dews.
And two things more, which I forgot to tell ye:
She neither must have bump in back nor belly.[273]
These are the faults that will not make her pass.
WARD And if I spy not these, I am a rank ass.
SORDIDO Nay, more; by right, sir, you should see her naked,
For that's the ancient order.[274]
WARD See her naked?
That were good sport, i'faith. I'll have the books turned over,
And if I find her naked on record,[275]
She shall not have a rag on. But stay, stay,
How if she should desire to see me so too?
I were in a sweet case[276] then; such a foul[277] skin!
SORDIDO But y'have a clean shirt, and that makes amends, sir.
WARD I will not see her naked for that trick,[278] though. *Exit*
SORDIDO Then take her with all faults, with her clothes on!
And they may hide a number with a bum-roll.[279]
Faith, choosing of a wench in a huge farthingale[280]
Is like the buying of ware under a great penthouse:[281]
What with the deceit of one

265 94 plaguey guess: shrewd judgment
266 95 'way: straight away
267 102 pearl in eye: cataract
268 102 ruby: pimple or spot
269 103 burn: a symptom of venereal disease
270 103 cut but . . . catalogue shows: "cut" was a term for female genitals; the Ward's wife should have no "cuts" but those that belong to a woman
271 107 hopper-rumped: with large, jiggling buttocks, like the hopper of a mill
272 109 drab: whore
273 113 bump in back nor belly: be neither hunchbacked nor pregnant
274 117 ancient order: the old custom
275 118–19 I'll have . . . on record: the Ward takes Sordido's reference to the "ancient order" as a reference to a commercial transaction, and vows to look in the record books to see if he can find an order for Isabella's nakedness
276 122 sweet case: a nice situation, with a pun on "case" meaning clothing
277 122 foul: blemished
278 124 for that trick: for fear of being stripped naked myself
279 126 bum-roll: stylish padding worn by women at hip level to hold out the back of their skirts
280 127 farthingale: a hoop-like frame worn around the waist to hold out women's skirts, hiding the body underneath
281 128 penthouse: a sloping roof over a door or window, sometimes used in shops to darken the room below, creating a "false light" that hid flaws in the wares

And the false light of th'other, mark my speeches,
He may have a diseased wench in's bed,
And rotten stuff[282] in's breeches. *Exit*
GUARDIANO It may take[283] handsomely.
LIVIA I see small hindrance.
How now, so soon returned?

Enter [SERVANT *with*] MOTHER

GUARDIANO She's come.
LIVIA That's well.
Widow, come, come, I have a great quarrel to you.
Faith, I must chide you, that you must be sent for!
You make yourself so strange,[284] never come at us;
And yet so near a neighbor, and so unkind!
Troth, y'are to blame. You cannot be more welcome
To any house in Florence, that I'll tell you.
MOTHER My thanks must needs acknowledge so much, madam.
LIVIA How can you be so strange, then? I sit here
Sometime whole days together without company
When business draws this gentleman from home,
And should be happy in society
Which I so well affect[285] as that of yours.
I know y'are alone too. Why should not we,
Like two kind neighbors, then, supply the wants
Of one another, having tongue-discourse,[286]
Experience in the world, and such kind helps
To laugh down time and meet age merrily?
MOTHER Age, madam? You speak mirth; 'tis at my door,
But a long journey from your ladyship yet.
LIVIA My faith, I'm nine and thirty, every stroke, wench;
And 'tis a general observation
'Mongst knights' wives or widows, we accompt[287]
Ourselves then old, when young men's eyes leave looking at's.
'Tis a true rule amongst us, and nev'r failed yet
In any but in one, that I remember:
Indeed, she had a friend[288] at nine and forty.
Marry, she paid well for him, and in th'end
He kept a quean[289] or two with her own money,
That robbed her of her plate and cut her throat.
MOTHER She had her punishment in this world, madam,
And a fair warning to all other women
That they live chaste at fifty.
LIVIA Ay, or never, wench.
Come, now I have thy company I'll not part with't
Till after supper.
MOTHER Yes, I must crave pardon, madam.

282 132 rotten stuff: rotting cloth; venereal disease
283 133 take: succeed
284 137 so strange: such a stranger
285 146 so well affect: enjoy so much
286 149 tongue-discourse: skill in conversation
287 156 accompt: account
288 160 friend: lover
289 162 quean: prostitute

LIVIA I swear you shall stay[290] supper. We have no strangers, woman;
None but my sojourners[291] and I, this gentleman
And the young heir his ward. You know our company.
MOTHER Some other time I will make bold with you,[292] madam.
GUARDIANO Nay, pray stay, widow.
LIVIA Faith, she shall not go.
Do you think I'll be forsworn?[293] *Table and chess [are brought on]*
MOTHER 'Tis a great while
Till supper time; I'll take my leave then now, madam,
And come again i'th'evening, since your ladyship
Will have it so.
LIVIA I'th'evening! By my troth, wench,
I'll keep you while I have you. You have great business, sure,
To sit alone at home; I wonder strangely[294]
What pleasure you take in't! Were't to me now,
I should be ever at one neighbor's house
Or other all day long. Having no charge,[295]
Or none to chide you if you go or stay,
Who may live merrier, ay, or more at heart's ease?
Come, we'll to chess or draughts;[296] there are an hundred tricks
To drive out time till supper, never fear't, wench.
MOTHER I'll but make one step home, and return straight, madam.
LIVIA Come, I'll not trust you; you use more excuses
To your kind friends than ever I knew any.
What business can you have, if you be sure
Y'have locked the doors? And that being all you have,
I know y'are careful on't. One afternoon
So much to spend here! Say I should entreat you now
To lie a night or two, or a week, with me,
Or leave your own house for a month together?
It were a kindness that long neighborhood
And friendship might well hope to prevail in.
Would you deny such a request? I'faith,
Speak truth, and freely.
MOTHER I were then uncivil, madam.
LIVIA Go to, then, set your men;[297] we'll have whole nights
Of mirth together ere we be much older, wench.
MOTHER [*Aside*] As good now tell her, then, for she will know't.
I have always found her a most friendly lady.
LIVIA Why, widow, where's your mind?
MOTHER Troth, ev'n at home, madam.
To tell you truth, I left a gentlewoman
Ev'n sitting all alone, which is uncomfortable,
Especially to young bloods.
LIVIA Another excuse!
MOTHER No, as I hope for health, madam, that's a truth;
Please you to send and see.

290 169 stay: stay for
291 170 sojourners: house-guests
292 172 make bold with you: take you up on your offer
293 174 forsworn: made a liar of
294 179 strangely: greatly
295 182 charge: person, such as a child, for whom one must care
296 185 draughts: board game also known as checkers
297 200 men: chessmen

LIVIA What gentlewoman? Pish!
MOTHER Wife to my son, indeed, but not known, madam,
To any but yourself.
LIVIA Now I beshrew you!
Could you be so unkind to her and me,
To come and not bring her? Faith, 'tis not friendly.
MOTHER I feared to be too bold.
LIVIA Too bold? Oh, what's become
Of the true hearty love was wont to be
'Mongst neighbors in old time?
MOTHER And she's a stranger,[298] madam.
LIVIA The more should be her welcome! When is courtesy
In better practice than when 'tis employed
In entertaining strangers? I could chide,[299] i'faith.
Leave her behind, poor gentlewoman, alone too!
Make some amends, and send for her betimes;[300] go.
MOTHER Please you command one of your servants, madam.
LIVIA Within there!

Enter SERVANT

SERVANT Madam.
LIVIA Attend the gentlewoman.
MOTHER [*Aside*] It must be carried wondrous privately
From[301] my son's knowledge; he'll break out in storms else.
Hark you, sir. [*She gives instructions; exit* SERVANT]
LIVIA [*Aside to* GUARDIANO] Now comes in the heat of your part.[302]
GUARDIANO [*Aside to* LIVIA] True, I know it, lady; and if I be out,[303]
May the duke banish me from all employments,
Wanton or serious.
LIVIA So, have you sent, widow?
MOTHER Yes, madam, he's almost at home by this.
LIVIA And faith, let me entreat you, that henceforward
All such unkind faults may be swept from friendship,
Which does but dim the luster. And think thus much:
It is a wrong to me, that have ability
To bid friends welcome, when you keep 'em from me.
You cannot set greater dishonor near me,
For bounty is the credit and the glory
Of those that have enough. I see y'are sorry,
And the good 'mends[304] is made by't.
MOTHER Here she's, madam.

Enter BIANCA *and* SERVANT

BIANCA [*Aside*] I wonder how she comes to send for me now?
LIVIA Gentlewoman, y'are most welcome, trust me y'are,
As courtesy can make one, or respect

298 216 a stranger: not from this city
299 219 chide: reproach you
300 221 betimes: right away
301 224–5 carried wondrous privately/From: kept carefully hidden from
302 226 the heat of your part: the crucial moment of your role
303 227 if I be out: if I forget my lines (playing on Livia's word "part")
304 239 'mends: amends

Due to the presence of you.
BIANCA I give you thanks, lady.
LIVIA I heard you were alone, and 't had appeared
An ill condition[305] in me, though I knew you not,
Nor ever saw you—yet humanity
Thinks ev'ry case her own—to have kept your company
Here from you, and left you all solitary.
I rather ventured upon boldness then
As the least fault, and wished your presence here—
A thing most happy motioned of[306] that gentleman,
Whom I request you, for his care and pity,
To honor and reward with your acquaintance:
A gentleman that ladies' rights stands for,[307]
That's his profession.[308]
BIANCA 'Tis a noble one,
And honors my acquaintance.
GUARDIANO All my intentions
Are servants to such mistresses.
BIANCA 'Tis your modesty,
It seems, that makes your deserts speak so low,[309] sir.
LIVIA Come, widow! Look you, lady, here's our business. [*Points to chess table*]
Are we not well employed, think you? An old quarrel
Between us, that will never be at an end.
BIANCA No?
And methinks there's men[310] enough to part you, lady.
LIVIA Ho! But they set us on.[311] Let us come off[312]
As well as we can, poor souls, men care no farther.
I pray, sit down, forsooth, if you have the patience
To look upon two weak and tedious gamesters.
GUARDIANO Faith, madam, set these by till evening;
You'll have enough on't then; the gentlewoman,
Being a stranger, would take more delight
To see your rooms and pictures.
LIVIA Marry, good sir,
And well remembered! I beseech you, show 'em her;
That will beguile time well. Pray heartily, do, sir;
I'll do as much for you.[313] Here, take these keys.
Show her the monument,[314] too—and that's a thing
Everyone sees not; you can witness that, widow.
MOTHER And that's worth sight indeed, madam.
BIANCA Kind lady,
I fear I came to be a trouble to you.
LIVIA Oh, nothing less, forsooth.
BIANCA And to this courteous gentleman,
That wears a kindness in his breast so noble

305 245 An ill condition: bad manners
306 251 motioned of: suggested by
307 254 stands for: defends; with the double entendre "has an erection for"
308 255 profession: occupation; creed
309 258 makes your . . . so low: makes you downplay your own merits
310 262 men: i.e. the chessmen
311 263 set us on: incite us to fight; sexually arouse us (punning on Bianca's reference to "men")
312 263 come off: come through the fight; achieve orgasm
313 273 I'll do . . . for you: I'll repay the favor by entertaining your guests in the future
314 274 monument: a carved figure in wood or stone

And bounteous to the welcome of a stranger.
GUARDIANO If you but give acceptance to my service,
You do the greatest grace and honor to me
That courtesy can merit.
BIANCA I were to blame else,
And out of fashion much. I pray you lead, sir.
LIVIA After a game or two w'are for you,[315] gentlefolks.
GUARDIANO We wish no better seconds[316] in society
Than your discourses, madam, and your partner's there.
MOTHER I thank your praise. I listened to you, sir,
Though when you spoke, there came a paltry rook[317]
Full in my way, and chokes up all my game. *Exit* GUARDIANO *and* BIANCA
LIVIA Alas, poor widow, I shall be too hard for thee.
MOTHER Y'are cunning at the game,[318] I'll be sworn, madam.
LIVIA It will be found so, ere I give you over.
She that can place her man well—
MOTHER As you do, madam.
LIVIA As I shall, wench, can never lose her game.
Nay, nay, the black king's mine.[319]
MOTHER Cry you mercy, madam.
LIVIA And this my queen.
MOTHER I see't now.
LIVIA Here's a duke
Will strike a sure stroke for the game anon;
Your pawn cannot come back to relieve itself.[320]
MOTHER I know that, madam.
LIVIA You play well the whilst.
How she belies her skill! I hold[321] two ducats
I give you check and mate to your white king:
Simplicity itself, your saintish king there.
MOTHER Well, ere now, lady,
I have seen the fall of subtlety; jest on.
LIVIA Ay, but simplicity receives two for one.[322]
MOTHER What remedy but patience!

Enter above GUARDIANO *and* BIANCA

BIANCA Trust me, sir,
Mine eye nev'r met with fairer ornaments.
GUARDIANO Nay, livelier, I'm persuaded, neither Florence
Nor Venice can produce.
BIANCA Sir, my opinion

315 285 w'are for you: we shall join you

316 286 seconds: companions; supporters

317 289 rook: the chess piece alternatively called the "castle." In early modern England, it was also known as the "duke," a fact upon which Middleton plays

318 292 game: the chess game, but with an innuendo on the word's secondary meanings of sexual intrigue and prostitution; this pun shapes the lines that follow

319 296 black king's mine: Livia implies that the mother has accidentally touched Livia's king

320 297–9 Here's a . . . relieve itself: Livia's "duke" moves against the mother's pawn, which cannot move backwards to escape, foreshadowing the duke's entrapment of Bianca

321 301 hold: wager

322 306 simplicity receives two for one: Livia appears to take two of the white pieces in response to the mother's taking one of hers

Takes your part highly.[323]
GUARDIANO There's a better piece[324]
Yet than all these.

[*Enter*] DUKE *above*

BIANCA Not possible, sir!
GUARDIANO Believe it.
You'll say so when you see't; turn but your eye now,
Y'are upon't presently.[325] *Exit*
BIANCA [*Seeing the* DUKE] Oh, sir!
DUKE He's gone, beauty!
Pish, look not after him; he's but a vapor
That, when the sun appears, is seen no more.
BIANCA Oh, treachery to honor!
DUKE Prithee, tremble not.
I feel thy breast shake, like a turtle[326] panting
Under a loving hand that makes much on't.
Why art so fearful? As I'm friend to brightness,[327]
There's nothing but respect and honor near thee.
You know me, you have seen me; here's a heart
Can witness I have seen thee.
BIANCA The more's my danger.
DUKE The more's thy happiness. Pish, strive not,[328] sweet!
This strength were excellent employed in love now,
But here 'tis spent amiss; strive not to seek
Thy liberty, and keep me still in prison.
I'faith, you shall not out till I'm released now.
We'll be both freed together, or stay still by't;[329]
So is captivity pleasant.
BIANCA Oh my lord!
DUKE I am not here in vain;[330] have but the leisure
To think on that, and thou'lt be soon resolved.
The lifting of thy voice is but like one
That does exalt his enemy,[331] who, proving high,[332]
Lays all the plots to confound him that raised him.
Take warning, I beseech thee. Thou seem'st to me
A creature so composed of gentleness
And delicate meekness, such as bless the faces
Of figures that are drawn for goddesses
And makes art proud to look upon her work;
I should be sorry the least force should lay
An unkind touch upon thee.
BIANCA Oh my extremity!
My lord, what seek you?

323 311 Takes your part highly: agrees with you completely
324 311 piece: artwork, with a punning reference to the penis
325 314 presently: immediately
326 318 turtle: turtle-dove
327 320 brightness: beauty
328 324 strive not: don't struggle; this line and the next ones suggest that Bianca is fighting physically to escape the duke's embrace
329 329 stay still by't: remain in prison together—that is, in one another's arms
330 331 I am . . . in vain: I won't leave without the pleasure I came for
331 333–4 The lifting . . . his enemy: Bianca's pleas only arouse the duke further
332 334 proving high: having gained power; having been aroused

DUKE Love.
BIANCA 'Tis gone already.
I have a husband.
DUKE That's a single comfort.
Take a friend to him.[333]
BIANCA That's a double mischief,
Or else there's no religion.
DUKE Do not tremble
At fears of thine own making.
BIANCA Nor, great lord,
Make me not bold with[334] death and deeds of ruin
Because they fear not you;[335] me they must fright,
Then am I best in health.[336] Should thunder speak
And none regard it, it had lost the name,
And were as good be still. I'm not like those
That take their soundest sleeps in greatest tempests;
Then wake I most, the weather fearfullest,
And call for strength to virtue.
DUKE Sure I think
Thou know'st the way to please me. I affect[337]
A passionate pleading 'bove an easy yielding,
But never pitied any; they deserve none
That will not pity me. I can command,
Think upon that; yet if thou truly knewest
The infinite pleasure my affection takes
In gentle, fair entreatings, when love's businesses
Are carried courteously 'twixt heart and heart,
You'd make more haste to please me.
BIANCA Why should you seek, sir,
To take away that you can never give?
DUKE But I give better in exchange: wealth, honor.
She that is fortunate in a duke's favor
Lights on a tree that bears all women's wishes.
If your own mother saw you pluck fruit there,
She would commend your wit and praise the time
Of your nativity. Take hold of glory!
Do not I know y'have cast away your life
Upon necessities, means merely[338] doubtful
To keep you in indifferent[339] health and fashion—
A thing I heard too lately,[340] and soon pitied—
And can you be so much your beauty's enemy
To kiss away a month or two in wedlock
And weep whole years in wants forever after?
Come, play the wise wench, and provide forever;
Let storms come when they list, they find thee sheltered.
Should any doubt arise, let nothing trouble thee;
Put trust in our love for the managing

333 345 Take a friend to him: take a lover in addition to him
334 348 Make me not bold with: don't make me careless about
335 349 they fear not you: they don't frighten you
336 350 best in health: Bianca equates her soul's health with her fear of sin
337 356 affect: love; am attracted to
338 373 merely: wholly
339 374 indifferent: tolerable
340 375 too lately: all too recently (since I could no longer prevent it)

Of all to thy heart's peace. We'll walk together,
And show a thankful joy for both our fortunes. *Exit above*
LIVIA Did not I say my duke would fetch you over,[341] widow?
MOTHER I think you spoke in earnest when you said it, madam.
LIVIA And my black king makes all the haste he can, too.
MOTHER Well, madam, we may meet with him in time yet.
LIVIA I have given thee blind mate[342] twice.
MOTHER You may see, madam,
My eyes begin to fail.
LIVIA I'll swear they do, wench.

Enter GUARDIANO

GUARDIANO [*Aside*] I can but smile as often as I think on't:
How prettily the poor fool was beguiled,
How unexpectedly! It's a witty age.
Never were finer snares for women's honesties
Than are devised in these days; no spider's web
Made of a daintier thread than are now practiced
To catch love's flesh-fly[343] by the silver wing.
Yet to prepare her stomach[344] by degrees
To Cupid's feast, because I saw 'twas queasy,[345]
I showed her naked pictures by the way,
A bit to stay the appetite.[346] Well, advancement!
I venture hard to find thee; if thou com'st
With a greater title set upon thy crest,
I'll take that first cross patiently, and wait
Until some other comes greater than that.
I'll endure all. [347]
LIVIA The game's ev'n at the best now. You may see, widow,
How all things draw to an end.
MOTHER Ev'n so do I,[348] madam.
LIVIA I pray, take some of your neighbors along with you.
MOTHER They must be those are almost twice your years, then,
If they be chose fit matches for my time, madam.[349]
LIVIA Has not my duke bestirred himself?
MOTHER Yes, faith, madam,
H'as done me all the mischief in this game.
LIVIA H'as showed himself in's kind.[350]
MOTHER In's kind, call you it?
I may swear that.
LIVIA Yes, faith, and keep your oath.
GUARDIANO [*Aside*] Hark, list! There's somebody coming down; 'tis she.

341 385 fetch you over: defeat you

342 389 blind mate: a situation in chess where one player checkmates the other, but does not see the mate, calling only "check." In this case, it is the mother who is blind to Bianca's situation

343 397 flesh-fly: the blow-fly, which leaves its eggs in animals' carcasses

344 398 stomach: sexual appetite

345 399 queasy: delicate; fastidious

346 401 stay the appetite: settle the stomach; make her hungry

347 402–6 if thou . . . endure all: Guardiano speaks ironically, saying that he will "endure" the bestowal of multiple honors and titles in exchange for his service to the duke

348 408 Ev'n so do I: the mother takes Livia's reference to the end of the game as an allusion to death and notes that she is close to it

349 409–11 I pray . . . time, madam: Livia seems to suggest that she, as the mother's friend and "neighbor," would like to die at the same time as her. The mother retorts that Livia is too young for death

350 414 in's kind: according to his nature

Enter BIANCA

BIANCA [*Aside*] Now bless me from a blasting![351] I saw that now
Fearful for any woman's eye to look on.
Infectious mists and mildews hang at's eyes,
The weather of a doomsday dwells upon him.
Yet since mine honor's leprous, why should I
Preserve that fair that[352] caused the leprosy?
Come, poison all at once! [*Aside to* GUARDIANO] Thou in whose baseness
The bane of virtue broods,[353] I'm bound in soul
Eternally to curse thy smooth-browed[354] treachery,
That wore the fair veil of a friendly welcome,
And I a stranger. Think upon't, 'tis worth it.
Murders piled up upon a guilty spirit
At his last breath will not lie heavier
Than this betraying act upon thy conscience.
Beware of off'ring the first-fruits to sin!
His weight is deadly[355] who commits with strumpets[356]
After they have been abased and made for use;
If they offend to th'death, as wise men know,
How much more they, then, that first made 'em so? [357]
I give thee that to feed on. I'm made bold now,
I thank thy treachery; sin and I'm acquainted,
No couple greater; and I'm like that great one
Who, making politic use of a base villain,
He likes the treason well, but hates the traitor.[358]
So I hate thee, slave.
GUARDIANO Well, so the duke love me,
I fare not much amiss then. Two great feasts[359]
Do seldom come together in one day;
We must not look for 'em.
BIANCA What, at it still, mother?
MOTHER You see we sit by't. Are you so soon returned?
LIVIA [*Aside*] So lively and so cheerful—a good sign, that.
MOTHER You have not seen all since,[360] sure?
BIANCA That have I, mother:
The monument and all. I'm so beholding
To this kind, honest, courteous gentleman,
You'd little think it, mother; showed me all,
Had me[361] from place to place, so fashionably—
The kindness of some people, how't exceeds!
Faith, I have seen that I little thought to see
I'th' morning when I rose.
MOTHER Nay, so I told you

351 417 a blasting: being blighted by infection, like a crop withered by disease
352 422 Preserve that fair that: strive to preserve that beauty which
353 424 broods: hatches
354 425 smooth-browed: pleasant-seeming; hypocritical
355 432 His weight is deadly: he commits a deadly sin
356 432 commits with strumpets: fornicates with whores
357 434–5 If they . . . 'em so?: if fornicators sin with strumpets, the people who first corrupted the strumpets are even more culpable
358 440 *He likes . . . the traitor*: the italics, which are in the original edition, indicate a proverbial saying
359 442 Two great feasts: both the duke's favor and Bianca's
360 447 since: already
361 451 Had me: took me, with a pun on sexual possession

Before you saw't, it would prove worth your sight.
I give you great thanks for my daughter, sir,
And all your kindness towards her.
GUARDIANO Oh good widow!
Much good may't do her— [*Aside*] forty weeks[362] hence, i'faith.

Enter SERVANT

LIVIA Now, sir?
SERVANT May't please you, madam, to walk in?
Supper's upon the table.
LIVIA Yes, we come.
Will't please you, gentlewoman?
BIANCA Thanks, virtuous lady—
[*Aside to* LIVIA] Y'are a damned bawd!—I'll follow you, forsooth;
Pray take my mother in. [*Aside to* LIVIA] An old ass go with you!—
This gentleman and I vow not to part.
LIVIA Then get you both before.
BIANCA There lies his art.[363] *Exeunt* [BIANCA, GUARDIANO, *and* SERVANT]
LIVIA Widow, I'll follow you. *Exit* [MOTHER]
Is't so, "damned bawd"?
Are you so bitter? 'Tis but want of use;
Her tender modesty is seasick a little,
Being not accustomed to the breaking billow
Of woman's wavering faith, blown with temptations.
'Tis but a qualm of honor, 'twill away:
A little bitter for the time, but lasts not.
Sin tastes at the first draught like wormwood water,[364]
But drunk again, 'tis nectar ever after.
Exit

Act III, scene i

Enter MOTHER

MOTHER I would my son would either keep at home,
Or I were in my grave!
She was but one day abroad, but ever since
She's grown so cutted[365] there's no speaking to her.
Whether the sight of great cheer at my lady's
And such mean fare at home work discontent in her,
I know not, but I'm sure she's strangely altered.
I'll nev'r keep daughter-in-law i'th'house with me
Again, if I had an hundred; when read I of any
That agreed long together, but she and her mother
Fell out in the first quarter? Nay, sometime
A grudging[366] of a scolding the first week, by'r Lady;

362 458 forty weeks: the duration of a pregnancy
363 465 There lies his art: that's what he's good at (as a pander who goes "before" his client)
364 473 wormwood water: a bitter-tasting medicinal drink prepared from the herb wormwood
365 4 cutted: curt; rude
366 12 A grudging: the first symptom of an illness

So takes the new disease,[367] methinks, in my house.
I'm weary of my part; there's nothing likes[368] her;
I know not how to please her here o'late.
And here she comes.

Enter BIANCA

BIANCA This is the strangest house
For all defects, as ever gentlewoman
Made shift withal to pass away her love in.
Why is there not a cushion-cloth of drawn work,[369]
Or some fair cut-work[370] pinned up in my bedchamber,
A silver-and-gilt casting bottle[371] hung by't?
Nay, since I am content to be so kind to you
To spare you for[372] a silver basin and ewer,
Which one of my fashion looks for of duty—
She's never offered under[373]—where she sleeps.
MOTHER She talks of things here my whole state's[374] not worth.
BIANCA Never a green silk quilt is there i'th'house, mother,
To cast upon my bed?
MOTHER No, by my troth, is there,
Nor orange tawny[375] neither.
BIANCA Here's a house
For a young gentlewoman to be got with child in!
MOTHER Yes, simple though you make it, there has been three
Got in a year[376] in't, since you move me to't,
And all as sweet-faced children and as lovely
As you'll be mother of; I will not spare you.
What, cannot children be begot, think you,
Without gilt casting bottles? Yes, and as sweet ones.
The miller's daughter brings forth as white[377] boys
As she that bathes herself with milk and bean-flour.[378]
'Tis an old saying, "one may keep good cheer
In a mean house"; so may true love affect[379]
After the rate of princes[380] in a cottage.
BIANCA Troth, you speak wondrous well for your old house here;
'Twill shortly fall down at your feet to thank you,
Or stoop when you go to bed, like a good child,
To ask you blessing. Must I live in want
Because my fortune matched me with your son?
Wives do not give away themselves to husbands

367 13 new disease: a common term in the period for a fever whose cause was unclear
368 14 likes: pleases
369 19 drawn work: ornamental patterns achieved by drawing out threads from woven fabric
370 20 cut-work: openwork lace created by cutting a pattern into the material
371 21 casting bottle: a bottle for scattering perfume
372 23 To spare you for: as not to ask you for
373 25 never offered under: never offered less
374 26 state: estate
375 29 orange tawny: a bright color usually associated with courtiers
376 31–2 three/Got in a year: three children conceived in a year (hyperbolic, unless the house was once shared with others or the widow herself had triplets)
377 37 white: beautiful; fair
378 38 milk and bean-flour: products that were supposed to whiten skin. Bathing in foodstuffs was a sign of great extravagance
379 40 affect: feel affection
380 41 After the rate of princes: just as well as princes

To the end to be[381] quite cast away; they look
To be the better used and tendered rather,[382]
Highlier respected and maintained the richer.
They're well rewarded else for the free gift
Of their whole life to a husband. I ask less now
Than what I had at home when I was a maid
And at my father's house; kept short of that
Which a wife knows she must have—nay, and will,
Will, mother, if she be not a fool born!
And report went of me that I could wrangle
For what I wanted when I was two hours old,
And by that copy this land still I hold.[383]
You hear me, mother. *Exit*
MOTHER Ay, too plain methinks;
And were I somewhat deafer when you spake,
'Twere nev'r a whit the worse for my quietness.[384]
'Tis the most sudden'st, strangest alteration,
And the most subtlest, that ev'r wit at threescore
Was puzzled to find out. I know no cause for't, but
She's no more like the gentlewoman at first
Than I am like her that nev'r lay with man yet;
And she's a very young thing, wherev'r she be.
When she first lighted[385] here, I told her then
How mean she should find all things; she was pleased, forsooth,
None better. I laid open[386] all defects to her;
She was contented still. But the devil's in her,
Nothing contents her now. Tonight my son
Promised to be at home. Would he were come once,[387]
For I'm weary of my charge, and life too.
She'd be served all in silver, by her good will,
By night and day; she hates the name of pewterer[388]
More than sick men the noise, or diseased bones
That quake at fall o'th'hammer, seeming to have
A fellow-feeling with't at every blow.
What course shall I think on? She frets me so. [*She moves away*]

Enter LEANTIO

LEANTIO How near am I now to a happiness
That earth exceeds not! Not another like it—
The treasures of the deep are not so precious
As are the concealed comforts of a man
Locked up in woman's love. I scent[389] the air
Of blessings when I come but near the house:
What a delicious breath marriage sends forth!

381 48 To the end to be: with the goal or intention of being
382 48–9 they look . . . tendered rather: on the contrary, they expect to be all the more kindly treated and cherished
383 59 Using a metaphor of legal title to land ("copy"), Bianca states that by virtue of her lifelong ability to fight ("wrangle") for what she wants, she will get her wishes again in this case
384 62 quietness: peace of mind
385 69 lighted: arrived
386 71 laid open: disclosed
387 74 once: at once
388 77 pewterer: a maker of pewter objects, cheaper than silver ones
389 86 scent: smell

The violet-bed's not sweeter. Honest wedlock
Is like a banqueting-house[390] built in a garden,
On which the spring's chaste flowers take delight
To cast their modest odors, when base lust
With all her powders, paintings, and best pride
Is but a fair house built by a ditch-side.[391]
When I behold a glorious dangerous strumpet,
Sparkling in beauty and destruction too,
Both at a twinkling, I do liken straight
Her beautified body to a goodly temple
That's built on vaults where carcasses lie rotting;
And so by little and little I shrink back[392] again,
And quench desire with a cool meditation,
And I'm as well, methinks. Now for a welcome
Able to draw men's envies upon man:
A kiss now that will hang upon my lip
As sweet as morning dew upon a rose,
And full as long.[393] After a five days' fast,
She'll be so greedy now, and cling about me,
I take care how I shall be rid of her.[394]
And here't begins.

[*Enter* BIANCA; MOTHER *comes forward*]

BIANCA Oh sir, y'are welcome home.
MOTHER Oh, is he come? I am glad on't.
LEANTIO Is that all?
[*Aside*] Why this? As dreadful now as sudden death
To some rich man that flatters all his sins
With promise of repentance when he's old,
And dies in the midway before he comes to't.
—Sure y'are not well, Bianca! How do'st, prithee?
BIANCA I have been better than I am at this time.
LEANTIO Alas, I thought so.
BIANCA Nay, I have been worse, too,
Than now you see me, sir.
LEANTIO I'm glad thou mend'st yet;
I feel my heart mend too. How came it to thee?
Has anything disliked[395] thee in my absence?
BIANCA No, certain, I have had the best content
That Florence can afford.
LEANTIO Thou makest the best on't.
Speak, mother, what's the cause? You must needs know.
MOTHER Troth, I know none, son; let her speak herself.
[*Aside*] Unless it be the same gave Lucifer
A tumbling-cast:[396] that's pride.

390 90 banqueting-house: semi-permanent banqueting-houses or gazebos were stylish features in Jacobean gardens and often rumored to be sites for sexual assignations
391 94 by a ditch-side: next to a sewer
392 100 shrink back: lose interest; lose an erection
393 106 full as long: just as long
394 108 I take . . . of her: I am not sure how I shall make her let go of me
395 120 disliked: displeased
396 126 tumbling-cast: a fall or throw in wrestling

BIANCA Methinks this house stands nothing to my mind.[397]
I'll have some pleasant lodging i'th'high street,[398] sir,
Or if 'twere near the court, sir, that were much better—
'Tis a sweet recreation for a gentlewoman
To stand in a bay-window and see gallants.[399]
LEANTIO Now I have another temper,[400] a mere stranger
To that of yours, it seems; I should delight
To see none but yourself.
BIANCA I praise not that.
Too fond is as unseemly as too churlish;[401]
I would not have a husband of that proneness[402]
To kiss me before company, for a world.
Beside, 'tis tedious to see one thing still,[403] sir,
Be it the best that ever heart affected—
Nay, were't yourself, whose love had power, you know,
To bring me from my friends, I would not stand thus
And gaze upon you always; troth, I could not, sir.
As good be blind and have no use of sight
As look on one thing still: what's the eye's treasure
But change of objects? You are learnèd, sir,
And know I speak not ill; 'tis full as virtuous
For woman's eye to look on several men
As for her heart, sir, to be fixed on one.
LEANTIO Now thou com'st home to me; a kiss for that word!
BIANCA No matter[404] for a kiss, sir; let it pass.
'Tis but a toy,[405] we'll not so much as mind it;
Let's talk of other business and forget it.
What news now of the pirates, any stirring?
Prithee, discourse a little.
MOTHER [*Aside*] I'm glad he's here yet
To see her tricks himself; I had[406] lied monstrously
If I had told 'em first.
LEANTIO Speak, what's the humor, sweet,
You make your lip so strange? This was not wont.[407]
BIANCA Is there no kindness betwixt man and wife
Unless they make a pigeon-house of friendship
And be still billing?[408] 'Tis the idlest fondness[409]
That ever was invented, and 'tis pity
It's grown a fashion for poor gentlewomen;
There's many a disease kissed in a year by't,
And a French curtsy[410] made to't. Alas, sir,
Think of the world, how we shall live; grow serious.

397 127 stands nothing to my mind: is not at all situated as I would like
398 128 high street: main commercial street of the city
399 131 stand in … see gallants: standing in a bay-window to see and be seen was an activity associated with prostitutes in Middleton's time
400 132 temper: disposition
401 135 churlish: miserly; crude
402 136 proneness: inclination
403 138 still: all the time
404 150 No matter: no need
405 151 toy: trifle
406 155 I had: he would have thought that I
407 157 was not wont: wasn't your custom in the past
408 160 billing: cooing; fawning on one another
409 160 idlest fondness: most pointless foolishness
410 164 French curtsy: elaborate gesture of deference; also an allusion to the "French pox," syphilis

We have been married a whole fortnight now.
LEANTIO How? A whole fortnight! Why, is that so long?
BIANCA 'Tis time to leave off dalliance; 'tis a doctrine
Of your own teaching, if you be remembered,
And I was bound to obey it.
MOTHER [*Aside*] Here's one fits him![411]
This was well catched, i'faith, son, like a fellow
That rids another country of a plague
And brings it home with him to his own house. *Knock within*
Who knocks?
LEANTIO Who's there now? Withdraw you, Bianca,
Thou art a gem no stranger's eye must see,
Howev'r thou please now to look dull on me. *Exit* [BIANCA]

Enter MESSENGER

Y'are welcome, sir; to whom your business, pray?
MESSENGER To one I see not here now.
LEANTIO Who should that be, sir?
MESSENGER A young gentlewoman I was sent to.
LEANTIO A young gentlewoman?
MESSENGER Ay, sir, about sixteen. Why look you wildly, sir?
LEANTIO At your strange error. Y'have mistook the house, sir;
There's none such here, I assure you.
MESSENGER I assure you, too;
The man that sent me cannot be mistook.[412]
LEANTIO Why, who is't sent you, sir?
MESSENGER The duke.
LEANTIO The duke!
MESSENGER Yes, he entreats her company at a banquet
At Lady Livia's house.
LEANTIO Troth, shall I tell you, sir,
It is the most erroneous business
That ev'r your honest pains was abused with.
I pray, forgive me if I smile a little—
I cannot choose, i'faith, sir, at an error
So comical as this—I mean no harm, though.
His grace has been most wondrous ill informed;
Pray so return it,[413] sir. What should her name be?
MESSENGER That I shall tell you straight, too: Bianca Capella.
LEANTIO How, sir, Bianca? What do you call th'other?
MESSENGER Capella, sir; it seems you know no such, then?
LEANTIO Who should this be? I never heard o'th'name.
MESSENGER Then 'tis a sure mistake.
LEANTIO What if you enquired
In the next street, sir? I saw gallants there
In the new houses that are built of late.
Ten to one, there you find her.
MESSENGER Nay, no matter.
I will return the mistake, and seek no further.
LEANTIO Use your own will and pleasure, sir; y'are welcome. *Exit* MESSENGER

411 170 fits him: punishes him fitly
412 183 be mistook: make a mistake
413 193 return it: report it to the sender

What shall I think of first? Come forth, Bianca.
Thou art betrayed, I fear me.

Enter BIANCA

BIANCA Betrayed? How, sir?
LEANTIO The duke knows thee.
BIANCA Knows me! How know you that, sir?
LEANTIO Has got thy name.
BIANCA [*Aside*] Ay, and my good name, too;
That's worse o'th'twain.
LEANTIO How comes this work about?
BIANCA How should the duke know me? Can you guess, mother?
MOTHER Not I, with all my wits; sure we kept house close.[414]
LEANTIO Kept close! Not all the locks in Italy
Can keep you women so. You have been gadding,[415]
And ventured out at twilight to th'court green yonder,
And met the gallant bowlers[416] coming home—
Without your masks,[417] too, both of you; I'll be hanged else!
Thou hast been seen, Bianca, by some stranger;
Never excuse it.
BIANCA I'll not seek the way, sir.
Do you think y'have married me to mew me up[418]
Not to be seen? What would you make of me?
LEANTIO A good wife, nothing else.
BIANCA Why, so are some
That are seen ev'ry day, else the devil take 'em.
LEANTIO No more then; I believe all virtuous in thee
Without an argument. 'Twas but thy hard chance
To be seen somewhere; there lies all the mischief.
But I have devised a riddance.
MOTHER Now I can tell you, son,
The time and place.
LEANTIO When, where?
MOTHER What wits have I?
When you last took your leave, if you remember,
You left us both at window.
LEANTIO Right, I know that.
MOTHER And not the third part of an hour after,
The duke passed by in a great solemnity
To St. Mark's Temple, and to my apprehension[419]
He looked up twice to th'window.
LEANTIO Oh, there quickened[420]
The mischief of this hour!
BIANCA [*Aside*] If you call't mischief,
It is a thing I fear I am conceived with.[421]
LEANTIO Looked he up twice, and could you take no warning?

414 210 kept house close: stayed hidden at home
415 212 gadding: roving abroad in search of pleasure
416 214 gallant bowlers: bowls were a popular pastime among courtiers in this period
417 215 masks: see I.ii. 74
418 218 mew me up: imprison me
419 231 to my apprehension: as it seemed to me
420 232 quickened: began
421 234 conceived with: made pregnant by (playing on the secondary meaning of Leantio's word "quickened")

MOTHER Why, once may do as much harm, son, as a thousand;
Do not you know one spark has fired an house
As well as a whole furnace?
LEANTIO My heart flames for't.
Yet let's be wise, and keep all smothered closely;
I have bethought a means. Is the door fast?[422]
MOTHER I locked it myself after him.
LEANTIO You know, mother,
At the end of the dark parlor there's a place
So artificially contrived for a conveyance[423]
No search could ever find it; when my father
Kept in for manslaughter,[424] it was his sanctuary.
There will I lock my life's best treasure up.
Bianca!
BIANCA Would you keep me closer yet?
Have you the conscience? Y'are best ev'n choke me up,[425] sir!
You make me fearful of your health and wits,
You cleave to such wild courses. What's the matter?
LEANTIO Why, are you so insensible of your danger
To ask that now? The duke himself has sent for you
To Lady Livia's—to a banquet, forsooth!
BIANCA Now, I beshrew you heartily! Has he so?
And you the man would never yet vouchsafe
To tell me on't till now. You show your loyalty
And honesty at once, and so farewell, sir.
LEANTIO Bianca, whither now?
BIANCA Why, to the duke, sir.
You say he sent for me.
LEANTIO But thou dost not mean to go, I hope.
BIANCA No? I shall prove unmannerly,
Rude and uncivil, mad, and imitate you.
Come, mother, come, follow his humor[426] no longer.
We shall be all executed for treason shortly.
MOTHER Not I, i'faith; I'll first obey the duke,
And taste of a good banquet; I'm of thy mind.
I'll step but up[427] and fetch two handkerchiefs
To pocket up[428] some sweetmeats, and o'ertake thee. *Exit*
BIANCA [*Aside*] Why, here's an old wench would trot into[429] a bawd now,
For some dry sucket[430] or a colt in marchpane.[431] *Exit*
LEANTIO Oh thou the ripe time of man's misery, wedlock,
When all his thoughts like over-laden trees
Crack with the fruits they bear, in cares, in jealousies.
Oh, that's a fruit that ripens hastily
After 'tis knit to marriage; it begins
As soon as the sun shines upon the bride

422 240 fast: secure
423 243 So artfully planned as a secret passage
424 245 Kept in for manslaughter: stayed hidden after committing manslaughter
425 248 Y'are best ev'n choke me up: you might as well just suffocate me
426 262 follow his humor: go along with his whims
427 266 step but up: just go upstairs
428 267 pocket up: wrap up to take away
429 268 trot into: willingly become
430 269 dry sucket: crystallized fruit or nuts
431 269 colt in marchpane: marzipan figure of a colt

A little to show color. Blessèd powers!
Whence comes this alteration? The distractions,
The fears and doubts it brings are numberless,
And yet the cause I know not. What a peace
Has he that never marries! If he knew
The benefit he enjoyed, or had the fortune
To come and speak with me, he should know then
The infinite wealth he had, and discern rightly
The greatness of his treasure by my loss.
Nay, what a quietness has he 'bove mine
That wears his youth out in a strumpet's arms,
And never spends more care upon a woman
Than at the time of lust; but walks away,
And if he find her dead at his return,
His pity is soon done: he breaks a sigh
In many parts, and gives her but a piece on't!
But all the fears, shames, jealousies, costs and troubles,
And still-renewed[432] cares of a marriage bed
Live in the issue[433] when the wife is dead.

Enter MESSENGER

MESSENGER A good perfection[434] to your thoughts!
LEANTIO The news, sir?
MESSENGER Though you were pleased of late to pin an error on me,
You must not shift another in your stead[435] too:
The duke has sent me for you.
LEANTIO How, for me, sir?
[*Aside*] I see then 'tis my theft; w'are both betrayed.
Well, I'm not the first has stol'n away a maid:
My countrymen have used it.[436]—I'll along with you, sir.

Exeunt

Act III, scene ii

A banquet prepared. Enter GUARDIANO *and* WARD

GUARDIANO Take you especial note of such a gentlewoman;
She's here on purpose. I have invited her,
Her father, and her uncle to this banquet.
Mark[437] her behavior well, it does concern you;
And what her good parts[438] are, as far as time
And place can modestly require[439] a knowledge of,
Shall be laid open to your understanding.
You know I'm both your guardian and your uncle;
My care of you is double, ward and nephew,
And I'll express it here.

432 293 still-renewed: ever-renewed
433 294 issue: children born of marriage
434 295 perfection: conclusion
435 297 shift another in your stead: try to pass yourself off as someone else
436 301 used it: done the same thing
437 4 Mark: note
438 5 parts: qualities
439 6 require: demand

WARD Faith, I should know her
Now by her mark[440] among a thousand women;
A little, pretty, deft, and tidy thing, you say?
GUARDIANO Right.
WARD With a lusty sprouting sprig[441] in her hair?
GUARDIANO Thou goest the right way still. Take one mark more:
Thou shalt nev'r find her hand out of her uncle's,
Or else his out of hers, if she be near him.
The love of kindred never yet stuck closer
Than theirs to one another; he that weds her
Marries her uncle's heart too. *Cornets*
WARD Say you so, sir?
Then I'll be asked i'th'church to[442] both of them.
GUARDIANO Fall back, here comes the duke.
WARD He brings a gentlewoman;
I should fall forward[443] rather.

Enter DUKE, BIANCA, FABRITIO, HIPPOLITO, LIVIA, MOTHER, ISABELLA, *and Attendants*

DUKE Come, Bianca,
Of purpose sent into the world to show
Perfection once in woman; I'll believe
Henceforward they have ev'ry one a soul too,
'Gainst all the uncourteous opinions
That man's uncivil rudeness ever held of 'em.[444]
Glory of Florence, light into[445] mine arms!

Enter LEANTIO

BIANCA Yon comes a grudging man will chide you, sir;
The storm is now in's heart, and would get nearer
And fall here if it durst; it pours down yonder.
DUKE If that be he, the weather shall soon clear;
List, and I'll tell thee how. [*Whispers to* BIANCA]
LEANTIO [*Aside*] A-kissing, too?
I see 'tis plain lust now, adultery boldened;[446]
What will it prove anon, when 'tis stuffed full
Of wine and sweetmeats, being so impudent fasting? [447]
DUKE [*To* LEANTIO] We have heard of your good parts, sir, which we honor
With our embrace and love. [*To* GENTLEMAN] Is not the captainship
Of Rouans' citadel,[448] since the late deceased,
Supplied[449] by any yet?
GENTLEMAN By none, my lord.
DUKE [*To* LEANTIO] Take it, the place is yours then; and as faithfulness

440 11 by her mark: by her distinctive characteristics
441 13 lusty sprouting sprig: large ornament in the shape of the sprig of a flowering plant (with a sexual innuendo)
442 20 asked i'th'church to: have the bans called for
443 22 fall forward: i.e. fall onto her (with a sexual connotation)
444 24–7 I'll believe . . . of 'em: there was controversy in Middleton's time over whether women had souls, since Genesis does not mention God breathing a soul into Eve
445 28 light into: come into
446 34 boldened: emboldened
447 36 impudent fasting: shameless when fasting
448 39 Rouans' citadel: probably alludes to a site in Florence that housed major forts, said to have been called "Ruinate," or "the ruinous"
449 40 Supplied: filled

And desert grows, our favor shall grow with't.
Rise now the captain of our fort at Rouans.
LEANTIO The service of whole life give your grace thanks.
DUKE Come, sit, Bianca.
LEANTIO [*Aside*] This is some good yet,
And more than ev'r I looked for: a fine bit[450]
To stay a cuckold's stomach.[451] All preferment
That springs from sin and lust, it shoots up quickly,
As gardeners' crops do in the rotten'st grounds.
So is all means[452] raised from base prostitution
Ev'n like a sallet[453] growing upon a dunghill.
I'm like a thing that never was yet heard of,
Half merry and half mad, much like a fellow
That eats his meat with a good appetite
And wears a plague-sore[454] that would fright a country;
Or rather like the barren,[455] hardened ass
That feeds on thistles[456] till he bleeds again[457]—
And such is the condition of my misery.
LIVIA Is that your son, widow?
MOTHER Yes, did your ladyship
Never know that till now?
LIVIA No, trust me, did I—
[*Aside*] Nor ever truly felt the power of love
And pity to a man till now I knew him.
I have enough to buy me my desires,
And yet to spare: that's one good comfort. [*To* LEANTIO] Hark you,
Pray let me speak with you, sir, before you go.
LEANTIO With me, lady? You shall; I am at your service.
[*Aside*] What will she say now, trow? More goodness yet?
WARD I see her[458] now, I'm sure. The ape's[459] so little
I shall scarce feel her; I have seen almost
As tall as she sold in the fair for ten pence.[460]
See how she simpers it, as if marmalade
Would not melt in her mouth! She might have the kindness, i'faith,
To send me a gilded bull from her own trencher,[461]
A ram, a goat, or somewhat to be nibbling.[462]
These women, when they come to sweet things once,
They forget all their friends, they grow so greedy—
Nay, oftentimes their husbands.
DUKE Here's a health[463] now, gallants,
To the best beauty at this day in Florence.
BIANCA Whoev'r she be, she shall not go unpledged, sir.

450 46 bit: morsel
451 47 stay a cuckold's stomach: to quell the cuckold's anger or nausea
452 50 So is all means: so are all gains
453 51 sallet: salad leaf
454 55 plague-sore: a sore symptomatic of the bubonic plague
455 56 barren: stupid
456 57 feeds on thistles: a proverb states, "The ass, though laden with gold, still eats thistles"
457 57 again: as a consequence
458 68 her: Isabella
459 68 ape: a diminutive term of endearment
460 69–70 I have . . . ten pence: i.e. Isabella is scarcely larger than a cheap doll sold at a public fair
461 73 trencher: plate
462 73–4 gilded bull . . . a goat: marzipan or candied animals; all of these beasts are associated with rampant male sexuality
463 77 health: toast

DUKE Nay, you're excused for[464] this.
BIANCA Who, I, my lord?
DUKE Yes, by the law of Bacchus,[465] plead your benefit;[466]
You are not bound to pledge your own health, lady.
BIANCA That's a good way, my lord, to keep me dry.[467]
DUKE Nay, then I will not offend Venus[468] so much,
Let Bacchus seek his 'mends[469] in another court.
Here's to thyself, Bianca. [*He drinks*]
BIANCA Nothing comes
More welcome to that name than your grace. [*She drinks*]
LEANTIO [*Aside*] So, so;
Here stands the poor thief now that stole the treasure,
And he's not thought on. Ours is near kin now
To a twin misery born into the world:
First the hard-conscienced worldling, he hoards wealth up;
Then comes the next, and he feasts all upon't.
One's damned for getting, th'other for spending on't. [470]
Oh, equal justice, thou hast met my sin
With a full weight; I'm rightly now oppressed:
All her friends' heavy hearts lie in my breast.[471]
DUKE Methinks there is no spirit amongst us, gallants,
But what divinely sparkles from the eyes
Of bright Bianca; we sat all in darkness
But for that splendor. Who was't told us lately
Of a match-making rite, a marriage tender?[472]
GUARDIANO 'Twas I, my lord.
DUKE 'Twas you, indeed. Where is she?
GUARDIANO This is the gentlewoman.
FABRITIO My lord, my daughter.
DUKE Why, here's some stirring yet.[473]
FABRITIO She's a dear child to me.
DUKE That must needs be: you say she is your daughter.
FABRITIO Nay, my good lord, dear[474] to my purse, I mean,
Beside my person;[475] I nev'r reckoned that.[476]
She has the full qualities of a gentlewoman;
I have brought her up to music, dancing, what not
That may commend her sex and stir her husband.
DUKE And which is he, now?
GUARDIANO This young heir, my lord.
DUKE What is he brought up to?

464 80 excused for: excused from
465 81 Bacchus: the Roman god of wine
466 81 plead your benefit: claim exemption from a duty or law
467 83 keep me dry: keep me thirsty or lacking in moistness (with a sexual connotation)
468 84 offend Venus: as goddess of love, Venus was associated with warmth and moistness
469 85 seek his 'mends: seek amends or legal remedies
470 89–93 Ours is . . . spending on't: Leantio likens himself to the miser who is damned for hoarding up wealth, and the duke to the heir who is damned for spending it all
471 95–6 I'm rightly . . . my breast: Leantio declares that his punishment is just, as he is now suffering the same sorrow as Bianca's friends, from whom he "stole" her
472 101 marriage tender: betrothal
473 104 some stirring yet: some excitement after all (with a suggestion of sexual excitement)
474 106 dear: expensive
475 107 Beside my person: apart from her physical debt to my body
476 107 reckoned that: included that in my calculations

HIPPOLITO [*Aside*] To cat and trap.[477]
GUARDIANO My lord, he's a great ward: wealthy, but simple.
His parts consist in acres.[478]
DUKE Oh, wise-acres!
GUARDIANO Y'have spoke him in a word, sir.
BIANCA 'Las, poor gentlewoman!
She's ill bestead,[479] unless sh'as dealt the wiselier
And laid in more provision for her youth;
Fools will not keep in summer.[480]
LEANTIO [*Aside*] No, nor such wives
From whores in winter.[481]
DUKE Yea, the voice too, sir?
FABRITIO Ay, and a sweet breast[482] too, my lord, I hope,
Or I have cast away my money wisely.
She took her pricksong[483] earlier, my lord,
Than any of her kindred ever did:
A rare child, though I say't, but I'd not have
The baggage[484] hear so much; 'twould make her swell[485] straight,
And maids of all things must not be puffed up.[486]
DUKE Let's turn us to a better banquet, then,
For music bids the soul of a man to a feast,
And that's indeed a noble entertainment,
Worthy[487] Bianca's self. [*To* BIANCA] You shall perceive, beauty,
Our Florentine damsels are not brought up idly.
BIANCA They are wiser of themselves,[488] it seems, my lord,
And can take gifts when goodness offers 'em. *Music*
LEANTIO [*Aside*] True, and damnation has taught you that wisdom;
You can take gifts, too. Oh, that music mocks me!
LIVIA [*Aside*] I am as dumb to any language now
But love's, as one that never learned to speak.[489]
I am not yet so old but he may think of me.
My own fault: I have been idle[490] a long time;
But I'll begin the week[491] and paint[492] tomorrow,
So follow my true labor[493] day by day.
I never thrived[494] so well as when I used it.
[*ISABELLA sings*]

477 112 cat and trap: See I.ii. 87 SD
478 114 His parts consist in acres: his only good qualities are his lands
479 116 ill bestead: badly situated
480 118 Fools will . . . in summer: Bianca puns on "fool," alluding to the cream-based dessert that will go bad in the heat
481 119 whores in winter: Leantio answers Bianca's pun, joking that wives like her will turn to hoar (frost), or whores, in winter
482 120 breast: singing voice
483 122 took her pricksong: learned to read written music, which was "pricked" into the paper (with a sexual pun on "prick")
484 125 baggage: derogatory term for a woman
485 125 swell: i.e. with pride (with a pun on swelling with child)
486 126 puffed up: proud or conceited; pregnant
487 130 Worthy: worthy of
488 132 of themselves: by nature
489 136–7 I am . . . to speak: I am so unable to speak of anything but love that I might as well be mute
490 139 been idle: not worked on my attractions
491 140 begin the week: start anew
492 140 paint: put on makeup
493 141 true labor: real vocation
494 142 thrived: succeeded romantically

Song

What harder chance can fall to woman,
Who was born to cleave to some man,
Than to bestow her time, youth, beauty,
Life's observance, honor, duty,
On a thing for no use good,
But to make physic work, or blood
Force fresh in an old lady's cheek?[495] *She that would be*
Mother of fools, let her compound with me.[496]

WARD Here's a tune indeed![497] Pish, I had rather hear one ballad sung i'th'nose[498] now, of the lamentable drowning of fat sheep and oxen, than all these simpering tunes played upon cat-guts and sung by little kitlings.[499]

FABRITIO How like you her breast now, my lord?
BIANCA [*Aside to* DUKE] Her breast?[500]
He talks as if his daughter had given suck
Before she were married, as her betters have.[501]
The next he praises, sure, will be her nipples.
DUKE [*Aside to* BIANCA] Methinks, now, such a voice to[502] such a husband
Is like a jewel of unvalued worth
Hung at a fool's ear.
FABRITIO May it please your grace
To give her leave to show another quality?
DUKE Marry, as many good ones as you will, sir:
The more, the better welcome.
LEANTIO [*Aside*] But the less,
The better practiced. That soul's black indeed
That cannot commend virtue; but who keeps it?[503]
The extortioner will say to a sick beggar,
"Heaven comfort thee," though he give none himself.
This good is common.
FABRITIO Will it please you now, sir,
To entreat your ward to take her by the hand,
And lead her in a dance before the duke?
GUARDIANO That will I, sir; 'tis needful.[504] Hark you, nephew.
FABRITIO Nay, you shall see, young heir, what y'have for your money,
Without fraud or imposture.
WARD Dance with her!
Not I, sweet guardianer, do not urge my heart to't;
'Tis clean against my blood.[505] Dance with a stranger!
Let whoso will, do't; I'll not begin first with her.

495 148–50 *a thing ... lady's cheek*: Isabella implies that the Ward can only provoke enough excitement to help medicine work (mild exercise was believed to do this), or to arouse a susceptible old lady

496 151 *compound with me*: agree with me; do like me

497 152 Here's a tune indeed: the Ward's lines may be spoken at the same time as Isabella's song (they appear side by side in the original text)

498 152 i'th'nose: nasally

499 154 kitlings: kittens; also a colloquial term for prostitutes

500 155 breast: though Fabritio alludes to Isabella's singing voice, Bianca takes up the more common meaning, "bosom"

501 156–7 as if ... betters have: as if Isabella had given birth to an illegitimate child before she was married, as many more nobly born women have done

502 159 to: compared to; given to

503 166 keeps it: practices it

504 171–2 lead her ... 'tis needful: the dance of the newly betrothed couple is treated as traditional or even compulsory, and soon becomes a metaphor for sex

505 176 blood: inclination; sexual desire

HIPPOLITO [*Aside*] No, fear't not, fool; sh'as took a better order.[506]
GUARDIANO Why, who shall take her, then?
WARD Some other gentleman.
Look, there's her uncle, a fine-timbered[507] reveler;
Perhaps he knows the manner of her dancing, too.
I'll have him do't before me—I have sworn, Guardianer;
Then may I learn the better.
GUARDIANO Thou'lt be an ass still.
WARD Ay, all that, uncle, shall not fool me out.[508]
Pish, I stick closer to myself[509] than so.
GUARDIANO I must entreat you, sir, to take your niece
And dance with her. My ward's a little willful;
He would have you show him the way.
HIPPOLITO Me, sir?
He shall command it at all hours; pray tell him so.
GUARDIANO I thank you for him; he has not wit himself, sir.
HIPPOLITO Come, my life's peace. [*Aside*] I have a strange office[510] on't here.
'Tis some man's luck to keep the joys he likes
Concealed for his own bosom,[511] but my fortune
To set 'em out now for another's liking,
Like the mad misery of necessitous[512] man
That parts from his good horse with many praises
And goes on foot himself. Need[513] must be obeyed
In ev'ry action; it mars[514] man and maid.

Music. A dance [*by* ISABELLA *and* HIPPOLITO], *making honors*[515] *to the* DUKE *and curtsy to themselves, both before and after*

DUKE Signor Fabritio, y'are a happy father.
Your cares and pains are fortunate, you see;
Your cost bears noble fruits. Hippolito, thanks.
FABRITIO Here's some amends for all my charges[516] yet:
She wins both prick and praise[517] wherev'r she comes.
DUKE How lik'st, Bianca?
BIANCA All things well, my lord,
But this poor gentlewoman's fortune; that's the worst.
DUKE There is no doubt, Bianca, she'll find leisure
To make that good enough: he's rich and simple.
BIANCA She has the better hope o'th'upper hand, indeed,
Which women strive for most.
GUARDIANO [*To* WARD] Do't when I bid you, sir.
WARD I'll venture but a hornpipe[518] with her, Guardianer,
Or some such married man's dance.

506 178 took a better order: made a better arrangement
507 180 fine-timbered: well built
508 184 fool me out: mock me into changing my mind
509 185 I stick closer to myself: I have more sense of self-interest (with an implied reference to masturbation)
510 191 office: duty
511 193 his own bosom: his own private enjoyment
512 195 necessitous: impoverished
513 197 Need: necessity
514 198 mars: ruins
515 198 SD *making honors*: bowing
516 202 charges: expenses
517 203 prick and praise: the highest praise; referring to the definition of "prick" as the center of the target in archery (with a pun on the word's sexual connotation)
518 210 hornpipe: a popular, lively dance; with a pun on the "horns" of the cuckold, hence the Ward calls this a "married man's dance"

GUARDIANO Well, venture something, sir.
WARD I have rhyme for what I do.
GUARDIANO [*Aside*] But little reason, I think.
WARD Plain men dance the measures,[519] the cinquepace[520] the gay;
Cuckolds dance the hornpipe, and farmers dance the hay;[521]
Your soldiers dance the round,[522] and maidens that grow big;
Your drunkards, the canaries;[523] your whore and bawd, the jig.[524]
Here's your eight kind of dancers; he that finds the ninth, let him pay the minstrels.
DUKE Oh, here he appears once in his own person![525]
I thought he would have married her by attorney,[526]
And lain with her so, too.
BIANCA Nay, my kind lord;
There's very seldom any found so foolish
To give away his part there.
LEANTIO [*Aside*] Bitter scoff!
Yet I must do't; with what a cruel pride
The glory[527] of her sin strikes by[528] my afflictions.
Music. WARD *and* ISABELLA *dance; he ridiculously imitates* HIPPOLITO
DUKE This thing[529] will make shift,[530] sirs, to make a husband,
For aught I see in him. How think'st, Bianca?
BIANCA Faith, an ill-favored shift, my lord. Methinks
If he would take some voyage when he's married,
Dangerous, or long enough, and scarce be seen
Once in nine year together, a wife then
Might make indifferent shift[531] to be content with him.
DUKE A kiss! That wit deserves to be made much on.
Come, our caroche.[532]
GUARDIANO Stands ready for your grace.
DUKE My thanks to all your loves. Come, fair Bianca,
We have took special care of you, and provided
Your lodging near us now.
BIANCA Your love is great, my lord.
DUKE Once more our thanks to all.
OMNES All blest honors guard you. *Cornets flourish. Exeunt all but* LEANTIO *and* LIVIA
LEANTIO Oh hast thou left me, then, Bianca, utterly?
Bianca! Now I miss thee; oh, return,
And save the faith of woman. I nev'r felt
The loss of thee till now. 'Tis an affliction
Of greater weight than youth was made to bear,
As if a punishment of after-life
Were fall'n upon man here. So new it is

519 213 measures: a slow, stately dance
520 213 cinquepace: a French dance popular with courtiers
521 214 hay: a country dance
522 215 round: a circling dance; also alludes to the "rounds" or watch of soldiers
523 216 canaries: a lively dance, said to have originated in the Canary Islands; also alludes to canary wine
524 216 jig: a vigorous dance often associated with sex
525 218 in his own person: apparently the Ward comes out to meet Isabella by this point
526 219 by attorney: by proxy
527 224 glory: boastfulness; vainglory
528 224 strikes by: casts aside
529 225 This thing: i.e. the Ward
530 225 make shift: make an attempt; try hard
531 231 make indifferent shift: just about manage
532 233 caroche: a luxurious coach

To flesh and blood, so strange, so insupportable
A torment—ev'n mistook,[533] as if a body
Whose death were drowning must needs therefore suffer it
In scalding oil.
LIVIA Sweet sir!
LEANTIO As long as mine eye saw thee,
I half enjoyed thee.
LIVIA Sir?
LEANTIO Canst thou forget
The dear pains my love took, how it has watched[534]
Whole nights together in all weathers for thee,
Yet stood in heart more merry than the tempests
That sung about mine ears—like dangerous flatterers
That can set all their mischief to sweet tunes—
And then received thee from thy father's window
Into these arms at midnight, when we embraced
As if we had been statues only made for't,[535]
To show art's life,[536] so silent were our comforts,
And kissed as if our lips had grown together!
LIVIA This makes me madder to enjoy him now.
LEANTIO Canst thou forget all this? And better joys
That we met after this, which then new kisses
Took pride to praise?
LIVIA I shall grow madder yet.—Sir!
LEANTIO This[537] cannot be but of some close[538] bawd's working.
—Cry mercy,[539] lady. What would you say to me?
My sorrow makes me so unmannerly,
So comfort bless me,[540] I had quite forgot you.
LIVIA Nothing but,[541] ev'n in pity to that passion,
Would give your grief good counsel.
LEANTIO Marry, and welcome, lady;
It never could come better.
LIVIA Then first, sir:
To make away[542] all your good thoughts at once of her,
Know most assuredly she is a strumpet.
LEANTIO Ha: most assuredly! Speak not a thing
So vild[543] so certainly, leave it more doubtful.
LIVIA Then I must leave all truth, and spare my knowledge:
A sin which I too lately found,[544] and wept for.
LEANTIO Found you it?
LIVIA Ay, with wet eyes.
LEANTIO Oh, perjurious friendship!
LIVIA You missed your fortunes when you met with her, sir.

533 246 mistook: inappropriate; unfair
534 250 watched: stayed awake; kept vigil
535 257 for't: for it (i.e. embracing)
536 258 To show art's life: to show how lifelike art can be
537 264 This: Bianca's abandonment of him
538 264 close: secret
539 265 Cry mercy: I beg your pardon
540 267 So comfort bless me: as truly as I hope to be blessed with comfort
541 268 Nothing but: nothing but that which
542 271 make away: do away with
543 274 vild: vile
544 276 found: discovered

Young gentlemen that only love for beauty,
They love not wisely. Such a marriage rather
Proves the destruction of affection:
It brings on want, and want's the key of whoredom.[545]
I think y'had small means with her.[546]
LEANTIO Oh, not any, lady.
LIVIA Alas, poor gentleman, what mean'st thou, sir,
Quite to undo thyself with thine own kind heart?
Thou art too good and pitiful to woman.
Marry, sir, thank thy stars for this blest fortune
That rids the summer[547] of thy youth so well
From many beggars[548] that had lain a-sunning
In thy beams only else,[549] till thou hadst wasted
The whole days of thy life in heat and labor.
What would you say now to a creature found
As pitiful to you, and as it were
Ev'n sent on purpose from the whole sex general[550]
To requite all that kindness you have shown to't?
LEANTIO What's that, madam?
LIVIA Nay, a gentlewoman, and one able
To reward good things; ay, and bears a conscience to't.[551]
Couldst thou love such a one, that—blow all fortunes[552]—
Would never see thee want?
Nay, more, maintain thee to thine enemies' envy,
And shalt not[553] spend a care for't, stir a thought,
Nor break a sleep, unless love's music waked thee;
No storm of fortune should. Look upon me,
And know that woman!
LEANTIO Oh, my life's wealth, Bianca!
LIVIA [*Aside*] Still with her name? Will nothing wear it out?
—That deep sigh went but for a strumpet, sir.
LEANTIO It can go for no other that loves me.
LIVIA [*Aside*] He's vexed in mind; I came too soon to him.
Where's my discretion now, my skill, my judgment?
I'm cunning in all arts but my own love.
'Tis as unseasonable[554] to tempt him now,
So soon, as a widow to be courted
Following her husband's corse,[555] or to make bargain
By the graveside, and take a young man there.
Her strange departure stands like a hearse[556] yet
Before his eyes, which time will take down shortly. *Exit*
LEANTIO Is she my wife till death, yet no more mine?
That's a hard measure;[557] then what's marriage good for?

545 282 want's the key of whoredom: poverty is the incitement to prostitution
546 283 I think you gained very little dowry from her
547 288 summer: prime
548 289 beggars: impoverished children
549 290 else: otherwise
550 294 whole sex general: entire female sex
551 297 bears a conscience to't: feels duty-bound to do so
552 298 blow all fortunes: come what may
553 301 and shalt not: and you shall not
554 311 unseasonable: ill-timed
555 313 corse: corpse
556 315 hearse: an ornamental framework built over a coffin, to be taken down before burial
557 318 measure: portion; treatment

Methinks by right I should not now be living,
And then 'twere all well. What a happiness
Had I been made of had I never seen her,
For nothing makes man's loss grievous to him
But knowledge of the worth of what he loses:
For what he never had, he never misses.
She's gone forever, utterly; there is
As much redemption of a soul from hell
As a fair woman's body from his palace.
Why should my love last longer than her truth?
What is there good in woman to be loved
When only that which makes her so has left her?
I cannot love her now but I must like[558]
Her sin, and my own shame too, and be guilty
Of law's breach with her,[559] and mine own abusing—
All which were monstrous. Then my fastest course
For health of mind and body is to turn
My heart and hate her, most extremely hate her;
I have no other way. Those virtuous powers
Which were chaste witnesses of both our troths
Can witness she breaks first—and I'm rewarded
With captainship o'th'fort! A place of credit,[560]
I must confess, but poor; my factorship
Shall not exchange means with't.[561] He that died last in't,
He was no drunkard, yet he died a beggar
For all this thrift. Besides, the place not fits me;
It suits my resolution, not my breeding.[562]

Enter LIVIA

LIVIA [*Aside*] I have tried all ways I can, and have not power
To keep from sight of him.—How are you now, sir?
LEANTIO I feel a better ease, madam.
LIVIA   Thanks to blessedness!
You will do well, I warrant you; fear it not, sir.
Join but your own good will to't; he's not wise
That loves his pain or sickness, or grows fond
Of a disease whose property is to vex[563] him
And spitefully drink his blood up.[564] Out upon't, sir;
Youth knows no greater loss. I pray, let's walk, sir.
You never saw the beauty of my house yet,
Nor how abundantly fortune has blessed me
In worldly treasure; trust me, I have enough, sir,
To make my friend a rich man in my life,
A great man at my death—yourself will say so.[565]
If you want anything, and spare to speak,
Troth, I'll condemn you for a willful man, sir.

558 331 but I must like: unless I like
559 332–3 be guilty/Of law's breach with her: share the guilt of adultery with her
560 340 credit: honor
561 341–2 my factorship . . . means with't: Leantio's old positon as a merchant's agent paid better than the captainship
562 345 The captainship may suit Leantio's bravery, but he has not been trained as a soldier
563 352 vex: afflict
564 353 drink his blood up: unrequited love was believed to dry up the lover's blood
565 359 yourself will say so: you will say so yourself

LEANTIO Why, sure this can be but the flattery of some dream.
LIVIA Now by this kiss, my love, my soul and riches,
'Tis all true substance. [*She kisses him*]
Come, you shall see my wealth; take what you list.[566]
The gallanter you go,[567] the more you please me.
I will allow you, too, your page and footman,
Your race horses, or any various pleasure
Exercised youth[568] delights in. But to me
Only, sir, wear your heart of constant stuff:[569]
Do but you love enough, I'll give enough.
LEANTIO Troth, then, I'll love enough and take enough.
LIVIA Then we are both pleased enough.

Exeunt

Act III, scene iii

Enter GUARDIANO *and* ISABELLA *at one door, and the* WARD *and* SORDIDO *at another*

GUARDIANO Now, nephew, here's the gentlewoman again.
WARD Mass, here she's come again! Mark her now, Sordido.
GUARDIANO This is the maid my love and care has chose
Out for your wife, and so I tender her to you.
Yourself has been eye-witness of some qualities
That speak a courtly breeding, and are costly.
I bring you both to talk together now;
'Tis time you grew familiar in your tongues.
Tomorrow you join hands, and one ring ties you,
And one bed holds you, if you like the choice.
Her father and her friends are i'th'next room,
And stay to see the contract[570] ere they part.
Therefore dispatch, good Ward; be sweet and short:
Like her or like her not, there's but two ways,
And one your body, th'other your purse pays.[571]
WARD I warrant you, Guardianer, I'll not stand all day thrumming,[572]
But quickly shoot my bolt[573] at your next coming.
GUARDIANO Well said! Good fortune to your birding,[574] then. [*Exit*]
WARD I never missed mark[575] yet.
SORDIDO Troth, I think, Master, if the truth were known,
You never shot at any but the kitchen-wench,
And that was a she-woodcock,[576] a mere innocent,[577]
That was oft lost and cried[578] at eight-and-twenty.
WARD No more of that meat, Sordido; here's eggs o'th'spit now,[579]

566 365 what you list: whatever you want
567 366 The gallanter you go: the more stylish you look
568 369 Exercised youth: an active young man
569 370 of constant stuff: of one constant—that is, faithful—color; contrasting with "changeable stuff," a glossy silk that changes color under different lights
570 12 contract: marriage contract
571 15 And one … purse pays: if you like her, you will pay for her with your body (that is, in sexual congress); if you refuse her, you will have to pay a fine to me
572 16 thrumming: strumming on a musical instrument; masturbating
573 17 shoot my bolt: speak my mind; ejaculate
574 18 birding: fowling (playing on "bird-bolt," an arrow used in fowling); pursuing women
575 19 mark: target; female genitalia
576 22 she-woodcock: easily seduced woman (woodcocks were seen as easy birds to catch)
577 22 innocent: simpleton
578 23 lost and cried: lost children were traditionally called for by the town crier
579 24 eggs o'th'spit: a delicate business to handle (eggs roasted on a spit had to be turned "gingerly" to keep them from breaking)

We must turn gingerly. Draw out the catalogue
Of all the faults of women.
SORDIDO How, all the faults! Have you so little reason, to think so much paper will lie in my breeches? Why, ten carts will not carry it, if you set down but the bawds.[580] All the faults? Pray, let's be content with a few of 'em; and if they were less, you would find 'em enough,[581] I warrant you. Look you, sir.
ISABELLA [*Aside*] But that I have th'advantage of the fool
As much as woman's heart can wish and joy at,
What an infernal torment 'twere to be
Thus bought and sold, and turned and pried into, when, alas,
The worst bit is too good for him! And the comfort is,
H'as but a cater's[582] place on't, and provides
All for another's table. Yet how curious[583]
The ass is, like some nice professor[584] on't
That buys up all the daintiest food i'th'markets,
And seldom licks his lips after[585] a taste on't!
SORDIDO Now to her, now y'have scanned all her parts over.
WARD But at what end shall I begin now, Sordido?
SORDIDO Oh, ever at a woman's lip, while you live, sir! Do you ask that question?
WARD Methinks, Sordido, sh'as but a crabbed[586] face to begin with.
SORDIDO A crabbed face? That will save money.
WARD How! Save money, Sordido?
SORDIDO Ay, sir, for having a crabbed face of her own, she'll eat the less verjuice[587] with her mutton. 'Twill save verjuice at year's end, sir.
WARD Nay, and your jests begin to be saucy once, I'll make you eat your meat without mustard.
SORDIDO And that in some kind is a punishment.
WARD Gentlewoman, they say 'tis your pleasure to be my wife, and you shall know shortly whether it be mine or no to be your husband; and thereupon thus I first enter upon you.[588] [*Kisses her*] Oh most delicious scent! Methinks it tasted as if a man had stepped into a comfit-maker's[589] shop to let a cart go by, all the while I kissed her. It is reported, gentlewoman, you'll run mad for me, if you have me not.
ISABELLA I should be in great danger of my wits, sir—
[*Aside*] For being so forward,[590] should this ass kick backward now![591]
WARD Alas, poor soul! And is that hair your own?[592]
ISABELLA Mine own? Yes, sure, sir; I owe nothing for't.
WARD 'Tis a good hearing;[593] I shall have the less to pay when I have married you.
[*To* SORDIDO] Look, does her eyes stand well?[594]
SORDIDO They cannot stand better
Than in her head, I think; where would you have them?

580 28 ten carts . . . the bawds: the paper needed to write up the faults of bawds alone would fill ten carts. Being paraded through the streets in a cart was a common punishment for women
581 29 and if . . . 'em enough: even if women's faults were fewer, you would still find the list long enough
582 36 cater's: the person who buys the "cates," or provisions, for a household
583 37 curious: picky
584 38 nice professor: fastidious expert
585 40 after: for
586 44 crabbed: ill-humoured
587 47 verjuice: a tart sauce, often made of crab-apples
588 53 enter upon you: make a start with you (with a sexual pun)
589 54–5 comfit-maker: confectioner
590 58 forward: quick to consummate her love with Hippolito
591 58 kick backward now: refuse to marry her
592 59 is that hair your own?: baldness was often seen as a symptom of venereal disease; wearing a wig was also read as a sign of vanity in women
593 61 'Tis a good hearing: I'm glad to hear it
594 62 does her eyes stand well?: are her eyes well placed?

And for her nose, 'tis of a very good last.[595]
WARD I have known as good as that has not lasted a year, though.
SORDIDO That's in the using of a thing; will not any strong bridge fall down in time, if we do nothing but beat[596] at the bottom? [597] A nose of buff[598] would not last always, sir, especially if it came into th'camp[599] once.
WARD But Sordido, how shall we do to make her laugh, that I may see what teeth she has? For I'll not bate her a tooth,[600] nor take a black one into the bargain.
SORDIDO Why, do but you fall in talk with her, you cannot choose but one time or other make her laugh, sir.
WARD It shall go hard, but I will. [*To* ISABELLA] Pray, what qualities have you beside singing and dancing? Can you play at shittlecock, forsooth?
ISABELLA Ay, and at stool-ball[601] too, sir; I have great luck at it.
WARD Why, can you catch a ball well?
ISABELLA I have catched two in my lap at one game.[602]
WARD What, have you, woman? I must have you learn
To play at trap too, then y'are full and whole.
ISABELLA Anything that you please to bring me up to[603]
I shall take pains to practice.
WARD 'Twill not do, Sordido; we shall never get her mouth opened wide enough.
SORDIDO No, sir? That's strange! Then here's a trick for your learning.

He yawns. [ISABELLA *yawns too, but covers her mouth with her handkerchief*]

Look now, look now; quick, quick there!
WARD Pox of that scurvy mannerly trick with handkerchief!
It hindered me a little, but I am satisfied.
When a fair woman gapes and stops her mouth so,
It shows like a cloth-stopple[604] in a cream-pot.
I have fair hope of her teeth now, Sordido.
SORDIDO Why, then y'have all well, sir. For aught I see,
She's right and straight enough now as she stands.
They'll commonly lie crooked;[605] that's no matter.
Wise gamesters[606] never find fault with that, let 'em lie still so.[607]
WARD I'd fain[608] mark how she goes,[609] and then I have all—for of all creatures, I cannot abide a splay-footed woman.[610] She's an unlucky thing to meet in a morning; her heels keep together so, as if she were beginning an Irish dance[611] still, and the wriggling of her bum playing the tune to't. But I have bethought a cleanly shift[612] to find it: dab[613] down as you see me, and peep of one side when her back's toward you. I'll show you the way.
SORDIDO And you shall find me apt enough to peeping;

595 64 last: shape
596 67 beat: pound; copulate
597 65–7 I have . . . the bottom: venereal disease caused the bone structure or "bridge" of the nose to collapse
598 67 buff: a tough and durable leather used for military tunics
599 68 camp: military camp; with a reference to prostitutes or "camp followers" giving or catching venereal disease amongst soldiers
600 70 bate her a tooth: accept one tooth less than a full set
601 75 stool-ball: an indoor game somewhat like cricket, especially popular amongst female players. Isabella picks up the excretory and sexual references of "shittlecock" with her references to "stool" and "ball[s]"
602 77 two in . . . one game: Isabella "catches" both the Ward and Hippolito through her marriage to the Ward
603 80 bring me up to: train me in; with a sexual implication that continues in Isabella's reference to her "practice" (with Hippolito)
604 88 cloth-stopple: a stopper made of cloth
605 92 lie crooked: sleep in a crooked position; cheat on their partners
606 93 gamesters: sexual partners
607 93 lie still so: go on lying that way
608 94 I'd fain: I'd like to
609 94 goes: walks
610 95 splay-footed woman: one who walks with her feet turned out. Witches were believed to be splay-footed; thus, the Ward finds this trait "unlucky"
611 96 Irish dance: traditional Irish dances often begin with the dancer's heels touching, or with one heel touching the other foot's instep
612 97 cleanly shift: honest trick
613 97 dab: duck

I have been one of them has seen mad sights
Under your scaffolds.[614]
WARD [*To* ISABELLA] Will it please you walk, forsooth,
A turn or two by yourself? You are so pleasing to me,
I take delight to view you on both sides.
ISABELLA I shall be glad to fetch[615] a walk to your love,[616] sir;
'Twill get affection a good stomach,[617] sir—
[*Aside*] Which I had need have, to fall to[618] such coarse victuals.
WARD Now, go thy ways for a clean-treading[619] wench,
As ever man in modesty peeped under!
SORDIDO I see the sweetest sight to please my master!
Never went Frenchman righter upon ropes[620]
Than she on Florentine rushes.[621]
WARD 'Tis enough, forsooth.
ISABELLA And how do you like me now, sir?
WARD Faith, so well,
I never mean to part with thee, sweetheart,
Under[622] some sixteen children, and all boys.
ISABELLA You'll be at simple[623] pains, if you prove kind,[624]
And breed 'em all in your teeth.[625]
WARD Nay, by my faith,
What serves your belly for? 'Twould make my cheeks
Look like blown bagpipes.

Enter GUARDIANO

GUARDIANO How now, ward and nephew,
Gentlewoman and niece! Speak, is it so or not?
WARD 'Tis so, we are both agreed, sir.
GUARDIANO In to your kindred, then;
There's friends, and wine, and music waits to welcome you.
WARD Then I'll be drunk for joy.
SORDIDO And I for company;
I cannot break my nose in a better action.[626]

Exeunt

Act IV, scene i

Enter BIANCA *attended by two* LADIES

BIANCA How goes your watches,[627] ladies? What's o'clock now?

614 101 scaffolds: raised wooden platforms for theatrical performances or public executions
615 104 fetch: take
616 104 to your love: for your pleasure
617 105 It will create a good sexual appetite
618 106 fall to: eat
619 107 clean-treading: straight walking
620 110 French performers were renowned for tightrope-walking
621 111 rushes: spread on floors as a covering
622 114 Under: with less than
623 115 simple: great (with a pun on "foolish")
624 115 kind: loving (with a pun on the Ward's "kind," or nature, as a "simpleton")
625 116 in your teeth: superstition held that loving husbands had toothache when their wives were pregnant
626 123 I cannot suffer in a better cause
627 1 watches: watches were expensive items of jewelry in Middleton's time. Women were often compared to them or to clocks, since both were held to be unreliable or unfaithful

1 LADY By mine, full nine.
2 LADY By mine, a quarter past.
1 LADY I set mine by St. Mark's.[628]
2 LADY St. Anthony's, they say,
Goes truer.
1 LADY That's but your opinion, madam,
Because you love a gentleman o'th'name.
2 LADY He's a true gentleman, then.
1 LADY So may he be
That comes to me tonight, for aught you know.
BIANCA I'll end this strife straight: I set mine by the sun.
I love to set by th'best; one shall not then
Be troubled to set often.
2 LADY You do wisely in't.
BIANCA If I should set my watch as some girls do,
By ev'ry clock i'th' town, 'twould nev'r go true;
And too much turning of the dial's point,
Or tampering with the spring,[629] might in small time
Spoil the whole work too. Here it wants of nine[630] now.
1 LADY It does indeed, forsooth; mine's nearest truth yet.
2 LADY Yet I have found her lying with an advocate, which showed
Like two false clocks[631] together in one parish.
BIANCA So now I thank you, ladies. I desire
A while to be alone.
1 LADY And I am nobody,
Methinks, unless I have one or other with me.
Faith, my desire and hers will nev'r be sisters. *Exit* LADIES
BIANCA How strangely woman's fortune comes about!
This was the farthest way[632] to come to me,
All would have judged, that knew me born in Venice
And there with many jealous eyes brought up,
That never thought they had me sure enough
But when they were upon me; yet my hap[633]
To meet it here, so far off from my birthplace,
My friends or kindred. 'Tis not good, in sadness,[634]
To keep a maid so strict in her young days;
Restraint breeds wand'ring thoughts, as many fasting days
A great desire to see flesh stirring[635] again.
I'll nev'r use any girl of mine so strictly;
Howev'r they're kept, their fortunes find 'em out—
I see't in me. If they be got[636] in court,
I'll never forbid 'em the country, nor the court
Though they be born i'th'country. They will come to't,
And fetch their falls a thousand mile about,[637]

628 3 St. Mark's: a church in Florence; watches were often set by church clocks, which were held to be the most accurate
629 13–14 dial's point . . . the spring: references to male and female genitalia
630 15 wants of nine: is not yet nine
631 18 two false clocks: the sexually unfaithful lady is as "false" as the advocate or lawyer, whose profession is seen as an intrinsically dishonest one
632 24 farthest way: most unlikely fate
633 28 hap: fortune
634 30 in sadness: seriously
635 32–3 fasting days . . . flesh stirring: Bianca alludes to strict laws against eating meat in Lent, but her references to "stirring" flesh are also full of sexual implications
636 36 got: begotten
637 39 Find a way to fall into sin, even if they have to go a thousand miles out of their way

Where one would little think on't.

Enter LEANTIO

LEANTIO [*Aside*] I long to see how my despiser looks,
Now she's come here to court. These are her lodgings;
She's simply[638] now advanced. I took her out
Of no such window, I remember, first:
That was a great deal lower, and less carved.
BIANCA [*Aside*] How now? What silkworm's[639] this, i'th'name of pride?
What, is it he?
LEANTIO A bow i'th'ham[640] to your greatness;
You must have now three legs,[641] I take it, must you not?
BIANCA Then I must take another;[642] I shall want[643] else
The service[644] I should have. You have but two there.
LEANTIO Y'are richly placed.
BIANCA Methinks y'are wondrous brave,[645] sir.
LEANTIO A sumptuous lodging.
BIANCA Y'ave an excellent suit there.
LEANTIO A chair of velvet.
BIANCA Is your cloak lined through,[646] sir?
LEANTIO Y'are very stately here.
BIANCA Faith, something proud,[647] sir.
LEANTIO Stay, stay, let's see your cloth-of-silver[648] slippers.
BIANCA Who's your shoemaker? H'as made you a neat[649] boot.
LEANTIO Will you have a pair? The duke will lend you spurs.[650]
BIANCA Yes, when I ride.[651]
LEANTIO 'Tis a brave life you lead.
BIANCA I could nev'r see you in such good clothes
In my time.
LEANTIO In your time?
BIANCA Sure, I think, sir,
We both thrive best asunder.
LEANTIO Y'are a whore.
BIANCA Fear nothing,[652] sir.
LEANTIO An impudent, spiteful strumpet.
BIANCA Oh sir, you give me thanks for your captainship;
I thought you had forgot all your good manners.
LEANTIO And to spite thee as much, look there, there read, [*He gives her a letter*]
Vex, gnaw! Thou shalt find there I am not love-starved.
The world was never yet so cold or pitiless

638 43 simply: absolutely
639 46 silkworm: someone ostentatiously dressed in silken finery
640 47 i'th'ham: from the waist
641 48 three legs: three bows; also implies two legs plus the "third leg," the penis
642 49 take another: another bow; another lover than Leantio
643 49 want: lack
644 50 service: deference; sexual service
645 51 brave: well-dressed
646 53 lined through: lined throughout (a sign of wealth)
647 54 proud: splendid
648 55 cloth-of-silver: expensive cloth interwoven with silver thread
649 56 neat: elegant; punning on "neat's leather," i.e. leather made from cowhide
650 57 lend you spurs: excite you sexually
651 58 when I ride: Bianca builds on Leantio's sexual innuendo
652 62 Fear nothing: speak freely

But there was ever still more charity found out
Than at one proud fool's door; and 'twere hard, 'faith,
If I could not pass[653] that. Read to thy shame there:
A cheerful and a beauteous benefactor too,
As ev'r erected the good works of love.[654]
BIANCA [*Aside*] Lady Livia!
Is't possible? Her worship was my pandress;
She dote, and send and give, and all to him?
Why, here's a bawd plagued home.[655] [*To him*] Y'are simply[656] happy, sir;
Yet I'll not envy you.
LEANTIO No, court saint,[657] not thou!
You keep some friend of a new fashion;
There's no harm in your devil, he's a suckling,[658]
But he will breed teeth[659] shortly, will he not?
BIANCA Take heed you play not then too long with him.
LEANTIO Yes, and the great one[660] too. I shall find time
To play a hot religious bout[661] with some of you,
And perhaps drive you and your course[662] of sins
To their eternal kennels.[663] I speak softly now;
'Tis manners in a noblewoman's lodgings,
And I well know all my degrees of duty.
But come I[664] to your everlasting parting[665] once,
Thunder shall seem soft music to that tempest.
BIANCA 'Twas said last week there would be change of weather
When the moon hung so, and belike you heard it.[666]
LEANTIO Why, here's sin made,[667] and nev'r a conscience put to't:[668]
A monster with all forehead and no eyes.[669]
Why do I talk to thee of sense or virtue,
That art as dark as death? And as much madness
To set light before thee, as to lead blind folks
To see the monuments,[670] which they may smell as soon
As they behold; marry, oft-times their heads
For want of light may feel the hardness of 'em.[671]
So shall thy blind pride my revenge and anger,
That canst not see it now; and it may fall
At such an hour when thou least see'st of all.[672]
So to an ignorance darker than thy womb

653 70 pass: surpass
654 72 As ever built a charitable institution (with a sexual innuendo)
655 75 plagued home: fitly punished
656 75 simply: extremely
657 76 court saint: idol of the court
658 78 a suckling: Leantio suggests that Bianca is a witch who suckles her familiar—perhaps implying the duke
659 79 he will breed teeth: his teeth will come in; he will grow up and become more dangerous
660 81 the great one: the devil (as well as his minion, the duke)
661 82 play a hot religious bout: fight a holy war
662 83 course: a pack of hounds used to hunt hares
663 84 eternal kennels: i.e. hell
664 87 come I: should I come
665 87 your everlasting parting: Bianca's final parting from the duke in death
666 89–90 'Twas said … heard it: Bianca pretends to take Leantio's fire-and-brimstone metaphor literally as small talk about the weather
667 91 made: raised to prominence
668 91 put to't: troubled
669 92 all forehead and no eyes: all effrontery and no conscience or foresight
670 96 monuments: impressive or holy sites
671 98 feel the hardness of 'em: bump into them
672 101 when thou … of all: when you are most blinded by sin

I leave thy perjured soul. A plague[673] will come. *Exit*
BIANCA Get you gone first, and then I fear no greater![674]
Nor thee will I fear long. I'll have this sauciness
Soon banished from these lodgings, and the rooms
Perfumed well after the corrupt air it leaves;
His breath has made me almost sick, in troth.
A poor base start-up![675] Life![676] Because h'as got
Fair clothes by foul means, comes to rail,[677] and show 'em.

Enter the DUKE

DUKE Who's that?
BIANCA Cry you mercy, sir.
DUKE Prithee, who's that?
BIANCA The former thing, my lord, to whom you gave
The captainship; he eats his meat with grudging still.
DUKE Still!
BIANCA He comes vaunting here of his new love,
And the new clothes she gave him: Lady Livia,
Who but she now his mistress?
DUKE Lady Livia?
Be sure of what you say.
BIANCA He showed me her name, sir,
In perfumed paper: her vows, her letter,
With an intent to spite me. So his heart said,
And his threats made it good—they were as spiteful
As ever malice uttered, and as dangerous,
Should his hand follow the copy.[678]
DUKE But that must not.
Do not you vex your mind; prithee to bed, go.
All shall be well and quiet.
BIANCA I love peace, sir.
DUKE And so do all that love. Take you no care for't;
It shall be still provided to your hand.[679] *Exit* [BIANCA]
Who's near us there?

Enter MESSENGER

MESSENGER My lord?
DUKE Seek out Hippolito,
Brother to Lady Livia, with all speed.
MESSENGER He was the last man I saw, my lord.
DUKE Make haste. *Exit* [MESSENGER]
He is a blood soon stirred;[680] and as he's quick
To apprehend a wrong,[681] he's bold and sudden
In bringing forth a ruin. I know likewise

673 103 A plague: divine retribution
674 104 no greater: no greater plague than you
675 109 start-up: upstart
676 109 Life: i.e. God's life!
677 110 rail: complain or criticize
678 122 Should his . . . the copy: should he put his threats into action
679 126 provided to your hand: given to you as a gift
680 130 a blood soon stirred: a young man easily angered
681 131 apprehend a wrong: perceive an insult

The reputation of his sister's honor's
As dear to him as life-blood to his heart.
Beside, I'll flatter him with a goodness[682] to her
Which I now thought on—but nev'r meant to practice,
Because I know her base—and that wind drives him.[683]
The ulcerous reputation feels the poise
Of lightest wrongs,[684] as sores are vexed with flies.
He comes.

Enter HIPPOLITO

Hippolito, welcome.
HIPPOLITO My loved lord.
DUKE How does that lusty widow, thy kind sister?
Is she not sped yet of[685] a second husband?[686]
A bed-fellow she has; I ask not that.
I know she's sped of him.[687]
HIPPOLITO Of him, my lord!
DUKE Yes, of a bed-fellow. Is the news so strange to you?
HIPPOLITO I hope 'tis so to all.
DUKE I wish it were, sir,
But 'tis confessed too fast;[688] her ignorant pleasures,
Only by lust instructed, have received
Into their services an impudent boaster:
One that does raise his glory from her shame,[689]
And tells the midday sun what's done in darkness—
Yet blinded with her appetite, wastes[690] her wealth,
Buys her disgraces at a dearer[691] rate
Than bounteous housekeepers purchase their honor.[692]
Nothing sads me so much as that, in love to thee
And to thy blood, I had picked out
A worthy match for her, the great Vincentio,
High in our favor and in all men's thoughts.
HIPPOLITO Oh thou destruction of all happy fortunes,
Unsated blood! Know you the name, my lord,
Of her abuser?
DUKE One Leantio.
HIPPOLITO He's a factor!
DUKE He nev'r made so brave a voyage,
By his own talk.[693]
HIPPOLITO The poor old widow's son!
I humbly take my leave.
DUKE [*Aside*] I see 'tis done.—

682 135 goodness: benefit; honor
683 137 that wind drives him: that idea will urge him on
684 138–9 The ulcerous . . . lightest wrongs: reputations that are already diseased are most sensitive to the pressure ("poise") of small blows
685 142 sped yet of: supplied yet with
686 142 a second husband: in fact, she has already had two, as she noted at I.ii. 52
687 144 she's sped of him: she's satisfied by him
688 147 confessed too fast: too widely known
689 150 One who draws honor from her dishonor (as a gardener raises flowers from manure)
690 152 wastes: she wastes
691 153 dearer: more expensive
692 154 honor: reputation for wealth and generosity
693 163 By his own talk: according to his own boasts

Give her good counsel, make her see her error;
I know she'll hearken to you.
HIPPOLITO Yes, my lord,
I make no doubt, as I shall take the course
Which she shall never know till it be acted;
And when she wakes to honor, then she'll thank me for't.
I'll imitate the pities of old surgeons[694]
To this lost limb, who, ere they show their art,
Cast one asleep,[695] then cut the diseased part.
So out of love to her I pity most,
She shall not feel him going till he's lost.
Then she'll commend the cure. *Exit*
DUKE The great cure's[696] past.
I count this done already; his wrath's sure,
And speaks an injury deep. Farewell, Leantio;
This place will never hear thee murmur[697] more.

Enter LORD CARDINAL *attended* [*by Servants*]

Our noble brother, welcome!
CARDINAL [*To Servants*] Set those lights down,
Depart till you be called. [*Exeunt Servants*]
DUKE [*Aside*] There's some serious business
Fixed in his look; nay, it inclines a little
To the dark color of a discontentment.—
Brother, what is't commands your eye so powerfully?
Speak; you seem lost.[698]
CARDINAL The thing I look on seems so
To my eyes: lost forever.
DUKE You look on me.
CARDINAL What a grief 'tis to a religious feeling
To think a man should have a friend so goodly,[699]
So wise, so noble—nay, a duke, a brother,
And all this certainly damned?
DUKE How!
CARDINAL 'Tis no wonder,
If your great sin can do't. Dare you look up
For thinking of a vengeance?[700] Dare you sleep
For fear of never waking but to death,
And dedicate unto a strumpet's love
The strength of your affections, zeal,[701] and health?
Here you stand now; can you assure your pleasures
You shall once more enjoy her, but once more?
Alas, you cannot. What a misery 'tis, then,
To be more certain of eternal death
Than of a next embrace! Nay, shall I show you
How more unfortunate you stand in sin

694 170 old surgeons: surgeons in olden times
695 172 Cast one asleep: put the patient to sleep with narcotics
696 175 great cure: major surgery
697 178 murmur: complain
698 184 lost: distracted
699 187 goodly: admirable; attractive
700 190–91 Dare you . . . a vengeance?: do you dare to look heavenwards without fearing God's vengeance on you?
701 194 zeal: energy; devotion

Than the low private man? All his offences,
Like enclosed grounds,[702] keep but about himself,
And seldom stretch beyond his own soul's bounds—
And when a man grows miserable, 'tis some comfort
When he's no further charged than with himself;
'Tis a sweet ease to wretchedness. But, great man,
Ev'ry sin thou commit'st shows like a flame
Upon a mountain:[703] 'tis seen far about,
And with a big wind made of popular breath[704]
The sparkles fly through cities. Here one takes,
Another catches there, and in short time
Waste all to cinders. But remember still,
What burnt the valleys first came from the hill.
Ev'ry offence draws his[705] particular pain,
But 'tis example[706] proves the great man's bane.
The sins of mean men lie like scattered parcels
Of an unperfect bill;[707] but when such[708] fall,
Then comes example, and that sums up all.[709]
And this your reason grants: if men of good lives,
Who by their virtuous actions stir up others
To noble and religious imitation,
Receive the greater glory after death—
As sin must needs confess[710]—what may they feel
In height of torments and in weight of vengeance,
Not only they themselves not doing well,
But sets[711] a light up to show men to hell?
DUKE If you have done, I have. No more, sweet brother.
CARDINAL I know time spent in goodness is too tedious;
This[712] had not been a moment's space in lust, now.
How dare you venture on[713] eternal pain,
That cannot bear a minute's reprehension?[714]
Methinks you should endure to hear that talked of
Which you so strive to suffer. Oh my brother!
What were you, if you were taken[715] now!
My heart weeps blood to think on't; 'tis a work
Of infinite mercy you can never merit
That yet you are not death-struck, no, not yet—
I dare not stay[716] you long, for fear you should not
Have time enough allowed you to repent in.
There's but this wall betwixt you and destruction,

702 202 enclosed grounds: fenced-off plots of land
703 207–8 flame/Upon a mountain: signal beacon, usually lit in times of invasion or war
704 209 popular breath: the gossip of the populace
705 214 his: its
706 215 example: being an example for others
707 216–17 scattered parcels . . . unperfect bill: the separated items of an untabulated bill
708 217 such: great men
709 218 Then comes . . . up all: the bad example they set makes their sins add up to a great sum
710 223 sin must needs confess: even the sinful must admit
711 226 sets: their example sets
712 229 This: the time we have spent in conversation
713 230 venture on: risk
714 231 reprehension: rebuke
715 234 taken: i.e. by death
716 238 stay: detain

When y'are at strongest, and but poor thin clay.[717]
Think upon't, brother. Can you come so near it[718]
For a fair strumpet's love, and fall into
A torment that knows neither end nor bottom
For beauty but the deepness of a skin,
And that not of their own[719] neither? Is she a thing
Whom sickness dare not visit, or age look on,
Or death resist? Does the worm shun her grave?
If not—as your soul knows it[720]—why should lust
Bring man to lasting[721] pain, for rotten dust?
DUKE Brother of spotless honor, let me weep
The first of my repentance in thy bosom,
And show the blest fruits of a thankful spirit;
And if I ev'r keep woman more unlawfully,
May I want penitence[722] at my greatest need—
And wise men know there is no barren place
Threatens more famine than a dearth in grace.
CARDINAL Why, here's a conversion is[723] at this time, brother,
Sung for a hymn in heaven; and at this instant
The powers of darkness groan, makes[724] all hell sorry.
First, I praise heaven; then in my work I glory.
Who's there attends without?

Enter SERVANTS

SERVANT My lord!
CARDINAL Take up those lights; there was a thicker darkness
When they came first. The peace of a fair soul
Keep with my noble brother.
DUKE Joys be with you, sir. *Exit* CARDINAL [*and* SERVANTS]
She lies alone tonight for't, and must still,
Though it[725] be hard to conquer; but I have vowed
Never to know her as a strumpet more,
And I must save my oath.[726] If fury fail not,
Her husband dies tonight, or at the most
Lives not to see the morning spent tomorrow;
Then will I make her lawfully mine own,
Without this sin and horror. Now I'm chidden
For what I shall enjoy then unforbidden,
And I'll not freeze in stoves.[727] 'Tis but a while
Live like a hopeful bridegroom, chaste from flesh,
And pleasure then will seem new, fair and fresh.
Exit

717 240–41 this wall . . . thin clay: the body was often imagined in early modern writing as a wall between the soul and eternity, and its frailty compared to that of breakable clay
718 242 it: damnation
719 246 not of their own: not natural; created by cosmetics
720 249 as your soul knows it: as you know in your soul to be true
721 250 lasting: everlasting
722 255 want penitence: lack access to confession
723 258 conversion is: conversion that is
724 260 makes: in a manner that makes
725 267 it: desire
726 269 save my oath: keep my word
727 275 freeze in stoves: be punished for behavior that I am able to enjoy

Act IV, scene ii

Enter HIPPOLITO

HIPPOLITO The morning so far wasted,[728] yet his baseness
So impudent? See if the very sun do not blush at him!
Dare he do thus much, and know me alive?
Put case[729] one must be vicious,[730] as I know myself
Monstrously guilty, there's a blind[731] time made for't.
He might use only that, 'twere conscionable:
Art,[732] silence, closeness,[733] subtlety, and darkness
Are fit for such a business. But there's no pity
To be bestowed on an apparent[734] sinner,
An impudent daylight lecher. The great zeal
I bear to her advancement in this match
With Lord Vincentio, as the duke has wrought it
To the perpetual honor of our house,
Puts fire in my blood to purge the air
Of this corruption, fear[735] it spread too far
And poison the whole hopes of this fair fortune.
I love her good so dearly that no brother
Shall venture farther for a sister's glory
Than I for her preferment.

Enter LEANTIO *and a* PAGE

LEANTIO Once again
I'll see that glistering[736] whore shines[737] like a serpent
Now the court sun's[738] upon her. Page!
PAGE Anon, sir!
LEANTIO I'll go in state, too. See the coach be ready.
I'll hurry away presently. *Exit* PAGE
HIPPOLITO Yes, you shall hurry,
And the devil after you. Take that at setting forth![739] [*Strikes* LEANTIO]
Now, and[740] you'll draw, we are upon equal terms, sir.
Thou took'st advantage of my name in honor
Upon my sister; I nev'r saw the stroke
Come till I found my reputation bleeding,
And therefore count it I no sin to valor
To serve thy lust so. Now we are of even hand,[741]
Take your best course against me. You must die.
LEANTIO How close sticks envy to man's happiness!

728 1 wasted: passed
729 4 Put case: even if we accept
730 4 vicious: sinful
731 5 blind: dark; secret
732 7 Art: strategy
733 7 closeness: secrecy
734 9 apparent: open
735 15 fear: for fear
736 20 glistering: glittering
737 20 shines: who shines
738 21 court sun: the favor of the court and of the duke
739 24 at setting forth: as you set out
740 25 and: if
741 30 of even hand: evenly matched

When I was poor and little cared for life,
I had no such means offered me to die;
No man's wrath minded me. [*Draws his sword*] Slave, I turn this to thee,
To call thee to account for a wound lately
Of a base stamp[742] upon me.
HIPPOLITO 'Twas most fit
For a base mettle.[743] Come and fetch one[744] now
More noble, then, for I will use thee fairer
Than thou hast done thine own soul, or our honor. [*They fight and* LEANTIO *falls*]
And there I think 'tis for thee.
[VOICES] WITHIN Help, help, oh part 'em!
LEANTIO False wife! I feel now th'hast prayed heartily for me.
Rise, strumpet, by my fall; thy lust may reign now.
My heart-string and the marriage knot that tied thee
Breaks both together. [*Dies*]
HIPPOLITO There I heard the sound on't,
And never liked string better.

Enter GUARDIANO, LIVIA, ISABELLA, WARD, *and* SORDIDO

LIVIA 'Tis my brother!
Are you hurt, sir?
HIPPOLITO Not anything.
LIVIA Blest fortune!
Shift for thyself;[745] what is he thou hast killed?
HIPPOLITO Our honor's enemy.
GUARDIANO Know you this man, lady?
LIVIA Leantio? My love's joy! [*To* HIPPOLITO] Wounds stick[746] upon thee
As deadly as thy sins! Art thou not hurt?
The devil take that fortune—and he dead!
Drop plagues into thy bowels without voice,[747]
Secret and fearful. [*To the others*] Run for officers,
Let him be apprehended with all speed,
For fear he 'scape away. Lay hands on him!
We cannot be too sure; 'tis willful murder.
You do heaven's vengeance, and the law just service.
You know him not as I do; he's a villain
As monstrous as a prodigy[748] and as dreadful.
HIPPOLITO Will you but entertain a noble patience
Till you but hear the reason, worthy sister!
LIVIA The reason! That's a jest hell falls a-laughing at!
Is there a reason found for the destruction
Of our more lawful loves? And was there none
To kill the black lust 'twixt thy niece and thee,
That has kept close[749] so long?
GUARDIANO How's that, good madam?

742 37 base stamp: low character (the phrase suggests a counterfeit impression made on a coin)
743 38 mettle: disposition, with a pun on "metal" (taking up Leantio's coin metaphor)
744 38 one: a wound
745 48 Shift for thyself: make your escape
746 50 Wounds stick: may wounds stick
747 53 without voice: silently
748 60 prodigy: unnatural occurrence; bad omen
749 67 close: hidden

LIVIA Too true, sir! There she stands; let her deny't.
The deed cries shortly in the midwife's arms,
Unless the parents' sins strike it still-born;
And if you be not deaf and ignorant,
You'll hear strange notes[750] ere long. [*To* ISABELLA] Look upon me, wench!
'Twas I betrayed thy honor subtly to him
Under a false tale; it lights[751] upon me now.
His arm has paid me home[752] upon thy breast,
My sweet, beloved Leantio!
GUARDIANO Was my judgment
And care in choice so devilishly abused,
So beyond shamefully? All the world will grin at me.
WARD Oh Sordido, Sordido, I'm damned, I'm damned!
SORDIDO Damned! Why, sir?
WARD One of the wicked—dost not see't?
A cuckold, a plain reprobate[753] cuckold!
SORDIDO Nay, and you be damned for that, be of good cheer, sir! Y'have gallant company of all professions. I'll have a wife next Sunday[754] too, because I'll along with you myself.
WARD That will be some comfort yet.
LIVIA [*To* GUARDIANO] You, sir, that bear your load of injuries,
As I of sorrows, lend me your grieved strength
To[755] this sad burthen,[756] who in life wore actions,
Flames were not nimbler.[757] We will talk of things
May have the luck to break our hearts together.
GUARDIANO I'll list[758] to nothing but revenge and anger,
Whose counsels I will follow.
Exeunt LIVIA *and* GUARDIANO
SORDIDO A wife, quoth'a!
Here's a sweet plum-tree[759] of your guard'ner's[760] grafting![761]
WARD Nay, there's a worse name belongs to this fruit yet, and[762] you could hit on't, a more open one:[763] for he that marries a whore looks like a fellow bound all his lifetime to a medlar-tree, and that's good stuff, 'tis no sooner ripe but it looks rotten—and so do some queans[764] at nineteen. A pox on't, I thought there was some knavery abroach,[765] for something stirred in her belly the first night I lay with her.
SORDIDO What, what, sir!
WARD This is she brought up so courtly! Can sing, and dance, and tumble[766] too, methinks! I'll never marry wife again that has so many qualities.[767]
SORDIDO Indeed, they are seldom good, master; for likely, when they are taught so many, they will have one trick more of their own finding out. Well, give me a wench but with one good

750 72 strange notes: unfamiliar sounds
751 74 lights: falls
752 75 paid me home: punished me for my crimes
753 81 reprobate: destined for damnation
754 83 next Sunday: choosing a wife on Sunday was seen as foolish because women in church passed themselves off as more virtuous than they really were
755 88 To: to carry
756 87 burthen: burden
757 87–8 who in . . . not nimbler: whose actions, while he was alive, were swifter than flame
758 90 list: listen
759 92 plum-tree: the plum was a common metaphor for female genitalia
760 92 guard'ner's: guardianer's (with a pun on "gardener's")
761 92 grafting: breeding fruit by artificially melding the tissues of two plants
762 93 and: if
763 93–4 a more open one: the fruit of the medlar-tree (a small, soft apple that appears rotten when ripe) was colloquially known as "open-arse" because of its deeply indented base
764 95 queans: whores
765 96 abroach: afoot
766 99 tumble: perform acrobatics; have sex
767 100 qualities: accomplishments

quality, to lie with none but her husband, and that's bringing up enough for any woman breathing.

WARD This was the fault, when she was tendered to me; you never looked to this.

SORDIDO Alas, how would you have me see through a great farthingale, sir! I cannot peep through a millstone,[768] or in the going,[769] to see what's done i'th'bottom.[770]

WARD Her father praised her breast; sh'ad the voice, forsooth! I marveled she sung so small[771] indeed, being no maid. Now I perceive there's a young chorister in her belly—this breeds a singing in my head,[772] I'm sure.

SORDIDO 'Tis but the tune of your wife's cinquepace, danced in a featherbed. Faith, go lie down, master—but take heed your horns do not make holes in the pillowberes.[773] [*Aside*] I would not batter brows with him for a hogshead of angels;[774] he would prick my skull as full of holes as a scrivener's[775] sand-box.[776] *Exeunt* WARD *and* SORDIDO

ISABELLA [*Aside*] Was ever maid so cruelly beguiled[777]
To the confusion[778] of life, soul, and honor—
All of one's woman's murdering! I'd fain bring
Her name no nearer to my blood than woman,
And 'tis too much of that.[779] Oh shame and horror!
In that small distance from yon man to me
Lies sin enough to make a whole world perish.
[*To* HIPPOLITO] 'Tis time we parted, sir, and left the sight
Of one another; nothing can be worse
To hurt repentance, for our very eyes
Are far more poisonous to religion
Than basilisks[780] to them. If any goodness
Rest in you, hope of comforts, fear of judgments,
My request is I nev'r may see you more;
And so I turn me from you everlastingly,
So is my hope to miss you.[781] But for her,
That durst so dally with a sin so dangerous,
And lay a snare so spitefully for my youth,
If the least means but favor my revenge,
That I may practice the like cruel cunning
Upon her life, as she has on mine honor,
I'll act it without pity.

HIPPOLITO Here's a care
Of reputation and a sister's fortune
Sweetly rewarded by her! Would a silence
As great as that which keeps among the graves
Had everlastingly chained up her tongue!
My love to her has made mine miserable.

Enter GUARDIANO *and* LIVIA

768 107 millstone: millstones were proverbially impossible to see through
769 107 in the going: while she is walking
770 107 i'th'bottom: in her private parts
771 108 small: softly; in a high pitch
772 110 singing in my head: the Ward suggests that Isabella's infidelity is giving him a headache thanks to the cuckold's horns he is growing
773 112 pillowberes: pillow cases
774 113 a hogshead of angels: a large barrel full of gold coins
775 114 scrivener's: scribe's
776 114 sand-box: box with a perforated top used by scribes to sprinkle sand on written pages in order to make ink dry faster
777 115 beguiled: tricked; seduced
778 116 confusion: destruction
779 119 'tis too much of that: even that is too close
780 126 basilisk: mythical reptile that could kill with a look
781 130 So is my hope to miss you: I hope to avoid you forever (including in the afterlife, where Isabella hopes they will not be damned together)

GUARDIANO [*Aside to* LIVIA] If you can but dissemble your heart's griefs now,
Be but a woman so far.[782]
LIVIA [*Aside to him*] Peace! I'll strive, sir.
GUARDIANO As I can wear my injuries in a smile,
Here's an occasion offered that gives anger
Both liberty and safety to perform
Things worth the fire it holds, without the fear
Of danger or of law; for mischiefs acted
Under the privilege[783] of a marriage-triumph[784]
At the duke's hasty nuptials will be thought
Things merely accidental: all's[785] by chance,
Not got of their own natures.[786]
LIVIA I conceive[787] you, sir,
Even to a longing for performance on't—
And here behold some fruits.[788] [*Kneels to* ISABELLA *and* HIPPOLITO]
Forgive me, both.
What I am now, returned to sense and judgment,
Is not the same rage and distraction
Presented lately to you; that rude form
Is gone forever. I am now myself,
That speaks all peace and friendship; and these tears
Are the true springs of hearty, penitent sorrow
For those foul wrongs which my forgetful[789] fury
Slandered your virtues with. This gentleman
Is well resolved[790] now.
GUARDIANO I was never otherways;[791]
I knew, alas, 'twas but your anger spake it,
And I nev'r thought on't more.
HIPPOLITO Pray rise, good sister.
ISABELLA [*Aside*] Here's ev'n as sweet amends made for a wrong now,
As one that gives a wound and pays the surgeon:
All the smart's nothing, the great loss of blood,
Or time of hindrance.[792] Well, I had a mother;
I can dissemble too. [*To* LIVIA] What wrongs have slipped
Through anger's ignorance, aunt, my heart forgives.
GUARDIANO Why, thus! Tuneful now!
HIPPOLITO And what I did, sister,
Was all for honor's cause, which time to come
Will approve[793] to you.
LIVIA Being awaked to goodness,
I understand so much, sir, and praise now
The fortune of your arm and of your safety;
For by his death y'have rid me of a sin

782 143 At least be enough of a woman (that is, in Guardiano's sense, enough of a liar) to hide your feelings
783 149 privilege: protection; cover
784 149 marriage-triumph: a masque or other spectacle held to celebrate a marriage
785 151 all's: all as if
786 151–2 by chance . . . own natures: not intentionally evil, but accidentally so
787 152 conceive: understand
788 154 fruits: results; offspring (a pun on the verb "conceive," with its secondary meaning of "become pregnant")
789 161 forgetful: distracted
790 163 resolved: reassured; freed from doubt
791 163 otherways: otherwise
792 169 time of hindrance: period during which the wound incapacitates its victim
793 174 approve: prove

As costly as ev'r woman doted on.
T'has pleased the duke so well, too, that—behold, sir— [*Gives him a letter*]
H'as sent you here your pardon, which I kissed
With most affectionate comfort; when 'twas brought,
Then was my fit just past: it came so well, methought,
To glad my heart.
HIPPOLITO I see his grace thinks on me.
LIVIA There's no talk now but of the preparation
For the great marriage.
HIPPOLITO Does he marry her, then?
LIVIA With all speed, suddenly, as fast as cost
Can be laid on with many thousand hands.
This gentleman and I had once a purpose
To have honored the first marriage of the duke
With an invention of his own;[794] 'twas ready,
The pains[795] well past, most of the charge bestowed on't.[796]
Then came the death of your good mother, niece,
And turned the glory of it all to black.
'Tis a device would fit these times so well, too:
Art's treasury not better.[797] If you'll join,
It shall be done; the cost shall all be mine.
HIPPOLITO Y'have my voice[798] first, 'twill well approve my thankfulness
For the duke's love and favor.
LIVIA What say you, niece?
ISABELLA I am content to make one.[799]
GUARDIANO The plot's full, then.
Your pages, madam, will make shift for[800] cupids.
LIVIA That will they, sir.
GUARDIANO You'll play your old part still.
LIVIA What, is't good? Troth, I have ev'n forgot it.
GUARDIANO Why, Juno Pronuba,[801] the marriage-goddess.
LIVIA 'Tis right, indeed.
GUARDIANO [*To* ISABELLA] And you shall play the nymph
That offers sacrifice to appease her wrath.
ISABELLA Sacrifice, good sir?
LIVIA Must I be appeased, then?
GUARDIANO That's as you list yourself, as you see cause.
LIVIA Methinks 'twould show the more state[802] in her deity
To be incensed.[803]
ISABELLA 'Twould, but my sacrifice
Shall take a course to appease you, or I'll fail in't—
[*Aside*] And teach a sinful bawd to play a goddess.
GUARDIANO For our parts, we'll not be ambitious, sir.[804]

794 190 an invention of his own: a theatrical composition or masque of Guardiano's devising
795 191 pains: effort
796 191 most of . . . bestowed on't: most of the money already spent on it
797 195 Art's treasury not better: the classic works of the past couldn't fit these times any better
798 197 voice: support
799 199 make one: participate
800 200 make shift for: manage to play the parts of
801 203 Juno Pronuba: Juno, wife of Jove and queen of the Roman gods, was the patroness of marriages—hence the soubriquet "Pronuba"
802 208 state: dignity
803 209 incensed: enraged
804 212 We will not demand dignified parts

Please you walk in and see the project drawn,[805]
Then take your choice.
HIPPOLITO I weigh not, so I have one.[806] [*Exeunt all but* LIVIA]
LIVIA How much ado have I to restrain fury
From breaking into curses! Oh, how painful 'tis
To keep great sorrow smothered! Sure, I think
'Tis harder to dissemble grief than love.
Leantio, here the weight of thy loss lies,
Which nothing but destruction can suffice.
[*Exit*]

Act IV, scene iii

Hoboys.[807] *Enter in great state the* DUKE *and* BIANCA, *richly attired, with Lords, Cardinals, Ladies, and other Attendants; they pass solemnly over. Enter* LORD CARDINAL *in a rage, seeming to break off the ceremony*

CARDINAL Cease, cease! Religious honors done to sin
Disparage[808] virtue's reverence, and will pull
Heaven's thunder upon Florence; holy ceremonies
Were made for sacred uses, not for sinful.
Are these the fruits of your repentance, brother?
Better it had been you had never sorrowed
Than to abuse the benefit, and return
To worse than where sin left you.
Vowed you then never to keep strumpet more,
And are you now so swift in your desires
To knit your honors and your life fast to her?
Is not sin sure enough to wretched man,[809]
But he must bind himself in chains to't? Worse!
Must marriage, that immaculate robe of honor,
That renders virtue glorious, fair, and fruitful
To her great master,[810] be now made the garment
Of leprosy[811] and foulness? Is this penitence,
To sanctify hot lust? What is it otherways
Than worship done to devils? Is this the best
Amends that sin can make after her riots?
As if a drunkard, to appease heaven's wrath,
Should offer up his surfeit[812] for a sacrifice!
If that be comely, then lust's offerings are
On wedlock's sacred altar.
DUKE Here y'are bitter
Without cause, brother. What I vowed, I keep
As safe as you your conscience, and this needs not.[813]
I taste more wrath in't than I do religion,
And envy more than goodness. The path now
I tread is honest, leads to lawful love,

805 213 drawn: written out; sketched
806 214 I weigh not, so I have one: I don't mind, as long as I have a part
807 0 SD *Hoboys*: oboes. The original text of the play places this direction before the new scene number, perhaps indicating a musical transition between these scenes
808 2 Disparage: degrade
809 12 sure enough to wretched man: a certain enough part of man's wretched lot
810 16 her great master: God
811 17 leprosy: corruption (also linked to venereal disease)
812 22 surfeit: over-indulgence; vomit
813 26 this needs not: this lecture is unnecessary

Which virtue in her strictness could not check.
I vowed no more to keep a sensual woman.[814]
'Tis done: I mean to make a lawful wife of her.
CARDINAL He[815] that taught you that craft,
Call him not master long; he will undo you.
Grow not too cunning for your soul, good brother.
Is it enough to use adulterous thefts,[816]
And then take sanctuary in marriage?
I grant, so long as an offender keeps
Close in a privileged temple,[817] his life's safe;
But if he ever venture to come out,
And so be taken, then he surely dies for't.
So now y'are safe; but when you leave this body,
Man's only privileged temple upon earth,
In which the guilty soul takes sanctuary,
Then you'll perceive what wrongs chaste vows endure
When lust usurps the bed that should be pure.
BIANCA Sir, I have read you over[818] all this while
In silence, and I find great knowledge in you,
And severe[819] learning; yet 'mongst all your virtues
I see not charity written, which some call
The first-born of religion, and I wonder
I cannot see't in yours. Believe it, sir,
There is no virtue can be sooner missed,
Or later welcomed; it begins the rest,
And sets 'em all in order. Heaven and angels
Take great delight in a converted sinner.
Why should you then, a servant and professor,[820]
Differ so much from them? If ev'ry woman
That commits evil should be therefore kept
Back in desires of goodness, how should virtue
Be known and honored? From a man that's blind
To take a burning taper, 'tis no wrong;
He never misses it. But to take light
From one that sees, that's injury and spite.
Pray, whether[821] is religion better served:
When lives that are licentious are made honest,
Than[822] when they still run through a sinful blood?
'Tis nothing Virtue's temples to deface;
But build the ruins,[823] there's a work of grace.
DUKE I kiss thee for that spirit; thou hast praised thy wit
A modest way. On, on there! *Hoboys*
CARDINAL Lust is bold,
And will have vengeance speak, ere't be controlled.[824]

Exeunt

814 31 sensual woman: mistress
815 33 He: the devil
816 36 use adulterous thefts: make a habit of stealing others' spouses
817 39 privileged temple: religious institution with the right to provide sanctuary
818 47 read you over: observed you carefully
819 49 severe: austere; judgmental
820 57 professor: a professed Christian; one who claims theological knowledge
821 65 whether: in which of these two cases
822 67 Than: or
823 69 build the ruins: restore something one has destroyed
824 72 controlled: brought to heel

Act V, scene i

Enter GUARDIANO *and* WARD

GUARDIANO Speak, hast thou any sense of thy abuse?
Dost thou know what wrong's done thee?
WARD I were an ass else!
I cannot wash my face, but I am feeling on't.[825]
GUARDIANO Here, take this galtrop,[826] then; convey it secretly
Into the place I showed you. Look you, sir,
This is the trap-door to't.
WARD I know't of old, uncle, since the last triumph;[827] here rose up a devil with one eye, I remember, with a company of fire-works at's tail.
GUARDIANO Prithee, leave squibbing[828] now. Mark me, and fail not; but when thou hear'st me give a stamp, down with't.[829] The villain's caught then.
WARD If I miss you,[830] hang me; I love to catch a villain, and your stamp[831] shall go current,[832] I warrant you. But how shall I rise up and let him down too, all at one hole? That will be a horrible puzzle. You know I have a part in't, I play Slander.
GUARDIANO True, but never make you ready for't.
WARD No? My clothes are bought and all, and a foul fiend's head with a long contumelious[833] tongue i'th'chaps[834] on't, a very fit shape for Slander i'th'out-parishes.[835]
GUARDIANO It shall not come so far; thou understand'st it not.
WARD Oh, oh!
GUARDIANO He shall lie deep enough ere that time,
And stick first upon those.[836]
WARD Now I conceive you, Guardianer.
GUARDIANO Away, list to the privy[837] stamp; that's all thy part.
WARD Stamp my horns in a mortar if I miss you, and give the powder in white wine to sick cuckolds:[838] a very present remedy for the headache. *Exit* WARD
GUARDIANO If this should any way miscarry now—
As,[839] if the fool be nimble enough, 'tis certain—
The pages that present[840] the swift-winged cupids
Are taught to hit him[841] with their shafts of love—
Fitting his part[842]—which I have cunningly poisoned.
He cannot 'scape my fury; and those ills
Will be laid all on fortune, not our wills.

825 3 feeling on't: feeling the pain of it; touching the cuckold's horns
826 4 galtrop: "an iron ball armed with four sharp prongs or spikes, placed like the angles of a tetrahedron, so that when thrown on the ground it has always one spike projecting upwards" (*OED* 2a)
827 7 triumph: court masque or pageant
828 9 squibbing: making silly comments (in this case, about fireworks or "squibs")
829 10 down with't: i.e. open the trapdoor
830 11 miss you: miss your signal
831 11 stamp: foot stomp; impression on a coin
832 11–12 go current: work well; be valid currency
833 15 contumelious: spiteful; insolent
834 16 chaps: jaws
835 16 out-parishes: suburbs. The Ward may imply that gossip is common there, or that old-fashioned morality plays featuring characters like Slander are likely to be performed there
836 20 those: the sharp points of the galtrop
837 21 privy: secret
838 22–3 Stamp my … sick cuckolds: horn was often used as an antidote for poison; the Ward imagines his horns curing the "headache" of other men's cuckoldry
839 25 As: whereas
840 26 present: play
841 27 him: Hippolito
842 28 Fitting his part: since Hippolito plays a lovesick shepherd, it will make sense for him to be hit by the cupids' arrows

That's all the sport on't—for who will imagine
That at the celebration of this night
Any mischance that haps can flow from spite?

Exit

Act V, scene ii

Flourish.[843] *Enter, above,*[844] DUKE, BIANCA, LORD CARDINAL, FABRITIO, *and other Cardinals, Lords, and Ladies, in state*

DUKE Now, our fair Duchess, your delight shall witness
How y'are beloved and honored; all the glories
Bestowed upon the gladness of this night
Are done for your bright sake.
BIANCA I am the more
In debt, my lord, to loves and courtesies
That offer up themselves so bounteously
To do me honored grace, without my merit.
DUKE A goodness set in greatness: how it sparkles
Afar off like pure diamonds set in gold!
How perfect[845] my desires were, might I witness
But a fair noble peace 'twixt your two spirits!
The reconcilement would be more sweet to me
Than longer life to him that fears to die.
[*To* CARDINAL] Good sir!
CARDINAL I profess[846] peace, and am content.
DUKE I'll see the seal upon't, and then 'tis firm.
CARDINAL You shall have all you wish. [*Kisses* BIANCA]
DUKE I have all indeed now.
BIANCA [*Aside*] But I have made surer work; this shall not blind me.
He that begins so early to reprove,
Quickly rid[847] him, or look for little love.
Beware a brother's envy; he's next heir,[848] too.
Cardinal, you die this night; the plot's laid surely.
In time of sports, Death may steal in securely;
Then 'tis least thought on.
For he that's most religious, holy friend,
Does not at all hours think upon his end;
He has his times of frailty, and his thoughts
Their transportations[849] too through flesh and blood,
For all his zeal, his learning, and his light,[850]
As well as we, poor soul, that sin by night. [FABRITIO *gives the* DUKE *a document*]
DUKE What's this, Fabritio?
FABRITIO Marry, my lord, the model[851]
Of what's presented.
DUKE Oh, we thank their loves!

843 0 SD *Flourish*: fanfare of trumpets
844 0 SD *above*: this stage direction from the first published edition suggests that the masque was originally staged on the main part of the stage, with the courtly spectators watching from the gallery above
845 10 perfect: fully satisfied
846 14 profess: teach; believe in
847 19 rid: get rid of
848 20 he's next heir: he will inherit his brother's titles and lands should the duke die
849 27 transportations: distractions
850 28 light: enlightenment
851 30 model: outline

Sweet duchess, take your seat, list to the argument.[852] [*He*] *reads*
There is a nymph that haunts the woods and springs,
In love with two at once, and they with her;
Equal it[853] *runs; but to decide these things,*
The cause to mighty Juno they refer,
She being the marriage goddess. The two lovers,
They offer sighs, the nymph a sacrifice,
All to please Juno, who by signs discovers[854]
How the event[855] *shall be, so that strife dies.*
Then springs a second, for the man refused
Grows discontent, and out of love abused
He raises Slander up, like a black fiend,
To disgrace th'other, which pays him[856] *i'th'end.*
BIANCA In troth, my lord, a pretty, pleasing argument,
And fits th'occasion well: envy and slander
Are things soon raised against two faithful lovers;
But comfort is, they are not long unrewarded.[857] *Music*
DUKE This music shows they're upon entrance[858] now.
BIANCA [*Aside*] Then enter all my wishes!

Enter HYMEN[859] *in yellow,* GANYMEDE[860] *in a blue robe powdered*[861] *with stars, and* HEBE[862] *in a white robe with golden stars, with covered cups in their hands. They dance a short dance; then, bowing to the* DUKE *&c.,* HYMEN *speaks:*

HYMEN [*Offering* BIANCA *a cup*] To thee, fair bride, Hymen offers up
Of nuptial joys this the celestial cup.
Take it, and thou shalt ever find
Love in thy bed, peace in thy mind.
BIANCA We'll taste you sure, 'twere pity to disgrace
So pretty a beginning. [*She drinks*]
DUKE 'Twas spoke nobly.
GANYMEDE Two cups of nectar have we begged from Jove;
Hebe, give that to innocence, I this to love.
[HEBE *gives her cup to the* CARDINAL; GANYMEDE *gives his to the* DUKE. *Both drink*]
Take heed of stumbling more; look to your way.
Remember still the Via Lactea.[863]
HEBE Well, Ganymede, you have more faults, though not so known;
I spilled one cup, but you have filched many a one.
HYMEN No more; forbear, for Hymen's sake.
In love we met, and so let's part. *Exeunt* [HYMEN, GANYMEDE, *and* HEBE]
DUKE But soft! Here's no such persons in the argument
As these three: Hymen, Hebe, Ganymede.
The actors that this model here discovers
Are only four: Juno, a nymph, two lovers.

852 32 argument: summary of the plot
853 35 *it*: the Nymph's love for both men
854 39 *discovers*: reveals
855 40 *event*: outcome
856 44 *pays him*: punishes him appropriately
857 48 unrewarded: unpunished
858 49 upon entrance: about to enter
859 50 SD HYMEN: the god of marriage; he is traditionally portrayed in yellow robes
860 50 SD GANYMEDE: Zeus's (Jove's) cupbearer and beloved
861 50 SD *powdered*: sprinkled. The stars reference the fact that Jove, in classical myth, made Ganymede a constellation
862 50 SD HEBE: a daughter of Zeus and goddess of youth, she too served as a cupbearer to the Olympian pantheon
863 60 Via Lactea: the Milky Way. A myth recounts that the Milky Way was created when Hebe stumbled upon a star and spilled the cup she was carrying

BIANCA This is some antemasque[864] belike, my lord,
To entertain[865] time. [*Aside*] Now my peace is perfect.[866]
[*To* DUKE] Let sports come on apace; now is their time, my lord. *Music*
Hark you, you hear from 'em!
DUKE The nymph indeed.

Enter two dressed like NYMPHS, *bearing two tapers lighted; then* ISABELLA *dressed with flowers and garlands, bearing a censer with fire in it. They set the censer and tapers on* JUNO*'s altar with much reverence, this ditty being sung in parts:*[867]

Ditty

Juno, nuptial goddess,
Thou that rul'st o'er coupled bodies,
Tie'st man to woman, never to forsake her,
Thou only powerful marriage-maker,
Pity this amazed[868] *affection;*
I love both, and both love me,
Nor know I where to give rejection,
My heart likes so equally,
Till thou set'st right my peace of life,
And with thy power conclude this strife.

ISABELLA Now with my thanks depart you to the springs,[869]
I to these wells[870] of love. [*Exeunt* NYMPHS]
Thou sacred goddess
And queen of nuptials, daughter to great Saturn,
Sister and wife to Jove, imperial Juno,
Pity this passionate conflict in my breast,
This tedious[871] war 'twixt two affections;
Crown one with victory, and my heart's at peace.

Enter HIPPOLITO *and* GUARDIANO, *like shepherds*

HIPPOLITO Make me that happy man, thou mighty goddess!
GUARDIANO But I live most in hope, if truest love
Merit the greatest comfort.
ISABELLA I love both
With such an even and fair affection,
I know not which to speak for, which to wish for,
Till thou, great arbitress 'twixt lovers' hearts,
By thy auspicious grace design[872] the man:
Which pity I implore.
BOTH We all implore it. LIVIA *descends*[873] *like* JUNO
ISABELLA And after sighs, contrition's truest odors,

864 69 antemasque: a short interlude, generally comic, performed before the masque proper—in this case, composed by Bianca herself and thus detached from Guardiano's plan
865 70 entertain: pass
866 70 perfect: complete
867 72 SD *in parts*: polyphonically
868 77 *amazed*: confused
869 83 springs: the home of the nymphs
870 84 wells: sources of love—perhaps alluding to the altars of Juno, or to the two suitors themselves
871 88 tedious: painful; drawn-out
872 96 design: point out
873 97 SD *descends*: in the first staging, Livia was presumably lowered from the upper canopy of the theatre in a chariot or other scenic vehicle. Her pages, dressed like cupids and armed with bows and arrows, may accompany her at this point or may enter later

I offer to thy powerful deity
This precious incense; may it ascend peacefully— [*Poisoned incense rises from the censer*]
[*Aside*] And if it keep true touch,[874] my good Aunt Juno,
'Twill try your immortality ere't be long;
I fear you'll never get so nigh heaven again
When you're once down.
LIVIA Though you and your affections
Seem all as dark to[875] our illustrious brightness
As night's inheritance, hell, we pity you,
And your requests are granted. You ask signs;
They shall be given you, we'll be gracious to you.
He of those twain which we determine for you
Love's arrows shall wound twice; the later wound
Betokens love in age: for so are all
Whose love continues firmly all their lifetime
Twice wounded at their marriage, else affection
Dies when youth ends. [*Aside*] This savor[876] overcomes me.
—Now for a sign of wealth and golden days,
Bright-eyed prosperity, which all couples love,
Ay, and makes love, take that! [*She throws flaming gold down on* ISABELLA]
Our brother Jove
Never denies us of his burning treasure,[877]
T'express bounty. [ISABELLA *falls and dies*]
DUKE She falls down upon't,
What's the conceit[878] of that?
FABRITIO As overjoyed, belike.
Too much prosperity overjoys us all,
And she has her lapful, it seems, my lord.
DUKE This swerves a little from the argument, though.
Look you, my lords!
GUARDIANO [*Aside*] All's fast.[879] Now comes my part to toll him hither;[880]
Then with a stamp given, he's dispatched as cunningly. [HIPPOLITO *discovers* ISABELLA*'s body*]
HIPPOLITO Stark dead! Oh treachery—cruelly made away! How's that? [GUARDIANO *falls through the trap door*][881]
FABRITIO Look, there's one of the lovers dropped away too.
DUKE Why, sure this plot's drawn false; here's no such thing.
LIVIA Oh, I am sick to th'death! Let me down quickly. [LIVIA *is lowered to the ground*]
This fume is deadly: oh, 't'has poisoned me!
My subtlety is sped;[882] her art has quitted me.[883]

874 101 keep true touch: prove trustworthy
875 105 to: compared to
876 114 savor: the scent of the poisoned incense
877 118 his burning treasure: Jove appeared to Danae in a shower of gold; he was also associated with lightning bolts. Livia's attack on Isabella may take either form
878 120 conceit: symbolic meaning
879 125 fast: securely in place
880 125 toll him hither: lure him here (with "toll" suggesting a death-knell)
881 126 SD and 127 SD HIPPOLITO *discovers . . . trap door.* O gives no stage directions here; the precise action is unclear. Perhaps Guardiano stamps on the floor himself, or perhaps Hippolito stamps when he discovers Isabella's death and causes the door to open at the wrong moment. This edition notes the likely moments of Hippolito's discovery and Guardiano's fall, but—like the original edition—leaves their interpretation open to those reading and staging the play
882 132 is sped: has succeeded (in killing Isabella); or, possibly, has been thwarted (by Isabella)
883 132 her art has quitted me: Isabella's "art" has requited Livia's "subtlety"

My own ambition pulls me down to ruin. [*Dies*]
HIPPOLITO [*To* ISABELLA] Nay, then I kiss thy cold lips, and applaud
This thy revenge in death. CUPIDS *shoot* [*at* HIPPOLITO]
FABRITIO Look, Juno's down too!
What makes she there? Her pride should keep aloft.
She was wont to scorn the earth in other shows;[884]
Methinks her peacock's feathers[885] are much pulled.
HIPPOLITO Oh, death runs through my blood in a wild flame too!
Plague of those cupids! Some lay hold on 'em;
Let them not 'scape! They have spoiled[886] me; the shaft's deadly.
DUKE I have lost myself[887] in this quite.
HIPPOLITO My great lords, we are all confounded.
DUKE How?
HIPPOLITO Dead; and I worse.[888] [*He points to* ISABELLA]
FABRITIO Dead? My girl dead? I hope
My sister Juno has not served me so.
HIPPOLITO Lust and forgetfulness has been amongst us,
And we are brought to nothing. Some blest charity
Lend me the speeding[889] pity of his sword
To quench this fire in blood. Leantio's death
Has brought all this upon us—now I taste it—
And made us lay plots to confound each other;
The event[890] so proves it, and man's understanding
Is riper at his fall than all his lifetime.
She,[891] in a madness for her lover's death,
Revealed a fearful lust in our near bloods,
For which I am punished dreadfully and unlooked for;[892]
Proved[893] her own ruin too: vengeance met vengeance
Like a set match,[894] as if the plagues of sin
Had been agreed to meet here all together.
But how her fawning partner[895] fell I reach not,
Unless by some springe[896] of his own setting—
For, on my pain,[897] he never dreamed of dying:
The plot was all his own, and he had cunning
Enough to save himself. But 'tis the property
Of guilty deeds to draw your wise men downward;
Therefore the wonder ceases. Oh, this torment!
DUKE Our guard below there!

884 137 in other shows: Juno appeared aloft in a number of other early modern masques and plays
885 138 peacock's feathers: in ancient mythology, peacocks drew Juno's chariot and were emblems of the goddess. Their feathers presumably feature in Livia's costume or props
886 141 spoiled: destroyed
887 142 I have lost myself: I am confused. The duke continues to be puzzled by the discrepancies between the "argument" he was given and the chaotic action of the masque
888 144 I worse: because of the agony of the poison; perhaps also because of the pain of Isabella's death
889 148 speeding: hastening
890 152 event: outcome
891 154 She: Livia
892 156 unlooked for: unexpectedly
893 157 Proved: it proved
894 158 set match: agreed criminal conspiracy
895 160 her fawning partner: Guardiano
896 161 springe: trap
897 162 on my pain: I swear on my suffering

Enter a LORD *with a Guard*

LORD My lord.
HIPPOLITO Run and meet death, then,
And cut off time and pain. [*Runs on Guard's weapon and dies*]
LORD Behold, my Lord,
H'as run his breast upon a weapon's point.
DUKE Upon the first night of our nuptial honors,
Destruction play her triumph,[898] and great mischiefs
Mask in[899] expected pleasures! 'Tis prodigious![900]
They're things most fearfully ominous; I like 'em not.
Remove these ruined bodies from our eyes.
BIANCA [*Aside*] Not yet? No change? When falls he[901] to the earth?
LORD Please but your excellence to peruse that paper,
Which is a brief confession from the heart
Of him[902] that fell first, ere his soul departed,
And there the darkness of these deeds speaks plainly.
'Tis the full scope, the manner and intent.
His ward, that ignorantly[903] let him down,[904]
Fear put to present[905] flight at the voice of him.
BIANCA [*Aside*] Nor yet?
DUKE [*To* CARDINAL] Read, read; for I am lost in sight and strength.
CARDINAL My noble brother!
BIANCA Oh, the curse of wretchedness!
My deadly hand is fall'n upon my lord.
Destruction take me to thee!—Give me way![906]
The pains and plagues of a lost soul upon him
That hinders me a moment!
DUKE My heart swells bigger yet; help here, break't ope!
My breast flies open next. [*Dies*]
BIANCA Oh, with the poison
That was prepared for thee, thee, Cardinal!
'Twas meant for thee.
CARDINAL Poor prince!
BIANCA Accursèd error!
Give me thy last breath, thou infected bosom,
And wrap two spirits in one poisoned vapor.
Thus, thus, reward thy murderer, and turn death
Into a parting kiss; my soul stands ready at my lips,
Ev'n vexed to stay one minute after thee.
CARDINAL The greatest sorrow and astonishment
That ever struck the general peace of Florence
Dwells in this hour.
BIANCA So, my desires are satisfied;
I feel death's power within me.
Thou hast prevailed in something, cursèd poison,

898 171 triumph: masque; celebratory pageant
899 172 Mask in: perform disguised in
900 172 prodigious: ill-omened
901 175 When falls he: Bianca is interested only in the death of the Cardinal
902 178 him: Guardiano
903 181 ignorantly: unintentionally
904 181 let him down: i.e. through the trap door
905 182 present: immediate
906 186 Give me way: move aside

Though thy chief force was spent in my lord's bosom.
But my deformity in spirit's more foul:
A blemished face[907] best fits a leprous soul.
What make I here? These are all strangers to me,
Not known but by their malice now th'art gone;
Nor do I seek their pities. [*She takes the poisoned cup and drinks from it*]
CARDINAL Oh, restrain
Her ignorant,[908] willful hand!
BIANCA Now do; 'tis done.
Leantio, now I feel the breach of marriage
At my heart-breaking! Oh, the deadly snares
That women set for women, without pity
Either to soul or honor! Learn by me
To know your foes. In this belief I die:
Like our own sex we have no enemy,[909] no enemy.
LORD [*To* LORD CARDINAL] See, my lord,
What shift sh'as made to be her own destruction.
BIANCA Pride, greatness, honors, beauty, youth, ambition,
You must all down together; there's no help for't.
Yet this my gladness is, that I remove[910]
Tasting the same death in a cup of love.[911] [*Dies*]
CARDINAL Sin, what thou art, these ruins show too piteously.
Two kings on one throne cannot sit together,
But one needs down, for his title's wrong;
So where lust reigns, that prince[912] cannot reign long.

Exeunt

FINIS.

907 205 blemished face: the poison may be causing sores to break out on Bianca's face, or she may scratch her own cheeks with her nails
908 209 ignorant: deliberately heedless
909 215 Like our . . . no enemy: we have no enemy like our own sex
910 220 remove: depart
911 221 cup of love: cup shared between two lovers or newlyweds
912 225 that prince: the prince of that state

12 Robert Armin, *The History of the Two Maids of More-clacke*

First performed 1607–08 (?)

First printed 1609

Edited by Richard Preiss

Robert Armin's *Two Maids of More-clacke* is the most canonical early modern play you have never heard of. Virtually unread today, and seemingly unloved even in its own day, its plot travesties what would become the most famous play of all time, William Shakespeare's *Hamlet*. This is not a strained connection: from 1599 onward Armin was the clown of Shakespeare's company, the Lord Chamberlain's/King's Men. He would have acted in *Hamlet* himself (likely as the First Gravedigger), as well as in nearly every Shakespeare play produced over the next decade, not to mention any earlier ones the company revived. *Two Maids* alludes to a staggering number of those plays, including *King Lear*, *Macbeth*, *Othello*, *Pericles*, *Julius Caesar*, *Love's Labor's Lost*, *The Merchant of Venice*, *As You Like It*, and *Romeo and Juliet*, but its parallels with *Hamlet* are by far the most sustained. It is both a witness to early modern dramatic canon formation and a victim of it.

For an actor and a solo comedian, Armin (c.1563–1615) was also a relatively prolific writer. He published an album of what may have been his stage routines (*Quips Upon Questions*, 1600), a jestbook about the real-life "natural" fools on whom his comic persona drew (*Foole Upon Foole* (1600), expanded in 1608 as *A Nest of Ninnies*), and a translation of a fable, *The Italian Taylor and His Boy* (c.1609). By the end of his career he had turned his energies to play writing. He is the author of a play printed in 1615 called *The Valiant Welshman*, and in 1609 he published *The Two Maids of More-clacke*. Elements of the latter, however, suggest that it may have spent a long time in development—perhaps too long.

The circumstances of the composition and performance of *Two Maids* are nebulous. In his prefatory epistle to the quarto of 1609, Armin mentions its having been lately acted by "the Boys of the Revels" (3)—presumably the Children of the King's Revels, named on the title page, who occupied the Whitefriars playhouse from 1607 to 1608. But he also hints that this was a revival, "sometime acted more naturally in the City" (3–4). We do not know if the actors in the earlier production were the same boys' company, a different one, or an adult one; neither does Armin disclose when this earlier production, if that is what it is, took place. He suggests only that he performed in the first ("I whilome pleased," 8–9), and had intended to appear in the second, but was prevented. As with so much about the play, we cannot tell if he is being sincere or facetious. He may imply that the play had changed hands from an adult company to a boy company, in whose plays adults did not perform; alternately, being of diminutive stature, he may have contemplated or even committed this very breach of theatrical decorum. As possibly the only early modern boys' play to have featured an adult, *Two Maids* already merits our attention.

An extended incubation, at any rate, would help explain the play's palimpsestic qualities. Topical allusions—to old plays and ballads; to law cases of yesteryear; to late Elizabethan public figures; to Queen Elizabeth herself, invoked as still the sitting monarch—appear to date parts of the play to the late 1590s, before Armin joined the Chamberlain's Men. At the same time, its main plot clearly engages with *Hamlet*, and may have been added later. Armin may have written *Two Maids* expressly for a boys' company: it was typical for their plays to imitate and satirize the fashions of the adults. Alternately, he may have felt bound (or entitled) to offer it first to his own company: although there is no record of the King's Men's staging it, its epilogue envisions performance at the Globe, bidding the audience to imagine "all the world were in your house" (V.iv. 350). If so, *Two Maids* would be the sole instance we have of a play the King's Men actually *rejected*. The surviving repertory of the King's Revels Children is thin, but it leans toward amateur and hack playwrights, whose plays a cash-strapped boys' troupe might have acquired cheaply. So both scenarios are possible—as is a third, in which Armin shopped his play around, continuously revising it to appeal to each company he approached.

The result is something of a hot mess, but a fascinating one. A brief plot summary will serve to illustrate. James Humil, presumed dead, returns to find his wife newly remarried to Sir William Vergir, a wealthy knight of More-clacke (present-day Mortlake, southwest of London). She recognizes James, and they begin a covert affair. Their son Humil does not recognize him, however, even when he discovers them in bed. Disgusted by her adultery, he betrays her to Sir William, hoping to win the hand of Sir William's daughter Mary. Yet Sir William now doubly wants rid of Humil. Not only must he silence him to suppress the scandal, but he thinks him a git, and beneath his daughter. Told he has hallucinated the tryst, Humil believes he is mad, and goes into exile. Restored to his conviction, he later returns disguised as an apothecary, and conspires with the vengeful Sir William to poison Lady Vergir. He is stayed by her revelation that James is his father; together they pretend to effect the poisoning, she fakes her death, and they accuse Sir William of murder. The subplot concerns the efforts of Sir William's daughters, Mary and Tabitha (the titular "two maids"), to marry their lovers, Toures and Filbon, against their father's wishes, by means of various ruses, elopements, and serendipitous fulfillments of prophecy. They are aided by the young men's fathers, by Sir William's rascal servant Tutch, and by the occasional convenient appearances of a local mental patient, John of the Hospital.

A jumble of genres and stock devices, *Two Maids* quickly reveals its limitations. As a clown, Armin rarely got to speak blank verse, and it shows: almost every long speech becomes mired in mixed metaphors and syntactic logjams, clouded by wandering pronouns and tortuous circumlocutions. Similar convolutions plague its plot, generating endless contradictions and missed opportunities. The play features no fewer than ten disguisings, often abandoned before they can realize their dramatic potential. Some are revealed too early, others too late, and still others not at all; some (like James's, if he is even disguised) are instantly obvious to one person (like Lady Vergir), yet elude others (like Humil). Characters agree to meet elsewhere (as in IV.i), yet in their next scene are still in the same place; conversely, scenes that appear continuous (like V.ii) prove not to be, jumping gaps in time. Motives remain bafflingly opaque, and plot twists almost willfully implausible. We never learn why James staged his death; Filbon's father urges his son's secret marriage, then inexplicably exposes it; Mary "dies" in a storm at sea that harms none of the ship's other passengers, and her miraculous awakening from her exhumed coffin is just as arbitrary. We await a tearful reunion between Humil and James, but never get it; when we next see them after Lady Vergir's confession, they are already calling each other father and son, as if the reunion has occurred off-stage. The play even forgets the very feigned poisoning on which its climax turns. First we are told the poison is a cosmetic Humil prepares for Lady Vergir, then a candy she will eat at a banquet—and the fateful moment of ingestion is then elided: one minute she is dancing, the next she is clutching her belly. *Two Maids* reads like the work of someone who had seen too many Shakespeare plays—because he was in them—yet never saw them from the outside, and thus failed to grasp how their parts form a whole.

So abundant are the play's lapses in continuity that they may be purposeful: had Armin sought to please a boys' company and their urbane clientele, his strategy may have pivoted to the avant-garde. Perhaps *Two Maids* is *trying* to be bad, flaunting the absurdity of dramatic convention and deliberately short-circuiting its expectations. When Lady Vergir asks James why he wrote to say he had died, or when James charges Sir William with a murder he immediately admits never happened, or when Mary's timely rescue entails that two men be out for a stroll in the storm her gravediggers have just fled, or when she sits up in her coffin, offers to tell her story, and then remembers she has amnesia, the joke is delivered so straight we cannot be sure it is a joke. A possible aesthetic analogue to plays like *The Knight of the Burning Pestle*, and an early modern forerunner of films like *The Room*, *Two Maids* inhabits an uncanny valley between pastiche and parody, subversion and schlock: it may be bumbling, or brilliant, or both.

But most pertinently for us, it stages something like *Hamlet* without the ghost—where a usurped father has *not* been murdered, and remains troublesomely alive. The result is comedy (or domestic melodrama) instead of tragedy, with all the commonplaces of *Hamlet* ironically rearranged to interrogate aspects of the original. Humil's stepfather rather than his father now becomes the object of his unswerving loyalty; the barrier to Humil's advancement, indeed, is his father's persistence, not his absence. In this version, the father *avoids* identifying himself to his son until the very end: Humil is here almost the *last* witness to James's return, rather than among the first—producing a burlesque inversion of *Hamlet*'s bedchamber scene, in which everyone sees the same figure Humil sees, but denies it. Stage directions such as "*Enter Humil sadly*" evoke Hamlet's melancholic disposition, and the soliloquies that follow seem garbled renditions of his sexual and sanitary neuroses. When Humil returns from exile, it is to destroy his mother, not the man who corrupted her or the man who deceived him. Put simply, Humil is a loser—a "humil"-iated Hamlet, irksome and creepy, ineffectual and overlooked—which may make us notice what a loser Hamlet is too. Which upsets Hamlet more, his father's death, or his mother's sexuality? How contingent is his filial devotion on thwarted ambition? Students have asked these questions for generations; they were already being asked in 1609.

Yet the real mystery of *Two Maids* is its other Shakespearean allusions, which seem unmoored to any thematic design. Beyond the clown called "Tutch," and the sea burial from *Pericles*, it teems with King's Men callbacks that would be all the more significant were it *not* a King's Men's play. A hopeful lover speaks in sonnets; another quotes the verses Costard sends Jaquenetta; Tutch's "her white is black" (III.ii. 44–5) recalls Iago's "a white that shall her blackness hit" (*Othello* II.ii. 133); Sir William's "Who knows the heart's affection by the face?" (III.v. 59) is nearly Duncan's "no art/To find the mind's construction in the face" (*Macbeth* I.iv. 11–12); Lady Vergir becomes Lady Macbeth, when her "sin blood red/Will not be washed hence with a sea of water" (III.v. 60–61); at his most Hamlet-like, Humil veers into Lear, crying "Blow, you swelled winds, and crack the battlements!" (III.v. 8). Armin's inexperience may have driven him to Shakespeare for lofty language, and as an actor, these lines may have caught his ear. But perhaps, again, they represent more: evidence of the widespread familiarity of the King's Men's catalogue, and—fifteen years before the Shakespeare First Folio—a fitful attempt to cram it into a single package. Precisely for being overcooked, *Two Maids* preserves formative pressures other texts rarely show us: a play in perpetual evolution, accreting material to the point of incoherence; a play in limbo between companies, repertories, and audiences, trying to market itself to each; as a result, a virtual map of theatrical London in the early seventeenth century, and an index of its favorite lines and motifs. Registering a decade of exposure to the period's most successful playwright, *Two Maids* gives us a stage-level view of Shakespeare's craft as seen by one of its key practitioners, and the pleasure of watching him write back.

The play also gave Armin himself, finally, a starring role. He tells us that he played John, an inmate of Christ's Hospital whom he had chronicled in *Foole Upon Foole*. He would also have played Tutch, whose disguise as a Welsh knight indulged another of Armin's specialties, stage-Welsh. When Tutch later impersonates John, Armin thus plays himself. The title-page woodcut depicts John (or Armin-as-John) bearded, with a flat cap, in the long blue coat worn by both servants and hospital residents; at his belt hang a pencase, an inkhorn, and a handkerchief. Today, the image is the play's sole claim to fame: however decontextualized, it is one of our few illustrations of early modern theater. That it promotes so minor a character speaks to what Armin thought would sell the play: his own celebrity. John's exploitation and abuse are hard to stomach, and remind us of our distance from early modern culture, where cruelty to the mentally disabled was considered entertainment. The difficulty of reconstructing what happens onstage in his scenes, meanwhile, reminds us of another gulf: that between the text of an early modern play and its performance.

Textual note

Never entered in the Stationers' Register, *The Two Maids of More-clacke* (STC 2nd edn/773) was printed by Nicholas Oakes for Thomas Archer. The 1609 quarto was its only printing; eleven copies survive. The copy-text used here (Q) is in the Huntington Library, supplemented by the copy in the British Museum. The manuscript was probably the author's foul papers, and the haphazard state of Q suggests no preparation for the press or stage. This is the first modern-spelling edition, and its chief task has been to restore as verse several hundred lines that Q sets as prose. Where meter is present, it has been lineated, but emendations are seldom introduced to regularize it. Scene divisions are imposed where a cleared stage is indicated or implied; act divisions are slightly more arbitrary, but follow major shifts in the plot. Otherwise, interventions have been kept minimal. Stage directions are expanded to supply missing speakers, or to clarify necessary action; speech-prefixes have been reassigned when a reading could not be found to justify them. Substantive emendations pose the greatest challenge to this policy, since Armin's knotted syntax and awkward vocabulary form an integral part of the play's interest. Punctuation has been added to aid comprehension, to separate ideas, or to lend emphasis; transposed or nonsensical phrases (e.g. "by seeking you that lost not what we find") have been adjusted where context dictates sense; where Q has misread its source (e.g. "Homers"), the closest plausible candidate ("Honor's") has been substituted. Cases where this proved impossible or self-defeating are discussed in the glosses.

Further reading

Editions

Liddie, Alexander S. (ed.) (1979) *An Old-Spelling, Critical Edition of The Two Maids of More-clacke*, New York: Garland.

Critical and contextual reading

Billington, Sandra (1984) *A Social History of the Fool*, New York: St. Martin's.

Bly, Mary (1998) "License Taken: Borrowed Prurience and the First Whitefriars Company," *Medieval and Renaissance Drama in England* 10: 149–78.

Cathcart, Charles (2005) "Authorship, Indebtedness, and the Children of the King's Revels," *Studies in English Literature* 45: 357–74.

Dahlberg, Sandra L., and Peter H. Greenfield (2016) "'To stirre vp liuing mens minds to the like good': Robert Armin, John in the Hospital, and the Representation of Poverty." *Medieval and Renaissance Drama in England* 29: 47–67.

Griffiths, Huw (2010) "'O, I Am Ignorance Itself in This!': Listening to Welsh in Shakespeare and Armin," in Willy Maley and Philip Schwyzer (eds), *Shakespeare and Wales: From the Marches to the Assembly*, Aldershot: Ashgate.

Henze, Catherine A. (2017) *Robert Armin and Shakespeare's Performed Songs*, London: Routledge.

Ingram, William (1985) "The Playhouse as an Investment, 1607–1614: Thomas Woodford and Whitefriars," *Medieval and Renaissance Drama in England* 2: 209–30.

Munro, Lucy (2011) *Children of the Queen's Revels: a Jacobean Theatre Repertory*, Cambridge: Cambridge University Press.

Preiss, Richard (2014) *Clowning and Authorship in Early Modern Theatre*, Cambridge: Cambridge University Press.

Wiggins, Martin, and Catherine Richardson, (2012–19) *British Drama 1533–1642: A Catalogue*, vol. V, Oxford: Oxford University Press.

The History of the Two Maids of More-clacke (1609)

Dramatis personae[1]

SIR WILLIAM VERGIR, a *widower and a wealthy knight of More-clacke*[2]
MARY, *his elder daughter*
TABITHA, *his younger daughter*
LADY VERGIR, *presumed widow of James Humil, now bride of Sir William*
JAMES HUMIL, *a citizen, first husband of Lady Vergir; presumed dead*
HUMIL, *son of James and Lady Vergir; suitor to Mary*
AUDITOR TOURES, *acquaintance of Sir William; auditor of one of the Queen's offices*
SIR ROBERT TOURES, *son of the Auditor, and suitor to Mary*
SIR RAFE FILBON, *acquaintance of Sir William and a friend of Auditor Toures*
FILBON, *son of Sir Rafe, and suitor to Tabitha*
EARL OF TUMULT, *friend of Sir William*
MASTER *of a ship*
GOVERNOR *of the Isles of Scilly, brother to Sir William*
HENRY, *a priest of Putney, a parish in the gift of Sir William*
TUTCH, *a clown and servant of Sir William*
MADGE, *a kitchen-maid in Sir William's house*
JOHN I'TH' HOSPITAL, *a natural,*[3] *and a ward at Christ's Hospital*
NURSE, *a woman appointed to attend John*
BOY, *another attendant of John*
WAT *and* FERRIS, *two watermen*

Messenger, Sailors, Gentlemen, Lords and Ladies, Servants, Musicians, Attendants

To the friendly peruser.

Gentlemen, Citizens, Rustics, or *quis non,*[4] I have boldly put into your hands a historical discourse, acted by the Boys of the Revels,[5] which perchance in part was sometime acted more naturally in the City, if not in the whole.[6] Howsoever, I commit it into your hands to be scanned, and you shall find verse, as well blank as crank,[7] yet in the prose let it pass for current.[8] I would have again enacted John myself, but *tempora mutantur in illis,*[9] & I cannot do as I would. I have

1 Dramatis personae: not in Q
2 *More-clacke*: present-day Mortlake, then a village southwest of London
3 *natural*: congenital simpleton; a mentally disabled person
4 2 *quis non*: who not, i.e. whoever (Latin)
5 3 Boys of the Revels: the Children of the King's Revels (named on the title page)
6 3–4 which perchance … the whole: which was once acted more naturally, perhaps in part if not in whole, in London. Armin may be contrasting the boys' production (at the Whitefriars, adjacent to if not quite within the city walls) with an earlier, adult production (at one of the suburban amphitheaters); "natural" may also pun on the role of John. Q prints "hole," possibly an allusion to the debtors' prison at Newgate
7 5 as well blank as crank: both blank verse (i.e. iambic pentameter) and lively
8 5 current: acceptable
9 6 *tempora mutantur in illis*: times change, and we with them (Latin)

therefore thought good to divulge him thus,[10] being my old acquaintance, Jack, whose life I knew,[11] and whose remembrance I presume by appearance likely.[12] Wherein I whilome[13] pleased: and being requested, both of Court and City, to shew him in private, I have therefore printed him in public, wishing thus much to everyone so delighting, I might put life into this picture, and naturally act him to your better contents; but since it may not be, my entreaty is that you would accept this dumb show,[14] and be well wishing to the substance.

Yours ever as he is merry and frolic,

Robert Armin.

[Act I, scene i]

Enter a MAID *strowing flowers, and a* SERVINGMAN *perfuming the door*[15]

MAID Strow, strow.
SERVINGMAN The muskadine[16] stays for the bride at church;
The priest and Hymen's[17] ceremonies 'ttend[18]
To make them man and wife.
MAID By my maidenhead,
A joyful time; I'll pave their way with flowers.
SERVINGMAN While I perfume.
MAID Some say this widow's rich.
SERVINGMAN I will not say as poor as Job,[19] but as bare
As January, when the trees look like
A girl whose color comes and goes as frost
Does in the milk.[20]
MAID 'Twas wont[21] to be a rich widow and a poor knight;
But now false, a knight rich and the widow poor.
SERVINGMAN However, honor is most rich, no matter who is poor.
MAID I would my fortune were no worse.
SERVINGMAN Thine may be better.
MAID So much if't be thy will:
If ever knight were gulled,[22] be it in me, in me I pray!

Enter HUMIL

HUMIL What, are the waits[23] of London come?
SERVINGMAN Yes sir.
HUMIL Play in their highest key, then.

10 7 divulge him thus: present him in this printed form
11 7–8 my old . . . I knew: Armin wrote about the historical John in *Foole Upon Foole* (1600)
12 8 whose remembrance . . . appearance likely: (1) whom I presume you will remember by his appearance (2) whose remembrance by you I presume likely (since, it appears, you are reading this)
13 8 whilome: once, formerly
14 12: dumb show: action without words (yet Armin apologizes for a text not enlivened by performance)
15 0 SD The servants perform customary preparations for a wedding reception
16 2 muskadine: muscatel wine
17 3 Hymen: classical god of matrimony
18 3 'ttend: attend
19 7 Job: Biblical figure tested by God with impoverishment and calamity
20 7–10 as bare . . . the milk: as poor as the bare trees in January, whose color changes as quickly as a girl's cheeks, the way frost comes and goes on the skin of milk
21 11 wont: usual
22 16 gulled: deceived
23 17 waits: small corps of wind musicians, maintained at public expense, who performed at civic occasions

SERVINGMAN Sound hoboys.[24] *Hoboys play*
HUMIL Make the gods dance, cause jovial mirth,
Music in heaven; for this earth's marriage
Is a triumphant concord to us all.
To me 'tis sealed by promise for his daughter,
Who in our blood shall sympathize,[25] says I.
She shall be ours, bedded. Although some
Menace a rivalship, yet the sure[26] card
Gives the trick ours, and we shall win,
Since in my mother it doth first begin.

Enter the solemn show of the marriage: SIR WILLIAM *Vergir,* EARL *of Tumult,* LORDS, AUDITOR, *Sir Robert* TOURES, SIR RAFE, FILBON, [*and*] *others*

Enter LADY; *Mistress* MARY, *Mistress* TABITHA; *and some other women for show* [*and exeunt*]

After all, enter JAMES [*disguised*], *a citizen, father to* HUMIL

JAMES Good morrow, sir.
HUMIL A good one to thyself;
To us 'tis seasoned.[27]
JAMES A marriage, sir?
HUMIL Aye, and a good one, friend.
JAMES Because 'tis rich?
HUMIL Good reach at stars;[28] i'faith 'tis true.
JAMES In whom,
Sir, if I may be bold?
HUMIL A knight of More-clacke,
To a London widow.
JAMES [*Aside*] My burdened soul, says I!
A knight of More-clacke to the widow Humil?
Just,[29] 'tis she.
HUMIL By this[30] the blessing of the holy rites
Relishes[31] in them. They are married—
At least, fare for it;[32] I must witness to't.
Farewell. *Exit*
JAMES How ignorance pleads nonage![33] In his eye
He knows me not. 'Tis not the lion's kind,[34]
Whose nature challenges[35] right property
Of perfect being; if it were,
Humil would Humil know that him begot
To be what now he is. Married again,
And her first husband living! Blame her not:

24 18 hoboys: oboes
25 23 sympathize: unify; Humil may mean his and Mary's blood, or perhaps his and Sir William's
26 25 sure: trump; Humil expects his mother's marriage to Sir William to put his own bid for Mary over the top
27 29 seasoned: spiced, prepared; already felicitous
28 31 reach at stars: (1) guess (2) the marriage itself is a "reach at stars," because Humil's mother is marrying above her station
29 35 Just: confirmed
30 36 this: now
31 37 Relishes: ferments, nears fulfillment (with an insinuation of sexual climax)
32 38 At least, fare for it: or, at least, are on their way
33 40 pleads nonage: attests to (Humil's) youth
34 41 the lion's kind: lions were reputedly able to see through disguises
35 42 challenges: asserts, affirms; the first of many ever-changing uses of this term in the play

'Tis my own project—thank[36] my letters,
That falsified our[37] death's black funeral
Into her mournful hearing.[38] Follow[39] it:
Think on thy soul. Divide that bitter band[40]
Knit by the closure of a mutual hand.

Exit

[Act I, scene ii]

Enter two Watermen[41] [WAT *and* FERRIS] *with luggage*

WAT I rest ye,[42] sir.

FERRIS At whose suit, Wat?

WAT At the bridegroom's. I'll not a foot further till I have eased my shoulders.

FERRIS No, nor I. We are asses[43] right: we carry provender, but are not the better for't.

WAT As how?

FERRIS Thou'lt not believe bread's bread till it be tasted. I say to thee, in this trunk is provender.

WAT Be an ass till thou prove it.

FERRIS Here's money which will buy it.

WAT O? By a figure,[44] I say to thee thou art an ass.

FERRIS How?

WAT By thy burthen.

FERRIS No, otherwise: that's not so good.

WAT Because thou hast ears.

FERRIS Are all asses, that have ears?

WAT Are all trunks laden with money, that are heavy?

FERRIS Indeed, I confess in that I am an ass; but I think so.

WAT By such a surmise thou mak'st it provender. We are watermen, and think because we see a man coming, and that I am his first man, he'll be my first fare, when another gets him.

Enter TUTCH *the Clown, writing* [*in a ledger*]

FERRIS Come, you are bookish.

WAT And thou blockish. Say right's right, and no more.

FERRIS See—sirrah, Mr. Tutch! What, an officer?[45]

WAT Yes, he's booking in.[46] Mr. Tutch! *Salve, sis salve!*[47]

FERRIS *Iubio te salvere, ave!*[48]

WAT He hears us not.

TUTCH [*To himself*] Let me see: capons,[49] turkeys, smallbirds, beefs, muttons, partridge, plover, woodcocks.

36 47 thank: thanks to
37 48 our: i.e. my
38 47–9 my letters . . . mournful hearing: one of a few cryptic references to the circumstances that led his wife to believe James dead; see also I.iii. 13 and I. vi. 6–7
39 49 Follow: pursue (the imperative of restoring his marriage)
40 50 band: bond, i.e. his wife's marriage to Sir William
41 0 SD *Watermen*: ferriers who taxied small craft across the river Thames
42 1 I rest ye: let's take a break (Ferris puns on "rest" and "arrest")
43 4 asses: because, argues Ferris, they are transporting the same money that will be used to pay them, like beasts made to carry their own feed
44 10 By a figure: figuratively
45 22 officer: one given an office to perform, as with a household servant; i.e. are you on an errand with which we can assist?
46 23 booking in: (1) looking in his book (2) filing charges, as a clerk or constable ("officer") might
47 23 *Salve, sis salve!*: Hail, a health to you! (Latin)
48 24 *Iubio te salvere, ave!*: I wish you health, greetings! (Latin)
49 26 capons: castrated roosters

WAT Meaning us?[50] [*To* TUTCH] Good morning, and many, sir.
FERRIS And many, Mr. Tutch.
TUTCH Are ye come, water-squirts,[51] are ye come?
WAT And why, sir, "water-squirts"?
TUTCH Because you shoot water, and so do they. But ha' ye that will do't,[52] my dainty element-dashers?
FERRIS Do't and stand to't, Mr. Tutch, if we might spend it sir.

Enter HUMIL

HUMIL Well said, honest knaves! Bear in.[53] But say, where's John i'th' Hospital, and's nurse?
WAT At hand, sir.
HUMIL 'Tis well. Away—and Tutch, touch the tips of their tongues with our cellar suckets.[54]
TUTCH I'll touch the tips of their tongues, and their tongues' tips; I'll baste their bellies and their lips till we have jerked the cat with our three whips.[55] [*Exeunt* WAT, FERRIS *and* TUTCH]
HUMIL Marrièd! 'Tis ended, and the next pull[56] mine—
At a fair fleece, a golden one.
The eldest daughter is my hope;
What then rests in it?[57] O, you wingèd lapwings,[58]
Farthest cry when we come nearest to it.
Quando pecus omnia sub umbra ruminat
antiquos paulilum vocitamus amores.[59] *Exit*

[Act I, scene iii]

[*Enter* JAMES]

JAMES 'Tis done—too late to ask why so.
Tardy intrusion, as a cipher placed,
Fills up but room, while substance in the other
Makes number precious; I am that round O,[60]
Which, with a sigh as sad as is my soul,
Grieves all too late. What now befits my moan
But black despair—and die in't, do?
To make thyself known but represents
Mellow fruit, falling into danger. O, I am that
Rotten, ruined, and unrelished substance
Which on my own upgrowing tree falls off;
By the time's negligence undone I am.
Would I had died indeed, and not in word:

50 28 Meaning us?: "woodcock" also meant "fool"
51 30 water-squirts: handheld water dispensers, as from a stick or hose
52 32 But ha' . . . do't: Tutch may be asking if they have enough money in their trunks to cover his expenditures; alternately, their cargo may be the items he has been tallying for the reception. Ferris's reply suggests a sexual innuendo
53 35 Bear in: carry in (your load)
54 37 suckets: candied preserves (usually fruit); Tutch's reply, however, takes this to mean liquor
55 38–9 baste their . . . three whips: all slang variations for "get drunk"; "to whip the cat" was proverbial
56 40 pull: turn, either to drink (continuing the previous image) or at cards
57 43 rests in it?: possibly a now-missing line connected "hope" to the bird imagery that follows, depicting Mary's heart as or in a nest
58 43 lapwings: birds thought to employ the diversion of pretending greater alarm the further an intruder moved from their nest, so as to conceal its location
59 45–6 *Quando pecus . . . vocitamus amores*: roughly, "when the herd grazes in the shade, we name over our loves" (Latin). The passage adapts the opening lines of Mantuan's first eclogue; also used in *Love's Labor's Lost* IV.ii. 92–3
60 2–4 Tardy intrusion . . . round O: James laments that his belated return makes his presence in the Vergir household superfluous, like a zero placed before a whole number, while Sir William's wealth and power ("substance in the other") holds all the value

These ill-tuned words like discords sounded harsh,
And yet were thought true music.[61] Well, well,
I'll take my stand,[62] and as she passes by
Note if her glories dash not all my hopes
With bare forgetfulness of what she was.
My picture[63] can she not forget, may be;
Old love may yet live in this new-born Lady.

Enter the solemn order of the bridegroom's return from Church,[64] *and as the bride goes by, she beholds* JAMES *the citizen with earnest eye, & speaks aside*

LADY [*Aside*] I am wonder-stricken in myself!
O you all-seeing, pardon my attempt:[65]
My second choice hath laid siege to my soul,
And my disloyalty hath in that witness[66]
Slain the concurrences of after-joy.[67]
Even so he look't, that had my maiden heart;
Even such was he, whose far-estrangèd[68] death
Gave me this license of ill liberty
To do, and undo. O, forgive me then,
Weak in my sex, my fault to the best of men. [LADY] *lets fall her glove;* JAMES *takes it up*
SIR WILLIAM New-wedded lady, and our morning's bride,
What is't that troubles ye?
LADY A loss, but being small.
EARL No matter for the loss;
You find a purchase equals any cross.[69]
LADY Let it go then. *Exeunt* [*all but* JAMES]
JAMES She knows me, and this constant accident[70]
Subscribes to't![71] How can she excuse
This double deed, this false neglect of love?
O women, how you dally in your trust,
How quickly you forget late-living life
And bury the remembrance in your smiles!
And ye this morning for the dead do sigh,
And shed your tears in bosom of new choice—
How have I sifted[72] your loose difference,[73]
Forever being precedent[74] against all.
Glad am I at this opportunity,

61 14–15 These ill-tuned ... true music: James presumably refers to the words of the letter that falsely announced his death, which (1) his wife believed true (2) seemed prudent to him at the time, possibly as a test of his wife's fidelity
62 16 stand: place, position in the receiving line
63 19 picture: face
64 20 SD *solemn order ... from Church*: the same procession that passed over the stage at I.i. 27 SD
65 22 attempt: act (i.e. her remarriage)
66 24 that witness: the sight of her first husband's face; it is not yet clear whether she thinks it merely an apparition, or understands that he is alive and returned
67 25 Precluded any enjoyment of the fruits of this marriage
68 27 far-estrangèd: (1) shocking and unexplained (2) alienating, severing her from him
69 34 By your marriage, you have gained sufficiently to outweigh any misfortune
70 36 constant accident: (1) purposeful accident (2) sign of (her) faithfulness (to me)
71 37 Subscribes to't: proves it
72 44 sifted: exposed
73 44 difference: (1) hypocrisy (2) indifference (with "loose")
74 45 precedent: uppermost (i.e. women are selfish and calculating before anything else)

Who[75] landed me even in the jaws of fear,
Swallowing my destined happiness
To utter ruin of herself and me.
If the unconstant air whistle abroad
That Humil lives, then Humil's widow dies
In desp'rate scandal, racked and tormented
In the remembrance of old wretchedness—
Which to prevent, plots cunningly contrived
Must buckler my repute,[76] so weakly wived.

Exit

[Act I, scene iv]

Enter Sir Robert TOURES *and young* FILBON

TOURES Lost her glove?
FILBON So she makes known.
TOURES I'll find it, to my ever-living glory,
And the next triumph[77] wear it in my helm,
Daring all gallants in defense to approve[78]
Sir William Vergir's lady owes[79] this glove. *Exit*
FILBON If my good fortune challenge such account[80]
To find it by my friend[81] or industry
I'll prick[82] it on a pole, and with my lance
Curvet[83] with nimble speed, in course of arms:[84]
And as I snatch it, by a curious[85] pass,
Cry in loud echo, "Here is for her love,
Who on her wedding day did lose this glove."

Exit

[Act I, scene v]

Enter the two maiden sisters, MARY *and* TABITHA

MARY The bride, our new-made mother, lost her glove.
TABITHA Aye, sister; so she says.
MARY I'll seek no further, for it is in vain.
TABITHA Especially when quicker eyes than ours
Arch in the brows of love's two votaries.[86]
Lord, how they'll brag to find it! Questionless,[87]
'Twill prove ransom of a thousand kisses,
Amorous glances, modest courtesy;
O, how these flatterers can insinuate,

75 47 Who: which
76 55 buckler my repute: protect my reputation (a buckler is a small shield)
77 3 triumph: tilt, tournament
78 4 to approve: to prove
79 5 owes: owns
80 6 challenge such account: produces a different version of events
81 7 by my friend: by means of a friend (possibly Tabitha)
82 8 prick: stick; Filbon refers to the chivalric sport of "running at the glove," here a variant of "running at the ring" with a lance on horseback
83 9 Curvet: an equestrian leap where the horse's hind legs kick up before its forelegs touch the ground
84 9 course of arms: the coming together of mounted combatants; Filbon now imagines a joust
85 10 curious: dextrous, skillful
86 5 love's two votaries: Toures and Filbon, whom Tabitha mocks for their earnest adherence to chivalric codes
87 6 Questionless: doubtless

And stretch an inch of length to an ell of width.[88]
Here's much in office for a little pay.
A glove, God wot!
MARY Aye, sister, so they say; go to, ye wanton you.
He that shall marry thee is matched, i'faith,
To English ratch[89]—or to a Dutch snap haunce;[90]
You will strike fire with words—
TABITHA Who, I? Now, as I live, sweet Moll,
If Filbon Marry me, as by this light—
MARY And wink.[91]
TABITHA 'Tis hard to juggle[92] with the devil! We maids
So simper in each other's quantity
As we know fashion ere it be devised.[93]
Forswear you one, and I'll forswear—
MARY The other:
Just, even so. Shall I be plain with thee?
TABITHA You'll answer no.[94]
MARY Aye.
TABITHA No, I.
MARY Aye, no.
TABITHA I know you will not therefore let him go.
I love my Filbon as men love good clothes,
Put them on every day.[95]
MARY And I love Toures as I love my sleep:
Embracing thus,[96] folding most dearly.
TABITHA Your lover nightly, as you wish him yearly.[97]
MARY In troth; in such a sort.
TABITHA As children play with stones,[98] to make them sport.
MARY You make me blush, Tabitha!
TABITHA At the thing ye wish?
Plague on the cat that loves nor milk nor fish.
We are all maidens' pictures:[99] fain we would,
Yet we cry "Away, away," when away we should.[100]
MARY Yet again?
TABITHA Never yet; ever so,
When so our matter's fit.[101]

Enter TOURES *and* FILBON

88 10 Exaggerate (an ell is a unit of cloth measurement equal to forty-five inches); in Q, the end of this line reads "ell of wide"
89 15 English ratch: a type of musket
90 15 Dutch snap haunce: a type of wheel-lock gun; Mary describes Tabitha as a pistol, a feisty maid with a sharp tongue
91 19 wink: Mary literalizes the metaphor in the oath "by this light": if Filbon married Tabitha, her intensity would make him blink, like one looking into a flame
92 20 juggle: conjure; Tabitha commends Mary's mercurial wit
93 20–22 We maids . . . be devised: "simper" and "quantity" are obscure here, but Tabitha means that they two are so attuned it is as if they can predict the future—indeed, they finish each other's sentences
94 25 answer no: i.e., to the offer to mutually forswear their suitors
95 27–8 I love . . . every day: I merely wear him like an attractive garment
96 30 thus: Mary presumably mimes a lover's embrace
97 31 yearly: a pun on "yarely," i.e. briskly, right away
98 33 stones: the word could also mean "testicles"
99 36 pictures: images, false fronts
100 36–7 fain we . . . we should: we women would gladly ("fain") gratify our desires, but we spurn men ("cry 'away'") when we should boldly go forth ("away we should")
101 38–9 Never yet . . . matter's fit: Tabitha seems to deny having been sexually free with Filbon, but adds that she will be when their marriage is secured (or when their genital "matters" come into contact)

MARY They are returned.
A glove or no?
TOURES No, but the glove I sought not, I ha' found.
MARY Where is't, man?
TOURES [*embracing her*] You're the glove which still I seek to wear.
Make me happy: match it to a pair.
MARY Be these forever matches.
TABITHA [*To* FILBON] How can ye find the glove was never lost?
FILBON [*embracing her*] By finding you that lost not what we sought.[102]
TABITHA Indeed, a willing loss is loss of gain
Where loving finders pity losers' pain—
I will not say enjoy; so much the rather
Because gift-giver cries out on the father.
But if I durst, I would; till when,
Unmatch our gloves, each take his own again.[103] [*They stand apart*]

Enter SIR WILLIAM, JAMES, EARL *of Tumult*, AUDITOR, SIR RAFE

SIR WILLIAM It is enacted by the bride's fair word:
Who finds her glove, is this day's governor,
To manage all our pastimes in the house;
And thou art he, the only conqueror
Of prize and honor: then, enjoy it.
JAMES You give, and I receive. Is this my office?
SIR WILLIAM Signed and delivered.
JAMES I take it on me. Music, triumphs, come!
Since fortune cast her favors in my fist,
I'll be most prodigal.
Yet, with modesty,[104] I am a citizen,
Unlooked for welcome, and unthinking come
To receive honor in a statesman's room;[105]
Yet to this presence[106] I will still address
Love, pains, and duty in this business. *Exit*
EARL In this is fortune blind, whose deeds are dangers,
Giving her graces not to friends but strangers.
TOURES [*Aside to* MARY] Prove on,[107] my fortunes; howsoe'er they stand,
I hold my fairest fortune in my hand. [*Surreptitiously takes her hand*]
MARY [*Aside to* TOURES] The like do I.

Enter young HUMIL[108]

FILBON [*Aside to* TABITHA] And all the fairest fortunes I would prove
Is only this: to enjoy my dearest love.
TABITHA [*Aside to* FILBON] The like I wish. [*They*] *speak aside*
HUMIL [*Aside*] All happiness live in thy choice; in hers[109]

102 47 Filbon's meaning is unclear, but he seems to hint at the loss of the maids' virginities. Q sets the line even more confusingly as "By seeking you that lost not what we find"

103 48–53 Indeed, a . . . own again: Tabitha coquettishly riffs on Filbon's innuendo: "It would be a boon to give that up willingly, because my pain would win your pity—if not your pleasure, because I who would give you this gift would be defying my father. If I could, I would; but until then, we must remain chaste"

104 64 with modesty: to speak modestly

105 65–6 Unlooked for . . . statesman's room: not expecting welcome, and accidentally receiving the honor reserved for a nobleman

106 67 presence: company (i.e. the wedding party)

107 71 Prove on: i.e. do your worst

108 73 SD Humil enters after the exchange between Toures and Mary, but reacts spitefully, as if he has overheard it; perhaps their clasped hands provoke him

109 77 thy choice; in hers: Tabitha's and Mary's respectively

All mischiefs, horrors, lest ourself
Participate in tender of our choice,[110]
Freely delivered in the sight of heaven.
SIR WILLIAM [*To* HUMIL] What news?
HUMIL The wedding dinner breathes his[111] last.
SIR WILLIAM And we will visit it; on, forward there.

Exeunt

[Act I, scene vi]

Enter JAMES *and* LADY

JAMES So fair and fortunate to be thus false,
Wedded to two. O you all-wond'ring eyes,
Gaze till your fires flame, your eyeballs droop
In moist imagination of this act!
Before the first be dead, to wed a second—O!
LADY Why writ you dead[112] in your last letters?
JAMES Sick was I, and no likelihood of life.[113]
What then, was that a just excuse
To varnish over this base counterfeiting?[114]
No, I'll make it known.
LADY I care not. I will thus excuse it:
All opposite of injury was yours,[115]
Putting to test our weakness by your letters—
Which, carrying credit, woman in her will
Guiltless is causer of this open ill.[116]
JAMES Had I been thus advised[117]—but all too late
Acquainted with your speed—I had prevented
What now is past and done.
LADY Why did you not? Bawd[118] to your own misdeed,
Three-quarters guilty of this accident,
That[119] might and would not stop the hazard,[120]
Will ye now heap up miracle[121]
And make it worse in note,[122] by adding to't
A bavin's blaze?[123] 'Tis not so soon extinct,
Being fierce of flame; quenched must it be
By water-course[124] of sounder policy.
JAMES I am from myself[125] in this. What shall I do?

110 78–9 lest ourself . . . our choice: unless I get to enjoy the offer (from Sir William) of my choice
111 81 his: its
112 6 writ you dead: cf. I.i. 47–9
113 7 Whether James's excuse for his letters is true is never made clear
114 9 counterfeiting: here, falsely advertising herself as marriageable when she did not know for certain her first husband was dead
115 12 You are not the injured party, but the offender
116 13–15 Putting to . . . open ill: Lady Vergir infers another motive for James's letters (which he never denies): that he was testing her fidelity. With no reason to doubt the information ("carrying credit"), she says, no woman could be held culpable of this public crime ("open ill")
117 16 thus advised: i.e. informed of her plan to remarry
118 19 Bawd: pimp
119 21 That: who
120 21 hazard: danger
121 22 heap up miracle: i.e. by miraculously returning to life
122 23 worse in note: more scandalous
123 24 bavin's blaze: a bavin is a pile of brush wood; she asks if the best solution is really to consume both their reputations in a wildfire of infamy
124 26 water-course: water channel, ditch
125 27 from myself: beside myself

O, I am mad, and mischief menaces,[126]
Unwitting of all purpose.
LADY Why did I cast my glove,
Proclaimed the finder stickler[127] of our sports,
But to appoint prevailing practice?[128]
JAMES I know not how.
LADY Leave all to me. Women that wade in sin
Have their wit's charter[129] to authorize it,
And they have antidotes that to digest[130]
Which better judgments lose themselves in.
Let me alone.
JAMES To lie with him the while?
LADY 'Tis true, to lie with him, but not in sheets:
To use the flourish of a woman's skill
In winds and turnings; other lying.
My new-made husband injures not the old.
As I am simply false,[131] I will be found
Constant to death, knowing my business
Is to heal up the fractures of the time,
And to salve virtue in her taint of ill.
JAMES I build on this.[132]
LADY Some month,[133]
While I possess the glory of my name,
Attendances according,[134] marry our son
Unto his eldest daughter—that's the point
Of all; regain my jointure[135] next—
'Tis not amiss to satisfy your debts;
These two achieved, the third is bedding.[136]
And if this brain beguile him not of that,
Say I am single.[137] No, since blame[138] sits nigh,
Behooves give care to use true policy.[139]

Enter HUMIL

JAMES [*To* LADY] Our son.
LADY Aside. *Exit* [JAMES]
HUMIL Mother, the noble guests expect ye;
The present meeting does neglect itself[140]
Where our fair bride is wanting.
Pray come in: you do them wrong.

126 28 mischief menaces: James probably means "menace (i.e. threaten) mischiefs," but he has just confessed to being distracted
127 31 stickler: referee, arbiter
128 32 appoint prevailing practice: devise a course of action that enables us to prevail
129 35 their wit's charter: law of their own cunning
130 36 that to digest: to digest that
131 43 simply false: innocently unfaithful
132 47 I build on this: i.e. this is a tolerable start, go on
133 47 Some month: (give me) a month or so
134 49 Attendances according: all the privileges belonging (to that name)
135 51 jointure: dower, i.e. lands and money entrusted to a wife for her future financial security (although it is unclear how Lady Vergir hopes to claim this from an illegitimate marriage)
136 53 Having achieved these two goals, only then will I take him into my bed
137 55 Say I am single: a boast: consider me altogether unmarried (i.e. divorce me)
138 55 blame: shame, calumny
139 56 Necessities (1) demand the commitment to set things right (2) require caution if we are to succeed
140 59 neglect itself: loses its definition (as a wedding reception)

LADY I am not well, and this commending air
Retains my health; I came to fetch it.
Wherefore, enriched with what was ours before,[141]
We yield[142] fresh duty, and attend them.
HUMIL Will you be mindful of our marriage, mother?
Begin so happily in yours.[143]
LADY I shall endeavor in it. Come.

Exeunt

[Act II, scene i]

Enter MARY, TABITHA, TOURES, *and* FILBON

TABITHA [*To* FILBON] Close and hushed, not a fly stirring.
While they feed hungrily, we, that love's deity
Does proclaim pardon[144] to presume[145] and speak,
Challenge liberty[146] now, by my maidenhead.
FILBON Swear[147] not, love.
TABITHA Can you forbid my oath? Sir, I will swear,
And till I lack it, say nought[148] shall confine me.
I had rather feast in fancy's pittance
Than to feed gagged with attention,
Soothing every bit with curiosity.[149]
No, I can fill my belly in a minute,
Satisfy my stomach in a breath:
Lovers digest their sighs, and chew their spleen,[150]
While other appetites fall hungry to't;
And let them greedily graze on.
MARY [*Aside to* TOURES] What's all this?
TOURES [*Aside to* MARY] Lovers talk anything.
FILBON I understand ye not.
TABITHA I would not that you should, for I speak Greek.
MARY Regard her not, for she talks idly, Filbon.
TABITHA Be you advised then, sister: I'm a fool,
Yet not so simple but I talk by rule.[151]
I say dine they that list,[152] I will not; for my dish,
Dressed to my hand,[153] is here. Here let me feed:
'Tis the maid's modicum.[154] God send us speed.
MARY In that I claim a part:
Whoever feeds this dish hath Mary's heart.
TABITHA So then said I well, ye wicked thing!

141 64 what was ours before: my recovered health (with a veiled reference to her returned first husband)
142 65 yield: submit to
143 67 Give yourself the happiness of beginning your marriage by arranging mine
144 3 proclaim pardon: grant license
145 3 presume: be forward and headstrong
146 4 Challenge liberty: demand freedom
147 5 Swear: make oaths (on your maidenhead, which Filbon would like to view as temporary)
148 7 say nought: (1) I vow that nothing (2) say nothing to me that
149 8–10 I had ... with curiosity: I would rather dine freely with you on the meager food of lovers' fantasies than eat with you in public, surrounded by those who would force me to conceal my thoughts with indirection ("curiosity")
150 13 spleen: in Galenic medicine, the organ that produced black bile, excess of which caused melancholy
151 21 by rule: to a purpose
152 22 list: wish (to do so)
153 23 Dressed to my hand: seasoned exactly to my tastes
154 24 modicum: (1) small portion (2) euphemism for female genitalia (in which case "Here let me feed" may be accompanied by a ribald gesture)

TOURES [*To* MARY] Mate[155] as I am of lovers' union,
Contracted to a solitary[156] life
By thus retaining singleness of heart,
Changing[157] all doubts that the world affords
But one, so to thy sweetest self,
Which only art idea of my thoughts,[158]
I vow a reconcilèd amity,[159]
Which violated, does command my life
To yield his interest to the shade of death.
May be your father alienates[160] our choice,
And shows as sunshine threatening rain[161]
To the all-hoping harvest present;
Which to make clear,[162] the honorable word
And fatherly regard in present office
Have passed their speed in our attention.[163]
I know your father will receive their[164] onset
Soldier-like, joying the siege begun,
Which though resisted bids them gladly come.
MARY Pause in that trust; give ear.

Enter JAMES *with the musicians*

JAMES Sound proclamation!
It is enacted by the bride and bridegroom
And by ourself chief in authority
That all receive their pleasures,
From the most high in this assembly
To the lowest. All pastimes are made free:[165]
Dancing, carding, dicing, reveling,
And other dues[166] of time's fit merriments.
Unto the bride and bridegroom's health!
TABITHA [*Aside to* FILBON] The day's short, and the night's—
FILBON Stop there.
TABITHA I will, to pleasure thee.
JAMES [*To musicians*] There, take your places,
And in your sweetest key of music strokes
Sound pleasant melody; echo those sounds
Which true-love hearts, in concord's chiefest grounds,
Have their blessed being. Use art in times[167]
Which may give welcome to our noble guests.

155 28 Mate: Q's "Mot" is obscure. "Mote," "moot," "mad," "made," and "not" are other possibilities, but make little grammatical or logical sense. "Mate" at least suits the theme of Toures's speech, which affirms his devotion to Mary
156 29 solitary: i.e. loving only one person
157 31 Changing: exchanging
158 33 Who (i.e. Mary) is the only perfect thing I contemplate
159 34 reconcilèd amity: contented friendship
160 37 alienates: severs us from
161 38 sunshine threatening rain: (1) pretending to be sunshine, but promising rain (2) rain that threatens the sunshine
162 40 Which to make clear: the evidence for which is that
163 40–42 the honorable . . . our attention: Sir William has exceeded his paternal responsibilities ("passed their speed") in scrutinizing our relationship
164 43 their: probably the lovers' intentions to marry, subsequently figured as a siege
165 52 made free: permitted
166 54 "dues" may be "activities appropriate to the occasion," but with "made free," connotes debt; V.iv. 98–102 likewise suggests an expectation that guests pay the bride and groom for their entertainment
167 62 times: time signatures; James requests up-tempo music

Enter HUMIL

TOURES We are betrayed: young Humil is at hand.
Dance, and excuse it so.[168]
FILBON [*To musicians*] Sound music there! [*Music*]
TOURES Content, a dance, and in again. [*They dance;* HUMIL *snatches* MARY *from* TOURES]
HUMIL Content, no dance, yet in again.
TOURES It is ungently done, to snatch her so.
HUMIL I snatch but that which promise says is mine.
Have I offended?
TOURES Aye.
HUMIL Right what is wrong.
TOURES Here?[169]
HUMIL Or where you dare; go seek in Brainford,[170] go.
TOURES Brainford? [*Music stops*]
JAMES Put up, or I shall be offending unto one.[171]
[*To* TOURES] Against the bride's son, dare ye?
HUMIL I repent not what is done. [*To* MARY] Come you with me.
TOURES So slaves by violence do hurry hence!
The rights of—
JAMES Peace! We on you do impose command;
Yield duty in it. Hall, a hall[172] there! Music sound,
And to the bride do consecrate this round. [*Music resumes*]

Enter all the train [SIR WILLIAM, LADY, AUDITOR, SIR RAFE, *others*] *to dance*

SIR WILLIAM [*To* JAMES] Squire of the day, cull out your gadding bucks,[173]
Select your light-heeled does; open[174] your rabbits,
Turn them to the toils;[175] we that are Venus' huntsmen
May partake the sports.
EARL You're a gallant woodsman, sir.
AUDITOR My son for one.
SIR RAFE And mine the other.
SIR WILLIAM Good!
My daughters for them both: a course[176] or so.
Go to, lead on; the bucks that have employment
For these does are not these giddy gamesters.
I'll be the forester, and look to't.
TOURES [*Aside to* MARY] Hear you that?
MARY A lightning before heat.[177]
FILBON [*Aside to* TABITHA] Your father's air is herald to his tongue.[178]

168 65 excuse it so: suddenly aware that he and Mary are standing too close, Toures suggests they pretend to have been dancing
169 71 Here?: i.e. right now? (since this is not the proper venue for a duel)
170 71 go seek in Brainford: a pleasure-resort town west of London; hence (1), fatuously, "go wait for me in Brainford then" (2) "go find yourself a whore in Brainford" (3) "go get yourself some brains"
171 73 Put away your sword, or I'll be the one to administer offense to one of you
172 79 Hall, a hall: traditional cry to clear space for dancing
173 81 cull out your gadding bucks: select your most vigorous young men; Sir William begins an extended analogy between the dance and a hunt
174 82 open: release
175 83 toils: traps, snares
176 87 course: chase; round; Sir William immediately qualifies his consent, and limits their coupling to one dance, going on to advise Auditor and Sir Rafe that their sons ("giddy gamesters") are not fit mates for his daughters
177 91 A lightning before heat: i.e. the flash before what is sure to be a heated argument
178 92 Sir William's demeanor signals his sentence on their match

TABITHA A' knows the coat, but thinks not who shall wear it.[179]
SIR WILLIAM There's two and two.
JAMES A couple more.
Two makes no show; our measure is for three.[180]
AUDITOR Why then, the bride.
SIR RAFE And bridegroom.
SIR WILLIAM [*To* JAMES] O sir, pardon me.
My joints were oiled to pleasure,[181] but now not.
JAMES Then I with her.
SIR WILLIAM You? O—your authority commands her.
JAMES Hark.[182]
LADY It gives his luster light.[183]
JAMES My warrant wins where his does lose the right.

[*The three couples,* TOURES *and* MARY, FILBON *and* TABITHA, JAMES *and* LADY, *begin to dance.*] HUMIL *snatches* MARY *from* TOURES *and dances* [*with her*]

SIR WILLIAM My son-in-law grows bold!
Good again: here's much to do[184] in love.
One[185] simply stands, not challenging his own—
And reason, Mary; chance is yet unknown.[186]
[*To* HUMIL] No, nor in you sir, though my son;
Words past contrive, but after deeds cry "done."[187]
AUDITOR [*To* TOURES] Brook'st thou this disgrace?
TOURES O sir, no remedy; what justice lives so free,
And to her own is friending.[188]
AUDITOR I am mad to think on't, boy, but—

[*The music swells,*[189] *and*] *they dance a measure* [HUMIL *with* MARY, FILBON *with* TABITHA, JAMES *with* LADY]

TOURES [*Aside*] How goddess-like the elder of the two
Stations[190] the measure! It is a jovial sight,
Where beauty gilds the pavement with her light.
How sullen Saturn[191] took her by the hand,
With frosty feeling, in whose icy touch
She shrunk her hold; but with a jealous eye
She glanced on me, fearful that standers-by
Should be enriched with't! Now she smiles me fair,
Gilding my torture with an after-hope.[192]
Thus moralized,[193] I season on my right,[194]
Her love thus challenged by inferior might. *The dance ends*

179 93 With ambiguous metaphor of "coat" as daughter or coat of arms: (1) he knows his daughters, but not who will marry them (2) he knows the value of his estate, but not who will inherit it
180 95 Two couples are not enough; our dance requires three
181 98 oiled to pleasure: limber enough for dancing
182 101 Hark: probably directed at the assembly, to validate James's assuming Sir William's place
183 102 It lends visibility to his (James's) ceremonial position
184 105 to do: zeal; intrigue
185 106 One: i.e. Toures
186 107 And for good reason, Mary, since your fate is as yet undetermined
187 109 Past words (promising you Mary) are theoretical; only deeds make a thing done
188 111–12 what justice . . . is friending: the phrasing is contorted, but Toures complains that power favors its own factions
189 113 SD *music swells*: some stage action appears to cut off Auditor's line
190 115 Stations: keeps
191 117 Saturn: i.e. Humil: astrologically, Saturn was associated with coldness and moroseness
192 122 after-hope: hope of some favor yet to come
193 123 moralized: glossed, interpreted
194 123 season on my right: renew my claim

Enter JOHN, NURSE, BOY, *all in blue coats*[195]

SIR WILLIAM After this dalliance here comes other sport.
Pray ye attend him, gallants. How now, John?
Tardi venientis,[196] John; you must be whipped.
Quaeso preceptor, non est tibi quid.[197]
This silly sot, my lords, so please you hear him,
Utters much hope of matter,[198] but small gain.
An old wife nursed him, which we call Blind Alice;
She, dying, left him to the city's keeping,
Which in their Hospital they thus nursed up,
Amongst the bounties of their other deeds,
Many besides.[199] Now you shall hear his fellow
Ask him such questions as his simpleness
Answers to any.[200] Sirrah, let me hear ye.
BOY John, how many parts of speech be there?
JOHN Eight: the vocative, and ablative; *caret nominativo*[201]—O!
BOY What say you to radish, Jack?
JOHN That it does bite. Ha ha ha!
BOY Where ha' you been, Jack?
JOHN At Paul's,[202] friend.
BOY Who saw you there?
JOHN Mr. Dean Nowell,[203] O he's a good man, truly.
BOY What did a'give thee, Jack?
JOHN A groat[204]—look here else.
BOY What wilt do with it?
JOHN Carry't home to my Nurse.
BOY I'll give thee a point,[205] Jack. What wilt do with it?
JOHN Carry't home to my Nurse.
BOY I'll give thee a fool's head,[206] Jack. What wilt do with it?
JOHN Carry't home to my Nurse.
BOY Carry a fool's head? What a fool art thou!
JOHN Should I go home without it? Who's fool now? *John tolls the bell, as if he pulled the rope*[207]
BOY Who tolls the bell for, John?
JOHN I know not.
BOY When died a?[208]
JOHN E'en now.
BOY Who, Jack, who?
JOHN My Nurse's chicken. Ha ha ha!
EARL [*To* SIR WILLIAM] A silly ignorant! Is a ever so?

195 124 SD *blue coats*: usual attire of staff and residents at Christ's Hospital, where John is a ward
196 127 *Tardi venientis*: you come late (Latin)
197 128 As your teacher, there is nothing I can do for you (Latin; "Quaeso" is an error for "quasi")
198 130 hope of matter: words merely resembling substantive discourse; nonsense
199 134–5 the bounties . . . Many besides: their many other charitable works
200 136–7 his simpleness . . . to any: he answers in the same idiotic way no matter to whom he speaks
201 139 *caret nominativo*: the nominative (case) is missing (Latin)
202 143 Paul's: St. Paul's Cathedral in London
203 145 Dean Nowell: Sir Alexander Nowell (1507–1602), Dean of St. Paul's from 1561 until his death
204 147 groat: silver coin worth fourpence
205 150 point: strip of lace used to support hose
206 152 fool's head: grotesque miniature of a human head at the end of a stick, carried by professional fools
207 155 SD: John mimes ringing church bells (historically, one of his hobbies)
208 158 a: he

SIR WILLIAM Never otherwise—a cleanly[209] idiot. What's put on him in his morning rise is as you see it.[210] This old woman is his nurse.

Enter MESSENGER

MESSENGER [*To* EARL] So please your honor, you are sent for to the court. The court goes from Richmond to Whitehall.
EARL We will attend her.[211] [*To* SIR WILLIAM *and* LADY] Kind Sir William Vergir,
Our time's bridegroom, to yourself and you
We wish as we have ever done, all love,
And for our present entertainment rest
Indebted to your bounty. If a court's amends
Have in it power of satisfaction,[212]
You command it; this acknowledged ever,
Your poor acquaintance[213] but an honorable friend.
AUDITOR We will attend your coach.
EARL [*To* SIR WILLIAM] Sir, be mindful of our servant Filbon;
What wants in him to weigh down love with gold[214]
Our favors shall supply. *Exeunt* [EARL, AUDITOR, *and* MESSENGER]
SIR WILLIAM [*Aside*] 'Tis a light weight.[215]
Their portions, if they poise no better,
Will to the world's belief grow less, not greater.[216]
But let them pass; I weigh them as they are.
Come, Nurse; follow us, John. *Exit* [*all but* NURSE *and* JOHN]
NURSE Wipe your nose. Fie, a sloven[217] still! Look ye be mannerly. Hold up your chin; let me see ye make your holiday leg.[218] So, my chucking: that's a good lamb. Do not cry for anything, John; if ye do—
JOHN No, Nurse, grace a-God, grace a-Queen.[219]

Exeunt

[Act II, scene ii]

Enter SIR WILLIAM *and his* LADY

SIR WILLIAM Shriek no more in my ear, I prithee, peace!
I grant I made such promise; but what then,
Shall I for that so set her on the rack,[220]
When her fair fortunes look a better way,
With the small proffer of your giddy son?
No, you shall pardon me.
LADY You'll let me have my jointure yet?

209 163 cleanly: thorough, complete
210 163–4 What's put . . . see it: This is no act; he gets up in the morning like this
211 167 her: i.e. Queen Elizabeth
212 171–2 If a . . . of satisfaction: if my position at Court should ever be able to recompense you
213 174 poor acquaintance: regrettably infrequent guest
214 177 What he lacks in money to add to his love. (Since Toures is the one with a rival, why the Earl should here vouch for Filbon—or anyone—is unclear)
215 178 light weight: Sir William ambiguously continues the image of balance scales: (1) a trifle compared to the sum needed to make these suitors acceptable (2) any sum would equal the worth of such loose ("light") wantons as his daughters
216 179–80 Their portions . . . not greater: his pronouns are undefined, but Sir William disparages his daughters and their suitors together: if they weigh themselves ("poise") worthy of such matches, their value in public opinion will only diminish
217 183 sloven: slob
218 184 holiday leg: elegant bow for formal occasions
219 186 John is perhaps practicing his polite language
220 3 set her on the rack: torture her (by marrying her to a wretched husband)

SIR WILLIAM Yes, that;
Three hundred by the year[221] 'tis thine.
But for your son to wed my eldest daughter—
LADY Why, he doth merit her in my accord.[222]
And 'tis no wrong in you, to dip her blood
In the self dye[223] that we are in.
SIR WILLIAM I grant his merit; but her shining value,
Made golden-glittering by my vauntings,[224]
Looks to a higher promontoria,[225]
From which tower when your son gazes
It affrights him, yields him planet-struck.[226]
LADY He shall not have her, then?
SIR WILLIAM Believe it, wife.
LADY He shall.
SIR WILLIAM Ha!
LADY I shall not bed with you till then.
SIR WILLIAM What?
LADY I ha' said it; and when posture of our word
Takes his base being,[227] I will die the death.
Into our wedding sheets shall mischief come
Before my body break your word with me,
Even on your wedding day.
SIR WILLIAM Nay then,
Up with the lists.[228] Again, it shall not be.
LADY I care not; think you I do?
Keep your word in that when I break mine.[229]
SIR WILLIAM No more! Be stranger to my bed: do, do.
Have I of nothing made thee much,[230] and wilt thou—
LADY Yes, I will.
Have you of protestations, oaths, and vows,
Made these loose fractures?[231] Lawful be it then
For me to shun the make-peace bed, since strife
Sets such division betwixt man and wife.
I am most firm in't.
SIR WILLIAM Very well, 'tis not amiss. [*Exit* LADY]

Enter AUDITOR, SIR RAFE, TOURES, FILBON

AUDITOR [*To* SIR WILLIAM] The night draws on, 'tis time to part.
SIR WILLIAM At your pleasures, gentlemen.
SIR RAFE Your gallant daughters will be next.[232]
SIR WILLIAM [*Aside*] Or not at all, for I am past it[233] now.

221 8 by the year: annually
222 10 accord: opinion
223 12 self dye: same mixture; i.e. if I deserved to marry you, my son deserves to marry your daughter
224 14 vauntings: boasts
225 15 Expects a superlative social station (here figured as a promontory or peak)
226 16–17 From which . . . planet-struck: which, should your son happen to look down from it, would make him terrified and dizzy
227 21–2 when posture . . . base being: when our vow lies down, i.e. is broken
228 26 lists: combats, as in a tournament; i.e. "the battle has begun"
229 28 Fulfill your original promise and then I'll break mine
230 30 made thee much: i.e. made you a gentlewoman
231 33 loose fractures: careless violations; destructive conflicts
232 40 next: i.e. to marry (implicitly, to their sons)
233 41 past it: (1) resolved (2) tired of thinking about it, to the point that I may deny them marriages at all

AUDITOR And we are prayed unto.[234] Our sons are gentlemen;
What resteth then, but we sail nearer to the point?
SIR WILLIAM What point?
SIR RAFE Of marriage, passed betwixt us in our promises.[235]
SIR WILLIAM Indeed, to one I promised her weight in gold;
Unto the other, which I love as dear,
Her weight in silver.[236] Now gentlemen, what goods
Have you to equal these large promises?
AUDITOR Why, all we have.
SIR WILLIAM But 'twill not serve:
The big avouchments[237] of my promises
Controls[238] you all, and all men else—yea, all
Under degrees of[239] earls, lords, or as potent;
To tool[240] them on I echo these large sums.
SIR RAFE Unvalued must your sums be to such choice;[241]
Honor looks high above such petty price.
SIR WILLIAM Look honor[242] high as heaven,
Our earthly reach[243] doth level in that eye,[244]
And with the embellishment[245] of richer worth
I'll buy, and out-buy, the imprisoned scope
Of reaching blood.[246] What will not value do
Where strong ability does reach his hand?[247]
And they have beauty too, which joined to riches
Will proffer fair—though not so quaint[248]
As courtly dames, or earth's bright treading stars;
They are maids of More-clacke, homely milkbowl things,
Such as I love and fain[249] would marry well.
SIR RAFE It was a promise in you to be kind.
SIR WILLIAM I'll forward with that promise. [*To* TOURES] You love my eldest—
TOURES With my soul.
SIR WILLIAM And pity to divide that love.
Then harken me: when she's dead and lives again
She's yours; not till then.
TOURES Then never but in death.
SIR WILLIAM [*To* FILBON] You love my youngest daughter?
FILBON And will ever.
SIR WILLIAM Pray ye, do; but when you are from yourself
A woman,[250] she is yours in marriage.[251]

234 42 prayed unto: beseeched (by their sons)
235 45 promises: Auditor and Sir Rafe evidently believe they have some prior agreement with Sir William, contradicting Toures's and Filbon's earlier doubts about their chances
236 46–8 Indeed, to . . . in silver: Sir William implies that he has named his daughters' dowries, not their recipients
237 51 big avouchments: lucrative assurances
238 52 Controls: excludes
239 53 Under degrees of: of lesser title than
240 54 tool: draw, entice
241 55 such choice: i.e. to those eminent nobles you desire (for whom honor matters more than money)
242 57 Look honor: let honor look
243 58 earthly reach: material wealth
244 58 doth level in that eye: (1) equals it (2) aspires to equal it
245 59 embellishment: reinforcement (through his daughters' marriages to rich men)
246 60–61 the imprisoned . . . reaching blood: those nobles who, possessing only titles ("blood"), are slaves to their honor
247 61–2 What will . . . his hand?: What cannot money accomplish when its possessor's will determines its reach?
248 64 quaint: elegant, fashionable
249 67 fain: gladly
250 74–5 from yourself/A woman: when you make a woman of yourself
251 68–75: Sir William's conditions typify the paradoxical formulae of prophecy in literary romance

FILBON Woman to woman joined—'twere wonderful;
But in more maze of wonder I should be
What I do challenge[252] to participate,
And from myself live to divide in other.[253]
SIR WILLIAM Faith, not till such a wonder.
SIR RAFE Is't not enough to scandal[254] thy true word,
But are we slighted thus with fantasies,
Impossibilities? Dead and alive again?
Manhood infused in woman? 'Tis not generous. *Exit*
AUDITOR Come, son: upon my blessing
Take from thy eyes thy heart-adoring shine;[255]
Offer no more thy altar-bearing thoughts
To one so giant-like, whose reach sits high
Above the compass of a gentle eye.[256] *Exit*
SIR WILLIAM You have your answers, gallants.
TOURES We like it not.
FILBON Nor will we so accept it.
SIR WILLIAM Forewarned: come near my house,
Rapes, felonies, and what may else be thought on,
I will with heavy impositions
Surcharge ye with, if not with pistol-shot;
I will defend myself and these I keep. *Exit*
TOURES Live I to hear this?
FILBON Convey[257] them from him, let us.
TOURES In disguise.
FILBON Or not at all.[258]
TOURES That way or none.

[*Exeunt*]

[Act II, scene iii]

Enter JAMES *and* HUMIL

HUMIL James, when I put thee from my thought,
Let me be hoodwinked from all fortune.
Thy partaking gentleness[259] is such
As I do love thee; troth, I do.
JAMES God continue this good league.
HUMIL Wot'st[260] what news?
JAMES No.
HUMIL The lovers are expulsed, and my fair hopes
Shine the clearer! What wilt say when I
Do marry this knight's eldest daughter?
JAMES That you are then possessed.[261]
HUMIL She is mine contracted, in her father's word.

252 78 challenge: consider, purpose
253 79 Transform myself into another person
254 81 scandal: disgrace, cheapen
255 86 shine: i.e. the light (in your eyes) that comes from your adoration (of Mary)
256 89 gentle eye: i.e. a gentleman such as yourself
257 97 Convey: steal
258 98 Or not at all: Filbon wholeheartedly agrees: by disguise or not at all
259 3 partaking gentleness: sympathy
260 6 Wot'st: do you know, i.e. have you heard
261 11 possessed: (1) well off (2) husbanded (3) crazy

JAMES New-broken, sir.
HUMIL Ha?
JAMES 'Tis true your mother challenged it:[262] but he,
As angry as the raging main[263]
Whose choler breathing[264] shakes high battlements,
Puts her off with a pause of contrary;[265]
I know it, sir. Her jointure is subscribed to—
Which else to do, sooner should earth to heaven
Presume a progress, than the grant make firm
What thy antecedent challenges.[266]
Your mother upon this abandons from his bed,
Vowing bold absence; he, enraged, gives way
To all malign and stubborn fashion of contempt.
Such a close[267] to day never had practice;[268]
Such a wedding night, till this sad first
Never had purchase. You shall well agree them,
Sir, to attune this jar;[269] use means, I pray you.
'Twill become ye well, when wrangling wrestles
With such violent injury; 'tis the son's office.
HUMIL 'Tis the devil's office, and not mine.
To hell[270] obedience if he break his word!
JAMES You had a father loved ye better.
HUMIL He loved me as a king in a play his servant,
Who, ne'er seeing him, gives kind applause,
But small utility.[271] My father in my childhood
Loved and left me to the world's eye
In bold necessity.[272] I thank him for it:
Since he died, my mother hath her chance;
Mine wants the proof.[273] Stand by, time's minion
And inconstancy![274] O!
JAMES Have patience.
HUMIL Yes—whereunto,[275] sith[276] all my hopes lie level
With despair? Such milksops in whose breasts
Lingers a lagging hope,
To them is patience sufferable.
But to me, horror and hell's black motions
Tickles[277] me on to mischief; and I will—[278] *Exit*
JAMES So,

262 14 challenged it: demanded that he keep it
263 15 main: ocean; Q reads "morne" here
264 16 choler breathing: furious (i.e. choleric) crashing
265 17 pause of contrary: obscure, but probably "abrupt refusal"
266 19–21 Which else … antecedent challenges: a knotted phrase: (but) to do more than this, it would be easier for the earth to travel to heaven than for her jointure to get your mother ("thy antecedent") what she wants (i.e. Humil's marriage to Mary)
267 25 close: conclusion
268 25 practice: precedent
269 28 attune this jar: harmonize this discord
270 32 To hell: to hell with
271 36 small utility: little money
272 38 bold necessity: in dire need; at the mercy of uncaring forces
273 40 wants the proof: remains to be seen
274 40–41 Stand by … And inconstancy!: a vague exhortation, possibly to Time's daughter ("minion") Truth, or to Fortune ("inconstancy"); depending on which, Humil calls for it either to "Stand by" him, or to stand aside
275 43 whereunto: to what end?
276 43 sith: since
277 48 Tickles: incites
278 48 and I will—: having worked himself into a passion, Humil evidently flies off in mid-sentence

Now swims upon the main such shipwracked souls
As the wind's rage splits on the rocks of danger.
I, my wife, and son, all three now heave,
And fear of sinking makes us timorous.
Should we be shelving[279] on the shallow beach,
The sea's rough gusts might scatter our intents;
So idle purchase might be gathered up[280]
From our so sudden shipwreck. No, my state
Stands yet secure: though maimed, yet is not foiled,
But salved by wise occasion, may make good
This sudden overflow of tide and flood.[281]

Exit

[Act II, scene iv]

Enter JOHN-'I-TH'-HOSPITAL [*eating bread*], *and a blue-coat* BOY[282] *with him*

BOY John, where hadst this bread and butter?
JOHN The crow did give it me.
BOY But take heed the kite[283] take't not from thee.
JOHN I'll choke first.
BOY John, shall's play at counter-hole-i'-th'-cloister?[284]
JOHN I ha' ne'er a counter.[285]
BOY I'll give thee one for a point.
JOHN Do, and I'll play hose-go-down.[286] O, Sir Willy is a good man truly. Here's good custard and capon, and good bread and butter too.
BOY Now, John, I'll cry[287] first.
JOHN And I'll cry lag![288] I was in hobbley's hole.[289] [BOY *takes a point off him, and* JOHN's *hose falls down*]
BOY I ha' won this, John; now for another.
JOHN I'll ha' it again, will I will. O! [JOHN *chases* BOY *and falls, crying*]

Enter NURSE

NURSE What's the matter? Making my sweet lamb cry? Come John, we must to London: on with your clean muckender,[290] and take leave of Sir William and his lady. Gods me! Your point! Where is it, John?
JOHN The crow has it, and did win it at counter-hole.
NURSE I'll whip ye for it! Take him up. Lose your point, lamb? Fie! Up with him, sirrah.
[BOY *lifts* JOHN *up and* NURSE *whips him*][291]
JOHN Good nurse now, no more truly! O, O!

279 53 shelving: washing up
280 55 Others might profit from our misfortune (who these others might be is unclear)
281 56–9 my state ... and flood: in a cascade of mixed metaphors, James consoles himself that his position ("my state"), though weakened, is not defeated but healed ("salved") by a prudent handling of the situation ("wise occasion"), which may turn this flood of accidents to advantage
282 0 SD *a blue-coat* BOY: this is the same Boy from II.i
283 3 kite: bird of prey
284 5 counter-hole-i'-th'-cloister: if not Armin's invention, a game (or some variant thereof) that has left no trace of its rules. It is difficult to reconstruct the stage action or humor, and the Boy appears to be simply making up excuses to take things from John
285 6 counter: in this context, any token used for keeping score; both "Counter" and "Hole" were names associated with London prisons
286 8 hose-go-down: apparently John's name for a game in which his trousers fall down
287 10 cry: go
288 11 cry lag: go last
289 11 hobbley's hole: meaning unknown
290 15 muckender: handkerchief (probably used as a bib)
291 18 SD BOY ... *whips him*: evidently Nurse, who earlier criticized John for his slovenliness, blames him for losing his hose-point

Enter Waterman [FERRIS]

FERRIS Where's this suck-egg?[292] Where's Jack-a-boy? Come, ye moveable matron,[293] where's this tuggage?[294] Away, away.
NURSE I'll take leave of Sir William, and go away. *Exit*
FERRIS Now, my John Juggler,[295] your nose is like Lothbery conduit,[296] that always runs waste.
BOY What's his name, John?
JOHN Sternigogilus.[297] Ha ha!
FERRIS Wat!
BOY A goggle eye, a wanton eye, a madcap—so a means.
FERRIS What?
WAT [*Within*] Hollo?[298]
FERRIS [*To Wat*] Trim boat, turn head:[299] we're at hand, mushrump.[300] We come, boy, we come.

Enter NURSE

NURSE Come John, our leave is taken. [JOHN] *sing*[*s*]
JOHN Have o'er the sea to Florida, and was not good King *Solomon*, *Tom Tyler*.[301]
FERRIS O, well sung, nightingale! Aboard, aboard there! Ha' rip there![302]

[*Exeunt*]

[Act III, scene i]

Enter TOURES *in a tawny coat like a tinker, and his* BOY[303] *with budget and staff*.[304] TOURES *tinks upon his pan, drinking*

TOURES Boy, you understand me? Though the liquor have rinsed[305] me, remember your business, boy.
BOY Yes master.
TOURES 'Tis rare to be a tinker, boy! Work enough, wench enough, and drink enough—is't not, boy?
BOY Aye, master.
TOURES Boy, where shall's have doings? I'll clout any woman's cauldron,[306] boy!
BOY Master, tink on. 'Tis time, for we ha' ne'er a penny.

292 20 suck-egg: term of endearment and paternal condescension; innocent lad
293 20–21 moveable matron: Ferris transports people, so everyone is "moveable" to him, but probably this carries some imputation of sexual looseness ("baggage" was slang for "whore")
294 21 tuggage: luggage (but with suggestion that he begins dragging John, who is back on the ground)
295 23 John Juggler: *Jack Juggler* was an early Elizabethan interlude, and the first known play written for children's performance; the term meant "trickster" or "imp"
296 23 Lothbery conduit: conduits were water fountains, connected to underground springs and to the city's above-ground sewer system; Lothbery (now Lothbury) Street was the site of a conduit at the intersection of Coleman Street
297 25 Sternigogilus: a nonce word; the Boy glosses it below
298 26–9: Ferris calls for his colleague ("Wat"), is misunderstood by the Boy to be asking "what?", and gets an explanation of the meaning of John's nickname; unsure why he is being spoken to, Ferris asks "what?"—and Wat now responds to what he thinks is his name
299 30 Trim boat, turn head: to trim a boat was to rig it for departure; to turn head was to turn a boat around
300 30 mushrump: mushroom (here, a term of familiarity)
301 33 Catches from popular ballads: "Was not good king Solomon" appears in *Love's Labours Lost*. (John/Armin may have sung more of each song than the text indicates; Q's truncation (and italics, reproduced here) may represent only a mnemonic shorthand)
302 34 Aboard, aboard … rip there! Ferris turns to the river, and calls for a water-taxi
303 0 SD *his* BOY: unlikely the same Boy who attends John (and whom we just saw depart), though a doubling of the actors is possible
304 0 SD *a tinker … and staff*: tinkers were itinerant handymen; the "budget" was a leather tool bag, and the "staff" a walking stick. Maligned for their drinking and petty thievery, they were (like unlicensed actors) subject to arrest under the Poor Laws of 1572
305 1 rinsed: drenched; i.e. (supposedly) intoxicated me. Toures is explaining the fiction they will enact
306 7 clout any woman's cauldron: strike (so as to repair) any housewife's cooking pot (with sexual suggestion). Toures here performs stereotypical tinker cant, hoping to attract attention

TOURES Pawn budget, boy; I'll ring in,[307] boy. [*Calls*] Ha' ye any work for a tinker? A ti- ti- tinker!

Enter MADGE

MADGE [*To* BOY] By my maidenhead! 'Tis he, the merry tinker of Twitnam,[308] boy, is't not?

BOY Yes, flower i'th' frying pan;[309] he stops holes[310] well. 'Tis he.

MADGE Has his old songs still, has he not?

BOY Yes, and new to boot.

MADGE And be not these tinkers knaves? Upon their backs they bear a long pick, with a staff i'th' end.[311] He shall ha' work; I'll break way for him, and call out the gentlewomen to hear him sing. [*Exit*]

BOY Let them all say what they can, [*sings*] *dainty, come thou to me.*[312] [*To* TOURES] We shall ha' work, master.

TOURES Draw, boy; *homo armatus*, boy.[313] [*Calls*] I'll pepper your pans! [*To* BOY] Where's my dog,[314] boy?

Enter SIR WILLIAM, HUMIL, LADY *Vergir*, MARY, TABITHA

BOY Your dame has him, and will meet you at Putney.[315]

HUMIL Indeed, what's a tinker without's wench,[316] staff, and dog?

LADY Is this the tinker you talk on?

HUMIL Aye, madam, of Twitnam. I have seen him lick out burning firebrands with's tongue, drink twopence from the bottom of a full pottle of ale, fight with a masty[317] and stroke his mustachoes with his bloody bitten fist, and sing as merrily as the sobrest chorister.[318]

[*Enter* MADGE]

MADGE Come, tinker; stop,[319] mend.

TOURES I'll tickle your holes.

SIR WILLIAM He's out of tune for singing now.

TOURES Out of tune, and temper too; thus can dainty liquor do. Sing, boy![320]

BOY Relish,[321] master, relish; a note above *ela*,[322] master. [*Sings*] *So, fa, me, re.*

TOURES *sings*[323]

307 9 Pawn budget … ring in: a joke that works in both realities: his tools are the last thing a tinker should pawn (and thus exactly what a drunken tinker would suggest); they don't need the tools anyway (because Toures is not a real tinker); ring in means "cry more loudly"

308 11 merry tinker of Twitnam: to his benefit, Madge mistakes Toures for a local celebrity tinker from Twickenham

309 13 flower i'th' frying pan: courteous epithet befitting a kitchen maid; apparently Armin's invention

310 13 stops holes: mends pots and pans (with sexual suggestion)

311 16–17 Upon their … i'th' end: Madge conflates tinkers with "hookers," who used long sticks fitted with hooks on the ends to swipe items from windows

312 19 *dainty, come thou to me*: title of a ballad; as at II.iv. 33, the actor may have sung more than just this line

313 21 Draw, boy; *homo armatus*, boy: (1) pour me (or yourself) another draught (2) draw your weapon (a more indirect drinking reference); *homo armatus* is Latin for "armed man." Toures is only pretending to be drunk, so this performance is for no one; the line may simply mean "prepare for battle"

314 22 my dog: perhaps the "tinker of Twitnam" was known for his dog, and Toures (jokingly) worries that he lacks one. Humil's first line suggests that companion dogs were part of the tinker image

315 23 meet you at Putney: Mary (among others) enters prior to this line, so it may be directed at her as code. Putney was a riverside village about two miles from Mortlake

316 24 wench: tinkers proverbially tried to seduce the housewives for whom they worked

317 27 masty: mastiff

318 26–8 I have … sobrest chorister: seemingly a catalogue of anecdotal, hyperbolic exploits associated with this particular tinker, or perhaps with tinkers in general

319 29 stop: (1) stay (2) stop up (holes)

320 32 Sing, boy!: Toures needs the boy's notes to find his pitch

321 33 Relish: with verve

322 33 *ela*: highest note in the gamut

323 33 SD *sings*: Toures's song has no ready textual source; its conceit seems to be that the girl, thought to be complaining of sickness (or love-sickness), is actually pregnant. "Stone" plays on "testicle"

TOURES *A maiden sitting all alone,*
Unto herself she made great moan;
Sorrow sat upon her cheek,
And she looked green as any leek:
Her friends did ask her cause of care,
But she cried out in her despair,
O stone, stone ne-ra, stone na-ne-ra, stone.
TABITHA Cold comfort in a stone.
TOURES *Doctors came her pulse to feel,*
And surgeons with their tools of steel,
To dig, to delve, to find her pain;
But all they did it was in vain.
Still on her back this maiden lies,
And with an open throat she cries,
O stone, stone na-ne-ra, stone ne-na-ne-ra, stone.
TABITHA Better and better, by my slipper.[324]
TOURES *Old wives they made answer thus:*
"Green sickness is most dangerous,
And oatmeal-eating[325] *is a food*
That never yet did maiden good.
Tut, tut, tut; 'tis nothing so."
Still she cried out with pain and woe,
O stone, stone ne-na-ne-ra, stone ne-na-ne-ra, stone,
Till she was delivered of a chopping[326] *boy,*
And all was as I am, omne bene.[327]

SIR WILLIAM What a disfiguring diet[328] drunkenness
Lays upon a man! A beastly appetite
Lingers[329] the body where such glutt'nous means
Swelters[330] in surfeit of desire and ease.
I am an enemy to myself to think
That man is slave so to continual drink.[331]
TOURES [*To* SIR WILLIAM] Knight, feast, knight! A good cellar-keeper,[332] knight. I'll cuss[333] thy daughter, knight.
MARY How's that?
TOURES Shall's not busse,[334] knight? Shall's not neb?[335] [TOURES *puts his arms around* MARY]
SIR WILLIAM Thou art in the straits, Moll, and the pirate's shot will sink thee; therefore yield.
TOURES [*as he kisses* MARY] I am thy Toures; being thus disguised, am come to steal thee; then be sudden, Moll.
MARY Nay then, i'faith.[336] *Exit*
TOURES Knight, shall's drink at door like beggars? No, I'll in, knight, see thy cellar; is thy

324 49 by my slipper: a mild but unusual oath
325 52 *oatmeal-eating*: oatmeal was associated with sexual appetite
326 57 *chopping*: healthy, lusty
327 58 *omne bene*: Latin: all (is) well
328 59 diet: constitution
329 61 Lingers: lingers in, afflicts
330 62 Swelters: festers. Sir William blames the lewdness of Toures's song on the mental and physical corruption that excessive drink has wrought in him
331 63–4 I am . . . continual drink: I do an injustice to myself to think that all men could have so little self-control
332 65 good cellar-keeper: i.e. the knight probably keeps a good wine cellar
333 65 cuss: kiss (perhaps gesturing at Mary, or seizing her)
334 68 busse: kiss
335 68 neb: nose, i.e. rub noses
336 72 Well, all right then

cellar in debt, knight? Dare he not show his face? Your blackjacks[337] are my elder brothers, knight; shall's not shake hands with our brothers, knight? *Exit, reeling*

SIR WILLIAM [*To* MADGE] Follow him: look he steal nothing.

MADGE Tinkers steal nought but drink and maidenheads; I'll watch him for one, if you allow loss of the other. [*Exit*]

SIR WILLIAM Where's Tutch?

Enter TUTCH

TUTCH Sir.

SIR WILLIAM Who wait you on?[338]

TUTCH On the world, sir.

SIR WILLIAM And what says the world to ye? [TUTCH] give[s] *her* [TABITHA] *the letter as he talks*[339]

TUTCH To me, sir?

SIR WILLIAM To you, sir—What, a message? Letters? Ha! Daughter, I'll be your secretary. Nay, hide not; juggle not with me. I'll once be secret to your thoughts, i'faith I will. [*He takes the letter*]

TABITHA 'Tis a card of lace, sir, which he[340] bought me.

TUTCH Aye, bone-lace,[341] sir.

SIR WILLIAM Bone-lace subscribed to like a letter?
Lace weaved of ten bones?[342] Is't so? Even so. [*He opens the letter and reads it silently*]

TABITHA O Tutch!

TUTCH O mistress, now am I tried on my own touch.[343]
I am true metal one way, but counterfeit another.[344]
O life, no life, but mess of public wrong;
Day turn to night, for I ha' lived too long.[345]

TABITHA From Filbon?

TUTCH Yes, from Filbon. Woe to the day, time, and hour!

TABITHA Wherefore?

TUTCH That I brought this news from your lover; therefore.[346]

SIR WILLIAM [*To* TUTCH] Pull off your coat.[347]

TUTCH I need not, sir; 'tis ready to fall off.[348] Yet if I do, 'tis the time of year: the fall of leaf, sir, and servingmen do drop their coats.[349] There, sir. *He pulls it off*

SIR WILLIAM Begone, come no more near my house; if thou do, thou art a felon. Are you the carrier, are ye indeed? Must love make you his Mercury?[350] Must Filbon send by you? My own betray my own, to him! You're a knave. They shuffle ye about; I'll deal the cards, and cut ye

337 74 blackjacks: leathern canteen pouches; wineskins

338 81 Who wait you on?: i.e. why are you here (since you were not summoned)?

339 83 SD *as he talks*: Q prints "*as she talks*," but Tabitha has no lines. She may mime dialogue with Lady Vergir and/or Humil as the scene proceeds, but "as he talks" makes better sense of Tutch's evasive answers to Sir William, enabling comic business as he tries to deliver the letter without detection

340 87 he: Tutch

341 88 bone-lace: lace made using a bobbin

342 90 ten bones: fingers; i.e. handwritten

343 92 tried on my own touch: a touchstone was black quartz or jasper used to test ("try") gold alloys by the streak they left behind when rubbed; punning on his own name, Tutch says that his baseness (as Sir William's servant, or as Tabitha's confidant) has been exposed

344 93 I am loyal to you and Filbon, but false to Sir William

345 94–5 O life … too long: Tutch riffs on a celebrated passage from Thomas Kyd's *The Spanish Tragedy* (c. 1587): "O eyes, no eyes, but fountains fraught with tears;/O life, no life, but lively form of death;/O world, no world, but mass of public wrongs,/Confused and filled with murder and misdeeds!" (III.ii. 1–4)

346 98–9 Wherefore? … therefore: Tutch misunderstands Tabitha as asking why he fears reprisal from Sir William, rather than why Filbon has written to her

347 100 Tutch is being stripped of his livery; servants wore coats marked according to the noble household to which they belonged

348 101 fall off: (1) it knows I don't deserve to wear it (2) I wanted to quit anyway (3) it is already in tatters

349 101–2 Yet if … their coats: punning on "fall," Tutch notes that servingmen are always let go with the falling of the leaves (before they get their annual salaries)

350 104 Mercury: messenger of the gods

from the deck. You understand me? Go.
TUTCH Gang is the word, and hang is the worst.[351] We are even: I owe you no service, and you owe me no wages. Short tale to make, the summer's day is long, the winter nights be short,[352] and brickle beds do hide our heads, as spital fields report.[353] *Exit Clown* [TUTCH]
SIR WILLIAM Wife, coop up our ginny hen,[354] that wants
This treading.[355] You, gossip![356] To your closet.[357]
Filbon shall, if we want will—yes, yes, what else?[358] [TABITHA *resists*]
LADY Come, daughter.
TABITHA I deny Filbon to his face; bring me to him. I will justify that all his actions are like apricocks;[359] they dangle, and I love them.[360]
SIR WILLIAM You do?

Enter MADGE

MADGE Alas, sir! Mistress Mary is with the tinker gone, and at the back door horsed; I saw the gelding, 'twas a dapple gray. [*Exit*]
HUMIL Hell and damnation! *Exit* HUMIL
SIR WILLIAM Death and torture!
TABITHA Christmas gambols, father; shoeing the wild mare.[361]
SIR WILLIAM Am I a jest to laugh at now? Indeed, indeed!

Enter HUMIL, [*running*] *after the* BOY

HUMIL O, not so fast, sir! I am for your race,[362]
And will outstrip ye if ye run no faster! [*Apprehends him*]
Speak, what was this tinker?
BOY Tinker, sir?
HUMIL Aye, thy master!
BOY My master is a knight who, Jove-like, in the shape of such a thing, came to see Danae in this shower of gold.[363]
SIR WILLIAM Toures, was it?
BOY *Etiam, ita, ego*:[364] aye, sir.
TABITHA Now fortune at the fairest go with thee!
Thou hast been cunning in this stratagem,
And I do give thee joy with all my heart.
SIR WILLIAM You do, huswife?[365]
TABITHA Wishing a whirlwind in the like disguise

351 107 Gang is ... the worst: Tutch consoles himself that going ("gang") is not as bad as hanging
352 108 winter nights be short: in fact, winter nights are long, but the oppositional structure leads Tutch into a clown's error
353 109 brickle beds ... fields report: the fields outside St. Mary's hospital (Spital Fields) were a clay-rich area used in brick-making, whose warm kilns attracted vagrants—thus producing a shanty town of "brickle beds"; Tutch implies he may go there
354 110 ginny hen: wanton, wayward girl
355 110–11 wants/This treading: (1) needs such enclosure (2) desires sexual defilement
356 111 gossip: frivolous woman prone to idle talk
357 111 closet: private bedchamber or study; i.e. go to your room
358 112 Sir William contemplates the threat Filbon poses; his trailing off and sudden turn of thought, "yes, yes, what else?", may mean either "if we do not check him, what else might he attempt?", or that he is cut off by Tabitha's insistent defense ("what else do you have to say?")
359 115 apricocks: apricots, an eroticized fruit
360 114–15 I deny ... love them: Tabitha's renunciation of Filbon inexplicably turns into defiant affirmation
361 121 Comparing the chaos of these events to holiday festivities, Tabitha gloats that Sir William's efforts to control Mary are as futile as putting horseshoes on a wild mare
362 123 for your race: a match for you
363 128–9 Jove-like ... of gold: Danae's father sealed her in a tower with no doors or windows; Jove, enamored of her, turned into a golden shower and rained down in her lap through the tower's open roof. It is unclear what prompts this grandiose analogy, but "Toures" means "tower," and cf. II.i. 115
364 131 *Etiam, ita, ego*: as Latin, this is nonsense; it might, however, be intended as a form of pig Latin, i.e. when the first letter in each word is dropped, the Boy appears to be saying "time to go" (Liddie, 1979)
365 135 huswife: maid, housewife; here used demeaningly, like the related term "hussy"

Fetch me hence smoothly! I am lawful prize.[366]
SIR WILLIAM [*To* LADY] Where's James?
LADY At London.
SIR WILLIAM I will thither too;
Since the devil drives, I am the second.[367]
Lock her up safe, be it your charge. *Exeunt ambo*[368] [LADY *with* TABITHA]
HUMIL What for this counselor,[369] concealing
Rape and ruin of your child?
SIR WILLIAM Whip him.
BOY I shall never endure it!
SIR WILLIAM Unless you do betray this trust, and tell us
To what cabinet[370] he hath conducted her.
BOY To Putney—O, to Putney, sir, where they'll be married.
SIR WILLIAM At my parsonage?[371] God amen!
No other hospital[372] to shadow them but mine?
Am I the patron of so hard mischance,
That my own of my own shall cozen me?
I'll thither. Son, your company! [*He starts to go*]
HUMIL No, I'll to Richmond,[373] sir, prevent[374] them there.
SIR WILLIAM No, sir, you shall with me:
That's the next office for yourself.
Delaying due, in other all things ready,
You will then serve yourself;[375] nor he nor you
Shall carve so to your appetites.[376]
HUMIL Your pleasure, sir.
Exeunt [SIR WILLIAM *and* HUMIL *together*, BOY *another way*]

[Act III, scene ii]

Enter FILBON *and* TUTCH

FILBON For my sake turned away?
TUTCH Yes, my master turns a new leaf, and so must I sir. 'Twas for your letter's sake.
FILBON Is there no hope?
TUTCH What do you call it when the ball, sir, hits the stool?
FILBON Why, "out."[377]
TUTCH Even so am I, out, out of all hope ever to come in to crumb my porridge at his table, sir.
FILBON Welcome to mine then, honest Tutch. But speak
Thy mind: thinkest thou she will continue firm?
TUTCH Firm, sir, yes; unless you take her for a joint-stool,[378] she'll continue firm. She feeds on

366 137 lawful prize: (1) unmarried and eligible (2) deserving of such extraordinary effort
367 141 Since the devil leads the way, I am only following
368 142 SD *ambo*: both (Latin)
369 143 counselor: accomplice
370 147 cabinet: hiding place
371 149 my parsonage: Sir William provides the house and stipend for the parson there
372 150 hospital: in the archaic sense of a place that offers hospitality to the needy
373 154 Richmond: about two miles from Mortlake, presumably arrived at before Putney via a different route
374 154 prevent: intercept
375 157–8 Delaying due ... serve yourself: an almost incomprehensibly elliptical reprimand of Humil's scattershot resolve: unwilling to do what must be done ("delaying due"), yet prepared to do everything else ("in other all things ready"), you are a slave to your poor instincts
376 158–9 nor he ... your appetites: neither of you will get to dictate matters
377 5 "out": a reference to stool-ball, an oft-mentioned but poorly understood early modern sport; in cricket, to which it may be related, when the ball hits the stump and dislodges the wickets, the batsman is "out"
378 9 joint-stool: ubiquitous home furnishing resembling a small table or bench; because one either sat on it or ignored it, to "take [someone] for a joint-stool" meant to take them for granted

ye, dreams on ye, hopes on ye, and relies on ye, telling her father what a friend you are, protesting and molesting[379] to the whole house of your good parts, vowing to God and man if she have not you, she will have nothing. For any man's pleasure, she'll not live if not for yours.
FILBON I stand resolved.
TUTCH She wishes that ye should, or she'll not trust to ye.

Enter SIR RAFE

SIR RAFE Son, see'st[380] thou young Toures?
FILBON Not since our last repulse in love; since when
I stand affected[381] unto singleness of life.
SIR RAFE Then art thou stable[382] in thy[383] thoughts.
But let me whisper to thee, boy:
Young Toures, in a tinker's habit, hath her stol'n
To whom his hearty adorations were
To this hour consecrate; she's gone,
And her old doting father got to complain him[384]
At the court. How 'twill work, I know not.
TUTCH Like wax:[385] she'll take any impression sir, she.
FILBON Like a tinker, say ye?
SIR RAFE Certainly,
Even so.
FILBON 'Twas my own project,[386] father!
He applauded it, knowing my fashion
Of that counterfeit[387] to be so sure
As no man could forego[388] me—
TUTCH —But himself, sir. 'Tis a point of law: arraign him upon *ipse facto*.[389]
FILBON And art thou stepped beyond me?[390]
Where tonight thou sleep'st, soft be thy pillow;
Easy be thy rest, and may thy bed be.[391]

Song.

TUTCH [*Sings*] *Mortal down, thistle soft,*
She laid herself under him, to keep him aloft;[392]
And ever she said "come turn thee to me,"
And was not this bonny lass Mary Ambree?[393]

Enter AUDITOR, *and doth whisper with* SIR RAFE

379 11 molesting: a malapropism
380 15 see'st: have you seen
381 17 stand affected: am inclined
382 18 stable: stoic; admirable
383 18 thy: Q reads "my" here
384 23 got to complain him: gone to complain
385 25 Like wax: Tutch completes the expression "'twill work like wax," i.e. effortlessly; Mary will (1) give herself to a man of any appearance (2) prove fertile
386 27 project: plan: Filbon complains (baselessly) that Toures stole the idea from him
387 28–9 my fashion/Of that counterfeit: my facility with that persona (of the drunken tinker)
388 30 forego: take precedence over
389 31 *ipse facto*: the fact itself (Latin); Tutch mockingly suggests that Filbon sue for copyright infringement
390 32 So, have you outdone me? (addressing Toures)
391 34 and may thy bed be: i.e. may your bed be easy as well
392 36 *aloft*: up; erect
393 35–8 *Mortal down . . . Mary Ambree*: Tutch parodies the popular ballad "Mary Ambree," which portrays her as chaste and virtuous; here she is lustful and controlling. Tutch's corrective to Filbon may be to imply that Mary was as much the author of her elopement as Toures

FILBON "Mary" indeed![394] She hath resigned to[395] me hard choice.
Near am I but as arrows afar off
Seems to the shooter neighbor to the mark,
Till it prove otherwise; so I
Furthest from favor am, though seeming nigh.[396]
TUTCH Change your mark: shoot at a white, will say "come stick me in the clout, sir." Her white is black:[397] 'tis crept into her eye,[398] and wenches with black eyes, the whites turned up[399] are but as custards—though they seem stone cold, yet greedily attempted, burning hot.[400] And such a wench is she, sir.
FILBON I know she loves me.
TUTCH Most affectionately; burns in desire for ye. But key-cold[401] through her father, she stands to freeze—while others are appointed to thaw the ice, not you.
FILBON I must use policy.[402]
TUTCH The only man[403]—I will assist you, sir.
FILBON I thank thee, and I will prevail in't.
AUDITOR [*To* SIR RAFE] I think, sir, if I see my house tonight,
There will come warrants to make open way
To their recovery, thinking they are with me—
Whom I protest I have not seen,
And unacquainted with her subtle stealth,
Am now as clear[404] as is the babe new-born.
I neither knew of it, nor where they are.
I do beshrew[405] their[406] hearts: right[407] I have in him for it.
SIR RAFE Sleep in my house, then,
So my word shall make your answer stronger.
I have a son: I wish him so possessed,[408]
But not with violence. Yet say he do climb high,
And reach the top bough with a stricter[409] course,
I knowing not the manner nor the means
Acquits me, and (God give them joy)
My oath is clear; and that's my warrant.[410]
AUDITOR Sir,
I will trouble[411] you tonight. By this sad time
His moan doth challenge comfort,[412] and the council

394 39 "Mary" indeed!: the somewhat thick Filbon seems to have grasped only that the names match
395 39 resigned to: given, left (me) with
396 40–43 Near am . . . seeming nigh: like the arrow that from far off looks closer to the mark than it is, I may be physically near Tabitha, but infinitely far from winning her
397 44–5 shoot at . . . is black: Tutch's advice misogynistically continues the language of archery: aiming for the center (the "white") of the target, a woman's virtue, will not do; a women's true "white" is her "black"—her genitals (black referring either to the color of pubic hair or to the vaginal cavity itself)
398 45 crept into her eye: you can see it in her eye (either Tabitha's or any woman's)
399 45 whites turned up: (1) if you look behind their eyes (2) when their eyes roll (in sexual pleasure)
400 46 but as . . . burning hot: Tutch shifts to a culinary simile: like a pie, a woman's outer crust may be hard and cold, but when penetrated ("greedily attempted"), they are piping hot inside (with an implication of venereal disease)
401 49 key-cold: cold as metal
402 51 policy: cunning, strategy
403 52 The only man: (1) now you sound like a man (2) I'm just the man to help you
404 59 clear: innocent
405 61 beshrew: curse
406 61 their: probably not Toures and Mary, whom Auditor has been encouraging; perhaps Sir William's bailiffs
407 61 right: justice; claim against Sir William for (1) wrongful search (2) (perhaps) theft of my son in turn (since children were their fathers' property)
408 64 possessed: i.e. of a rich bride, in particular of the other Vergir daughter
409 66 stricter: more prudent
410 69 warrant: justification, defense
411 70 trouble: inconvenience (Auditor accepts Sir Rafe's invitation)
412 70–71 By this . . . challenge comfort: by now Sir William's complaint will have demanded ("challenged") satisfaction

Whose loves he hath so often visited,
Heartened on by the Earl of Tumult's means,
They will add present purpose[413] as he begs it.
SIR RAFE But if the Earl know of my son's discharge,[414]
Signed by his careless answer,[415] 't'would allay
His hot endeavors with a cold responsal.[416]
But cease that; the time shall come—
FILBON 'Tis mine,
The cause and all; pine let me in them.
If the sun of hope shine
As a troubled meteor in the sky,
'Tis our fate's fortune, and no matter cause,
No remedy.[417]
AUDITOR True vauntings of resolve.
'Tis late, and custom challenges no right[418]
In me to be so hurtful to myself;
The evening's air is raw and cold.
SIR RAFE Filbon,
Follow us; be you more temperate.[419]
You see what hurry threatens in this misdeed;[420]
Wounds deep are dangerous, though they hardly bleed.
FILBON Sir, I am lessoned. *Exeunt* [*all but* TUTCH]
TUTCH As the boys at school
Practice their knowledge: by contrary rule![421]

[*Exit*]

[Act III, scene iii]

Enter HUMIL, *sadly*[422]

HUMIL O, I am slain with wonder!
Hath this life left in it a little breath
To blow out[423] treason?[424] Reek, ye clouds of shame,
Putrify all imagination! Hold her at stern:[425]
There let her sink, never to win again
Honor's recovery! Shall I say and think it?
O!
Have I not been in bed tonight, and so
Talk idly, wanting sleep; or rose from rest,
As many troubled do, acting like life,[426]

413 74 present purpose: urgency, swiftness of action
414 75 discharge: rejection
415 76 Signed by his careless answer: as signified by Sir William's haughty dismissal of Filbon's suit
416 76–7 't'would allay . . . cold responsal: Sir William's heat would receive a cold response from the Earl
417 80–83 If the . . . No remedy: with a pun on sun/son, "if the sun turns malignant, there is nothing to be done," i.e. what will be will be. Filbon attempts to discourage the fathers' intervention, urging that his problems are his own ("pine let me in them," i.e. let me alone pine over my misfortunes)
418 84 custom challenges no right: honor does not require
419 87 more temperate: i.e. than Toures was
420 88 You see (1) what turmoil threatens to issue from Toures's crime (2) how hastiness in such an enterprise can threaten it
421 91 contrary rule: seizing on Filbon's "lessoned," Tutch wryly interprets for the audience: schoolboys always do the opposite of what they are told
422 0 SD *sadly*: Humil in this speech is strongly reminiscent of Hamlet, parodying his soliloquies and melancholic disposition
423 2–3 Hath this . . . blow out: (1) does this world have any virtue left to defeat (2) does this breathless body have enough strength in it left to decry
424 3 treason: treachery
425 4 Hold her at stern: if the antecedent is "imagination," perhaps "hold off," but it is Lady Vergir whose honor needs recovering, so the phrase may mean "drop her over the edge" (like a ship's anchor)
426 10 acting like life: i.e. sleepwalking

A waking dead? For in that flattering fear[427]
Perchance her reputation may be saved.
No, I am certain in my fear: 'tis true.
In yond black closet[428] lies a woman
(I will not say my mother; that name's lost)
In the twined bracings[429] of the slave her man,
In James his[430] arms. And shall I suffer it?
O!
To blab it were to herald out my shame
In quartered scutcheon of black obloquy;[431]
To murder one were most impartial;[432]
Again to turn hills on[433] this sin
Would write me bawd.[434] But to be nobly satisfied
Is a content licensed from equity.[435]
The knight shall know it: I will write to him,
Startle his bold imagination with pale fear,
Rouse his revengeful spirit on them both,
And make me hopeful of his love neglected.
Forgive me world: heaven's justice puts me on,[436]
And though a son, I'll punish both or none.

Exit

[Act III, scene iv]

Enter EARL, LORD, SIR WILLIAM, [*other*] *Lords, and Sir William's two men* [SERVANTS] *bearing torches*

EARL [*To* SIR WILLIAM] You that bind up in secrets of the night,
Day's benefits going to rest
As peaceful birds lodged in a sanctuary,
Smile at our courtiers' care, whose industry
Rules in the silent and all-shadowing night.
Suits that are breathless in a troubled day
Have their abiding in our cares at night—
Hard-censured, and atoned by late advice,
Salving the world's scars—as we would your care,
Knew we the burthen of it.[437]
LORD With us the morn is mated with[438] the moon,
And we are retrograde[439] to what you do,
Esteeming conscience, benefit and good,

427 11 flattering fear: i.e. that through either sleep deprivation or somnambulism he hallucinated what he saw
428 14 closet: bedroom
429 16 twined bracings: entwined embraces
430 17 James his: James's
431 19–20 herald out . . . black obloquy: since his mother's shame extends to him, "herald" operates as both "publicize" and "heraldry," emblazoning his dishonor; an escutcheon was a shield ornamented with a family's heraldic devices, often subdivided into four parts ("quartered")
432 21 impartial: partial, biased; i.e. it would be unfair to murder only one of the lovers
433 22 turn hills on: to bury (in dirt); to pretend to ignore
434 23 write me bawd: define me as a pimp or pander to my mother's infidelity
435 23–4 But to . . . from equity: yet to vindicate my honor is a resolution permitted by law ("equity")
436 29 puts me on: drives me
437 1–10 You that . . . of it: a speech so tortuous it demands a full paraphrase: "You who sleep through nocturnal intrigues, your daily pleasures dozing as thoughtlessly as kept birds, appreciate the business of us courtiers, whose toil becomes visible only by dark. Petitions that are never spoken of during the hectic day fill our nightly labors—where they are arbitrated with difficulty, and resolved with long reflection, thereby healing the world's wounds—as we would do with yours, if we knew its theme"
438 11 mated with: indistinguishable from
439 12 are retrograde: travel paths opposite

Challenged in[440] service of our country.
Sir, though our blood affirm us labor-free,
It binds thee[441] more to busy industry;
Wonder not at our late up-sitting therefore.
SIR WILLIAM Your humors toil in our extremities,
But we unthankful merit contrary;
Think it a want and weakness in our kind.[442]
I post and labor in a toil[443] myself,
Seeking my own: midnight to me is noon,
And all the hours of dull-paced night
Sunshine-eclipses,[444] that do much molest me—
Pardon me, that I am so tedious.
EARL Seeking your own?
SIR WILLIAM My eldest daughter is conveyed from me—
Hurried away, as thieves by violence
Convey their booties from the true man's store.
Auditor Toures' son hath done this deed:
A rescue, noble lords!
EARL Rescue, and right.[445] Challenge the benefit.[446]
SIR WILLIAM A warrant, for a general search;
Restraints for Cinque Ports,[447] and all passages
That thievish water doth despoil us of.
EARL It shall be signed i'th' morning.
Draw the contents as you affect the means,[448]
And let attendance urge the early act.[449]
LORD Good night.
EARL Good morrow, is it not?
SIR WILLIAM Betwixt them both: the moral
Of my misery,[450] seeking too late
That to recover which I lost too soon.
LORD And yet in each you stand indifferent.[451]
SIR WILLIAM I must, till perfected[452] by you:
Either late loss, or timely victory,
Recovering what I fear is past advantage.[453]
EARL Hope the best, sir. Things at worst
Season in their decay, as children mend:[454]
Bent in their eye to ruin, yet they pause
Resting in grace, does reobtain at will

440 14 Challenged in: obligated to
441 16 thee: "us" makes far better sense, but he may mean "we ensure the stability of your enterprises"
442 18–20 Your humors ... our kind: your energies are devoted to our desperate circumstances, and they are undeserving who do not thank you; consider this ingratitude a weakness of character
443 21 in a toil: frantically
444 24 Sunshine-eclipses: i.e. eclipses
445 32 right: right the wrong (by doing so)
446 32 Challenge the benefit: demand whatever aid from me you require
447 34 Restraints for Cinque Ports: orders to bar all ships from leaving the five port towns of southeastern England (Hastings, Romney, Hythe, Dover, and Sandwich)
448 37 Draft the documents to include whatever you think will help
449 38 (1) Take care to do it soon (2) May our cooperation get the job done quickly
450 40–41 the moral/Of my misery: a metaphor for my woeful predicament
451 43 in each ... indifferent: you are seeking as keenly as you feel that loss
452 44 perfected: assisted, reinforced
453 45–6 Either late ... past advantage: (1) (I must experience) either a last-minute loss or a dramatic victory, recovering what I thought was beyond hope (2) whether I experience a late loss or a timely victory, I cannot hope to recover what I fear I have lost
454 47–8 Things at ... children mend: (1) things at their most chaotic point always recover, like children (2) things improve ("season") with their own corruption, the way children recover (see next note)

Opinion in rash judgement, dooming ill.[455]
LORD Good rest, for we go to't.
SIR WILLIAM The peace of happiness be with ye.
I will retire to my inn, and wish
Hours as short as momentary breath;
For till the morning, minutes hours be,
And hours years. Such is[456] revenged to me,
Might I enjoy it! [*Exeunt all but* SIR WILLIAM *and* SERVANTS]

[*Enter* MESSENGER]

MESSENGER Sir.
SIR WILLIAM My man, a midnight messenger?
What, is thy haste in Lethe[457] steeped? Speak.
Is that all, one?[458] One all, that we call daughter,[459]
Gone too is she?
MESSENGER No, sir.
SIR WILLIAM Wherefore starest thou so wildly?
Say, were't thou asleep and wakened?
Com'st to us here without thy better part,[460]
And sent abroad, leaving thy wits at home?
MESSENGER Your son, sir—in all haste, sends you his tales,[461]
Wishes your wit and judgement suddenly:
Read and regard, sir. [*Gives him* HUMIL's *letter*]
SIR WILLIAM [*To* SERVANT] Give me the torch.
[*Reads*] "If you will see my mother and your wife
Fellowed in bed, make haste. James your man
Writes on your pillow, &c.[462]
My eyes are witness to their adultery."
1 SERVANT [*To* MESSENGER] What's the news?
MESSENGER Plague on these jauntings![463]
Once we shall be old, and then this trotting life
Will linger in our bones. All hours are nights!
We dally with our own destruction.
SIR WILLIAM It cannot be. Or if, or if—what if?
If it be so, I am undone. Poisoned
Am I with fair promises. No marvel though[464]
You do forswear my bed; if yet again, if—
What make I here when treason is at home?
Away!

[*Exeunt*]

455 49–51 Bent in … dooming ill: though rebelliously inclined to self-destruction, children pause at a moment of grace and recover their senses, which instantly repairs the rash judgment of general opinion (or the general opinion of their formerly rash judgment) that had judged them poorly
456 57 Such is: such as is
457 61 Lethe: river in Hades whose waters caused forgetfulness
458 62 one?: daughter, i.e. have I lost only one today?
459 62 that we call daughter: of the remaining offspring that I can still call my daughter
460 67 better part: brain
461 69 tales: summons (an archaic legalism)
462 74 &c.: *et cetera*; here, perhaps a cue for the actor to continue reading silently, with the final line spoken aloud by Sir William as to himself (since he would presumably not want it overheard)
463 76 jauntings: journeys
464 82 though: that

[Act III, scene v]

Enter young HUMIL

HUMIL The bird that greets the dawning of the day
Signs[465] with his wings the midnight's 'parture,[466]
And the sleety dew, moistening the cheeks
Of morrow's welcome, gives earnest of the morn;
Yet all secure, adulterate lust does sleep,
And I, the hatched young of this trodden hen,[467]
Stands sentinel to her idolatry.
Blow, you swelled winds, and crack the battlements![468]
Rouse their incestuous[469] luxury with fear
Of what's to come! Yet that were my mishap:
No, silent air fan on them bawdy breath,
That as they reek in their licentious love
Devil may seal sure, and Morpheus so pleased,[470]
May to their pastime add affliction
Delivered by the hand of him that's wronged,
And stands[471] indebted to his destiny.[472]
Yet are they as the hour, whose sandy minutes
Runs out at pleasure till the period[473] comes,
Fast sleeping, and enjoy their quiet.
Rouse thee, black mischief, from thy ebon[474] cell:
Land in the bosoms of this twin in lust
Him whose heaped wrong calls vengeance to be just.[475]
SIR WILLIAM [*within*] Lock fast that door and leave me.
Give me your light.[476] Son Humil?

Enter SIR WILLIAM *and his men*

HUMIL Father.
SIR WILLIAM Thou see'st I am obedient at thy call. *Exit Servants*
I come as messengers that bring their bale[477]
Signed in their looks. Be well advised:
Thou mak'st a challenge goes[478] beyond all grace
Should it be false.
HUMIL It is my love to you that makes me step
Heart-deep in disobedience to my mother—
Wretch that I am to think her so.[479]

465 2 Signs: signals
466 2 'parture: departure
467 6 trodden hen: i.e. Lady Vergir; cf. III.i. 111–12
468 8 Compare *King Lear*, III.ii. 1: "Blow, wind, and crack your cheeks!"
469 9 incestuous: Humil has no reason to use this word, which here recalls *Hamlet* I.ii. 157, "incestuous sheets," and I.v. 83, "A couch for luxury and damnèd incest"
470 13 so pleased: (1) pleased by (2) pleased with (their lethargy). Morpheus was the god of sleep and dreams
471 16 stands: who stands
472 16 indebted to his destiny: entitled by destiny to his revenge
473 18 period: end, conclusion
474 20 ebon: ebony
475 21–2 Land in . . . be just: place directly between these two adulterers the one (i.e. Sir William) whose accumulated injuries call on vengeance for justice
476 23–4 Lock fast . . . your light: Sir William instructs his servants offstage; curiously, they still enter with him
477 26 bale: sorrow; messengers proverbially wore their bad news in their facial expressions
478 28 goes: that goes
479 32 think her so: i.e. to think of her as my mother

It makes me desperate of priority,[480]
Forethinking my beginning to be base,
Conceived in such mistrust and frailty;
My front hath that impression still,[481]
Adding a blush to my distemperature,[482]
And I am crestfall'n in sanguinity.[483]
Pray ye believe me, would it were not so.
SIR WILLIAM Enough: watch, and be secret. I will enter,
Sit as the night-raven or the screeching owl
Over my portal,[484] menacing ill chance
To all within; for death[485] is to my blood
A blessing, while this fever kills
Almost my intellect or better part.
Yet she's thy mother, and no son but hates
His own disgrace so highly merited,[486]
And I believe thee.
HUMIL Sir, truth is truth. My conscience and religion
Binds up[487] in me; and since I do proclaim
Detraction from my blood by her misdeed,
Give me leave to report a fly a fly[488]
If it offend the virtue of mine eye.
SIR WILLIAM 'Tis true.
And yet methinks it should not be:
How hardly will this scandal take impression
Where resolved Christianity does dwell![489]
But I will try the gold; perhaps 'tis base.[490]
Who knows the heart's affection by the face? *Exit*
HUMIL Scarlet is scarlet, and her sin blood red
Will not be washed hence with a sea of water.[491]
Is this my hand? Or is the fire fire
Whose scorching heat dissolves relenting metal
Whenas[492] it tries the substance? Yes, and I
Make known my mother is an alien
From my blood, so to fall off and perish[493]
Even in her pride of bliss. Damned be the slave[494]
That so attempts her spotless chastity[495]
To ruin! I know that yet-smooth look
Plotted, contrived, and won her with device.
She never knew a double character[496] till now,

480 33 desperate of priority: fearful of my (true) ancestor
481 36 (1) My forehead is still flush with the thought of my potential bastardy (2) My face resembles my mother's (which makes me ashamed)
482 37 distemperature: queasiness, discombobulation
483 38 crestfall'n in sanguinity: humiliated by my blood (or blood relations)
484 42 portal: door
485 43 death: presumably James's and Lady Vergir's, but ambiguous
486 46–7 no son . . . highly merited: any son would hate an act that so plainly disgraces him
487 50 Binds up: are inseparable; stiffen
488 52 report a fly a fly: i.e. call a spade a spade
489 56–7 How hardly . . . does dwell!: how deep an impact will this scandal make in a Christian community!
490 58 I will test the truth of your report, by analogy with goldsmithing; cf. III.i. 92–3
491 60–61 her sin . . . water: compare *Macbeth* II.ii. 63–4, "Will all great Neptune's ocean wash this blood/Clean from my hand?"
492 64 Whenas: when
493 66 so to . . . and perish: i.e. to cut (her) off and (let her) perish. "Fall off" was also a euphemism for sexual incontinence
494 67 slave: i.e. James
495 68 chastity: sexual fidelity
496 71 knew a double character: practiced duplicity

But single singler[497] she ever ruled;
Even modesty herself, Vesta,[498] resigned to her
And virtue, hand-in-hand at barley-break,
Ran the swift course.[499] None but a hound of hell
Hunted this fawn of fortune to his kennel.
But my mother, forgetting her degree,
Does captivate love, life, and liberty
By one deed's practice:[500] wicked—nay far worse,
Fatal—disgrace, honor's cheated course.[501]

Enter SIR WILLIAM [*on another part of the stage*]

SIR WILLIAM [*To himself*][502] Fool, fool, fool!
HUMIL Ha?
SIR WILLIAM [*To himself*] Light bubble,[503] swell and break!
Would'st thou believe all this, and give a gloss[504]
To slander's cruelty, ripening reproach itself[505]
With thy fond ear? O Humil, Humil!
HUMIL Sir?
SIR WILLIAM Thou art a villain, and hast cast up hills
Against heaven itself.[506] When sons unto
Their mothers are so false, O where is grace?
Hoodwinked from honor, shamed to show her face.
HUMIL Is it not so?
SIR WILLIAM Trust thy own eyes. Go: thou shalt see a sight
Will melt thy stubborn spleen[507] in pity.
Sweetly she sleeps, whose innocent respect[508]
Smiles in her dreams. They childlike govern,[509]
Laughing loud in their simplicity,
While waking mischief seeks that to undo
Which truth required stands sentinel unto.[510]
Go, and return with shame.
HUMIL With shame? Devil of mischance, what's this?
Did I not see their culted guilt look big?[511]
Was I in trance of my belief? Ha, was I?
Can be no juggling[512] in it—can there? *Exit*

497 72 single singler: with singular transparency, i.e. without any duplicity ("double character") at all
498 73 Vesta: virgin Roman goddess of the hearth, a protector of households
499 74–5 And virtue . . . swift course: "barley-break" was similar to the game of tag, in which couples chased and tried to capture each other; Humil suggests that Lady Vergir's figurative partner in this game was virtue itself
500 78–9 Does captivate . . . deed's practice: Humil extends the "barley-break" analogy: with one indiscretion, she has taken prisoner love, her own life, and her own freedom
501 80 honor's cheated course: vague, but suggests that Lady Vergir has played the game falsely
502 81 SD *To himself*: we do not yet know that Sir William has decided to trick Humil into believing his allegations were false. Depending on how much it wishes to reveal, this exchange can thus unfold in three ways: (1) Sir William addresses Humil throughout (2) unaware of him, Sir William enters genuinely grieving his cuckoldry, but by Humil's "Ha?" remembers himself, and begins scolding him (3) *pretending* to be unaware of Humil, he addresses both speeches to himself, feigning soliloquy for Humil's (and our) benefit. The present text adopts (3) as the most theatrically interesting possibility
503 83 Light bubble: empty-headed nitwit
504 84 give a gloss: prejudicially translate; condone
505 85 ripening reproach itself: validating the very epitome of evil
506 87–8 cast up . . . heaven itself: (1) hidden the face of heaven by your sinning (2) declared war on heaven itself
507 93 spleen: cf. II.i. 13; organ also associated with anger
508 94 respect: respectability
509 95 They childlike govern: i.e. her innocent dreams are all that occupy her mind
510 98 Over which dutiful truth stands guard; in Q the beginning of the line reads "Which true required"
511 101 culted guilt look big: secret ("culted," or occulted) shame exposed
512 103 juggling: magic, misdirection (Humil may refer either to what he saw or to Sir William's denial)

SIR WILLIAM No, thou art constant as the northern star;
And I as giddy[513] as the untamed leopard
That sees no means but dire destruction,
Flinging his foam to poison in his way
Man's mischief, plotted to his overthrow.[514]
He told me true—O, that I live to think so,
Or they so wretched to deserve the thought.[515]
Soundly they slept, whose slumbers killed me waking.
Yet to recover half-slain reputation,
Done have I what to purpose practiseth.[516]
If it prevail, our honor so preserved
Will kick at[517] all malignant cruelty
That taints our name with ever-living scorn.
Fortune[518] be for me, I will that recover
Which devil himself cries "guilty" to: my fame.[519]
The flight it wings imps feathers of renown;[520]
That lost, all's lost, my birthright tumbles down.

Enter HUMIL *amazed*

HUMIL Sir, I am sorry.
SIR WILLIAM How can they excuse
Such wanton looseness? Know they I stand here
To thunder vengeance on their luxury?[521]
HUMIL My mother's fast asleep, and I awake
Am in a transive[522] maze, unwitting how
To make my peace with God, herself, and you.
SIR WILLIAM Why, are they not together?
HUMIL Not in bed.
SIR WILLIAM Thou should'st with Argus'[523] hundred eyes
Search in the corners round about.
It cannot be but he is extant there.
Ha? Is he not?
HUMIL I am confounded in the search.
Please your justice be my torture:[524] I have
Murdered innocence. Sorrow is not the way,
Death is the least;[525] I challenge[526] cruelty, and urge
The exactest point of peril, slave that I am to live.
SIR WILLIAM A son, a son, to do so to a mother!
HUMIL Fare ye well; rather than be a witness of my wrong,

513 105 giddy: usually "dizzy," but here "frantic," like a hunted animal

514 105–8 untamed leopard . . . his overthrow: the claws and saliva of the leopard were believed to be laced with toxins; Sir William, desperate to evade his tormentors, says that he runs wildly, leaving a trail of poison behind him

515 109–10 O, that . . . the thought: Sir William savors the irony that the lovers should be mentioned in the same breath as the word "true"

516 113 I have done what will serve my purpose

517 115 kick at: defend against (but sometimes with a connotation of futile struggling)

518 117 Fortune: if fortune

519 118 That (i.e. my reputation) for whose loss the Devil would admit responsibility

520 119 The flight of my fame must be maintained with borrowed feathers (to "imp" means to graft feathers onto a broken wing)

521 121–3 How can . . . their luxury?: Sir William may say this to Humil sarcastically, since he continues a mock-performance of indignation further on, or he may continue to speak in aside, oblivious to Humil's entrance—only later recovering by pretending to have been teasing Humil the whole time

522 125 transive: trance-like (Armin's coinage)

523 128 Argus: a giant with a hundred eyes, charged by Hera to guard the nymph Io from Zeus's sexual advances

524 132 Please . . . torture: if it please you, judge what torture I ought to receive

525 133–4 Sorrow is . . . the least: my mere remorse is insufficient punishment; death is the least I deserve

526 134 challenge: demand

I will not see myself in't.
SIR WILLIAM Go, thou worse than—[527]
I'll sacrifice to the devil that tempted thee;
All[528] thy distempered thoughts, cry mercy to her sex.[529]
To spotless innocence be free:[530] say all thy treasons
Build on slippery ice, and thou art frozen cruelty.
HUMIL Sir, for your wrongs, if you remit[531] black torture
'Tis my hell, and I appeal to stern rigor. O you sons
Whose true obedience shines in majesty,
While mine more ugly is than Vulcan's stithy,[532]
Smells ranker than despisèd hemlock!
Curse and ban him;[533] I am your subject to't.
And every mother, whose snow innocence
Feels soft and tender as the down on palm,[534]
Rate[535] my rebellion with a blissless name,
And for my sake give misadventure aim.[536]
Guide 'em[537] to me: say I am such a son,
Through whom a mother is so soon undone.
SIR WILLIAM Let me not see thee while thou liv'st: away.
Let thy repentance show itself in this,
Not to be seen where thou hast done amiss.
Caitiff,[538] depart.
HUMIL I will; this tongue that slanderèd—
SIR WILLIAM Be her slander still.[539]
HUMIL It is too much already. Was I bewitched,
That thus at hoodman-blind[540] I dallied
With her I honored? O you times, how have you
Nursed me! But no more—Humil hath branded
On his mother's name an Ethiop's[541] blackness,
And a spotted stain; forgive me that, and all! *Exit*
SIR WILLIAM What need I to afflict revenge on him
That on himself exasperates?[542] Farewell,
Thou pride of sons, who to a father
In supposition only, and by law,[543]
Art all so loving that, thy mother dallying
With wantonness (as girls with gauds[544]), thou not
Respect'st the womb that brought thee forth,

527 138 Go thou worse than: Sir William starts to curse Humil, then breaks off
528 140 All: for all
529 140 cry mercy to her sex: beg the forgiveness of all women
530 141 be free: confess yourself fully (to the innocence you have wronged)
531 143 remit: rescind
532 146 Vulcan's stithy: Vulcan was the blacksmith of the gods; his stithy was his anvil or his forge itself, a symbol of filth
533 148 him: me (Humil here seems to drift into the self-dissociation promised earlier)
534 150 down on palm: goat willow or pussy willow, a tree whose long, downy catkins were carried instead of palm branches on Palm Sunday in northern Europe (hence its erroneous folkname)
535 151 Rate: (1) equate, esteem (2) berate
536 152 give misadventure aim: aim (like an arrow) misfortune at me
537 153 'em: antecedent unclear, but probably "misadventure[s]" from the previous line
538 158 Caitiff: wretch; slave (a corruption of "captive")
539 159 (1) You continue to slander her (2) Be quiet
540 161 hoodman-blind: a game of hide-and-seek played with a bag over the seeker's head; thus Humil says he has blindly and stupidly molested his mother's honor
541 164 Ethiop: Ethiopians epitomized dark-skinned Africans in the early modern English imagination, just as blackness symbolized moral impurity
542 167 exasperates: aggravates, intensifies (his own suffering)
543 168–9 a father . . . by law: a father in expectation only (had Humil wed Mary)—and (at present) just a step-father
544 171 gauds: toys, trinkets

But ill attempting so, and so thou rumor'st—
As the fault, ripe in act, is blown to air—
And, though her son, thou utter'st what they were.[545]
Thou shalt not lose by't. Now it fits
I challenge from the offense some right,[546]
And add confine[547] to this adultery.
Wife, wife! Rise, and come forth.

Enter LADY *in her night gown, and night attire*

LADY Call ye, sir?
SIR WILLIAM Yes, take my closet key[548]—let forth your lover.
Give me some ease by way of reason[549] yet,
And 'twill allay our discontent. [*Exit* LADY *with the key*]
O God, so new to marriage, and so stale!
Couldst thou so soon revolt, so soon, ha?

Enter JAMES *unready*,[550] *in his night-cap, garterless, with the* LADY

JAMES I must acknowledge all.
LADY O no, some better loose:[551]
This will but add to mischief torture.[552]
Use patience now; be reconciled to fear;
Be dove-like humble, and leave that to me.
JAMES How can I, when the brand is on my brow,[553]
But by exclaim?[554] Give ease to torture?
My brain is seared, and I am liveless in't! [JAMES *kneels, followed by* LADY]
SIR WILLIAM Kneel not.
JAMES AND LADY A sentence; let us die.
SIR WILLIAM No marvel though you vow this abstinence
When, deputed[555] by him, you shun my bed.
You do deserve your jointure well,
To admit a fellow in a true man's place.
I thank ye for it, yes.
LADY Sir—
SIR WILLIAM No, no: words I know you can alledge[556]—
The devil has scripture for his damnèd ill,
And this does neighbor[557] it. Go and attire ye.
Be smileful, and express no grief in sighs;
Rather be tickling sportful,[558] topped in[559] pleasure,

545 173–5 But ill . . . they were: Sir William marvels at his stepson's devotion to him—who, when his mother attempts evil, divulges it ("blown to air") the instant it occurs ("ripe in act")
546 177 I demand some compensation from my offenders
547 178 confine: confinement, penalty
548 181 closet key: Sir William has evidently spirited James into his own bedchamber (even though that would seem to require exiting Lady Vergir's)
549 182 Give me some reasons (for your actions) that will ease my mind
550 185 SD *unready*: disheveled
551 187 loose: release (as in archery), i.e. some more prudent confession; she does not want James to reveal his true identity
552 188 add to mischief torture: i.e. add torture (whatever punishment would follow upon the revelation of her bigamy) to our mischief
553 191 brand is on my brow: (1) the mark of my sin (2) the horns of my *own* cuckoldry (the rest of James's speech sustains either reading)
554 192 by exclaim: by exclaiming, confessing
555 197 deputed: appropriated; mastered; whored
556 201 alledge: add to your cause
557 203 neighbor: resemble
558 205 tickling sportful: giggly, merry
559 205 topped in: overtopped with, brimming with; like "tickling," Sir William's terms are bitterly sexual, since to be "topped" was also to have intercourse

Than daunted any way. That me concerns.[560]
To use the madman's guise—but I am past it.
Since what is done, no reference hath to wish;[561]
I am for credit' sake supportable.[562] All's well.
Content am I to be sensible, and feel
My fortunes as I may, ranking myself
With such as sometime lived in my repute
Most base.[563] Faith, all is well, believe it.
I am satisfied: I know you do repent,
And that's my remedy. Other amends
I look not for. In, and attire ye;
[*To* JAMES] But stay you with me.
LADY I am obedient. *Exit* LADY
SIR WILLIAM Go thou, shame, never till now possessed
And in a breath confounded.[564] Sir, you see
Your wrongs shine through the horn,[565] as candles
In the eve, to light out others.[566] Think you
This mideed merits salvation?
JAMES I must acknowledge contrary.
SIR WILLIAM Wilt thou, for all this spite, yet use me
Kindly in the next?[567]
JAMES Command me, sir.
SIR WILLIAM Not for the second:[568] this mistake me not.
Rather to bind thee from it. If hereafter
Fashion of frailty summon us to fear[569]—
I must be plain. And therefore thus:
Look whensoever I hold up this finger,
Signing my lips with it, and cry "begone,"[570]
Even then be speedy to depart the land.
If not, all power of mischief that I can,[571]
I will, and so resolve.
JAMES Sir, I am ready to the minute.
SIR WILLIAM It may be other reasons will restrain me,
As causeless motives, not seeing guiltiness;[572]
In needy sequences[573] perhaps our heart
Will in itself take truce[574] with this mischance—
Or if it do not, yet attend our spleen.[575]

560 206 That me concerns: that's all that concerns me
561 208 Thanks to the steps I have already taken (to contain the scandal), it is irrelevant
562 209 I am . . . sake supportable: my reputation is temporarily secure
563 210–13 Content am . . . Most base: I am content to experience my emotions, and adopt a stoic attitude, viewing myself like all those other cuckolds in my predicament, who have had to live in disgrace
564 218–19 Go thou . . . breath confounded: a valediction to his wife, whom he could not even possess sexually before she ruined her honor in an instant
565 220 the horn: (1) the lantern ("lanthorne") Sir William holds (2) the proverbial cuckold's horn Sir William now wears
566 221 light out others: discover other crimes
567 224–5 use me . . . the next: (1) do me a kindness on another occasion (2) cuckold me again ("kindly," i.e. in the same kind). Even James seems unsure which he means, and offers a safe answer
568 226 second: i.e. I am not commanding you to cuckold me a second time
569 227–8 If hereafter . . . to fear: if your proclivity to moral lapse gives me cause for insecurity
570 230–31 Look whensoever . . . cry "begone": Sir William holds a finger to his lips; it is unclear whether the accompanying verbal command is actually spoken, or just a translation of the gesture
571 233 can: i.e. can summon
572 237 Such as random whims, or forgetfulness of your guilt
573 238 needy sequences: (1) longed-for moments (2) the necessary passage of time
574 239 take truce: be reconciled
575 240 attend our spleen: be watchful of my ill will

It will be better for ye.[576]
JAMES In humble duty.
SIR WILLIAM Go, give copies of good countenance[577]
To our friends; think all is well, for so it is.
I that am all in grief, am all in suffering,
I forgive the reason.[578] Fare ye well. *Exit* [JAMES]
What I will do is barred up in this closet;[579]
The key that opens it is my revenge,
Turned by a hand whose palm does itch with fire
Till all consume. A cuckold, a cuckold
Sir William is: it's even so. Would I
Were yet the last, or least; but not by thousands.
Go to, then: am I all alone in this?
Who is't that tongue calls man[580] that is assured
Of his wife's condition? None: or if any,
There the phoenix lives unfellowed.[581]
Be his fate renowned, while mine is mockery,
And a jestive stock to all that knows me.
O you stars, blaze fire,
Till this abuse be quenched by my desire!

Exit

[Act IV, scene i]

Enter TUTCH *like a Welsh knight,*[582] *and* FILBON *as a servant, waiting* [*upon him*]

TUTCH Hark ye, Morris!
FILBON Aye, sir?
TUTCH Where is tailor?[583] Dudge me,[584] will knog his pad![585] What, is chirken with cold button[586] done, say you?
FILBON Excellent! This is Welsh indeed, O my honest Tutch.
TUTCH Saucebox![587] Rowly-powly! Am I not your master?
FILBON You are, sir; pray ye pardon me.
TUTCH You must have your left eye diameter-wise, fix't on my right heel; and all the offices a servant owes in duty to his master, perform as naturally as if the forty-shilling time[588] were come—lest I leave talking Welsh, and crack your pate in English.
FILBON I shall obey, sir.

576 241 It will . . . for ye: unclear, since Sir William has just outlined two different eventualities
577 242 copies of good countenance: cheerful facial expressions
578 245 reason: cause
579 246 this closet: i.e. in his heart, or bosom
580 253 Who is't . . . calls man: i.e. what man can be called a man
581 255 The phoenix is a mythical, unique bird that consumes itself in flame and is reborn from its own ashes; Sir William's point is that any man who can trust his wife must be similarly unique
582 0 SD *like a Welsh knight*: save for Armin's other play, *The Valiant Welshman*, representations of Welsh knights were rare on the English stage; how Tutch's Welshness is conveyed visually remains uncertain
583 3 tailor: Tutch asks (or pretends to ask) for his tailor
584 3 Dudge me: an oath; possibly a variant of "dudgeon," i.e. to take offense (from Welsh *dygen*, "anger"), or an invented compound of "damn me" and "cudgel me"
585 3 knog his pad: knock his pate (head). In stage-Welsh, voiceless consonants tend to get voiced and vice versa; the best-known example is Fluellen in Shakespeare's *Henry V*
586 3–4 chirken with cold button: jerkin (jacket) with gold button
587 6 Saucebox: impudent person, smartass (they are only rehearsing, but Tutch refuses to drop character)
588 9 forty-shilling time: time of year when servants were paid their wages, and thus the most solicitous

Enter AUDITOR *in a merchant's habit,*[589] *with* TABITHA

AUDITOR Fairest of beauties, love her seemly self—
For thy two eyes are Cupids, which do shoot
From thy enamored brow shafts all of gold,
Headed with metal of immortal proof[590]—
In thy fair bosom lives two hearts relenting:[591]
Thine penetrable, through atoning pity;[592]
Mine longing by desire to scale the fort
Of love's fair presence. Make me happy,
Sign to[593] my suit. But[594] ye—for 'tis thy censure
Makes me thus bold—pronounce fair judgement,
Either of life or death, I that plead love,
Doubly devoted, challenge from thy deity
A maiden answer. Let it come bright fire,
To try the substance[595] of my love's resolve.[596]
TABITHA Sir, in sooth and verity believe me.
That I am fair, 'tis credible; but to shoot
Arrows whose heads have such immortal proof
'Tis most erroneous and false.
AUDITOR 'Sfoot, you're a Puritan:[597]
A citizen, I'm sure, her canvas curran bags
Stuffed with sweet cinnamon and cloves.[598]
TABITHA Good sir, you are deceived in me;
I'm country plain.[599] Without[600] this nicety:
"And do you love me, yes?" Then crave
An answer, without ceremony
Fetched from proud Ovid and his *Arte Amandi.*[601]
I do not like it, I.
TUTCH Ples you, latie[602]—
TABITHA [*To* AUDITOR] Sir, and you tell me of Cupid's eyes,
Shot from enamored bows, with hearts relenting,
Doubly devoted, and I know not what—
TUTCH Ples you, firgin[603]—
TABITHA [To AUDITOR] No sir, no. Give me plain courtesy,
Drawing on love's white hand a glove of warmth—

589 11 SD *in a merchant's habit*: we never learn how or why Auditor has been recruited into Filbon's scheme, or what practical purpose his guise as a merchant is intended to serve

590 14–15 shafts all . . . immortal proof: arrows tipped with gold were thought to penetrate any armor; the "metal" is thus both "immortal" and mortal to the victim

591 16 relenting: soft, yielding

592 17 atoning pity: pity "atones" by softening her heart, making it "penetrable"

593 20 Sign to: accept

594 20 But: until, unless

595 24–5 Let it . . . the substance: another goldsmithing metaphor: let your answer be a fire that tests the metal (or mettle) of my devotion

596 12–25 Fairest of . . . love's resolve: this passage, a sonnet (though only intermittently rhymed), is a litany of Petrarchan love-poetry clichés

597 30 Puritan: (1) frigid, austere (ironically, the very type of the Petrarchan mistress) (2) excessively literal, owing to the Puritan sects' strictly literal interpretations of scripture

598 31–2 A citizen . . . and cloves: currans are raisins, yet her "curran bag" carries cinnamon and cloves; perhaps his way of teasing her for being a "city" girl, practical and unromantic, taking things in the wrong sense

599 34 Country plain: on the contrary, being a country girl, I demand even more plainness of style

600 34 Without: do without

601 37 Ovid . . . *Amandi*: also known as *Ars Amatoria* (*The Art of Love*), a collection of elegies by the Roman poet Ovid. Considered lewd and dangerous, it claimed to teach the best manners of courtship and intercourse, and was an essential reource for hack love poets

602 38 Ples you, latie: bless you, lady (Tutch tries to interrupt)

603 42 firgin: virgin

Not cheveril, stretching to such profanation![604]
You overthrow love's deity in this,
And putrify his altars with bad breath.
I am a dairy huswife,[605] no such wanton
So easily flattered with far-fetched replies.
Yet I esteem this worthless person[606] free,
And though not fair, yet something fortunate.
TUTCH —Harg[607] ye now, Latie!
TABITHA Sir, cry you mercy.
TUTCH Was[608] a knight, marg you, of Englise in Wales, Welse blood; and 'tis no mock in en to marry in Welse blood, is it? [609]
TABITHA Sir, all the smiles a modest maid
Can in this kind make proffer of are yours,
In your fair welcome. Blame me not,
Though his unkindness made me negligent
In your kind entertain.[610]
AUDITOR [*To* TABITHA] Neglect me so?
TABITHA [*To* AUDITOR] Wives unto citizens[611] are tradesmen's daughters.
I am a blood of gentle composition;
My mind does equal it. I must be coached,[612]
Banqueted everywhere, courted abroad,[613]
At home flattered. For my private use
I must have fancies;[614] playfellows as[615] apes,
Monkeys, baboons; muffs, fans, receipts,[616]
Costly habiliments of several suits;[617]
Will ye give this? 'Twill break[618] you, sir,
And crack your credit's fair condition. No,
Citizens would, but cannot answer so.
TUTCH [*To* TABITHA] Harg you, marry with her,[619] and God dudge me, all is yours. Was a knight: have land, and a great deal of rishes, will maintain you well, say you.
TABITHA [*To* AUDITOR] This gentleman or this,[620] before a citizen;
[*To* TUTCH] You sir, pardon me, I will ha' none.
AUDITOR Then whom you will. Call you this modesty,
To be so waspish? Given to slight men off
With incivility? Give me leave to remember—
TABITHA What you please.
All the world except one or two[621] are eye-motes,[622]

604 45 Cheveril, i.e. kid-leather, was buttery soft, and thus associated with moral flexibility
605 48 dairy huswife: milkmaid
606 50 this worthless person: i.e. myself
607 52 Harg: hark
608 54 Was: (I) am. The Welsh were thought to use only the past tense of the verb "to be"
609 54–5 a knight . . . is it?: Tutch introduces himself as a knight of England in Wales, of Welsh blood, and asks (rhetorically) if Tabitha thinks it ridiculous for one ("en") to marry a Welshman
610 60 entertain: entertainment, greeting
611 61 Wives unto citizens: the proper wives for citizens (such as you)
612 63 coached: driven in a horse-drawn carriage
613 64 abroad: out of the house
614 66 fancies: amusements; light music (e.g. ballads and airs)
615 66 playfellows as: such playthings as
616 67 receipts: (1) receptions (2) recipes (as for cosmetics)
617 63–8 I must . . . several suits: Tabitha satirizes the frivolous and extravagant lifestyles of aristocratic ladies
618 69 break: bankrupt
619 72 marry with her: Tutch means "marry me"; another convention of stage-Welsh was the use of "her" for almost all personal pronouns
620 74 This gentleman or this: Tabitha indicates Tutch, then his page (Filbon/Morris)
621 80 one or two: i.e. just a few men
622 80 eye-motes: specks of dust in one's eye, i.e. irritating

That trouble but my sight. Filbon for me:
Man else,[623] but mere illusion and idolatry,
Vain worship; images of molten metal
Which, to dross dissolved, appear as nothing
To my judgment. But his worth, beyond compare,
Gentle and suffering as the silent air,
That though it brook the buffets of base breath[624]
Yet in itself is heavenly, free from earth.
TUTCH Harg you, was knight in house called Sir William Perger?[625]
TABITHA Vergir, sir?
TUTCH Morris, was say true;[626] give a ducket.[627] Look you tuck it: is mark, mark you that? And mark is thirteen shillings fourpence, good currans[628] money. And how do you? Well![629] [*To* TABITHA] Whan was Sir Robert Morgan; mik you latie,[630] grace-a-God!
AUDITOR You, sir?
TUTCH Was[631] I lie, pray you?

Enter SIR WILLIAM, SIR RAFE, [*and*] HENRY, *a Priest of Putney* [*at the other end of the stage*]

SIR WILLIAM Think you Master Auditor knew nothing, sir?
SIR RAFE Upon my soul, I think it.
I did wind[632] him subtly, as hounds the game
New got on foot.[633] For instance, he lamented oft
His son's proceedings, neglecting[634] his own house,
Lest you in quest of her should search it.
Believe me sir, I tell you what I know.
SIR WILLIAM 'Tis likely: sons in these doting days
Will from their fathers alienate,[635] differ still
From love's obedience,[636] and in heart's affection
Join hand to hand, though beggary neighbor it.[637]
And let them go.
HENRY Sir, I am free then from your fear?[638]
SIR WILLIAM Aye, good sir Henry; I was wrong informed.[639]
I am your patron in all love.
HENRY Long may ye live so, sir. I find you gentle,
And a good benefactor to poor scholars;
We ha' few such—many, rather, we have,

623 82 Man else: i.e. any other man (is)
624 87 brook the . . . base breath: suffer the exhalations of vile creatures
625 89 Perger: Stage-Welsh usually replaces "v" with "f" (cf. "firgin"); the homophony with "perjure" may be a private joke at the expense of Tutch's former master
626 91 was say true: I told you so
627 91 ducket: ducat. Tutch exploits the situation to extract increasing sums of money: Filbon/Morris hands him a ducat (a coin worth about four shillings sixpence), which Tutch tells him to pocket ("tuck it"), insisting that the fictional "bet" was really for one mark (coin worth two-thirds of a pound)
628 92 currans: current
629 92 And how do you? Well!: Tutch here converses with his coin, speaking one or the other half of the exchange as the coin itself; such ventriloquism was one of Armin's specialties
630 93 Whan was . . . you latie: I am Sir Robert Morgan, (and will) make you a lady
631 95 Was: do
632 98 wind: twist, wring; to draw out secrets
633 98–9 as hounds . . . on foot: the way hounds patiently stalk the quarry at the beginning of a hunt
634 100 neglecting: avoiding
635 104 alienate: (1) become estranged (2) stray
636 104–5 differ still/From love's obedience: deviate from the duty they owe their parents
637 106 Marry, even though such unsanctioned marriages make beggars of them
638 107 free then from your fear: (1) forgiven of my crime, and free of your wrath (2) innocent of the crime you fear
639 108 wrong informed: it is unclear what new information (or misinformation) Sir William has gotten from Sir Rafe; he knows Mary and Toures have eloped, but seems to believe they were not married by Henry, as the Boy told him in III.i

That sell the church rights than[640] maintain them;
And in my next stanza[641] I shall tickle[642] them.
SIR WILLIAM Speak conscience, and no more.
HENRY Nay as for that, sir, pardon me:
I seldom exercise[643] without that thought.[644]
What my text[645] leads me to, I will pronounce,
Maugre the devil of judgment.[646]
SIR WILLIAM Soft.
AUDITOR [*Coming forward*] Bless you, gallant knight: a merchant, sir,
Of London am I—my estate secure,
And so it please you; covet[647] this fair maid
In marriage, nothing else.
SIR WILLIAM Know you him, Sir Rafe?
SIR RAFE Not well, sir, but by guess
He is indifferent[648] rich; has broke[649] three times,
Made his head whole by means;[650] and that, say I,
As this world shapes,[651] is secure policy.
What think you, sir?
SIR WILLIAM I do not think it so;
Though common practice finds it furthering,
Shifts do the devil resemble,[652]
And bankrupt baseness makes good credit tremble.
I like it not.
TUTCH [*To* SIR WILLIAM] Plese you Aunt,[653] harg you now: knight was love this firgin, and God will, must make her wife; shall be her latie,[654] go in Wales great worship, God willing.
SIR WILLIAM [*To* SIR RAFE] O, know: this knight, he was created t'other day.[655]
SIR RAFE Sir Robert Morgan? O sir, such a one,
Whose reputation reacheth to the best,
Merits a good conjunction![656]
Were't my daughter, she should have him.
O, beware when majesty shines in a man's estate.[657]
They long stand firm, spread wide, regenerate;
And though base born, yet honor makes them swell
Like clustered grapes,[658] till mature sweetness brings
Luscious conclusion.

640 113 than: rather than; Henry refers to simony, specifically the selling of church benefices
641 114 stanza: sermon (an odd usage)
642 114 tickle: finger, needle
643 117 exercise: perform religious services
644 117 that thought: i.e. Sir William's advice to "speak conscience"
645 118 my text: i.e. scripture
646 119 In spite of any harsh judgment it might provoke
647 123 covet: I covet
648 126 indifferent: modestly, unexceptionally
649 126 broke: gone bankrupt
650 127 Made his . . . by means: recouped his losses through sharp practice
651 128 shapes: goes
652 130–31 Though common . . . devil resemble: although everyday conduct may find it advantageous, craftiness ("shifts") is a vice
653 134 Aunt: malaprop term of familiarity, like "cousin," but with accidental insult; Tutch may again be improvising Welsh idiom to get away with disrespect to his former master
654 135 shall be her latie: (she) shall be my lady
655 136 O know . . . t'other day: Sir William nudges Sir Rafe: this "knight" looks like he was given his title ("created") yesterday
656 139 conjunction: union, marriage
657 141 when majesty . . . man's estate: when (a man's) nobility resides only in his hereditary titles
658 142–4 They long . . . clustered grapes: by contrast, those who, like grapevines, stand rooted firmly in themselves, will prosper and create themselves ("regenerate"); though of low birth, their honor builds them up

SIR WILLIAM I have some mind to[659] him.
[*To* TUTCH] Sir, you receive kind welcome;
Let it store your thoughts with those sweet motions[660]
Lovers wish to enjoy. She may, perchance,
All things concluded on, be for ye.
TUTCH Was a clad[661] man! Morris, fetch trunk of 'pparel.[662] Was lie here a four week,
will not out now.[663] Was welcome, plague on you, was love ye!
SIR WILLIAM [*To* AUDITOR] Sir, as for you: being city-proud,[664]
My daughter's look sits on[665] a courtier's brow.
What say'st, my girl?
TABITHA O sir, a courtier!
On my life, I love to sit up late,
Lie long i'th' morning; rot with sweetmeats,
And to play at shuttlecock;
Methinks the game's now in mine arms. [TUTCH *or* FILBON *makes a sign*[666] *to her*]
In any hand,[667] a courtier's wife—and why not?
His black jet[668] shows best about beauty's neck,
And I am proud of such a suitor.
If I understand not his Welsh, like a good piece of ord'nance[669]
I shall lie fast upon the bulwark,[670] and discharge
My obedient English. Must be a lady, sir.[671]
SIR WILLIAM [*To* AUDITOR] Yet welcome, sir; let it not grieve you.
AUDITOR Signior, no. [*To* TUTCH] You're welcome to the wife I woo.
HENRY And mistress, might I be the man to strike the stroke?[672]
TABITHA You, or else none, Sir Henry.
SIR WILLIAM Troth, she says true— [*Aside to* HENRY] but listen me[673] for that.
Come, gallants, enter with me:
We will feast. There's little labor lost
Where trial bids presumption sire the cost.[674] [*Exit*]
HENRY [*Aside*] Right to a hair.[675] 'Tis mine, and I must do't;
I see my fees, my rich advantage. Sirrah boy,
Shall we have work, in faith, and shall we?[676] *Exit*
AUDITOR Conclude: I'll busy him, Sir Rafe.[677]
SIR RAFE [*To* FILBON] Son,

659 145 have some mind to: am taking an interest in
660 147 motions: inclinations, ideas (of winning Tabitha)
661 150 clad: glad
662 150 'pparel: apparel
663 150–51 Was lie ... out now: I will reside with you for four weeks; I won't leave ("out") now
664 152 city-proud: too proud to consort with a mere citizen
665 153 look sits on: affection has lighted on
666 158 SD *makes a sign*: Tabitha's speech abruptly changes tone, from sarcastic to eager, suggesting the ruse is revealed to her. (Its success entails her complicity at some point, since she would never consent to Sir Robert otherwise, yet Q omits this crucial communication.) Tutch or Filbon (or both) may react with increasing alarm as her tenor drifts toward rejection; she needs, and apparently gets, some sign to tell her to play along
667 159 In any hand: in any case
668 160 jet: polished black coal used in jewelry; Tabitha imagines a necklace. Its cheapness is her point: his gems may be ordinary, but my beauty will make them more lustrous
669 162 ord'nance: ordinance, i.e. artillery
670 163 I shall ... the bulwark: entrench myself on the front line
671 164 Must be a lady, sir: such are the sacrifices a lady must make
672 167 strike the stroke: perform the ceremony
673 169 listen me: await my instructions; still distrustful, Sir William is hedging his bets
674 172 trial bids ... the cost: i.e. a test of (the groom's) pretense (to wealth) requires my footing the bill (for the feast)
675 173 to a hair: i.e. to the smallest degree
676 175 Henry either apostrophizes himself in diminutive terms, or addresses Filbon
677 176 This is probably Tabitha's and the audience's first (however unceremonious) indication that the merchant is really Auditor in disguise

You see to what a happy issue[678] this disguise
Speaks fair.[679] You know the plots. Boldly proceed:
'Tis ours in action, but your own the deed.
I must shun all suspicion
By my presence.[680] Look to't, boy:
If thou failest now, forever lose thy joy. *Exeunt* [AUDITOR *and* SIR RAFE]

TUTCH Ha, ha! Master, I a Welshman? A hangman![681] [TUTCH *and* FILBON *remove their disguises*]

TABITHA A trick! Now, on my maidenhead, I did
Mistrust[682] it. Come, leave the rest to me;
This priest shall marry us incontinent.[683]

FILBON Aye, if I were the Welshman,[684] because your father gave him light[685] thereto. [*To* TUTCH] Therefore come, sirrah: we'll shift clothes. [*To* TABITHA] Meet us at Putney; else my father shall mistrust ye.[686]

TABITHA I will, excusing your departure till anon.

FILBON Do, gentle love;
Heaven on our venture smiles, this to approve.

TABITHA O, it cannot choose;
Fathers are fortunate in this good news.
Go, ye drones: do ye not love the hive
There's[687] honey in't? 'Tis a sweet thing to win.

TUTCH I must break the ice for ye; if I slip up to the chin now, you will pull me out, save me from drowning, mistress?[688]

TABITHA Fear it not. *Exit*

TUTCH I would be loath betwixt Welsh and English to be hanged, mistress; I cannot live on the bargain.[689] Come, sir: I'll shift with them, and now I must shift with you.[690]

FILBON Aye: clothes, good Tutch.

TUTCH And use me no worse, being your man, than I used you being mine.

FILBON O, better, better.

TUTCH O love, thou art a beggar; yet I am thy debtor.[691]

Exeunt

[Act IV, scene ii]

Enter [TOURES, *the* MASTER *of a ship, and*] *two Sailors with a trunk, wherein is Mistress* MARY *in her winding sheet; others with a pick-axe and spades, as on the sands*[692]

TOURES [*To Sailors*] Set down the heaviest load
That ever true affection underwent.

678 177 issue: outcome
679 178 Speaks fair: promises
680 181 presence: i.e. by attending Sir William within
681 183 A hangman!: i.e. it is as absurd to mistake me for one as the other
682 185 Mistrust: suspect
683 186 incontinent: immediately
684 187 if I were the Welshman: Filbon explains, or perhaps realizes, that he and Tutch must now swap disguises (a complication that might have been avoided had he played Sir Robert)
685 187 light: permission
686 188–9 Meet us . . . mistrust ye: no reason is ever given why Sir Rafe might still distrust Tabitha
687 196 There's: when there's
688 197–8 I must . . . drowning, mistress?: i.e. I initiated this stratagem, so remember to save me if it goes awry
689 200–01 I would . . . the bargain: i.e. if I get caught between my English and Welsh selves, I'll end up dead
690 201 I'll shift . . . with you: with a pun on "shift" as "deceive" and "change clothes"
691 205 Tutch mocks the desperate extremes to which lovers are driven, yet he is love's "debtor" because it has provided him gainful employment
692 0 SD *the sands*: a beach. This scene and the next take place on one of the Isles of Scilly, sparsely inhabited islands west of the English Channel; the location may have been chosen because its waters were notoriously treacherous, but we soon learn that the cause of Mary's demise was a storm at sea

To you, 'tis like the anchor of your ship—
Heavy at first, but easily weighed,[693] seems light;
To me, that not supports her body's weight,
'Tis heart-deep in the burden, and too ponderous
Sad. Heavy is that load, whose leaden poise[694]
Is as a sullen sorrow too, too pressing.
MASTER Sir, I would wish you to be brief.
TOURES Dig ho[695] this golden beach, whose glitt'ring sands
Shows with the sun as diamonds set in gold;
Fitly[696] entombs a jewel of much worth,
Whose living beauty stained all lapidary.[697]
MASTER She was most gentle, which[698] was worth all riches.
TOURES And this night's tempest did a cruel deed,
To take from me a value of such price.[699]
MASTER Sir, though our seas kill women with their frowns,
Us[700] their bugbear threats are womanish;
And so we leave 'em.[701]
TOURES Leaving yourself and all, sometime?[702]
MASTER Even so. No safer in our beds
Or on the land, but under death's black stroke;
And he that is the surest, sits in state,
Dyingly tended by the hand of Fate.[703]
TOURES And yet methinks death should not
Take her from me, being scarce mine own,
But newly wed, never bedded yet:
So that, the ceremony burning bright,
Hymen yet hath his tapers flaming red,[704]
And the bold boastings[705] of that good man's breath,
That all religiously made one of two,
Hardly digested[706] in the freezing cold.
Little I thought the priest's word, being ever,[707]
Should find his period[708] in so short a time.
MASTER Sir, but the gift was given ye on condition:
"Till death d'ye part," "better or worse."
Methinks this catechizing little needs
To human guiding:[709] and to you the less,
Knowing what openly you do confess.[710]

693 4 weighed: lifted, carried; Toures says that to the sailors Mary's coffin is, like an anchor, just another object they can get used to hauling
694 7 poise: weight
695 10 Dig ho: the actors must pretend to dig with their spades while Toures and Master converse
696 12 Fitly: (it) fittingly
697 13 stained all lapidary: made all other gems seem dirty and dull by comparison
698 14 which: who
699 16 value of such price: a prize of such value
700 18 Us: to us
701 19 And so we leave 'em: and thus we bury men who die at sea (i.e. in obscure plots on the nearest beach)
702 19 Leaving yourself and all, sometime?: i.e. and do you yourself expect to be left like this at some point?
703 22–3 And he … of Fate: even a king, who seems the most secure ("surest") from death surrounded by his pomp ("state"), is unknowingly moving toward death, guided by the hand of Fate
704 28 Hymen was the god of matrimony; for Toures the candles ("tapers") of the ceremony still burn (like his passion)
705 29 bold boastings: the priest's benedictions and pronouncements
706 31 Hardly digested: (1) barely realized (2) painfully interpreted
707 32 being ever: (1) potent forever (2) the word "ever" itself
708 33 period: expiration, completion
709 36–7 Methinks this … human guiding: I don't think (1) people need these formalities to remind them of their mortality (2) you need my tedious arguments to be reminded of the conditionality of a marriage contract
710 37–8 and to … do confess: you least of all, since I know what you've freely admitted (that you abducted her)

TOURES Bear wi' me, Master. He that pines in grief
Lives as you sailors do, thinking at sea
Every storm ends, when flattery flouts ye;
So to our lovesick sorrows comes a calm
By ease of fancies, when 'tis furthest;[711]
And many times the weapon that doth wound
Is salve and surgeon both, to make all sound.[712]
MASTER Are ye ready, sir?
TOURES All fitted. Let me take my last farewell.
I am all jelly in my tears and sighs,
Wasted by wailing her untimely loss;
So long I did consume in drops of woe
That contrary I laugh to think it so.[713]
He that weeps much, having no tears to spend,
Smiles out the rest, but inwardly does rend.[714]
O God! That I, vent'ring so hard a chance,[715]
Should lose my dice before my hand be out!
'Tis even so: in all things man intends
The loss is ours, the winnings not our friends.[716]
MASTER For charity, be brief. Should the wind
Turn his beak into the southern side,[717]
Our ship would leave us. Dally not with grief.
Once, and no more, let sorrow rule as chief.
TOURES Then thus, and this the last.
Moll,[718] I take leave yet on thy hearsèd self—
Dead self, and self slain.[719] Moll deceased,
I am thy morning music,[720] call thee up
To wedded rites; I lead thee to the church,
And there receive thee; dine with thee at noon,
Dance all the after-day; bring thee at night
Into the wedding chamber—this[721] is it.
And here I leave thee to thy virgin slumber,
Never attempted, as thy birth bestowed;[722]
"Maiden" beginning, take it in thy end.[723]
So live, thus die, onely:[724] my married friend
And nothing else.[725] Gone art thou to a power
Which will with welcomes take thee; left I am
To the world's cross, thy father, who, enraged,
Will bitterly revenge thy death on me.

711 39–43 He that . . . 'tis furthest: men in grief are like men at sea, who delude themselves that the storm is about to end; our imaginations bring false hope, telling us a calm is on the horizon, when it is actually farthest away
712 44–5 And many . . . all sound: love cures the wounds it inflicts
713 50–51 So long . . . it so: I have so exhausted my tears that now I can only laugh
714 53 rend: break (oneself) in two
715 54 vent'ring so hard a chance: taking such a dangerous risk
716 57 winnings not our friends: i.e. no friend to us, never ours
717 59 Turn northerly, threatening a storm
718 63 Moll: familiar diminutive of "Mary"
719 64 Dead self, and self slain: Toures speaks of himself, implying that he feels just as bereft of life
720 65 morning music: music to wake up to (since Toures proceeds to narrate their imaginary wedding day), but with obvious, poignant pun on "mourning"
721 69 this: i.e. the coffin
722 71 Never violated, and thus intact as you were born
723 72 Having entered the world as a maiden, you may take that title with you as you leave
724 73 onely: singly
725 74 nothing else: because the marriage was never consummated

But I will prove his martyr.[726] See thee,[727] Moll—
Fool that I am to say so—here is all:
Gowns, tire,[728] all habiliments of thine.
No rag shall rest remembrant in my view[729]
To stir the embers of thy dying fire.
I kiss thy key-cold corpse, and with this key[730]
Lock thee forever up. Farewell, farewell:
My mouth the church, my voice thy parting knell;[731]
All ears that live and hear this bell to toll,
Christian-like bid peace unto her soul.
MASTER Amen.
[*Sailors lower the coffin and begin to cover it*][732]
Be speedy, mates: see ye not? Look,
The blueness of yon cloud does threaten wind.
If it rise fair, we shall be lodged in France;
But not, where please the Fates. Dispatch!
A cry within
WITHIN[733] Aboard, aboard! Hey!
MASTER Hollo! Linger no time! Aboard, you hear?
[*To Toures*] With me, ho! Will the rest stay? How, a year?[734]
[*Exit* TOURES]
O God, that man should leave behind,
And live, the love of soul and mind.
Exeunt, and leave the pickaxe and spades behind

[Act IV, scene iii]

Enter GOVERNOR *and a* GENTLEMAN [*with a spyglass*]

GOVERNOR Sir, welcome to Scilly.
Where I command,[735] my brother's friends[736] have welcome;
But now my flattery[737] gets you on this beach,
Where you prospectively[738] see many countries.
Learn this of me: where danger shoots her string,[739]
We, in our neighbor-nearness,[740] ought to fear,
But armed by our foresight, make bold resist
Against the brags[741] of foreign enemies.
GENTLEMAN I have not seen a better glass to look in.
What country call you yon, whose cliffs are as
The clouds' smoke, and all-shadowing mists?
GOVERNOR Sir, that is France, a fair-beseeming friend.
On yonder continent[742] stands Ireland;

726 78 prove his martyr: suffer my ordeal with faith and dignity
727 78 See thee: look here (Toures immediately regrets his choice of words)
728 80 tire: attire
729 81 remembrant in my view: to remind me of you
730 83 key: evidently Toures locks the coffin, to protect the finery inside from graverobbers
731 85 My words are the only funeral rites you will receive
732 88 SD The coffin is presumably lowered into the stage trapdoor
733 93 SP WITHIN: i.e. voices call from off-stage, as though from the ship
734 95 Will the . . . a year? Do you expect the rest of the crew to wait for you? For how long, a year?
735 2 command: govern
736 2 my brother's friends: the Gentleman is never named, and we never learn how he is connected to the Vergirs
737 3 flattery: persuasion
738 4 prospectively: through a perspective glass (a spyglass or telescope)
739 5 where danger shoots her string: (here), where the bowstring of danger is constantly drawn back (i.e. imminent)
740 6 neighbor-nearness: proximity (to so many warring kingdoms)
741 8 brags: threats
742 13 continent: landmass

On this side Britain, and on that side Garsey;[743]
Islands besides of much hostility,
Which are as sunshine sometimes splendeous,[744]
Anon disposed to alt'ring frailty.[745]
We, that all neighbor, must so strength our being,
As fearless we may frolic yet not seeing.[746]
GENTLEMAN I understand ye, sir.
GOVERNOR Now, let my longing have content in you
With the report of them you lately saw,
My brother Vergir and his children.
Is he a widower still at More-clacke?
GENTLEMAN Married, sir, unto a London cast-away,[747]
One whose decayèd husband left to live,
Though poorly:[748] yet your brother's lady.
GOVERNOR It is his choice, and I subscribed[749] to't.
But for his daughters, sir?
GENTLEMAN Alas, in them he is unhappy.
One is haled[750] from him by stol'n practices;
The other lives as though she were not his—
A goodly gentlewoman, but her own in heart.
She will be gone too, for her government
Stands upon will, as men stand on the beach,
Seeing the sea wherein they must be drowned,
Yet fearless venture on the ruthless main.[751]
She will, regardless of her father, marry,
And does (as most) long for the misery
Signed[752] to them in their cradles.
GOVERNOR Sorry am I.
—Ha? What scrambled ends[753] heap up confusedly!
New digged and ripped up is this plot of ground:
Some shipwreck, on my life, hid to deceive
The Queen[754] and me of our advantages.
GENTLEMAN Likely, sir;
And see, our sudden coming scared from hence
Into new ending[755] such as piled this heap:
Behind them have they left their implements
Which did the theft. What think ye, sir, if we
Re-dig the ground? Should we depart and leave it,
At midnight would they fetch their borrowings.

743 14 Garsey: the Isle of Jersey, at the time a lawless pirate sanctuary
744 16 splendeous: splendid, i.e. friendly
745 17 Just as quickly prone to the political weakness of changed ("alt'ring") allegiances
746 18–19 must so . . . not seeing: must fortify ourselves to appear harmless, as though we do not see the danger
747 25 cast-away: widow
748 26–7 whose decayèd . . . though poorly: (1) whose husband of declining ("decayed") fortunes died ("left to live") in debt (2) whose dead husband left her to live in poverty
749 28 subscribed: consented
750 31 haled: carried
751 34–7 for her . . . ruthless main: she is ruled by her own will, which, as infirm as the beach men stand on before they set sail, will take her recklessly to her own destruction
752 40 Signed: assigned, fated
753 41 scrambled ends: aborted designs
754 44 Queen: Elizabeth I, for whom governors collected tariffs
755 47 new ending: a different conclusion (from what they had planned). Governor and Gentleman imagine either a pirate crew that has buried its loot for later recovery, or a shipwrecked crew that has done the same, and been scared off by the men's arrival

GOVERNOR I like your purpose. I'll make one.[756]

[*They take up the spades and begin to dig*]

GENTLEMAN What do you think it is, sir?
GOVERNOR No body buried: it is sure some goods,
Wracked on the sea; money, or rich commodity.
GENTLEMAN Tobacco then?
GOVERNOR 'Tis likely, for with us men smoke their lands
Through their nostrils.[757] Shall I tell ye, sir,
'Tis a commodity may well be spared.[758]
GENTLEMAN Good luck![759] A God's name, sir, it is a trunk.
GOVERNOR Lift it, sir.

They lift it out

GENTLEMAN 'Tis quick[760]: it heaved as I heaved it.
GOVERNOR I'faith, I think so too! In heart of hope,
I will be all so bold as to break way.

They break the trunk open, and she [MARY] *sits up*[761]

GENTLEMAN Ha!
MARY If you be men, and born of that weak sex
Which I myself profess, being woman,
Pity the living sorrow of a maid
Buried for dead—but back again recalled
By the divinity of heavenly power.
Amaze not:[762] I am creature, flesh and blood—
Not as I seem, a pale and earthly[763] ghost.
The story, when you hear it, shall make plain
The woeful chance of life so lately slain.[764]
GOVERNOR I had acquaintance with this voice—my cousin?
GENTLEMAN 'Tis she, sir—'tis Mistress Mary Vergir!
I know her.
MARY My name recalls my memory,
And I am such a creature. O, my uncle!
Where am I? Return again:[765]
Death, thou art wanton in a lover's pain.[766]
GOVERNOR Cousin, I will not question the particulars.
The time calls on a present comfort,[767]
And your life, half spent,
Makes true necessity delay no longer.
Therefore come: at leisure we shall hear
The dying story of your misery.[768]
However, glad I am that such a chance
Landed in Scilly, not in neighboring France!

[*Exeunt* GOVERNOR *and* GENTLEMAN *together bearing* MARY *away*]

756 52 I'll make one: i.e. count me in
757 57–8 men smoke . . . their nostrils: i.e. waste all their money on tobacco
758 59 Introduced into England through New World trade, tobacco was by the 1590s as controversial as it was popular; Governor articulates the standard critique, which stressed its expense and noisesomeness
759 60 Good luck!: i.e. we are in luck!
760 61 quick: alive; i.e. something alive is inside
761 63 SD *sits up*: miraculous survival in coffins is a romance convention; Shakespeare uses it in *Pericles*
762 70 Amaze not: i.e. don't be astonished or frightened
763 71 earthly: mouldy, as one risen from the earth
764 73 The misfortune that befell this person ("life") who recently died
765 78 Return again: (1) return me to the grave (2) return again, Death
766 79 Death, the pain you bring lovers knows no limit
767 81 Your situation demands immediate relief
768 85 dying story of your misery: a poetic inversion, since Mary's misery, not her story, is a "dying" one

[Act V, scene i]

Enter FILBON *in Welsh attire, and* TUTCH *in servingman's, like one another;*[769] *with them* SIR RAFE, AUDITOR, *and* TABITHA[770]

AUDITOR [*To* FILBON] If ever you used speed, be swift as lightning,
Shoot as the stars in their celestial spheres;
Go and return as Paris did from Greece
With that matchless Helen.[771] Tell the priest
It must be done: he will believe your haste,
Because 'twas quickened with the former grant[772]
And promised by the knight himself.
SIR RAFE Let me alone to make the way; follow you, son. *Exit*
FILBON And if I do not, let me lose my prize.
AUDITOR [*To* TABITHA] Where's the knight?
TABITHA Busy with one
Who comes as[773] conjured up from Cupid's quiver,
Struck deep in love: he is a 'pothecary.[774]
TUTCH I know him; his mother was a—[775]
AUDITOR —Peace.
Him will I busily attend; go you dispatch
While I detain the father. If this prove,
'Tis comic pleasure in the school of love. *Exit*
FILBON We must be quick and sudden: come.
TUTCH Slip like your eel.
TABITHA If any man know any lawful cause
Why these two may not marry, now speak,
Or else forever mum;[776] I am gone, i'faith. *Exit*
TUTCH Master, remember, you ha' my tongue.[777]
FILBON Yes, and thou mine. Let me alone to counterfeit.[778]

Exeunt

[Act V, scene ii]

Enter SIR WILLIAM *with* HUMIL, [*dressed*] *like a Pothecary*

SIR WILLIAM Think on[779] your oath.
HUMIL Sir, if I do not, let me die.
When I have poisoned her with this confection,[780]

769 0 SD *like one another*: i.e. each wearing the outfit the other had worn in IV.i

770 0 SD *with them* . . . *and* TABITHA: despite the urgency with which IV.i concluded, this scene resumes where the other left off, and no one has left for Putney yet

771 3–4 Paris did . . . matchless Helen: Paris abducted Helen from Sparta and took her to Troy; an inauspicious example, since Helen was already married, and the abduction caused Troy's ruin

772 6 quickened with the former grant: sparked by Sir William's earlier approval

773 11 as: as if; like one

774 12 'pothecary: apothecary, a purveyor of herbs, drugs, medical advice, cosmetics, and (in plays) illicit poisons

775 13 I know . . . was a—: a premature joke, since the audience has not yet seen the apothecary to know that it is Humil in disguise (and thus cannot appreciate the ironic truth of what Tutch is prevented from saying)

776 19–21 If any . . . forever mum: Tabitha is not rehearsing the priest's lines; more likely she mocks Filbon and Tutch, whom she suggests are enjoying the bonding experience of this "buddy" caper a bit too much

777 22 (1) you are to speak as me (i.e. as Sir Robert) (2) you, as my "master" in this fiction, must give me permission to speak

778 23 counterfeit: dissemble; rehearse; despite this build-up, we never see Filbon-as-Robert's conversation with Henry, which would seem to be the whole reason for engineering the role reversal

779 1 Think on: remember; apparently this is Sir William's second conversation with Humil/Pothecary, not the one Tabitha reported in V.i, and some time has passed

780 3 confection: (1) a prepared dish or delicacy, e.g. a sugary preserve (2) a medicinal mixture compounded of various drugs, beaten into a paste (3) a poison. Humil's sense obviously includes (3); the play, however, vacillates between (1) and (2), offering evidence for both. This scene intimates that Humil will administer the poison to Lady Vergir in a cosmetic paste; thereafter, the expectation seems to be that she will consume it in a candy at the banquet

Be you cloudy, killed with sorrow;[781] 'tis a skin
Will draw to purpose on the straitest glove.[782]
But then, your promisèd reward.
SIR WILLIAM My daughter and my goods;
I have no other son but you, all is thine.
Question not the reason why this[783] is:
For I have many, and amongst them one
'Sides all the rest that, known to thee,
Will rather hasten death than pity it.
Go: I will bid my guests forth to this feast.
Shall she[784] have noble poison,[785] 'twill cause fear,
Useless suspicion, and my mortal hate
Shall itself kennel in the pride of state.[786]
HUMIL Give order for the banquet.
SIR WILLIAM Within there!

Enter LADY

LADY Sir, what is your will?
SIR WILLIAM To murder thee. *He speaks aside*
HUMIL [*Aside to* SIR WILLIAM] She dies, sir, if I live; I am a 'pothecary,
And can knead the paste to purpose. She is gone
Had she a thousand lives laid up in one.
SIR WILLIAM Wife, I must have thee paint,[787] and set
A gloss upon this lovely front,[788] to move
And to attract all eyes. Look as the summer,
Which glads all hearts with his blood-'creasing[789] spring;
Use thy best graces, though most proudly
I will have it so,[790] seat thee to all state,[791]
Decked in thy choicest ornament. Shine, glow-worm,
In the noon of night, for at this supper
I will have more than all our friends,
Music several,[792] masques[793] and revelings,
In which thou shalt be mounted[794] as the bride,
And I the jolly bridegroom will tend on thee,
As duty and the time commands me.
LADY Whereof comes this cost?
SIR WILLIAM Examine not,
But lay your best end now to't.[795]

781 4 Be you . . . with sorrow: be sure to look pallid and stricken, as though dead with sadness
782 4–5 a skin . . . straitest glove: i.e. it will ensure the desired effect, like a hand slipping into the narrowest glove
783 9 this: i.e. why I want my wife murdered
784 14 Shall she: if she should
785 14 noble poison: a poison that is otherwise inert and chemically undetectable
786 14–16 'twill cause . . . of state: Sir William envisions Lady Vergir's death setting off a panic among his guests, allowing his bloodlust ("mortal hate") to conceal itself ("kennel") in his authority ("pride of state")
787 22 paint: apply cosmetics
788 23 front: face
789 25 blood-'creasing: blood-increasing; springtime proverbially quickened the pulse and thickened the blood
790 26–7 though most . . . it so: (1) though I take excessive pride in you, I will have it so (2) use your best graces, even with excessive pride in your appearance
791 27 seat thee to all state: i.e. give you pride of place
792 31 several: of diverse kinds
793 31 masques: exclusive dances at which the guests wore masks to conceal their identities; also a court entertainment that combined such dancing with a lavish, spectacular, allegorical scripted drama
794 32 mounted: exalted, celebrated
795 36 Devote your full energies to its achievement

Counsel with this 'pothecary, which I sent for
To the business. Pray ye use your art,
For I am bent to this consumption.[796]
Where's our servant James?
LADY Within, sir; shall I call him?
SIR WILLIAM No, I will wait on him; for 'tis my duty.
[*Aside*] Such as would spend in feasts are but the slaves,
T'attend the pleasures of consuming knaves.
And I am one of those;[797] he is the flower
That I must crop, too, in this fatal hour.[798]
[*To* HUMIL] Pray ye appoint,[799] sir: she will fit you well.
My purse shall purvey what you determine.
What we will be wasteful sometime, and our own,
We uncontrolled may dispose of.[800] [*Aside*] 'Tis our love[801]—
Rather our destiny, hath joined to this brow
A horn that draws on death, no matter how.[802] [*Exit*]
LADY Sir, in my closet serve yourself with sugars,[803]
There are spices of the purest; use them
In this cost.[804] What else you want, please you command.
They shall attend you.
HUMIL I want virtue in a mother. Are you one?
LADY I was mother to an absent son,
But not to virtue wanting;[805] wrong me not.
HUMIL Wrong not yourself.
LADY I never will.
HUMIL You have. *He discovers himself to his mother*
LADY Humil! O, my shame and not my son;
By thee a mother is made miserable.[806]
HUMIL By my black sin? No, by thine own neglect,
Made perfect by my true intelligence,[807]
And whoever[808] cunning[809] masked and donned
The vizard[810] that so muffled me. I knew not
Who was in the bed![811]
LADY Your eyes were witnesses?
HUMIL And holy ones.
LADY Found you the man you looked for?
HUMIL No, 'twas a subtle train so hoodwinked truth.[812]

796 39 I am (1) inclined to incur this expense (2) determined on your destruction
797 45 those: i.e. those who slavishly spend money to provide "consuming knaves" with pleasure
798 45–6 he is . . . fatal hour: this is Sir William's sole mention of a separate plan to murder James; it never materializes
799 47 appoint: (1) see the Lady to her chamber (2) begin your preparations
800 49–50 What we . . . dispose of: what we are sometimes wasteful of, if ("and") it is ours, we may dispose of as we please
801 50 our love: my wife
802 51–2 Rather our . . . matter how: or rather, (it is) my destiny (that I am disposing of), which fatalistically compels me to avenge my cuckolding
803 53 sugars: candies
804 54–55 use them/In this cost: enjoy them as a privilege due an honored guest
805 59 but not . . . wanting: but not the author ("mother") of a deficient virtue
806 61–2 It is unclear what Lady Vergir has been told about Humil's exile; she may know he accused her of infidelity, but evidently does not know he saw her in bed with James
807 64 Proven by my conclusive information
808 65 whoever: i.e. Sir William, with her and James's complicity
809 65 cunning: cunningly
810 66 vizard: mask, i.e. deceived me
811 66–7 I knew . . . the bed!: (1) said sarcastically, i.e. "as if I didn't know who was in that bed!" (2) or with more poetic compression, i.e. "I thought I saw a crime between only two, but I didn't realize Sir William would cover it up, and that you were all in bed together"
812 69 'twas a . . . hoodwinked truth: it was a devious ploy ("train") used to cheat the truth

I am a traitor if I did not see
James, your man, fast in your arms.
LADY Thou art a traitor then, if any James[813] were there.
He was no man of mine; he was thy father.
[HUMIL][814]
LADY Marvel not. At leisure I will tell thee all:
His late return; the trick to place him here;
My stay,[815] and his continuing in this house—which known,
Thou wilt no sin account, to keep our own.[816]
HUMIL O you prophetic fairies,[817] how dally you
In concaves of our hearts! Shamed at my error,
I thought forever to be from your sight.[818]
But thinking truth was blinded, I forethought
Some following business: thus I altered,
Coming as one disguised to save her life—
Damned for that fact.[819]
LADY My life?
HUMIL You must be poisoned at this feast;
'Tis I must do the deed. O mother,
How are you blessed in my return from travel!
I, that to light bring your offense (so thought),
Must be the pardon at your judgment brought.[820]
LADY Ah, me!
HUMIL No more: much secrecy calls on[821] us.
Acquaint me with my father; plead my guilt.[822]
We shall with cunning so unfold this business
That our hopes shall strengthen as they perish.[823]
No idle practice, but a serious toil,
Must bring home conquest from this long-wished spoil.[824]

Exeunt

[Act V, scene iii]

Enter HENRY, FILBON, TABITHA, SIR RAFE, TUTCH

HENRY If I lock up[825] this treason, let me perish!
No, sir, my breast is yet an uncorrupt

813 72 any James: (1) just any James; (2) the James you mean (and the one accused of adultery)
814 74 Q gives the Lady two speeches in a row, and seems to elide a line spoken by Humil. This may be a printing error, or it may indicate a dramatic pause, in which Humil stares dumbfounded, or it may indicate that he starts to speak, but is immediately interrupted
815 77 My stay: i.e. my remaining in this house (as Sir William's wife)
816 78 You cannot deem it a sin for me to keep my own husband
817 79 O you prophetic fairies: upon learning the truth of his father's murder, Hamlet exclaims "O my prophetic soul!" (I.v. 40); in this instance, Humil has just realized his error, and this line may begin a complicated attempt to disavow it
818 80–81 Shamed at … your sight: Humil cannot mean Lady Vergir, since he moments ago re-accused her; he may still be addressing the "prophetic fairies," whom he imagines like the Furies, chthonic gods of vengeance
819 82–5 But thinking … that fact: suspecting the truth was being hidden, I hatched a plan: I came disguised as one whose profession nurtures life (when my intent was opposite)—a deed for which I am condemned. Lady Vergir's reply interprets this differently: she is "damned" for her act, and Humil has returned to save her
820 89–90 I, that … judgment brought: I, who revealed your alleged offense, am now the pardon brought to your trial
821 91 calls on: is demanded of
822 92 plead my guilt: beg his forgiveness of me
823 94 perish: diminish, i.e. if we ("with cunning") let Sir William believe the poisoning has occurred, our chances of success will improve even as they appear to weaken
824 96 Spoils are brought home from conquest, not vice versa, but since there is nothing to be won here except "spoil"—ruining the banquet and Sir William—perhaps the transposition is apt
825 1 lock up: conceal

And holy house, that harbors in it nought
But honesty; and to do this wrong
To my patron, *per deum atque hominem fidem*[826]—
TABITHA No matter if you tell it now, 'tis done:
"*Finis*," men say, concludes the ancient work,[827]
And this,[828] though newly done, cries "so be it."
HENRY If [to] keep secrets can be but offense,[829]
And so 'tis now, may be I lose my place.[830]
But there's a friend which turning calls detraction—
At his heels lives hope—whose cunning quickens
Every fault to favor.[831]
FILBON Why, true, and we shall as we may excuse it.
'Twas a deed done in Welsh: you understood it not.
TABITHA Let me alone to buckler[832] thee, Sir Henry.
HENRY Can ye ward[833] yourself?
TABITHA This was a pass,[834] 'twas fencer's play;
And for the after-venny,[835] let me use my skill.
SIR RAFE However, girl, thou art my daughter now.
What thou shalt lose in father from thy own,
Thou uncontrolled[836] shalt find as much in his;[837]
And I am he.
TABITHA And I acknowledge both.
This[838] is my lord, my head, my husband:
At whose bed I am obedient,
At whose board I am obedient,
All in all. I am the wife of Filbon,
Whose rough Welsh hath got a constering[839] English.
Parse[840] it, boy: nouns, pronouns, verbs, adverbs,
And God-give-thee-joy.[841]
TUTCH With vocative "O," your father hears it.[842]
TABITHA And ablative *caret*,[843] takes his daughter.
HENRY Then, *in pluraliter*,[844] ah, he has a son.
FILBON So, singular and plural, all is done.

826 5 *per deum atque hominem fidem*: by the faith of God and man (Latin)
827 7 (1) men write "finis" ("the end") at the end of old books (2) the word "finis" concludes old books, according to the men who (unlike me) read them
828 8 this: i.e. Filbon and Tabitha's marriage
829 9 If keeping secrets can only be an offense (Q omits "to," here given in brackets)
830 10 place: position
831 11–13 But there's ... to favor: there is a potential ally, the rhetorical figure called distraction, whose slipperiness converts offense to advantage. Henry hopes to equivocate, deflect Sir William's questions, and pretend ignorance
832 16 buckler: shield, protect (as in combat)
833 17 ward: defend
834 18 This was a pass: our secret wedding was but a thrust in a larger fencing match
835 19 after-venny: a "venny" was a fencing match; Tabitha imagines the subsequent confrontation with her father as the "after-venny"
836 22 uncontrolled: i.e. like it or not
837 22 his: Filbon's
838 25 This: Filbon
839 29 constering: construing, understanding; also translating (which cues the ensuing game). Tabitha jokes that she will be a skilled interpreter of her husband's wishes, since she has already had to interpret for him
840 30 Parse: decline (grammatically). The figuring of social relationships in schoolroom grammar categories is a particularly Shakespearean conceit; cf. *Merry Wives of Windsor* IV.i. 13–85 and *Love's Labour's Lost* V.i
841 31 God-give-thee-joy: whatever else you please
842 32 Tutch uses Latin grammatical cases to narrate the events to come: your father will greet the news with a cry of "O" (the conventional marker of the vocative case)
843 33 ablative *caret*: the ablative marks movement away, and for things moving away from each other, lacks a preposition ("caret," missing); Sir William takes his daughter away (from Filbon)
844 34 *in pluraliter*: in plural form; nevertheless, Sir William will still gain a son (or, if too late, a grandson)

Enter AUDITOR, [*dressed*] *like a merchant still*

AUDITOR If ever you were swift, be nimble now.
What, ha' ye married, tied this knot?
TABITHA Aye, and the earnest blow[845] given: fear it not.
HENRY Sir, I have set my hand to't, sealed the deed;
Pray God it cancel not in me.[846]
AUDITOR Then part, and everyone be silent.
There is a feast appointed at the knight's.
TABITHA Our marriage dinner, is it?
AUDITOR A gallant one: much cost is threatened,[847]
And the good old knight unbuckles from his back
The liberal load of honor; does proclaim
Triumphs and welcome unto all; calls for his wife,
Charges her care; commands his servant James
To invite his guests, which in a roll[848] stands quoted.
There's a new-come 'pothecary, and he bribes
Even grace herself in this assembly,[849]
And does promise his furtherance in the business.[850]
On the sudden, you are missed: "Daggers and devils,"
The knight cries, "Where's my daughter?"
One up ascends to search the chambers;
Another runs to seek for this lost daughter.
I, knowing more than much in this her absence,
Singled myself[851] to warn you of his search:
Hither will he come, for he fears[852] young Filbon,
Missing the suitors, calling for the merchant.
I answered not (being absent);[853]
In this heat,[854] "The Welshman, where is he?"
None can be found; cries out he knows not what;
And all his word is now "A plot, a plot, a plot!"
SIR RAFE [*To Filbon and Tabitha*] What will ye do?
TABITHA Kiss and part.
Till fit occasion of our next salute,
Filbon, farewell; my husband, think on me.
I am thy treasure, but thou bear'st the key. *Exit*
SIR RAFE I will home. [*Exit*]
AUDITOR And I will see the rest.
What will you, sir, do?
HENRY Nay, I ha' done enough; I am undone in myself. *Hei mihi, quod nullus,* I must do this deed;[855] 'twas I! *Pauca* the rest,[856] I'll home, sir, I. [*Exeunt* AUDITOR *and* HENRY *in separate directions*]
TUTCH What rests[857] for Welsh Sir Robert Morgan? By God, was crag de pen, and the hangman

845 38 earnest blow: the kiss that ends the ceremony, but suggestive of sexual consummation
846 40 (1) I hope I have done nothing to mar it (2) I hope it does not prove the end of me
847 44 threatened: levied
848 49 roll: scroll, i.e. the guest list
849 50–51 he bribes . . . this assembly: obscure, but Humil/Pothecary seems to be obsequiously flattering the guests
850 52 (1) Seeks to aid in the festivities (2) may prove useful to our scheme
851 58 Singled myself: separated myself, slipped away
852 59 fears: suspects
853 61 (being absent): Auditor seems here to realize that he is reporting speech he could not have heard
854 62 heat: vein (of panic), i.e. something like this
855 71–2 *Hei mihi* . . . this deed: Henry mixes Latin and English: woe is me, that none but I should have done this deed
856 72 *Pauca* the rest: *Pauca* is Latin for "few"; the whole phrase means "To say the rest in a few words," i.e. "To sum up"
857 73 What rests: what remains

calls to me. Da-hum-a, da-hum-a![858]
FILBON I will be at this feast in some disguise.
TUTCH I'll fit ye,[859] sir; 'tis here.[860] I am Tutch, right—*hic et ubique*,[861] everywhere.

Exeunt

[Act V, scene iv]

Enter SIR WILLIAM *Vergir*

SIR WILLIAM Now smiles the instant,[862] and wrath's wrinkles seem
As smoothèd curls upon a wanton stream.
My hopes grow big, and their delivery
Is by our midwife time brought to true birth.
I will not be a pointing-stock[863] to th'world:
No, if this gossip Rumor publish it,
It shall be christened with revenge and death.[864]
Why, when?[865] Are we grown sluggards now?
Tardy in bounty,[866] shall we niggard[867] it?

Enter HUMIL[868] *in white sleeves and apron,*[869] *and others posting over the stage with boxes* [*and bringing a table, chairs, dishes, and glasses*]

HUMIL [*To attendants*] Be quick, carry those sweetmeats[870] in.
[*To* SIR WILLIAM] Bid them that in this business have to do
That they attend this rich confectionery
With no common care; the cost commands
More love and duty.
Sir, we are fitting to occasion.
Would all your guests were come!
SIR WILLIAM 'Tis the feast's duty to attend.
Thou art a willing mischief. Hast thou fitted
Our purpose to the proof?[871]
HUMIL Have I? Think you I am slack,
Pushed on with hope of beauty and reward?
She dies, had she a life more dear
Than the last spring, sole comfort of the year.
But I will cover,[872] and prepare. *Exit*
SIR WILLIAM Do, do. My daughter's thine, my goods, my all;
Blessèd beginning to my sorrow's fall.
Where's my lady?

858 73–4 was crag . . . da-hum-a!: Tutch resumes his Welsh: "I am crag-de-pen," seems to connote the judge's scratching of a death sentence onto parchment; "da-hum-a" may be meant to evoke the creaking sound of swinging from the gallows, perhaps accompanied by grim comic gestures
859 76 I'll fit ye: I'll provide whatever you need
860 76 'tis here: i.e. I've got it
861 76 *hic et ubique*: Latin: here and everywhere; the same phrase is used to describe the ghost in *Hamlet* (I.v. 159)
862 1 Now smiles the instant: the moment appears favorable
863 5 pointing-stock: laughing stock
864 6–7 No, if . . . and death: Sir William modifies his childbirth metaphor: when word of his deed spreads, the story of his cuckoldry will become known ("christened") as the story of his revenge. (Since his cuckoldry remains a secret, of course, murdering Lady Vergir only publicizes it)
865 8 Why, when?: Sir William may express impatience with himself, or he may direct the next two lines at his attendants within, cueing the elaborate stagecraft that must follow
866 9 bounty: hospitality, generosity
867 9 niggard: be stingy with
868 9 SD *Enter* HUMIL: Since Humil enters again eighteen lines later, he may pass over the stage several times, supervising preparations
869 9 SD *white sleeves and apron*: an outfit that ambiguously implies both food and drug preparation; cf. V.ii. 3 and note
870 10 sweetmeats: candies, bonbons
871 18–19 Hast thou . . . the proof: have you effected our design, i.e. (1) given her the poison (2) prepared the poison for her?
872 24 cover: spread the tablecloth

LADY [*within*] Here.

Enter LADY, *gallant and brave,*[873] *while* HUMIL [*who re-enters*] *and others* [*including* JAMES] *prepare*

SIR WILLIAM [*Aside*] That one so heavenly fair should earthly be
Slave to misfortune, base in luxury![874]
LADY Sir, for to please your eye, I am thus quaint;[875]
Good faith, I am ashamèd in myself.
SIR WILLIAM [*Aside*] How, and a woman?
Come, blaze thy affections to immodesty:[876]
And though thy virtues contradict the deed,[877]
Be Venus' wanton,[878] smile with Helen's eye,[879]
For I will have it so.
LADY I was not so brought up; I shall endeavor,
Though my cheeks put on sensuable[880] dye
Of other bashfulness.
JAMES Sir, your honorable guests are come.
SIR WILLIAM [*To* LADY] Nay, then you wrong me most of all.
Show not these signs of fear: all's past,
And I am dead in old remembrance.[881]
Troth, I am: forget it, as I do. [*To* JAMES] Say on.
JAMES Coaches so fill the pavements of your door
That scarce can passage give the footmen way.
'Tis not amiss you go to meet them, sir.
SIR WILLIAM Why, well said; spoke with courage. And I will,
Jovial like a bridegroom. Lady, you see:
They wait on us, and all attend on thee.
LADY Worthless I am, but since it is your will,
I borrow light from sunshine of your beams.
[*Aside*] Who glisters so, gives splendor nothing proud,
Darkened by fear, half-hidden in a cloud.[882]
SIR WILLIAM Nay, hand in hand. In faith, James, pardon me,
That dally with the darling of your heart. *Exeunt* [SIR WILLIAM *and* LADY]
JAMES Even so. But little thinking such a thing,
Small gain springs from that toil, where industry
Sweats in the brows of others' victory.[883]

Enter HUMIL *busily still*

HUMIL Father, be mindful.[884] This presuming knight

873 27 SD *gallant and brave*: sumptuous and beautiful
874 29 luxury: lust
875 30 quaint: pretty, dainty; curiously attired or made up
876 33 Display your emotions unashamedly
877 34 thy virtues contradict the deed: your inner character does not match your appearance
878 35 wanton: minion
879 35 Appear as lascivious and seductive as possible (Sir William wants her to look like the whore he believes she is)
880 38 sensuable: sensible, perceptible. Lady Vergir claims her make-up is noticeably counteracted by her blushing, as she thinks of her past infractions
881 43 The ancient memory of that is dead in me
882 53–4 Who glisters . . . a cloud: who projects such false radiance ("glisters") does not at all convey pride, but is (1) tinged with obscure menace (2) hiding their fear (Lady may be describing Sir William or herself)
883 57–9 But little . . . others' victory: uncertain, but since James will shortly reveal knowledge of Humil's plot, he may console himself: Sir William little imagines all the industry he devotes to his banquet, and all the labor he forces James to undertake, merely create sweat on the brow of James's victory—and no gain for Sir William
884 60 Father, be mindful: Humil has overheard James during his stage transits. Inexplicably, Armin omits their reunion, which might have been one of the play's emotional climaxes; unseen, Humil and James have already met as father and son

Plays with the flame, burns in the candle-light;
When[885] we shall furnish to disfurnish him
Of what he yet enjoys.
JAMES Humil, 'tis cunningly contrived, and I attend it. *Exit*
HUMIL [*To attendants*] For charity, be swift!
Place your plate, and pile your vitrial[886] bowls
Nest upon nest. These for wines and beer;
The other tend the call of altering diet.[887]
"Sirrah," quoth he, "we shall fit, I trow,
The pleasant purpose of love's appetite;
At hand, i'faith, and welcome to the feast,
Whose food is pleasure, dainties but a jest!"[888]
And I provide it for ye.[889]

Enter EARL, LORDS, LADIES, *as many as may be* [*including* JAMES]; SIR WILLIAM *and his* LADY *in complement*[890]

SIR WILLIAM Right noble and my heart's endearèd friends,
To preach your welcome were to drown the sea
With floods of water. Be it known unto ye
That your coming, solemnly invited,
Hath that attendance appertaining as the gods
In their selected bacchanals command;[891]
Marry, the nectar wants, and the ambrosia
Smiles in the presence of such earthly wines
As the world's compound furnishes withal,
Though it come short of luscious surfeiting.[892]
Yet willing furtherance makes the value meet.[893]
In her best suit of entertain,[894] sit then,
And let our music relish to the ear
Such care and cost as love and welcome gives.
Not to profane the best, accept the least,
As prologue to begin this worthless feast.
EARL Sir, we are easily won to fawn on friendship
Spaniel-like, yet with the smiles of men,
Which re-delivers love for love:
What we receive are treasures safely stored,
And shall with interest be repaid again.
You're free, yet frugal, without lavishing.
Nor come we to make boot of[895] courtesy,
But value kindness in her best of love.[896]
So we dwell, in your bounty.
SIR WILLIAM Rent-free, welcome.

885 62 When: at which time
886 66 vitrial: vitreous; of transparent glass
887 68 The second (set of bowls) should remain empty, awaiting whatever fare the rest of the menu prescribes
888 69–72 "Sirrah . . . a jest!": Humil bitterly mocks Sir William's smug pomposity, pretending to greet a guest
889 73 Seemingly a servant's grumbling, but Humil may hint at his coming revenge—as well as the "dainties" (perhaps) that Sir William believes contain his own revenge
890 73 SD *in complement*: together, as one (possibly they hold hands)
891 77–9 That your . . . bacchanals command: the gods do not command a more august audience at their private festivals
892 80–83 Marry, the . . . luscious surfeiting: admittedly, the food ("nectar") is imperfect, and our ambrosia deigns to be earthly wine, gathered from the world over, despite being finite in amount
893 84 Your indulgence makes the offering worthy of its recipients
894 85 suit of entertain: display of welcome (that the world has to offer)
895 96 make boot of: profit from, take advantage of
896 97 Take your generosity in the best spirit

If you think this your receptacle,[897] then
Landlord I am, and shall so soundly prove:
As, fines forgiven, you lease free-borne[898] our love.
Welcome our tenants, landlady.[899]
LADY I do; my duty tenders it.
Sit then and frolic, for to my heart's liking
Is this day consecrated; blessed the means
That added to it such prosperity. [LADY *unwraps the candy and reads*[900]]
While we sat sighing on the banks of bale,[901]
Bliss kissed her cheek,[902] *and bids her joy: all hail!* [*All applaud, and* LADY *eats the candy*[903]]
SIR WILLIAM [*Aside*] Aye, such a storm as, when the shower is past,
It drives destruction to thy soul.
Moral, in faith: enigmas riddle so.
Music, fall to! Wife, I will seat thee here—
With pardon of thy betters.[904] [*Music plays*]
EARL In yours, she is the best, and does command
Place and priority i'th' upper hand.
Besides, her beauty merits as the best
To overshine stars, were they here possessed.[905]
LADY Well mocked, my lord.
EARL No, not a whit;
My judgment errs if otherwise I censure[906] it.
Sit, sirs; for I, although invited, challenge[907] here
Full-flowing welcome—from his[908] lips that lends
As unto me, so much to all my friends.
And I begin unto ye. *The* EARL *sits, and all do follow him*
SIR WILLIAM [*Aside*] There's a cockerel,[909] right,
That learns to crow from others. Good my Earl—
If that my boldness may challenge thy own—
Engaged unto thy nobleness forever,
I promise whose performance lightly gives,[910]
Heart-willingness to boot.[911] Gods me, fill wine!

[SIR WILLIAM] *fills two glasses, gives her* [LADY] *one*

Skink[912] and carouse! Wife, charge[913] this common shot.[914]

897 99 receptacle: resting place, home
898 101 free-borne: by native right; unbeholden
899 102 Sir William bids Lady Vergir to welcome the guests
900 106 SD LADY … *reads*: the ensuing couplet seems out of place, but Lady Vergir may be reading: a "frolic" was a sweetmeat wrapped in paper, on which was written a little poem, and her use of "frolic" three lines earlier may obliquely announce that she is about to open one
901 107 *bale*: woe; the lines seem largely non-referential, describing in stylized pastoral terms a shift from sadness to joy
902 108 *Bliss kissed her cheek*: "her" has no obvious antecedent; whose cheek "Bliss" kisses is unclear
903 108 SD LADY *eats the candy*: if the supposed "poison" is a candy, Q fails to specify when it is introduced; Sir William's reaction suggests he believes this is that moment
904 113 With apologies to your social superiors (a deliberately cruel reference to the fact that she is only a Lady by virtue of her marriage to him)
905 117 possessed: present, seated
906 119 censure: deem, pronounce
907 120 challenge: offer
908 121 his: i.e. Sir William's
909 124 cockerel: young rooster
910 128 I liberally give performance to that which I have promised
911 129 Heart-willingness to boot: wholeheartedly as well
912 130 Skink: pour
913 130 charge: fill
914 130 common shot: here, a game in which the lady chooses someone on whom she will bestow either her glass, or her "piercing eye" (a favorable glance), or both; the nobles vie for her favor by praising the deadly power of her beauty (Sir William overlays a conceit of gunnery)

Level point-blank; see who thy piercing eye
Can mark to hit. If they be bullet-free
They scape the under-daunt of courtesy.[915]
EARL They say he's cursed that by a cannon dies;
May I be blessed in such a destiny!
For of all other, I were only happy
Being the eye-mark of so fair a shot.
1 LORD Discharge, bright beauty, and shoot home;
Make me the man so happy.
2 LORD Aye, or me.
EARL Or any: 'mongst so many lives free choice
To one as principal; to each a voice.[916]
LADY [*To Earl*] Then to the worthiest: to yourself, my lord,
By figure of the rest. 'Tis understood
By the king's nod he greets his subjects freely,
Though his eye settle upon one.[917]
EARL Even so to me, I answer and acknowledge
Receipt of compliment, bestowed about
On every willing and right-welcome guest.[918]
Pray ye all memories.[919]
ALL We do so, and he gives a duty
To gratulate such seeming courtesy!

Enter FILBON *and* TUTCH *in blue,*[920] *like* NURSE *and* JOHN I'TH' HOSPITAL

SIR WILLIAM Nurse, John! Unlooked for, better welcome![921]
This is kindly visitation, faith.
FILBON Sir, 'tis my duty, and my beggared boldness
Makes me presume to trouble ye.
Knowing how you affect this ignorant,[922]
I brought him to give welcome to your guests—
Hearing at London of this preparation.
SIR WILLIAM At London? Is it got so far abroad?
[*To all*] You see a niggard's[923] bounty how it spreads,
Like to a nine days' wonder,[924] gentlemen!
And much the more, because 'tis seldom seen
That covetous misers are so plentiful.[925]
Faith, 'tis much in me!
EARL We find it so, Sir William.
SIR WILLIAM [*To* JOHN] Now, my suck-egg, tell me: what's the news at London? You hear all.
TUTCH That honest men want, and knaves get money, I ha' nothing, nurse has some, dogs are

915 131–3 see who . . . of courtesy: whoever escapes wounding by your glance loses the valor of being inflicted with such honor
916 140–41 'mongst so . . . a voice: she who is first has free choice among so many, though they all have a claim
917 143–5 By figure . . . upon one: By casting her glance on Earl, she does so on all, because he is their figurehead; likewise, when a king nods at one he is recognizing everyone
918 147–8 bestowed about . . . right-welcome guest: the Earl receives and redistributes the Lady's courtesy to all, just as she bestowed it
919 149 Seemingly a call to cheer
920 151 SD *in blue*: Filbon plays the Nurse and Tutch John, possibly substituting their blue hospital outfits (cf. II.i. 124 SD) with blue servingmen's uniforms. Aside from its convenience, the device allows Armin (who in the original production doubled Tutch and John) to play both roles at once
921 152 Unlooked for, better welcome!: your arrival is all the more welcome because unexpected
922 156 affect this ignorant: are fond of this fool
923 160 niggard's: miser's (with false modesty)
924 161 nine days' wonder: short-lived popular sensation or attraction
925 163 plentiful: generous

let loose, and the bears undone.[926] Ha ha ha!
SIR WILLIAM Came ye by foot, John, or by water?
TUTCH A-horseback, i'th' boat.
SIR WILLIAM Art not galled[927] with riding, John?
TUTCH No, but weary with sitting. Nurse shall sing a Geneva psalm,[928] and bid these beggars welcome.[929]
SIR WILLIAM How "beggars," John?
TUTCH All the world is so. Ha ha ha!
EARL He says true; chide him not. We are no less.

Enter TABITHA

SIR WILLIAM Daughter, welcome. Nurse all day, at night be your bedfellow![930]
TABITHA My nurse, indeed, my bedfellow forever. *Speaks aside*
My Filbon welcome; welcome as my husband,
My last and forever best belovèd.
SIR WILLIAM James, to season this good meeting,
Take hand in hand with our fair wife and dance.
Gallants, my man can trick it[931] with my lady;
You shall see else. Make not[932] squeamish: to't.
It is my will, and what I will shall be.
JAMES Beseech ye, sir.
SIR WILLIAM Befool ye, sir, will't be.[933] Wife, make not coy.
LADY Since you command it, I am ready.
SIR WILLIAM [*Aside to* HUMIL] I trow so. But I trust a potion pleads
By this time to true purpose, does it not?
HUMIL I would not be so sped. For all the world,
'Tis done; too late; 'tis past. [LADY *and* JAMES *dance*]
SIR WILLIAM [*Aside*] Good i'th' beginning,[934] let her dance her last:
Who fronts[935] me with a cornucopian[936] wreath,
Were she a wife sprung from the race of kings,
Such bitter breathing[937] follows.
Now, ye lamps of spotted Nemesis,[938]
Burn blue! Let fall the light on mischief's self,
That dallied[939] lately in our wretchedness;
Tell her sad sorrow, tombs, and epitaphs attend
Her amazing obsequies; and then live free,
Thou wrongèd soul,[940] from slander's cruelty.
LADY [*To* JAMES] I am not well, sir; pray ye, leave the dance.

926 167–8 dogs are . . . bears undone: Tutch/John alludes to bear-baiting, a popular London pastime
927 171 galled: chafed
928 172 Geneva psalm: a psalm as translated in the Geneva Bible (1560); psalms were often sung recreationally
929 172–3 Nurse shall . . . beggars welcome: Tutch/John announces that Filbon/Nurse will sing—probably prompting a terrified look from Filbon, whose voice would give him away
930 177 Nurse all . . . your bedfellow!: Sir William's wisecrack that Tabitha take Nurse to bed seems coarse and gratuitous, but it creates an irony on which Tabitha seizes. It is unclear how she can instantly recognize Filbon, but the obviousness of his disguise seems to be a running gag
931 183 trick it: turn a step neatly; dance well
932 184 Make not: (1) don't be (2) don't pretend to be
933 187 will't be: it will be (me making a fool of you rather than your beseeching me)
934 193 Good i'th' beginning: i.e. Lady Vergir (whose former virtue Sir William contrasts with her impending death)
935 194 Who fronts: whoever crowns, places on my forehead
936 194 cornucopian: the cornucopia (Latin: "horn of plenty") was a symbol of abundance, but could also represent cuckoldry
937 196 bitter breathing: presumably the respiratory distress he thinks he observes in Lady Vergir
938 197 Nemesis: Greek goddess of revenge (who was not "spotted," but Sir William addresses the stars)
939 199 dallied: delighted
940 202 Thou wrongèd soul: Sir William now apostrophizes himself

SIR WILLIAM Not well? James, begone.[941]
JAMES Sir, you shall pardon me, unless with[942] her being not well.
SIR WILLIAM Ha?
JAMES Think you I will, what, leave my country, sir,
Upon a slight, a trifle? 'Tis more dear to me.
SIR WILLIAM Was't not thy promise?
JAMES Pugh!
SIR WILLIAM Pugh![943]
TABITHA Madam, lean on me; I'll bring you to your chamber.
LADY Prithee, daughter. Faith, I'm passing ill.
[*To* EARL] Your honor and the rest must bear with[944] us.
'Tis nothing usual:[945] a queasy fit.
EARL The mother?[946]
LADY No, the husband.
Good faith, I am not woman-sick, though woman,
But earnest ill,[947] clogged at the stomach with
A sudden qualm. I fear me 'tis my death.
SIR WILLIAM Nurse, help to bring her to her closet, do.
FILBON [*To* TABITHA]: Excellent fit,[948] supported by us two.
[*Exeunt* FILBON *and* TABITHA, *carrying* LADY; *followed by* JAMES *and* HUMIL]

TUTCH [*Aside*] Plague on't, shall I be left alone? Master, make haste! But 'tis my deed, I am author of this shift.[949] He's where he would be now; I'm where I should be too, but not well-backed.[950] Yes, now I am.

Enter SIR RAFE[951]

SIR RAFE Beseech ye, pardon me.
Sir William, I am wronged, and to this company
I make it known. By coming of thy daughter,
Is my son made her endearèd husband?[952]
Shall I suffer it? Call you this courtesy?
'Tis simple craft![953] Cloaked under thy denial,
Is this well, to engraft with us unknown,[954]
And so to join younkers to heirs?[955] He is
My only all—and married unto thy daughter?

Enter FILBON [*still disguised*] *and* TABITHA

941 204 begone: presumably he holds a finger to his lips, the promised signal for James to banish himself (cf. III.v. 229–32)
942 205 unless with: because of
943 209 Pugh! Pugh!: they (1) spit (2) make some other noise of disgust: probably mutually, but Sir William's may only be an incredulous repetition of James's, as if flabbergasted by his defiance
944 212 bear with: forgive, excuse
945 213 usual: habitual (i.e. this isn't like me!)
946 214 The mother?: "a fit of the mother" was a term for hysteria (from the Greek word for "uterus"), whose symptoms included panicked breathing; Earl asks if Lady Vergir is menstruating or pregnant
947 215–16 I am … earnest ill: although I am a woman, my sickness is not gender-specific, but a serious one indeed
948 219 Excellent fit: Filbon puns rather tastelessly on Lady Vergir's "fit," remarking either that he and Tabitha make a good team, or that their carrying her off affords them opportunity to be together
949 221 author of this shift: i.e. it was my decision for us to adopt these (very public) disguises
950 222 well-backed: supported (he is thus relieved at the arrival of a diversion in Sir Rafe)
951 222 SD *Enter* SIR RAFE: Sir Rafe earlier gave no reason to expect his return, so his motive for crashing the banquet and feigning outrage over his son's marriage remains unclear. Perhaps it is to repay Sir William by rejecting his daughter, but outing Filbon's disguise is unnecessary
952 225–6 By coming … endearèd husband?: By your welcoming your daughter, am I to infer your approval of her marriage to my son?
953 228 simple craft: outright malpractice
954 229 engraft with us unknown: to marry into my family (1) without my knowledge (2) someone of no account
955 230 younkers to heirs: oddly, "heirs" is pejorative here: a "younker" was a young lord, whereas Sir Rafe implies that Tabitha's only distinction is the money she stands to inherit

SIR WILLIAM Ha? Married? Nurse, how is't within?
FILBON She's very ill, sir, and I fear—
SIR RAFE —That your disguise is known. Come, juggle not:
Call you this "Nurse?" O, thou dissembling boy! [SIR RAFE *discovers* FILBON]
SIR WILLIAM Are you married?
TABITHA Sir, I must needs confess it:
He's my husband. And the reason?[956]
SIR WILLIAM No matter for the reason: I ha' done.[957] God buy ye.[958]
Coneycatched by a trick, and so persuaded good![959]
SIR RAFE I am abused!
SIR WILLIAM Yes, questionless[960] you are; I have all right.
FILBON You have no wrong, sir. I do affirm your word:
"When I was woman and from man, I should."[961] And now
I trust my shape does challenge but[962] your promise. [TUTCH *discovers himself*]
TUTCH I played but "John come kiss me now says she":[963] I am Tutch your *quondam*[964] servant, sir, thrust out to thrust them in.[965] A lawful marriage is no mockery, sir; I counterfeited Welsh to join this const'ring English.

Enter AUDITOR *and his son* TOURES

EARL What, at a gaze,[966] Sir William? Cannot be recalled?[967]
SIR WILLIAM No, no! More mischief? Nay, come all together!
Welcome!
AUDITOR Thank ye, sir.
My son, returned, surrenders to your doom[968]
His life, for yours so lately lost, deputed
In your daughter.[969] For she is dead, sir,
Buried in the Isle of Scilly.
SIR WILLIAM Not amiss;[970]
What's the next, pagan?[971] All the craft[972] of this is known.
TOURES Sir, had I two hearts to melt,
This frozen fear would thaw with passion.
The drops distilled from our tormented brain,
Witnessed by the sailors that interred her,
Knows how I parted with her when she died.
EARL Is mistress Mary dead?
TOURES She is.

956 237 And the reason?: (1) (with startling dismissiveness) and why do you ask? (2) Q's question mark may be emphatic, i.e. "and let me tell you why!"
957 238 I ha' done: I'm through (asking you questions)
958 238 God buy ye: God be with you, i.e. good-bye (said dismissively)
959 239 Sir William may speak in aside or to Tabitha: (1) First they dupe me, and then try to convince me it is for the best! (2) You've been deceived (into marriage), and are now defending it! "Coneycatching" was slang for scamming, by analogy with sprung rabbit (coney) traps; the pronunciation "cunny-catching" also made suggestive reference to the female genitals
960 241 questionless: doubtless
961 243 "When I . . . I should": see II.ii. 71–9
962 244 challenge but: perfectly fulfill the terms of
963 245 "John come . . . says she": title of a popular ballad
964 245 *quondam*: sometime; former (Latin)
965 246 thrust out . . . them in: (1) expelled from your service in order to gain them admission (2) forced onstage in order to force them together (with sexual insinuation)
966 248 at a gaze: in a stupor
967 248 recalled: snapped out of it, restored to lucidity
968 252 doom: judgment, sentence
969 253–4 for yours . . . your daughter: i.e. in exchange for the life you lost that resided in your daughter
970 255 Not amiss: naturally (with sarcasm)
971 256 What's the next, pagan?: what will you tell me next, pagan? (i.e. unbeliever, hence not to be believed)
972 256 craft: trickery, deceit

SIR WILLIAM Well. [*To* EARL] Shall I have justice for her death?
EARL Command it, sir.
SIR WILLIAM To prison with him then: for she is murdered.
Sir, 'cause[973] you knew your rapine[974] and your theft
Tied to your runaway legs that clog,[975]
You were uncertain of her portion
And our love; therefore, to rid that fear,
You rid me thus of her, to me most dear—
My own, my only eldest of my daughters. O!
AUDITOR I'll be his bail.[976]
SIR WILLIAM Sir, tell me not of bail.
For my assurance[977] pleads in his life,
And he shall die.
EARL You have no precedent for that.
SIR WILLIAM Yes: remember Donnington's man Grimes,
Who for an heir so stol'n and marrièd
Was hangèd, and the sergeant-at-arms
For assisting them did lose his place;[978]
[*To* TOURES][979] If this were done, your theft will hardly scape.
EARL I thought of that indeed.

Enter JAMES *and* HUMIL, [HUMIL] *disguised still*[980]

JAMES Murder! Murder! Murder!
EARL Ha? By whom?
JAMES By this fair counterfeit of husband.[981]
Here's my witness, and the deputy
In such a mischief.
SIR WILLIAM Nay then!
JAMES My wife is made away,[982] poisoned here,
And you that should be just are witnesses.
EARL We follow; speak, explain this mystery.
SIR WILLIAM Your wife, sir?
JAMES Yes.
Supposed for dead, as[983] risen from my grave
I came to More-clacke but a little late,
Even when[984] the lying priest did call her thine.
She knew it, and devisèd with her glove
To repossess me of the house she challenged.[985]
So honored, I slept with my own—but, thought

973 266 'cause: because
974 266 rapine: plunder
975 267 clog: heavy block of wood tied to someone's legs to confine them; Sir William accuses Toures of having killed Mary to escape the burden of having kidnapped her
976 272 I'll be his bail: Auditor offers either money for the commutation of Toures's sentence, or himself in his son's place
977 273 assurance: restitution, satisfaction
978 275–8 Donnington's man … his place: Sir William may refer to an actual 1597 case in which one "Dinington" abducted and married a woman; noting that even the accessories to that crime were hanged, he cites it as precedent for charging Toures with a capital offense
979 279 SD *To* TOURES: Sir William views both suitors' crimes as property theft, so he could just as easily direct this line to Filbon, with emphasis on "your"
980 280 SD James may drag Humil/Pothecary onstage to reinforce the illusion that he has confessed, but the fiction is soon dropped
981 282 this fair counterfeit of husband: i.e. Sir William
982 286 made away: gone; stolen from me
983 291 as: as if
984 293 Even when: at the very instant that
985 295 challenged: here, something like "commanded"; "house" cannot be Sir William's, which James never possessed and to which he has no right, so perhaps it means "her body"

The contrary,[986] you know what happenèd.
That son that so betrayed his parents, thus disguised,[987]
Fearing ensuing mischief, wrought by you
To have poisoned his dear mother.
'Twas your bidding: therefore, murder.
But the will of heaven bade otherwise,
And yet she lives. Wife, what say you?

Enter LADY

LADY That all is so.
HUMIL And I affirm it true: [HUMIL *discovers himself*]
My shape cast off does answer, sir, in few.[988]
SIR WILLIAM Pretty,[989] i'faith. [*To* LADY] No marvel you foreswore my bed,
When you had substance for a property.[990]
[*To* JAMES] Sir, you must have your own; who can deny it?
And I must, as the story runs,[991] be mum,
Fooled in myself, by my own slights undone.
But what's this to my daughter? Where is she?
MARY [*Within*] Here, sir.

Enter GOVERNOR, MARY, *and others*[992]

GOVERNOR Brother Vergir.
SIR WILLIAM Brother George from Scilly! What's the news?
GOVERNOR That your dear daughter, dead and buried, sir,
By miracle was thus preserved: which at
More leisure I shall manifest. Pray ye,
Forgive her fault. Come, there's some wanton blood
Left yet says aye;[993] ye will,[994] I know,
And wrongs past all remedy the world must undergo.
MARY My Toures! The dead does live; I am thy wife, Mary.
TOURES Or her ghost; a shadow, or a substance?
TABITHA Sister, I will teach ye medicine
To make a shadow substance. Lie with him
Tonight, as I will with my Filbon,
And by the morning, think but what is past,[995]
And he will rightly reckon[996] you.
He'll hold you three-to-one my med'cine's true.
SIR WILLIAM Methinks I have a tickling in my blood
Crosses[997] all anger. Malediction, hence;
Hence, thou ill-tempered fear:
This comical event seasons the true applause.[998]

986 296–7 thought/The contrary: my sleeping with her being perceived otherwise than lawful
987 298 thus disguised: disguised himself thus
988 305 in few: in few words
989 306 Pretty: i.e. how nice
990 307 substance for a property: source of income or security
991 309 as the story runs: as the saying goes; as this comic situation demands of butts like me
992 312 SD *others*: it is unclear who the "others" are; the scene already prescribes "as many as may be" (73 SD)
993 318–19 there's some . . . says aye: there must still be some youthful whimsy left in you that will allow you to say "yes"
994 319 ye will: i.e. forgive her
995 326 think but what is past: (1) reflect on your experiences (2) considering what you've spent the night doing
996 327 reckon: recognize
997 330 Crosses: i.e. that crosses
998 332 This happy ending makes approval the only appropriate response

Since welcome is the word, i'faith,
I know not what to say; fain I would.[999]
And yet a lazy lagging apprehends
With doubt[1000]—but well I know not what.
In me it lies to punish or to pardon:
I will be generally laughed at once,[1001]
In sooth I will. I am a widower,
Gallants, and you, meet[1002] at marriages
And funerals, so think it[1003] pray ye.
I abridge all compliments,[1004] bar all opponents,[1005]
And resolve to favor you, you, you,[1006]
And challenge from your love persuasion
To this purpose. Since our fate makes us
The world's fond idiot, be it so;
Youth and your fortune was prodigious to[1007] it,
And my best of spirit binds up in[1008] this—
All is but thankless merit.[1009]
EARL [*Coming forward*] Then Epilogue am I.
Imagine all the world were in your house,[1010]
And hearing this report with wond'ring brain;
I thus excuse[1011] it. Gentlemen, you see
How fortune favors in extremity:[1012]
If any botched-up ill have show of good,
And is not in the sequel understood,
Yet bear with all, as this old knight has done,[1013]
Losing a wife, redoubled in a son.
What you shall want in judgement, seeing this,
Think every act is subject to amiss.[1014]
So said, so done, will bring to true delight;
Hands meeting thus,[1015] to sign[1016] this blessèd night.

[*Exeunt*]

FINIS.

999 334 fain I would: I would gladly welcome her
1000 335–6 apprehends/With doubt: fills (me) with doubt
1001 338 once: i.e. presuming to punish or pardon
1002 340 meet: skilled (since he has witnessed three false marriages and the false report of his daughter's death); he reminds them that widowers have experienced weddings and funerals in earnest
1003 341 so think it: i.e. remember that I am a widower
1004 342 abridge all compliments: suspend all ceremonies
1005 342 bar all opponents: renounce all conflicts
1006 343 you, you, you: assuming at least two are Mary and Tabitha, it is unclear who the third is; possibly each "you" indicates a group of characters standing together
1007 347 prodigious to: an omen of; Sir William concedes that youth and luck are irresistible foes
1008 348 binds up in: (1) is summed up by (2) falls short of expressing
1009 349 thankless merit: probably "gifts for which I cannot properly give thanks"
1010 350 Possibly an allusion to the Globe theater (whose "house" fancifully holds "all the world"); if so, this suggests that if the King's Men did not initially perform the play, Armin at least expected them to
1011 352 excuse: apologize for; moralize
1012 353 fortune favors in extremity: i.e. our fortunes often reverse when they are most desperate
1013 354–6 If any … has done: if any evil thing with the appearance of good does not eventually ("in the sequel") expose its true nature, be patient and it will do so. Ironically this maxim describes the opposite of Sir William's experience
1014 358–9 What you … to amiss: (1) even if you lack judgment, seeing this play you will learn that every action is liable to miscarry (2) if your judgment of this play is wanting, think that every act in it was misperformed
1015 361 Hands meeting thus: possibly the actors join hands; more likely, a cue for the audience to applaud
1016 361 sign: seal

13 Anonymous, *The Fair Maid of the Exchange*

First performed c. 1601–02 (?)

First printed 1607

Edited by Genevieve Love

The text of *The Fair Maid of the Exchange* begins with an unusual document: a doubling chart showing how "eleven actors may easily play" the comedy by taking on multiple roles. Some actors, such as the one playing Cripple, are assigned only one part; others have up to four. We know the doubling of parts was a practice in the early modern theater, though only two such printed charts are extant today. Unfortunately, *Fair Maid*'s doubling chart doesn't quite work: on at least one occasion, characters supposed to be played by the same actor appear on stage at the same time. But the framing of this particular play by a doubling chart calls our attention to the ways it is structured, like many comedies, around pairings, parallels, likenesses, exchanges—and to the differences that may lie outside these linked patterns.

A city comedy, *The Fair Maid of the Exchange* is set in what seems to be a contemporary London, and engaged with the interlinked matters of economic and romantic striving. The play's schematic structure is anchored by two young women, Phyllis Flower and Moll Berry, both of whom work as seamstresses in the Exchange, a kind of shopping arcade. Each has parents or a parent—Mistress and Master Flower, and Master Berry—concerned with her plans for marriage. Phyllis, the "fair maid" of the title, is wooed by three brothers, Ferdinand, Anthony, and Frank Golding; Moll by a pair of friends, Bowdler and Bernard. Phyllis and Moll negotiate their marital options in a cityscape cut across by economic rivalries and necessities.

Fair Maid's pairings (or triplings) and parallels may all seem very neat, but their neatness is disrupted (even as it is underwritten) by the play's central character, an unusual figure called Cripple. Cripple, like Phyllis and Moll, works in the Exchange. He has a physical disability—an undefined limb difference in his legs—and uses crutches. Cripple speaks of a time "before the visitation of my legs" (that is, before he acquired this impairment) but, unlike other physically disabled characters in early modern drama, he is not referred to by a proper name. Central to the development and resolution of all the play's plots, he orchestrates the romantic lives of both Phyllis and Moll, through both personal interactions with them and his close relationships with their suitors. His power in the play seems akin to the power of the author: to make the play's conflicts resolve as playgoers are made to feel they properly should. Given that the author of the play remains unknown, Cripple's "authorial" power is especially interesting. His place in the world of the play is enigmatic: as a dedicated laborer in the economic world of the Exchange, he seems both very much a part of that realm and distant from it, orchestrating the play's outcomes but not participating in them. Cripple's disability also links him to the play itself: the apology that ends the Prologue compares the play to a "cripple" in need of playgoers' "alms for charity" in order to flourish. This connection reminds us of his dramaturgical likeness to the role of the author who designs the play's outcomes.

Ideas about similarity and likeness play out all around Cripple. He is the nexus of *Fair Maid*'s interest in a key problem of theatrical representation: unique among art forms, plays use live bodies to represent other bodies. Cripple's job in the Exchange is to provide grounds for representational similitude: he is a "drawer," which means he traces patterns on cloth for others to complete in embroidery. The play also suggests a linkage between doubleness and his disability. His prosthetic crutches give him four legs rather than two, suggesting that his is a kind of double body, like the theatrical body that is always both actor and character. Finally, and perhaps most importantly, Cripple becomes the site of imitation when Frank needs to impersonate him in order to succeed in wooing Phyllis. The play begins with events that set up a pair of debts. Phyllis is attacked by two thieves and Cripple rescues her; the thieves then attack Cripple, and Frank comes to the rescue. The three become bound in debt: Phyllis to Cripple, a debt she feels as romantic attachment, and Cripple to Frank, a bond that will reach its apotheosis in the strange episode in which Frank impersonates Cripple to express his desire for Phyllis. Since Phyllis has loved Cripple since the play's opening scene, the only way for the comedy's apparent romantic hero to win her is to take on the persona of Cripple.

The play's elevation of a disabled character, and in particular its placement of disability as a crucial site of imitation, is one of its most intriguing features. In recent years, critical interest in the play has focused on Cripple as a central early modern disability representation. He is economically successful, known and liked by nearly all the characters in the play, and desired (almost) to the end by Phyllis. On the other hand, the play's conclusion seems to erase him. He enters the final scene desiring to speak with Phyllis, but is never answered and never speaks again; Phyllis seems silently to acquiesce to marrying Frank even once he's not in disguise as Cripple. Whether the play presents a powerful figure of a disabled person, or exploits disability as a performed state rather than an element of lived experience, or both, is a matter for debate. Of course, Frank's theatrical imitation of disability echoes the practice of the play itself, as the role of Cripple was presumably performed by an able-bodied actor. A relationship between disability and imitation reverberates through many layers of the play's story and its imagination of itself as a theatrical event.

The play's interest in both imagination and the repetitions and doublings creative representation involves is reflected in Master Flower's refrain, one which he begins almost as soon as he enters the play: "it is a good conceit." What he means by the phrase, which he uses to refer to many things, is that something is a cool idea, a sound plan. The linkage of "conceit" to ideas and planning reminds us of Cripple's role in the play: he seems to be the only one with long-term plans, or the ability to carry them out. Another meaning of "conceit," as a fanciful turn of thought or metaphor, echoes the play's interest in playful doublings and figurations. We might say that the play explores the many things "good conceit" might be: a fine idea, an ingenious representation, a cutting letter, an appropriate imitation. The play's last lines express Master Flower finding one of his "good conceits"—his supplying of a loan to the false "Captain Racket"—bringing him "to infamy." In comedy, outlandish, fanciful ideas often lead to unexpected success. This play ends with a kind of debunking of that idea. That might make us wonder: what about Frank's imitation of Cripple? Is this a good conceit, an apposite metaphor? Or is it infamy, borrowing the signs of Cripple's identity only to dispense with them after gaining sympathy?

Master Flower's pleasure in the kind of verbal wit suggested by "a good conceit"—often matched and elevated by Fiddle's rhetorical engagement with whatever he says—suggests the degree to which the play takes an interest in the verbal exchange of wit. Alongside the economic exchange of goods and money and the theatrical exchange of disguise, characters exchange language. One of Cripple's most significant relationships in the play is with his friend Bowdler. They enter the play bantering, and most of their scenes are taken up with back-and-forth exchanges that don't really advance the plot but that suggest a long-term, ongoing relationship based in part around the trading of insults, some of them anti-Semitic. As Jean Howard notes, Bowdler deploys a number of abusive terms that relate Cripple to Judaism ("dog," "dog of Israel," "cur," and reference to his "nose"). Cripple is also associated with provident business as against improvident Christian social behavior—for example, the dance that Bowdler and Bernard pressure Cripple to join them in attending in II.ii—a distinction that echoes other plays of the period featuring Jewish people, such as *The Merchant of Venice*.

Cripple doesn't seem to acknowledge the anti-Semitism or the ableism of Bowdler's insults, but instead deflects them and other slurs directed at him by returning to any of his various labors in the play: his work pattern-drawing in the Exchange, his work orchestrating the play's matters of marital exchange. In the end, despite what seems to be a close bond of friendship with Bowdler, Cripple orchestrates the marriage of Moll to Bernard rather than Bowdler: why? Cripple, like other vaguely omniscient outsider figures in plays of the period, such as Moll Cutpurse in *The Roaring Girl*, seems to be motivated to preserve existing class distinctions; he assists rising members of the moneyed middle class such as Master Berry in their economic victimization of wastrel debtor gallants such as Bernard. A side benefit for Cripple, perhaps, is that Bowdler will remain available for their homosocial exchanges of wit—which stand in contrast to Bowdler's failed ones with Moll.

Cripple's strange manipulation of Moll to choose Bernard over Bowdler—seemingly unmotivated by her in any way, and involving peculiar claims that are hard to reconcile within the world of the play—raises the question of the power of the play's young women against Cripple's dramaturgical power and the patriarchal aims with which his authorial power may be aligned. Phyllis and Moll seem to operate quite independently of their parents: we see them alone, doing business, relating to others for most of the play, before we ever see them with their parents. We see Moll master Bowdler rhetorically and Phyllis master her shop, including with physical threats to her boy servant. Yet in the end their fates seem to be at the whims of Cripple, who reinforces the generic insistence that comedies end in marriage. Phyllis must marry Frank, because he is clearly the hero; Moll must marry Bernard rather than Bowdler because that will have the plot-friendly result of absolving Bernard's unfortunate debt to Moll's father. To the degree that Moll and Phyllis both end up in marriages toward which their independent actions do not seem to have been leading, we are reminded of the possibility that women may be treated as commodities similar to the articles they vend at their places of work. To what degree is the "fair maid" Phyllis a participant in the Exchange, and to what degree is she herself an object of exchange—if not by her parents, then at the hands of plotty Cripple?

Cripple seems capable of managing many forms of exchange. In addition to his successful business in the Exchange and his management of marital exchanges, he also exercises control over the movement of letters—of textual fragments—in the play. *The Fair Maid of the Exchange* includes several kinds of letters: the real love letters written from Anthony and Ferdinand to Phyllis, which never get delivered; the wooing letters written to Phyllis's parents by the same two; the false letters from Phyllis rebuffing their love. Important in this mix, and explained in an unusual soliloquy, is Cripple's apparent possession of a portfolio of all-purpose letters. His ownership of these texts seems to reflect and mark his ownership of the play itself. He's in control of both verbal and written texts, and the interface between them, a control that reflects his work in the Exchange, tracing patterns based on verbal instructions that will later become physically rendered.

These correspondences themselves are rendered in different ways in early texts of the play—sometimes in italics, introduced with "A Letter"; sometimes in quotation marks—differences preserved in this edition. The differences in textual presentation serve to remind us not only of the unstable and variable state of the early text, but of the differing status of letters in the play. Like the paratextual material of the Prologue and doubling chart, the play's letters—set apart typographically from the play's dialogue—are both part and not-part of its text. In this they are like Cripple himself, so central to the play's action and movements and yet silenced and, though on stage, seemingly disregarded at its end. He is thus also perhaps akin to the technology of his pattern-drawing, in which he draws fine dots using a powder that can be traced, after which it can be blown away. Is Cripple, like this powder, dispelled from the play? If so, perhaps his pattern, a powerful model for early modern disabled embodiment, remains.

Textual note

The copy-text for this edition is the EEBO copy of the quarto of 1607 held in the Henry E. Huntington Library. While the playtext proper in the quarto begins with the heading "Scene. I.," the play as printed in Q is otherwise undivided into acts or scenes. This edition divides the play into acts and scenes in accord with a conventional five-act structure.

Further reading

Editions

Snyder, Karl (ed.) (1980) *A Critical Edition of The Faire Maid of the Exchange, by Thomas Heywood*, New York: Garland.

Critical and contextual reading

Baker, Naomi (2016) "'Happy, and Without a Name': Prosthetic Identities on the Early Modern Stage," *Textual Practice* 30: 1309–26.

Green, Juana (2000) "The Sempster's Wares: Merchandising and Marrying in *The Fair Maid of the Exchange* (1607)," *Renaissance Quarterly* 53: 1084–118.

Howard, Jean (2006) *Theatre of a City: The Places of London Comedy* 1598–1642, Philadelphia: University of Pennsylvania Press.

Love, Genevieve (2018) *Early Modern Theatre and the Figure of Disability*, London: Bloomsbury.

Row-Heyveld, Lindsay (2013) "Disability and Masculine Commerce in *The Fair Maid of the Exchange*," *Allegorica* 29: 88–105.

Waswo, Richard (2004) "Crises of Credit: Monetary and Erotic Economies in the Jacobean Theater," in Dieter Mehl, Angela Stock and Anne-Julia Zwierlein (eds), *Plotting Early Modern London: New Essays on Jacobean City Comedy*, Burlington: Ashgate, 55–73.

Williams, Katherine Schaap (2015) "'More Legs Than Nature Gave Thee': Performing Cripple in *The Fair Maid of the Exchange*," *English Literary History* 82: 491–519.

The Fair Maid of the Exchange (c. 1601–2)

Eleven may easily act this comedy[1]

MASTER BERRY, *an old man* BOBBINGTON, *a thief* RICHARD GARDINER, *a young gentleman* OFFICERS	For one
MOLL BERRY, *Master Berry's daughter*	For one
MASTER FLOWER, *a humorous*[2] *old man* WILLIAM BENNET, *a young gentleman* SCARLET, *a thief* RALPH, *Bowdler's servant*	For one
CRIPPLE	For one
BERNARD, *a gentleman* MISTRESS FLOWER, *Master Flower's wife* BOY, PHYLLIS' *servant* URSULA, PHYLLIS' *assistant*	For one
ANTHONY GOLDING, *gentleman, brother of Ferdinand and Frank*	For one
FERDINAND GOLDING, *gentleman, brother of Anthony and Frank* MASTER WOOD	For one
FRANK GOLDING, *gentleman, brother of Anthony and Ferdinand*	For one
BOWDLER, *a humorous gallant*[3]	For one
PHYLLIS FLOWER, *the fair maid, daughter of Master and Mistress Flower*	For one
FIDDLE, *the clown, servant to Master Flower*	For one

1 Eleven may . . . this comedy: the cast list in the 1607 Quarto (given here with some additional information to clarify relationships in the play) shows the breakdown of roles among actors; so, for example, one actor plays Master Berry, Bobbington, Gardiner, and Officers, and one actor plays only Moll Berry. Some of the doublings given here don't work: for example, Mistress Flower and Bernard are on stage together in the final scene, as are Master Berry and Officers

2 *humorous*: whimsical, odd

3 *gallant*: young man of fashion and pleasure; a ladies' man

Prologue

The humble sock[4] that true comedians wear
Our muse hath donned, and to your favoring eyes,
In lowest plainsong[5] doth herself appear,
Borrowing no colors from a quaint[6] disguise.
If your fair favors cause her spirit to rise,
She to the highest pitch her wings shall rear,
And proud cothurnic[7] action shall devise,
To win your sweet applause she deems so dear.

Meanwhile shore up our tender pamping twig,[8]
That yet on humble ground doth lowly lie.
Your favor's sunshine gilding once this sprig,
It may yield nectar for the gods on high.
Though our invention lame imperfect be,
Yet give the cripple[9] alms for charity.[10]

Exit

[Act I, scene i]

Enter SCARLET *and* BOBBINGTON

SCARLET Even now the welcome twilight doth salute
Th' approaching night, clad in black sable weeds:[11]
Black as my thoughts, that harbor naught but death,
Thefts, murders, rapes, and suchlike damnèd acts,
The infant babes to whom my soul is nurse.
Come, Bobbington, this star-bespangled sky
Bodeth[12] some good: the weather's fair and dry.
BOBBINGTON My scarlet-hearted Scarlet, gallant blood,
Whose bloody deeds are worthy memory
Of after-ages, let me embrace thee. So,
So, now methinks I fold[13] a richer gem
Than wealthy India can afford to Spain.
There lies my treasure, and within thy arms
Security that never breedeth harms.
SCARLET Brave resolution! I am proud to see
So sweet a graft upon a wormwood tree,[14]
Whose juice is gall, but yet the fruit most rare.
Who recks[15] the tree, if that the fruit be fair?

4 1 sock: thin-soled shoe, ancient symbol of comedy
5 3 lowest plainsong: most humble, simplest melody
6 4 quaint: elaborate
7 7 cothurnic: tragic, from *cothurnus*, the thick-soled boot that is the ancient symbol for tragedy. The author seems to be promising that if this comic play is successful, he will write a tragedy next
8 9 shore up . . . pamping twig: prop up this immature, vulnerable play; "pamping" means tendril-like, as the young shoot of a vine
9 13–14 our invention . . . the cripple: both "invention" and "cripple" refer to the play itself. The metaphorical use of disability anticipates the appearance of Cripple, the play's central character
10 14 alms for charity: i.e. applause
11 2 black sable weeds: dark clothing
12 7 Bodeth: portends
13 11 fold: enclose
14 16 Such admirable behavior in a disreputable person
15 18 recks: cares about

Therefore, resolve: if we a booty[16] get,
It boots not[17] whence, from whom, when, where, or what.
BOBBINGTON Well (God forgive us) here let's take our stands.
We must have gold although we have no lands.

Enter PHYLLIS *and* URSULA

PHYLLIS Stay, Ursula. Have you those suits of ruffs,
Those stomachers, and that fine piece of lawn
Marked with the letters double C and S?[18]
URSULA I have.
PHYLLIS If your forgetfulness cause any defect,
You're like to pay for't; therefore look unto it.
URSULA I would our journey had as safe an end,
As I am sure my lady's ruffs are here,
And other wares which she bespoke of[19] you.
PHYLLIS 'Tis good. But stay; give me thy hand, my girl.
'Tis somewhat dark; come, let us help each other.
She passed her word one of her gentlemen
Should meet us at the bridge, and that's not far.
I muse they are not come.[20] I do assure thee,
Were I not much beholding to her ladyship
For many kindnesses, Mile-End[21] should stand
This gloomy night unvisited for[22] us.
But come! Methinks I may discern the bridge,
And see a man or two. In very deed
Her word, her love, and all is honorable.
BOBBINGTON [*Aside to* SCARLET] A prize, young Scarlet! Oh, a gallant prize.
And we are pirates that will seize the same
To our own uses.
SCARLET But hold, man, not too fast:
As far as I can gather by their words,
They take us for my lady's[23] gentlemen,
Who, as it seems, should meet them on their way.
Then, if thou sayest the word, we'll seem[24] those men,
And by those means withdraw them from their way,
Where we may rifle them of[25] what they carry:
I mean both goods and their virginity.
BOBBINGTON 'Tis well-advised. But, Scarlet, give me leave
To play the gentleman and welcome them.
SCARLET Enjoy thy wish.
BOBBINGTON [*To* PHYLLIS *and* URSULA] Welcome, you sacred stars,
That add bright glory to the sable night.
SCARLET [*Aside*] Excellent, by heaven.

16 19 booty: money or goods taken in a robbery
17 20 boots not: doesn't matter
18 23–5 suits of . . . and S: decorative clothing pieces Phyllis and Ursula are to deliver: neck ruffs (frilly detachable neckpieces) with matching wrist cuffs, ornamental coverings for the bodices of womens' garments, and delicate linen embroidered with, perhaps, initials
19 31 bespoke of: ordered from
20 36 muse they are not come: wonder why they haven't arrived
21 38 Mile-End: a suburb of London
22 39 for: by
23 47 my lady's: i.e. Phyllis's customer's
24 49 seem: pretend to be
25 51 rifle them of: steal from them

BOBBINGTON I am sorry your beauty's so discomfited,[26]
Treading so many tedious, weary steps,
And we not present to associate[27] you.
SCARLET [*Aside*] Oh, blessed Bobbington.
PHYLLIS Sir, I do thank you for this taken pains:
That, as your worthy lady promised me,
We now enjoy your wishèd company.
SCARLET [*Aside*] She's thine own, boy, I warrant thee.
BOBBINGTON And I am proud, too proud, of this employment.
Come, Master Scarlet, take you that pretty sweet.
You see my lady's care: she promised one
But hath sent two.
PHYLLIS 'Tis honorably done.
BOBBINGTON This is your way.
PHYLLIS That way? Alas, sir, no.
BOBBINGTON Come, it is. Nay, then! It shall be so.
PHYLLIS What mean you, gentlemen?
URSULA Oh, he will rob me.
PHYLLIS Look to the box,[28] Ursula.
PHYLLIS AND URSULA Help, help! Murder, murder!

Enter the CRIPPLE

CRIPPLE Now, you supporters[29] of decrepit[30] youth,
That mount this substance 'twixt fair heaven and earth,
Be strong to bear that huge deformity.[31]
And be my hands as nimble to direct them,[32]
As your desires to waft[33] me hence to London.
PHYLLIS AND URSULA Help, help! He'll ravish me!
CRIPPLE Methinks I hear the sound of ravishment.
PHYLLIS AND URSULA Help, help!
CRIPPLE Marry, and will, knew I but where and how.
What do I see?
Thieves full of lust beset[34] virginity!
Now stir thee, Cripple, and of thy four legs[35]
Make use of one to do a virgin good.
Hence, ravening curs![36] What, are you at a prey?
Will nothing satisfy your greedy chaps[37]
But virgin's flesh? I'll teach you prey on carrion.[38]
Pack,[39] damnèd ravishers! Hence, villains! *Fight & beat them away*
PHYLLIS Thanks, honest friend, who from the gates of death
Hath set our virgin souls at liberty.

26 58 discomfited: uneasy
27 60 associate: escort
28 73 box: money-box
29 75 you supporters: Cripple addresses his crutches
30 75 decrepit: enfeebled
31 76–7 this substance . . . that huge deformity: both refer to Cripple's body
32 78 them: i.e. the crutches
33 79 waft: convey
34 85 beset: attack
35 86 four legs: two legs and two crutches
36 88 ravening curs: bloodthirsty, worthless dogs
37 89 chaps: jaws
38 90 carrion: rotting flesh
39 91 Pack: be off

CRIPPLE Give God the glory that gave me the power.
PHYLLIS I do, kind sir, and think myself much bound
To him above, to thee that treads this ground.
And for this aid I'll ever honor thee.
My honor you have saved, redeemed it home,[40]
Which, were't not done, by this time had been gone.
CRIPPLE Hereafter more of this. But tell me now
The cause of these events, the effect, and how.
PHYLLIS I'll tell you, sir. But let us leave this place,
And onward on our way.

Enter SCARLET *and* BOBBINGTON

BOBBINGTON [*Aside to* SCARLET] It shall be so. See where they walk along?
I'll cross the other way and meet them full.[41]
Keep thou this way, and when thou hear'st us chat,
Come thou behind him, snatch away his crutches,
And then thou know'st he needs must fall to ground.
And what shall follow, leave the rest to me. *Exit* BOBBINGTON
SCARLET [*Aside*] About it, then.
CRIPPLE I' faith she is an honorable lady,
And I much wonder that her ladyship
Gives entertain to[42] such bad men as these.

Enter BOBBINGTON

BOBBINGTON Stand thou, that hast more legs than nature gave thee!
CRIPPLE Mongrel, I'll choose.[43]
SCARLET Then go to,[44] sir, you shall.
ALL Murder, murder!

Enter FRANK *Golding*

FRANK Stay there, my horse.
Whence comes this echo of extremity?
ALL Help, help!
FRANK What do I hear, a virgin call for help?
Hands off, damned villains, or by heaven I swear
I'll send you all to hell. *Fight and drive them away*
CRIPPLE Hold, forbear!
I came in rescue of virginity.
PHYLLIS He did, he did, and freed us once from thrall.[45]
But now, the second time, they wrought[46] his fall.
FRANK Now, you distressèd objects, do you tell
Upon what mount of woe your sorrows dwell.
PHYLLIS First get we hence away, and, as we go,
Kind gentleman, our fortunes you shall know.
CRIPPLE Thanks, worthy sir. May but the cripple be

40 98 home: completely
41 105 full: directly
42 113 Gives entertain to: maintains in her service
43 115 choose: do what I like
44 115 Then go to: all right, then
45 124 thrall: captivity
46 125 wrought: caused

Of power to gratify this courtesy,
I then shall think the heavens favor me.
PHYLLIS No more now. For God's sake, let us hence!
CRIPPLE If I do live, your love I'll recompense.[47]

Exeunt

[Act I, scene ii]

Enter MOLL *Berry*

MOLL Now, for my true love's handkercher: these flowers
Are pretty toys,[48] are very pretty toys.
Oh, but methinks the peascod would do better:
The peascod and the blossom,[49] wonderful!
Now, as I live, I'll surely have it so.
Some maids will choose the gillyflower, some the rose,
Because their sweet scents do delight the nose;
But very fools they are, in my opinion.
The very worst, being drawn by cunning art,
Seems in the eye as pleasant to the heart.[50]
But here's the question: whether my love, or no,
Will seem content? Aye, there the game doth go.
And yet I'll pawn my head[51] he will applaud
The peascod and the flower, my pretty choice.
For what is he, loving a thing in heart,
Loves[52] not the counterfeit,[53] though made by art?
I cannot tell how others' fancies stand,
But I rejoice sometime to take in hand
The simile[54] of that I love. And, I protest,
That pretty peascod likes my humor[55] best.
But I'll unto the drawer's;[56] he'll counsel me.
Here is his shop. Alas, what shall I do?
He's not within; now all my labor's lost.
See, see, how forward[57] love is ever crossed.[58]
But stay, what gallant's this?

Enter Master BOWDLER

BOWDLER A plague on this drawer! He's never at home.
Good morrow, sweetheart. Tell me how thou dost?
MOLL Upon what acquaintance?[59]

47 134 recompense: repay
48 2 toys: trifling, foolish amusements
49 4 peascod and the blossom: Moll's choice of pea-pod and pea's blossom as the decorations to be embroidered on the handkerchief for her "true love" refers both to a rustic custom of the pea-pod as a love-token and to the male and female genitalia: the man's "pod" and the woman's "blossom"; "peascod" is also an inversion of "codpiece," an ornamental article of clothing meant to emphasize the male genitals
50 6–10 Some maids . . . the heart: since embroidered decorations don't give off scents, Moll muses, girls are foolish to select visual ornaments based on the good smells of real flowers; all embroidered flowers, no matter how their real-life counterparts smell, are beautiful
51 13 pawn my head: bet my virginity (maidenhead)
52 16 Loves: i.e. That loves
53 16 counterfeit: picture, image
54 19 simile: likeness
55 20 likes my humor: matches my inclination
56 21 drawer's: the pattern-drawer's shop. Pattern-drawers sketched designs on cloth, outlines that could then be embroidered
57 24 forward: bold
58 24 crossed: frustrated
59 28 Upon what acquaintance?: based on what relationship?

BOWDLER That's all one,[60] once I love thee. Give me thy hand, and say amen.
MOLL Hands off, sir knave, and wear it for a favor.[61]
BOWDLER What? Dost thou mean thy love, pretty fool?
MOLL No, fool! [*Aside*] The knave. Oh gross!
A gentleman and of so shallow wit!
BOWDLER I know thou cam'st to the drawer.
MOLL —How then?
BOWDLER Am I not the properer man?
MOLL Yes, to make an ass on.
BOWDLER Will you get up and ride?
MOLL No, I'll lackey[62] by his side, and whip the ass.
BOWDLER Come, come, leave your jesting. I shall put you down.[63]
MOLL With that face? Away, you want-wit.
BOWDLER By this hand, I shall.
MOLL By this[64] ass-head, you shall not.
BOWDLER Go to, you are a woman.
MOLL Come, come, ye are a man.
BOWDLER I have seen as fair.
MOLL I have heard as wise.
BOWDLER As fair as Moll Berry.
MOLL As wise as young Bowdler.
BOWDLER As Master Bowdler.
MOLL Heyday, come up.
BOWDLER Go thou down, [65] then.
MOLL No, good ass, bate an ace of that.[66]

Enter BERNARD

BERNARD What, Master Bowdler, will it ne'er be otherwise?
Still, still a-hunting; every day wenching?
BOWDLER Faith, sir, the modest behavior of this gentlewoman
Hath insinuated my company.[67]
MOLL Lord, how eloquence flows in this gentleman!
BOWDLER Faith, I shall put you down[68] in talk. You were best to yield.
MOLL No, sir, I will hold out as long as I may,
Though in the end you bear the fool away.[69]
BOWDLER Mean you by me? You gull[70] me not?
MOLL No, by this night, not I.
BOWDLER For if you did,[71] it would intoxicate my head.
MOLL Yea, I dare swear you'll go a fool to bed.
BOWDLER Mean you by me? You gull me not?
BERNARD No, I dare swear the gentlewoman means well.
MOLL And so I do indeed, himself can tell.

60 29 That's all one: it doesn't matter
61 30 wear it for a favor: show the mark of my hand as a token of my affection (i.e. I'll slap you)
62 38 lackey: do service as a lackey, e.g. attend on, run errands for
63 36–9 make an . . . you down: in this exchange, Bowdler responds to Moll's insults with sexual suggestions
64 42 this: i.e. your
65 50–51 come up . . . thou down: in this exchange, Moll challenges Bowdler to keep "up" his witticisms, and he responds with another sexual suggestion that she lie "down"
66 52 bate an ace of that: an expression of incredulity, "forget that"
67 56 insinuated my company: charmed me
68 58 put you down: defeat you
69 60 bear the fool away: since fools were often depicted riding an ass, she is again calling him an ass
70 61 gull: dupe, deceive
71 63 if you did: if you did let me bear you away (sexually)

But this it is: speak maidens what they will,
Men are so captious,[72] they'll ever conster ill.[73]
BERNARD To her, sir, to her! I dare swear she loves you.
BOWDLER Well then, fair Moll, you love me as you say.
MOLL I never made you promise; did I, pray?
BOWDLER All in good time. You will do, else you lie!
Will you not?
MOLL No, forsooth, not I.
BOWDLER Bernard, she gulls me still.
BERNARD 'Tis but your misconceit;[74] try her again.
You know by course all women must be coy.
To her again; then she may haply[75] yield.
BOWDLER Not I, in faith.
MOLL Then mine shall be the field.[76]
Wisdom, adieu. Once more, faint heart, farewell.
Yet if thou seest the drawer, I prithee[77] tell him
Moll Berry hath more work for him to do.
And for yourself, learn this when you do woo:
Arm you with courage, and with good take-heed,[78]
For he that spares to speak must spare to speed.[79]
And so farewell. *Exit*
BOWDLER Call her again, Bernard.
BERNARD She's too swift for me.
Why, this is the right course of gullery.[80]
What did you mean, having so fair an aim
So fondly to let slip so fair a game?[81]
Bowdler, become a man, for maids will stand,[82]
And then strike home.[83] Art thou not young and lusty,
The minion of delight, fair from thy birth,
Adonis's playfere,[84] and the pride of earth?
BOWDLER I know it, but a kind of honest blood
Tilts[85] in my loins with wanton appetites.
She bade me do a message to the drawer,
And I will do it. There will come a day
When Humphrey Bowdler will keep holiday.[86]
Then, Moll, look to yourself; see that you be sped,[87]
Or by this light I'll have your maidenhead.
BERNARD Spoke like a gallant, spoke like a gentleman, spoke like yourself!
Now do I see some sparks of manhood in you:

72 69 captious: disposed to find fault
73 69 conster ill: infer the worst
74 76 misconceit: misunderstanding
75 78 haply: perhaps
76 79 mine shall be the field: I win
77 81 prithee: pray you
78 84 good take-heed: good sense, prudence
79 85 speed: succeed
80 88 right course of gullery: the way trickery works
81 90 So foolishly let such a nice piece of prey escape
82 91 stand: assume a defensive position
83 92 strike home: make an effective thrust with a weapon
84 94 Adonis's playfere: the playmate of Adonis, the archetype of a handsome young man
85 96 Tilts: combats
86 99 keep holiday: take a day off
87 100 sped: prepared

Keep in that key, keep in the self-same song;
I'll gage[88] my head you'll have her love ere long.

Exeunt

[Act I, scene iii]

Enter FERDINAND *and* FRANK

FRANK Wilt thou not tell me, brother Ferdinand?
Now, by this light, I'll haunt thee like a sprite[89]
Until I know whence springs this melancholy.
FERDINAND Oh, brother!
Thou art too young to reach the depth of grief
That is immured[90] within my heart's deep closet.
A thousand sighs keep daily sentinel
That beat like whirlwinds all my comfort back;
As many sobs guard my distressèd heart,
That no relief comes near to aid my soul.
Millions of woes, like bands of armèd men
Stop up the passage of my sweet relief.
And art thou then persuaded that thy words
Can any comfort to my soul afford?
No, no, good Frank. Dear brother, then forbear,[91]
Unless with grief in me you'll take a share.
FRANK Grief me no griefs,[92] but tell me what it is
Makes[93] my sweet Ferdinand thus passionate.
I'll conjure grief,[94] if grief be such an evil,
In spite of fortune, fates, or any devil.
FERDINAND Wilt thou not leave me to myself alone?
FRANK Brother, you know my mind.
If you will leave your dumpish melancholy,
And, like myself, banish that puling humor,[95]
Or satisfy my expectation
By telling whence your sorrow doth proceed,
I will not only cease to trouble you,
But, like a true skillful physician,
Seek all good means for your recovery.
FERDINAND Well, brother, you have much importuned me,[96]
And for the confidence I have in you
That you'll prove secret, I will now unfold
The load of care that presseth down my soul.
Know then, good Frank, love is the cause thereof.
FRANK How, love? Why, what's that love?
FERDINAND A child. A little, little boy that's blind.[97]
FRANK And be o'ercome by him! Plagued by him!

88 105 gage: bet
89 2 sprite: spirit, ghost
90 6 immured: walled
91 15 forbear: refrain
92 17 Grief me no griefs: don't talk to me about grief
93 18 Makes: that makes
94 19 conjure grief: make grief disappear
95 24 puling humor: whiny, childish mood
96 30 much importuned me: asked me persistently
97 36 A little . . . that's blind: i.e. Cupid, the god of desire and attraction

Driven into dumps[98] by him! Put down by a boy!
Mastered by love? Oh, I am mad for anger.
By a boy!
Is there no rosemary and bays in England
To whip the ape?[99] By a boy!
FERDINAND Aye, such a boy as thou canst never see,
And yet ere long may'st feel his tyranny.
He's not visible, yet aims at the heart;
Woe be to those that feel his wounding dart.[100]
And one of them I am: wounded so deep,
That in my passions I no mean[101] can keep.
Unhappy time, woe to that dismal hour,
When love did wound me with fair Phyllis Flower.
Oh, Phyllis, Phyllis, of flowers sweetest flower
That ever garnished any princely bower![102]
Farewell, farewell, my woes will ne'er remove,
Till I enjoy fair Phyllis for my love. *Exit*
FRANK What's here?[103] Phyllis and love, and love and Phyllis!
I have seen Phyllis, and have heard of love;
I will see Phyllis and will hear of love.
But neither Phyllis, nor the power of love,
Shall make me bondslave to a woman's beck.[104]

Enter ANTHONY

Who's here, my second brother malcontent?[105]
I'll stand aside and note his passions.
ANTHONY Oh, love, that I had never known thy power.
FRANK [*Aside*] More lovers yet! What the devil is this love?
ANTHONY That[106] these my wandering eyes had kept their stay;
That I myself had still been like myself;
That my poor heart had never felt the wound
Whose anguish keeps me in a deadly sound.[107]
Oh, how deluding dreams, this night o'erpassed,[108]
Drenched my sad soul in pleasure's floating sea!
Methought I clasped my love within my arms,
And, circling her, saved her from threatening harms.
Methought there came an hundred in an hour
That sought to rob me of my sweetest flower.
But, like a champion, I did keep her still
Within this circle,[109] free from every ill.
But when I waked and missed my Phyllis there,

98 38 dumps: depression
99 41–2 no rosemary . . . the ape: rosemary and bay leaves are symbols of constancy and victory, respectively. Frank suggests that Ferdinand "should be brought back to his normal attitude toward life by chastising him with rosemary (reminding him that he should be constant to his own self) and bays (reminding him to be victorious over his passions)" (Snyder, 1980)
100 46 dart: arrow
101 48 mean: moderation
102 52 bower: a shady recess, overarched with branches or shrubs
103 55 What's here?: what's all this about?
104 59 bondslave to a woman's beck: complete servant to a woman's will
105 60 malcontent: discontented
106 64 That: i.e. I wish that
107 67 deadly sound: death-like swoon
108 68 this night o'erpassed: last night
109 75 this circle: the embrace of my arms

All my sweet joys converted into fear.
FRANK What, brother Anthony, at prayers so hard?
Tell me what saint it is thou invocat'st?[110]
Is it a male, or female? Howsoever,
God bless thee, brother, th' art in a good mind;
But now I remember me, thy saint is blind.
ANTHONY How, blind?
FRANK Aye, brother, blind. I heard thee talk of love,
And love is blind, they say.
ANTHONY I would[111] it were as blind as ebon[112] night,
That love had never hit my heart so right.
But what is love, in your opinion?
FRANK A voluntary motion[113] of delight,
Touching the superficies[114] of the soul.
A substance less divine than is the soul,
Yet more than any other power in man,
Is that which loves; yet neither is enforced,
Nor doth enforce the heart of man to love.[115]
Which motion, as it unbeseems a man,
So by the soul and reason which adorn
The life of man, it is extinguishèd,
Even at his pleasure that it doth possess.[116]
ANTHONY Thus may the free man jest at manacles,[117]
The fur-clad citizen laugh at a storm,
The swarthy Moor,[118] diving to gather pearl,
Challenge the scalding ardor of the sun,
And agèd Nestor,[119] sitting in his tent,
May term wounds sport, and war but merriment.
FRANK 'Tis true, 'fore God it is, and now methinks
My heart begins to pity hearts in love.
Say once more, Anthony: tell me thy griefs,
Let me have feeling of thy passion,
Possess me deeply of thy melting[120] state,
And thou shalt see—
ANTHONY That thou wilt pity me.
FRANK No, by my troth, if ever a tale of love,
Or love itself, or fool-bewitching beauty
Make me cross-arm myself, study ah-mes,
Defy my hat-band, tread beneath my feet
Shoe-strings and garters, practice in my glass
Distressèd looks, and dry my liver up
With sighs enough to wind an argosy[121]—

110 79 invocat'st: call in prayer
111 86 would: wish
112 86 ebon: black
113 89 motion: emotion; show, illusion
114 90 superficies: surface
115 93–4 neither is . . . to love: love can't be controlled, but also can't force us to its ways
116 95–8 Which motion . . . doth possess: the force of love ("Which motion"), when it makes a man act foolishly ("unbeseems a man"), can be extinguished at will ("at his pleasure") if he uses reason ("that it doth possess")
117 99 manacles: shackles for the hands
118 101 Moor: person from North Africa, now Morocco and part of Algeria
119 103 Nestor: member of the Greek army in Homer's *Iliad*, famed for his age and wisdom
120 109 melting: emotionally tender
121 113–17: Make me . . . an argosy: Frank describes the typical habits and appearance of a melancholy lover: with crossed arms, the archetypal lover sighs ("ah-me") and makes mopey faces in the mirror ("glass"). His sighs are so forceful they could power (by their "wind") a large ship ("argosy"). "The

If ever I turn thus fantastical,[122]
Love plague me; never pity me at all.

Enter PHYLLIS

ANTHONY Yonder she comes that holds me prisoner.
FRANK What? Phyllis, the fair maid of the Exchange?
Is she god Cupid's judge over men's hearts?
Brother, I'll have one venny[123] with her tongue,
To breathe my wit and jest at passion.
By your leave, Mistress Flower.
PHYLLIS Your rude behavior scarce offers you welcome.
FRANK I prithee tell me, Phyllis: I hear say
Thou keepest love captive in thy maiden thoughts.
PHYLLIS That is a thought beyond your reach to know.
FRANK But shall I know it?
PHYLLIS On what acquaintance? Then might you deem me fond,[124]
If, as you say, love be at my command.
FRANK May not your friend command as great a matter?
PHYLLIS I'll know him well first, for that friend may flatter.
FRANK Why, I hope you know me.
PHYLLIS That's a question.
FRANK Well, if you do not, you shall before I stir.[125]
Know you yonder lump of melancholy,
Yonder bundle of sighs, yonder wad[126] of groans?
The same and I were chickens of one brood.
And if you know him, as I am sure you do,
Being his brother, you needs must know me too.
PHYLLIS I partly have a guess of yonder gentleman.
His name is Master Golding, as I take it.
ANTHONY Golding I am, and thine, sweet fair, I am.
And yet not thine, but a most wretched man.
Thou knowest my cause of grief, my wound of woe.
And, knowing it, why wilt thou see it so?
Put salves of comfort to my grief's unrest,
So may'st thou heal my sore of heaviness.
FRANK Hark you, fair maid: are you a surgeon?
I prithee, give my brother Anthony
Somewhat[127] to heal the love-sore of his mind.
And yet 'tis pity that he should have help.
A man as free as air, or the sun's rays,
As boundless in his function as the heavens,
The male and better part of flesh and blood,
In whom was poured the quintessence[128] of reason,
To wrong the adoration of his maker
By worshipping a wanton female skirt

hatband, shoestrings, and garters were the portions of attire most decorated by the city gallant; thus they would be the articles of wearing apparel to be neglected and abandoned by the lover in his melancholy state" (Snyder, 1980)

122 118 fantastical: irrational
123 123 venny: bout or encounter, as in fencing
124 131 deem me fond: judge me foolishly over-affectionate
125 136 stir: leave
126 138 wad: heap
127 152 Somewhat: something
128 157 quintessence: purest and most perfect form

And making love his idol! Fie, dotard,[129] fie!
I am ashamed of this apostasy.[130]
[*Aside*] I'll talk with her to hinder his complaints.
—Phyllis, a word in private ere you go!
I love ye, sweet.
PHYLLIS Sour, it may be so.
FRANK Sour and sweet! Faith, that doth scarce agree.
PHYLLIS Two contraries, and so be we.
FRANK A plague on this courting! Come, we'll make an end.[131]
PHYLLIS I am sorry for it, since you seem my friend.
FRANK Aye, but thou canst not weep.
PHYLLIS Then had I a hard heart.
FRANK How say you? Come, brother, now to your part.
ANTHONY At your direction? No, this merry glee,
Good brother, sorts not with my melancholy.
Love covets[132] private conference; so my sorrow
Craveth your absence, which I fain would borrow.[133]
FRANK No marvel then we say that love is blind,
If it still revel in obscurity.
I will depart; I will not hinder love;
I'll wash my hands. Farewell, sweet turtle-dove. [*Begins to exit*]
PHYLLIS [*To* ANTHONY] I' faith your brother is a proper[134] man.
FRANK [*Returning*] What's your will with me?
PHYLLIS Even what you please.
FRANK Did you not call me back?
PHYLLIS Not to my knowledge.
FRANK No? 'Sblood, somewhat[135] did. Farewell, farewell! [*Begins to exit*]
PHYLLIS [*To* ANTHONY] He is a very, very proper man.
FRANK [*Returning*] I am in haste. Pray, urge me not to stay.
PHYLLIS The man doth dote.[136] Pray God he hits his way![137]
FRANK 'Fore God, there's not a maid in all this town
Should sooner win me, but my business calls me.
Give me thy hand. Next time I meet with thee,
Lesser entreaty shall woo my company.
PHYLLIS I' faith, i' faith.
FRANK [*Aside*] I' faith, this was the hand. What means my blood?
Do I not blush, nor look extremely pale?
Is not my head afire, my eyes, nor heart?
Ha, art thou here? I feel thee, love, i' faith,
By this light.—Well, *via*,[138] farewell, farewell. *Exit*
ANTHONY Now he is gone, and we in private talk,
Say, wilt thou grant me love, wilt thou be mine?
For all the interest in[139] my love is thine.
PHYLLIS Your brother Ferdinand hath vowed as much.

129 160 dotard: stupid person
130 161 apostasy: abandonment of principles
131 167 make an end: conclude this conversation
132 174 covets: longs for
133 175 fain would borrow: would like to make use of
134 180 proper: well-mannered
135 183 somewhat: something
136 186 dote: act deranged
137 186 hits his way: gets going
138 196 *via*: onward
139 199 interest in: claim on

Nay, more: he swears what man soe'er he be,
Presumes to be corrival[140] in his love,
He will revenge it as an injury
And clothe the thief in basest obloquy.[141]
ANTHONY Aye, is my brother my competitor?
I'll court my love and will solicit thee,
Were Ferdinand himself in company.
What sayst thou to my suit?
PHYLLIS Time may do much. What I intend to do
I mean to pause upon.[142]
ANTHONY Let it be so.
If that my brother's hinderance be all,[143]
I'll have thy love though by my brother's fall. *Exit*
PHYLLIS Two brothers drowned in love! Aye, and the third,
For all his outward habit of neglect,
If I judge rightly, if I did not dream,
Hath dipped his foot, too, in love's scalding stream.
Well, let them plead and perish if they will.
Cripple, my heart is thine, and shall be still!

Exit

[Act I, scene iv]

Enter FRANK

FRANK I am not well, and yet I am not ill.
I am—what am I? Not in love, I hope!
In love! Let me examine myself. Who should I love? Who did I last converse with? With Phyllis. Why should I love Phyllis? Is she fair? Faith, so-so. Her forehead is pretty, somewhat resembling the sign of the Maidenhead Inn, &c.[144] What's her hair? Faith, to Bandora-wires[145] there's not the like simile.[146] Is it likely yet that I am in love? What's next? Her cheeks. They have a reasonable scarlet; never a dyer's daughter in the town goes beyond her. Well, yet I am not in love. Nay, she hath a mole in her cheek, too; Venus' mole was not more natural. But what of that? I am Adonis, and will not love.[147] Good Venus, pardon me. Let us descend. Her chin. Oh Helen, Helen, where's your dimple, Helen? It was your dimple that bewitched Paris,[148] and without your dimple I will not love you, Helen. No, yet I am safe. Her hand, let's handle that. I saw her hand, and it was lily-white. I touched her palm, and it was soft and smooth. And then, what then? Her hand did then bewitch me; I shall be in love now out of hand. In love! Shall I, that ever yet have profaned love, now fall to worship him? Shall I, that have jested at lovers' sighs, now raise whirlwinds? Shall I, that have flouted[149] ah-mes once a quarter[150] now practice ah-mes every minute? Shall I defy hatbands, and tread garters and shoestrings under my feet?

140 201–02 what man . . . be corrival: whatever man presumes to be a rival
141 204 obloquy: slander
142 210 mean to pause upon: intend to take time to consider
143 211 If that . . . be all: if all I need to do is obstruct my brother
144 5 Maidenhead Inn, &c: Perhaps the "actor was allowed to extemporize at this point," comparing Phyllis's forehead "to the picture on the sign of whichever inn happened to be near the theatre" (Snyder, 1980)
145 5 Bandora-wires: the strings of a guitar-like instrument
146 6 not the like simile: nothing more similar
147 8–9 Venus' mole . . . not love: In myth, Venus, the goddess of love, falls in love with the beautiful hunter Adonis, who refuses her
148 10 Helen, Helen . . . bewitched Paris: In myth, Helen, the most beautiful woman in the world, is taken from her husband Menelaus by Paris of Troy, giving rise to the Trojan War
149 15 flouted: scoffed at
150 15 once a quarter: once every fourth part of the year (or perhaps every fourth part of an hour)

Shall I fall to falling-bands and be a ruffin[151] no longer? I must. I am now liege-man[152] to Cupid, and have read all these informations in his book of statutes, the first chapter, page *millisimo-nono*.[153] Therefore, hat-band, avaunt![154] Ruff, regard yourself! Garters, adieu! Shoestrings—so and so![155] I am a poor enamorate,[156] and enforced, with the poet, to say: love overcomes all, and I that love obey.

Exit

[Act II, scene i]

Enter MASTER FLOWER

MASTER FLOWER Now, afore God, a very good conceit![157]
But too much sleep hath overtaken me;
The night hath played the swift-foot runaway:[158]
A good conceit, a very good conceit.
What, Fiddle! Arise, Fiddle; Fiddle, I say!

Enter FIDDLE

FIDDLE Here's a fiddling, indeed. I think your tongue be made of nothing but fiddlestrings! I hope the fiddle must have some rest as well as the fiddlestick. Well, crowd,[159] what say you to Fiddle now?
MASTER FLOWER Fiddle, it is a very good conceit.
FIDDLE It is indeed, master.
MASTER FLOWER What dost thou mean?
FIDDLE To go to bed again, sir.
MASTER FLOWER No, Fiddle. That were no good conceit, Fiddle.
FIDDLE What a fiddling do you keep! Are you not ashamed to make such music? I hope, sir, you will christen me anew shortly, for you have so worn this name, that ne'er a wench in all the town but will scorn to dance after my fiddle.[160]
MASTER FLOWER Well, Fiddle, thou art an honest fellow.
FIDDLE That's more than you know, master.
MASTER FLOWER I'll swear for thee, Fiddle.
FIDDLE You'll be damned then, master.
MASTER FLOWER I love thee, Fiddle.
FIDDLE I had rather your daughter loved me.
MASTER FLOWER 'Tis a rare conceit,[161] i' faith.
FIDDLE I hold with you, master, if my young mistress would like so well of my music that she would dance after nobody's instrument[162] but mine.
MASTER FLOWER No, Fiddle, that were no good conceit.
FIDDLE A shame on you, I thought you would not hear on that side.[163]

151 17 ruffin: "ruffian," gallant; someone who wears (i.e. is "in") a "ruff"
152 17 liege-man: faithful servant and follower
153 19 *millisimo-nono*: nine-thousandth, a tiny number
154 19 avaunt!: begone!
155 20 so and so!: whatever!
156 20 enamorate: lover
157 1 a very good conceit: what a great idea, what a fanciful notion, what a witty thought. Master Flower constantly repeats this phrase, and variations of it, in reference to ideas and phrasings expressed by himself and others
158 3 The morning came too quickly
159 7 crowd: fiddle; Fiddle is also probably addressing the audience
160 15–16 so worn . . . my fiddle: Master Flower has spoken Fiddle's name so much that it has become worn out, meaning that no women will be attracted to Fiddle's penis (his "instrument," line 25)
161 23 rare conceit: an unusually good idea, here meant ironically
162 25 instrument: i.e. penis
163 27 I thought . . . that side: I didn't think you'd hear my offensive comment about your daughter since I spoke it toward your deafer ear

MASTER FLOWER Fiddle, thou told'st me Master Golding was in love with my daughter.
FIDDLE True, master; therein you say well.
MASTER FLOWER And he entreats me to meet him at the Star, in Cheap,[164] to talk concerning the match.
FIDDLE True still, master.
MASTER FLOWER And I have sent for my neighbor, Master Berry, to bear me company.
FIDDLE True, all this is most natural truth.
MASTER FLOWER And now, Fiddle, I am going on my way.
FIDDLE Nay, that's a lie; that hath marred all. Was your conceit so tired you could tell truth no longer?
MASTER FLOWER Why, Fiddle, are we not going?
FIDDLE No indeed, sir, we are not; we stand still. Your conceit failed in that.
MASTER FLOWER 'Fore God, 'tis true—I am not ready yet. What's he?

Enter BOBBINGTON

BOBBINGTON By your leave, sir, I would crave a word in secret, sir.
MASTER FLOWER At your pleasure. Here's none but my man Fiddle.
FIDDLE Aye, sir, Master Fiddle is my name. Sir Lawrence Lyre was my father.
BOBBINGTON Sir, this is my business. My name is Racket;[165] I have a ship of my own upon the river.
MASTER FLOWER By your leave, sir, Captain Racket is your name.
BOBBINGTON Some call me so, indeed, sir.
MASTER FLOWER It is a good conceit. I pray, proceed.
BOBBINGTON Sir, I am now bound to sea, and wanting some money for the better furnishing of my wants.
MASTER FLOWER Oh, you would borrow money of me.
BOBBINGTON That's my suit, indeed.
MASTER FLOWER That's no good conceit.
BOBBINGTON Nay, hear me, sir. If you will supply me with ten pound[166] till my return from Barbary,[167] I will leave in your hands a diamond of greater value than the money.
MASTER FLOWER A diamond! Is it a diamond, or but a counterfeit? Fiddle, my spectacles.
BOBBINGTON [*Handing him a diamond*] 'Tis right,[168] I assure you, sir.
MASTER FLOWER Then 'tis a good conceit—my spectacles.
FIDDLE Here, sir.
MASTER FLOWER Where, sir?
FIDDLE You cannot see, master, but I can.
MASTER FLOWER Oh, 'tis good! It is a good conceit. Well, sir, ten pound.
You are content if, at three months' end,
You bring me not ten pound in English coin,
This diamond shall be my proper own?
BOBBINGTON I am, sir. Shall I receive the money now?
MASTER FLOWER Aye, here it is, and 'tis a good conceit.
Will you go near, sir? Fiddle, make him drink.[169]
FIDDLE Will you approach, *cavaliero*?[170] If I speak not in season,[171] 'tis because I was never in the salt country,[172] where you sea-captains use to march.

164 30 the Star, in Cheap: i.e. the Star Inn, in Cheapside, a major London market thoroughfare
165 44 Racket: the thief Bobbington is impersonating a sea-captain to con unsuspecting marks out of money
166 54 ten pound: quite a bit of money today, at least $2,000
167 54–5 till my . . . from Barbary: until my return from the northern African coast laden with valuable goods
168 57 right: real
169 68 make him drink: take him into the cellar to have a drink (a customary gesture of hospitality)
170 69 *cavaliero*: gallant
171 69 in season: in the correct way
172 70 salt country: the ocean, punning on the foregoing "salt" as "season"ing

BOBBINGTON You are very eloquent, sir—I'll follow you.
FIDDLE Let me alone, then, for leading my men. *Exeunt* BOBBINGTON *and* FIDDLE
MASTER FLOWER A diamond worth forty, for ten pound!
If he return not safe from Barbary.
'Tis good, a very good conceit.

Enter MASTER BERRY

MASTER BERRY By your leave, Master Flower.

MASTER FLOWER Welcome, good Master Berry. I was bold to entreat your company to speak with a friend of mine. It is some trouble, but the conceit is good.

MASTER BERRY No trouble at all, sir. Shall we be going?

MASTER FLOWER With all my heart, sir, and, as we go,
I'll tell you my conceit. Come, Master Berry.

Exeunt

[Act II, scene ii]

Enter at one door CRIPPLE, *at the other* BOWDLER

BOWDLER Well-met, my dear bundle of rue, well-met.

CRIPPLE As much to thee, my humorous blossom.

BOWDLER A plague on thee for a dog! Have I found thee? I hate thee not, and yet by this hand I could find in my heart[173]—but, sirrah[174] Crutch, I was encountered.[175]

CRIPPLE Who became your bail?

BOWDLER You filthy dog! I was encountered by a wench, I say.

CRIPPLE In a wench's counter![176] I thought no less. What, sirrah, didst thou lie in the knight's ward, or on the master's side?

BOWDLER Neither, neither, i' faith.

CRIPPLE Where then? In the hole?[177]

BOWDLER By this hand, Cripple, I'll bombast thee![178]

CRIPPLE My crutch, you mean, for wearing out my clothes.[179]

BOWDLER Thy nose, dog, thy nose![180] A plague on thee! I care not for thee, and yet I cannot choose but love thee. Sirrah, Moll Berry was here about work thou hast of hers. Hadst thou been here to have heard how I spurred the wench with incantations,[181] thou wouldst have given me the praise for a jester.

CRIPPLE True, master Bowdler; I yield it you. I hold you for the absolutest jester. Oh, mistake me not: I mean to jest upon, a juggling gull, a profound-seeing man of shallow wit,[182] that Europe (nay, the world), I think, affords.

BOWDLER Well, thou art a Jew, sirrah. I'll cut out that venomous tongue of thine one of these days.

173 1–4: In these lines we see the repartee that characterizes Cripple and Bowdler's long-standing relationship: Bowdler thinks Cripple is melancholy and aggressive; Cripple, that Bowdler is whimsical and irresponsible (see Introduction)

174 4 sirrah: a somewhat condescending term of address

175 4 encountered: met; put in the Counter, a debtor's prison (in-Counter-ed). Cripple suggests the latter, punning meaning in the next line

176 7 counter: cunt

177 7–10 knight's ward … the hole?: "knight's ward," "master's side," and "hole" refer to parts of the debtor's prison, from most to least comfortable, as well as, with innuendo, to Bowdler's sexual "encounter"

178 11 bombast thee: "baste" your "bum," i.e. kick your butt

179 12 My crutch … my clothes: Cripple turns Bowdler's word, "bombast," to an alternate meaning. "Bombast" also means "stuff"; Cripple suggests that Bowdler should pad the top of his crutch so it doesn't wear out his shirt

180 13 Thy nose, dog, thy nose!: Bowdler's taunting of Cripple's "nose" anticipates his association of Cripple with Judaism; see Introduction

181 15 spurred the wench with incantations: excited Moll with charming words

182 18 I mean … shallow wit: Cripple insults Bowdler with oppositional language: he's a jest-er in the sense that he's the source of jests, not their origin; a trickster that gets tricked, someone who thinks he sees deeply but is actually shallow

CRIPPLE Do it in time, or I'll crush the heart of thy wit till I have strained forth thy infectious humor to a drop, i' faith.

Enter MOLL *Berry*

BOWDLER [*Aside*] Here comes my amorous vessel. I'll board[183] her, i' faith.—Well-encountered, Moll. How dost thou, wench, how dost thou?
MOLL What's that to you, sir?
BOWDLER Why, I ask thee in kindness.
MOLL Why then, in kindness, you are a fool for asking.
BOWDLER Is the fool your livery?[184]
MOLL Not so, for then you wearing that livery would term yourself my fool.
BOWDLER Meaning me? You gull me not, if you do!
MOLL What then?
BOWDLER Oh, vile! I would take you down.
MOLL Alas, it wants wit; his wit is too narrow.
BOWDLER I'll stretch my wit, but I will take you down.
MOLL How, upon the tenters?[185] Indeed, if the whole piece were so stretched, and very well-beaten with a yard of reformation,[186] no doubt it would grow to a goodly breadth.
BOWDLER By this hand.
MOLL Away, you ass. Hinder not my business.
CRIPPLE Finely put off, wench, i' faith.
MOLL By your leave, master drawer.
CRIPPLE Welcome, Mistress Berry. I have been mindful of your work.
MOLL Is it done?
CRIPPLE Yes, and here it is.
MOLL Here is your money.
Cripple, ere long I'll visit thee again.
I have some ruffs and stomachers to draw.[187]
CRIPPLE At your pleasure.
BOWDLER By thy leave, Moll, a word.
MOLL Away, you bundle of nothing, away. *Exit* MOLL
CRIPPLE She hath a wit as sharp as her needle.
BOWDLER Alas, myself have been her whetstone[188] with my conference in th' Exchange any time these many years.
CRIPPLE In th' Exchange! I have walked with thee there, before the visitation of my legs, and my expense in timber,[189] at the least a hundred times, and never heard thee speak to a wench.
BOWDLER That's a lie! Thou wert by when I bought these gloves of a wench.
CRIPPLE That's true, they cost thee an English shilling at a word.[190] Marry, it follows in the text[191] that your shilling proved but a harper,[192] and thou wert shamefully arraigned for it.
BOWDLER Good, but I excused myself.
CRIPPLE True, that thou thoughtst it had been a shilling. Marry, thou hadst never another, nor so much as a shilling more to change it.[193] Thou, talk in th' Exchange!

183 24 board: a) accost; b) mount, as onto a boat ("vessel")
184 29 Do your servants wear motley (traditionally the costume of a fool) as a uniform?
185 36 tenters: a device on which cloth was stretched
186 36–7 the whole ... of reformation: Moll compares Bowdler's "wit" to a piece of cloth, expanded by being put on the tenters and beaten with a paddle
187 46 to draw: i.e. for you to draw outlines on
188 51 whetstone: sharpening device
189 53–4: before the ... in timber: before the onset of my disability and my purchase of wooden crutches
190 56 at a word: frankly, truthfully
191 56–7 it follows in the text: what happened next was
192 57 harper: an Irish shilling, worth less than an English one. "People who tried to pass them as of equal value were subject to prosecution" (Snyder, 1980)
193 59–60 thou hadst ... change it: you didn't have another harper, or shilling to exchange for the harper

BOWDLER Indeed, my best gift is in the morning when the maids visit my chamber, with such necessaries as I usually buy of them.
CRIPPLE Oh, thou art one of those that if an honest maid be sent to thy chamber with her mistress' goods, and return as honest and chaste as the moon, sirrah, you are one of those that will slander the poor wenches, by speaking liberally of their proneness[194] to love. And, withal, brag how cheap you have bought their ware metaphorically, when, indeed, they depart as honest as they came thither, and leave you all the day after to sigh at the sight of an ill bargain.
BOWDLER When wilt thou spit out this serpent's tongue of thine?
CRIPPLE When wilt thou cast off this antic garment of ostentation?[195] Do it, do it, or by the Lord, I will impress[196] thy vanities and so anatomize[197] the very bowels of thy absurdities, that all the world shall take notice of thee for a fool, and shun thee as the pox, or the pestilence.

Enter BERNARD

BERNARD News, news, news!
BOWDLER Sweet rogue, what's the matter?
BERNARD By Jesu, the rarest dancing in Christendom!
BOWDLER Sweet rascal, where?
Oh, do not kill my soul with such delays.
Tell me, kind rogue! Oh, tell me where it is.
BERNARD At a wedding in Gracious Street.[198]
BOWDLER Come, come, away! I long to see the man
In dancing art that does more than I can.
BERNARD Than you, sir? He lives not.
BOWDLER Why, I did understand thee so.
BERNARD You only excepted, the world besides
Cannot afford more exquisite dancers
Than are now capering in that bride-ale house.[199]
BOWDLER I will behold them. Come, Crutch, thou shalt with us.
CRIPPLE Not I.
BOWDLER Down, dog! I'll have thy company.
CRIPPLE I have business.
BOWDLER By this hand, thou shalt go with us.
CRIPPLE By this leg, I will not.
BOWDLER A lame oath! Never stand to that.
CRIPPLE By this crutch, but I will.
BERNARD Come, you lose time. Supper is done long since,
And they are now a-dancing.

Enter MASTER BERRY *and* FIDDLE

MASTER BERRY Stay, Fiddle, with thy torch. Gentlemen, good even.
BERNARD Master Berry!
BOWDLER Master Berry, I wish you well, sir. Master Fiddle, I am yours for a congee.[200]
FIDDLE After the French salutation, I am yours for the like courtesy.
MASTER BERRY Master Bernard, tomorrow is your day
Of payment, sir. I mean the hundred pound

194 65 proneness: inclination
195 69 antic garment of ostentation: grotesque pretentious behavior
196 70 impress: force into my service
197 70 anatomize: lay open for analysis
198 78 Gracious Street: a street in the same neighborhood as Cripple's shop in the Exchange
199 85 bride-ale house: house where the marriage feast is taking place
200 98 congee: French term for a bow, here meant as a greeting

For which I have your bond. I know 'tis sure;[201]
You will not break an hour. Then, if you please
To come to dinner, sir, you shall be welcome.
BERNARD Sir, I did mean to visit you at home,
Not to pay down the money, but entreat
Two months' forbearance.[202]
MASTER BERRY How? Forbear my money?
Your reason why I should forbear my own?
BERNARD You know at first the debt was none of mine;
I was a surety,[203] not the principal.
Besides, the money that was borrowed
Miscarried in the venture: my friend died.
And once already have you prisoned me
To my great charge (almost my overthrow),
And somewhat raised the debt by that advantage.
These things considered, you may well forbear,
For two months' space, so small a sum as this.
MASTER BERRY How? I may forbear? Sir, I have need of money.
I may indeed sit moneyless at home,
And let you walk abroad, spending my coin.
This I may do; but, sir, you know my mind.
If you do break your day,[204] assure yourself
That I will take the forfeit of your bond.[205]
CRIPPLE The forfeit of his bond!
MASTER BERRY Aye, sir, the forfeit! 'Tis no charity
To favor you that live like libertines.[206]
Here's a crew![207]
ALL A crew! What crew?
MASTER BERRY A crew of unthrifts, careless dissolutes,
Licentious prodigals, vild[208] tavern-tracers,
Night-watching money-wasters[209]—what should I call ye?
Oh, I want words for to define you rightly.
But this I know, London never fostered such
As Bernard, Bowdler, and this paltry crutch.
CRIPPLE And[210] you want words, sirrah, I'll teach thee words.
Thou shouldst have come to every one of us
As thus:[211] "Thou wretch, thou miser, thou vild slave
And drudge to money, bondman to thy wealth,
Apprentice to a penny, thou that hoards up
The fry[212] of silver pence and half-pennies,
With show of charity to give the poor,

201 102 'tis sure: your word is reliable
202 106–7 entreat/Two months' forbearance: to ask for a two-month extension
203 110 I was a surety: I borrowed the money on behalf of someone else
204 122 break your day: fail to repay me on time
205 123 forfeit of your bond: penal fine for breaking our contract
206 126 like libertines: amorally, promiscuously
207 127 crew: group, mob, with derogatory connotation
208 129 vild: vile, possibly also including the sense "wild"
209 128–30 A crew . . . money-wasters: most of these terms are virtual synonyms, describing the group as poor at managing money (unthrifts, dissolutes, prodigals, money-wasters). Master Berry also calls them more generally unrestrained (careless, licentious), staying up all night on bar crawls (night-watching tavern-tracers)
210 134 And: if
211 136 As thus: while Cripple says this is what Master Berry should have said, the speech that follows is actually directed at Master Berry himself
212 139 fry: offspring

But put'st them to increase,[213] where in short time
They grow a child's part, or a daughter's portion—[214]
Thou that invents new clauses for a bond
To cozen simple plainness! Oh, not a dragon,
No, nor the devil's fangs are half so cruel
As are thy claws!" Thus, thus thou shouldst have railed.
The forfeit of his bond! Oh, I could spit
My heart into his face! Thou bloodhound that dost hunt
The dear, dear life of noble gentry.
MASTER BERRY Cripple, 'tis known I am an honest man!
But for thy words, Bernard shall fare the worse.
As for thyself—

FIDDLE Who, he, sir? Never regard him. I know the vildest thing by[215] him. Oh, 'tis abominable!

MASTER BERRY Dost thou so, Fiddle? Speak: hold, take thou that. [*Gives money*] Speak of his shame. Speak freely; I'll protect thee.

FIDDLE I tell you, sir, 'twill make your hair stand on end, as stiff as a rubbing-brush, to hear his villainies. What's this you have given me?

MASTER BERRY A shilling, Fiddle.

FIDDLE Have you any skill in arithmetic?

MASTER BERRY Why dost thou ask?

FIDDLE Sir, I would have you to multiply. Could you not make this one shilling two or three? I would not be known to beg, but if out of your cunning you can do this trick of multiplication, I shall speak the better.

MASTER BERRY Oh, there's another shilling for thee. Now let me hear what villainies thou canst charge the cripple with.

FIDDLE So, sir, this is multiplication. Now, sir, if you know the rule of addition, you are an excellent scholar. Can you not add?

MASTER BERRY What dost thou mean?

FIDDLE Another shilling, sir.

MASTER BERRY There is another shilling. Now, Fiddle, speak.

FIDDLE Why, then, attend, you hills and dales, and stones so quick of hearing: this cripple is—

ALL What is he, villain?

FIDDLE An honest man, as any is in all the town.

MASTER BERRY An honest man!

FIDDLE Aye, by this silver, and as good a fellow as ever went upon four legs. If you would multiply until midnight,[216] I would never speak otherwise.

MASTER BERRY Fiddle, thou art a knave, and so is he!
Come, let us home. Bernard, look to thy bond.
If thou do break the day, I do protest,
By yon chaste moon—

FIDDLE The chaste moon? Why, the moon is not chaste.

MASTER BERRY How prov'st thou that?

FIDDLE Why, sir, there's a man in the middle of her. How can she be chaste, then?

MASTER BERRY Then, by my life, I swear I'll clap[217] him up
Where he shall see neither the sun nor moon,
Till I be satisfied the utmost penny.
And so farewell. *Exit*

213 141 putst them to increase: by charging interest on his loans, Master Berry creates money from money, in the manner of biological reproduction
214 142 Your investments increase enough to fund an inheritance or a dowry
215 153 by: about
216 177 multiply until midnight: i.e. keep giving me money all day
217 185 clap: shut

FIDDLE Gallants, good night. If time and place were in prosperity, I were yours for an hour's society. I must after yon mulberry[218] with my torch. Adieu, dear hearts, adieu.

Exit

BOWDLER Come, Bernard, let's to the dancing! Let's tickle it tonight, for tomorrow thy heels may be too heavy.
BERNARD All's one! My heart shall be as light as fire.
Come, shall we go?
BOWDLER Cripple, will you along?
CRIPPLE My business stays me here.
BOWDLER Farewell, then, dog of Israel, farewell! *Exeunt* [BOWDLER *and* BERNARD]
CRIPPLE "All's one! My heart shall be as light as fire."
'Sblood, were I indebted a hundred pound,
My fortunes failed, and fled, as Bernard's are,
Not worth a hundred pence, as Bernard is,
I should be now devising sentences
And caveats,[219] for posterity to carve
Upon the inside of the Counter wall!
Therefore I'll now turn provident.[220] I'll to my shop
And fall to work.

Enter PHYLLIS

PHYLLIS [*Aside*] Yonder's his shop. Oh, now, you gods above,
Pity poor Phyllis' heart, that melts in love!
Instruct the cripple to find out my love,
Which I will shadow under the conceit
Of my invention for this piece of work.[221]
Oh, teach him how to yield me love again,
A little, little love; a dram[222] of kind affection.
His many virtues are my true direction.
—By your leave, master drawer!
CRIPPLE Welcome, Mistress Flower. What's your pleasure?
PHYLLIS My cause of coming is not unknown to you.
Here is bespoken work[223] which must be wrought
With expedition;[224] I pray, have care of it.
The residue I refer to your direction[225]—
Only this handkercher a young gentlewoman
Wished me acquaint you with her mind herein:
In one corner of the same, place wanton Love,[226]
Drawing his bow, shooting an amorous dart.
Opposite against him an arrow in a heart;
In a third corner picture forth disdain,
A cruel fate unto a loving vein.
In the fourth, draw a springing laurel tree,[227]

218 190 yon mulberry: i.e. Master Berry
219 202–3 sentences/And caveats: maxims and warnings
220 205 turn provident: plan for my (financial) future
221 210–11 shadow under . . . of work: disguise in my fanciful description of the design I'd like him to draw
222 213 dram: tiny amount, as of medicine or liquor
223 218 bespoken work: i.e. work ordered by Phyllis's customers
224 218–19 wrought/With expedition: quickly and skillfully completed
225 220 The residue . . . your direction: I'll leave the rest of the work for you to design
226 223 wanton Love: naughty Cupid
227 228 laurel tree: symbol of triumph; made into a wreath (see line 233), the leaves are a victory crown

Circled about with a ring of poesy.[228] And thus it is:
Love wounds the heart and conquers fell disdain.
Love pities love, seeing true love in pain.
Love seeing love how faithful love did breathe,
At length impaled[229] *love with a laurel wreath.*
Thus you have heard the gentlewoman's mind.
I pray be careful that it be well done!
And so I leave you. More I fain would[230] say,
But shame forbids and calls me hence away. *Exit*
CRIPPLE Sweet fair, I pity you, yet no relief
Harbors within the closet of my soul.[231]
This Phyllis bears me true affection,
But I detest the humor of fond love.[232]
Yet I am hourly solicited
As now you see,[233] and fain she would make known
The true perplexion of her wounded heart.
But modesty, checking her forwardness,
Bids her be still. Yet she in similes
And love-comparisons, like a good scholar,
By figures makes a demonstration
Of the true love enclosèd in her heart.
I know it well, yet will not tell her so.
Fancy shall never marry me to woe.
Take this of me: a young man's never marred,
Till he by marriage from all joy be barred.

Exit

[Act II, scene iii]

Enter FRANK *singing*

FRANK *Ye gods of love that sit above*
And pity lovers' pain,
Look from your thrones upon the moans
That I do now sustain.

Was ever man thus tormented with love?

Ye little birds that sit and sing
Amidst the shady valleys,
And see how Phyllis sweetly walks
Within her garden alleys:[234]
Go, pretty birds, about her bower!
Sing, pretty birds, she may not lour.[235]
Ah me, methinks I see her frown!
Ye pretty wantons,[236] *warble.*

228 229 poesy: poetry
229 233 *impaled*: crowned
230 236 fain would: would like to
231 238–9 no relief . . . my soul: I do not have it in me (i.e. I do not have the capacity or the inclination) to relieve her suffering
232 241 humor of fond love: whimsical nature of infatuated, foolish love
233 242–3 hourly solicited . . . you see: constantly courted in this way
234 9 *alleys*: narrow walkways between flower beds
235 11 *lour*: look gloomy
236 13 *wantons*: playful birds

Go tell her, through your chirping bills,
As you by me are bidden,
To her is only known my love,
Which from the world is hidden.
Go, pretty birds, and tell her so!
See that your notes strain[237] *not too low.*
For still methinks I see her frown.
Ye pretty wantons, warble.

Go tune your voices' harmony,
And sing, I am her lover!
Strain loud and sweet, that every note
With sweet content may move her.
And she that hath the sweetest voice,
Tell her I will not change my choice!
Yet still methinks I see her frown.
Ye pretty wantons, warble.

Oh, fly! Make haste! See, see, she falls
Into a pretty slumber.
Sing round about her rosy bed
That waking, she may wonder.
Say to her, 'tis her lover true,
That sendeth love to you, to you!
And when you hear her kind reply,
Return with pleasant warblings.

Avaunt, delusion! Thoughts cannot win my love.
Love, though divine, cannot divine[238] my thoughts.
Why to the air, then, do I idle here
Such heedless words, far off, and ne'er the near.[239]
Hie[240] thee, young Frank, to her that keeps thy heart;
There let sweet words thy sweeter thoughts impart.
But stay! Here comes my melancholy brothers both.
I'll step aside, and hear their conference. *Exit aside*

[*Enter* ANTHONY *at one door,* FERDINAND *at the other*]

ANTHONY [*Aside*] What? Is my brother Ferdinand so near?
He is my elder; I must needs give place.
Anthony, stand by, and list[241] what he doth say.
Haste calls me hence, yet I will brook[242] delay.
FERDINAND Shall I exclaim 'gainst fortune and mishap,
Or rail on[243] Nature, who first framèd me?
Is it hard chance that keeps me from my love?
Or is this heap of loathed deformity[244]
The cause that breeds a blemish in her eye?

237 19 *strain*: sing
238 39 divine: interpret
239 40–41 idle here . . . the near: vainly express these words, unworthy of attention, which are not bringing me any closer to Phyllis
240 42 Hie: go quickly
241 48 list: listen to
242 49 brook: tolerate
243 51 rail on: complain about
244 53 this heap . . . loathed deformity: this body, i.e. himself

I know not what to think, or what to say!
Only one comfort yet I have in store,
Which I will practice, though I ne'er try more.
ANTHONY [*Aside*] Oh, for to hear that comfort I do long;
I'll turn it to a strain[245] to right my wrong.
FERDINAND I have a brother, rival in my love;
I have a brother hates me for my love;
I have a brother vows to win my love;
That brother, too, he hath incensed[246] my love,
To gain the beauty of my dearest love.
What hope remains, then, to enjoy my love?
ANTHONY [*Aside*] I am that brother rival in his love;
I am that brother hates him for his love;
Not his, but mine, and I will have that love,
Or never live to see him kiss my love.
What thou erst[247] said, I am that man alone
That will depose you, brother, from love's throne.
I am that man, though you my elder be,
That will aspire beyond you one degree.
FERDINAND I have no means of private conference,
So narrowly[248] pursues my hinderer.
No sooner am I entered the sweet court
Of lovely rest, my love's rich mansion,[249]
But rival love to my affection
Follows me, as a soon-enforcèd straw,
The drawing virtue of a sable jet.[250]
This therefore's my determination:
Within the close womb of a sealed paper,
Will I write down, in bloody characters,
The burning zeal of my affection;
And by some trusty messenger or other,
Convey the same into my love's own hand.
So shall I know her resolution,
And how she fancies my affection.
ANTHONY [*Aside*] Yet, subtle fox, I may perchance to cross you.
—Brother, well met! Whither away so fast?
FERDINAND About affairs that do require some haste.
ANTHONY 'Tis well done, brother; you seek still for gain.[251]
FERDINAND [*Aside*] But you would reap the harvest of my pain.
—Farewell, good brother! I must needs be gone.
I have serious business now to think upon.
[*Aside*] Yet for I fear my brother Anthony,
I'll step aside, and stand a while unseen.
I may perchance descry[252] which way he goes.
Thus policy[253] must work 'twixt friends and foes. [*Stands*] *aside*
ANTHONY So, he is gone. I scarcely trust him neither.

245 59 turn it to a strain: make Ferdinand's "comfort" into my own musical accompaniment
246 63 incensed: kindled
247 70 erst: just now
248 75 narrowly: closely
249 76–7 the sweet . . . rich mansion: i.e. Phyllis's presence
250 79–80 as a . . . .sable jet: in the same way a piece of straw is attracted to the black mineral jet (when it is charged with static electricity)
251 92 you seek still for gain: you are always working hard to make money
252 98 descry: catch a glimpse of
253 99 policy: trickery

For 'tis his custom, like a sneaking fool,
To fetch a compass of a mile about,
And creep[254] where he would be. Well, let him pass.
I heard him say, that since by word of mouth
He could not purchase his sweet mistress' favor,
He would endeavor what his wit might do
By writing, and by tokens. Oh, 'tis good
Writing with ink! Oh, no, but with his blood!
Well, so much for that. Now I know his mind,
I do intend not to be far behind.
He'll send a letter; I will write another.
Do what you can, I'll be before you, brother!
I'll intercept his letter by the way,
And as time serves, the same I will bewray.[255]
Mine being made,[256] a porter[257] I'll procure,
That shall convey that heart-enticing lure.
About it, then! My letter shall be writ,
Though not with blood, yet with a reaching wit.[258] *Exit*
FERDINAND And shall it so, good brother Anthony?
Were you so near when we in secret talked?
Will it ne'er be otherwise? Will you dog me still? [FRANK *comes forward*]
Welcome, sweet Frank! Such news I have to tell
As cannot choose but like[259] thee passing well.
Thou know'st my love to Phyllis?
FRANK Brother, say on.
FERDINAND Thou likewise art acquainted with my rival,
And I do build upon your secrecy.
FRANK 'Sblood, and[260] I thought you did not, I'd retire.[261]
Brother, you know I love you as my life.
FERDINAND I dare profess as much, and thereupon
Make bold to crave thy furtherance,[262] in a thing
Concerns me much.
FRANK Out with it, brother.
If I shrink back, repose trust in some other.
FERDINAND Then thus it is. My brother all in haste
Is gone, to write a letter to my love,
And thinks thereby to cross me in my suit,
Sending it by a porter to her hand.
If ever, therefore, thou wilt aid thy brother,
Help me in this, who seeks help from no other.
FRANK By the red lip of that dainty saint, I'll aid thee all I may.
FERDINAND It is enough. Then, brother, I'll provide
A porter's habit, alike in every point.[263]
Will you but[264] so much humble your estate

254 102–3 fetch a . . . And creep: take a circuitous route and sneak unobserved
255 114 bewray: reveal
256 115 Mine being made: my letter having been written
257 115 porter: one employed to convey goods and letters
258 118 reaching wit: intellectual quickness that achieves its goals
259 123 like: please
260 127 and: if
261 127 retire: retreat, give up
262 130 crave thy furtherance: ask your assistance
263 141 A porter's . . . every point: attire in all ways like a porter's uniform
264 142 Will you but: if you will only

To put yourself in that so base attire,
And, like so mean[265] a person, wait his coming
About[266] his door, which will not be o'erlong,
Thou shalt forever bind me to thy love.
FRANK Brother, 'tis a base task, by this light.
But to procure a further force of love,
I'll do't, i' faith, I will, sweet Ferdinand.
About it, then, provide thee some disguise!
But see you stay not long in any wise.[267]
Here shall you find me. Go, dispatch!
FERDINAND For this I'll love thee everlastingly. [*Exit*]
FRANK Meantime I'll cross your love and if I can.
Here's no villainy 'twixt us three brothers.
My brother Ferdinand he would have the wench,
And Anthony he hopes to have her too.
Then what may I? Faith, hope well, as they do.
Neither of them know that I love the maid.
Yet by this hand I am half-mad for love.
I know not well what love is, but 'tis sure
I'll die if I have her not; therefore,
Good brothers mine, beguile[268] you one another,
Till you be both gulled[269] by your younger brother.

Enter FERDINAND

FERDINAND Here is a porter's habit. On with it, brother.
FRANK Your hand then, brother, for to put it on. [*Puts on porter's habit*]
So now 'tis well. Come brother, what's my task?
FERDINAND This first, that thou make haste to Anthony's.
Ask for a burden,[270] and thou shall be sure
To have his letter to my dear love Phyllis.
Deliver it not, but keep it to thyself,
Till thou has given this paper to her hands, [*Gives* FRANK *his letter*]
Whose lines do intimate my chaste desires.
This is the sum of all. Good Frank, make haste!
Love burns in me, and I in love do waste. *Exit*
FRANK Waste still, but let me in my love increase.
Now would not all the world take me for a porter?
How strangely I am metamorphosèd!
And yet I need not be ashamèd neither.
Jove,[271] when his love-scapes[272] he attempted, ever
Transformed himself, yet ever sped[273] in love.
Why may not I, then, in this strange disguise?
This habit may prove mighty in love's power,
As beast, or bird, bull or swan, or golden shower.[274]

265 144 mean: low-born
266 144–5 wait his coming/About: await Anthony near
267 151 wise: way
268 163 beguile: deceive
269 164 gulled: duped
270 169 a burden: employment
271 180 Jove: the god Jupiter, or Zeus
272 180 love-scapes: amorous adventures
273 181 sped: succeeded
274 184 golden shower: Zeus appeared to women in many forms, including as golden rain

Enter ANTHONY

ANTHONY Within the center of this paper square,
Have I wrote down in bloody characters,
A pretty posy of[275] a wounded heart.
Such is love's force, once burst into a flame,
Do what we can, we cannot quench the same.
Unless the tears of pity move compassion,
And so quench out the fire of affection,
Whose burning force heats me in every vein,
That I to love for safety must complain.
This is my orator, whose dulcet[276] tongue
Must plead my love to beauteous Phyllis.
Now for a trusty messenger, to be
Employed herein betwixt my love and me!
And, in good time, I see a porter nigh.
Come hither, fellow! Dwellst thou hereabout?
FRANK [*Disguised*] Sir, my abiding is not far from hence,
And Trusty John men call me by my name.
ANTHONY Canst thou be trusty, then, and secret, too,
Being employed in weighty business?
FRANK Sir, I was never yet disproved in either.
ANTHONY Then mark[277] me well. In Cornhill,[278] by th' Exchange,
Dwells an old merchant, Flower they call his name.
He hath one only daughter, to whose hands,
If thou conveniently canst give this letter,
I'll pay thee well, make thee the happiest porter
That ever undertook such business.
FRANK Sir, give me your letter. If I do it not,
Then let your promised favor be forgot.
ANTHONY Anthony Golding is my name, my friend.
About it, then! Thy message being done,
Make haste to me again. Till when, I leave thee. *Exit*
FRANK And so fare thee well, loving brother!
It had been better you had sent some other.
Let me consider what is best be done.
Shall I deliver his letter? No!
Shall I convey it to my rival brother? Nor so!
Shall I tear the same? No, not for a million.
What shall I then do? Marry, like a kind brother,
Open the book; see what is written there.
If naught but love, in love have thou a share.
Brother, by your leave, I hope you'll not deny
But that I love you. [*Opens letter*] God bless my eyesight!
A sonnet[279] 'tis, in verse. Now, on my life,
He hath perused all the impressions[280]
Of sonnets since the fall of Lucifer,

275 187 posy of: poem about
276 194 dulcet: sweet
277 205 mark: attend to
278 205 Cornhill: i.e. Cornhill Street
279 227 sonnet: poem
280 228 impressions: printed copies

And made some scurvy,[281] quaint collection
Of fustian[282] phrases, and uplandish[283] words.

A Letter
Fair glory of virtue! Thy enamorate
Pleads loyally in pure affection.
Whose passion, Love, do thou exonerate,[284]
And he shall live by thy protection.
Nor from thy love shall he once derogate,[285]
For any soul under this horizon.
Yield thou to love, and I will fail in neither.
So love and truth shall always live together.
Yours devoted, Anthony Golding.

Before God, excellent good poetry!
'Sblood, what means he by this line:
"For any soul under this horizon"?
No matter for his meaning. Mean what he will,
I mean his meaning shall not be delivered,
But for my other trust, my other letter,
That shall come short too of fair Phyllis' hands.
There is a cripple dwelling here at hand,
That's very well acquainted with the maid.
And for I once did rescue them from thieves,
Swore, if he lived, he would requite that kindness.
To him I will for counsel; he shall be
My tutor by his wit and policy.[286]

Exit

[Act III, scene i]

Enter BOY *in a shop cutting of square parchments,*[287] *to him enter* PHYLLIS

PHYLLIS Why, how now, sirrah? Can you find naught to do
But waste the parchment in this idle sort?[288]
BOY I do but what my mistress gave in charge.
PHYLLIS Your mistress! In good time.[289] Then, sir, it seems
Your duty cannot stoop but to her lure.[290]
Sir, I will make you know that in her absence
You shall account to my demand. Your mistress!
And your mistress' will is thus! And thus you'll do.
But answer to the motion I have made,[291]
Or you shall feel you have another mistress now.
Speak! Why, when, I say?

281 230 scurvy: shabby, worthless
282 231 fustian: pompous
283 231 uplandish: outlandish, foreign
284 234 *do thou exonerate*: if you relieve
285 236 *derogate*: fall away
286 253 policy: strategy
287 0 SD *square parchments*: i.e. to be used as wrapping paper
288 2 sort: way
289 4 In good time: really? (expressing ridicule)
290 5 Your duty . . . her lure: i.e. "you only obey the boss's directions" (a metaphor from falconry)
291 9 the motion I have made: my prompting

BOY Indeed I know your glory;[292]
Your pride's at full in this authority.
But, were it not for modest bashfulness,
And that I dread a base contentious name,
I would not be a by-word to[293] th' Exchange,
For everyone to say (myself going by),
"Yon[294] goes a vassal to authority."
PHYLLIS You would not, sir; had I the yard[295] in hand,
I'd measure your pate[296] for this delusion,
And by my maiden chastity I swear,
Unless— *Reach for the yard, and the* BOY *stay her hand*[297]
BOY What unless? I know your wilfulness!
These words are but to show the world your humor.[298]
I often use to square these parchment pieces
Without occasion.[299] I am sure you are not witting[300]
The lawns[301] you lately bought of Master Brooks
Are new come home, brought by the merchant's servant.
I know you are short-membered,[302] but not so short
Of your remembrance, that this is news to you.
PHYLLIS Y'are best to brave me[303] in a taunting humor.
Wilt please you ope the door?[304] Where's Ursula?
Oh, here's good stuff![305] My back's no sooner turned,
But she must needs be gadding,[306] and where, I pray?
BOY She's gone to Master Palmer's, on th' other side.[307]
PHYLLIS On great occasions, sir, I doubt it not. *Sit and work in the shop*

Enter Master Richard GARDINER *booted,*[308] *and Master William* BENNET, *two gentlemen, at one end of the stage*

BENNET Kind Dick, thou wilt not be unmindful of my duty
To that same worthy arts-master, Lionel Barnes.[309]
GARDINER Thy love, sweet Will, hath chained it to my memory.
BENNET Then with this kind embrace I take my leave,
Wishing thou wert as safe-arrived at Cambridge,[310]
As thou art at this present near the Exchange.
GARDINER And well remembered, kind Will Bennet.
Others' affairs made me oblivious

292 12 glory: boastful nature
293 16 by-word to: object of scorn in
294 18 Yon: there
295 19 yard: measuring-stick
296 20 measure your pate: i.e. beat you about the head
297 22 SD *Reach for . . . her hand*: Phyllis starts to grab the measuring-stick and the boy stops her hand
298 24 humor: whims
299 26 occasion: giving offense
300 26 witting: aware
301 27 lawns: lengths of fine fabric
302 29 are short-membered: have a short memory
303 31 You are . . . brave me: good job defying me (sarcastic)
304 32 Wilt please . . . the door?: they have been talking through the open top half of the door; the bottom half has been closed, with the boy inside the shop and Phyllis outside
305 33 Oh, here's good stuff!: oh, great! (sarcastic)
306 34 gadding: wandering idly
307 35 on th' other side: i.e. the other side of the square walk of the Exchange building
308 36 SD *booted*: wearing riding boots, indicating that he's about to travel
309 37–8 Bennet is asking Gardiner (who is on his way to Cambridge) to give his regards to Bennet's former teacher ("arts-master") Lionel Barnes; it is unclear whether Barnes was a real person or simply a name the author invented for this play
310 41 Cambridge: i.e. Cambridge University

Of mine own. I pray thee go to the Exchange.
I have certain bands,[311] and other linen to buy.
Prithee accompany me.
BENNET With all my heart.
GARDINER Sure, this is a beauteous gallant walk.
Were my continual residence in London,
I should make much use of such a pleasure.
Methinks the glorious virgins of this square[312]
Gives life to dead-struck youth.[313] [*Seeing* PHYLLIS] Oh, heavens!
BENNET Why, how now, Dick?
GARDINER By my sweet hopes of an hereafter bliss,
I never saw a fairer face than this.
Oh, for acquaintance with so rich a beauty!
BENNET Take thy occasion; never hadst thou better.
GARDINER Have at her, then.
PHYLLIS What lack you,[314] gentlemen?
GARDINER Faith, nothing, had I thee.
For in thine eye all my desires I see.
PHYLLIS My shop you mean, sir. There you may have choice
Of lawns, or cambrics,[315] ruffs well-wrought, shirts,
Fine falling-bands of the Italian cut-work,[316]
Ruffs for your hands, waistcoats wrought with silk,
Nightcaps of gold, or suchlike wearing linen,
Fit for the chapman[317] of whate'er degree.[318]
GARDINER Faith, virgin,
In my days, I have worn and out-worn much,
Yea, many of these golden necessaries.
But such a gallant beauty, or such a form[319]
I never saw, nor never wore the like.
Faith, be not then unkind, but let me wear
This shape of thine, although I buy it dear.[320]
PHYLLIS What, hath the tailor played his part so well,
That with my gown you are so far in love?
GARDINER Mistake not, sweet! Your garment is the cover
That veils the shape and pleasures of a lover.
PHYLLIS That argues, then, you do not see my shape.
How comes it then you are in love with it?
GARDINER A garment made by cunning arts-men's skill
Hides all defects that Nature's swerving hand
Hath done amiss, and makes the shape seem pure.
If then it grace such lame deformity
It adds a greater grace to purity.[321]
PHYLLIS Oh, short-lived praise! Even now I was as fair

311 46 bands: shirt-collars or ruffs
312 51 glorious virgins of this square: attractive young female shopkeepers in this part of the Exchange
313 52 dead-struck youth: fatigued young men
314 58 What lack you: what are you shopping for? (conventional shopkeeper's question)
315 62 cambrics: fine white linens
316 63 Lacy flat collars
317 66 chapman: customer
318 66 degree: rank
319 70 such a form: i.e. Phyllis's shape
320 72–3 let me … it dear: let me put your body on mine, as if putting on clothing, even if I have to pay a lot for it
321 80–84 A garment … to purity: a well-made garment hides any natural defects; if it can improve the appearance ("grace") of someone unattractive ("lame deformity"), it will add that much more to your natural beauty ("purity")

As anything—now, fouler nothing.
Dissembling men! What maid will credit them?
GARDINER How misconstruction leads your thoughts awry!
BENNET I prithee, Dick, have done. Think on thy journey.
PHYLLIS You counsel well, sir. I think the gentleman
Comes but to whet his wit, and 'tis but need.
'Tis blunt enough; he may ride far upon't.[322]
GARDINER Marry, gip, minx![323]
PHYLLIS A fine word in a gentleman's mouth!
'Twere good your back were towards me; there can I
Read better content than in the face of lust.
GARDINER Now you display your virtues as they are.
PHYLLIS What am I? You cipher, parenthesis of words,[324]
Stall-troubler, prater![325] What, sit I here for naught?
Bestow your lustful courtships on your minions;[326]
This place holds none. You and your companion,
Get you down the stairs, or, I protest,
I'll make this squarèd walk[327] too hot[328] for you.
Had you been, as you seemed in outward show,
Honest gentlemen, such terms of vild abuse
Had not been proffered to virginity.
But swains[329] will quickly show their base descent.
GARDINER This is no place for brawls, but if it were,
Your impositions[330] are more than I would bear.
BENNET Come, she's a woman; I prithee leave her. *Exeunt* GARDINER *and* BENNET
PHYLLIS Nay, sure a maid, unless her thoughts deceive her.
God speed you well! Sirrah, boy!
BOY Anon![331]
PHYLLIS Go to the starcher's[332] for the suit of ruffs,
For Master Bowdler's bands, and Master Golding's shirts;
Let's have a care to please our provèd friends.[333]
As for our strangers, if they use us well,
For love and money, love and ware we'll sell.

Exeunt

[Act III, scene ii]

Enter FRANK [*in disguise as a porter*]. *The* CRIPPLE *at work*

FRANK Now fortune be my guide. This is the shop!
And in good time,[334] the cripple is at work.

322 91–2 Comes but . . . far upon't: although Gardiner seems to want to "sharpen" his wit through banter with Moll, she suggests that Gardiner's wit is "wide" or "blunt" like a fat horse, more comfortable to ride than a thin one
323 93 Marry, gip, minx: well, get out, you flirt!
324 98 You cipher, parenthesis of words: you nothing, you irrelevance
325 99 Stall-troubler, prater: you pompous chatterer disturbing my shop window
326 100 minions: mistresses
327 103 squarèd walk: the upper arcade of the Exchange
328 103 hot: uncomfortable
329 107 swains: country bumpkins
330 109 impositions: accusations
331 113 Anon!: coming!
332 114 starcher's: the shop of the person who stiffens cloth with starch
333 116 provèd friends: regular customers
334 2 in good time: fortunately

God speed you, sir.
CRIPPLE Welcome, honest friend. What's thy will with me?
FRANK I would entreat you, read a letter for me.
CRIPPLE With all my heart.
I know the maid to whom it is directed.
FRANK I know you do, Cripple, better than you think.
CRIPPLE I pray you, what gentleman writ the same?
FRANK Sir, a gentleman of good learning, and my friend.
To say the truth, 'twas written for[335] myself,
Being somewhat overtaken with fond love,
As many men be, sir.
CRIPPLE Why, art thou persuaded, or hast thou any hope,
So beautiful a virgin as she is,
Of such fair parentage, so virtuous,
So gentle, kind, and wise as Phyllis is,
That she will take remorse of[336] such base stuff?[337]
I think not so! But let me see: what's thy name?
FRANK Trusty John men call me, sir.
CRIPPLE How comes it, then, your blinded secretary
Hath writ another name unto the letter?
"Yours devoted, Anthony Golding."
But sure this letter is no right of thine:
Either thou foundst the same by happy chance,
Or, being employèd as a messenger,
Play'dst legerdemain[338] with him that sent the same.
Wherefore, the maid well-known unto myself,
I will reserve the letter to her use,[339]
That she, if by the name herein set down,
She know the gentleman that doth wish her well,
She may be grateful for his courtesy.
FRANK Nay, then, I see I must disclose myself.
Sir, might I build upon your secrecy,
I would disclose a secret of import.
CRIPPLE Assure thyself, I will not injure thee.
FRANK Then, Cripple, know: I am not what I seem,
But took this habit to deceive my friend:
My friend indeed, but yet my cruel foe.
Foe to my good, my friend in outward show.
I am no porter, as I seem to be,
But younger brother to that Anthony.
And, to be brief, I am in love with Phyllis,
Which[340] my two elder brothers do affect.
The one of them seeks to defeat the other.
Now if that I, being their younger brother
Could gull them both, by getting of the wench,
I would requite it with love's recompense.
Cripple, thou once didst promise me thy love,
When I did rescue thee on Mile-End Green;

335 11 for: on behalf of
336 18 take remorse of: take pity on
337 18 such base stuff: i.e. a lower class person, a mere porter
338 27 Play'dst legerdemain: performed sleight of hand
339 29 reserve the . . . her use: save the letter for her
340 44 Which: whom

Now is the time, now let me have thy aid,
To gull my brothers of[341] that beauteous maid.
CRIPPLE Sir, what I promised I will now perform.
My love is yours, my life to do you good,
Which to approve,[342] follow me but in all:
We'll gull your brothers in the wench and all.
FRANK Sayst thou me so, friend? For that very word,
My life is thine: command my hand and sword.
CRIPPLE Then let me see this letter it should seem
You undertook to carry from your brother
To the maid.
FRANK I did, and from my brother Ferdinand,
This other letter to the same effect.
CRIPPLE Well, list to me, and follow my advice:
You shall deliver neither of them both,
But frame[343] two letters of your own invention,
Letters of flat[344] denial to their suits.
Give them to both your brothers as from Phyllis,
And let each line in either letter tend
To the dispraise of both their features.
And the conclusion I would have set down:
A flat resolve, bound with some zealous oath,
Never to yield to either of their suits.
And if this sort not well to your content,
Condemn the cripple.
FRANK But this will ask much time,
And they by this time look for my return.
CRIPPLE Why, then, myself will fit[345] you presently.
I have the copies in my custody
Of sundry[346] letters to the same effect.
FRANK Of thy own writing?
CRIPPLE My own, I assure you, sir.
FRANK Faith, thou hast robbed some sonnet-book or other,
And now wouldst make me think they are thine own.
CRIPPLE Why, think'st thou that I cannot write a letter,
Ditty,[347] or sonnet with judicial[348] phrase,
As pretty, pleasant, and pathetical,
As the best Ovid-imitating dunce
In all the town?
FRANK I think thou canst not.
CRIPPLE Yea, I'll swear I cannot.
Yet, sirrah, I could coney-catch[349] the world,
Make myself famous for a sudden[350] wit,
And be admired for my dexterity,[351]

341 52 gull my brothers of: trick my brothers out of
342 55 approve: make good
343 66 frame: compose
344 67 flat: absolute
345 77 fit: supply
346 79 sundry: various
347 84 Ditty: short, simple song
348 84 judicial: persuasive
349 89 coney-catch: dupe, deceive
350 90 sudden: quick, ready
351 91 dexterity: cleverness

Were I disposed.[352]
FRANK I prithee, how?
CRIPPLE Why thus: there lived a poet in this town—
If we may term our modern writers poets—
Sharp-witted, bitter-tongued, his pen of steel;
His ink was tempered[353] with the biting juice,[354]
And extracts of the bitterest weeds that grew.
He never wrote but when the elements
Of fire and water tilted[355] in his brain.
This fellow, ready to give up his ghost
To Lucia's bosom,[356] did bequeath to me
His library, which was just nothing,
But rolls, and scrolls, and bundles of cast[357] wit,
Such as durst[358] never visit Paul's churchyard.[359]
Amongst them all, I happened on a quire
Or two of paper[360] filled with songs and ditties,
And here and there a hungry epigram.[361]
These I reserve to my own proper use,
And, pater-noster-like, have conned[362] them all.
I could now, when I am in company,
At alehouse, tavern, or an ordinary,[363]
Upon a theme make an extemporal[364] ditty
(Or one at least should seem extemporal)
Out of th' abundance of this legacy,
That all would judge it, and report it, too,
To be the infant of a sudden wit,
And then were I an admirable fellow.
FRANK This were a piece of cunning.
CRIPPLE I could do more, for I could make inquiry
Where the best-witted gallants use to dine,
Follow them to the tavern, and there sit
In the next room with a calf's head and brimstone,[365]
And overhear their talk, observe their humors,
Collect their jests,[366] put them[367] into a play,
And tire them too with payment,[368] to behold
What I have filched[369] from them. This I could do.
But oh, for shame, that men should so arraign

352 92 If I wanted to
353 97 tempered: mixed
354 97 the biting juice: gall, bile
355 100 tilted: engaged in combat
356 101–2 ready to . . . Lucia's bosom: i.e. on his deathbed
357 104 cast: discarded
358 105 durst: dared
359 105 Paul's churchyard: the center of the book trade around St. Paul's cathedral
360 106–7 a quire . . . of paper: a couple of gatherings of sheets of paper
361 108 hungry epigram: appetizing short poem
362 110 Have learned them all, as I learned the Lord's Prayer
363 112 ordinary: pub or tavern that serves food
364 113 extemporal: improvised
365 123 calf's head and brimstone: obscure; a calf's head was generally a special centerpiece dish; "brimstone" is possibly a term for strong drink
366 125 jests: bantering talk
367 125 them: i.e. the jests
368 126 tire them too with payment: exhaust the gallants' finances, by charging them to watch the play
369 127 filched: stolen

Their own fee-simple wits, for verbal theft![370]
Yet men there be that have done this and that,
And more by much more than the most of them.[371]
FRANK But to our purpose, Cripple—to these letters.
CRIPPLE I have them ready for you; here they be.
Give these to your two brothers; say that Phyllis
Delivered them with frowns, and though her name
Be not subscribed[372] (which may not well be done[373])
It may perhaps give them occasion
To think she scorned them so much grace and favor.
This done, return to me, and let me know
Th'occurents of this practice as they grow.[374]
And so farewell! I can no longer stand
To talk with you: I have some work in hand. *Exit*
FRANK Farewell, mad cripple. Now, Frank Golding, fly,
To put in practice this new policy.
But soft, here comes the maid. I will assay

Enter PHYLLIS *and* FIDDLE

To plead my own love by a stranger way.
—By your leave, sir.
FIDDLE Porter, I am not for you;[375] you see I am perambulating[376] before a female.
FRANK I would crave but a word with you.
FIDDLE Speak in time, then, porter; for otherwise I do not love to answer you, and be as brief as you can, good porter.
FRANK I pray you, sir, what gentlewoman is this?
FIDDLE Certes,[377] porter, I serve a gentleman. That gentleman is father to this gentlewoman. This gentlewoman is a maid. This maid is fair. And this fair maid belongeth to the Exchange. And the Exchange hath not the like fair maid. Now, porter, put this all together, and tell me what it spells.
FRANK I promise you, sir, you have posed[378] me.
FIDDLE Then you are an ass, porter. 'Tis the fair maid of the Exchange.
FRANK Her name, I pray you, sir.
FIDDLE Her name, porter, requires much poeticality in the subscription,[379] and no less judgment in the understanding. Her name is Phyllis. Not Phyllis that same dainty lass that was beloved of Amintas, nor Phyllis she that doted on that comely youth Demophoön,[380] but this is Phyllis, that most strange[381] Phyllis, the flower of the Exchange.
PHYLLIS What, would that porter anything with me?
FRANK Yes, mistress. Since by chance I meet you here,
I'll tell you, though it not concerns myself,
What I this morning saw. There is a gentleman,

370 128–9 that men ... verbal theft: that anyone would find fault ("arraign") with his own ("fee-simple") wit by stealing witty words from others ("verbal theft"). Cripple "could do" this, but he wouldn't
371 130–31 Yet men ... of them: it's difficult to understand what Cripple means here. Frank's next line seems to indicate that he's not sure what Cripple is talking about in these last two lines; he changes the subject
372 136 Be not subscribed: isn't undersigned
373 136 may not well be done: wouldn't be right to do
374 140 The progress of this trickery as it develops
375 148 I am not for you: I do not have time for you
376 148 perambulating: walking
377 153 Certes: certainly
378 157 posed: perplexed
379 160 subscription: signature
380 161–2 Not Phyllis ... youth Demophoön: Fiddle alludes to two mythological Phyllises
381 163 strange: exceptional, rare

One master Golding, the youngest of three brothers:
They call him Frank. Oh, this man lies very sick:
I being at his house, perchance, inquired
What his disease was, of a servant there,
Who said, the doctors cannot tell themselves,
But in his fits he ever calls on love,
And prays to love for pity, and then names you,
And then names love again, and then calls "Phyllis!"
And sometimes starts,[382] and would forsake his bed,
And being asked whither, he says he would go to Phyllis.
My business called me hence, but I heard say
His friends do mean to entreat you to take the pains
To visit him, because they do suppose
The sick man loves you, and thence his sickness grows.
PHYLLIS Porter, is this true?
Or art thou hired to this? I prithee tell me.
FRANK Mistress, not hired—my name is Trusty John.
If I delude you, never trust me more.
PHYLLIS I thank thee, porter, and thank love withal,
That thus hath wrought the tyrant Golding's fall.
He once scorned love, jested at wounded hearts,
Challenged almighty beauty, railed at passion,
And is he now caught by the eyes and heart?
Now, by Diana's milk-white veil, I swear,
The goddess of my maiden-chaste desires,[383]
I am as glad of it as glad may be.
And I will see him, if but to laugh at him,
And torture him with jests. Fiddle, along!
When we return, if they do send for me,
I'll arm myself with flouts[384] and cruelty.
FIDDLE Porter, we commit you. If you be a crafty knave, and lay in the wind for a vantage,[385] you have your answer. Mark her last words: "I'll arm myself with flouts and cruelty."

Exeunt [FIDDLE *and* PHYLLIS]

FRANK "I'll arm myself with flouts and cruelty."
Will you so, Phyllis? What a state am I in!
Why I of all am furthest from her love.
'Sblood, if I now should take conceit[386] at this,
Fall sick with love indeed, were not my state
Most lamentable? Aye, by this hand, were it!
Well, heart, if thou wilt yield, look to thyself:
Thou wilt be tortured. Well, what remedy?

Enter ANTHONY

Here comes my brother Anthony; I am for[387] him.
ANTHONY Porter, what news? Spake you with Phyllis?
FRANK Aye, too late,[388] to my grief.

382 176 starts: rises suddenly
383 191–2 Diana's milk-white . . . maiden-chaste desires: Diana is the virgin goddess of the moon
384 197 flouts: jeers, scoffs
385 198 lay in . . . a vantage: place yourself in the most advantageous position (a metaphor from sailing)
386 203 take conceit: become ill
387 208 for: ready for
388 210 late: lately, recently

Spoke with her, sir? I' faith I think I have.
Here's a letter for you, and by that
You shall be judge if I did speak with her.
[*Aside*] Now, Cripple, shall we prove[389] your learnèd wit!
ANTHONY [*Reading the letter*] Zounds, am I mad, or is she mad that writ this?
I'll read it over again:

A Letter

Sir, I did never like you; I do not now think well of you; and I will never love you. I choose my husband with my eyes, and I have seen some especial fault in you, as the color of your hair, the elevating of your head to an affected proportion, as if you fainted for want of air, and stood in that manner to suck it into your nose; your neck is too long; and, to be short, I like no part in or about you. And the short and the long, boy, is that I will never love you, and I will never marry but one I love.

Not yours, but her own.

ANTHONY Blank! I am struck blank,[390] and blind, and mad withal.[391]
Here is a flat denial to my suit,
A resolution never to be won.
What shall I do? Assist me, god of love;
Instruct me in thy school-tricks! Be my guide
Out of this labyrinth of love and fear,
Unto the palace of fair Phyllis' favor.
I have it: I will intimate[392] her mother
In my behalf, with letters and with gifts.
To her I'll write to be my advocate.
Porter, farewell! [*Giving money*] There's for thy pains—
Thy profit by this toil passeth my gains.[393] *Exit*
FRANK You have your answer, and a kind one, too.
Cripple, I'll make thee crutches of pure silver
For this device. Thou hast a golden wit.
Now, if my brother Ferdinand were here
To read his absolution[394]—here he comes!

Enter FERDINAND

Brother!
FERDINAND Frank!
What, hast thou given the letter to her hand,
And stayed[395] my brother Anthony's withal?
FRANK I have done both, and more than that. Behold,
Here is an answer to your letter, brother.
FERDINAND Frank, I will love thee whiles I live, for this.
FRANK [*Aside*] Scarce, when you read what there containèd is.

[FERDINAND *reads*]

A Letter

Gallant, that write for love, if you had come yourself you might perchance have sped. I do not counsel you, neither, to come yourself, unless you leave your head at home, or wear a vizard,[396]

389 214 prove: test
390 225 Blank! I am struck blank: there's no signature! I'm completely confused
391 225 withal: besides
392 232 intimate: solicit
393 236 You're getting more out of this than I am
394 241 absolution: dismissal
395 245 stayed: kept back
396 252 *vizard*: mask

or come backwards, for I never look you in the face but I am sick. And so, praying God to continue my health, by keeping you from me, I leave you.

FERDINAND Oh, unkind answer to a lover's letter!
Let me survey the end once more.
"For I never look you in the face but I am sick. And so, praying God to continue me in health, by keeping you from me—"
Is she so far from yielding? Is this fort
Of her chaste love yet so impregnable?
What shall I do? This is the furthest way,
A labor of impossibilities.
This way to win her! I will once again
Challenge the promise that her father made me.
To him I'll write, and he, I know, will plead
My love to Phyllis, and so win the maid. *Exit*
FRANK Farewell, poor tortured heart! Was ever known
Two loving brothers in such misery?
Let me consider of my own estate.
What profit do I reap by this delusion?
Why, none! I am as far from Phyllis' heart
As when she first did wound me with her eyes.
Cripple, to thee I come: 'tis thou must be
My counselor in this extremity.[397]

Exit

[Act III scene iii]

Enter CRIPPLE, BOWDLER, *and* BERNARD

CRIPPLE Sirrah Bowdler, what makes thee in this merry vein?[398]
BOWDLER Oh Lord, sir, it is your most elevated humor[399] to be merry. To be concise, set up the collar, and look thus with a double chin,[400] like Diogenes[401] peering over his tub, is too cynical,[402] the sign of melancholy, and indeed the mere effect of a salt rheum.[403]
CRIPPLE Who would think this gentleman's yesterday's distemperature[404] should breed such motions?[405] I think it be restorative to activity. I never saw a gentleman caper[406] so excellent, as he did last night.
BOWDLER Mean you me, sir?
CRIPPLE Your own self, by this hand.
BOWDLER You gull me not?
CRIPPLE How, gull you?
Methinks a man so well-reputed of,
So well-commended for your qualities
In schools of nimble activeness,[407]
And places where divinest choristers

397 274 extremity: urgent condition
398 1 what makes . . . merry vein?: why are you in such a good mood?
399 2 elevated humor: exalted temperament
400 2–3 To be . . . double chin: to be inexpressive, to turn up one's collar (with a possible pun on choler = anger), and look down one's nose, like this
401 3 Diogenes: Greek philosopher and one of the founders of Cynicism, who slept in a barrel or tub in the marketplace
402 4 cynical: surly, contemptuous of pleasure
403 4 salt rheum: a runny nose, sign of a humoral imbalance
404 5 yesterday's distemperature: drunkenness last night
405 6 motions: passions
406 6 caper: dance in a frolicsome way
407 14 schools of nimble activeness: sites of silly dance practice and performance

Warble enchanting harmony,[408] to such
As think there is no heaven on earth but theirs,
And knowing yourself to be the genius[409]
Of the spectators, and the audience' hearts,
You wrong your worthy self intolerably,
To think our words savor of flattery.

BOWDLER Sirrah, dog! How didst thou like my last caper, and turn o' the toe?

CRIPPLE Before God, passing well.

BERNARD I know his worship made it,[410] 'tis so excellent.

BOWDLER It was my yesterday's exercise.

CRIPPLE After the working of your purgation,[411] was it not?

BOWDLER What purgation, you filthy cur?

CRIPPLE After the purging of your brain, sir.

BOWDLER Be still, dog; bark not. Though by misfortune
I was last night somewhat distemperèd,
I will not be upbraided.[412] 'Twas no more
But[413] to refine my wit. But tell me truly,
How dost thou like my caper?

CRIPPLE Far better than I can commend[414] it.

BOWDLER Now, as I am a gentleman
My tutor was not witting of the same.
And in my opinion 'twill do excellent.[415]
Oh, this air! Here's a most eloquious air for the memory;[416]
I could spend the third part of my arms[417] in silver,
To be encountered by some good wit or other.

CRIPPLE What say you to your sweetheart, Moll Berry?

BOWDLER Peace, Cripple! Silence; name her not. I could not endure the career[418] of her wit for a million; she is the only she-Mercury[419] under the heavens. Her wit is all spirit; that spirit fire; that fire flies from her tongue, able to burn the radix[420] of the best invention. In this element, she is the abstract and brief[421] of all the eloquence since the incarnation of Tully.[422] I tell thee, Cripple, I had rather encounter Hercules with blows than Moll Berry with words. And yet, by this light, I am horribly in love with her.

Enter MOLL *Berry*

CRIPPLE See where she comes. Oh, excellent!

BOWDLER Now have I no more blood than a bulrush.[423]

BERNARD How now! What ail you, sir?

CRIPPLE What's the matter, man?

BOWDLER See, see, that glorious angel doth approach. What shall I do?

408 15–16 places where . . . enchanting harmony: taverns where gallants sing drinking songs (meant ironically)
409 18 be the genius: embody the spirit
410 24 his worship made it: meaning unclear
411 26 purgation: vomiting
412 31 upbraided: scolded
413 31–2 no more/But: only
414 34 commend: praise
415 36–7 My tutor . . . do excellent: my dance teacher didn't acknowledge how great my "caper" was, but I think it was really superior
416 38 Bowdler breathes in deeply, associating the eloquent ("eloquious") air with his recollection of his great dancing the night before
417 39 arms: family wealth
418 42 career: charge, as in battle
419 43 she-Mercury: female form of the god of eloquence
420 44 radix: origin
421 45 abstract and brief: summary
422 45 Tully: Cicero, considered one of Rome's greatest orators
423 49 bulrush: a fragile reed

CRIPPLE She is a saint indeed. Zounds—to her, court her, win her, wear her,[424] wed her, and bed her, too.
BOWDLER I would it were come to that. I win her! By heaven, I am not furnished of a courting phrase to throw at a dog.
CRIPPLE Why, no, but at a woman you have! Oh, sir, seem not so doltish now; can you make no fustian?[425] Ask her if she'll take a pipe of tobacco.
BOWDLER It will offend her judgment. Pardon me.
CRIPPLE But hear you, sir. Reading so much as you have done,
Do you not remember one pretty phrase,
To scale the walls of a fair wench's love?
BOWDLER I never read anything but *Venus and Adonis*.
CRIPPLE Why, that's the very quintessence[426] of love.
If you remember but a verse or two,
I'll pawn my head, goods, lands, and all, 'twill do.
BOWDLER Why, then, have at her!
"Fondling, I say, since I have hemmed thee here,
Within the circle of this ivory pale,
I'll be a park—"
MOLL Hands off, fond sir!
BOWDLER "—And thou shalt be my deer![427]
Feed thou on me, and I will feed on thee,
And Love shall feed us both."[428]
MOLL Feed you on woodcocks;[429] I can fast a while.
BOWDLER "Vouchsafe,[430] thou wonder, to alight[431] thy steed."
CRIPPLE Take heed, she's not on horseback.
BOWDLER Why then, she is alighted!
"Come, sit thee down, where never serpent hisses;
And, being set, I'll smother thee with kisses."
MOLL Why, is your breath so hot? Now God forbid
I should buy kisses to be smotherèd.
BOWDLER Mean you me? You gull me not?
MOLL No, no, poor Bowdler, thou dost gull thyself.
[*Aside*] Thus must I do to shadow the hid fire,[432]
That in my heart doth burn with hot desire.
Oh, I do love him well, whate'er I say,
Yet will I not myself self-love bewray.[433]
If he be wise he'll sue[434] with good take-heed.
Bowdler, do so, and thou art sure to speed.
I will fly hence to make his love the stronger,
Though my affection must lie hid the longer.
—What, Master Bowdler, not a word to say?
BOWDLER No, by my troth, if[435] you stay here all day.

424 53 win her, wear her: possess her
425 57–8 can you . . . no fustian?: can't you speak pompously?
426 64 quintessence: perfect expression, form
427 68–72 "Fondling, I . . . my deer!": slightly altered quotation from Shakespeare's narrative poem, *Venus and Adonis* (lines 229–31), published in 1593. These are Venus's words to Adonis, whom she's pursuing; the "ivory pale" is the circle of Venus's white arms, which has "hemmed" Adonis
428 73–4 "Feed thou . . . us both": these lines are not in Shakespeare's poem. The lines quoted in lines 76 and 79–80 are taken from *Venus and Adonis* lines 13–18
429 75 woodcocks: a) birds; b) fools or simpletons
430 76 Vouchsafe: show a gracious willingness
431 76 alight: dismount
432 85 shadow the hid fire: conceal the secret passion
433 88 bewray: reveal
434 89 sue: pursue (me)
435 94 if: even if

MOLL Why then, I'll bear the bucklers hence away.[436] *Exit*

CRIPPLE What, Master Bowdler, have you let her pass unconquered?

BOWDLER Why, what could I do more? I looked upon her with judgment; the strings of my tongue were well in tune; my embraces were in good measure; my palm of a good constitution; only the phrase was not moving. As, for example, Venus herself with all her skill could not win Adonis with the same words. Oh, heavens! Was I so fond,[437] then, to think that I could conquer Moll Berry? Oh, the natural fluence[438] of my own wit had been far better!

Enter FIDDLE

Good-den,[439] good fellow.

FIDDLE God give you the time of the day. Pardon me, gallants, I was so near the middle that I knew not which hand to take.[440]

BOWDLER A very good conceit.

FIDDLE And yet because I will be sure to give you a true salutation, Cripple, *quomodo vales*?[441] Good morrow, Cripple; good-den good Master Bernard; Master Bowdler, *bonos noches*,[442] as they say, good night! And thus you have heard my manner of salutation.

CRIPPLE You are very eloquent, sir. But Fiddle, what's the best news abroad?

FIDDLE The best news I know not, sir, but the newest news is most excellent, i' faith.

BERNARD Prithee, let's hear it.

FIDDLE Why, this it is: the sergeants are watching to arrest you at Master Berry's suit.[443]

BERNARD 'Swounds, where?

FIDDLE Nay, I know not where. Alas, sir, there is no such matter.[444] I did but say so much to make you warm the handle of your rapier.[445] But, Master Bowdler, I have good news for you.

BOWDLER Let me hear it, my sweet russeting.[446]

FIDDLE How, russeting?

BOWDLER Aye, my little apple-john.[447]

FIDDLE You are a—

BOWDLER A what?

FIDDLE You are a—Oh, that I could speak for indignation!

BOWDLER Nay, what am I?

FIDDLE You are a pippinmonger[448] to call me russeting or apple-john.

BOWDLER Sirrah Russeting, I'll pare your head off.

FIDDLE You pippinmonger, I'll cut off your legs, and make you travel so near the mother earth, that every boy shall be high[449] enough to steal apples out of thy basket—call me Russeting!

CRIPPLE Nay, be friends, be friends.

FIDDLE As I am a gentleman, Cripple, I meant him no harm, but the name of Russeting to Master Fiddle, that many times travels under the arm in velvet, but for the most part in leather trussed with calfskin points,[450] 'tis most tolerable,[451] and not to be endured. Flesh and

436 95 Then I'll depart as the winner
437 100 fond: foolish
438 101 fluence: flow
439 102 Good-den: i.e. good evening
440 103–4: God give . . . to take: "Fiddle means he knows it is about noon, but he is not sure whether he should say, 'Good morning,' or 'Good afternoon'" (Snyder, 1980)
441 106 *quomodo vales*?: how are you? (Latin)
442 107 *bonos noches*: good night (Spanish)
443 112 at Master Berry's suit: on account of Master Berry's legal petition
444 114 there is no such matter: I was just kidding
445 115 warm the . . . your rapier: put your hand on your sword handle
446 116 russeting: russet apple; simple person
447 118 apple-john: shriveled apple
448 123 pippinmonger: apple merchant
449 126 high: tall
450 129–30 under the . . . calfskin points: Fiddle objects that he wears fine clothing, not the coarse woolen "russet" cloth of country people; points are cords used for fastening clothing
451 130 tolerable: a malapropism for "intolerable"

blood cannot bear it.
CRIPPLE Come, come, all shall be well.
BOWDLER Fiddle, give me thy hand. A plague on thee, thou knowest I love thee.
FIDDLE Say you so? Why, then, anger avoid the room; melancholy march away; choler[452] to the next chamber. And here's my hand; I am yours to command from this time forth, your very mortal friend and loving enemy, master Fiddle.
BOWDLER Now, tell us, what is the news you had for me?
FIDDLE Oh, the sweet news! Faith, sir, this it is: that I was sent to the cripple from my young mistress. Master Cripple, you know I have spent some time in idle words, therefore be you compendious,[453] and tell me if my mistress' handkercher be done or no.
CRIPPLE Fiddle, 'tis done, and peace[454] it is. Commend me to thy mistress.
FIDDLE After the most humble manner, I will. And so, gentlemen, I commit[455] you all: you, Cripple, to your shop; you, sir, to a turnip and dish of capers;[456] and lastly, you, Master Bernard, to the tuition of the Counter-keeper.[457] There's an item[458] for you, and so farewell!

Exit

CRIPPLE Master Bowdler, how do you like his humor?
BOWDLER By this light, I had not thought the clod[459] had had so nimble a spirit. But Cripple, farewell. I'll to Moll Berry. Come, Bernard, along with me.
CRIPPLE Farewell, sweet signiors both. Farewell, farewell!

Exeunt

[Act IV, scene i]

Enter MASTER FLOWER *at one door reading a letter from* FERDINAND, *at the other* MISTRESS FLOWER, *with a letter from* ANTHONY

MASTER FLOWER [*Aside*] The conceit is good: Ferdinand entreats[460] a marriage with my daughter. Good, very good! For he is a gentleman of good carriage: a wise man, a rich man, a careful man, and therefore worthy of my daughter's love. It shall be so.
MISTRESS FLOWER [*Aside*] Marry, and shall,[461] kind gentleman. My furtherance,[462] sayest thou? Yes, Anthony, assure thyself; for, by the motherly care that I bear to my daughter, it hath been a desire that long hath lodged within my careful breast, to match her with thy well-deserving self. And to this end have I sent for my daughter, and charged my servants, that presently, upon her repair[463] hither from her mistress's, that she enter this private walk, where and with whom I will so work, that, doubt it not, dear son, but she shall be thine.
MASTER FLOWER [*Aside*] And I will make her jointure[464] of a hundred pounds by year. It is a very good conceit, and why? Because the worthy portion betters my conceit, which, being good in conceiving well of the gentleman's good parts, the proffered jointure adds to my conceit, and betters it.[465] Very good.

452 134 choler: irritability
453 140 compendious: brief
454 141 peace: perhaps a misprint for "here."
455 142 commit: deliver, hand over
456 143 turnip and dish of capers: Fiddle punningly sends Bowdler to do more dancing: a "turn-up" and "capers"
457 144 tuition of the Counter-keeper: custody of the jailer
458 144 item: hint
459 146 clod: blockhead, dolt
460 1 entreats: asks for
461 4 Marry, and shall: indeed you shall
462 4 furtherance: assistance
463 8 repair: return
464 10 jointure: dowry
465 11–13 It is . . . betters it: Master Flower reflects that it makes sense to give Phyllis a big dowry, because not only is Ferdinand a "good" man, as Flower already thought, but he is also rich (he has a "worthy portion")—just as Ferdinand's "portion" adds to his "good"ness, so Phyllis's large "jointure" will appropriately match Ferdinand's "portion"

MISTRESS FLOWER [*Aside*] A thousand crowns[466] for you to make the match! Pretty heart, how love can work! By God's blessed mother, I vow she shall be thine, if I have any interest in my daughter.

MASTER FLOWER *smiles reading the letter, they snatch the letter from each other*

But stay, whom have I espied? My husband likewise reading of a letter, and in so good an humor? I'll lay my life, good gentleman, he hath also wrought with him[467] for his good will. And for I long to know the truth thereof, my sudden purpose shall experience it.[468]—What's here, husband? (*She reads privately, and frowns*) A letter from master Ferdinand, to entreat a marriage with your daughter?

MASTER FLOWER And here the like to you, from Anthony,
To that effect. This is no good conceit.
If she be mine, she shall be Ferdinand's.
MISTRESS FLOWER If she respect her mother's favor,
'Tis Anthony shall be her love.
MASTER FLOWER How, wife?
MISTRESS FLOWER Even so, husband.
MASTER FLOWER You will not cross my purpose, will you?
MISTRESS FLOWER In this you shall not bridle[469] me, I swear.
MASTER FLOWER Is she not my daughter?
MISTRESS FLOWER You teach me, husband, what your wife should say.
I think her life is dearest unto me,
Though you forget the long extremity
And pain which I endured, when forth this womb,
With much ado, she did enjoy the life
She now doth breathe; and shall I now suffer
Her destruction?
MASTER FLOWER Yea, but conceit me, wife.
MISTRESS FLOWER A fig for[470] your conceits!
In this I know there can be none of that.[471]
Say he[472] be his father's eldest son,
And a merchant of good wealth.
Yet my dear Anthony's as rich as he.
What though his portion[473] was but small at first,
His industry hath now increased his talent.[474]
And he that knoweth the getting of a penny
Will fear to spend. She shall have him, if any.
MASTER FLOWER By the Mary God, wife, you vex me.
MISTRESS FLOWER 'Tis your own impatience—you may choose.[475]
MASTER FLOWER I will not wed my daughter to that Anthony.
MISTRESS FLOWER By this—[476]
MASTER FLOWER Hold, wife, hold. I advise thee, swear not.
For, by him that made me, first I vow,

466 14 A thousand crowns: two or three times the amount Master Flower mentioned
467 18 he hath . . . with him: Anthony has also worked on Master Flower
468 19 my sudden . . . experience it: I am determined to quickly find out
469 30 bridle: restrain
470 39 A fig for: I couldn't care less about
471 40 With respect to our daughter's marriage, let's leave your "conceits" out of it
472 41 he: i.e. Ferdinand
473 44 portion: share of his father's estate
474 45 talent: wealth
475 49 may choose: can decide how to feel
476 51 by this—: Mistress Flower is about to swear on something, perhaps her hand

She shall not touch the bed of Anthony.
MISTRESS FLOWER And may I never live (so God me help)
If ever she be wed to Ferdinand.
MASTER FLOWER The devil's in this woman. How she thwarts me still!
MISTRESS FLOWER Fret on, good husband. I will have my will!
MASTER FLOWER But conceit me, wife: suppose we should consent our daughter should wed either of them both,[477] and she dislike the match. Were that a good conceit?
MISTRESS FLOWER All's one for that. I know my daughter's mind
If I but say the word.
MASTER FLOWER I would be loath to wed her against her will.
Content thee, wife. We'll hear her resolution,
And as I find her, to her own content
To either of them, she shall have my consent.
MISTRESS FLOWER Why, now old Flower speaketh like himself.
MASTER FLOWER Agreed. And, faith, wife, 'tis a good conceit.

Enter PHYLLIS

And see where my daughter comes! Welcome, girl.
How doth your mistress, Phyllis? God bless thee, Phyllis! [PHYLLIS *kneels*]
Rise.
PHYLLIS God have the glory, in perfect health she is.
MASTER FLOWER 'Tis good. I am glad she doth so well.
But list, my daughter! I have golden news
To impart unto thee.
A golden Golding, wench, must be thy husband.
Is't not a good conceit?
PHYLLIS Father, I understand you not.
MASTER FLOWER Then, my girl, thy conceit is very shallow.
Master Ferdinand Golding is in love with thee.
MISTRESS FLOWER No, daughter, 'tis thine Anthony.
MASTER FLOWER Ferdinand is rich, for he hath store of gold.
MISTRESS FLOWER Anthony is rich, yet is not so old.
MASTER FLOWER Ferdinand is virtuous, full of modesty.
MISTRESS FLOWER Anthony's more gracious, if more may be.
MASTER FLOWER Ferdinand is wise. Being wise, who would not love him?
MISTRESS FLOWER Anthony more wise. Then, girl, desire to prove him.[478]
MASTER FLOWER In Ferdinand is all the beauty that may be.
MISTRESS FLOWER He is deceived. 'Tis in thine Anthony.
PHYLLIS Dear parents, you confound me with your words.
I pray, what mean these hot persuasions?
MASTER FLOWER Thy good, my daughter.
MISTRESS FLOWER If but ruled by me.
MASTER FLOWER But for thy ill fare—
MISTRESS FLOWER If she tend[479] to thee.
MASTER FLOWER The truth is this: that each of us hath ta'en
A solemn vow, that thou, my loving daughter
Shalt wed with one of those two gentlemen;
But yet refer the choice unto thyself.
One thou shalt love. Love Ferdinand, if me.
MISTRESS FLOWER If love thy mother, love thine Anthony.

477 60 either of them both: i.e. either of the two of them
478 87 prove him: put him to the test
479 93 If she tend: should she listen

PHYLLIS In these extremes, what shall become of me?
I pray you give me respite to consider
How to digest[480] these impositions.
You have imposed a business of such weight,
Pray God your daughter may discharge herself.[481]
MASTER FLOWER Think on't, my girl. We will withdraw a while. *They walk*
PHYLLIS [*Aside*] A little respite fits my resolution.
Those gentles[482] sue too late: there is another
Of better worth, though not of half their wealth.
What though deformed? His virtue mends that miss.
What though not rich? His wit doth better[483] gold,
And my estate shall add unto his wants.
I am resolved, good father and dear mother:
Phyllis doth choose a cripple, and none other.
But yet I must dissemble.[484]
MASTER FLOWER How now, my soul's best hope? Tell me, my girl,
Shall Ferdinand be he?
PHYLLIS I pray, a word in private.
MASTER FLOWER Marry, with all my heart.
PHYLLIS [*Aside to* MASTER FLOWER] In all the duty that a child can show,
The love that to a father it doth owe,
I yield myself to be at your command,
And vow to wed no man but Ferdinand.
But, if you please, at your departure hence,
You may enforce[485] dislike to cloud your brow,
To avoid my mother's anger and suspicion.
MASTER FLOWER [*Aside to* PHYLLIS] Before God, a very good conceit.
—Hence, baggage,[486] out of my sight!
Come not within my doors! Thou hadst been better
Run millions of miles barefooted, than
Thus by your coy disdain to have deluded me.
[*Aside*] Oh, mine own flesh and blood, the mirror[487] of wit!
Now will I hence, and, with all the speed I may,
Send for my son. I'll have it done this day. *Exit* [MASTER] FLOWER[488]
MISTRESS FLOWER [*Aside*] What, is he gone? And in so hot a chase?
Well, let him go. I need not question why.
For well I wot his suit is cold;[489] 't'must die.
—Daughter, I gather by these pleasant smiles
Thy mother hath more interest in thy love
Than discontented Flower, thy agèd father.
PHYLLIS Mother, you have, for when I well consider
A mother's care unto her dear-bought child,
How tenderly you nursed and brought me up,
I could not be so much unnatural

480 102 digest: settle in my mind
481 104 discharge herself: perform this duty responsibly
482 107 Those gentles: the gentlemen Ferdinand and Anthony
483 110 better: surpass
484 114 dissemble: pretend
485 124 enforce: cause, compel
486 127 baggage: disreputable woman
487 131 mirror: exemplar
488 133 SD in Q, this stage direction reads "*Exit old Flow.*"
489 136 I wot . . . is cold: I know his request that Phyllis marry Ferdinand will go no further

As to refuse the love you proffer[490] me,
Especially being for my chiefest good.
Therefore, when married I intend to be,
My loyal husband shall be Anthony.
MISTRESS FLOWER Live ever, then, my dear, dear daughter Phyllis!
Let me embrace thee in a mother's arms.
Thus, thus, and thus I'll ever hug my daughter.
Him[491] hence thou send'st with frowns, me hence with laughter.
Come, Phyllis, let us in. *Exit* MISTRESS FLOWER
PHYLLIS Forsooth, I'll follow you.
—Am I not a good child, think you,
To play with both hands thus against my parents?
Well, 'tis but a trick of youth. Say what they will,
I'll love the cripple, and will hate them still.

Exit

[Act IV, scene ii]

Enter CRIPPLE *in his shop, and to him enters* FRANK

FRANK Mirror of kindness, extremity's best friend,
While I breathe, sweet blood, I am thine.
Entreat me—nay, command thy Francis'[492] heart,
That wilt not suffer my ensuing smart.[493]
CRIPPLE Sweet signior, my advice in the reservation[494] of those letters,
Which I will have you hide from eye of day,
Never to feel the warmth of Phoebus'[495] beams,
Till myself's care, most careful of your weal,[496]
Summon those lines unto the bar of joy.[497]
FRANK I will not err, dear friend, in this command.
CRIPPLE So much for that. Now listen further, Frank.
Not yet two hours' expiration
Have taken final end, since beauty's pride
And nature's better part of workmanship,
Beauteous Phyllis, was with me consorted,[498]
Where she, 'mongst other pleasing conference,
Burst into terms of sweet affection,
And said ere long she would converse with me
In private at my shop; whose wounded soul
Struck with love's golden arrow lives in dread,
Till she do hear the sentence of my love,
Or be condemned by judgment of fell[499] hate.
Now, since that gracious opportunity
Thus smiles on me, I will resign the same

490 144 proffer: offer
491 151 Him: i.e. Master Flower
492 3 thy Francis': my (Francis is Frank's full name)
493 4 Who will not allow me to suffer further love-pangs
494 5 reservation: keeping-back
495 7 Phoebus': the sun's
496 8 careful of your weal: concerned for your well-being
497 9 Summon those . . . of joy: ask you to bring the letters forth, in the manner of legal documents, as part of our success in your love-pursuits
498 12–15 Not yet . . . me consorted: it's been less than two hours since Phyllis came to speak with me
499 22 fell: cruel

To you,[500] my friend, knowing my unworthy self
Too foul for such a beauty, and too base
To match in brightness with that sacred comet,[501]
That shines, like Phoebus, in London's element,[502]
From whence inferior stars derive their light.
Wherefore I will immediately you take
My crooked habit,[503] and in that disguise
Court her, yea, win her, for she will be won.
This will I do to pleasure you, my friend.
FRANK For which my love to thee shall never end.
CRIPPLE About it,[504] then. Assume this shape of mine;
Take what I have, for all I have is thine!
Supply my place, to gain thy heart's desire;
So may you quench two hearts that burn like fire.
She's kind to me; be she as kind to you,
What admiration[505] will there then ensue?
Frank, I will leave thee. Now be thou fortunate,
That we will joy your loves may consummate.
Farewell, farewell. When I return again,
I hope to find thee in a pleasing vein.[506] *Exit*
FRANK [*Disguised as* CRIPPLE][507] Farewell, dear friend.
—Was ever known a finer policy?
Now, brothers, have amongst you[508] for a third part,
Nay, for the whole, or, by my soul, I'll lose all.
What though my father did bequeath his lands
To you, my elder brethren, the movables[509] I sue for
Were none of his. And you shall run through fire,
Before you touch one part of my desire.
Am I not like myself in this disguise?
Crooked in shape, and crooked in my thoughts?
Then am I a cripple right.[510] Come, wench, away!
Thy absence breeds a terror to my stay.[511]

Enter PHYLLIS

Yonder she comes. Now frame thy hands to draw:[512]
A worser workman never any saw.
PHYLLIS Yea, yonder sits the wonder of mine eye.
I have not been the first whom destiny
Hath thwarted thus. Imperious love,
Either withdraw the shaft that wounds my heart,
Or grant me patience to endure my smart![513]

500 24–5 resign the same/To you: give over to you these favorable circumstances
501 27 that sacred comet: i.e. Phyllis
502 28 element: sky
503 30–31 Wherefore I . . . crooked habit: for which reason I'll have you put on my garment and assume my deformed shape at once
504 35 About it: get to work
505 40 admiration: wonder
506 44 vein: mood
507 45 SD *Disguised as* CRIPPLE: Frank impersonates Cripple throughout this scene
508 47 have amongst you: watch out
509 50 movables: properties (i.e. Phyllis)
510 55 right: altogether, fully
511 56 Your absence makes waiting terrible
512 57 frame thy hands to draw: pretend you're drawing
513 63 smart: pain

Remorseless love, had any but thyself
Been privy to my direful passion,
How I consume and waste myself in love,
They would have been, yea, much more pitiful.
But all avails not.[514] Demanding for my work[515]
Shall be a means to have some conference. *She speaks to* FRANK
Good morrow to you. Is my handkercher done?
FRANK Yea, Mistress Flower, it is finishèd.
PHYLLIS [*Aside*] How sweetly tunes the accent of his voice!
—Oh, do not blame me, dearest love alive!
Though thus I dote in my affection.
I toil, I labor, and I fain would thrive;[516]
And thrive I may, if thou wouldst give direction.
Thou art the star whereby my course is led;
Be gracious, then, bright sun, or I am dead.
FRANK Fair mistress Phyllis, such wanton toys[517] as these
Are for young novices that will soon be pleased.[518]
The careful thoughts that hammer in my brain
Bid me abandon wanton love. 'Tis vain.
PHYLLIS For me it is.
FRANK Is my ungarnished,[519] dark, and obscure cell[520]
A mansion fit for all-commanding love?
No, if thou wilt sport with love,
And dally with that wanton amorous boy,[521]
Hie thee[522] unto the odoriferous groves.[523]
PHYLLIS There is no groves more pleasant unto me,
Than to be still[524] in thy society.
FRANK There, of the choicest fragrant flowers that grow,
Thou may'st devise sweet roseate coronets,[525]
And with the nymphs that haunt the silver streams,
Learn to entice the affable young wag.[526]
There shalt thou find him, wandering up and down,
Till some fair saint impale him[527] with a crown.
Be gone, I say, and do not trouble me;
For, to be short, I cannot fancy thee.
PHYLLIS For, to be short, you cannot fancy me?
Oh, cruel word, more hateful than pale death.
Oh, would to God it would conclude my breath.
FRANK Forbear, forbear! Admit[528] that I should yield:
Think you your father would applaud your choice?

514 68 But all avails not: But there's no help for it
515 68 my work: i.e. the patterning work she ordered from Cripple
516 75 fain would thrive: would like to succeed
517 79 wanton toys: playful, trivial words
518 80 that will soon be pleased: who seek immediate gratification
519 84 ungarnished: unfurnished
520 84 cell: small room
521 87 wanton amorous boy: i.e. Cupid
522 88 Hie thee: go quickly
523 88 odoriferous groves: sweet-smelling country woods
524 90 still: always
525 92 devise sweet roseate coronets: make aromatic flower crowns
526 94 affable young wag: friendly mischievous boy, i.e. Cupid
527 96 impale him: encircle his head
528 102 Admit: suppose for the sake of argument

PHYLLIS Doubt not thereof. Or, if he do not, all's one,[529]
So you but grant to my affection.
FRANK I am too base.[530]
PHYLLIS My wealth shall raise thee up.
FRANK I am deformed.
PHILLLIS Tut, I will bear with that.
FRANK Your friends'[531] dislike brings all this out of frame.[532]
PHYLLIS By humble suit, I will redress[533] the same.
FRANK [*Aside*] Now to employ the virtue of my shape!
—Fair mistress,
If heretofore I have remorseless been,
And not esteemed your undeservèd love[534]
(Whereby, in the glass of your affection,
I see my great unkindness), forgive what's past.
And here I proffer all the humble service
Your high-prized love doth merit at my hands,
Which, I confess, is more than I (unable)
Can gratify. Therefore command my toil,
My travail,[535] yea, my life, to pleasure you.
PHYLLIS I take thee at thy word, proud of thy service.
But yet no servant shalt thou be of mine:
I will serve thee. Command, and I'll obey.
This doth my soul more good—yea, ten times more—
Than did thy harsh denial harm before.
Let us embrace like two united friends;
Here love begins, and former hatred ends!

Enter FERDINAND *and* ANTHONY *walking together*

FERDINAND Brother Anthony! What news from Venice?
Are your ships returned? [*Aside*] I had rather
Hear news from Phyllis. Oh, brother Frank,
Thy absence makes me burn in passion.
ANTHONY Sir, I had letters from my factors[536] there
Some three days since. [*Aside*] But the return of one,
Of one poor letter, yet not answerèd,[537]
Makes me stark mad. A plague upon that porter!
Damned may he be for thus deluding me. FERDINAND *spies* PHYLLIS *and turns back*
—How now, brother! Why retire you so?
FERDINAND Yonder's a friend of mine acquaintance,
With whom I would gladly have some conference.
I pray thee, stay; I will return immediately. *Go to* PHYLLIS *and court her to themselves*[538]

529 104 all's one: it doesn't matter
530 106 base: low-born
531 108 friends': family's
532 108 brings all . . . of frame: makes our courtship inappropriate
533 109 redress: correct
534 113 And not valued your love, which I don't deserve
535 120 travail: labor
536 132 factors: agents, representatives
537 134 one poor . . . not answerèd: Anthony's complaint here ignores the rejection letter he received near the end of III.ii, supposedly from Phyllis (actually written by Cripple)
538 140 SD *to themselves*: i.e. Ferdinand and Phyllis talk apart from Anthony

ANTHONY [*Aside*] Of your acquaintance! Is she so, good brother?
Only with you acquainted, and no other?
Faith, I'll try that; take heed, sir, what you do.
If you begin to court, I needs must woo. *Go to her too*
—Brother, have you done?
FERDINAND But two words more, at most.
[*To* PHYLLIS] You have not then received any such letter?
A vengeance take the lazy messenger!
[*Aside*] Brother,[539] if I live, I'll quittance[540] thee for this.
FRANK [*Aside*] Good words, dear brother; threatened men live long.[541]
ANTHONY You have done?
FERDINAND Yes.
ANTHONY Then, by your leave, brother.
You had one word; I must have another. *Talk in private*
FERDINAND [*Aside*] I know our business tends to one effect.[542]
Oh, that villain Frank! It mads my soul
I am so wronged by such a foolish boy.
FRANK [*Aside*] That foolish boy may chance prove to be witty!
What, and the elder brothers fools? Oh, 'tis pity!
ANTHONY [*Aside*] That villain porter hath deluded me.
Confusion guerdon[543] his base villainy.
FRANK [*Aside*] What, are you cursing, too? Then we catch no fish!
Comes there any more, here's two snipes to a dish.[544]
FERDINAND [*Aside*] Well, since I have such opportunity,
I'll trust no longer to uncertainty. *He courts her again in private*
ANTHONY [*Aside*] At it so hard, brother? Well, woo apace;[545]
Awhile I am content to give you place.
FRANK [*Aside*] Well, to her both; both do the best you can!
I fear young Frank will prove the happier man.
PHYLLIS [*To* FERDINAND] You have your answer; trouble me no more.
FERDINAND Yet this is worse than my suspense before.
For then I lived in hope; now hope is fled.
ANTHONY What, malcontent? Is Ferdinand struck dead?
Fortune, be blithe,[546] and aid the second brother. *Talk in private*
FRANK [*Aside*] Think you to have more favor than another?
To her, a' God's name! Live not in suspense.
While you two strive, I needs must get the wench.
PHYLLIS [*To* ANTHONY] I am resolved, and, sir, you know my mind.
FRANK [*Aside*] What, you repulsed too? Phyllis is too unkind!
PHYLLIS Here sits my love, within whose lovely breast
Lives my content, and all my pleasures rest.
And for a further confirmation,
Which, to approve, even in sight of both you here present,
I give my hand, and, with my hand, my heart,
Myself, and all to him! And with this ring
I'll wed myself.
FRANK I take thy offering,

539 149 Brother: i.e. Frank
540 149 quittance: pay you back
541 150 threatened men live long: proverbial, meaning that threats are often not carried out, and those on their guard are in less danger
542 155 tends to one effect: shares the same goal
543 161 guerdon: reward
544 163 here's two . . . a dish: here are two "stupid birds" (Snyder, 1980) ready to be plucked and eaten
545 166 apace: quickly
546 174 blithe: kind

And for the gift you gave to me, take this,
And let us seal affection with a kiss.
FERDINAND Oh, sight intolerable!
ANTHONY A spectacle worse than death!
FRANK Now, gentlemen, please you draw near and listen to the cripple. *Give them the letters and they stamp and storm*
Know you that letter? Sir, what say you to this?
BOTH How came they to your hands?
FRANK Sirs, a porter even of late left them with me,
To be delivered to this gentlewoman.
ANTHONY A plague upon that porter! If ever I meet him,
My rapier's point with a death's wound shall greet him. *Exit*
FERDINAND Frank, thou art a villain; thou shalt know't ere long,
For proferring me such undeservèd wrong. *Exit*
FRANK [*Aside*] So! Vomit forth the rheum of all your spite.
These threats of yours procure me more delight.
PHYLLIS Now, gentle love, all that I have to say
Is to entreat you seek without delay
My father's kind consent, for thou hast mine.
And, though he storm, yet will I still be thine.
Make trial then; 'tis but thy labor lost,
Though he deny thee. It requires no cost.
FRANK I will assail with expedition.[547]
PHYLLIS God and good fortune go with thee. Farewell! *Exit*
FRANK Well, I will go, but not in this disguise.
Arm thee with policy, Frank; Frank must be wise.
Now, would the substance of this borrowed shape
Were here in presence—and see where he comes.

Enter the CRIPPLE

Poor in the well-framed limbs of nature, but
Rich in kindness beyond comparison.
Welcome, dear friend! The kindest soul alive!
Here I resign thy habit[548] back again,
Whereby I prove the happiest man that breathes.
CRIPPLE Hast thou then, sweet blood, been fortunate? *Whisper in private*

Enter BOWDLER, MOLL *Berry, and* RALPH, BOWDLER *capers and sings*

RALPH Faith, sir, methinks of late you are very light.[549]
BOWDLER As a feather, sweet rogue, as a feather.
Have I not good cause? Sweet Moll, sweet Moll!
Hath she not caused the same? Well, if I live, sweet wench,
Either by night or day I will requite your kindness.
FRANK [*To* CRIPPLE] Now I will take my leave, to put the same in practice.[550] *Exit* FRANK
CRIPPLE Good fortune wait on thee!
BOWDLER Moll, thou art mine, by thine own consent!
How sayest thou, Moll?

547 208 assail with expedition: attempt (to talk to your father) right away
548 217 resign thy habit: return your clothing
549 220 light: cheerful
550 225 put the same in practice: do what we just planned

MOLL Yes, forsooth.
RALPH I am witness, sir.
BOWDLER But that is not sufficient, Moll. If thou art content, Moll, here's a rogue hard by, a friend of mine, whom I will acquaint with our loves, and he shall be partaker of the match.[551]
RALPH Nay, sir, if you mean to have partners in the match, I hope Ralph can help to serve your wife's turn as well as another, whate'er he be. How say you, mistress?
MOLL All's one to me, whom he please.
BOWDLER Come, then, sweet Moll. We'll to the drawer,
There to dispatch what I further intend.
MOLL And well remembered, husband.
RALPH A forward maiden, by this light. "Husband" before the clerk hath said Amen!
MOLL He hath work of mine; I pray forget it not.
BOWDLER I will not, Moll. Now, you lame rogue, where is this maiden's work? My wife's work, you rascal! Quick, give it her!
CRIPPLE Sweet signior, the sweet nymph's work is almost finished, but, sweet blood, you drive me into admiration with your latter words. Your sweet wife's work! I admire it.[552]
BOWDLER Aye, ye halting rascal, my wife's work! She's my wife before God and Ralph. How sayest thou, Moll, art thou not?
MOLL Yes, forsooth. And to confirm the same,
Here in this presence, I plight[553] my faith again;
And speak again what erst before was said:
That none but you shall have my maidenhead.
BOWDLER A good wench, Moll! I' faith, now will I to thy father for his good will. Cripple, see you remember what is past, for I will call thee in question for a witness, if need require. Farewell, cur; farewell, dog! *Exit* BOWDLER *and* RALPH
CRIPPLE Adieu, fond humorist, parenthesis of jests,[554]
Whose humor like a needless cipher fills a room!
But now, Moll Berry, a word or two with you.
Hast thou forgotten Bernard? Thy thoughts were bent on him.
MOLL On him, Cripple? For what? Was it for marriage?
CRIPPLE It was for love; why not for marriage? Oh, monstrous!
Were I a maid and should be so bewitched,
I'd pull my eyes out that did lend me light,
Exclaim against my fortune, ban my stars,[555]
And tear my heart, so yielding her consent
To Bowdler's love, that froth of compliment.[556]
MOLL Cripple, you lose[557] your time, with your fair tears
To circumvent my heart. Bowdler, I love thee;
Bernard I hate; and thou shalt never move me.
CRIPPLE I will! Thou dost love Bernard, and I can prove it.
MOLL That I love Bernard? By heavens, I abhor him.
CRIPPLE Thou lov'st him. Once again I say, thou lov'st him,
For all thou hast borne Bowdler still in hand.[558]
MOLL What, wilt thou make me mad? I say I hate him.
CRIPPLE I say thou lov'st him. Have not I been at home,
And heard thee in thy chamber praise his person,
And say he is a proper little man,

551 232 partaker of the match: i.e. witness to our marriage
552 243–4 you drive . . . admire it: Cripple expresses astonishment at hearing Bowdler call Moll his wife
553 248 plight: pledge, as a marriage vow
554 254 parenthesis of jests: speaker of irrelevant banter
555 262 ban my stars: curse my destiny
556 264 froth of compliment: unsubstantial flatterer
557 265 lose: waste
558 271 borne Bowdler still in hand: led Bowdler on

And pray that he would be a suitor to thee?
Have I not seen thee in the bay window
To sit cross-armed, take counsel of thy glass,[559]
And prune thyself to please young Bernard's eye?
Sometimes curling thy hair, then practicing smiles;
Sometimes rubbing thy filthy butter-teeth,[560]
Then pull the hairs from off thy beetle-brows,[561]
Painting the veins upon thy breasts with blue;
An hundred other tricks I saw thee use,
And all for Bernard.
MOLL For Bernard? 'Twas for Bowdler.
CRIPPLE I say, for Bernard.
Nay, more: thou know'st I lay one night at home,
And in thy sleep, I heard thee call on Bernard
Twenty times over.
MOLL Will you be sworn I did?
CRIPPLE Aye, I will swear it!
And art thou not ashamed thus to be changed,
To leave the love of a kind gentleman
To dote on Bowdler? Fie, fie, reclaim thyself!
Embrace thy Bernard; take him for thy husband,
And save his credit,[562] who is else undone
By thy hard father's hateful cruelty.
MOLL Cripple, if thou canst prove that ever I
Did fancy Bernard, I will love him still.
CRIPPLE Why, I'll be sworn thou didst.
MOLL And that I doted on him in my sleep?
CRIPPLE I'll be sworn I could not sleep all night
In the next room, thou didst so rave on him.
MOLL I cannot tell; I may well be deceived.
I think I might affect him in my sleep,
And yet not know it. Let me look on him.
I' faith, he is a pretty handsome fellow.
'Tis pity he should waste himself in prison.
Hey, ho![563]
CRIPPLE What's the matter, wench?
MOLL Cripple, I will love him.
CRIPPLE Wilt thou, i' faith?
MOLL I' faith, I will.

Enter two SERGEANTS [*with* BERNARD *and* BOWDLER *following*]

CRIPPLE Give my thy hand. A bargain! 'Tis enough.
MOLL But how shall he know I love him?
CRIPPLE Why, thus. I will entreat the sergeants
To go with him along unto thy father.
And by the way I'll send young Bowdler from us,
And then acquaint my Bernard with thy love.

559 278 take counsel of thy glass: consult your mirror
560 281 butter-teeth: front teeth
561 282 beetle-brows: bushy eyebrows
562 295 save his credit: fix his money problems
563 308 Hey, ho!: an expression of surprise

He shall accept it and avouch the same[564]
Unto thy father. Wench, do thou the like,
And then I hope his bonds[565] are cancelèd.
BERNARD Cripple, shall we have your company?
CRIPPLE My friends, hold here. There's money for your pains.
Walk with your prisoner but to Master Berry,
And ye shall either find sufficient bail,
Or else discharge the debt—or, I assure you,
We'll be your aid to guard him safe to prison.
SERGEANT Well, we are willing, sir. We are content
To show the gentleman any kind of favor.
CRIPPLE Along, then! Hark, Master Bowdler!
Exeunt

[Act V, scene i]

Enter MASTER FLOWER, MISTRESS FLOWER, MASTER BERRY, *and* FIDDLE

MASTER FLOWER Welcome, good Master Berry! Is your stomach up,[566] sir? It is a good conceit, i' faith.
FIDDLE It is indeed, sir.
MASTER FLOWER What, Fiddle?
FIDDLE If his stomach be up, to go to dinner.
MASTER FLOWER Fiddle, bid Master Berry welcome.
FIDDLE What else, master? With the best belly in my heart, the sweetest strain in my music, and the worst entertainment that may be, Fiddle bids your worship *adesdum*.[567]
MASTER BERRY Thanks, Fiddle. And Master Flower, I am much beholden to your courtesy.
MISTRESS FLOWER Fiddle, I wonder that he stays so long.[568]
Thou toldst me Anthony would follow thee.
FIDDLE Aye, and he'll be here, I warrant you.
MASTER FLOWER I'll tell you, sir. It is a rare conceit.
My wife would have her marry Anthony,
The younger brother, but against her mind
I will contract her unto Ferdinand,
And I have sent for you and other friends
To witness it. And 'tis a good conceit!
MISTRESS FLOWER Fiddle, are all things ordered well within?
FIDDLE All's well, all's well! But there wants some saffron[569] to color the custards withal.
MISTRESS FLOWER Here, take my keys.[570] Bid Susan take enough.
MASTER FLOWER Fiddle, are all our guests come yet?
FIDDLE Aye, sir, and here comes one more than you looked for. *Exit*

Enter FRANK

FRANK God save you, Master Flower. As much to you, Master Berry.
MASTER FLOWER Welcome, Master Golding; you are very welcome, sir.
FRANK My brother Ferdinand commends him to you,[571]

564 319 avouch the same: confirm your love for him
565 321 bonds: debts
566 1 Is your stomach up: a) are you in a bad temper?; b) are you hungry?
567 8 *adesdum*: come here (Latin)
568 10 he stays so long: Anthony is so delayed
569 20 saffron: used to tint food, liquor, etc. an orange-yellow color
570 22 keys: to the household cupboard where supplies are stored
571 27 commends him to you: sends his regards

And here's a letter to you from himself.
MASTER FLOWER A letter, sir? It is a good conceit.
I'll read it straight.[572] FRANK *gives the other letter to* MISTRESS FLOWER

"Master Flower, I am beholding to you for your kindness, and your furtherance in my love-suit, but my mind is changed, and I will not marry your daughter. And so farewell."
This is no good conceit! What, Ferdinand,
Delude old Flower, make me deceive my friends,
Make my wife laugh, and triumph in her will?
What think you, Fiddle?
FIDDLE Why, sir, I think it is no good conceit.
MASTER FLOWER Thou sayest true, Fiddle; 'tis a bad conceit.
But hear you sir— [*Talks to* FRANK *aside*]
MISTRESS FLOWER *reads her letter*
MISTRESS FLOWER [*Aside*] "I understand by Fiddle your forwardness in my suit to your daughter. But, nevertheless, I am determined to draw back, and commit your daughter to her best fortunes, and yourself to God. Farewell."
Why, this is like my husband's bad conceit.
Have you o'erreached me, Flower, you crafty fox?
This is your doing, but, for all your sleight,[573]
I'll cross you, if my purpose hit aright.
FRANK [*Aside to* MASTER FLOWER] Tut, tell not me, sir; for my credit and reputation is as it is; and there's an end. If I shall have her, why so.
MASTER FLOWER [*Aside to* FRANK] Sir, the conceit is doubtful. Give me leave
But to consider of it by myself.
FRANK [*Aside to* MASTER FLOWER] With all my heart. [FRANK *and* MISTRESS FLOWER *speak aside*]
MISTRESS FLOWER Master Golding, a word, I pray, sir.
You know my daughter Phyllis, do you not?
FRANK Mistress, I do.
MISTRESS FLOWER She is a star, I tell you.
FRANK She is no less, indeed.
MISTRESS FLOWER I tell you, sir, upon the sudden now,
There came an odd conceit into my head.
Are you a bachelor?
FRANK I am, indeed.
MISTRESS FLOWER And are you not promised?
FRANK Not yet, believe me.
MASTER FLOWER Master Golding!
MISTRESS FLOWER Well, do you hear, sir? If you will be pleased
To wed my daughter Phyllis, you shall have her.
FRANK To wed your daughter? Why, she loves me not!
MISTRESS FLOWER All's one for that. She will be ruled by me!
Disdain her not because I proffer her.
I tell you, sir, merchants of great account
Have sought her love, and gentlemen of worth
Have humbly sued to me in that behalf.
To say the truth, I promised her to one,
But I am crossed and thwarted by my husband,
Who means to marry her unto another.
Now, sir, to cry but quittance for his guile,[574]

572 30 straight: right away
573 45 sleight: trickery
574 73 cry but . . . his guile: get even with him for his deceit

I offer her to you. If you accept her,
I'll make her dowry richer by a pair
Of hundred pounds, than else it should have been.
FRANK [*Aside*] Why, this is excellent, past all compare!
Sued to to have her!—Gentle Mistress Flower,
Let me consider of it.
MISTRESS FLOWER Nay, nay; defer no time if you will have her.
I'll search my coffers[575] for another hundred.
FRANK Say I should yield: your husband will withstand it?
MISTRESS FLOWER I'll have it closely[576] done, without his knowledge!
Is it a match?
FRANK Well, well, I am content.
MISTRESS FLOWER Why, then, old Flower, I'll cross your close intent.[577]
MASTER FLOWER [*Aside*] It shall be so! And 'tis a good conceit.
It shall be so, if but to cross my wife. [FRANK *and* MASTER FLOWER *speak aside*]
Hark, Master Golding, the conceit doth like me.
You love my daughter—so methought you said.
You said, moreover, that she loves you well.
This love on both sides is a good conceit.
But are you sure, sir, that my daughter loves you?
FRANK For proof thereof, show her this ring.
MASTER FLOWER A ring of hers! 'Tis well.
FRANK Aye, but conceit me:
If I had wooed her in my proper shape,
I do believe she never would have liked me.
Therefore since I shall have her, give me leave
To come and court her in my borrowed shape.[578]
MASTER FLOWER With all my heart, and 'tis a good conceit.
And here's my hand, son Golding: thou shalt have her.
FRANK Then, father Flower, I rest upon your promise.
I'll leave you for a while, till I put on
My counterfeited shape, and then return. *Exit*
MASTER FLOWER [*Aside*] Welcome, good son! 'Tis well. By this conceit
My wife will be prevented of her will.
I would not, for the half of all my wealth,
My cross-word wife had compassed her intent.[579]
—Now, wife!
MISTRESS FLOWER Now, husband!
MASTER FLOWER You still maintain the suit for Anthony?
You'll have your will, and I must break my word?
MISTRESS FLOWER Jest on, old Flower, be cross, and do thy worst.
Work the best means thou canst, yet whiles I live
I swear she never shall wed Ferdinand.
MASTER FLOWER What, shall she not?
MISTRESS FLOWER No, that she shall not.
MASTER FLOWER I say she shall.
MISTRESS FLOWER I' faith, she shall not.
MASTER FLOWER No!
MISTRESS FLOWER No.

575 81 coffers: a coffer is a strongbox for money; "coffers" refers to financial resources in general
576 83 closely: secretly
577 85 close intent: secret purpose
578 98 in my borrowed shape: i.e. in disguise as Cripple
579 107 cross-word wife . . . her intent: contrary wife had achieved her aims

MASTER FLOWER Well, wife, I am vexed, and by God's precious—
MASTER BERRY Oh, sir, be patient. Gentle Mistress Flower,
Cross not your husband; let him have his will.
MISTRESS FLOWER His will!
MASTER FLOWER Hear'st thou, wife, be quiet. Thou knowest my humor
Thus to be crossed, it is no good conceit.
MISTRESS FLOWER A fig for your conceit! [*Aside*] Yet forbecause
I know I shall prevent him of the match
That he intends, henceforth I will dissemble.
—Well, Master Flower, because it shall be said,
And for kind Master Berry may report
The humble loyalty I bear to you,
Such as a wife should do unto her husband,
I am content to yield to your desires,
Protesting, whiles I live, I nevermore
Will speak that Anthony may marry her.
MASTER FLOWER Wife, speak'st thou with thy heart?
MISTRESS FLOWER Husband, I do.
MASTER FLOWER Dost thou, indeed?
MISTRESS FLOWER Indeed, forsooth, I do.
MASTER FLOWER Then 'tis a good conceit! Ha, ha!
I see 'tis sometimes good to look aloft.[580]
Come hither, wife. Because thou art so humble,
I'll tell thee all. I have received a letter
From Ferdinand, wherein he sends me word
He will not marry with my daughter Phyllis.
And therefore I was full determinèd
To cross thy purpose, that his brother Frank
Should marry her—and so I still intend.
Whay sayest thou, wife? Dost thou assent thereto?
MISTRESS FLOWER [*Aside*] That Frank should marry her! I have sworn he shall;
And since this falls so right, I'll not disclose
That I did mean so much.[581] But now I'll yield,
That it may seem my true humility.
—Husband! Because hereafter you may say
And think me loving, loyal, and submiss,[582]
I am content. Frank shall have my consent.
MASTER FLOWER Why, now thou show'st thyself obedient,
And thou dost please me with thy good conceit.

Enter BERNARD, MOLL, *and two* SERGEANTS

BERNARD By your leave, Master Flower!
Berry! I am arrested at your suit.
MASTER BERRY And I am glad of it with all my heart!
Hold, friends. [*Giving money to* SERGEANTS] There's somewhat more for you to drink.[583]
Away with him to prison!
BERNARD Stay, Master Berry; I have brought you bail.
MASTER BERRY What, bail? Where is your bail? Here's none I know
Will be your bail. Away with him to prison!

580 140 look aloft: be ambitious
581 151 did mean so much: wanted the same thing
582 154 submiss: i.e. submissive, obedient
583 161 somewhat more . . . to drink: some more money for you

MOLL Yes, I, forsooth, father! I'll be his bail,
Body for body. Think you I'll stay at home,
And see my husband carried to the jail?
MASTER BERRY How, thy husband?
MOLL My husband, I assure you.
Father, these sergeants both can witness it.
SERGEANT We saw them both contracted man and wife,
And therefore thought it fit to give you knowledge,
Before we carried him unto the prison.
MASTER BERRY But I'll undo this contract. On my blessing,
Daughter, come from him. He's a reprobate![584]
MOLL He is my husband.
MASTER BERRY But thou shalt not have him.
MOLL Faith, but I will. Bernard, speak for thy self.
BERNARD Why, Master Berry, 'tis well-known to you
I am a gentleman, though by misfortune
My ventures in the world have somewhat failed me.
Say that my wealth disables my desert;
The difference of our blood supplies that want.[585]
What though my lands be mortgaged? If you please,
The dowry you intend to give your daughter
May well redeem them. You perhaps imagine
I will be wild, but I intend it not.
What shall I say? If you will give consent,
As you redeem my lands, so I my time ill-spent
Mean to redeem with frugal industry.
I'll be your counsel's pupil, and submit
My follies to your will, mine to your wit.
MASTER BERRY What think you, Master Flower?
MASTER FLOWER Faith, Master Berry,
Bernard speaks well, and with a good conceit.
Dost thou love him, Moll?
MOLL Yes, sir. And here protest
Of all in London I love Bernard best.
MASTER FLOWER Then, Master Berry, follow my conceit.
Cancel his bond and let him have your daughter.
MASTER BERRY Well, Bernard, since I see my daughter loves thee,
And for I hope thou wilt be kind and loving,
Regard thy state,[586] and turn an honest man,
Here, take my daughter. I'll forgive thee in thy bond,
Redeem thy lands, and, if thou please me well,
Thou shalt not want. All that I have is thine.
BERNARD I am love-bound to her, to you in duty;
You conquer me with kindness, she with beauty.
SERGEANT Then, Master Berry, I think we may depart.
MASTER BERRY Aye, when you please. You see the matter ended,
The debt discharged, and I can ask no more.
SERGEANT Why, then, we take our leaves. *Exeunt* SERGEANTS
MASTER FLOWER Now, wife, if young Frank Golding were come back,
To sum our wish, it were a good conceit.

584 175 reprobate: degenerate, rogue
585 181–2 Say that . . . that want: if my financial insolvency detracts from my rank, my higher social class makes up for it
586 200 Regard thy state: be mindful of your rank

Enter PHYLLIS

Why, how now, Phyllis! Sad? Come, tell me, wench,
Art thou resolved yet for to have thy husband?
PHYLLIS A golden Golding! 'Tis a good conceit.
That golden Golding is but loathsome dross,[587]
Nor is it gold that I so much esteem.
Dust is the richest treasure that we have,
Nor is the beauty of the fairest one
Of a higher price or value unto me
Than is a lump of poor deformity.[588]
Father, you know my mind, and what I said,
Which if you grant not, I will rest a maid.[589]

Enter FIDDLE

MASTER FLOWER To die a maid! That is no good conceit.
FIDDLE Master! Where's my master? Here's one would couple a brace of words[590] with you.
MASTER FLOWER With me, sir?
FIDDLE No, sir, with my young mistress.
MASTER FLOWER What is he, knave?
FIDDLE A crooked knave, sir. 'Tis the cripple.
MASTER FLOWER What would he have? He hath no good conceit;
'Tis he that hath bewitched my daughter's heart.
He is a knave. Go send him packing hence.
PHYLLIS As you respect the welfare of your child,
Dear father, let me speak with him.
MASTER FLOWER Speak with him! No, it is no good conceit.
I know he comes to run away with thee.
FIDDLE Run away with her? Well may she carry him; but if he run away with her, I'll never trust crutch more.
MASTER FLOWER Thou say'st true, Fiddle; 'tis a good conceit.
Go, call him in! [*Aside*] Frank Golding, it is he, *Exit* FIDDLE
In the lame knave's disguise. A good conceit!

Enter FRANK [*disguised as* CRIPPLE]

Now, sir, what's the news with you? You come to speak with my daughter?
FRANK Yea, sir, about a little work I have of hers.
MASTER FLOWER What work, you knave? No, thou hast some conceit
To rob me of my daughter! But away!
I like not that conceit. Out of my doors.
PHYLLIS Unhappy Phyllis, and unfortunate.
FRANK Sir, I am content. I'll not move your patience.
PHYLLIS Life of my living body, if thou go,
Though not alive, take me hence dead with woe. *She swoons*
MASTER BERRY In troth, sir, you are to blame.
MASTER FLOWER What? Is she dead? It is no good conceit.
Speak to me, Phyllis! Oh, unhappy time!

587 215 loathsome dross: disgusting rubbish
588 220 a lump of poor deformity: i.e. Cripple
589 222 rest a maid: remain unmarried, and a virgin
590 224 couple a brace of words: put a few words together, i.e. talk. The image is from hunting: to couple a brace of hounds is to attach two dogs to the same leash

Sweet girl, dear daughter! Oh, my only joy.
Speak to thy father, wench, in some conceit.
What, not a word?
MASTER BERRY Now may you see what fell impatience
Begets upon[591] such tender plants as these.
MISTRESS FLOWER Now may we see the folly of old age,
Governed by spleen,[592] and overweening[593] rage.
MASTER FLOWER Speak to me, daughter,
And thou shalt have—what not? Covet'st thou gold?
Thou shalt not want for crowns;[594] thou shalt have all.
Oh, was my fury author[595] of thy trance?
Did I deny thy love's access to thee?
Speak but one word and thou shalt be his wife.
By heaven, thou shalt!
PHYLLIS [*Reviving*] I take you at your word. It is no pain
To die for love, and then revive again.
MASTER BERRY Now, Master Flower, how like you this conceit?
Hath she not overreached[596] you?
MASTER FLOWER My word is past,[597] and yet, for all my rage,
I rather choose to fail in my conceit,
And wed thee, Phyllis, to thine own content.
Here, take my daughter, Cripple; love her well,
Be kind to her, and I'll be kind to thee.
Thou art but poor; well, I will make thee rich.
And so God bless you with a good conceit.
FRANK I thank you. When I leave to love my wife,
Heaven hasten death, and take away my life.
MASTER FLOWER [*Aside to* FRANK] 'Tis well done, Frank. I applaud thy wit,
And now I know I fail not in conceit.

Enter CRIPPLE, FERDINAND, ANTHONY, BOWDLER

CRIPPLE Gentlemen, sweet bloods, or brethren of familiarity,
I would speak with Phyllis. Shall I have audience?
PHYLLIS Help me, dear father! Oh, help me, gentlemen!
This is some spirit! Drive him from my sight!
FRANK Were he the devil, thou shalt not budge a foot.
BOWDLER Zounds, two cripples! Two dogs, two curs! 'Tis wonderful!
FRANK Fear not, dear heart.
PHYLLIS Hence, foul deformity!
Nor thou, nor he shall my companion be.
If cripples dead the living seem to haunt,
I'll neither of either.[598] Therefore, I say, avaunt![599]
Help me, father.
FRANK Dear heart, revoke these words. [*Removes his disguise*]
Here are no spirits, nor deformities.

591 256–7 what fell . . . Begets upon: how cruel irascibility affects
592 259 spleen: irritable temper
593 259 overweening: immoderate
594 262 crowns: money (coins with the imprint of a crown)
595 263 author: cause
596 270 overreached: gotten the better of
597 271 My word is past: I've given my pronouncement
598 290–91 If cripples . . . of either: if cripples return as ghosts, I won't marry either the "living" or the "dead" cripple
599 291 avaunt!: be gone!

I am a counterfeit cripple now no more,
But young Frank Golding, as I was before.
Amaze not, love, nor seem not discontent;
Nor thee, nor him, shall ever this repent.
FERDINAND Master Flower, I come to claim your promise.
ANTHONY [*To* MISTRESS FLOWER] I come for yours—your daughter I do mean.
MASTER FLOWER [*To* FERDINAND] My promise? Why, sir, you refused my promise,
And sent me word so in your letter.
MISTRESS FLOWER [*To* ANTHONY] And so you did to me, and now 'tis past.[600]
Your brother Frank hath both our free consents.
FERDINAND Sir, sir, I wrote no letter.
ANTHONY By heaven, nor I.
FRANK But I did for you both! I was your scribe,
The whilst you went to see your house a-fire!
And you (as I remember) I did send
To see your sister drowned at London Bridge.[601]
FERDINAND I' faith, good brother, have you o'erreached us so?
ANTHONY So cunningly, that none of us could know?
FERDINAND For all this cunning, I will break the match.
ANTHONY And so will I.
FRANK Why, brothers, she's mine, by her father's gift.
FERDINAND Brother, you lie; you got her with a shift.[602]
FRANK I was the first that loved her.
FERDINAND That's not so! 'Twas I.
ANTHONY Catch that catch can![603] Then, brothers both, you lie.
MASTER FLOWER Yea, but conceit me, gentlemen. What, do you mean to spoil my daughter?[604] You claim her, and I have given her your younger brother! This is no good conceit. Why, how now, Phyllis? Still drooping? Cheer thee, my girl! See, a company of gentlemen are at strife for thy love! Look up, and in this fair assembly make thine own choice. Choose where thou wilt, and use thine own conceit.
PHYLLIS But will my father then applaud my choice?
MASTER FLOWER I will.
PHYLLIS And will these worthy gentlemen be pleased,
However my dislike or liking prove?
ALL We will.
PHYLLIS I must confess, you all have taken pains,
And I can give but all[605] for that pains taken.
And all my all is but a little love,
And of a little, who can make division?
I would I knew what would content you all!
FERDINAND Thy love.
ANTHONY Thy life and love.
FRANK Thy life, thy love, thy self, and all for me;
For if I want but one, I then want thee.
PHYLLIS If, then, I give what either[606] of you crave,
Though not what you desire, will it suffice?
FERDINAND I wish but love.
PHYLLIS And, as a friend, you have it.

600 302 'tis past: that's over
601 305–8 I was . . . London Bridge: i.e. I sent you on wild goose chases
602 314 shift: fraudulent strategy
603 317 Catch that catch can!: every man for himself!
604 318–19 spoil my daughter: treat my daughter as the spoils (plunder) of your conflict
605 329 give but all: only give everything I have
606 337 either: any

ANTHONY I, life and love.
PHYLLIS And, as your friend, I vow
To love you whilst I live, as I do now.
FRANK I ask but all, for I deserve no more.
PHYLLIS And thou shalt have thy wish. Take all my store,[607]
My love, myself.
FRANK By heaven, I ask no more.
Brothers, have done! And, Dad, to end all strife,
Come, take her hand, and give her for my wife.
MASTER FLOWER With all my heart, and 'tis a good conceit.
BOWDLER Gentlemen, patience is your fairest play.
FERDINAND Impatience[608] pulls me hence. For this disdain[609]
I am resolved never to love again. *Exit*
ANTHONY Stay, brother Ferdinand. I'll follow thee.
Farewell all love! 'Tis full of treachery. *Exit*
BOWDLER By heavens, Frank, I do commend thy wit.
Come, Moll, shall thou and I ask blessing too, for company?[610]
MOLL You and I, sir? Alas, we are not playfellows,[611] though we be turtles.[612] I am provided.[613]
BOWDLER Provided! Why, am I not thy Menelaus?
MOLL Aye, sir. But this[614] is my Paris.[615] I am resolved,
And what I do is by authority.
BOWDLER Is it even so? Is Helen stol'n by Paris?
Then thus, in arms, will Menelaus mourn,
Till Troy be sacked, and Helena return. *Exit*

Enter Master WOOD, *and* OFFICERS

WOOD This is the man. Officers, attach[616] him upon felony!
OFFICER Master Flower, I arrest you upon felony, and charge you to obey.
MASTER FLOWER Arrest me upon felony! At whose suit?
WOOD Sir, at mine! Where had you that diamond on your finger? It was stole from me, and many other jewels, to the value of a hundred pound.
MASTER FLOWER This is no good conceit! Hath Captain Racket
Bandied old Flower to such an exigent?[617]
I hope my credit somewhat will assist me.
Well, whither must I go?
WOOD Straight to the bench,[618] where now the judges are
To give you speedy trial.
MASTER FLOWER Words here are little worth. Wife, and friends, all
Go with me to my trial. You shall see
A good conceit now brought to infamy.

Exeunt

FINIS.

607 343 all my store: i.e. all that I have
608 349 Impatience: irritation
609 349 For this disdain: because of this rejection
610 354 for company: to be sociable
611 355 playfellows: sexual playmates
612 355 turtles: affectionate friends
613 355 provided: i.e. with a husband
614 357 this: i.e. Bernard
615 356–7 am I . . . my Paris: in myth, Menelaus was the husband of Helen, who was taken by Paris of Troy, giving rise to the Trojan War
616 362 attach: arrest
617 368 Struck (as with a racket) me into this crisis
618 371 the bench: the seat where justice is administered

14 George Chapman, Ben Jonson, and John Marston, *Eastward Ho*

First performed 1605

First printed 1605

Edited by Katherine Schaap Williams

Eastward Ho is most recognizable as the kind of play Shakespeare didn't write. Composed in triple collaboration by George Chapman, Ben Jonson, and John Marston, the plot features a master and apprentices, marriage plots that turn on status and social advancement, and a failed Virginia venture that is also a double-crossing cuckoldry attempt gone awry. Above all, it vividly represents early modern London: from the shopkeeper's cry, "What do ye lack, sir?" in the opening scene, to Slitgut's narration of the shipwrecked travelers scattered at various points along the Thames from his perch above the river, to the final lines that compare the audience in the theater to a crowd of citizens eagerly waiting for the annual civic pageant on the Lord Mayor's Day. The genre is city comedy, popular in the first two decades of the seventeenth century, a kind of play that idealized and satirized London life. City comedies depict the excitement of new economic possibilities and speculative risk, explore the mutual disdain of impoverished spendthrift aristocrats and prosperous hardworking citizens, and dramatize labor and hierarchy in the pecking order of the city's guilds. *Eastward Ho* is poised between documentary and sitcom as it self-reflexively celebrates and mocks the social world outside—and also inside—the theater.

The play begins at the shop of William Touchstone, a goldsmith for whom thrift is the great citizen virtue. Adapting the biblical parable of the prodigal son, the opening scenes juxtapose Golding and Quicksilver, Touchstone's two apprentices, who model divergent responses to their master's work ethic. In early modern London, trades were organized and regulated within a system of guilds: craftsmen took on the training of young apprentices who, after a typical period of seven years, became "free" to practice their own trade and participate in urban governance as citizens. In the fourth act, the play offers a fantasy version of this guild structure when Golding attains his freedom and is promoted from apprentice to alderman's deputy immediately, reinforcing Touchstone's civic values. Touchstone's emphasis on pious industry and prudent frugality are shared by the dutiful Golding and Mildred, Touchstone's daughter (indeed, in the 2002 Royal Shakespeare Company production, Golding and Mildred completed each other's proverbs, a vision of love at first aphorism).

Quicksilver, by contrast, bucks the confines of his apprenticeship. As the younger son of an aristocratic family who resents his lack of inheritance, he wants to live like a gallant. This lifestyle entails wearing velvets and silks instead of prescribed work clothes, and spending money on leisure activities such as gambling and attending the theater. These profligate delights are supported by dubious financial practices, the get-rich-quick schemes that Quicksilver shares with other characters in the play, from Security's "parchment toils" as a usurer, earning profit from interest on loans, to the fraud Sir Petronel employs to bilk his new wife out of her inheritance. Quicksilver's rebellion is echoed by Gertrude, Touchstone's other daughter, who chafes at citizen proscriptions, and wants to marry a knight so that she will have a title and a coach. Gertrude's longings are what early modern medical theory would call a humor, a kind of physiological compulsion legible as gripping desire. *Eastward Ho* associates these humors with status, fashion, and sex, and the play conflates female appetites with the consumption of luxury goods (and, conversely, dramatizes male anxieties about being exposed as bankrupt or cuckolded).

Critical debates about *Eastward Ho* have often focused on the ending, asking: does the play bear out Touchstone's citizen morals? In the final scene, Quicksilver sings a ballad of confession, composed while in prison, to win Touchstone's forgiveness. Early critics argued that Touchstone's closing lines in the play—which reference the biblical parable of the lost sheep—confirm Quicksilver's reformation since Touchstone welcomes his repentant return to the social community epitomized by the goldsmith's shop. In this reading, Touchstone is the arbiter and standard—true to his name, which denotes the black stone used to test metals to determine their worth. Touchstone's testing affirms both the worth of Golding and the lesson learned by Quicksilver, whose name signifies the liquid metal mercury, associated with swift, "mercurial" changes. From another perspective, however, Quicksilver offers a virtuosic demonstration of performance and improvisation across literary registers and vocabularies. Quicksilver, who has learned to speak from plays, has the greatest verbal range of any character: he can shift into verse to concoct a double-crossing with Sir Petronel; lament in soliloquy after the shipwreck; reassure his stranded companions with a fast-talking display of pseudo-scientific alchemical jargon; and craft a song that adapts a popular confessional form. In the final scene, his ballad parodies the conventions of repentance and successfully wins over, perhaps even hoodwinks, Touchstone, his most skeptical spectator. In this reading, Touchstone's relentless moralizing is just as much a target for the play's critique because he cannot perceive how easily his axioms might be counterfeited.

Rather than finally adjudicating the question of a single character's sincerity, however, *Eastward Ho* invites us to notice that performance is a risky endeavor that may return high dividends. It is no surprise that one of the play's key words is "venture," part of a whole range of terms, including "credit" and "commodity," that acquire new economic meanings in the early modern period. "Venture" shifts from a primary sense of risk and fortune (as in "adventure," like the chivalric quests central to medieval prose romances, a genre beloved by Gertrude) to speculative commercial enterprise, one that may entail economic loss. *Eastward Ho* employs "venture" in both senses, and the Virginia expedition is the plot element most associated with this dynamic early modern vocabulary. England's colonizing ambitions are an important backdrop: Queen Elizabeth approved attempts to settle the Roanoke colonies in the 1580s; the East India Company received a royal charter in 1600; and the first permanent English settlement would be established in Jamestown, Virginia, in 1607, a mere two years after *Eastward Ho* was performed. The pun on Virginia as a "maidenhead" ready for taking exposes the violence of imperial domination at the heart of Petronel's prospective endeavor. Yet unlike other plays that strive to dramatize exotic locales, *Eastward Ho* does not let its travelers make it beyond the Thames. Virginia is less a feasible destination than it is a set of literary conventions taken from narratives of actual and fictional travel. When Seagull, Spendall, and Scapethrift envision Virginia over tavern beer, their fantasy of startling wealth—lifted from Hakluyt's *Principal Navigations* and Thomas More's *Utopia*—evokes the literary tropes that encouraged and were employed to justify brutal colonization across the Atlantic.

The imagined elsewhere of Virginia also offers the means to critique the here and now of the play, for *Eastward Ho*'s satire resulted in imprisonment for two of the three playwrights, and censorship of the text. One passage contains a jibe about "industrious Scots," with a punchline about wishing that the Scots currently in England were in Virginia instead. King James VI of Scotland had been crowned as King James I of England in 1603, bringing with him Scottish nobility, who were often mocked for their thick accents; James was also widely known for allowing the purchase of knighthoods (hence the joke, IV.i. 125–6, about Sir Petronel being a "thirty-pound-knight," or someone who bought his title). Although James promoted the concept of a united kingdom in Britain, the play's brief references to being "one country" evoke deep cultural divisions. Sir James Murray, a Scottish courtier, complained to King James about the play, and letters survive written by Jonson and Chapman from prison appealing for release, which was eventually granted. We do not know whether Marston escaped imprisonment or was imprisoned elsewhere; nor do we know whether the complaint about these lines was provoked by seeing the play in performance or reading it in print. Still, the incident suggests that theatrical use of topical political humor could function as a powerful critique—and that satire on the Jacobean stage (or page) could be perceived as dangerously subversive.

As a collaborative text, *Eastward Ho* also offers a compelling study of the ventures of professional playwrights. Just a few years earlier, in the so-called "Poets' War," from about 1599–1601, Jonson and Marston had attacked each other, and other rivals, by caricaturing competing writers and their works. In Jonson's *Poetaster* (in this volume), for example, Horace gives Crispinus an emetic that causes him to vomit Marston's distinctive vocabulary. By 1605, however, they collaborated on *Eastward Ho* with Chapman, in response to Thomas Dekker and John Webster's 1604 *Westward Ho* (which Dekker and Webster followed with *Northward Ho*, probably performed in late 1605 in response to *Eastward Ho*). The titles of these plays allude to the cries of the watermen on the Thames, whose boats carried passengers eastward and westward, and they echo as a competition between theater companies. *Westward Ho* was performed by the Children of Paul's, and *Eastward Ho* was performed by the Children of the Queen's Revels, the other predominant company of boy actors, at the Blackfriars theater, an indoor playhouse known for posh crowds entertained with biting wit. The three London plays constitute a rivalrous conversation across playwrights and acting companies, associating the plays with cardinal directions as theaters strive to attract and reorient audience attention.

Eastward Ho was printed three times in 1605, a popularity suggesting the impact of the play's social and political commentary, and also, perhaps, the pleasures of a good meme. The play is packed to bursting with quotations, allusions, parodies, ballads, proverbs, and tales. These borrowed texts appear in bits and snatches, making the theater a fund of jokes old and new. Touchstone's signature line is thus emblematic of the play's approach to the texts and textures of London: *work upon that now*. Spoken eight times in the first act alone, this catchphrase appears more than fifteen times in the play, always printed in italics, as if to signal that it functions as a comment on the plot, a kind of proverb, and a command at the same time. Identified with Touchstone's character but exceeding him, repeated and undermined by Quicksilver, the line cycles through dramatic contexts and accrues different meanings with each successive setting. Likewise, Security's catchphrase adapts a biblical verse that, once released into circulation, is further adapted by other characters (and is also printed in italics every time it appears in the quarto).

As the play invokes and repurposes other texts, it often reflects on its own theatrical experiments, drawing the audience into a dense network of references. When Touchstone asks spectators to remember the familiar emblem of the "horn of suretyship," he draws upon a commonplace image of debt. In this depiction, a man falls into the big end of a horn only to be squeezed out of the small end, showing that debt is easy to get into and difficult to get out of—a lesson that, as Touchstone says, "you all know." Touchstone's appeal to the offstage audience to participate in his lesson about financial solvency by calling the emblem to mind works across verbal and visual registers, and is one of the play's many explicitly metatheatrical gestures.

Above all, *Eastward Ho* reworks other plays. Quicksilver quotes key lines from theatrical hits. Touchstone derides these snippets as "play ends," comparing them to "gold ends," leftover bits that a skilled goldsmith might melt down for future remaking. His point is that Quicksilver is shirking his duties, but the image succinctly captures how the early modern theater decomposes plays into their constitutive parts so that words, lines, characters, and dramatic conventions may be recycled. Touchstone's name evokes a character from Shakespeare's *As You Like It*, but *Eastward Ho* sends up *Hamlet* in particular: through the character of Gertrude, repeated allusion to the thrifty re-use of cold meats in wedding celebrations, and a one-off scene with a frenetic servant named Hamlet.

The play lets us see how it works upon its audience too. Although there is no speech prefix for the final lines, every modern editor assigns it to Quicksilver, who detains Touchstone with a gesture to the city of London itself. The play's last move is to incorporate audience members into its farewell, urging them to return to the theater, in the hope that "contentment" can profitably convert a crowd into regular spectators. *Eastward Ho* channels three writers into the category of "author," multiple registers of literary borrowing into the category of "text," and the city of London itself into the category of "play," asking us to think about the early modern theater as essentially collaborative in its acts of making and remaking.

Textual note

This edition is based primarily upon the second issue of the first quarto of 1605, in a copy held at the Folger Shakespeare Library (STC 4971), and incorporates material from the first issue of Q1 (STC 4970, Dyce Collection via EEBO). The first issue of Q1 contains the offending lines about the Scots (III.iii. 26–31); the second issue's cancel replaces this material with two words and adds a sentence (III.iii. 35–6), presumably to fill space left blank by the deleted lines. With respect to the emended material, editors typically choose to follow the text of the first issue, subordinating the replacement material of the second issue in an explanatory footnote. This edition, however, conflates the first and second issues in III.iii, supplying the lines that were both deleted and added, to make the act of textual censorship and substitution visible on the page.

Editorial tradition has held that Marston wrote the beginning of the play (I.i–II.i), Chapman wrote the middle (II.ii–III.iii), and Jonson wrote the end (IV.ii–V.v), with all three contributing to IV.i; recent editors Gossett and Kay find evidence that all three authors worked on many scenes of the play, suggesting that *Eastward Ho*'s collaborative writing is impossible to demarcate with certainty. This edition follows editorial tradition in regularizing speech prefixes, introducing scene divisions, and standardizing entrances (the quarto marks only act divisions and often masses character-entrances at the beginning of the act); it also preserves shifts in stage directions, especially in Sir Petronel's title attribution, which signals his status inconsistently throughout the play. The quarto consistently prints language that circulates (quotations from other plays, *sententiae*, songs, proverbs, and catchphrases) in italics, as if to highlight shared commonplaces and intertextual borrowings. This edition retains this textual feature as much as possible, indicating quotations and proverbs with quotation marks, and preserving songs and Touchstone's catchphrase in italics.

Further reading

Editions

Kay, W. David, and Suzanne Gossett (eds) (2012) "*Eastward Ho!*" in David Bevington, Martin Butler, and Ian Donaldson (eds), *The Cambridge Edition of the Works of Ben Jonson*, vol. 2, Cambridge: Cambridge University Press.

Van Fossen, R.W. (ed.) (1979) *Eastward Ho!*, Manchester: Manchester University Press.

Critical and contextual reading

Donley, Marin L. (2013) "The Mechanics of Virtue: Quicksilver's 'Repentance,' the Test of the Audience, and Social Change in *Eastward Ho*," *Renaissance Drama* 41: 25–55.

Gossett, Suzanne (2004) "Marston, Collaboration, and *Eastward Ho!*," *Renaissance Drama* 33: 181–200.

Hirschfeld, Heather (2004) *Joint Enterprises: Collaborative Drama and the Institutionalization of the English Renaissance Theater*, Amherst: University of Massachusetts Press.

Ingram, Jill Phillips (2006) *Idioms of Self Interest: Credit, Identity and Property in English Renaissance Drama*, London: Routledge.

Kay, W. David (2012) "Parodic Wit and Social Satire in Chapman, Jonson, and Marston's *Eastward Ho!*," *English Literary Renaissance* 42: 391–424.

Lake, Peter, with Michael Questier (2002) *The Antichrist's Lewd Hat: Protestants, Papists and Players in Post-Reformation England*, New Haven: Yale University Press.

Munro, Lucy (2005) *Children of the Queen's Revels: A Jacobean Theatre Repertory*, Cambridge: Cambridge University Press.

Shapiro, Michael (1977) *Children of the Revels: The Boy Companies of Shakespeare's Time and Their Plays*, New York: Columbia University Press.

Stage, Kelly J. (2015) "*Eastward Ho* and the Strength of Weak Ties for Playwrights and Patrons," *Ben Jonson Journal* 22: 208–28.

Stage, Kelly J. (2018) *Producing Early Modern London: A Comedy of Urban Space, 1598–1616*, Lincoln: University of Nebraska Press.

Turner, Henry S. (2006) *The English Renaissance Stage: Geometry, Poetics, and the Practical Spatial Arts 1580–1630*, Oxford: Oxford University Press.

Walsh, Brian (2016) *Unsettled Toleration: Religious Difference on the Shakespearean Stage*, Oxford: Oxford University Press.

West, William (2013) "Intertheatricality," in Henry S. Turner (ed.), *Early Modern Theatricality*, Oxford: Oxford University Press, 151–72.

Eastward Ho (1605)

Dramatis personae[1]

WILLIAM TOUCHSTONE, *a goldsmith with a shop in Cheapside*
MISTRESS TOUCHSTONE, *his wife, a gentlewoman*
GERTRUDE, *their elder daughter*
MILDRED, *their younger daughter*
FRANCIS QUICKSILVER } *his apprentices*
GOLDING } *his apprentices*
SINDEFY, *lover of Quicksilver, later the companion of Gertrude*
SIR PETRONEL FLASH, *a newly dubbed knight, engaged to Gertrude*
SECURITY, *an old usurer, host to Sindefy*
WINIFRED, *young wife of Security*
BRAMBLE, *a lawyer*
POLDAVY, *a tailor*
CAPTAIN SEAGULL, *ship's captain hired for Petronel's Virginia venture*
SCAPETHRIFT } *adventurers with Petronel*
SPENDALL } *adventurers with Petronel*
DRAWER, *at the Blue Anchor Tavern at Billingsgate*
MISTRESS FOND } *wives of London citizens*
MISTRESS GAZER } *wives of London citizens*
BETTRICE, *a maid*
HAMLET, *a footman*
POTKIN, *a tankard-bearer*
SLITGUT, *a butcher's apprentice*
MASTER WOLF, *prison-keeper at the Counter*
HOLDFAST, *a prison guard*

Scrivener, Coachman, Prisoners, Friend, Page to Petronel Messenger, Constable, Officers

Prologus

Not out of envy, for there's no effect
Where there's no cause; nor out of imitation,
For we have evermore been imitated;
Nor out of our contention to do better
Than that which is opposed to ours in title,[2]
For that was good, and better cannot be.
And for the title, if it seem affected
We might as well have called it, "God you good even,"[3]

1 Dramatis personae: not in Q
2 5 that which . . . in title: a reference to the play *Westward Ho*, written by Thomas Dekker and John Webster in 1604
3 8 God you good even: God give you a good evening

Only that[4] eastward westwards still exceeds[5]—
Honor the sun's fair rising, not his setting.
Nor is our title utterly enforced,[6]
As by the points we touch at[7] you shall see.
Bear with our willing pains,[8] if dull or witty;
We only dedicate it to the City.

Act I, scene i

Enter Master TOUCHSTONE, *and* QUICKSILVER *at several*[9] *doors,* QUICKSILVER *with his hat, pumps,*[10] *short sword, and dagger, and a racket*[11] *trussed*[12] *up under his cloak. At the middle door, enter* GOLDING *discovering*[13] *a goldsmith's shop, and walking short turns before it*

TOUCHSTONE And whither with you now? What loose[14] action are you bound for? Come, what comrades are you to meet withal?[15] Where's the supper? Where's the rendezvous?

QUICKSILVER Indeed, and in very good sober truth, sir—

TOUCHSTONE "Indeed, and in very good sober truth, sir"? Behind my back thou wilt swear faster than a French footboy[16] and talk more bawdily than a common midwife, and now "indeed, and in very good sober truth, sir"! But if a privy search should be made,[17] with what furniture[18] are you rigged[19] now? Sirrah, I tell thee: I am thy master William Touchstone,[20] goldsmith, and thou my prentice, Francis Quicksilver,[21] and I will see whither you are running. *Work upon that now!*[22]

QUICKSILVER Why, sir, I hope a man may use his recreation[23] with his master's profit.

TOUCHSTONE Prentices' recreations are seldom with their masters' profit. *Work upon that now.* You shall give up your cloak, though you be no alderman.[24] TOUCHSTONE *uncloaks* QUICKSILVER

Heyday, Ruffians' Hall![25] Sword, pumps, here's a racket, indeed!

QUICKSILVER *Work upon that now*!

TOUCHSTONE Thou shameless varlet,[26] dost thou jest at thy lawful master contrary to thy indentures?[27]

QUICKSILVER Why, 'sblood, sir, my mother's a gentlewoman and my father a justice of peace and of quorum,[28] and though I am a younger brother and a prentice, yet I hope I am my father's

4 9 Only that: except that
5 9 still exceeds: always surpasses
6 11 enforced: constrained (i.e. only by the direction of east, and by answering *Westward Ho*)
7 12 points we touch at: compass points (as in east and west); subject matter of the play
8 13 pains: efforts
9 0 SD *several*: different
10 0 SD *pumps*: low-heeled shoes for dancing
11 0 SD *hat, pumps . . . a racket*: accessories of a gallant, including tennis racket
12 0 SD *trussed*: tied
13 0 SD *discovering*: revealing the entrance to the shop in the rear of the stage
14 1 loose: immoral, dissolute
15 2 withal: besides
16 5 footboy: a page employed to attend a footman
17 6 a privy . . . be made: if you were searched to find what you are concealing
18 6 furniture: belongings
19 7 rigged: equipped
20 7 Touchstone: a black stone used to test the quality of gold and silver
21 8 Quicksilver: another name for mercury, a metal known for its extreme volatility
22 8–9 *Work upon that now*: Touchstone's signature phrase appears in italics throughout Q; this edition preserves that textual feature
23 10 use his recreation: seek entertainment
24 12 alderman: an elected civic officer of London (editors sometimes emend "no" to "an" to make sense of this phrase)
25 13 Ruffians' Hall: a London field known for duels and fights
26 15 varlet: rascal
27 16 indentures: the contract by which an apprentice is bound to his master in the trade
28 18 quorum: a select group of distinguished justices of the peace

son; and by God's lid,[29] 'tis for your worship and for your commodity[30] that I keep company. I am entertained among gallants, true; they call me "cousin Frank," right; I lend them monies, good; they spend it, well. But when they are spent, must not they strive to get more? Must not their land fly?[31] And to whom? Shall not your worship ha' the refusal? Well, I am a good member of the city if I were well considered! How would merchants thrive, if gentlemen would not be unthrifts?[32] How could gentlemen be unthrifts if their humors[33] were not fed? How should their humors be fed but by white meat[34] and cunning secondings?[35] Well, the city might consider us. I am going to an ordinary[36] now: the gallants fall to play; I carry light gold[37] with me; the gallants call, "cousin Frank, some gold for silver"; I change, gain by it; the gallants lose the gold; and then call, "cousin Frank, lend me some silver." Why—

TOUCHSTONE Why? I cannot tell. Seven score pound art thou out in the cash,[38] but look to it; I will not be gallanted out of my monies. And as for my rising by other men's fall, God shield me. Did I gain my wealth by ordinaries? No. By exchanging of gold? No. By keeping of gallants' company? No. I hired me a little shop, bought[39] low, took small gain, kept no debt book, garnished[40] my shop—for want of plate[41]—with good, wholesome, thrifty sentences,[42] as "Touchstone, keep thy shop, and thy shop will keep thee"; "Light gains makes heavy purses"; "'Tis good to be merry and wise." And when I was wived, having something to stick to, I had the horn of suretyship[43] ever before my eyes. [*To the audience*] You all know the device of the horn, where the young fellow slips in at the butt end, and comes squeezed out at the buccal. And I grew up, and I praise providence, I bear my brows[44] now as high as the best of my neighbors. [*To* QUICKSILVER] But thou—well, look to the accounts. Your father's bond lies for you;[45] seven score pound is yet in the rear.[46]

QUICKSILVER Why, 'slid, sir, I have as good as proper gallants' words for it as any are in London: gentlemen of good phrase, perfect language, passingly behaved; gallants that wear socks[47] and clean linen, and call me "kind cousin Frank," "good cousin Frank," for they know my father. And by God's lid, shall not I trust 'em? Not trust?

Enter a PAGE *as inquiring for* TOUCHSTONE*'s shop*

GOLDING [*To the* PAGE] What do ye lack, sir?[48] What is 't you'll buy, sir?

TOUCHSTONE Ay, marry, sir, there's a youth of another piece. There's thy fellow prentice, as good a gentleman born as thou art; nay, and better meaned.[49] But does he pump it, or racket it?[50] Well, if he thrive not, if he outlast not a hundred such crackling bavins[51] as thou art, God and

29 19 God's lid: God's eyelid
30 19 commodity: advantage
31 22 fly: be mortgaged for cash
32 24 unthrifts: spendthrifts, prodigals
33 24 humors: desires, whims
34 25 white meat: dairy foods, such as milk and eggs (Quicksilver shifts from gallants' whims to what they eat)
35 25 secondings: a) second courses; b) reinforcement of their desires
36 26 ordinary: tavern; also a gambling game
37 26–7 light gold: coins of lighter weight, and therefore lower value
38 29 art thou . . . the cash: Quicksilver already has a debt to Touchstone
39 32 bought: Q reads "fought"; emended here, following Van Fossen, but other editors have preserved Q's reading, or emended to "sought"
40 33 garnished: decorated
41 33 want of plate: lack of gold
42 33 sentences: proverbial maxims (like those that follow: throughout Q, proverbial sayings are italicized; in this edition they are put in quotation marks)
43 36 horn of suretyship: a familiar emblem of debt in which a man falls into the big end of the horn, and is squeezed out the buccal, the smaller end with the mouthpiece; the image shows that it is easy to get into, and difficult to get out of, financial obligations brought on by overspending
44 38 bear my brows: hold up my head
45 39 bond lies for you: presumably a cash bond from Quicksilver's father for his apprenticeship
46 40 in the rear: in arrears (owed by Quicksilver)
47 43 socks: light slippers
48 45 What do ye lack, sir: shopkeeper's call to prospective customers
49 47 better meaned: wealthier
50 47 pump it, or racket it: use dancing shoes or a tennis racket; show off with expensive pastimes
51 48 crackling bavins: bundles of brushwood easily kindled

men neglect industry.

GOLDING (*To the* PAGE) It is his shop, and here my master walks.

TOUCHSTONE With me, boy?

PAGE My master, Sir Petronel Flash, recommends his love to you, and will instantly visit you.

TOUCHSTONE To make up the match with my eldest daughter, my wife's dilling,[52] whom she longs to call madam.[53] He shall find me unwillingly ready, boy. *Exit* PAGE

[*To the audience*] There's another affliction, too. As I have two prentices, the one of a boundless prodigality, the other of a most hopeful industry, so have I only two daughters: the eldest of a proud ambition and nice[54] wantonness, the other of a modest humility and comely soberness. The one must be ladyfied, forsooth, and be attired just to the court cut and long tail.[55] So far is she ill-natured to the place and means of my preferment and fortune that she throws all the contempt and despite hatred itself can cast upon it. Well, a piece of land she has, 'twas her grandmother's gift. Let her, and her Sir Petronel, flash out that. But as for my substance,[56] she that scorns me, as I am a citizen and tradesman, shall never pamper her pride with my industry, shall never use me as men do foxes: keep themselves warm in the skin, and throw the body that bare it to the dung-hill. I must go entertain this Sir Petronel. [*To* GOLDING] Golding, my utmost care's for thee, and only trust in thee: look to the shop. [*To* QUICKSILVER] As for you, Master Quicksilver, think of husks, for thy course is running directly to the prodigal's hogs' trough.[57] Husks, sirrah![58] *Work upon that now.* *Exit*

QUICKSILVER Marry, faugh, goodman flat-cap![59] 'Sfoot,[60] though I am a prentice I can give arms,[61] and my father's a justice o' peace by descent, and 'sblood—

GOLDING Fie, how you swear!

QUICKSILVER 'Sfoot, man, I am a gentleman and may swear by my pedigree, God's my life! Sirrah, Golding, wilt be ruled by a fool? Turn, good fellow, turn swaggering gallant, and "let the welkin roar, and Erebus also."[62] Look not westward to the fall of Don Phoebus,[63] but to the east: eastward ho!

"Where radiant beams of lusty Sol appear,
And bright Eous makes the welkin clear."[64]

We are both gentlemen, and therefore should be no coxcombs;[65] let's be no longer fools to this flat-cap, Touchstone. Eastward, bully! This satin-belly and canvas-backed[66] Touchstone. 'Slife[67] man, his father was a malt-man, and his mother sold gingerbread in Christ Church![68]

GOLDING What would ye ha' me do?

QUICKSILVER Why, do nothing; be like a gentleman, be idle! The curse of man is labor. Wipe thy bum with testons,[69] and make ducks and drakes with shillings.[70] What, eastward ho! Wilt thou cry, "what is 't ye lack?" Stand with a bare pate, and a dropping nose, under a wooden

52 53 dilling: darling

53 54 longs to call madam: Mistress Touchstone is eager to address Gertrude as "madam," since she will have a title when she marries Sir Petronel

54 57 nice: ignorant; fussy; lascivious

55 58 court cut and long tail: dress influenced by the fashion of the court, with sweeping trains

56 61 substance: wealth and goods

57 66–7 prodigal's hogs' trough: Touchstone alludes to the biblical parable of the prodigal son, who squanders his wealth and is forced to tend pigs, where he is tempted to share their husks for food

58 67 sirrah: term of reprimand or contempt

59 68 Marry, faugh, goodman flat-cap: an exclamation of disgust at Touchstone that mocks his position as master and his citizen appearance

60 68 'Sfoot: by God's foot, an oath

61 68–9 give arms: display my family's coat of arms

62 72–3 "let the . . . Erebus also": a line from Shakespeare's *2 Henry IV* (II.iv. 152–3), slightly misquoted

63 73 Don Phoebus: the sun

64 75–6 "Where radiant . . . welkin clear": unidentified, although these lines about the sun rising and dawn's clear skies sound like another of Quicksilver's "play ends"

65 77 coxcombs: a cap worn by a fool, shaped like a rooster's comb; also a vain and foolish person

66 78 satin-belly and canvas-backed: Touchstone's clothing is made of fine fabric in front, and cheap cloth in back, for thrift

67 78 'Slife: by God's life

68 79 malt-man . . . Christ Church: a man who sells malt for brewers; Christ Church was a London parish with Newgate prison (Quicksilver mocks Touchstone's parents for their unrefined occupations and low status)

69 82 testons: sixpence pieces

70 82 make ducks . . . with shillings: spend money carelessly ("ducks and drakes" is a game of skipping stones across water)

penthouse,[71] and art a gentleman? Wilt thou bear tankards, and may'st bear arms? Be ruled, turn gallant, eastward ho! [*Sings*] *Ta, ly re, ly re, ro!* "Who calls Jeronimo? Speak, here I am."[72] God's so, how like a sheep thou look'st! O' my conscience, some cowherd begot thee, thou Golding of Golding Hall! Ha, boy?

GOLDING Go, ye are a prodigal coxcomb! I a cowherd's son, because I turn not a drunken whore-hunting rakehell[73] like thyself?

QUICKSILVER Rakehell? Rakehell?

[QUICKSILVER] *offers to draw*[74] *and* GOLDING *trips up his heels and holds*[75] *him*

GOLDING Pish! In soft terms: ye are a cowardly bragging boy. I'll ha' you whipped.

QUICKSILVER Whipped? That's good, i'faith. Untruss[76] me!

GOLDING No, thou wilt undo thy self. Alas, I behold thee with pity, not with anger. Thou common shot-clog,[77] gull of all companies, methinks I see thee already walking in Moorfields[78] without a cloak, with half a hat, without a band,[79] a doublet with three buttons, without a girdle, a hose with one point and no garter,[80] with a cudgel under thine arm, borrowing and begging threepence.

QUICKSILVER Nay, 'slife, take this[81] and take all. As I am a gentleman born, I'll be drunk, grow valiant, and beat thee. *Exit*

GOLDING Go, thou most madly vain, whom nothing can recover but that which reclaims atheists, and makes great persons sometimes religious: calamity. As for my place and life, thus I have read:

"Whate'er some vainer youth may term disgrace,
The gain of honest pains is never base:
From trades, from arts, from valor, honor springs;
These three are founts of gentry, yea, of kings."[82]

[*Exit*]

[Act I, scene ii]

Enter GERTRUDE, MILDRED, BETTRICE, *and* POLDAVY, *a tailor;* POLDAVY *with a fair gown, Scotch farthingale, and French fall*[83] *in his arms,* GERTRUDE *in a French head attire and citizen's gown,* MILDRED *sewing, and* BETTRICE *leading a monkey after her*

GERTRUDE For the passion of patience, look if Sir Petronel approach, that sweet, that fine, that delicate, that—for love's sake, tell me if he come! O sister Mil, though my father be a low-capped tradesman, yet I must be a lady; and I praise God my mother must call me medam.[84] Does he come? Off with this gown, for shame's sake, off with this gown! Let not my knight take me in the city cut[85] in any hand: tear it, pax[86] on't. Does he come? [*She takes off the gown*] Tear

71 84 penthouse: sloping roof (imagined here as a shopfront canopy)
72 85 "Who calls . . . I am": a line from Thomas Kyd's popular play *The Spanish Tragedy* (II.v. 4)
73 89 rakehell: dissolute scoundrel
74 90 SD *offers to draw*: attempts to draw his sword
75 90 SD *holds*: restrains
76 92 Untruss me: free me; let me go
77 94 common shot-clog: unwelcome companion, only tolerated because he pays the bill for others in the group
78 94 Moorfields: a park on the north side of London known for its population of poor and homeless people (Golding imagines Quicksilver's appearance as he begs there)
79 95 band: collar
80 96 hose with . . . no garter: a pair of stockings with only one string to tie them up, and no band to keep the stockings from falling down
81 98 this: i.e. his sword
82 103–6 "Whate'er some . . . of kings": Golding's rhyming proverb has not been traced to another source; the theme of citizen virtue suggests it is original to the play
83 0 SD *Scotch farthingale, and French fall*: a farthingale is a hooped petticoat; a fall is a fashionable women's collar
84 3 medam: i.e. madam; because Gertrude marries a knight, Mistress Touchstone will have to defer to her; the spelling may suggest an affected pronunciation (as with "chitty" below)
85 5 cut: fashion
86 5 pax: euphemism for "pox," i.e. syphilis

it off! [*Sings*] *Thus whilst she sleeps, I sorrow, for her sake, etc.*[87]
MILDRED Lord, sister, with what an immodest impatiency and disgraceful scorn do you put off your city tire.[88] I am sorry to think you imagine to right your self, in wronging that which hath made both you and us.
GERTRUDE I tell you I cannot endure it. I must be a lady! Do you wear your coif[89] with a London licket,[90] your stammel petticoat with two guards,[91] the buffin gown with the tuftaffety cape,[92] and the velvet lace. I must be a lady, and I will be a lady. I like some humors of the city dames well: to eat cherries only at an angel a pound,[93] good; to dye rich scarlet black, pretty; to line a grogram gown clean through with velvet, tolerable; their pure linen, their smocks of three pounds a smock are to be borne withal.[94] But your mincing niceries, taffeta pipkins,[95] durance[96] petticoats, and silver bodkins[97]—God's my life, as I shall be a lady, I cannot endure it. Is he come yet? Lord what a long[98] knight 'tis! [*Sings*] *And ever she cried "shoot home!"*—and yet I knew one longer—[*Sings*] *And ever she cried "shoot home!" fa, la, ly, re, lo, la.*[99]
MILDRED Well, sister, those that scorn their nest oft fly with a sick wing.
GERTRUDE Bow-bell![100]
MILDRED Where titles presume to thrust before fit means to second them, wealth and respect often grow sullen, and will not follow. For sure, in this, I would for your sake I spake not truth. "Where ambition of place goes before fitness of birth, contempt and disgrace follow." I heard a scholar once say that Ulysses, when he counterfeited himself mad, yoked cats and foxes and dogs together to draw his plough, while he followed and sowed salt. But sure, I judge them truly mad that yoke citizens and courtiers, tradesmen and soldiers, a goldsmith's daughter and a knight! Well, sister, pray God my father sow not salt too.
GERTRUDE Alas, poor Mil! When I am a lady, I'll pray for thee yet, i'faith. Nay, and I'll vouchsafe to call thee "sister Mil" still, for though thou are not like to be a lady as I am, yet sure thou art a creature of God's making, and mayest peradventure[101] to be saved as soon as I. Does he come? [*Sings*] *And ever and anon she doubled in her song.* Now, Lady's my comfort, what a profane ape's here![102] Tailor Poldavy, prithee fit it, fit it. [*She puts on the new clothes*] Is this a right Scot?[103] Does it clip close? And bear up round?
POLDAVY Fine and stiffly, i'faith; 'twill keep your thighs so cool and make your waist so small. Here was a fault in your body, but I have supplied the defect with the effect of my steel instrument,[104] which, though it have but one eye, can see to rectify the imperfection of the proportion.
GERTRUDE Most edifying tailor! I protest you tailors are most sanctified members,[105] and make many crooked things go upright. How must I bear my hands? Light? Light?[106]

87 6 *Thus whilst . . . sake, etc*: lines from John Dowland's song, "Sleep, wayward thoughts," in *First Book of Songs or Airs* (1597)
88 8 city tire: attire appropriate to a citizen's rank
89 10 coif: close-fitting cap
90 11 licket: ribbon to tie the cap
91 11 stammel petticoat with two guards: a petticoat made of coarse red cloth, with two ornamental borders to prevent fraying
92 11–12 buffin gown . . . tuftaffety cape: a gown worn by middle-class women, with a cape made from a kind of taffeta with a tufted pile (Gertrude is mocking Mildred's thrifty citizen attire)
93 13 an angel a pound: a shockingly high price (an angel is a gold coin worth ten shillings)
94 15 borne withal: endured likewise (Gertrude cites examples of profligate expense)
95 15 taffeta pipkins: hats fashionable at court until the 1590s, and therefore outdated
96 16 durance: thick and durable woolen fabric
97 16 bodkins: ornamental pins for fastening women's hair
98 17 long: late; well-endowed (with a pun on "night" and "knight")
99 18 *And ever . . . lo, la*: presumably lines from ballads, with bawdy puns
100 20 Bow-bell: born within the sound of the bells of St. Mary-le-Bow Church (or "Bow Church") in Cheapside, and thus a Cockney: a gibe at a citizen
101 30 peradventure: possibly
102 32 profane ape's here: presumably Gertrude responds to some action of Bettrice's monkey, perhaps something irreverent or indecent
103 33 right Scot: tight fit, referring to the Scotch farthingale
104 35–6 steel instrument: needle, with a bawdy insinuation that continues in the following lines
105 38 sanctified members: reference to Puritans, also extending the bawdy wordplay
106 39 Light: nimbly; also, with reference to women, promiscuous

POLDAVY O, ay, now you are in the lady-fashion, you must do all things light.
Tread light, light, ay and fall so: *She trips about*[107] *the stage*
That's the court amble.
GERTRUDE Has the court ne'er a trot?
POLDAVY No, but a false gallop,[108] lady.
GERTRUDE [*Sings*] *And if she will not go to bed—*
BETTRICE The knight's come, forsooth!

Enter SIR PETRONEL, MASTER TOUCHSTONE, [GOLDING,] *and* MISTRESS TOUCHSTONE

GERTRUDE Is my knight come? O the lord, my band! Sister, do my cheeks look well? Give me a little box o' the ear that I may seem to blush: now, now! [MILDRED *slaps* GERTRUDE's *face*] So, there, there, there! Here he is: O, my dearest delight! Lord, lord, and how does my knight?
TOUCHSTONE Fie, with more modesty!
GERTRUDE Modesty! Why, I am no citizen now. Modesty? Am I not to be married? Y'are best to keep me modest now I am to be a lady!
SIR PETRONEL Boldness is good fashion, and court-like.
GERTRUDE Ay, in a country lady I hope it is, as I shall be. And how chance ye came no sooner, knight?
SIR PETRONEL Faith, I was so entertained in the progress[109] with one Count Epernoum, a Welsh knight. We had a match at balloon,[110] too, with my Lord Whachum, for four crowns.
GERTRUDE At baboon?[111] Jesu! You and I will play at baboon in the country, knight?
SIR PETRONEL O, sweet lady, 'tis a strong play with the arm.
GERTRUDE With arm, or leg, or any other member, if it be a court sport. And when shall's be married, my knight?
SIR PETRONEL I come now to consummate it, and your father may call a poor knight son-in-law.
TOUCHSTONE Sir, ye are come. What is not mine to keep, I must not be sorry to forgo. A hundred pound land[112] her grandmother left her, 'tis yours; herself, as her mother's gift, is yours. But if you expect aught from me, know my hand and mine eyes open together. I do not give blindly. *Work upon that now.*
SIR PETRONEL Sir, you mistrust not my means? I am a knight.
TOUCHSTONE Sir, sir; what I know not, you will give me leave to say I am ignorant of.
MISTRESS TOUCHSTONE Yes, that he is a knight! I know where he had money to pay the gentlemen ushers and heralds their fees. Ay, that he is a knight; and so might you have been too, if you had been aught else than an ass, as well as some of your neighbors. And[113] I thought you would not ha' been knighted, as I am an honest woman, I would ha' dubbed[114] you myself. I praise God I have wherewithal! But as for you, daughter—
GERTRUDE Ay, mother, I must be a lady tomorrow. And by your leave, mother—I speak it not without my duty, but only in the right of my husband—I must take place of[115] you, mother.
MISTRESS TOUCHSTONE That you shall, lady-daughter, and have a coach as well as I, too.
GERTRUDE Yes, mother. But by your leave, mother—I speak it not without my duty, but only in my husband's right—my coach-horses must take the wall of[116] your coach-horses.

107 41 SD *trips about*: dances around
108 44 false gallop: canter, continuing the wordplay on a horse's gait with a comment on the court's immorality
109 56 progress: royal progress, the monarch's travel to the countryside
110 57 balloon: a game of hitting a large leather ball fastened to wooden paddles
111 58 baboon: Gertrude misunderstands the word, and her subsequent comments continue a pattern of language with sexually suggestive double meanings
112 65 hundred pound land: the land yields one hundred pounds annually
113 72 And: if
114 73 dubbed: paid for your knighthood (with the reference to "fees" above, glances at King James's practice of granting knighthood in return for money); also with a suggestion of cuckoldry
115 76 take place of: have a higher social standing than
116 79 take the wall of: have the privileged inside position when passing in the street

TOUCHSTONE Come, come, the day grows low; 'tis supper time. Use my house; the wedding solemnity is at my wife's cost.[117] Thank me for nothing but my willing blessing, for—I cannot feign—my hopes are faint. And sir, respect my daughter: she has refused, for you, wealthy and honest matches, known good men, well moneyed, better traded, best reputed.

GERTRUDE Body o' truth, chitizens,[118] chitizens! Sweet knight, as soon as ever we are married, take me to thy mercy out of this miserable chitty; presently carry me out of the scent of Newcastle coal, and the hearing of Bow-bell.[119] I beseech thee, down with me,[120] for God's sake!

TOUCHSTONE Well, daughter, I have read that old wit sings:[121]
"The greatest rivers flow from little springs.
Though thou art full, scorn not thy means at first;
He that's most drunk may soonest be athirst."
Work upon that now. *All but* TOUCHSTONE, MILDRED, *and* GOLDING *depart*

No, no! Yond stand my hopes: Mildred, come hither, daughter! And how approve you your sister's fashion? How do you fancy her choice? What dost thou think?

MILDRED I hope, as a sister, well.

TOUCHSTONE Nay but, nay but, how dost thou like her behavior and humor?[122] Speak freely.

MILDRED I am loath to speak ill, and yet—I am sorry of this—I cannot speak well.

TOUCHSTONE Well, very good, as I would wish; a modest answer. Golding, come hither; hither, Golding! How dost thou like the knight, Sir Flash? Does he not look big?[123] How lik'st thou the elephant?[124] He says he has a castle in the country.

GOLDING Pray heaven the elephant carry not his castle on his back.[125]

TOUCHSTONE 'Fore heaven, very well. But seriously, how dost repute him?

GOLDING The best I can say of him is: I know him not.

TOUCHSTONE Ha, Golding! I commend thee, I approve thee, and will make it appear my affection is strong to thee. My wife has her humor, and I will ha' mine. Dost thou see my daughter here? She is not fair, well-favored[126] or so, indifferent,[127] which modest measure of beauty shall not make it thy only work to watch her, nor sufficient mischance to suspect her.[128] Thou art towardly,[129] she is modest;[130] thou art provident,[131] she is careful. She's now mine; give me thy hand, she's now thine. *Work upon that now!*

GOLDING Sir, as your son, I honor you, and as your servant, obey you.

TOUCHSTONE Sayest thou so? Come hither, Mildred. Do you see yond fellow? He is a gentleman, though my prentice, and has somewhat to take to: a youth of good hope, well friended, well parted.[132] Are you mine? You are his. *Work (you) upon that now.*

MILDRED Sir, I am all yours. Your body gave me life; your care and love, happiness of life. Let your virtue still direct it, for to your wisdom I wholly dispose myself.

TOUCHSTONE Say'st thou so? Be ye two better acquainted. Lip her,[133] lip her, knave! So, shut up shop: in! We must make holiday. *Exeunt* GOLDING *and* MILDRED

117 81 at my wife's cost: paid for by my wife
118 84 chitizen: an affected pronunciation of "citizen," with a suggestion of "shit"
119 85–6 scent of . . . of Bow-bell: the smell of coal and the sound of the church bells that define life in the city of London
120 86 down with me: take me to the country (where Gertrude believes he has a castle); take me to bed
121 87 old wit sings: wise saying which declares
122 95 humor: inclination
123 98 big: important
124 99 elephant: proverbially associated with pride
125 100 elephant carry . . . his back: joking that Sir Petronel may own nothing more than the clothes he is wearing; in chess, the piece known as the rook was often depicted as an elephant with a castle on its back
126 105 well-favored: good-looking
127 105 indifferent: neutral; neither good nor bad
128 105–6 modest measure . . . suspect her: because she is not very beautiful, you will not have to devote all of your time to watching her or suspecting that she is unfaithful (because other men will not find her attractive)
129 107 towardly: promising
130 107 modest: demure
131 107 provident: frugal
132 112 well parted: of good character
133 115 Lip her: kiss her

This match shall on, for I intend to prove
Which thrives the best: the mean or lofty love?
Whether fit wedlock vowed twixt like and like,[134]
Or prouder hopes, which daringly o'erstrike
Their place and means. 'Tis honest time's expense,
When seeming lightness bears a moral sense.[135]
Work upon that now.

Exit

Act II, scene i

[*Enter*] TOUCHSTONE; GOLDING *and* MILDRED *sitting on either side of the stall*

TOUCHSTONE Quicksilver! Master Francis Quicksilver! Master Quicksilver!

Enter QUICKSILVER [*hiccupping*]

QUICKSILVER Here, sir (*ump*).[136]
TOUCHSTONE So, sir. Nothing but flat[137] "Master Quicksilver," without any familiar addition,[138] will fetch you! Will you truss my points,[139] sir?
QUICKSILVER Ay, forsooth[140] (*ump*).
TOUCHSTONE How now, sir? The drunken hiccup, so soon this morning?
QUICKSILVER 'Tis but the coldness of my stomach, forsooth.
TOUCHSTONE What? Have you the cause natural for it? Y'are a very learned drunkard; I believe I shall miss some of my silver spoons with your learning.[141] The nuptial night will not moisten your throat sufficiently, but the morning likewise must rain her dews into your gluttonous weasand.[142]
QUICKSILVER An't please you, sir, we did but drink (*ump*) to the coming off[143] of the knightly bridegroom.
TOUCHSTONE To the coming off on him?
QUICKSILVER Ay, forsooth: we drunk to his coming on (*ump*) when we went to bed; and now we are up, we must drink to his coming off. For that's the chief honor of a soldier, sir; and therefore we must drink so much the more to it, forsooth (*ump*).
TOUCHSTONE A very capital reason, so that you go to bed late and rise early to commit drunkenness? You fulfill the scripture[144] very sufficient wickedly, forsooth.
QUICKSILVER The knight's men, forsooth, be still o' their knees[145] at it, (*ump*) and because 'tis for your credit, sir, I would be loath to flinch.
TOUCHSTONE I pray sir, e'en to 'em again, then! Y'are one of the separated crew,[146] one of my wife's faction, and my young lady's, with whom, and with their great match,[147] I will have nothing to do.
QUICKSILVER So, sir, now I will go keep my (*ump*) credit with 'em, an't please you, sir.

134 119 like and like: people of similar status
135 121–2 'Tis honest . . . moral sense: matchmaking, which seems frivolous, is a good use of time when it teaches a moral lesson
136 2 *ump*: Quicksilver's hiccups are marked with this stage direction throughout
137 3 flat: plain
138 3–4 familiar addition: casual address (i.e. Quicksilver only arrives when called with the formal term "Master")
139 4 truss my points: tie the laces that fasten my hose to my doublet
140 5 forsooth: truly
141 8–9 very learned . . . your learning: you seem to know everything, so I should keep an eye on my valuables around you
142 11 gluttonous weasand: greedy throat
143 12 coming off: as if leaving a field of military triumph, with suggestion of sexual conquest
144 19 fulfill the scripture: Touchstone alludes to Isaiah 5:11: "Woe unto them that rise up early to follow drunkenness, and to them that continue until night, till the wine do inflame them" (Geneva Bible, 1560)
145 20 o' their knees: kneeling down to drink toasts
146 22 separated crew: a phrase generally used to refer to Puritans; used here to refer to the division in Touchstone's family
147 23 great match: i.e. Gertrude's marriage to Sir Petronel

TOUCHSTONE In any case, sir, lay one cup of sack[148] more o' your cold stomach, I beseech you.

QUICKSILVER Yes, forsooth. *Exit* QUICKSILVER

TOUCHSTONE [*To the audience*] This is for my credit? Servants ever maintain drunkenness in their master's house for their master's credit? A good idle serving-man's reason! I thank Time the night is past; I ne'er waked to such cost. I think we have stowed more sorts of flesh in our bellies than ever Noah's ark received: and for wine, why, my house turns giddy with it, and more noise in it than at a conduit.[149] Ay me, even beasts condemn our gluttony! Well, 'tis our city's fault, which because we commit seldom, we commit the more sinfully. We lose no time in our sensuality, but we make amends for it. O, that we would do so in virtue, and religious negligences![150] But see, here are all the sober parcels[151] my house can show. I'll eavesdrop, hear what thoughts they utter this morning. [TOUCHSTONE *withdraws and* GOLDING *and* MILDRED *come forward*]

GOLDING But is it possible that you, seeing your sister preferred[152] to the bed of a knight, should contain your affections in the arms of a prentice?

MILDRED I had rather make up the garment of my affections in some of the same piece[153] than, like a fool, wear gowns of two colors, or mix sackcloth with satin.

GOLDING And do the costly garments, the title and fame of a lady, the fashion, observation, and reverence proper to such preferment, no more inflame you, than such convenience[154] as my poor means and industry can offer to your virtues?

MILDRED I have observed that the bridle given to those violent flatteries of fortune is seldom recovered. They bear one headlong in desire from one novelty to another, and where those ranging appetites reign, there is ever more passion than reason: no stay, and so no happiness.[155] These hasty advancements are not natural. Nature hath given us legs to go to our objects, not wings to fly to them.

GOLDING How dear an object you are to my desires I cannot express, whose fruition[156] —would my master's absolute consent and yours vouchsafe me—I should be absolutely happy. And though it were a grace so far beyond my merit that I should blush with unworthiness to receive it, yet thus far both my love and my means shall assure your requital:[157] you shall want nothing fit for your birth and education. What increase of wealth and advancement the honest and orderly industry and skill of our trade will afford in any,[158] I doubt not will be aspired by me; I will ever make your contentment the end of my endeavors; I will love you above all; and only your grief shall be my misery, and your delight my felicity.

TOUCHSTONE [*Aside*] *Work upon that now.* By my hopes, he woos honestly and orderly; he shall be anchor of my hopes. Look, see the ill-yoked[159] monster, his fellow!

Enter QUICKSILVER *unlaced,*[160] *a towel about his neck, in his flat cap,*[161] *drunk*

QUICKSILVER Eastward ho! "Holla, ye pampered Jades of Asia!"[162]

TOUCHSTONE [*Aside*] Drunk now, downright, o' my fidelity!

148 26 sack: an imported white wine
149 33 conduit: public fountain, known for noise
150 36 negligences: neglect (i.e. that we would be as excessive in making up for neglect of religion and virtue)
151 36 parcels: members (of the household)
152 38 preferred: advanced
153 40–41 some of the same piece: cut from the same cloth (i.e. of the same social status)
154 43 convenience: mode of living
155 45–7 I have . . . no happiness: a horsemanship metaphor to describe how desire for advancement and material goods must be reined in by self-control, like a rider checking a horse; without self-restraint, it is impossible to be content
156 50 fruition: attainment (of my desires, i.e. marriage)
157 53 requital: repayment or reward
158 55 afford in any: enable for anyone
159 59 ill-yoked: wearing the neck towel like a harness; unsuited for work
160 59 SD *unlaced*: with his doublet's laces untied
161 59 SD *flat cap*: hat worn by an apprentice
162 60 "Holla, ye . . . of Asia": a line from Christopher Marlowe's *2 Tamburlaine* (IV.iii. 1)

QUICKSILVER (*Ump*) Pulldo, Pulldo![163] "Showse," quoth the caliver.[164]

GOLDING Fie, fellow Quicksilver, what a pickle are you in!

QUICKSILVER Pickle? Pickle in thy throat! Zounds, pickle? Wa ha ho![165] Good morrow, Knight Petronel; 'morrow, Lady Goldsmith! Come off, knight, with a counterbuff,[166] for the honor of knighthood!

GOLDING Why, how now, sir? Do ye know where you are?

QUICKSILVER Where I am? Why, 'sblood, you jolthead,[167] where I am?

GOLDING Go to, go to![168] For shame, go to bed and sleep out this immodesty. Thou sham'st both my master and his house.

QUICKSILVER Shame? What shame? I thought thou wouldst show thy bringing up.[169] An[170] thou wert a gentleman as I am, thou wouldst think it no shame to be drunk. Lend me some money, save my credit;[171] I must dine with the servingmen and their wives—and their wives, sirrah!

GOLDING E'en who you will; I'll not lend thee threepence.

QUICKSILVER 'Sfoot, lend me some money! "Hast thou not Hyren here?"[172] [TOUCHSTONE *comes forward*]

TOUCHSTONE Why how now, sirrah? What vein's[173] this, hah?

QUICKSILVER "Who cries on murder? Lady, was it you?"[174] How does our master? Pray thee: cry "Eastward ho!"

TOUCHSTONE Sirrah, sirrah, y'are past your hiccup now. I see y'are drunk.

QUICKSILVER 'Tis for your credit, master.

TOUCHSTONE And hear you keep a whore in town.

QUICKSILVER 'Tis for your credit, master.

TOUCHSTONE And what you are out in cash, I know.

QUICKSILVER So do I. My father's a gentleman: *work upon that now*. Eastward ho!

TOUCHSTONE Sir, "Eastward ho!" will make you go "Westward ho."[175] I will no longer dishonest[176] my house, nor endanger my stock with your license.[177] There, sir, there's your indenture [*Hands* QUICKSILVER *the document*]; all your apparel—that I must know[178]—is on your back, and from this time my door is shut to you. From me be free,[179] but for other freedom, and the moneys you have wasted, "Eastward ho!" shall not serve you.

QUICKSILVER Am I free o' my fetters? Rent,[180] fly with a duck in thy mouth![181] And now I tell thee, Touchstone—

TOUCHSTONE Good sir.

QUICKSILVER "When this eternal substance of my soul"[182]—

TOUCHSTONE Well said: change your gold ends[183] for your play ends.[184]

163 62 Pulldo: unknown; editors suggest the cry of rowers, or Quicksilver's belch

164 62 "Showse," quoth the caliver: "Bang went the gun" (Schelling, quoted in Van Fossen, 1979)

165 64 Wa ha ho: falconer's call

166 65 counterbuff: blow given in return

167 68 jolthead: blockhead

168 69 Go to, go to: come, come

169 71 show thy bringing up: sobriety is a virtue proverbially associated with citizens

170 71 An: if

171 73 credit: finances; social reputation

172 76 "Hast thou not Hyren here?": line that imitates Pistol in Shakespeare's *2 Henry IV* (II.iv. 154)

173 77 vein's: style or kind of speech

174 78 "Who cries . . . it you?": this line also appears in George Chapman's play *The Blind Beggar of Alexandria* (ix. 49) and *Poetaster* (III.iv. 184)

175 86 "Westward ho!": in the direction of the gallows at Tyburn

176 87 dishonest: dishonor

177 87 license: unrestrained and immoral behavior

178 88 that I must know: articles of clothing masters are required to provide to apprentices; the clothing that Touchstone knows Quicksilver has

179 89 free: legally released from the bond of apprenticeship

180 91 Rent: wages

181 91 fly with . . . thy mouth: a figure for money earning interest; he will make money without being an apprentice

182 94 "When this . . . my soul": in this and the following quotations, Quicksilver declaims lines from the opening of *The Spanish Tragedy* (I.i. 1–2, 4–5)

183 95 gold ends: bit and broken pieces of gold

184 95 play ends: lines from plays

QUICKSILVER "Did live imprisoned in my wanton flesh"—

TOUCHSTONE What then, sir?

QUICKSILVER "I was a courtier in the Spanish court, and Don Andrea was my name."

TOUCHSTONE Good master Don Andrea, will you march?

QUICKSILVER Sweet Touchstone, will you lend me two shillings?

TOUCHSTONE Not a penny.

QUICKSILVER Not a penny? I have friends, and I have acquaintance. I will piss at thy shop posts, and throw rotten eggs at thy sign. *Work upon that now.* *Exit staggering*

TOUCHSTONE Now, sirrah, you! Hear you? You shall serve me no more neither, not an hour longer.

GOLDING What mean you, sir?

TOUCHSTONE I mean to give thee thy freedom;[185] and with thy freedom, my daughter; and with my daughter, a father's love. And with all these, such a portion[186] as shall make Knight Petronel himself envy thee. Y'are both agreed, are ye not?

GOLDING AND MILDRED With all submission, both of thanks and duty.

TOUCHSTONE Well, then, the great power of heaven bless and confirm you. And Golding, that my love to thee may not show less than my wife's love to my eldest daughter, thy marriage feast shall equal the knight's and hers.

GOLDING Let me beseech you: no, sir. The superfluity[187] and cold meat left at their nuptials will with bounty furnish ours. The grossest prodigality[188] is superfluous cost of the belly. Nor would I wish any invitement of states or friends; only your reverend presence and witness shall sufficiently grace and confirm us.

TOUCHSTONE Son to mine own bosom, take her and my blessing! The nice fondling,[189] my lady sir-reverence,[190] that I must not now presume to call daughter, is so ravished with desire to hansel[191] her new coach, and see her knight's eastward castle, that the next morning will sweat with her busy setting forth. Away will she and her mother, and while their preparation is making, ourselves, with some two or three other friends, will consummate the humble match we have in God's name concluded:
'Tis to my wish, for I have often read:
"Fit birth, fit age, keeps long a quiet bed."
'Tis to my wish, for tradesmen (well 'tis known)
Get[192] with more ease than gentry keeps his own.

Exeunt

[Act II, scene ii]

[*Enter*] SECURITY *alone*

SECURITY My privy[193] guest, lusty Quicksilver, has drunk too deep of the bride-bowl,[194] but with a little sleep, he is much recovered, and I think is making himself ready to be drunk in a gallanter likeness. My house is, as 'twere, the cave where the young outlaw hoards the stolen vails[195] of his occupation. And here, when he will revel it in his prodigal similitude, he retires to

185 107 freedom: conclude his apprenticeship term, promoting Golding to guild membership
186 108 portion: dowry
187 114 superfluity: leftovers, as thrift (a parody of Shakespeare's *Hamlet* (I.ii. 180–81))
188 115 grossest prodigality: most wasteful extravagance
189 118 fondling: foolish person
190 119 sir-reverence: with all respect for (Touchstone's mocking tone suggests he may also mean the term in its other sense: human excrement)
191 120 hansel: experience for the first time (to Gertrude, the coach is the first sign of the advancement in status that accompanies marriage to a knight)
192 127 Get: make money
193 1 privy: trusted; secret
194 1 bride-bowl: celebratory toast shared by wedding guests
195 4 vails: profits

his trunks and (I may say softly) his punks.[196] He dares trust me with the keeping of both, for I am security itself: my name is Security, the famous usurer.[197]

Enter QUICKSILVER *in his prentice's coat and cap,* [*and*] *his gallant breeches and stockings, gartering himself*[198]

QUICKSILVER Come, old Security, thou father of destruction. Th' indented sheepskin[199] is burned wherein I was wrapped, and I am now loose, to get more children of perdition[200] into thy usurous bonds. Thou feed'st my lechery, and I thy covetousness; thou art pander[201] to me for my wench, and I to thee for thy cozenages.[202] "Ka me, Ka thee,"[203] runs through court and country.

SECURITY Well said, my subtle Quicksilver. These K's[204] ope the doors to all this world's felicity; the dullest forehead sees it. Let not Master Courtier think he carries all the knavery[205] on his shoulders. I have known poor Hob in the country, that has worn hobnails on's shoes, have as much villainy in's head as he that wears gold buttons in's cap.[206]

QUICKSILVER Why, man, 'tis the London highway to thrift; if virtue be used, 'tis but as a scrap[207] to the net of villainy. They that use it simply, thrive simply, I warrant. "Weight and fashion makes goldsmiths cuckolds."

Enter SINDEFY, *with Quicksilver's doublet, cloak, rapier, and dagger*

SINDEFY Here, sir, put off the other half[208] of your prenticeship.

QUICKSILVER Well said, sweet Sin! Bring forth my bravery;[209]
Now let my trunks shoot forth their silks concealed.
I now am free, and now will justify
My trunks and punks. Avaunt,[210] dull flat cap, then!
Via,[211] the curtain that shadowed Borgia![212] [*He sheds the rest of his apprentice attire and dresses as a gallant*]
There lie, thou husk of my envasselled[213] state.
I, Samson[214] now, have burst the Philistines' bands,
And in thy lap, my lovely Dalida,
I'll lie, and snore out my enfranchised[215] state.

196 5 punks: prostitutes
197 6 usurer: moneylender, known for often charging an excessive rate of interest
198 6 SD *gartering himself*: Q reads "*Securitie following*" after this description of Quicksilver; editors typically delete this phrase because Security is already onstage from his introductory speech (perhaps suggesting that the opening soliloquy was a later addition to the play, intended to clarify that the action has shifted to a new location)
199 7 indented sheepskin: parchment on which the articles of indenture were written
200 8 perdition: irredeemable wickedness (the victims will be ruined)
201 9 pander: a go-between in secret love affairs; a pimp
202 10 cozenages: deceptions, frauds
203 10 "Ka me, Ka thee": proverbial ("one good turn deserves another")
204 12 K's: keys (he puns on "ka," pronounced the same way)
205 13 knavery: trickery
206 14–15 poor Hob . . . in's cap: the proverbial country bumpkin is just as capable of plotting evil as a courtier
207 17 scrap: small bit; here a lure used to bait the net of villainy
208 19 other half: i.e. the clothing of an apprentice
209 20 bravery: finery
210 23 Avaunt: begone
211 24 *Via*: away
212 24 Borgia: Cesare Borgia, fifteenth-century Italian noble and example of political ambition for Niccolo Machiavelli's *The Prince*, noted for his use of disguise
213 25 envasselled: subjugated; subordinated
214 26 Samson: in the biblical story, Samson is a man of great strength, who cannot be held captive by the Philistines; his undoing, which Quicksilver does not relate, comes when his lover Delilah (here, the archaic "Dalida") cuts his hair and deprives him of strength
215 28 enfranchised: free; released from confinement

[*Sings*]
When Samson was a tall young man
His power and strength increasèd then:[216]
He sold no more, nor cup, nor can,
But did them all despise.
Old Touchstone, now write to thy friends
For one to sell thy base gold ends;
Quicksilver now no more attends
Thee, Touchstone.
[*To* SECURITY] But dad,[217] hast thou seen my running gelding dressed[218] today?
SECURITY That I have, Frank: the ostler, o' th' Cock,[219] dressed him for a breakfast.
QUICKSILVER What, did he eat him?
SECURITY No, but he eat[220] his breakfast for dressing him, and so dressed him for breakfast.
QUICKSILVER "O witty age, where age is young in wit,
And all youths' words have gray beards full of it!"[221]
SINDEFY But alas, Frank, how will all this be maintained[222] now? Your place maintained it before.
QUICKSILVER Why, and I maintained my place. I'll to the court, another manner of place for maintenance, I hope, than the silly city. I heard my father say, I heard my mother sing, an old song and a true: "Thou art a she-fool, and know'st not what belongs to our male wisdom."[223] I shall be a merchant, forsooth! Trust my estate in a wooden trough[224] as he does? What are these ships but tennis balls for the winds to play withal? Tossed from one wave to another; now under-line,[225] now over the house; sometimes brick-walled against a rock, so that the guts[226] fly out again; sometimes struck under the wide hazard;[227] and farewell, Master Merchant!
SINDEFY Well, Frank, well; the seas, you say, are uncertain. But he that sails in your court seas[228] shall find 'em ten times fuller of hazard, wherein to see what is to be seen is torment more than a free spirit can endure. But when you come to suffer, how many injuries swallow you? What care and devotion must you use to humor an imperious lord? Proportion your looks to his looks, smiles to his smiles, fit your sails to the wind of his breath?
QUICKSILVER Tush, he's no journeyman[229] in his craft that cannot do that.
SINDEFY But he's worse than a prentice that does it, not only humoring the lord, but every trencher-bearer, every groom, that by indulgence and intelligence[230] crept into his favor and by panderism[231] into his chamber. He rules the roost, and when my honorable lord says it shall be thus, my worshipful rascal, the groom of his close stool,[232] says it shall not be thus, claps the door after him, and who dares enter? A prentice, quoth you? 'Tis but to learn to live, and does that disgrace a man? "He that rises hardly stands firmly; but he that rises with ease, alas,

216 29–30 *When Samson . . . increasèd then*: opening lines of a popular ballad, upon which Quicksilver improvises
217 37 dad: form of address to an older man; also a euphemistic oath (as Quicksilver will use it later)
218 37 dressed: groomed (a second meaning is "prepared as food," as Quicksilver puns)
219 38 ostler, o' th' Cock: groom at the Cock tavern
220 40 eat: ate, i.e. earned his meal by caring for the horse
221 42–3 "O witty . . . of it!" Quicksilver's couplet is perhaps a proverbial saying or improvisational reworking of Touchstone's earlier lines about "old wit" (see I.ii. 87)
222 44 maintained: afforded, also used in the following lines to mean living like a gallant, to which Quicksilver has become accustomed
223 48 "Thou art . . . male wisdom": Quicksilver may speak or sing this casually misogynistic line, untraced to sources beyond the inheritance he relates
224 49 wooden trough: i.e. a ship
225 51 under-line: below the level of the sea for a ship, and below the line on the tennis court (Quicksilver develops an extended comparison between merchant seafaring and a tennis match)
226 52 guts: goods that the ship carries
227 52 the wide hazard: on an indoor tennis court, the hazard is an opening in the wall; to strike under the hazard is to lose a point
228 54–5 sails in your court seas: becomes a courtier
229 59 journeyman: one who has advanced beyond apprentice and is a skilled craftsman
230 61 indulgence and intelligence: the lord's lenience and desire for news and gossip
231 62 panderism: acting as pimp
232 63 groom of his close stool: attendant with the task of emptying the lord's chamber pot, a privileged position at court

falls as easily."

QUICKSILVER A pox on you, who taught you this morality?

SECURITY 'Tis 'long of[233] this witty age, Master Francis. But indeed, Mistress Sindefy, all trades complain of inconvenience, and therefore 'tis best to have none. The merchant, he complains, and says, "traffic[234] is subject to much uncertainty and loss." Let 'em keep their goods on dry land with a vengeance, and not expose other men's substances to the mercy of the winds, under protection of a wooden wall, as Master Francis says, and all for greedy desire, to enrich themselves with unconscionable gain, two for one, or so; where[235] I and such other honest men, as live by lending money, are content with moderate profit, thirty or forty i' th' hundred,[236] so we may have it with quietness, and out of peril of wind and weather, rather than run those dangerous courses of trading, as they do.

QUICKSILVER Ay, dad, thou may'st well be called Security, for thou takest the safest course.

SECURITY Faith, the quieter, and the more contented, and, out of doubt, the more godly. For merchants in their courses are never pleased but ever repining[237] against heaven. One prays for a westerly wind to carry his ship forth; another for an easterly, to bring his ship home; and at every shaking of a leaf, he falls into an agony, to think what danger his ship is in on such a coast, and so forth. The farmer, he is ever at odds with the weather: sometimes the clouds have been too barren; sometimes the heavens forget themselves, their harvests answer not their hopes; sometimes the season falls out too fruitful, corn will bear no price; and so forth. Th' artificer,[238] he's all for a stirring[239] world; if his trade be too full and[240] fall short of his expectation, then falls he out of joint; where we, that trade nothing but money, are free from all this. We are pleased with all weathers: let it rain or hold up, be calm or windy, let the season be whatsoever, let trade go how it will. We take all in good part, e'en what please the heavens to send us, so the sun stand not still, and the moon keep her usual returns, and make up days, months, and years.

QUICKSILVER And you have good security?

SECURITY Ay, marry, Frank, that's the special point.

QUICKSILVER And yet, forsooth, we must have trades to live withal, for we cannot stand without legs, nor fly without wings, and a number of such scurvy[241] phrases. No, I say still, he that has wit, let him live by his wit; he that has none, let him be a tradesman.

SECURITY Witty Master Francis! 'Tis pity any trade should dull that quick brain of yours. Do but bring Knight Petronel into my parchment toils[242] once, and you shall never need to toil in any trade, o' my credit! You know his wife's land?

QUICKSILVER Even to a foot, sir; I have been often there. A pretty fine seat,[243] good land, all entire within itself.

SECURITY Well wooded?

QUICKSILVER Two hundred pounds worth of wood ready to fell, and a fine sweet house that stands just in the midst on't, like a prick[244] in the midst of a circle. Would I were your farmer, for a hundred pound a year.

SECURITY Excellent Master Francis, how I do long to do thee good! How I do hunger and thirst[245] to have the honor to enrich thee; ay, even to die, that thou mightest inherit my living.

233 68 'long of: on account of
234 70 traffic: the transportation of merchandise for trade
235 73 where: whereas
236 74–5 thirty or . . . th' hundred: i.e. thirty or forty percent (the maximum legal rate of interest was 10%)
237 79 repining: complaining
238 85 artificer: artisan; craftsman
239 85 stirring: changing (i.e. with supply and demand enough to keep him busy)
240 85 and: some editors change this word to "or"
241 94 scurvy: worthless; contemptible
242 97 parchment toils: paper snares; he puns on the labor of drawing up bonds
243 99 seat: estate
244 103 prick: the bulls-eye mark at the center of an archery target, with bawdy suggestion
245 105–6 hunger and thirst: Security's catchphrase borrows from Matthew 5:6 ("blessed are those who hunger and thirst for righteousness" in the Geneva Bible) and, like Touchstone's catchphrase, is italicized in Q whenever it appears

Even hunger and thirst! For o' my[246] religion, Master Francis—and so, tell Knight Petronel—I do it to do him a pleasure.

QUICKSILVER Marry, dad, his horses are now coming up, to bear down his lady. Wilt thou lend him thy stable to set 'em in?

SECURITY Faith, Master Francis, I would be loath to lend my stable out of doors.[247] In a greater matter I will pleasure him, but not in this.

QUICKSILVER A pox of your hunger and thirst! Well, dad, let him have money. All he could any way get is bestowed on a ship, now bound for Virginia, the frame[248] of which voyage is so closely conveyed that[249] his new lady nor any of her friends know it. Notwithstanding, as soon as his lady's hand[250] is gotten to the sale of her inheritance, and you have furnished him with money, he will instantly hoist sail and away.

SECURITY Now a frank[251] gale of wind go with him, Master Frank! We have too few such knight adventurers. Who would not sell away competent certainties to purchase, with any danger, excellent uncertainties? Your true knight venturer ever does it. Let his wife seal today, he shall have his money today.

QUICKSILVER Tomorrow she shall, dad, before she goes into the country; to work her to which action, with the more engines,[252] I purpose presently to prefer[253] my sweet Sin here to the place of her gentlewoman, whom you (for the more credit[254]) shall present as your friend's daughter, a gentlewoman of the country new come up with a will for a while to learn fashions forsooth, and be toward[255] some lady. And she shall buzz pretty devices[256] into her lady's ear, feeding her humors so serviceably, as the manner of such as she is, you know—

SECURITY True, good Master Francis.[257]

QUICKSILVER That she shall keep her port open to anything she commends to her.

SECURITY O' my religion, a most fashionable[258] project. As good she spoil[259] the lady as the lady spoil her, for 'tis three to one of one side. [*To* SINDEFY] Sweet Mistress Sin, how are you bound to Master Francis! I do not doubt to see you shortly wed one of the head men[260] of our city.

SINDEFY But, sweet Frank, when shall my father Security present me?

QUICKSILVER With all festination.[261] I have broken the ice to it already, and will presently to the knight's house, whither, my good old dad, let me pray thee with all formality to man[262] her.

SECURITY Command me, Master Francis; I do hunger and thirst to do thee service. Come, sweet Mistress Sin, take leave of my Winifred and we will instantly meet frank Master Francis at your lady's.

Enter WINIFRED *above*

WINIFRED Where is my Cu[263] there? Cu?

SECURITY Ay, Winnie.

246 107 o' my: on my
247 111 out of doors: to strangers
248 114 frame: scheme
249 115 closely conveyed that: secretly planned that neither
250 116 hand: signature
251 118 frank: steady
252 123 engines: trickery; plots
253 123 prefer: advance
254 124 credit: believability
255 126 be toward: serve in attendance on
256 126 devices: ideas
257 128 Master Francis: a stage direction in Q at this point reads "*Enter Sindefie.*" Editors typically delete it because no exit is marked earlier in the scene: whether and when Sindefy exits during this scene would radically alter her complicity with their scheme
258 130 fashionable: following the fashion (Gertrude will want to have a companion, just as she imagines a lady should); capable of being molded or shaped
259 130 spoil: destroy; ruin by indulging
260 132–3 head men: chief citizens; cuckolds
261 135 festination: haste
262 136 man: escort
263 140 Cu: Winifred's nickname for Security

WINIFRED Wilt thou come in, sweet Cu?
SECURITY Ay, Winnie, presently. *Exeunt* [WINIFRED *above*, SECURITY *and* SINDEFY *below*]
QUICKSILVER "Ay, Winnie," quod he? That's all he can do, poor man; he may well cut off her name at Winnie.[264] O 'tis an egregious pander! What will not an usurous knave be, so he may be rich? O 'tis a notable Jew's trump![265] I hope to live to see dog's meat made of the old usurer's flesh, dice of his bones, and indentures of his skin. And yet his skin is too thick to make parchment; 'twould make good boots for a peterman[266] to catch salmon in. Your only smooth skin to make fine vellum[267] is your Puritan's skin; they be the smoothest and slickest knaves in a country.
[*Exit*]

[Act II, scene iii]

Enter SIR PETRONEL *in boots, with a riding wan*[*d;*] [*enter* QUICKSILVER]

PETRONEL I'll out of this wicked town as fast as my horse can trot! Here's now no good action for a man to spend his time in. Taverns grow dead, ordinaries are blown up,[268] plays are at a stand, houses of hospitality at a fall; not a feather waving, nor a spur jingling anywhere. I'll away instantly!
QUICKSILVER Y'had best take some crowns in your purse, knight, or else your eastward castle will smoke but miserably.[269]
PETRONEL O Frank! My castle? Alas, all the castles I have are built with air, thou know'st.
QUICKSILVER I know it, knight, and therefore wonder whither your lady is going.
PETRONEL Faith, to seek her fortune, I think. I said I had a castle and land eastward, and eastward she will without contradiction: her coach and the coach of the sun must meet full butt.[270] And the sun being outshined with her ladyship's glory, she fears he goes westward to hang himself.
QUICKSILVER And I fear, when her enchanted castle becomes invisible, her ladyship will return and follow his example.
PETRONEL O, that she would have the grace, for I shall never be able to pacify her when she sees herself deceived so!
QUICKSILVER As easily as can be. Tell her she mistook your directions, and that shortly, yourself will down[271] with her to approve it. And then, clothe but her crupper[272] in a new gown, and you may drive her any way you list,[273] for these women, sir, are like Essex calves: you must wriggle 'em on by the tail still,[274] or they will never drive orderly.
PETRONEL But alas, sweet Frank, thou know'st my ability[275] will not furnish her blood with those costly humors.[276]
QUICKSILVER Cast that cost on me, sir. I have spoken to my old pander, Security, for money or commodity,[277] and commodity, if you will, I know he will procure you.
PETRONEL Commodity! Alas, what commodity?
QUICKSILVER Why, sir, what say you to figs and raisins?

264 144–5 That's all . . . at Winnie: a play on her nickname, suggesting that Security is capable only of whinnying (i.e. impotent)
265 146 Jew's trump: musical instrument (a Jew's harp), and a derogatory term for a usurer
266 148 peterman: fisherman
267 149 vellum: the best parchment, made from calf-skin
268 2 blown up: out of business; ruined
269 6 smoke but miserably: produce smoke; i.e. not have enough money to build a fire in the hearth
270 11 full butt: head-on
271 18 down: go down to the site
272 18 crupper: rump (used in relation to a horse's hindquarters)
273 19 list: wish
274 20 wriggle 'em . . . tail still: mode of directing cattle (with sexual suggestion)
275 21 ability: financial capacity
276 21–2 furnish her . . . costly humors: supply enough to satisfy her expensive longings
277 24 commodity: goods sold on credit by a usurer to a needy person, who then resells them, sometimes to the usurer, at a lower price for cash

PETRONEL A plague of figs and raisins, and all such frail commodities! We shall make nothing of 'em.
QUICKSILVER Why then, sir, what say you to forty pound in roasted beef?
PETRONEL Out upon't, I have less stomach to that than to the figs and raisins. I'll out of town, though I sojourn with a friend of mine, for stay here I must not. My creditors have laid[278] to arrest me, and I have no friend under heaven but my sword to bail me.
QUICKSILVER God's me, knight, put 'em in sufficient sureties[279] rather than let your sword bail you. Let 'em take their choice, either the King's Bench or the Fleet, or which of the two Counters[280] they like best, for by the Lord, I like none of 'em.
PETRONEL Well, Frank, there is no jesting with my earnest necessity. Thou know'st if I make not present money to further my voyage begun, all's lost, and all I have laid out about it.
QUICKSILVER Why then, sir, in earnest: if you can get your wise lady to set her hand to the sale of her inheritance, the bloodhound Security will smell out ready money for you instantly.
PETRONEL There spake an angel! To bring her to which conformity, I must feign myself extremely amorous and, alleging urgent excuses for my stay behind, part with her as passionately as she would from her foisting[281] hound.
QUICKSILVER You have the sow by the right ear,[282] sir. I warrant there was never child longed more to ride a cockhorse,[283] or wear his new coat, than she longs to ride in her new coach. She would long for everything when she was a maid, and now she will run mad for 'em. I lay my life she will have every year four children, and what charge[284] and change of humor you must endure while she is with child, and how she will tie you to your tackling[285] till she be with child, a dog would not endure. Nay, there is no turnspit dog bound to his wheel[286] more servilely than you shall be to her wheel. For as that dog can never climb the top of his wheel but when the top comes under him, so shall you never climb the top of her contentment, but when she is under you.
PETRONEL 'Slight, how thou terrifiest me!
QUICKSILVER Nay, hark you, sir? What nurses, what midwives, what fools, what physicians, what cunning women[287] must be sought for—fearing sometimes she is bewitched, sometimes in a consumption—to tell her tales, to talk bawdy to her, to make her laugh, to give her glisters,[288] to let her blood[289] under the tongue and betwixt the toes! How she will revile and kiss you, spit in your face and lick it off again; how she will vaunt[290] you are her creature, she made you of nothing; how she could have had thousand mark jointures;[291] she could have been made a lady by a Scotch knight, and never ha' married him;[292] she could have had panadas[293] in her bed every morning; how she set you up, and how she will pull you down.[294] You'll never be able to stand of your legs to endure it.
PETRONEL Out of my fortune, what a death is my life bound face-to-face to! The best is, a

278 32 laid: set a watch
279 33 sufficient sureties: full certainty, either through reassurance of payment or because you are in prison
280 34–5 King's Bench . . . two Counters: all four are London prisons, located throughout the city
281 42 foisting: farting
282 43 You have . . . right ear: Quicksilver adapts a proverb ("have the right sow by the ear," i.e. "you have understood correctly") to reassure Petronel about his course of action
283 44 cockhorse: hobbyhorse
284 46 charge: costs
285 47 tie you to your tackling: keep you in harness; i.e. make you work incessantly
286 48 turnspit dog . . . his wheel: dog tied to the roasting spit, running in circles to turn it
287 54 cunning women: women who practice magic
288 55 glisters: enemas
289 56 to let her blood: cut open a vein to extract blood, a common medical treatment
290 57 vaunt: boast
291 58 jointures: marriage settlements
292 59 by a . . . married him: Scots were believed to have a custom of common-law marriage by cohabitation
293 59 panadas: a boiled paste of bread, with sugar, nutmeg, and other flavorings (emended, following editorial tradition, from Q's "poynados," small daggers)
294 60 set you . . . you down: both financial (making him rich through marriage and impoverishing him through spending) and sexual (arousing him and causing his erection to subside)

large, time-fitted conscience is bound to nothing.[295] Marriage is but a form[296] in the school of policy,[297] to which scholars sit fastened only with painted chains.[298] Old Security's young wife is ne'er the further off with[299] me.

QUICKSILVER Thereby lies a tale, sir. The old usurer will be here instantly with my punk Sindefy, whom you know your lady has promised me to entertain for her gentlewoman, and he, with a purpose to feed on you, invites you most solemnly, by me, to supper.

PETRONEL It falls out excellently fitly. I see desire of gain makes jealousy venturous.[300]

Enter GERTRUDE

See, Frank, here comes my lady. Lord, how she views thee! She knows thee not, I think, in this bravery.[301]

GERTRUDE How now? Who be you, I pray?

QUICKSILVER One Master Francis Quicksilver, an't please your ladyship.

GERTRUDE [*Aside*] God's my dignity! As I am a lady, if he did not make me blush so that mine eyes stood a-water. Would I were unmarried again!

Enter SECURITY *and* SINDEFY

Where's my woman, I pray?

QUICKSILVER See, madam, she now comes to attend you.

SECURITY God save my honorable knight and his worshipful lady. [*He removes his hat*]

GERTRUDE Y'are very welcome. [*To* SECURITY] You must not put on your hat yet![302]

SECURITY No, madam; till I know your ladyship's further pleasure, I will not presume.

GERTRUDE And is this a gentleman's daughter new come out of the country?

SECURITY She is, madam, and one that her father hath a special care to bestow in some honorable lady's service, to put her out of her honest humors, forsooth, for she had a great desire to be a nun, an't please you.

GERTRUDE A nun? What nun? A nun substantive? Or a nun adjective?[303]

SECURITY A nun substantive, madam, I hope, if a nun be a noun. But, I mean, lady, a vowed maid of that order.

GERTRUDE I'll teach her to be a maid of the order, I warrant you. [*To* SINDEFY] And can you do any work belongs to a lady's chamber?

SINDEFY What I cannot do, madam, I would be glad to learn.

GERTRUDE Well said! Hold up, then; hold up your head, I say! Come hither, a little. [*Inspects* SINDEFY]

SINDEFY I thank your ladyship.

GERTRUDE And hark you— [*To* SECURITY] good man, you may put on your hat now, I do not look on you— [*To* SINDEFY] I must have you of my faction now, not of my knight's, maid.

SINDEFY No, forsooth, madam; of yours.

GERTRUDE And draw all my servants in my bow,[304] and keep my counsel, and tell me tales, and put me riddles, and read on a book sometimes when I am busy, and laugh at country gentlewomen, and command any thing in the house for my retainers,[305] and care not what you

295 62–3 The best . . . to nothing: thankfully, an unrestrained, adaptable sense of right and wrong is not bound to social conventions

296 63 form: classroom bench

297 64 policy: cunning

298 64 painted chains: imagined or artificial restraint

299 65 ne'er the further off with: not unattainable for me (even though she is married)

300 69 venturous: willing to engage in risk

301 71 this bravery: these fine clothes

302 79 You must . . . hat yet: Security removes his hat as a sign of respect; rather than swiftly concluding the show of hierarchy and status, Gertrude prolongs it

303 85 A nun . . . nun adjective: Gertrude mishears "nun" as "noun" and asks a grammatical question (which of the two kinds of noun?); with sexual innuendo, for "nun" can also mean "prostitute"

304 96 in my bow: according to my inclination or will (proverbial)

305 98 retainers: servants (Gertrude imagines her aristocratic household)

spend, for it is all mine; and in any case, be still a maid whatsoever you do, or whatsoever any man can do unto you.

SECURITY I warrant your ladyship for that.

GERTRUDE Very well, you shall ride in my coach with me into the country tomorrow morning. [*To* PETRONEL] Come knight, pray thee, let's make a short supper and to bed presently.

SECURITY Nay, good madam, this night I have a short supper at home waits[306] on his worship's acceptation.

GERTRUDE By my faith, but he shall not go, sir. I shall swoon and he sup from[307] me!

PETRONEL Pray thee, forbear; shall he lose his provision?[308]

GERTRUDE Ay, by Lady, sir, rather than I lose my longing. Come in, I say; as I am a lady, you shall not go.

QUICKSILVER [*Aside*] I told him what a burr he had gotten.

SECURITY If you will not sup from your knight, madam, let me entreat your ladyship to sup at my house with him.

GERTRUDE No, by my faith, sir; then we cannot be abed soon enough after supper.

PETRONEL [*Aside*] What a medicine[309] is this!—Well, Master Security, you are new married as well as I; I hope you are bound as well.[310] We must honor our young wives, you know.

QUICKSILVER [*Aside to* SECURITY] In policy,[311] dad, till tomorrow she has sealed.

SECURITY I hope in the morning, yet, your knighthood will breakfast with me?

PETRONEL As early as you will, sir.

SECURITY Thank your good worship; I do hunger and thirst to do you good, sir.

GERTRUDE Come, sweet knight, come; I do hunger and thirst to be abed with thee.

Exeunt

Act III, scene i

Enter PETRONEL, QUICKSILVER, SECURITY, BRAMBLE, *and* WINIFRED

PETRONEL Thanks for our feast-like breakfast, good Master Security. I am sorry, by reason of my instant[312] haste to so long a voyage as Virginia, I am without means by any kind amends to show how affectionately I take your kindness, and to confirm, by some worthy ceremony, a perpetual league[313] of friendship betwixt us.

SECURITY Excellent knight, let this be a token betwixt us of inviolable friendship. I am new married to this fair gentlewoman, you know, and, by my hope to make her fruitful, though I be something in years, I vow faithfully unto you to make you godfather (though in your absence) to the first child I am blessed withal. And henceforth call me gossip;[314] I beseech you, if you please to accept it.

PETRONEL In the highest degree of gratitude, my most worthy gossip! For confirmation of which friendly title, let me entreat my fair gossip, your wife here, to accept this diamond, and keep it as my gift to her first child, wheresoever my fortune, in event of my voyage, shall bestow me. [PETRONEL *gives* WINIFRED *the jewel*]

SECURITY [*To* WINIFRED] How now, my coy wedlock?[315] Make you strange of so noble a favor? Take it, I charge you, with all affection, and, by way of taking your leave, present boldly your lips to our honorable gossip.

QUICKSILVER [*Aside*] How venturous he is to him, and how jealous to others!

306 104 waits: that waits
307 106 and he sup from: if eats supper away from
308 107 lose his provision: have provided supper for nothing
309 114 medicine: disagreeable but necessary thing to submit oneself to
310 115 bound as well: joined as happily; bound for bed
311 116 In policy: be shrewdly diplomatic; keep up the trick
312 2 instant: urgent
313 4 perpetual league: eternal covenant
314 8 gossip: godparent
315 14 coy wedlock: shy wife

PETRONEL [*Kisses* WINIFRED] Long may this kind touch of our lips print in our hearts all the forms of affection! And now, my good gossip, if the writings be ready to which my wife should seal, let them be brought this morning before she takes coach into the country, and my kindness shall work her to dispatch it.

SECURITY The writings are ready, sir. My learned counsel here, Master Bramble the lawyer, hath perused them, and within this hour I will bring the scrivener,[316] with them, to your worshipful lady.

PETRONEL Good Master Bramble, I will here take my leave of you then. God send you fortunate pleas, sir, and contentious clients!

BRAMBLE And you foreright[317] winds, sir, and a fortunate voyage. *Exit*

Enter a MESSENGER

MESSENGER Sir Petronel, here are three or four gentlemen desire to speak with you.

PETRONEL What are they?

QUICKSILVER They are your followers in this voyage, knight: Captain Seagull and his associates. I met them this morning and told them you would be here.

PETRONEL Let them enter, I pray you. I know they long to be gone, for their stay is dangerous.

Enter SEAGULL, SCAPETHRIFT, *and* SPENDALL

SEAGULL God save my honorable colonel!

PETRONEL Welcome, good Captain Seagull and worthy gentlemen. If you will meet my friend Frank here, and me, at the Blue Anchor Tavern by Billingsgate this evening, we will there drink to our happy voyage, be merry, and take boat to our ship with all expedition.[318]

SEAGULL[319] Defer it no longer, I beseech you, sir. But as your voyage is hitherto carried closely[320] and in another knight's name, so, for your own safety and ours, let it be continued, our meeting and speedy purpose of departing known to as few as is possible, lest your ship and goods be attached.[321]

QUICKSILVER Well advised, captain; our colonel shall have money this morning to dispatch all our departures. Bring those gentlemen at night to the place appointed, and with our skins full of vintage,[322] we'll take occasion by the vantage and away.

SEAGULL We will not fail but be there, sir.

PETRONEL Good morrow, good captain and my worthy associates! [*To* WINIFRED] Health and all sovereignty to my beautiful gossip! For you, sir [*To* SECURITY], we shall see you presently with the writings.

SECURITY With writings and crowns[323] to my honorable gossip. I do hunger and thirst to do you good, sir!

Exeunt

Act III, scene ii

Enter a COACHMAN *in haste, in his frock, feeding*[324]

316 23 scrivener: notary
317 27 foreright: favorable, straight on the course
318 36 expedition: haste
319 37 SP SEAGULL: Q contains the ghost speech prefix "Spoyl" (presumably for a character named "Spoil-all"), changed here to "Seagull" because the captain speaks for all
320 37–8 carried closely: undertaken secretly
321 40 attached: seized by the authorities, presumably because Petronel is in debt (see also IV.ii. 166–7, when Touchstone suggests that Quicksilver has stolen five hundred pounds from his business in order to finance the Virginia venture)
322 42–3: skins full of vintage: bodies full of wine, with a pun on the wineskins that hold wine
323 48 crowns: coins worth five shillings each
324 0 SD *feeding*: eating

COACHMAN Here's a stir when citizens ride out of town, indeed, as if all the house were afire! 'Slight, they will not give a man leave to eat 's breakfast afore he rises.

Enter HAMLET, *a footman, in haste*

HAMLET What, coachman! My lady's coach! For shame! Her ladyship's ready to come down. [*Exit* COACHMAN]

Enter POTKIN, *a tankard-bearer*

POTKIN 'Sfoot Hamlet, are you mad? Whither run you now? You should brush up my old mistress.[325] [*Exit* HAMLET]

Enter SINDEFY

SINDEFY What, Potkin! You must put off your tankard, and put on your blue coat, and wait upon Mistress Touchstone into the country. *Exit*

POTKIN I will, forsooth, presently! *Exit*

Enter MISTRESS FOND *and* MISTRESS GAZER

FOND Come, sweet Mistress Gazer, let's watch here, and see my Lady Flash take coach.

GAZER O' my word, here's a most fine place to stand in. Did you see the new ship launched last day,[326] Mistress Fond?

FOND O God, and we citizens should lose[327] such a sight?

GAZER I warrant[328] here will be double as many people to see her take coach as there were to see it take water.

FOND O, she's married to a most fine castle i'th'country, they say.

GAZER But there are no giants in the castle, are there?

FOND O no, they say her knight killed 'em all, and therefore he was knighted.

GAZER Would to God her ladyship would come away![329]

Enter GERTRUDE, MISTRESS TOUCHSTONE, SINDEFY, HAMLET, [*and*] POTKIN

FOND She comes, she comes, she comes!

GAZER AND FOND Pray heaven bless your ladyship!

GERTRUDE Thank you, good people. My coach, for the love of heaven, my coach! In good truth, I shall swoon[330] else.

HAMLET Coach, coach, my lady's coach! *Exit*

GERTRUDE As I am a lady, I think I am with child already, I long for a coach so! May one be with child afore they are married, mother?

MISTRESS TOUCHSTONE Ay, by'r lady, madam, a little thing does that. I have seen a little prick no bigger than a pin's head[331] swell bigger and bigger, till it has come to an ancome,[332] and e'en so 'tis in these cases.[333]

Enter HAMLET

325 4–5 brush up my old mistress: brush off, or freshen, Mistress Touchstone's clothing
326 11 last day: yesterday
327 12 lose: miss
328 13 warrant: am certain
329 18 come away: leave (so they can see her in the coach)
330 22 swoon: faint
331 27 prick no . . . pin's head: small cut, with an obvious pun on "prick" as "penis"
332 27 ancome: a boil or ulcerous swelling
333 28 cases: instances, but also slang for the vagina, continuing the sexually suggestive wordplay

HAMLET Your coach is coming, madam.
GERTRUDE That's well said. Now, heaven! Methinks I am e'en up to the knees in preferment.[334]
[*Sings*]
But a little higher, but a little higher, but a little higher,
There, there, there lies Cupid's fire.[335]
MISTRESS TOUCHSTONE But must this young man, an't please you, madam, run by your coach all the way afoot?
GERTRUDE Ay, by my faith, I warrant him; he gives no other milk, as I have another servant does.[336]
MISTRESS TOUCHSTONE Alas! 'Tis e'en pity, methinks. For God's sake, madam, buy him but a hobby-horse; let the poor youth have something betwixt his legs to ease 'em. Alas, we must do as we would be done to.
GERTRUDE Go to! Hold your peace, dame; you talk like an old fool, I tell you.

Enter PETRONEL *and* QUICKSILVER

PETRONEL Wilt thou be gone, sweet honeysuckle, before I can go with thee?
GERTRUDE I pray thee, sweet knight, let me. I do so long to dress up[337] thy castle afore thou com'st. But I marvel how my modest sister occupies herself this morning, that she cannot wait on me to my coach as well as her mother!
QUICKSILVER Marry, madam, she's married by this time to prentice Golding. Your father, and some one more, stole to church with 'em in all the haste, that the cold meat left at your wedding might serve to furnish their nuptial table.[338]
GERTRUDE There's no base fellow, my father, now, but he's e'en fit to father such a daughter. He must call me daughter no more now, but "madam," and "please you, madam," and "please your worship, madam," indeed. Out upon him! Marry his daughter to a base prentice?
MISTRESS TOUCHSTONE What should one do? Is there no law for one that marries a woman's daughter against her will? How shall we punish him, madam?
GERTRUDE As I am a lady an't[339] would snow, we'd so pebble 'em with snowballs[340] as they come from church. But sirrah, Frank Quicksilver?
QUICKSILVER Ay, madam.
GERTRUDE Dost remember since thou and I clapped what d' ye' call-its[341] in the garret?
QUICKSILVER I know not what you mean, madam.
GERTRUDE
[*Sings*]
His head as white as milk,
All flaxen was his hair:
But now he is dead,
And laid in his bed,
And never will come again.[342]
God be at your labor.
PETRONEL [*Aside*] Was there ever such a lady?

Enter TOUCHSTONE, GOLDING, [*and*] MILDRED *with rosemary*

334 31 preferment: advancement, since she has a coach
335 32–3 *But a . . . Cupid's fire*: refrain from a song in Thomas Campion's *A Book of Airs* (1601)
336 36–7 he gives . . . servant does: he serves no other function, as I have another servant for other duties (with sexual suggestion, echoed in Mistress Touchstone's comment on the hobby-horse and "ease" that follow); to have a footman is a sign of prestige
337 43 dress up: prepare
338 47–48 cold meat . . . nuptial table: see II.i. 114–15
339 54 an't: if it
340 54 pebble 'em with snowballs: pelt them with snowballs like pebbles
341 57 what d' ye' call-its: perhaps referring to a game, but suggesting a past sexual encounter, since this phrase commonly sets up jokes about genitals
342 59–63 *His head . . . come again*: parodying and conflating Ophelia's song in *Hamlet* IV.v

QUICKSILVER See, madam, the bride and bridegroom.
GERTRUDE God's my precious! God give you joy, Mistress What-lack-you! Now out upon thee, baggage! My sister married in a taffeta hat? Marry, hang you! Westward with a wanion[343] t'ye! Nay, I have done wi'ye, minion;[344] then, i'faith, never look to have my countenance any more, nor anything I can do for thee! Thou ride in my coach? Or come down to my castle? Fie upon thee! I charge thee, in my ladyship's name: call me sister no more!
TOUCHSTONE An't please your worship, this is not your sister. This is my daughter, and she calls me father, and so does not your ladyship, an't please your worship, madam.
MISTRESS TOUCHSTONE No, nor she must not call thee father by heraldry,[345] because thou mak'st thy prentice thy son as well as she. [*To* GOLDING] Ah, thou misproud[346] prentice, dar'st thou presume to marry a lady's sister?
GOLDING It pleased my master, forsooth, to embolden me with his favor. And though I confess myself far unworthy so worthy a wife (being in part her servant, as I am your prentice), yet, since I may say it without boasting, I am born a gentleman, and by the trade I have learned of my master, which I trust taints not my blood, able with mine own industry and portion[347] to maintain your daughter, my hope is heaven will so bless our humble beginning that in the end I shall be no disgrace to the grace with which my master hath bound me his double prentice.
TOUCHSTONE "Master" me[348] no more, son, if thou think'st me worthy to be thy father.
GERTRUDE Sun?[349] Now, good Lord, how he shines and you mark him! He's a gentleman?
GOLDING Ay, indeed, madam, a gentleman born.
PETRONEL Never stand o' your gentry, master bridegroom: if your legs be no better than your arms,[350] you'll be able to stand upon neither shortly.
TOUCHSTONE An't please your good worship, sir, there are two sorts of gentlemen.
PETRONEL What mean you, sir?
TOUCHSTONE Bold to put off my hat[351] to your worship [TOUCHSTONE *removes his hat*]—
PETRONEL Nay, pray forbear, sir, and then forth with your two sorts of gentlemen.
TOUCHSTONE If your worship will have it so. I say there are two sorts of gentlemen: there is a gentleman artificial, and a gentleman natural.[352] Now, though your worship be a gentleman natural—*work upon that now.*
QUICKSILVER Well said, old Touchstone! I am proud to hear thee enter a set speech, i'faith. Forth, I beseech thee.
TOUCHSTONE Cry you mercy,[353] sir, your worship's a gentleman I do not know. If you be one of my acquaintance, y'are very much disguised, sir.
QUICKSILVER Go to, old quipper! Forth with thy speech, I say.
TOUCHSTONE What, sir, my speeches were ever in vain to your gracious worship, and therefore, till I speak to you gallantry indeed, I will save my breath for my broth anon. Come, my poor son and daughter. Let us hide ourselves in our poor humility and live safe. Ambition consumes itself with the very show. *Work upon that now.* [*Exeunt* TOUCHSTONE, GOLDING, *and* MILDRED]
GERTRUDE Let him go, let him go, for God's sake! Let him make his prentice his son, for God's sake; give away his daughter, for God's sake! And when they come a-begging to us, for God's sake, let's laugh at their good husbandry,[354] for God's sake! Farewell, sweet knight; pray

343 68 wanion: plague; vengeance
344 69 minion: originally meaning a favorite, here "hussy"
345 74 by heraldry: according to rank
346 75 misproud: arrogant
347 80 industry and portion: hard work and share of profit
348 83 "Master" me: call me master
349 84 Sun: Gertrude's pun on Touchstone's "son" emphasizes Golding's ascendancy
350 87 arms: coat of arms, a sign of status
351 90 put off my hat: raising or removing a hat was a sign of respect to nobility (Touchstone is following exactly, and even exaggerating, the protocols of deference to his son-in-law)
352 93 natural: by birth; foolish
353 97 Cry you mercy: I beg your pardon
354 106 husbandry: household management; frugality and thrift

thee make haste after.
PETRONEL What shall I say? I would not have thee go.
QUICKSILVER [*Sings*] *Now, O now, I must depart, parting though it absence move*[355]—This ditty, knight, do I see in thy looks in capital letters:
[*Sings*] *What a grief 'tis to depart,*
And leave the flower that has my heart!
My sweet lady, and alack, for woe,
Why should we part so?
Tell truth, knight, and shame all dissembling lovers: does not your pain lie on that side?
PETRONEL If it do, canst thou tell me how I may cure it?
QUICKSILVER Excellent easily: divide your self in two halves, just by the girdlestead.[356] Send one half with your lady, and keep the tother[357] yourself. Or else do as all true lovers do: part with your heart and leave your body behind, I have seen't done a hundred times. 'Tis as easy a matter for a lover to part without a heart from his sweetheart, and he ne'er the worse, as for a mouse to get from a trap and leave her tail behind her. See, here comes the writings.[358]

Enter SECURITY *with a* SCRIVENER

SECURITY Good morrow to my worshipful lady. I present your ladyship with this writing, to which, if you please to set your hand[359] with your knight's, a velvet gown shall attend your journey o'my credit.
GETRUDE What writing is it, knight?
PETRONEL The sale, sweetheart, of the poor tenement[360] I told thee of, only to make a little money to send thee down furniture for my castle, to which my hand shall lead thee.
GERTRUDE Very well. Now give me your pen, I pray. [*She signs*]
QUICKSILVER [*Aside*] It goes down without chewing,[361] i'faith.
SCRIVENER Your worships deliver this as your deed?
GERTRUDE AND PETRONEL We do.
GERTRUDE So now, knight, farewell till I see thee!
PETRONEL All farewell to my sweetheart!
MISTRESS TOUCHSTONE God b'w'ye,[362] son knight.
PETRONEL Farewell, my good mother.
GERTRUDE Farewell, Frank; I would fain take thee down[363] if I could.
QUICKSILVER I thank your good ladyship. Farewell, Mistress Sindefy.
Exeunt [GERTRUDE, MISTRESS TOUCHSTONE, SINDEFY, HAMLET, *and* POTKIN]
PETRONEL O tedious voyage, whereof there is no end! What will they think of me?
QUICKSILVER Think what they list! They longed for a vagary[364] into the country, and now they are fitted.[365] So a woman marry to ride in a coach, she cares not if she ride to her ruin. 'Tis the great end[366] of many of their marriages. This is not the first time a lady has rid a false journey in her coach, I hope.
PETRONEL Nay, 'tis no matter; I care little what they think. He that weighs men's thoughts has his hands full of nothing. A man in the course of this world should be like a surgeon's

355 109 *Now, O . . . absence move*: from John Dowland's *The First Book of Songs or Airs* (1597)
356 117 girdlestead: waist
357 118 tother: other
358 121 writings: mortgage bond for Gertrude's land
359 123 hand: signature
360 126 poor tenement: insignificant property
361 129 without chewing: she swallows the story whole
362 134 God b'w'ye: God be with you
363 136 down: with me to the castle, with sexual suggestion
364 139 vagary: excursion
365 140 fitted: satisfied; appropriately punished
366 141 end: aim

instrument: work in the wounds of others, and feel nothing himself. The sharper and subtler, the better.

QUICKSILVER As it falls out[367] now, knight, you shall not need to devise excuses, or endure her outcries when she returns; we shall now be gone before, where they cannot reach us.

PETRONEL [*To* SECURITY] Well, my kind compeer,[368] you have now th' assurance we both can make you. Let me now entreat you the money we agreed on may be brought to the Blue Anchor, near to Billingsgate, by six o'clock, where I and my chief friends, bound for this voyage, will with feasts attend you.

SECURITY The money, my most honorable compeer, shall without fail observe your appointed hour.

PETRONEL Thanks, my dear gossip. I must now impart
To your approvèd love a loving secret,
As one on whom my life doth more rely
In friendly trust, than any man alive.
Nor shall you be the chosen secretary[369]
Of my affections for affection only;
For I protest, if God bless my return,
To make you partner in my action's gain
As deeply as if you had ventured with me
Half my expenses. Know then, honest gossip:
I have enjoyed, with such divine contentment,
A gentlewoman's bed, whom you well know,
That I shall ne'er enjoy this tedious voyage,
Nor live the least part of the time it asketh,
Without her presence: so I[370] "thirst and hunger"
To taste the dear feast of her company!
And if the "hunger" and the "thirst" you vow
(As my sworn gossip) to my wishèd good
Be—as I know it is—unfeigned and firm,
Do me an easy favor in your power.

SECURITY Be sure, brave gossip, all that I can do,
To my best nerve,[371] is wholly at your service.
Who is the woman, first, that is your friend?

PETRONEL The woman is your learnèd counsel's wife:
The lawyer, Master Bramble, whom would you
Bring out this even,[372] in honest neighborhood,[373]
To take his leave, with you, of me, your gossip,
I, in the meantime, will send this my friend
Home to his house, to bring his wife disguised
Before his face, into our company.
For love hath made her look for such a wile,[374]
To free her from his tyrannous jealousy,
And I would take this course before another
In stealing her away, to make us sport,
And gull his circumspection the more grossly.[375]
And I am sure that no man like yourself

367 147 falls out: happens
368 149 compeer: partner
369 159 secretary: confidant
370 169 so I: so much do I
371 176 best nerve: greatest power
372 180 even: evening
373 180 neighborhood: friendly neighborliness
374 185 wile: cunning trick
375 189 gull his . . . more grossly: outwit his vigilance more fully, i.e. cheat him right under his nose

Hath credit with him[376] to entice his jealousy
To so long stay abroad, as may give time
To her enlargement[377] in such safe disguise.
SECURITY A pretty, pithy, and most pleasant project!
Who would not strain a point[378] of neighborhood,
For such a point-device[379] that, as the ship
Of famous Draco[380] went about the world,
Will wind about the lawyer, compassing
The world himself. He hath it[381] in his arms,
And that's enough, for him, without his wife.
A lawyer is ambitious, and his head
Cannot be praised nor raised too high,
With any fork[382] of highest knavery.
I'll go fetch him straight. *Exit*
PETRONEL So, so. Now Frank, go thou home to his house,
'Stead of his lawyer's, and bring his wife hither,
Who, just like to the lawyer's wife, is prisoned
With his stern, usurous jealousy, which could never
Be overreached thus, but with overreaching.[383]

Enter SECURITY

SECURITY And Master Francis, watch you th'instant time
To enter with his exit.[384] 'Twill be rare:
Two fine horned[385] beasts, a camel and a lawyer! *[Exit]*
QUICKSILVER How the old villain joys in villainy!

Enter SECURITY

SECURITY And hark you, gossip, when you have her here,
Have your boat ready; ship her to your ship
With utmost haste, lest Master Bramble stay[386] you.
To o'erreach that head that outreacheth all heads?
'Tis a trick rampant,[387] 'tis a very quiblin![388]
I hope this harvest to pitch cart with lawyers,
Their heads will be so forkèd.[389] "This sly touch
Will get apes[390] to invent a number such." *Exit*
QUICKSILVER Was ever rascal honeyed[391] so with poison?
"He that delights in slavish avarice
Is apt to joy in every sort of vice."

376 191 Hath credit with him: is sufficiently trusted by him
377 193 enlargement: release from confinement
378 195 strain a point: exceed the bounds
379 196 point-device: perfect plot
380 197 Draco: Sir Francis Drake, known for his circumnavigation of the globe
381 199 it: i.e. the world
382 203 fork: horn, of a cuckold and of a devil (i.e. the ambition characteristic of lawyers justifies the trickery)
383 209 overreached thus, but with overreaching: outwitted, except through cheating
384 211 enter with his exit: attend to the timing, and enter the house just as Bramble leaves
385 212 horned: camels were imagined to have horns; the lawyer has the horns of a cuckold
386 216 stay: detain (and outwit)
387 218 rampant: vigorous, lusty
388 218 quiblin: excellent trick
389 219–20 this harvest . . . so forkèd: the long horns on the foreheads of cuckolded lawyers will serve instead of pitchforks to fill carts when we harvest
390 221 Will get apes: will prompt imitators
391 222 rascal honeyed: scoundrel flattered

Well, I'll go fetch his wife, whilst he the lawyer.
PETRONEL But stay, Frank, let's think how we may disguise her upon this sudden.[392]
QUICKSILVER God's me, there's the mischief! But hark you, here's an excellent device[393]—'fore God, a rare one! I will carry her a sailor's gown and cap, and cover her, and a player's beard.
PETRONEL And what upon her head?
QUICKSILVER I tell you, a sailor's cap! 'Slight, God forgive me, what kind of figent[394] memory have you?
PETRONEL Nay then, what kind of figent wit hast thou?
A sailor's cap? How shall she put it off[395]
When thou present'st her to our company?
QUICKSILVER Tush[396] man, for that, make her a saucy[397] sailor.
PETRONEL Tush, tush, 'tis no fit sauce for such sweet mutton.[398] I know not what t'advise.

Enter SECURITY, *with his wife's gown*

SECURITY Knight, knight, a rare device!
PETRONEL [*Aside*] Zounds, yet again.
QUICKSILVER What stratagem have you now?
SECURITY The best that ever. You talked of disguising?
PETRONEL Ay, marry gossip, that's our present care.
SECURITY Cast care away, then; here's the best device
For plain Security (for I am no better),
I think, that ever lived. Here's my wife's gown,
Which you may put upon the lawyer's wife,
And which I brought you, sir, for two great reasons:
One is, that Master Bramble may take hold
Of some suspicion that it is my wife,
And gird me[399] so, perhaps, with his law wit.
The other (which is policy[400] indeed)
Is, that my wife may now be tied at home,
Having no more but her old gown abroad,
And not show me a quirk, while I firk others.[401]
Is not this rare?[402]
QUICKSILVER AND PETRONEL The best that ever was.
SECURITY Am I not born to furnish[403] gentlemen?
PETRONEL O my dear gossip!
SECURITY Well, hold Master Francis, watch when the lawyer's out, and put it in.
And now—I will go fetch him. [*Begins to*] *Exit* [*and pauses*]
QUICKSILVER [*Aside*] O my dad! He goes as 'twere the devil to fetch the lawyer; and devil shall he be, if horns will make him.
PETRONEL Why, how now gossip, why stay you there musing?
SECURITY A toy,[404] a toy runs in my head, i'faith.

392 226 upon this sudden: on the spur of the moment
393 227 device: trick, strategem
394 231 figent: restless (here, forgetful)
395 234 put it off: take off the hat (to greet the sailors)
396 236 Tush: come now, an exclamation of impatience
397 236 saucy: insolent (i.e. one who doesn't doff his hat when introduced); wanton
398 237 sweet mutton: tender meat, picking up on "sauce"; "mutton" is slang for prostitute
399 250 gird me: jest at me
400 251 policy: advantage
401 254 Not give me a turn (i.e. cuckold me), while I cheat others
402 255 rare: excellent
403 257 furnish: provide or pander for
404 264 toy: idle fancy

QUICKSILVER [*Aside*] A pox of that head! Is there more toys yet?
PETRONEL What is it, pray thee, gossip?
SECURITY Why, sir? What if you should slip away now with my wife's best gown, I having no security[405] for it?
QUICKSILVER For that, I hope, dad, you will take our words.
SECURITY Ay, by th'mass, your word: that's a proper staff
For wise Security to lean upon!
But 'tis no matter. Once I'll trust my name
On your cracked credits;[406] let it take no shame.[407]
Fetch the wench, Frank. *Exit*
QUICKSILVER [*Aside*] I'll wait upon you, sir.
And fetch you over; you were ne'er so fetched.
[*To* PETRONEL] Go to the tavern, knight; your followers
Dare not be drunk, I think, before their captain. *Exit*
PETRONEL Would I might lead them to no hotter[408] service,
Till our Virginian gold were in our purses.
Exit

[Act III, scene iii]

Enter SEAGULL, SPENDALL, *and* SCAPETHRIFT, *in the tavern with a* DRAWER

SEAGULL Come, drawer, pierce your neatest hogsheads,[409] and let's have cheer, not fit for your Billingsgate tavern but for our Virginian colonel![410] He will be here instantly.
DRAWER You shall have all things fit, sir. Please you have any more wine?
SPENDALL More wine, slave?[411] Whether we drink it or no, spill it, and draw more!
SCAPETHRIFT Fill all the pots in your house with all sorts of liquor, and let 'em wait on us here like soldiers in their pewter coats.[412] And though we do not employ them now; yet we will maintain 'em till we do.
DRAWER Said like an honorable captain! You shall have all you can command, sir. *Exit* DRAWER
SEAGULL Come boys, Virginia longs till we share the rest of her maidenhead.[413]
SPENDALL Why, is she inhabited already with any English?
SEAGULL A whole country of English is there, man, bred of those that were left there in '79.[414] They have married with the Indians, and make 'em bring forth as beautiful faces as any we have in England, and therefore the Indians are so in love with 'em that all the treasure they have, they lay at their feet.
SCAPETHRIFT But is there such treasure there, captain, as I have heard?
SEAGULL I tell thee, gold is more plentiful there than copper is with us, and for as much red copper as I can bring, I'll have thrice the weight in gold. Why man, all their dripping pans and their chamber pots are pure gold; and all the chains, with which they chain up their streets, are massy[415] gold; all the prisoners they take are fettered in gold. And for rubies and diamonds, they go forth on holidays and gather 'em by the seashore, to hang on their children's coats,

405 267–8 slip away . . . no security: you might steal the gown if you have given me no collateral
406 273 cracked credits: utterly ruined reputations
407 273 let it take no shame: live up to the credit which I extend to you
408 279 hotter: uncomfortable or dangerous; Petronel echoes Quicksilver's injunction, as "hot" is also slang for drunk or tipsy
409 1 pierce your neatest hogsheads: open your finest barrels of wine
410 2 Virginian colonel: i.e. Petronel, leading the expedition to Virginia
411 4 slave: rascal
412 6 like soldiers . . . pewter coats: i.e. the pewter mugs will be arranged in rows, like soldiers in armor
413 9 maidenhead: here a pun on "Virginia" as a virgin woman and an untouched land
414 11 '79: Seagull either fabricates or misremembers: there was no English settlement in 1579 (the "Lost Colony" of the English in Virginia was in 1587)
415 19 massy: immense, massive

and stick in their caps, as commonly as our children wear saffron-gilt[416] brooches and groats[417] with holes in 'em.[418]

SCAPETHRIFT And is it a pleasant country withal?

SEAGULL As ever the sun shined on; temperate and full of all sorts of excellent viands.[419] Wild boar is as common there as our tamest bacon is here; venison, as mutton. And then you shall live freely there, without sergeants, or courtiers, or lawyers, or intelligencers[420]—only a few industrious Scots, perhaps, who, indeed, are dispersed over the face of the whole earth. But as for them, there are no greater friends to Englishmen and England, when they are out on't,[421] in the world, than they are. And for my part, I would a hundred thousand of 'em were there, for we are all one countrymen now, ye know, and we should find ten times more comfort of them there than we do here.[422] Then for your means to advancement there, it is simple and not preposterously mixed. You may be an alderman[423] there, and never be scavenger;[424] you may be a nobleman,[425] and never be a slave. You may come to preferment[426] enough, and never be a pander; to riches and fortune enough, and have never the more villainy, nor the less wit. Besides, there we shall have no more law than conscience, and not too much of either: serve God enough, eat and drink enough, and "enough is as good as a feast."[427]

SPENDALL God's me! And how far is it thither?

SEAGULL Some six weeks' sail, no more, with any indifferent good wind. And if I get to any part of the coast of Africa, I'll sail thither with any wind. Or when I come to Cape Finisterre,[428] there's a foreright wind continually wafts us till we come at Virginia. See, our colonel's come.

Enter SIR PETRONEL[429]

PETRONEL Well met, good Captain Seagull, and my noble gentlemen! Now the sweet hour of our freedom is at hand. Come, drawer, fill us some carouses[430] and prepare us for the mirth that will be occasioned presently. Here will be a pretty wench, gentlemen, that will bear us company all our voyage.

SEAGULL Whatsoever she be, here's to her health, noble colonel, both with cap and knee. [*He removes his hat and kneels to drink a toast*]

PETRONEL Thanks, kind Captain Seagull. She's one I love dearly, and must not be known till we be free from all that know us. And so, gentlemen, here's to her health.

SPENDALL AND SCAPETHRIFT Let it come, worthy colonel: we do hunger and thirst for it.

PETRONEL Afore heaven, you have hit the phrase of one that her presence will touch,[431] from the foot to the forehead,[432] if ye knew it.

SPENDALL Why then, we will join his forehead with her health, sir; and Captain Scapethrift, here's to 'em both! [*They kneel and drink a toast*]

416 21 saffron-gilt: imitation gold
417 21 groats: silver coins
418 16–22 I tell … in 'em: borrows heavily from Hakluyt's *Principal Navigations* on the value of copper, and Book 2 of Sir Thomas More's *Utopia* in the description of common goods made of gold and jewels
419 24 viands: foods
420 26 intelligencers: spies; informers
421 28 out on't: out of England
422 26–31 only a … do here: this passage about the Scots, as discussed in the Introduction, was excised in the first print run for its offense
423 32 alderman: senior civic official, chosen from the leaders of the guilds
424 32 scavenger: street sweeper
425 33 a nobleman: in the second issue of the Quarto, this phrase is replaced by "any other officer"
426 33 preferment: advancement, promotion
427 34–6 Besides, there … a feast: these lines were inserted in the second issue of the Quarto when the lines above about the Scots (26–31) were removed
428 39 Cape Finisterre: a peninsula on the west coast of Spain
429 41 SD the second issue of the Quarto adds the phrase "*with his Followers*" to Sir Petronel's entrance direction perhaps to fill space; editors typically delete because no new characters speak or are introduced in the scene
430 43 carouses: full cups of liquor (to be drunk for toasts)
431 50 touch: hurt
432 51 from the … the forehead: fully (with an allusion to the cuckold's horns)

Enter SECURITY *and* BRAMBLE

SECURITY See, see, Master Bramble, 'fore heaven their voyage cannot but prosper! They are o'their knees for success to it.
BRAMBLE And they pray to god Bacchus.[433]
SECURITY God save my brave colonel, with all his tall captains and corporals! See, sir, my worshipful learned counsel, Master Bramble, is come to take his leave of you.
PETRONEL Worshipful Master Bramble, how far do you draw us into the sweet briar of your kindness? Come, Captain Seagull, another health to this rare Bramble, that hath never a prick[434] about him.
SEAGULL I pledge his most smooth disposition, sir. Come, Master Security, bend your supporters[435] and pledge this notorious[436] health here.
SECURITY Bend you yours likewise, Master Bramble, for it is you shall pledge me.
SEAGULL Not so, Master Security; he must not pledge his own health.
SECURITY No, Master Captain?

Enter QUICKSILVER *with* WINIFRED *disguised*

Why then, here's one is fitly come to do him that honor.
QUICKSILVER Here's the gentlewoman your cousin, sir, whom with much entreaty I have brought to take her leave of you in a tavern; ashamed whereof, you must pardon her if she put not off her mask.[437]
PETRONEL Pardon me, sweet cousin: my kind desire to see you before I went made me so importunate to entreat your presence here.
SECURITY How now, Master Francis? Have you honored this presence with a fair gentlewoman?
QUICKSILVER Pray, sir, take you no notice of her, for she will not be known to you.
SECURITY But my learned counsel, Master Bramble here, I hope may know her?
QUICKSILVER No more than you, sir, at this time; his learning must pardon her.
SECURITY Well, God pardon her for my part, and I do, I'll be sworn. And so, Master Francis, here's to all that are going eastward tonight, towards Cuckold's Haven;[438] and so to the health of Master Bramble.
QUICKSILVER I pledge it, sir [*He kneels*]. Hath it gone round, captains?
SEAGULL It has, sweet Frank, and the round closes with thee.
QUICKSILVER Well sir, here's to all eastward and toward cuckolds,[439] and so to famous Cuckold's Haven so fatally[440] remembered. QUICKSILVER [*drinks and*] *rises*
PETRONEL [*To* WINIFRED, *who weeps*] Nay, pray thee coz, weep not.—Gossip Security?
SECURITY Ay, my brave gossip?
PETRONEL A word, I beseech you, sir. [*Aside to* SECURITY] Our friend, Mistress Bramble here, is so dissolved in tears that she drowns the whole mirth of our meeting. Sweet gossip, take her aside and comfort her.
SECURITY [*Aside to* WINIFRED] Pity of all true love, Mistress Bramble. What, weep you to enjoy your love? What's the cause, lady? Is't because your husband is so near and your heart earns[441] to have a little abused him? Alas, alas, the offence is too common to be respected. So great a grace hath seldom chanced to so unthankful a woman: to be rid of an old

433 56 god Bacchus: the god associated with wine and revelry
434 60–1 hath never a prick: has no thorns; a pun on Bramble's name that is meant to suggest he is impotent
435 62–3 bend your supporters: kneel down
436 63 notorious: notable
437 70 her mask: Winifred's disguise, which must include a covering that hides her face from her husband
438 79 Cuckold's Haven: a point on the Thames about a mile from London Bridge, known for a pole erected with a pair of horns at the top
439 83 eastward and toward cuckolds: all those going eastward, toward Cuckold's Haven; imminent cuckolds (such as Security)
440 84 fatally: ominously
441 92 earns: grieves

jealous dotard,[442] to enjoy the arms of a loving young knight, that, when your prickless Bramble is withered with grief of your loss, will make you flourish afresh in the bed of a lady.

Enter DRAWER

DRAWER Sir Petronel, here's one of your watermen come to tell you it will be flood these three hours; and that 'twill be dangerous going against the tide, for the sky is overcast; and there was a porpoise[443] even now seen at London Bridge, which is always the messenger of tempests, he says.

PETRONEL A porpoise? What's that to th' purpose? Charge him, if he love his life, to attend us. Can we not reach Blackwall (where my ship lies) against the tide, and in spite of tempests? Captains and gentlemen, we'll begin a new ceremony at the beginning of our voyage, which I believe will be followed of all future adventurers.

SEAGULL What's that, good colonel?

PETRONEL This, Captain Seagull: we'll have our provided supper brought aboard Sir Francis Drake's ship that hath compassed the world,[444] where with full cups and banquets we will do sacrifice[445] for a prosperous voyage. My mind gives me[446] that some good spirits of the waters should haunt the desert ribs of her,[447] and be auspicious to all that honor her memory, and will with like orgies[448] enter their voyages.

SEAGULL Rarely conceited! One health more to this motion, and aboard to perform it. He that will not this night be drunk, may he never be sober!

They compass in[449] WINIFRED, *dance the drunken round, and drink carouses*

BRAMBLE Sir Petronel and his honorable captains, in these young services we old servitors[450] may be spared. We only came to take our leaves, and with one health to you all, I'll be bold to do so. Here, neighbor Security: to the health of Sir Petronel, and all his captains! [*Drinks a toast*]

SECURITY You must bend then, Master Bramble [*They kneel*]; so, now I am for you [*Drinks a toast*]. I have one corner of my brain, I hope, fit to bear one carouse more. Here, lady, to you that are encompassed there, and are ashamed of our company. [*Drinks a toast to* WINIFRED] Ha, ha, ha! By my troth, my learned counsel Master Bramble, my mind runs so of Cuckold's Haven tonight, that my head runs over[451] with admiration.

BRAMBLE [*Aside to* SECURITY] But is not that your wife, neighbor?

SECURITY [*Aside to* BRAMBLE] No, by my troth, Master Bramble. Ha, ha, ha! A pox of all cuckold's havens, I say.

BRAMBLE [*Aside to* SECURITY] O'my faith, her garments are exceeding like your wife's.

SECURITY [*Aside to* BRAMBLE] *Cucullus non facit monachum*,[452] my learned counsel; all are not cuckolds that seem so, nor all seem not that are so. Give me your hand, my learned counsel; you and I will sup somewhere else than at Sir Francis Drake's ship tonight. [*To* PETRONEL] Adieu, my noble gossip.

BRAMBLE Good fortune, brave captains; fair skies God send ye!

ALL Farewell, my hearts, farewell!

PETRONEL Gossip, laugh no more at Cuckhold's Haven, gossip!

SECURITY I have done, I have done, sir. Will you lead, Master Bramble? Ha, ha, ha!

[*Exeunt* SECURITY *and* BRAMBLE]

442 94 dotard: person who has become senile with age

443 98 porpoise: understood as a warning or omen of a storm when one appears in the Thames, a rarity

444 105–6 Sir Francis … the world: Drake's ship, the *Golden Hind*, which made a voyage around the globe from 1577–80, was docked in London on the Thames at Deptford, upon its return, where it remained a venue for tourism

445 106–7 do sacrifice: eat and drink as at a ritual feast

446 107 My mind gives me: I have the idea

447 108 desert ribs of her: i.e. the empty ship

448 109 like orgies: similar ceremonial celebrations

449 111 SD *compass in*: surround

450 112 servitors: servants, here continuing the sense of military service

451 119 runs over: overflows

452 124 *Cucullus non facit monachum*: the cowl does not make the monk (proverbial Latin phrase)

PETRONEL Captain Seagull, charge[453] a boat.

ALL A boat, a boat, a boat! *Exeunt* [DRAWER *remains*]

DRAWER Y'are in a proper taking,[454] indeed, to take a boat, especially at this time of night and against tide and tempest. They say yet, "drunken men never take harm." This night will try the truth of that proverb.

Exit

[Act III, scene iv]

Enter SECURITY

SECURITY What, Winnie! Wife, I say! Out of doors at this time? Where should I seek the gadfly?[455] Billingsgate, Billingsgate, Billingsgate! She's gone with the knight, she's gone with the knight; woe be to thee, Billingsgate! A boat, a boat, a boat; a full hundred marks for a boat![456]

Exit

Act IV, scene i

Enter SLITGUT, *with a pair of ox horns, discovering Cuckold's Haven above*[457] [*in a storm*]

SLITGUT All hail, fair haven of married men only, for there are none but married men cuckolds! For my part, I presume not to arrive here but in my master's behalf, a poor butcher of Eastcheap,[458] who sends me to set up, in honor of Saint Luke,[459] these necessary ensigns of his homage. And up I got this morning, thus early, to get up to the top of this famous tree that is all fruit and no leaves,[460] to advance this crest of my master's occupation. Up then! Heaven and Saint Luke bless me, that I be not blown into the Thames as I climb, with this furious tempest. 'Slight, I think the devil be abroad in likeness of a storm, to rob me of my horns. Hark, how he roars. Lord! What a coil[461] the Thames keeps! She bears some unjust burden, I believe, that she kicks and curvets thus to cast it.[462] Heaven bless all honest passengers that are upon her back now, for the bit is out of her mouth, I see, and she will run away with 'em. So, so [*He attaches and adjusts the horns*], I think I have made it look the right way; it runs against London Bridge, as it were, even full butt. And now let me discover, from this lofty prospect, what pranks the rude Thames plays in her desperate lunacy.[463] O me, here's a boat has been cast away hard by. Alas, alas, see one of her passengers, laboring for his life to land at this haven here; pray heaven he may recover it. His next land[464] is even just under me [*Calling to the man*]: hold out yet a little, whatsoever thou art, pray, and take a good heart to thee! [*To the audience*] 'Tis a man: [*To the man*] take a man's heart to thee. Yet a little further; get up o' thy legs, man; now 'tis shallow enough. So, so, so! [*To the audience*] Alas, he's down again. [*To the man*] Hold thy wind, father! [*To the audience*] 'Tis a man in a nightcap. So! Now he's got up again; now he's past the worst; yet, thanks be to heaven, he comes toward me pretty and strongly!

453 132 charge: order

454 134 proper taking: excellent condition (ironic)

455 2 gadfly: wandering woman

456 3 A boat . . . a boat: Security's cry parodies Shakespeare's *Richard III*, "A horse, a horse; my kingdom for a horse!" (V.iv. 7)

457 0 SD *discovering Cuckold's Haven above*: Slitgut could be above the stage, as if at the top of the pole at Cuckold's Haven—a bankside point overlooking the Thames river—with a pair of ox horns to fasten to the pole; he may also climb one of the stage's balcony posts

458 3 Eastcheap: market known especially for butchers, who maintained the horns on the pole at Cuckold's Haven

459 3 Saint Luke: biblical figure whose symbol was an ox

460 4–5 this famous . . . no leaves: the pole was known as a "tree"; "fruit" suggests both the sexual act of cuckolding and illegitimate offspring

461 8 coil: disturbance, as a noisy fuss

462 8–9 she kicks . . . cast it: the image is of the river as a horse kicking and leaping ("curvets") against a bridle (the "bit" of the next line), trying to unseat ("cast") a rider

463 13 lunacy: fit of folly

464 15 next land: closest shore

Enter SECURITY *without his hat, in a nightcap, wet band,*[465] *etc.*

SECURITY Heaven, I beseech thee, how have I offended thee! Where am I cast ashore now, that I may go a righter way home by land? Let me see. O, I am scarce able to look about me! Where is there any sea-mark[466] that I am acquainted withal?

SLITGUT Look up, father: are you acquainted with this mark?[467]

SECURITY What! Landed at Cuckold's Haven? Hell and damnation! I will run back and drown myself. *He falls down*

SLITGUT Poor man, how weak he is! The water has washed away his strength.

SECURITY Landed at Cuckold's Haven? If it had not been to die twenty times alive, I should never have scaped death.[468] I will never arise more; I will grovel[469] here, and eat dirt till I be choked; I will make the gentle earth do that which the cruel water has denied me.

SLITGUT Alas, good father, be not so desperate. Rise, man: if you will, I'll come presently and lead you home.

SECURITY Home? Shall I make any know my home that has known me thus abroad? How low shall I crouch away, that no eye may see me? I will creep on the earth while I live, and never look heaven in the face more. *Exit creep[ing]*

SLITGUT What young planet reigns now, trow,[470] that old men are so foolish? What desperate young swaggerer would have been abroad such a weather as this, upon the water? Ay me, see another remnant of this unfortunate shipwreck, or some other. A woman! I'faith, a woman. Though it be almost at Saint Katherine's,[471] I discern it to be a woman, for all her body is above the water and her clothes swim about her most handsomely. O they bear her up most bravely! Has not a woman reason to love the taking up of her clothes the better while she lives, for this? Alas, how busy the rude Thames is about her! A pox o'that wave! It will drown her, i'faith; 'twill drown her! Cry God mercy, she has scaped it! I thank heaven she has scaped it. O, how she swims like a mermaid. Some vigilant body look out and save her! That's well said: just where the priest fell in,[472] there's one sets down a ladder, and goes to take her up. God's blessing o'thy heart, boy; now take her up in thy arms and to bed with her. She's up, she's up! She's a beautiful woman, I warrant her; the billows durst not[473] devour her.

Enter the DRAWER *in*[474] *the tavern before, with* WINIFRED

DRAWER How fare you now, lady?

WINIFRED Much better, my good friend, than I wish, as one desperate of her fame[475] now my life is preserved.

DRAWER Comfort yourself; that power that preserved you from death can likewise defend you from infamy, howsoever you deserve it. Were not you one that took boat late this night, with a knight and other gentlemen, at Billingsgate?

WINIFRED Unhappy that I am, I was.

DRAWER I am glad it was my good hap[476] to come down thus far after you, to a house of my friend's here in Saint Katherine's, since I am now happily made a mean to your rescue from the ruthless tempest, which, when you took boat, was so extreme, and the gentleman that brought you forth so desperate and unsober, that I feared long ere this I should hear of your shipwreck;

465 20 SD *band*: the neck-band or collar of his nightshirt
466 23 sea-mark: landmark for guidance in navigation
467 24 this mark: the post and horns at Cuckold's Haven
468 28–9 If it . . . scaped death: i.e. I have lived only to die multiple times from the shame of being a cuckold
469 29 grovel: lie prone on the ground in humiliation
470 36 trow: do you suppose
471 39 Saint Katherine's: a dockside district in east London known for its hospital
472 44–5 just where . . . fell in: allusion to this event appears in several texts of the period, but further details are unknown
473 47 billows durst not: waves dare not
474 47 SD *in*: from
475 49 desperate of her fame: having lost hope of her reputation
476 55 hap: luck

and therefore, with little other reason, made thus far this way. And this I must tell you, since perhaps you may make use of it: there was left behind you at our tavern, brought by a porter (hired by the young gentleman that brought you) a gentlewoman's gown, hat, stockings, and shoes, which, if they be yours, and you please to shift you,[477] taking a hard bed here in this house of my friend, I will presently go fetch you.

WINIFRED Thanks, my good friend, for your more than good news. The gown with all things bound with it are mine; which, if you please to fetch as you have promised, I will boldly receive the kind favor you have offered till your return, entreating you—by all the good you have done in preserving me hitherto—to let none take knowledge of what favor you do me, or where such a one as I am bestowed, lest you incur me much more damage in my fame than you have done me pleasure in preserving my life.

DRAWER Come in, lady, and shift yourself. Resolve that nothing but your own pleasure shall be used[478] in your discovery.

WINIFRED Thank you, good friend. The time may come I shall requite you. *Exeunt* [WINIFRED *and* DRAWER]

SLITGUT See, see, see! I hold my life, there's some other a-taking up at Wapping[479] now! Look, what a sort of people cluster about the gallows there! In good troth, it is so. O me! A fine young gentleman! What, and taken up at the gallows? Heaven grant he be not one day taken down[480] there. O' my life,[481] it is ominous. Well, he is delivered for the time. I see the people have all left him. Yet will I keep my prospect awhile, to see if any more have been shipwrecked.

Enter QUICKSILVER *bareheaded*

QUICKSILVER Accursed that ever I was saved or born!
How fatal is my sad arrival here!
As if the stars and Providence spake to me,
And said, "the drift[482] of all unlawful courses
(Whatever end they dare propose themselves,
In frame of their licentious policies[483])
In the firm order of just destiny,
They are the ready highways to our ruins."
I know not what to do; my wicked hopes
Are, with this tempest, torn up by the roots.
O, which way shall I bend my desperate steps,
In which unsufferable shame and misery
Will not attend them? I will walk this bank,
And see if I can meet the other relics[484]
Of our poor shipwrecked crew, or hear of them.
The knight, alas, was so far gone with wine,
And th'other three, that I refused their boat,
And took the hapless woman in another,
Who cannot but be sunk, whatever Fortune
Hath wrought upon the others' desperate lives. [*Exit*]

Enter PETRONEL *and* SEAGULL *bareheaded*

PETRONEL Zounds, captain, I tell thee, we are cast up o'the coast of France. 'Sfoot, I am not

477 62 shift you: change your clothes
478 70–71 pleasure shall be used: wishes shall be followed
479 73 a-taking up at Wapping: coming ashore at Wapping (on the north bank of the Thames; the place of execution for pirates)
480 75 taken down: i.e. taken down from the gallows after being hanged
481 76 O' my life: on my life
482 81 drift: current; natural progress
483 83: To justify immoral practices
484 91 relics: remnants; survivors

drunk still, I hope! Dost remember where we were last night?

SEAGULL No, by my troth, knight, not I; but methinks we have been a horrible while upon the water, and in the water.

PETRONEL Ay me, we are undone for ever! Hast any money about thee?

SEAGULL Not a penny, by heaven.

PETRONEL Not a penny betwixt us, and cast ashore in France?

SEAGULL Faith, I cannot tell that; my brains, nor mine eyes, are not mine own yet.

Enter two GENTLEMEN

PETRONEL 'Sfoot, wilt not believe me? I know't by th' elevation of the pole,[485] and by the altitude and latitude of the climate. See, here comes a couple of French gentlemen; I knew we were in France. Dost thou think our Englishmen are so Frenchified that a man knows not whether he be in France or in England, when he sees 'em? What shall we do? We must e'en to 'em, and entreat some relief[486] of 'em. Life is sweet, and we have no other means to relieve our lives now but their charities.

SEAGULL Pray you, do you beg on 'em, then; you can speak French.

PETRONEL *Monsieur, plaist-il d'avoir pitie de nostre grande infortunes? Je suis un poure chevalier d'Angleterre qui a souffri l'infortune de naufrage.*[487]

GENTLEMAN 1 *Un poure chevalier d'Angleterre?*[488]

PETRONEL *Oui, monsieur, il est trop vraye; mais vous sauves bien, nous sommes toutes subject à fortune.*[489]

GENTLEMAN 2 A poor knight of England? A poor knight of Windsor,[490] are you not? Why speak you this broken French when y'are a whole Englishman? On what coast are you, think you?

PETRONEL On the coast of France, sir.

GENTLEMAN 1 On the coast of Dogs, sir. Y'are i' th' Isle o' Dogs,[491] I tell you. I see y'ave been washed in the Thames here, and I believe ye were drowned in a tavern before, or else you would never have took boat in such a dawning as this was. Farewell, farewell, we will not know you for shaming of you. [*To* GENTLEMAN 2] I ken the man weel; he's one of my thirty pound knights.[492]

GENTLEMAN 2 No, no, this is he that stole his knighthood o'the grand day[493] for four pound, giving to a page all the money in's purse, I wot[494] well. *Exeunt* [GENTLEMEN]

SEAGULL Death, colonel, I knew you were overshot.[495]

PETRONEL Sure, I think now, indeed, Captain Seagull, we were something overshot.

Enter QUICKSILVER

What! My sweet Frank Quicksilver! Dost thou survive to rejoice me? But what, nobody at thy heels, Frank? Ay me, what is become of poor Mistress Security?

QUICKSILVER Faith, gone quite from her name, as she is from her fame, I think. I left her to the mercy of the water.

SEAGULL Let her go, let her go. Let us go to our ship at Blackwall and shift us.[496]

485 106 elevation of the pole: the pole-star for navigation; he fails to see the pole at Cuckold's Haven, which would orient him
486 110 entreat some relief: beg some aid
487 113–14 *Monsieur, plaist-il . . . de naufrage:* "Sir, will you please to have pity on our great misfortune? I am a poor knight of England who has suffered the misfortune of a shipwreck"; Petronel's French is notably bad; the misspellings reflect his grammatical errors
488 115 *Un poure chevalier d'Angleterre*: A poor knight of England
489 116–17 *Oui, monsieur . . . à fortune*: Yes, sir, it is too true; but you know well that we are all subject to fortune
490 118 knight of Windsor: shorthand for a pauper
491 122 Isle o' Dogs: the Isle of Dogs, a peninsula on the Thames river, known for its swampy land and for being a refuge for debtors
492 125–6 I ken . . . pound knights: suggesting a Scottish accent, and a contemptuous reference to King James's practice of selling knighthoods
493 127 grand day: the coronation of King James I in 1603
494 128 wot: know
495 129 overshot: mistaken; out of your depth (in trying to guess their location); drunk
496 135 shift us: change our clothes

PETRONEL Nay, by my troth, let our clothes rot upon us, and let us rot in them. Twenty to one our ship is attached by this time! If we set her not under sail this last tide, I never looked for any other. Woe, woe is me; what shall become of us? The last money we could make the greedy Thames has devoured, and if our ship be attached, there is no hope can relieve us.

QUICKSILVER 'Sfoot, knight, what an unknightly faintness transports thee? Let our ship sink, and all the world that's without us[497] be taken from us, I hope I have some tricks, in this brain of mine, shall not let us perish.

SEAGULL Well said, Frank, i'faith! O my nimble-spirited Quicksilver, 'fore God, would thou hadst been our colonel.

PETRONEL I like his spirit rarely, but I see no means he has to support that spirit.

QUICKSILVER Go to, knight, I have more means than thou art aware of. I have not lived amongst goldsmiths and goldmakers all this while but I have learned something worthy of my time with 'em. And, not to let thee stink where thou stand'st,[498] knight, I'll let thee know some of my skill presently.

SEAGULL Do, good Frank, I beseech thee.

QUICKSILVER I will blanch copper so cunningly that it shall endure all proofs but the test: it shall endure malleation; it shall have the ponderosity of Luna, and the tenacity of Luna, by no means friable.[499]

PETRONEL 'Slight, where learn'st thou these terms, trow?

QUICKSILVER Tush, knight, the terms of this art every ignorant quacksalver[500] is perfect in. But I'll tell you how yourself shall blanch copper thus cunningly. Take arsenic, otherwise called realga (which indeed is plain ratsbane[501]), sublime[502] him[503] three or four times, then take the sublimate of this realga, and put him into a glass, into chymia,[504] and let him have a convenient decoction natural, four and twenty hours, and he will become perfectly fixed. Then take this fixed powder, and project him upon well-purged copper, *et habebis magisterium*.[505]

PETRONEL AND SEAGULL Excellent Frank, let us hug thee!

QUICKSILVER Nay, this I will do besides: I'll take you off twelvepence from every angel, with a kind of *aqua fortis*, and never deface any part of the image.[506]

PETRONEL But then it will want weight.[507]

QUICKSILVER You shall restore that thus: take your *sal alchyme*[508] prepared, and your distilled urine, and let your angels lie in it but four and twenty hours, and they shall have their perfect weight again. Come on, now; I hope this is enough to put some spirit into the livers[509] of you; I'll infuse more another time. We have saluted the proud air long enough with our bare sconces. Now will I have you to a wench's house of mine at London, there make shift to shift us, and after, take such fortunes as the stars shall assign us.

PETRONEL AND SEAGULL Notable Frank, we will ever adore thee!

Exeunt [QUICKSILVER, PETRONEL, *and* SEAGULL]

Enter DRAWER *with* WINIFRED, *new attired*

497 141 the world that's without us: everything of value that is external to us (i.e. our possessions)
498 148 stink where thou standest: proverbial; so you do not soil yourself with fear or anxiety
499 151–3 I will . . . means friable: I will whiten copper to the color of silver so well that the counterfeit will be undetectable except for testing in the furnace; it will have the weight and strength of silver, and will not be easily ground to dust
500 155 quacksalver: person faking medical knowledge, and a kind of pun on his name (to claim his knowledge of alchemy is real, Quicksilver offers further specious examples of alchemical jargon in the following lines)
501 157 ratsbane: rat poison
502 157 sublime: convert a substance from solid to vapor by heating
503 157 him: it
504 158 chymia: a laboratory glass
505 160 *et habebis magisterium*: and you will have the philosopher's stone
506 162–3 I'll take . . . the image: I'll strip a tenth of the value from a gold coin, using an acid solution, without marring the image stamped on the coin (profiting from the extracted gold and the counterfeit coin)
507 164 want weight: i.e. be devalued
508 165 *sal alchyme*: dry salt
509 167 livers: the organ regarded as the site of cowardice; Quicksilver hopes his speech has inspired courage

WINIFRED Now, sweet friend, you have brought me near enough your tavern,[510] which I desired I might with some color[511] be seen near, inquiring for my husband—who, I must tell you, stale[512] thither last night with my wet gown we have left at your friend's (which, to continue your former honest kindness, let me pray you to keep close from the knowledge of any). And so, with all vow of your requital, let me now entreat you to leave me to my woman's wit, and fortune.

DRAWER All shall be done you desire; and so, all the fortune you can wish for attend you! *Exit*

Enter SECURITY

SECURITY I will once more to this unhappy tavern before I shift one rag of me more, that I may there know what is left behind, and what news of their passengers. I have bought me a hat and band with the little money I had about me, and made the streets a little leave staring[513] at my nightcap.

WINIFRED O, my dear husband! Where have you been tonight? All night abroad at taverns? Rob me of my garments? And fare as one run away from me? Alas! Is this seemly[514] for a man of your credit?[515] Of your age? And affection to your wife?

SECURITY What should I say? How miraculously sorts this?[516] Was not I at home, and called thee last night?

WINIFRED Yes, sir, the harmless sleep you broke; and my answer to you would have witnessed it, if you had had the patience to have stayed and answered me. But your so sudden retreat made me imagine you were gone to Master Bramble's, and so[517] rested patient and hopeful of your coming again, till this your unbelieved[518] absence brought me abroad, with no less than wonder, to seek you where the false knight had carried you.

SECURITY Villain and monster that I was, how have I abused thee! I was suddenly gone indeed, for my sudden jealousy transferred[519] me. I will say no more but this: dear wife, I suspected thee.

WINIFRED Did you suspect me?

SECURITY Talk not of it, I beseech thee. I am ashamed to imagine it. I will home, I will home, and every morning, on my knees, ask thee heartily forgiveness. *Exeunt* [WINIFRED *and* SECURITY]

SLITGUT Now will I descend my honorable prospect, the farthest seeing sea-mark of the world [*He climbs down*]; no marvel, then, if I could see two miles about me.[520] I hope the red tempest's anger be now overblown, which sure I think heaven sent as a punishment for profaning holy Saint Luke's memory with so ridiculous a custom.[521] Thou dishonest satire,[522] farewell to honest married men; farewell, to all sorts and degrees of thee! Farewell, thou horn of hunger, that call'st th' Inns o' Court to their manger.[523] Farewell, thou horn of abundance,[524] that adornest the headsmen[525] of the commonwealth. Farewell, thou horn of direction, that is the city lanthorn.[526]

510 172 near enough your tavern: Winifred and the Drawer are back in Billingsgate
511 173 color: pretense
512 173 stale: stole
513 180 made the . . . leave staring: made passersby stare at me less
514 183 seemly: appropriate
515 184 credit: reputation
516 185 sorts this: does this turn out
517 189 so: so I
518 190 unbelieved: incredible
519 193 transferred: transported
520 199 no marvel . . . about me: the height of the pole has allowed him to survey characters in locations along the Thames (Cuckold's Haven, St. Katherine's, Wapping, Isle of Dogs, and Billingsgate)
521 201 ridiculous a custom: i.e. the ritual of putting horns on the pole
522 201 dishonest satire: i.e. the ox-horns, which comment on the lack of chastity in marriage; the series of horns that follow pun on the horns of the cuckold
523 202–3 horn of . . . their manger: the call to dinner for law students
524 203 horn of abundance: cornucopia
525 204 headsmen: a) distinguished citizens; b) cuckolds who have horns on their foreheads
526 204 city lanthorn: lantern hung in the streets to light the way

Farewell, thou horn of pleasure,[527] the ensign of the huntsman. Farewell, thou horn of destiny,[528] th' ensign of the married man. Farewell, thou horn tree, that bearest nothing but stonefruit.[529]

Exit

[Act IV, scene ii]

Enter TOUCHSTONE

TOUCHSTONE Ha, sirrah! Thinks my knight adventurer we can[530] no point of our compass? Do we not know north-north-east? North-east-and-by-east? East-and-by-north? Nor plain east-ward? Ha! Have we never heard of Virginia? Nor the *Cavallaria*? Nor the *Colonaria*?[531] Can we discover no discoveries? Well, mine errant Sir Flash, and my runagate[532] Quicksilver, you may drink drunk, crack cans, hurl away a brown dozen of Monmouth caps[533] or so in sea-ceremony to your *bon voyage*, but for reaching any coast save the coast of Kent or Essex[534] with this tide, or with this fleet, I'll be your warrant for a Gravesend[535] toast. There's that gone afore[536] will stay your admiral and vice-admiral and rear-admiral, were they all (as they are) but one pinnace,[537] and under sail, as well as a remora,[538] doubt it not; and from this sconce,[539] without either powder or shot. *Work upon that now.* Nay, and you'll shew tricks, we'll vie with you a little. My daughter, his lady, was sent eastward by land to a castle of his i' the air (in what region I know not), and, as I hear, was glad to take up her lodging in her coach, she and her two waiting women, her maid and her mother, like three snails in a shell and the coachman atop on 'em, I think. Since, they have all found the way back again by Weeping Cross,[540] but I'll not see 'em. And for two on 'em, madam and her malkin,[541] they are like to bite o' the bridle for William,[542] as the poor horses have done all this while that hurried 'em, or else go graze o' the common.[543] So should my Dame Touchstone too, but she has been my cross[544] these thirty years and I'll now keep her, to fright away sprites, i' faith. I wonder I hear no news of my son Golding! He was sent for to the Guildhall[545] this morning betimes, and I marvel at the matter. If I had not laid up comfort and hope in him, I should grow desperate of all. See, he is come i' my thought!

Enter GOLDING

How now, son? What news at the Court of Aldermen?[546]

GOLDING Troth, sir, an accident somewhat strange, else it hath little in it worth the reporting.

TOUCHSTONE What? It is not borrowing of money, then?

527 205 horn of pleasure: hunting horn
528 205 horn of destiny: cuckold's horns
529 206 horn tree ... but stonefruit: the pole at Cuckold's Haven, with a pun on "stone" as testicles
530 1 can: know
531 3 *Cavallaria*? Nor the *Colonaria*: Latin terms related to the feudal practice of tenants furnishing soldiers for war and cultivating the land (Touchstone mocks Petronel's Virginia plan)
532 4 runagate: runaway; vagrant
533 5 brown dozen of Monmouth caps: full dozen of sailors' caps
534 6 Kent or Essex: counties to the southeast and northeast, respectively, of London; i.e. they will not get very far
535 7 Gravesend: a port further east on the Thames; with a pun on "graves"
536 7 that gone afore: Touchstone hints he has intervened to intercept the ship
537 8 your admiral ... one pinnace: admiral ships, and their variations here, are ships that carry the commanding officers in a fleet; a pinnace is a small ship with two masts
538 9 remora: a sucking fish that attaches to a ship's hull, thought to slow its movement
539 9 this sconce: my brain (i.e. this plan would stay the knight's voyage, even if they were in flagships and not a small ship, as they are)
540 14 by Weeping Cross: with sorrowful repentance (proverbial)
541 15 malkin: female servant, with derogatory connotation of low status and sexual activity
542 15 to bite ... for William: go hungry for all I care (proverbial)
543 16 graze o' the common: as the horses graze on common land; they will have to live on charity
544 17 cross: burden to bear
545 19 Guildhall: the hall of the Corporation of the City of London, where the aldermen assemble for civic business
546 21 Court of Aldermen: the ruling civic body

GOLDING No sir, it hath pleased the worshipful commoners of the city to take me one i'their number at presentation of the inquest[547]—

TOUCHSTONE Ha!

GOLDING And the alderman of the ward[548] wherein I dwell, to appoint me his deputy—

TOUCHSTONE How!

GOLDING In which place, I have had an oath ministered me[549] since I went.

TOUCHSTONE Now, my dear and happy son! Let me kiss thy new worship,[550] and a little boast mine own happiness in thee. What a fortune was it—or rather, my judgment, indeed—for me first to see that in his disposition which a whole city so conspires to second?[551] Ta'en into the livery of his company the first day of his freedom![552] Now, not a week married, chosen commoner and alderman's deputy in a day! Note but the reward of a thrifty course. The wonder of his time! Well, I will honor Master Alderman for this act, as becomes me, and shall think the better of the Common Council's wisdom and worship, while I live, for thus meeting, or but coming after me, in the opinion of his desert.[553] Forward, my sufficient[554] son, and as this is the first, so esteem it the least[555] step to that high and prime honor that expects[556] thee.

GOLDING Sir, as I was not ambitious of this, so I covet no higher place; it hath dignity enough if it will but save me from contempt. And I had rather my bearing, in this or any other office, should add worth to it, than the place give the least opinion to me.

TOUCHSTONE Excellently spoken! This modest answer of thine blushes, as if it said, "I will wear scarlet[557] shortly." Worshipful son! I cannot contain myself; I must tell thee, I hope to see thee one o'the monuments of our city,[558] and reckoned among her worthies to be remembered the same day with the Lady Ramsey[559] and grave Gresham,[560] when the famous fable of Whittington and his puss[561] shall be forgotten, and thou and thy acts become the posies[562] for hospitals; when thy name shall be written upon conduits, and thy deeds played i'thy lifetime by the best companies of actors, and be called their get-penny.[563] This I divine. This I prophesy.

GOLDING Sir, engage not your expectation farther than my abilities will answer. I, that know mine own strengths, fear 'em; and there is so seldom a loss in promising the least, that commonly it brings with it a welcome deceit.[564] I have other news for you, sir.

TOUCHSTONE None more welcome, I am sure?

GOLDING They have their degree of welcome, I dare affirm. The colonel and all his company, this morning putting forth drunk from Billingsgate, had like to have been cast away o'this side Greenwich, and (as I have intelligence by a false brother[565]) are come dropping to town, like so many masterless men,[566] i'their doublets and hose, without hat, or cloak, or any other—

TOUCHSTONE A miracle! The justice of heaven! Where are they? Let's go presently and lay for[567] 'em.

547 24–5 it hath . . . the inquest: Golding has been elected to the Common Council
548 27 alderman of the ward: chief officer of the city district
549 29 had an oath ministered me: taken the oath confirming my appointment
550 30 worship: person or position of distinction
551 32 second: confirm my opinion
552 33 Ta'en into . . . his freedom: appointed to a senior position in the guild on the first day he is no longer an apprentice
553 36–7 for thus . . . his desert: for agreeing with me, or at least following me, in valuing his worth
554 37 sufficient: capable
555 38 esteem it the least: think of it as the most insignificant
556 38 expects: awaits
557 43 scarlet: the prescribed color of an Alderman's robes
558 44 monuments of our city: distinguished or eminent citizens
559 45 Lady Ramsey: Lady Mary Ramsey, with her husband, Sir Thomas Ramsey, was known as a sixteenth-century philanthropist
560 45 grave Gresham: Sir Thomas Gresham was a sixteenth-century merchant and financier, known for building London's Royal Exchange
561 45–6 Whittington and his puss: the rags-to-riches story of Richard Whittington, who rose from poverty to become Lord Mayor of London, with the help of a skilled rat-catching cat
562 46 posies: memorial engravings
563 48 get-penny: reliable hit, moneymaker
564 50–51 promising the . . . welcome deceit: setting expectations deliberately low and far exceeding them
565 55 false brother: informant
566 56 masterless men: unemployed men who are vagrants
567 58 lay for: set a trap for

GOLDING I have done that already, sir, both by constables and other officers, who shall take 'em at their old Anchor, and with less tumult or suspicion than if yourself were seen in't, under color[568] of a great press[569] that is now abroad, and they shall here be brought afore me.
TOUCHSTONE Prudent and politic son! Disgrace 'em all that ever thou canst; their ship I have already arrested. How to my wish it falls out, that thou hast the place of a justicer upon 'em! I am partly glad of the injury done to me, that thou may'st punish it. Be severe i'thy place, like a new officer o'the first quarter,[570] unreflected.[571] You hear how our lady is come back with her train from the invisible castle?
GOLDING No, where is she?
TOUCHSTONE Within, but I ha' not seen her yet, nor her mother, who now begins to wish her daughter undubbed,[572] they say, and that she had walked a foot-pace with[573] her sister. Here they come; stand back.

[*Enter*] MISTRESS TOUCHSTONE, GERTRUDE, MILDRED, [*and*] SINDEFY

God save your ladyship; 'save your good ladyship! Your ladyship is welcome from your enchanted castle; so are your beauteous retinue.[574] I hear your knight errant is traveled on strange adventures. Surely, in my mind, your ladyship "hath fished fair, and caught a frog," as the saying is.
MISTRESS TOUCHSTONE Speak to your father, madam, and kneel down.
GERTRUDE Kneel? I hope I am not brought so low yet. Though my knight be run away, and has sold my land, I am a lady still.
TOUCHSTONE Your ladyship says true, madam; and it is fitter, and a greater decorum, that I should curtsy to you, that are a knight's wife and a lady, than you be brought o' your knees to me, who am a poor cullion[575] and your father.
GERTRUDE Law![576] My father knows his duty.
MISTRESS TOUCHSTONE O child!
TOUCHSTONE And therefore I do desire your ladyship, my good Lady Flash, in all humility, to depart my obscure cottage[577] and return in quest of your bright and most transparent castle, "however presently concealed to mortal eyes."[578] And as for one poor woman of your train[579] here, I will take that order; she shall no longer be a charge unto you, nor help to spend your ladyship. She shall stay at home with me and not go abroad, not put you to the pawning of an odd coach-horse, or three wheels, but take part with the Touchstone. If we lack, we will not complain to your ladyship. And so, good madam, with your damosel[580] here, please you to let us see your straight backs in equipage;[581] for truly, here is no roost for such chickens as you are or birds o'your feather, if it like your ladyship.
GERTRUDE Marry, fist[582] o' your kindness! I thought as much. Come away, Sin, we shall as soon get a fart from a dead man as a farthing[583] of courtesy here.
MILDRED O good sister!
GERTRUDE Sister, sir-reverence? [*To* SINDEFY] Come away, I say. "Hunger drops out at his

568 61 color: pretext
569 61 great press: conscription as soldiers, especially of men found to be unemployed
570 65 o'the first quarter: in the first term (three months) of service
571 65 unreflected: not diverted from punishment; also punning on the first quarter of the moon
572 69 undubbed: i.e. not married to Sir Petronel
573 69 walked a foot-pace with: walked at the same speed as (i.e. made a similar choice in her husband)
574 72 retinue: group of attendants accompanying a noble person
575 80 cullion: literally, testicle; here, as a term of contempt, a base fellow
576 81 Law: an expression of surprise and emphatic confirmation
577 84 obscure cottage: dark and humble house
578 85 "however presently . . . mortal eyes": perhaps another proverbial formulation or quotation
579 85 one poor . . . your train: i.e. Mistress Touchstone
580 89 damosel: maid in waiting (originally associated with rank, but by this time a slight)
581 90 your straight backs in equipage: i.e. you riding away from us in your fancy dress
582 92 fist: fart
583 93 farthing: a coin worth a quarter of a penny

nose."[584]

GOLDING O madam, "fair words never hurt the tongue."

GERTRUDE How say you by that? You come out with your gold ends[585] now!

MISTRESS TOUCHSTONE Stay, lady-daughter! Good husband!

TOUCHSTONE Wife, no man loves his fetters, be they made of gold. I list not[586] ha' my head fastened under my child's girdle; as she has brewed, so let her drink, o' God's name. She went witless[587] to wedding, now she may go wisely a-begging. It's but honeymoon yet with her ladyship; she has coach-horses, apparel, jewels yet left; she needs care for no friends, nor take knowledge of father, mother, brother, sister, or anybody. When those are pawned or spent, perhaps we shall return into the list[588] of her acquaintance.

GERTRUDE I scorn it, i'faith. Come, Sin.

MISTRESS TOUCHSTONE [*Weeping*] O madam, why do you provoke your father thus?

Exeunt GERTRUDE [*with* SINDEFY]

TOUCHSTONE Nay, nay, e'en let pride go afore; shame will follow after, I warrant you. Come, why dost thou weep now? Thou art not the first good cow hast had an ill calf, I trust.

Enter CONSTABLE

What's the news with that fellow?

GOLDING Sir, the knight and your man Quicksilver are without. Will you ha' 'em brought in?

TOUCHSTONE O, by any means. [*Exit* CONSTABLE]

And son, here's a chair [*Offers a chair to* GOLDING]; appear terrible unto 'em on the first interview. Let them behold the melancholy of a magistrate, and taste the fury of a citizen in office.

GOLDING Why sir, I can do nothing to 'em, except you charge 'em with somewhat.[589]

TOUCHSTONE I will charge 'em, and recharge 'em, rather than authority should want foil[590] to set it off.

GOLDING [*Refusing the chair*] No, good sir, I will not.

TOUCHSTONE Son, it is your place; by any means.

GOLDING Believe it, I will not, sir.

Enter KNIGHT PETRONEL, QUICKSILVER, CONSTABLE, [*and*] OFFICERS

PETRONEL How misfortune pursues us still in our misery!

QUICKSILVER Would it had been my fortune to have been trussed up[591] at Wapping, rather than ever ha' come here!

PETRONEL Or mine to have famished in the island!

QUICKSILVER Must Golding sit upon[592] us?

CONSTABLE You might carry an "M" under your girdle[593] to Master Deputy's worship.

GOLDING What are those, Master Constable?

CONSTABLE An't please your worship, a couple of masterless men I pressed for the low countries,[594] sir.

GOLDING Why do you not carry 'em to Bridewell,[595] according to your order, they[596] may be

584 95–6 "Hunger drops ... his nose": a proverb about poverty (here, suggesting miserliness)
585 98 gold ends: i.e. the proverbs, just like Touchstone
586 100 list not: do not wish to
587 102 witless: thoughtlessly
588 105 list: catalogue
589 116 somewhat: something
590 117 foil: the gold backing by which a jewel's luster is enhanced
591 123 trussed up: hanged
592 126 sit upon: pass verdict on
593 127 carry an ... your girdle: i.e. address Golding respectfully, as "Master," given his position (proverbial)
594 129–30 pressed for the low countries: conscripted as soldiers to fight in Holland
595 131 Bridewell: a workhouse
596 131 they: so that they

shipped away?
CONSTABLE An't please your worship, one of 'em says he is a knight, and we thought good to show him to your worship, for our discharge.
GOLDING Which is he?
CONSTABLE This, sir.
GOLDING And what's the other?
CONSTABLE A knight's fellow, sir, an't please you.
GOLDING What, a knight and his fellow thus accoutred?[597] Where are their hats and feathers, their rapiers and their cloaks?
QUICKSILVER [*Aside*] O, they mock us.
CONSTABLE Nay, truly, sir; they had cast[598] both their feathers and hats, too, before we see[599] 'em. Here's all their furniture,[600] an't please you, that we found. They say knights are now to be known without feathers, like cockerels by their spurs,[601] sir.
GOLDING What are their names, say they?
TOUCHSTONE [*Aside*] Very well, this. He should not take knowledge of 'em in his place,[602] indeed.
CONSTABLE This is Sir Petronel Flash.
TOUCHSTONE How!
CONSTABLE And this Francis Quicksilver.
TOUCHSTONE Is't possible? I thought your worship had been gone for Virginia, sir; you are welcome home, sir. Your worship has made a quick return, it seems, and no doubt a good voyage. Nay, pray you be covered,[603] sir. How did your biscuit[604] hold out, sir? Methought I had seen this gentleman afore. Good Master Quicksilver! How a degree to the southward has changed you!
GOLDING Do you know 'em, father? [*To the prisoners*] Forbear your offers[605] a little; you shall be heard anon.
TOUCHSTONE Yes, Master Deputy. I had a small venture with them in the voyage, a thing, called a son-in-law, or so.—Officers, you may let 'em stand alone; they will not run away, I'll give my word for them. A couple of very honest gentlemen. One of 'em was my prentice, Master Quicksilver, here, and when he had two year to serve, kept his whore and his hunting nag, would play his hundred pound at gresco, or primero,[606] as familiarly (and all o' my purse) as any bright piece of crimson[607] on 'em all; had his changeable trunks of apparel standing at livery with his mare, his chest of perfumed linen, and his bathing tubs,[608] which when I told him of, why he—he was a gentleman, and I a poor Cheapside groom.[609] The remedy was, we must part. Since when he hath had the gift of gathering up some small parcels[610] of mine, to the value of five hundred pound, dispersed among my customers, to furnish this his Virginian venture; wherein this knight was the chief, Sir Flash—one that married a daughter of mine, ladyfied her, turned two thousand pounds' worth of good land of hers into cash within the first week, bought her a new gown and a coach, sent her to seek her fortune by land whilst himself

597 139 accoutred: dressed
598 142 cast: cast off
599 142 see: saw
600 143 furniture: clothing and accessories
601 144 spurs: cockerel are young roosters without spurs; the gallants have lost their feathers (with a further dig at Petronel's lack of accoutrement, since spurs were associated with rank, and knights could wear golden spurs)
602 146 place: position
603 153 be covered: put your hat back on (though Petronel has lost his hat in the storm)
604 153 biscuit: dry bread packed by sailors for a voyage
605 156 Forbear your offers: stop trying to speak
606 162 gresco, or primero: card and dice games, with gambling
607 163 bright piece of crimson: well-dressed gallant
608 163–4 changeable trunks . . . bathing tubs: Touchstone catalogues Quicksilver's lavish lifestyle by the objects that suggest leisure and pleasure: multiple changes of clothing, expensive cloth goods, and more than one device for bathing (possibly to treat venereal disease)
609 165 groom: servingman
610 166 parcels: sums of money

prepared for his fortune by sea, took in fresh flesh[611] at Billingsgate for his own diet, to serve him the whole voyage—the wife of a certain usurer called Security, who hath been the broker for 'em in all this business. Please, Master Deputy, *work upon that now*!

GOLDING If my worshipful father have ended—

TOUCHSTONE I have, it shall please Master Deputy.

GOLDING Well then, under correction[612]—

TOUCHSTONE [*Aside to* GOLDING] Now son, come over 'em with some fine gird,[613] as thus, "Knight, you shall be encountered," that is, had to the Counter; or "Quicksilver, I will put you in a crucible,"[614] or so.

GOLDING Sir Petronel Flash, I am sorry to see such flashes[615] as these proceed from a gentleman of your quality and rank. For mine own part, I could wish I could say I could not see them, but such is the misery of magistrates and men in place, that they must not wink at[616] offenders. [*To* OFFICERS] Take him aside. [*To* PETRONEL] I will hear you anon, sir.

TOUCHSTONE [*Aside*] I like this well. Yet there's some grace i'the knight left; he cries.

GOLDING Francis Quicksilver, would God thou hadst turned quacksalver, rather than run into these dissolute and lewd courses. It is great pity. Thou art a proper young man, of an honest and clean face, somewhat near a good one—God hath done his part in thee—but thou hast made too much and been too proud of that face, with the rest of thy body; for maintenance of which in neat and garish attire, only to be looked upon by some light housewives,[617] thou hast prodigally consumed much of thy master's estate, and being by him gently admonished, at several times, hast returned thyself haughty and rebellious in thine answers, thundering out uncivil comparisons, requiting all his kindness with a coarse and harsh behavior, never returning thanks for any one benefit, but receiving all as if they had been debts to thee and no courtesies. I must tell thee, Francis, these are manifest signs of an ill nature, and God doth often punish such pride and *outrecuidance*[618] with scorn and infamy, which is the worst of misfortune.—My worshipful father, what do you please to charge them withal?—From the press I will free 'em, Master Constable.

CONSTABLE Then I'll leave your worship, sir.

GOLDING No, you may stay; there will be other matters against 'em.

TOUCHSTONE Sir, I do charge this gallant, Master Quicksilver, on suspicion of felony; and the knight as being accessary, in the receipt of my goods.

QUICKSILVER O God, sir!

TOUCHSTONE Hold thy peace, impudent varlet, hold thy peace! With what forehead or face dost thou offer to chop logic[619] with me, having run such a race of riot as thou hast done? Does not the sight of this worshipful man's fortune and temper confound thee, that was thy younger fellow in household, and now come to have the place of a judge upon thee? Dost not observe this? Which of all thy gallants and gamesters,[620] thy swearers and thy swaggerers, will come now to moan thy misfortune, or pity thy penury? They'll look out at a window, as thou rid'st in triumph to Tyburn, and cry, "Yonder goes honest Frank, mad Quicksilver." "He was a free boon companion[621] when he had money," says one. "Hang him, fool," says another, "he could not keep it when he had it." "A pox o' the cullion, his master," says a third, "he has brought him to this"—when their pox of pleasure and their piles of perdition would have been better bestowed upon thee, that hast ventured for 'em with the best, and by the clew[622] of thy

611 171 flesh: slang for a prostitute (referring here to Winifred)
612 176 under correction: subject to correction, a formula expressing response to the charge
613 177 gird: sharp blow; jest
614 179 crucible: vessel for melting and testing metal
615 180 flashes: showy failures; with the pun on his name, suggesting superficiality and vanity
616 182 wink at: close their eyes to
617 189 light housewives: hussies
618 195 *outrecuidance*: arrogance (the word is borrowed from French)
619 204 chop logic: argue
620 207 gamesters: gamblers
621 210 free boon companion: generous good fellow
622 213 clew: winding threads

knavery, brought thyself weeping to the cart of calamity.[623]

QUICKSILVER Worshipful master!

TOUCHSTONE Offer not to speak, crocodile;[624] I will not hear a sound come from thee. Thou hast learnt to whine at the play yonder.—Master Deputy, pray you commit 'em both to safe custody, till I be able farther to charge 'em.

QUICKSILVER O me, what an unfortunate thing am I!

PETRONEL Will you not take security,[625] sir?

TOUCHSTONE Yes, marry will I, Sir Flash, if I can find him, and charge him as deep as the best on you. He has been the plotter of all this; he is your enginer,[626] I hear. Master Deputy, you'll dispose of these? In the meantime, I'll to my Lord Mayor, and get his warrant to seize that serpent Security into my hands, and seal up both house and goods to the king's use,[627] or my satisfaction.

GOLDING Officers, take 'em to the Counter.

QUICKSILVER AND PETRONEL O God!

TOUCHSTONE Nay, on, on! You see the issue of your sloth: of sloth cometh pleasure, of pleasure cometh riot,[628] of riot comes whoring, of whoring comes spending, of spending comes want, of want comes theft, of theft comes hanging; and there is my Quicksilver fixed.[629]

Exeunt

Act V, scene i

[*Enter*] GERTRUDE [*and*] SINDEFY

GERTRUDE Ah, Sin! Hast thou ever read i'the chronicle[630] of any lady and her waiting woman driven to that extremity that we are, Sin?

SINDEFY Not I, truly, madam, and if I had, it were but cold comfort should come out of books now.

GERTRUDE Why, good faith, Sin, I could dine with a lamentable story now. [*Sings*] *O hone, hone, o no nera, etc.*[631] Canst thou tell ne'er a one, Sin?

SINDEFY None but mine own, madam, which is lamentable enough. First to be stol'n from my friends, which were worshipful[632] and of good accompt,[633] by a prentice in the habit and disguise of a gentleman, and here brought up to London and promised marriage, and now likely to be forsaken, for he is in possibility to be hanged.

GERTRUDE Nay, weep not, good Sin. My Petronel is in as good possibility as he. Thy miseries are nothing to mine, Sin. I was more than promised marriage, Sin: I had it, Sin, and was made a lady, and by a knight, Sin, which is now as good as no knight, Sin. And I was born in London, which is more than brought up, Sin; and already forsaken, which is past likelihood, Sin. And instead of land i'the country, all my knight's living lies i'the Counter, Sin; there's his castle now!

SINDEFY Which he cannot be forced out of, madam.

GERTRUDE Yes, if he would live hungry a week or two. "Hunger," they say, "breaks stone walls." But he is e'en well enough served, Sin, that so soon as ever he had got my hand to the sale of my inheritance, run away from me, and[634] I had been his punk, God bless us. Would the

623 214 cart of calamity: cart carrying convicted criminals to execution
624 216 crocodile: proverbially said to weep falsely before devouring someone who is deceived by the show of sorrow
625 220 take security: Petronel asks if Touchstone will take bail, but Touchstone, in a deliberate misunderstanding, refers to the character Security in the answer that follows
626 222 enginer: person who designed the scheme
627 224 to the king's use: goods to be seized by the state
628 229 riot: the pursuit of an extravagant lifestyle
629 231 fixed: caught, and also a joke on Quicksilver's name: a fixed substance is no longer volatile and responsive
630 1 chronicle: historical record
631 5–6 *O hone . . . etc*: refrain from a popular lament or ballad
632 8 worshipful: distinguished
633 8 accompt: esteem
634 19 and: as if

Knight o' the Sun or Palmerin of England have used their ladies so, Sin? Or Sir Lancelot? Or Sir Tristram?[635]

SINDEFY I do not know, madam.

GERTRUDE Then thou know'st nothing, Sin. Thou art a fool, Sin! The knighthood nowadays are nothing like the knighthood of old time. They rid[636] a-horseback; ours go afoot. They were attended by their squires; ours by their lackeys.[637] They went buckled in their armor; ours muffled in their cloaks. They traveled wildernesses and deserts; ours dare scarce walk the streets. They were still pressed[638] to engage their honor; ours still ready to pawn their clothes. They would gallop on at sight of a monster; ours run away at sight of a sergeant. They would help poor ladies; ours make poor ladies.

SINDEFY Ay, madam, they were knights of the Round Table at Winchester, that sought adventures; but these of the square table at ordinaries,[639] that sit at hazard.[640]

GERTRUDE True, Sin; let him vanish. And tell me, what shall we pawn next?

SINDEFY Ay marry, madam, a timely consideration, for our hostess, profane[641] woman, has sworn by bread and salt she will not trust us another meal.[642]

GERTRUDE Let it stink in her hand, then; I'll not be beholding to her. Let me see: my jewels be gone, and my gowns, and my red velvet petticoat that I was married in, and my wedding silk stockings, and all thy best apparel, poor Sin. Good faith, rather than thou shouldst pawn a rag more, I'd lay my ladyship in lavender,[643] if I knew where.

SINDEFY Alas, madam, your ladyship?

GERTRUDE Ay, why? You do not scorn my ladyship, though it is in a waistcoat?[644] God's my life, you are a peat[645] indeed! Do I offer to mortgage my ladyship for you, and for your avail, and do you turn the lip and the "alas"[646] to my ladyship?

SINDEFY No, madam, but I make question who will lend anything upon it?

GERTRUDE Who? Marry, enow,[647] I warrant you, if you'll seek 'em out. I'm sure I remember the time when I would ha' given a thousand pound (if I had had it) to have been a lady, and I hope I was not bred and born with that appetite alone. Some other gentle-born o' the city have the same longing, I trust. And for my part, I would afford 'em a penn'orth:[648] my ladyship is little the worse for the wearing, and yet I would bate[649] a good deal of the sum. I would lend it—let me see—for forty pound in hand, Sin; that would apparel us, and ten pound a year. That would keep me, and you, Sin, with our needles,[650] and we should never need to be beholding to our scurvy[651] parents. Good lord, that there are no fairies nowadays, Sin!

SINDEFY Why, madam?

GERTRUDE To do miracles, and bring ladies money. Sure, if we lay in a cleanly house, they would haunt it, Sin. I'll try! I'll sweep the chamber soon at night, and set a dish of water o'the hearth. A fairy may come, and bring a pearl or a diamond; we do not know, Sin. Or, there may be a pot of gold hid o'the backside,[652] if we had tools to dig for't. Why may not we two rise early i'the morning, Sin, afore anybody is up, and find a jewel i'the streets, worth a hundred pound?

635 20–21 Knight o' the Sun … Sir Tristram: all knightly heroes, from sixteenth-century romances translated from Spanish and Portuguese (Knight o'the Sun and Palmerin of England), and from Arthurian romance set in Britain's mythic past (Sir Lancelot and Sir Tristram)

636 24 rid: rode

637 25 lackeys: footmen, but with a sense of servility and obsequiousness

638 27 still pressed: always striving

639 31 square table at ordinaries: gambling table at taverns

640 31 hazard: a game of dice

641 33 profane: irreverent

642 34 trust us another meal: give us another meal on credit, without payment

643 38 lay my ladyship in lavender: pawn my title

644 40 waistcoat: short garment, suggesting low class when worn without a gown

645 41 peat: proud woman

646 42 turn the … the "alas": show signs of scorn

647 44 enow: enough

648 47 penn'orth: a penny's worth

649 48 bate: discount

650 50 with our needles: working as seamstresses

651 51 scurvy: discourteous

652 56 backside: i.e. behind the house

May not some great court lady, as she comes from revels at midnight, look out of her coach as 'tis running, and lose such a jewel, and we find it? Ha?
SINDEFY They are pretty waking dreams, these.
GERTRUDE Or may not some old usurer be drunk overnight, with a bag of money, and leave it behind him on a stall? For God's sake, Sin, let's rise tomorrow by break of day, and see. I protest, law, if I had as much money as an alderman, I would scatter some on't[653] i'th'streets for poor ladies to find, when their knights were laid up. And, now I remember my song o'the "Golden Shower." Why may not I have such a fortune? I'll sing it, and try what luck I shall have after it.
[*Sings*]
Fond fables tell of old,
How Jove in Danae's lap
Fell in a shower of gold,
By which she caught a clap.[654]
O had it been my hap,
Howe'er the blow[655] *doth threaten;*
So well I like the play,
That I could wish all day
And night to be so beaten.

Enter MISTRESS TOUCHSTONE

O, here's my mother! Good luck, I hope. Ha' you brought any money, mother? Pray you, mother, your blessing. [MISTRESS TOUCHSTONE *weeps*] Nay, sweet mother, do not weep!
MISTRESS TOUCHSTONE God bless you! I would I were in my grave.
GERTRUDE Nay, dear mother, can you steal no more money from my father? Dry your eyes, and comfort me. Alas, it is my knight's fault, and not mine, that I am in a waistcoat, and attired thus simply.
MISTRESS TOUCHSTONE Simply? 'Tis better than thou deserv'st. Never whimper for the matter: "Thou shouldst have looked before thou hadst leaped." Thou wert afire to be a lady, and now your ladyship and you may both "blow at the coal," for aught I know. "Self do, self have." "The hasty person never wants woe," they say.
GERTRUDE Nay then, mother, you should ha' looked to it. A body would think you were the older! I did but my kind, I. He was a knight, and I was fit to be a lady. 'Tis not lack of liking, but lack of living, that severs us. And you talk like yourself and a citiner[656] in this, i'faith. You show what husband you come on, iwis.[657] You smell o' the Touchstone, he that will do more for his daughter that he has married[658] a scurvy gold-end man and his prentice, than he will for his tother daughter that has wedded a knight and his customer! By this light, I think he is not my legitimate father.
SINDEFY O good madam, do not take up[659] your mother so.
MISTRESS TOUCHSTONE Nay, nay, let her e'en alone. Let her ladyship grieve me still with her bitter taunts and terms. I have not dole[660] enough to see her in this miserable case, I? Without her velvet gowns, without ribands,[661] without jewels, without French wires,[662] or cheat-bread,[663]

653 63 on't: of it
654 67–70: *Fond fables … a clap*: in classical myth, Jove (i.e. Jupiter) raped Danae in the form of a shower of gold, and she became pregnant with Perseus; "clap" is also gonorrhea
655 72 blow: thrust in sexual intercourse
656 88 citiner: citizen
657 89 iwis: certainly
658 90 married: i.e. married to
659 93 take up: reprimand
660 95 dole: grief
661 96 ribands: ribbons
662 96 French wires: the frame to support a French ruff
663 96 cheat-bread: a kind of wheat bread

or quails, or a little dog, or a gentleman usher, or anything, indeed, that's fit for a lady—
SINDEFY [*Aside*] Except her tongue.
MISTRESS TOUCHSTONE And I not able to relieve her neither, being kept so short[664] by my husband. Well, God knows my heart. I did little think that ever she should have had need of her sister Golding.
GERTRUDE Why, mother, I ha' not yet. Alas, good mother, be not intoxicate[665] for me; I am well enough. I would not change husbands with my sister, I: "the leg of a lark is better than the body of a kite."[666]
MISTRESS TOUCHSTONE I know that. But—
GERTRUDE What, sweet mother? What?
MISTRESS TOUCHSTONE It's but ill food, when nothing's left but the claw.
GERTRUDE That's true, mother. Ay, me! [*She weeps*]
MISTRESS TOUCHSTONE Nay, sweet ladybird, sigh not. Child, madam! Why do you weep thus? Be of good cheer. I shall die, if you cry and mar your complexion thus.
GERTRUDE Alas, mother, what should I do?
MISTRESS TOUCHSTONE Go to thy sister's, child: she'll be proud thy ladyship will come under her roof. She'll win thy father to release thy knight and redeem thy gowns, and thy coach, and thy horses, and set thee up again.
GERTRUDE But will she get him to set my knight up, too?
MISTRESS TOUCHSTONE That she will, or anything else thou'lt ask her.
GERTRUDE I will begin to love her, if I thought she would do this.
MISTRESS TOUCHSTONE Try her, good chuck,[667] I warrant thee.
GERTRUDE Dost thou think she'll do't?
SINDEFY Ay, madam, and be glad you will receive it.
MISTRESS TOUCHSTONE That's a good maiden; she tells you true. Come, I'll take order for[668] your debts i'the alehouse.
GERTRUDE Go, Sin, and pray for thy Frank, as I will, for my Pet.

[*Exeunt*]

[Act V, scene ii]

Enter TOUCHSTONE, GOLDING, [*and*] WOLF

TOUCHSTONE I will receive no letters, Master Wolf; you shall pardon me.
GOLDING Good father, let me entreat you.
TOUCHSTONE Son Golding, I will not be tempted. I find mine own easy nature,[669] and I know not what a well-penned subtle letter may work upon it. There may be tricks, packing;[670] do you see? Return with your packet, sir.
WOLF Believe it, sir, you need fear no packing here. These are but letters of submission, all.
TOUCHSTONE Sir, I do look for no submission. I will bear myself in this like blind Justice.[671] *Work upon that now*. When the sessions[672] come, they shall hear from me.
GOLDING From whom come your letters, Master Wolf?
WOLF An't please you, sir: one from Sir Petronel, another from Francis Quicksilver, and a third from old Security, who is almost mad in prison. There are two to your worship: one from Master Francis, sir, another from the knight.
TOUCHSTONE I do wonder, Master Wolf, why you should travail thus, in a business so

664 99 kept so short: so strictly confined, and without access to money
665 102 intoxicate: distressed
666 104 kite: bird of prey (also figuratively a term of reproach)
667 118 chuck: chick, a term of endearment
668 121–2 take order for: settle up
669 3 find mine own easy nature: am aware that I am easily moved
670 4 packing: plotting
671 7 blind Justice: justice is often personified as a woman blindfolded, to represent impartiality
672 8 sessions: court hearing to determine causes

contrary to kind,[673] or the nature o' your place! That you, being the keeper of a prison, should labor the release of your prisoners! Whereas, methinks, it were far more natural and kindly in you to be ranging about for more, and not let these scape you have already under the tooth. But they say you wolves, when you ha' sucked the blood once, that[674] they are dry, you ha' done.

WOLF Sir, your worship may descant[675] as you please o' my name, but I protest I was never so mortified[676] with any men's discourse or behavior in prison; yet I have had of all sorts of men i' the kingdom under my keys, and almost of all religions i' the land: as Papist, Protestant, Puritan, Brownist, Anabaptist, Millenary, Family o' Love, Jew, Turk, Infidel, Atheist, Good Fellow, etc.[677]

GOLDING And which of all these, thinks Master Wolf, was the best religion?

WOLF Troth, Master Deputy, they that pay fees best; we never examine their consciences farther.

GOLDING I believe you, Master Wolf. [*Reading the letters*] Good faith, sir, here's a great deal of humility i' these letters.

WOLF Humility, sir? Ay, were your worship an eyewitness of it, you would say so. The knight will i' the Knights' Ward,[678] do what we can, sir, and Master Quicksilver would be i' the Hole, if we would let him. I never knew or saw prisoners more penitent, or more devout. They will sit you up all night singing of psalms, and edifying the whole prison (only Security sings a note too high, sometimes, because he lies i' the Twopenny Ward, far off, and cannot take his tune[679]). The neighbors cannot rest for[680] him, but come every morning to ask what godly prisoners we have.

TOUCHSTONE Which on 'em is't is so devout, the knight or the tother?

WOLF Both, sir. But the young man especially! I never heard his like! He has cut his hair,[681] too. He is so well given, and has such good gifts! He can tell you almost all the stories of the *Book of Martyrs*,[682] and speak you all the *Sick Man's Salve*[683] without book.[684]

TOUCHSTONE Ay, if he had had grace, he was brought up where it grew, iwis. On, Master Wolf.

WOLF And he has converted one Fangs, a sergeant, a fellow could neither write nor read; he was called the Bandog[685] o' the Counter, and he has brought him already to pare[686] his nails, and say his prayers, and 'tis hoped he will sell his place[687] shortly, and become an intelligencer.[688]

TOUCHSTONE No more; I am coming[689] already. If I should give any farther ear, I were taken. Adieu, good Master Wolf.—Son, I do feel mine own weaknesses; do not importune me. Pity is a rheum[690] that I am subject to, but I will resist it.—Master Wolf, "fish is cast away that is cast in

673 14 kind: natural inclination (i.e. befitting the name "Wolf")

674 17 that: so that

675 18 descant: a) pun; b) discuss and criticize

676 19 mortified: prompted to spiritual discipline

677 20–22 all religions ... Good Fellow, etc.: Wolf's list of prisoners ranges from divisions within Christianity, such as Catholic (Papist) and Protestant (Puritans and sects such as Brownists, who followed the separatist Robert Browne; Anabaptists, a German sect that believed in adult baptism; Millenarists, believers in the thousand-year reign of Christ; and Family of Love, a sect founded by a mystic, and suppressed in England), to non-Christian and non-religious "sorts," such as Infidel (meaning unbeliever, usually Muslim), and Good Fellow (hedonist)

678 29 Knights' Ward: prison housing ranged on a spectrum of price and rank: the Masters' Ward was the best, followed by the Knights' Ward, the Twopenny Ward, and the Hole, the worst of the dungeons (i.e. both men choose worse housing than they could have, a sign of penitence)

679 33 tune: pitch

680 33 for: because of

681 36 cut his hair: like a Puritan, in contrast to the long hair of courtiers

682 37–8 *Book of Martyrs*: a common title for John Foxe's popular *Actes and Monuments* (1563), a history of Protestant suffering under Catholic authorities

683 38 *Sick Man's Salve*: Thomas Becon's *The Sick Man's Salve* (1561), a very popular Protestant text, was a dialogue about conversion and preparation for death

684 38 without book: from memory

685 42 Bandog: ferocious bloodhound

686 42 pare: trim

687 43 sell his place: sell his position of sergeant, paid to make arrests, to another person

688 43 intelligencer: informer

689 44 coming: relenting

690 46 rheum: a) tears; b) a watery secretion from the eyes, associated with disease

dry pools."[691] Tell hypocrisy it will not do; I have touched and tried[692] too often. I am yet proof,[693] and I will remain so. When the sessions come, they shall hear from me. In the meantime, to all suits, to all entreaties, to all letters, to all tricks, I will be deaf as an adder and blind as a beetle, lay mine ear to the ground,[694] and lock mine eyes i' my hand, against all temptations. *Exit*

GOLDING You see, Master Wolf, how inexorable[695] he is. There is no hope to recover him. Pray you commend me to my brother knight, and to my fellow Francis; present 'em with this small token of my love. [*Gives money*] Tell 'em I wish I could do 'em any worthier office, but in this, 'tis desperate. Yet I will not fail to try the uttermost of my power for 'em. And, sir, as far as I have any credit with you, pray you let 'em want nothing, though I am not ambitious they should know so much.

WOLF Sir, both your actions and words speak you to be a true gentleman. They shall know only what is fit, and no more.

Exeunt

[Act V, scene iii]

[*Enter*] HOLDFAST [*and*] BRAMBLE

HOLDFAST Who would you speak with, sir?

BRAMBLE I would speak with one Security, that is prisoner here.

HOLDFAST You are welcome, sir. Stay there; I'll call him to you. Master Security?

[SECURITY *appears at a window grating in the prison*]

SECURITY Who calls?

HOLDFAST Here's a gentleman would speak with you.

SECURITY What is he? Is't one that grafts my forehead, now I am in prison, and comes to see how the horns shoot up and prosper?[696]

HOLDFAST [*To* BRAMBLE] You must pardon him, sir. The old man is a little crazed with his imprisonment.

SECURITY What say you to me, sir? Look you here. My learned counsel, Master Bramble! Cry you mercy, sir; when saw you my wife?

BRAMBLE She is now at my house, sir, and desired me that I would come to visit you, and inquire of you your case, that we might work some means to get you forth.

SECURITY My case,[697] Master Bramble, is stone walls and iron grates. You see it;[698] this is the weakest part[699] on't. And, for getting me forth, no means but hang myself, and so to be carried forth, from which they have here bound me in intolerable bands.

BRAMBLE Why, but what is't you are in for, sir?

SECURITY For my sins, for my sins, sir, whereof marriage is the greatest. O, had I never married, I had never known this purgatory, to which hell is a kind of cool bath in respect.[700] My wife's confederacy, sir, with old Touchstone, that she might keep her jubilee,[701] and the feast of her new moon.[702] Do you understand me, sir?

691 46–7 "fish is . . . dry pools": proverbial, though Touchstone wants to keep his eyes dry
692 47 touched and tried: puns on his craft, testing and refining gold
693 48 proof: invulnerable
694 49–50 deaf as . . . the ground: proverbial behavior of animals; the adder put its head to the ground to block its ear
695 52 inexorable: unable to be moved
696 7 horns shoot up and prosper: proverbial horns of a cuckold, as if they were newly implanted and growing on his forehead (Security thinks someone must be having sex with his wife, and coming to mock him in prison)
697 14 case: condition; legal suit; place that contains me
698 14 it: the prison
699 15 weakest part: i.e. the window grating, though which Security speaks
700 19 in respect: by comparison
701 20 jubilee: a time of celebration prescribed in the Hebrew Bible, announced with a ram's horn
702 21 feast of her new moon: alluding to the "horns" of the new moon, and pagan festival of sex and fertility; another reference to Security's fear of being cuckolded

Enter QUICKSILVER

QUICKSILVER Good sir, go in and talk with him. The light does him harm, and his example will be hurtful to the weak prisoners. Fie, father Security, that you'll be still so profane;[703] will nothing humble you? [*Exeunt* QUICKSILVER, BRAMBLE, *and* HOLDFAST]

[*As they depart,*] *enter two* PRISONERS, *with a* FRIEND

FRIEND What's he?
PRISONER 1 O, he is a rare young man. Do you not know him?
FRIEND Not I. I never saw him I can remember.
PRISONER 2 Why, it is he that was the gallant prentice of London, Master Touchstone's man.
FRIEND Who, Quicksilver?
PRISONER 1 Ay, this is he.
FRIEND Is this he? They say he has been a gallant indeed.
PRISONER 2 O, the royallest[704] fellow that ever was bred up i'the city! He would play you his thousand pound a night at dice; keep knights and lords company; go with them to bawdy houses; had his six men in a livery; kept a stable of hunting horses, and his wench in her velvet gown and her cloth of silver. Here's one knight with him here in prison.
FRIEND And how miserably he is changed!
PRISONER 1 O, that's voluntary in him. He gave away all his rich clothes as soon as ever he came in here among the prisoners, and will eat o' the basket, for humility.[705]
FRIEND Why will he do so?
PRISONER 2 Alas, he has no hope of life. He mortifies himself. He does but linger on, till the sessions.
PRISONER 1 O, he has penned the best thing, that he calls his "Repentance," or his "Last Farewell," that ever you heard. He is a pretty poet, and for prose—you would wonder[706] how many prisoners he has helped out, with penning petitions[707] for 'em, and not take a penny. Look, this is the knight, in the rug gown.[708] Stand by.

Enter PETRONEL, BRAMBLE, [*and*] QUICKSILVER

BRAMBLE Sir, for Security's case, I have told him. Say he should be condemned to be carted,[709] or whipped for a bawd, or so, why I'll lay an execution[710] on him o' two hundred pound; let him acknowledge a judgment (he shall do it in half an hour), they shall not all fetch him out without paying the execution, o' my word.
PETRONEL But can we not be bailed, Master Bramble?
BRAMBLE Hardly; there are none of the judges in town, else you should remove yourself, in spite of him, with a *habeas corpus*.[711] But if you have a friend to deliver your tale sensibly to some justice o' the town, that he may have feeling of it, do you see, you may be bailed. For as I understand the case, 'tis only done *in terrorem*,[712] and you shall have an action of false imprisonment against him when you come out, and perhaps a thousand pound costs.

Enter WOLF

703 23 profane: impious
704 32 royallest: most magnificent
705 38 eat o' the basket, for humility: eat out of the communal alms basket, scraps of food collected for the prisoners, as an act of voluntary self-abasement
706 43 wonder: be amazed at
707 44 petitions: pleas of appeal
708 45 rug gown: a gown of coarse woolen cloth, worn in penitence
709 47 carted: carried in a cart, on public display, as punishment
710 47 lay an execution: a legal scheme; Bramble will deploy a writ of execution that shows Security owes a debt, and cannot be removed from prison until the debt is paid
711 52 *habeas corpus*: a writ requiring the person restrained to appear before a judge or court to determine whether the restraint is lawful
712 54 *in terrorem*: in fright or terror (Latin); as a warning to terrify or deter others

QUICKSILVER How now, Master Wolf? What news? What return?[713]

WOLF Faith, bad all: yonder will be no letters received. He says the sessions shall determine it. Only, Master Deputy Golding commends him to you and, with this token [*Gives the money to* QUICKSILVER], wishes he could do you other good.

QUICKSILVER I thank him. Good Master Bramble, trouble our quiet no more. Do not molest us in prison thus, with your winding devices;[714] pray you, depart. [*Exit* BRAMBLE] For my part, I commit my cause to him that can succor me; let God work his will. Master Wolf [*Returning the money*], I pray you let this be distributed among the prisoners, and desire 'em to pray for us.

WOLF It shall be done, Master Francis. [*Exit* QUICKSILVER]

PRISONER 1 An excellent temper!

PRISONER 2 Now God send him good luck. *Exeunt* [PRISONERS *and* FRIEND]

PETRONEL But what said my father-in-law, Master Wolf?

Enter HOLDFAST

HOLDFAST Here's one would speak with you, sir.

WOLF I'll tell you anon, Sir Petronel— [*To* HOLDFAST] Who is't? [*Exit* PETRONEL]

HOLDFAST A gentleman, sir, that will not be seen.

Enter GOLDING

WOLF Where is he? Master Deputy! Your worship is welcome—

GOLDING Peace!

WOLF [*To* HOLDFAST] Away, sirrah. [*Exit* HOLDFAST]

GOLDING Good faith, Master Wolf, the estate[715] of these gentlemen, for whom you were so late[716] and willing a suitor, doth much affect me. And because I am desirous to do them some fair office,[717] and find there is no means to make my father relent so likely as to bring him to be a spectator of their miseries, I have ventured on a device, which is to make myself your prisoner, entreating you will presently go report it to my father, and, feigning an action at suit of some third person, pray him by this token [*Gives* WOLF *a ring*], that he will presently, and with all secrecy, come hither for my bail. Which train,[718] if any, I know will bring him abroad,[719] and then having him here, I doubt not but we shall be all fortunate in the event.

WOLF Sir, I will put on my best speed to effect it. Please you, come in?

GOLDING Yes, and let me rest[720] concealed, I pray you.

WOLF [*To audience*] See here a benefit truly done, when it is done timely, freely, and to no ambition. [*Exeunt*]

[Act V, scene iv]

Enter TOUCHSTONE, *Wife* [MISTRESS TOUCHSTONE], *Daughters* [MILDRED, GERTRUDE], SINDEFY, [*and*] WINIFRED

TOUCHSTONE I will sail by you and not hear you, like the wise Ulysses.[721]

713 56 return: response
714 61 winding devices: wily counsel
715 75 estate: condition
716 76 late: recently
717 76–7 fair office: kind service
718 81 train: snare
719 82 abroad: out
720 84 rest: stay
721 1 wise Ulysses: in Homer's *Odyssey*, Odysseus (Latin: Ulysses) commands his men to plug their ears with wax and ties himself to the mast in order to sail past the sirens (see line 6) without changing course

MILDRED Dear father!
MISTRESS TOUCHSTONE Husband!
GERTRUDE Father!
WINIFRED *and* SINDEFY Master Touchstone!
TOUCHSTONE Away, sirens![722] I will immure[723] myself against your cries, and lock myself up to your lamentations.
MISTRESS TOUCHSTONE Gentle husband, hear me.
GERTRUDE Father, it is I, father, my Lady Flash. My sister and I am friends.
MILDRED Good father!
WINIFRED Be not hardened,[724] good Master Touchstone.
SINDEFY I pray you, sir, be merciful.
TOUCHSTONE I am deaf, I do not hear you; I have stopped mine ears with shoemaker's wax, and drunk Lethe[725] and mandragora[726] to forget you. All you speak to me I commit to the air.[727]

Enter WOLF

MILDRED How now, Master Wolf?
WOLF Where's Master Touchstone? I must speak with him presently; I have lost my breath for haste.
MILDRED What's the matter, sir? Pray all be well.
WOLF Master Deputy Golding is arrested upon an execution, and desires him presently to come to him, forthwith.
MILDRED Ay me! Do you hear, father?
TOUCHSTONE [*Not listening*] Tricks, tricks, confederacy,[728] tricks! I have 'em in my nose; I scent 'em.
WOLF Who's that? Master Touchstone?
MISTRESS TOUCHSTONE Why, it is Master Wolf himself, husband.
MILDRED Father!
TOUCHSTONE I am deaf still, I say. I will neither yield to the song of the siren, nor the voice of the hyena,[729] the tears of the crocodile, nor the howling o' the wolf. Avoid my habitation, monsters!
WOLF Why, you are not mad, sir? I pray you look forth, and see the token I have brought you, sir.
TOUCHSTONE Ha! What token is it?
WOLF [*Shows him the ring*] Do you know it, sir?
TOUCHSTONE My son Golding's ring! Are you in earnest, Master Wolf?
WOLF Ay, by my faith, sir. He is in prison, and required me to use all speed and secrecy to you.
TOUCHSTONE My cloak there! Pray you be patient; I am plagued for my austerity.[730] My cloak! At whose suit, Master Wolf?
WOLF I'll tell you as we go, sir.

Exeunt

[Act V, scene v]

Enter FRIEND [*and*] PRISONERS

722 6 sirens: mythical monsters, part woman and part bird, said to lure sailors to their doom through song
723 6 immure: wall in, shut oneself up
724 11 hardened: callously unsympathetic
725 14 Lethe: the mythical river in Hades that, when drunk, produces forgetfulness
726 14 mandragora: a medicinal preparation of mandrake root, with a sedative effect
727 14 air: editors typically insert an exit for Touchstone here, to explain why he does not respond to the women, and then insert his re-entrance at line 30. Possibly, however, he retreats into the discovery space (i.e. his shop), or remains onstage but renders himself unable to hear them—an opportunity for physical comedy (suggested by his reference to earplugs, and his earlier assertion, V.ii. 49–50, that he will be as deaf as the adder)
728 22 confederacy: conspiracy (of the women)
729 27–8 voice of the hyena: said to imitate human cries in order to lure victims to death
730 36 austerity: sternness

FRIEND Why, but is his offence such as he cannot hope of life?
PRISONER 1 Troth,[731] it should seem so; and 'tis great pity, for he is exceeding penitent.
FRIEND They say he is charged but on suspicion of felony yet.
PRISONER 2 Ay, but his master is a shrewd[732] fellow; he'll prove great matter against him.
FRIEND I'd as lief as[733] anything I could see his "Farewell."
PRISONER 1 O, 'tis rarely written. Why, Toby may get him to sing it to you; he's not curious[734] to anybody.
PRISONER 2 O, no. He would that all the world should take knowledge of his repentance, and thinks he merits[735] in't, the more shame he suffers.
PRISONER 1 Pray thee; try what thou canst do.
PRISONER 2 I warrant you: he will not deny it, if he be not hoarse with the often repeating of it. *Exit* PRISONER 2
PRISONER 1 You never saw a more courteous creature than he is, and the knight too; the poorest prisoner of the house may command 'em. You shall hear a thing admirably penned.
FRIEND Is the knight any scholar too?
PRISONER 1 No, but he will speak very well, and discourse admirably of running horses and Whitefriars,[736] and against bawds, and of cocks, and talk as loud as a hunter, but is none.

Enter WOLF *and* TOUCHSTONE

WOLF Please you stay here, sir; I'll call his worship down to you. [*Exit*]

Enter QUICKSILVER *and* PETRONEL [*with* PRISONER 2; *enter also* WOLF *and* GOLDING, *who stand apart so* TOUCHSTONE *does not see them*]

PRISONER 1 [*To* FRIEND] See, he has brought him, and the knight too. Salute him, I pray. [*To* QUICKSILVER] Sir, this gentleman, upon our report, is very desirous to hear some piece of your "Repentance."
QUICKSILVER Sir, with all my heart, and as I told Master Toby, I shall be glad to have any man a witness of it. And the more openly I profess it, I hope it will appear the heartier,[737] and the more unfeigned.
TOUCHSTONE [*Aside*] Who is this? My man, Francis? And my son-in-law?
QUICKSILVER Sir, it is all the testimony I shall leave behind me to the world and my master, that I have so offended.
FRIEND Good sir!
QUICKSILVER I writ it when my spirits were oppressed.
PETRONEL Ay, I'll be sworn for you, Francis.
QUICKSILVER It is in imitation of Mannington's, he that was hanged at Cambridge, that cut off the horse's head at a blow.[738]
FRIEND So, sir.
QUICKSILVER To the tune of "I wail in woe, I plunge in pain."[739]
PETRONEL An excellent ditty it is, and worthy of a new tune.
QUICKSILVER
[*Sings*] *In Cheapside, famous for gold and plate,*
Quicksilver, I did dwell of late:

731 2 Troth: truly
732 4 shrewd: severe
733 5 as lief as: wish more than
734 6 curious: difficult; unsociable
735 9 merits: earns merit
736 16 Whitefriars: area known for prostitution and petty crime
737 22 heartier: expressing unrestrained feeling
738 30–31 imitation of . . . a blow: based on "A woeful Ballad, made by Mr. George Mannynton, an houre before he suffred at Cambridge Castell," entered into the Stationers' Register in 1576, and reprinted in Clement Robinson's *A Handful of Pleasant Delights* in 1584
739 33 "I wail . . . in pain": this is the first line of Mannington's song; the ballad tune, extant, is known as "Labandala Shot"

I had a master, good and kind,
That would have wrought[740] *me to his mind.*
He bade me still: "Work upon that."
But alas, I wrought I know not what.
He was a touchstone, black but true,
And told me still what would ensue.
Yet, woe is me, I would not learn;
I saw, alas, but could not discern.

FRIEND Excellent, excellent well!

GOLDING [*Aside to* WOLF *about* TOUCHSTONE] O let him alone; he is taken[741] already.

QUICKSILVER
[*Sings*] *I cast my coat and cap away;*
I went in silks and satins gay;
False metal[742] *of good manners I*
Did daily coin unlawfully.
I scorned my master, being drunk;
I kept my gelding and my punk;
And with a knight, Sir Flash by name,
Who now is sorry for the same—

PETRONEL I thank you, Francis.

QUICKSILVER
[*Sings*] *I thought by sea to run away,*
But Thames and tempest did me stay.

TOUCHSTONE [*Aside*] This cannot be feigned, sure! Heaven pardon my severity. "The ragged colt may prove a good horse."

GOLDING [*Aside*] How he listens, and is transported! He has forgot me.

QUICKSILVER
[*Sings*] *Still "Eastward ho!" was all my word,*
But westward I had no regard; [743]
Nor never thought, what would come after,
As did, alas, his youngest daughter.
At last the black ox[744] *trod o' my foot,*
And I saw then what longed unto't,[745]
Now cry I, "Touchstone, touch me still,[746]
And make me current[747] *by thy skill."*

TOUCHSTONE [*Aside*] And I will do it, Francis.

WOLF [*To* GOLDING] Stay him, Master Deputy. Now is the time; we shall lose[748] the song else. [*They move toward* TOUCHSTONE]

FRIEND I protest it is the best that ever I heard.

QUICKSILVER How like you it, gentlemen?

ALL O admirable, sir!

QUICKSILVER This stanza now following alludes to the story of Mannington, from whence I took my project[749] for my invention.

FRIEND Pray you go on, sir.

QUICKSILVER

740 38 *wrought*: shaped, as in the goldsmith's craft
741 46 taken: absorbed (by Quicksilver's song)
742 49 *false metal*: counterfeit money
743 62 *westward I had no regard*: I had no thought of punishment (the gallows at Tyburn lay to the west)
744 65 *black ox*: proverbial figure of adversity
745 66 *longed unto't*: belonged unto it (i.e. adversity, perhaps also Touchstone's virtue)
746 67 *touch me still*: test me further
747 68 *make me current*: turn me into genuine metal (or coin, in contrast to the "false metal")
748 70 lose: ruin
749 76 project: idea

[*Sings*] *O Mannington, thy stories show*
Thou cutt'st a horse-head off at a blow;
But I confess, I have not the force
For to cut off the head of a horse.
Yet I desire this grace to win:
That I may cut off the horse-head of Sin.
And leave his body in the dust
Of sin's highway and bogs of lust.
Whereby I may take Virtue's purse,
And live with her, for better, for worse.

FRIEND Admirable, sir, and excellently conceited![750]

QUICKSILVER Alas, sir.

TOUCHSTONE [*Aside to* GOLDING *and* WOLF] Son Golding and Master Wolf, I thank you. The deceit is welcome, [*To* GOLDING] especially from thee, whose charitable soul in this hath shown a high point of wisdom and honesty. Listen! I am ravished with his "Repentance," and could stand here a whole prenticeship to hear him.

FRIEND Forth, good sir.

QUICKSILVER
This is the last, and the "Farewell."
[*Sings*] *Farewell, Cheapside; farewell, sweet trade*
Of goldsmiths all, that never shall fade;
Farewell, dear fellow prentices all;
And be you warnèd by my fall.
Shun usurers, bawds,[751] *and dice, and drabs:*[752]
Avoid them as you would French scabs.[753]
Seek not to go beyond your tether,[754]
But cut your thongs unto your leather;[755]
So shall you thrive by little and little,
Scape Tyburn, Counters, and the Spital.[756]

TOUCHSTONE [*Revealing himself to the prisoners*] And scape them shalt thou, my penitent and dear Francis!

QUICKSILVER Master!

PETRONEL Father! [QUICKSILVER *and* PETRONEL *kneel to* TOUCHSTONE]

TOUCHSTONE I can no longer forbear to do your humility right.[757] Arise, and let me honor your repentance with the hearty and joyful embraces of a father and friend's love. Quicksilver, thou hast eat into my breast,[758] Quicksilver, with the drops of thy sorrow, and killed the desperate opinion I had of thy reclaim.[759]

QUICKSILVER O sir, I am not worthy to see your worshipful face.

PETRONEL Forgive me, father.

TOUCHSTONE Speak no more; all former passages[760] are forgotten, and here my word shall release you. Thank this worthy brother, and kind friend, Francis.—Master Wolf, I am their bail.

A shout in the prison [*and* SECURITY *appears at the window grate*]

SECURITY Master Touchstone! Master Touchstone!

750 88 excellently conceited: composed with wit and ingenuity
751 100 *bawds*: pimps
752 100 *drabs*: prostitutes
753 101 *French scabs*: scars from syphilis
754 102 *tether*: limit
755 103 *cut your . . . your leather*: proverbial ("live within your means")
756 105 *Spital*: the Spital was a hospital for the poor, known for treating venereal diseases
757 110 do your humility right: acknowledge and honor your humility
758 112 thou hast . . . my breast: just as drops of mercury corrode metal, Quicksilver's sorrow has eaten away at Touchstone's resolve not to forgive him
759 113 reclaim: redemption
760 116 passages: events

TOUCHSTONE Who's that?
WOLF Security, sir.
SECURITY Pray you, sir; if you'll be won with a song, hear my lamentable tune, too:

SONG[761]
O Master Touchstone,
My heart is full of woe.
Alas, I am a cuckold:
And why should it be so?
Because I was a usurer,
And bawd, as all you know,
For which, again I tell you,
My heart is full of woe.

TOUCHSTONE Bring him forth, Master Wolf, and release his bands. [*Exit* WOLF]
This day shall be sacred to mercy, and the mirth of this encounter in the Counter.

[*Enter* WOLF *with* SECURITY]

See, we are encountered with more suitors.

Enter MISTRESS TOUCHSTONE, GERTRUDE, MILDRED, SINDEFY, [*and*] WINIFRED

[*To the women*] Save your breath, save your breath! All things have succeeded to your wishes, and we are heartily satisfied in their events.
GERTRUDE [*To* PETRONEL] Ah, runaway, runaway! Have I caught you? And how has my poor knight done all this while?
PETRONEL Dear Lady-wife, forgive me!
GERTRUDE As heartily as I would be forgiven, knight. Dear father, give me your blessing, and forgive me too. I ha' been proud and lascivious,[762] father, and a fool, father; and being raised to the state of a wanton coy[763] thing called a Lady, father, have scorned you, father, and my sister, and my sister's velvet cap, too; and would make a mouth[764] at the city, as I rid through it; and stop mine ears at Bow-bell. I have said your beard was a base one, father; and that you looked like Twierpipe, the taborer;[765] and that my mother was but my midwife.
MISTRESS TOUCHSTONE Now God forgi' you, child Madam!
TOUCHSTONE No more repetitions. What is else wanting, to make our harmony full?
GOLDING Only this, sir: that my fellow Francis make amends to Mistress Sindefy with marriage.
QUICKSILVER With all my heart.
GOLDING And Security give her a dower,[766] which shall be all the restitution he shall make of that huge mass[767] he hath so unlawfully gotten.
TOUCHSTONE Excellently devised! A good motion.[768] What says Master Security?
SECURITY I say anything, sir, what you'll ha' me say. Would I were no cuckold!
WINIFRED Cuckold, husband? Why, I think this wearing of yellow[769] has infected you.
TOUCHSTONE Why, Master Security, that should rather be a comfort to you than a corrosive.[770] If you be a cuckold, it's an argument you have a beautiful woman to your wife.

761 121 SD *SONG*: Q marks Security's composition with this heading
762 139 lascivious: inclined to lustful desire
763 140 wanton coy: undisciplined and rude
764 141 make a mouth: make a contemptuous face
765 143 Twierpipe, the taborer: a famous minstrel who played the tabor, a small drum
766 149 dower: money or property that a bride brings into marriage
767 150 huge mass: i.e. of money
768 151 motion: proposal
769 153 yellow: the color of jealousy, also the color of prisoners' clothing
770 155 corrosive: consuming worry

Then, you shall be much made of; you shall have store of friends, never want money; you shall be eased of much o'your wedlock pain; others will take it for you. Besides, you being a usurer, and likely to go to hell, the devils will never torment you; they'll take you for one o' their own race. Again, if you be a cuckold and know it not, you are an innocent;[771] if you know it and endure it, a true martyr.

SECURITY I am resolved, sir. Come hither, Winnie.

TOUCHSTONE Well then, all are pleased, or shall be anon. Master Wolf, you look hungry, methinks. Have you no apparel to lend Francis to shift him?[772]

QUICKSILVER No sir, nor I desire none, but here make it my suit: that I may go home through the streets in these, as a spectacle—or rather, an example—to the children of Cheapside.

TOUCHSTONE Thou hast thy wish. Now, London, look about,
And in this moral see thy glass[773] run out:
Behold the careful father, thrifty son;
The solemn deeds, which each of us have done;
The usurer punished, and from fall so steep
The prodigal child reclaimed, and the lost sheep.[774]

[*All begin to*] *Exeunt*

Epilogus

[QUICKSILVER] [*To* TOUCHSTONE] Stay, sir, I perceive the multitude are gathered together, to view our coming outat the Counter. See, if the streets and the fronts of the houses be not stuck with[775] people, and the windows filled with ladies,as on the solemn day of the pageant![776]
[*To the audience*] O may you find, in this our pageant here, The same contentment which you came to seek: And as that show but draws you once a year, May this attract you hither once a week.

FINIS.

771 159 innocent: a) free of guilt; b) simpleton
772 163 shift him: enable him to change out of his prison clothes
773 167 glass: mirror; hourglass
774 171 prodigal child . . . lost sheep: biblical parables of loss and restoration
775 3 stuck with: packed full of
776 3 pageant: annual show celebrating London and the election of the Lord Mayor

15 Thomas Dekker, *If This Be Not a Good Play, The Devil Is In It*

First performed 1611–12

First printed 1612

Edited by David McInnis

Thomas Dekker's *If This Be Not A Good Play, The Devil Is In It* was first performed by Queen Anne's Men at the Red Bull, c.1611–12. When the play was printed in 1612, Dekker's prefatory note (which he dedicated to the Queen's Men) implies that he had previously offered it to the Prince's Men at the Fortune, but that they had rejected it: "when Fortune in her blind pride set her foot upon this imperfect building, as scorning the foundation and workmanship, you gently raised it up on the same columns, the frontispiece only a little more garnished" (14–17).

Despite the Prince's men's reluctance to take it on, *If This Be Not A Good Play* would have seemed a prudent repertorial acquisition for a commercial company. Devil-dramas were a staple of the London playhouses' offerings; the King's company had recently (1606) added Barnabe Barnes's *The Devil's Charter* to their repertory, and reprised *The Merry Devil of Edmonton* (c.1603, possibly also by Dekker) at their Blackfriars playhouse after 1609 and at court in 1612–13. The specific subject matter of Dekker's play would have been familiar to London playgoers, drawing as it does on the "Friar Rush" legend, in which a devil enters a monastery in the guise of a holy man and plays pranks. The earliest surviving printed version of the story is from 1620 but the legend was dramatized in 1602 as "Friar Rush and the Proud Woman of Antwerp" by John Day and William Haughton (with alterations by Henry Chettle), and acquired by Henslowe for the then-Admiral's company at their recently built Fortune playhouse (see *Lost Plays Database*; Matusiak). It is remotely possible that that play was still in repertory at the Fortune in 1611; F. G. Fleay conjectured that this might be the reason why the Prince's Men rejected Dekker's newer play on the subject (Fleay, 1981: 1.133). Ben Jonson subsequently wrote a play for the King's company on a similar theme of devils visiting earth in the hope of gathering souls: *The Devil is an Ass* (1616). Each of these plays makes use of the popular idea that London is so vicious and sinful that it frightens off the devils themselves. As Cyrus Hoy notes, the affinities between hell and London provided the playwright and his peers with a favorite subject matter, which Dekker returns to frequently (Hoy, 1980: 3. 78–9).

Dekker's play speaks not just to these Friar Rush-inspired dramas, but to that most famous example of stage devilry, Marlowe's *Doctor Faustus* (c.1588). A version of that play was reprinted in 1611, the year Dekker was writing *If This Be Not A Good Play*. In a passage in scene v of *If This Be Not A Good Play*, Bartervile, Naples' official receiver of tribute monies, assumes a distinctly Faustian stance when he contrives to trick a gentleman into forfeiting his mortgaged lands:

1 GENTLEMAN Damned wretch, thou wilt go quick to hell I fear.
BARTERVILE No sir, the devil shall fetch me when I go.
LURCHALL [Aside] That's all my errand.
2 GENTLEMAN   We are cheated both.
BARTERVILE Proceed in your chancery suit. I have begun your bill:
"Humbly complaining—"
1 GENTLEMAN   Of thee, villain, I'll complain,
That sells thy soul for money; devils on earth dwell
And men are nowhere, all this world is hell.

(v. 142–8)

Bartervile invokes Faustus's final lamentation as he is resigned to his fate ("the date is expired, the time will come, and he [Mephistopheles] will fetch me," xvi. 31), and the first Gentleman clearly labels Bartervile as a Faustian "type" who sells his soul, before recalling the metaphysical dispute between Faustus and Mephistopheles on the ontology of hell ("Why, this is hell, nor am I out of it," I.iii. 74). Bartervile is not the only Neapolitan to succumb to diabolical temptation; in Dekker's play, courtiers, merchants and religious men are equally corrupted.

Besides its moral meditations, Dekker's play capitalizes on spectacle, offering some of the most extravagant stage directions of the period. The devil Ruffman produces "*Fireworks on lines*" to impress the Neapolitan court (iv. 190 SD) and Pluto/Lucifer blasts a yew-tree with fireworks to mark it (xi. 113–14). A group of devils, accompanied by "*Rain, thunder and lightning*" (xi. 25 SD), appears on a heath reminiscent of the one occupied by the witches in *Macbeth*, whilst the abbey's cook hides up a tree on stage and watches in disbelief. Elsewhere, devils "*Sink down, above flames*" (xvi. 146 SD) or "*rise up*" from "*under the ground in several places*" (xvii. 0 SD). A singing and dancing Italian zany (clown), accompanied by "*five or six courtesans*," seeks to distract the solemn Subprior from studying at his desk where he contemplates "*a death's head, a cloak and a cross*" (xiii. 0 SD). On two occasions (vi. 73 and viii. 119) the "golden head" of Glitterback (a golden devil) ascends from under the stage—perhaps recalling another supernatural play, Robert Greene's *Friar Bacon and Friar Bungay* (1589), and the brazen head at the centre of its protagonist's magical aspirations. François Ravaillac, the man who assassinated Henri IV of France, appears as a tormented soul in hell, his "*Hand burnt off*" before our eyes (xvii. 38 SD). A demented Guy Fawkes dances about the stage attempting to ignite barrels of gunpowder in hell, and a "*coal-black*" ghost of a Puritan makes a cameo appearance (xvii. 249 SD). As Dekker himself acknowledges in the preface, this was a challenging play to stage, making great demands on the "cost, counsel and labor" of the company (13).

For all its apparent extravagance, *If This Be Not A Good Play* is typical of plays from the London commercial theaters inasmuch as it offers a new spin on a well-known subject, takes full advantage of the spectacular technologies and capabilities of the public theaters, and offers a clear response to a number of plays in the repertories of rival companies. On the other hand, *If This Be Not A Good Play* is somewhat unusual for Dekker in being a sole-authored play: only a handful of other examples exist, including *The Shoemaker's Holiday* (1599), *Old Fortunatus* (1599), *Satiromastix* (1601), *The Second Part of The Honest Whore* (1605) and *The Whore of Babylon* (1606). Dekker's dramatic output during the early years of his career, by contrast, was both collaborative and plentiful, averaging around ten plays per year at the turn of the century, most of which are now lost. When Philip Henslowe, manager of the Rose playhouse and theatrical impresario, ceased recording details of dramatic activity in 1603, our knowledge of Dekker's work habits becomes limited. *The Whore of Babylon* was followed by a period of writing plague texts and satirical pamphlets before examples of Dekker's dramatic writing can again be found with *The Bloody Banquet* (c.1610, with Thomas Middleton) and *The Roaring Girl* (1611, also with Middleton). This hardly seems sufficient to earn a living, and indeed there may have been other plays written by Dekker about which no evidence exists. Whatever his writing habits, they do not seem to have met his financial needs; Dekker was arrested in early 1613 and spent seven years imprisoned in the King's Bench for his substantial debts, during which time his dramatic output all but ceased. He wrote a pageant that he offered for inclusion in the Lord Mayor's pageant in 1617, but it was rejected and Dekker was paid £4 for his efforts. Upon his release from prison, he collaborated with Philip Massinger in writing a Roman tragedy, *The Virgin Martyr* (1620). Around 1621, he may have written a (now-lost) play on "The Jew of Venice" and he was collaborating again (this time with John Ford, William Rowley, and maybe one other) on *The Witch of Edmonton*, which dramatized recent, sensational events. He probably also wrote his *Match Me in London* that year, and *The Wonder of a Kingdom* and *The Noble Spanish Soldier* the following year. He wrote a handful of other plays, many lost, in subsequent years, but fell on hard times again and turned once more to pamphleteering and pageant-writing whilst in debt; his literary output apparently ceased by 1632, and it is likely that it was Thomas Dekker the playwright who was buried at St James, Clerkenwell in August of that year.

Textual note

The copy-text for this edition is the only early edition of the play: the quarto printed in 1612. I have consulted the Library of Congress's copy, which has not been collated previously. Fredson Bowers imposed act divisions on the play, but Q is undivided and Dekker's usual habit was to value scenic units but not the five-act structure of classical drama (see for example the partial through-scene-numberings but lack of act divisions in *1 Honest Whore*, 1604). Accordingly, I have divided the play into a prologue, scenes 1–17, and an epilogue, following Dekker's implied divisions as marked by group exits and new entrances. Dekker's reference to the "frontispiece" having been "garnished" suggests that the play as it was printed had been enlarged, and probably refers to the first scene in hell—the only scene in which Lurchall is referred to by an alternative name, "Grumball," and the scene in which, along with the closing scene, the character called "Lucifer" in xi is called by the revised name of "Pluto" (see Fleay, 1891: 1.134; Hoy, 1980: 3.81). For clarity, this edition substitutes "Pluto" for Q's "Lucifer" in speech-prefixes and stage directions. That the manuscript behind the printed playbook was authorial, probably holograph, is implied by the presence of the playwright's name at the end of the dedication. But the text also bears marks of theatrical origin: stage directions anticipate the need for "*A confused noise to come pressing in*" and "*A noise to come in*" (xvii. 248, 270), and in scene xiv, Q adds "*Iouinelli here,*" which appears to be a prompter's note to ensure the relevant actor was ready for his character's entrance (see Bowers, 1958: 3. 116). A number of stage directions are printed in roman type, seemingly as continuations of a character's speech, suggesting that perhaps the manuscript had been marked up somewhat unclearly, confusing the typesetter.

It is hard to account for the significant number of errors in speech prefixes and directions. Dialogue beginning with the word "Pluto" is wrongly assigned *to* Pluto (i. 44); Scumbroth's criticism of Shackle-Soul is assigned *to* Shackle-Soul (iii. 37); Jovinelli is given an individual entrance in Scene ii after he has already spoken thirteen times in the scene, and long after receiving the group entrance at the start of that scene; and the printed text assigns two consecutive speeches to Brisco (iv. 33–38 and 39), to name but a few examples. On a number of occasions, verse is set as prose in Q; following Bowers in most instances, I have converted these back to verse. Despite these copious and confusing errors, the text was evidently playable, and the layers of revision or alteration indicated by the playwright's prefatory dedication to the company and the inconsistencies of the printed text can perhaps be regarded as a testament to the fluidity of performance in the period.

Most perplexing for an editor is Q's inconsistent handling of the names of the three devils whom Pluto sends to earth to corrupt court, church and trade. When Ruffman disguises himself as Shalkan Bohor, a Helvetian courtier, he is identified consistently throughout in speech prefixes and stage directions by his devil name rather than his disguise name. When Shackle-Soul disguises himself as Friar Rush, his entrances and speeches are sometimes given as "Shackle-Soul" and sometimes as "Rush." The third devil is given the speech prefix "Lurchall" consistently throughout, even when Pluto initially calls him "Grumball"—at i. 82, before he assumes the disguise of a merchant, and again at i. 115 shortly after he appears in the disguise. In the context of the latter exchange, it appears that the devil's name is Grumball and his merchant disguise-name is Lurchall. Q should therefore have given "Grumball" as the speech prefixes on the first occasions at least, if not throughout, to be consistent with its treatment of Ruffman and Shackle-Soul, but it does not. The situation is further complicated by the fact that the character oddly refers to himself as "Lurchall" from the secure vantagepoint of an aside in which he explicitly discusses playing the role of the merchant: "But Lurchall, now thou'rt in and for years bound/To play the merchant" (v. 10–11). Perhaps he is simply absorbed in his role, for other characters (Bartervile and his servant), who know him only as the merchant he purports to be, call him Lurchall in that same scene, confirming that Lurchall is clearly the name he goes by as a merchant. This edition emends Q's speech prefixes to reflect the devil's true name, "Grumball," until he appears fully fledged as "Lurchall" in scene v, in keeping with Q's practice of using both "Shackle-Soul" and "Rush" as speech prefixes for the same individual. I have emended the Ruffman/Bohor speech prefixes accordingly.

Further reading

Editions

Bowers, Fredson (1958) *The Dramatic Works of Thomas Dekker*, vol. 3, Cambridge: Cambridge University Press.

Critical and contextual reading

Conover, James H. (1969) *Thomas Dekker: An Analysis of Dramatic Structure*, The Hague: Mouton.

Equestri, Alice (2018) "A New Suggestion for Robert Armin's alias 'Grumball'," *Notes and Queries* 65: 101–5.

Fleay, F. G. (1891) *A Biographical Chronicle of the English Drama*, 2 vols, London: Reeves and Turner.

Freeman, Arthur (1965) "The Date of Dekker's *If This Be Not a Good Play, The Devil Is In It*," *Philological Quarterly* 44: 122–4.

Griffith, Eva (2013) *A Jacobean Company and its Playhouse: The Queen's Servants at the Red Bull Theatre (c. 1605–1619)*, Cambridge: Cambridge University Press: 204–8.

Herford, Charles H. (1886) *Studies in the Literary Relations of England and Germany in the Sixteenth Century*, Cambridge: Cambridge University Press.

Hoy, Cyrus (1980) *Introductions, Notes, and Commentaries to texts in 'The Dramatic Works of Thomas Dekker', Edited by* Fredson Bowers, *4 vols*, Cambridge: Cambridge University Press.

Knutson, Roslyn L., David McInnis, and Matthew Steggle (eds) (2009–) *Lost Plays Database*, Washington, DC: Folger Shakespeare Library https://lostplays.folger.edu.

Marcus, Leah S. (1986) *The Politics of Mirth: Jonson, Herrick, Milton, Marvell, and the Defense of Old Holiday Customs*, Chicago: University of Chicago Press.

Matusiak, Christopher (2014) "Lost Stage Friars and Their Narratives" in David McInnis and Matthew Steggle (eds), *Lost Plays in Shakespeare's England*, Basingstoke: Palgrave Macmillan: 208–28.

Wiggins, Martin (2012–) *British Drama, 1533–1642: A Catalogue*, 11 vols, Oxford: Oxford University Press.

If This Be Not a Good Play, the Devil is In It (1611–12)

To My Loving and Loved Friends and Fellows, the Queen's Majesty's Servants.

Knowledge and Reward dwell far asunder.[1] Greatness lay once between them, but in his stead, Covetousness now: an ill neighbor, a bad benefactor, no paymaster to poets. By this hard housekeeping (or rather, shutting up of Liberality's doors), Merit goes a-begging, and Learning starves. Books had wont to have[2] patrons and now patrons have books. The snuff[3] that is lighted consumes that which feeds it: a sign the world hath an ill ear, when no music is good, unless it strikes up[4] for nothing. I have sung so but will no more. A hue and cry[5] follow his wit that sleeps when sweet tunes are sounding. But 'tis now the fashion. Lords look well, knights thank well, gentlemen promise well, citizens take well, gulls swear well, but none give well. I leave therefore all for you, and all that this can be to you. Not in hope to have, but in recognition of what I have (as I think) already: your loves.

Acknowledgement is part of payment sometimes, but it neither is nor shall be (between you and me) a canceling. I have cast mine eye upon many but find none more fit, none more worthy, to patronize this than you, who have protected it. Your cost, counsel, and labor had been ill-spent if a second[6] should by my hand snatch from you this glory. No: when Fortune in her blind pride set her foot upon this imperfect building,[7] as scorning the foundation and workmanship, you gently raised it up on the same columns, the frontispiece only a little more garnished.[8] To you therefore deservedly is the whole frame consecrated, for I durst swear if wishes and curses could have become witches, the neck of this harmless devil had long ago been broken.[9]

But I am glad that Ignorance (so insolent for being flattered) is now stripped naked and her deformities discovered, and more glad that Envy sits maddingly[10] gnawing her own snakes, whose stings she had armed to strike others. Feed let her so still. So, still let the other be laughed at. Whilst I, pitying the one and not dreading the other, send these my wishes flying into your bosoms: that the god of poets may never pester your stage with a Choerilus,[11] nor a Suffenus[12] (males eminent in nothing but in long ears,[13] in kicking, and in

1 1 asunder: apart

2 4 had wont to have: used to have

3 4 snuff: portion of candle wick that is consumed to give light

4 6 strikes up: begins to play

5 6 hue and cry: outcry demanding the pursuit of a criminal

6 14 a second: i.e. a second patron; one who would share the glory with the first (Queen Anne's Men), and by doing so, diminish it

7 15 this imperfect building: Dekker's play, which had been offered to but rejected by the Prince's Men at the Fortune playhouse, and which was subsequently acquired for performance by Queen Anne's Men at the Red Bull

8 16–17 the frontispiece . . . more garnished: a reference to minor alterations, apparently to the opening scene of the play, when it was performed at the Red Bull

9 17–19 I durst swear . . . been broken: i.e. if every wish or curse uttered during the writing of this play were a witch (i.e. able to perform supernatural acts), the play would have been produced sooner (breaking a neck being a swift end)

10 21 maddingly: acting madly, in a frenzy

11 24 Choerilus: epic poet who was harshly criticized by Horace

12 25 Suffenus: like Choerilus, a poet who was ridiculed (by Catallus)

13 25 eminent in . . . long ears: i.e. ass-like

bragging out calumnies) upon whose cruppers[14] may be aptly pinned that moral of poor Ocnus,[15] making ropes in hell whilst an ass stands by and (as he twists) bites them in sunder. But if his versifying deity sends you any, I wish they may be such as are worthy to sit at the Table of the Sun.[16] None else.

I wish a fair and fortunate day to your next new play[17] (for the maker's sake and your own) because such brave triumphs of poesy and elaborate industry, which my worthy friend's muse hath there set forth, deserve a theater full of very muses themselves to be spectators. To that fair day I wish a full, free, and knowing auditor. And to that full audience, one honest door-keeper.[18] So, farewell.

Yours, Tho. Dekker.

Dramatis personae[19]

PLUTO, *prince of devils; sometimes referred to as Lucifer*
CHARON, *Hell's ferryman*
A PRODIGAL, *damned in Hell*
RUFFMAN, *a devil; disguises himself as Shalkan* BOHOR, *a Helvetian courtier*
SHACKLE-SOUL, *a devil; disguises himself as Friar* RUSH
GRUMBALL, *a devil; disguises himself as* LURCHALL, *a merchant*
ALFONSO, *newly crowned King of Naples*
OCTAVIO, *uncle to Alfonso*
ASTOLFO, *uncle to Alfonso*
NARCISSO, *a count*
JOVINELLI, *a count*
BRISCO, *a count*
SPENDOLA, *a count*
FARNEZE, *a courtier*
DUKE OF CALABRIA
ERMENHILD, *Princess of Calabria, the Duke's daughter*
SCUMBROTH, *the abbey's cook*
ALPHEGE, *a Capuchin friar*
PRIOR *of the Capuchin*
SUBPRIOR *of the Capuchins; also known as Father Clement*
HILARY, *a Capuchin friar*
BARTERVILE, *the official receiver of Naples*
GLITTERBACK, *a golden devil*
FRANÇOIS RAVAILLAC, *the assassin who killed Henri IV of France; a damned soul in Hell*
GUY FAWKES, *Gunpowder Plot conspirator; a damned soul in Hell*
MINOS, *the just judge of Hell*
AEACUS, *the severe judge of Hell*
RHADAMANTH, *the temperate judge of Hell*

Prologue, a Spirit accompanying Grumball, Capuchin Friars, Two Pilgrims, a One-legged Soldier, a Scholar, a Mariner, a Bravo, an Italian Zany, Furies, Ladies and others attending Ermenhild, Two Servants attending Bartervile (one named Carlo), Bartervile's Factors, Gentlemen (one named Innocentio), Devils, Courtesans, Calabrian Soldiers, a Guard, Two Gunmen, Brokers, a Puritan Ghost, Epilogue

14 26 cruppers: leather straps buckled to the back of a saddle to prevent it slipping forward on the horse
15 26 Ocnus: a figure of hesitation or unprofitable use of time, condemned to the underworld where he wove rope that was consumed by an ass as quickly as the rope was made
16 28 Table of the Sun: proverbially well-provided. According to legend, it was a field in Ethiopia, furnished with various meats overnight, and available to hungry and poor travelers by day
17 30 next new play: possibly Webster's *The White Devil*
18 33–4 one honest door-keeper: playgoers' entrance fees were collected by door-keepers
19 Dramatis personae: not in Q

Prologue

Would 'twere a custom that at all new plays
The makers sat o' th' stage, either with bays[20]
To have their works crowned, or beaten in with hissing.
Pied[21] and bold idiots durst not then sit kissing
A muse's cheek. Shame would base changelings[22] wean
From sucking the mellifluous Hippocrene,[23]
Who write as blind men shoot: by hap, not aim.
So fools by lucky throwing oft win the game.
Phoebus[24] has many bastards, true sons few
(I mean of those whose quick, clear eyes can view).
Poesy's pure essence, it being so divine
That the sun's fires (even when they brightest shine),
Or lightning when most subtly Jove does spend it,
May as soon be approached, weighed, touched, or comprehended.
But 'tis with poets now, as 'tis with nations:
Th' ill-favord'st vices are the bravest fashions.
A play whose rudeness Indians would abhor
If't fill a house with fishwives, "Rare!" they all roar.
It is not praise is sought for now but pence,
Though dropped from greasy-apron[25] audience.
Clapped may he be with thunder that plucks bays[26]
With such foul hands and with squint-eyes does gaze
On Pallas' shield,[27] not caring (so he gains
A crammed third day[28]) what filth drops from his brains.
Let those that love Pan's pipe dance still to Pan,
They shall but get long ears by it.[29] Give me that man
Who, when the plague of an impostumed[30] brain's
Breaking out infects a theater and hotly rains,
Killing the hearers' hearts, that the vast rooms
Stand empty like so many dead-men's tombs,
Can call the banished auditor home and tie
His ear with golden chains to his melody;
Can draw with adamantine[31] pen even creatures
Forged out of th' hammer,[32] on tiptoe, to reach up
And from rare silence clap their brawny hands
T'applaud what their charmed soul scarce understands.
That man give me, whose breast, filled by the muses
With raptures, into a second[33] them infuses;

20 2 bays: in ancient Rome poetic achievement was marked by a crown made of bay leaves (a laurel crown)
21 4 Pied: patched, motley; the "idiots" of this line are poets who write incoherent works, perhaps assembling incongruous scraps from other poets
22 5 changelings: impostors
23 6 Hippocrene: a spring on Mount Helicon, sacred to the muses
24 9 Phoebus: the sun god (Apollo in the Roman tradition), famed for his many loves
25 20 greasy-apron: a pejorative term for the working class; foul linen and greasy aprons were signs of manual labor
26 21 thunder that plucks bays: bay leaves supposedly protected against thunder, but as the laurels (see line 2) are unmerited, the unnatural punishment applies
27 23 Pallas' shield: Pallas (Athena) gave Perseus a polished shield in which he could see Medusa's reflection without gazing directly at her and turning to stone
28 24 crammed third day: the playwright's benefit (percentage of receipts) from the third performance
29 25–6 Let those … by it: the Phrygian King Midas preferred Pan's rustic pipe playing to Apollo's skill with the lyre, and was accordingly punished by having his human ears replaced by the long ears of an ass as a marker of stupidity
30 27 impostumed: swollen, ulcerated
31 33 adamantine: unbreakable, like the strong rock adamant
32 33–4 creatures … of th' hammer: Hoy suggests the mythological Cyclops, a race of one-eyed giants famed for their craftsmanship, who lived a rustic existence
33 38 into a second: i.e. into someone else's breast

Can give an actor sorrow, rage, joy, passion,
Whilst he again by self-same agitation
Commands the hearers, sometimes drawing out tears,
Then smiles, and fills them both with hopes and fears.
That man give me, and to be such a one
Our poet this day strives, or to be none.
Lend not him hands for pity but for merit:
If he please, he's crowned; if not, his fate must bear it.

[Scene i]

Enter at the sound of hellish music, PLUTO[34] *and* CHARON

PLUTO Ha!
CHARON So.
PLUTO What so?
CHARON I'll be thy slave no longer.
PLUTO What slave?
CHARON Hell's drudge, her galley-slave.[35] I ha' wore
My flesh to th' bones, bones marrowless, at the oar
Tugging to waft to thy Stygian[36] empire souls
Which, but for Charon, never had come in shoals,
Yet (swarmed they ne'er so) them on shore I set.
Hell gets by[37] Charon, what does Charon get?
PLUTO His fare.[38]
CHARON Scurvy fare, I'll first cry garlic.[39]
PLUTO Do!
And make Hell stink, as that does hither.
CHARON If I do!
Some like that smell. My boat to shore I'll pull,
Not work a stroke more.
PLUTO How?
CHARON Not touch a scull.[40]
PLUTO Why?
CHARON I have no doings;[41] Gravesend barge[42] has more,
And carries as good as any are in Hell.
I fear th' infernal rivers are frozen o'er,
So few by water come: else the whores that dwell
Next door to Hell go about.[43] Besides, 'tis thought
That men to find Hell, now, new ways have sought,
As Spaniards did to the Indies. Pluto, mend

34 0 SD PLUTO: Pluto seems to be a name used by Dekker for the character also assigned the speech-prefix "Lucifer" in sc.xi in Q; the changed name may thus be the product of Dekker's "more garnished frontispiece" (i.e. revised framing) for the Queen's company. This edition standardizes the character's name as Pluto

35 2 galley-slave: a particularly painful type of slavery, working the oar in the galley of a boat

36 4 Stygian: infernal (having to do with the Styx, one of the rivers of the classical underworld)

37 7 gets by: benefits from

38 8 fare: Charon was the ferryman of the underworld, carrying souls across the rivers dividing the worlds of the living and dead, for a fee

39 8 cry garlic: Charon regards his monetary fare for ferrying souls across the underworld river as too low; he puns here on "fare" as "food," suggesting its shabbiness needs rectifying through the provision of flavoring (garlic)

40 11 scull: a kind of oar

41 12 no doings: nothing to do; Hell has a shortage of souls for Charon to ferry

42 12 Gravesend barge: the point of departure from London to the continent

43 16 go about: prostitutes plying their trade are keeping damned souls too busy to find their way to Hell. Possibly "go about" is also intended in the nautical sense of setting on the opposite tack, or executing an about turn, i.e. even those once close to Hell have set a new course for themselves and won't be ferried to the underworld

My wages, or row thy self.
PLUTO Ugly, grumbling slave,
Have I not raised thy price? Yet still dost crave?
Such bold brave beggars (heard of ne'er before)
Are thy fares now, they teach thee to beg more.
Thy fare was first a halfpenny, then the souls gave thee
A penny, then three halfpence. We shall have thee
(As market-folks in dearth[44]) so damnèd dear,
Men will not come to Hell, crying out they're here
Worse racked than they're in taverns. Why dost howl?
CHARON For money. I'll have two pence for each soul
I ferry over. I'm old, crazed stiff, and lamed.
That soul that's not worth two pence, would 'twere damned.
PLUTO Thou shalt not.
CHARON I will have it or lie still.
If Charon fill Hell, Hell shall Charon fill,
For ghosts now come not thronging to my boat
But drop by one and one in. None of note
Are fares now: I had wont brave fellows to ply,
Who, hacked and mangled, did in battles die.[45]
But now these gallants which do walk Hell's rounds
Are fuller of diseases than of wounds.
If wounded any take my boat, they roar,
Being stabbed, either drunk or slain about some whore.
That's all the fight now.
PRODIGAL (*Within*) Charon.
PLUTO Get thee gone:
Thou'rt called for.
PRODIGAL [*Within*] Charon.
CHARON Bawl not. I'll come anon.
Hags of Hell gnaw thee with their foul furred[46] gums.
Pluto, no wonder if so few hither comes?
[PLUTO] Why?
[CHARON] Gingerly: see, see,
One of thine own promoters[47] (with hawks' eyes,
That should for prey be watching) here snoring lies.
PLUTO With a mischief![48] Cabined![49] A fury.[50]
CHARON I'll ferret out more.

RUFFMAN *comes up,* [*a*] FURY *enters*

CHARON Another! Look, dancing[51] a bawd on's knee.

Enter SHACKLE-SOUL, *comes up*

SHACKLE-SOUL I do enquire if rich bawds carted[52] be

44 25 market-folks in dearth: vendors raising prices during times of low supply
45 35–6 had wont . . . battles die: Charon had previously been accustomed to applying himself to ferrying the souls of men who died valiantly in battle
46 43 furred: encrusted with morbid matter
47 47 promoters: one who prosecutes or informs; a professional accuser
48 49 With a mischief: exclamation of impatience
49 49 Cabined: confined in a narrow space (i.e. the promoter is sleeping snuggled up tight)
50 49 fury: avenging deity sent from Tartarus to punish crime
51 51 dancing: dandling, bouncing
52 52 carted: carried in a cart as punishment

On earth as well as poor ones? I sleep not, Pluto.
PLUTO Twist stronger-knotted whips, I'll wake you, slaves! GRUMBALL[53] *and another spirit comes up*
CHARON Two of thy sumners[54] dead-drunk here too.
GRUMBALL Thou liest.
[PRODIGAL (*Within*)] Charon.
CHARON I come. If I must work, let these
Thy prentices ply their occupation;
T'uphold Hell's kingdom, more must work than one. *Exit*
PLUTO Ha! Are there whipping-posts for such as dwell
In idleness on Earth, and yet shall Hell
(As if we took bribes here too) let such pass?
I'll have you tawed.[55] Is not the world as 'twas?
Once mother of rapes, incests, and sodomies,
Atheism and blasphemies; plump boys indeed,
That sucked our dam's breast. Is she now barren? Ha!
Is there a dearth of villains?
OMNES[56] More now than ever!
PLUTO Is there such penury[57] of mankind hellhounds,
You can lie snoring?
RUFFMAN Each land is full of rakehells.[58]
SHACKLE-SOUL But shoals of sharks eat up the fish at sea.
GRUMBALL Brave pitchy villains there.
PLUTO Yet you playing here.
OMNES No, no, most awful Pluto.
PLUTO Were you good hellhounds, every day should be
A Simon-and-Jude,[59] to crown our board with feasts
Of black-eyed souls each minute. Were you honest devils,
Each officer in Hell should have at least
A brace of whores to his breakfast; above us dwell
Devils braver and more subtle than in Hell.
OMNES We'll fill thy palace with them.
PLUTO I'll try[60] that. Go
Ruffman, take instantly a courtier's shape
Of any country: choose thine own disguise
And return swiftly.
RUFFMAN Yes. *Exit*
PLUTO Shackle-Soul, wear thou
A friar's grave habit.
SHACKLE-SOUL Well. *Exit*
PLUTO Grumball, walk thou
In treble-ruffs[61] like a merchant.
GRUMBALL So. 'Tis done. *Exit*
PLUTO The bars of our litigious courts had wont
To crack with thronging pleaders, whose loud din

53 54 SD GRUMBALL: see Introduction on the naming of Grumball/Lurchall in Q
54 55 sumners: men employed to summon persons to court
55 62 tawed: whipped or thrashed
56 66 SP OMNES: all (Latin)
57 67 penury: dearth
58 68 rakehells: scoundrels
59 73 Simon-and-Jude: a feast day (October 28) during which soul cakes were prepared in anticipation of the feast of All Souls; Simon and Jude were apostles who were martyred together
60 78 try: ascertain the truth of
61 83 treble-ruffs: particularly elaborate detachable frills worn around and standing out from the neck

Shook the infernal Hell, as if't had been
An earthquake bursting from the deep abyss,
Or else Jove's thunder, thrown at the head of Dis
(The god of gold) for hiding it below,
Thereby to tempt churls hither. Nor did we know
What a vacation meant: continual term
Fattened Hell's lawyers, and shall so again.

Enter RUFFMAN, SHACKLE-SOUL *and* GRUMBALL [*all now disguised*]

RUFFMAN Here.
SHACKLE-SOUL Here.
LURCHALL Command us.
PLUTO Fly into the world:
As y'are in shapes transformed, be so in name,
For men are outsides only. Be you the same.
Hie thee to Naples, Ruffman; thou shalt find
A prince there, newly crowned, aptly inclined
To any bendings.[62] Lest his youthful brows
Reach at stars only, weigh down his loftiest boughs
With leaden plummets,[63] poison his best thoughts with taste
Of things most sensual; if the heart once waste,
The body feels consumption. Good or bad kings
Breed subjects like them; clear streams flow from clear springs.
Turn therefore Naples to a puddle with a civil,
Much-promising face and (well-oiled)[64] play the court devil.
RUFFMAN I'll do't in bravery. If as deep as Hell
Thy large ears hear a land curse me, my part's played well.
PLUTO Fly, Shackle-Soul.
SHACKLE-SOUL Whither?
PLUTO To the friary
Best-famed in Naples for strict orders. Throw
What nets thou seest can catch them. Amongst 'em sow
Seeds of contention or whatever sin
They most abhor. Sweat thou to bring that in.
SHACKLE-SOUL A wolf in lambskin leaps into the rout,[65]
Bell, book, or candle[66] cannot curse me out:
I'll curse faster than they.
PLUTO Do. Grumball!
GRUMBALL Here.
PLUTO Be thou a city-devil, make thy hands
Of harpies' claws, which being on courtiers' lands
Once fastened, ne'er let loose; the merchant play,
And on the Burse,[67] see thou thy flag display
Of politic bankruptism.[68] Train up[69] as many
To fight under it as thou canst, for now's not any
That break (they'll break their necks first). If beside

62 97–8 aptly inclined/To any bendings: open to any suggestion/manipulation
63 100 leaden plummets: balls or lumps of lead
64 105 well-oiled: figuratively, operating smoothly
65 113 rout: flock of animals (typically used of wild animals such as wolves)
66 114 Bell, book, or candle: referring to the closing lines of a popular form of excommunication
67 119 the Burse: meeting place for merchants
68 120 politic bankruptism: judicious or contrived bankruptcy
69 120 Train up: lure

Thou canst not through the whole city meet with pride,
Riot, lechery, envy, avarice, and such stuff,
Bring 'em all in, coached; the gates are wide enough.
The spirit of gold instruct thee: hence all.
OMNES Fly!
PLUTO Stay, lest you should want helpers, at your calling
Any devils shall come: Starch-Hound,[70] Tobacco-Spawling,[71]
Upshotten,[72] Suckland,[73] Glitterback[74] or any
Whom you shall need to employ. But call not many,
There's but few good in Hell. And stay, remember
We all meet to hear how you prosper.
OMNES Where?
PLUTO The tree
Blasted with goblins, that about whose root
Five mandrakes grow, i' th' grove by Naples there.
Meet there.
OMNES We shall.
PLUTO Our blessings with you bear.
RUFFMAN Dread King of Ghosts,[75] we'll ply our thrift so well,
Thou shalt be forced to enlarge thy jail of Hell.
PLUTO Be quick thou'rt best, let saucy mortals know
Howe'er they sleep, there's one wakes here below.

Exeunt

[Scene ii]

Enter ALFONSO (*King of Naples*) *crowned, wearing robes imperial; swords of state, maces etc. being borne before him by* OCTAVIO [*and*] ASTOLFO (*two uncles*), NARCISSO, JOVINELLI [*and*] BRISCO (*Counts*), *with others; Count* SPENDOLA *meeting them*

SPENDOLA One of those gallant troops went forth[76] to meet
Your admired mistress (Ermenhild the fair)
Hath left your convoy with her on the way.
ALFONSO And brings glad news of her being here this day.
Let cannons tell in thunder her arrival,
When she's at hand ourself will meet her.
OMNES On. [*Flourish.*] *He takes his seat; all kneel*
ALFONSO Pray rise. Until about our brows were thrown
These sparkling beams, such adoration
Was not bestowed on us: whom does the knee
Thus lowly worship? This idol, gold; or me?
Indeed 'tis the world's saint. If that you adore,
Go, pray to your coffers. None to us shall bow,
Give God your knees.
OCTAVIO Whose own voice does allow
That subjects should to those who are supreme
Bend, as to God, all kings being like to him.
ASTOLFO Thou wonder of thy time, I'll pay no more
To thee of duty than has been before

70 128 Starch-Hound: the name probably alludes to gallants using excessive starch in their clothing (i.e. being overly concerned about their appearance)
71 128 Tobacco-Spawling: spitting and spawling (to spit copiously, coarsely) were common methods of taking tobacco
72 129 Upshotten: uncertain meaning
73 129 Suckland: the name has connotations of exploiting or draining resources (sucking the land dry)
74 129 Glitterback: presumably so named because his back shines brilliantly. As will be clear in Scene viii, he is a demon of gold
75 136 Ghosts: i.e. devils, spirits
76 1 troops went forth: i.e. troops that went forth

And ever shall be paid to those sit high.
ALFONSO Pray mock not me with such idolatry.
Kings gods are, I confess, but gods of clay,
Brittle as you are, you as good as they,
Only in weight they differ this poor dram,[77]
Yet all but flesh and blood; and such I am.
If such, pray let me eat, drink, speak and walk,
Not looked clean through with superstitious eyes,
Not stared at like a comet. As you go
Or speak, or feed unwondered at, let me so.
OCTAVIO Not kings of ceremony?[78]
ALFONSO Uncle, what then?
Still are they kings.[79]
OCTAVIO But show like common men.
ALFONSO Good uncle know, no sun in this our sphere
Shall rule but we. Let others shine as clear
In goodness, none in greatness shall.
ASTOLFO Blessed reign!
The golden world[80] is molding new again.[81]
ALFONSO All that I crave is this, and 'tis not new:
Pay unto Caesar only Caesar's due.
OCTAVIO We owe thee loyal hearts and those we'll pay
Each minute, mirror of kings.
JOVINELLI Mark, the old lords promise their hearts, but no money.
OCTAVIO Here are the names of bold conspirators,
Young Catilines[82] and far more desperate,
Who in your father's days kindled the fires
Of hot rebellion.
ALFONSO Which are now burnt out.
OCTAVIO Who knows that?[83] Embers in dead ashes lie.
King, set thy hand to this, let traitors die.
ASTOLFO 'Tis fit you should do so.
OCTAVIO Sound policy.
ALFONSO Men many things hold fit that are not good:
A young beginner and set up in blood![84]
Butchers can do no more. Shall records say
Being crowned, he played the tyrant the first day?
How should that chronicler be cursed? Your paper.
When such a fatal book comes in my sight,
I'll with Vespasian[85] wish I could not write.
Their bond is canceled, I forgive the debt.
See that at liberty they all be set.
OMNES A princely act.
OCTAVIO If wisely, 'tis well done.

77 22 dram: i.e. a small amount (from the measure used by apothecaries)

78 28 Not kings of ceremony: i.e. you do not want to be like those kings who insist, through formalities and ceremoniousness, on their difference from "common men" (line 29)? See Shakespeare, *Henry V*: "what have kings that privates have not too,/Save ceremony" (IV.i. 230–31)

79 28–9 Uncle, what . . . they kings: what of it? Even without ceremony, kings are still kings

80 33 golden world: time of prosperity (golden age)

81 33 molding new again: forming anew

82 40 Catilines: Catiline was a Roman senator who conspired to overthrow the Republic in 63 BC

83 43 Who knows that?: how can we be certain?

84 47 Just a novice and already have blood on my hands!

85 52 Vespasian: Roman emperor, reigned AD 69–79, who bestowed gifts on writers (who in turn praised him in their writings) and punished those who did not represent him favorably

SPENDOLA That reign must boast, which mercy has begun.
ALFONSO Bear witness all, what pace the chariot wheels
Of our new-gilded sovereignty shall run.
BRISCO A main gallop[86] I hope.
ALFONSO And here I vow to end as 'tis begun.
ASTOLFO Heaven fill thee full of days, but (being all told)
Ending no worse, their sum we'll write in gold.
OCTAVIO The course you'll take dear lord?
ALFONSO This: pray observe it.
JOVINELLI Call you this Coronation Day? Would I were i' th' streets where the conduits run claret wine,[87] there's some good fellowship.
OCTAVIO Peace.
ALFONSO Each week within the year shall be a book
Which each day I'll read o'er: I well may do't,
The book being but six leaves (six days), the seventh
Be his that owes[88] it. Sacred is that and high;
And who profanes one hour in that, shall die.
SPENDOLA How many will be left alive then, this day fortnight?
OCTAVIO First, beat all taverns down, then—souls are lost
(Being drowned in surfeits) on that seventh day most.
Stay, best of kings, mine own hand shall set down
What laws thou mad'st first day thou wor'st a crown.
Begin, begin thy week.
ALFONSO Write Monday.
OCTAVIO So, so— [*Writes*] Monday.
JOVINELLI They say Monday's Shoemakers' holiday, I'll fall to that trade.
OCTAVIO I have writ it down, my liege.
JOVINELLI Peace, harken to your lesson.
ALFONSO That day, from morn till night, I'll execute
The office of a judge, and weigh outlaws
With even scales.
JOVINELLI That's more than grocers do.
ALFONSO The poor and rich man's cause
I'll peise[89] alike: it shall be my chief care
That bribes and wrangling be pitched o'er the bar.[90]
JOVINELLI We shall have old[91] breaking of necks then.
ALFONSO Down with that first.
OCTAVIO [*Writing*] Oh, for a pen of gold!
You'll have no bribes.
ALFONSO None.
OCTAVIO Yet term-time[92] all the year!
A good strong lawsuit cannot now cost dear.
ALFONSO Have you done?
OCTAVIO [*Writing*] I'm at bribes, and wrangling; done presently.
NARCISSO We must all turn pettifoggers,[93] and instead of gilt rapiers, hang buckram-bags[94] at our girdles.

86 59 main gallop: full gallop
87 64–5 conduits run claret wine: fountains and conduits of wine were a tradition at royal entries and mayoral pageants in London
88 70 owes: owns, i.e. the seventh day belongs to God
89 88 peise: weigh
90 89 pitched o'er the bar: thrown out of court
91 90 old: great
92 92 term-time: the period in which a law court is in session
93 96 pettifoggers: inferior lawyers dealing with petty cases
94 96 buckram-bags: specifically, lawyers' bags

JOVINELLI All my clients shall be women.
SPENDOLA Why?
JOVINELLI Because they are easiest fetched over: there's something to be gotten out of them.
OCTAVIO Thy Monday's task is done. What's next?
JOVINELLI Sunday, if the week goes backward.
ALFONSO Tuesdays we'll sit to hear the poor-man's cries,
Orphans' and widows'; our own princely eyes
Shall their petitions read. Our progress then
Shall be to hospitals which good-minded men
Have built to pious use for lame, sick, and poor.
We'll see what's given, what spent and what flows o'er.
Churls[95] with God's money shall not feast, swill wine,
And fat their rank guts whilst poor wretches pine.
JOVINELLI This is a brave world for beggars, if it hold.
OCTAVIO [*Writing*] Poor wretches pine, so are they left. To the next.
ALFONSO Wednesdays we'll spend—
JOVINELLI In fish dinners.
ALFONSO —in th'affairs
Of foreign states, treat[96] with embassadors,
Hear them and give them answers. Thursday, for wars.
JOVINELLI That's well: better be together by th' ears,[97] than to go halting to hospitals.
ALFONSO Our Neapolitan youths that day shall try
Their skill in arms. Poor scornèd soldiers
Shall not be suffered beg here as in some lands,
Nor stoop, slave-like, to captains' proud commands,
Starve and lie nasty, when the self-same pay
The soldier fights for keeps the leaders gay.
Nor shall he through ice and fire make grey his head,
Wear out new moons, only to earn his bread;
Wade up to th' beard in torrents and be drowned
All save the head; march hard to meet a wound
I' th' very face and even his heart-strings crack
To win a town, yet not to clothe his back.
And the black storm of troubles being gone,
Shunned like a creditor, not looked upon
But as court-palates when bright day draws nigh,
Rolled up in some dark corner is thrown by.[98]
Uncle write that.
OCTAVIO [*Writing*] Fast as my pen can trot.
SPENDOLA What a number of tottered rogues will be turned into brave fellows at this new change of the moon.
JOVINELLI The braver they are, the sooner are mercers undone.[99]
OCTAVIO Soldiers are down too.
ALFONSO Down with[100] learning next.
For Friday shall be spent i' th' reverend schools,
Where we'll sift bran from flour, hiss babbling fools

95 110 Churls: term of disparagement for the lower class
96 115 treat: speak, negotiate
97 117 together by th' ears: fighting
98 132–3 court-palates . . . thrown by: perhaps a reference to elitist taste in clothes, worn to extravagant evening events but less appropriate by the light of day (hence "thrown by")
99 137 Mercers trade in cloth and fabrics; "braver" thus puns on "having courage" and being "finely dressed," while "undone" puns on "being brought to ruin" and "becoming unfastened or untied"
100 138 Down with: write down

But crown the deep-brained disputant. None shall hold
Three or four church-livings (got by simonious[101] gold)
In them, to fat himself as in a sty,
When greater scholars languish in beggary
And in thin, thread-bare cassocks[102] wear out their age
And bury their worth in some by[103] vicarage:
This we'll see mended.
JOVINELLI Tithe-pigs,[104] you'll smoke for this.
ALFONSO So set it down.
OCTAVIO [*Writes*] Scholars languish in beggary—so:
Thy Friday's law is writ; for Saturday, what?
ALFONSO Aye, marry sir, all our cares now for that.
Well to begin and not end so were base,
The winning of the goal crowns each man's race.

NARCISSO *stepping in before in the scene,*[105] *enters here*

NARCISSO Sir, there's a stranger newly arrived your court,
And much importunes to behold your highness.
ALFONSO What is he?
NARCISSO Of goodly presence.
ALFONSO Let him see us.

RUFFMAN [*disguised as Shalkan* BOHOR, *a Helvetian courtier*] *brought in by all*

BOHOR The powers that guide me, guard thee. I have heard thy name
In regions far hence, where it does resound
Louder than here at home; to touch this ground
I ha' passed through countries into which none here
Would willingly sail, I think, and with me bring
My love and service, which to your grace I tender.
ALFONSO What are you, and whence come you?
BOHOR From Helvetia.[106]
SPENDOLA What hell says he?
JOVINELLI Peace, you shall know hot hell time enough.
BOHOR I am an Helvetian born, the house from which I am descended, ancient and well known to many princes. Bohor is my name.
JOVINELLI [*Aside*] Zounds! Bohor! H'as struck two of my teeth out[107] with his name.
BOHOR A Shalkan Tartar[108] being my grandfather,
Men call me Shalkan Bohor. About the world
My travels make a girdle perfect round,
So that what wonders kings on earth ever found
I know, and what I know is yours.
ALFONSO Brave Helvetian,
We give you thanks and welcome: your arrival
Is fair and to our wish. Of all those days
Which Time sets down, to number up a week,

101 142 simonious: pertaining to the selling of ecclesiastical preferments (e.g. pardons)
102 145 cassocks: loose gowns worn by poor scholars
103 146 by: out of the way
104 148 Tithe-pigs: pigs taken as tithe (the tenth part of annual agricultural produce, due as payment in support of religious establishments)
105 154 SD *stepping in . . . the scene*: Narcisso is visible to the playgoers before he assumes a role in the action
106 164 Helvetia: i.e. Switzerland
107 169 struck two of my teeth out: the sense seems to be that the mere utterance of Bohor's name has dealt a blow to Jovinelli, knocking out two teeth
108 170 Shalkan Tartar: a member of a people who lived near the Caspian Sea

Every day have we tasked, save only one.
How in these courts of kings, through which you have gone,
Do princes waste their hours?
BOHOR How but in that
For which they are born kings? Pleasure. Every man's aim
Is to hit pleasure; only 'tis changed in name,
That's all the difference. Are kings tyrants? Blood
Is then their pleasure. Thirst they after wars?
Ambition tickles them. That for which man most cares,
Good or bad, 'tis his pleasure, and to gain it
His soul must compass it, though hell restrain it.
To this mark all men's thoughts creation drew,
That all might strive for a thing that's got by few:
Who are those few but kings? And 'tis fit they
Should have it, because true pleasure does soon decay.
ALFONSO How like you his counsel?
OMNES Rarely.
OCTAVIO What ruffian's this?
ALFONSO Bohor, th'ast warmed our young blood. All cares of state
Shall that day sleep; to ourself we'll Saturday have.
Pleasure, the slave of kings, shall then be our slave.
Lords, let there be a proclamation drawn,
What man soever, strange or native born,
Can feast our spleen[109] and heighten our delight,
He shall have gold and be our favorite.
Tilts, tourneys, masques, plays, dancing, drinking deep
Though ere noon all Naples lie dead-drunk asleep.
OCTAVIO How, King?
ALFONSO We'll have it so, uncle.
OMNES Down with that too.
JOVINELLI Print Saturday in great text letters.
OCTAVIO Well, well, it shall.
[*Aside*] Our swan turns crow, poisoned with one drop of gall.
ALFONSO I'll have this proclamation forthwith drawn.
NARCISSO And publish all the days.
BRISCO And Saturday.
JOVINELLI Especially that at large if you can, in red, like a Dominical letter.[110]
ALFONSO Go see it done.
JOVINELLI My task. *Exit*
ALFONSO Why sigh you? Of six days would you not spare me one?
OCTAVIO Thine own laws from thine own mouth we'll proclaim,
If thine own words thou eat'st, be't thine own shame.

Enter JOVINELLI *hastily*

JOVINELLI Your long expected happiness is arrived,
The Princess of Calabria.
ALFONSO Thou crown'st me again.
Dear uncle, honored lords, with our whole court
Honor her hither. I am rapt with joy,
And lost till I behold her. Fetch me my love.
OCTAVIO I fear deep whirlpools though it run smooth above.

109 198 spleen: the organ associated with laughter and mirth
110 211 Dominical letter: the letter used to denote Sundays in a particular year was printed in red (or larger type)

ALFONSO To our worthy friend, your welcomes. *Exeunt* OCTAVIO *and* ASTOLFO
JOVINELLI But pray sir, tell us, mean you that we indeed
Shall have but one playing day through the whole week?
ALFONSO All Jovinelli, we'll be jovial all.
BRISCO Till Saturday came, we lived in terrible fear.
Thank Bohor, who your dead spirits up did rear.
ALFONSO Had I (as first I did begin) gone on,
I like a schoolboy should have worn my crown,
As if I had borrowed it.
BOHOR Had been most vile.
ALFONSO I'll be a sea: boundless.
SPENDOLA Thou art a sun,
And let no base clouds muffle thee.
ALFONSO Brave kings all!
Crown, scepter, court, city, country, are at your call.
JOVINELLI There spake young Jove indeed.
BRISCO The tide now turns.
NARCISSO And now we'll swim.
ALFONSO And laugh, though the whole world mourns. *Flourish*
OMNES Tantara,[111] hey. *Trumpets.* ERMENHILD *brought in*

Enter OCTAVIO *and* ASTOLFO, *ushering* ERMENHILD,[112] *attended by Ladies and others*

NARCISSO Call up your lustiest[113] spirits: the lady's come.
ALFONSO O my earthly bliss! Embraces! Kisses! How sweet
Are you to parted lovers when they meet?
That entertainment which the duke your father
Lent royally (late to me) I now can pay
At a king's charge. To our Neapolitan court
None, brightest Ermenhild, can come longed for
More than yourself. You have stol'n upon us, lady.
ERMENHILD You have good law against me, playing the thief;
Your grace may keep me prisoner.
ALFONSO In these arms;
From whence not Jove shall ransom thee. We twain
Will wed, and bed, and get a prince shall reign
In Naples bravely when we both lie dead:
Till then, pleasure's wings to their full breadth be spread.
Exeunt

[Scene iii]

Enter SCUMBROTH, *ringing a bell;* ALPHEGE (*a friar*), *and* SHACKLE-SOUL [*as Friar* RUSH], *in a friar's weed,*[114] *with cloth to lay*[115]

SCUMBROTH A mangier, a mangier, a mangier—I must needs have a mangy voice, when I do nothing but bawl for a company of hungry scabs. A mangier—
ALPHEGE You must be nimble Rush.

111 237 Tantara: imitating the trumpet fanfare
112 237 SD *ushering* ERMENHILD: this apparently redundant entrance direction for Ermenhild (see "ERMENHILD *brought in*" immediately above) may be explained by the fact that the MS behind Q appears authorial with theatrical markings; alternatively she might enter and then be escorted further down the stage by the others
113 238 lustiest: merriest, most pleasing
114 0 SD *weed*: garment
115 0 SD *cloth to lay*: i.e. a tablecloth

RUSH As a drawer in a new tavern, first day the bush[116] is hung up.
SCUMBROTH A mangier, a manger, a mangier . . . *Exit*
ALPHEGE So, the Lord Prior's napkin here, there the Subprior's, his knife and case of pick-tooths thus. As for the convent, let them lick their fingers instead of wiping, and suck their teeth instead of picking.
RUSH What other duty, sir, must I call mine?
ALPHEGE As you are novice,[117] you are to say grace demurely, wait on the Prior's trencher[118] soberly, steal away a mouthful cunningly, and munch it up in a corner hungrily. Ply your office, Rush. *Exit*
RUSH Thanks, good Friar Alphege. Yes, Shackle-Soul will ply
The task he's set to: devils never idle lie.
Friar Rush! Ha, ha! Y'have now an excellent choir
To sing in Hell, the devil and the friar.

Enter PRIOR, SUPBRIOR, ALPHEGE, HILARY[119] *and other friars. All sit. Dishes brought in before*

PRIOR Where's Rush, our junior novice?
RUSH Here, Lord Prior.
PRIOR Stand forth and render thanks.
RUSH Hum, hum.
For our bread, wine, ale and beer,
For the piping hot meats here;
For broths of sundry tastes and sort,
For beef, veal, mutton, lamb, and pork;
Green sauce[120] with calf's head and bacon,
Pig and goose, and crammed-up capon.
For paste raised stiff with curious art,[121]
Pie, custard, Florentine, and tart,
Baked rumps, fried kidneys, and lamb-stones,[122]
Fat sweetbreads, luscious marrowbones,
Artichoke, and oyster pies,
Buttered crab, prawns, lobsters' thighs:
Thanks be given for flesh and fishes,
With this choice of tempting dishes.
To which preface, with blithe[123] looks sit ye,
Rush bids this convent, much good do't ye.
PRIOR How dar'st thou mock us, thou ill-nurtured slave?
SUBPRIOR Contemn'st thou our order and religious fare?
[SCUMBROTH] He has spoken treason to all our stomachs.
OMNES Down with the villain.
SUBPRIOR Mischief on us waits
If we feed so vile a wretch.
PRIOR Thrust him out at gates.
RUSH I do conjure you by my hallowed beads
To hear me speak.
PRIOR Canst thou excuse thyself?
RUSH Alas, my lord, I thought it had been here

116 4 bush: a vintner's bush, hung at a tavern door, advertised the availability of wine to drink
117 10 novice: candidate for admission into a religious order
118 11 trencher: a flat board or wooden plate
119 16 SD HILARY: only speaks collectively with the other friars
120 23 Green sauce: a sauce made from herbs (especially sorrel), vinegar, and sugar; eaten with meat
121 25 paste raised . . . curious art: pastry dough molded into ornate shapes
122 27 lamb-stones: lamb testicles
123 33 blithe: kind, friendly

As in the neighboring churches, where the poor'st vicar
Is filled up to the chin with choice of meats,
Yet seeks new ways to whet dull appetite,
As there with holy spells men's souls they cherish,
So with delicious fare, they themselves nourish.
Nor want they argument for sweet belly-cheer
To prove it lawful.
SUBPRIOR Most profane and fearful.
RUSH But since your order, pious and reverend,
Tied to religious fasts, spends the sad day
Wholly in meagre contemplation,
I absolution[124] beg on both my knees
For what my tongue offended in. 'Las![125] Poor Rush
(See't by his cheeks) eats little. I can feed
On roots and drink the water of the spring
Out of mine own cup. Make an anatomy
Of my most sinful carcass, then pardon me.
PRIOR Thy ignorance is thy pardon, we believe thee.
RUSH *Gratias, reverende domine Prior.*[126]
PRIOR But do our brethren in parts more remote
Feed so delicious say'st thou?
RUSH Rush cannot lie.
SUBPRIOR Thou falsely dost accuse those holy men.
PRIOR How can it stand with their profession?
SUBPRIOR Thou say'st, vile youngman, they have arguments
To prove it lawful gluttonously to feed.
OMNES Rush, answer the Subprior.
RUSH *Audite, fratres*:[127] they do not only prove it lawful, but make it palpable, that he who eats not good meat is damned.
SUBPRIOR *Benedicite.*[128]
SCUMBROTH What shall become of all us then?
PRIOR Thou art distracted, whence canst thou force argument?
RUSH From silly[129] reason, would you hear me speak?
PRIOR Speak freely and be bold. Listen.
OMNES Hum, hum, hum.
RUSH He that eats not good meat is damned; *sic disputo.*[130]
If he that feeds well hath a good soul, then *e contra.*[131]
No, he that feeds ill hath a bad and a poor soul.
SCUMBROTH That's we.
RUSH And so consequently is damned, for who regards poor souls? And if they be not regarded, they are cast forth, and if cast forth, then they are damned.
SUBPRIOR I deny your minor;[132] he that feeds well hath a good soul.
RUSH *Sic probo*:[133] the soul follows the temperature of the body, he that feeds well hath a good temperature of body, *ergo*,[134] he that feeds well hath a good soul.

124 53 absolution: forgiveness
125 54 'Las: i.e. alas
126 60 Thanks, reverend father Prior (Latin)
127 68 *Audite fratres*: Listen, brothers (Latin)
128 70 Bless you (Latin)
129 73 silly: plain, simple
130 76 *sic disputo*: I argue it thus (Latin)
131 77 *e contra*: conversely (Latin)
132 82 minor: minor premise (of Shackle-Soul's syllogistic argument)
133 83 *Sic probo*: I prove it thus (Latin)
134 84 *ergo*: therefore

PRIOR A full and edifying argument.
OMNES Hum, hum, hum.
SUBPRIOR I deny that the soul follows the temperature of the body.
RUSH *Anima sequitur temperaturam corporis,*[135] it is a principle, *et contra principia non est disputandum.*[136]
[SCUMBROTH All we.][137]
PRIOR It's most apparent.
SCUMBROTH Oh most learned Rush!
SUBPRIOR A shallow sophister, hear me farther.
PRIOR Subprior, we'll hear the rest disputed at our leisure: you take too much upon you.
SCUMBROTH Shall I take this upon me my lord?
PRIOR Hence with this trash. We have too long forborne to taste heaven's blessings fully, which to our duty had more enabled us. Rush, thou'rt some angel.
SUBPRIOR Rather some devil sent to bewitch our souls.
PRIOR Subprior, no more.
SUBPRIOR I must speak. Hear me brethren,
Shall we, bound by solemn oaths t'abjure the world
And all her sorceries, to whom night and day
Are as one hour of prayer, whose temperance makes us
Endure what full-filled belly-gods[138] admire;
Shall we, by zealous patrons tied to observe
Dirges and requiems for their peaceful souls,
In gluttonous riot bury sacred alms?
Turn sanctimonious zeal and charity
To loathsome surfeit? And those well-got goods
Our benefactors saved by their own fasts
And moderate living, shall we feed upon,
Full-gorging us till we vomit? Forefend it heaven!
By all the saints, by him first taught our order
What temperance was, here shall poor Clement feed,
Till his o'er-wearied life takes her last leave
Of this all-tempting world where all sins breed.
PRIOR How's this? Are you become our confessor?
Best thrust us out at gates, lock up the cloister,
And call in whom you like. Be you the Prior.
Speak: are you agreed Rush be our master-cook?
SCUMBROTH You have my voice.
ALPHEGE And mine.
PRIOR Do you all consent?
OMNES Yes, all.
SUBPRIOR First send this fiend to banishment.
PRIOR We have most voices on our side.
SUBPRIOR You may;
'Las! Most men covet still the broadest way.
PRIOR Give Rush his charge then. Scumbroth, you must resign.
SCUMBROTH With a good maw[139]—I shall have a fatter office[140] to be his scullion.[141]

135 88 *Anima . . . corporis*: Latin translation of the previous line, "the soul follows the temperature of the body"
136 88–9 *et contra . . . est disputandum*: and there is no disputing the principle (Latin)
137 90 [SCUMBROTH All we]: meaning obscure. In Q, these lines are erroneously printed as part of Rush's Latin speech immediately preceding. Bowers attributes them to Scumbroth, presumably because they echo his "That's we" at line 79. Possibly Scumbroth simply does not understand what Rush has just said but replies as though he does; or possibly this phrase was intended for another part of the scene (e.g. following line 81) and misprinted
138 103 belly-gods: gluttons; those who make gods of their bellies
139 125 maw: appetite, inclination
140 125 fatter office: position or post with greater opportunity or reward
141 125 scullion: kitchen servant

RUSH Worthy Lord Prior, hear me yet.
I must not my profession let[142]
To Scumbroth. What I know I'll teach:
To make caudles,[143] jellies, leach
Syrup of violets and of roses,
Cowslip salads and kick-choses,[144]
Preserve the apricot and cherry,
Damson pear-plum,[145] raspberry;
Potatoes eke[146] if you shall lack,
To corroborate[147] the back.
A hundred more shall Rush devise,
And yet to early matins[148] rise,
Our Lady's Office[149] sing at prime,
At evensong, and at compline time;[150]
Chant anthems, anniversaries, dirges,
And the doleful *de profundis*.[151]
PRIOR Thou shalt not change thy order. Sirrah cook,
From Rush take lessons against night, for fare
Abundant and delicious.
SCUMBROTH I shall be greedy to learn of him sir; since your lordship is turned, our very jack and his spits[152] shall turn too. *Exit*

Enter two PILGRIMS

PRIOR What men are these?
SUBPRIOR Welcome, good holy fathers.
BOTH Thanks reverend master.
1 PILGRIM Blessed sir, according to the church's rite,
We, pilgrims to Jerusalem bound this night,
Desire repose and pious charity
In your most holy convent.
PRIOR You are most welcome.
Alphege, go lead 'em in.
RUSH By no means.
PRIOR Why?
RUSH 'Tis mortal sin.
SUBPRIOR Oh, black impiety!
PRIOR How? Sin to feed religious votaries!
RUSH Rather to nourish idle vagabonds:
The clergy of other lands have with much piety
And thrift destroyed those drones[153] that lazily
Live eating up the labors of the bee.
A churchman there cares but to feed the soul,

142 127 let: leave
143 129 caudle: a thin (spiced or sweet) gruel, mixed with alcohol and served to the sick
144 131 kick-choses: from French, *quelque chose*; a fancy dish in cookery
145 133 Damson pear-plum: small plum of Syrian (Damascan) origins
146 134 eke: also, in addition
147 135 corroborate: strengthen
148 137 matins: service preceding first mass of the day
149 138 Our Lady's Office: divine service or worship of the Virgin Mary
150 139 compline time: the last service of the day
151 141 *de profundis*: first words of the Latin version of Psalm 130
152 145–6 jack and his spits: a jack was a machine used for turning spit roasts
153 160 drones: non-working male honey-bees

He makes that charge his office. Alms-deeds?[154] Alas!
They through the lawyers' hands are fitt'st to pass.
SUBPRIOR Can you hear this devil?
RUSH Besides, my reverend lord,
These maunderers[155] here are spies and soon bear word
To princes' ears of what they hear and see.
PRIOR Ha, Rush! Thou speak'st right.
SUBPRIOR Damned iniquity!
PRIOR Hence with those runagates.[156]
OMNES Come, hence.
PRIOR Spurn 'em away.
SUBPRIOR Oh, had mine eyes dropped out ere seen this day.
Stay, comfortless poor souls, my pitying tears
Shall speak what my tongue dares not. Hear, holy men:
You ne'er shall say when next we meet again,
Friar Clement to the hungry 'grudged his meat
Or to the weary pilgrim lodging; this makes you eat,
And when you have relieved your fainting limbs,
Commend me in your prayers, and midst your hymns
Thus wish, that he who did your journey further
May never live to break his holy order.
PRIOR Old superstitious dotard;[157] beat hence these beggars.
1 PILGRIM Many old men's curses will on his soul be spent,
Who thus defaces Charity's monument. *Exeunt*
RUSH I told you they were curs that cease to bark
No longer than you feed them.
PRIOR Friar, thou speak'st right:
Make haste with fare delicious, we'll crown the night. *Exeunt. Manet*[158] RUSH
RUSH Ha, ha! Laugh Lucifer,[159] dance grim fiends of Hell,
Of souls thou judge just, but most terrible,
I must exact a double pay from thee.
Ne'er hadst thou journeyman deserved such fee.[160]
Let me cast up my reckonings, what I ha' won
In this first voyage. Charity! She's undone:
Fat gluttony broke her back. Next her stepped in
Contention, who shakes churches; now the sweet sin
Sallow[161] lechery should march after. Avarice,
Murder, and all sins else Hell can devise
I'll broach. The head's in, draw the body after,
Begin thy feast in full cups, end in slaughter.
That damned'st Fury:[162] oh, but Friar Clement's free!
True: hast no snare t'intrap him? Let me see.
He's old, choke him with gold; hold on[163] thy revels,

154 163 Alms-deeds: charitable acts; acts of giving alms
155 166 maunderers: professional beggars
156 169 runagates: vagabonds
157 180 dotard: imbecile
158 185 SD *Manet* RUSH: Shackle-Soul (as Rush) remains on stage when the others exit
159 186 Lucifer: the original name assigned to the character subsequently renamed "Pluto" after Dekker altered the play for the Queen's company
160 189 You've never had a laborer so deserve his pay
161 194 Sallow: sickly yellow or brown complexion
162 198 That damned'st Fury: unclear; possibly a reference to the fury and other spirit-servants found napping or intoxicated at i.49ff, when Shackle-Soul makes his first appearance, but it is unclear why Shackle-Soul (as Rush) should be cursing him now
163 200 hold on: carry on with, continue

Pluto makes Shackle-Soul president[164] of Devils.

Exeunt

[Scene iv]

Enter King ALFONSO, OCTAVIO [*carrying a table*[165]], NARCISSO, JOVINELLI, [*and*] SPENDOLA

ALFONSO What picture's that, uncle Octavio?
OCTAVIO The picture of thy state, drawn by thyself.
This is that book of statutes were enacted[166]
In the high parliament of thy royal thoughts
Where wisdom was the speaker. And because
Thy subjects shall not be abused by laws
Wrapped up in characters, crabbed and unknown,
These thine own language speak.
ALFONSO Hang 'em up, uncle.
OCTAVIO What says the king?
JOVINELLI You must hang up the laws.
OCTAVIO Like cobweb in foul rooms through which great flies
Break through; the less, being caught by the wing, there dies.
No, no, thy laws I'll fix full in thy sight *Hangs a table*[167] *up*
Like sea-marks,[168] that if this great ship of sway
And kingly ventures lose her constant way
I' th' bottomless gulf of state (beaten by the storms
Of youthful folly, raging in the monstrous forms),
She may be saved from sinking and from wrack,
Steered by this compass, for the points of it
Shall guide her so, on rocks she cannot split.
ALFONSO You are our careful pilot. In this voyage
Of government, be you our admiral.
Wisdom and age being props, realms seldom fall.

Enter BRISCO

OCTAVIO Oraculous[169] is thy voice.
ALFONSO How now, Count Brisco?
Methinks I read a comedy in thy looks.
NARCISSO H'as met some merry painter, he's drawn so lively.
OMNES Come, Count, your news.
BRISCO I shall bestow them freely.
The physic of your proclamation works:
Your gilded pills (rolled up in promises
Of princely favors to his wit who highest
Can raise your pleasures) slip so smoothly down
Your subjects' throats that all, upon a sudden,
Are loosely given.
ALFONSO How? Loosely given? Why, Count?

164 201 president: probably in the sense of "The head of a religious house . . .; (also) a person who presides over the chapter of a cathedral or collegiate" (*OED*)—an ironic title, since Shackle-Soul has been "Friar Rush"
165 0 SD *table*: i.e. a tablet or board for writing upon
166 3 were enacted: that were enacted
167 12 SD *table*: see 0 SDn above
168 13 sea-marks: conspicuously visible signals to guide sailors navigating at sea
169 23 Oraculous: full of wisdom

BRISCO Name but what sport your highness would have acted,
I'm prologue to't. Your court must have more gates
To let in ruffling[170] Saturday. Without now waits
Music in some ten languages: each one swears
By Orpheus' fiddle-case[171] they will tickle your ears
If they can do't with scraping.[172]
NARCISSO There's seven-score noise[173] at least of English fiddlers.
JOVINELLI Seven score! They are able to eat up a city in very scraps.[174]
BRISCO Very base-vile[175] men, most of 'em: besides whole swarms of Welsh harps, Irish
bagpipes, Jews' trumps,[176] and French kits.[177]
All these made I together play,
But their damnèd caterwauling
Frighted me away.
OCTAVIO These sports to please
A prince's eyes?
BRISCO How like you then of these?
The city water-bearers,[178] trimly dight[179]
With yellow ochre tankards[180] pinned upright
Like brooches in their hats, in their fresh loves
A May-game bring, all wearing dog-skin gloves,
Made not to shrink i' th' wetting.
ALFONSO Bid these poor men
Drink well, and so be gone.
BRISCO What will you have then?
Will you see the turners'[181] show, bravely prepared
With colors, drums, and guns with rust half-marred,
Bearing that of which they long have been deprived?
ALFONSO What is't?
BRISCO Their daring giant, newly revived.[182]
OMNES For Jove's sake, let's see that.
OCTAVIO Oh, fie, Prince, fie!
In thy court, painted monsters (they come not here)
Ride forth; thou shalt meet giants everywhere.
Methinks, young lords, your souls being new refined
With beams of honor, should not be declined
To sports so low and vulgar. But since the king
Of birds (the eagle) lets you spread a wing
So near his own, you should put up such game[183]
As fits an eagle, and pursue the same.
And not like ravens, kites, or painted jays

170 35 ruffling: arrogant, swaggering
171 37 Orpheus' fiddle-case: fiddle refers to a stringed instrument (usually a violin, but Orpheus played the lyre)
172 38 scraping: used disparagingly to describe the playing of a fiddle
173 39 seven-score noise: a large band or company of musicians
174 40 They are … very scraps: unclear; probably conveys the idea that musicians (traditionally poor and hungry—see, e.g. *Romeo and Juliet* IV.iv) will devour as much food as they can get when invited to play at court
175 41 base-vile: with a pun on "bass-viol," a stringed instrument for playing the bass part
176 42 trumps: trumpets
177 42 kits: small fiddles, used especially by dancing masters
178 47 water-bearers: those employed to carry water from a spring or well for domestic use
179 47 dight: clothed
180 48 tankards: vessels for carrying water (or drinking water from), here pinned upright in the manner that brooches in a hat are pinned upright
181 53 turners: those who fashion (turn) objects out of wood, metal, etc.
182 56 daring giant, newly revived: presumably from a newly revived stage romance in which a champion must be found to overcome an audacious giant holding a kingdom for ransom
183 64 put up such game: rouse game (animals or birds hunted for sport), causing them to emerge from cover

Soar high, yet light on dunghills for stinking preys.
JOVINELLI Old lord, you rave.
NARCISSO What sports would you devise?
OCTAVIO Most fit for kings. Were I before his eyes
To present objects, they should all be rare:
Of Roman triumphs, laden with the spoils of war,
Or lions, and wild boars killed by active force.
Or sea-fights, or land-battles on foot, or horse:
Such fights as these kindle in kings brave fire,
And meeting spirits that dare mount, mount 'em higher,
Where[184] apish pastimes lay our souls down flat
Groveling on earth, base and effeminate.
BRISCO I have bowls of this bias too, for your lordship's alley.[185]
ALFONSO Trundle 'em out before him.
BRISCO The wooden-leg soldier
Waits to present you with his show of war.
OCTAVIO Aye, marry, my liege.
BRISCO The scholar has his device, the mariner his.
OCTAVIO These are kings' sports indeed.
BRISCO Will you see these?
ALFONSO Faith, be it so; because we'll now rather please
Our uncle than ourself, pray fetch in these.
The rest cashier.[186]
SPENDOLA Send the fiddlers merrily home.
BRISCO And yet pay 'em scurvily! 'Tis impossible.
JOVINELLI And bid the water-bearers cleanse the city;
There's many a foul thing in it.
ALFONSO Marshall 'em in.
OCTAVIO I'll fetch these worthy spirits in myself.
BRISCO No, no, we'll aid you sir.
JOVINELLI March! And give us room. *Exeunt* [JOVINELLI, OCTAVIO, BRISCO]
ALFONSO 'Sdeath! If these doting greybeards might have their wills,
We never shall have ours. Let us cross them
As they cross us.
OMNES How, how!
ALFONSO Every device
Their ningles[187] bring in, abuse with scurvy jest,
Be it ne'er so good.
OMNES Agreed.
NARCISSO If ninnies,[188] bring away the nest.
ALFONSO Teach Jovinelli and Brisco when to give fire.

Drums and trumpets sounding, enter OCTAVIO, JOVINELLI, BRISCO, RUFFMAN [*as* BOHOR], *the* SOLDIER, SCHOLAR, MARINER

SOLDIER I am a soldier.

184 76 Where: i.e. whereas
185 78 I have similar spectacles you will like. Brisco's metaphor is from the game of bowls, where the "bias" is the way a ball's construction leads it to swerve when rolled
186 87 cashier: discharge, dismiss
187 96 ningles: close male friends, confidants
188 99 ninnies: simpletons, fools ("nest" was often used as the collective noun)

JOVINELLI We know that by your legs.
SOLDIER Does my stump grieve you?
BRISCO Not if you bestir your stumps nimbly sir.
NARCISSO What hotshot's[189] this?
SOLDIER A soldier sir, that's all:
That's more than, sir, I think you dare be. Zounds! Baffled[190]
For my limbs lost in service! Your noble father
Has clapped[191] this buff-jerkin,[192] when this stump of wood
Has up to th' knee stuck three hours in French blood,
When such as you, with your spangled roses,[193] that day
Bravely bestirred their heels, and ran away.
I'll stand to't, I.
SPENDOLA With one leg.
SOLDIER Yes, with one.
OCTAVIO Young lords, thus to scorn soldiers, 'tis ill done.
ALFONSO Uncle, here's no man scorns 'em; must we be braved
By a staring fellow for a little fighting? Go.
SOLDIER Fighting! I cannot halt, I, but speak plain.
No king on earth baffles me. I'd baffle again
Th' whole race of great Turks, had I 'em i' th' field. I ha' brought
With me a hundred soldiers, old servitors
Poor as myself in clothes. Pick out five hundred
Of such silk-stocken[194] men; if they beat us, hang us.
'Sblood if we toss not them, hang 's again. A fort
We ha' built without and manned it: this was the sport
A soldier would ha' given thee. My one hundred[195]
Had taught thee all the rules i' th' school of war.
ALFONSO All this I'll read without maim, wound or scar.
SOLDIER What say you to an engine,[196] that at once
Shall spoil some thirty men?
JOVINELLI Thirty men! Nothing.
SOLDIER If nothing, hast thou been beat for this? Farewell.
JOVINELLI I can fetch twenty scriveners[197] have done more
With a bare goose-quill.[198]
SOLDIER May'st thou but live to need
A soldier's arm, that laughed to see him bleed. *Exit*
BRISCO You have lost the day sir, for your soldiers fly.
ALFONSO Fly to the devil, let 'em.
JOVINELLI Your leaders before.
SPENDOLA You fight all under one colors,[199] do you not?
SCHOLAR Sir, these pleasures to the king which I prefer,
Flow from Jove's brain.
NARCISSO Heyday![200] Here's one has beaten out Jove's brains.

189 105 hotshot: reckless or hot-headed person
190 106 Baffled: disgraced or mocked
191 108 clapped: embraced
192 108 buff-jerkin: close-fitting jacket of buff-leather, worn by soldiers
193 110 spangled roses: large silk roses worn on shoes (Hoy, 1980)
194 121 stocken: stocking
195 124 My one hundred: i.e. his hundred soldiers (line 119), who will best the five hundred "silk-stocken men" (line 121)
196 127 engine: a machine or contraption (or perhaps a cunning device, a trap)
197 130 scriveners: scribes
198 131 goose-quill: pen made from a goose's feather
199 135 one colors: one flag or ensign carried by an armed force; Spendola implies that the mariner, scholar, and soldier have a common objective
200 138 Heyday: exclamation of surprise or wonder

MARINER [*Aside*] Would I had thee hung up at our main kite.[201]
SCHOLAR No sir, Jove's brain, Minerva queen of wit;[202]
If all the muses and the arts can fit
With their high tunes such choice and princely ears,
Apollo, father to them all, appears—
JOVINELLI Apollo was an ass; he let a wench whom he loved to be turned into a bay tree,[203] and now she's glad for a penny to stick[204] alehouse windows and wind dead corpses.[205]
BRISCO Let Apollo go and lie with his own daughters.
ALFONSO Are you a scholar, sir?
JOVINELLI A schoolmaster, as I take it and comes to present a very pretty show of his scholars in broken Latin.
OCTAVIO Can we be dumb and see this?
SCHOLAR Oh, hapless learning!
Fly and complain to heaven, where thou wert born,
That thou, whom kings once nursed, are now their scorn. *Exit*
NARCISSO How blows the wind sir?
MARINER Wind! 'Tis nor-nor-west.
NARCISSO To hoise[206] your sails up too, I think 'tis best.
MARINER A black gust[207] is coming: up alow[208] there, hey! A young man[209] up to th' topmast-head,[210] and lookout! Stand to your sails! Stand to your topsails! Let go your harriars,[211] let go, amaine,[212] lower amaine, quick, quick, goodfellows.
OMNES He's mad.
MARINER Who's at helm? Bear up[213] hard! And hard up! And[214] thou be'st a man, bear up; starboard, port again! Off with your drabblers,[215] and your banners; out with your courses! Ho: I spy two ships yonder, that yaw[216] to and again, they have both sprung a leak, I think the devil is sucking tobacco, here's such a mist. Out with your boat, and you boatsmen, cut down mast by th' board;[217] bear up!
I'm a blunt fellow you see, all I say is this,
You that scorn seamen shall a seaman miss. *Exit*
OCTAVIO Now by my life I have patient stood too long,
To see rich merit and love paid with base wrong.
Learning! And arms! And traffic! The triple wall
That fortifies a kingdom, race[218] 'em down all!
This seaman, he that dearest earns his bread,
Had rigged and manned four galleys bravely furnished
With soldiers, rowers, and fireworks for a sea-fight.
ALFONSO You are full of squibs too; pray go fire 'em all.
OCTAVIO Must I be then cashiered too? Marry and shall.

201 139 main kite: one of the highest sails of a ship
202 140 Alludes to Minerva/Athena (the goddess of wisdom), who was born out of the head of Jove (Jupiter)/Zeus
203 144 he let . . . bay tree: Daphne was transformed into a laurel tree so that she did not have to have sex with Apollo
204 145 stick: unclear; perhaps either to fasten the windows in position or to fix a sign, bill, broadsheet, etc. to the window
205 145 wind dead corpses: bodies were wrapped in a shroud called a winding sheet
206 155 hoise: raise
207 156 gust: sudden violent blast of wind
208 156 alow: aloft; towards the lower part of a vessel
209 156 young man: in colloquial nautical use, a junior member of the ship's crew
210 156–7 topmast-head: the top of the topmast
211 157 harriars: obsolete form of "halyards" (rope or tackle used for raising and lowering sails)
212 158 amaine: lower the topsail
213 160 Bear up: to sail in a certain direction
214 160 And: if
215 161 drabblers: additional piece of canvas laced to the bottom of a sail for greater depth
216 162 yaw: deviate from course
217 164 by th' board: down by the ship's side, overboard
218 170 race: tear down or demolish; to raze

To save thy sinking honor, I'll send hence
These men with thanks, with praise, and recompense. *Exit*
OMNES Pray, do.
ALFONSO Brave Shalkan Bohor, all this while
Our eye has followed yours and seen it smile
As 'twere in scorn of what these men could do,
Which made us slight them off.[219] To engross[220] you
(Our best and richest prize) i'th' courts of kings
Through which you ha' passed, you ha' seen wonders; show 'em.
BOHOR I shall at opportune hours. If your grace
Arride[221] the toys they bragged of (fireworks,
And such light stuffs), sit fearless without danger
Of murd'ring shot, which villains might discharge
In idle counterfeit sea-fights. You shall see
At opening of this hand a thousand balls
Of wild-fire, flying round about the air—there! *Fireworks on lines*[222]
OMNES Rare, rare.
ALFONSO 'Tis excellent. 'Sdeath, from whence flew they?
BRISCO Hell, I think.
JOVINELLI Hell! Nay, if any that are in Hell skip up ever so nigh heaven, as these devils that spit fire did, I'll drink nothing but gunpowder.
BOHOR Ha, ha, a trifle this. Your scholar there,
Come with his arts and muse's shallow, leaden brain,
Your swaggering soldier, led a tottered train
Of ruffianly boot-halers:[223] I noted all
These feasts for kings i' th' garden of variety,
The vast world! You are starved midst your satiety;
Pluck no one apple from the golden tree,
But shake the fruit of every pleasure down.
ALFONSO Thanks Bohor; why else wears a king his crown?
Shalkan, all Naples shall not buy thee from me.
BOHOR Nor you and these from me.
ALFONSO Ask what thou wilt have
But to stay here.
BOHOR Lo, this is all I crave.
ALFONSO Thou hast our fast embraces.
BOHOR Swift as man's thought,
Various delights shall be each minute born,
And die as fast that fresh may rise; we scorn
To serve up one dish twice, be't ne'er so rare;
Will you that 'gainst tomorrow I prepare
A feast of strange mirth for you?
ALFONSO Dear Bohor, do.
BOHOR I shall. Nor do I thus your love pursue
With servile hopes of gold; I need it not.
If out the jaws of Hell gold may be got,
Black arts are mine to do't, and what delights
Those work be yours.
ALFONSO Thou art gracious in our sight.

Exeunt

219 181 slight them off: to treat with disdain or disrespect
220 181 engross: absorb, entertain
221 185 Arride: laugh or smile at, especially in mockery or derision
222 190 SD *on lines*: i.e. on strings
223 198 boot-halers: highwaymen or marauding soldiers

[Scene v]

A table is set out by [two] young fellows like merchants' men, books of account upon it, small desks to write upon. They sit down to write tickets,[224] [GRUMBALL *as*] LURCHALL *with them*

1 SERVANT Come fellow Lurchall, write.
LURCHALL Fuh, stay not for me,
I shall out-go you all.
2 SERVANT I hold[225] five crowns
We all leave you behind us.
LURCHALL Done; but I
Must not leave you behind me. [*Aside*] What pains a poor devil
Takes to get into a merchant! He's so civil
One of Hell must not know him.[226] With more ease
A devil may win ten gallants than one of these;
Yet a merchant's wife, before these ten, is won
To entertain her devil, if Pride be one.
But Lurchall, now thou'rt[227] in and for years bound
To play the merchant, play him right: th'ast found
A master, who more villainy has by heart
Than thou by rote; see him but play his own part
And thou doest Hell good service. Bartervile,
There's in thy name a harvest makes me smile.
BARTERVILE (*Within*) Lurchall!
OMNES My master calls.
LURCHALL Ay.

Enter BARTERVILE. *Men to and fro, bring in bags and have bills.*[228] *Exit*

BARTERVILE Oh, art there?
This day 'twixt one and two, a gallant's bound
To pay four hundred crowns to free his lands
Fast mortgaged to me. Lurchall, get thee up high
Into my turret, where thou may'st espy
All comers every way; if by thy guess,
Thou see'st the gull, make hither—
LURCHALL So, sir.
BARTERVILE —that, his hour
Lie gasping, at the last minutes, let him beat at door;
Within, I'll beat his heart out.
LURCHALL I'll let him stand.
BARTERVILE Do, take my watch, go faster. All his land
Is summed[229] with these two figures (two and one[230]).
At past one, his strike but two, 'tis mine own.[231]
LURCHALL I'll turn the wheels and spin the hours up faster.

224 0 SD *tickets*: notes of money received on credit
225 2 hold: bet
226 5–6 He's so … know him: i.e., it is difficult for a devil to spend time with him because he's so civil (educated, cultured, respectable), unlike the showy "gallants" of line 7
227 10 now thou'rt: i.e. now that thou art
228 16 SD *bills*: paper bills (written documents, letters, etc.)
229 26 summed: reckoned, counted up
230 26 two and one: referring to "deuce-ace," a roll of the dice that turns up two and one and is thus a poor throw or bad luck, but also referring to the gallant's fate hinging on the events scheduled to unfold between one and two o'clock in the afternoon
231 25–7: Do, take … mine own: the general gist is that the gentleman who has mortgaged his lands to Bartervile and owes money as a result will forfeit his lands if the money is not repaid by the appointed time; in this scene, Bartervile is attempting to prevent the gentleman from repaying the debt on time

BARTERVILE The city clocks then strike, and kill thy master.
Would all the city sextons,[232] at my cost,
Were drunk this day four hours.
LURCHALL Troth, so would I,
And we their Jacks[233] a' th' clock-house.
BARTERVILE We'd strike merrily.
Fly up to th' top o' th' house.
LURCHALL There sir, I'll sit.
[*Aside*] And croak like a raven, to damn thee in Hell's pit. *Exit*

BARTERVILE *set amongst his men, reading a long scroll*[234]

BARTERVILE How goes this month?
OMNES Much shorter than the last.
BARTERVILE Weddings this month: twelve thousand. Not worth the scoring.[235]
But think there's little marrying, we ha' so much whoring.
Grinding mills, so much used; about the city
Such grinding, yet no more money. Suits in law,
Full brought to an end this month, no more but ten:
This law will beggar us. Had I the bags again
I bought this cumbrous[236] office with, the king
Should make his best of't: he that did farm't before
Had it for less than I, yet received more. [237]
How much remains of the salt tribute[238] due?
1 SERVANT Seven thousand crowns.
BARTERVILE That's well: a savory sum.
These, our Italian tributes, were well devised.
Methinks 'tis fit a subject should not eat
But that his prince from every dish of meat
Should receive nourishment: for, being the head,
Why should he pine, when all the body is fed?
Besides, it makes us more to awe a king
When at each bite we are forced to think on him.

Enter a BRAVO[239] *with money*

1 SERVANT What payment's this?
BRAVO The pension of the stews;[240] you need not untie it, I brought it but now from the sealer's office.[241] There's not a piece there but has a hole in't, because men may know where 'twas had[242], and where it will be taken again. Bless your worship. Stew-money sir, stew-prune[243] cash sir.
BARTERVILE They are sure, though not the soundest paymasters;
Read what's the sum.

232 30 sextons: officers responsible for church property; their duties included bell-ringing
233 32 Jacks: a "Jack" or a knave is a figure of a man who strikes the bell on the outside of a clock
234 34 SD In Scene ix it is made explicit that Bartervile is "receiver/Of all our tribute monies" (1–2) and holds the Office of Receiver (157); here he is keeping his accounts
235 36 scoring: recording debts by using notches in a tally
236 42 cumbrous: obsolete form of "cumbersome"
237 43–4 he that . . . received more: the last person to hold the office of receiver paid less for the privilege but reaped a greater financial benefit
238 45 salt tribute: a levy on salt, probably with a pun on "salt" meaning "lecherous," suggesting that Bartervile might benefit from a tax on lecherous behavior
239 53 SD *a* BRAVO: a villain; a hired assassin or soldier
240 55 pension of the stews: a taxation on or collection from the brothels ("stews"; originally heated rooms used for vapor baths but subsequently associated with their frequent use for prostitution purposes)
241 56 sealer's office: a sealer is one who inspects goods and attaches an official seal of quality or approval to them
242 56–7 not a piece . . . 'twas had: every coin (piece) has a hole in it, so that men know it came from a brothel (there is a pun on "hole" meaning "genitals"
243 57–8 stew-prune: stewed prune; associated with brothels (Hoy, 1980)

1 SERVANT But bare two hundred crowns.
BRAVO They are bare crowns[244] indeed sir, and they came from animals and vermin that are more bare. We that are clerks of these flesh-markets have a great deal of rotten mutton[245] lying upon our hands, and find this to be a sore payment.
BARTERVILE Well, well, the world will mend.
BRAVO So our surgeons tell 'em every day; but the pox of mendment[246] I see.
BARTERVILE Do not your gallants come off roundly then?
BRAVO Yes sir, their hair comes off fast enough, we turn away cracked French crowns every day. I have a suit to your worship in behalf of all our dealers in small wares, our free-whores sir; you know my meaning.
BARTERVILE If your whores are known, what's thy suit?
BRAVO I should have brought a petition from 'em, but that 'tis put off sir, till cleansing-week,[247] that they may all be able to set to their hands, or else a whore's mark.
BARTERVILE Well, well, what's their request?
BRAVO Marry sir, that all the she-tobacco-shops,[248] that creep up daily in every hole about the city, may be put to silence.
BARTERVILE Why, pray thee, honest fellow? [*Offers gold*]
BRAVO I thank your good worship, I had not such a sweet bit[249] given me this seven years,[250] honest fellow. Marry sir, I'll open to you your suppliants' cases: they that had wont to spend a crown about a smock,[251] have now their delight dog-cheap, but for spending one quarter of that money in smoke. Besides, sir, they are not contented to rob us of our customs only, but when their pipes are foul with spitting and driveling in those foresaid shops, they have no place to burn 'em in, but our houses.
BARTERVILE Draw their petition, and we'll see all cured.
BRAVO Let a frost come first, sir. I thank your venerable worship; the pox gnaw out so many small guts as have paid thee crowns. *Exit*

Enter LURCHALL, *running*

LURCHALL The tide's against you sir, the crowns are come.
BARTERVILE How goes my watch?
LURCHALL As most watches use to go sir; sleepily, heavily.
BARTERVILE Not reached to one yet; wert thou to be hanged,
The hour had galloped.
LURCHALL I spurred it all that I could.
BARTERVILE 'Sdeath, keep his hour, heaven help poor citizens
If gentlemen grow thus wary. Let him in. *Exit* LURCHALL
Barren now, that hast in craft so fruitful been.[252]

Enter [LURCHALL] *with two* GENTLEMEN

Your business, sir, to me.
1 GENTLEMAN Do you not know me, sir?
BARTERVILE No, in good truth, sir.
1 GENTLEMAN To know you I am bold sir;

244 61 bare crowns: alluding to one symptom of syphilis, which is hair-loss
245 62 mutton: slang term for prostitutes (or female genitals)
246 65 mendment: amendment
247 71–2 cleansing-week: the week of purification that makes up the first week of Lent in the liturgical calendar
248 74 she-tobacco-shops: Hoy (1980) compares with *Roaring Girl* II.i. 10, where it is implied that women, in direct response to the rise in brothels, would gladly open tobacco shops
249 77 bit: thieves' slang for money
250 77 seven years: a proverbially long time
251 79 spend a . . . a smock: spend money on a prostitute
252 93 Bartervile laments his present lack of inspiration for outfoxing his client, Innocentio

You have lands of mine in mortgage. This is my day,
And here's your crowns.
BARTERVILE Signor Innocentio;
My memory had quite lost you. Pray, sit both.
A bowl of wine here.
1 GENTLEMAN Sir, it shall not need.
Please you to fetch my evidence, whilst we tell.
BARTERVILE What needs this forward spring? Faith, two months hence
Had been to me as welcome.
1 GENTLEMAN Sir, I thank you.
2 GENTLEMAN Your hour draws on, Signor Innocentio.
BARTERVILE [*Aside to* LURCHALL] Go beat a drum i' th' garret, that no tongues
Of clocks be heard but mine.[253]
LURCHALL Little past one.
BARTERVILE Wind, wind.
LURCHALL [*Aside*] Thus wind'st thou to damnation.
2 GENTLEMAN I'll part with none, sir, pardon me, till I see
Your writings: will you fetch the evidence, sir?
BARTERVILE What evidence, sir, have I of yours?
1 GENTLEMAN My friend sir,
Whose money he lends me to redeem my mortgage.
BARTERVILE Which you would have for your security.
2 GENTLEMAN 'Tis so sir?
BARTERVILE No, Sir Innocentio,
Tomorrow on your bare word will I lend you thirty crowns more. I love you sir, and wish you beware whose hands you fall into: the world's a serpent.
2 GENTLEMAN This does but spend the hour,[254] sir; will you take your money?
BARTERVILE With all my heart.
1 GENTLEMAN Let him see my writings then.
BARTERVILE Have you such covenant from me? I remember none.
1 GENTLEMAN Your conscience is sufficient covenant, sir.
BARTERVILE Ha! What's that conscience? I know no law-terms I,
Talk to me as to a citizen.
2 GENTLEMAN We'll dally no longer;
We knew what snake would sting us, and therefore brought
Our medicine 'gainst his venom: you'll keep the writings,
And we'll i' th' Court of Conscience[255] tender your crowns,
Whither this writ[256] does summon you.
LURCHALL A fox, and o'ertaken?
BARTERVILE Serve writs upon me, yet keep my money too?
[*Aside to* LURCHALL] Dull slave, hast thou no brain?
LURCHALL Brain! Try this. [*Whispers*]
BARTERVILE Peace.
2 GENTLEMAN Will you as fits a Christian give us in
What is our right and take your crowns, sir, yet?
BARTERVILE 'Tis good to try men's patience. Fetch me down
Those writings on my pillow, there they ha' slept
These two hours for you. Must not friends jest? Ha! *Exit* LURCHALL

253 104–5 Go beat … but mine: in a desperate bid to cause the gentleman to lose track of time and forfeit his lands, Bartervile asks Lurchall to beat a drum in the tower as a distraction from the striking clocks
254 115 spend the hour: the second gentleman sees through Bartervile's time-wasting stratagem
255 123 Court of Conscience: a small-debt court
256 124 writ: the Gentleman produces a legal document compelling Bartervile to attend court

BOTH Yes sir. Let your men tell, just four hundred crowns.
BARTERVILE Besides the use.[257]
1 GENTLEMAN The use is there too.
BARTERVILE Hold:
I'll take it without telling, put it up.
BOTH Not till we see the writings.

Enter LURCHALL

BARTERVILE Dare you touch it?
BOTH Dare? Yes sir, and dare stab him to the heart,
Offers to take it from us.
BARTERVILE Who stabs first? *Flings money amongst it*[258]
Now touch it if you dare: there's gold of mine
And if they lay one finger on't, cry thieves.
They come to rob me; touch it if you dare.
1 GENTLEMAN Damned wretch, thou wilt go quick to hell I fear.
BARTERVILE No sir, the devil shall fetch me when I go.
LURCHALL [*Aside*] That's all my errand.
2 GENTLEMAN We are cheated both.
BARTERVILE Proceed in your chancery suit. I have begun your bill:
"Humbly complaining—"
1 GENTLEMAN Of thee, villain, I'll complain,
That sells thy soul for money; devils on earth dwell
And men are nowhere, all this world is hell. *Exeunt* [*two* GENTLEMEN]
BARTERVILE I kiss thy forehead, my witty Oedipus[259]
That canst unfold such riddles. *One rings. Exit* 1 SERVANT
LURCHALL Sir, I am bound
To do you all service— [*Aside*] till I you all confound.

[*Enter* 1 SERVANT]

1 SERVANT Master Silverpen the proctor,[260] sir, sends word, if you come not in tomorrow and personally depose[261] your payment of the two hundred crowns, you'll be non-suited.[262]
BARTERVILE That is a law-draught[263] goes down coldly.[264]
LURCHALL Why sir? 'Tis but your swearing the money is paid.
BARTERVILE If oaths had backdoors to come in at, without danger of damnation, to catch a man's soul by th' back, swearing were brave.
1 SERVANT What answer shall I give the proctor's man?
LURCHALL Tell him my master shall come in and swear. *Exit* [1 SERVANT] *and enters* [*again*]
BARTERVILE Do, tell him.[265] On thee I'll build. Now all my fear
Is for appearance at the Chancellor's Court.
No trick to save that?

257 133 use: interest
258 137 SD: Lurchall's strategy, evidently whispered at line 127, is for Bartervile to mix his own money with the gentleman's and accuse him of theft if he tries to take any of the resultant mix; the gentlemen are thus unable to resolve the situation within the crucial time period and Bartervile appears set to retain both the mortgaged lands and the 400 crowns
259 148 witty Oedipus: the mythological Greek king who solved the riddle of the Sphinx
260 151 proctor: a professional who represents others in a court of canon or civil law
261 152 depose: put down, deposit
262 152 non-suited: subjected to the stoppage of a suit by the judge on the grounds of insufficient evidence or a failed legal case
263 153 law-draught: legal written order for the drawing (withdrawing) of money
264 153 goes down coldly: with a pun on draught, meaning "drink," which in this case offers cold comfort
265 159 Do, tell him: addressed to the exiting servant

LURCHALL I have a brave one for't.
Bring in a pottle[266] of wine. *Exit* 1 SERVANT *for wine; bring't in*[267]
Will Carlo here,
My fellow, depose a truth if he see it, to help his master?
BARTERVILE Would thou not, honest Carlo?
2 SERVANT Yes sir.

Enter [1 SERVANT] *with wine*

1 SERVANT Here's the wine.
LURCHALL Set this to your head anon sir; when 'tis there,
Away you, and tomorrow thou may'st swear
Before the chancellor, and swear true, if he
Were in that case thou left'st him, 'twere in vain
To hope he could live, till thou cam'st back again.[268]
BARTERVILE All Knights o'th' Post[269] learn this trick: the fit's upon me[270] now.
LURCHALL Take a good draught,'twill help you sir. [2 SERVANT *drinks*] It gulps,
He's almost breathless, Carlo, away.
2 SERVANT I am gone. *Exit*
LURCHALL He's gone, he's gone sir.
BARTERVILE One gulp more had choked me;
This wine has washed my fears off, th'ast given me power
To make me dote upon thee. Carlo's gone?
LURCHALL Yes and will swear his heart out, to your good.
[*Aside*] Swear let him; be thyself and he damned too.
BARTERVILE So I may get by it. In my bosom sleep
My dove, my love; prosper but thou and I.
LURCHALL And let all else sink.
BARTERVILE Let 'em: so I kiss gold,
The young man's whore, the saint of him that's old.
Exeunt

[Scene vi]

Enter PRIOR, ALPHEGE, HILARY *and friars with pruning knives, spades, etc., met by* SUBPRIOR *and* SHACKLE-SOUL [*as Friar* RUSH]

SUBPRIOR Whither, madmen, run you?
OMNES To our vines.
SUBPRIOR Your vines?
The tree of sin and shame? This serpent here
Has with that liquorish[271] poison so set on fire
The brains of Nicodeme and Silvester,
That they in drunken rage have stabbed each other.
PRIOR Stabbed!
RUSH Yes, they bleed a little, but have no harm.
Their young blood with the grapes' juice being made warm,
They brawled and struck, but I kept off the blows;

266 162 pottle: tankard or pot
267 162 SD *bring't in*: probably a playhouse annotation to the text, since the servant's actual entrance with wine is provided at line 168 below
268 166–70: Set this … back again: syntax is unclear, but the general sense is that the servant is to become inebriated so that he can plausibly testify falsely on behalf of his master
269 171 Knights o'th' Post: notorious perjurers who made their livings by providing false depositions
270 171 fit's upon me: drink has successfully produced a state of temporary inactivity
271 3 liquorish: pleasant to the palate; sweet, tempting or attractive

Yet the Subprior says from me their quarrel rose.
SUBPRIOR It did.
RUSH In very deed (for I not swear)
It did not sir. To me you malice bear,
As if that all such mischief done were mine,
But 'cause yourself shall see how I repine
To see vice prosper, pardon me good Lord Prior,
If I a telltale be of what mine eyes
Beheld with water in them: sin will rise
In holy circles I see sometimes.
PRIOR What sin?
SUBPRIOR What hast thou seen?
RUSH Would present I had not been,
But till I utter it, my clogged conscience bears
A man upon a woman.
OMNES Ha!
RUSH I speak't in tears:
Scumbroth (our cook) and a female I beheld
Kissing in our orchard: on her lips he dwelled
I think some half hour.
SUBPRIOR Shame to our reverend order!
A woman in our convent! Sin black as murder.
PRIOR Our cook shall be severely punished. A woman,
A tempter here!
OMNES Abominable!
PRIOR Rush, thou'lt rebuke sin.
RUSH Though, my lord, I'm bad,
I'm not given that way.
PRIOR Let us some plagues invent
To lay on this lecherous knave.
RUSH Some light punishment,
Good my Lord Prior: suppose 'twere your own fault,
Whip as you would be whipped, the best's naught.
SUBPRIOR He shall be punished and then lose his place.
PRIOR That, sir, shall be as we will. To our vines, away.
SUBPRIOR For shame give o'er. Dare you profane this day
That is to holy uses consecrate?
PRIOR Why? What day is this?
OMNES Lambert the martyr.[272]
PRIOR No matter,
To vex thee deeper, this whole day we'll spend
Only about our vines.
SUBPRIOR You vex not me,
But heaven: what warrants you to this?
PRIOR Our will.
SUBPRIOR Thou hast thy will, thy wish thou ne'er shalt have,
In sight of heaven who sees and punishes
Men's black impieties, and in sight of these
Sharers in thy full sin, and in his light,
T'express whose villainies, there's no epithet.
PRIOR No matter what he says, Rush.
RUSH I'm known what I am.

272 36 Lambert the martyr: September 17 is the feast of St. Lambert of Maastricht, who was murdered in Liege in AD 706 after denouncing the affair of Pepin II, Duke and Prince of the Franks with a Frankish noblewoman named Alpaida

SUBPRIOR To thee I prophesy, vicious old man, to thee
Who erst[273] with lift-up hands and down-bowed knee,
Seemest t'have had work in heaven; now, full of spite,
Only to sate a liquorish appetite,
Digg'st our religious[274] wales up, planting there
Luxurious fruits to pamper belly-cheer:
For all thy pains to dress it, of this vine
Thy lustful lips shall never taste the wine.
PRIOR Distracted fool, instead of my just anger,
Thou only hast my pity. Thou prophesy?
OMNES Ha, ha.
SUBPRIOR Laugh on, but since nor prayers prevail nor tears,
I'll pour my grief into my prince's ears. *Exit*
RUSH He'll go and complain to the king.
PRIOR Let him complain,
Kings cannot subjects of their food restrain. *Exeunt. Manet* [RUSH, *now as*] SHACKLE-SOUL
Away!
SHACKLE-SOUL Engender sin with sin, that wine's rich heat
May bring forth lust, lust murder may beget;
But here strike sail, this bark[275] awhile hale in,[276]
And launch into the deep a brighter sin.[277]
Ho, Glitterback, ascend to Shackle-Soul,
To Shackle-Soul ascend, ho Glitterback!
Thou richest spirit, thrust up thy golden head
From Hell thus high. When?[278] Art imprisonèd
In misers' chests so fast thou canst not come?
Or fear'st thou thieves, or cutpurses? Here be some
Can save thee from their fingers. When? Arise,
And dazzle th'approaching night with thy glist'ring eyes. *A golden head ascends*
GLITTERBACK Here.
SHACKLE-SOUL How thou sweat'st with coming! Save me those drops
(Gold's pure elixir) stilling[279] from thy locks:
Shake from thy brows and hair that golden shower. [GLITTERBACK *shakes gold onto the stage*]
So. Get home, quick; to Hell, lest Hell grow poor
If rich men's paws once fasten thee, and beware
I' th' way thou meet'st no lawyers: they'll pull thee bare.
Hence, down!
GLITTERBACK I'm gone. *Descends*
SHACKLE-SOUL Cool night will call Friar Clement forth anon.
Angels,[280] be you his strong temptation;
Wine's lustful fires him warm not. At this spring,
Scorned by the rest for him, spread thy gilt wing
Full in his eye; as he drinks water down
In streams of avarice, let his weak soul drown.
Exit

273 47 erst: at first
274 50 religious: holy, sacred. It is unclear what "wales" refers to, other than something that could be dug up to enable planting of fruits
275 64 bark: small ship
276 64 hale in: draw up, hoist sail
277 62–5 Engender sin . . . brighter sin: the bark is a metaphor for free will and, in this case, deliberately choosing (steering a course towards) immorality
278 69 When?: an exclamation of impatience
279 76 stilling: trickling down in minute drops; distilling
280 84 Angels: a pun on the golden coins featuring the Archangel Michael

[Scene vii]

Enter the King [ALFONSO], NARCISSO, BRISCO, SPENDOLA, JOVINELLI, RUFFMAN [*as* BOHOR], *followed by* ASTOLFO

ASTOLFO I do beseech your highness, yet turn back
And comfort the sad lady, whose fair eyes
Are worn away with weeping.
JOVINELLI If her eyes be worn away, what should a man do with a blind wife? Kill her with flies?[281]
ALFONSO I cannot abide a woman that's fond of me.
SPENDOLA Nor I.
NARCISSO I would love a woman but as I love a walnut, to crack it, and peel it, eat the meat, and then throw away the shell.
JOVINELLI Or as noblemen use their great horses, when they are past service: sell 'em to brewers and make 'em dray-horses.[282] So use a woman.
ASTOLFO So, so.
BOHOR The Indians are warm without clothes, and a man is best at ease without a woman; or if your highness must needs have one,
Have factors[283] to buy the fairest, dote not any,[284]
But like the Turk regard none, yet keep many.
ALFONSO You hear the jury's verdict.
ASTOLFO Whose foreman's the devil?
These counsel thee to thy destruction.
ALFONSO Destruction? Why? Though heaven can abide but one sun, I hope we on earth may love many men's daughters. Tell Erminhilda so: send her home to the duke her father, and tell him too, because the disease of marriage brings the stone[285] with it, I hate a woman. I love not to be cut:[286] enclosed grounds are too rank.[287]
BOHOR Best feeding on the commons then.
ASTOLFO Will you not marry this chaste lady?
ALFONSO No sir, and will you now my reason have?
A woman is an insatiate grave,
Wherein he's damnèd that lies burièd.
OMNES On, on, away.
BOHOR Brave battles! Fight you, but I'll win the day. *Exeunt. Manet* ASTOLFO

Enter OCTAVIO *and* ERMENHILD

ERMENHILD I heard the story, tell't not o'er again,
'Twere cruelty to wound men, being half-slain.
OCTAVIO 'Tis cruelty too much, and too much shame
That one of your high birth, youth, beauty, name,
And virtues shining bright, should hence be sent
Like some offender into banishment,
Abused by a king, and his luxurious train
Of parasites, knaves, and fools (a kingdom's bane),

281 4–5 If her . . . with flies: proverbially, "the blind eats many a fly" (that is, are unable to anticipate unwelcome situations or circumstances); Heywood wrote a play with this name in 1603
282 11 dray-horses: large, powerful horses used for drawing a dray (wheeled sled or cart, such as those used by brewers)
283 15 factors: agents who buy and sell
284 15 dote not any: do not dote on any one in particular
285 21 stone: kidney (or similar) stones
286 22 love not to be cut: I do not want to be castrated (i.e. emasculated by a wife)
287 22 enclosed grounds are too rank: referring to the enclosure of common grounds (cf. line 24) by landowners so as to make pasture, resulting (negatively) in rampant or monstrous growth; marriage is likened to enclosure in opposition to the liberty of common grounds

For them, by him not cared for; you came not so,
But as his bride, his queen, and bedfellow.
ERMENHILD And yet am neither. From my father's court
Came I (being sued by princes too) for this?
To see him, his subjects' scorn, and myself his?
Once thought I that his love had been (as fate)
Unmovable; and is't now turned to hate?
Yes, yes, he's wavering as the running stream,
And far more idle than a madman's dream.
ASTOLFO Send to the duke your father, let him enforce
Your plighted marriage.
ERMENHILD Worse than a divorce.
No, to his eyes since hateful I am grown,
I'll leave his court and him, and die unknown. *Exit*
ASTOLFO All runs I see to ruin.
OCTAVIO If he pursue
These godless courses, best we leave him too.
That land to itself must a quick downfall bring,
Whose king has lost all but the name of king.

Exeunt

[Scene viii]

Enter SUBPRIOR *with an earthen pot and a lantern;* SCUMBROTH *with him with a piece*[288]

SUBPRIOR Get thee to bed thou foolish man and sleep.

SCUMBROTH How? Sleep? No sir, no, I am turned a tyrant and cannot sleep. I stand *sentinel perdu,*[289] and somebody dies if I sleep; I am possessed with the devil and cannot sleep.

SUBPRIOR What devil possesses thee?

SCUMBROTH The fencer's devil, a fighting devil. Rush has committed a murder upon my body, and his carcass shall answer it; the cock of my revenge is up.

SUBPRIOR Murder! What murder?

SCUMBROTH He has taken away my good name, which is flat manslaughter, and half-hanged me, which is as much as murder; he told the Lord Prior and you that I was kissing a wench: it's a lie. I give him the lie and he shall fight with me at single pistol against my caliver.[290] Do I look like a whoremonger? When have you seen a wencher[291] thus hairy as I am? Rush, thou diest for this treason against my member's[292] concupiscentiality.[293]

SUBPRIOR Thou would not kill him, would thou?

SCUMBROTH No, but I'll make him know what 'tis to boil a cook in's own grease. I am scalding hot, I am charged with fury, I carry a heart-burning within me. I kiss a whore? I shall have boys cry out to me, now who kissed Mary? No Rush, Scumbroth shall give thee sugar pellets to eat, I will not be danced upon.

SUBPRIOR Let me persuade thy peace of mind tonight.
Get thee to rest; if Rush have thee belied,
Rejoice, by wrongs to have thy patience tried.
He shall forgiveness ask thee.

SCUMBROTH Let me but have one blow at's head with my cleaver i' th' kitchen, and I freely forgive him, or let me bounce at him.

288 0 SD *piece*: firearm
289 2–3 *sentinel perdu*: a sentinel position so dangerous that death is inevitable (French)
290 10 caliver: a light musket
291 11 wencher: one who associates with common women
292 12 member's: penis's
293 12 concupiscentiality: lustfulness (Scumbroth attempts to speak in bombastic legal jargon)

SUBPRIOR These bloody thoughts will damn thee into hell.
SCUMBROTH Do you think so? What becomes of our roaring boys[294] then that stab healths one to another, do you think they will be damned up too?
SUBPRIOR I think so, for I know it, dear son to prayer,
Two sins beset thee, murder and despair;
I charge thee meet me at my cell anon,
To save thee will I spend my orison.[295]
In name of heaven I charge thee to be gone.
SCUMBROTH Well sir, the cold water of your counsel has laid[296] the heat of my fury: he had met with his match, but I will shoot off my anger, I will be gone, and why? Look you, because the moon is up and makes horns at one of us. As the nobleman's coach is drawn by four horses, the knight's by two, and the cuckold by three, even so am I drawn away with none at all. *Vale, bonos noctis.*[297] I am possessed still: it buzzes here. *Vale.* *Exit*
SUBPRIOR Blessed star of light, stuck there to illuminate
This world darkened o'er with sin: thou watchest late,
To guide man's coming home, showing thereby
Heaven's care of us, seeing how we tread awry.
We have two great lights, for midnight and for noon,
Because black deeds at no time should be done.
All hail to thee (now my best guide) be given,
What needs I earth's candle, having the lamp of heaven?
Now, *benedicite*![298] Where am I?

Enter [SHACKLE-SOUL, *disguised as*] RUSH[299][, *aloof*]

Oh whither am I going? Which way came I?
[*He sees the gold*] Ah welladay,[300] I come to fill my pot
With water, not with thee; thou art misbegot,
Else wouldst thou not lie there. What orphan's blood
Hast thou sucked out to make this golden flood?
None drink this well but I; how is it then
Thou thus waylay'st me, thief to the soul of man?
Would some poor wretch by loss of law undone
Had thee. Go do him good; me canst thou none.
My wholesome cup is poisoned, it flows o'er
With man's damnation, gold. Drink there no more.
RUSH [*Aside*] Not taste what all men thirst for? Old and so brave;
When money assaults, one combat more I'll have.

Enter SCUMBROTH

SCUMBROTH So, ho, ho, father Subprior.
SUBPRIOR Who's there? What art thou call'st me?
SCUMBROTH One that feeds the hungry, the cook sir, Scumbroth.
SUBPRIOR Come hither, I have for thee a golden prize.
RUSH [*Aside*] Ha, ha! He'll take it.

294 25 roaring boys: young men given to riotous or drunken behavior
295 30 orison: prayer
296 32 laid: allayed
297 35–6: *Vale, bonos noctis*: Goodbye, goodnight (Latin)
298 45 *benedicite*: bless me (Latin)
299 45 SD RUSH: why Q specifies the devil's disguise-name here is unclear; perhaps Shackle-Soul approaches with caution lest he be observed, and deems the Rush disguise the safest option. At lines 144ff below there is no need for the disguise when Shackle-Soul calls from off-stage and then enters to speak exclusively with Glitterback
300 47 welladay: an exclamation

Villains and fools will ha' gold, though got from hell,
But they who do so, as thou shalt, pay for't well. *Exit*

SCUMBROTH But stay, father Subprior, before we go one step farther, what do you think I have done since I went from you?

SUBPRIOR No hurt, I hope. Say hast thou?

SCUMBROTH Hurt? If I did hurt in that, how much harm do almanac makers, who lie coldly quivering at it all the year long? I did do nothing but stand staring at the man in the moon.

SUBPRIOR And what good thoughts bred that within thee?

SCUMBROTH This: I thought to myself, what a happy fellow that man in the moon was, to see so many fools and knaves here below, and yet never to be troubled with 'em, nor meddle with 'em.

SUBPRIOR He's happy that meddles not with this world indeed.

SCUMBROTH If that man in the moon should write a prognostication,[301] oh he should not need to tell astronomical lies to fill his book, nor talk in gibberish no man understands, of quartiles,[302] aspects,[303] stations,[304] retrogradations,[305] peragrations;[306] centrical,[307] eccentrical,[308] cosmical,[309] acronical,[310] and such palquodical,[311] solar, lunar, lunatical[312] vaulting over the rails of heaven, that no Christian dare look upon their tricks, for fear his wit break his neck.

SUBPRIOR Thou put'st into a sea thou canst not sound,
Ignorance still is foe to arts profound.
Come hither man, come hither.

SCUMBROTH Arts profound? Arts make men as very asses as women do. I have no art, and yet I know this moon that shines tonight sees more than you or I do, for all your spectacles.

SUBPRIOR True, 'tis the eye of heaven.

SCUMBROTH Which of the eyes? 'Tis but the left eye and the sun is the right. And yet the left sometimes sees more than the right, and the right as much as the left; there's paxonism for you father, globical paxonism.[313]

SUBPRIOR I understand thee not.

SCUMBROTH No, why here's the oyster opened: I say the sun sees much knavery in a year, and the moon more in a quarter. The moon sees men carried by a quarreling watch to prison, and the sun sees the constable and the bookkeeper share fees the next morning.

SUBPRIOR That's not well.

SCUMBROTH Yes, but they swear 'tis well: the moon sees bastards come bawling into the world, and the sun sees 'em shifted and shuffled in dossers[314] away to nurse, and that's the cause we have so many dosser-heads.[315] The moon sees old curmudgeons[316] come reeling from taverns with sipping of half-pints of sack,[317] and the sun sees the same churls the next day, soberly cutting any man's throat for a penny.

SUBPRIOR Enough of this: come hither. Look what here lies.

SCUMBROTH What here lies: marry, father Subprior, the devil and some usurer's money have

301 77 prognostication: a prediction or prophecy
302 78 quartiles: designating the aspect of two celestial objects which are a quarter of a circle (90 degrees) apart in the sky
303 79 aspects: the relative positions of the heavenly bodies as they appear to an observer on the earth's surface at a given time
304 79 stations: the apparent stationary position in the sky of a planet when its motion changes from prograde to retrograde or vice versa
305 79 retrogradations: an apparent motion of a planet or other celestial object in a reverse direction to that which is normal
306 79 peragrations: the action of completing a circuit of the zodiac
307 79 centrical: of, relating to, or characterized by a center
308 79 eccentrical: not concentric with another circle (e.g. an eccentric orbit around the sun)
309 79 cosmical: occurring at sunrise, coincident with the rising of the sun
310 80 acronical: occurring at or just after sunset
311 80 palquodical: a nonsense word; Scumbroth may be getting confused with his terminology
312 80 lunatical: a nonsense word, playing on "lunatic" (i.e. one influenced or driven mad by the moon)
313 89–90 paxonism for . . . globical paxonism: Scumbroth continues to use scientific-sounding nonsense words
314 97 dossers: baskets carried on the back
315 98 dosser-heads: foolish persons
316 98 curmudgeons: avaricious or miserly people
317 99 sack: general name for white wines from Spain and the Canaries

been here at their lechery, and see what goodly children they have begot. If you will, I'll keep the bastards at nurse.
SUBPRIOR I am content that half this gold be thine,
If it be asked for never, for 'tis not mine,
So thou wilt promise t'other half to give
To such as I appoint.
SCUMBROTH By this gold, I will lay it out bravely, as you appoint me.
SUBPRIOR Look not to prosper if thou deal'st amiss;[318]
Good works are keys opening the gates of bliss.
That golden key thou in that heap may'st find,
If with it thou relieve the lame, sick, blind
And hungry.
SCUMBROTH I will do it I protest.
SUBPRIOR One half bestowed so, take thyself the rest.
So fare thee well. *Exit*
SCUMBROTH Farewell good father—
Fool! I'll give the blind a dog to lead 'em, the lame shall to the whipping-post, the sick shall die in a cage, and the hungry leap at a crust. I feed rogues? The pox shall. The world is changed: a beggar yesterday and full of gold today. An ass today and a proud scab[319] tomorrow. *Golden head ascends*
GLITTERBACK Stay, stand.
SCUMBROTH Stand? Cannot a gentleman grow rich, but he must keep knaves about him?
GLITTERBACK That gold is none of thine.
SCUMBROTH But all the craft in that great head of yours cannot get it out of my fangers.[320] Zounds, who the devil art thou?
GLITTERBACK A spirit sent up from Hell to make thee rich.
SCUMBROTH Thank Hell for it: Hell makes worse fools rich in a year.
GLITTERBACK That gold I laid there for thee.
SCUMBROTH When do you lay again, that I may have more of these eggs?
GLITTERBACK Spend those, I charge thee, first.
SCUMBROTH Yes, Head.
GLITTERBACK And bravely, I charge thee.
SCUMBROTH What need you be at such charges? I'll do't: but shall the poor be a penny the better for me, as the old fellow charge me, yea, or no?
GLITTERBACK No.
SHACKLE-SOUL (*Within*) No.
SCUMBROTH Who's that?
GLITTERBACK 'Tis thine own genius[321] cries unto thee "no."
SCUMBROTH My genius? I am a cook, my genius then belike is a scullion; but when this is spent, can my genius tell me whither I shall have more?
SHACKLE-SOUL More.
GLITTERBACK More. } *Within*
1 [DEVIL] More. } *In a big voice*
2 [DEVIL] More.
SCUMBROTH Because my genius keeps company with a great man, I'll take all their words, and his bond.
GLITTERBACK When thou hast spent all that, I charge thee come
To the black tree that stands in Naples' grove,
Climb boldly to the top and keep fast hold,
For there I'll rain on thee a shower of gold.

318 110 deal'st amiss: do wrong, act erroneously
319 119 scab: scurvy fellow, scoundrel
320 123 fangers: something that catches hold, e.g. a tooth or a claw
321 137 genius: one of two opposed spirits (good or evil) imagined to accompany and influence a person throughout his or her lifetime

If what thou seest there, thou to any tell,
Devils shall tear thee.
SHACKLE-SOUL [*Within*] Away.
OMNES Away.
SCUMBROTH Farewell. *Exit*

Enter SHACKLE-SOUL *laughing*

SHACKLE-SOUL Ha, ha! Down, down, bright spirit, thou would be missed anon, Hell mint[322] stands idle.
GLITTERBACK Lose not that fool.
SHACKLE-SOUL Be gone.
GLITTERBACK Have care to meet at next infernal court:
The day draws nigh. *Goes down*
SHACKLE-SOUL I thank thee for this, spirit.
Exit

[Scene ix]

Enter ALFONSO, RUFFMAN [*as* BOHOR], NARCISSO, SPENDOLA, BRISCO, JOVINELLI[, BARTERVILE, *two* GENTLEMEN, GRUMBALL (*as* LURCHALL), *and* FARNEZE]

ALFONSO You that complain 'gainst Bartervile, receiver
Of all our tribute monies, speak your wrongs;
Nay you have deafed our ears too much already,
He does confess your crowns, paid and received,
But to give back your writings there's no clause;
If them you'll win, fight it out by our laws.
BARTERVILE I humbly thank your highness. A gracious doom.[323]
1 GENTLEMAN One day, to try this plea,[324] to hell thou'lt come. *Exeunt 2* [GENTLEMEN]
ALFONSO To th' next, we ha' business of our own, to th' next:
O Bartervile! For these two hundred crowns.
BARTERVILE I paid 'em to that man.
FARNEZE Now afore the king
And his lords here, thou liest: th'ast paid me none.
ALFONSO Your choler's, sirrah, too high.
FARNEZE Though my collar stand[325]
So high, it scarce bears up this falling band.[326]
Thou say'st thou'lt swear th'ast paid it: 'ods nails[327] swear so,
And the foul fiend go with't. Two hundred crowns?
I ha' lost as much at loggets.[328] Swear but to revel
And spend 't in hell, gallop thee and that to th' devil.
LURCHALL Man, wherefore dost not swear?
ALFONSO Reach me a book.
BARTERVILE Let me, before I swear, on my notes look,

322 152 Hell mint: because Glitterback is made entirely of gold
323 7 doom: judgment
324 8 try this plea: ascertain the truth of the matter through judicial examination
325 13 Your choler's … collar stand: choler is the hot and dry bodily humor thought to produce irritability; Farneze willfully misinterprets Alfonso's remark as referring to the collar around his neck
326 14 falling band: a band of fabric fastened at the neck (a style of collar), sometimes worn under a ruff; with a possible pun on "band" meaning "bond" (Hoy, 1980)
327 15 'ods nails: by God's nails (a mild oath)
328 17 loggets: an old game, the object of which is to throw loggets (missiles) closest to a wooden stake fixed into the ground

I'll tell you the very day; pray hold my staff
Till I draw out my false eyes.[329]
FARNEZE Draw thy heart out an't[330] would: thou may'st well say thy false eyes.
BARTERVILE The day: August 14.
FARNEZE That's now. Be damned, and so away.
BARTERVILE On this day, August 14, I swear I paid
Into these hands two hundred crowns in gold.
FARNEZE Zounds! Nor in silver: by this book I had none.
ALFONSO One of you two is perjuriously forsworn.
FARNEZE He, he, as I am true Christian man.
JOVINELLI He swears
To your own hands he paid them.
BARTERVILE Else let that eye,
Which sees me play false, scourge my perjury
With fearful stripes. [*He falls in a trance*]
FARNEZE Oh, justice! Fall'n down dead! LURCHALL *and* BOHOR *about him*[331]
Would I had lost all, though I had been cozened,
Rather than thou thy soul.
OMNES He bleeds at mouth.
FARNEZE See his staff beating the earth (for heaven loves truth)
Is burst in shivers, and that gold he swore
Was paid to me, lies scattered on the floor. [*He begins to recover*]
BOHOR He comes again, the devil will not receive him.
ALFONSO Take him away, we'll punish him for this crime.
BOHOR Beg his office:[332] you a courtier?
SPENDOLA I have a suit to your highness.
ALFONSO What is't, Count Spendola?
LURCHALL Master, look up man,
In this black trance had thy soul flown away,
I had wrought hard and made a holiday.
BOHOR Lose not a minute, puck-fellow,[333] leave him not yet,
I have whales here too, lie playing in the net. *Exit*
FARNEZE I'll take this gold at venture,[334] sweet young King,
For all this hellhound owes me.
ALFONSO Do, and be gone.
FARNEZE I am paid: the devil's turned Puritan,[335] I fear,
He hates (methinks) to hear his own child swear. *Exit*
ALFONSO The office of this perjured Bartervile
I frankly give away, dividing it
To the Count Spendola and our worthy friend
Brave Bohor here; farm it to whom you please.
BOTH We thank your highness.
SPENDOLA Who bids most, he buys it.
ALFONSO If to his life the devil gives longer lease,
To build more work for hell, go see, and from him
Exact a strict account of what he owes us.
BOHOR That strict account I'll take. *Exit* [*with* BARTERVILE]
ALFONSO Show him no favor.

329 22 false eyes: spectacles
330 23 an't: if it
331 33 SD *about him*: i.e. they attend to him
332 41 Beg his office: ask to be given the position of receiver
333 47 puck-fellow: a mischievous spirit (Puck; Robin Goodfellow)
334 49 at venture: as chance directs; recklessly, at random
335 51 Puritan: refers to a group of English Protestants known for their strict, austere observance of morality and religious practice; see also xv. 250–77

Enter OCTAVIO *with petitions*

OCTAVIO If now thou art a just king, keep thy word
With thy poor subjects.
ALFONSO How now, uncle, why?
OCTAVIO This is thy day to hear the poor man's cry,
And yonder's crying enough, at thy court gates;
Five hundred white heads, and scarce ten good hats,
Yet haberdashers too, of all trades some,
Crying out they are undone.
OMNES Undone by whom?
OCTAVIO Marry, look: by such as you are, who go gay,[336]
Wear't out, book down[337] more, set to their hands[338] but never pay.
Never in dear years[339] was there such complaining
Of poor starved servants, or when plagues are reigning,
Mourn orphans so and widows, as those do
That owe[340] these sorrowful papers.
ALFONSO Pray how can I
To their complainings add a remedy?
OCTAVIO I'll tell thee how: are any here in debt
To merchants, mercers, tailors? Let 'em jet[341]
In their own satins, pay for what they ha' ta'en,
And these will go less brave, t'other less complain.
OMNES Ha, ha!
OCTAVIO The mighty wrongs the weak, the rich the poor,
This man should have his own, could he grease more
His too-fat lawyer; that wretch for's coat does sue,
But his coat's gone, and his skin flayed off too,
If his purse be o'er-match'd. These gross impure
And rank diseases, long unto[342] thy cure
(Thy word's in pawn for't): these are the poor's cries,
How wilt thou stop their throats?
ALFONSO With halters.
OMNES Hang 'em.
OCTAVIO Hang 'em! Any halters here? Is't so set down?
This law-book speaks not so, yet 'tis thine own.
ALFONSO Still braving me with this? Burn it.
OCTAVIO Yes do.
If you burn all the week, burn Saturday too.
Do one good day's deed first, read poor men's plaints.
ALFONSO Hell's plagues confound 'em in their heads and thine.
Vex me no more.
OCTAVIO I warrant thee I'll save mine. *Meets the* SUBPRIOR
Holy Saint, pardon me; 'las good father, my brain
So wild is I forgot thee, but I'll to him again,
'Tis but an old man's head off. King take it,
I'll speak whilst this stands on my shoulders.
ALFONSO But that you are—

336 70 go gay: go about finely dressed
337 71 book down: purchase more clothing on credit
338 71 set to their hands: make a promise (e.g. by writing their names) to pay
339 72 dear years: years of dearth (Hoy, 1980)
340 75 owe: own
341 78 jet: strut, swagger
342 87 long unto: belong to, are part of

OCTAVIO An honest man, thou'dst have this. Oh, I beseech
Thy attention to this reverend Subprior,
Who 'plains against disorders of this house;
Where once devotion dwelt and charity,
There's drunkenness now, gluttony and lechery.
Tell thou the tale.
SUBPRIOR Bad story soon is told;
Because 'tis foul, that leaf[343] does all enfold.
Their sins grow high, and fearful, and strike at heaven,
Punish them Thou,[344] whose power from thence is given.
ALFONSO Your friar's so lusty!
JOVINELLI All the barbers[345] in Naples tell news of that priory.
BRISCO I would your grace would let me purge this house of her infection; bestow the livings of it on me, I'll sweeten it in one month.
JOVINELLI He'll lay it in lavender.[346]
ALFONSO The convent, the demesnes,[347] immunities,[348]
Rents, customs, charters, what to this house of Baal[349]
Soever is belonging—Brisco, 'tis thine.
OCTAVIO Would rob the church too, now th'ast nothing left
Scarce for thyself?
SUBPRIOR Oh, heaven forfend such theft!
ALFONSO Bestow it at thy pleasure.
OCTAVIO Woe to those days
When to raise upstarts, the poor church decays.
SUBPRIOR Call back thy gift, O King, and ere these eyes
Behold unhallowed hands to tyrannize
Where many a good man has his orisons said
And many a requiem been sung out for the dead,
Till I am thrust out by death, oh let me have
My dwelling there. There let me dig my grave
With mine own nails, shut up from worldly light
Between two walls, and die an anchorite.[350]
ALFONSO I refer you to your patron there.
BRISCO That's I:
Show me first where your abbey-gold sleeps, then go die.
SUBPRIOR I fear religion's fall: alack, I see
This world's a city built by the most high,
But kept by man, God's greatest enemy. *Exit*
OCTAVIO Let ill news fly together; thou art full of tears,
But I more full of woes, of cares, of fears. *Exit*

Enter ASTOLFO

ALFONSO 'Sdeath shall we have yet fair weather?
JOVINELLI Here's one storm more.
ASTOLFO Calabria's duke demands of you a daughter.
ALFONSO Let me but lie with's wife, I'll give him a son.

343 108 leaf: a single sheet of (metaphorical) paper or parchment; the story it contains is necessarily brief
344 110 Thou: i.e., God
345 112 barbers: i.e. barber-surgeons; practitioners of surgery and dentistry, and thus acquainted with disease treatment
346 115 in lavender: in pawn (Hoy, 1980)
347 116 demesnes: properties; land or estate
348 116 immunities: exemptions or privileges, in particular from lay jurisdiction or secular liabilities
349 117 Baal: a false god
350 130 anchorite: hermit

ASTOLFO He sends for Ermenhild.
ALFONSO Deliver her.
ASTOLFO She's not to be found.
ALFONSO You're an old fool,
To ask for that which is not.
ASTOLFO Thus he says,
Deny her and look for wars.
ALFONSO So, go your ways.
ASTOLFO I'm quickly gone. *Exit*

Enter RUFFMAN [*as* BOHOR] *and* BARTERVILE

ALFONSO With sack I'll swear you are.[351]
This was short and sweet. Seems then we shall ha' wars,
Bohor. The drum must scold, the cannon thunder;
Fighting about a wench.
OMNES Tush, that's no wonder,
ALFONSO Who bailed him out of hell? Damned perjured caitiff!
Out of mine eye.
BOHOR I never begged before,
Pardon his crime, I entreat, and back restore
Both your high favor to him and his place.
BARTERVILE Let me want life, rather than want your grace.
SPENDOLA Do you think I'll lose the king's gift?
BARTERVILE I'll send you gold.
SPENDOLA That stops my mouth. Pray let him still, sir, hold
This office of Receiver;[352] I resign
That part which I have in it.
BOHOR And I all mine.
ALFONSO Sirrah, thank these lords.
BARTERVILE I shall their loves deserve.
ALFONSO Bartervile, we have wars; I'll have thee lend me
Some thirty thousand chequeens[353] at least.
BARTERVILE Take all my gold.
ALFONSO Well, get you home: with your bags, sir, we'll make bold.
BARTERVILE Your majesty shall have what bags you will.
[*Aside*] Bags only, but I'll keep my money still. *Exit*

Enter OCTAVIO *and* ASTOLFO

ALFONSO Now Shalkan, some new spirit.
BOHOR A thousand wenches
Stark nak'd, to play at leap-frog.
OMNES Oh, rare sight!
JOVINELLI Your uncle—
ALFONSO 'Sdeath, still haunted with this grey sprite.
OCTAVIO You need no tailors now, but armorers.
There's a dear reckoning for you all to pay
About a lady; the Calabrian duke
Is on a march. The lightning flashes now,
You'll hear the crack anon. Before the star

351 146 I'll swear you are: i.e. you are "gone" due to drinking sack (wine)
352 157 Receiver: official appointed to receive monies on behalf of someone else
353 161 chequeens: gold coins of Italy and Turkey

To call whom up the wakeful cock doth sing,
Be twice more seen abroad, at your city gates
The devil's pursuivant[354] will beat the cannon.
Will these brisk leaders, stuck with ostrich feathers,
Go brave your enemy now and beat him back?
Save thee, thy kingdom, and themselves from wrack?
ALFONSO Dotard, I scorn to take prescription
From any breath to which ours is supreme;
Stood devils with fireworks on your battlements,
A thousand armèd Joves at your proud walls
Hurling forked thunder and the gates rammed[355] up
With piles of citizens' heads, our springtide pleasures
No adverse winds, no torrent shall resist.
Midst flames we'll dance, and die a Neronist.[356] *Exit*
OMNES Fight you, y'are good for nothing else. *Exit*
ASTOLFO They mock us.
OCTAVIO All stark mad: let us be wise
And fly from buildings falling to th' surer side;
If we can his safety, if not, our own provide.
Exeunt

[Scene x]

Enter BARTERVILE *like a Turk* [*and* GRUMBALL *as*] LURCHALL

BARTERVILE Thou hadst like t' ha' sent me swearing into hell.
I'll weave my nets myself, how doest thou like me?
Is not this habit Turk-merchant-like?
LURCHALL A mere[357] Turk sir, none can take you for less.
BARTERVILE King borrow thirty thousand chequeens of me! Ha, ha!
LURCHALL But pray sir, what is't turns you into a Turk?
BARTERVILE That for which many their religion,
Most men their faith, all change their honesty:
Profit, that gilded god Commodity.
He that would grow damned rich, yet live secure,
Must keep a case of faces: sometimes demure,
Sometimes a grum-surly[358] sir; now play the Jew,
Then the precisian.[359] Not a man we'll view
But varies so. Myself, of bashful nature,
Am thus supplied by art.
LURCHALL Mine own dear creature.
But sir, your aims and ends in this?
BARTERVILE Marry, these—
A hundred thousand florins[360] fill my coffers,
Some of it is mine own and some the king's,
Some taken up at use of sundry merchants
To pay at six six-months on mine own band;[361]

354 175 pursuivant: herald
355 183 rammed: forced in or compacted by ramming
356 186 Neronist: imitator of the Roman emperor Nero, who was said to have fiddled while Rome burned
357 4 mere: pure
358 12 grum: gloomy, morose
359 13 precisian: Puritan
360 17 florins: gold coins
361 20 band: bond

Sue that,[362] I'll keep the monies in my hand.
LURCHALL You'll break sir.
BARTERVILE Not mine own neck, but their backs;
To get their monies, Bartervile must die,
Make will, name an executer, which am I.
LURCHALL Rare!
BARTERVILE Given out his kinsman, lately employed
By him in Turkey.
LURCHALL What will hence befall?
BARTERVILE Like an executer will I cozen all.
Make creditors orphans and widows spend those tears
They saved from their late husbands' burials;
They get not two pence i' th' pound.
LURCHALL They'll tell the king.
BARTERVILE The king? Ha, ha!
The king is going this way; he means to borrow,
If the wars hold, my gold. Yes. When? Tomorrow.
All debts of mine on him shall be conferred.
I ha' briefs and tickets which from time to time
Show what large sums his minions ha' fetched from me.
His tribute money has paid it. That's no matter,
The world bites these dead, whom alive they flatter.
And so must I. Then give it out I left
A complete state, but the king's death bereft
Me of those sums he owed.
LURCHALL Say the king prevails?
BARTERVILE With that wind must I likewise shift my sail:[363]
And where the fox gets nothing, will turn ape,
Make legs, crouch, kiss my paw, present some stale
Device of virtue's triumph to express
How much I joy him safe, wish nothing less.
LURCHALL But how can you excuse your turning Turk?
BARTERVILE Easiest of all: I'll swear this saved my life.
Pursued by kennels of barking creditors
For my much love to him and thus being forced
To walk obscure, my credit fell to wrack,
Want of return made all my factors break
In parts remote;[364] to recompense which loss,
And that[365] with safety I may give direction
To my disturbed state, crave I the king's protection.
LURCHALL Protection! What's that?
BARTERVILE A merchant, and yet know'st not
What a protection[366] is? I'll tell thee.
LURCHALL Pray sir, for I never broke with any man.
BARTERVILE It is a buckler of a large fair compass
Quilted within with fox-skins: in the midst
A pike sticks out, sometimes of two years long,
And sometimes longer. And this pike keeps off

362 21 Sue that: follow that (i.e. following Bartervile's scheme)
363 42 shift my sail: Bowers emends to "sails," presumably to rhyme with "prevails" in the previous line; but "sail" is most typically used in the singular in conjunction with "shift" = change of direction (see *OED*)
364 52–3 Want of return . . . parts remote: a lack of profit on investments caused my agents ("factors") in distant lands ("parts remote") financial hardship
365 54 that: so that
366 57 a protection: a letter or certificate of protection guaranteeing exemption or immunity to the person it specifies

Sergeants and bailiffs, actions and arrests:
'Tis a strong charm 'gainst all the noisome[367] smells
Of counters, jailors, garnishes,[368] and such hells.
By this a debtor crazed so lusty[369] grows,
He may walk by and play with his creditor's nose.
Under this buckler, here I'll lie and fence.
LURCHALL You have outreached me.
BARTERVILE I'll outreach the devil.
But I tempt danger: go thou and fetch some friar
As if, at point of death, I did desire
(No, Bartervile did desire) to make confession:
If any creditors beat or rail at door,
Up starts this Turk and answers them.
LURCHALL Why fetch I a friar?
BARTERVILE I have a reaching[370] plot in that, boy; hasten,
That we may smile in our securer port,
Seeing others sea-tossed. Why, 'tis but a sport
For him that's safe to see the proud waves swallow
Whole fleets of wretched souls: it needs must follow,
Nature sent man into the world, alone,
Without all company, but to care for one,[371]
And that I'll do.
LURCHALL True city doctrine, sir.
BARTERVILE Away, thy haste our richest love shall earn.
LURCHALL I came to teach, but now (methinks) must learn.

Exeunt

[Scene xi]

Enter SCUMBROTH *like a beggar*

SCUMBROTH What says the prodigal child in the painted cloth?[372] When all his money was spent and gone, they turned him out unnecessary; then did he weep and wist not what to don, for he was in's hose and doublet verily.[373] The best is, there are but two batches of people molded in this world, that's to say gentlemen and beggars, or beggars and gentlemen, or gentlemanlike beggars, or beggarlike gentlemen. I rank with one of these, I am sure, tag and rag,[374] one with another. Am I one of those whom Fortune favors? No, no, if Fortune favored me, I should be full, but Fortune favors nobody but garlic,[375] nor garlic neither now, yet she has strong reason to love it; for though garlic made her smell abominably in the nostrils of the gallants, yet she had smelled and stunk worse but for garlic: one filthy scent takes away another. She once smiled upon me like a lamb, when she gave me gold, but now she roars upon me like a lion. Stay: what said Head?[376] Spend this bravely and thou shalt have more: can any prodigal new-come upstart spend it more bravely? And now to get more, I must go into the grove of Naples (that's here) and get into a black tree. Here's a black tree too, but art thou he?

367 64 noisome: harmful, injurious, noxious
368 65 garnishes: slang (garnish money) for money extorted from a new prisoner
369 66 lusty: healthy, confident
370 76 reaching: far-reaching, far-sighted
371 82 one: i.e. oneself
372 1 painted cloth: evidently a well-known tapestry depicting a biblical scene (here the parable of the prodigal son, Luke 15: 11–32) and displayed on a wall
373 1–3 When all ... doublet verily: with the tapestry of the prodigal son, Scumbroth seems also to recall an accompanying poem (set as prose in Q) that describes the action; "don" is an archaic form of "do," used here to rhyme with "gone"
374 5 tag and rag: the masses, those of lower social status
375 7 Fortune favors nobody but garlic: apparently an allusion to a lost jig called "Garlic," performed by the Prince's company, presumably at the Fortune, by 1611
376 11 Head: i.e. Glitterback

GLITTERBACK (*Within*) He.
SCUMBROTH Ha, ha, where art thou, my sweet great Head?
GLITTERBACK Head.
SCUMBROTH Oh, at the head, that's to say at the top. How shall I get up? For 'tis hard when a man is down in this world to get up. I shall never climb high.
GLITTERBACK High.
SCUMBROTH I will hie me[377] then, but I am as heavy as a sow of lead.[378] [*Climbs tree*]
GLITTERBACK Lead.
SCUMBROTH Yes, I will lead (big Head) whatsoever follows,
Many a gallant for gold has climbed higher on a gallows.
The storm, even as Head nodded, is coming. Cook, lick thy fingers; now or never.
GLITTERBACK Now or never.

Rain, thunder, and lightning. Enter PLUTO *and devils*

OMNES Oooh.
PLUTO This is the tree.
SCUMBROTH [*Aside*] On which would you all were hanged, so I were off it and safe at home.
PLUTO And this—I am sure 'tis this—the horrid grove
Where witches broods engender,[379] our place of meeting.
SCUMBROTH [*Aside*] Do witches engender here? Zounds, I shall be the devil's bawd whilst he goes to his lechery.
PLUTO And this the hideous black infernal hour.
Ha! No appearance yet? If their least minute
Our vassals[380] break, sink shall these trees to Hell.
SCUMBROTH [*Aside*] Alas!
PLUTO This grove I'll turn into a brimstone lake
Which shall be ever-burning.
SCUMBROTH [*Aside*] The best is, if I be a match in the devil's tinderbox, I can stink no worse than I do already.
PLUTO Not yet come? Oooh!

Enter SHACKLE-SOUL, RUFFMAN, *and* GRUMBALL *at several doors with other devils. Embrace*

OMNES Oooh, oooh!
SCUMBROTH [*Aside*] Sure these are no Christian devils, they so love one another.
PLUTO Stand forth. [*Devils sit*] *under the tree all about him*[381]
SCUMBROTH [*Aside*] Friar Rush amongst 'em!
PLUTO And here unlade[382] you of that precious freight
For which you went: men's souls. What voyage is made?
OMNES No saving voyage, but a damning.
PLUTO Good.
SCUMBROTH [*Aside*] I thought the devil was turned merchant, there's so many pirates at sea.
RUFFMAN I' th' court of Naples have I prospered well,
And brave souls shall I shortly ship to Hell
In sensual streams. Courtier and king I ha' crowned,
From whence war is flowing, whose tide shall all confound.

377 20 hie me: hurry
378 20 sow of lead: an oblong mass of metal as formed by molten metal run from a furnace and allowed to solidify
379 30 Where witches broods engender: i.e. where witches go to produce offspring
380 35 vassals: servants or slaves
381 44 SD In Q this stage direction reads "*Sits under the tree all about him*"
382 46 unlade: to remove a burden

SCUMBROTH [*Aside*] Are there gentlemen devils too? This is one of those, who studies the black art; that's to say, drinks[383] tobacco.
PLUTO Are all then good i' th' city?
GRUMBALL No, Pluto.
SCUMBROTH [*Aside*] No, nor scarce i' th' suburbs.
GRUMBALL Great Prince of Devils, thy hests I have obeyed,
I am bart'ring for one soul, able to lade[384]
An argosy;[385] if city-oaths, if perjuries,
Cheatings, or gnawing men's souls by usuries,
If all the villanies that a city can,
Are able to get thee a son, I ha' found that man.
PLUTO Serve him up. *Stands up*
SCUMBROTH [*Aside*] Alas, now, now.
GRUMBALL Damnation gives his soul but one turn more,
Cause he shall be enough.
SCUMBROTH [*Aside*] It's no marvel if markets be dear, when the city is bound to find the devil roast meat.
PLUTO Has Rush lain idle?
SHACKLE-SOUL Idle? No Pluto.
SCUMBROTH [*Aside*] All the world is turned devil. Rush is one too.
SHACKLE-SOUL Idle? I have your nimblest devil been,
In twenty shapes begetting sin.
SCUMBROTH [*Aside*] One was to get me thrust out of the priory.
SHACKLE-SOUL I am fishing for a whole school of friars.
All are gluttoning or muttoning,[386] stabbing or swelling.
There's only one lamb 'scapes my killing,
But I will have him. Then there's a cook—
SCUMBROTH [*Aside*] Whose arse makes buttons.[387]
SHACKLE-SOUL —of whom I some revenge have took.
SCUMBROTH [*Aside*] The devil choke you for't.
SHACKLE-SOUL He mickle scath[388] has done me,
And the knave thinks to outrun me.
SCUMBROTH [*Aside*] Not too fast.
PLUTO Kick his guilty soul hither.
SHACKLE-SOUL I'll drive him to despair,
And make him hang himself.
SCUMBROTH [*Aside*] For hanging I stand fair.
PLUTO Go, ply your works, our sessions are at hand.
ALL 3[389] We fly to execute thy dread command. *Exeunt* [*the*] *3*
SCUMBROTH [*Aside*] Would I could fly into a bench-hole.[390]
PLUTO But what have you done? Nothing.
1 DEVIL We have all like bees
Wrought in that hive of souls, the busy world;
Some ha' lain in cheesemongers' shops, paring leaden weights.[391]
SCUMBROTH [*Aside*] Would I were there but with a paring[392] of cheese.

383 55 drinks: smokes
384 59 lade: fill with cargo
385 60 argosy: merchant-vessel of the largest size
386 76 muttoning: whoring (Hoy, 1980)
387 79 Whose arse makes buttons: i.e. who is worried or frightened (and thus involuntarily defecating)
388 82 mickle scath: much hurt
389 89 SP ALL 3: i.e. Shackle-Soul, Ruffman, and Grumball
390 90 bench-hole: toilet
391 93 paring leaden weights: shaving (i.e. deceitfully adjusting) the cheesemonger's weights
392 94 paring: sliver

1 DEVIL For one half-ounce, we had a chandler's soul.
SCUMBROTH [*Aside*] If he melted tallow, he smelled sweetly as I do.
1 DEVIL Walk round Hell's shambles,[393] thou shalt see there sticks
Some four butchers' souls, puffed quaintly up with pricks.[394]
SCUMBROTH [*Aside*] Four sweetbreads,[395] I hold my life; that devil's an ass.
1 DEVIL Tailors o'er-reach us, for to this 'tis grown:
They scorn thy hell, having better of their own.[396]
SCUMBROTH [*Aside*] They fear not satin[397] nor all his works.
1 DEVIL I have with this fist beat upon rich-men's hearts
To make 'em harder: and these two thumbs thrust
(In open churches) into brave dames' ears,
Damming up attention; whilst the loose eye peers
For fashions of gown-wings,[398] laces, purls,[399] ruffs,
Falls,[400] cauls,[401] tires,[402] wires,[403] caps, hats, and muffs, and puffs.
For so[404] the face be smug, and carcass[405] gay,
That's all their pride.
PLUTO 'Twill be a festival day
When those sweet ducks comes to us. Lose 'em not: go.
More souls you pay to Hell, the less you owe.
This yew-tree blast with your hot-scorching breath,
A mark (to th' witch who next sits here) of death. *Fireworks.* SCUMBROTH *falls*
OMNES Ooooh. *Exeunt omnes*
SCUMBROTH Call you this raining down of gold? I am wet to th' skin in the shower, but 'tis with sweating for fear: had I now had the conscience that some vintners and innholders[406] have, here might I have gotten the devil and all. But two sins have undone me: prodigality and covetousness; and three P's have peppered[407] me: the punk, the pot, and pipe of smoke, out of my pocket my gold did soak. I cannot swear now, "zounds I am gallant," but I can swear as many of the ragged regiment do, "zounds I have been a gallant." But I am now down, dejected and debashed,[408] and can better draw out a thirdendeal[409] gallant (that's to say, a gallant that wants of his true measure) than any tapster can draw him out of his scores.[410] Thus he sets up, and thus he's pulled down; thus is he raised, and thus declined:[411]

Singulariter:
Nominativo, *hic*: *Gallantus*, a Gallant.
Genetivo, *huius*: brave.
Dativo huic, If he gets once a lick,

393 97 shambles: part of town where meat is sold
394 98 pricks: skewers used by butchers to pin fat to lean meat, thereby increasing saleability (Hoy, 1980)
395 99 Four sweetbreads: i.e. the four butchers' souls fattened artificially. A sweetbread is the pancreas of an animal, used for food
396 101 their own: "tailor's hell" refers to that part of a tailor's shop into which shreds or offcuts of material are thrown
397 102 satin: silk fabric (marker of seventeenth-century dandyism), with a pun on "Satan"
398 107 gown-wings: a pair of lateral projecting pieces of a garment on or near the shoulder
399 107 purls: thread or cord made of twisted loops used for borders and embroidering
400 108 Falls: Hoy suggests "falling bands" (a style of collar/broad band of fabric fastened at the neck and lying flat against the body)
401 108 cauls: a close-fitting cap or net for the hair, usually ornamental and worn by women
402 108 tires: head-dresses
403 108 wires: wire frames used to support the hair or similar frame used to support a ruff
404 109 so: as long as
405 109 carcass: body
406 117 innholders: innkeepers
407 119 peppered: inflicted suffering or punishment
408 122 debashed: abashed
409 122 thirdendeal: literally the third part of anything, but often in the context of a "thirdendeal pot" of beer (sometimes three pints in measure)
410 123 scores: tavern bill (Hoy, 1980)
411 124 thus is . . . thus declined: with a pun on the grammatical sense of "declined": to inflect a noun, adjective, or pronoun through its different cases. In the list of articles that follows, Scumbroth directly follows (and parodies) the introduction of the eight parts of Latin speech in William Lily's Latin Grammar, a staple of English education

Accusativo hunc, Of a taffety punk.[412]
Accusativo hanc, His cheeks will grow lank,
Hunc, hanc, et hoc, With lifting up her smock.
Vocativo, O! He's gone if he cries so.
Ablativo, ab hoc, Away with him, he has the pock.[413]
Pluraliter:
Nominativo, hi gallanti, If the pox he can defy,
Genetivo, horum, Yet he's a beggar in coram.[414]
Dativo, his: His gilt rapier he does miss.
Accusativo hos: Without his cloak he goes.
Accusativo has, To the counter[415] he must pass.
Hos, has, et hæc, With two catchpoles[416] at his back.
Vocativo, O! A hole he desired, and to th' hole[417] he must go.
Ablativo, ab his, Thus many a gallant declinèd is.

Exit

[Scene xii]

Enter ERMENHILD *to the* SUBPRIOR

SUBPRIOR What art thou?
ERMENHILD Daughter to the Calabrian duke.
The hapless troth-plight[418] wife to your sad king.
SUBPRIOR Alack! What notes are these I hear you sing?
Pardon me, madam.
O lady! Want of you has bred much woe;
Calamity does everywhere o'erflow,
All long of[419] your strange absence. *Drums afar off, marching*
ERMENHILD I confess,
Loaden with your king's contempt, and loath to bear
Shame to my country, who from thence came freighted
With many glorious honors, I preferred
An obscure life before a public shame;
Oh then, good father, be it not my blame
If my supposed death on the king have thrown
Dangers which from himself are merely grown.
SUBPRIOR What, princely maiden, would you wish me do?
ERMENHILD I do conjure you sir, by all the bonds
Tie[420] you to pious acts, you would make way
To my incensèd father; give him these lines,
This ring, pledge of that blessing he delivered me
At our last parting. Add unto these, if ever
His daughter's memory to him were dear,
To wound the prince let his rash hand forbear:
Since through each wound he gives him, I am slain.
If the sad king you meet, venture to tell him

412 129 taffety punk: a prostitute wearing the characteristic dress of taffeta (i.e. overdressed)
413 133 pock: i.e. the pox (venereal disease)
414 136 in coram: called to account (from the Latin preposition meaning "before, in the presence of," frequently used in legal discourses)
415 139 counter: one of the two City prisons, one in Cheapside, the other in the Poultry (Hoy, 1980)
416 140 catchpoles: petty officers of the justice
417 141 th' hole: the name of one of the worst apartments in the Counter prison in Wood street, London
418 2 troth-plight: bound by solemn promise or engagement
419 7 long of: on account of (Hoy, 1980)
420 16–17 bonds/Tie: i.e. bonds that tie

That more for him, than he for me, I bide,
And am his subject still, though not his bride.
SUBPRIOR This shall I do. How shall we meet again?
ERMENHILD Fears follow me so, I know not where nor when.
SUBPRIOR Hark how the sound of horror beats the air.
Your father's up in arms and does prepare
Sharp vengeance for this city, woe is me. Trust you
To me, who ne'er made much of woman yet;
Rest here sweet maid, till an old friar beget
What joys he can to comfort thee. Is Clement grown
A woman's man now? No, I am not mine own
Where your command may sway me: much more in this,
Where heaven, through virtue's trial, makes you his.

Exeunt

[Scene xiii]

A table is set out with a candle burning, a death's head,[421] *a cloak and a cross.* SUBPRIOR *sits reading. Enter* SHACKLE-SOUL, *leading in an Italian* ZANY,[422] *five or six courtesans, every one holding a jewel*

SHACKLE-SOUL [*Aside to* ZANY *and courtesans*]
That's he, and there's your golden hire to charm him.
Your fees I'll treble, let but lust's flame be felt;
The alpine snow at the sun's beams does melt,
So let your beauties thaw his frozen age,
First t'act an old lecher, then a devil on Hell's black stage.
Strike, strike your silver strings, brave set of whores! *Music*
At your striking up, devils dance and all Hell roars. ZANY *and courtesans fall into a short dance*
SUBPRIOR What sound offends mine ear? Soul of temptation?
Enchanters I defy ye, get you gone;
I'm blind to your enticements, from this I learn
At how dear rate the careless world does earn
That thing called pleasure. How many souls do fall,
Sold for a little gilt to daub this wall?[423]
Hence with your witchcrafts, the sight of this drives hence
All thoughts besieging our voluptuous sense.
SHACKLE-SOUL [*Aside*] Another bait, at this he will not bite.

The ZANY *sings;* SUBPRIOR *holds his head down as fast asleep*

ZANY *Will you have a dainty girl? Here 'tis.*
Coral lips, teeth of pearl: here 'tis.
Cherry cheeks, softest flesh; that's she.
Breath like May, sweet and fresh; she, she.
Be she white, black, or brown,
Pleasure your bed shall crown,
Choose her then, use her then,
Women are made for men.
Pretty, pretty waist,
Sweet to be embraced.
Pretty leg, oh pretty foot,
To beauty's tree the root,

421 0 SD *death's head*: symbolic skull, reminder of mortality
422 0 SD ZANY: usually a comic performer or parasite attending a mountebank, acrobat, etc. (here a courtesan), imitating their master's actions awkwardly
423 13 gilt to daub this wall: the Subprior refers to the courtesans' make-up, the "gilt" with which they "daub" the "wall" of flesh

This is she shall do't,
Or she shall do't, or she shall do't, she shall do't, she shall do't,
Kiss, kiss, play, play, come and dally,
Tumble, tumble, tumble, in beauty's valley.
SHACKLE-SOUL [*Aside to* ZANY *and courtesans*] His soul is chained in pleasures, bind it fast,
If he break your charms, the strongest spell comes last. *Exit*

All wake him

SUBPRIOR Hence devils incarnate, 'tis not the sorcery
Of your deceitful tunes shuts up mine eye,
Mine ears are likewise stopped. Hence, hence I say.
OMNES Ha, ha! A man of ice, a clod of clay. *Exeunt*

Enter SHACKLE-SOUL, *or some spirit*[424] *in a frightful shape*

SUBPRIOR Are all thy incantations spent now? Art come again?
Base workmanship of heaven, what other train?[425]
Were all hell's frightful horrors stuck in thy look,
Thou canst not shake me.
SHACKLE-SOUL I can.
SUBPRIOR Thou liest, thou shalt not.
SHACKLE-SOUL I bring thee tidings of thy death this night.
SUBPRIOR How dost thou know that hour of my last fight?
False herald, minister of despair and lies.
SHACKLE-SOUL I know too how many minutes thy days must rise.
SUBPRIOR Who gives thee the number?
SHACKLE-SOUL All things to us are known,
Whatever have been, are, or shall be done.
SUBPRIOR I'll pose[426] thee presently. What's this, thou fiend,
Which now I have turned to? Do but tell me that
And I'll believe thee.
SHACKLE-SOUL I scorn to be thy slave.[427]
SUBPRIOR Down, down, and sink into thy damnèd cave:
Look here, dost fly thou, hellhound? I dare thee stand,
O'er thee by these holy spells have I strong command,
Thy batteries[428] are too weak. By goodmen's prayers,
The continence[429] of saints (by which as stairs,
They ascend to heaven), by virgins' chastity,
By martyrs' crowned deaths, which recorded lie
In silver leaves, above: I charge thee down.
Howl where th'art bound in slavery, till the last doom.
SHACKLE-SOUL Storms, thunder, lightning, rip up the earth's womb.
SUBPRIOR Eternal power, thanks on my humbled knee,
Thou still to constant breasts giv'st victory. *Exit*
SHACKLE-SOUL No way to conquer thee? I'll give thee o'er:
Ne'er fished I so, yet lost a soul, before.

Exit

424 38 SD *or some spirit*: Q appears to be based on an authorial MS marked up in the theatre; this imprecise SD enables the actor playing Shackle-Soul to quickly change and re-enter, or provides an alternative whereby another actor can play this role
425 40 train: trick or scheme designed to entrap
426 49 pose: question, interrogate
427 50–51 turned to? … thy slave: the Subprior tests Shackle-Soul's professed knowledge of all things by turning his thoughts to something and asking Shackle-Soul to read his mind; Shackle-Soul refuses to play along
428 55 batteries: assaults
429 56 continence: self-restraint

[Scene xiv]

Alarums. Enter ALFONSO, RUFFMAN [*as* BOHOR], SPENDOLA, BRISCO, *with drawn weapons*

ALFONSO Black horrors, mischief, ruin, and confusion
Affright us, follow us.
BOHOR Dare them to the face,
And you fright them.
SPENDOLA No safety but to fly.
ALFONSO Whither Spendola, whither? Better stay, and die.

Enter NARCISCO [*to the*] *King; alarums afar off*

OMNES What hope? What news?
ALFONSO Is my uncle fled?
NARCISCO He's gone—
And fights against you.
ALFONSO Follow him damnation,
That leaves his prince so in distress, in misery;
O bane of kings! Thou enchanting flattery,
Thy venom now I feel, eating my heart,
More mortal than an Indian's poisoned dart.
BOHOR Y'are too dejected; gather head and fight it out.
ALFONSO The head's here, where are hands to lay about?

Enter JOVINELLI

JOVINELLI Where is the king?
ALFONSO The man that title mocks
Is here, thou sad-visage man. Are any hired
To kill me or betray me? Let 'em come:
Grief's growing extreme, death is a gentle doom.
JOVINELLI Prepare then for the worst.
ALFONSO I am armed for't: show it.
JOVINELLI Thy kingdom is a weak ship, bruised, split, sinking;
Nor hast thou any pilot to waft us o'er
Out of this foul sea to some calmer shore.
Thy people's hearts are turned to rocks of flint,
The scholar, soldier, and the mariner,
Whom (as themselves say) once thou trod'st upon,
Now serve as wheels of thy destruction.
ALFONSO Flying swiftly backward, the kingly lion's quailed;[430]
What shall the weaker herds do, if he fall?
SPENDOLA Let's fly.
OMNES Zounds, whither?
BRISCO So we may be safe—
JOVINELLI But where?
SPENDOLA At Bartervile: the churl's to me beholden,
His house so stands, we may enter without fear.
OMNES Be't so, to Bartervile.
SPENDOLA What will your highness do?
ALFONSO Die, Spendola, a miserable king,
None here can hinder us of that.
SPENDOLA How? Die?

430 25 quailed: trembling, frightened

[*To others*] Ha' you any stomach to death sirs?
OMNES Not I.
SPENDOLA Nor I.
Troth's,[431] though you grow desperate, we'll grow wise.
OMNES Farewell sir, we'll save one. *Exeunt*
ALFONSO Oh, my cruel'st enemies!
Stabs Brutus[432] at me too?
BOHOR [*Aside*] Now mine own or never.
ALFONSO Why art not thou gone?
BOHOR Aye, I'll stick to you ever:
I am no courtier, sir, of Fortune's making.
ALFONSO Thou art no wiseman to prefer thy love
To me before thy life; pray thee leave me.
BOHOR Not I.
ALFONSO I shall not hate the world so readily
As else I would. Oh, had the ancient race
Of men (who had long leases of their lives)
Been wretched as we are, no recompense
Could the gods have given them for their being here,
But now more pitiful wise Nature grows,
Who cuts off man's years to cut off his woes.
BOHOR True sir, and teaches him a thousand ways
To lead him out this horrid giddy maze.
ALFONSO I apprehend thee: a small dagger's point
Opens the veins to cure our pleurisy.[433]
BOHOR Than to be made your foe's slave, better die.
ALFONSO A hundred thousand deaths, than like a captive
Be chained to grace proud Caesar's chariot wheel.[434]
BOHOR Much less a petty duke's.
ALFONSO Fetch me, dear friend,
An armed pistol and mouth it[435] at my breast:
I'll make away myself, and all my sorrows
Are made away.
BOHOR The best and nobler spirits
Have done the like.
ALFONSO Your bravest men at arms
Have done the like.
BOHOR Philosophers have done it.
ALFONSO Great peers have done it.
BOHOR Kings have done the like.
ALFONSO And I will do it.
BOHOR Nay it shall ne'er be said,
I lived a minute after you: here, here.
ALFONSO I embrace thee, noblest friend.
BOHOR Let's sail together.
ALFONSO Content, brave Bohor. Oh! But whither? Whither?
BOHOR From hell (this world), from fiends (in shapes of men).
ALFONSO No: into Hell, from men to be damned black with fiends.
Methinks I see Hell yawn to swallow us.

431 34 Troth's: truth is
432 36 Brutus: Alfonso alludes to Caesar's betrayal (and assassination) by Brutus
433 51 pleurisy: overabundance or excess of something
434 54 Caesar's chariot wheel: being forced to follow Caesar's chariot was a mark of humiliation or debasement
435 56 mouth it: point its mouth

BOHOR Fuh, this is but the swimming of your brain,
By looking downwards with a timorous eye.
ALFONSO My soul was sunk too low to look more high.
Forgiveness, heaven. *Alarums*
BOHOR The whips of furies lash me, the foe comes on.
ALFONSO And we will meet him, dare confusion[436]
And the world's mixed poisons; there is a hand
That fights for kings, and under that we'll stand.

Alarum still afar off. Enter a FRIAR *running*

BOHOR Whither runs this friar?
FRIAR To save my wretched life,
From th'insolent soldier threat'ning the city's spoil.[437]
ALFONSO Of what house art thou?
FRIAR Of Father Clement's order,
The Capuchin's Subprior: a quick messenger
Fetched me to be rich Bartervile's confessor,
Who lies a-dying.
ALFONSO A-dying!
FRIAR He does, but I
Have come thus far, with so much jeopardy
That could I safely get to the lee shore,[438]
Him nor the priory would I see more.
For charity's sake, direct me and defend me.
ALFONSO To help distressèd men, religion binds me.
Shouldst thou in this hot broils[439] be met abroad,
It will be judged you leave your priory
Carrying gold and silver with you.
FRIAR 'Las, I have none.
ALFONSO But friar, if you be thus taken, your life is gone.
Here, here, cast off thy habit, better that lie
I' th' streets than thou, poor wretch; wear mine, and away: [*They exchange clothes*]
Strike[440] down that lane.
FRIAR Thanks master, for your lives I'll pray. *Exit*
ALFONSO This, Bohor, shall disguise me; whither wilt thou fly?
BOHOR I'll shift I warrant: haste thou to th' priory.
ALFONSO If we ne'er meet again, best friend, farewell.
BOHOR [*Aside*] Not meet? Yes, I hope: you must not thus cheat Hell. *Exit*
ALFONSO I will not trust this fellow. To th' priory? No,
Bartervile's confessor:[441] if to betray
Thou findst the churl apt, leave him, if not, there stay;
The downfall of that prince is quick and steep,
Who has no heart to leave, nor power to keep.

Exit

436 74 dare confusion: defy (and possibly welcome) chaos and destruction
437 78 the city's spoil: to spoil (sack) the city
438 84 lee shore: shore that affords shelter
439 88 hot broils: furious battle
440 94 Strike: make your way
441 100 Bartervile's confessor: I will go serve (in disguise) as Bartervile's confessor

[Scene xv]

Enter BARTERVILE [*disguised as a Turk*] *and* [GRUMBALL *as*] LURCHALL, *with the courtiers*

LURCHALL Make the door sure, the house is round beset.
OMNES Beset!
BARTERVILE Put up: fear nothing. Armies, should they enter,
Cannot here find you.
OMNES How shall we escape?
BARTERVILE Send for your trunks and jewels, I'll ship you this night. Meantime, this unknown way leads to a cellar, where a world cannot fetch you forth. In, in, if danger pursue you, in a dry-fat[442] I'll pack you hence.
OMNES Zounds, into the dungeon?
BARTERVILE So to Sardinie:[443]
Your cloaks and your gilt rapiers down, down, down. *Exeunt* [*the courtiers*]

Enter King [ALFONSO] *as a friar*[, *aloof*]

ALFONSO How soon meets Babel's pride confusion?
LURCHALL What nest of birds are these new-killed with fear?
BARTERVILE Fowl cannot last long sweet, therefore kept there
In my cold cellar; stay, house beset? What foes?
LURCHALL Such as strike dead the heart, yet give no blows. Sergeants.
BARTERVILE This—*foutre*[444] for 'em! Proclamations Lurchall?
Six thousand crowns are his, can these betray,
Soon earned, we'll share. Fetch the Calabrian hither.
They are here: say "Damn 'em."
LURCHALL You shall be damned together. *Exit*
[*King comes forward*]

ALFONSO Where's that devout sickman desires to take
Leave of this world? *Deus hic*[445] to all now here.
BARTERVILE Now Domine[446] Friar; what I to you confess
You are bound by oath to keep.
ALFONSO I aver no less.
BARTERVILE Keep then this close: I am no Turk, not I,
But Bartervile disguised in policy.
ALFONSO Are you the sickman?
BARTERVILE Sick of a disease
Bad as a plague to citizens: I must break,
Play a bankrupt's part. I have money of the king's,
Of merchants'; I'll keep all, these are city springs.[447]
Here lies sergeants leaguer[448] about my doors:
My house to me is an hospital, they the sores
Which run upon me vilely, peep I but out.
To raise this Dunkirk siege,[449] thus cast I about.
ALFONSO Let's hear, pray how?

442 6 dry-fat: large barrel or vessel used to store dry things
443 7 Sardinie: i.e. the western Mediterranean island of Sardinia
444 14 *foutre*: French expression of contempt, which roughly translates to English "fuck"
445 19 *Deus hic*: God be here (i.e. a standard Latin blessing)
446 20 Domine: respectful term of address to the clergy
447 27 springs: snares, traps
448 28 Here lies sergeants leaguer: i.e. sergeants lie in wait (to arrest him for debt) outside of Bartervile's doors. To "lie leaguer" was a military term for besieging a city
449 31 raise this Dunkirk siege: to raise a siege is to abandon it or withdraw from it; Dunkirk, in northern France and held by the Spanish, had been besieged as recently as 1600 by the Dutch with assistance from the English (an event probably dramatized in a lost Admiral's men play of 1603)

BARTERVILE Thus, thus, sweet Domine Friar:
I'll be like you, a Capuchin. So, by your Prior,
Subprior, and convent, I may be fetched hence,
Spite of all shoulder-clappers'[450] violence.
Though the king should lay hands on me, I would not tarry.
ALFONSO You need not.
BARTERVILE You are my guard, my sanctuary.
ALFONSO But what your level[451] in this, when this is done?
BARTERVILE Alas! What level but pure devotion?
ALFONSO [*Aside*] The devil you have.
BARTERVILE When I die there, take all:
Will you go to your Prior and tell this? *A march afar*[452]
ALFONSO Yes I shall.
BARTERVILE I'll send him an earnest penny[453] (a hundred crowns)
As the first stone my charity builds upon.
What drum's this? Come, dispatch Friar, and be gone.
ALFONSO [*Aside*] Out of this hell thou meanest. Yes, I'll fly from thee
As from the devil's hangman: thou'lt else betray me.
World! To what crest of villainy art thou grown,
When of good men whole kingdoms scarce breed one? *Exit*

[BARTERVILE *removes his disguise. Enter* LURCHALL, *bound, and the Duke of* CALABRIA, *with* ASTOLFO *and soldiers*]

LURCHALL Here's the Duke of Calabria, sir. If you have made me tell a lie, they'll send me of a voyage to the island of hogs and devils (the Bermudas). The Duke, sir.
BARTERVILE His grace is welcome. 'Las! I had more need
To have physicians and apothecaries
Than fighters at my gates. Lurchall, why come they?
CALABRIA Deliver up those monsters in thy house,
That have devoured a kingdom and the king.
'Tis death to thee, and him, if thou detain'st 'em.
BARTERVILE I detain 'em here, here, here.
ASTOLFO Reward if thou deliver'st them.
BARTERVILE I'm past rewarding in this world, I look
Only for good men's prayers. There's the key, Lurchall.
CALABRIA Unbind him. Stay, why did thy house receive them?
BARTERVILE Full sore against my will: the bed I rise from
Count I my deathbed; for each minute I look
When angels (heaven's good porters) will let me in,
Yet like my betters, I'm heavy laden with sin.
And being thus sick, and at last gasp, I sent for my
Nearest cousin, my executor,
Who seeing brave fellows beating at my gates,
Took 'em for honest men, let 'em in simply,
And undertook this night, to ha' shipped 'em hence;
My faithful servant telling me this, in zeal
To you and my country, I bid him all reveal.
CALABRIA Th'ast played a subject's part in't.
BARTERVILE He'll lead you to them.
CALABRIA My lord, take force and seize 'em, ne'er stand upon

450 35 shoulder-clappers': a shoulder-clapper is an officer charged with the arrest of an offender
451 38 what your level: what is your purpose, or aim
452 41 SD *A march afar*: the sound of Calabria's drums (see line 44), heard as though far away
453 42 earnest penny: sum paid in earnest to secure a bargain (Hoy, 1980)

Mere trials; give 'em speedy execution.
ASTOLFO Come, fellow. *Exeunt* ASTOLFO *and* LURCHALL *cum militibus*[454]
BARTERVILE Your grace has done with me?
CALABRIA Go, look to thy health:
The crowns the proclamation promised
Shall to thy man be paid.
BARTERVILE Thanks to your grace:
'Las, what I did in this, was for no hire. *Exit*
CALABRIA Ha ha, the rent of a cellar never was so dear.
On beat the drum.

As they go off, enter OCTAVIO *with* RUFFMAN [as BOHOR] *and a guard*

OCTAVIO Are the rest ta'en?
CALABRIA Yes.
OCTAVIO The grand pirate's here.
Here's the devil's bellows, kindled all those fires
Which now are burning. This is the snake whose sting,
Being kept warm in the bosom of a king,
Struck him to th' heart. This he, who by the force
Of his damned arguments, was the first divorce
Of the king's love. This is Bohor.
CALABRIA This that serpent?
Y'have all, like traitors, wrought a prince's fall,
And all shall taste one death.
OCTAVIO Sirrah, where's the king?
BOHOR Warrant me life, I'll bring you to the place
Where you shall take him.
OCTAVIO Wilt thou betray him slave?
BOHOR Yes.
CALABRIA Thou shalt have life.
BOHOR And you the king shall have.
OCTAVIO And the gallows shall have thee, else hang me. Away.
Exeunt

[Scene xvi]

Enter SCUMBROTH [*to the* SUBPRIOR]

SCUMBROTH Alas, where's the Subprior?
SUBPRIOR Here; what ailest[455] thou?
SCUMBROTH Can you pick nothing out of my face?
Is there not a death's head standing on my shoulders?
SUBPRIOR Why, what's the matter?
SCUMBROTH The Lord Prior is called away.
SUBPRIOR Whither, by whom?
SCUMBROTH By the great head; I think he cozened me. He is gone to the black squib-tree, to Judas' Oak, set by the devil. I told you then, I saw Friar Rush spit fire amongst other hellcats, and ye would not believe me. Now I tell you that the Prior is choked; will his choking go down your throat?
SUBPRIOR How, choked?
SCUMBROTH Yes, choked: that of which men die o'ernight, and are well the next morning;

454 76 SD *cum militibus*: with soldiers (Latin)
455 2 what ailest: what troubles

wine has killed the Lord Prior. He would in a bravery taste the liquor of our vines, because you threatened he should never lick his lips after. And the kernel of a grape stopped his windpipe, for want of a scouring-stick.[456]
SUBPRIOR Art thou sure he is dead?
SCUMBROTH How, dead? Because I would be sure, I cut his throat of purpose, to take out the kernel.
SUBPRIOR Most fearful and prodigious, whither runst thou?
SCUMBROTH To see more throats cut. An execution of certain gallants is this morning, and I came running to see them. Who, like a whore, spoils every good thing that comes into his hand? The hangman. I leave you to the gallows.

Enter BARTERVILE *like a friar, brought in by the* SUBPRIOR,[457] *the King* [ALFONSO],[458] SHACKLE-SOUL [*as Friar* RUSH], *and* [GRUMBALL *as*] LURCHALL, *with others* [*as friars*]

RUSH Welcome dear brother: now your heed must be
Not to look back at this world's vanity,
Riches, and pleasures. You have laid aside
That garment, and must now be mortified.[459]
BARTERVILE I am mortified, I warrant you.
ALFONSO [*Aside*] So is the devil.
SUBPRIOR Your gold and silver; you must see no more.
BARTERVILE Oh, fie! Give it, every farthing, to the poor,
When I have sent for't hither.
LURCHALL [*Aside*] That will be never.
RUSH Your money shall be spent in pious sort.
BARTERVILE I know that: let my soul be the better for't,
That's all I crave for, after I am dead.
SUBPRIOR Many a requiem for it shall be said. [*Drum sounds*]
OMNES What drum is this?
RUSH Friars, stand upon your guard:
The priory is beset with armèd men,
Of which some troops are entered.
ALFONSO I am betrayed.
BARTERVILE Lurchall, I feel my weasand-pipe[460] cut.
LURCHALL I warrant you.

Enter CALABRIA, OCTAVIO, ASTOLFO, [*and*] RUFFMAN [*as* BOHOR] *led by two holding pistols; soldiers, drums and colors*[461]

CALABRIA Guard the abbey gates, let not a friar go forth:
You have a king amongst you, which is he?
OMNES A king!
SUBPRIOR I know of none here.
CALABRIA Villains, you lie!
OCTAVIO This caitiff[462] does delude you: torture him.
CALABRIA Hang him and these up o'er the abbey walls,
Our wrath shall smite like thunder where it falls.
BARTERVILE I shall, like a dog, die without money, Lurchall.

456 16 scouring-stick: a sponge or scourer for cleaning out the bore of a gun
457 23 SD SUBPRIOR: the Subprior has been on stage for the entire scene; perhaps he facilitates the others' entrance here?
458 23 SD ALFONSO: the king is still disguised in the friar's clothes
459 27 mortified: purified of sin and worldly desires
460 40 weasand-pipe: throat, wind-pipe
461 41 SD *colors*: flags or ensigns carried by a military regiment
462 45 caitiff: wretch or villain (i.e. Bartervile)

LURCHALL I warrant you.
ALFONSO Tyrant, that royal hart[463] thou hunt'st is here.
Stand from me all, you have betrayed me all,
And I'll trust none of you; if the lion must fall,
Fall shall he like a lion. Think'st thou, base lord,
Because the glorious sun behind black clouds
Has awhile hid his beams, he's darkened forever?
Eclipsed never more to shine, yes, and to throw
Fires from his sparkling eyes, thee to confound?
Touch not that noble friend of mine (it seems,
For my sake, marked for danger); let your arrows,
Dipped in rank poison, be shot all at me.
Since all is lost, die nobly, and lose life too.
O uncle! Must the first dart fly from you?
OCTAVIO Into thy bosom fly I.
ALFONSO To betray me?
OCTAVIO To fight for thee till I can fight no more:
Hadst thou possessed this kingly spirit before,
We ne'er had left thee: what makes Judas here?
ASTOLFO Here's he that to the duke thy life betrayed.
ALFONSO Bohor!
OCTAVIO Aye, Bohor.
BOHOR I told him where you were.
OCTAVIO I tell thee th'art a traitor and I'll have
Thy head off, or thou mine.
BOHOR Head?
OCTAVIO Th'art a slave!
Thou seest, Duke, what to trust to.
BARTERVILE I have confessed, and shall be hanged. The king?
CALABRIA Our fair game come to this? Our swords I see
Must from your heart's-blood let out all my wrongs.
A murdered daughter for just vengeance cries,
Whom to appease, your lives we'll sacrifice:
Beat the drum. [*Drum beats*]
ALFONSO Thunder mock thunder, beat ours. [*Another drum beats*]
SUBPRIOR Oh, let these fires be quenched out with my tears
If waters cannot. Duke, I bind thy rage
With this strong charm, and this. [*Gives ring and letter to* CALABRIA] Read o'er that spell,
And let thy hard breast grow more flexible. *Exit*
ALFONSO Where's Jovinelli, and that bastard crew
Of my false friends?
OCTAVIO Beheaded.
ALFONSO They have their due.
CALABRIA The ring I gave her, and her hand.[464] Old man—
Where's the old friar delivered these?
OMNES He's gone.
CALABRIA Make after him, 'tis some delusion.

Enter SUBPRIOR *and* ERMENHILD

ERMENHILD 'Tis no delusion, father; am I the ground
Of this your quarrel, which must both confound

463 50 hart: male deer
464 84 hand: her handwriting (i.e. a letter)

If you go on. Your battles thus I'll part.
The first blow given shall run clean through my heart.
ALFONSO O noble constant maid, forgive my wrongs,
The warmth of heaven to a pining spring
Cannot such comfort give as thy glad presence
Does to my bosom.
OCTAVIO Will you fight or no?
CALABRIA 'Twere madness to wish storms when fair winds blow:
Will you your faith yet keep?
ALFONSO Inviolate.
CALABRIA Then here end all my wars.
ALFONSO And all my hate.
Haste all these friars up to the abbey walls,
And with shrill voices, this our peace proclaim.
Stay, holy father, Bohor. See you this done.
BOHOR Vengeance, I have now lost more than I have won. *Exit*
BARTERVILE I shall go scot-free, Lurchall.
LURCHALL Passing well?
BARTERVILE They do not smell me, yet myself I smell. *Exit*
OCTAVIO Why sends your highness thus these friars to play
Your heralds' parts in publishing this peace?
ALFONSO There's in't a riddle, uncle, which by none
But by these friars only, can be done.

Enter [BARTERVILE *and*] *friars above*

So: are you mounted? Sing now.
OMNES Sing?
ALFONSO Yes sing,
Like swans before your deaths: there you all shall die.
Give fire to this most damnèd priory.
SUBPRIOR Alack for pity!
ALFONSO Father, but for thee,
Thunder from heaven had long ere this to dust
Grinded these hellish buildings. That hand was just
Which struck your vicious Prior, so is our doom:
That synagogue[465] of devils, let fire consume.
BARTERVILE But means the king that I shall burn here too?
ALFONSO Thou? The grand villain, give him a villain's due.
BARTERVILE I am no friar, see: I'm poor Bartervile.
OMNES How? Bartervile?
ALFONSO He lies, the slave's a Turk.
BARTERVILE A Christian, by this hand, your officer.
ALFONSO The city canker, the court's cozener,
A devil in shape of man.
BARTERVILE Half that I have
I freely give, so you my life will save.
I'll lend your highness thirty thousand chequeens.
ALFONSO Ten kingdoms cannot buy thee; were there ten hells,
Th'art damned in all. 'Sdeath! Fire that house of devils.
ALL 3 DEVILS [*Removing their disguises*] Do: let's not want light to set forth our revels.
RUFFMAN King, little dost thou know, whom all this while
Thy court, this convent, and this Bartervile

465 115 synagogue: in post-Reformation use, refers disparagingly to abbeys

Have entertained: of Hell, three spirits we are.
OMNES How?
RUFFMAN Sent to catch souls for Pluto, our prince and master.
OMNES Defend us heavens!
RUFFMAN Thyself hast burst those bands
In which I once held thee: these are in our hands.
BARTERVILE If you be right sergeants, for money you'll let me go.
Five thousand crowns I'll give but to go home.
ALL 3 DEVILS No.
BARTERVILE I'll put in four brokers[466] to be my bail: I hope they'll be taken.
RUFFMAN Yes, as thou art, to Hell, you dog; leave howling.
This pile of green young devils needs no fire
Of mortals' kindling to consume these frames,
You shall with us to Hell ride, all in flames.
SHACKLE-SOUL Catch.
ALL 3 DEVILS Come.
RUFFMAN Let every spirit his own prize bear.
ALL 3 DEVILS They are so heavy with sin, they'll soon be there.
RUFFMAN Away then and be damned, would you all were here.
OMNES Oooh! *Sink down, above flames*
ALFONSO Immortal thanks for our deliverance:
Raze to the ground those walls: no stone shall stand
To tell such place was ever in our land.
What wealth can there be found, give to the poor.
Another house we'll build and thee restore
To former virginity.[467] Weep not for these ruins,
Thou shalt from us have honors.[468] Here we begin
Our reign anew, which golden threads shall spin.
Justice shall henceforth sit upon our throne
And virtue be your king's companion.
War here resigns his black and horrid stage
To sportful Hymen, god of marriage.

Exeunt

[Scene xvii]

The play ending, as they go off, from under the ground in several places rise up spirits; to them enter, leaping in great joy, RUFFMAN, SHACKLE-SOUL, *and* GRUMBALL, *discovering behind a curtain* RAVAILLAC,[469] GUY FAWKES,[470] BARTERVILE, *[and] a* PRODIGAL, *standing in their torments*

ALL DEVILS Ha, ha, ha.
ALL DAMNED SOULS Torments inutterable! Oh! Damned for nothing?
RAVAILLAC Terrors incomprehensible.
GUY FAWKES Back, y'are blown up else.
BARTERVILE Whooh! Hot, hot, hot! Drink! I am heart-burnt.
PRODIGAL One drop, a bit!
GUY FAWKES Now, now, now.
BARTERVILE I am parboiled, I am stewed, I am sod in a kettle of brimstone pottage. It scalds!
It scalds! It scalds! It scalds! Whooh!
ALL DEVILS Ha, ha, ha!

466 138 brokers: pawnbrokers. Dekker and other playwrights frequently associate pawnbrokers and second-hand dealers (especially of clothing) with Hell
467 152 virginity: the mode of life characterized by religious chastity
468 151–3 Another house . . . have honors: addressed to the Subprior
469 0 SD RAVAILLAC: François Ravaillac, the assassin who killed Henri IV of France (14 May 1610)
470 0 SD GUY FAWKES: principal conspirator in the failed Gunpowder Plot to destroy Parliament in November 1605

PRODIGAL But one half-crumb, a little, little drop, a bit.
GUY FAWKES Towers, towers, towers, towers, pinnacles and towers, battlements and pinnacles, steeples, abbeys, churches, and old chimneys.
BARTERVILE Zounds, drink! Shall I choke in mine inn? Drink.
ALL DAMNED SOULS Drink, drink, oh! One drop, one drop to cool us.
RUFFMAN So many tapsters in Hell, and none fill drink here!
ALL DEVILS Bawl no more, you shall be liquored. *Exeunt*
RAVAILLAC Why art thou damned to th' horrors of one hell,
Yet feel'st ten thousand?
GUY FAWKES Wherefore is thy soul
Made sensible of tortures which, each minute,
Kill thee ten thousand times, yet canst not die?
BARTERVILE Some sack.
PRODIGAL Why for a few sins that are long hence past,
Must I feel torments that shall ever last?
Ever, ever.
BARTERVILE Let the sack be mulled.[471]
RAVAILLAC Why is the devil (if man be born good)
Suffered to make him evil?
BARTERVILE Man is an ass, if he sit broiling thus i' th' glass-house[472] without drink: two links of my chain for a three-halfpenny[473] bottle of mother conscience's ale: drink.
ALL DAMNED SOULS One drop of puddle water to cool us.

Enter SHACKLE-SOUL *with a burning torch and a long knife,* GRUMBALL *with a handful of snakes, a third spirit with a ladle full of molten gold. All three make a stand, laughing*

ALL DEVILS Leave howling and be damned.
SHACKLE-SOUL Here's drink for thee, royal villain. *Stabs* RAVAILLAC
RAVAILLAC Oh!
SHACKLE-SOUL Is't not good!
For blood th'ast thirsted, and thy drink is blood.
Strikes it so cold to thy heart? Here's that shall warm thee. *[Stabs] again*
RAVAILLAC Damnation, Furies, firebrands! *Hand burnt off*[474]
ALL DEVILS Ha, ha, ha.
PRODIGAL One drop of moisture, but one crumb.
GRUMBALL Art hungry? Eat this adder. Dry? Suck this snake.
PRODIGAL Suck and be damned thyself: I'll starve first. Away.
BARTERVILE Is not this all waters? Ruby water,[475] some ruby water, or else a bottle of postern water[476] to save charges, or else a thimbleful of lemon water, to cool my stomach.
3 DEVIL The ruby is swilled up all, here's lemon down with't. *[Offers molten gold]*
BARTERVILE Foh, the great devil or else some aqua-vitae woman has made water, it scalds me.
ALL DAMNED SOULS Oooh.
ALL DEVILS Ha, ha, ha. *Curtains are drawn over them*

Enter RUFFMAN

RUFFMAN Hell grins to hear this roaring. Where's this black

471 26 mulled: warmed and spiced
472 29 glass-house: building where glass is made (and which therefore, like Hell, is notable for its fires)
473 30 three-halfpenny: depreciatory epithet of anything held in small esteem; literally worth three halfpence
474 38 SD *Hand burnt off*: As Hoy (1980) notes, the hand with which the historical Ravaillac killed Henry IV of France was plunged into a furnace and burned off in an attempt to solicit a confession
475 43 Ruby water: uncertain meaning; perhaps a red-hued liquor or juice; "postern water" below suggests something inferior to clean drinking water, but lemon water (mentioned subsequently) implies a tonic for the stomach
476 44 postern water: meaning somewhat unclear; perhaps rainwater collected in a bowl fastened to a gatepost

Child of fathomless[477] perdition, rarest devil
That ever hold in[478] Barathrum?[479] [GUY FAWKES *comes forward*] Hear, dear pupil,
Of a new damnation's stamp; saucer-eyed Lucifer[480]
Has drunk to thee this deep infernal bowl off,[481]
Wilt pledge his ugliness?
GUY FAWKES Reach it me.[482]
RUFFMAN Choke with it.
ALL DEVILS Ha, ha, ha!
GUY FAWKES Give fire, blow all the world up.
RUFFMAN Bounce![483] 'Tis done. Ha, ha, ha! *Fires the barrel-tops*[484]
GUY FAWKES I shall be grinded into dust; it falls, I am mad.
ALL DAMNED SOULS (*Within*) I am mad, I am mad.
ALL DEVILS Ha, ha, ha.
OTHER DEVILS (*Below*) Ho, ho, ho.

Enter PLUTO, *attended by* MINOS, AEACUS, *and* RHADAMANTH, *and three* FURIES

PLUTO Fetch whips of poisoned steel, strung with glowing wires,
And lash these saucy hellhounds: duck their souls
Nine times to th' bottom of our brimstone lakes,
From whence up pull them by their singèd hair,
Then hang 'em in ropes of ice nine times frozen o'er.
Are they scarce hot in Hell, and must they roar?
What holiday's this, that here's such grinning, ha!
Is Hell a dancing school? Y'are in extremes,
Snoring, or else horn-mad?[485] Who are set on shore,
On this vast land of horror, that it resounds
With laughter 'stead of shrieks, who are come to our bounds? Ha!
RUFFMAN Dread lord of this lower tartary,[486] to thy jail
Have we thy busy catchpoles prisoners brought:
Souls, for whose coming all Hell long hath sought.
PLUTO Their names? Is Ward and Dansiker[487] then come?
RUFFMAN Yes: Dansiker is come.
PLUTO Where's the Dutch *schellum*?[488] Where's Hell's factor? Ha?
RUFFMAN Charon has bound him for a thousand years,
To tug at's oar: he scoured the seas so well,
Charon will make him ferryman of Hell.
PLUTO Where's Ward?
SHACKLE-SOUL The merchants are not pilled nor pulled[489] enough,
They are yet but shaven; when they are flayed, he'll come,
And bring to Hell fat booties of rich thieves,

477 50 fathomless: unable to be measured
478 51 hold in: has been kept in
479 51 Barathrum: the abyss, Hell
480 52 Lucifer: alternative name (and the original name Dekker provided) for Pluto
481 53 He has drunk the entire bowl
482 55 Reach it me: pass it to me
483 59 Bounce: imitating the sound of a gun
484 59 SD *Fires the barrel-tops*: ignites the barrels of gunpowder
485 72 horn-mad: enraged, possibly at having been made a cuckold
486 75 tartary: hell
487 78 Ward and Dansiker: John Ward (an English pirate and apostate) and Simon Dansiker (a Dutch pirate) were the subjects of Robert Daborne's *A Christian Turned Turk* (1611, printed 1612). Dansiker died in 1611 and was thus a timely inclusion in Hell; Ward was still alive, and hence not "ripe for damning" (line 89)
488 80 *schellum*: skelm; rascal, scoundrel, villain
489 85 pilled nor pulled: stripped bare, pillaged (Hoy, 1980)

A crew of swearers and drinkers, the best that lives.
RUFFMAN Ward is not ripe for damning yet.
PLUTO Who is it then?
Cutlar the sergeant?[490] Ha! He come?
RUFFMAN Yes, Pluto:
Cutlar has been here long, sent in by a carman,[491]
But his stern looks the fiends did so displease,
Bound hand and foot, he howls in little ease,
Having only mace to comfort him. He does yell
And rave, because he cannot rest in Hell.
SHACKLE-SOUL 'Tis not for him, that we this holiday hold.
PLUTO The bawd of Shoreditch,[492] is that hellcat come?
RUFFMAN No: but she's been a long time launching forth
In a rosa solis-bark.[493]
PLUTO Devils! Who is it then?
Moll Cutpurse[494]—is she come?
RUFFMAN Our cousin come? No.
SHACKLE-SOUL 'Tis not yet fit Moll Cutpurse here should howl,
She has been too late a sore-tormented soul.
PLUTO Where is our daughter? Ha? Is she idle?
RUFFMAN No.
She was beating hemp in Bridewell to choke thieves,
Therefore to spare this she-ramp[495] she beseeches,
Till like herself all women wear the breeches.
GRUMBALL Moll Cutpurse plies her task and cannot come.
PLUTO For whom then is this wild Shrove Tuesday kept?
RUFFMAN See, king of gloomy shades, what souls resort
To this, thy most just and least-trying[496] court.
PLUTO Stay, since our jail is with brave fellows stored,
Bid Charon that no more yet come aboard.
Seeing our judges of Hell here likewise are
Sit, call a sessions: set the souls to a bar.[497]
Minos the just, Rhadamanth the temperate,
And Aeacus the severe, each take his state.
MINOS Not an officer here?
OMNES A fury.
ALL 3 JUDGES Make an oyez![498]
FURY Oyez! All manner of souls, if they love their own quietness, keep out of Hell, unless they have horrible business at this infernal sessions, upon pain of being damnably plagued for their lustiness. Back there, let those shackled rakehells show their faces.
BROKERS (*Within*) Room here, we must come into the court.

490 90 Cutlar the sergeant: untraced; a cutler is one who fashions or deals in blades, but Dekker clearly intends "Cutlar" to be the proper name of an apparently infamous sergeant

491 91 carman: carter, carrier

492 97 bawd of Shoreditch: a pander (go-between) or prostitute from the district of Shoreditch in north London, famed for its taverns, theatres, and brothels. Possibly the "bawd" in question is a specific individual such as Rose Flower, who appears in the *Gesta Grayorum* and in the works of Thomas Nashe as a moderately famous prostitute who worked in Shoreditch in the late sixteenth century

493 99 rosa solis-bark: rosa solis is an alcoholic cordial made with the juice of the sundew plant, used as a medicine. A "bark" is a boat (slowly launching towards Hell)

494 100 Moll Cutpurse: Mary Frith (1584/9–1659), a notorious thief and cross-dresser; dramatized by Dekker and Middleton in *The Roaring Girl* (also performed at the Fortune playhouse, in 1611)

495 105 she-ramp: bold, wanton, or lively woman; tomboy

496 110 least-trying: Q's "least-fying" remains unintelligible; as a conjectural emendation, "least-trying" is at least consistent with the scene's legal terminology

497 114 bar: barrier at which all the business of the court is transacted

498 117 Make an oyez: call for silence and attention

PLUTO What damnèd fiends are those, dare make this noise?
SHACKLE-SOUL A jury of brokers empanelled and deeply sworn
To pass[499] on all the villains in Hell.
RHADAMANTH Evil Conscience[500] be their keeper.
FURY Look to the jury: Evil Conscience look to the brokers.
PLUTO Now proceed.
AEACUS Stay, let the King of Ghosts have first a view
Of those who are doomed to pains horrid but new,
Then produce those who came to your prison untried.
FURY Peace there.
OMNES Here's one Hell's tortures does deride. RAVAILLAC [*brought in*]
RAVAILLAC Arraign me, rend me piecemeal, I'll confess nothing.
RUFFMAN Peace, thou shalt bawl thy throat out.
RAVAILLAC Merciless hangmen! To tyrannize over so brave a Roman spirit.
PLUTO Ho, ho, what country devil is this?
RAVAILLAC Thine own.
RUFFMAN A French.
The eagerest bloodhound that e'er came from thence;
Is there a king to be murdered, whilst he does stand
Colossus-like, supporting a whole land,
And when by his fall that land most fears a wrack,
Send forth this devil: his name is Ravaillac.
RAVAILLAC Ravaillac: I am Ravaillac, that laughs at tortures, spurns at death, defies all mercy.
Gibbets, racks, fires, pincers, scalding oil, wild horses; I spit in the face of all.[501]
FURY Peace.
RAVAILLAC No: were my tongue torn out with burning flesh-hooks, Fame's thousand tongues shall thunder out Ravaillac's name, extol it, eternize it, chronicle it! Canonize it! Oh!
MINOS Down with this devil to th' dungeon, there let him howl.
RAVAILLAC Worlds shall applaud my act, and crown my soul. *Exit*
PLUTO Another.
OMNES Come you lean dog.

PRODIGAL *brought in*

PRODIGAL One drop, a bit.
PLUTO What's he? What starveling's this?
PRODIGAL One that lacks a medicine for hunger: I am fallen away.
OMNES From heaven.
ALL 3 JUDGES To th' common jail with him.
FURY He must feed on beggary's basket: leave bawling, sirrah.
PRODIGAL Shall I be undone for a little drink?
GRUMBALL No, th'art undone for drinking.
PLUTO Starve him away. *Exit* PRODIGAL
What was he when he lived?
GRUMBALL A prodigal,
Who, in one year, spent on whores, fools, and slaves
An army's maintenance, now begs for crumbs, and raves
To see his sumptuous buildings, pastures, woods,
That stood in uplands, drowned in Rhenish floods.[502]
PLUTO Is here all?

499 124 pass: i.e. pass judgment
500 125 Evil Conscience: apparently the keeper of the jury of brokers in Hell
501 145 Gibbets, racks . . . of all: tortures to which the historical Ravaillac was subjected
502 165 Rhenish floods: "Rhenish" pertains to the Rhine river, which flows from the Swiss Alps through Germany and the Netherlands

SHACKLE-SOUL All! No, the arch-hellhound's here.

GUY FAWKES *enters*

PLUTO What Peter Gunner's[503] this?
GUY FAWKES Speak softly, within an inch of giving fire, within an inch.
SHACKLE-SOUL Had all thy grey devils in their highest lust sat
T'have littered Furies, they could not have begot
One to match this: i'th dark he groped damnation—
GUY FAWKES Now, now.
SHACKLE-SOUL Digged cellars to find where Hell stood and has found it;
There was but one villainy unborn, and he crowned it.
GUY FAWKES So: all the billets[504] lie close. Glorious bonfire? Pontifical bonfire? Brave heads to contrive this; gallant souls to conspire in't; resolute hand to seal this with my blood, through fire, through flint; ha, ha, ha. Whither fly myself to heaven? Friends to honor, none to the halter, enemies to massacre, ha, ha. Dismal tragical comedy now?
PLUTO What does he?
SHACKLE-SOUL As he thinks, giving fire to powder;
Ne'er in any land could devils have found such walks
As he was beating out.
PLUTO His name?
OMNES Guy Fawkes.
GUY FAWKES Who calls? Damnation stop's[505] throat.
ALL 3 JUDGES Let it stop thine.
GUY FAWKES Am I betrayed? Give fire, now, now, give fire.
OMNES To burn thine own soul, villain.
PLUTO Pay him his hire: *Exit* [GUY FAWKES]
He has a desperate rakehell's face.
SHACKLE-SOUL Had his plot ta'en fire,
One realm before any other had doomsday seen,
Kings who in tombs lay at rest had wakened been.
He was within twelve hours of hewing down
A whole land at one blow, and at once drown
In a flood of flames an ark-royal with his whole fleet
Of nobility and clergy; in a leaden sheet,
Law and her children had been hotly wrapped;
Millions ere this had in our sail been clapped,[506]
For damnèd arts not known now, which had then
Been rife, but now lie dead (th'acts with the men).
PLUTO Make much of this our ningle: for the rest,
Deliver 'em to our head-hangman.
OMNES When?
PLUTO In a twinkling.
MINOS How applauds Pluto
Our enginous[507] tortures and most rigorous doom?
PLUTO Minos, thy doom is just. But you, ill-faced caitiffs:
What fish in your infernal nets drew you up
I' th' Naples court, city, and friary?
We charged you sail thither: is mischief's river there dry?

503 167 Peter Gunner: derogatory term for an incompetent shooter
504 175 billets: thick pieces of wood appropriate for fuel
505 183 stop's: stop his
506 195 had in . . . been clapped: had been shipped to Hell
507 201 enginous: clever, crafty, deceitful

RUFFMAN Dry, no: fat preys for Hell we all did meet,
In court, city, country, nay, in every street,
In every house, within-him and without-him.
He that wore best clothes had some devil about him:
Courtiers from Naples hither in shoals are come,
Some for Ambition, for Flattery, and Envy some.
Some, who each meal eat subjects up, and wore
Whole families in their shoestrings; such, and others more,
Being here, have been examining (ever since
They came) by Hell's clerk, Spotted-Conscience.
MINOS Till the next sessions, these we must defer.
PLUTO None come fro' th' city, so many bad being there!
GRUMBALL Yes, king of endless horror, see who's here: BARTERVILE [*brought in*]
PLUTO Rich men in Hell! They are welcome. What's the greybeard?
BARTERVILE One that can buy thee and ten such as thou art out of thy sea-coal[508] pits here. Is not this Newcastle?
GRUMBALL No, covetous wretch: 'tis Hell, thy black soul's prison.
BARTERVILE Soul in prison! I never had any soul to speak on.
GRUMBALL Now thou shalt find th'ast one.
BARTERVILE Can angels[509] bail me?
MINOS Not all the wealth which the world's back does bear
Can bail thy wretched soul hence, now 'tis here.
BARTERVILE A thousand pounds—
FURY Where is't, fool?
RHADAMANTH Thy wealth's now gone,
Thy hands still catch at bags, but they grip none.
BARTERVILE What's this?
OMNES Ha, ha, ha.
AEACUS Air, shadows, things imaginary:
That is thy torment now, which was thy glory.
BARTERVILE If you give me bags full of sawdust instead of money, my ghost shall walk.
ALL 3 JUDGES To thy grim Father of Hell.
BARTERVILE No, to my old brother, Sir Achitophel Pinch-Gut.[510] Shall I? Shall I?
PLUTO Hence with him, the churl's mad:
In Lethe's flood[511] drowned all the wealth he had.
BARTERVILE My chain! Let me hang in chains, so it be my gold chain; thieves, thieves, thieves. *Exit* [*led by three devils*]
MINOS Throw him headlong into our boiling lake,
Where molten gold runs.
GRUMBALL His thirst it cannot slake,
Seas could not quench his dropsy.[512] Gold to get
He would hang a city, starve a country. Even yet
Raves he for bonds and encumbers:[513] to save whose soul,
(Though he fed none living) sausages were his dole.[514] *A confused noise to come pressing in*

508 220 sea-coal: mineral coal (i.e. a soft coal, as distinct from charcoal, which is hard)

509 225 angels: i.e. the gold coins of that name

510 238 Sir Achitophel Pinch-Gut: the biblical Achitophel deserted David and sided with Absolom, but commited suicide after the betrayal; a "pinch-gut" is a miserly purser, one who deprives another of food (hence "pinch-gut money" is nautical slang for an allowance given to sailors when provisions are inadequate)

511 240 Lethe's flood: Lethe was one of the five rivers of the underworld, associated with forgetfulness or oblivion

512 245 dropsy: insatiable thirst

513 247 encumbers: mortgages

514 248 sausages were his dole: most likely a reference to the "chains" (line 241) that Bartervile will be hung in, i.e. even in Hell Bartervile raves for "bonds and encumbers" (247), financial instruments that entangle other men, so his eternal sorrow ("dole") will be the "sausages" that bind him. *OED* provides some instances (from 1650 and after) of "sausages" being used as a word for things that resemble a string of sausages, e.g. chains. See also *The Sea Voyage* (in this volume) I.iv. 47: "here's two chains, suppose 'em sausages"

OMNES What coil[515] is that? *A noise*

Enter a [PURITAN] *ghost, coal-black*

PURITAN 'Tis a burning zeal must consume the wicked, and therefore I will not be kept out, but will chastise and correct the foul fiend.

ALL 3 JUDGES What's this black incubus?

SHACKLE-SOUL An arch-great Puritan once.

OMNES Ha! How? A Puritan?

MINOS An arch-great Puritan! How comes thy soul so little?

PURITAN I did exercise too much with a lively spirit.[516]

PLUTO Are there any more of his synagogue?

RUFFMAN Yes, a whole hoy-full[517] are landed.

OMNES Ha!

PLUTO Are they all so black as he is?

OMNES Worse.

MINOS Sirrah, why, being a Puritan, is your soul so black?

PURITAN We were all smoked out of our own country, and sent to Rotterdam.

MINOS How cam'st thou lame and crooked, why dost halt?

PURITAN All the brethren and sisters for the better part are crooked, and halt: for my own part, I never went upright.

ALL 3 JUDGES And yet a Puritan? Hence with him.

PURITAN Alack!
How can I choose but halt, go lame and crooked,
When I pulled a whole church down upon my back?

MINOS Hence with him, he will pull all Hell down too. *A noise to come in*

PURITAN Let in the brethren, to confound this wicked assembly.

ALL 3 JUDGES Thrust him out at Hell gates. *Exit* [PURITAN]

PLUTO They'll confound our kingdom
If here they get but footing. Rise therefore, away;
Keep the jury of brokers till our next court day.

MINOS Adjourn this.

FURY Oyez! Sessions is deferred.
Because of Puritans, Hell cannot be cleared.

PLUTO Set forward to our hall paved all with brass.
Judges, we thank you: let our officers drink
I' th' bottom of Hell's cellar, for their good service.
Since to this height our empire up you rear,
Hell shall hold triumphs and, that's done, prepare
Again to walk your circuits o'er the earth.
Souls are Hell's subjects, and their groans our mirth.

FINIS.

Epilogue

If't be not good, the devil is in't (they say);
The devil was in't, this then is no good play
By that conclusion; but hereby is meant,

515 249 coil: noisy disturbance

516 256 exercise too ... lively spirit: exercise my religion with too much zeal; the line also suggests (satirizing Puritan hypocrisy) that the Puritan has had too much sex and squandered his vital spirit (the "soul" of line 255 and/or semen)

517 258 hoy-full: a hoy is a small vessel carrying passengers and goods short distances on the sea-coast

If for so many noons and midnights spent
To reap three hours of mirth, our harvest-seed
Lies still and rot, the devil's in't then indeed.
Much labor, art, and wit make up a play,
As it does a ship, yet both are cast away,
When bravely they have passed the humorous seas,
At landing. What black Fates curseth both these?
Sail it or sink it, now 'tis forth and near
The haven at which it longs t'arrive: if there
It suffers wrack, the spitefuller rocks shoot forth,
Yet none may bring it home laden with much worth.
By wonted[518] gentle gale, sweet as the balm,
Or by extending your fair liberal palm
To fan away all storms, if you see it lours,[519]
The air shall ring thanks, but the glory's yours.

518 15 wonted: accustomed
519 17 it lours: the sky is threatening a storm

16 John Fletcher and Philip Massinger, *The Sea Voyage*

First performed 1622

First printed 1647

Edited by Claire M. L. Bourne

The Sea Voyage reads—and plays—like a social experiment. We are made to witness what happens when a ship carrying French pirates, self-styled gallants, and a woman kidnapped by the captain wreck on an uninhabited island without any material possessions or the proofs of social status those possessions bring with them. Lacking food, medical supplies, and sources of pleasure and distraction beyond their own withering wit, the men struggle to sustain themselves. At first, they complain of pangs in their stomachs and yearn for something—anything—to eat. Then, they imagine rocks and mud turning into food, especially the sorts of dishes that were thought in early modern England to enhance sexual performance. Here, as throughout the play, hunger is code for sexual appetite. Nowhere is this correlation more visceral than in what is arguably the play's most disturbing set-piece: growing ever more desperate, Lamure, Morillat, and Franville enlist the Surgeon to help them cannibalize the famished Aminta after she falls asleep. They fantasize about how she will taste and joke about whether they should wake her and kill her "in a chase" because hunting her for sport would make her flesh taste "sweeter" (III.i. 116). The shipmaster arrives just in time to preempt the violence, and the situation he sees looks a lot like attempted rape: "They would have ravished her upon my life" (III.i. 159). Aminta, who woke up of her own accord and has been trying to reason with the men for almost thirty lines, responds: "Forgive 'em; 'twas their hungers" (160).

Aminta's quickness to excuse the men's bad behavior is symptomatic of the play as a whole. *The Sea Voyage* is a tragicomedy that brings its male characters to the brink of death only to save them. At the same time, it celebrates female skill, legitimizes female anger, and validates female self-governance only to deny its female characters any real agency in the end. In this second plot, a "commonwealth" of Portuguese women—modeled, we are told, on a now-vanished community of indigenous Amazons—is thriving on a fertile, neighboring island that the French captain Albert "discovers" on his quest for food. These women live according to their own set of laws and harness the natural world for sustenance. Forbidden by their matriarch Rosella to consort with men, their community is irrevocably destabilized when Albert washes ashore. The women agree to bring food to the starving men on the other island and, aroused by the sight of Albert and after much pleading with Rosella, are permitted to "enjoy" his fellows (II.ii. 245) for one month only. But the sexual exchange never happens. The men offer the women jewels to remunerate them for their promise of food and sex, and Rosella immediately recognizes the jewelry as that she and the others lost years ago when they wrecked on the island. Suspecting the men of being the pirates who drove them from their plantations and of harming the male relatives she thought had perished in the wreck, Rosella arrests them and makes plans to sacrifice them in an elaborate ritual. Her rites are interrupted when two Portuguese men (who turn out to have given Albert and his compatriots the treasure) appear and reveal themselves to be none other than Rosella's husband and nephew, the men she had given up for dead. Rosella willingly abdicates her power, and the self-governing women are quickly brought into the patriarchal fold.

While *The Sea Voyage* does not feature any English characters, it is typically read as a commentary on England's relatively recent, and expanding, colonial ventures. The play patches together descriptions of New World exploration that were circulating in print and manuscript at the time of its composition in the 1620s—not only first-hand observations of "bouncing Amazons" and "Cannibals that each other eat" (to borrow phrases from Shakespeare) but also harrowing accounts of events like the Jamestown massacre (1622) and a famine that came to be known as "the starving time" in the Virginia colony (1609–10). Unlike the sites of contact and colonization featured in this news from abroad, however, the setting of *The Sea Voyage*—a pair of islands, one sterile and one fruitful—is geographically unlocated. It is also devoid of—that is, no longer home to—indigenous people, thus perpetuating the myth of New World "discovery" and "virgin" land. There are no Calibans to curse European sovereignty; instead, the play figures the hostile environment coupled with unchecked male prerogative as obvious dangers to the success of colonial settlement.

The play's only would-be cannibals are the French gallants, and they justify their appetite for human flesh by citing precedent, that is, the very narratives that served as source material for the play. Morillat begins, "I have read in stories —" Lamure interjects, "Of such restoring meats, we have examples,/Thousand examples" (III.i. 101–3). Without creature comforts or status symbols to manage their behavior, the men are as quick to revel in the pile of useless jewels—a miscalculation that results in the loss of their ship—as they are to try to eat Aminta—a situation that leads the more restrained Tibalt to respond with an exceptionally violent, morbid joke about their incompetence: why wouldn't they eat one another and "spare the woman to beget more food on"? (III.i. 169). Women, it turns out, are not expendable. However extreme this seems, it is not far off from one of the play's key messages: successful sexual performance (often regardless of consent) perpetuates family lines, personal legacies, *and* colonial enterprises. It is a key characteristic of good housekeeping.

In contrast to the men who model their behavior on stories they have read, the Portuguese women learn to live as Amazons directly "[b]y . . . example" from the "warlike women" who lived on the island "heretofore" but whose society presumably died out because they could not procreate (although foul play is never definitively ruled out—see II.ii. 202–10). The resulting commonwealth, in which each woman acts in the general interest of the group, offers a viable alternative to the monarchical, paternalistic model of rule that neither the men nor the play can shake off entirely. In the end, *The Sea Voyage* is deeply conservative in its reestablishment of patriarchal order, even as it shows this model to be problematic and potentially deadly.

The Sea Voyage is very likely a collaboration between John Fletcher and Philip Massinger, even though it was published for the first time in the 1647 folio collection as a "Beaumont and Fletcher" play. It was licensed by deputy Master of the Revels John Astley on June 22, 1622, for performance at the Globe and staged by the King's Men shortly thereafter. At the time, Fletcher had been the company's house playwright for almost a decade. The Globe, with its elevated gallery space, would have allowed for the vertical staging sequences required early in the play, especially in the storm scene where the action shifts among different levels of the ship, and on the island when characters seek higher ground for a better view of their unfamiliar surroundings. It is unclear whether the play was a hit since no further accounts of its presence in the company's repertory survive.

We do know that *The Sea Voyage* was revived after the Restoration. The diarist and drama-enthusiast Samuel Pepys issued a tepid review when he saw it performed to a packed house at the Theatre Royal at Bridges Street on September 25, 1667: "It is 'The Storme,' a play of Fletcher's; which is but so-so, methinks; only there is a most admirable dance at the end, of the ladies, in a military manner, which indeed did please me mightily" (qtd in Van Lennep, 1965: 118); so much did this dance (which is not explicitly called for in the earliest extant texts of the play) delight Pepys, that he took his wife to see the play the very next night. It was still in the repertory a year later, when he records having seen it twice more, now preoccupied with Elizabeth Knepp, one of his favorite actresses, for "doing her part of sorrow so well" (qtd in Van Lennep, 1965: 136)—she played the kidnapped Aminta. Less than twenty years later, Thomas D'Urfey adapted *The Sea Voyage* as *A Common-wealth of Women*. D'Urfey's version was first performed by the United Company at Drury Lane soon after being licensed on September 11, 1685, and was revived several times in the early eighteenth century (Van Lennep, 1965: 338). There is also some evidence to suggest that *The Sea Voyage* itself was staged again sometime between 1690 and 1692 (Downes, 1708: 43).

The influence of Fletcher's earlier collaborator Francis Beaumont is evident in the play's tragicomic form, especially its surprise ending. The play also bears some resemblance to key moments in the Shakespearean corpus. The separation of family members as the result of a shipwreck (and the assumption that they perished) echoes *Twelfth Night*, as does the fact that the relative presumed dead is named Sebastian. Fletcher and Massinger also seem to have been thinking about *A Midsummer Night's Dream*: like *Dream*, *The Sea Voyage* is preoccupied with husbandry; both plays treat fertile female bodies as ships venturing for merchandise (and vice versa); and Rosella, like Titania and Hippolita, is a resilient female leader of women who is ultimately restrained by the bonds of marriage. The love-triangle subplot among Albert, Aminta, and Rosella's daughter Clarinda has the hallmarks of Shakespearean romantic comedy, where the final couplings are products of coercion as much as they are the result of consent.

As the playwright John Dryden stressed in the preface to his own adaptation of *The Tempest*, it is that play with which *The Sea Voyage* most obviously shares dramaturgical DNA:

> Our excellent *Fletcher* had so great a value for [*The Tempest*], that he thought fit to make use of the same Design, not much varied, a second time. Those who have seen his *Sea-Voyage*, may easily discern that it was a Copy of *Shakespear's Tempest:* the Storm, the desart Island, and the Woman who had never seen a Man, are all sufficient testimonies of it.
>
> (Dryden and Davenant, 1670: sig. A2v)

Both plays open with a shipwreck, feature nobles who struggle in vain to make the environment work for them, and present women's desire for men as innate (both Miranda and Clarinda are titillated by their first glimpse of a virile male body). But *The Sea Voyage* departs from Shakespeare's play in its erasure of native inhabitants from the islands where the action is set. By side-stepping the option to dramatize the interplay between European self-rule and white rule over an indigenous population, the playwrights use the island setting as a control site to explore one practicable (if ultimately unsustainable) alternative to the patriarchal-monarchical model of governance upheld in *The Tempest*: the commonwealth.

Still, Rosella's passing mention of the vanished Amazons serves as a latent reminder that European colonial ventures almost always demanded the absence—and, often, violent erasure—of the people native to these so-called "new" lands.

In terms of performance, *The Sea Voyage* makes exciting demands on the representational capacities of theatrical space, and it requires a good deal of resolve from its audience: we must keep tabs as the conspicuous absence of the island's first inhabitants and morally abhorrent set-pieces chafe against quasi-utopian ones without any idea of how things will turn out until they do. Like many tragicomedies of the period, the play ends without making clear whether it endorses colonial projects or critiques them. The play is bookended by the violent end of one voyage—the opening shipwreck—and the promise of another, more salutary one—the journey "home." But the meaning of "voyage" in Sebastian's final line (one of only two places the word appears in the play) is much more slippery—and capacious:

When a while
We have here refreshed ourselves, we'll return
To our several homes; and well that voyage ends
That makes of deadly enemies faithful friends.
(V.iv. 110–13)

The rhymed couplet signals resolution and finality, but the future tense suggests that the "voyage" of the play's title—and all the dangers and ambiguities it has entailed thus far—might extend far beyond the actions dramatized here.

Textual note

The Sea Voyage was one of the thirty-five "Never Before Published" plays to appear in *Comedies and Tragedies* (1647), a large folio volume attributed to Beaumont and Fletcher, even though it contained plays written by a number of different playwrights. A lightly emended text of the play appeared in the expanded and reordered folio collection of 1679. The very small changes clarify some localized textual difficulties found in F1647 but also introduce new errors.

This edition takes F1647—specifically, the copy housed in the Eberly Family Special Collections Library at The Pennsylvania State University (PR2420 1647 Q)—as its copy-text. I defer to F1679 in cases where the F1647 text is erroneous or obscure and the later text offers a reasonable solution or clarification. I have also consulted F1679 for the placement of stage directions. Often, the F1679 text better articulates the sequence of dialogue and action because many stage directions (especially entrances) are set on their own lines. In F1647, these same directions are cramped and distributed over several lines to the right of the dialogue, allowing for the flexible timing of stage business but also making it more difficult to tell precisely what happens when. In F1679, *The Sea Voyage* also acquired a title page, where it is labeled a "Comedy"; a list of *dramatis personae*; and a list of five actors who were active with the King's Men in the early 1620s and probably performed in the play's 1622 premiere. Those paratexts are reprinted here. The text in both early editions is divided into acts but not into scenes. I have added scene divisions every time the stage clears and marked these interventions with square brackets.

Further reading

Editions

Colman, George, Jr. (ed.) (1778) "*The Sea Voyage*," in George Colman Jr. (ed.) *The Dramatick Works of Beaumont and Fletcher*, vol. 9, London: T. Sherlock for T. Evans, et al.

Dyce, Alexander (ed.) (1845) "*The Sea Voyage*," in Alexander Dyce (ed.), *The Works of Beaumont and Fletcher*, London: Edward Moxon.

Hoy, Cyrus (ed.) (1994) "*The Sea Voyage*," in Fredson Bowers (ed.), *The Dramatic Works in the Beaumont and Fletcher Canon*, vol. 9, Cambridge: Cambridge University Press.

Sympson, John, and Thomas Seward (eds) (1750) "*The Sea Voyage*," in Seward and Sympson (eds), *The Works of Mr. Francis Beaumont and Mr. John Fletcher*, vol. 9, London: Tonson and Draper.

Weber, Henry William (ed.) (1812) "*The Sea Voyage*," in Henry William Weber (ed.), *The Works of Beaumont and Fletcher*, vol. 7, Edinburgh: James Ballantyne for F. C. and J. Rivington, et al.

Critical and contextual reading

Akhimie, Patricia (2009) "Travel, Drama, and Domesticity: Colonial Huswifery in John Fletcher and Philip Massinger's *The Sea Voyage*," *Studies in Travel Writing* 13: 153–66.

Banerjee, Rita (2013) "Gold, Land, and Labor: Ideologies of Colonization and Rewriting *The Tempest* in 1622," *Studies in Philology* 110: 291–317.

Brown, Alison and Jason Denman (2018) "*The Sea Voyage* and Accounts of Famine in Colonial Virginia," *Notes and Queries* 65: 119–22.

Downes, John (1708) *Roscius Anglicanus*, London: H. Playford.

Dryden, John and William Davenant (1670) *The Enchanted Island*, London: Henry Herringman [Wing S2944].

D'Urfey, Thomas (1686) *A Common-wealth of Women*, London: Richard Bentley and John Hindmarsh [Wing D2715].

Feerick, Jean (2006) "'Divided in Soyle': Plantation and Degeneracy in 'The Tempest' and 'The Sea Voyage'," *Renaissance Drama* 35: 27–54.

Hattaway, Michael (1996) "'Seeing things': Amazons and Cannibals," in Jean-Pierre Maquerlot and Michèle Willems (eds), *Travel and Drama in Shakespeare's Time*, Cambridge: Cambridge University Press: 179–92.

Jowitt, Claire (2001) "'Her flesh must serve you': Gender, Commerce and the New World in Fletcher's and Massinger's *The Sea Voyage* and Massinger's *The City Madam*," *Parergon* 18: 93–117.

Langbaine, Gerard (1711) "Introduction," in *The Works of Mr. Francis Beaumont and Mr. John Fletcher*, London: J. Tonson.

Lesser, Zachary (2007) "Tragical-Comical-Pastoral-Colonial: Economic Sovereignty, Globalization, and the Form of Tragicomedy," *English Literary History* 74: 881–908.

Mason, John Monck (1798) *Comments on the Plays of Beaumont and Fletcher*, London: V. Griffiths for E. Harding.

Shahani, Gitanjali (2012) "Of 'Barren Islands' and 'Cursèd Gold': Worth, Value, and Womanhood in 'The Sea Voyage'," *Journal for Early Modern Cultural Studies* 12: 5–27.

Sutherland, Julie (2012) "'What Beast is This Lies Wallowing in His Gore?' The Indignity of Man and the Animal Nature of Love in *The Sea Voyage*," *Modern Language Review* 107: 88–107.

Van Lennep, William (ed.) (1965) The London Stage, 1660–1800: A Calendar of Plays, Entertainments & Afterpieces, Together with Casts, Box-receipts and Contemporary Comment, Part 1: 1660–1700, Carbondale, IL: Southern Illinois University Press.

The Sea Voyage (1622)

The Persons Represented in the Play[1]

Men
ALBERT, *a French pirate, in love with Aminta*
TIBALT *du-pont, a merry Gentleman, friend to Albert*
MASTER *of the ship, an honest merry man*
LAMURE, *an usuring merchant*
FRANVILLE, *a vain-glorious gallant*
MORILLAT, *a shallow-brained gentleman*
BOATSWAIN, *an honest man*
SEBASTIAN, *a noble gentleman of Portugal, husband to Rosella*
NICUSA, *nephew to Sebastian, both cast upon a desert island*
RAYMOND, *brother to Aminta*
SURGEON
SAILORS
[*Gentlemen*]

Women
AMINTA, *mistress to Albert, a noble French virgin*
ROSELLA, *governess of the Amazonian Portugals*
CLARINDA, *daughter to Rosella, in love with Albert*
HIPPOLITA
CROCALE
JULETTA
} *three ladies, members of the female common-wealth*

The Scene

First at sea, then in the desert islands[2]

The Principal Actors were

Joseph Taylor *Joh*[*n*] *Lowin*
William Eglestone *John Underwood*[3]
Nich[*olas*] *Toolie*

Act I, scene i

A Tempest. Thunder and Lightning. Enter MASTER *and two* SAILORS

1 The Persons . . . the Play: the following list of dramatis personae is adapted from F2; it is not in F1
2 The Scene . . . desert islands: adapted from F2; not in F1
3 The Principal . . . *Underwood*.: all actors in the King's Men when the play was first performed; printed in F2; not in F1

MASTER Lay her[4] aloof![5] The sea grows dangerous:
How it spits against the clouds, how it capers,[6]
And how the fiery element frights it back!
There be devils dancing in the air. I think
I saw a dolphin hang i'th' horns of the moon[7]
Shot from a wave—Hey day! Hey day![8]
How she kicks and yerks![9]
Down with the main mast, lay her at hull,[10]
Farle up[11] all her linens, and let her ride it out.
1 SAILOR She'll never brook it, master.
She's so deep laden that she'll bulge.[12]
MASTER Hang her.
Can she not buffet with a storm a little?
How it tosses her! She reels like a drunkard.
2 SAILOR We have discovered the land, sir.
Pray, let's make in. She's so drunk, else
She may chance to cast up[13] all her lading.
1 SAILOR Stand in, stand in! We are all lost else, lost and perished.
MASTER Steer her a starboard there.
2 SAILOR Bear in with all the sail we can. See, master,
See what a clap of thunder there is:
What a face of heaven, how dreadfully it looks!
MASTER Thou rascal, thou fearful rogue, thou hast been praying;
I see't in thy face. Thou hast been mumbling
When we are split, you slave. Is this a time
To discourage our friends with your cold orisons?[14]
Call up the boatswain! [*Exit* SAILOR] —How it storms! Holla!

[*Enter* SAILOR *again with* BOATSWAIN]

BOATSWAIN What shall we do, master?
Cast over all her lading? She will not swim
An hour else.

Enter ALBERT, FRANVILLE, LAMURE, TIBALT, [*and*] MORILLAT

MASTER The storm is loud—
We cannot hear one another—
What's the coast?
BOATSWAIN We know not yet. Shall we make in?
ALBERT What comfort, sailors?
I never saw, since I have known the sea,
(Which has been this twenty years)[15] so rude a tempest.

4 1 her: i.e. the ship
5 1 aloof: towards the wind
6 2 capers: dances
7 5 horns of the moon: points of the crescent moon
8 6 Hey day!: an exclamation of surprise and wonder
9 7 yerks: jerks
10 8 at hull: the state of moving with no assistance from the sails
11 9 Farle up: furl up; bundle
12 11 The ship is so full of cargo that it might spring a leak
13 16 cast up: vomit (because "drunk")
14 25 orisons: prayers
15 36 Unless otherwise noted, parentheses in this edition are original to F1 and typically indicate asides and guarded speech

In what state are we?
MASTER Dangerous enough, captain.
We have sprung five leaks, and no little ones.—
Still rage!—Besides, her ribs are open,
Her rudder almost spent. Prepare yourselves,
And have good courages: death comes but once,
And let him come in all his frights.
ALBERT Is't not possible,
To make in to th'land? 'Tis here before us.
MORILLAT Here hard by, sir.
MASTER Death is nearer, gentlemen.
Yet do not cry. Let's die like men.
TIBALT Shall's hoise the boat out,[16]
And go all at one cast?[17] The more the merrier.

Enter AMINTA

MASTER You are too hasty, monsieur.
Do ye long to be i'th'fish-market before your time?—
Hold her up there.
AMINTA O miserable fortune!
Nothing but horror sounding in mine ears;
No minute to promise to my frighted soul.
TIBALT Peace, woman!
We ha' storms enough already. No more howling.
AMINTA Gentle master—
MASTER Clap this woman under hatches.
ALBERT Prithee, speak mildly to her.
AMINTA Can no help?
MASTER None that I know.
AMINTA No promise from your goodness?
MASTER Am I a god?—For heaven's sake, stow this woman!
TIBALT Go! Take your gilt prayer book,
And to your business: wink[18] and die.
There[19] an old haddock[20] stays for ye.
AMINTA Must I die here in all the frights, the terrors,
The thousand several shapes death triumphs in?
No friend to counsel me?
ALBERT Have peace, sweet mistress.
AMINTA No kindred's tears upon me? O my country!
No gentle hand to close mine eyes?
ALBERT Be comforted. Heaven has the same
Power still, and the same mercy.
AMINTA O! That wave will devour me!
MASTER Carry her down, captain,
Or, by these hands, I'll give no more direction.
Let the ship sink or swim! We ha' ne'er better luck
When we ha' such stowage[21] as these trinkets with us,

16 47 Shall we lower the row boat into the water
17 48 at one cast: in a single motion or stroke
18 62 wink: close your eyes; sleep
19 63 There: under water; below the deck
20 63 old haddock: fish; shriveled (i.e. impotent) man
21 75 stowage: cargo

These sweet sin-breeders. How can heaven smile on us,
When such a burden of iniquity[22]
Lies tumbling like a potion in our ship's belly? *Exit* [MASTER, BOATSWAIN, *and* SAILORS]
TIBALT Away with her, and if she have a prayer
That's fit for such an hour, let her say't quickly,
And seriously. *Exeunt* [*all but* ALBERT *and* AMINTA]
ALBERT Come. I see it clear, lady. Come in,
And take some comfort. I'll stay with ye.
AMINTA Where should I stay? To what end should I hope?
Am I not circled round with misery?
Confusions in their full heights dwell about me.
O Monsieur Albert, how am I bound to curse ye,
If curses could redeem me. How to hate ye!
You forced me from my quiet, from my friends,
Even from their arms that were as dear to me
As daylight is, or comfort, to the wretched.
You forced my friends from their peaceful rest.
Some your relentless sword gave their last groans—
Would I had there been numbered—
And to Fortune's[23] never-satisfied afflictions,
Ye turned my brother and those few friends I'd left,
Like desperate creatures, to their own fears
And the world's stubborn pities. O merciless!
ALBERT Sweet mistress—
AMINTA And whether they are wandered to avoid ye,
Or whether dead and no kind earth to cover 'em—
Was this a lover's part? But heaven has found ye,
And in his loud voice, his voice of thunder,
And in the mutiny of his deep wonders,[24]
He tells ye now, ye weep too late.
ALBERT Let these tears tell how I honor ye.
Ye know, dear lady, since ye were mine,
How truly I have loved ye, how sanctimoniously[25]
Observed your honor. Not one lascivious word,
Not one touch, lady. No, not a hope that might not render me
The unpolluted servant of your chastity.
For you I put to sea to seek your brother—
Your captain, yet your slave—that his redemption,
If he be living where the sun has circuit,
May expiate your rigor,[26] and my rashness.
AMINTA The storm grows greater! What shall we do?
ALBERT Let's in,
And ask heaven's mercy. My strong mind yet presages,
Through all these dangers, we shall see a day yet
Shall crown your pious hopes, and my fair wishes. *Exit* [ALBERT *and* AMINTA]

Enter MASTER, SAILORS, BOATSWAIN, SURGEON, *and gentlemen*

22 77 iniquity: sin; wickedness
23 95 Fortune: goddess of chance and luck
24 104 in the . . . deep wonders: in heaven's own revolt against its ability to work miracles (i.e. the storm that leaves no hope of survival)
25 108 sanctimoniously: sacredly; or in a manner that pretends piety
26 115 expiate your rigor: make amends for your distress

MASTER It must all overboard.
BOATSWAIN It clears to the seaward mast.
Fling o'er the lading there, and let's lighten her—
All the meat and the cakes. We are all gone else.—
That we may find her leaks, and hold her up—
Yet save some little biscuit for the lady,
'Til we come to the land.
LAMURE Must my goods over, too?
Why, honest master? Here lies all my money:
The money I ha' racked[27] by usury,[28]
To buy new lands and lordships[29] in new countries,
'Cause I was banished from mine own.
I ha' been this twenty years a-raising it.
TIBALT Out with it.
The devils are got together by the ears[30] who shall have it,
And here they quarrel in the clouds.
LAMURE I am undone, sir.
TIBALT And be undone. 'Tis better than we perish.
LAMURE O save one chest of plate.[31]
TIBALT Away with it lustily,[32] sailors!
It was some pawn that he has got unjustly.
Down with it low enough, and let crabs breed in't.
MASTER Over with the trunks, too.

Enter ALBERT

ALBERT Take mine and spare not!
MASTER We must over with all.
FRANVILLE Will ye throw away my lordship
That I sold, put it into clothes and necessaries,
To go to sea with?
TIBALT Over with it! I love to see a lordship sink.
Sir, you left no wood upon't to buoy it up.[33]
You might ha' saved it else.
FRANVILLE I am undone forever!
ALBERT Why, we are all undone. Would you be only happy?
LAMURE Sir, you may lose, too.
TIBALT Thou liest! I ha' nothing but my skin,
And my clothes; my sword here, and myself;
Two crowns[34] in my pocket; two pair of cards;
And three false dice. I can swim like a fish,
Rascal, nothing to hinder me.
BOATSWAIN In with her of all hands![35]
MASTER Come, gentlemen!—Come, captain!—Ye must help, all.
My life now for the land:'

27 127 racked: raked in
28 127 usury: lending money at interest
29 128 lordships: titles
30 131 got together by the ears: fighting over
31 134 plate: gold or silver coins; or, serving vessels and utensils
32 134 lustily: energetically
33 142–3 I love … it up: i.e. by selling his lordship (with pun on *ship*) for goods, Franville dispensed with the very timber that might have now saved those goods
34 150 crowns: coins, each worth five shillings
35 153 Everyone pitch in to help!

'Tis high, and rocky, and full of perils.
ALBERT However, let's attempt it.
MASTER Then cheer lustily, my hearts.[36]

Exeunt[37]

[Act I, scene ii]

Enter SEBASTIAN *and* NICUSA [*above*][38]

SEBASTIAN Yes, 'tis a ship. I see it now, a tall ship.
She has wrought[39] lustily for her deliverance.
Heaven's mercy, what a wretched day has here been?
NICUSA To still and quiet minds that knew no misery,
It may seem wretched, but with us 'tis ordinary.
Heaven has no storm in store, nor earth no terror,
That can seem new to us.
SEBASTIAN 'Tis true, Nicusa.
If Fortune were determined to be wanton,[40]
And would wipe out the stories of men's miseries,
Yet we two living, we could cross her purpose,
For 'tis impossible she should cure us.
We are so excellent in our afflictions,
It would be more than glory to her blindness,[41]
And style her power beyond her pride, to quit us.
NICUSA Do they live still?
SEBASTIAN Yes, and make to harbor.
NICUSA Most miserable men. I grieve their fortunes.
SEBASTIAN How happy had they been, had the sea covered 'em!
They leap from one calamity to another:
Had they been drowned, they had ended all their sorrows. [*Shouts within*]
What shouts of joy they make!
NICUSA Alas, poor wretches,
Had they but once experience of this island,
They'd turn their tunes to wailings.
SEBASTIAN Nay, to curses
That ever they set foot on such calamities.
Here's nothing but rocks and barrenness,
Hunger, and cold to eat; here's no vineyards
To cheer the heart of man, no crystal rivers
After his labor to refresh his body
If he be feeble, nothing to restore him
But heavenly hopes. Nature, that made those remedies,
Dares not come here, nor look on our distresses,
For fear she turn wild, like the place, and barren.
NICUSA O uncle, yet a little memory of what we were,
'Twill be a little comfort in our calamities:
When we were seated in our blessèd homes,

36 157 my hearts: form of address emphasizing courage and bravery
37 157 SD F1's *Exit* has been emended to *Exeunt* here and silently throughout when the stage clears
38 0 SD Sebastian's "let's descend" at line 62 suggests that he and Nicusa are elevated (probably in the gallery space) as they observe the approach of the ship and its crew
39 2 wrought: worked
40 8 wanton: extravagant; jovial
41 13 her blindness: Fortune was sometimes depicted veiled or blindfolded

How happy in our kindreds, in our families,
In all our fortunes—
SEBASTIAN Curse on those French pirates that displanted us;
That flung us from that happiness we found there;
Constrained[42] us to the sea to save our lives, honors, and our riches,
With all we had, our kinsmen and our jewels,
In hope to find some place free from such robbers,
Where a mighty storm severed our barks,[43]
That,[44] where my wife, my daughter,
And my noble ladies that went with her,
Virgins and loving souls, to scape those pirates—
NICUSA They are living yet. Such goodness cannot perish.
SEBASTIAN But never to me, cousin;[45]
Never to me again. What bears their flag-staves?[46]
NICUSA The arms[47] of France, sure.
Nay, do not start,[48] we cannot be more miserable.
Death is a cordial[49] now, come when it will.
SEBASTIAN They get to shore apace. They'll fly as fast
When once they find the place. What's that which swims there?
NICUSA A strong young man, sir, with a handsome woman
Hanging about his neck.
SEBASTIAN That shows some honor.—
May thy brave charity, whate'er thou art,
Be spoken in a place that may renown thee
And not die here.
NICUSA The boat it seems turned over,
So forcèd to their shifts,[50] yet all are landed.
They're pirates, on my life.[51]
SEBASTIAN. They will not rob us,
For none will take our misery for riches.
Come, cousin, let's descend and try[52] their pities;
If we get off,[53] a little hope walks with us.
If not, we shall but load this wretched island
With the same shadows still that must grow shorter.[54]

Exeunt

[Act I, scene iii]

Enter ALBERT, AMINTA, TIBALT, MORILLAT, LAMURE, MASTER, FRANVILLE, SURGEON, [BOATSWAIN,] *and sailors*

42 39 Constrained: forced
43 42 barks: ships
44 43 That: so that
45 47 cousin: kinsman; relative. F1's "cozen" is also viable: Sebastian tells Nicusa not to cheat or deceive him by pretending Sebastian's wife and daughter are still alive
46 48 What bears their flag-staves?: what flags are flying on the ship's poles?
47 49 arms: emblem; coat of arms
48 50 start: be startled
49 51 cordial: a comforting or curative medicine
50 59 forcèd to their shifts: brought to an extremity, i.e. swimming
51 60 on my life: I swear
52 62 try: test
53 63 get off: succeed, with the possible implication of escaping the island
54 65 that must grow shorter: i.e. with age

TIBALT Wet come[55] ashore, my mates. We are safe arrived yet.
MASTER Thanks to heaven's goodness, no man lost.
The ship rides fair, too, and her leaks in good plight.[56]
ALBERT The weather's turned more courteous.—How does my dear?
Alas, how weak she is and wet!
AMINTA I am glad yet, I 'scaped with life;
Which certain, noble captain, next to heaven's goodness,
I must thank you for, and which is more,
Acknowledge your dear tenderness, your firm love
To your unworthy mistress, and recant, too,
(Indeed I must) those harsh opinions,
Those cruel unkind thoughts, I heaped upon ye.
Farther than that, I must forget your injuries.
So far I am tied and fettered[57] to your service,
Believe me, I will learn to love.
ALBERT I thank ye, madam,
And it shall be my practice to serve.—
What cheer,[58] companions?
TIBALT No great cheer,[59] sir: a piece of soused[60] biscuit
And half a hard egg, for the sea has taken order.[61]
Being young and strong, we shall not surfeit,[62] captain.
For mine own part, I'll dance 'til I'm dry.
Come, surgeon, out with your clyster-pipe,[63]
And strike a galliard.[64]
ALBERT What a brave[65] day again,
And what fair weather, after so foul a storm!
LAMURE Ay, an't[66] pleased the master, he might ha' seen[67]
This weather, and ha' saved our goods.
ALBERT Never think on 'em. We have our lives and healths.
LAMURE I must think on 'em, and think
'Twas most maliciously done to undo me.
FRANVILLE And me, too. I lost all.
I haven't another shirt to put upon me, nor clothes
But these poor rags. I had fifteen fair suits,
The worst[68] was cut upon taffety.[69]
TIBALT I am glad you ha' lost. Give me thy hand—
Is thy skin whole? Art thou not purled[70] with scabs?
No ancient monuments of Madam Venus?[71]

55 1 Wet come: i.e. welcome. All previous editions preserve this phrase, justifying it as an instance of Tibalt's "droll character" (Sympson, 1750)
56 3 plight: condition
57 14 fettered: bound with chains or shackles
58 17 What cheer: how do you feel
59 18 cheer: provisions; food and drink
60 18 soused: pickled (by the sea water)
61 19 the sea has taken order: i.e. the sea has successfully taken the rest
62 20 surfeit: indulge to excess
63 22 clyster-pipe: syringe used to administer an enema for sustenance or to cleanse the bowels. Here, the only "instrument" available
64 23 galliard: a piece of music to accompany a lively dance of the same name
65 23 brave: splendid
66 25 an't: if it
67 25 seen: anticipated
68 33 worst: least valuable
69 33 taffety: taffeta, a glossy silk fabric
70 35 purled: i.e. embroidered
71 36 monuments of Madam Venus: i.e. scars from venereal disease

Thou hast a suit, then, will pose the cunning'st tailor,[72]
That will never turn fashion,[73] nor forsake thee,
'Til thy executors, the worms, uncase[74] thee.
They take off glorious suits, Franville. Thou art happy;
Thou art delivered of 'em. Here are no brokers,
No alchemists, to turn 'em into metal,[75]
Nor leathered captains[76] with ladies to adore 'em.
Wilt thou see a dogfish rise in one of thy brave doublets,
And tumble like a tub[77] to make thee merry,
Or an old haddock rise with thy hatched sword[78]
Thou paid'st a hundred crowns for?
A mermaid in a mantle[79] of your worship's,
Or a dolphin in your double ruff?
FRANVILLE Ye are merry, but if I take it thus,
If I be foisted[80] and jeered[81] out of my goods—
LAMURE Nor I, I vow thee.
Nor master nor mate, I see your cunning.
ALBERT O be not angry, gentlemen.
MORILLAT Yes, sir, we have reason.
And some friends I can make.[82]
MASTER What I did, gentlemen, was for the general safety.
If ye aim at me, I am not so tame—
TIBALT Pray take my counsel, gallants.
Fight not 'til the surgeon be well.
He's damnable sea-sick, and may spoil all.
Besides, he has lost his fiddlestick, and the best
Box of boar's grease[83]—Why do you make such faces,
And hand your swords?
ALBERT Who would ye fight with, gentlemen?
Who has done ye wrong? For shame, be better tempered.
No sooner come to give thanks for our safeties,
But we must raise new civil broils amongst us,
Inflame those angry powers to shower new vengeance on us?
What can we expect for these unmanly murmurs,
These strong temptations of their holy pities,
But plagues in another kind, a fuller[84] so dreadful
That the singing storms are slumbers to it?
TIBALT Be men and rule your minds.
If you will needs fight, gentlemen,
And think to raise new riches by your valors,
Have at ye. I have little else to do now

72 37 pose the cunning'st tailor: transcend the abilities of (or suggest the workmanship of) the most skilled tailor
73 38 turn fashion: become unfashionable
74 39 uncase: strip; undress
75 41–2 Here are … into metal: i.e. there is no way (by alchemy or pawning) to transform your clothes into money ("metal"). F1's "mettle" (the substance of one's character; courage) is also viable
76 43 leathered captains: men in military attire
77 45 like a tub: i.e. like a fish ("tub" is the name of a fish); clumsily
78 46 hatched sword: a sword with an engraved, gilded, or otherwise decorated hilt
79 48 mantle: a loose, sleeveless cloak
80 51 foisted: cheated
81 51 jeered: mocked; derided
82 56 some friends I can make: Morillat threatens to lead a mutiny
83 62–3 fiddlestick, and … boar's grease: his "what-do-you-call-it" (a reference to the clyster-pipe in line 22) and the lubricant needed to administer it; Tibalt suggests that the gallants need purging
84 71 a fuller: i.e. a worse plague

I have said my prayers. You say you have lost,
And make your loss your quarrel,
And grumble at my captain here, and the master,
Two worthy persons, indeed: too worthy for such rascals,
Thou galloon-gallant,[85] and Mammon,[86] you
That build on golden mountains, thou money-maggot.
Come, all draw your swords! Ye say ye are miserable—
ALBERT Nay, hold, good Tibalt.
TIBALT Captain, let me correct 'em—
I'll make ye ten times worse—I will not leave 'em—
For look ye, fighting is as nourishing to me as eating.
I was born quarreling.
MASTER Pray, sir—
TIBALT I will not leave 'em skins to cover 'em—
Do ye grumble when ye are well, ye rogues?
MASTER Noble du-Pont—
TIBALT Ye have clothes now, and ye prate.[87]
AMINTA Pray, gentlemen, for my sake be at peace.
Let it become me to make all friends.[88]
FRANVILLE You have stopped our angers, lady.
ALBERT This shows noble.
TIBALT 'Tis well. 'Tis very well. There's half a biscuit—
Break't amongst ye all, and thank my bounty.
This is clothes and plate, too. Come, no more quarreling.

Enter SEBASTIAN *and* NICUSA

AMINTA But ha! What things are these?
Are they human creatures?
TIBALT I have heard of sea-calves.[89]
ALBERT They are no shadows,[90] sure; they have legs and arms.
TIBALT They hang but lightly on though.
AMINTA How they look! Are they men's faces?
TIBALT They have horse tails growing to 'em,
Goodly long manes.
AMINTA Alas, what sunk eyes they have!
How they are crept in, as if they had been frighted!
Sure they are wretched men.
TIBALT Where are their wardrobes? [SEBASTIAN *and* NICUSA *kneel*]
Look ye, Franville, here are a couple of courtiers.
AMINTA They kneel. Alas, poor souls.
ALBERT What are ye? Speak. Are ye alive,
Or wand'ring shadows, that find no peace on earth,
'Til ye reveal some hidden secret?
SEBASTIAN We are men as you are,
Only our miseries make us seem monsters.
If ever pity dwelt in noble hearts—

85 81 galloon-gallant: i.e. a gallant whose clothing is trimmed with braided ribbon or thread
86 81 Mammon: the inordinate desire for wealth; an avaricious person
87 90 prate: speak foolishly; inform against someone
88 92 In F1, this line is assigned to Lamure. In F2, the speech prefix for Lamure is omitted. This line makes little sense coming from the combative Lamure and aligns better with Aminta's peace-making efforts in the previous line
89 98 sea-calves: seals
90 99 shadows: illusions; ghosts

ALBERT We understand 'em too. Pray, mark 'em, gentlemen.
SEBASTIAN Or that heaven is pleased with human charity;
If ever ye have heard the name of friendship,
Or suffered in yourselves the least afflictions,
Have gentle fathers that have bred ye tenderly,
And mothers that have wept for your misfortunes,
Have mercy on our miseries.
ALBERT Stand up, wretches,
Speak boldly, and have release. [*They stand*]
NICUSA If ye be Christians
And, by that blessed name, bound to relieve us,
Convey us from this island.
ALBERT Speak, what are ye?
SEBASTIAN As you are, gentle born. To tell ye more
Were but to number up our own calamities,
And turn your eyes wild with perpetual weepings.
These many years, in this most wretched island
We two have lived, the scorn and game of Fortune.
Bless yourselves from it, noble gentlemen.
The greatest plagues that human nature suffers
Are seated here: wildness and wants innumerable.
ALBERT How came ye hither?
NICUSA In a ship, as you do, and as you might have been
Had not heaven preserved ye for some more noble use,
Wracked[91] desperately, our men and all consumed
But we two, that still live, and spin out
The thin and ragged threads[92] of our misfortunes.
ALBERT Is there no meat above?[93]
SEBASTIAN Nor meat nor quiet;
No summer here, to promise anything;
Nor autumn, to make full the reaper's hands;
The earth, obdurate to the tears of heaven,
Lets nothing shoot[94] but poisoned weeds;
No rivers, nor no pleasant groves, no beasts.
All that were made for man's use fly this desert.
No airy fowl dares make his flight over it,
It is so ominous:
Serpents, and ugly things, the shames of nature,
Roots of malignant tastes, foul standing waters.
Sometimes we find a fulsome sea-root,
And that's a delicate;[95] a rat sometimes,
And that we hunt like princes in their pleasure;
And when we take a toad, we make a banquet.
AMINTA For heaven's sake, let's aboard.
ALBERT D'ye know no farther?
NICUSA Yes, we have sometimes seen the shadow
Of a place inhabited, and heard the noise of hunters,
And have attempted to find it. So far as a river,
Deep, slow, and dangerous, fencèd with high rocks,

91 135 Wracked: shipwrecked; also, ruined, more generally
92 137 threads: i.e. the threads of life
93 138 above: further inland; at higher elevations
94 142 shoot: germinate; grow
95 150 delicate: delicacy; treat

We have gone, but not able to achieve that hazard,
Return to our old miseries.
If this sad story may deserve your pities—
ALBERT Ye shall aboard with us. We will relieve your miseries.
SEBASTIAN Nor will we be unthankful for this benefit.
No, gentlemen, we'll pay for our deliverance.
Look ye that plough the seas for wealth and pleasures,
That outrun day and night with your ambitions,
Look on those heaps. They seem hard ragged quarries.
Remove 'em and view 'em fully.[96]
MASTER O heaven, they are gold and jewels.
SEBASTIAN Be not too hasty.
Here lies another heap.
MORILLAT And here another. All perfect gold.
ALBERT Stand farther off. You must not be your own carvers.[97]
LAMURE We have shares, and deep ones.
FRANVILLE Yes, sir, we'll maintain't.—Ho, fellow sailors!
LAMURE Stand all to your freedoms. I'll have all this—
FRANVILLE And I this—
TIBALT You shall be hanged first.
LAMURE My losses shall be made good.[98]
FRANVILLE So shall mine, or with my sword I'll do't.—
All that will share with us, assist us.
TIBALT Captain, let's set in.
ALBERT This money will undo us, undo us all.
SEBASTIAN This gold was the overthrow of my happiness.
I had command, too, when I landed here,
And led young, high, and noble spirits under me.
This cursed gold enticing 'em, they set upon their captain,
On me that owned this wealth, and this poor gentleman;
Gave us no few wounds; forced us from our own;
And then their civil swords,[99] who should be owners
And who lords over all, turned against their own lives,
First in their rage consumed the ship,
That poor part of the ship that 'scaped the first wrack,
Next their lives by heaps. O be you wise and careful.
LAMURE We'll ha' more, sirrah,[100] come show it.
FRANVILLE Or ten times worse afflictions than thou speak'st of—
ALBERT Nay, and ye will be dogs— *Beats 'em out*
TIBALT Let me come, captain:
This golden age must have an iron ending.[101]
Have at the bunch— [TIBALT] *beats 'em off.* [AMINTA, SEBASTIAN, *and* NICUSA *remain*]
AMINTA O Albert! O gentlemen! O friends! *Exit* [AMINTA]
SEBASTIAN Come, noble nephew, if we stay here, we die.
Here rides their ship, yet all are gone to th' spoil.
Let's make a quick use.[102]

96 166–7 Look on … 'em fully: Sebastian reveals piles of treasure (perhaps by drawing the curtain of the discovery space) and invites the men to move them into better view (onto the stage)
97 170 be your own carvers: take or choose a portion for yourself
98 175 I'll recuperate what I lost in the storm
99 186 civil swords: i.e. swords used against people on the same side
100 191 sirrah: a contemptuous term of address
101 194 iron ending: i.e. with the other men either dead by the stroke of a sword, or taken prisoner (in fetters)
102 198: make a quick use: take advantage of the situation

NICUSA Away, dear uncle.
SEBASTIAN This gold was our overthrow.
NICUSA It may now be our happiness.

Exeunt

[Act I, scene iv]

Enter TIBALT *and* [ALBERT, *pursuing*] *the rest* [MORILLAT, LAMURE, FRANVILLE, MASTER, BOATSWAIN, SURGEON, *and* SAILORS]

TIBALT You shall have gold. Yes, I'll cram it int'ye.
You shall be your own carvers. Yes, I'll carve[103] ye.
MORILLAT I am sore. I pray, hear reason.
TIBALT I'll hear none.
Covetous, base minds have no reason.
I am hurt myself, but whilst I have a leg left,
I will so haunt your gilded[104] souls!—How d'ye, captain?
Ye bleed apace. Curse on the causers on't.
Ye do not faint?
ALBERT No, no, I am not so happy.
TIBALT D'ye howl? Nay, ye deserve it,
Base greedy rogues.—Come, shall we make an end of 'em?
ALBERT They are our countrymen. For heaven's sake, spare 'em.
Alas, they are hurt enough, and they relent now.

[*Enter*] AMINTA *above*

AMINTA O captain, captain!
ALBERT Whose voice is that?
TIBALT The lady's.
AMINTA Look, captain, look, ye are undone. Poor captain,
We are all undone, all, all. We are all miserable!
Mad, willful men, ye are undone: your ship, your ship!
ALBERT What of her?
AMINTA She's under sail and floating.
See where she flies. See to your shames, you wretches,
Those poor starvèd things that showed you gold. [*Exit*]

LAMURE, FRANVILLE[, *and* SAILORS] *go up to see the ship*

1 SAILOR [*Above*] They have cut the cables,
And got her out. The tide too has befriended 'em.
MASTER Where are the sailors that kept her?
BOATSWAIN Here, here in the mutiny to take up money,
And left no creature; left the boat ashore too.
This gold, this damned enticing gold.
2 SAILOR [*Above*] How the wind drives her,
As if it vied to force her from our furies!
LAMURE [*Above*] Come back, good old men!
FRANVILLE [*Above*] Good honest men, come back!
TIBALT The wind's against ye: speak louder.
LAMURE [*Above*] Ye shall have all your gold again.—They see us!
TIBALT Hold up your hands, and kneel,
And howl, ye blockheads. They'll have compassion on ye.

103 2 carve: i.e. stab or cut with his sword
104 6 gilded: covered in, or adorned with, gold (also, possibly, blood)

Yes, yes, 'tis very likely. Ye have deserved it.
D'ye look like dogs now? [*Exeunt* LAMURE, FRANVILLE, *and* SAILORS]
Are your mighty courages abated?[105]
ALBERT I bleed apace, Tibalt.
TIBALT Retire, sir, and make the best use of our miseries.
They but begin now.

Enter AMINTA

AMINTA Are ye alive still?
ALBERT Yes, sweet.
TIBALT Help him off, lady,
And wrap him warm, in your arms.—
Here's something that's comfortable.—Off with him handsomely.
I'll come to ye straight, but vex[106] these rascals a little. *Exit* ALBERT [*and*] AMINTA

[*Enter* LAMURE, FRANVILLE, *and* SAILORS]

FRANVILLE O! I am hungry, and hurt, and I am weary.
TIBALT Here's a pestle[107] of portague,[108] sir:
'Tis excellent meat, with sour sauce.
And here's two chains, suppose 'em sausages.
Then there wants[109] mustard,[110]
But the fearful surgeon will supply ye[111] presently.
LAMURE O for that surgeon! I shall die else.
TIBALT Faith, there he lies in the same pickle, too.
SURGEON My salves,[112] and all my instruments are lost,
And I am hurt, and starved.
Good sir, seek for some herbs.
TIBALT Here's herb graceless.[113] Will that serve?—
Gentlemen, will ye go to supper?
ALL Where's the meat?
TIBALT Where's the meat? What a veal voice[114] is there?
FRANVILLE Would we had it, sir, or anything else.
TIBALT I would now cut your throat, you dog,
But that I wo' not[115] do you such a courtesy
To take you from the benefit of starving.
O! What a comfort will your worship have
Some three days hence? Ye things beneath pity,
Famine shall be your harbinger;[116]
You must not look for down beds here,

105 36 abated: diminished
106 43 vex: harass; irritate
107 45 pestle: the leg of an animal, used as food
108 45 portague: a sixteenth-century Portuguese gold coin
109 48 wants: lacks
110 48 mustard: seasoning; also, anything that is caustic or strong
111 49 supply ye: provide you with mustard, here either medicinal powders or strong remedies to quell the strength of their hunger
112 52 salves: healing ointments
113 55 herb graceless: an inversion of herb o'grace, the colloquial name for rue (an herb associated with regret or repentance)
114 58 veal voice: i.e. a loud and shrill voice (cf. *The Mad Lover*, "vociferating veals" II.ii. 12)
115 61 wo' not: i.e. would not
116 64–5 Ye things … your harbinger: "harbinger" in this context means "host"; the reading of 64–5 given here is from F2; F1 reads "Yea things beneath pitty shall be your harbinger"

Nor hangings,[117] though I could wish ye strong ones;[118]
Yet here be many lightsome[119] cool star-chambers,[120]
Open to every sweet air, I'll assure ye,
Ready provided for ye, and so I'll leave ye.
Your first course is served: expect the second. *Exit*
FRANVILLE A vengeance on these jewels.
LAMURE O! This cursèd gold.
Exeunt

[Act II, scene i]

Enter ALBERT [*and*] AMINTA

ALBERT Alas, dear soul, ye faint.
AMINTA You speak the language
Which I should use to you. Heaven knows, my weakness
Is not for what I suffer in myself,
But to imagine what you endure, and to what fate
Your cruel stars reserve ye.
ALBERT Do not add to my afflictions
By your tender pities. Sure we have changed sexes:
You bear calamity with a fortitude
Would become[121] a man; I, like a weak girl, suffer.
AMINTA O but your wounds:
How fearfully they gape! And every one
To me is a sepulcher.[122] If I loved truly
(Wise men affirm that true love can do wonders[123]),
This[124] bathed in my warm tears would soon be cured,
And leave no orifice[125] behind. Pray, give me leave
To play the surgeon and bind 'em up.
The raw air rankles 'em.[126]
ALBERT Sweet, we want[127] means.
AMINTA Love can supply all wants. [AMINTA *cuts her hair and binds his wounds with it*]
ALBERT What have ye done, sweet?
O sacrilege to beauty.[128] There's no hair
Of these pure locks by which the greatest king
Would not be gladly bound and love his fetters.
AMINTA O Albert, I offer this sacrifice of service
To the altar of your staid temperance[129] and still adore it.
When, with a violent hand, you made me yours,
I cursed the doer, but now I consider

117 67 hangings: curtains surrounding a bed to prevent drafts
118 67 strong ones: i.e. strong halters for hanging (presumably leading to quick death)
119 68 lightsome: full of light; elegant
120 68 star-chambers: i.e. rooms in the shape of, or decorated with, stars (Tibalt speaks ironically about how the gallants will have to learn to sleep out of doors)
121 9 Would become: that would suit
122 12 sepulcher: tomb; grave
123 13 do wonders: F2 emends to "do noe wonders"
124 14 This: i.e. one of Albert's wounds
125 15 orifice: opening, scar
126 17 rankles 'em: causes the wounds to fester
127 17 want: lack
128 19 sacrilege to beauty: i.e. a sin against beauty
129 23 staid temperance: dignified self-restraint

How long I was in your power and with what honor
You entertained me (it being seldom seen,
That youth and heat of blood could e'er prescribe
Laws to itself), your goodness is the Lethe,[130]
In which I drown your injuries and now live
Truly to serve ye. How do you, sir?
Receive you the least ease from my service?
If you do, I am largely recompensed.
ALBERT You good angels,
That are engaged when man's ability fails
To reward goodness, look upon this lady.
Though hunger gripes[131] my croaking entrails,
Yet when I kiss these rubies, methinks
I'm at a banquet, a refreshing banquet.
Speak, my blessèd one, art not hungry?
AMINTA Indeed, I could eat to bear you company.
ALBERT Blush, unkind Nature!
If thou hast power or being to hear
Thyself, and by such innocence accused,
Must print[132] a thousand kinds of shames upon
Thy various[133] face. Canst thou supply a drunkard
And with a prodigal[134] hand reach choice of wines
'Til he cast up thy blessings, or a glutton,
That robs the elements to soothe his palate
And only eats to beget appetite,
Not to be satisfied, and suffer here
A virgin, which the saints would make their guest,
To pine for hunger? *Horns within*
Ha! If my sense
Deceive me not, these notes take being
From the breath of men. Confirm me, my Aminta. [*Horns again*]
Again, this way the gentle wind conveys it to us.
Hear you nothing?
AMINTA Yes, it seems free hunters' music.[135] [*Horns again*]
ALBERT Still, 'tis louder, and I remember the Portugals
Informed us they had often heard such sounds,
But ne'er could touch the shore from whence it came.
Follow me, my Aminta!—My good genius,[136]
Show me the way still!— [*Horns again*]
Still we are directed.
When we gain the top of this near rising hill
We shall know further. *Exeunt, and enter above*
Courteous Zephyrus[137]
On his dewy wings carries perfumes to cheer us.
The air clears, too:
And now we may discern another island,

130 29 Lethe: river in Hades whose waters caused those who drank them to forget the past
131 36 gripes: afflicts
132 44 Must print: hearing it must print
133 45 various: changeable; capricious
134 46 prodigal: extravagant
135 56 free hunters' music: i.e. the sound of horns signaling the chase (possibly the hunters are "free" because they can roam anywhere, or the music is "free" because it is not conventional?)
136 60 genius: attending and guiding spirit
137 63 Zephyrus: i.e. Zephyr, the god of the west wind

And, questionless,[138] the seat of fortunate men.
O that we could arrive there!
AMINTA No, Albert, 'tis not to be hoped.
This envious torrent's[139] cruelly interposed.[140]
We have no vessel that may transport us,
Nor hath nature given us wings to fly.
ALBERT Better try all hazards,[141]
Than perish here remediless. I feel
New vigor in me, and a spirit that dares
More than a man to serve my fair Aminta.
These arms shall be my oars, with which I'll swim,
And my zeal to save thy innocent self,
Like wings, shall bear me up above the brackish[142] waves.
AMINTA Will ye then leave me?
ALBERT 'Til now I ne'er was wretched.—
My best Aminta, I swear by goodness
'Tis nor hope nor fear of myself that invites me
To this extreme. 'Tis to supply thy wants, and believe me,
Though pleasure met me in most ravishing[143] forms,
And happiness courted me to entertain her,
I would nor eat nor sleep 'til I returned
And crowned thee with my fortunes.
AMINTA O but your absence—
ALBERT Suppose it but a dream, and as you may,
Endeavor to take rest; and when that sleep
Deceives your hunger with imagined food,
Think you have sent me for discovery
Of some most fortunate[144] continent, yet unknown,
Which you are to be queen of.—
And now ye powers that e'er heard lovers' prayers,
Or cherished pure affection, look on him
That is your votary,[145] and make it known
Against all stops,[146] you can defend your own.

Exeunt

[Act II, scene ii]

Enter HIPPOLITA, CROCALE, [*and*] JULETTA [*with bows and arrows*]

HIPPOLITA How did we lose Clarinda?
CROCALE When we
Believed the stag was spent[147] and would take soil,[148]
The sight of the black lake, which we supposed
He chose for his last refuge, frighted him more

138 67 questionless: i.e. without question; undoubtedly
139 70 torrent: forcefully flowing stream of water
140 70 interposed: i.e. situated between this island and the other island
141 73 try all hazards: brave all dangers
142 79 brackish: salty
143 84 ravishing: entrancing; overpowering
144 92 fortunate: i.e. prosperous; full of resources
145 96 votary: worshipper
146 97 stops: impediments
147 2 spent: exhausted
148 2 take soil: seek safety in the water

Than we that did pursue him.
JULETTA That's usual,
For death itself is not so terrible
To any beast of chase.[149]
HIPPOLITA Since we lived here, we ne'er could force one to it.[150]
CROCALE 'Tis so dreadful!
Birds that with their pinions[151] cleave[152] the air
Dare not fly over it. When the stag turned head,
And we even tired with labor, Clarinda, as if
She were made of air and fire and had
No part of earth in her, eagerly pursued him.
Nor need we fear her safety: this place yields not
Fauns nor satyrs,[153] or more lustful men.
Here we live secure,
And have among ourselves a commonwealth,[154]
Which in ourselves begun,[155] with us must end.
JULETTA Ay, there's the misery.
CROCALE But being alone,
Allow me freedom but to speak my thoughts.
The strictness of our governess that forbids us
On pain of death the sight and use of men
Is more than tyranny.[156] For herself, she's past
Those youthful heats[157] and feels not the want
Of that which young maids[158] long for. And her daughter,
The fair Clarinda, though in few years
Improved in height and large proportion,[159]
Came here so young
That, scarce remembʼring that she had a father,
She never dreams of man, and should she see one,
In my opinion, a[160] would appear a strange beast to her.
JULETTA 'Tis not so with us.
HIPPOLITA For my part, I confess it, I was not made
For this single life, nor do I love hunting so,
But that I had rather be the chase[161] myself.
CROCALE By Venus[162] (Out upon me![163] I should have sworn
By Diana![164]), I am of thy mind too, wench.
And though I have ta'en an oath, not alone[165]
To detest but never to think of man,

149 7 beast of chase: i.e. hunted animal
150 8 it: i.e. the black lake
151 10 pinions: the wings of a bird in flight
152 10 cleave: adhere, cling to; slice through
153 16 Fauns nor satyrs: both hybrid human-goat creatures characterized by their lust
154 18 commonwealth: a body politic, or independent community, in which the people have a voice and interest
155 19 in ourselves begun: i.e. which we founded
156 24 tyranny: i.e. absolute rule and therefore in conflict with the community's status as a commonwealth
157 25 heats: desires
158 26 maids: virgins
159 27–8 in few . . . large proportion: i.e. she has grown up quickly
160 32 a: he
161 36 the chase: i.e. the one being hunted, pursued
162 37 Venus: goddess of beauty and love
163 37 Out upon me: i.e. curses upon me. In lines 37–8 as they appear in F1, only "Out upon me" is enclosed in parentheses, suggesting that it is the only part of these lines spoken aside. Colman (1778) was the first to suggest enclosing "I should . . . By Diana" as well
164 38 Diana: the moon-goddess; patroness of hunting and virginity
165 39 not alone: i.e. not only

Every hour something tells me I am forsworn.[166]
For I confess imagination helps me sometimes,
And that's all is left[167] for us to feed on.
We might starve else, for if I have any pleasure
In this life but when I sleep, I am a pagan.[168]
Then, from the courtier to the country clown,
I have strange visions—
JULETTA Visions, Crocale?
CROCALE Yes, and fine visions, too;
And visions I hope in dreams are harmless,
And not forbid by our canons.[169] The last night
(Troth 'tis a foolish one, but I must tell it)
As I lay in my cabin betwixt sleeping and waking—
HIPPOLITA Upon your back?
CROCALE How should a young maid lie, fool,
When she would be entranced?[170]
HIPPOLITA We are instructed. Forward, I prithee.[171]
CROCALE Methought a sweet young man
In years, some twenty, with a downy chin
Promising a future beard, and yet no red one,[172]
Stole slyly to my cabin all unbraced,[173]
Took me in his arms, and kissed me twenty times,
Yet still[174] I slept.
JULETTA Fie! Thy lips run over, Crocale.
But to the rest?
CROCALE Lord, what a man is this, thought I,
To do this to a maid!
Yet then, for my life, I could not wake.
The youth, a little daunted,[175] with a trembling hand
Heaved up the clothes.[176]
HIPPOLITA Yet still you slept.
CROCALE I'faith I did.
And when methoughts he was warm by my side,
Thinking to catch him, I stretched out both mine arms,
And when I felt him not, I shrieked out
And waked for anger.
HIPPOLITA 'Twas a pretty dream.
CROCALE Ay, if it had been a true one.

Enter ALBERT [*as if washed up on the shore*][177]

JULETTA But stay, what's here cast o'th'shore?
HIPPOLITA 'Tis a man.

166 41 forsworn: perjured
167 43 all is left: i.e. all that is left
168 45 a pagan: i.e. uncivilized; an unbeliever
169 50 canons: laws
170 54 When she wants to be thrown into a trance? (i.e. a state of ecstasy, with an implication of sexual pleasure)
171 55 Forward, I prithee: continue, please
172 58 no red one: a red beard, figuratively associated with Judas, was taken to be a sign of evil or dishonesty
173 59 unbraced: i.e. with his clothes unfastened or loosened
174 61 still: without movement; continually
175 66 daunted: apprehensive
176 67 clothes: bedsheets; garments
177 72 SD: the placement of Albert's entrance follows F2. In F1, it is situated to the right of Hippolita's "pretty dream"

Shall I shoot him?
CROCALE No, no! ’Tis a handsome beast.
Would we had more o’the breed. Stand close, wenches,
And let’s hear if he can speak.
ALBERT Do I yet live?
Sure it is air I breathe. What place is this?
Sure something more than human[178] keeps residence here,
For I have past the Stygian[179] gulf,[180]
And touch upon the blessed shore![181] ’Tis so:
This is the Elysian shade; these, happy spirits
That here enjoy all pleasures.
HIPPOLITA He makes towards[182] us.
JULETTA Stand, or I’ll shoot.
CROCALE Hold! He makes no resistance.
ALBERT Be not offended, goddesses, that I fall
Thus prostrate at your feet; or, if not such,
But nymphs of Dian’s train[183] that range[184] these groves
Which you forbid to men. Vouchsafe[185] to know
I am a man, a wicked sinful man, and yet not sold
So far to impudence[186] as to presume
To press[187] upon your privacies, or provoke
Your heavenly angers. ’Tis not for myself
I beg thus poorly, for I am already wounded,
Wounded to death, and faint. My last breath
Is for a virgin comes as near yourselves
In all perfection, as what’s mortal may
Resemble things divine. O pity her,
And let your charity free her from that desert,[188]
If heavenly charity can reach to hell,
For sure that place comes near it, and where’er
My ghost shall find abode,
Eternally I shall pour blessings on ye.
HIPPOLITA By my life, I cannot hurt him.
CROCALE Though I lose my head for it, nor I.
I must pity him and will.

Enter CLARINDA

JULETTA But stay.[189]—Clarinda!
CLARINDA What new game[190] have ye found here? Ha!
What beast is this lies wallowing[191] in his gore?
CROCALE Keep off.

178 78 more than human: i.e. divine. F1’s “humane” is also viable
179 79 Stygian: relating to the river Styx; infernal, hellish
180 79 gulf: an impassible gap symbolizing eternal separation (Luke 16:26); a profound depth in the ocean or a river
181 80 blessed shore: i.e. Elysium, where the blessed (as opposed to the damned) would go after death
182 82 makes towards: approaches
183 86 train: retinue; entourage
184 86 range: roam
185 87 Vouchsafe: receive in a gracious manner; deign to accept
186 89 impudence: boldness; audacity
187 90 press: impose (perhaps with sexual innuendo)
188 97 desert: uninhabitable, barren wilderness; punishment
189 104 stay: wait
190 105 game: animal caught or killed for sport; pleasurable activity or dalliance (with an unwitting erotic implication)
191 106 wallowing: rolling around

CLARINDA Wherefore, I pray? I ne'er turned
From a fell[192] lioness robbed of her whelps,[193]
And shall I fear dead carrion?[194]
JULETTA O but—
CLARINDA But what is't?
HIPPOLITA It is infectious.
CLARINDA Has it not a name?
CROCALE Yes,
But such a name from which, as from the devil,
Your mother commands us fly.
CLARINDA Is it a man?
CROCALE It is.
CLARINDA What a brave[195] shape it has in death.
How excellent would it appear had it life!
Why should it be infectious? I have heard
My mother say I had a father,
And was not he a man?
CROCALE Questionless, madam.
CLARINDA Your fathers, too, were men?
JULETTA Without doubt, lady.
CLARINDA And without such it is impossible
We could have been.
HIPPOLITA A sin against nature to deny it.
CLARINDA Nor can you or I have any hope to be a mother
Without the help of men?
CROCALE Impossible.
CLARINDA Which of you then most barbarous, that knew
You from a man had being, and owe to it
The name of parent, durst[196] presume to kill
The likeness of that thing by which you are?
Whose arrows made these wounds? Speak, or by Dian,
Without distinction,[197] I'll let fly[198] at ye all.
JULETTA Not mine.
HIPPOLITA Nor mine.
CROCALE 'Tis strange to see her moved thus.—
Restrain your fury, madam. Had we killed him,
We had but performed your mother's command.
CLARINDA But if she command unjust and cruel things,
We are not to obey it.
CROCALE We are innocent.
Some storm did cast him shipwrecked on the shore,
As you see, wounded, nor durst we be surgeons
To such your mother doth appoint for death.
CLARINDA Weak excuse. Where's pity?
Where's soft compassion? Cruel and ungrateful!
Did providence offer to your charity
But one poor subject to express it on,
And in't to show our wants, too; and could you

192 108 fell: fierce
193 108 whelps: cubs
194 109 dead carrion: a corpse; decaying flesh
195 114 brave: handsome
196 126 durst: dared
197 129 Without distinction: i.e. without distinguishing the person responsible from the rest
198 129 let fly: shoot (arrows)

So carelessly neglect it?
HIPPOLITA For aught I know,
He's living yet, and you may tempt your mother,
By giving him succor.[199]
CLARINDA Ha! Come near, I charge ye.
So, bend his body softly, rub his temples.—
Nay, that shall be my office.[200] How the red
Steals into his pale lips!— [*To* HIPPOLITA] Run and fetch the simples[201]
With which my mother healed my arm
When last I was wounded by the boar.
CROCALE Do!—
But remember[202] her to come after ye,
That she may behold her daughter's charity. *Exit* HIPPOLITA
CLARINDA Now he breathes;
The air passing through the Arabian groves[203]
Yields not so sweet an odor. Prithee, taste it.
Taste it, good Crocale. Yet I envy thee
So great a blessing. 'Tis not sin to touch
These rubies,[204] is it?
JULETTA Not, I think.
CLARINDA Or thus to live chameleon-like?[205] I could
Resign my essence to live ever thus.

Enter HIPPOLITA [*with the simples*]

O welcome! Raise him up gently. Some soft hand
Bound up these wounds. A woman's hair.—What fury,
For which my ignorance does not know a name,
Is crept into my bosom? But I forget
My pious work.—Now, if this juice hath power,
Let it appear. [*She applies the medicine*] His eyelids ope. Prodigious![206]
Two suns break from these orbs.
ALBERT Ha! Where am I? What new vision's this?
To what goddess do I owe this second life?
Sure thou art more than mortal,
And any sacrifice of thanks or duty
In poor and wretched man to pay, comes short
Of your immortal bounty. But to show
I am not unthankful, thus in humility
I kiss the happy ground you have made sacred
By bearing of your weight.
CLARINDA No goddess, friend,
But made of that same brittle mold as you are,
One too acquainted with calamities,
And, from that, apt to pity. Charity ever
Finds in the act reward, and needs no trumpet

199 147 succor: assistance; shelter
200 150 office: duty
201 151 simples: medicines composed of a single ingredient, i.e. plants or herbs used for medicinal purposes
202 154 remember: remind
203 157 Arabian groves: i.e. trees known for their fragrance
204 161 rubies: i.e. his lips
205 162 live chameleon-like: chameleons were proverbially said to live on nothing but air—as Clarinda imagines she could live on Albert's breath
206 169 Prodigious!: wonderful!

In the receiver.[207] O forbear this duty!
I have a hand to meet with yours,
And lips to bid yours welcome.
CROCALE [*Aside*] I see that, by instinct,
Though a young maid hath never seen a man,
Touches have titillations, and inform her.[208]

Enter ROSELLA

But here's our governess.
—Now I expect a storm.
ROSELLA Child of my flesh,
And not of my fair unspotted[209] mind,
Unhand this monster.
CLARINDA Monster, mother?
ROSELLA Yes,
And every word he speaks, a siren's note,[210]
To drown the careless hearer. Have I not taught thee
The falsehood and the perjuries of men,
On whom, but for a woman to show pity,
Is to be cruel to herself? The sovereignty[211]
Proud and imperious[212] men usurp upon[213] us,
We confer on ourselves, and love those fetters
We fasten to our freedoms. Have we, Clarinda,
Since thy father's wrack, sought liberty
To lose it uncompelled?[214] Did Fortune guide,
Or rather destiny,[215] our bark to which
We could appoint no port,[216] to this blessed place,
Inhabited heretofore[217] by warlike women[218]
That kept men in subjection? Did we then
By their example, after we had lost
All we could love in man, here plant ourselves
With execrable[219] oaths never to look
On man but as a monster? And wilt thou
Be the first precedent[220] to infringe those vows
We made to heaven?
CLARINDA Hear me, and hear me with justice,
And as ye are delighted in the name
Of mother, hear a daughter that would be like you.
Should all women use this obstinate abstinence
You would force upon us, in a few years
The whole world would be peopled only with beasts.

207 182–4 Charity ever . . . the receiver: the act of charity is enough of a reward in itself that the recipient does not need to draw further attention to it
208 188 i.e. physical contact with Albert stimulates Clarinda's senses and teaches her about men (with strong erotic overtones)
209 191 unspotted: pure
210 193 siren's note: song of mythological creatures, half woman and half bird, that was supposed to lure sailors to destruction
211 197 sovereignty: dominion; authority
212 198 imperious: domineering; dictatorial
213 198 usurp upon: unjustly or illegally seize from
214 202 uncompelled: voluntarily
215 203 destiny: i.e. destine, preordain
216 204 appoint no port: find no place to dock
217 205 heretofore: before this time
218 205 warlike women: i.e. Amazons; this is the play's first and only reference to an indigenous population
219 209 execrable: fearful; involving a curse if broken
220 211 precedent: example

HIPPOLITA We must and will have men.
CROCALE Ay, or we'll shake off all obedience.
ROSELLA Are ye mad? Can no persuasion alter ye?
Suppose you had my suffrage[221] to your suit.
Can this shipwrecked wretch supply them all?[222]
ALBERT Hear me, great lady?[223]
I have fellows in my misery. Not far hence,
Divided only by this hellish river,
There live a company of wretched men
Such as your charity may make your slaves.
Imagine all the miseries mankind
May suffer under, and they groan beneath 'em.
CLARINDA But are they like to you?
JULETTA Speak they your language?
CROCALE Are they able, lusty men?
ALBERT They were, good ladies;
And in their May of youth, of gentle blood,[224]
And such as may deserve ye. Now, cold and hunger
Hath lessened their perfection, but restored
To what they were, I doubt not they'll appear
Worthy of your favors.
JULETTA This is a blessing
We durst not hope for.
CLARINDA Dear mother, be not obdurate.[225]
ROSELLA Hear, then, my resolution, and labor not
To add to what I'll grant, for 'twill be fruitless.[226]
You shall appear as good angels to these wretched men.
In a small boat we'll pass o'er to 'em,
And bring 'em comfort. If you like their persons,
And they approve of yours (for we'll force nothing),
And since we want ceremonies,[227]
Each one shall choose a husband and enjoy
His company a month; but that expired
You shall no more come near 'em. If you prove fruitful,[228]
The males ye shall return to them, the females
We will reserve ourselves.[229] This is the utmost
Ye shall e'er obtain. As ye think fit,
Ye may dismiss this stranger,
And prepare tomorrow for the journey. *Exit*
CLARINDA Come, sir, will ye walk?
We will show ye our pleasant bowers,[230]
And something ye shall find to cheer your heart.
ALBERT Excellent lady,
Though 'twill appear a wonder one near starved

221 221 suffrage: vote, consent
222 222 supply them all: i.e. with children
223 223 F1 & F2's question mark has typically been emended by previous editors to a colon or comma. I maintain the question mark to preserve the possible apprehension in Albert's tone
224 232 of gentle blood: noble by birth; also, mild in temperament
225 237 obdurate: resistant; hardened against persuasion
226 239 fruitless: unsuccessful; also suggesting the failure to conceive and procreate
227 244 want ceremonies: lack established rituals
228 247 prove fruitful: conceive and procreate
229 248–9 The males … reserve ourselves: we'll give male children to the men and keep the female children
230 254 bowers: spaces enclosed or overarched by trees and other plants; arbors

Should refuse rest and meat, I must not take
Your noble offer. I left in yonder desert
A virgin almost pined.
CLARINDA She's not your wife?
ALBERT No, lady, but my sister ('tis now dangerous
To speak truth). To her I deeply vowed
Not to taste food or rest, if fortune brought it me,
'Til I blessed her with my return. Now if you please
To afford me an easy passage to her,
And some meat for her recovery,
I shall live your slave, and thankfully
She shall ever acknowledge her life at your service.
CLARINDA You plead so well, I can deny ye nothing.
I myself will see you furnishèd
And, with the next sun, visit and relieve thee.
ALBERT Ye are all goodness—

Exeunt

[Act III, scene i]

Enter severally LAMURE, FRANVILLE, [*and*] MORILLAT

LAMURE O! What a tempest have I in my stomach!
How my empty guts cry out! My wounds ache.
Would they would bleed again that I might get
Something to quench my thirst.
FRANVILLE O Lamure, the happiness my dogs had
When I kept house at home! They had a storehouse,
A storehouse of most blessèd bones and crusts.
Happy crusts! O! How sharp hunger pinches me! *Exit* FRANVILLE
MORILLAT O my importunate[231] belly, I have nothing
To satisfy thee. I have sought,
As far as my weak legs would carry me,
Yet can find nothing, neither meat nor water
Nor anything that's nourishing.
My belly's grown together like an empty satchel.

Enter FRANVILLE [*with a handful of mud*]

LAMURE How now what news?
MORILLAT Hast any meat yet?
FRANVILLE Not a bit that I can see.
Here be goodly quarries,[232] but they be cruel hard
To gnaw. I ha' got some mud. We'll eat it with spoons.
Very good thick mud, but it stinks damnably.
There's old rotten trunks of trees, too,
But not a leaf nor blossom in all the island.
LAMURE How it looks!
MORILLAT It stinks, too.
LAMURE It may be poison.
FRANVILLE Let it be anything,
So I can get it down. Why, man,

231 9 importunate: insistent to the point of being annoying
232 18 quarries: large masses of stone or rock suitable for excavation, with reference to the term's other meaning—a heap of animals killed during the hunt

Poison's a princely dish.
MORILLAT Hast thou no biscuit?[233]
No crumbs left in thy pocket? Here's my doublet.[234]
Give me but three small crumbs.
FRANVILLE Not for three kingdoms,
If I were master of 'em!—O Lamure,
But one poor joint of mutton we ha' scorned, man!
LAMURE Thou speakest of paradise!
FRANVILLE Or but the snuffs of those healths[235]
We have lewdly at midnight flung away.
MORILLAT Ah! But to lick the glasses.

Enter SURGEON

FRANVILLE Here comes the surgeon.—What hast thou discovered?
Smile, smile, and comfort us.
SURGEON I am expiring.
Smile they that can. I can find nothing, gentlemen.
Here's nothing can be meat without a miracle.
O that I had my boxes and my lints[236] now,
My stupes,[237] my tents,[238] and those sweet helps of nature.
What dainty dishes could I make of 'em.
MORILLAT Hast ne'er[239] an old suppository?
SURGEON O would I had, sir.
LAMURE Or but the paper where such a cordial,
Potion, or pills hath been entombed.
FRANVILLE Or, the blessed[240] bladder where a cooling-glister[241]—
MORILLAT Hast thou no cerecloths[242] left?
Nor any old poultice?[243]
FRANVILLE We care not to what it hath been ministered.[244]
SURGEON Sure, I have none of these dainties, gentlemen.
FRANVILLE Where's the great wen[245]
Thou cutt'st from Hugh the sailor's shoulder?
That would serve now for a most princely banquet.
SURGEON Ay, if we had it, gentlemen.
I flung it overboard, slave that I was.
LAMURE A most unprovident villain.
SURGEON If I had anything that were but supple[246] now!
I could make salads of your shoes, gentlemen,
And rare ones. Anything unctuous[247]—
MORILLAT Ay, and then we might fry the soles i'th'sun.

233 27 biscuit: flat, dry, crispy bread
234 28 doublet: jacket
235 33 snuffs of those healths: the last sips of drinks
236 40 lints: dressings for wounds
237 41 stupes: soft cloths dipped in hot water and medicated to relieve pain and inflammation
238 41 tents: pieces of absorbent material administered to a wound or bodily orifice to keep it open
239 43 Hast ne'er: i.e. You don't even have
240 47 blessed: F2 emends to "best"
241 47 glister: i.e. clyster
242 48 cerecloths: textiles used for wrapping dead bodies; winding-sheets
243 49 poultice: soft, moist mass of material (usually made from plants or flour) applied to the body to help relieve pain and inflammation
244 50 ministered: applied
245 52 wen: boil or other growth on the skin
246 58 supple: of a soft and yielding consistency; not hard
247 60 unctuous: greasy

The soles would make a second dish.
LAMURE Or, souse 'em in the salt-water,
An inner sole well soused—

Enter AMINTA

FRANVILLE Here comes the woman.
It may be she has meat and may relieve us.
Let's withdraw and mark and then be ready.
She'll hide her store[248] else, and so cozen us. [*They step aside*]
AMINTA How weary and how hungry am I;
How feeble and how faint is all my body!
Mine eyes, like spent lamps glowing out,[249] grow heavy,
My sight forsaking me; and all my spirits,
As if they heard my passing bell[250] go for me,
Pull in their powers and give me up to destiny.
O! For a little water, a little, little meat,
A little to relieve me ere I perish.
I had whole floods of tears awhile that nourished me,
But they are all consumed for thee, dear Albert;
For thee they are spent, for thou art dead;
Merciless fate hath swallowed thee.
O—[251]I grow heavy. Sleep is a salve for misery.
Heaven look on me, and either take my life,
Or make me once more happy. [*She falls asleep*]
LAMURE She's fast asleep already.
Why should she have this blessing, and we wake still,
Wake to our wants?
MORILLAT This thing[252] hath been our overthrow,
And all these biting mischiefs that fall on us
Are come through her means.
FRANVILLE True, we were bound, ye all know,
For happy places and most fertile islands,
Where we had constant promises of all things.
She turned the captain's mind,
And must have him go in search, I know not of who,
Nor to what end: of such a fool her brother,
And such a coxcomb[253] her kinsman,
And we must put in everywhere.[254]
She has put us in now i'faith.
LAMURE Why should we consume[255] thus, and starve,
Having nothing to relieve us,
And she live there that bred all our miseries,
Unroasted or unsod?[256]
MORILLAT I have read in stories—
LAMURE Of such restoring meats, we have examples,

248 68 store: supply
249 71 glowing out: i.e. decreasing in light and heat
250 73 passing bell: death knell
251 81 F1 & F2's dash suggests non-verbal business, perhaps Aminta sitting down or swooning
252 86 This thing: i.e. Aminta
253 95 coxcomb: a vain, conceited man
254 96 put in everywhere: enter every harbor or port, causing the ship to deviate from its intended course
255 98 consume: waste away
256 101 unsod: unboiled; uncooked

Thousand examples and allowed for excellent:
Women that have eat their children;
Men, their slaves, nay their brothers. But these are nothing:
Husbands devoured their wives (they are their chattels[257]);
And of a schoolmaster that, in time of famine,
Powdered up[258] all his scholars.
MORILLAT She's young and tidy.[259]
In my conscience, she'll eat delicately,[260]
Just like young pork, a little lean.
Your opinion, surgeon?
SURGEON I think she may be made good meat,
But look we shall want salt.
FRANVILLE Tush, she needs no powdering.
SURGEON I grant ye.
But to suck out the humorous[261] parts, by all means,
Let's kill her in a chase. She'll eat the sweeter.[262]
LAMURE Let's kill her any way, and kill her quickly,
That we might be at our meat.
SURGEON How if the captain—
MORILLAT Talk not of him. He's dead, and the rest famished.—
Wake her, surgeon, and cut her throat,
And then divide her, every man his share.
FRANVILLE She wakes herself.
AMINTA Holy and good things keep me!
What cruel dreams have I had!—Who are these?
O they are my friends.—For heaven's sake, gentlemen,
Give me some food to save my life,
If ye have aught[263] to spare,
A little to relieve me. I may blesse ye,
For, weak and wretched, ready to perish,
Even now I die.
MORILLAT You'll save a labor then.
You bred these miseries, and you shall pay for 't.
We have no meat, nor where to have we know not,
Nor how to pull ourselves from these afflictions.
We are starved, too, famished, all our hopes deluded,
Yet ere we die thus, we'll have one dainty meal.
AMINTA Shall I be with ye, gentlemen?
LAMURE Yes, marry,[264] shall ye, in our bellies, lady.
We love you well—
AMINTA What said you, sir?
LAMURE Marry, we'll eat your ladyship.
FRANVILLE You that have buried us in this base island,
We'll bury ye in a more noble monument.[265]
SURGEON Will ye say your prayers, that I may perform, lady?

257 106 chattels: i.e. property
258 108 Powdered up: salted; seasoned
259 108 tidy: in good condition; also, in season, or opportune
260 109 I am certain she'll taste delicious; also, possibly, eating her will not weigh on my conscience
261 115 humorous: juicy (a reference to the humors, or bodily fluids)
262 116 She'll eat the sweeter: i.e. they will enjoy eating her more after a hunt because of the sport of it
263 127 aught: anything
264 137 marry: an expression used for emphasis; indeed
265 141 a more noble monument: i.e. their bodies

We are wondrous sharp set.[266] Come, gentlemen,
Who are for the hinder parts?[267]
MORILLAT *and* FRANVILLE I.
LAMURE And I.
SURGEON Be patient;
They will not fall to every man's share.
AMINTA O hear me.
Hear me, ye barbarous men.
MORILLAT Be short and pithy,
Our stomachs cannot stay a long discourse.
SURGEON And be not fearful, for I'll kill ye daintily.
AMINTA Are ye not Christians?
LAMURE. Why, do not Christians eat women?
AMINTA Eat one another? 'Tis most impious.

Enter TIBALT [*and*] MASTER, [*with*] *sailors*[268]

SURGEON Come, come—
AMINTA O, help, help, help!
TIBALT The lady's voice!—Stand off, slaves.
What do you intend villains?
I have strength enough left me, if you abuse this soul,
To—[269]
MASTER They would have ravished her upon my life.—
Speak, how was it, lady?
AMINTA Forgive 'em; 'twas their hungers.
TIBALT Ha, their hungers!
MASTER They would have eaten her.
TIBALT O damnèd villains, speak. Is it true?
SURGEON I confess an appetite.
TIBALT An appetite? I'll fit ye for an appetite.
Are ye so sharp set that her flesh must serve you?
Murder's a main[270] good service[271] with your worships.
Since ye would be such devils, why did you not
Begin with one another handsomely,
And spare the woman to beget more food on?[272]
AMINTA Good sir—
TIBALT You shall grow mummy,[273] rascals.
I'll make you fall to[274] your brawns[275] and your buttocks,
And worry[276] one another like keen bandogs.[277]
AMINTA Good sir, be merciful.
TIBALT You shall know what 'tis to be damned cannibals.

266 143 sharp set: hungry
267 144 hinder parts: buttocks
268 152 SD In F1, the SD is situated to the right of lines 151–3. In F2, it appears after line 151
269 158 F1 & F2's dash here suggests non-verbal business, possibly Tibalt physically threatening Franville, Morillat, Lamure, and the Surgeon
270 166 main: exceedingly
271 166 good service: benefit; advantage
272 167–9 why did . . . food on?: i.e. why didn't you start properly ("handsomely") by killing each other so that you could then use her to produce ("beget") more food?
273 171 grow mummy: become flesh (for each other to eat)
274 172 fall to: begin eating voraciously
275 172 brawns: fleshy, muscular parts of the body
276 173 worry: seize by the throat with the teeth
277 173 bandogs: i.e. dogs chained up because of their ferocity

Enter ALBERT

AMINTA O my best friend!
ALBERT Alas, poor heart! Here—
Here's some meat and sovereign[278] drink to ease you.
Sit down, gentle sweet.
AMINTA I am blessed to see you.
TIBALT Stir not within forty foot of this food,
If you do, dogs—
ALL O captain, captain, captain!
ALBERT Ye shall have meat, all of you.
TIBALT Captain, hear me first. Hark, 'tis so inhumane!—
I would not ha' the air corrupted with it. [*Whispers*]
ALBERT O barbarous men!—Sit down, du-Pont,
Good master, and honest sailors.
TIBALT But stand you off,
And wait upon our charity. I'll wait on[279] you else.
And touch nothing but what's flung ye, as if you were dogs.
If you do, I'll cut your fingers, friends.
I'll spoil your carving.
AMINTA There, wretches, there— [*She throws food to them*]
TIBALT Eat your meat handsomely now,
And give heaven thanks.
ALBERT There's more bread— [*He throws more food to them*]
TIBALT See, they snarl like dogs.—
Eat quietly, you rascals, eat quietly.
ALBERT There is drink, too.
TIBALT Come, come, I'll fill you each your cups— [*He serves them drink*]
Ye shall not surfeit.
AMINTA And what have you discovered?
ALBERT Sweet, a paradise,
A paradise inhabited with angels,
Such as you are. Their pities make 'em angels.
They gave me these viands[280] and supplied me
With these precious drinks.
AMINTA Shall not we see 'em?
ALBERT Yes, they will see you.
Out of their charities, having heard our story,
They will come and comfort us, come presently.
We shall no more know wants nor miseries.
AMINTA Are they all women?
ALBERT All, and all in love with us.
AMINTA How!
ALBERT Do not mistake. In love with our misfortunes,
They will cherish and relieve our men.
TIBALT [*To the gallants*] Do you shrug now,
And pull up your noses? You smell comfort.—
See, they stretch out their legs, like dottrels,[281]

278 177 sovereign: effective; beneficial
279 186 wait on: serve you (with the threat of violence)
280 201 viands: meats
281 213 dottrels: plovers; silly people

Each like a new Saint Denis.[282]
ALBERT Dear mistress,
When you would name me, and the women hear,
Call me your brother. You, I'll call my sister,
And pray observe this all—
Why do you change color, sweet?
AMINTA Eating too much meat.
ALBERT Sauced with jealousy.—
Fie, fie, dear saint, i'faith ye are too blame.[283]
Are ye not here? Here, fixed in my heart? [*Horns within*]
ALL Hark, hark!

Enter ROSELLA, CLARINDA, CROCALE, HIPPOLITA, [*and*] JULETTA

ALBERT They are come. Stand ready, and look nobly,
And with all humble reverence receive 'em.
Our lives depend upon their gentle pities,
And death waits on their anger.
MORILLAT Sure they are fairies.
TIBALT Be they devils, devils of flesh and blood,
After so long a lent[284] and tedious voyage,
To me they are angels.
FRANVILLE O for some eryngoes![285]
LAMURE Potatoes[286] or cantharides.[287]
TIBALT Peace, you rogues that buy abilities of your 'pothecaries,[288]
Had I but took the diet of green cheese,[289]
And onions[290] for a month, I could do wonders.
ROSELLA Are these the jewels[291] you run mad for?
What can you see in one of these
To whom you would vouchsafe a gentle touch?
Can nothing persuade you
To love yourselves and place your happiness
In cold and chaste embraces of each other?
JULETTA This is from the purpose.
HIPPOLITA We had your grant[292] to have them as they were.
CLARINDA [*Aside*] 'Tis a beauteous creature,
And to myself, I do appear deformed
When I consider her, and yet she is
The stranger's sister. Why then should I fear?
She cannot prove my rival.
ROSELLA When you repent[293]
That you refused my counsel, may it add

282 214 Each like … Saint Denis: acting according to the needs of their bodies, not their heads. Also, they are acting like martyrs: after he was beheaded in Paris, Saint Denis is said to have walked several miles with his head in his hands
283 220 too blame: blameworthy; apt to suspect guilt
284 228 lent: period of abstinence
285 230 eryngoes: candied roots of sea holly (a thistle-like plant); regarded as an aphrodisiac
286 230 Potatoes: also thought to have aphrodisiac properties
287 230 cantharides: a kind of dried beetle, or Spanish fly; also used as an aphrodisiac
288 231 buy abilities of your 'pothecaries: i.e. purchase substances to enhance sexual performance
289 232 green cheese: likely being cited as a sexual stimulant
290 233 onions: also believed to stimulate sexual performance
291 234 jewels: i.e. the precious men
292 241 grant: permission
293 246 repent: i.e. regret

To your afflictions that you were forward,[294]
Yet leaped into the gulf of your misfortunes.
But have your wishes.
MASTER Now she makes to us.
AMINTA I am instructed, but take heed, Albert,
You prove not false.
ALBERT Ye are your own assurance,
And so acquainted with your own perfections,
That weak doubts cannot reach you. Therefore, fear not.
ROSELLA That you are poor and miserable men
My eyes inform me: that without our succors,
Hope cannot flatter you[295] to dream of safety.
The present plight you are in can resolve[296] you
That to be merciful is to draw near
The heavenly essence. Whether you will be
Thankful, I do not question, nor demand
What country bred you, what names, what manners.
To us, it is sufficient we relieve
Such as have shapes of men; and I command you,
As we are not ambitious to know
Farther of you, that on pain of death
You presume not to enquire what we are
Or whence derived.[297]
ALBERT In all things we obey you,
And thankfully we ever shall confess
Ourselves your creatures.
ROSELLA You speak as becomes you.
First, then, and willingly, deliver up
Those weapons we could force from you.
ALBERT We lay 'em down most gladly at your feet.
TIBALT I have had many a combat with a tall wench,
But never was disarmed before.
ROSELLA And now hear comfort:
Your wants shall be supplied, and though it be
A debt women may challenge to be sued to,
Especially from such they may command,[298]
We give up to you that power, and therefore
Freely each make his choice.
FRANVILLE Then here I fix—
MORILLAT Nay, she is mine. I eyed her first.
LAMURE This mine—
TIBALT Stay, good rascals.—
You are too forward, Sir Gallant.
You are not giving order to a tailor
For the fashion of a new suit.—
Nor are you in your warehouse, Master Merchant.—
Stand back and give your betters leave—your betters—
And grumble not. If ye do, as I love meat,

294 248 forward: eager; immodest. Sympson (1750) suggested "forwarnd," i.e. "forewarned"
295 257 Hope cannot flatter you: you cannot have enough hope even
296 258 resolve: inform; persuade
297 268 whence derived: where we come from
298 276–8 though it . . . may command: although women can exact a penalty for sexual advances, especially from the men they control

I will so swinge[299] the salt itch[300] out on[301] you.—
Captain, master, and the rest of us
That are brothers and good fellows, we have been
Too late by the ears[302] and yet smart[303] for our follies.
To end therefore all future emulation,[304] if you please
To trust to my election, you shall say
I am not partial to myself. I doubt not
Give content to all.[305]
ALL Agreed, agreed.
TIBALT Then but observe how learnèd and discreetly
I will proceed, and as a skillful doctor
In all the quirks belonging to the game,
Read over your complexions.[306]—For you, captain,
Being first in place and therefore first to be served,
I give my judgment thus: for your aspect[307]
Y'are much inclined to melancholy, and that tells me
The sullen Saturn had predominance
At your nativity,[308] a malignant planet,
And, if not qualified by a sweet conjunction
Of a soft and ruddy wench born under Venus,[309]
It may prove fatal. Therefore to your arms,
I give this rose-cheeked virgin.
CLARINDA To my wish.
'Til now I never was happy.
AMINTA [*Aside*] Nor I accursed.
TIBALT Master, you are old,
Yet love the game. That I perceive, too.
And, if not well spurred up,[310] you may prove rusty.
Therefore, to help ye, here's a Bradamanta,[311]
Or I am cozened in my calculation.
CROCALE A poor old man allotted to my share.
TIBALT Thou wouldst have two, nay, I think twenty.
But fear not, wench, though he be old he's tough.
Look on's making. He'll not fail, I warrant thee.
ROSELLA A merry fellow,
And were not man a creature I detest,
I could endure his company.
TIBALT Here's a fair herd of does before me.
And now for a barren one,
For though I like the sport, I do not love

299 289 swinge: beat
300 289 salt itch: restless desire; also, venereal disease
301 289 on: of
302 291–2 we have . . . the ears: we have been fighting with each other until very recently
303 292 yet smart: still feel the pain
304 293 emulation: rivalry
305 295–6 I doubt . . . to all: i.e. I am sure the pairings I make will please everyone
306 300 complexions: dispositions of mind and body, thought to have been controlled by the (im)balance of humors, or bodily fluids, and reflected in the face and behavior
307 302 aspect: facial expression
308 304–5 sullen Saturn . . . your nativity: because of its distance from the sun, Saturn was supposed to cause coldness, slowness, and melancholy in those born under its influence
309 307 Venus: the second planet from the sun, therefore warm; also, the Roman goddess of beauty and love
310 313 spurred up: i.e. equipped for riding (with sexual innuendo)
311 314 Bradamanta: i.e. Bradamante, a female knight featured in Ariosto's *Orlando Furioso*

To father children. Like the Grand Signor,[312]
Thus I walk in my seraglio,[313]
And view 'em as I pass. Then, draw I forth
My handkercher, and having made my choice,
I thus bestow it—
ROSELLA On me?
TIBALT On you.—Now my choice is made,
To it, you hungry rascals.
ALBERT Excellent.
AMINTA As I love goodness,
It makes me smile i'th'height of all my fears.
CLARINDA What a strong contention you may behold
Between my mother's mirth and anger.
TIBALT Nay, no coyness. Be mistress of your word.
I must and will enjoy you.
ROSELLA Be advised, fool.
Alas, I am old. How canst thou hope content
From one that's fifty?
TIBALT Never talk on't.
I have known good ones at threescore[314] and upwards.
Besides, the weather's hot, and men
That have experience fear fevers.
A temperate diet is the only physic.
Your juleps[315] nor guajacum,[316] prunellos,[317]
Camphor[318] pills, nor gourd water,[319]
Come not near your old woman.[320]
Youthful stomachs are still craving,
Though there be nothing left to stop their mouths with.
And believe me I am no frequent giver of those bounties.[321]—
Laugh on, laugh on, good gentlemen, do.
I shall make holiday and sleep, when you
Dig in the mines till your hearts ache.[322]
ROSELLA A mad fellow!—
Well, sir, I'll give you hearing and, as I like,
Your wooing and discourse, but I must tell ye, sir,
That rich widows look for great sums in present,[323]
Or assurances of ample jointures.[324]
TIBALT That to me is easy,
For instantly I'll do it.—Hear me, comrades.
ALBERT What say'st thou, Tibalt?
TIBALT Why, that to woo a wench with empty hands
Is no good heraldry.[325] Therefore let's to the gold,

312 326 Grand Signor: Ottoman Sultan
313 327 seraglio: the part of a Muslim nobleman's palace reserved for women; a harem
314 341 threescore: sixty
315 345 juleps: sweet drinks used as a vehicle for medicine
316 345 guajacum: a drug prepared from a genus of trees native to the West Indies; used as a cure for syphilis
317 345 prunellos: small plums
318 346 Camphor: bitter, translucent pharmaceutical derived from plants; thought to quell sexual desire
319 346 gourd water: rain water (collected in a hollowed-out gourd)
320 347 Are not nearly as good as old women for relieving fever (i.e. sexual desire)
321 350 I am . . . those bounties: i.e. I do not have sex often
322 353 Have sex until you are exhausted
323 357 great sums in present: large amounts of money as gifts
324 358 jointures: the shared use of property between two parties (especially husband and wife)
325 362 heraldry: display of pedigree, with reference to familial coats of arms

And share it equally. 'Twill speak for us
More than a thousand compliments or cringes,[326]
Ditties stol'n from Petrarch,[327] or discourse from Ovid.[328]
Besides, 'twill beget us respect
And, if ever Fortune friend us with a bark,
Largely supply us with all provision.
ALBERT Well advised. Defer it not.
TIBALT Are ye all contented?
ALL We are!
TIBALT Let's away then.—
Straight we'll return, and you shall see our riches. *Exit* [*with all the men*]
ROSELLA Since I knew[329] what wonder and amazement was,
I ne'er was so transported.[330]
CLARINDA [*To* AMINTA] Why weep ye gentle maid?
There is no danger here to such as you.
Banish fear, for with us I dare promise,
You shall meet all courteous entertainment.
CROCALE We esteem ourselves most happy in you.
HIPPOLITA And bless fortune that brought you hither.
CLARINDA Hark in your ear:
I love you as a friend already;
Ere long you shall call me by a nearer name.[331]
I wish your brother well. I know you apprehend me.
AMINTA [*Aside*] Ay, to my grief, I do.—
Alas, good ladies, there is nothing left me
But thanks to pay ye with.
CLARINDA That's more
Than yet you stand engaged for.

Enter ALBERT, TIBALT, *and the rest with treasure*

ROSELLA So soon returned!
ALBERT Here—see the idol of the lapidary.[332]
TIBALT These pearls for which the slavish negro
Dives to the bottom of the sea.
LAMURE To get which the industrious merchant
Touches at either pole.[333]
FRANVILLE The never-failing purchase
Of lordships and of honors.
MORILLAT The world's mistress
That can give everything to the possessors.
MASTER For which the sailors scorn tempestuous winds,
And spit defiance in the sea.
TIBALT Speak, lady. Look we not lovely now?
ROSELLA Yes, yes.—O my stars,

326 364 cringes: deferential acts
327 365 Petrarch: the influential Italian Renaissance poet well known for his love sonnets, which served as inspiration for English Renaissance poets
328 365 Ovid: the ancient Roman poet whose *Metamorphoses* and *Ars Amatoria* ("The Art of Love") were well known to early modern poets and playwrights and cited throughout the period
329 372 knew: this is F2's reading; F1 reads "know"
330 372–3 Since I … so transported: Sympson reassigns these lines to Clarinda, suggesting that they are out of character for Rosella. All other editors follow F1 and F2 by assigning it to Rosella
331 381 a nearer name: i.e. sister-in-law
332 387 idol of the lapidary: i.e. treasure that a stone cutter or connoisseur of precious stones would worship
333 391 Touches at either pole: i.e. circumnavigates the globe; searches high and low

Be now for ever blessed, that have brought
To my revenge these robbers.—[*To the women*] Take your arrows,
And nail these monsters to the earth.
ALBERT What mean ye, lady?
In what have we offended?
ROSELLA O my daughter!
And you, companions with me in all fortunes,
Look on these caskets and these jewels.
These were our own when first we put to sea
With good Sebastian, and these the pirates
That not alone deprived him of this treasure,
But also took his life.
CROCALE Part of my present[334]
I well remember was mine own.
HIPPOLITA And these were mine.
JULETTA Sure, I have worn this jewel.
ROSELLA Wherefore do ye stay[335] then,
And not perform my command?
ALBERT O heaven!
What cruel fate pursues us?
TIBALT I am well enough served,
That must be offering jointures, jewels,
And precious stones more then I brought with me.
ROSELLA Why, shoot ye not?
CLARINDA Hear me, dear mother,
And when the greatest cruelty is justice,
Do not show mercy. Death to these starved wretches
Is a reward, not punishment. Let 'em live
To undergo the full weight of your displeasure.
And that they may have sense to feel the torments
They have deserved, allow 'em some small pittance[336]
To linger out their tortures.
ROSELLA 'Tis well counseled,
And we'll follow it.
ALL[337] Hear us speak—
ROSELLA. Peace dogs.—
Bind 'em fast. When fury hath given way to reason,
I will determine of their sufferings,
Which shall be horrid. Vengeance, though slow paced,
At length o'ertakes the guilty, and the wrath
Of the incensèd powers will fall most sure
On wicked men when they are most secure.

Exeunt

Act IV, scene i

Enter RAYMOND, SEBASTIAN, NICUSA, [*and*] SAILORS

1 SAILOR Here's nothing, sir, but poverty and hunger:

334 408 my present: i.e. among the treasure given to me just now by the master
335 411 stay: hesitate
336 422 pittance: allowance of food and drink
337 424 SP ALL: i.e. the men

No promise of inhabitance,[338] neither tract[339] of beast,
Nor foot of man. We have searched
All this rocky desert, yet cannot discover any assurance[340]
Here is or hath been such men.
2 SAILOR Not a relic of anything they wore,
Nor mark left by 'em, either to find relief
Or to warn others from the like misfortune.
Believe it: these fellows[341] are both false,
And to get a little succor in their misery,
Have framed this cunning tale.
RAYMOND The ship, I know, is French, and owned by pirates,
If not by Albert, my arch enemy.
You told me, too, there was a woman with 'em,
A young and handsome woman.
SEBASTIAN There was so, sir.
RAYMOND And such and such young gallants.
NICUSA We told ye true, sir,
That they had no means to quit this island.
RAYMOND And that amidst their mutiny to save your lives
You got their ship.
SEBASTIAN All is most certain, sir.
RAYMOND Where are they then? Where are these men
Or woman? We are landed where your faiths
Did assure us we could not miss their sights.
For this news, we took ye to our mercy;
Relieved ye when the furious sea and famine
Strove which should first devour ye;
Clothed and cherished ye;
Used ye as those ye say ye are.
Fair gentlemen, now keep your words,
And show us this company your own free pities spoke of,
These men ye left in misery, the woman.
Men of those noble breedings you pretend to
Should scorn to lie or get their food with falsehood.
Come, direct us.
SEBASTIAN Alas, sir, they are gone,
But by what means or providence, we know not.
2 SAILOR Was not the captain
A fellow of fiery, yet brave nature,
A middle stature, and of brown complexion?
NICUSA He was, sir.
RAYMOND 'Twas Albert,
And my poor wretched sister.
1 SAILOR 'Twas he certain.
I ha' been at sea with him; many times at sea.
RAYMOND Come, show us these men.
Show us presently, and do not dally with us.[342]
SEBASTIAN We left 'em here.—What should we say, sir?—
Here, in this place.

338 2 inhabitance: shelter
339 2 tract: track; trace
340 4 assurance: certainty
341 9 these fellows: i.e. Sebastian and Nicusa
342 43 dally with us: waste our time; play tricks on us

2 SAILOR The earth cannot swallow 'em.
They have no wings; they cannot fly sure.
RAYMOND You told us, too,
Of heaps of treasure, and of sums concealed,
That set their hearts afire. We see no such thing,
No such sign. What can ye say to purge ye?[343]
What have ye done with these men?
NICUSA We, sir?
RAYMOND You, sir,
For certain I believe ye saw such people.
SEBASTIAN By all that's good, by all that's pure and honest,
By all that's holy—
RAYMOND I dare not credit ye,
Ye have so abused my hope that now I hate ye.
1 SAILOR Let's put 'em in their ragged clothes again, captain,
For certain they are knaves. Let's e'en deliver 'em
To their old fruitful[344] farm. Here, let 'em walk the island.
SEBASTIAN If ye do so, we shall curse your mercies.
NICUSA Rather put us to sea again.
RAYMOND Not so.
Yet this I'll do, because ye say ye are Christians,
Though I hardly credit it.—Bring in the boat,
And all aboard again, but these two wretches,
Yet leave 'em four days' meat.—If in that time,
(For I will search all nooks of this strange island)
I can discover any tract of these men,
Alive or dead, I'll bear ye off, and honor ye.
If not, ye have found your graves. So, farewell. *Exit* [*with* SAILORS]
NICUSA That goodness dwells above,[345] and knows us innocent,
Comfort our lives, and at his pleasure quit[346] us.
SEBASTIAN Come, cousin, come. Old time will end our story,
But no time (if we end well) ends our glory.

Exeunt

[Act IV, scene ii]

Enter ROSELLA, CLARINDA, CROCALE, HIPPOLITA, [*and*] JULETTA

ROSELLA Use 'em with all the austerity[347] that may be.
They are our slaves. Turn all those pities,
Those tender reluctations[348] that should become your sex,
To stern anger, and when ye look upon 'em,
Look with those eyes that wept those bitter sorrows,
Those cruelties ye suffered by their rapines.[349]
Some five days hence that blessèd hour comes,
Most happy to me, that knit this hand to my dear husband's,
And both our hearts in mutual bands. That hour, ladies—
CLARINDA What of that hour?

343 50 purge ye: i.e. free yourselves from suspicion
344 58 fruitful: fertile (said ironically)
345 69 That goodness dwells above: i.e. may that goodness that dwells above
346 70 quit: deliver; acquit
347 1 austerity: sternness; severity
348 3 reluctations: pleas against cruelty
349 6 rapines: forceful seizing of others' property

ROSELLA Why, on that hour, daughter,
And in the height of all our celebrations,
Our dear remembrances of that dear man
And those that suffered with him, our fair kinsmen,
Their lives shall fall a sacrifice to vengeance,
Their lives that ruined his. 'Tis a full justice.
I will look glorious in their bloods,
And the most noble spirit of Sebastian,
That perished by the pride of these French pirates,
Shall smile in heaven, and bless the hand that killed 'em.
Look strictly all unto your prisoners,
For he that makes a 'scape beyond my vengeance,
Or entertains a hope by your fair usage—
Take heed, I say—she that deceives my trust—
Again take heed—her life—and that's but light neither—
Her life in all the tortures my spirit can put on.
ALL We shall be careful.
ROSELLA Do so. *Exit* ROSELLA
CLARINDA You are angry mother, and ye are old, too,
Forgetting what men are, but we shall temper ye.[350]—
How fare your prisoners, ladies? In what forms
Do they appear in their afflictions?
JULETTA Mine fare but poorly, for so I am commanded.
'Tis none of their fault.
CLARINDA Of what sort are they?
JULETTA They say they are gentlemen, but they show mongrels.[351]
CLARINDA How do they suffer?
JULETTA Faith, like boys.
They are fearful in all fortunes. When I smile,
They kneel and beg to have that face continued
And, like poor slaves, adore the ground I go on.
When I frown, they hang their most dejected heads,
Like fearful sheephounds. Show 'em a crust of bread,
They'll saint me presently and skip like apes
For a sup[352] of wine. I'll whip 'em like hackneys,[353]
Saddle 'em, ride 'em, do what I will with 'em.
CLARINDA Tush, these are poor things.
Have they names like Christians?
JULETTA Very fair names: Franville, Lamure, and Morillat;
And brag of great kindreds,[354] too. They offer very handsomely,
But that I am a fool and dare not venture.
They are sound, too, i'my conscience,
Or very near upon't.
CLARINDA Fie, away fool.
JULETTA They tell me if they might be brought before you,
They would reveal things of strange consequence.
CLARINDA Their base poor fears.
JULETTA Ay, that makes me hate 'em, too,
For if they were but manly to their sufferance,

350 29 temper ye: i.e. moderate your anger (by treating the prisoners well)
351 34 show mongrels: look like monrels (i.e. of mixed blood, of dubious origin)
352 42 sup: sip
353 42 hackneys: horses; also, menial laborers
354 47 great kindreds: noble families

Sure I should strain a point or two.[355]
CLARINDA An hour hence I'll take a view of 'em
And hear their business.—Are your men thus, too?
CROCALE Mine? No, gentle madam, mine were not cast
In such base molds. Afflictions, tortures
Are names and natures of delight to my men.
All sorts of cruelties they meet like pleasures.
I have but two: the one they call du-Pont,
Tibalt du-Pont, the other, the shipmaster.
CLARINDA Have they not lives and fears?
CROCALE Lives they have, madam,
But those lives never linked to such companions
As fears or doubts.
CLARINDA Use 'em nobly;
And where you find fit subjects for your pities
Let it become ye to be courteous.
My mother will not always be thus rigorous.
HIPPOLITA Mine are sailors, madam,
But they sleep soundly and seldom trouble me,
Unless it be when they dream sometimes
Of fights and tempests. Then, they roar and whistle
For cans of wine, and down they fling me,
And in that rage (for they are violent fellows),
They play such reaks.[356] If they have meat, they thank me.
If none, they heartily desire to be hanged quickly.
And this is all they care.
CLARINDA Look to 'em diligently, and where your pities tell ye
They may deserve, give comfort.
ALL We will. *Exeunt [all but* CLARINDA]

Enter AMINTA

CLARINDA Come hither, be not frighted.
Think not ye steal this liberty, for we give it.
Your tender innocence assures me, virgin,
Ye had no share in those wrongs these men did us.
I find ye are not hardened in such mischiefs.
Your brother was misled sure, foully misled.
AMINTA [*Aside*] How much I fear these pities!
CLARINDA Certain he was, so much I pity him,
And for your sake, whose eyes plead for him,
Nay, for his own sake—
AMINTA Ha!
CLARINDA For I see about him—
Women have subtle eyes, and look narrowly—
Or I am much abused, many fair promises,
Nay, beyond those, too many shadowed virtues.
AMINTA I think he is good.
CLARINDA I assure myself he will be,
And out of that assurance take this comfort,
For I perceive your fear hath much dejected ye.
I love your brother—

355 56 strain a point or two: go further than permitted
356 79 reaks: pranks; tricks

AMINTA Madam.
CLARINDA Nay, do not take it for a dreamt-of favor,
That comforts in the sleep, and awake vanishes.
Indeed, I love him.
AMINTA Do ye, indeed?
CLARINDA You doubt still, because ye fear his safety.
Indeed, he is the sweetest man I e'er saw.
I think, the best. Ye may hear without blushes,
And give me thanks, if ye please, for my courtesy.[357]
AMINTA Madam, I ever must.
(Yet, witness, heaven, they[358] are hard pulled from me.)
Believe me, madam, so many imperfections I could find
(Forgive me, grace, for lying), and such wants
('Tis to an honest use), such poverties,
Both in his main proportion[359] and his mind, too.
There are a hundred handsomer (I lie lewdly).
Your noble usage, madam, hath so bound me to ye,
That I must tell ye[360]—
CLARINDA Come, tell your worst.
AMINTA He is no husband for ye.
I think ye mean in that fair way.
CLARINDA Ye have hit it.
AMINTA (I am sure ye have hit my heart.)[361]
You will find him dangerous, madam,
As fickle as the flying air, proud, jealous,
Soon glutted in your sweets, and soon forgetful.
I could say more, and tell ye I have a brother,
Another brother, that so far excels this,
Both in the ornaments of man, and making.
CLARINDA If you were not his sister, I should doubt ye mainly,[362]
Doubt ye for his love,[363] ye deal so cunningly.
Do not abuse me. I have trusted ye with more than life,
With my first love. Be careful of me.
AMINTA In what use, madam?
CLARINDA In this, lady:
Speak to him for me. You have power upon him.
Tell him I love him, tell him I dote on him.
It will become[364] your tongue.
AMINTA [*Aside*] Become my grave.
O fortune! O cursed fortune!
CLARINDA Tell him his liberty,
And all those with him, all our wealth and jewels—
Good sister, for I'll call ye so—
AMINTA I shall, lady—
Even die, I hope.

357 109 courtesy: considerateness
358 111 they: i.e. my thanks
359 115 proportion: physical form
360 117–18 Your noble … tell ye: i.e. your fair treatment of me obligates me to tell you (the truth)
361 121 Implied as an aside by Colman (1778). Explicitly marked as an aside by Weber (1812) and Dyce (1845). Hoy (1994) adds parentheses to extend the typographic strategy in F1's presentation of Aminta's last long speech. This edition follows previous editors, but it should be noted that this line does not necessarily have to be guarded speech
362 128 doubt ye mainly: suspect you considerably
363 129 Doubt ye for his love: i.e. suspect you were his lover, in love with him
364 135 become: suit

CLARINDA Here's meat and wine.—Pray, take it.
And there he lies. Give him what liberty you please
But, still concealed, what pleasure you shall please, sister.
He shall ne'er want again. Nay, see an[365] you'll take it.
Why do you study thus?
AMINTA To avoid mischiefs,
If they should happen.
CLARINDA Go and be happy for me. [*Exit*]
AMINTA O blind fortune!
Yet happy thus far, I shall live to see him,
In what strange desolation lives he here now?
Sure, this curtain will reveal— [*Draws a curtain*]

Enter ALBERT

ALBERT Who's that? Ha!
Some gentle hand, I hope, to bring me comfort.
Or if it be my death, 'tis sweetly shadowed.[366]
AMINTA Have ye forgot me, sir?
ALBERT My Aminta?
AMINTA She, sir,
That walks here up and down an empty shadow,[367]
One that for some few hours
But wanders here, carrying her own sad coffin,
Seeking some desert place to lodge her griefs in.
ALBERT Sweet sorrow, welcome. Welcome, noble grief.
How got you this fair liberty to see me,
For sorrows in your shape are strangers to me?[368]
AMINTA I come to counsel ye.
ALBERT Ye are still more welcome,
For good friends in afflictions give good counsels.
Pray, then, proceed.
AMINTA Pray, eat first. Ye show faint.
Here's wine to refresh ye, too— [*Hands him food and wine*]
ALBERT I thank ye, dear. [*He drinks*]
AMINTA Drink, again.
ALBERT Here's to our loves.— [*He drinks again*]
How, turn and weep!—
Pray, pledge it.[369] This happiness we have yet left:
Our hearts are free—Not pledge it? Why?
And, though beneath the axe,[370] this health[371] were holy—
Why do ye weep thus?
AMINTA I come to woo ye.
ALBERT To woo me, sweet? I am wooed and won already.
You know I am yours. This pretty[372] way becomes ye.
But you would deceive my sorrows. That's your intent.
AMINTA I would I could. I should not weep, but smile.

365 143 an: if
366 151 shadowed: impersonated; acted
367 153 shadow: i.e. without substance; a spirit; also, an actor
368 159 sorrows in . . . to me: i.e. I am not accustomed to feeling sorrow when I see you
369 166 it: i.e. our love
370 168 beneath the axe: i.e. under threat of death
371 168 health: drink
372 171 pretty: crafty; cunning

Do ye like your meat and wine?
ALBERT Like it?
AMINTA Do you like your liberty?
ALBERT All these I well may like.
AMINTA Then pray like her that sent 'em.
Do ye like wealth, and most unequaled beauty?
ALBERT Peace, indeed, you'll make me angry.
AMINTA Would I were dead that ask it,
Then ye might freely like, and I forgive ye.
ALBERT What like? And who? Add not more misery
To a man that's fruitful in afflictions.
Who is't you would have me like? Who sent these comforts?
AMINTA I must tell.
ALBERT   Be bold.
AMINTA   But be you temperate.
If you be bold, I die. The young fair virgin
(Sorrow hath made me old)—O hearken,
And wisely hark: the governess' daughter,
That star that strikes this island full of wonder,
That blooming sweetness—
ALBERT   What of her?
AMINTA She sent it, and with it
(It must be out), she dotes on ye,
And must enjoy ye, else no joy must find ye.
ALBERT And have you the patience to deliver this?
AMINTA A sister may say much, and modestly.
ALBERT A sister?
AMINTA   Yes, that name undid ye,
Undid us both. Had ye named wife,[373] she had feared ye,
And feared the sin she followed. She had shunned. Yea,
Her virgin modesty had not touched at ye.
But thinking you were free hath kindled a fire[374]
I fear[375] will hardly be extinguished.
ALBERT Indeed, I played the fool.
AMINTA O my best sir, take heed,
Take heed of lies. Truth, though it trouble some minds,
Some wicked minds that are both dark and dangerous,
Yet it preserves itself, comes off pure, innocent,
And like the sun, though never so eclipsed,
Must break in glory. O sir, lie no more.
ALBERT Ye have read me a fair lecture,
And put a spell upon my tongue for feigning.
But how will you counsel now?
AMINTA Ye must study to forget me.
ALBERT   How?
AMINTA   Be patient.
Be wise and patient. It concerns ye highly.
Can ye lay by[376] our loves? But why should I doubt it?
Ye are a man, and men may shift affections.
'Tis held no sin. To come to the point:

373 198 named wife: i.e. called me your wife
374 201 Thinking that you were unmarried filled her with desire
375 202 I fear: that I fear
376 215 lay by: put aside

Ye must lose me. Many and mighty reasons—
ALBERT Hear me, Aminta.
Have you a man that loves you, too, that feeds ye,
That sends ye liberty? Has this great governess
A noble son, too, young and apt to catch ye?
Am I, because I am in bonds and miserable,
My health decayed, my youth, and strength half-blasted,
My fortune like my waning self, for this despised?
Am I for this forsaken? A new love chosen,
And my affections, like my fortunes, wanderers?
Take heed of lying, you that chid me for it,
And showed how deep a sin it was, and dangerous.
Take heed, yourself. You swore you loved me dearly,
No few, nor little oaths you swore, Aminta.
Those sealed with no small faith, I then assured myself.
O seek no new ways to cozen truth.
AMINTA I do not.
By love itself, I love thee,
And ever must, nor can all deaths dissolve it.
ALBERT Why do you urge me thus then?
AMINTA For your safety,
To preserve your life.
ALBERT My life, I do confess, is hers. She gives it,
And let her take it back. I yield it.
My love's entirely thine. None shall touch at it.
None, my Aminta, none.
AMINTA Ye have made me happy,
And now I know ye are mine.—Fortune, I scorn thee.—
Go to your rest, and I'll sit by ye.
Whilst I have time, I'll be your mate and comfort ye,
For only I am trusted. You shall want nothing,
Not a liberty that I can steal ye.
ALBERT May we not celebrate our loves, Aminta?
And where our wishes cannot meet—
AMINTA You are wanton,
But with cold kisses I'll allay that fever.
Look for no more, and that in private, too.
Believe me I shall blush else.
But let's consider: we are both lost else.
ALBERT Let's in, and prevent fate.[377]

Exeunt

[Act IV, scene iii]

Enter CROCALE [*and*] JULETTA [*with*] TIBALT [*and*] MASTER

TIBALT You do well to air us, ladies, we shall be musty else.
What are your wise wills now?
CROCALE You are very crank[378] still.
TIBALT As crank as a holy friar fed with hailstones.
But do ye bring us out to bait like bulls?[379]

377 253 prevent fate: try to stop the inevitable
378 2 crank: merry; lusty; cocky
379 4 bait like bulls: i.e. be tormented by the women's lust; an allusion to the sport of bull-baiting, where dogs attacked a bull tethered to a stake

MASTER Or are you weary of the charge ye are at?
Turn us abroad again. Let's jog, ladies.
We are gross and coarse,[380] unfit for your sweet pleasures.
TIBALT Knock off our shoes, and turn 's to grass.[381]
CROCALE You are determined
Still to be stubborn then? It well becomes ye.
TIBALT An humor,[382] lady, that contents a prisoner.
A sullen fit sometimes serves for a second course.[383]
JULETTA Ye may as well be kind,
And gain our favors. Gain meat, and drink,
And lodging to rest your bones.
TIBALT My bones have bore me thus long,
And had their share of pains, and recreations.
If they fail now, they are no fair companions.
CROCALE Are ye thus harsh to all our sex?
MASTER We cannot be merry without a fiddler.
Pray strike up your tabors,[384] ladies.
CROCALE The fools despise us.
JULETTA We know ye are very hungry now.
TIBALT Yes, 'tis very wholesome,[385] ladies,
For we that have gross bodies must be careful.
Have ye no piercing air[386] to stir our stomachs?[387]
We are beholding[388] to ye for our ordinary.[389]
JULETTA Why slaves, 'tis in our power to hang ye.
MASTER Very likely.
'Tis in our powers then to be hanged, and scorn ye.
Hanging's as sweet[390] to us, as dreaming to you.[391]
CROCALE Come, be more courteous.
JULETTA Do, and then ye shall be pleased, and have all necessaries.
TIBALT Give me some ratsbane[392] then.
CROCALE And why ratsbane, monsieur?
TIBALT We live like vermin here, and eat up your cheese,[393]
Your moldy cheese, that none but rats would bite at.
Therefore, 'tis just[394] that ratsbane should reward us.
We are unprofitable, and our ploughs are broken.[395]
There is no hope of harvest this year, ladies.
JULETTA Ye shall have all content.[396]
MASTER Ay, and we'll serve your uses.

380 7 gross and coarse: fat and unrefined
381 8 turn 's to grass: i.e. put us out to pasture
382 11 humor: mood
383 12 course: another reference to bear and bull baiting; each time the animal was baited was called a "course"
384 21 tabors: drums
385 24 wholesome: conducive to good health
386 26 air: melody
387 26 stir our stomachs: give us an appetite; arouse us
388 27 beholding: i.e. beholden
389 27 ordinary: daily allowance of food
390 31 sweet: sexually satisfying
391 31 as dreaming to you: i.e. the women have only been able to dream about sex; perhaps with an unknowing reference to Crocale's description of her erotic dream at II.ii. 46–72
392 34 ratsbane: rat poison; arsenic
393 36 cheese: slang alluding to the female body
394 38 just: appropriate
395 39 We are unable to perform sexually
396 41 all content: i.e. everything you ask for

I had rather serve hogs. There's more delight in't.
Your greedy appetites are never satisfied.
Just like hungry camels, sleeping or waking,
You chew the cud still.
CROCALE By this hand, we'll starve ye.
MASTER 'Tis a noble courtesy.
I had as lief[397] ye should famish me, as founder[398] me.
To be jaded to death is only fit for a hackney.[399]
Here be certain tarts of tar about me,
And parcels of potargo[400] in my jerkin,[401]
As long as these last—
JULETTA Which will not last ever.
TIBALT Then we'll eat one another like good fellows:
A shoulder of his for a haunch of mine.
JULETTA 'Tis excellent.
TIBALT 'Twill be as we'll dress it, ladies.
CROCALE Why sure ye are not men.
MASTER Ye had best come search us,
A seaman is seldom without a salt eel.[402]
TIBALT I am bad enough,
And in my nature a notorious wencher,
And yet ye make me blush at your immodesty.—
Tell me, good master, didst ever see such things?
MASTER I could like 'em, though they were lewdly given,
If they could say no. But fie on 'em.
They gape like oysters.
TIBALT Well, ye may hang, or starve us,
But your commanding impudence shall never fear[403] us.
Had ye by blushing signs, soft cunnings, crept into us,
And showed us your necessities, we had met your purposes,
Supplied your wants. We are no saints, ladies.
I love a good wench, as I love my life,
And with my life I will maintain my love.
But such a sordid impudence I'll spit at—
Let's to our dens again. Come, noble master.—
You know our minds, ladies.
This is the faith in which we'll die. *Exit* TIBALT *and* MASTER
CROCALE I do admire 'em.
JULETTA They are noble fellows,
And they shall not want, for this.[404]

Enter CLARINDA

CROCALE But see, Clarinda comes.
Farewell, I'll to my charge. [*Exit*]
CLARINDA Bring out those prisoners now,
And let me see 'em and hear their business.

397 49 lief: gladly
398 49 founder: cause to break down or go lame (often said of horses); drown
399 50 Dying from overuse (being "jaded") is only suitable for a horse ("hackney"); with sexual implications
400 52 potargo: salted and dried fish roe; perhaps a reference to the spotted design of his jacket
401 52 jerkin: jacket
402 58 salt eel: the end of a rope used for flogging; slang for penis
403 66 fear: i.e. frighten
404 76–7 They are . . . for this: i.e. the men will be rewarded for acting like "noble fellows"

JULETTA I will, madam. *Exit*
CLARINDA I hope she hath prevailed upon her brother.
She has a sweet tongue, and can describe the happiness
My love is ready to fling on him.
And, sure, he must be glad, and certain wonder,[405]
And bless the hour that brought him to this island.
I long to hear the full joy that he labors with.

Enter JULETTA [*with*] MORILLAT, FRANVILLE, [*and*] LAMURE. [*The men kneel*]

MORILLAT Bless thy divine beauty.
FRANVILLE Mirror of sweetness.
LAMURE Ever-springing brightness.
CLARINDA Nay, stand up, gentlemen, and leave your flatteries.
MORILLAT She calls us gentlemen. Sure we shall have some meat now.
CLARINDA I am a mortal creature.
Worship heaven and give these attributes
To their divinities. Methinks ye look but thin.
MORILLAT O we are starved, immortal beauty.
LAMURE We are all poor starved knaves.
FRANVILLE Neither liberty nor meat, lady.
MORILLAT We were handsome men, and gentlemen, and sweet men,
And were once gracious in the eyes of beauties,
But now we look like rogues, like poor starved rogues.
CLARINDA What would ye do if ye were to die now?
FRANVILLE Alas, we were prepared. If you will hang us,
Let's have a good meal or two to die with,
To put 's in heart.[406]
MORILLAT Or if you'll drown us,
Let's be drunk first, that we may die merrily,
And bless the founders.[407]
CLARINDA Ye shall not die so hastily.
What dare ye do to deserve my favor?
LAMURE Put us to any service.
FRANVILLE Any bondage,
Let's but live.
MORILLAT We'll get[408] a world of children,
For we know ye are heinously[409] provided[410] that way.
And ye shall beat us when we offend ye,
Beat us abundantly, and take our meat from us.
CLARINDA [*To* JULETTA] These are weak abject things that show ye poor ones.[411]—
What's the great service ye so oft have threatened,
If ye might see me, and win my favor?
JULETTA That business of discovery.
MORILLAT O, I'll tell ye, lady.
LAMURE And so will I.
FRANVILLE And I.
Pray let me speak first.

405 86 certain wonder: certainly marvel
406 106 To put 's in heart: to put us in good spirits
407 108 the founders: those who drown us
408 112 get: i.e. beget; father
409 113 heinously: atrociously; grievously
410 113 provided: F2 emends to "unprovided"
411 116 It reflects badly on you that you desire such pathetic men

MORILLAT Good, no confusion.
We are before a lady that knows manners,
And by the next,[412] meat I shall eat, 'tis certain.
This little gentlewoman that was taken with us—
CLARINDA Your captain's sister, she you mean?
MORILLAT Ay, ay, she's the business that we would open to ye.
You are cozened in her.
[CLARINDA] } How! What is't you would open?[413]
FRANVILLE } She is no sister.[414]
MORILLAT Good sirs, how quick you are.
She is no sister, madam.
FRANVILLE She is his—[415]
MORILLAT Peace, I say.
CLARINDA What is she?
MORILLAT Faith, sweet lady,
She is, as man would say, his—
CLARINDA What?
LAMURE His mistress.
MORILLAT Or, as some new translators read, his—
CLARINDA O me!
MORILLAT And why he should delude you thus,
Unless he meant some villainy?[416] These ten weeks
He has had her at sea for his own proper appetite.
LAMURE His cabin-mate, I'll assure ye.
CLARINDA No sister, say ye?
MORILLAT No more than I am brother to your beauty.
I know not why he should juggle[417] thus.
CLARINDA Do not lie to me.
MORILLAT If ye find me lie,[418] lady, hang me empty.
CLARINDA How am I fooled!—
Away with 'em, Juletta, and feed 'em.
But hark ye, with such food as they have given me.—
New misery!
FRANVILLE Nor meat, nor thanks[419] for all this. *Exit* [FRANVILLE, MORILLAT, *and* LAMURE]
CLARINDA Make 'em more wretched.—
O I could burst! Curse and kill now,
Kill any thing I meet!—Juletta, follow me,
And call the rest along.
JULETTA We follow, madam.
Exeunt

412 123 next: i.e. next mealtime or day

413 128 How! What . . . would open: this line is assigned to Lamure in F1 & F2, a choice supported by Morillat's "Good sirs" at 129. Colman (1778) was the first to assign the line to Clarinda, with all subsequent editors following suit. "Sirs" was often used in the period to address more than one person, regardless of gender

414 128 F1's brace indicates that both lines are delivered at the same time

415 130 his—: the dash here, like those at lines 132 and 133, was supplied for the first time by Langbaine (1711). They suggest interruption, hesitation, the typographic erasure of an unspeakable word (perhaps "whore"?), or a lewd gesture to stand in for the missing word. However, this exchange still makes sense without the dashes, as it is presented in F1

416 136 villainy: injury; treatment of a degrading nature

417 140 juggle: deceive

418 142 find me lie: i.e. find out I am lying

419 146 Nor meat, nor thanks: neither meat, nor thanks

[Act IV, scene iv]

Enter ALBERT *and* AMINTA

AMINTA I must be gone now, else she may suspect me.
How shall I answer her?
ALBERT Tell her directly.
AMINTA That were too sudden, too improvident.
Fires of this nature must be put out cunningly.
They'll waste all come[420] near 'em else.
Farewell once more.
ALBERT Farewell—
And keep my love entire.
Nay, kiss me once again—methinks we should not part.
AMINTA O be wise, sir.
ALBERT Nay, one kiss more—
AMINTA Indeed, you're wanton.
We may be taken, too.

Enter CLARINDA, JULETTA, CROCALE, [*and*] HIPPOLITA

CLARINDA Out, thou base woman.—
By heaven, I'll shoot 'em both.
CROCALE Nay, stay, brave lady, hold.
A sudden death cuts off a nobler vengeance.
CLARINDA Am I made bawd[421] to your lascivious meetings?
Are ye grown so wise in sin?—Shut up that villainy!—
And, sirrah, now expect my utmost anger.—
Let him there starve.
ALBERT I mock at your mischiefs. *Exit* [CROCALE *with* ALBERT]
CLARINDA Tie that false witch unto that tree.
There, let the savage beasts gnaw off her sweetness,
And snakes embrace her beauties. Tie her, and watch
That none relieve her. [AMINTA *is tied to a tree*]
HIPPOLITA We could wish ye better fortune, lady,
But dare not help ye.
AMINTA Be your own friends, I thank ye. [*Exeunt all but* AMINTA]
Now only my last audit,[422] and my greatest:
O heaven, be kind unto me,
And if it be thy will, preserve—

Enter RAYMOND

RAYMOND Who is this?
Sure 'tis a woman. I have trod this place,
And found much footing.[423] Now I know 'tis peopled.
Ha, let me see! 'Tis her face.
O heaven!—Turn this way, maid.
AMINTA O Raymond! O brother!
RAYMOND Her tongue, too. 'Tis my sister. What rude hand—

420 5 waste all come: destroy all who come
421 17 bawd: one who facilitates prostitution; pander
422 27 audit: settling of accounts
423 31 much footing: many footprints

Nay, kiss me first. O joy!
AMINTA Fly, fly, dear brother,
You are lost else.

Enter JULETTA, CROCALE, [*and*] CLARINDA[424]

JULETTA A man, a man, a new man.
RAYMOND What are these?
CROCALE An enemy, an enemy.
CLARINDA Dispatch him,
Take him off, shoot him straight.
RAYMOND I dare not use my sword, ladies,
Against such comely foes.
AMINTA O brother, brother!
CLARINDA Away with 'em, and in dark prisons bind 'em!—
One word replied, ye die both.—Now, brave mother, follow thy noble anger,
And I'll help thee.

Exeunt

Act V, scene i

Enter ROSELLA, CLARINDA, CROCALE, JULETTA, [*and*] HIPPOLITA

ROSELLA I am deaf to all your entreaties. She that moves me
For pity or compassion to these pirates
Digs up her father's, or her brother's tomb,
And spurns[425] about their ashes.—
Could'st thou remember what a father thou hast once,
'Twould steel[426] thy heart against all foolish[427] pity.
By his memory and the remembrance of his dear embraces,
I am taught that, in a noble cause, revenge is noble.
And they shall fall[428] the sacrifices to appease
His wandering ghost, and my incensèd[429] fury.
CLARINDA The new-come prisoner, too?
ROSELLA Him, too. Yet that we may learn
Whether they are the same, or near allied
To those that forced me to this cruel course,
Better their poor allowance[430] and permit 'em
To meet together and confer
Within the distance of your ear. Perhaps
They may discover[431] something that may kill
Despair in me, and be a means to save 'em
From certain ruin.
CROCALE That shall be my charge.
ROSELLA Yet to prevent
All hope of rescue (for this new-come captain
Hath both a ship and men not far off from us,

424 37 SD In F1, the entrance direction is situated to the right of line 38. In F2, it is erroneously situated after Raymond's half of that line
425 4 spurns: kicks
426 6 steel: fortify
427 6 against all foolish: this is F2's reading; F1 reads "against foolish"
428 9 fall: serve as
429 10 incensèd: kindled; enflamed
430 15 Better their poor allowance: allow them to have more food and drink
431 18 discover: reveal

Though ignorant to find the only port,
That can yield entrance to our happy island),
Guard the place strongly, and ere the next sun
Ends his diurnal[432] progress, I will be
Happy in my revenge, or set 'em free.

Exeunt

[Act V, scene ii]

Enter CROCALE, JULETTA, [*and*] HIPPOLITA. *A table furnished*[433] [*with food*]

CROCALE So serve it plentifully,
And lose not time to enquire the cause.[434]
There is a main design[435] that hangs upon[436] this bounty.
See the table furnished with wine, too,
That discovers secrets which tortures cannot open.
Open the doors, too, of the several prisons,
And give all free entrance into this room.
Undiscovered, I can here mark all. [*Exeunt* JULETTA *and* HIPPOLITA. CROCALE *steps aside*]

Enter TIBALT [*and*] MASTER

Here's Captain Careless, and the tough shipmaster.
The slaves are nosed like vultures. How wild they look.
TIBALT Ha! the mystery of this,
Some good hobgoblin[437] rise and reveal.
MASTER I am amazed at it, nor can I sound[438] the intent.
TIBALT Is not this bread,
Substantial bread, not painted?
MASTER But take heed,
You may be poisoned.
TIBALT I am sure I am famished;
And famine[439] as the wise man says,
Gripes the guts as much as any mineral.
This may be treacle[440] sent to preserve me
After a long fast, or be it viper's spittle,
I'll run the hazard.
MASTER We are past all fear. I'll take part with ye.
TIBALT Do. [*They eat*] —And now i'faith, how d'ye feel yourself?
I find great ease in't. What's here?—
[*Drinks*] Wine, and it be thy will,
Strong lusty wine. Well, fools may talk
Of mithridate,[441] cordials, and elixirs.

432 27 diurnal: daily
433 0 SD *furnished*: set forth
434 2 Don't waste time asking why
435 3 design: scheme; plot
436 3 hangs upon: depends on
437 12 hobgoblin: mischievous sprite
438 13 sound: fathom, ascertain
439 17 famine: F2 adds this word; it is not in F1
440 19 treacle: salve; remedy
441 27 mithridate: antidote to poison

But from my youth this was my only physic.[442]
Here's a color!
What lady's cheek, though cerused[443] over, comes near it?
It sparkles, too: hangs out diamonds.
O my sweetheart, how I will hug thee, again, and again!
They are poor drunkards, and not worth thy favors,
That number thy moist kisses in these crystals.[444]
MASTER But monsieur,
Here are suckets[445] and sweet dishes.
TIBALT Tush, boy's meat.
I am past it. Here's strong food fit for men:
Nectar, old lad.—Mistress of merry hearts,
Once more I am bold with you— [*Drinks*]
MASTER Take heed, man.
Too much will breed distemper.
TIBALT Hast thou lived at sea
The most part of thy life, where to be sober
While we have wine aboard is capital treason,
And dost thou preach sobriety?
MASTER Prithee, forbear,
We may offend in it. We know not for whom
It was provided.
TIBALT I am sure for me. Therefore, footra.[446]
When I am full, let 'em hang me. I care not.
MASTER [*Aside*] This has been his temper ever.—
See provoking dishes, candied eringoes,
And potatoes.
TIBALT I'll not touch 'em. I will drink— [*Drinks*]
But not a bit on a march.[447] I'll be an eunuch[448] rather.

Enter ALBERT, AMINTA, RAYMOND, LAMURE, MORILLAT, [*and*] FRANVILLE *severally*

MASTER Who are these?
TIBALT Marry, who you will. I keep my text here— [*Drinks*]
ALBERT Raymond!
RAYMOND Albert!
TIBALT Away, I'll be drunk alone— [*Drinks*]
Keep off, rogues, or I'll belch ye into air.
Not a drop here.
AMINTA Dear brother, put not in your eyes such anger.
Those looks, poisoned with fury, shot at him,
Reflect on me. O brother, look milder, or
The crystal[449] of his temperance
Will turn 'em on yourself.
ALBERT Sir, I have sought ye long
To find your pardon. You have ploughed the ocean

442 28 physic: medicine
443 30 cerused: painted over with a white cosmetic
444 33–4 They are . . . these crystals: i.e. wine is more valuable than diamonds, and those who would liken wine to diamonds have "poor" (or no) taste
445 36 suckets: sweetmeats of candied fruit
446 46 footra: i.e. fuck it (from the French *foutre*)
447 51 not a bit on a march: not a bite to eat moving forward (i.e. I will drink but will not eat from here on out)
448 51 an eunuch: castrated
449 60 crystal: i.e. brightness; purity; iciness

To wreak your vengeance on me for the rape[450]
Of this fair virgin. Now our fortune guides us
To meet on such hard terms that we need rather
A mutual pity of our present state,
Than to expostulate of breaches[451] past,
Which cannot be made up. And though it be
Far from your power to force me to confess
That I have done ye wrong; or, such submission
Failing to make my peace, to vent your anger,
You, being yourself slaved, as I, to others;
Yet for your sister's sake, her blessèd sake,
In part of recompense of what she has suffered
For my rash folly, the contagion
Of my black actions catching hold upon
Her purer innocence, I crave your mercy;
And wish, however several motives kept us
From being friends while we had hope to live,
Let death, which we expect and cannot fly from,
End all contention.
TIBALT Drink upon't. 'Tis a good motion.
Ratify[452] it in wine, and 'tis authentical.[453]
RAYMOND When I consider
The ground of[454] our long difference, and look on
Our not-to-be-avoided miseries,
It doth beget in me, I know not how,
A soft religious tenderness, which tells me,
Though we have many faults to answer for
Upon our own account, our fathers' crimes
Are in us punished. O Albert, the course
They took to leave us rich was not honest,
Nor can that friendship last, which virtue joins not.[455]
When first they forced the industrious Portugals,
From their plantations in the happy islands—
CROCALE [*Aside*] This is that I watch for.
RAYMOND And did omit no tyranny, which men
Inured[456] to spoil and mischief could inflict,
On the grieved sufferers; when, by lawless rapine,
They reaped the harvest, which their labors sowed;
And not content to force 'em from their dwelling,
But laid for 'em at sea, to ravish from 'em
The last remainder of their wealth; then, then,
After a long pursuit, each doubting other,
As guilty of the Portugals' escape,
They did begin to quarrel like ill men
(Forgive me, piety, that I call 'em so).
No longer love or correspondence holds,
Than it is cemented with prey or profit.
Then did they turn those swords they oft had bloodied

450 64 rape: kidnapping
451 68 breaches: ruptures; assaults
452 84 Ratify: validate
453 84 authentical: legally valid
454 86 ground of: reason for
455 94 which virtue joins not: i.e. which is not founded on virtuous behavior
456 99 Inured: accustomed

With innocent gore upon their wretched selves,
And paid the forfeit of their cruelty
Shown to Sebastian and his colony
By being fatal enemies to each other.
Thence grew Aminta's rape, and my desire
To be revenged. And now observe the issue:
As they, for spoil, ever forgot compassion
To women (who should be exempted
From the extremities of lawful war),
We now, young able men, are fall'n into
The hands of women that, against the soft
Tenderness familiar to their sex,
Will show no mercy. CROCALE [*comes forward*]
CROCALE None, unless you show us
Our long-lost husbands.
We are those Portugals you talked of.
RAYMOND Stay.
I met upon the sea, in a tall ship,
Two Portugals, famished almost to death.
TIBALT Our ship, by this wine!
And those the rogues that stole her
Left us to famish in the barren islands.
RAYMOND Some such tale they told me,
And something of a woman, which I find
To be my sister.
CROCALE Where are these men?
RAYMOND I left 'em,
Supposing they had deluded me with forged tales,
In the island where they said
They had lived many years, the wretched owners
Of a huge mass of treasure.
ALBERT The same men, and that the fatal muck[457]
We quarreled for.
CROCALE They were Portugals, you say.
RAYMOND So they professed.
CROCALE They may prove such men as may save your lives,
And so much I am taken with fair hope
That I will hazard life to be resolved[458] on't.
How came you hither?
RAYMOND My ship lies by the river's mouth,
That can convey ye to these wretched men,
Which you desire to see.
CROCALE Back to your prisons,
And pray for the success. If they be those
Which I desire to find, you are safe.
If not, prepare to die tomorrow,
For the world cannot redeem ye.
ALBERT However,[459] we are armed for either fortune. *Exeunt* [*all but* CROCALE *and* TIBALT]
TIBALT What must become of me now that I am not dismissed?
CROCALE O sir, I purpose to have your company.

457 139 muck: refuse; excrement; corrupting wealth
458 144 resolved: satisfied; informed
459 153 However: whatever happens

TIBALT Take heed wicked woman, I am apt to mischief now.
CROCALE You cannot be so unkind to her that gives you liberty.
TIBALT No, I shall be too kind, that's the devil on't.
I have had store of good wine, and when I am drunk,
Joan is a lady to me,[460] and I shall
Lay about me like a lord.—I feel strange motions.
Avoid me, temptation.
CROCALE Come sir, I'll help ye in.

Exeunt

[Act V, scene iii]

Enter SEBASTIAN, *and* NICUSA

NICUSA What may that be that moves upon the lake?
SEBASTIAN Still, it draws nearer, and now I plainly can discern it.
'Tis the French ship.
NICUSA In it a woman, who seems to invite us to her.
SEBASTIAN Still, she calls with signs of love to hasten to her.
So lovely hope doth still appear.
I feel nor age nor weakness.
NICUSA Though it bring death,
To us 'tis comfort and deserves a meeting,
Or else Fortune, tired with what we have suffered,
And in it overcome, as it may be,
Now sets a period to our misery.

Exeunt

[Act V, scene iv]

Enter severally RAYMOND, ALBERT, [*and*] AMINTA. *Horrid music*

RAYMOND What dreadful sounds are these?
AMINTA Infernal music,
Fit for a bloody feast.
ALBERT It seems prepared
To kill our courages, ere they divorce
Our souls and bodies.
RAYMOND But they that fearless fall
Deprive them of their triumph.

Enter ROSELLA, CLARINDA, JULETTA, HIPPOLITA, *&c. An altar prepared*

AMINTA See the furies,
In their full trim[461] of cruelty.
ROSELLA 'Tis the last
Duty that I can pay to my dead lord:
Set out the altar, I myself will be
The priest, and boldly do those horrid rites
You shake to think on. Lead these captains nearer,
For they shall have the honor to fall first
To my Sebastian's ashes.—And now, wretches,

460 159–60 when I . . . to me: a variation on the proverbial "Joan is as good as my lady in the dark" (also the title of a now-lost play)
461 6 trim: adornment; state of being ready to sail

As I am taught already that you are,
And lately by your free confession,
French pirates, and the sons of those I hate,
Even equal with the devil, hear with horror,
What 'tis invites me to this cruel course,
And what you are to suffer. No Amazons, we,
But women of Portugal, that must have from you
Sebastian and Nicusa. We are they
That groaned beneath your fathers' wrongs.
We are those wretched women,
Their injuries pursued, and overtook,
And from the sad remembrance of our losses
We are taught to be cruel. When we were forced
From that sweet air we breathed in, by their rapine,
And sought a place of being as the seas
And winds conspired with their ill purposes
To load us with afflictions in a storm
That fell upon us, the two ships that brought us
To seek new fortunes in an unknown world
Were severed. The one bore all the able men,
Our treasure, and our jewels. In the other,
We women were embarked and fell upon,
After long tossing in the troubled main,
This pleasant island. But in a few months,
The men that did conduct us hither died.
We long before had given our husbands lost.
Rememb'ring what we had suffered by the French,
We took a solemn oath never to admit
The cursed society of men. Necessity
Taught us those arts not usual to our sex,
And the fertile earth yielding abundance to us,
We did resolve thus shaped like Amazons
To end our lives. But when you arrived here,
And brought as present to us our own jewels,
Those which were borne in the other ship,
How can ye hope to scape our vengeance?
AMINTA It boots not,[462] then, to swear our innocence?
ALBERT Or that we never forced it from the owners?
RAYMOND Or that there are a remnant of that wrack,
And not far off?
ROSELLA All you affirm, I know,
Is but to win time.[463] Therefore, prepare your throats,
The world shall not redeem ye; and that your cries
May find no entrance to our ears,
To move pity in any, bid loud music sound
Their fatal knells. If ye have prayers use 'em quickly,
To any power will own ye[464]—

Enter CROCALE, SEBASTIAN, NICUSA, [*and*] TIBALT

But ha!

462 49 boots not: does no good
463 53 win time: stall
464 58 ye: this is F2's reading; F1 reads "yea"

Who are these? What spectacles of misfortune?
Why are their looks so full of joy and wonder?
CROCALE O! Lay by these instruments of death, and welcome
To your arms what you durst never hope to embrace.
This is Sebastian; this, Nicusa, madam:
Preserved by miracle.—Look up, dear sir,
And know your own Rosella. Be not lost
In wonder and amazement, or if nature
Can, by instinct, instruct you what it is
To be blessed with the name of father,
Freely enjoy it in this fair virgin.
SEBASTIAN Though my miseries
And many years of wants I have endured
May well deprive[465] me of the memory
Of all joys past, yet looking on this building,
This ruined building of a heavenly form
In my Rosella, I must remember
I am Sebastian.
ROSELLA O my joys!
SEBASTIAN And here,
I see a perfect model of thyself,
As thou wert when thy choice first made thee mine.
These cheeks and front,[466] though wrinkled now with time,
Which art cannot restore, had equal pureness
Of natural white and red and as much ravishing,
Which by fair order and succession
I see descend on her; and may thy virtues
Wind into her form, and make her a perfect dower,[467]
No part of thy sweet goodness wanting to[468] her.
I will not now, Rosella, ask thy fortunes,
Nor trouble thee with hearing mine.
Those shall hereafter serve to make glad hours
In their relation.—All past wrongs forgot.
I am glad to see you, gentlemen; but most,
That it is in my power to save your lives.
You saved ours when we were near starved at sea.
And I despair not, for if she be mine,
Rosella can deny Sebastian nothing.
ROSELLA She does give up herself,
Her power and joys, and all, to you,
To be discharged of 'em as too burdensome.
Welcome in any shape.
SEBASTIAN [*To* RAYMOND] Sir, in your looks,
I read your suit of my Clarinda. She is yours.—
And, lady, if it be in me to confirm
Your hopes in this brave gentleman,
Presume I am your servant.
ALBERT We thank you, sir.
AMINTA O happy hour!
ALBERT O my dear Aminta,

465 72 deprive: this is F2's reading; F1 reads "deprave"
466 79 front: forehead
467 84 dower: endowment; dowry
468 85 wanting to: lacking in

Now all our fears are ended.
TIBALT Here I fix.[469] She's mettle,
Steel to the back, and will cut my leaden dagger,
If not used with discretion.
CROCALE You are still no changeling.[470]
SEBASTIAN Nay.
All look cheerfully, for none shall be
Denied their lawful wishes. When a while
We have here refreshed ourselves, we'll return
To our several homes; and well that voyage ends
That makes of deadly enemies faithful friends.

Exeunt

FINIS.

469 105 Here I fix: I will attach myself to her (i.e. Crocale)
470 108 You are intractable

17 James Shirley, *The Bird in a Cage*

First performed 1633

First printed 1633

Edited by Clare McManus

"This is the piece made up of all performance" (II.i. 406): the duke's description of Rolliardo, the disguised Philenzo, also encapsulates *The Bird in a Cage*. Shirley's play is a remarkable survey of early modern performance culture. First printed and staged at the Phoenix, or Cockpit, in Drury Lane in 1633, it showcases the diversity of early modern theatricality inside and outside the playhouses. A pastiche of theatrical tropes and performance modes, its action consists of disguise, magic, spectacular props, and tricks played on both characters and audience. Its characters—male and female—live by performance, whether they are courtiers seeking edification or entertainment or those who, like Bonamico disguised as the mountebank Altomaro, scrabble for a living. This is not the bitter metatheatricality of Elizabethan and Jacobean plays like Thomas Kyd's *Spanish Tragedy* (1585) or Thomas Middleton's *Revenger's Tragedy* (1606); Shirley's comedy is an altogether lighter meditation on a culture saturated with performance, and it shows early modern theater in all its vitality.

The play is a tightly constructed comedy in which Eugenia is imprisoned in a tower by her tyrannical father, the duke of Mantua, who has banished her beloved, Philenzo, so that he can marry her to the prince of Florence. The main action, including both Philenzo's/Rolliardo's wager that he can gain access to Eugenia and Bonamico's deception of Grutti and Dondolo with an invisibility trick, consists of the male courtiers' efforts to infiltrate the tower. Strikingly, the play is structured around homosocial communities. The predominantly masculine stage picture is punctuated by two scenes of the women in the tower (III.iii and IV.ii) and, with the exception of IV.ii, when Eugenia and Philenzo are reunited and the audience at last learns that he was disguised as Rolliardo all along, male and female characters appear on stage together only in the opening and closing scenes. In the former, the women are sentenced to imprisonment; in the latter, the comic ending is so governed by convention rather than narrative that it does not even identify the couples who are apparently reunited—this must be decided in performance.

The Bird in a Cage is remarkably specific about the performance practices that it gathers into itself. In reworking the old narrative of imprisoned or enclosed women, it innovatively adapts the Jupiter and Danae myth as well as John Fletcher's earlier use of the trope in *Women Pleased* (*c.* 1619–23). What's more, it is saturated with the commercial theater repertory: there are direct quotations from *The Spanish Tragedy* (III.iv. 28–9), and unmissable nods towards *The Merchant of Venice* (II.i. 448). There are reconfigured scenes: IV.ii reworks from Shakespeare's *1 Henry IV*; V.ii reworks *Romeo and Juliet* by way of the "resurrection" scenes of Fletcher's *Tamer Tamed* (V.iv) and Middleton's *Chaste Maid in Cheapside* (V.iv); and, in the play's final lines, the image of love as the partner-swapping game of barley-break is a comic version of that game's tragic deployment at the end of Thomas Middleton and William Rowley's *The Changeling* (1622). Finally, the playful way in which Shirley keeps the audience ignorant of the key dramatic fact of Rolliardo's true identity is a powerful manipulation of comic structure along the lines of Jonson's revelation of Epicene's identity at the very end of his 1609 play of that name. Yet Shirley's play reaches far beyond the commercial stages. Imprisoned in the tower, the noblewomen's dances and songs (III.iii), and their improvised play of Jupiter and Danae (IV.ii) reflect women's performance in the courts of Charles I and his wife, Queen Henrietta Maria (Britland, 2006; Gough, 2003). Morello, sentenced to perform as a punishment for cross-dressing to get into the tower, is alternatively jester, crier, and ballad singer, reflecting the court's interest in popular entertainment. Popular street performance is there in Bonamico's disguise as Altomaro, stage magician, mountebank and con artist, and in talk of puppet plays in Hyde Park (II.i. 455). The spectacular birdcage prop that drives the plot and allows Rolliardo/Philenzo to infiltrate the tower hidden in its large interior pillar (IV.ii) echoes the miraculous "devices" displayed by the famous engineer Soloman de Caus through the courts of Europe and is compared to the pageant cars of London's civic pageantry. Dialogue is packed with references to performing animals like the birds in the cage (IV.i. 126–70), the horse that snorts when Spain is mentioned (IV.i. 155–6), and exotic displays like a bird from Peru (II.i. 96–8), as well as to the spectacle of "monstrous" performers, both human and animal. Most strikingly, Morello's inadequate performance of his female character transforms him into an hermaphrodite (III.i. 75–6), half man, half woman. A twenty-first-century audience may see anti-trans prejudice at work here; an early modern audience delighted in bodily difference, commodifying such bodies as spectacles ("monster" comes from the Latin "monstrare," to show). All of seventeenth-century theatrical life is digested in this play.

The stage and print histories of *The Bird in a Cage* are driven by controversy over theatrical fashion and, in early 1633, nothing was more controversial than Puritan attacks against theater, the court, and women's performance. Shirley wrote for the commercial theaters in London and Dublin (1636–40) and for the court. He had particularly close connections with the Queen's Men, the company patronized by Henrietta Maria, and with the queen herself. In February 1633, William Prynne, an outspoken Puritan antitheatricalist, was imprisoned for attacking "women-actors, notorious whores" in his sprawling book, *Histrio-Mastix: the Player's Scourge, or the Actor's Tragedy*. Prynne's troubles did not stem from attacking women, *per se*, but from the fact that he seemed to be making a direct attack on Henrietta Maria's masquing and—more controversially—her acting, including, in January 1633, in Walter Montagu's pastoral *The Shepherds' Paradise*. Prynne was in the Tower awaiting trial when Shirley wrote his taunting dedication and changed his play's title from "*The Bewties*" to better mock Prynne's predicament (Senescu, 1980: lvii; Sanders, 2002: 23). Prynne would eventually be pilloried, fined, and imprisoned, and would see his book burnt by the hangman: his ears would be cut off and his cheeks branded (Senescu, 1980: lvi). Three potential responses from Shirley survive; the first two, his mocking anti-dedicatory letter and new title, cruelly capitalize on Prynne's notoriety; the third, the play itself, is a celebratory exercise in the very theatricality that Prynne so detested.

Most striking of all the theatrical contexts which *Bird* celebrates is—as the dedicatory letter stresses—women's performance. Far from impossible or illicit, women's performance was widespread beyond the commercial theaters, and Shirley invokes Caroline courtly theatricals and the broader European context of performances by Spanish, French, and Italian actresses. The depiction of women's playing as it is translated from the court to the commercial Cockpit playhouse using boy actors—established practitioners in female roles for decades—is too complex for straightforward flattery. Shirley exploits the association of "playing" with sexuality: Donella asserts "I ha' known men ha' been insufficient, but women can play their parts" (III.iii. 29–30) and complains to Eugenia, "had you not waked as you did, madam, I should ha' forgot myself and played Jupiter indeed with you" (IV.ii. 158–9). But Shirley also protects his characters from the opprobrium associated with playing; their play is spontaneous, extemporized, and lacks both audience and stage. In contrast to Henrietta Maria's noblewomen, who were criticized in 1626 for cross-dressing and wearing beards to act male roles in Racan's court pastoral *Artenice* (Tomlinson, 1992: 189), Mardona, playing Danae's father Acrisius, is told, "No matter for properties—we'll imagine, madam, you have a beard" (IV.ii. 16). This distances Mardona from the fearful metamorphosis suffered by Morello in III.i, the frightening early modern fantasy of the loss of identity in a theatrical role, and the tensions surrounding the proximity of character and self (Barker). Morello's performative failure is mocked, as is that of the improvising women who fail to meet either the standard set by the court for both men and women or—not incidentally—that set by the Queen's Men's boy actors. The boy-actors in Shirley's play walk a tightrope throughout: playing performing courtly women on a commercial London stage, they embody the tensions surrounding women's performance while displaying their own skill.

The embedded play also gestures to the connections between English and continental theater. The women's skills of improvisation, song, dance, and eloquence reflect the acting in which Queen Henrietta Maria was trained as a child in France. Italy, too, is a key influence: improvisation was a central skill for *commedia* actresses, and Shirley's improvising women display the performance skills of celebrated actresses like Isabella Andreini in improvised scenarios such as the 1589 *Madness of Isabella* (Brown, 2012). In his feigned insanity (II.i. 389–97), Philenzo/Rolliardo also reuses Italianate conventions, spouting the kind of macaronic absurdity used by Andreini in 1589. Even Morello's inept cross-dressing evokes anecdotes of Spanish men cross-dressing to infiltrate the women-only audience section in the Madrid playhouses (Thacker, 2014: 59). Women's performance in Shirley's play might be safely sequestered inside the New Prison tower, but it was a thriving part of the Caroline performance context.

The multiple lives of an early modern play extend beyond composition and performance into the print house and readership. The 1633 quarto of *The Bird in a Cage* is not primarily a record of performance but a print artifact, and it cuts across audience experience by introducing an apparatus for its readers. For instance, Philenzo's/Rolliardo's identity is revealed in the *dramatis personae*, though the quarto continues to use the speech prefix "Rolliardo" to the end. The lengthy paratextual letter to Prynne and the introduction of onstage letters and songs with headers rather than stage directions also work to remind us that this is a reader's text. Yet as readers of the quarto we can never be sure that we are reading what was performed in the Cockpit, or even what Shirley wrote. The 1633 quarto is not really one text at all but rather a closely related set of texts that must be untangled, and textual critics have identified four different phases ("states") of revision and correction. Early modern plays were usually sold in cheap quartos; errors introduced by a compositor (or typesetter) were corrected as printing progressed but those corrected sheets were still bound into quartos to be sold, meaning that one could buy more accurate texts later in a print run. The copy-text for this edition (held by the Folger Shakespeare Library) was produced late: the type is worn and letters are breaking, but most if not all corrections have been made (Senescu, 1980: vi). Compositors didn't necessarily work with authorial corrections, and often introduced their own errors; so, while the corrected quarto does not necessarily bring us closer to what Shirley intended, it does reveal the processes of early modern printing.

One place these processes can best be seen is in Philenzo/Rolliardo's speech on the five senses at I.i. 208–11. The fate of the phrase "the small birds dare not peep for him" shows that the compositor took three attempts to get this speech right. State 1 omits the phrase completely, but still binds these sheets into copies for sale. In state 2, the compositor adds the missing phrase in the wrong place (at line 208 rather than 209) before, a little further through the printing, correcting that mistake too. Some other major errors are corrected in the errata page, "The Printer to the Reader," but still more remain at large (there is even a catchword abbreviation for a non-existent character at IV.ii. 23). In all of this, the 1633 quarto bears the marks of speedy printing intended to exploit the sensation of the queen's theatricals and is testament to the rich early modern dramatic culture that contributed to the making of a play.

Textual note

This edition is based on the 1633 quarto held in the Folger Shakespeare Library (STC 22436). *The Bird in a Cage* has been reprinted from the mid-eighteenth century onwards (edited by Dodsley, Gifford, Hill, Senescu, and Sanders). My edition adopts several of these later editors' emendations, and it owes a particular debt to Sanders's 2006 edition. The play's many proverbs are glossed using R.W. Dent's work (1981 and 1984).

Further reading

Editions

Dodsley, Robert (1744) *A Select Collection of Old Plays*, vol. 9, London: R. Dodsley.

Gifford, William (1833) *The Dramatic Works and Poems of James Shirley*, vol. 2, London: John Murray.

Hill, Artis Neal, Jr. (1974) *Critical Old-Spelling Edition of James Shirley's The Bird in a Cage*, Texas Tech University, unpublished Ph.D. thesis.

Sanders, Julie (ed.) (2006) "*The Bird in a Cage*," in Hero Chalmers, Julie Sanders, and Sophie Tomlinson (eds), *Three Seventeenth-Century Plays on Women and Performance*, Manchester: Manchester University Press.

Senescu, Frances Frazier (ed.) (1980) *James Shirley's The Bird in a Cage*, New York: Garland.

Critical and contextual reading

Barker, Roberta (2015) "The 'Play Boy,' the Female Performer, and the Art of Portraying a Lady," *Shakespeare Bulletin* 33: 83–97.

Britland, Karen (2006) *Drama at the Courts of Queen Henrietta Maria*, Cambridge: Cambridge University Press.

Brown, Pamela Allen (2012) "'Cattle of this colour': Boying the Diva in *As You Like It*," *Early Theatre* 15: 145–166.

Carr, Morwenna (2018) "'We'll Imagine, Madam, You Have a Beard': Beards and Early Female Playwrights," in Jennifer Evans and Alun Withey (eds), *New Perspectives on the History of Facial Hair: Framing the Face*, Basingstoke: Palgrave Macmillan.

Dent, R.W. (1981) *Shakespeare's Proverbial Language: An Index*, Berkeley: University of California Press.

Dent, R.W. (1984) *Proverbial Language in English Drama Exclusive of Shakespeare, 1495–1616*, Berkeley: University of California Press.

Deutermann, Allison K. (2015) "Literary Celebrity and Theatrical Culture in Shirley's *Bird in a Cage*," in Ronda Arab, Michelle M. Dowd, Adam Zucker, and Phyllis Rackin *(eds), Historical Affects and the Early Modern Theater*, New York: Routledge.

Gough, Melinda (2003) "'Not as Myself': The Queen's Voice in *Tempe Restored*," *Modern Philology* 101: 48–67.

Prynne, William (1633) *Histrio-Mastix: The Player's Scourge, or, Actor's Tragedy*, London: Michael Sparke.

Sanders, Julie (2002) "'Powdered with Golden Rain': The Myth of Danae in Early Modern Drama," *Early Modern Literary Studies* 8: 1–23.

Stern, Tiffany (2009) *Documents of Performance in Early Modern England*, Cambridge: Cambridge University Press.

Thacker, Jonathan (2014) "Staging and Performance," in Robert Henke and M.A. Katritzky (eds), *European Theatre Performance Practice, 1580–1750*, Farnham: Ashgate: 55–76.

Tomlinson, Sophie (1992) "'She That Plays the King': Henrietta Maria and the Threat of the Actress in Caroline Culture," in Gordon McMullan and Jonathan Hope (eds), *The Politics of Tragicomedy*, London: Routledge.

Traub, Valerie (1992) "The (In)Significance of 'Lesbian' Desire in Early Modern England," in Susan Zimmerman (ed.), *Erotic Politics: Desire on the Renaissance Stage*, London: Routledge.

Walker, Kim (1991) "New Prison: Representing the Female Actor in Shirley's *The Bird in a Cage* (1633)," *English Literary Renaissance* 21: 385–400.

The Bird in a Cage (1633)

The Persons[1]

FULVIO, ORPIANO — *Noblemen*
MORELLO, DONDOLO[2], GRUTTI — *Courtiers*
GENTLEMEN USHERS[3]
DUKE OF MANTUA
EUGENIA, *the Duke's daughter*
PERENOTTO, *Captain of his Guard*
DONELLA, KATHERINA, MARDONA, CASSIANA, FIDELIA — *ladies attendant on the princess*
PHILENZO, *lover of Eugenia, under the disguise and name of* ROLLIARDO
BONAMICO, *a mountebank*[4] *or decayed*[5] *artist disguised as* ALTOMARO
CARLO, *servant to Bonamico*
AMBASSADOR *of Florence*

Guards, Courtiers, Attendants

To Master William Prynne,[6] Utter[7] Barrister of Lincoln's Inn.

Sir,

The fame of your candor and innocent love to learning—especially to that musical part of human knowledge, poetry—and in particular to that which concerns the stage and scene (yourself as I hear, having lately written a tragedy[8]) doth justly challenge from me this dedication. I had an early desire to congratulate your happy retirement,[9] but no poem could tempt me with so fair a circumstance as this in the title,[10] wherein I take some delight to think (not without imitation of yourself, who have ingeniously fancied such elegant and apposite names for your own

1 The Persons: Q gives this heading for the dramatis personae; the list of characters here is adapted from the list given in Q
2 DONDOLO: Italian name for a gull or fool
3 GENTLEMEN USHERS: courtiers who control entry to the duke's presence
4 *mountebank*: traveling performer who staged shows in streets and piazzas to sell medicines
5 *decayed*: fallen on hard times
6 0 To Master William Prynne: Shirley's sarcastic dedicatory letter cruelly mocks Prynne's imprisonment for sedition: Prynne's antitheatricalist tract, *Histrio-Mastix* (1633), attacked Queen Henrietta Maria's performances in court masques and pastorals
7 0 Utter: junior
8 3–4 yourself as . . . a tragedy: a reference to *Histrio-Mastix*'s full title, *The Player's Scourge, or, Actor's Tragedy*
9 5 retirement: i.e. Prynne's 1633 imprisonment
10 6 title: the play was entered in the Stationers' Register as *The Beawties*; Shirley perhaps renamed it to mock Prynne's imprisonment

compositions, as *Health's Sickness*,[11] *The Unloveliness of Love-locks*,[12] etc.) how aptly I may present you at this time, with *The Bird in a Cage*, a comedy which wanteth, I must confess, much of that ornament which the stage and action lent it, for it comprehending also another play, or interlude, personated by ladies.[13] I must refer to your imagination the music, the songs, the dancing, and other varieties which I know would have pleased you infinitely in the presentment. I was the rather inclined to make this oblation,[14] that posterity[15] might read you a patron to the Muses[16] and one that durst, in such a critical age, bind up the wounds which ignorance had printed upon wit and the professors. Proceed, inimitable Maecenas,[17] and having such convenient leisure and an indefatigable Pegasus[18]—I mean your prose, which scorneth the road of common sense and despiseth any style in his way—travel still in the pursuit of new discoveries which you may publish, if you please, in your next book of digressions. If you do not happen presently to convert the organs,[19] you may in time confuse the steeple and bring every parish to one bell.[20]

This is all I have to say at this time and, my own occasions not permitting my personal attendance, I have entreated a gentleman to deliver this testimony of my service. Many faults have escaped[21] the press, which your judgment will no sooner find than your mercy correct, by which you shall teach others a charity to your own volumes, though they be all errata.[22] If you continue where you are,[23] you will every day enlarge your fame and, beside the engagement of other poets to celebrate your Roman constancy,[24] in particular oblige the tongue and pen of your devout honorer,

James Shirley

Act I, scene i

Enter FULVIO [*and*] ORPIANO, *passing*[25]

ORPIANO He does not mean this building for a college, I hope?
FULVIO That were an ill foundation. There are more scholars than can live one by another already; 'tis pity we should have more plenty of learned beggars.
ORPIANO 'Tis past all my conjecture why he built it.
FULVIO Signor Peronotto, captain o'th' guard, is of counsel only with the duke in't.

Enter MORELLO

MORELLO Signor Orpiano, and Fulvio.
FULVIO My spark![26] Whither in such haste? Let us change air[27] a little.
MORELLO You are traveling to your mistress?[28]
ORPIANO Madam Donella is newly returned to court.

11 8 *Health's Sickness*: published 1628, attacking drunkenness; a "health" is a toast
12 8 *The Unloveliness of Love-locks*: published 1628, criticizing men for long, styled, and "womanish" hair
13 11 personated by ladies: the play was in fact staged in an indoor playhouse, the Phoenix (or Cockpit), by the Queen's Men; female roles were played by boy actors. Shirley is hinting at the performance of women at court that Prynne attacked in *Histrio-Mastix* (see Introduction)
14 13 oblation: an offering to a deity
15 13 that posterity: so that future generations
16 14 Muses: the goddesses of learning and the arts
17 15 Maecenas: ironic reference to the patron of the classical poets Virgil and Horace
18 16 Pegasus: ironic invocation of the classical winged horse
19 19 organs: *Histrio-Mastix* inveighs against church music and organs as distracting from worship, 280–81
20 19–20 confuse the . . . one bell: i.e. to shame the church ("steeple") and reduce its music and ceremonies to a single "bell"
21 23 escaped: i.e. come out from
22 24 errata: errors
23 25 where you are: the Tower of London
24 26 Roman constancy: 1) stoicism; 2) Shirley, servant to a Catholic queen, taunts Prynne with a reference to Roman Catholicism
25 0 SD *passing*: i.e. walking across the stage
26 7 spark: gallant, fop
27 7 change air: exchange air, i.e. converse
28 8 mistress: beloved, a woman he serves romantically, perhaps sexually

FULVIO With the princess?
ORPIANO She was but late retired into the country. What's the matter?
MORELLO Your lordships, I hope, have heard. The duke sent post[29] for them, as they say. There is something in't.
FULVIO What?
MORELLO Does not your lordship know?
FULVIO Not I.
MORELLO Your lordship's wisdom and mine is much about a scantling[30] then; yet, for aught I hear, there be others of the court as ignorant as we. Your honors' pardon, I beseech you: I must in all haste to the princess's lodging.
ORPIANO Farewell, signor—your amorous lock[31] has a hair out of order.
MORELLO Um! What an oversight was this of my barber! I must return now and have it corrected, dear signor. *Ex*[*it* MORELLO]
FULVIO Here's a courtier that will not miss a hair of his complement[32] when he is to appear before his mistress. Every morning does this fellow put himself upon the rack[33] with putting on's apparel, and manfully endures his tailor when he screws and wrests his body into the fashion of his doublet.[34] But that the court cannot subsist without a fool, I should marvel what this fellow does to follow it.
ORPIANO There are more have much about his parcel of brains; the benefit of youth and good clothes procured their places, and ignorance and impudence have since maintained 'em.
FULVIO Two great helps as the world goes.

Enter GENTLEMEN USHERS, DONDOLO, GRUTTI

GENTLEMEN USHERS Clear the presence![35] The duke is entering!

Enter DUKE, EUGENIA, PERENOTTO, [*and*] *attendants*

EUGENIA [*To* DUKE] I ever was obedient—
DUKE 'Tis for thy honor, which I know
Is to thy self a precious sound. That building
I late erected, then, shall be thy palace.
EUGENIA Or my prison, sir, if I do rightly understand.
DUKE That name
Is too unworthy of it, my Eugenia.
Nor will it seem restraint to my loved daughter
Since, free to all delights, thy mind shall be
Its own commander. Every day shall strive
To bring thee in fresh rarities; Time shall be
Delighted with thy pleasures and stay with thee.
EUGENIA Indeed, I shall think Time has lost his wings[36]
When I am thus caged up.
DUKE Thou shalt give
To him feathers when thou pleasest. Mantua
Shall pour her raptures on thee. Why have I
A crown, but to command what thou canst wish for,
My dear Eugenia?

29 12 post: with speed, in haste
30 17 much about a scantling: similarly scanty
31 20 amorous lock: love lock, a fashionably long, curled lock worn in the fringe; see "To Master William Prynne" (n12)
32 23 not miss . . . his complement: omit no accessory or preparation
33 24 rack: torture device
34 26 doublet: jacket
35 31 presence: presence chamber
36 44 wings: emblems of Time were traditionally winged

EUGENIA A deer it seems,
For, as you had suspicion of my wildness,
You'll measure out my walk.[37]
DUKE I am thy father
Who, by example of the wisest kings,[38]
But build a place to lay my treasure in
Safe from the robber, where I'll place a guard—
EUGENIA Do you suspect I shall break prison?
DUKE To keep off violence and soliciting,[39]
Which may disturb thy pleasures, until we
Shall find out one to match thy birth[40] and virtues—
My dukedom is too poor that way.[41] Maintain
Thy father's soul: thou hast no blood to mix
With any beneath prince.[42] Forget, as I shall,
Thy love was ever falling[43] from thy greatness
Into the arms of one carries[44] but style of honor.
EUGENIA Sir, I am your daughter.
DUKE Thou'st deserved my blessing, and thy obedience
In this new crowns thy father. I see I need not
Urge what I am to move thee, and lay force;[45]
Thy understanding does appear convinced
And loving duty teaches thee to more
Than[46] the command.—Perenotto!
EUGENIA [*Aside*] What narrow ground I tread! I know he is
Too passionate to be denied his will,
And yet to yield will make me miserable.
'Tis my misfortune to be born so great:
Each common man and woman can enjoy
The air, when the condition of a princess
Makes me a prisoner. But I must obey
In hope it will not last. [*To* DUKE] I have a soul
Is full of grateful duty, nor will suffer me
Further dispute your precept. You have power
To steer me as you please.
DUKE All the graces
Speak in my girl! Each syllable doth carry
A volume of thy goodness; all my cares
So well rewarded do convert to sweetness.
I thank thy filial piety. Know, my girl,
That place wherein I lock so rich a jewel,[47]
I do pronounce again, shall be thy paradise—
Thy paradise, my Eugenia!—saving that
In this man only finds no being. Other
Delights shall stream themselves into thy bosom

37 49–51 A deer … my walk: deer belonged to the monarch; Eugenia's comparison highlights her lack of autonomy and her father's strict control
38 52 wisest kings: the confinement of elite women by men, usually fathers, is a common trope of early modern romance
39 56 soliciting: courting, begging favor
40 58 one to match thy birth: a husband worthy of your lineage
41 59 is too poor that way: lacks anyone of such quality
42 60–61 no blood … beneath prince: her family is too exalted to marry a prince of lesser standing
43 62 was ever falling: i.e. had ever fallen
44 63 one carries: i.e. one that carries
45 66–7 I see … lay force: I don't need to remind you that I am your father and ruler, nor coerce you, in order to persuade you
46 69–70 teaches thee to more/Than: i.e. drives you to outdo
47 86 jewel: a common image for female virtue and virginity

And those that pass shall flow again t'invite
Thy sense to tasting.—Perenotto?
PERENOTTO Your grace's pleasure?
DUKE Admit those ladies that attend.
FULVIO [*To* ORPIANO] The duke shows much indulgence.
ORPIANO [*To* FULVIO] Observe the issue.[48]
DUKE We will not limit thy companions:
Elect what Mantuan beauties thou canst best
Delight in, they shall serve thee; or, if some
Of your own train,[49] whom we have thought most proper
To be your personal guard, affect[50] you, they
Attend our pleasures.

Enter DONELLA, KATHERINA, MARDONA[, CASSIANA] *and* FIDELIA

See, they are ignorant
Yet of our purpose. If to any, thy
Affection be not free, thy breath[51] discharge them
And 'point[52] thy own attendants.
EUGENIA [*To* DUKE] I shall be pleased with your appointment.
—Ladies, I know you love me. *She goes to the ladies*
DONELLA Doth your grace hold suspicion any of us
Serve you not with our heart?
EUGENIA I do not doubt,
Or, if I did, you now approach a trial.
For my sake can you be content to be
All prisoners?
LADIES Prisoners?
EUGENIA Yes, shut up close prisoners,[53] and be barred[54]
The conversation, nay the sight, of men.
KATHERINA Marry,[55] heaven defend! Wherein have we offended that we must lose the sweet society[56] of men?
MARDONA How have we forfeited our freedom?
DUKE No man argue—'tis our pleasure.
DONELLA 'Las madam, I am new contracted[57] to a handsome signor.
KATHERINA I have but newly entertained a servant[58] that gave me these gloves. They smell of him still—a sweet courtier.
DONELLA Not one man among so many ladies? Not a gentleman usher, nor a page?[59] How shall we do, madam?
MARDONA I beseech your grace, let me be exempted. If I have committed an offense deserves[60] your anger, let one of your lords cut off my head rather—Signor Dondolo?
FIDELIA Shall we express so cold a duty to her highness? Fie, ladies!
EUGENIA You shall but suffer with me. I partake

48 95 Observe the issue: wait and see what happens
49 99 train: retinue
50 100 affect: appeal to
51 103 breath: word
52 104 'point: appoint
53 112 shut up close prisoners: i.e. to be held in strict confinement
54 112 barred: denied
55 114 Marry: a gentle oath, invoking the Virgin Mary
56 115 society: company
57 118 contracted: perhaps engaged, probably a looser romantic connection
58 119 entertained a servant: accepted a suitor
59 121 page: young male servant
60 124 deserves: i.e. that deserves

As much severity as any of you shall.
DUKE I will expect your duties, lords, in silence.
—Orpiano, you shall to Florence[61] with
Our daughter's picture. Your commission's sealed.
—Now, fair ladies,
I hope y'are fixed to wait upon Eugenia.
If your restraint be a burden, it shall be
In her power to enlarge you and elect
New friends into your places.
LADIES 'Tis our duties to obey your grace and her.
DUKE Perenotto, are all things prepared?
PERENOTTO They are, my lord.
DUKE [*To women*] For once, then, let us[62] usher you.
KATHERINA [*To* PERENOTTO] Whither do we go?
PERENOTTO I'll tell you.
DONELLA Whither?
PERENOTTO To take physic,[63] madam. The duke has prepared to stay all looseness[64] in your bodies. You must be all fast:[65] stone walls and mortar will bind.
FIDELIA Come, follow with a courage.
DONELLA I hope we shall be allowed our little dogs and monkeys.[66]
DONDOLO Sweet madam! *Ex*[*eunt*] *omn*[es.] *Man*[*ent*][67] FULVIO, ORPIANO, DONDOLO [*and*] GRUTTI
GRUTTI Madam Katherina? They are gone, signor.
DONDOLO Would I had known this afore!
FULVIO The duke will be censured for this act.
ORPIANO 'Tis very strange. Good lady![68] I read a forced obedience in her eye, which hardly held up rain.[69]

Enter MORELLO

MORELLO Save you, dear signor. Which way went the ladies?
GRUTTI News, signor. News!
MORELLO I beseech you I may partake.
FULVIO Have you forgot there was suspicion she[70] affected[71] Signor Philenzo, the Cardinal's nephew?
ORPIANO Alas, poor gentleman, he suffers for't.
FULVIO By this restraint he[72] would make her sure, his jealousy is not yet over—Signor Morello, is your lock rectified? You have missed your lady but a hair's breadth.
MORELLO Nay, but my lords and gentlemen, where are the ladies gone indeed?
GRUTTI We ha' told you.
MORELLO What, committed to New Prison?[73]
FULVIO Very true, signor.

61 129 Florence: Q has "*Ferrara*" but the errata page, "The Printer to the Reader," added after printing was completed, replaces it with "*Florence*" (see Introduction)
62 139 us: me (the royal plural)
63 143 physic: medicine
64 143 stay all looseness: constrain all immorality; the self-control women were believed to lack will be imposed by their enclosure in the New Prison
65 144 fast: fixed, steadfast, confined
66 146 dogs and monkeys: exotic pets of Caroline courtiers
67 147 SD *Man*[*ent*]: they remain (Latin); used to indicate that multiple characters stay on stage while other characters exit
68 151 lady: i.e. Eugenia
69 151–2 hardly held up rain: i.e. she scarcely stopped herself crying
70 156 she: i.e. Eugenia
71 156 affected: favored, loved
72 159 he: the duke
73 163 New Prison: the building's name becomes the title for the women's play (IV.ii. 22–3)

DONDOLO Our dancing days are done. Shut up close, not a man must enter.
MORELLO Would I were a mouse then! Why, but is the duke mad?
ORPIANO Take heed what you say, signor! Though we be no informers, yet walls have ears.
MORELLO Ears? Would I had left mine behind me.[74] Here's news indeed!
FULVIO And you'd come a little sooner, you might ha' taken your leave, but 'twas your barber's fault.
MORELLO Would he had left me i'th' suds[75] an hour ago! What shall we do, gentlemen? 'Tis a hard case, when a man that has an intention to marry and live honest—

Enter [PHILENZO *disguised as*] ROLLIARDO

How now, what art thou?
PHILENZO Anything, nothing. Yet a man, yet no man, for I want.
MORELLO What? Th' art no capon,[76] I hope.
PHILENZO Money, sir. Will you spare any from your precious sins?
GRUTTI Th' art very free.[77]
PHILENZO Yet, sir, I am in debt.
DONDOLO What dost owe?
PHILENZO Nobody harm.
FULVIO Whence cam'st?
PHILENZO I dropped from the moon.[78]
ORPIANO So methinks, thou talk'st very madly. Thou'st much humor in thee.
PHILENZO Ha' ye anything to do that ye account[79] impossible, gentlemen?
FULVIO Why, wilt thou do't?
PHILENZO And you'll pay for't. Let me have money enough[80] and I'll do anything.
ORPIANO Hold,[81] hold.
PHILENZO Yes, I will hold.
MORELLO I'll lay[82] with thee. What wilt hold?[83]
PHILENZO Why, paradoxes.[84]
GRUTTI AND DONDOLO Paradoxes?
MORELLO I hold you a paradox.
FULVIO Let's hear some.
PHILENZO There are no beasts but cuckolds[85] and flatterers; no cold weather but i'the dog days;[86] no physic to[87] a whore, no fool to an alderman, no scholar to a justice of peace, nor no soldier to a belt and buff[88] jerkin.
ORPIANO A smart fellow.

Enter DUKE

MORELLO The duke!
DUKE [*Aside*] So, my fears are over. In her restraint I bury all my jealousies.—How now? What

74 168 Ears? . . . behind me: prefigures the cropping of Prynne's ears (see Introduction)
75 171 i'th' suds: with soap in my hair; i.e. left his grooming unfinished
76 175 capon: a castrated cock, playing on Philenzo's "no man" in the previous line
77 177 free: i.e. with his words, disrespectful
78 182 from the moon: i.e. he is a lunatic, a madman
79 184 account: believe
80 186 Let me have money enough: Philenzo's catchphrase
81 187 Hold: wait, hush
82 189 lay: bet
83 189 hold: wager
84 190 paradoxes: witty, contradictory sayings; punning on "a pair of doxies," i.e. wenches or prostitutes
85 194 cuckolds: cheated husbands
86 194–5 dog days: the hottest, unhealthiest time of year
87 195 to: i.e. compared to
88 196 buff: yellow brown, like buff leather

fellow's this?

FULVIO Such an humorist as I never before conversed withal. It seems he makes himself free of all places.[89]

DUKE What would he have?

PHILENZO Thy pardon, mighty man. If it be no treason to pray for thee, save thee, wilt employ me? 'Tis vacation[90] and I want work. Ask me not what I can do: let me have money enough and I'll do anything.

DUKE You have your senses?[91]

PHILENZO Five, I take it. I can see greatness big with an impostume,[92] yet[93] towering in the air like a falcon; the small birds dare not peep for him.[94] I can hear a man swear, "I am thy eternal slave, and will serve thee," when—if opportunity were offered—for price of a plush cloak[95] he will be the first shall strip thee to the very soul. I can taste wine that another man pays for, and relish anything that comes of free cost. I can smell a knave through a barred gown,[96] a politician through a surplice,[97] a fool through a scarlet outside.[98] I can touch a wench better than a lute, and tell money with a secretary[99] to show I ha' not lost my feeling.[100] Tush, all's nothing! I have a humor to do something to be talked on, nothing can come amiss to me. Let me have money enough and—my life to a cheese paring—I'll do anything.

DUKE You'll except somewhat.[101]

PHILENZO Not to do o'er the seven wonders of the world and demolish 'em when I ha' done. Let me have money enough, what star so high but I will measure by this Jacob's staff?[102] Divine money, the soul of all things sublunary![103] What lawyer's tongue will not be tipped with silver? And will not money with a judge make it a plain case? Does not gouty greatness[104] find ease with *aurum palpabile*?[105] And he's a slight physician[106] cannot[107] give a golden clyster[108] at a dead lift.[109] Money, I adore thee! It comes near the nature of a spirit and is so subtle it can creep in at a cranny, be present at the most inward councils[110] and betray 'em. Money! It opens locks, draws curtains, buys wit, sells honesty, keeps courts, fights quarrels, pulls down churches, and builds almshouses.[111]

DUKE A wild fellow.

FULVIO Will your grace have him punished for this insolence?

DUKE No, his humor is good mirth to us.[112] [*To* PHILENZO] Whence art?[113]

PHILENZO I am of no country.

DUKE How?

PHILENZO I was born upon the sea.

89 201–2 free of all places: Fulvio is surprised Rolliardo has gained access to the court
90 205 vacation: when the courts and Inns of Court are closed and young male students are idle
91 207 Are you sane?
92 208 impostume: a swelling or cyst; figuratively, swelling pride
93 208 yet: still
94 209 peep for him: make a noise for fear of the falcon
95 208–11 Five, I . . . plush cloak: this section reveals the accidents of the printing process (see Introduction)
96 212 barred gown: a robe ornamented with bars of gold lace, worn by judges
97 213 politician through a surplice: i.e. see the scheming plotter through the religious clothing
98 213 scarlet outside: scarlet gowns, worn by members of the legal profession
99 214 tell money with a secretary: i.e. pay the wench's pimp
100 214 feeling: sense
101 217 except somewhat: exclude something
102 219 Jacob's staff: a sixteenth-century surveying instrument, named for the pilgrim staff of St. James (Latin, "Jacobus")
103 220 sublunary: between the earth and the moon, in the lower sphere of the Ptolomaic universe; hence terrestrial, mundane, mortal
104 221 gouty greatness: the elite who eat rich diets
105 222 *aurum palpabile*: tangible, material gold; punning on *aurum potabile*, or drinkable gold, used in medicine; i.e. money eases the cares of the wealthy
106 222 slight physician: weak doctor
107 222 cannot: i.e. that cannot
108 222 clyster: enema
109 222–3 at a dead lift: in extremity, when one can do no more. Physicians were notorious for extorting money from patients
110 224 inward councils: secret or intimate gatherings
111 226 almshouses: charity homes for the poor or infirm
112 229 his humor . . . to us: Rolliardo is a licensed fool to entertain the duke
113 229 Whence art?: where are you from?

DUKE When?
PHILENZO In a tempest, I was told.
MORELLO A blustering fellow.
DUKE Thy name?
PHILENZO Rolliardo.
DUKE And how long hast thou been mad thus?
PHILENZO Your highness may be merry, and if you have no employment for me, I am gone.
DUKE Stay, we command you. And bethink again
What to except in[114] your bold undertaking.
PHILENZO I except nothing; nothing, Duke. It were no glory not to be general, active in all. Let me have money enough and I'll do anything.
DUKE You shall.
FULVIO Will your grace set him awork?
PHILENZO Name the action!
DUKE What say you to a lady?
PHILENZO I will fall upon her, as Jupiter on Danae. Let me have a shower of gold, Acrisius's brazen[115] tower shall melt again.[116] Were there an army about it, I would compass[117] her in a month or die for't.
DUKE Ha! A lady without guard would try your wit and money to get her love.
PHILENZO A toy,[118] a toy.
DUKE Through a credulity[119] you may too much
Traduce[120] the sex, and merit such a justice
No money will buy off. Admit some branches
Grow not so straight and beautiful as nature
Intended them, will you disgrace the stem?
Or for some woman's lenity[121] accuse
That fair creation? Money buy their love?
Promise a salary of that sacred flame
Themselves cannot direct, as guided by
Divine intelligence.[122]
PHILENZO Your highness, pardon. If you prohibit I must not undertake. But let me have freedom and money enough (for that's the circle I walk in) and if I do not conjure up a spirit hot enough to inflame a frozen Lucrece'[123] bosom, make mummy[124] of my flesh and sell me to the apothecaries. Try me with some masterpiece! A woman's love is as easy as to eat dinner without saying grace,[125] getting of[126] children, or going to bed drunk. Let me have money enough and tax[127] me to the purpose.
FULVIO AND ORPIANO He's constant.[128]
DUKE Admit[129] there be a lady, whom a prince
Might court for her affection, of a beauty

114 241 except in: exclude from
115 249 brazen: bronze
116 248–9 as Jupiter . . . melt again: Acrisius imprisoned his daughter Danae in a tower; Jupiter impregnated her in the form of a shower of gold
117 249 compass: surround, take possession of
118 252 toy: trifle
119 253 a credulity: credulousness
120 254 Traduce: defame, slander
121 258 lenity: gentleness, mercifulness; sexual generosity
122 260–62 Promise a . . . Divine intelligence: i.e. you may as well reward yourself with ("Promise a salary of") the sacred flame of chastity, which women cannot control but is instead "guided" by the gods
123 265 frozen Lucrece: the Roman Lucrece was proverbial for female chastity; raped by Tarquin, she killed herself to dispel her shame
124 265 mummy: powdered mummified flesh, often from Egypt, was a prized medicinal ingredient
125 267 grace: prayer before eating
126 267 getting of: begetting
127 268 tax: instruct
128 269 constant: persistent, unchanging
129 270 Admit: i.e. let me admit

Great as her virtue; add unto them birth
Equal to both, and all three but in her
Not to be matched. Suppose this miracle,
Too precious for man's eye, were shut up where
A guard more watchful than the dragons[130] did
Forbid access to mankind; men picked out[131]
Between whose souls and money were antipathy
Beyond that which we know,[132] and you as soon
Might bribe to be a saint. What would you do
With your enough of money, were your life
Engaged to win her love?
PHILENZO The sky may fall and aldermen cry larks[133] about the city.
DUKE The fellow's impudent! Sirrah, thou hast landed thyself upon a rock; you shall have sense of what you would contemn[134]—a life. Put on a most fortified resolution, you shall need it.
We have a daughter thus locked up[135]—
FULVIO [*To* ORPIANO] What does the duke mean?
DUKE —A virgin.
ORPIANO [*To* FULVIO] He is in passion.
DUKE Shalt not[136] engage thee on a work so much
Impossible as procurement of her love?
Make it appear with all the art thou canst.
Get but access to her—a month, we limit.
But take heed, boaster: if you fail, your life
Shall only satisfy our charge, and teach
All other mountebanks[137] to be at distance
With such bold undertakings. You shall expect
A severe justice. By this I shall try
The fidelity of those are trusted.
PHILENZO 'Tis a match! I shall have money enough?
DUKE You shall. What d' ye call enough?[138]
PHILENZO I will not be particular[139] and agree o'th' sum. You look I should die if I perform not, and I'll look to be merry and want nothing while I live. I'll not take the advantage on you, because I hope to receive credit by it:[140] if I use now and then a round[141] sum, set me up o'th' ticket[142] for't. But who shall pass[143] his word, if I do this feat, you'll let me keep my head o' my shoulders?
DUKE Our royal word secure thee.
PHILENZO 'Tis enough.
FULVIO What security can your grace expect for his forthcoming, if he fail?
DUKE We ha' studied that—
'Tis but the loss of some superfluous crowns.
Let the end carry what success fate please,
All the expense will not be lost to try

130 276 the dragons: perhaps a reference to the myth of the golden fleece of Colchis, sought by Jason and guarded by a dragon
131 277 picked out: chosen
132 278–9 Between whose … we know: whose souls despise money more than we could imagine
133 283 aldermen cry larks: street sellers touted their wares with cries, hence—paradoxically—respected merchants might sell cheap wares in the streets
134 285 contemn: slight, treat disparagingly
135 286 The duke shifts from angry prose to sententious verse
136 290 Shalt not: i.e. shall you not
137 296 mountebanks: frauds, adventurers. In Act II, Bonamico poses as a literal mountebank, a seller of fake medicines and charms
138 301 enough?: Q gives the duke additional lines, but "The Printer to the Reader" cuts them (see Introduction)
139 302 particular: fastidious, fussy
140 303–4 I'll not … by it: i.e. I won't take advantage of you because I hope to gain your favor by completing the task
141 304 round: full, goodly
142 304–5 o'th' ticket: on account; i.e. the duke will pay the costs
143 305 pass: pronounce

The faith of those we shall employ in this:
Our city's strong; the river that environs
On three parts shall be carefully attended;
A wall makes safe the fourth, which shall be guarded;
Our vigils[144] shall be so exact he shall
Deserve his liberty if he escape us.
[*To* PHILENZO] We are constant, sir.
FULVIO Would he might pay for his curiosity.
PHILENZO I'll wait upon your highness for some earnest. I have a month—good. Let me have fair play and my bargain, money enough. If I do come short, let my head be too heavy for my shoulders; if I do more than is expected, you'll believe it possible hereafter—when a man has money enough he may do anything.
DUKE [*To* PHILENZO] Maintain your humor still. Attend us.

Exeunt [DUKE, FULVIO, ORPIANO, *and* PHILENZO]
Manent MORELLO, DONDOLO *and* GRUTTI

MORELLO Here's a mad fellow! Does he mean to get in to the ladies?
DONDOLO It seems so.
GRUTTI Or I would not be in his taking[145] when the moon changes.
MORELLO Our best course then is to observe and humor him—he may have a trick more than we know. He seems to be a good fellow. Let's be drunk together, and get him to confess it, ha?
DONDOLO AND GRUTTI A match!
MORELLO Like errant knights, our valiant wits must wrestle
To free our ladies from the enchanted castle.

Exeunt

Act II, scene i

Enter BONAMICO [*from the house, disguised as* ALTOMARO *the mountebank, with a false beard and costume*] *and* [CARLO, *his*] *servant*

CARLO D'ye think this hair[146]
And habit will sufficiently disguise you
From your inquiring creditors?
BONAMICO No question.
Have you dispersed my bills about the city?
Does every public place carry the scroll[147]
As I commanded?
CARLO I have been careful.
BONAMICO What do they say abroad?[148] Do they not wonder?
CARLO They are stricken dumb at reading. He that has
The use of tongue employs it to express
His admiration of your art, your deep,
Invisible art.
BONAMICO There's hope, then, we shall prosper
In this believing age. Italy is full
Of juggling mountebanks that show tricks with oils
And powders. Here an empiric[149] dares boast

144 318 vigils: watches
145 329 taking: state, plight
146 1 hair: i.e. false beard, a common prop for disguise or for a young actor playing older men
147 4–5 my bills . . . the scroll: paper advertisements for medicines and performances
148 7 abroad: i.e. about town
149 14 empiric: a doctor who believed practice should be observation-based, not theory-based

Himself a Paracelsian[150] and dawb
Each post with printed follies,[151] when he went
O'th ticket with[152] some midwife or old woman
For his whole stock of physic.[153] Here a fellow
Only has skill to make a handsome periwig,[154]
Or to sow teeth i'th' gums of some stale madam[155]—
Which she coughs out again when so much phlegm
As would not strangle a poor flea provokes her—
Proclaims himself a rectifier of nature,
And is believed so; getteth more by keeping
Mouths in their quarterly reparations
Than knowing men for all their art and pains
I'th' cure of the whole body. Shall we doubt
To be made rich—rich, Carlo!—by our art
Whereof I am the first and bold professor[156]
In Italy? We shall grow fat and purchase,
Dost not think so?

CARLO To go invisible?
Who will not learn at any rate?[157]

BONAMICO True, Carlo.
There may be in the throng of our admirers
Some will presume't above the power of art
To make men walk and talk invisible.
But we can clear the mystery, and make
Mantua in the proof acknowledge it
A matter feasible.

Enter [PHILENZO *disguised as*] ROLLIARDO

Here's some customer.
[*Aside*] Ha! 'Tis the humorist, the undertaker,[158]
The bird I spread my art for.[159] He has money
Enough,[160] and's apt to prove a fortune to me.

PHILENZO [*Aside*] So, the covenants are sealed. I am like a famous cathedral with two rings of bells: a sweet chime o' both sides. Now 'tis noised[161] I ha' money enough, how many gallants of all sorts and sexes court me? Here's a gentleman ready to run himself in the kennel[162] for haste to give me the wall;[163] this cavalier will kiss my hand, while th'other signor crinkles i'th' hams,[164] as he were studying new postures against[165] his turn comes to salute me. As I walk, every

150 15 Paracelsian: a follower of Paracelsus (*c.* 1493–1541), whose medical teaching was based on observation; hence, even lowly physicians can give themselves a fancy name
151 15–16 dawb . . . printed follies: hang misleading posters on every surface
152 16–17 went/O'th' ticket with: went into debt to, bought on credit from
153 18 stock of physic: stores or provisions of medicine
154 19 periwig: stylised hairpiece
155 20 stale madam: old or sexually worn-out woman, perhaps also a pimp
156 29 first and bold professor: pre-eminent and most public practitioner
157 32 rate: cost
158 39 undertaker: someone who undertakes a task or challenge
159 40 The bird . . . art for: the one I seek to trap (i.e. like a bird in a net)
160 40–41 money/Enough: Rolliardo's catchphrase is common knowledge
161 43 noised: reported, rumored
162 44 kennel: gutter
163 45 give me the wall: ceding the pavement near the wall rather than the gutter was a sign of deference
164 45 crinkles i'th' hams: bends his knees in a bow
165 46 against: in preparation for when

window is glazed with eyes, as some triumph[166] were in the street: this *madonna*[167] invites me to a banquet for my discourse; t'other *bona roba*[168] sends me a spark; a third a ruby; a fourth an emerald, and all but in hope to put their jewels to usury, that they may return again with precious interest. Thus far it goes well, very well. What's next?—

BONAMICO Save you, signor.

PHILENZO What art thou?

BONAMICO One appointed by fate to do you service, sir.

PHILENZO But I gave fate no commission to take you up for me. I ha' more followers than the duke already. Prithee have me commended to the Lady Destinies,[169] and tell 'em I am provided.

BONAMICO Mistake me not. He speaks to you has power[170]
To make you happy.

PHILENZO Prithee, make thyself happy with a warm suit first; thy house is but poorly thatched. And[171] thou be'st so good at making happy, why hast no better clothes?

BONAMICO 'Tis no felicity; or admit, the sun
Dispenseth a rich warmth about the world
Yet hath no heat itself.

PHILENZO Philosophy![172]

BONAMICO To omit circumstance, I know what you
Have undertaken to the general
Amazement: upon penalty of death,
You must procure access to the fair princess.
'Tis in my art to help, to perfect what
The duke holds so impossible.

PHILENZO How canst thou assist me?

BONAMICO Although my outside promise not, my brain
Is better furnished. I ha' gained by study
A secret will advance the work you labor with:
I'll teach you, sir, to go invisible—

PHILENZO How! Thou'st no cloven foot, I scent no brimstone:[173]
And thou be'st a devil, tell me.

BONAMICO I trifle not. I am a man whose fame
Shall outlive time in teaching you this mystery,
For which I must expect reward. You are—
Loud noise[174] proclaims it—able, and can pay me
Out of the duke's exchequer, being yourself
His walking treasury.

PHILENZO You'll teach me to go invisible, you say?

BONAMICO I can, and with your safety, for I deal not
With magic to betray you to a faith
Black and satanical.[175] I abhor the devil—

PHILENZO Very like so.

BONAMICO —which some have conjured into a ring[176]
To effect the wonder. I admit of no

166 47 triumph: royal entry or pageant, common early modern public performance forms
167 47 *madonna*: lady
168 48 *bona roba*: wench, "showy wanton" (*OED*; Hill, 1974)
169 55 Lady Destinies: the classical goddesses controlling birth, life, and death
170 56 He speaks to you has power: he who speaks to you has the power
171 59 And: if
172 62 Philosophy: i.e. pointless theorizing
173 74 no cloven . . . no brimstone: none of the devil's marks
174 79 noise: report
175 83–5 I deal . . . and satanical: Bonamico claims his feats are based on science rather than blasphemous knowledge
176 87 conjured into a ring: circles were used to summon and contain the devil (see Marlowe, *Doctor Faustus* iv. 8–13)

Suffumigation,[177] incense offered to
Infernal spirits, but by art, whose rules
Are lawful and demonstrative[178]—

PHILENZO You think I admire you all this while. Hark, when did you eat? Or do you hope again, that you are put to this pitiful and desperate exigent?[179] I see you, my would-be-invisible, fine knave!

BONAMICO D'ye mock me, sir?

PHILENZO I'll tell you a better project, wherein no courtier has prefooled you. Stick your skin with feathers, and draw the rabble of the city for pence a piece to see a monstrous bird brought from Peru:[180] baboons have passed for men already, been taken for usurers i'their furred gowns and nightcaps.[181] Keep a fool in pay,[182] to tell the multitude of a gentle faith that you were caught in a wilderness, and thou may'st be taken for some far country howlet.[183]

BONAMICO Do you despise my art?

PHILENZO Art? But such another word and I shall mar the whole expectation of your invisible traffic.[184] In to your nest and leave me! Distinguish[185] men before you practice on 'em, 'tis wholesome caution.

BONAMICO I leave you to the misery of your unbelief. When you hear of me hereafter, you will curse your fortune to have thus neglected me. Fare you well, sir. *Ex[eunt* BONAMICO *and* CARLO]

Enter PERENOTTO, *with three or four of the* GUARD

PHILENZO [*Aside*] This is Perenotto, captain of the guard.

PERENOTTO [*To* GUARDS] Not yet attempted you?[186]

1 GUARD We have not seen him, my lord.

PERENOTTO He's here!

2 GUARD Is that he that has gold enough? Would I had some of his yellowhammers.[187]

PHILENZO [*To* 1 GUARD] D'ye hear, you are one of the list?[188]

1 GUARD A poor halberd[189] man, sir.

PHILENZO Poor? Hold thee, there's gold for thee [*Offers him money*]. Thou wilt be honest now?

1 GUARD Oh, yes, sir.

PHILENZO [*Takes back the money*] Not a penny! And thou hadst not been a fool, thou wouldst ha' been a knave, and so thou might'st have got by me.[190] Yet, by those scurvy legs, there's some hope thou'lt be converted [*Gives him money*]. At all adventures, take it.

1 GUARD I will be what you please, sir.

PHILENZO [*Indicating* PERENOTTO] Tell me, what condition is that signor of? Is he rich?

1 GUARD He loves money.

PHILENZO Come, shalt be my pensioner[191] [*Gives him money*]. Here's more gold for

177 89 Suffumigation: incense used in incantations and magic
178 91 demonstrative: provable
179 93 exigent: extremity; state of need
180 97–8 monstrous bird brought from Peru: displays of exotic creatures trafficked from colonized territories in the Americas were common in European street performance
181 98–9 baboons have . . . and nightcaps: an anti-Semitic comparison between usurers, who were usually Jewish and often dressed in "furred gowns," and performing apes
182 99 Keep a fool in pay: i.e. pay a performing clown
183 100 howlet: owl
184 103 traffic: trade
185 103 Distinguish: i.e. distinguish between
186 108 Hasn't he attempted you yet? (i.e. hasn't Rolliardo tried to get past the guards yet?)
187 111 yellowhammers: small English birds; slang for gold coins
188 112 one of the list: member of the guard
189 113 halberd: battle-axe carried by lowly foot soldiers
190 118 got by me: got money from me
191 123 pensioner: dependent

thee. And will he take a bribe?
1 GUARD D'ye make question of that, sir? He bought his office[192] and therefore may sell his conscience: he has sold two hundred on's twice over.[193] He was brought up at court and knows what belongs to his place, I warrant you.
PHILENZO Good.
1 GUARD Am I not a knave now, sir?
PHILENZO I like thee.
1 GUARD [*Aside*] To your cost.—I hope you won't tell him what I say but, if you do, and he chance to turn me out of my office, your gold is restorative.
PERENOTTO To your stations, and be circumspect! *Ex*[*eunt*] GUARDS
PHILENZO [*To* PERENOTTO] Noble sir, you are the only man I have ambition to honor.
PERENOTTO I should be proud to merit such a phrase.
PHILENZO 'Tis in your power to oblige my soul—we're private?
I am jealous of the wind lest it convey
Our noise too far. This morn I had some traffic
With a jeweler and, if my judgment err not,
He's richly furnished me.
[*Shows him a jewel*] What says your lordship to this diamond?
PERENOTTO 'Tis a glorious one!
PHILENZO Does it not sparkle most divinely, signor?
A row of these stuck in a lady's forehead
Would make a Persian stagger in his faith
And give more adoration to this light
Than to the sunbeam.[194] I ha' fellows to 'em,[195]
A nest of bright ones.
PERENOTTO This box is studded like a frosty night with stars.
PHILENZO You have outbid their value. Make me a gainer
In changing[196] them for your commends.[197]
PERENOTTO How, sir!
PHILENZO I'm serious.
PERENOTTO I never shall deserve this bounty. If
You'd point me out some service to begin my gratitude—
PHILENZO You have a noble soul.
I'll teach you how to merit more.
PERENOTTO I am covetous of such a knowledge.
PHILENZO Make but my path a smooth one to the princess.
I am brief—you know my undertaking.
PERENOTTO So I should be a traitor?
PHILENZO It comes not near the question of a life.[198] Do't! I'll enable you to buy another dukedom, state and title.
PERENOTTO Although 'twere necessary in the affairs
Of such high consequence to deliberate
Yet, for this once, I'll be as brief as you:
I won't do't.
PHILENZO How!
PERENOTTO No, indeed, signor, you shall pardon me
At this time. And I'll keep your jewels, too,
For they are gifts. Hereafter you will know me.

192 125 office: rank, post
193 126 sold two . . . twice over: i.e. sold it four hundred times already
194 144–7 A row . . . the sunbeam: Muslims were mistakenly imagined to be sun-worshippers
195 147 fellows to 'em: companions for them, i.e. more
196 151 changing: exchanging
197 151 commends: remembrances, compliments
198 162 It comes . . . a life: your life won't be called into question; i.e. you won't be hung for treason

So, fare you well, sir. *Exit*
PHILENZO Was I not told this officer was corrupt?
I want[199] faith to believe the miracle.[200]
Sure, he does but jest with me, ha?

Enter MORELLO, DONDOLO, GRUTTI

MORELLO The guard will accept no moncy.
DONDOLO What an age do we live in, when officers will take no bribes?
GRUTTI Not the golden one.
DONDOLO Here's Rolliardo!
PHILENZO [*Aside*] I'm quite lost.
GRUTTI 'Tis he.
PHILENZO [*Aside*] Yet he keeps my jewels, there may be some hope.
I'll to him again. 'Tis but his modesty
At first not to seem easy, he must be courted:
Statesmen, like virgins, first should give denial.
Experience and opportunity make the trial.
—Save you, gallants.
MORELLO And you go thereto, save yourself: you are in a worse pickle than we are.
DONDOLO And how is't wi' ye, signor?
GRUTTI Do you thrive in your hopes?
PHILENZO I do not despair, gentlemen. You see I do not wear my hat in my eyes,[201] crucify my arms,[202] or entreat your lordship's brain to melt[203] in a petition for me.
MORELLO I did but jest, I know you have a way to the wood[204] in your pericranium.[205] What is't? We are honest, simple-minded lords.
PHILENZO I think so.
GRUTTI Nay, nay, impart.
DONDOLO We tell no tales.
MORELLO Would we were whipped and[206] we do.
PHILENZO Why shall I tell you? You are three—
MORELLO Very secret—
PHILENZO Coxcombs![207]
ALL THREE How!
PHILENZO A miserable leash[208] of court mimics.
MORELLO Mimics? What's that?
PHILENZO You perfumed goats!
MORELLO Oh, is that it? I never heard what a mimic was before.
PHILENZO D'ye think I am so wretched in a point that concerns my life and honor, to trust my ways and purposes to you that have no souls?[209]
DONDOLO No souls?
MORELLO Peace, how comes he to know that?
GRUTTI [*To* MORELLO] Why hast thou none?
MORELLO 'Twas more than ever I could see in myself yet.

199 174 want: lack
200 174 miracle: i.e. of Perenotto's sudden virtue
201 191 wear my hat in my eyes: a sign of a melancholic lover
202 191–2 crucify my arms: cross arms were a conventional posture of melancholy
203 192 melt: sweat, i.e. labor
204 193 way to the wood: plan; from the proverb "there be more ways to the wood than one"
205 193 pericranium: head
206 198 and: if
207 201 Coxcombs: fools
208 203 leash: hunting term for a set of three
209 208 souls: consciences, morality

PHILENZO Things that have forfeited their creation. And, had not your tailors took compassion on you, you had died to all men's thoughts, who long since would ha' forgotten that ever there were such things in nature.

DONDOLO Shall we suffer this?

PHILENZO Yes, and make legs[210] in token of your thankfulness. If I were at leisure, I would make you show tricks now. [*Seizes* MORELLO]

MORELLO Do I look like a Johnanapes?[211]

PHILENZO [*Lets* MORELLO *go*] But I won't.

MORELLO It were not your best course.[212]

PHILENZO How?

MORELLO Alas, sir, I should but shame myself, and be laughed at afore all this company.

PHILENZO When you see me next, avoid me as you would do your poor kindred when they come to court. Get you home. Say your prayers and wonder that you come off without beating, for 'tis one of my miracles. [*Exit*]

MORELLO Had we not better ha' gone to tavern, as I plotted at first? He could not ha' been more valiant in his drink.

GRUTTI I'm glad he's gone.

DONDOLO I know not what to make on him.

MORELLO "Make on him," quotha?[213] He made little reckoning of us, but and he had not gone as he did, I should ha' made—

DONDOLO What?

MORELLO Urine in my breeches—he squeezed me, I think I was ready to melt o' both sides.

GRUTTI But hark you, signor, we forget the ladies still!

MORELLO Well remembered.

DONDOLO Let's consult to purpose about that, shall we?

MORELLO No. Everyone think what he can by himself. My thoughts shall be private and not free at this time; everyone scratch his own head.

GRUTTI And he that gets the first hint, communicate—

DONDOLO A match!

MORELLO Let me see—umh.

DONDOLO What if I did—nothing! My brains are dull.

GRUTTI Ten to one, but if I did—let it alone. A pox on't! I were best drink some sack,[214] they say it helps invention.

MORELLO Oh, rare!

BOTH Rub, rub! Out with it!

MORELLO No, 'tis gone back again. I drunk buttered sack[215] this morning and it slipped back when 'twas almost at my tongue's end—but it was a delicate project, whatsoever it was.

GRUTTI Recover it with thy finger.

DONDOLO Follow it, Morello.

MORELLO Now, now, now! Let me alone. Make no noise, 'tis coming again. I ha't, I ha't!

DONDOLO Hold it fast, now!

GRUTTI Lose it not! Thou art great[216] with wit: let us deliver thee. What is't?

MORELLO Some wiser than some.[217] *They follow him up and down for discovery*[218]

DONDOLO Wilt not tell us?

GRUTTI Didst not promise?

MORELLO No haste, as occasion serves. It cost more than so, yet you may know't.

210 217 make legs: bow
211 219 Johnanapes: ape, ridiculous upstart
212 221 course: i.e. of action
213 231 quotha?: say you?
214 244 sack: white wine from Spain or the Canaries
215 248 buttered sack: spiced wine with melted butter
216 254 great: pregnant
217 255 Some wiser than some: i.e. I know something you don't know
218 255 SD *for discovery*: i.e. trying to discover his project

DONDOLO Well said.
MORELLO Hereafter, but not now. Away, do not tempt me! I will eat the sweat of my own brain. Oh, rare! Never was such a strain[219] of wit invented.—D'ye hear, gentlemen? If you will command me any service to the ladies, I do purpose to visit 'em—with quirk![220] Hey!
GRUTTI How?
MORELLO Marry, do I!
DONDOLO Nay, Morello.
MORELLO Gentlemen, as I told you, if you have anything to the ladies before I go, I am the messenger. There is a crotchet[221] and so forth—a carriwitchet[222] is found out. Your ears! I will do such a stratagem as never the like was heard of in the world. Oh, rare! *Exit*
DONDOLO He's mad.
GRUTTI So am I, that he is so reserved.[223]
What shall's do?

Enter BONAMICO, [*newly*] *disguised*

BONAMICO Save you, signors. Pray, whereabouts is the sign of the invisible man?[224]
DONDOLO AND GRUTTI The invisible man?
BONAMICO Cry ye mercy,[225] now I see it. *Exit*
DONDOLO See't? He does more than we can. The gentleman's mistaken; here's no such sign. Yet he went in there.
GRUTTI He has better eyes than we to distinguish it.

Enter [CARLO], *disguised*

CARLO This, aye, this is it.
DONDOLO What is it, pray?
CARLO What's that to you?
GRUTTI In courtesy we ask.
CARLO Then, by the sign, this is the house whither I am going to enquire for a gentleman that teaches men to walk invisible.
GRUTTI That would be seen! This is news!
CARLO News? Either you have slept long, or you are gentlemen of very small intelligence![226] Examine the next paper[227] you see advanced and inform yourselves. Farewell, gallants. *Exit*
DONDOLO He's entered there, too.
GRUTTI Teach men to walk invisible? A very fine trade!
DONDOLO Would 'twere true, we should desire no other device to get into the ladies.

Enter BONAMICO *and* [CARLO] *in other disguises*[*, passing*]

GRUTTI 'Tis impossible—see, see, more gentlemen! Prithee, let's to him: this will be a trick worth our learning. [*Exeunt* BONAMICO *and* CARLO *into the house*]
DONDOLO Stay, we are not acquainted. Let's knock first [*Knocks*].

Enter [CARLO, *as himself*]

219 261 strain: class, kind
220 262 quirk: a trick, subterfuge
221 267 crotchet: fanciful device or plan
222 267 carriwitchet: quibble, conundrum
223 270 reserved: uncommunicative
224 272 sign of the invisible man: businesses were advertised by emblematic signs
225 274 Cry ye mercy: I beg your pardon
226 285 intelligence: news, information; the courtiers are preoccupied with staying ahead of courtly intrigue
227 286 paper: poster, advertisment. In performance, Carlo might offer a paper proclaiming Altomaro (see line 306)

CARLO Your pleasures, gentlemen?
DONDOLO Pray, sir, what sign is this?
CARLO The invisible man, sir.
GRUTTI Man? I see no man.
DONDOLO Here's nothing but a cloud.
CARLO Right, sir, and he's behind it. The man's invisible.
DONDOLO Pretty, faith! It may be the man i'the moon[228] for aught we know.
CARLO Would ye anything with my master?
GRUTTI He does teach to walk invisible, they say?
CARLO He is the only professor of the miraculous invisible art.
DONDOLO May we change a little discourse[229] with him?
CARLO There are some gentlemen with him, but I'll tell him—I am prevented, he's coming forth himself!

Enter BONAMICO[, *disguised as* ALTOMARO]

DONDOLO Signior Altomaro,[230] I take it?
BONAMICO 'Tis my name, sir. A poor artist, not warm[231] in these parts of Italy.
GRUTTI And[232] you were not too busy, sir—
BONAMICO Please you, walk in; I am now alone. Your persons will grace my poor habitation.
DONDOLO We saw four or five enter but now.
BONAMICO I ha' dispatched 'em; they are fresh departed.
DONDOLO Which way?
GRUTTI Here's not a man! Are they not sunk?[233] Came they out here?
BONAMICO Upon my credit, sir, no other way.
DONDOLO Then they went invisible.
BONAMICO Right, sir. They came hither to that purpose; their designs[234] required haste.
GRUTTI This man can do't, I see already.
DONDOLO Sir, if you can assure us this invisible walking—for we are not so ignorant as we seem, we ha' seen the play of the *Invisible Knight*, and—
BONAMICO That of *The Ring*[235] too, ha' ye not?
DONDOLO Yes.
BONAMICO The one was magic, and t'other an imposture.[236] What I do is by art fair and natural. Are you in debt and fear arresting? You shall save your money in protections,[237] come up to the face of a sergeant, nay, walk by a shoal of these mankind horse-leeches[238] and be mace-proof.[239] If you have a mind to rail[240] at 'em, or kick some o' their loose flesh out, they shall not say "blacks your eye,"[241] nor with all their lynxes' eyes[242] discover you. Would you see, when the mercer's[243] abroad, how his man plays the merchant at home with his mistress Silkworm, and deals underhand for commodity? Would yourself talk with a lady in secret; sit down, play with

228 299 man i'the moon: i.e. an imaginary person
229 303 change a little discourse: exchange some conversation
230 306 Altomaro: Dondolo perhaps learns his name from the showbill (see line 286)
231 307 warm: perhaps referring to Mantua's northern position; or, his fame is not hot, i.e. he is not well-known
232 308 And: if
233 313 sunk: into the earth, i.e. vanished
234 316 designs: plans
235 319–20 *Invisible Knight . . . The Ring*: only the titles survive but these plays probably come from the commercial stage in or around Shirley's time
236 322 imposture: deception, fraud
237 323 protections: extortion under threat of violence
238 324 mankind horse-leeches: insatiable human bloodsuckers
239 324–5 mace-proof: safe from arrest; the guard carried maces as weapons
240 325 rail: complain, rant
241 326 "blacks your eye": a charm wishing a bruised eye on the unseen attackers
242 326 lynxes' eyes: lynxes were known for their sharp-sightedness
243 327 mercer's: a fabric and textile dealer, often trading costly materials

her, ravish[244] a diamond from her finger, and bind her soft wrist with a bracelet? Kiss her abroad, at home, before her servants, in the presence of her jealous husband? Nay, truss her up when the tame lord is abed with her, and to his eyes be undiscovered as the wind? Signor, do you suspect your mistress plays double?[245] Would you hear how she entertains the t'other's love and know what she does i'the closet with the smooth page?[246] Would you be present at secret counsels? Betray letters? See how such a lord paints his thighs,[247] this perfume his breath, t'other marshal his fine French teeth?[248] See this statesman's eyes put out[249] with a bribe, how that officer cozens[250] the duke, and his secretary abuses 'em both? This lawyer takes fees o' both sides, while the judge examines the fertility and price of the manor before the witnesses, and then decrees who shall have the land? Would you see justice employ her scales to weigh light gold[251] that comes in for fees or corruption, and flourish with her sword like a fencer to make more room for causes i'the court?

DONDOLO All this and more may be done, if we can but go invisible, but how can you assure us of that?

GRUTTI I would fain see any man go invisible once.

BONAMICO See him, sir?

GRUTTI *Video pro intelligo*,[252] I mean, sir.

BONAMICO Nay, sir, you need not distinguish,[253] for it is possible to see a man invisible. Observe me: you see me now perfectly, in every part; if I should walk before you without a body—

GRUTTI How!

BONAMICO —my head only visible and hanging in the air like a comet.

DONDOLO That were a strange sight!

BONAMICO Sometimes nothing shall be seen but my arm; another while one of my legs, hopping without a body.

GRUTTI This is admirable.

BONAMICO When I please, I will have nothing conspicuous but my hand, nay, perhaps my little finger.

DONDOLO Do not you conjure[254] then?

GRUTTI Come, you will cast a mist before our eyes.

BONAMICO 'Tis a mystery indeed, but a safe[255] one, signors.

DONDOLO Why, look you, sir, if you will be pleased that we may see you first walk invisible, we shall not only credit your art, but at any rate be ambitious to be your disciples.

BONAMICO Why, gentlemen, you speak but justice; you shall have experiment.[256] I will be invisible first but, as to other in this kind, I will not demonstrate without half in hand. Let me have fifty crowns apiece, I'll 'point[257] you a day when I will be invisible.

GRUTTI Can you not do it presently?[258]

BONAMICO I can be invisible in a twinkling, but what assurance can you have that I am here at the same instant when you see no part of me? I may deceive you.

DONDOLO He says true.

BONAMICO I do purpose therefore to give you reality and proof. For I will walk invisible, all

244 329 ravish: steal, with sexual implications
245 332 plays double: is unfaithful
246 333 smooth page: male servant too young for a beard
247 334 paints his thighs: perhaps refers to colorful silk breeches worn by courtiers at Charles I's court
248 335 marshal his fine French teeth: affects a French accent
249 335 eyes put out: blinded, figuratively
250 336 cozens: deceives
251 338 light gold: a forged or clipped coin lacking the legal amount of gold
252 345 *Video pro intelligo*: I see [because] I know (Latin)
253 346 distinguish: i.e. between his meanings
254 357 conjure: deceive, trick
255 359 safe: i.e. not blasphemous or devilish
256 362 experiment: proof
257 364 'point: appoint
258 365 presently: immediately

but—my hand!
BOTH Your hand?
BONAMICO Only my hand. You shall touch it, see every line in't, and the rest of my body be to you invisible. This will require a little time for preparation and when, with the consent of your eyes and understandings, I keep my promise in this point, you will think your moneys well expended to be taught the mystery.
DONDOLO This is very fair.
GRUTTI The crowns shall be ready, sir.
DONDOLO Expect 'em within this hour.

Enter [PHILENZO *disguised as*] ROLLIARDO

BONAMICO At your own pleasures—[*Aside*] Ha, Rolliardo? I must not be seen.—Gentlemen.
Exeunt [BONAMICO *and* CARLO]
BOTH Farewell, incomparable signor.
GRUTTI What luck had we to light upon this artist! He shall not publish it.[259] We'll buy the whole secret at any value and then get him remove into some other province[260]—who's this?
PHILENZO [*Aside*] Am not I mad? Sure I am, though I do not know it, and all the world is but a bedlam, a house of correction to whip us into our senses.[261] I ha' known the time when jewels and gold had some virtue in 'em. The generation of men now are not subject to corruption: Democritus,[262] the world's refined.[263]
DONDOLO [*To* GRUTTI] 'Tis Rolliardo! He looks melancholy; let's have a fling at[264] him—Give you joy of the great lady, sir! Which is the next way to the moon, pray?[265]
PHILENZO Bolt upright, musk-cat,[266] and if you make haste you may be one of her calves.[267] Next time she appears, you shall see her beckon to you with a pair of horns[268] just o'the size of those are preparing for your forehead, my precious animal.
DONDOLO Ha, ha, ha! The fellow's mad.
GRUTTI Can you tell, sir, what became of all the swallows, cuckoos, and small birds we had here last summer?
PHILENZO Marry, sir, they went to sea to aid the cranes, and there have been mustering ever since. But for want of a woodcock[269] they ha' left behind 'em, they dare not venture upon the pygmies.[270] You may do well to overtake the buzzard and relieve the army, sir.[271]
GRUTTI Ha, ha, ha! *Ex*[*eunt* DONDOLO *and* GRUTTI]
PHILENZO I shall be grinned to death as I walk the streets! 'Tis no policy to be dull and modest. But let me see, which way to compass[272] my work and put myself out of the common laughter? The very children will jeer me shortly, I think, and point me out with stones: "the precious undertaker!" I might have had more wit than to run myself into this calamity[273]—whom have we next?

259 381 publish it: make it public
260 382 get him . . . other province: pay him to go to another part of the country
261 384 bedlam . . . our senses: Bedlam (i.e. Bethlehem) hospital, an asylum for the mentally ill originally located in Bishopsgate, London, was known for the cruel treatment of its inmates
262 386 Democritus: Greek philosopher (fifth century BCE), who proposed that the world was made of unchanging matter; Philenzo claims that this matter has been purified
263 386 refined: purified
264 387 have a fling at: taunt, mock
265 388 Which is . . . the moon, pray?: a nonsense question, associating Rolliardo with lunacy, as at I.i. 182
266 389 musk-cat: fop
267 389 calves: literally, offspring; a play on "mooncalf" or simpleton
268 390 pair of horns: i.e. the points of the crescent moon; horns were the traditional sign of the cuckold, a man whose wife is unfaithful
269 396 woodcock: also a word for "fool"
270 397 pygmies: mythical diminutive tribe. Homer and Aristotle write of a battle between pygmies and birds; Shirley takes it from Antonio de Torquemada's *Spanish Mandeville of Miracles* (1618)
271 389–97 Bolt upright . . . army, sir: a conventional nonsense speech to perform madness (see Introduction)
272 400 compass: plan, design
273 399–402 I shall . . . this calamity: the audience sees Rolliardo perform madness, not his true identity

Enter the DUKE, AMBASSADOR, FULVIO, DONDOLO, GRUTTI[,] *Attendants,* [*and*] COURTIERS

[*Aside*] The duke! What stranger's that?[274] I must not seem dejected.
AMBASSADOR Is this he your highness discoursèd of?
DUKE This is the piece made up of all performance,
The man of anything without exception.
Give him but gold, king's daughters and their heirs,
Though locked in towers of brass, are not safe from him.
Nay, though I play the chemist with my trust
And, from a million of sure confidences
I draw the spirit of honesty into a few,[275]
He can corrupt 'em.
PHILENZO You are my prince, great sir, and you have spoke
Not much unlike a brave one.—
DONDOLO He'll jeer the duke, too!
PHILENZO —If my head
Come to be paid to you before sunset
That day when it is forfeit, I ha' cleared with[276] you
And shall depart out of your royal debt:
There's all you can demand. A good sharp sword
Will make an even reckoning.
AMBASSADOR He seems confident!
1 COURTIER [*To* DUKE] With your grace's leave, let me come to him.
PHILENZO Now, a fierce dog!
1 COURTIER What came into thy mind, thou daring madman—
"Fool" is a word of favor to thee—
PHILENZO So, sir.
1 COURTIER —to undertake such an impossible task?
PHILENZO Mushroom![277] I'll cast away a few words on thee.
Had I another life, I'd undertake yet—
Though I be low in all opinion—
To venture it with the riches I have spread
To corrupt others, to make thee my parasite.[278]
I would engage my life to wear[279] no steps
To thy white[280] daughter. Thou and thy grave matron
Most humbly should present her, when I was pleased, too,
For fear I should refuse the sport[281] you brought me.
DUKE I never knew man bear his scorn so high. To him, some other!
GRUTTI Not I, sir. You shall excuse me; 'twas the last thing I did.
1 COURTIER In the position general, I'll not touch him.
For money may be said to purchase all things
But to aspire to my good sovereign's daughter
Of blessèd memory—
PHILENZO She's not dead, I hope.
1 COURTIER There gold and trash was impudently inferred,[282]

274 404 What stranger's that?: Who is that foreigner? (referring to the ambassador)
275 410–12 I play . . . a few: the duke imagines himself as a "chemist," refining ("drawing") his courtiers' natures by separating out their component qualities through the alchemical process of sublimation
276 419 cleared with: paid my debt to
277 429 Mushroom: upstart
278 433 parasite: i.e. dependent upon his money and approval
279 434 wear: wear out
280 435 white: pure, chaste
281 437 sport: sexual pleasure
282 444 inferred: bestowed

And 'twas a task too insolent. In that point
You'd willingly give a pound of your proud flesh,
To be released.
PHILENZO I heard a pound of flesh, a Jew's demand[283] once;
'Twas gravely now remembered of your lordship. Released?
Fortune and courtesy of opinion
Gives many men nobility of birth
That never durst do nobly, nor attempt
Any design but fell below their honors,[284]
Cased up in chambers,[285] scarcely air themselves
But at a horse-race,[286] or i'th' Park[287] with puppets.[288]
That for which I'm your laughter—I speak to
You flattering tribe of courtiers, to you glow-worms[289]—
Is my chief glory. That perhaps being sprung
From humble parentage, dare yet attempt
A deed too far above me, that sets all
Your wisdoms in combustion. You may think
I've made a sorry bargain for my life:
Let scorners know in aiming at her only,[290]
My memory after death receives more honor
Than all your marble pinnacles[291] can raise you,
Or alabaster figures, whiter far
Than e'er your souls were, and, that hour I die,
If you dare look upon me without fainting
(Which I much fear) you shall see death so scorned—
I mean for any terror—you shall think him
My slave to take my upper garment off.
DONDOLO I told your highness how you should find him.
AMBASSADOR A brave resolution!
DUKE Be this the prologue to the mirth, my lord,
Attends to[292] entertain you. Set on, we'll leave him. Ha, ha, ha! [*Flourish*][293]

Exeunt [*omnes*]. [PHILENZO, *disguised as*] ROLLIARDO *pulls* FULVIO *back*

PHILENZO Sir, I observed you noble, and not apt
To throw derision on me with the rest,
Which does encourage me to ask you a question.
FULVIO Name it, sir.
PHILENZO Pray, what stranger's that walked with the duke?
FULVIO 'Tis an ambassador from Florence, sir.
PHILENZO An ambassador? His design, I pray?
FULVIO To treat of marriage betwixt our princess
And the great duke's son, desired much by our master,

283 448 pound of . . . Jew's demand: an allusion to Shakespeare's *The Merchant of Venice*
284 453 Any plan except those that dishonor them
285 454 Cased up in chambers: i.e. Who, cooped up indoors
286 455 horse-race: a fashionable Caroline pursuit
287 455 Park: Hyde Park, a fashionable 1630s location
288 455 puppets: puppet plays were commonly performed at fairs and in Hyde Park
289 457 glow-worms: i.e. base insects that shine brightly
290 463 know in aiming at her only: know that, merely by aiming at her
291 465 pinnacles: ornate tombs
292 475 Attends: that waits
293 475 SD *Flourish*: a trumpet or cornet fanfare, usually off-stage. The SD, found in an early state of the 1633 Quarto, was corrected later in the print-run. It may document stage practice

Who has some hope 'twill be effected, too.
He's brought rich presents to her.
PHILENZO This is all?
FULVIO You have it freely.
PHILENZO You've honored me. *Exit* [FULVIO]
Married to Tuscany? So, if my ambition had been fortunate, I might have been his taster,[294] but my stars[295] want influence, they are too dull and weary of my fate. Rolliardo then must forfeit! Why, that's the worst on't! I will make a glorious blaze in death and, while I live, make the duke's treasure pay for't, nor shall he accuse me I exhaust him poorly. I'll study out some noble way to build me a remembrance.[296] Ha!—A church or college? Tedious! My glass[297] has but few sands; I must do something I may live to finish. I ha't! I will send to all the prisons i'th' city and pay the poor men's debts[298] for 'em: the world wants[299] such a precedent. I ha' money enough: since I fail in my other ends, I will do some good deeds before I die. So shall I be more sure of prayers than if I built a church, for they are not certain to continue their foundation.[300] Fate, I despise thee! I sink under no cheap and common action, but sell my life to fame in catching my death by so brave an aspiring.
If I obtain a monument, be this all:
Write on my grave, "This man climbed high to fall."
Exit

Act III, scene i

Enter [*three*] GUARDS

1 GUARD Come, gentlemen, we must watch still, that none run away with the princess.
2 GUARD He must have an excellent stomach,[301] that can break these stone walls to come to her.
3 GUARD Beside this moveable wall of flesh which we carry.
2 GUARD One makes toward us—'tis a lady.

Enter MORELLO[, *disguised*] *like a lady*

MORELLO [*Aside*] So, now am I as valiant as Hercules when he turned spinster.[302] Great Jupiter, the patron of scapes,[303] assist my petticoat and, at my return, I will sacrifice my linen breeches to thee. Here be the men, the men of mettle. Now, Venus,[304] I beseech thee, and they be men, they will let a lady enter without many questions.
1 GUARD Save you, sweet lady, your affairs this way?
MORELLO I go but in to the princess.
1 GUARD From whom?
MORELLO From the duke's grace.
1 GUARD What may be your ladyship's name?
MORELLO [*Aside*] I never thought to give myself a name!—My name is Madam—um—my

294 488 taster: someone to test food for poison, hence the first to enjoy access to Eugenia
295 489 stars: i.e. those that ruled over his birth
296 492 remembrance: memorial, legacy
297 492 glass: hourglass
298 494 poor men's debts: debtors were often imprisoned
299 494 wants: lacks
300 496 for they … their foundation: religious controversies abounded in the 1630s; Philenzo suggests that any "church" (religious group or building) has an uncertain future
301 2 stomach: courage
302 6 Hercules when he turned spinster: Hercules was emasculated by Omphale, the queen of Libya, and made to cross-dress and spin thread
303 7 scapes: dangerous or scandalous escapades, often for seduction
304 8 Venus: goddess of love

name is something, an odd name, but—I do not stand upon't[305]—my name's Thorn.[306]

1 GUARD Indeed, Madam Thorn, if his grace have sent you to such a purpose, you must show something for our discharge.[307]

MORELLO Why, hark you, it was but forgotten of the duke to send his signet.[308] But I ha' brought some of his highness's deputies[309] wi' me, I hope that will satisfy.

As he takes out money[, *he*] *discovers*[310] [*his*] *breeches*

2 GUARD [*To* 3 GUARD] By this gold, breeches!

3 GUARD [*To* 2 GUARD] No, they are but silk.[311] Here will be sport, I have a hint already.

1 GUARD [*To* MORELLO] Say you so? 'Tis very well. But, madam, we are many, and we would be loath to venture.[312] Deal ingeniously, sweet lady; have you no more gold in your breeches?

MORELLO Not a doit,[313] as I am virtuous and sinful.

1 GUARD Pass, but, d'ye hear, and[314] you should not be secret, now—

MORELLO As I am a gentleman.

3 GUARD A gentleman? Dost hear him? I'll put him to't.

MORELLO I have left some crowns with your fellow.

2 GUARD Tush, that won't satisfy me!

MORELLO Indeed, I ha' no more money.

2 GUARD You have commodity. Hang this transitory gold! Give me [*Grabs* MORELLO's *hand*]—what's this?

MORELLO Nothing but a wart o' my little finger.

2 GUARD A wart? Let me see't. *Pulls off his glove*

MORELLO 'Tis a diamond. 'Twas my mother's legacy, or else—

2 GUARD Is it your will[315] I should have it?

MORELLO It was my mother's will I should wear it. Her ghost will haunt me and I should give it away.

2 GUARD You know the way back, lady.

MORELLO You will give me my gold again?

1 GUARD Not a doit, as I am virtuous and sinful. Stand with him for a toy,[316] and know you've no warrant from the duke. 'Tis in our power.

MORELLO D'ye hear, sir, and it were a diamond of gold, you should have it. [*Gives him the ring*]

2 GUARD Lady, I kiss your hand.

MORELLO You've kissed the ring off o' my finger, I'm sure.

2 GUARD Use your fortune, pass.

MORELLO [*Aside*] If I get to the ladies, somebody shall pay for this, that's my comfort.

3 GUARD Can you wrestle, madam? *Takes him by the shoulder*

MORELLO Ah! Wrestle, sir? Ladies do not use to wrestle.

3 GUARD They are thrown down with their good wills, then? Come, you and I will have a bout; I must hug your little body.

1 GUARD Humor him and you're past danger.

MORELLO Would you ha' me tear my clothes?

305 16 stand upon't: insist on it
306 16 Thorn: a suitably phallic name for a cross-dressed man
307 18 discharge: release from obligation
308 19 signet: ring with the duke's seal
309 20 deputies: coins carrying the duke's image
310 20 SD *discovers*: reveals
311 22 silk: portraiture shows Caroline courtiers wearing silk breeches, mistaken for female underwear
312 25 venture: risk, hazard
313 27 doit: small coin or sum of money
314 28 and: if
315 39 will: wish
316 44 Stand with . . . a toy: "haggle . . . for a trifle" (Sanders, 2006)

1 GUARD I'll persuade him.

2 GUARD To tell you true, madam, this fellow is an abominable lecher, there is no scaping[317] him without a fall.[318] A very satyr,[319] he leaps[320] all comes near him! If your ladyship's modesty can dispense with a private favor—you understand. For our parts, we are satisfied otherwise and our lips are sewed up. Take him o'th' side and see how you can mollify[321] him. He's a cock o' the game,[322] and will tread[323] you and you were ten thorns.

MORELLO Mollify him? Doth he use ladies so? He will mollify me!

2 GUARD And you were his sister, all's one to him. The devil is not more hot and robustious[324] where he finds opposition to the sport; therefore the duke made choice of him, as suspecting some lord might come disguised o' this fashion, to prevent dishonor to the princess and ladies. Use your own discretion.

MORELLO [*Aside*] What will become of me? If he be such a wencher,[325] he'll ravish[326] me and discover all! What a rascal was I to venture thus! [*To* 1 AND 2 GUARD] I'll give thee my fan to persuade him—Help! Help!

3 GUARD Nay, then. *He throws him down, and discovers his breeches*

Why, how now? Breeches?

1 GUARD This is a man!

2 GUARD Sure, 'tis a woman!

MORELLO To tell you true, gentlemen, I am neither a man nor a woman: I am an hermaphrodite.

1 GUARD How! An hermaphrodite? What would you do among the ladies then?

2 GUARD An hermaphrodite!

3 GUARD Let's search[327] him.

MORELLO Ah!

1 GUARD Stay, let's be advised. If he be such a monster,[328] our best way is to carry him to the duke.

2 AND 3 GUARD Agreed!

MORELLO [*Aside*] I shall be undone!—D'ye hear, noble friends, 'tis but a folly to dissemble. I am no such thing. I am no hermaphrodite, I am a friend of yours.

ALL Of ours?

2 GUARD Your name, I beseech you?

MORELLO I did but jest all this while. The duke himself put me upon't to see whether I could cozen[329] you. My name's Morello.

1 GUARD Signor Morello? 'Tis not possible!

MORELLO As I am virtuous, I am. I am no hermaphrodite. No matter for the gold or diamonds, 'tis your own. I'll acquaint his grace how careful I found you, and if he do not reward you beside, I'll say he's the poorest duke in Christendom [*Starts to leave*]. I'll tell him presently.[330]

3 GUARD Noble signor, we'll wait upon you to him.

MORELLO No, no! 'Tis better for me to go alone.

1 GUARD Your pardon. You shall tell how careful you found us; we'll relate to him how cunningly you carried the business.

317 58 scaping: escaping
318 59 fall: sexual encounter
319 59 satyr: mythical creature, half man, half goat, typically lustful
320 59 leaps: flings himself on
321 61 mollify: placate, appease
322 62 cock o' the game: a game-cock; a sexually overconfident man
323 62 tread: have sex with
324 64 robustious: sturdy, exuberant
325 68 wencher: a man who associates with common women or prostitutes
326 68 ravish: assault; rape
327 79 search: i.e. his clothes and body; women were "searched" to confirm virginity
328 81 monster: prodigy, marvel, spectacle (from Latin, "monstrare" to show); human and animal "monsters" were displayed in early modern touring shows, making Morello another kind of performer
329 89 cozen: trick
330 93 presently: immediately

MORELLO Nay, d'ye hear, gentlemen?
ALL It must be so, sir. Come, sweet, effeminate signor!

Exeunt

[Act III, scene ii]

Enter FULVIO [*and*] AMBASSADOR

AMBASSADOR You've done me a noble office, signor, in this discovery. Where now lives her[331] banished lover?
FULVIO My kinsman[332] lives in Florence. But two days since I received letters from him.
AMBASSADOR In Florence, too?
FULVIO Sir, you may censure me
But my affection to the injured lord,
And not without respect unto the honor
Of your master, too, hath been the cause of
My free language.
AMBASSADOR Trust me, signor,
We are all engaged to study you a recompense;
But Mantua was unjust to banish him
For being too much a servant.[333]
FULVIO Sir, when princes resolve to punish—
AMBASSADOR Virtue shall be treason.
'Twas tyranny.[334] Why now is she thus caged?
FULVIO I can conjecture nothing but his jealousy,
Which will be ever active. By that love
We interchanged at Pisa when we grew
Together in our studies, I conjure
Your nobleness to silence me.[335]
AMBASSADOR You will dishonor me by suspicion: I am charmed.[336]

Enter PERENOTTO, DONDOLO, [*and*] GRUTTI

PERENOTTO [*To* AMBASSADOR] My honored lord.
AMBASSADOR Signor Perenotto.
FULVIO [*To* DONDOLO *and* GRUTTI] My gentle sparks.
DONDOLO AND GRUTTI Your servants.
FULVIO You are all courtship.
PERENOTTO Is your lordship for this wonder?
AMBASSADOR What wonder, my lord?
PERENOTTO These pair of gentlemen have discoursed me into admiration. There's one has undertaken to go invisible.
AMBASSADOR Invisible?
PERENOTTO This hour expected, and in this place.
FULVIO How?
DONDOLO With a trick that he has.
FULVIO Do you believe him, gentlemen?
GRUTTI You shall see't.

331 2 her: i.e. Eugenia's
332 3 kinsman: i.e. Philenzo; Fulvio gives the Florentine ambassador false information about Philenzo's whereabouts
333 12 servant: i.e. lover
334 15 tyranny: the duke is accused of overstepping legitimate sovereign powers
335 20 silence me: i.e. before I go too far
336 21 charmed: enchanted; he will keep Fulvio's secret

DONDOLO We were heretics[337] in that point, but our understandings are convinced: he did demonstrate.[338]
GRUTTI And because you shall know the truth of his art, he will be invisible—all but his hand. What think you of that? The rarest fellow in Christendom!
AMBASSADOR Nothing visible but his hand?
DONDOLO As sure as we have given him a hundred crowns in hand.
AMBASSADOR Why is not the duke presented with this novelty?
DONDOLO He's[339] traveling to the emperor[340] first. Only, as he goes, for our sake, he will show us a figary[341] of his art.

Enter [PHILENZO, *disguised as*] ROLLIARDO

Here's Rolliardo. He's somewhat costive[342] on t'other side; wants[343] faith.
PHILENZO Save you, nest of courtiers. Smooth faces, rich clothes, and sublime compliments make you amorous[344] in sight of your ladies. *Donzel del Phebo* and *Rosicleer*,[345] are you there? What pestilent diseases have you got, that you wear so much musk and civet[346] about you? Oh for a priest of Cupid to sacrifice you now! How your breeches would burn like incense and your hair, disguised in sweet powder,[347] leave your bodies in a mist, while your bones were inwardly consuming with the fire of Dame Venus' altar![348]
DONDOLO The same humorist,[349] still.
PHILENZO I heard say we shall have strange apparitions i'th' air and yet invisible wonders. A hand must appear as fatal to some as that hung o'er the Capitol[350]—for there is a suspicion some purses will be juggled empty—and as silent as the moon, no bright Sol[351] appearing, nor a piece of pale-faced silver[352] in your silken hemispheres.[353]
GRUTTI He is an infidel![354]
PHILENZO Right Yehochanan![355] Right, my precious Jew! We are all infidel that won't believe the court catechism.[356]—My lord ambassador, you are welcome from Florence. Does the great duke[357] pick salads[358] still? I mean, continue his assize,[359] return into his exchequer once in seven years the wealth of Tuscany? Vespasian was held covetous for ordaining vessels to receive the beneficial public urine, but 'tis heathenism among Christians not to hold *Dulcis odor lucri e re qualibet*.[360]

337 37 heretics: unbelievers
338 38 demonstrate: offer proof
339 44 He's: i.e. Bonamico as Altomaro
340 44 emperor: Ferdinand II, Habsburg Holy Roman Emperor until 1637; his court was in Vienna
341 45 figary: trifle, whim
342 46 costive: reluctant to speak or believe; literally, constipated
343 46 wants: lacks
344 48 amorous: loving, worthy of love
345 48 *Donzel del Phebo* and *Rosicleer*: characters in the Spanish romance *The Mirrour of Princely Deedes and Knighthood*, translated by Margaret Tyler (1578); Philenzo mocks the courtiers' exaggerated, foolish devotion (Sanders, 2006)
346 49 musk and civet: perfumes masking diseased corruption
347 51 sweet powder: perfumed hair powder
348 52 fire of Dame Venus's altar: the burning symptoms of syphilis caused by worshipping Venus, goddess of love
349 53 humorist: cynical melancholic
350 55 as that hung o'er the Capitol: i.e. those fatal omens that appeared in Rome the night before Julius Caesar's murder (Shakespeare, *Julius Caesar* II.ii. 13–26)
351 56 bright Sol: the sun, gold, a French coin
352 56–7 piece of pale-faced silver: coin
353 57 silken hemispheres: their purses (Senescu, 1980); perhaps also their breeches (see III.i. 21–2)
354 58 infidel: unbeliever
355 59 Yehochanan: an "archetypal Jewish name" (Sanders, 2006), used to mock Grutti as a fanatical follower of the court. For the play's antisemitism, see II.i. 448
356 60 catechism: memorized articles of belief
357 61 great duke: the Medici dynasty famously ruled Florence
358 61 pick salads: i.e. gather from everywhere
359 61 assize: setting of taxes
360 63–4 *Dulcis … qualibet*: "The smell of gain is good, come from what it may"; said to be uttered by the Roman emperor Vespasian to his son Titus, when he questioned the imposition of a tax on public toilets (Senescu, 1980)

AMBASSADOR He's mad!

PHILENZO Signor Perenotto, it has puzzled my understanding, how you can subsist at court without making use of the common sins, flattery, and corruption? Take heed, you're a great man and 'tis ominous to die in your bed, a sign your children are like to inherit but weak brains. Thou may'st go to heaven, but thy heir had rather thou shouldst make a journey to Erebus, for the proverb's sake: happy is that son whose father goes to the devil. Why, when comes out my *Don Invisible*?[361] Maybe he's here already, for we cannot see him. [*To* DONDOLO] What says my squirrel?[362] Thou look'st dull and physical,[363] methinks; the crowns will return again invisibly, never fear it. [*To* GRUTTI] And how does my grave gymnosophist,[364] whose ambition it is to be registered an honest lord, though thou be'st buried upon alms,[365] carried to church with four torches and have an inscription on thy marble worse than the ballad of the devil and the baker,[366] and might be sung to as vild[367] a tune, too.—Gentlemen, I'll invite you shortly to see my head cut off, and do only entreat you would not laugh at me when I am dead. 'Twill show but poorly in you and I shall revenge it with my ghost-walking.

FULVIO Either he is very confident to achieve his design or late grown desperate, he talks so wildly.

DONDOLO I wonder Signor Altomaro forgets us.

Enter [CARLO]

Now, now, ye shall hear. This is his servant; I know he is not far off. [*To* CARLO] Where is thy master?

CARLO He is invisible. This letter is directed to you. [*Gives* DONDOLO *the letter*]

DONDOLO [*Reads*][368] "Gentlemen, that you may perceive I deal plainly with you, I am now invisible; all but my hand,[369] and here it is. You may with ease read every line, as I promised upon the receipt of your crowns."—His hand?

CARLO Ay, sir, 'tis his own hand, I can assure you.

OMNES Ha, ha, ha!

DONDOLO He does not mean to serve us so, thou dost but jest! Where is he invisible?

CARLO Here, I think, for I cannot see him; nor do I know when I shall, or where he will be visible again. Upon diligent search I found this paper,[370] but my master is not to be found.

FULVIO Then he is invisible, indeed.

PHILENZO All but his hand! Ha, ha!

GRUTTI I do incline to believe that we are cheated.

PERENOTTO "With a trick that he has!" Ha, ha, ha!

AMBASSADOR You were heretics in that point, till he did demonstrate. Ha, ha, ha!

PHILENZO I cannot contain my merry spleen.[371] Ha, ha!

FULVIO [*To* AMBASSADOR] Come, my lord, let's leave them now to be their own derision. *Exeunt* AMBASSADOR [*and*] FULVIO

Enter GUARDS *with* MORELLO[*, disguised as before*]

DONDOLO Signor Morello! Ha, ha, ha! How came he in a petticoat?

361 71 *Don Invisible*: a mocking Spanish pronunciation (see line 48)

362 72 squirrel: an overly familiar insult

363 72 physical: in need of physic, i.e. medicine

364 73 gymnosophist: member of an ancient austere Hindu sect

365 74 upon alms: by charity

366 75–6 ballad of … the baker: Sanders (2006) notes that Shirley refers to this ballad in *Hyde Park* (II.iv) but that it hasn't been found. A later version perhaps exists: *The Gelding of the Devil* promises news "Betwixt the Baker and the Devil of Hell" (1674–79) (UC Santa Barbara Early English Ballads Archive)

367 76 vild: vile

368 85 SD *Reads*: instead of a direction and speech prefix ("DONDOLO"), Q has "*The Letter*" (see Introduction)

369 86 my hand: handwriting

370 92 paper: letter

371 98 spleen: the seat of laughter or mirth

MORELLO Carry me away quickly, they will laugh me out of my little wit.
PHILENZO No, no! Do not, gentlemen. Remember yourselves.
1 GUARD We won't, then.
PERENOTTO Morello? I'll wait upon him to the duke myself.
MORELLO What wise man in Italy would be in my coat now?

Ex[eunt GUARDS, MORELLO *and* PERENOTTO]

PHILENZO I was costive and an infidel? You are Christian coxcombs and so, while I see what will become of the mirth that is gone before, I leave your wise signorships to the mercy of your garters,[372] which is a speedy way, after a little time, to make yourselves invisible indeed. Fare you well. *Exit*
DONDOLO Signor Grutti, we are gulled.[373]
GRUTTI I always thought he would cheat us. What shall's do to prevent more laughter?
CARLO [*Aside*] I am resolved: I shall get no more money by him.—Gentlemen, be not head-hung. Droop not. 'Tis in this sconce[374] to revenge yourselves and, it may be, recover your crowns,[375] too.
DONDOLO How, prithee?
CARLO My master—
DONDOLO Is invisible, we know't too well.
CARLO What will you give me, if I discover him to your eyes again? Nay, give him to your possession?
DONDOLO This.
GRUTTI And this—oh, quickly! [*They*] *give him money*
CARLO Then first know, my master is not that man you took him for: no Altomaro he, but Bonamico, the decayed artist; he that made properties,[376] and grew poor for want of pictures,[377] who for fear of his creditors left his dwelling and, in this quaint disguise, set up the trade of cozening such wise gentlemen as you are.
GRUTTI AND DONDOLO Bonamico?
CARLO The same.
DONDOLO Oh, that we could reach him again!
CARLO Follow me close, and I will bring you within an hair's breadth of his false beard immediately.
GRUTTI That will be excellent.
DONDOLO Nimbly, good Mercury,[378] nimbly!

Exeunt

[Act III, scene iii]

Enter EUGENIA, FIDELIA, MARDONA, DONELLA, KATHERINA [*and*] CASSIANA

FIDELIA Madam, you are too passive. If you be dejected, what must we, whose hopes and blisses depend upon your fortune?
DONELLA Oh liberty, liberty! Are all the Roman spirits[379] extinct? Never a Brutus[380] in nature, to deliver poor ladies from this captivity?

372 108–9 the mercy of your garters: Philenzo suggests that they hang themselves
373 111 gulled: deceived, mocked
374 114 sconce: head
375 115 crowns: completes the speech's puns on "head"
376 124 properties: spectacular theatrical devices (see Introduction)
377 124 pictures: theatrical tableaux or dumbshows with spectacular props; pictures of rulers on coins
378 133 Mercury: messenger of the gods
379 3 Roman spirits: Romans were famed for resisting tyranny
380 3 Brutus: invokes two characters opposed to tyranny: Julius Caesar's assassin and Lucius Junius Brutus, who initiated the Roman republic

CASSIANA Since there is no probability of our enlargement,[381] let's be merry and despise our sufferings; laugh, tell tales, sing, dance, anything to cozen[382] our melancholy.
EUGENIA There are some thoughts that stick upon my memory I would fain discharge.
KATHERINA Shall we try our lutes,[383] madam?
EUGENIA And voices, if you please.
DONELLA Yes, you may try. They say music built the walls of Thebes:[384] it were a greater miracle if you could charm these to fall. I shall never endure to live an anchorite[385] thus, and[386] it were not for the happiness that I do sometimes dream of a man, I should leap the battlement. Now would I give all my jewels for the sight of a pair of breeches, though there were nothing in 'em. [*They sing*][387]
DONELLA This but feeds our dullness. Shall we dance, madam, and stir ourselves?
CASSIANA I am for that music. We shall grow to the ground and[388] we use no more activity.
EUGENIA With all my heart.
DONELLA None o' your dull measures. There's no sport but in your country figaries. A nimble dance will heat and make us merry. *They dance, which done, a bell rings*
EUGENIA Hark, the bell! *Exit* DONELLA, *and enters again with a letter* [*and jewels*]

DONELLA Some news from the duke. A letter, madam, and these jewels.
EUGENIA Ha! Whence? From Florence? (*reads*) This is my father's practice.[389] I'll peruse the paper. *Exit*
DONELLA I have an excellent hint, ladies, of a mirth cannot but please the princess.
FIDELIA What is't?
DONELLA It will require everyone's endeavor. What if we play some pretty, comic story?
KATHERINA A play?
CASSIANA Shall we?
DONELLA We? Do not distrust your own performance! I ha' known men ha' been insufficient, but women can play their parts.[390]
MARDONA I like it, t'will be new.
DONELLA We will not present it to the princess, but engage her person in the action; we shall be too few, else. Some pretty interlude[391] to square with our number—d'ye allow it?
ALL Willingly.
DONELLA Come, I'll acquaint you with a plot, then, instantly. Refer yourselves to me for your parts. We can receive no disparagement, our spectators cannot jeer us, for we'll speak but to the people in the hangings,[392] and they have as much judgment as some men that are but clothes at most, but walking pictures.
FIDELIA I shall be on't.
CASSIANA What part will you give me? I'll be a king!
KATHERINA Thou'lt play a tyrant bravely.
DONELLA Let me alone. I'll fit you all, I warrant you.

Exeunt

381 5 enlargement: being set free
382 6 cozen: deceive
383 8 lutes: courtly women were trained musicians; music was associated with female sexuality and lutes, in particular, with the alluring courtesan
384 10 music built . . . of Thebes: the music of Amphion, son of Zeus, built the city walls
385 11 anchorite: recluse, hermit
386 12 and: if
387 14 SD *They sing*: missing lyrics indicate that the printer was "given lyrics . . . on separate papers," lost before printing (Stern, 2009: 154). Q has "*Song*," a print marker not a stage direction (see Introduction)
388 16 We shall . . . ground and: We'll take root if
389 22 practice: plotting
390 30 parts: theatrical roles; also body parts
391 33 interlude: play, inter-act entertainment
392 37 people in the hangings: images in the tapestries

[Act III, scene iv]

Enter DONDOLO *and* GRUTTI

DONDOLO Now our invisible merchant is caged, we may redeem our opinion and pass again in the rank of discreet[393] courtiers.
GRUTTI I think now, to most of the beholders, he is invisible all but his head, for he has but a small grate to look out at.
DONDOLO He shall gull no more with his art, I warrant him.
GRUTTI Nay, he is like to lie by't[394] for, I hear since, all his creditors, like so many crows, have light[395] upon him and they'll leave him but a thin carcass.
DONDOLO Let 'em pick out his eyes, what care we?
GRUTTI He sent me an epistle to take pity on him.
DONDOLO But I hope thou hast more wit than to show thyself a Christian to such a rascal as he is?
GRUTTI I returned him my court compliment:[396] that I was sorry I could not serve him; I would do him any office[397] that stretched not to mine own prejudice; that we had taken order with his keeper, upon payment of our sums disbursed, he might be enlarged.
DONDOLO Which is impossible.

Enter BONAMICO [*behind,*] *brave*[398]

[*To* GRUTTI] Prithee, let me see his letter. In what submissive language the rogue does beseech us! [*He reads*] "Most heroic signors,"—Good—"I throw myself at the feet of your mercy; for, to your justice, I beg I may not be made a sacrifice"—Nay, we'll make him beg ere we ha' done.
GRUTTI At the grate.
DONDOLO [*Reads*] "I confess I ha' done you wrong."—Does he so? It shall not serve the turn.—"There is no hope I shall ever satisfy you."—All the better. Lie and rot!—"If I be known a prisoner to my creditors, I am irrecoverably lost. Oh compassionate[399] a miserable man, who otherwise must soon forfeit his daylight and die in a dungeon!" Ha, ha, ha!
BONAMICO [*To* DONDOLO *and* GRUTTI] Save you, noble signors.
GRUTTI Ha!
DONDOLO 'Tis he!
GRUTTI Did he not die in prison, and his ghost haunts us? Brave! 'Tis not he.
BONAMICO "When this eternal substance of my soul
Did live imprisoned in my wanton flesh—"[400]
and so forth. And how d'ye like Don Andrea, gentlemen? Poor snake! But he has cast his skin and recovered a new coat o'th' Destinies' spinning.[401] The bird is flown again.
DONDOLO How the devil came he at liberty?
GRUTTI And thus gallant?[402]
BONAMICO The slave does not beg of your heroic signorship a court compassion: debts must be paid. There is no danger of the grate as the case goes, nor of "forfeiting his daylight in a dungeon," if I mistake not, my illustrious pair of wigeons,[403] my serene smooth-faced coxcombs, whose brains are curdled this hot weather. Will your neat[404] worship sell your cloak, ha? Or you

393 2 discreet: judicious
394 6 lie by't: i.e. in prison
395 7 light: descended
396 12 court compliment: the conventional excuse of an unreliable courtier
397 13 office: service
398 15 SD *brave*: splendidly or finely dressed
399 22 compassionate: pity
400 28–9 "When this . . . wanton flesh": the famous first lines of Don Andrea's ghost to Revenge in Kyd's *Spanish Tragedy* (1585)
401 31 o'th' Destinies' spinning: spun by the fates
402 33 gallant: finely dressed
403 36 wigeons: simpletons, literally a duck
404 37 neat: elegant

that superfluous double-hatched rapier?[405] There be sums in nature to lend you, upon security that I shall like of.

DONDOLO He jeers us!

GRUTTI Would we durst beat him.

BONAMICO You see me now, gentlemen, perfectly. What if I should walk before you without a body, my head hanging in the air like a comet?

Enter [PHILENZO *disguised as*] ROLLIARDO

GRUTTI Would thou wert hanged anyway.
DONDOLO Here's Rolliardo, too. Let's be gone.
BONAMICO Or shall I appoint you a day when I will be invisible, all but my hand?
DONDOLO No, I thank you, sir. We have some business at this present.
GRUTTI Let's to the prison, and know the wonder better. [*To* BONAMICO] Noble signor.
BONAMICO For your crowns—
DONDOLO We are glad we had 'em for you,[406] dear signor. Talk no more on 'em.
Exeunt [DONDOLO *and* GRUTTI]
BONAMICO Farewell phantasmas,[407] then—Ha! 'Tis he! [*To* PHILENZO] Sir.
PHILENZO Keep your way.
BONAMICO You do not know me
But I ha' brought a life[408] which, by your means,
Has been preserved from wretchedness. Your bounty
Deserves[409] you should dispose it.
PHILENZO What are you?
BONAMICO I was the object of a charity
We seldom meet in mankind: from a prison
You sent a sum to free me.
PHILENZO Prithee, friend, if thou'st received a benefit, go home and say thy prayers.
I would forget it.
BONAMICO 'Mong many whom your nobleness enlarged,
I came to make you tender[410] of my service:
Despise not, sir, my gratitude.
PHILENZO D'ye mock me?
BONAMICO May my soul want[411] heaven's mercy, then. To you,
Next my creator,[412] I do owe this, my being.
I have a soul is full of thanks: but name
Employment to assure you,[413] and you make me twice happy.
PHILENZO I ha' nothing to say to you.
BONAMICO Then I ha' something to say to you.
PHILENZO How?
BONAMICO And you shall hear it, too, and give me thanks:
You've sowed your charity in a fruitful ground,
Which shall return it tenfold; nay, one hundred.
What you have done for me, you shall acknowledge,
I will deserve to th' height.[414]

405 38 double-hatched rapier: an ornamented sword
406 50 We are . . . for you: a courteous formula of dismissal
407 51 phantasmas: illusions
408 54 brought a life: i.e. to offer it to Philenzo
409 56 Deserves: i.e. merits that
410 63 tender: offer
411 65 want: lack
412 66 Next my creator: i.e. second only to God
413 68 assure you: make you safe
414 75 to th' height: to the utmost

PHILENZO Thou'rt liberal in language.
BONAMICO I'll be active—off with this sullen face,
It scurvily[415] becomes you, d'ye hear?
I studied for you, since you paid my debts.
I'll do you a courtesy and save your life,
Which your attempt upon the princess has
Left desperate—a happy fancy,[416] sir,
If heaven will please to prosper it, and you
Not be your own enemy to refuse it.
PHILENZO Ha, ha, ha! What mean'st?
BONAMICO Nay, you shall laugh, and heartily, ere I ha' done wi' ye.
The duke does love his daughter, sends her all
Rarities are presented to him.
PHILENZO His soul's not dearer to him, what of that?
BONAMICO Why, then, you shall be admitted into the castle of comfort, that's all. The conceit is in my brain, and would you could as probably get her consent to untie her virgin zone,[417] as I dispose your access to her, it shall not cost you much. If I fail, instead of saying of my prayers I'll curse the Destinies and die with you.
PHILENZO D'ye hear? I ha' bestowed three hundred crowns already to set your heels at liberty; if you do mock me, it shall cost me five hundred, but I'll ha' you clapped up again, where you shall howl all day at the grate for a meal at night from the basket.[418]
BONAMICO You are in earnest now?
PHILENZO Yes.
BONAMICO By all that you have threatened, so am I.
Have but the patience to walk and hear me.
PHILENZO Can thy art procure this?
BONAMICO My art? Why look you, I made this watch [*Gives* PHILENZO *a watch*]. I'll bestow it on you.
PHILENZO What to do? To reckon the hours I ha' to live?
BONAMICO It shan't cost me so much trouble as that toy did to make you master of your wishes still, if heaven prosper it. Come let's talk privately, you shall ha' the plot.
He that doth many good deeds, it may fall,
Among the rest, one may reward them all.
I long to be discoursing it. Pray, lead the way.
PHILENZO Provide again you mock me not. Come on, sir.

[*Exeunt*]

Act IV, scene i

Enter DONDOLO *and* GRUTTI

DONDOLO Rolliardo pay his debts? Sure, the fellow that never saw much money in's life, now by the duke made master of so many sums, is grown mad with 'em!
GRUTTI Many other he hath discharged,[419] they say.
DONDOLO He'll undo[420] the exchequer and[421] he hold on. He shall be chronicled[422] for't.
GRUTTI He has some cause to imagine himself short-lived, and that makes him so desperately charitable toward his end. (*Enter* PERENOTTO) Signor Perenotto.

415 78 scurvily: sorrily, unsatisfactorily
416 82 fancy: invention, design
417 91–2 untie her virgin zone: take her virginity
418 96 basket: charitable donations of food for prisoners were delivered in a basket
419 3 discharged: paid their debts
420 4 undo: ruin
421 4 and: if
422 4 chronicled: memorialized (i.e. the deed will be recorded in historical chronicles)

PERENOTTO Dondolo and Grutti! News, news for ye!

DONDOLO What, we beseech you?

PERENOTTO You have lost the best mirth in Italy in your absence. Your companion, Morello—

DONDOLO Was carried to the duke in a petticoat, in which he attempted a passage to the sequestered ladies. What's the issue?[423]

PERENOTTO Mirth in abundance.

GRUTTI How came he off?[424]

PERENOTTO Nay, 'tis on still. The duke, to make himself sport, would call a council, before whom the poor signor must be arraigned. Not to hold you in circumstance,[425] the business was merrily discussed and the pitiful projector[426] was judged—

DONDOLO How? How?

PERENOTTO To wear the petticoat for a month. If he appear without it during the term,[427] he incurs his perpetual exile from court.

DONDOLO AND GRUTTI Ha, ha, ha!

PERENOTTO You may imagine with what variety of lamentable faces the courtier heard his unexpected sentence. Some would have pleaded for him but for laughter, which continued so long and so high that he had time to collect his scattered senses and, instead of swooning, which was expected, he grew fortified and most humbly besought the duke, since his sentence had passed so definitive,[428] he would be so merciful to admit him that course of a moon[429] to be his jester; that, since he could not shake off the fool's coat, that he might have that favorable pretense to keep it on.

GRUTTI Very good—

PERENOTTO 'Twas easily granted but, ever since, to the astonishment of the hearers, he is grown so jocund and airy,[430] nay, as if he had been born with a song in's head. He talks everlasting ballad. No man laughs at him but he lashes him in rhyme worse than a satyr.[431] The duke has privileged his mirth, made him fool-free, and now he plays the tyrant—

Enter MORELLO, *like a jester*

—He's here already.

MORELLO O yes, o yes, o yes![432]
If there be anyone in city or in town
Can show me a wise man, I'll please him for his pain.

PERENOTTO Disgrace has made him witty.

DONDOLO [*To* MORELLO] What will you say to him will show you a wise man?

MORELLO Marry, if he go far, he is not so wise as he should be. Dondolo! Grutti! Old acquaintance, how is't? How is't?

GRUTTI The case is altered[433] with you.

MORELLO It does appear so. But nothing can make me proud; I'll know my fellows.

PERENOTTO How do you mean, Morello?

MORELLO Your lordship may make one at football,
'Tis all the sport nowadays.
[*Sings*] *What other is the world than a ball,*

423 11 issue: outcome
424 13 How did he fare?
425 15 hold you in circumstance: detain you with circumstantial detail
426 16 projector: entrepreneur
427 18 term: month (i.e. the term of the sentence)
428 25 definitive: i.e. definitively
429 25 course of a moon: a month
430 30 jocund and airy: merry and dismissive
431 31 satyr: see III.i. 59. Morello plays a satirical fool, Rolliardo a satirical madman
432 34 Cry of the town crier
433 41 The case is altered: your situation has changed; "*case*" refers to clothes

Which we run after with whoop and with hollow,[434]
He that doth catch it is sure of a fall,
His heels tripped up by him that doth follow.
DONDOLO Do not women play, too?
GRUTTI They are too light,[435] quickly down.[436]
MORELLO Oh, yes! [*Sings*] *They are the best gamesters of all*
For, though they often lie on the ground,
Not one amongst a hundred will fall
But under her coats the ball will be found.
"With a fading."[437]
But we be three of old— [*To* PERENOTTO] without exception to your lordship—only with this difference: I am the wisest fool, for you play the fool in your old clothes and I have a new coat on.
PERENOTTO Does it not become him?
DONDOLO Rarely well. Do you ever mean to resign it?
GRUTTI 'Twere pity, but he should have a patent[438] for't to him and his posterity.
MORELLO Hark you, gentlemen, d'ye hear the news?
DONDOLO News? What news?
MORELLO D'ye not hear on't yet? Why 'tis in a ballad already.
GRUTTI And thou canst sing it?
MORELLO 'Twas well guessed, and I can but hit o'th' tune.
[*Sings*] *There was an invisible fox by chance*
Did meet with two visible geese,[439]
He led 'em a fine invisible dance
For a hundred crowns a piece.
Invisible all but his hand he would go
But when it came to be tried,
Not only his hand which was left he did show,
But a fair pair of heels beside.
Invisible since their wits have been,
But yet there is hope of either,
Their wit and their crowns may return again,
Invisible altogether. *Exit*
GRUTTI And[440] he continue thus but a moon, he'll make the court mad.
PERENOTTO Oh, 'twill be excellent! Since it is not safe for a wise man to speak truth, 'twere pity fools should lose their privilege.—The duke!

Enter DUKE, FULVIO, *and* COURTIERS

FULVIO My lord.
DUKE What is't?
FULVIO Here's an important suitor calls himself
An artist, humbly craves admittance with
A present which he'd tender[441] to your acceptance
And, if my judgment err not, a most pleasing one.
DUKE Let us see him and his present;
It will reward my daughter's patience,

434 47 *hollow*: a loud shout, of encouragement or for the hunt
435 51 light: wanton
436 51 quickly down: ready and willing to lie down (i.e. for sex)
437 56 *With a fading*: the refrain of a sexual song; an Irish dance; "*fading*" means orgasm
438 62 patent: right, title
439 69 *geese*: easily deceived birds
440 80 And: if
441 87 tender: offer

Love, and obedience. All the rarities
Ten kingdoms yield shall not be thought too weighty
That she may shift each solitary hour
With a fresh object.[442]

Enter BONAMICO. *A cage discovered*[443][*, filled with birds*]

DONDOLO [*To* GRUTTI] Bonamico?
GRUTTI [*To* DONDOLO] 'Tis he!
DUKE By my love to goodness,
It is a masterpiece; 'twill feed the eye
With plenty of delight.
BONAMICO [*Aside*] I am as jocund, since I am admitted; I talk as glib, methinks, as he that farms the monuments.[444]
DUKE Is't not, sirs?
PERENOTTO My lord, I ha' not seen so much delight
In any piece these seven years.
DUKE Where's the master of this work?
BONAMICO My lord, I am the constable that put all these in the cage, and you may call it a point of injustice, for they never kept late hours.[445] Though they all wear feathers, there's not a roarer[446] amongst 'em and, yet, were they suffered, they'd fly high, for some of 'em are very lofty minded.
DUKE A pleasant fellow, too.
BONAMICO Oh, my lord, we're all born in our degrees to make one another merry: the birds make me merry, I make my wife merry, the fool makes your courtiers merry, and the courtiers make your grace merry.
DUKE And whom do I make merry?
BONAMICO The whole commonwealth,[447] if you govern handsomely.
DUKE There's salt in's mirth—
I'll ha' this fellow wait i'th' court.
BONAMICO I shall be kicked out by the pages.
DUKE Why so?
BONAMICO Because I cannot flatter.
DUKE A conceited[448] thing.
We lack the humorist Rolliardo here.
DONDOLO We see[449] him i'th' court ere while, my lord.
DUKE This humor would ha' been a gadfly[450] to him
And stung him to the quick.
BONAMICO [*Aside*] Not altogether so, duke.
GRUTTI [*To* BONAMICO] Fellow, what bird is that?
BONAMICO "Fellow?" Cry mercy, I'd forgot you, fellow. I'll tell thee. D'ye not know him? 'Tis an Arabian woodcock, the same that carried a bunch of grapes in January last to Bethlem Gabor.[451]

442 93–4 shift each . . . fresh object: pass each hour with a new delight
443 94 SD *discovered*: revealed
444 98–9 he that farms the monuments: makes money from tours of the monuments in St. Paul's and Westminster Abbey (Gifford, 1833)
445 105 never kept late hours: i.e. they do not live riotously, like the "roarer" of the following line
446 106 roarer: a riotous, expensively dressed reveler
447 113 commonwealth: state in which "the whole people have a voice" (*OED*). Bonamico satirizes the duke's tyranny
448 119 conceited: witty, full of conceits
449 121 see: will see
450 122 gadfly: a biting fly; a torment
451 127–8 Bethlem Gabor: Gábor Bethlen, prince of Transylvania (1613–29). Transylvania was an Ottoman tributary, hence "Arabian." The bird catalogue reflects the Protestant and Catholic conflict of the Thirty Years' War (1618–48), for which Bethlen was famous, and that between Christian Europe and the Islamic Ottoman Empire.

DONDOLO [*Indicating a bird*] And what call you this?
BONAMICO This was the Duke of Venice his own bullfinch, and taken by the Turks.[452]
DUKE By the Turks say'st thou? He droops indeed.
BONAMICO Since his captivity, the wretch endured
Much misery by the infidel:[453] it had nothing
But bread and water for three months.
FULVIO A shrewd calamity.[454]
DUKE I do affect this fellow's prate.[455]
PERENOTTO [*Indicating a bird*] What's this?
BONAMICO This is the blackbird, which was hatched that day
Gondomar[456] died, and which was ominous;
About that time Spinola's thrush[457] forsook him.
PERENOTTO Was this he?
BONAMICO Yes.
DUKE [*Indicating another bird*] And what was this?
BONAMICO This was the pigeon was so shrewdly handled
For carrying letters at the siege of Bergen.[458]
PERENOTTO Alas, pretty bird.
BONAMICO This a wagtail[459] of the city, which a silkman
So dearly loved he called it wife, but could not
(Though in much jealousy he had caged her up)
Keep her from flying out. This was a rail,[460]
Bred up by a zealous brother in Amsterdam
Which, being sent unto an English lady,
Was ta'en at sea by Dunkirks.[461] Name but Rome
And straight she gapes as she would eat the Pope.
A bird to be made much on: she and the horse
That snorts at Spain by an instinct of nature
Should ha' shown tricks together.[462] I could run over[463]—
But, your gracious pardon.
DUKE How, our pardon?
BONAMICO I'm now another man, and know my distance.
DUKE This man is good at all.
BONAMICO My buffoon[464] face is off. I did but show
The impudent condition of a mountebank
That sets off base toys with miraculous lies.
Thus far I'll boast: they[465] are the only choice[466]

452 130 taken by the Turks: for decades Venice skirmished with the Ottoman Empire. While those "taken by the Turks" could be imprisoned as galley slaves, many were better treated and some converted to Islam
453 133 infidel: a non-Christian, i.e. Muslim
454 135 shrewd calamity: Fulvio notes the covert reference to Eugenia's situation
455 136 prate: chatter, prattle
456 139 Gondomar: Diego Sarmiento de Acuña, Conde de Gondomar, Spanish ambassador to the Jacobean court, unsuccessfully negotiated for marriage between the future Charles I and the Infanta María. He was satirized in Middleton's hugely popular *A Game at Chess* (1624) as the Black Knight, hence the blackbird
457 140 Spinola's thrush: Ambrogio Spinola, Marqués de Balbases, general of Spanish forces in the Netherlands (1602–28). Thrushes were proverbial innocents, caught in traps made from their own droppings; Bonamico perhaps refers to Spinola's ruin in Spanish service
458 145 siege of Bergen: Spinola unsuccessfully laid siege to the Dutch town Bergen-ap-Zoom (Hill, 1974)
459 147 wagtail: a small, fluttering bird; a profligate or inconstant woman
460 150 rail: a kind of bird; punning on the ranting ("railing") of "extreme Protestant sects from Amsterdam" (Sanders, 2006)
461 153 Dunkirks: pirates from the French town
462 155–7 she and … tricks together: touring performers displayed trained animals; the examples given here seem intended to pander to English anti-Catholicism in the midst of the Thirty Years' War
463 157 run over: keep talking
464 161 buffoon: clown, street performer
465 164 they: the birds
466 164 only choice: choicest

Italy and other parts of Europe yield.
For the work, if it prove so fortunate
To receive grace from your divine acceptance,
The workmanship (so duty suffer not)
I freely tender.
DUKE No, that were to quench
The fire in all deservers[467]—Fulvio.
FULVIO My lord?
DUKE Pay the cost double. I'll send it to my daughter.
BONAMICO [*Aside*] It takes, as art could wish it!
DUKE I know it is a present the sweet soul
Will raise much joy in.—Signor Perenotto?
PERENOTTO My lord? [*They speak aside*]
BONAMICO [*To* DONDOLO *and* GRUTTI] There are two birds I ha' not named.
DONDOLO [*To* BONAMICO] What are they?
BONAMICO [*To* DONDOLO *and* GRUTTI] A pair of gulls,[468] which you may share between you.
PERENOTTO [*To* DUKE] It shall, my lord.
DUKE If Florence now keep touch,[469] we shortly shall
Conclude all fear with a glad nuptial.

Exeunt

[Act IV, scene ii]

Enter EUGENIA, FIDELIA, MARDONA, DONELLA, CASSIANA [*and*] KATHERINA

DONELLA Ye like this story best, then?
EUGENIA That of Jupiter and Danae[470] comes near our own.
DONELLA Be it so. We are all perfect in[471] the plot, I think.
EUGENIA You shall dispose the rest.[472]
DONELLA You will not be ambitious, then, and quarrel about the parts, like your spruce actor that will not play out of the best clothes, and the fine young prince who, if he fight, 'tis six to four he kills all and gets the lady?[473]
FIDELIA We are constant. You shall appoint 'em.
DONELLA [*To* EUGENIA] Then, madam, without ceremony, you shall play Danae, that is shut up in the brazen tower.
EUGENIA Well, I'm contented. 'Twill suit with my present fortune.
DONELLA I need not to instruct you in the character. [*To* MARDONA] You shall be the king, Acrisius, her father; a jealous, harsh, crabbed[474] man who, in fear of the oracle, commands her to be thus enclosed.
MARDONA So. I'll fit you for a vinegar[475] king.
DONELLA No matter for properties—we'll imagine, madam, you have a beard.
FIDELIA What shall I play?
DONELLA [*To* FIDELIA, CASSIANA, *and* KATHERINA] You must be ladies whom the king leaves to keep her company. Entertain what humor you please.
CASSIANA AND KATHERINA This is our own parts, indeed!

467 170 deservers: the duke insists on paying; European courts spent lavishly on art to boost princely magnificence
468 179 gulls: dupes
469 182 keep touch: remain true
470 2 Jupiter and Danae: see I.i. 248–9
471 3 are all perfect in: have all memorized
472 4 the rest: like an experienced player, Donella organizes casting, props, audience, and musical effects
473 5–7 your spruce . . . the lady: mocking dramatic conventions
474 13 crabbed: irritable, churlish
475 15 vinegar: acidic

DONELLA Ye will play it the more naturally. And let me alone to play the thunderer; I'll wanton Jove it! Now, whet your inventions and about it. Imagine our scene expressed and "The New Prison," the title, advanced in form.[476]

EUGENIA "The New Prison?" Why?

DONELLA Oh, 'tis an excellent name, where spectators throng together, as ours do, methinks, in the arras already.[477] The music ha' their part.[478] Dispose yourselves for your entrances while I speak the prologue to our mixed audience of silk and cruel[479] gentlemen in the hangings. Hem![480]

KATHERINA Let it be a confident prologue, howsoever. *Music*[481]

DONELLA [*As Prologue*] *You're welcome to New Prison! We have still*
Our ancient keeper, and we fear he will
Speak in his old key, too. But do not look for
Choice diet for, alas, we play the cook for
All you are like to feed on. Let your palate
Expect at most, then, but a root or salad
Picked from the prison garden. We know you are
Judicious hangings, and well seen; nor dare
We lift you up—too bold!—lest we incense
Your green and spreading wits with impudence.
As I began, let me conclude in rhyme:
Hang still, you learnèd critics of the time.
[*To* EUGENIA, CASSIANA *and* KATHERINA] Now, Danae and the ladies.[482]

[DONELLA *partly hides behind the arras*]

EUGENIA [*As Danae*] *Was ever father to his child*
So unkind? It makes me wild
When, to beguile a tedious hour
From the top of this high tower,
I see every other creature,
Enjoy a liberty by nature.
Can the silver running fountains
And the cloud-aspiring mountains,
Every grove and flowery field,
But a new affliction yield?

DONELLA This is excellent! She has played the part before.

CASSIANA [*As Lady*] *Waste not yourself in woeful plaint;*
Sorrow will not help restraint.
Think, madam, all is but a dream
That we are in—Now I am out[483]—*Beam? Cream?*[484]
Help me, Katherina! I can make no sense rhyme to't.

DONELLA "Cream" is as good a rhyme as your mouth can wish. Ha, ha, ha!

CASSIANA Does not the arras laugh at me? It shakes, methinks.

KATHERINA It cannot choose; there's one behind[485] does tickle it.

476 23 the title, advanced in form: play titles were advertised on placards

477 25–6 where spectators . . . arras already: i.e. in embroidered tapestry figures; the Cockpit audience's rich clothes are imagined as the hangings of a Whitehall court chamber (see III.iii. 37)

478 26 The music ha' their part: Q omits musical directions

479 27 cruel: puns on "crewel" embroidery (Sanders, 2006)

480 27 Hem!: she clears her throat

481 28 SD the music accompanying *New Prison* goes without comment by the characters: but see "To Master William Prynne," 11–13. The Cockpit musicians played between acts. Alternatively, the silent Fidelia might play a lute: see III.iii. 8

482 41 Now . . . ladies: Donella acts like a prompter

483 56 out: out of my part, i.e. I have forgotten my lines

484 56 *Beam? Cream?*: a weak improviser, Cassiana runs through the alphabet (see line 113)

485 60 one behind: i.e. Donella

EUGENIA [*As Danae*] *A dream? Alas, 'tis no relief*
For us to flatter so much grief.
Fancy[486] *wants power to delight*
Or, if we could think it might,
Such a dream so sad would make us,
That it could not choose but wake us.
DONELLA My lady has helped her pretty well out of her dream.
KATHERINA [*As Lady*] *The sun with glittering golden rays*
May appear one of these days.
You know always after winter,
Comes the spring and pleasant summer.
DONELLA "Winter" and "summer?" Ha, ha, ha!
MARDONA "Winter" and "summer"? By my faith, that's well; there's but half a year between! There be some call themselves poets, make their rhymes straddle so wide[487] a twelvemonth will hardly reconcile 'em; and, I hope, a lady may straddle a little by poetical licence.
CASSIANA [*As Lady*] *Madam, your father, King Acrisius!*
MARDONA Must I enter already? Hum!
EUGENIA [*As Danae*] *This is his hour to visit us.*
MARDONA [*as Acrisius*] *How fares our daughter?*
CASSIANA What voice is that?
DONELLA The king speaks through a trunk.[488]
MARDONA [*As Acrisius*] *How is't, heroic birth?*[489] *What dullness, cold*
As Saturn's,[490] *dwells on thy forehead? Be bold*
To give thy grief a tongue: instruct, child
My paternal nature, lest I grow wild
As the rude North.[491] *Thought of thee makes my hairs*
Silver, my blood is curdled with my cares.
DONELLA Most high and mighty nonsense! Sure, the king has swallowed pills[492] and, his stomach not able to digest 'em, does vomit 'em up again.
MARDONA [*As Acrisius*] *Is thy organ*[493] *dumb?*
Or am I grown cheap in majesty? Trivial fool!
Shall I reap crabbed thistles in neglect for rich love?
CASSIANA Crabbed language, I am sure.
DONELLA Sure, my lady does not understand him.
EUGENIA [*As Danae*] *If my brow so sad appear,*
My fortune's livery[494] *I wear.*
MARDONA [*As Acrisius*] *Weep no more, thy eyes pave the ground with pearl.*
My power is 'rased,[495] *my crown thy tribute, girl.*
Here is nothing to want.
EUGENIA [*As Danae*] *Nothing to want, indeed! To be*
A prisoner speaks all misery.
MARDONA [*As Acrisius*] *Curse not thy soft stars, but take thy fair bliss*
With comfort; free from loud noise and fear is

486 63 *Fancy*: imagination
487 74 make their … so wide: place their rhymes so far apart; "straddle" has sexual connotations, especially when repeated in the next line
488 81 trunk: tube to project sound
489 82 *birth*: i.e. my daughter
490 82–3 *cold/As Saturn's*: the god Saturn was associated with melancholia
491 86 *North*: North wind
492 88 pills: medicine; perhaps also testicles and so gestures to Mardona's femininity, Acrisius's masculinity, and the boy actor playing both
493 90 *organ*: i.e. of speech
494 96 *livery*: uniform, clothing identifying a servant's household
495 98 *'rased*: i.e. erased

Thy gaudy station. When I have unscrewed[496]
Mystic oracles which—not understood—
Do perplex with involved sense, I shall then
Enlarge thy person, Danae. 'Till when,
If aught else do clog thy thoughts with unkind
Thoughts, unload the dark burden of thy mind;
Pronounce thy grief aloud, my amorous darling
And I will—
CASSIANA [*To* EUGENIA] Let him[497] choose his rhyme, I beseech you, madam!
MARDONA Uh, uh—Cold phlegm[498] obstructs my language—"Barling? Carling?"
DONELLA Ha, ha! 'Tis time to make an end; he was almost choked with his own phrase.
MARDONA And you get me[499] to play an old man again—
DONELLA We'll have a young one for thee. Twenty one and a coat is a double game.[500]—My turn comes next! [*Exit* DONELLA. MARDONA *withdraws*]
EUGENIA [*As Danae*] *He's gone, and leaveth us behind*
To tell our passions to the wind.
Ha? What o'th' sudden doth surprise
My active motion? On my eyes
What dark and heavy cloud doth sit
To persuade me it is night?
It is some charm; I cannot keep
These windows[501] *open—I must sleep.* [*She lies on a couch*]

Enter [*DONELLA, as*] *Jupiter*

CASSIANA This was well passionated! Now comes Jupiter to take my lady napping. We'll sleep, too;[502] let the wanton[503] have her swinge[504]—would she were a man, for her[505] sake!
DONELLA [*As Jupiter*] *Let the music of the spheres*[506]
Captivate these mortal ears,
While Jove descends into this tower
In a golden streaming shower,
To disguise him from the eye
Of Juno,[507] *who is apt to pry*
Into my pleasures. I today
Have bid Ganymede[508] *go play,*
And thus stole from heaven to be
Welcome on earth to Danae.
And see where the princely maid
On her easy couch is laid,
Fairer than the Queen of Love's,[509]
Drawn about with milky doves.

496 104 *unscrewed*: interpreted, untangled
497 112 him: the male character, not Mardona the actress
498 113 Cold phlegm: Mardona is coughing
499 115 And you get me: i.e. If you ever get me
500 116 Twenty one . . . double game: perhaps the French card game *vingt-et-un*
501 125 *windows*: i.e. eyes
502 126–7 We'll sleep, too: we won't stop her
503 127 wanton: lustful, indulgent person
504 127 swinge: will, liberty
505 127 her: Eugenia's or Donella's
506 128 *music of the spheres*: celestial, divine music, created by the moving spheres of Renaissance cosmology
507 133 *Juno*: Jove's jealous wife
508 135 *Ganymede*: a beautiful young boy, cupbearer to Jove and object of his desire
509 140 *Queen of Love's*: Venus's

To thee let Paphian[510] *altars smoke,*
Priests thy better name invoke.
When Hymen[511] *lights his holy fires,*
Thou, that canst infuse desires
In the gods, from thy lip
Let Jove heavenly nectar sip
And translate,[512] *by kissing thee,*
Into thy breast his deity.
But I rob myself of treasure:
This[513] *is but the gate of pleasure.*
To dwell here, it were a sin,
When Elysium[514] *is within.*
Leave off then this flattering kisses,
To rifle[515] *other greater blisses—* *Bell* [*rings*] *within*
EUGENIA The bell! News from my father.
CASSIANA Then your play is interrupted, Jove!—Madam, I'll see. [*Exit*]
DONELLA Beshrew[516] the bellman! And you had not waked as you did, madam, I should ha' forgot myself and played Jupiter indeed with you. My imaginations were strong upon me, and you lay so sweetly— [*Enter* CASSIANA] How now?
CASSIANA A present, madam, from the duke: one of the finest pieces of pageantry[517] that e'er you saw. 'Tis a cage with variety of birds in it. It moves on wheels—your assistance, ladies, to bring it in. [*Exeunt* LADIES]
EUGENIA A cage! If from Florence, it shall to the fire,
Or whencesoe'er. It cannot be intended
But as a mockery of my restraint.
I'm very sad o'th' sudden. [*They bring in the cage*] Ha! 'Tis so!
Break it to pieces!
DONELLA 'Twere pity, madam, to destroy so much art.
EUGENIA Yet spare the workmanship. In the perusal
There's something pleads for mercy. I feel within[518]
Some alteration, I know not what.
Let me entreat your absence for some minutes.
I am in earnest; pray do, without reply.
Your eyes shall feed with plenteous satisfaction
On this gay[519] object when I call you.
LADIES We obey you. [*Exeunt* LADIES]
EUGENIA Yet can't I say I am alone, that have
So many partners in captivity!
[*To the birds*] Sweet fellow prisoners! 'Twas a cruel art,
The first invention to restrain the wing,
To keep th'inhabitants o'th' air close captive
That were created to sky-freedom. Surely
The merciless creditor took his first light[520]

510 142 *Paphian*: from Paphos, i.e. Cyprus; the island was the mythical birthplace of Venus
511 144 *Hymen*: god of marriage
512 148 *translate*: convey
513 151 *This*: i.e. kissing
514 153 *Elysium*: paradise
515 155 *rifle*: search thoroughly, plunder
516 158 Beshrew: curse
517 161 pieces of pageantry: the mobile pageant cars of London's civic performances, such as the Lord Mayor's show, or Shirley's 1634 court masque, *The Triumph of Peace* (Sanders, 2006)
518 171 within: i.e. within herself
519 176 gay: brilliant, showy
520 184 light: inspiration

And prisons their first models from such bird loops?[521]
I know yon nightingale[522] is not long-lived;
See how that turtle[523] mourns, wanting her mate.
And doth the duke, my father, think I can
Take comfort either in restraint, or in
The sight of these that every moment do
Present it to me? Were these tendered[524] me?
They shall no more be prisoners to please me,
Nor shall the woods be robbed of so much music.

She opens the cage and [PHILENZO, *disguised as*] ROLLIARDO *comes* [*out*] *from the pillar*[525]

PHILENZO I take you at your word, fair princess;
I am the truest prisoner! Tremble not!
Fear flies the noble mind, for injury dares not come near.
EUGENIA Sir, what are you?
PHILENZO The humblest of your servants.
EUGENIA You are not mine, for in this bold attempt
You have undone me.
PHILENZO You see I keep at distance.
EUGENIA Y'are too near. [*Starts to leave*] I will discover you, though
I fall myself by your presumption.
PHILENZO Hold, be counseled rather
But to calm silence for a pair of minutes
And none shall perish. You shall save him, too,
That would for your sake lose himself for ever.
EUGENIA For my sake? What relation has my birth,
Or any passion I call mine, to you?
PHILENZO Nor doom me unto scorn. I am a gentleman,
And when my inimitable resolution
In those attempts—whose very sounds breeds earthquakes
In other hearers—shall your knowledge fill
With wonder and amaze,[526] you will at least
Think I fall too low, if I love beneath you.
EUGENIA Ha! This is a strange accident.[527]
PHILENZO Was it less
Than death, dear princess, to adventure hither?
EUGENIA It will be death, however.
PHILENZO You're deceived, lady.
EUGENIA How! I'm perplexed.
PHILENZO It had been death:
Your sight gives me a lease of longer life;
My head stands fast.
EUGENIA [*Aside*] He speaks all mystery.
I shall not get him off,[528] I fear, without some stain.[529]
PHILENZO The truth is, princess, if you now discover[530] me—

521 185 bird loops: snares for catching birds
522 186 nightingale: an image of female mourning; in classical mythology, Philomel, raped by Tereus, transformed into the bird to sing her lament
523 187 turtle: turtle dove; proverbially faithful and monogamous
524 191 tendered: offered
525 193 SD *pillar*: the cage includes a pillar big enough to conceal Philenzo and an opening through which he emerges onto the stage
526 212 amaze: amazement
527 214 accident: occurrence
528 220 get him off: get rid of him
529 220 stain: i.e. on her honor
530 221 discover: reveal

Though I made nice[531] at first to put your fright by—
You cannot harm me much. I ha' done my task.
Do you fear me still? Why is there such a space
Betwixt us, lady? Can you keep that man
At so unkind a distance, that for your sake
Has in his undertaking swallowed danger,
Robbed death of all his fears?
EUGENIA For my sake?
PHILENZO Yours. Fair princess, dare you so far trust me yet
To let me kiss your hand?
EUGENIA Audacious sir,
I shall grow loud if you forget your distance,
Nor that you may hold long—
[*Aside*] I'm studying how I should be rid of him
Without their[532] knowledge. Yet that's dangerous too,
And might show guilt in me, for he will boast on't.
PHILENZO Such was the duke your gracious father's care,
He would put confidence in none about him
But saw me brought himself.
EUGENIA This is a fine paradox!
PHILENZO Which must be to high purpose. Come, be wise
And keep me while you have me. [*Aside*] 'Tis but reaping
This fruitless harvest from my cheek and chin[533]
And you can form the rest.[534] [*To* EUGENIA] Y'are young and beautiful:
Lose not the blessing of your youth, sweet princess;
Fair opportunity waits upon your pleasure.
You want but the first knowledge of your joy.
Your blood is ripe. Come, I am confident.
Your will[535] is but controlled by upstart fears,
Like advanced beggars that will check their princes.[536]
My safest way is yours now, to conceal me;
It may be thought I have enjoyed you else.
Ill censure soon takes fire. Nay, perhaps
To be revenged of your stern cruelty,
I'll swear myself I have possessed you freely.
Play your game wisely, then; your honor lies
Full at my mercy. Come, 'tis in your love
To lead me to a secret couch.
EUGENIA Bold villain!
[*Starts to leave*] For these uncivil, most unhallowed words,
I'll die but I'll undo thee.
PHILENZO Stay, and let me circle in mine arms
All happiness at once! I have not soul
Enough to apprehend my joy; it spreads
Too mighty for me. Know, excellent Eugenia,
I am the Prince of Florence,[537] that owe heaven
More for thy virtues than his own creation.
I was born with guilt enough to cancel

531 222 made nice: scrupled, hesitated
532 234 their: i.e. her women's
533 241–2 reaping . . . and chin: i.e. removing his false ("fruitless") beard
534 243 you can form the rest: i.e. you will be able to recognize me
535 248 will: sexual desire
536 249 As if a monarch were controlled by pushy commoners
537 264 I am . . . of Florence: audiences may believe this statement; the prince is referred to at I.i. 129–30 and II.i. 481–8

My first purity, but so chaste a love
As thine will so refine my second being,
When holy marriage frames us in one piece,
Angels will envy me.
EUGENIA Ha! The Prince of Florence?
PHILENZO I ha' made no travail[538] for so rich a blessing.
Turn me to pilgrimage, divinest beauty,
And when I ha' put a girdle 'bout the world,[539]
This purchase will reward me.
EUGENIA Purchase? I am not bought and sold, I hope?
PHILENZO Give it what name you will, you're mine, Eugenia.
EUGENIA Yours, prince? I do not know
By what title you pretend this claim;
I never yet remember that I saw you,
And if I had any interest in myself,[540]
Produce your witness, when I gave it you.
I have possession yet; ere I deliver it,
You must show stronger evidence.
PHILENZO Are we not contracted?
EUGENIA Contracted?
When? Where? Good prince, I pity your abuse.
PHILENZO 'Tis firm between our fathers.
EUGENIA Mine cannot give away my heart.
PHILENZO Cannot?
EUGENIA Shall not, prince.
It is not your travail and your trouble,
With this conceit[541] to boot—were it your own
Invention, with all your birds about you—
That can take me.
PHILENZO Is it my person, madam,
You hold unworthy? For my birth and fortune
Cannot deserve your scorn.
EUGENIA It takes not from
The greatness of your state or blood, my lord,
To say I cannot love you, since affection
Flows uncompelled and rests in the clear[542] object.
Nor do I rob your person of just value
If to me other[543] seem as fair and comely;
Form may apparel and become what we
Affect,[544] not cause true love. You have enough
To promise you a happier choice: attempt
A nobler fate and leave me to myself
And humble destiny. For know, Florentine,
I have but one faith, one love, and though my father
Lock up my person, 'tis beyond his will
To make me false to him I gave my faith to,
And y'are not noble now if you proceed.
Be then what you were born, and do not tempt

538 271 travail: labor (i.e. work or childbirth); travel
539 273 put a . . . the world: circumnavigated the globe
540 280 interest in myself: stake in my own future
541 290 this conceit: the bird cage
542 297 clear: virtuous
543 299 other: i.e. another
544 300–01 Form may . . . Affect: outer show might furnish and grace the inner qualities that we love

A woman to commit a sacrilege:
For when I give my heart to any other
Than my Philenzo, I commit that sin.
PHILENZO If you'll not pardon, I'll deliver up
Philenzo to be punished for this trial (*He discovers himself*[545]) See, lady!
EUGENIA [*Kneels*] My dear banished Philenzo!
PHILENZO Oh, let not such a glorious building[546] stoop,
[*Kneels*] It is my duty.
EUGENIA I will make it mine.
PHILENZO I have a double duty, for I owe
Your constancy as much respect and reverence
As your most princely person. [*They stand*]
EUGENIA What for our safety?
PHILENZO Oh, with what willingness could I be lost
In this distracted wilderness of joy!
Tomorrow, madam, I go to my arraignment.[547]
EUGENIA How?
PHILENZO Spend no fear upon't,
Your story shall be pleasing. I ha' much
To tell you. For your ladies—
EUGENIA They are mine; what should our innocence
Fear in their knowledge? I desire to hear
The circumstance of this wonder.
PHILENZO It attends.[548]
The story past, we must some counsel find;[549]
The puzzle of our fate is still behind.[550]

Exeunt

Act V, scene i

Enter DONDOLO, MORELLO, GRUTTI

DONDOLO We are sorry we gave thee distaste. Come, let's be friends, you did apprehend too nicely.[551]
MORELLO Nicely? It might ha' been your own case.
GRUTTI Come, you were unkind to rub[552] us before the duke so.
MORELLO Be wise hereafter, and make the fool[553] your friend; 'tis many an honest man's case at court. It is safer to displease the duke than his jester: every sentence the one speaks flatterers make an oracle, but let the impudent fool bark never so absurdly, other men ha' the wit to make a jest on't. 'Tis policy in state to maintain a fool at court to teach great men discretion.
DONDOLO AND GRUTTI Great men? We are none.
MORELLO No, but you may be, by the length of your wit and shortness of your memory; for if you have but wit enough to do mischief, and oblivion enough to forget good turns, you may come to great places in time. Keep a fool o'your own, and then you are made—
DONDOLO Made what?

545 314 SD the audience finally sees Philenzo's true identity; he may remove his false beard
546 316 building: temple, body
547 323 arraignment: trial
548 329 attends: waits to be told
549 330 some counsel find: seek out advice
550 331 behind: to come
551 1–2 apprehend too nicely: feel it too sensitively
552 4 rub: irritate, annoy
553 5 fool: jester

MORELLO Cuckolds, if my lady take a liking to the innocent.[554] Oh, your fool is an excellent fellow upon all occasions!

[*Sings*] *Among all sorts of people*
The matter, if we look well to,
The fool is the best, he from the rest,
Will carry away the bell,[555] *too.*
All places he is free of[556]
And fools it without blushing.
At masques and plays, is not the bays[557]
Thrust out, to let the plush[558] *in?*
Your fool is fine, he's merry,
And of all men doth fear least,
At every word he jests with my lord,
And tickles[559] *my lady in earnest.*
The fool doth pass the guard now,
He'll kiss his hand and leg it.[560]
When wise men prate and forfeit their state,
Who but the fine fool will beg it?
He without fear can walk in
The streets that are so stony;
Your gallant sneaks, your merchant breaks,[561]
He's a fool that does owe no money.

Enter [PHILENZO *disguised as*] ROLLIARDO

PHILENZO The duke, where is the duke?
MORELLO He's forthcoming; there's no more money i'th' exchequer.
PHILENZO I come to give up my accounts and reckon with him, somebody tell him so.
MORELLO And you do not reckon well with him, he'll be even with you. I'll do your message.
PHILENZO Do, and say I sent a fool o' my errand. [*Exit* MORELLO]
Prithee, cry mercy, such an office would ha' become either of you gentlemen.
DONDOLO His tongue moves circular in abuses.
GRUTTI The duke!

Enter DUKE, FULVIO, PERENOTTO, [*and Attendants*]

DUKE How now, what day is't?
PHILENZO 'Tis holiday.
DUKE How?
PHILENZO Therefore we are preparing a morris[562] to make your grace merry. They have chosen me for the hobby-horse,[563] and if I do not deceive their expectation, they will laugh at me extremely before I die.
DUKE Do you come like one prepared for death?
PHILENZO Not so well, I hope, as I may be hereafter, unless you will be unjust, and have a

554 14 innocent: a halfwit, i.e. the fool
555 19 *carry away the bell*: to win the prize; proverbial
556 20 *is free of*: has access to
557 22 *bays*: laurel wreaths awarded in poetry competitions
558 23 *plush*: velvet; fashion is rewarded over intellectual ability
559 27 *tickles*: makes laugh, with a sexual innuendo
560 29 *leg it*: bow
561 34 *breaks*: is bankrupted
562 47 morris: English folk dance
563 48 hobby-horse: horse costume worn by morris dancers

desire to be clapped into the chronicles[564] with some o' your predecessors for cutting off heads when you do not like their complexion. 'Tis but laying one block upon another,[565] and I am quickly sent of a headless errand.
DUKE Unjust? Do you remember what sums you owe for? Do not jest away your life.
PHILENZO I crave no longer day for't, and I prove not myself free from my engagements.
DUKE How?
PHILENZO For, although I had not the art to go invisible as these wise courtiers, nor could counterfeit another sex so becomingly as t'other gaudy signor, to introduce me to the ladies, yet, with your princely licence, I may say, 'tis done.
DUKE Done? What is done?
PERENOTTO He's mad, sir.
PHILENZO I come not to petition for a mercy
But to cry up my merit for a deed
Shall drown all story; and posterity,
When it shall find in her large chronicle
My glorious undertaking, shall admire it
More than a Sybil's leaf,[566] and lose itself
In wonder of the action. Poets shall
With this make proud their muses, and apparel it
In ravishing numbers,[567] which the soft-haired virgins—
Forgetting all their legends and love tales
Of Venus, Cupid, and the scapes of Jove—
Shall make their only song, and in full choir
Chant it at Hymen's feast.
DUKE What means this boasting?
FULVIO Rolliardo?
PHILENZO You think I am a lost man, and your gay things,[568]
That echo to your passions and see through
Your eyes all that's presented, do already
Tickle their very souls with expectation
To see me beg most miserably for life.
But you are all deceived. Here I pronounce
The great work done that cancels all my debts:
I have had access unto the fair Eugenia,
Your princely daughter; stayed, discoursed with her.
More, she has entertained me for her servant.[569]
PERENOTTO Sir, do you believe him?
DUKE Thou hast profaned a name will strike thee dead!
PHILENZO It cannot be, for if you mean your daughter,
'Tis that is my preserver: blest Eugenia,
To whose memory my heart does dedicate
Itself an altar, in whose very mention
My lips are hallowed, and the place a temple
Whence the divine sound came. It is a voice
Which, should our holy churchmen use it, might
Without addition of more exorcism
Disenchant houses, tie up nightly spirits
Which fright the solitary groves. Eugenia,

564 52 chronicles: histories
565 53 laying one block upon another: putting one's head ("block") on the executioner's block
566 68 Sybil's leaf: the Sibyl, a classical prophetess, delivered divinations written on palm leaves
567 71 numbers: poetic meter
568 77 gay things: lavishly dressed courtiers
569 86 entertained me for her servant: accepted him as a suitor

When I have named, I needs must love my breath
The better after it.
DUKE Thou hast undone
Thyself i'th' repetition, and in this
Wherein thou cunningly wouldst beg our pity,
Thou hast destroyed it and not left a thought
To plead against our anger. Where before
Thy life should have been gently invited forth,[570]
Now, with a horrid circumstance, death shall
Make thy soul tremble, and, forsaking all
The noble parts, it[571] shall retire into
Some angle of thy body and be afraid
To inform thy eyes, lest they let in a horror
They would not look on.
PHILENZO I am still the same.[572] And let me be so bold
To plead your royal word: 'twas my security.
Nor shall you take mine to induce your faith
To what is done. I have more pregnant evidence.
[*Gives* DUKE *a letter*] Your highness knows that character.[573]
DUKE Ha! 'Tis not so. I'll not believe my eyes.
Come hither, Fulvio, Perenotto: read [*Gives* PERENOTTO *the letter*]
But not too loud. Does she not write to me,
"It is unjust you let Rolliardo die
Unless Eugenia bear him company"?
Give me the paper!
PERENOTTO 'Tis counterfeit, my lord. Cut off my head
If this be not a jig[574] of his invention.
DUKE My soul is in a sweat. I feel my blood
Heave in my veins. He looks as he had seen her.
More, my prophetic thoughts do whisper to me.
FULVIO Believe it not, sir.
DUKE I won't.—Perenotto! [*Takes* PERENOTTO *aside*]
DONDOLO I know not what to think.
GRUTTI The duke's perplexed. Observe.
PHILENZO [*To* DONDOLO *and* GRUTTI] Will either of you speak for me, gentlemen, if the justice of my cause should fail me? I'll pay you for't. I know courtiers that live upon countenance[575] must sell their tongues: what is the price of yours, pray?
GRUTTI Humble yourself, you coxcomb!
DUKE [*To* PERENOTTO] Away— [*Exit* PERENOTTO]
and let not him stir, I charge you.
[*Aside*] This does entrench[576] too much upon her person.
Have my endeavors to preserve Eugenia,
Of whom I thought so many men unworthy,
Ruined themselves? Human invention
Could not instruct me to dispose her where
She could be more defensed[577] from all men's eyes;
An anchorite lives not prisoned in a wall

570 105 gently invited forth: taken without violence
571 108 it: i.e. your soul
572 112 still the same: unmoved, constant
573 116 character: handwriting; identity or personality; theatrical role
574 124 jig: sport, cheat
575 132–3 upon countenance: by feigned show or outward appearance
576 136 entrench: trespass or infringe upon
577 141 defensed: defended

With more security. 'Tis not possible!
Why am I troubled thus? My fear abuses me.
In such a cause I would check[578] an oracle.
And shall his dexterous forgery unsettle
My confidence? I won't show a guilt
Of so much weakness in me—Fulvio
And gentlemen, we'll speak to you anon.
PHILENZO [*Aside*] I ha' spoke too much already, it seems. Sure he has sent for her.
I dare repose my life on her to whose trust I gave my heart: she is a thousand witnesses in herself.
FULVIO [*To* DUKE] It will be mirth, sir.
PHILENZO [*Aside*] I like not this consulting, they break off pleasantly. Now, in the name of Mercury, what crotchet?[579]
DUKE [*To* PHILENZO] I see it is in vain
To interrupt our fate; what is decreed
Above becomes not mortals to dispute.
Sit there [*Indicates the throne*]. Nay, be not modest; you were born to't
And therefore take your place. [PHILENZO *sits*] Nay, nay, be covered:[580]
Imagine that[581] a crown, and these[582] your subjects
As, when I die, you know 'twill come to that,
In right of my sole daughter[583]—so, does he not
Look like a prince indeed? Appears he not
A pretty lump of majesty?
DONDOLO He's studying some speech, I'll lay my life—
DUKE Against[584] his coronation, to thank all
His loving subjects, that as low as earth
Thus offer him their duties. [COURTIERS] *draw their swords* [*against* PHILENZO]

[*Enter*] EUGENIA *and* PERENOTTO

EUGENIA Hold, I beseech you!
[*To* DUKE] Let not my duty suffer misconstruction
If, while my knee doth beg your blessing, here
I throw my arms and circle, next to heaven,
What must be dearest to me. [*She kneels and embraces* PHILENZO]
DUKE Ha!
EUGENIA [*To* PHILENZO] My joy of life!
DUKE Destroy me not!
EUGENIA [*To* DUKE] Alas, I would preserve all; am so far from killing
That would I die myself rather than see
One drop of blood forced from his crimson fountain,
Or but one tear racked from your eye. Oh hear me,
And after let your anger strike two dead,
So you would let us dwell both in one grave.
And did you know[585] how near we were in life,
You would not think it fitting that in death
Our ashes were divided. You have heard,

578 145 check: reject, refute
579 155 crotchet: fanciful device or plan
580 160 covered: keep your hat on
581 161 that: i.e. his hat
582 161 these: the courtiers
583 162–3 when I . . . sole daughter: Philenzo's descendents would inherit the dukedom
584 167 Against: in preparation for
585 181 did you know: if you knew

When the poor turtle's[586] ravished[587] from her mate,
The orphaned dove doth groan away her life
In widow's solitude: let me call him husband
And tell yourself the rest.
DUKE Kill not thy father with one word, Eugenia:
Thy husband?
EUGENIA I do beseech you, hear me.
DUKE Beg thou may'st be forgotten. 'Tis sin
'Bove my forgiveness—this a match for thee?
What man can bring me a certificate
He had a father, or was christened? He?
We all are in a dream: awake me, thunder!
PHILENZO Temper[588] your passion, sir.
DUKE Some tortures, to enforce confession from him
How he procured access.
PHILENZO They shall not need: you sent me, sir, yourself.
DUKE We?
PHILENZO The cage was my conveyance.
PERENOTTO [*To* DUKE] That was presented lately with the birds. You gave command.
DUKE Be dumb! I dare not hear you.
DONDOLO This was a "Bird in a Cage" indeed!
DUKE [*To* GRUTTI] Search for the traitor Bonamico presently;
He has betrayed me. They shall suffer both
Before the noise[589] be spread to our dishonor. [*Exit* GRUTTI]
EUGENIA Yet will you hear me?
DUKE I hear too much. Thou hast forgot thy birth,
Thy fortunes, and thy father. Were my cares
So wondered at abroad, censured at home,
Worthy of nothing but contempt from thee
For whom they were begotten? Thou hast ploughed
Upon my face;[590] canst thou undo a wrinkle
Or change but the complexion of one hair?
Yet thou hast grayed a thousand; taken from me,
Not added to my comforts, more than what,
Like an indulgent parent, I have flattered
Myself into.

Enter BONAMICO [*and* GRUTTI]

GRUTTI Here is the other traitor, sir.
DUKE Away with 'em to death.
EUGENIA Let me go too.
DUKE It needs not; thou art dead already, girl,
And, in thy shame, I and the dukedom suffer.
Thou may'st remember—false to thy own vow—
Philenzo, whom I banished for thy sake.
The title of my subject,[591] and thy love
To him, pulled our displeasure on him. Since,

586 184 turtle's: turtle dove (see IV.ii. 187)
587 184 ravished: stolen, encompassing kidnap and rape
588 195 Temper: moderate
589 206 noise: report
590 212–3 ploughed/Upon my face: i.e. carved wrinkles of worry or distress into his face
591 225 title of my subject: i.e. his status as the duke's subject

We studying to add more height to thee,
Thou hast made thyself less, and, for aught we know,
Clasped with the son of earth[592] to cool the fever
Of hot sin in thy veins, ingrateful to
Philenzo, cold already in thy memory.
PHILENZO 'Tis happiness enough that you have mentioned him,
And, whether to your mercy or your justice,
See that Philenzo kneel! [*He reveals himself and kneels*]
OMNES Lord Philenzo!
FULVIO My noble cousin, so near me and concealed?
EUGENIA [*Kneels*] Your daughter's knees join with his bended heart
To beg your pardon.
DUKE Philenzo? Were not you banished, sir?
PHILENZO It was your sentence.
DUKE In pain of death not to return. Blest fate,
Thou hast relieved me: had'st thou died before
By our command, it would have been thought tyranny—
Though none durst tell us so. Now we have argument
Of justice, and our every breath is law
To speak thee dead at once. We shall not need
To study a divorce: thy second exile
Shall be eternal—death.
PHILENZO You do me honor.
DUKE [*To* BONAMICO] Be it your punishment, as you preferred[593] him
By art to her, now by another art
Forever to divide 'em: be's executioner,
And, after, make him higher by the head[594]
To cure's[595] ambition. See't advanced.
PHILENZO Ere I go, dread sir,
I have an humble suit. It is not life
I'll ask, for that I give up willingly
And call it mercy in you to immortalize
The affection I shall owe Eugenia.
Your other banishment is only death:
You new-create me now. It was my aim,
And my attempt you thought so bold, I made
To serve this end: that since I could not live
I might die for her. Pray, reprieve my breath
But till I take my leave. One minute does it:
It shall be a very short and silent farewell.

Enter AMBASSADOR

DUKE 'Tis granted.
FULVIO My lord Ambassador.
DUKE [*Aside to* FULVIO] Not the least whisper of Philenzo, as you value our regard—Oh my good lord, welcome.
AMBASSADOR [*Gives* DUKE *letters*] Letters to your grace.
DUKE They are grateful as my comfort.—Perenotto: let them withdraw, her vein[596] will

592 229 Clasped with the son of earth: had sex with a laborer
593 248 preferred: advanced, presented
594 251 make him ... the head: display his head on a spike, a spectacular punishment for traitors
595 252 cure's: i.e. cure his
596 270 vein: humor, complaint

be discovered—[*Aside to* FULVIO] Fulvio, follow and part 'em. Give order for his execution: off with his head instantly.—I can read no more for joy!—Perenotto, use your best oratory on my daughter to forget that traitor and prepare to marry Florence. 'Tis concluded to be solemnized by proxy.[597] [*Exeunt* PERENOTTO *with* EUGENIA *and* PHILENZO, *with* FULVIO *and* BONAMICO *following*]

DONDOLO I'll see the execution. *Exit*

DUKE Now, to the rest.

[*Reads*] "Your last letters were acceptable, and our son before had intention to finish the marriage in his person. But, lately receiving intelligence that one Philenzo of noble birth, now in exile, though without your consent had long since interest in your daughter's affection, we thought meet rather to advise for his repeal than proceed to our dishonor. Where the hearts meet, there only marriages are sacred, and princes should be exemplary in all justice. Although we disclaim in this design,[598] on our parts we will continue all other princely correspondence."

[*Aside*] I am justly punished and have run myself
Into a labyrinth, from whence no art
Can bring me off with safety. [*To* AMBASSADOR] —My lord, you may
Please to retire yourself. [*Exit* AMBASSADOR]
[*Aside*] A thousand wheels
Do move preposterous[599] in my brain. What cure?
I lose myself! [*To* GRUTTI] Run with a haste thou wouldst
Preserve my life, and stay the execution.
I will not have a drop of blood fall from
Philenzo for my dukedom. Fly, I say!
Thou shouldst be there already! [*Exit* GRUTTI]

Enter DONDOLO

How now? Has Philenzo still a head on?
DONDOLO Yes, my lord.
DUKE Follow him and, with that nimbleness thou wouldst
Leap from thy chamber when the roof's a-fire,
Proclaim aloud our pardon to Philenzo
And bring him back to us.
DONDOLO 'Tis too late, sir: Philenzo's dead already.
He saved the executioner that trouble.
The voice[600] is, he is poisoned.

Enter FULVIO

DUKE Poisoned? How?
[*To* FULVIO] Where is Philenzo?
This fool reports him poisoned: what circumstance?
FULVIO He had no sooner parted from Eugenia
But, suddenly, he fainted. At which fall
Of his own spirit, he seemed grieved with shame
To shew so little courage near his death,
Which he called martyrdom, and presently—
Whether supplied by other or prepared
By himself, we know not—he had a vial

597 274 by proxy: using a substitute for the prince of Florence
598 282 disclaim in this design: i.e. reject this plot or plan
599 288 preposterous: backwards, contrary to nature
600 302 voice: report

Of water sovereign[601]—as was pretended—
To enliven his dull heart. He drank it up
And soon showed cheerful in his eyes. We led
Him smiling forward but, before we could
Approach the place of death, he sunk again
But irrecoverably, for in vain we applied
Our help. By which we did conclude he had
Drunk poison.
DUKE All this talk is such,[602] and through
My ear I take it in with as much danger:
I feel it active in my brain already.
Call our physicians! I will hang 'em all
Unless they can recover him. It shall be
Death to save any man hereafter, if
They suffer him to perish.

Enter PERENOTTO [*and*] EUGENIA

FULVIO Sir, your daughter.
It seems the accident has arrived at[603] her.
DUKE Arrived at her? Fame will soon spread it, Fulvio,
About the world, and we shall be their mockery.
—He's dead they tell me, girl; poisoned, they say, too.
EUGENIA Oh my Philenzo!

Enter GRUTTI [*and* BONAMICO.] PHILENZO's *body is brought in* [*by Attendants*], *and laid upon a carpet*

DUKE Eugenia, shalt not marry Florence now,
Nor any other, since Philenzo's dead.
But, thou wilt not believe me, had he lived
He had been thine; that minute took him hence,
Wherein I first resolved to ha' given thee to him.
EUGENIA Oh, do not mock me, sir, to add to my
Affliction: you ne'er would give me to him.
DUKE May heaven forgive me never then; but what
Avails too late compunction? [*To* PHILENZO's *body*] Noble gentleman,
Thou shalt have princely funeral, and carry
On thy cold marble the inscription of
Our son in death, and my Eugenia's husband.
FULVIO [*To* EUGENIA] Madam, this sorrow for his loss is real.
We met the Florentine ambassador,
Who told me the expectation[604] of that prince
Was now dissolved, and messengers were sent
To stay the execution.
DUKE Who now
Shall marry my Eugenia? I have undone
The hope of our posterity![605]
EUGENIA Not so, sir.
If yet you'll give me leave to make my choice,

601 312 sovereign: potent, powerful
602 319 such: i.e. poison
603 326 the accident has arrived at: news of the poisoning has reached
604 345 expectation: in marriage
605 349 posterity: descendants

I'll not despair to find a husband.
DUKE Where?
EUGENIA [*Indicates* PHILENZO*'s body*] Here, royal sir: Philenzo is not dead
But made by virtue of a drink to seem so,
Thus to prevent his suffering, that I might—
Or other friend by my confederacy—
By begging of his body fit for burial,
Preserve him from your anger.
DUKE Dost not mock me?
EUGENIA Let me beg your pardon.
Confident of your change to mercy, I have
Confessed what terror could not force me to.

Enter MORELLO, [FIDELIA, MARDONA, DONELLA, CASSIANA] *and* [KATHERINA]

GRUTTI This is pretty, Dondolo!
DUKE [*To* EUGENIA] Blessings fall doubly on thee!
EUGENIA He expects
Not such a full stream of happiness. Heaven dispose him
To meet it quickly. [*Music plays*]
PERENOTTO Here are strange turnings: see, he stirs!
PHILENZO [*Waking*] Where am I now? No matter where I be,
'Tis heaven if my Eugenia meet me here.
She made some promise, sure, to such a purpose.
This music sounds divinely. Ha, Eugenia!
'Tis so. Let's dwell here for eternity.
If I be dead, I won't live again;
If living— [*Sees* DUKE] Ha! I'm lost, lost for ever!
DUKE Not found till now. Take her, a gift from me,
And call me father.
PHILENZO I am not yet awake!
EUGENIA Thou art, Philenzo, and all this is truth:
My father is converted.
PHILENZO 'Tis a miracle.
DUKE You must believe it.
In sign how we are pleased, to proclaim this day
Through Mantua a pardon to all offenders,[606]
As amply[607] as when we took our crown.
MORELLO Then my petticoat is discharged.
DONDOLO [*To lady*] Now, lady, you are free.
GRUTTI [*To lady*] Make me happy to renew my suit.
MORELLO [*To lady*] And mine. [*To couples*] Shall's to barley-break?[608]
I was in hell[609] last, 'tis little less to be in a petticoat sometimes.
PHILENZO [*To* EUGENIA] Madam, vouchsafe him kiss your hand, [*Indicating* BONAMICO]
We owe him much.
DUKE We'll take him to our service.
BONAMICO I am too much honored.
DUKE [*To* EUGENIA *and* PHILENZO] And you into our bosom. [*To all*] This day shall
Be consecrate to triumph. And may Time,

606 379 offenders: criminals
607 380 amply: generously
608 384 barley-break: a game played by three mixed-sex couples, one of whom tries to catch the others; couples can swap partners when in difficulty. The text is silent about the pairings and whether the women accept the men: this must be decided in performance
609 385 hell: the "den," or place from which one couple playing barley-break try to catch the others

When 'tis decreed the world shall have an end,
By revolution of the year make this
The day that shall conclude all memories.

Exeunt omnes

FINIS.

The Printer to the Reader

Gentle reader, let me desire thy favorable correction of these places, *viz*:
Act. I, page the fifth:[610] for "Ferrara" read "Florence."
Page the tenth:[611] leave out these words, "Yet it shall be under twenty thousand crowns, I will not leave the pawn for twice so much."
Act. 4, in a song:[612] for "two invisible," read "two visible."
Many other errors, though for the most part literal,[613] thou shalt meet, which thou canst not with safety of thy own interpret a defect in the author's judgment, since all books are subject to these misfortunes.
Vale et mitius interpretare[614]

610 2 Act. I . . . the fifth: I.i. 129
611 3 Page the tenth: I.i. 301
612 5 Act. 4, in a song: IV.i. 69
613 6 literal: i.e. of the letters that make up the words, hence the printer's or compositor's errors
614 9 *Vale et mitius interpretare*: "Farewell, and interpret kindly" (Hill, 1974)